CLASSICAL
AND MEDIEVAL
LITERATURE
CRITICISM

Guide to Gale Literary Criticism Series

For criticism on	Consult these Gale series
Authors now living or who died after December 31, 1999	*CONTEMPORARY LITERARY CRITICISM (CLC)*
Authors who died between 1900 and 1999	*TWENTIETH-CENTURY LITERARY CRITICISM (TCLC)*
Authors who died between 1800 and 1899	*NINETEENTH-CENTURY LITERATURE CRITICISM (NCLC)*
Authors who died between 1400 and 1799	*LITERATURE CRITICISM FROM 1400 TO 1800 (LC)* *SHAKESPEAREAN CRITICISM (SC)*
Authors who died before 1400	*CLASSICAL AND MEDIEVAL LITERATURE CRITICISM (CMLC)*
Authors of books for children and young adults	*CHILDREN'S LITERATURE REVIEW (CLR)*
Dramatists	*DRAMA CRITICISM (DC)*
Poets	*POETRY CRITICISM (PC)*
Short story writers	*SHORT STORY CRITICISM (SSC)*
Literary topics and movements	*HARLEM RENAISSANCE: A GALE CRITICAL COMPANION (HR)* *THE BEAT GENERATION: A GALE CRITICAL COMPANION (BG)*
Asian American writers of the last two hundred years	*ASIAN AMERICAN LITERATURE (AAL)*
Black writers of the past two hundred years	*BLACK LITERATURE CRITICISM (BLC)* *BLACK LITERATURE CRITICISM SUPPLEMENT (BLCS)*
Hispanic writers of the late nineteenth and twentieth centuries	*HISPANIC LITERATURE CRITICISM (HLC)* *HISPANIC LITERATURE CRITICISM SUPPLEMENT (HLCS)*
Native North American writers and orators of the eighteenth, nineteenth, and twentieth centuries	*NATIVE NORTH AMERICAN LITERATURE (NNAL)*
Major authors from the Renaissance to the present	*WORLD LITERATURE CRITICISM, 1500 TO THE PRESENT (WLC)* *WORLD LITERATURE CRITICISM SUPPLEMENT (WLCS)*

ISSN 0896-0011

Volume 67

CLASSICAL AND MEDIEVAL LITERATURE CRITICISM

Criticism of the Works of World
Authors from Classical Antiquity through the
Fourteenth Century, from the First Appraisals
to Current Evaluations

Janet Witalec
Project Editor

GALE®

Detroit • New York • San Diego • San Francisco • Cleveland • New Haven, Conn. • Waterville, Maine • London • Munich

Classical and Medieval Literature Criticism, Vol. 67

Project Editor
Janet Witalec

Editorial
Jessica Bomarito, Jenny Cromie, Kathy D. Darrow, Julie Keppen, Jelena O. Krstović, Michelle Lee, Ellen McGeagh; Thomas J. Schoenberg, Marie Toft, Lawrence J. Trudeau, Russel Whitaker

Data Capture
Francis Monroe, Gwen Tucker

Indexing Services
Synapse, the Knowledge Link Corporation

Rights and Acquisitions
Peg Ashlevitz, Lori Hines, Shalice Shah-Caldwell

Imaging and Multimedia
Robert Duncan, Lezlie Light, Kelly A. Quin

Composition and Electronic Capture
Kathy Sauer

Manufacturing
Rhonda Williams

LIBRARY OF CONGRESS CATALOG CARD NUMBER 88-658021

ISBN 0-7876-6770-6
ISSN 0896-0011

Printed in the United States of America
10 9 8 7 6 5 4 3 2 1

Contents

Preface

Since its inception in 1988, *Classical and Medieval Literature Criticism* (*CMLC*) has been a valuable resource for students and librarians seeking critical commentary on the works and authors of antiquity through the fourteenth century. The great poets, prose writers, dramatists, and philosophers of this period form the basis of most humanities curricula, so that virtually every student will encounter many of these works during the course of a high school and college education. Reviewers have found *CMLC* "useful" and "extremely convenient," noting that it "adds to our understanding of the rich legacy left by the ancient period and the Middle Ages," and praising its "general excellence in the presentation of an inherently interesting subject." No other single reference source has surveyed the critical reaction to classical and medieval literature as thoroughly as *CMLC*.

Scope of the Series

CMLC provides an introduction to classical and medieval authors, works, and topics that represent a variety of genres, time periods, and nationalities. By organizing and reprinting an enormous amount of critical commentary written on authors and works of this period in world history, *CMLC* helps students develop valuable insight into literary history, promotes a better understanding of the texts, and sparks ideas for papers and assignments.

Each entry in *CMLC* presents a comprehensive survey of an author's career, an individual work of literature, or a literary topic, and provides the user with a multiplicity of interpretations and assessments. Such variety allows students to pursue their own interests; furthermore, it fosters an awareness that literature is dynamic and responsive to many different opinions. Early commentary is offered to indicate initial responses, later selections document changes in literary reputations, and retrospective analyses provide the reader with modern views. The size of each author entry is a relative reflection of the scope of the criticism available in English.

An author may appear more than once in the series if his or her writings have been the subject of a substantial amount of criticism; in these instances, specific works or groups of works by the author will be covered in separate entries. For example, Homer will be represented by three entries, one devoted to the *Iliad*, one to the *Odyssey*, and one to the Homeric Hymns.

CMLC continues the survey of criticism of world literature begun by Thomson Gale's *Contemporary Literary Criticism* (*CLC*), *Twentieth-Century Literary Criticism* (*TCLC*), *Nineteenth-Century Literature Criticism* (*NCLC*), *Literature Criticism from 1400 to 1800* (*LC*), and *Shakespearean Criticism* (*SC*).

Organization of the Book

A *CMLC* entry consists of the following elements:

■ The **Author Heading** cites the name under which the author most commonly wrote, followed by birth and death dates. Also located here are any name variations under which an author wrote, including transliterated forms for authors whose native languages use nonroman alphabets. If the author wrote consistently under a pseudonym, the pseudonym will be listed in the author heading and the author's actual name given in parenthesis on the first line of the biographical and critical information. Uncertain birth or death dates are indicated by question marks. Single-work entries are preceded by a heading that consists of the most common form of the title in English translation (if applicable) and the original date of composition.

■ The **Introduction** contains background information that introduces the reader to the author, work, or topic that is the subject of the entry.

- A **Portrait of the Author** is included when available.

- The list of **Principal Works** is ordered chronologically by date of first publication and lists the most important works by the author. The genre and publication date of each work is given. In the case of foreign authors whose works have been translated into English, the list will focus primarily on twentieth-century translations, selecting those works most commonly considered the best by critics. Unless otherwise indicated, dramas are dated by first performance, not first publication. Lists of **Representative Works** by different authors appear with topic entries.

- Reprinted **Criticism** is arranged chronologically in each entry to provide a useful perspective on changes in critical evaluation over time. The critic's name and the date of composition or publication of the critical work are given at the beginning of each piece of criticism. Unsigned criticism is preceded by the title of the source in which it appeared. All titles by the author featured in the text are printed in boldface type. Footnotes are reprinted at the end of each essay or excerpt. In the case of excerpted criticism, only those footnotes that pertain to the excerpted texts are included. Criticism in topic entries is arranged chronologically under a variety of subheadings to facilitate the study of different aspects of the topic.

- A complete **Bibliographical Citation** of the original essay or book precedes each piece of criticism.

- Critical essays are prefaced by brief **Annotations** explicating each piece.

- An annotated bibliography of **Further Reading** appears at the end of each entry and suggests resources for additional study. In some cases, significant essays for which the editors could not obtain reprint rights are included here. Boxed material following the further reading list provides references to other biographical and critical sources on the author in series published by Thomson Gale.

Cumulative Indexes

A **Cumulative Author Index** lists all of the authors that appear in a wide variety of reference sources published by the Thomson Gale, including *CMLC*. A complete list of these sources is found facing the first page of the Author Index. The index also includes birth and death dates and cross references between pseudonyms and actual names.

Beginning with the second volume, a **Cumulative Nationality Index** lists all authors featured in *CMLC* by nationality, followed by the number of the *CMLC* volume in which their entry appears.

Beginning with the tenth volume, a **Cumulative Topic Index** lists the literary themes and topics treated in the series as well as in *Nineteenth-Century Literature Criticism, Twentieth-Century Literary Criticism,* and the *Contemporary Literary Criticism* Yearbook, which was discontinued in 1998.

A **Cumulative Title Index** lists in alphabetical order all of the works discussed in the series. Each title listing includes the corresponding volume and page numbers where criticism may be located. Foreign-language titles that have been translated into English are followed by the titles of the translation—for example, *Slovo o polku Igorove* (*The Song of Igor's Campaign*). Page numbers following these translated titles refer to all pages on which any form of the titles, either foreign-language or translated, appear. Titles of novels, dramas, nonfiction books, and poetry, short story, or essay collections are printed in italics, while individual poems, short stories, and essays are printed in roman type within quotation marks.

Citing *Classical and Medieval Literature Criticism*

When citing criticism reprinted in the Literary Criticism Series, students should provide complete bibliographic information so that the cited essay can be located in the original print or electronic source. Students who quote directly from reprinted criticism may use any accepted bibliographic format, such as University of Chicago Press style or Modern Language Association style.

The examples below follow recommendations for preparing a bibliography set forth in *The Chicago Manual of Style,* 14th ed. (Chicago: The University of Chicago Press, 1993); the first example pertains to material drawn from periodicals, the second to material reprinted from books:

Sealey, R. J. "The Tetralogies Ascribed to Antiphon." *Transactions of the American Philological Association* 114, (1984): 71-85. Reprinted in *Classical and Medieval Literature Criticism.* Vol. 55, edited by Lynn M. Zott, 2-9. Detroit: Gale, 2003.

Bourne, Ella. "Classical Elements in *The Gesta Romanorum.*" In *Vassar Medieval Studies* edited by Christabel Forsyth Fiske, 345-76. New Haven: Yale University Press, 1923. Reprinted in *Classical and Medieval Literature Criticism.* Vol. 55, edited by Lynn M. Zott, 81-92. Detroit: Gale, 2003.

The examples below follow recommendations for preparing a works cited list set forth in the *MLA Handbook for Writers of Research Papers,* 5th ed. (New York: The Modern Language Association of America, 1999); the first example pertains to material drawn from periodicals, the second to material reprinted from books:

Sealey, R. J. "The Tetralogies Ascribed to Antiphon." *Transactions of the American Philological Association* 114. (1984): 71-85. Reprinted in *Classical and Medieval Literature Criticism.* Ed. Lynn M. Zott. Vol. 55. Detroit: Gale, 2003. 2-9.

Bourne, Ella. "Classical Elements in *The Gesta Romanorum.*" *Vassar Medieval Studies.* Ed. Christabel Forsyth Fiske. New Haven: Yale University Press, 1923. 345-76. Reprinted in *Classical and Medieval Literature Criticism.* Ed. Lynn M. Zott. Vol. 55. Detroit: Gale, 2003. 81-92.

Suggestions are Welcome

Readers who wish to suggest new features, topics, or authors to appear in future volumes, or who have other suggestions or comments are cordially invited to call, write, or fax the Project Editor:

Project Editor, Literary Criticism Series
Thomson Gale
27500 Drake Road
Farmington Hills, MI 48331-3535
1-800-347-4253 (GALE)
Fax: 248-699-8054

Acknowledgments

The editors wish to thank the copyright holders of the criticism included in this volume and the permissions managers of many book and magazine publishing companies for assisting us in securing reproduction rights. We are also grateful to the staffs of the Detroit Public Library, the Library of Congress, the University of Detroit Mercy Library, Wayne State University Purdy/Kresge Library Complex, and the University of Michigan Libraries for making their resources available to us. Following is a list of the copyright holders who have granted us permission to reproduce material in this volume of *CMLC*. Every effort has been made to trace copyright, but if omissions have been made, please let us know.

COPYRIGHTED MATERIAL IN *CMLC*, VOLUME 67, WAS REPRODUCED FROM THE FOLLOWING PERIODICALS:

American Benedictine Review, v. 35, December, 1984; v. 36, March, 1985; v. 43, March, 1992. Copyright © 1984, 1985, 1992 *American Benedictine Review.* All reproduced by permission.—*American Journal of Philology,* v. 111, 1990. Copyright © 1990 by The Johns Hopkins University Press. Reproduced by permission.—*Anglo-Norman Studies,* v. 6, 1984. Copyright © by Walter Frohlich. Reproduced by permission.—*Anselm Studies: An Occasional Journal,* v. 2, 1988 for "St. Augustine and the *Orationes sive Meditationes* of St. Anselm" by Thomas H. Bestul. Copyright © 1988 Individual Contributors. All rights reserved. Reproduced by permission of the author.—*Archives d'histoire doctrinale et littéraire du moyen age,* v. 58, 1992. Copyright © Librairie Philosophique J. VRIN, 1992. Reproduced by permission.—*Arctos,* v. 26, 1992. Copyright © 1992 *Arctos.* Reproduced by permission.—*Arethusa,* v. 26, spring, 1993. Copyright © 1993 by The Johns Hopkins University Press. Reproduced by permission.—*Contemporary Literature,* v. 27, winter, 1986. Copyright © 1986 by the Board of Regents of the University of Wisconsin System. Reproduced by permission.—*Critical Inquiry,* v. 13, summer, 1987. Copyright © 1993 by The University of Chicago. Reproduced by permission.—*Deutsche Vierteljahrs Schrift für Literaturwissenschaft und Geistesgeschichte,* v. 61, June, 1987. Copyright © 1987 *Deutsche Vierteljahrs Schrift für Literaturwissenschaft und Geistesgeschichte.* Reproduced by permission.—*Downside Review,* July, 1981; v. 100, January, 1982; v. 103, July, 1985. Copyright © 1981, 1982, 1985 *Downside Review.* All reproduced by permission.—*ELH,* v. 61, spring, 1994. Copyright © 1994 by The Johns Hopkins University Press. Reproduced by permission.—*Eranos,* v. 84, 1986. Copyright © 1986 *Eranos.* Reproduced by permission.—*Euphorion,* v. 82, 1988. Copyright © 1988 *Euphorion.* Reproduced by permission.—*European Legacy,* v. 7, February, 2002. Copyright © 2002 International Society for the Study of European Ideas. Reproduced by permission.—*Fifteenth-Century Studies,* v. 17, 1990. Copyright © 1990 William C. McDonald and Guy R. Mermier. All rights reserved. Reproduced by permission.—*Laval théologique et philosophique,* v. 42, February, 1986. Copyright © 1985 Université Laval. All rights reserved. Reproduced by permission.—*Leeds Studies in English,* v. 7, 1974. Copyright © 1974 *Leeds Studies in English.* Reproduced by permission.—*Medium Aevum,* v. 63, 1974. Copyright © *Medium Aevum.* Reproduced by permission.—*Michigan Academician,* v. 18, spring, 1986. Copyright © The Michigan Academy of Science, Arts, and Letters, 1986. All rights reserved. Reproduced by permission.—*Modern Language Review,* v. 93, April, 1998. Copyright © 1998 The Modern Humanities Research Association. All rights reserved. Reproduced by permission.—*Proceedings of the PMR Conference,* vs. 16/17, 1992-1993. Copyright © 1992-1993 Villanova University. Reproduced by permission.—*Rivista di Letterature moderne e comparate,* v. 40, September, 1987. Copyright © by Pacine Editore. Reproduced by permission.—*Scottish Journal of Theology,* v. 32, 1979. Copyright © 1979 *Scottish Journal of Theology.* Reprinted with the permission of Cambridge University Press.—*Transactions of the American Philological Association,* v. 124, 1994. Copyright © 1994 *Transactions of the American Philological Association.* Reproduced by permission.—*Translation Review,* 1990. Copyright © *Translation Review.* Reproduced by permission.—*Victorian Poetry,* v. 21, 1983 for "Morris' Radical Revisions to the *Laxdaela Saga*" by Florence S. Boos. Copyright © 1983 *Victorian Poetry*/v. 28, Spring, 1990 for "Swinburne's Sappho: The Muse as Sister-Goddess" by Joyce Zonana. Copyright © 1990 West Virginia University. Both reproduced by permission of the respective authors.

COPYRIGHTED MATERIAL IN *CMLC*, VOLUME 67, WAS REPRODUCED FROM THE FOLLOWING BOOKS:

Arent, A. Margaret. From an introduction to *The Laxdoela Saga.* Translated by A. Margaret Arent. University of Washington Press, 1964. Copyright © 1964 by the University of Washington Press. Renewed 1992. Reproduced by permission.—Bevington, David. From "Introduction to *Sappho and Phao*," in *John Lyly: 'Campaspe' and 'Sappho and Phao.'*

Edited by G. K. Hunter and David Bevington. Manchester University Press, 1991. Copyright © David Bevington 1991. All rights reserved. Reproduced by permission.—Dubois, Page. From *Sappho Is Burning.* University of Chicago Press, 1995. Copyright © 1995 by The University of Chicago. All rights reserved. Reproduced by permission.—Foote, Peter. From an introduction to *The Laxdale Saga.* Translated by Muriel Press. J. M. Dent & Sons Ltd, 1964. Copyright © J. M. Dent & Sons Ltd, 1964. All rights reserved. Reproduced by permission.—Law, Richard. From "The *Proslogion* and Saint Anselm's Audience," in *Faith Seeking Understanding: Learning and the Catholic Tradition.* Edited by George C. Berthold. Saint Anselm College Press, 1991. Copyright © Order of Saint Benedict of New Hampshire, 1991. All rights reserved. Reproduced by permission.—Losoncy, Thomas A. From "Language and Saint Anselm's *Proslogion* Argument," in *Acta Conventus Neo-Latini Bononiensis: Proceedings of the Fourth International Congress on Neo-Latin Studies.* Edited by R. J. Schoeck. Medieval & Renaissance Texts & Studies, 1985. Copyright © 1985. Reproduced by permission.—Louis-Jensen, Jonna. From "A Good Day's Work: *Laxdaela Saga,* ch. 49," in *Cold Counsel: Women in Old Norse Literature and Mythology.* Edited by Sarah M. Anderson. Routledge, 2002. Copyright © 2002 by Routledge. All rights reserved. Reproduced by permission of the publisher and the author.—Madelung, A. Margaret Arent. From **The Laxdoela Saga***: Its Structural Patterns.* University of North Carolina Press, 1972. Copyright © by University of North Carolina Studies in the Germanic Languages and Literatures. Reproduced by permission of the publisher.—Magnussen, Magnus. From an introduction to *Laxdaela Saga.* Translated by Magnus Magnussen and Hermann Pálsson. Penguin Books, 1969. Copyright © 1969 Penguin Books. Reproduced by permission of Penguin Books, a division of Penguin Putnam Inc.—Schach, Paul. From *Icelandic Sagas.* Twayne Publishers, 1984. Copyright © 1984 by G. K. Hall & Company. All rights reserved. Reproduced by permission.—Snyder, Jane McIntosh. From *Lesbian Desire in the Lyrics of Sappho.* Columbia University Press, 1997. Copyright © 1997 Columbia University Press. All rights reserved. Reproduced by permission.—Thomas, J. W. From an introduction to *Eilhart von Oberge's* **Tristant.** Translated by J. W. Thomas. University of Nebraska Press, 1978. Copyright © 1978 by the University of Nebraska Press. All rights reserved. Reproduced by permission.—Van Fleteren, Frederick. From "Augustine and Anselm: Faith and Reason," in *Faith Seeking Understanding: Learning and the Catholic Tradition.* Edited by George C. Berthold. Saint Anselm College Press, 1991. Copyright © Order of Saint Benedict of New Hampshire, 1991. All rights reserved. Reproduced by permission.—Warren, Rosanna. From "Sappho: Translation as Elegy," in *The Art of Translation: Voices from the Field.* Edited by Rosanna Warren. Northeastern University Press, 1989. Copyright © 1989 by Rosanna Warren. All rights reserved. Reproduced by permission.—Whitehead, Frederick. From "The Early Tristan Poems," in *Arthurian Literature in the Middle Ages: A Collaborative History.* Edited by Roger Sherman Loomis. Oxford University Press, 1959. Copyright © Oxford University Press 1959. Reproduced by permission of Oxford University Press.—Wiesmann-Wiedemann, Friederike. From "From Victim to Villain: King Mark," in *The Expansion and Transformations of Courtly Literature.* Edited by Nathaniel B. Smith and Joseph T. Snow. University of Georgia Press, 1980. Copyright © 1980 by the University of Georgia Press. Reproduced by permission.—Worthen, J. F. From "Augustine's *De trinitate* and Anselm's *Proslogion*: 'Exercere Lectorum'," in *Collectanea Augustiniana.* Edited by Joseph T. Lienhard, Earl C. Muller, and Roland J. Teske. Peter Lang, 1993. Copyright © Peter Lang Publishing, Inc., New York, 1993. All rights reserved. Reproduced by permission.

PHOTOGRAPHS AND ILLUSTRATIONS APPEARING IN *CMLC*, VOLUME 67, WERE RECEIVED FROM THE FOLLOWING SOURCES:

Illuminated manuscript depicting Tristan kidnapping Isolde, 15th century. Copyright © Archivo Iconografico, S.A./Corbis. Reproduced by permission.—Manuscript page from *Laxdaelasaga in Modruvallabok.* Written around the year 1350. Courtesy of the Arni Magnusson Institute in Iceland, AM 132 fol.—Sappho, bronze sculpture. The Library of Congress.—St. Anselm of Canterbury, woodcut. The Library of Congress.

Gale Thomson Literature Product Advisory Board

The members of the Thomson Gale Literature Product Advisory Board—reference librarians from public and academic library systems—represent a cross-section of our customer base and offer a variety of informed perspectives on both the presentation and content of our literature products. Advisory board members assess and define such quality issues as the relevance, currency, and usefulness of the author coverage, critical content, and literary topics included in our series; evaluate the layout, presentation, and general quality of our printed volumes; provide feedback on the criteria used for selecting authors and topics covered in our series; provide suggestions for potential enhancements to our series; identify any gaps in our coverage of authors or literary topics, recommending authors or topics for inclusion; analyze the appropriateness of our content and presentation for various user audiences, such as high school students, undergraduates, graduate students, librarians, and educators; and offer feedback on any proposed changes/enhancements to our series. We wish to thank the following advisors for their advice throughout the year.

St. Anselm of Canterbury
1033/34–1109

Italian-born Anglo-Norman theologian.

INTRODUCTION

Saint Anselm, Archbishop of Canterbury from 1093 to 1109, is considered an important figure in the field of medieval Scholasticism, a theological school of thought that emphasized the close relationship between faith and reason and dominated Western philosophy for centuries. In practice, Anselm has become best known for his two works on the primary nature of God, the *Monologion* (1076) and *Proslogion* (1077–78)—the latter containing his famous ontological argument for God's existence. Both works are of particular interest in the history of church doctrine for their argumentative use of reason as the sole means of explaining the mysteries of revelation, as well as defining the characteristics of God without recourse to direct quotation of past authority. Anselm's other outstanding works include writings on Christian redemption, especially his *Cur Deus Homo* (1094–98) and his principal devotional compositions collected as *Orationes sive Meditationes* (1060–78). An innovative thinker and spiritual leader, Anselm also contributed to the development of Christian Platonism in the Middle Ages and was often involved in the eleventh- and twelfth-century disputes between ecclesiastical and secular authorities in the granting of high church offices known as the investiture controversy. Canonized in 1163, he was named a Doctor of the Roman Catholic Church in 1720.

BIOGRAPHICAL INFORMATION

Anselm was born in Aosta, a town in the Piedmont region of northern Italy, in either 1033 or 1034. His parents were members of the continental nobility; his mother, Ermenberga, belonged to a landholding family in Burgundy, and his father, Gondolfo, was a Lombard aristocrat. Schooled in classical languages and the theological doctrines of the period, the young Anselm excelled in Latin and opted to pursue monastic life upon completion of his education. He departed Aosta in 1057, stopping at monasteries in southern and central France before joining the order of Benedictine monks at Bec in Normandy in 1060. There he hoped to serve under Lanfranc, a distinguished cleric who had recently

returned from Rome. Lanfranc's departure to Caen in 1063 opened the way for Anselm's elevation to prior of the monastery at Bec; he was later be made Abbot in 1078. During this period, Anselm began to compose his theological and devotional writings, the first outstanding achievement of which was his *Monologion*. Undertaken at the request of his fellow monks, the *Monologion* was sent by Anselm to his superior, Lanfranc, in order to win his approval. The Abbot's reaction to Anselm's work, however, was one of thinly disguised disapproval, principally for the work's failure to quote authority in the accepted tradition of theological inquiry and argumentation. Undaunted by Lanfranc's lack of enthusiasm, Anselm began composition of a follow-up work that was far more ambitious in scope. Shortly after its appearance, the *Proslogion* sparked a vehement challenge by the monk Gaunilo of Marmoutier, who in his *Liber pro insipiente* questioned Anselm's arguments. In response, the Abbot of Bec composed the *Liber apologeticus contra Gaunilonem* (1078), which essentially restates the original thesis of the *Proslogion.* Meanwhile, the Norman conquest of England in 1066 placed lands on the far side of the English Channel under the ecclesiastical authority of Bec, lands Anselm visited several times in the ensuing years. His strong relationship to the region culminated in his being named Archbishop of the See at Canterbury in England by William Rufus, son of William the Conqueror, in March of 1093. Despite Anselm's reluctance to transfer his authority to a region devastated by Norman occupation, he accepted the promotion in December of that same year, filling a position previously held by Lanfranc until his death in 1089. Tension between Anselm and William II in regard to the transfer of monies from church possession to the King's treasury erupted in a dispute between the Norman ruler and Pope Urban II regarding ecclesiastical investiture. Two years later, in 1095, English bishops decided in favor of their King, and Anselm was expelled from England. The overall investiture issue remained unresolved. Returning to Italy, Anselm completed work on his *Cur Deus Homo* (1094–98). The death of William II in the spring of that year prompted Anselm to return to England in support of William's brother Henry I. Continuing controversy over lay versus ecclesiastical investiture raged between 1103 and 1106, however, forcing Anselm to again leave Canterbury. Anselm's return in 1107 was followed by two years of relative calm before his death in April of 1109. The events of Anselm's life were first recorded by the devout monk Eadmer in his *Vita Anselmi,* completed in the early years of the twelfth century. Later, under the authority of Thomas Becket of Canterbury, Anselm was referred for canonization in 1163. His official sanctification as a Doctor of the Roman Catholic Church was affirmed in 1720 by Pope Clement XI.

TEXTUAL HISTORY

In accordance with Anselm's high ecclesiastical position and sweeping influence on medieval thought, numerous manuscript editions of his works have survived into the modern era. Principal among these is the complete collection of Anselm's writings housed in the British Library, London. Another extant collection, the Hereford Cathedral manuscript, was bequeathed to the Augustinian abbey at Cirencester in the mid-twelfth century and there preserved. A fourteenth-century compilation comprising Anselm's *Proslogion* and several of his dialogues can be found at the Library of the University of Cambridge. In addition to these texts, many other editions containing portions of Anselm's collected works, including diverse letters written by the cleric, are available from the late medieval period. The standard Latin critical edition of Anselm's oeuvre, the six-volume *Sancti Anselmi Opera Omnia,* was edited by

Franciscus S. Schmitt and published in the middle of the twentieth century. Various English translations of Anselm's major and most of his minor writings also abound.

MAJOR WORKS

Principal among Anselm's early works are a series of devotional writings collected in his *Orationes sive Meditations* (*Prayers and Meditations of St. Anselm*), most of which were composed before Anselm became abbot of Bec in 1078. They include a number of pious exhortations that insist on the sinners' finding repentance through their acceptance of the boundless love of God. Outstanding among these works is Anselm's "Meditation on Human Redemption," written somewhat later than the other prayers, which encapsulates the monk's intense devotional spirit. Scholars regard Anselm's first groundbreaking work, the *Monologion,* as a meditation on the subject of faith combined with a philosophical inquiry into the existence of God. Based upon reason alone, without appeal to authority, Anselm's early treatise outlines his conception of God as the ultimate standard of perfection conceivable by human beings. In the early chapters of its companion work, the *Proslogion,* which originally bore the subtitle *Fides Quarens Intellectum* ("faith seeking understanding"), Anselm lays out his famous ontological argument for the existence of God. Like the *Monologion,* this work completely eschews traditional appeals to authority in favor of a meditative understanding of divine nature. Building upon Anselm's definition of God as "something a greater than which cannot be conceived" (*"aliquid quo nihil maius cogitari posit"*), the *Proslogion* employs the device of a questioning Fool who denies God's existence. Using this format, Anselm argues in the work that God necessarily exists precisely because of His presences in such diverse conceptual frames as those of the Fool, the author himself, and by logical extension all beings capable of thought. Anselm's contributions to soteriology rest on the arguments of his *Cur Deus Homo* (*Why God Became Man*), in which he offers his view of human redemption through the death of Christ. Articulating a theory of satisfaction atonement, Anselm's treatise forwards a conception of justice that mirrors the hierarchical moral and social orders of medieval feudalism. Just as individuals in feudal society demand recompense for harm done based upon their position within the social hierarchy (i.e., a king may claim far greater satisfaction than a peasant if he is wronged), so does God demand the highest possible level of atonement for the sins of humankind against him—an infinitude. Such an amount can only be equaled by an act of God Himself, namely the act of sacrificing Christ. Another notable work, the *Epistola de Incarnatione*

Verbi (1094) contains Anselm's response to the monk Roscelin of Compiègne, an outspoken critic of ecclesiastical authority, and was drafted in the form of a letter to Pope Urban II. The treatise condemns Roscelin's theory distinguishing the three persons of the Trinity as separate entities, calling this conceptualization heretical. Anselm's additional writings comprise a series of theological discourses composed as dialogues. Scholars are quick to point out that despite the seeming dialectical character of this literary form, Anselm's dialogues instead fall squarely into the Platonic tradition. Rather than making distinctions between rival points of view or schools of thought in order to come to a synthetic conclusion, Anselm's dialogues generally offer a convenient form in which to organize his essentially monologic thought. Representative of these works, *De Libertate Arbitrii* (1085) defines freedom in human obedience to God and *De Concordia Praescientiae Praedestinationis et Gratiae Dei cum Libero Arbitrio* (1007–08) presents arguments against theological fatalism. Finally, Anselm's extant *Correspondence* (c. 1089–1109) contains some 400 letters written over the course of his career as Abbot of Bec and Archbishop at Canterbury.

CRITICAL RECEPTION

Long venerated as a seminal figure of Scholastic thought and a promulgator of church orthodoxy as a Doctor of Roman Catholicism, Saint Anselm has continued to elicit considerable scholarly interest in the contemporary era. Primarily, critics have been drawn to his arguments for the existence of God in the *Proslogion* and its precursor the *Monologion,* as well as to the soteriological theories of his *Cur Deus Homo.* Regarding his well-known ontological argument, numerous theologians and philosophers have sought to either champion or condemn Anselm's methodology in arguing for God's existence. Generally, critics have acknowledged that Anselm's argument fails to withstand rigorous logical analysis, noting his tacit assumption of divine existence in the opening portions of the proof. Thus, some have accused Anselm's ontological argument of failure on the grounds that it "begs the question" by postulating elements of its final conclusion, or otherwise have suggested that it derives false conclusions from inaccurate assumptions. Critics have usually recognized its greatest logical flaw in its implication that because God exists on a conceptualized level, He must necessarily also exist in reality. Most commentators sympathetic to Anselm, however, urge that the general methods and ideas of Anselm's ontological argument, rather than the specifics of his logical proof, are the principal issues at stake in these works. His reliance on reason to produce a compelling description of God's characteristics, then,

constitutes the work's main value for such scholars. These views notwithstanding, many critics have continued to maintain that Anselm's writings, despite their clarity of purpose, remain deficient in logical precision, and are thus open to a thorough rational critique. Other areas of critical interest are his intensely felt and highly personal devotional writings, particularly his *Orationes sive Meditationes,* which have also been studied in the context of similar works by St. Augustine. Likewise, the intellectual relationship between Anselm and Augustine, and particularly the influence of Augustine's *De trinitate* and other writings on Anselm's thought has fascinated many scholars. Anselm's unique and fundamental articulation of the relationship between faith and reason, which posits the primacy of faith as a necessity to the exercise of rational thought, has also been viewed as a formative and enduring contribution to the tradition of Scholasticism in the Middle Ages.

PRINCIPAL WORKS

Orationes sive Meditationes (meditations) c. 1060-78

Monologion (theology) 1076

Proslogion (theology) 1077–78

Liber Apologeticus Contra Gaunilonem (theology) c. 1078

Disputatio Inter Christianum et Gentilem (theology) c. 1079

De Casu Diaboli (theology) c. 1085-90

De Grammatico (theology) c. 1085-90

De Libertate Arbitrii (theology) 1085

De Veritate (theology) c. 1085

Correspondence (letters) c. 1089-1109

De Humanis Moribus per Similitudines (theology) c. 1090

Cur Deus Homo (theology) 1094–98

Epistola de Incarnatione Verbi (theology) 1094

De Conceptu Virginali et de Originali Peccato (theology) 1099–1100

Meditatio Redemptionis Humanae (theology) 1099–1100

De Processione Spiritus Sancti (theology) 1102

Epistola de Sacramentis Ecclesiae ad Walerannum (theology) c. 1106–07

Epistola de Sacrificio Azimi et Fermentati (theology) c. 1106–07

De Concordia Praescientiae Praedestinationis et Gratiae Dei cum Libero Arbitrio (theology) c. 1107–08

Meditatio ad Concitandum Timorem (theology) 1108

Opera [et] Tractatus Beati Anselmi (theology) 1491

Sancti Anselmi Opera Omnia. 6 vols. [edited by Franciscus S. Schmitt] (theology, meditations, correspondence, and miscellaneous writings) 1938–51

Principal English Translations

The Devotions of St. Anselm (edited by Clement C. J. Webb) 1903

Proslogium; Monologium; An Appendix, in Behalf of the Fool, by Gaunilon; and Cur Deus Homo (translated by Sidney Norton Deane) 1903

De Grammatico *of St. Anselm: The Theory of Paronymy* (translated by Desmond P. Henry) 1964

St. Anselm's Proslogion *with, A Reply on Behalf of the Fool, by Gaunilo, and the Author's Reply to Gaunilo* (translated by M. J. Charlesworth) 1965

Theological Treatises. 3 vols. (edited and translated by Jasper Hopkins and Herbert Richardson) 1965–67

Truth, Freedom, and Evil; Three Philosophical Dialogues (translated by Jasper Hopkins and Herbert Richardson) 1967

Why God Became Man, and The Virgin Conception and Original Sin (translated by Joseph M. Colleran) 1969

Trinity, Incarnation, and Redemption; Theological Treatises (translated by Jasper Hopkins and Herbert Richardson) 1970

Prayers and Meditations of St. Anselm (translated by Sister Benedicta Ward) 1973

Anselm of Canterbury (translated by Jasper Hopkins and Herbert Richardson) 1974

A New, Interpretive Translation of St. Anselm's Monologion *and* Proslogion (translated by Jasper Hopkins) 1986

Letters of Saint Anselm of Canterbury (translated by Walter Fröhlich) 1990

Confessions of a Rational Mystic: Anselm's Early Writings (translated by Gregory Schufreider) 1994

Monologion; and, Proslogion: with the Replies of Gaunilo and Anselm (translated by Thomas Williams) 1996

Anselm of Canterbury: Major Works (translated by Brian Davies and G. R. Evans) 1998

Complete Philosophical and Theological Treatises of Anselm of Canterbury (translated by Jasper Hopkins and Herbert Richardson) 2000

Three Philosophical Dialogues (translated by Thomas Williams) 2002

CRITICISM

Hugh R. Smart (essay date 1949)

SOURCE: Smart, Hugh R. "Anselm's Ontological Argument: Rationalistic or Apologetic?" *Review of Metaphysics* 3 (1949): 161-66.

[*In the following essay, Smart argues that Anselm's ontological argument offers a combination of rational proof and spiritual revelation about the existence of God.*]

In this paper I propose to consider two possible interpretations of Anselm's ontological argument. According to the first interpretation the argument is purely rational; according to the second, reason *and* faith together form the foundation of the argument.

The ontological argument, as understood by the first interpretation, runs as follows: The concept of God is the concept of a being than which nothing greater can be conceived. This latter concept includes the concept of a being which exists necessarily, for necessary existence is one of the perfections of an absolutely perfect being; that is, the concept of God is the concept of a being which exists necessarily. God then must be conceived as existing necessarily, and hence we must attribute to his essence necessary existence. According to the first interpretation, this inference from concepts alone constitutes the whole of the ontological argument. The argument is thus analytic and purely rational.

The second interpretation to be considered here admits the correctness of this interpretation, so far as it goes. Reason can proceed to the required conclusion in the way suggested by the first interpretation, but only upon a prior basis given by faith. According to this interpretation, Anselm's attitude is radically misunderstood if it is thought of as being purely philosophical and theoretical. His real aim is practical, polemical, apologetic. He is engaged in combatting scepticism—the scepticism of the fool who says in his heart, "There is no God". Against this position Saint Anselm advances the view that not only does God exist, He exists with an absolute necessity which excludes the possibility of His being even *conceived* correctly as possibly not existing. In pursuit of such a purpose Anselm might legitimately use any order of cognition he thought sound and he might therefore be expected to depend on faith at least in part; only had his end been pure philosophic speculation would such an appeal to the supra-rational have been out of court.

We may consider the evidence in the text for this second interpretation of Anselm's argument. In the first place the interpretation seems to receive support from Chapter II of the *Proslogium:* Quod vere sit Deus, etsi insipiens dixit in corde suo: *Non est Deus.* This title would seem to suggest that the chapter is intended as a piece of Christian apologetic; and the suggestion is especially important because this chapter contains what the first school of interpretation regards as the essence of the ontological argument.

The argument as well as the title of the chapter suggests an apologetic purpose. Anselm first states what he would like to believe:

> Ergo, Domine, qui das fidei intellectum, da mihi, ut, quantum scis expedire, intelligam quia es, sicut credi-

mus; et hoc, quod credimus. Et quidem credimus te esse aliquid, quo nihil majus cogitari possit.[1]

Then Anselm states the purpose of his ontological argument—to maintain this position against the doubt raised by the atheist:

> An ergo non est aliqua talis natura, quia *dixit insipiens in corde suo: Non est Deus?*[2]

In the rest of this chapter Anselm is concerned to answer the fool. Thus his animus is that of a Christian apologist, not that of a philosopher pure and simple.

The same conclusion is suggested by the preceding chapter, which is not to be understood as having no relation to the argument from the idea of God which follows this chapter. The concluding passage is especially significant:

> Non tento, Domine, penetrare altitudinem tuam; quia nullatenus comparo illi intellectum meum, sed desidero aliquatenus intelligere veritatem tuam, quam credit et amat cor meum. Neque enim quæro intelligere, ut credam; sed credo, ut intelligam. Nam et hoc credo quia nisi credidero, non intelligam.[3]

This attitude seems clearly to be that of a *defensor fidei*—a defender whose apologetic proceeds rationally from faith, not by reason alone. It is not likely that, after thus making faith fundamental to reason, Anselm immediately went on to present his ontological argument as a purely rational argument; if such an interpretation is made, it requires special evidence.

The relations of the passage quoted to what goes before it should also be noticed. The passage is the culmination of a section which shows that the ontological argument is in part the product of anguish and prayer:

> Quid faciet, altissime Domine, quid faciet iste tuus longinquus exsul?[4] . . . Anhelat videre te et nimis abest illi facies tua . . .
>
> Heu! quid perdidit, et quid invenit??[5] . . . Perdidit beatitudinem ad quam factus est, et invenit miseriam propter quam factus non est[6] . . .
>
> Doce me quærere te, et ostende, te quærenti; quia nec quærere te possum, nisi tu doceas, nec invenire, nisi te ostendas.[7]

It thus appears to be a mistake[8] to separate Anselm's proof from its history, for its history is in reality an essential part of it; unless God reveals Himself to us, we cannot truly conceive the necessity of His existence.

In the Preface also Anselm suggests that for him reason is subordinate to faith; here he speaks of himself as having written the **Proslogium** "sub persona . . .

quærentis intelligere quod credit."[9] The same subordination is also suggested by the original title of the **Proslogium:** fides quærens intellectum.[10]

One further consideration seems to suggest that Anselm's ontological argument has a religious basis. In the **Monologium,** where Anselm seems to argue from reason alone concerning the existence of God,[11] he thinks it necessary to preface his treatise by the explicit statement that in this particular work he proposes to use reason alone.

> quatenus auctoritate Scripturæ penitus nihil in ea persuaderetur; sed quidquid per singulas investigationes finis
>
> assereret, id ita esse plano stylo et vulgaribus argumentis, simplicique disputatione, et rationis necessitas breviter cogeret, et veritatis claritas patenter ostenderet.[12]

But in the **Proslogium** Anselm makes no such statement. Instead, he begins with prayer and supplication, and it seems that he thus proceeds because he has found the rationalistic method of the **Monologium** to be inadequate. Hence his desire for something better:

> . . . cœpi mecum quærere si forte posset inveniri unum argumentum, quod nullo alio ad se probandum, quam se solo indigeret: et solum ad astruendum quia Deus vere est . . .[13]

The *unum argumentum* of the **Proslogium** satisfies Anselm because it is not a merely rational argument, such as those of the **Monologium,** but is rather a rational working out of what is implied in the certitudes of faith.

The crux of Anselm's argument, therefore, seems to be this: the argument is not about the *concept* God, but about His *idea,* which is something very different. Anselm does not argue from the concept of God as an absolutely perfect being to the concept of God as a being which cannot be conceived not to exist. Rather, when he has a clear and distinct idea of the essential nature of God—obtained through purification and the grace of God—he is able to affirm that His nature is such as to involve His necessary existence. The fool is such, not because he does not have a concept of a necessary being, but because he does not have an idea of such a being—he is a fool because he is a conceptualist. It is true that Gaunilon and Kant, among others, consider Anselm to be a conceptualist and condemn his argument on the ground that it argues from a mere concept to real existence. But one may ask whether such critics have not read their own theory of universals into Anselm. If it be agreed that Anselm stands in the Platonico-Augustinian tradition[14] and that both Plato and Augustine are strong anti-conceptualists who regard all true knowledge as a mental apprehension of what is *not* mere concept, one may well wonder at the frequent easy assumption that Anselm's ontological argument is conceptualistic. That interpretation, if it is to be maintained, calls for a special proof demonstrating that in this special case Anselm departs from his general theory.

Anselm does not make the presuppositions of his ontological argument as clear as might be desired, but on the whole the evidence of the text seems to indicate that the argument is best interpreted as being based upon both reason and faith and not upon reason alone.

Notes

1. *Patrologiæ latinæ,* Migne, tom. CLVIII. col. 227.

2. *Ibid.*

3. *Ibid.*

4. *Ibid.,* col. 225.

5. *Ibid.,* col. 225-6.

6. *Ibid.,* col. 226.

7. *Ibid.,* col. 227.

8. As Gilson suggests it is. "Certes, sa formule se déploie tout entière sur le plan de l'entendement, mais c'est le cœur qui l'a trouvée: pour en faire une *res per se nota,* il faut le considérer en dehors de ce qui le prépare et le rend intelligible: purification du cœur, foi, appel à Dieu, illumination de la pensée par grâce. La *res per se nota* que critique la Somme, c'est la peau morte de l'argument de saint Anselme, ce qui en reste lorsqu'on l'isole de son milieu naturel, l'augustinisme, pour le transporter dans l'intellectualisme de saint Thomas" (É. Gilson, *Études sur le rôle de la pensée médiévale dans la formation du système cartésien,* p. 218).

9. *Patrologiæ latinæ,* Migne, tom. CLVIII. col. 224.

10. *Ibid.,* col. 225.

11. Chapters I-V.

12. *Ibid.,* col. 143.

13. *Ibid.,* col. 223.

14. I might in particular suggest, although I cannot here work out the suggestion in detail, that Anselm's religious quest for the idea of God rather closely resembles the Platonic Socrates' quest for the divine Ideas.

Norman Malcolm (essay date 1960)

SOURCE: Malcolm, Norman. "Anselm's Ontological Arguments." *Philosophical Review* 69 (1960): 41-62.

[*In the following essay, Malcolm considers whether Anselm's ontological arguments stand up to the scrutiny of logic as well as of faith.*]

I believe that in Anselm's **Proslogion** and **Responsio editoris** there are two different pieces of reasoning which he did not distinguish from one another, and that a good deal of light may be shed on the philosophical problem of "the ontological argument" if we do distinguish them. In Chapter 2 of the **Proslogion**[1] Anselm says that we believe that God is *something a greater than which cannot be conceived.* (The Latin is *aliquid quo nihil maius cogitari possit.* Anselm sometimes uses the alternative expressions *aliquid quo maius nihil cogitari potest, id quo maius cogitari nequit, aliquid quo maius cogitari non valet.*) Even the fool of the Psalm who says in his heart there is no God, when he hears this very thing that Anselm says, namely, "something a greater than which cannot be conceived," understands what he hears, and what he understands is in his understanding though he does not understand that it exists.

Apparently Anselm regards it as tautological to say that whatever is understood is in the understanding (*quidquid intelligitur in intellectu est*): he uses *intelligitur* and *in intellectu est* as interchangeable locutions. The same holds for another formula of his: whatever is thought is in thought (*quidquid cogitatur in cogitatione est*).[2]

Of course many things may exist in the understanding that do not exist in reality; for example, elves. Now, says Anselm, something a greater than which cannot be conceived exists in the understanding. But it cannot exist *only* in the understanding, for to exist in reality is greater. Therefore that thing a greater than which cannot be conceived cannot exist only in the understanding, for then a greater thing could be conceived: namely, one that exists both in the understanding and in reality.[3]

Here I have a question. It is not clear to me whether Anselm means that (a) existence in reality by itself is greater than existence in the understanding, or that (b) existence in reality and existence in the understanding together are greater than existence in the understanding alone. Certainly he accepts (b). But he might also accept (a), as Descartes apparently does in *Meditation III* when he suggests that the mode of being by which a thing is "objectively in the understanding" is *imperfect.*[4] Of course Anselm might accept both (a) and (b). He might hold that in general something is greater if it has both of these "modes of existence" than if it has either one alone, but also that existence in reality is a more perfect mode of existence than existence in the understanding.

In any case, Anselm holds that something is greater if it exists both in the understanding and in reality than if it exists merely in the understanding. An equivalent way of putting this interesting proposition, in a more current terminology, is: something is greater if it is both conceived of and exists than if it is merely conceived of. Anselm's reasoning can be expressed as follows: *id quo maius cogitari nequit* cannot be merely conceived of and not exist, for then it would not be *id quo maius cogitari nequit.* The doctrine that something is greater if it exists in addition to being conceived of, than if it is only conceived of, could be called the doctrine that *existence is a perfection.* Descartes maintained, in so many words, that existence is a perfection,[5] and presumably he was holding Anselm's doctrine, although he does not, in *Meditation V* or elsewhere, argue in the way that Anselm does in *Proslogion* 2.

When Anselm says, "And certainly, that than which nothing greater can be conceived cannot exist merely in the understanding. For suppose it exists merely in the understanding, then it can be conceived to exist in reality, which is greater,"[6] he is claiming that if I conceived of a being of great excellence, that being would be *greater* (more excellent, more perfect) if it existed than if it did not exist. His supposition that "it exists merely in the understanding" is the supposition that it is conceived of but does not exist. Anselm repeated this claim in his reply to the criticism of the monk Gaunilo. Speaking of the being a greater than which cannot be conceived, he says:

> I have said that if it exists merely in the understanding it can be conceived to exist in reality, which is greater. Therefore, if it exists merely in the understanding obviously the very being a greater than which cannot be conceived, is one a greater than which can be conceived. What, I ask, can follow better than that? For if it exists merely in the understanding, can it not be conceived to exist in reality? And if it can be so conceived does not he who conceives of this conceive of a thing greater than it, if it does exist merely in the understanding? Can anything follow better than this: that if a being a greater than which cannot be conceived exists merely in the understanding, it is something a greater than which can be conceived? What could be plainer?[7]

He is implying, in the first sentence, that if I conceive of something which does not exist then it is possible for it to exist, and *it will be greater if it exists than if it does not exist.*

The doctrine that existence is a perfection is remarkably queer. It makes sense and is true to say that my future house will be a better one if it is insulated than if it is not insulated; but what could it mean to say that it will be a better house if it exists than if it does not? My future child will be a better man if he is honest than if he is not; but who would inderstand the saying that he will be a better man if he exists than if he does not? Or who understands the saying that if God exists He is more perfect than if He does not exist? One might say, with some intelligibility, that it would be better (for oneself or for mankind) if God exists than if He does not—but that is a different matter.

A king might desire that his next chancellor should have knowledge, wit, and resolution; but it is ludicrous to add that the king's desire is to have a chancellor who exists. Suppose that two royal councilors, A and B, were asked to draw up separately descriptions of the most perfect chancellor they could conceive, and that the descriptions they produced were identical except that A included existence in his list of attributes of a perfect chancellor and B did not. (I do not mean that B put nonexistence in his list.) One and the same person could satisfy both descriptions. More to the point, any person who satisfied A's description would *necessarily* satisfy B's description and *vice versa*! This is to say that A and B did not produce descriptions that differed in any way but rather one and the same description of necessary and desirable qualities in a chancellor. A only made a show of putting down a desirable quality that B had failed to include.

I believe I am merely restating an observation that Kant made in attacking the notion that "existence" or "being" is a "real predicate." He says:

> By whatever and by however many predicates we may think a thing—even if we completely determine it—we do not make the least addition to the thing when we further declare that this thing *is*. Otherwise, it would not be exactly the same thing that exists, but something more than we had thought in the concept; and we could not, therefore, say that the exact object of my concept exists.[8]

Anselm's ontological proof of *Proslogion* 2 is fallacious because it rests on the false doctrine that existence is a perfection (and therefore that "existence" is a "real predicate"). It would be desirable to have a rigorous refutation of the doctrine but I have not been able to provide one. I am compelled to leave the matter at the more or less intuitive level of Kant's observation. In any case, I believe that the doctrine does not belong to Anselm's other formulation of the ontological argument. It is worth noting that Gassendi anticipated Kant's criticism when he said, against Descartes:

> Existence is a perfection neither in God nor in anything else; it is rather that in the absence of which there is no perfection. . . . Hence neither is existence held to exist in a thing in the way that perfections do, nor if the thing lacks existence is it said to be imperfect (or deprived of a perfection), so much as to be nothing.[9]

II

I take up now the consideration of the second ontological proof, which Anselm presents in the very next chapter of the *Proslogion.* (There is no evidence that he thought of himself as offering two different proofs.) Speaking of the being a greater than which cannot be conceived, he says:

> And it so truly exists that it cannot be conceived not to exist. For it is possible to conceive of a being which cannot be conceived not to exist; and this is greater than one which can be conceived not to exist. Hence, if that, than which nothing greater can be conceived, can be conceived not to exist, it is not that than which nothing greater can be conceived. But this is a contradiction. So truly, therefore, is there something than which nothing greater can be conceived, that it cannot even be conceived not to exist.
>
> And this being thou art, O Lord, our God.[10]

Anselm is saying two things: first, that a being whose nonexistence is logically impossible is "greater" than a being whose nonexistence is logically possible (and therefore that a being a greater than which cannot be conceived must be one whose nonexistence is logically impossible); second, that *God* is a being than which a greater cannot be conceived.

In regard to the second of these assertions, there certainly is *a* use of the word "God," and I think far the more common use, in accordance with which the statements "God is the greatest of all beings," "God is the most perfect being," "God is the supreme being," are *logically* necessary truths, in the same sense that the statement "A square has four sides" is a logically necessary truth. If there is a man named "Jones" who is the tallest man in the world, the statement "Jones is the tallest man in the world" is merely true and is not a logically necessary truth. It is a virtue of Anselm's unusual phrase, "a being a greater than which cannot be conceived,"[11] to make it explicit that the sentence "God is the greatest of all beings" expresses a logically necessary truth and not a mere matter of fact such as the one we imagined about Jones.

With regard to Anselm's first assertion (namely, that a being whose nonexistence is logically impossible is greater than a being whose nonexistence is logically possible) perhaps the most puzzling thing about it is the use of the word "greater." It appears to mean exactly the same as "superior," "more excellent," "more perfect." This equivalence by itself is of no help to us, however, since the latter expressions would be equally puzzling here. What is required is some explanation of their use.

We do think of *knowledge,* say, as an excellence, a good thing. If A has more knowledge of algebra than B we express this in common language by saying that A has a *better* knowledge of algebra than B, or that A's knowledge of algebra is *superior* to B's, whereas we should not say that B has a better or superior *ignorance* of algebra than A. We do say "greater ignorance," but here the word "greater" is used purely quantitatively.

Previously I rejected *existence* as a perfection. Anselm is maintaining in the remarks last quoted, not that existence is a perfection, but that *the logical impossibility of nonexistence is a perfection.* In other words, *necessary existence* is a perfection. His first ontological proof uses the principle that a thing is greater if it exists than if it does not exist. His second proof employs the different principle that a thing is greater if it necessarily exists than if it does not necessarily exist.

Some remarks about the notion of *dependence* may help to make this latter principle intelligible. Many things depend for their existence on other things and events. My house was built by a carpenter: its coming into existence was dependent on a certain creative activity. Its continued existence is dependent on many things: that a tree does not crush it, that it is not consumed by fire, and so on. If we reflect on the common meaning of the word "God" (no matter how vague and confused this is), we realize that it is incompatible with this meaning that God's existence should *depend* on anything. Whether we believe in Him or not we must admit that the "almighty and everlasting God" (as several ancient prayers begin), the "Maker of heaven and earth, and of all things visible and invisible" (as is said in the Nicene Creed), cannot be thought of as being brought into existence by anything or as depending for His continued existence on anything. To conceive of anything as dependent upon something else for its existence is to conceive of it as a lesser being than God.

If a housewife has a set of extremely fragile dishes, then as dishes they are *inferior* to those of another set like them in all respects except that they are *not* fragile. Those of the first set are *dependent* for their continued existence on gentle handling; those of the second set are not. There is a definite connection in common language between the notions of dependency and inferiority, and independence and superiority. To say that something which was dependent on nothing whatever was superior to ("greater than") anything that was dependent in any way upon anything is quite in keeping with the everyday use of the terms "superior" and "greater." Correlative with the notions of dependence and independence are the notions of *limited* and *unlimited.* An engine requires fuel and this is a limitation. It is the same thing to say that an engine's operation is *dependent* on as that it is *limited* by its fuel supply. An engine that could accomplish the same work in the same time and was in other respects satisfactory, but did not require fuel, would be a *superior* engine.

God is usually conceived of as an *unlimited* being. He is conceived of as a being who *could not* be limited, that is, as an absolutely unlimited being. This is no less than to conceive of Him as *something a greater than which cannot be conceived.* If God is conceived to be an absolutely unlimited being He must be conceived to be unlimited in regard to His existence as well as His operation. In this conception it will not make sense to say that He depends on anything for coming into or continuing in existence. Nor, as Spinoza observed, will it make sense to say that something could *prevent* Him from existing.[12] Lack of moisture can prevent trees from existing in a certain region of the earth. But it would be contrary to the concept of God as an unlimited being to suppose that anything other than God Himself could prevent Him from existing, and it would be self-contradictory to suppose that He Himself could do it.

Some may be inclined to object that although nothing could prevent God's existence, still it might just *happen* that He did not exist. And if He did exist that too would be by chance. I think, however, that from the supposition that it could happen that God did not exist it would follow that, if He existed, He would have mere duration and not eternity. It would make sense to ask, "How long has He existed?," "Will He still exist next week?," "He was in existence yesterday but how about today?," and so on. It seems absurd to make God the subject of such questions. According to our ordinary conception of Him, He is an eternal being. And eternity does not mean endless duration, as Spinoza noted. To ascribe eternity to something is to exclude as senseless all sentences that imply that it has duration. If a thing has duration then it would be merely a *contingent* fact, if it was a fact, that its duration was endless. The moon could have endless duration but not eternity. If something has endless duration it will *make sense* (although it will be false) to say that it will cease to exist, and it will make sense (although it will be false) to say that something will *cause* it to cease to exist. A being with endless duration is not, therefore, an absolutely unlimited being. That God is conceived to be eternal follows from the fact that He is conceived to be an absolutely unlimited being.

I have been trying to expand the argument of *Proslogion* 3. In *Responsio* 1 Anselm adds the following acute point: if you can conceive of a certain thing and this thing does not exist then if it *were* to exist its nonexistence would be *possible.* It follows, I believe, that if the thing were to exist it would depend on other things both for coming into and continuing in existence, and also that it would have duration and not eternity. Therefore it would not be, either in reality or in conception, an unlimited being, *aliquid quo nihil maius cogitari possit.*

Anselm states his argument as follows:

> If it [the thing a greater than which cannot be conceived] can be conceived at all it must exist. For no one who denies or doubts the existence of a being a greater than which is inconceivable, denies or doubts that if it did exist its non-existence, either in reality or in the understanding, would be impossible. For otherwise it would not be a being a greater than which cannot be conceived. But as to whatever can be conceived but does not exist: if it were to exist its non-existence either in reality or in the understanding would be possible. Therefore, if a being a greater than which cannot be conceived, can even be conceived, it must exist.[13]

What Anselm has proved is that the notion of contingent existence or of contingent nonexistence cannot have any application to God. His existence must either be logically necessary or logically impossible. The only intelligible way of rejecting Anselm's claim that God's existence is necessary is to maintain that the concept of God, as a being a greater than which cannot be conceived, is self-contradictory or nonsensical.[14] Supposing that this is false, Anselm is right to deduce God's necessary existence from his characterization of Him as a being a greater than which cannot be conceived.

Let me summarize the proof. If God, a being a greater than which cannot be conceived, does not exist then He cannot *come* into existence. For if He did He would either have been *caused* to come into existence or have *happened* to come into existence, and in either case He would be a limited being, which by our conception of Him He is not. Since He cannot come into existence, if He does not exist His existence is impossible. If He does exist He cannot have come into existence (for the reasons given), nor can He cease to exist, for nothing could cause Him to cease to exist nor could it just happen that He ceased to exist. So if God exists His existence is necessary. Thus God's existence is either impossible or necessary. It can be the former only if the concept of such a being is self-contradictory or in some way logically absurd. Assuming that this is not so, it follows that He necessarily exists.

It may be helpful to express ourselves in the following way: to say, not that *omnipotence* is a property of God, but rather that *necessary omnipotence* is; and to say, not that omniscience is a property of God, but rather that *necessary omniscience* is. We have criteria for determining that a man knows this and that and can do this and that, and for determining that one man has greater knowledge and abilities in a certain subject than another. We could think of various tests to give them. But there is nothing we should wish to describe, seriously and literally, as "testing" God's knowledge and powers. That God is omniscient and omnipotent has not been determined by the application of criteria: rather these are requirements of our conception of Him. They are internal properties of the concept, although they are also rightly said to be properties of God. *Necessary existence* is a property of God in the *same sense* that *necessary omnipotence* and *necessary omniscience* are His properties. And we are not to think that "God necessarily exists" means that it follows necessarily from something that God exists *contingently*. The a priori proposition "God necessarily exists" entails the proposition "God exists," if and only if the latter also is understood as an a priori proposition: in which case the two propositions are equivalent. In this sense Anselm's proof is a proof of God's existence.

Descartes was somewhat hazy on the question of whether existence is a property of things that exist, but at the same time he saw clearly enough that *necessary existence* is a property of God. Both points are illustrated in his reply to Gassendi's remark, which I quoted above:

> I do not see to what class of reality you wish to assign existence, nor do I see why it may not be said to be a property as well as omnipotence, taking the word property as equivalent to any attribute or anything which can be predicated of a thing, as in the present case it should be by all means regarded. Nay, necessary existence in the case of God is also a true property in the strictest sense of the word, because it belongs to Him and forms part of His essence alone.[15]

Elsewhere he speaks of "the necessity of existence" as being "that crown of perfections without which we cannot comprehend God."[16] He is emphatic on the point that necessary existence applies solely to "an absolutely perfect Being."[17]

III

I wish to consider now a part of Kant's criticism of the ontological argument which I believe to be wrong. He says:

> If, in an identical proposition, I reject the predicate while retaining the subject, contradiction results; and I therefore say that the former belongs necessarily to the latter. But if we reject subject and predicate alike, there is no contradiction; for nothing is then left that can be contradicted. To posit a triangle, and yet to reject its three angles, is self-contradictory; but there is no contradiction in rejecting the triangle together with its three angles. The same holds true of the concept of an absolutely necessary being. If its existence is rejected, we reject the thing itself with all its predicates; and no question of contradiction can then arise. There is nothing outside it that would then be contradicted, since the necessity of the thing is not supposed to be derived from anything external; nor is there anything internal that would be contradicted, since in rejecting the thing

itself we have at the same time rejected all its internal properties. "God is omnipotent" is a necessary judgment. The omnipotence cannot be rejected if we posit a Deity, that is, an infinite being; for the two concepts are identical. But if we say, "There is no God," neither the omnipotence nor any other of its predicates is given; they are one and all rejected together with the subject, and there is therefore not the least contradiction in such a judgment.[18]

To these remarks the reply is that when the concept of God is correctly understood one sees that one cannot "reject the subject." "There is no God" is seen to be a necessarily false statement. Anselm's demonstration proves that the proposition "God exists" has the same a priori footing as the proposition "God is omnipotent."

Many present-day philosophers, in agreement with Kant, declare that existence is not a property and think that this overthrows the ontological argument. Although it is an error to regard existence as a property of things that have contingent existence, it does not follow that it is an error to regard necessary existence as a property of God. A recent writer says, against Anselm, that a proof of God's existence "based on the necessities of thought" is "universally regarded as fallacious: it is not thought possible to build bridges between mere abstractions and concrete existence."[19] But this way of putting the matter obscures the distinction we need to make. Does "concrete existence" mean contingent existence? Then to build bridges between concrete existence and mere abstractions would be like inferring the existence of an island from the concept of a perfect island, which both Anselm and Descartes regarded as absurd. What Anselm did was to give a demonstration that the proposition "God necessarily exists" is entailed by the proposition "God is a being a greater than which cannot be conceived" (which is equivalent to "God is an absolutely unlimited being"). Kant declares that when "I think a being as the supreme reality, without any defect, the question still remains whether it exists or not."[20] But once one has grasped Anselm's proof of the necessary existence of a being a greater than which cannot be conceived, no question remains as to whether it exists or not, just as Euclid's demonstration of the existence of an infinity of prime numbers leaves no question on that issue.

Kant says that "every reasonable person" must admit that "all existential propositions are synthetic."[21] Part of the perplexity one has about the ontological argument is in deciding whether or not the proposition "God necessarily exists" is or is not an "existential proposition." But let us look around. Is the Euclidean theorem in number theory, "There exists an infinite number of prime numbers," an "existential proposition"? do we not want to say that *in some sense* it asserts the existence of something? Cannot we say, with equal justification, that the proposition "God necessarily exists" asserts the existence of something, *in some sense*? What we need to understand, in each case, is the particular sense of the assertion. Neither proposition has the same sort of sense as do the propositions, "A low pressure area exists over the Great Lakes," "There still exists some possibility that he will survive," "The pain continues to exist in his abdomen." One good way of seeing the difference in sense of these various propositions is to see the variously different ways in which they are proved or supported. It is wrong to think that all assertions of existence have the same kind of meaning. There are as many kinds of existential propositions as there are kinds of subjects of discourse.

Closely related to Kant's view that all existential propositions are "synthetic" is the contemporary dogma that all existential propositions are contingent. Professor Gilbert Ryle tells us that "Any assertion of the existence of something, like any assertion of the occurrence of something, can be denied without logical absurdity."[22] "All existential statements are contingent," says Mr. I. M. Crombie.[23] Professor J. J. C. Smart remarks that "Existence is not a property" and then goes on to assert that "There can never be any *logical contradiction* in denying that God exists."[24] He declares that "The concept of a logically necessary being is a self-contradictory concept, like the concept of a round square. . . . No existential proposition can be logically necessary," he maintains, for "the truth of a logically necessary proposition depends only on our symbolism, or to put the same thing in another way, on the relationship of concepts" (p. 38). Professor K. E. M. Baier says, "It is no longer seriously in dispute that the notion of a logically necessary being is self-contradictory. Whatever can be conceived of as existing can equally be conceived of as not existing."[25] This is a repetition of Hume's assertion, "Whatever we conceive as existent, we can also conceive as non-existent. There is no being, therefore, whose non-existence implies a contradiction."[26]

Professor J. N. Findlay ingeniously constructs an ontological *dis*proof of God's existence, based on a "modern" view of the nature of "necessity in propositions": the view, namely, that necessity in propositions "merely reflects our use of words, the arbitrary conventions of our language."[27] Findlay undertakes to characterize what he calls "religious attitude," and here there is a striking agreement between his observations and some of the things I have said in expounding Anselm's proof. Religious attitude, he says, presumes *superiority* in its object and superiority so great that the worshiper is in comparison as nothing. Religious attitude finds it "anomalous to worship anything *limited* in any thinkable manner. . . . And hence we are led on irresistibly to demand that our religious object should have an *un-*

surpassable supremacy along all avenues, that it should tower *infinitely* above all other objects" (p. 51). We cannot help feeling that "the worthy object of our worship can never be a thing that merely *happens* to exist, nor one on which all other objects merely *happen* to depend. The true object of religious reverence must not be one, merely, to which no *actual* independent realities stand opposed: it must be one to which such opposition is totally *inconceivable*. . . . And not only must the existence of *other* things be unthinkable without him, but his own non-existence must be wholly unthinkable in any circumstances" (p. 52). And now, says Findlay, when we add up these various requirements, what they entail is "not only that there isn't a God, but that the Divine Existence is either senseless or impossible" (p. 54). For on the one hand, "if God is to satisfy religious claims and needs, He must be a being in every way inescapable, One whose existence and whose possession of certain excellences we cannot possibly conceive away." On the other hand, "modern views make it self-evidently absurd (if they don't make it ungrammatical) to speak of such a Being and attribute existence to Him. It was indeed an ill day for Anselm when he hit upon his famous proof. For on that day he not only laid bare something that is of the essence of an adequate religious object, but also something that entails its necessary non-existence" (p. 55).

Now I am inclined to hold the "modern" view that logically necessary truth "merely reflects our use of words" (although I do not believe that the conventions of language are always *arbitrary*). But I confess that I am unable to see how that view is supposed to lead to the conclusion that "the Divine existence is either senseless or impossible." Findlay does not explain how this result comes about. Surely he cannot mean that this view entails that nothing can have necessary properties: for this would imply that mathematics is "senseless or impossible," which no one wants to hold. Trying to fill in the argument that is missing from his article, the most plausible conjecture I can make is the following: Findlay thinks that the view that logical necessity "reflects the use of words" implies, not that nothing has necessary properties, but that *existence* cannot be a necessary property of anything. That is to say, every proposition of the form "*x* exists," including the proposition "God exists," must be *contingent*.[28] At the same time, our concept of God requires that His existence be *necessary*, that is, that "God exists" be a necessary truth. Therefore, the modern view of necessity proves that what the concept of God requires *cannot* be fulfilled. It proves that God *cannot* exist.

The correct reply is that the view that logical necessity merely reflects the use of words cannot possibly have the implication that every existential proposition must be contingent. That view requires us to *look at* the use of words and not manufacture a priori theses about it. In the Ninetieth Psalm it is said: "Before the mountains were brought forth, or ever thou hadst formed the earth and the world, even from everlasting to everlasting, thou art God." Here is expressed the idea of the necessary existence and eternity of God, an idea that is essential to the Jewish and Christian religions. In those complex systems of thought, those "languages-games," God has the status of a necessary being. Who can doubt that? Here we must say with Wittgenstein, "This language-game is played!"[29] I believe we may rightly take the existence of those religious systems of thought in which God figures as a necessary being to be a disproof of the dogma, affirmed by Hume and others, that no existential proposition can be necessary.

Another way of criticizing the ontological argument is the following. "Granted that the concept of necessary existence follows from the concept of a being a greater than which cannot be conceived, this amounts to no more than granting the *a priori* truth of the *conditional* proposition, 'If such a being exists then it necessarily exists.' This proposition, however, does not entail the *existence* of *anything,* and one can deny its antecedent without contradiction." Kant, for example, compares the proposition (or "judgment," as he calls it) "A triangle has three angles" with the proposition "God is a necessary being." He allows that the former is "absolutely necessary" and goes on to say:

> The absolute necessity of the judgment is only a conditional necessity of the thing, or of the predicate in the judgment. The above proposition does not declare that three angles are absolutely necessary, but that, under the condition that there is a triangle (that is, that a triangle is given), three angles will necessarily be found in it.[30]

He is saying, quite correctly, that the proposition about triangles is equivalent to the conditional proposition, "If a triangle exists, it has three angles." He then makes the comment that there is no contradiction "in rejecting the triangle together with its three angles." He proceeds to draw the alleged parallel: "The same holds true of the concept of an absolutely necessary being. If its existence is rejected, we reject the thing itself with all its predicates; and no question of contradiction can then arise."[31] The priest, Caterus, made the same objection to Descartes when he said:

> Though it be conceded that an entity of the highest perfection implies its existence by its very name, yet it does not follow that that very existence is anything actual in the real world, but merely that the concept of existence is inseparably united with the concept of highest being. Hence you cannot infer that the existence of God is anything actual, unless you assume that that highest being actually exists; for then it will actually contain all its perfections, together with this perfection of real existence.[32]

I think that Caterus, Kant, and numerous other philosophers have been mistaken in supposing that the proposition "God is a necessary being" (or "God necessarily exists") is equivalent to the conditional proposition "If God exists then He necessarily exists."[33] For how do they want the antecedent clause, "*If* God exists," to be understood? Clearly they want it to imply that it is *possible* that God does *not* exist.[34] The whole point of Kant's analysis is to try to show that it is possible to "reject the subject." Let us make this implication explicit in the conditional proposition, so that it reads: "If God exists (and it is possible that He does not) then He necessarily exists." But now it is apparent, I think, that these philosophers have arrived at a self-contradictory position. I do not mean that this conditional proposition, taken alone, is self-contradictory. Their position is self-contradictory in the following way. On the one hand, they agree that the proposition "God necessarily exists" is an a priori truth; Kant implies that it is "absolutely necessary," and Caterus says that God's existence is implied by His very name. On the other hand, they think that it is correct to analyze this proposition in such a way that it will entail the proposition "It is possible that God does not exist." But so far from its being the case that the proposition "God necessarily exists" entails the proposition "It is possible that God does not exist," it is rather the case that they are *incompatible* with one another! Can anything be clearer than that the conjunction "God necessarily exists but it is possible that He does not exist" is self-contradictory? Is it not just as plainly self-contradictory as the conjunction "A square necessarily has four sides but it is possible for a square not to have four sides"? In short, this familiar criticism of the ontological argument is self-contradictory, because it accepts *both* of two incompatible propositions.[35]

One conclusion we may draw from our examination of this criticism is that (contrary to Kant) there is a lack of symmetry, in an important respect, between the propositions "A triangle has three angles" and "God has necessary existence," although both are a priori. The former can be expressed in the conditional assertion "If a triangle exists (and it is possible that none does) it has three angles." The latter cannot be expressed in the corresponding conditional assertion without contradiction.

IV

I turn to the question of whether the idea of a being a greater than which cannot be conceived is self-contradictory. Here Leibniz made a contribution to the discussion of the ontological argument. He remarked that the argument of Anselm and Descartes

> is not a paralogism, but it is an imperfect demonstration, which assumes something that must still be proved in order to render it mathematically evident; that is, it

is tacitly assumed that this idea of the all-great or all-perfect being is possible, and implies no contradiction. And it is already something that by this remark it is proved that, assuming that God is possible, he exists, which is the privilege of divinity alone.[36]

Leibniz undertook to give a proof that God is possible. He defined a *perfection* as a simple, positive quality in the highest degree.[37] He argued that since perfections are *simple* qualities they must be compatible with one another. Therefore the concept of a being possessing all perfections is consistent.

I will not review his argument because I do not find his definition of a perfection intelligible. For one thing, it assumes that certain qualities or attributes are "positive" in their intrinsic nature, and others "negative" or "privative," and I have not been able clearly to understand that. For another thing, it assumes that some qualities are intrinsically simple. I believe that Wittgenstein has shown in the *Investigations* that nothing is *intrinsically* simple, but that whatever has the status of a simple, an indefinable, in one system of concepts, may have the status of a complex thing, a definable thing, in another system of concepts.

I do not know how to demonstrate that the concept of God—that is, of a being a greater than which cannot be conceived—is not self-contradictory. But I do not think that it is legitimate to demand such a demonstration. I also do not know how to demonstrate that either the concept of a material thing or the concept of *seeing* a material thing is not self-contradictory, and philosophers have argued that both of them are. With respect to any particular reasoning that is offered for holding that the concept of seeing a material thing, for example, is self-contradictory, one may try to show the invalidity of the reasoning and thus free the concept from the charge of being self-contradictory *on that ground.* But I do not understand what it would mean to demonstrate *in general,* and not in respect to any particular reasoning, that the concept is not self-contradictory. So it is with the concept of God. I should think there is no more of a presumption that it is self-contradictory than is the concept of seeing a material thing. Both concepts have a place in the thinking and the lives of human beings.

But even if one allows that Anselm's phrase may be free of self-contradiction, one wants to know how it can have any *meaning* for anyone. Why is it that human beings have even *formed* the concept of an infinite being, a being a greater than which cannot be conceived? This is a legitimate and important question. I am sure there cannot be a deep understanding of that concept without an understanding of the phenomena of human life that give rise to it. To give an account of the latter is beyond my ability. I wish, however, to make one suggestion (which should not be understood as autobiographical).

There is the phenomenon of feeling guilt for something that one has done or thought or felt or for a disposition that one has. One wants to be free of this guilt. But sometimes the guilt is felt to be so great that one is sure that nothing one could do oneself, nor any forgiveness by another human being, would remove it. One feels a guilt that is beyond all measure, a guilt "a greater than which cannot be conceived." Paradoxically, it would seem, one nevertheless has an intense desire to have this incomparable guilt removed. One requires a forgiveness that is beyond all measure, a forgiveness "a greater than which cannot be conceived." Out of such a storm in the soul, I am suggesting, there arises the conception of a forgiving mercy that is limitless, beyond all measure. This is one important feature of the Jewish and Christian conception of God.

I wish to relate this thought to a remark made by Kierkegaard, who was speaking about belief in Christianity but whose remark may have a wider application. He says:

> There is only one proof of the truth of Christianity and that, quite rightly, is from the emotions, when the dread of sin and a heavy conscience torture a man into crossing the narrow line between despair bordering upon madness—and Christendom.[38]

One may think it absurd for a human being to feel a guilt of such magnitude, and even more absurd that, if he feels it, he should *desire* its removal. I have nothing to say about that. It may also be absurd for people to fall in love, but they do it. I wish only to say that there *is* that human phenomenon of an unbearably heavy conscience and that it is importantly connected with the genesis of the concept of God, that is, with the formation of the "grammar" of the word "God." I am sure that this concept is related to human experience in other ways. If one had the acuteness and depth to perceive these connections one could grasp the *sense* of the concept. When we encounter this concept as a problem in philosophy, we do not consider the human phenomena that lie behind it. It is not surprising that many philosophers believe that the idea of a necessary being is an arbitrary and absurd construction.

What is the relation of Anselm's ontological argument to religious belief? This is a difficult question. I can imagine an atheist going through the argument, becoming convinced of its validity, acutely defending it against objections, yet remaining an atheist. The only effect it could have on the fool of the Psalm would be that he stopped saying in his heart "There is no God," because he would now realize that this is something he cannot meaningfully say or think. It is hardly to be expected that a demonstrative argument should, in addition, produce in him a living faith. Surely there is a level at which one can view the argument as a piece of logic, following the deductive moves but not being touched religiously? I think so. But even at this level the argument may not be without religious value, for it may help to remove some philosophical scruples that stand in the way of faith. At a deeper level, I suspect that the argument can be thoroughly understood only by one who has a view of that human "form of life" that gives rise to the idea of an infinitely great being, who views it from the *inside* not just from the outside and who has, therefore, at least some inclination to *partake* in that religious form of life. This inclination, in Kierkegaard's words, is "from the emotions." This inclination can hardly be an *effect* of Anselm's argument, but is rather presupposed in the fullest understanding of it. It would be unreasonable to require that the recognition of Anselm's demonstration as valid must produce a conversion.

Notes

1. I have consulted the Latin text of the *Proslogion,* of *Gaunilonis Pro Insipiente,* and of the *Responsio editoris,* in S. Anselmi, *Opera Omnia,* edited by F. C. Schmitt (Secovii, 1938), vol. I. With numerous modifications, I have used the English translation by S. N. Deane: *St. Anselm* (LaSalle, Illinois, 1948).

2. See *Proslogion* 1 and *Responsio* 2.

3. Anselm's actual words are: "Et certe id quo maius cogitari nequit, non potest esse in solo intellectu. Si enim vel in solo intellectu est, potest cogitari esse et in re, quod maius est. Si ergo id quo maius cogitari non potest, est in solo intellectu: id ipsum quo maius cogitari non potest, est quo maius cogitari potest. Sed certe hoc esse non potest." *Proslogion* 2.

4. Haldane and Ross, *The Philosophical Works of Descartes,* 2 vols. (Cambridge, 1931), I, 163.

5. *Op. cit.,* p. 182.

6. *Proslogion* 2; Deane, p. 8.

7. *Responsio* 2; Deane, pp. 157-158.

8. *The Critique of Pure Reason,* tr. by Norman Kemp Smith (London, 1929), p. 505.

9. Haldane and Ross, II, 186.

10. *Proslogion* 3; Deane, pp. 8-9.

11. Professor Robert Calhoun has pointed out to me that a similar locution had been used by Augustine. In *De moribus Manichaeorum* (Bk. II, ch. xi, sec. 24), he says that God is a being *quo esse aut cogitari melius nihil possit* (*Patrologiae Patrum Latinorum,* ed. by J. P. Migne, Paris, 1841-1845, vol. 32: *Augustinus,* vol. 1).

12. *Ethics,* pt. I, prop. 11.

13. *Responsio* 1; Deane, pp. 154-155.

14. Gaunilo attacked Anselm's argument on this very point. He would not concede that a being a greater than which cannot be conceived existed in his understanding (*Gaunilonis Pro Insipiente,* secs. 4 and 5; Deane, pp. 148-150). Anselm's reply is: "I call on your faith and conscience to attest that this is most false" (*Responsio* 1; Deane, p. 154). Gaunilo's faith and conscience will attest that it is false that "God is not a being a greater than which is inconceivable," and false that "He is not understood (*intelligitur*) or conceived (*cogitatur*)" (*ibid.*). Descartes also remarks that one would go to "strange extremes" who denied that we understand the words "*that thing which is the most perfect that we can conceive;* for that is what all men call God" (Haldane and Ross, II, 129).

15. Haldane and Ross, II, 228.

16. *Ibid.,* I, 445.

17. E.g., *ibid.,* Principle 15, p. 225.

18. *Op. cit.,* p. 502.

19. J. N. Findlay, "Can God's Existence Be Disproved?," *New Essays in Philosophical Theology,"* ed. by A. N. Flew and A. MacIntyre (London, 1955), p. 47.

20. *Op. cit.,* pp. 505-506.

21. *Ibid.,* p. 504.

22. *The Nature of Metaphysics,* ed. by D. F. Pears (New York, 1957), p. 150.

23. *New Essays in Philosophical Theology,* p. 114.

24. *Ibid.,* p. 34.

25. *The Meaning of Life,* Inaugural Lecture, Canberra University College (Canberra, 1957), p. 8.

26. *Dialogues Concerning Natural Religion,* pt. IX.

27. Findlay, *op. cit.,* p. 154.

28. The other philosophers I have just cited may be led to this opinion by the same thinking. Smart, for example, says that "the truth of a logically necessary proposition depends only on our symbolism, or to put the same thing in another way, on the relationship of concepts" (*supra*). This is very similar to saying that it "reflects our use of words."

29. *Philosophical Investigations* (New York, 1953), sec. 654.

30. *Op. cit.,* pp. 501-502.

31. *Ibid.,* p. 502.

32. Haldane and Ross, II, 7.

33. I have heard it said by more than one person in discussion that Kant's view was that it is really a misuse of language to speak of a "necessary being," on the grounds that necessity is properly predicated only of propositions (judgments) not of *things.* This is not a correct account of Kant. (See his discussion of "The Postulates of Empirical Thought in General," *op. cit.,* pp. 239-256, esp. p. 239 and pp. 247-248.) But if he had held this, as perhaps the above philosophers think he should have, then presumably his view would not have been that the pseudo-proposition "God is a necessary being" is equivalent to the conditional "If God exists then He necessarily exists." Rather his view would have been that the genuine proposition "'God exists' is necessarily true" is equivalent to the conditional "If God exists then He exists" (*not* "If God exists then He *necessarily* exists," which would be an illegitimate formulation, on the view imaginatively attributed to Kant).

"If God exists then He exists" is a foolish tautology which says nothing different from the tautology "If a new earth satellite exists then it exists." If "If God exists then He exists" were a correct analysis of "'God exists' is necessarily true," then "If a new earth satellite exists then it exists" would be a correct analysis of "'A new earth satellite exists' is necessarily true." If the *analysans* is necessarily true then the *analysandum* must be necessarily true, provided the analysis is correct. If this proposed Kantian analysis of "'God exists' is necessarily true" were correct, we should be presented with the consequence that not only is it necessarily true that God exists, but also it is necessarily true that a new earth satellite exists: which is absurd.

34. When summarizing Anselm's proof (in part II, *supra*) I said: "If God exists He necessarily exists." But there I was merely stating an entailment. "If God exists" did not have the implication that it is possible He does not exist. And of course I was not regarding the conditional as *equivalent* to "God necessarily exists."

35. This fallacious criticism of Anselm is implied in the following remarks by Gilson: "To show that the affirmation of necessary existence is analytically implied in the idea of God, would be . . . to show that God is necessary if He exists, but would not prove that He does exist" (E. Gilson, *The Spirit of Medieval Philosophy,* New York, 1940, p. 62).

36. *New Essays Concerning the Human Understanding,* Bk. IV, ch. 10; ed. by A. G. Langley (LaSalle, Illinois, 1949), p. 504.

37. See *Ibid.,* Appendix X, p. 714.

38. *The Journals,* tr. by A. Dru (Oxford, 1938), sec. 926.

R. W. Southern (essay date 1963)

SOURCE: Southern, R. W. "The Monk of Bec." In *Saint Anselm and His Biographer: A Study of Monastic Life and Thought 1059-c. 1130,* pp. 27-76. Cambridge: Cambridge University Press, 1963.

[*In the following excerpt, Southern describes the content of Anselm's early works, the* Monologion *and* Proslogion, *the latter of which features his arguments concerning the existence of God.*]

The Early Treatises

Until he became archbishop, Anselm's life for over thirty years was one of monastic peace disturbed only by the occasional enmities inseparable from the life of men living in close proximity in a small community, and by material cares which weighed less heavily upon him, as some thought, than they ought to have done. All his writings of this period are the witnesses of this peace: his intimate correspondence with friends at Canterbury and elsewhere, his prayers and meditations, his *Proslogion* and *Monologion*—themselves meditations on the nature of God—and his philosophical and theological dialogues, which were the product of his teaching in the cloister. In all this body of work there is scarcely a word of controversy. The only controversy was with the remarkable Gaunilo over the argument of the *Proslogion,* and it was conducted with such mutual regard and identity of purpose that it is hard to realize that a new philosophical issue had suddenly sprung into existence. Nothing could be more peaceful or more withdrawn from the storms and controversies which, in the realm of government, were rending the Empire and Papacy of Henry IV and Gregory VII, or which, in the realm of theology, in 1079 produced the final condemnation of Berengar of Tours. The idea that the task of the theologian was to reconcile apparent contradictions arose from the controversies of this time. It influenced the future in countless ways. But this was not Anselm's method: there is never in his works a moment of indecision, of poise between two opposites, and a final resolution of the point at issue. If ever there was a moment of irresolution we are not allowed to see it: in all his writings, he appears on the field already a victor, ready to explain, perhaps to demonstrate, but not to fight. None of the paraphernalia of *pro* and *contra,* of *distinguo* and *respondeo* had any place in his thought. For him the points about which others argued were the points which were settled before arguments began.

It may therefore seem strange that so much of his work was cast in the form of dialogue, which of all forms seems most to suggest the existence of opposing points of view. It was not so with Anselm. Indeed when Anselm came up against two concrete opponents, Roscelin and the Greeks, he dropped the dialogue form. For him, the dialogue was a form of art, used, as Plato had used it, to draw out his meaning and to give structure to thoughts which might otherwise have seemed to tumble out with too little disposition towards a system; it was not an expression of two rival bodies of thought. The protagonists in his dialogues were always a master and his pupil, never the representatives of two schools of thought.

Although most of the treatises which Anselm wrote at Bec are in dialogue form, the two earliest works, written shortly after the main body of his prayers and meditations, are extended meditations. They grew out of the earlier writings and have many similarities with them. They could be read, and to some extent they must be read, as religious exercises: we shall have especially to remember this in discussing the argument of the *Proslogion,* which begins in the manner of one of Anselm's earlier prayers:

> Come now, little man, put aside your business for a while, take refuge for a little from your tumultuous thoughts; cast off your cares, and let your burdensome distractions wait. Take some leisure for God; rest awhile in him. Enter into the chamber of your mind; put out everything except God and whatever helps you to seek Him; close the door and seek him. Say now to God with all your heart: 'I seek thy face, O Lord, thy face do I seek.'[1]

But, however strong their connexions with his earlier prayers, the treatises we are now to examine were much more ambitious than anything previously attempted by Anselm. They place him at once in the front rank of theologians and philosophers, and despite all his depreciatory gestures it is impossible not to see that he knew this.

The passage in which Eadmer describes Anselm's first appearance as a theologian is the best introduction to these treatises. Eadmer's words at this point have almost the authority of autobiography, for there can be no doubt that Anselm was their source, and it is very likely that he read and at first approved what Eadmer had written:

> He also composed another small book, which he called the *Monologion* because in this he alone spoke and argued with himself. Here, putting aside all authority of

Holy Scripture, he inquired into and discovered by reason alone what God is, and proved by invincible reason that God's nature is what the true Faith holds it to be, and that it could not be other than it is. Afterwards it came into his mind to try to prove by one single and short argument the things which are believed and preached about God—that he is eternal, unchangeable, omnipotent, omnipresent, incomprehensible, just, righteous, merciful, true, as well as truth, goodness, justice and so on; and to show how all these qualities are united in Him. And this, as he himself would say, gave him great trouble, partly because thinking about it took away his desire for food, drink and sleep, and partly—and this was more grievous to him—because it disturbed the attention which he ought to have paid to Matins and to Divine service at other times. When he was aware of this, and still could not entirely lay hold on what he sought, he supposed that this line of thought was a temptation of the devil and he tried to banish it from his mind. But the more vehemently he tried to do this, the more these thoughts crowded in on him. Then suddenly one night during Matins, the grace of God shone on his heart, the whole matter became clear to his mind, and a great joy and jubilation filled his inmost being.[2]

The two works thus described, the *Monologion* and *Proslogion,* belong to the years 1077 and 1078. They are closely related in plan and subject-matter. They both consist, broadly speaking, of proofs of God's existence followed by meditations on God's qualities. But whereas the first, the *Monologion,* is concerned with the qualities of the Trinity, and is closely dependent on Augustine's *De Trinitate,* the *Proslogion* is chiefly concerned with the qualities of God as Unity; it is only very slightly dependent on Augustine, and it is altogether more personal and more vivid in expression than the earlier treatise.

There is also a notable difference in Anselm's intellectual posture in the two works: although they both contain proofs which Anselm regards as wholly convincing, the *Monologion* is a philosophical soliloquy, while the *Proslogion* is a prayer. The distinction is important. The *Monologion* was in form a highly original work, but in substance it had the authority of Augustine behind it. In it Anselm speaks, with the confidence of a man with all the best cards in his hand, with a secret source of authority; there is in his opening words a youthful confidence, as if it were the easiest thing in the world to prove, even to those of mediocre intelligence, that those things which we believe about God are necessarily true.[3] But in the *Proslogion* he was on his own; he had reached the furthest limits of his thought; he still trembled with the awe of a new discovery. The *Proslogion* contains Anselm's most original contribution to philosophy, but it should be approached, as Anselm approached it, through the *Monologion.*

(1) The Monologion

The first words of the **Monologion** laid down a principle of inquiry from which he never afterwards departed.

> Some of my brethren have persistently asked me to write down some of the things which I have proposed to them in talk for meditation on the divine essence and certain associated topics . . . with this condition that I should persuade them of nothing on the authority of scripture, but plainly and simply put down whatever the argument might require, without overlooking any objections, however fatuous.[4]

It would be hard to imagine a more complete break with the past than this. To Lanfranc, the whole enterprise appeared misguided. Yet the younger spirits were ready for the change. Anselm was not a reformer speaking odious truths to a generation unwilling to listen to him. He was a conservative, reluctantly writing what he would have preferred to leave to the spoken word, speaking perhaps what he would have preferred to leave unsaid, driven on by eager pupils. That the pupils were eager there is every reason to believe: their existence was not a literary fiction. They only needed the signal for a freer and more speculative approach to the problems of theology.

Anselm himself assumed an attitude of indifference towards the fate of his work. He sent it to Lanfranc asking him, as if casually, to approve it or to destroy it; and if he approved, to give it a name.[5] The casualness was deceptive. Lanfranc did not approve, though he did not condemn outright. He made suggestions which would have altered the whole nature of the work. Anselm did not follow them. Nor did Anselm destroy the work. Instead, he himself turned to the question of giving his treatise a name. Ostensibly, he had left the work without a title and without an author's name because it was unworthy of such ornaments; but another reason seems to have been the difficulty of finding the right name. At first he called it an 'Example of meditating about the substance of faith (*de ratione fidei*)', but he still left it anonymous. Then he called it a '*Monoloquium* on the substance of faith'. Finally he dropped the descriptive phrase and, introducing a literary refinement after the fashion of the time, abandoned the hybrid *Monoloquium* in favour of the more elegant **Monologion**.[6] And so, with many hesitations, but also with a considerable show of firmness, not to say obstinacy, this first treatise was launched into the world.

The work was quite unlike any other of recent times and substantially unlike any other work of any earlier period. The most striking point which separated it from other writings of this period was its entire lack of any quotation of authorities. This omission was not designed by Anselm as a *tour de force:* it was a deliberately

chosen method and it sets him apart from all his contemporaries, except those who came under his immediate influence, and from the main line of development of medieval scholastic thought. By nature Anselm was anything but a rebel, but in this one respect he may be accounted one. The whole articulation of medieval thought came about through the collection of authorities, through the work of arranging and examining them, and through the task of harmonizing the vast and confusing mass of authoritative texts. The process of accumulation, of arrangement, and even—though as yet only feebly—of criticism, had already begun. It was against all this that Anselm set his face. There is no one in these centuries more conscious of his philosophic mission: he will not repeat other men's words.

Anselm at first called the **Monologion** an example of meditating about the substance of faith, *de ratione fidei.* This is an ambiguous phrase, and he soon dropped it from the title of his work. Nevertheless it was a phrase to which he reverted on several occasions and it contains the best description of what he was trying to do throughout the whole of his writings. It therefore requires careful examination.

First of all then the **Monologion** is an *exemplum meditandi,* a meditation. This was a form of writing which Anselm made peculiarly his own. 'Meditatio' and 'meditare' are words which occur very rarely in the Rule of St. Benedict, and then with a sense very different from that in which they are used by Anselm: they refer to such activities as learning the Psalter, or preparing the Lessons or the music for the Offices, not to the free excursion of the mind among problems of theology.[7] St. Augustine also has very little to say about meditation. It is not until the twelfth century, and especially among writers of the Cistercian school, that meditation came to have a well defined place as a philosophical activity.[8] But we need not go into the technical meaning attached to the word to see that it suggests a form of reasoning which claims a certain freedom of development, letting the mind take what turns it will, ignoring the exigencies of scholastic debate. All this is well brought out by the twelfth century writer Hugh of St. Victor in his account of the place of meditation among the arts:

> Meditation has its foundation in reading, but it is constrained by no rules or order of reading. It rejoices to run freely in an open space where it can fix its gaze on the truth without hindrance, and investigate now this, now that problem until nothing is left doubtful or obscure.[9]

It was Anselm who did more than anyone else to fix this later, freer tradition of meditation, and to use it as a basis both for extended private prayer and for philosophical inquiry. The inquiry was scarcely distinguishable from the prayer, since the aim of both was to shake off the torpor of the mind and see things as they are in their essential being.

Secondly, the **Monologion** is a meditation *de ratione fidei*. What this phrase means is not very easy to say. It comes from St. Paul, who in the Epistle to the Romans admonishes his readers, if they have the gift of prophecy, to prophesy *secundum rationem fidei*.[10] St. Paul seems to mean by this that their words are to be accommodated to the measure of their faith, but this cannot be Anselm's meaning. Perhaps the best translation would be 'a meditation on the rationale of the Faith', and this is a fair description of most of Anselm's theological works.

Anselm soon dropped the phrase *de ratione fidei* from the title of his work. He probably did so only for reasons of literary elegance. But he must have known that the conjunction of the two words 'reason' and 'faith' raised a problem. It was inevitable from the nature of his inquiries that he should soon say something about the relations between them, if only to allay the misgivings and suspicions which his method and the absence of authorities in his work aroused.

Faith and Reason

This is a subject on which a great deal of confusion can be avoided by making an immediate distinction between two senses of the word 'faith': in the first sense it is a mode of knowledge, an activity; in the second, it is an object of knowledge, a state of affairs capable of being expressed in a set of propositions. We know 'by faith' and what we know is 'the Faith'. About faith in the first sense Anselm has very little to say. He has no psychology of belief; he feels no difficulties. The holding of the propositions of the Catholic faith was an obligation on all who had been baptized:

> Our Faith is to be defended by reason against unbelievers, not against those who profess to rejoice in the name of Christians. From the latter, it may justly be demanded that they hold inviolate the pledges made for them in baptism . . . The Christian ought to progress through faith to understanding, and not through understanding to faith. Let him rejoice if he is able to attain understanding; and if he cannot, let him revere what he cannot apprehend.[11]

This is a blunt statement of his position and should be kept in mind, but it is open to some misunderstanding. It suggests that knowing by faith is a mere passive act of receptivity; but it is this only at a very low level of understanding. The man who believes is impelled to raise his mind to God. He does this by means of reason. But reason is itself a spiritual gift, by which man is made in the image of God: reason is not a machine for performing a plodding series of mechanical acts; it is a kindling of the spirit, a throwing off of the chains of the flesh, a rising above the world of material things. Hence it is not inappropriate that Anselm uses in his philosophical discourses the same phrases of mental excitation which he uses in his prayers. This is most evident in the **Proslogion.** Here prayer and philosophy are most intimately combined; yet the philosophical starting point is strictly a problem of grammar and logic, and not one of faith in the narrow sense at all. It was not an accident that he chose this moment to assert the necessity of faith for understanding, and to coin the famous phrase which better than any other describes his theological programme: *Fides quaerens intellectum.*[12] Reason is the activity of faith. Hence, at the most primitive level, those who fail to discern the reality of universals fail before they begin to think: they are slaves of their corporeal images; they are like bats disputing with the eagle about the rays of the noonday sun; they are incapable of ascending to the plane of rational truth, which is the plane of incorporeal essences.[13] Indeed it is clear that if the objects of reason are incorporeal essences inaccessible to the senses, some sort of act of faith is necessary before the processes of reason can begin at all. If anyone does not admit the existence of such essences, he lacks both faith and an object in which to exercise his reason. Nothing can be done about him except oblige him to keep silence. One way of achieving this was by authority; the other way was to convict him of a logical contradiction in asserting that something is *not,* which by logical necessity *is*. Anselm hoped that he had achieved the second of these results. But whether or not he was justified in this hope, it is plain that faith and reason, considered simply as activities, are much more closely related than the dogmatic statement which has been quoted would suggest.

Similarly, the objects of faith and reason are the same. St. Augustine expressed this identity of aim in two images when he said that reason is to the heart as the eye is to the body, and faith glows in the eye of the heart as gold in the eye of the body.[14] Reason, therefore, is the eye of the spirit, and faith is the most glorious of the objects presented to it. But, just as the eye does not change the nature of the object presented to it, so the nature of faith is not altered by the scrutiny of reason. This view, with all the consequences which follow from it, is also Anselm's, and his attitude is sharply distinguishable from that of St. Thomas Aquinas. Professor Gilson has remarked that for St. Thomas when something has been proved it ceases to be an object of faith; it is an object of demonstration. For Anselm it is not so. Reason makes faith intelligible; it does not supersede it. Faith becomes intelligible in two ways. In the first place, the interrelation between the various tenets of faith becomes plain: system emerges from a mass of details.

Secondly, the rationality of faith is established: that is to say, what is known by faith is shown to be rationally necessary.

Why then is faith not swallowed up in demonstration? For two reasons. Firstly, because (as we have seen) the demonstration is only convincing to a man in a state of spiritual elevation, which if not identical with faith is closely related to it. Secondly, because the demonstrations of reason are in varying degrees provisional. In Anselm's theology they are provisional in the same way that explanations in natural science are provisional. If the explanation accounts for all observed events in the field it purports to explain, it may be said to have a high degree of probability. But, even supposing that no unobserved events could exist, and that all observed events have been correctly observed, it would still be possible for another explanation to fit them and for the other explanation to be the right one.

Of course, scientific explanations are doubly provisional, because the facts are never either complete nor reported with complete accuracy. Anselm would not have admitted that the theologian was faced with this double hazard: the Faith, enshrined in the dogmas of the Church, is certain, and, within the limits of its subject-matter, complete. But to compensate for this, it is supremely difficult to grasp intellectually, and full of apparent contradictions between God's foreknowledge and man's free will, God's mercy and God's justice, the goodness of the Creator and the existence of evil, and so on. The distance by which any explanation, however bound together by 'necessary reasons', falls short of giving a complete explanation of these apparent contradictions in the Christian faith, is the measure of the provisional character of all reasoning on these subjects.

(II) THE PROSLOGION

When Lanfranc failed either to approve or give a name to the **Monologion,** Anselm's reaction shows that the author in him in some degree predominated over the monk. He neither altered nor destroyed the work. Instead, he straightway wrote another which not only had the characteristic which Lanfranc had found offensive in the **Monologion**—an absence of all authorities—but even went further in the same direction, in that it could not be said in any sense to provide a simplified account of St. Augustine's thoughts. It is on this work that Anselm's philosophical, as distinct from his theological, reputation will always chiefly rest. It was written in a state of philosophical excitement which (it is probably safe to say) had never before been experienced so intensely in any Benedictine monastery, and was probably never again to be repeated in Benedictine history.[15] This excitement is chiefly to be associated

with the first three chapters of the treatise in which the famous, so-called ontological, argument for the existence of God is set out. Although everything Anselm wrote is stamped with his personal quality, these chapters are in a special sense his own. The proof they contain was his own discovery; and it is the only philosophical discovery of the early Middle Ages which has survived to excite the interest of modern philosophers who have no other interest in the period.

Whether it is true or false, nothing is more surprising than the way in which this proof has united, at least temporarily, men of the most diverse temperaments and outlooks—a tenuous link across vast seas of spiritual difference. Among living philosophers none is perhaps further removed from Anselm in outlook, though perhaps not so far in qualities of mind, than he who remembers:

> the precise moment, one day in 1894, as I was walking along Trinity Lane, when I saw in a flash (or thought I saw) that the ontological argument is valid. I had gone out to buy a tin of tobacco; on my way back, I suddenly threw it up in the air, and exclaimed as I caught it: 'Great Scott, the ontological argument is sound'.[16]

Leave out Trinity Lane, the tobacco and the 'Great Scott' (delightful evocation of an age more remote in spirit than the eleventh century) and substitute Bec, Matins, and *Deo gratias,* and it was just so that the argument came to Anselm in 1078:

> Behold, one night during Matins, the grace of God shone in his heart and the matter became clear to his understanding, filling his whole being with immense joy and jubilation.[17]

We can well believe that the argument came, as Eadmer describes, in a flash of illumination after days or weeks of frustrated gropings and reluctant distraction in the midst of the daily offices. Yet it did not come from nowhere. Its distant ancestor must be judged to be St. Augustine, but only in a remote and ineffectual way. Its immediate parents are the grammar and logic of Anselm's day, but applied with an otherwise unknown subtlety. As we shall see, what Anselm needed for this argument was a definition of God on which he could build a logical structure of a peculiar kind. He did not find this in Augustine, whose language—so similar to that of Anselm in some respects—lacked the precision of the logician. He could find in Augustine that:

> God is not really known in the sound of these two syllables (*Deus*), but this sound, when it strikes the ears of all who know Latin, moves them to thinking of some most excellent and immortal nature. . . . For when God is thought of, our thought tries to reach something than which nothing is better or more sublime.[18]

This has the germ of what he needed—the concentration on the word *Deus,* and the connexion between this word and a nature 'than which nothing is better or more sublime'. But there is no basis here for a proof of God's existence. Strangely enough, the form of words Anselm needed for his proof were lying in a most unlikely place. He may have noticed them. In the Introduction to Seneca's *Quaestiones Naturales*—a rare book, but a book of which there were two copies at Bec in the twelfth century[19]—there is a definition of God: 'God is that than which nothing greater can be thought'.[20] Seneca used these words in a sense very different from Anselm: he was speaking only of physical magnitude, and was certainly innocent of any philosophical intention. But for Anselm, whether he found this phrase in Seneca or coined it himself, these words were full of exciting possibilities. They gave him a starting-point for his argument.[21]

He begins with the Fool, described by the Psalmist as one who thinks 'there is no God'. What, Anselm asks, is God? He is 'something than which nothing greater can be thought'. The Fool, then, has this *something* 'in intellectu' but denies that it exists 'in re'.

Let us suppose the Fool is right. Then God does not exist outside the mind. But still it would be possible to think of another Being, also having the quality of being 'that than which nothing greater can be thought', who exists not only in the mind but also outside the mind. Such a Being would be greater than the Being existing only in the mind. The Being existing only in the mind is therefore not 'that than which nothing greater can be thought'; such a Being therefore is by definition not God. Thus the Fool asserts that 'God is not-God', which is nonsense. God, therefore, exists not only in the mind but also outside the mind.

Now we can go a step farther. God exists both 'in intellectu' and 'in re'. But many other things exist outside the mind which do not exist necessarily. There is no logical necessity in the existence of physical objects. Not so with God: he exists outside the mind, and *cannot* be thought not to exist outside the mind.

The Fool is now reduced to a very pitiable state. He thought he understood the meaning of words like 'God' and of sentences like 'God does not exist'. But if the argument is valid, it has been shown that he uses words without understanding the things to which they refer, and constructs sentences without understanding the verbal contradictions they contain. Not only has he no understanding of things, but he does not even grasp words and sentences in their basic grammatical and logical connexions. Although Anselm nowhere says so formally, we can see in the progression of his argument that there are three stages of knowledge:

> *cogitatio* at the level of words and sentences (grammar and logic);

> *intellectus* at the level of entities, the things to which words refer (philosophy);

> *sapientia* in the apprehension of the Supreme Being (theology).

The Fool of course lacked *sapientia*, being by definition *insipiens*. Anselm has tried to show that he consequently lacks *intellectus* and even the power of *cogitatio*: he must be silent like a beast. Meanwhile, the right-thinking person has risen from understanding the word 'God' (*cogitatio*), to understanding the thing for which the word stands 'God outside the mind' (*intellectus*), to a knowledge of God's necessary Being (*sapientia*).

It has been necessary to express the well-known argument in this way in order to bring out its grammatical and logical foundations. For it is clear that though Anselm's argument is to be placed in the same class as that of Descartes, yet Anselm's presuppositions, his method of proceeding, and even his conclusion is different from that of his successor. It is only in a careless way that Anselm's proof can be called a proof that God exists. It is rather a demonstration of the manner of God's existence; for that he has some kind of existence, the mere fact that it is possible to attach some meaning to the word 'God' is sufficient to show. What the proof undertakes to show is that the existence of God is external to the mind, and that it cannot be thought of in any other way.

That the argument can be refuted has been shown again and again. But the argument continues to attract defenders and opponents, and this suggests that the refutations are never quite complete, or that the argument has some hidden source of life. Instead, therefore, of entering on a refutation, we may ask what conditions would have to be satisfied for the argument, as Anselm states it, to be valid. In this way we may hope to discover something which, whether or not of any philosophical value, is of value for understanding the mind and presuppositions of Anselm.

It is evident at once that there are two conditions which have to be satisfied before the argument can have any claim to validity. The first condition is that when we say that something is 'greater' than something else, we can mean—and in this context *do* mean—that it is 'greater' in having a greater degree of being; and that 'existence only in the mind' and 'existence both in the mind and outside the mind' are related in respect of degrees of being. If this were not so, then the criticism of all who have attacked the argument from Anselm's day to the present would be clearly justified: God *in re* would not be greater than God *in intellectu*. He would just be something entirely different, even though the same word 'God' is used, in different senses, in both phrases. There must therefore be degrees of being, such that 'being in the mind' and 'being in the mind and outside the mind' are related as lesser to greater. Moreover, Anselm evidently attaches a special degree of being to that which not only exists *in intellectu et in re* but also cannot be thought of as not existing. The degrees of being are thus, in ascending order: *esse in intellectu esse in intellectu et in re esse in intellectu et in re et non posse cogitari non esse.*

The second condition is a consequence of the first: in the phrases 'it exists in the mind' and 'it exists outside the mind', it must be possible for the subject to be really, and not merely grammatically, the same in both sentences. If this were not so, we should be talking about different things in the two sentences; and to arrange them in series, as if the second sentence referred to the same thing as the first, would be to fall into the simplest form of blunder arising from an identity of grammatical structure.

For Anselm there is only a difference of degree between the existence of a thing and the existence of the idea of a thing. The idea in the mind and its object outside the mind are strictly related as ascending powers in a scale of existence. But this interchangeability between idea and thing is only plausible if there is a still higher degree of being, of which both the idea and its object are lower powers; and this higher degree of being can only be in the mind of God himself. We know from the *Monologion* that this is in fact what Anselm thought: things have their highest degree of being in the mind of God; a lower degree in their own objective existence; a still lower degree in our idea of them.[22]

This is of course a form of Platonism. There seems to be no proof that Anselm had read even that amount of Plato which was accessible in his day, but he had imbibed the elements of Platonic thought from St. Augustine, and there can be no doubt that his essential philosophical ideas are Platonic—so much so that he seems to think that any other type of philosophy must not only lead to heresy but even gives evidence of hopeless intellectual blindness.

The *Proslogion* is intended both as a meditation for the believer and a proof for the unbeliever. The proof for the unbeliever does not, as has sometimes been thought, depend upon the previous acceptance of certain theological truths, but it does depend on a previous acceptance of certain philosophical principles which appear on analysis to commit the unbeliever to a view of knowledge which necessitates the existence of God. A proof which demands, in however subtle and roundabout a way, assent to its conclusion before it begins will rightly be thought to be no proof at all in the ordinary sense of the word.[23]

Whether Anselm was conscious of this limitation in his argument we cannot tell. He seems to have thought that the account of knowing which his argument presupposed was the only possible one and that since the unbeliever could produce no other he would effectively be reduced to silence. This is a possible and—despite many difficulties of which Anselm could not have been aware—a consistent point of view: consistent both in itself and within the framework of the theological programme announced at the beginning of the *Proslogion: Fides quaerens intellectum.* The argument returns, and must always return in Anselm's thought to its point of origin, the Faith from which it starts. But, for the purpose of this argument, the Faith is not the Christian faith but a philosophical faith which Anselm seems, wrongly, to have thought an essential part of any coherent system of thought.

To most people all these preliminary conditions will appear unacceptable, and all refutations of the argument are based on the rejection of these preliminaries. In the common view, horses exist and unicorns do not exist; and it does not seem an adequate description of the difference between the existence of the one and the nonexistence of the other to allege that both exist, but one more than the other, because one exists *in re et in intellectu* while the other exists only *in intellectu.* Similarly most people who believe that God exists will not think that the existence of God is in any way affected by our ability or inability to think of Him as not existing. But since Anselm certainly himself accepted these preliminary conditions of his argument, we must ask what the status of the argument will be if his conditions are accepted. The answer is clear: the argument will then be irrefutable, but irrefutable only because it requires the conclusion to be accepted before the argument starts.

Anselm's philosophical outlook was not destined to command any wide body of assent, at least for a long time to come. It was not until the thirteenth century that the proofs for the existence of God engaged the serious attention of theologians and the weight of opinion was then against the validity of Anselm's argument.[24] Among Anselm's immediate friends and disciples no one except Eadmer so much as mentions the argument. Of the others Gilbert Crispin repeats the definition on which the argument was based, but he did not build upon it. We know that Lanfranc disapproved of the *Monologion;* we do not know what he thought of the *Proslogion,* but it is hard to think that—if he ever read it—he approved. In the immediate future the peculiar mixture of linguistic analysis and Augustinian philosophy on which the argument, as Anselm stated it, was based was replaced by newer methods and by a different conception of the purpose of theological study. Yet if Anselm's argument did not meet with acceptance, the two treatises *Monologion* and *Proslogion* made his name known far and wide. In 1085 he could no longer have spoken of himself as he did ten years earlier as a man unknown to the world. Within a year or two of their composition the two works were known not only in Normandy and in Canterbury, but at Poitiers, Tours, and Lyons.[25]

It is very common for authors to say that they have been obliged to write by the demands of their pupils, but there is no reason to doubt that Anselm is telling the truth when he says this. At Bec and elsewhere he had an eager audience. A generation had grown up in the monasteries of men who were connoisseurs in theological debate. Yet it did not produce monastic successors to Anselm. Philosophical interests soon became centred on the universities and the age of Anselm remained the highest point of philosophical culture in the history of the Benedictine Order. Unlike the later schoolmen, the monastic philosophers and theologians have left comparatively little record of their interests. Anselm's first critic therefore deserves a special mention. Gaunilo, monk of Marmoutier near Tours, is entirely unknown except for three or four pages in which he criticized Anselm's argument. These pages also would no doubt have been lost if Anselm had not given directions for the inclusion of the criticism and his reply to it in all future copies of the *Proslogion.* Since all the earliest copies include Gaunilo's criticism, it must have been written very soon after the composition of the treatise. It is so familiar a text that it is hard to realize how unlikely it was to survive. It is a very notable piece of writing. Though not quite conclusive as an attack on Anselm, it is urbane and intelligent, and strikingly anticipates later lines of attack on the ontological argument. Its existence is a warning against underestimating the level of philosophical cultivation in communities which have left little trace of their intellectual attainments.

Of all the arguments for the existence of God, the one which Anselm first formulated is the most refined and the least capable of a finally satisfactory statement. It draws its strength from an ambiguity, which appears to be an ambiguity in language, but is more deeply an ambiguity in human experience. If God exists, there must be a level of experience at which it is impossible to think of God as not existing. But at what level can this impossibility be made to appear? Must the demonstration await the experience of the Beatific Vision? Or can it, at the very opposite extreme, be made out at the level of linguistic-logical analysis? Whether valid or not, the first three chapters of the *Proslogion* were the first piece of writing in which this problem was raised and a solution proposed which will probably never be finally buried. It may be agreed that Descartes put it better, because more simply and with fewer philosophical presuppositions. He had the advantage, which Anselm lacked, of inheriting, if only to reject, a long

philosophical tradition. The Augustinian and grammatical background of Anselm's thought, which made it possible for him to formulate the argument, also burdened it with limitations. But these pages of Anselm must be placed among the most deeply interesting pieces of reasoning ever written The early chapters of the *Proslogion,* in which the argument was first expressed, will never be read without excitement, nor thought about without appearing to be more cogent than they are. For the most extraordinary thing about the argument is that it loses nothing of its power, its freshness, or even in a curious way its persuasiveness, by being refuted. The *Proslogion* may not set forth a valid argument for belief in God, and even if it were valid it is doubtful whether it would ever persuade an unbeliever; but in its subtlety, and in a certain unsubstantial, ethereal quality which antagonizes men of robust common sense, it perfectly reflects the quality and mystery of Anselm's personality.

The *Monologion* and *Proslogion* were the product of two remarkable years in Anselm's life, 1077-8, his last years as Prior of Bec. In sheer force of philosophical originality he never rose to these heights again. For the next fifteen years before he became archbishop of Canterbury he was occupied in monastic administration and in the composition of four works (all of them Dialogues) which display his talent and originality, but could not in themselves have formed the basis of his reputation, as the *Monologion* and *Proslogion* standing by themselves could have done. They were years in which his reputation in the world slowly grew, in which the number of his pupils—men who had become monks at Bec mainly because of his influence and presence—increased, and in which his monastic peace was disturbed only by necessary journeys to courts and synods and tours of inspection of his lands in England.

Notes

1. *Proslogion,* cap. 1.

2. *VA* 1, xix.

3. *Monologion,* cap. 1.

4. *Ibid.* prologus.

5. Ep. 72 [i, 63]. Lanfranc's letter of criticism does not exist—it is interesting that Anselm, who preserved some other letters of Lanfranc, should not have preserved this—but its contents can be gathered from Anselm's reply, Ep. 77 [i, 68].

6. For the stages in the development of the title, see *VA* I, xix n.

7. *Regula,* cap. 8, 48, 58. (See the note on these passages in B. Linderbauer, *S. Benedicti Regula Monachorum herausgegeben und philologisch erk-*

lärt, 1922). For the use of the word 'meditation' in this sense, see Bede, *Hist. Eccl.* III, vi: 'meditari . . . id est, aut legendis scripturis, aut psalmis discendis operam dare' (ed. Plummer, p. 136).

8. See, for example, Alcher of Clairvaux, *De Spiritu et Anima* (printed among the works of St. Augustine, *PL* XL, 779) cap 28: 'Sensus parit imaginationem, imaginatio cogitationem, cogitatio meditationem. Meditatio acuit ingenium, ingenium rationem; ratio conduct ad intellectum, intellectus ad intelligentiam, intelligentia per contemplationem ipsam veritatem admiratur, et per caritatem in ea delectatur.'

9. *Didascalicon,* iii, 10 (ed. Buttimer, p. 59).

10. Romans xii, 6.

11. Ep. 136 [ii, 41].

12. This wonderful phrase was the original title of the work. It was later dropped for the more enigmatic title *Proslogion,* but the programme is expressed in the body of the work, though less attractively: 'Neque enim quaero intelligere ut credam, sed credo ut intelligam.'

13. *Epistola de Incarnatione Verbi,* i (Schmitt, ii, p. 8).

14. Dedit tibi Deus oculos in corpore, rationem in corde (*Hom.* 32, 11); Sicut lucet aurum ad oculos corporis, sic lucet fides ad oculos cordis (De decem chordis, x); Fides gradus est intelligendi, intellectus meritum fidei (*Hom.* 32, 1). Many similar passages can be found in which this union of faith, reason and understanding is expressed in various ways.

15. For the history of the discovery, see *VA* 1, xix.

16. Bertrand Russell, *My mental development,* in P. A. Schilpp, *The Philosophy of Bertrand Russell,* 1944, p. 10.

17. *VA* 1, xix.

18. *De Doctrina Christiana,* I, vii.

19. G. Becker, *Catalogi Bibliothecarum antiqui,* p. 202, no. 104; p. 266, no. 136. Of these two volumes, the first came to Bec in the twelfth century; but the second may have been there in Anselm's time. The only other reference to this work in the catalogues printed by Becker is at St. Gall in the ninth century (p. 35).

20. I am indebted to Schmitt, i, 102 n. for this quotation: 'Quid est Deus? quod vides totum et quod non vides totum. Sic demum magnitudo sua illi redditur, qua nihil maius excogitari potest' (*Senecae Opera,* ed. F. Haase, i, 159).

21. The following paragraphs summarize the argument of the first four chapters of the *Proslogion.* I have tried to preserve what, for want of a better word, may be called Anselm's *tone,* but it is more difficult to do this here than in any other part of Anselm's writings.

22. *Monologion,* xxxvi: Restat igitur ut (creatae substantiae) tanto verius sint in seipsis quam in nostra scientia . . . Cum ergo et hoc constat, quia omnis creata substantia tanto verius est in Verbo, id est in intelligentia creatoris, quam in seipsa. . . .

23. There is, however, at this point an interesting affinity between Anselm's argument and G. E. Moore's proof of an external world, which—having the same problem of arguing from what is 'inside the mind' to what is 'outside the mind'— ends in the same predicament; the proof is only a proof for those who, in the last resort, accept as a premiss the conclusion which the argument purports to prove (G. E. Moore, *Philosophical Papers,* 1959, p. 150).

24. The essential texts for the thirteenth century are collected in A. Daniels, *Gottesbeweise im xiii Jahrhundert mit bes. Rücksicht auf dem ontologischen Argument* (*BGPM,* viii, 1909).

25. Epp. 83 [i, 74], 109 [ii, 17].

Richard Campbell (essay date 1979)

SOURCE: Campbell, Richard. "Anselm's Theological Method." *Scottish Journal of Theology* 32 (1979): 543-48.

[*In the following excerpt, Campbell asserts that critics of Anselm's ontological argument have misrepresented his point, which is simply to demonstrate "that it cannot be said that God is not."*]

The study of Anselm's **Proslogion** argument on the existence of God which I recently undertook[1] emerged out of a growing conviction that commentator after commentator had been guilty of serious misrepresentation of its structure. Traditionally, Anselm has been taken as presenting in **Proslogion** 2 the first version ever to be formulated fully of the 'Ontological Argument'. The reasoning in **Proslogion** 2 was—and often still is—supposed to proceed from an alleged definition of God as something-than-which-nothing-greater-can-be-thought, through inferences designed to show that, unless he exists in reality, he would not be something than which nothing greater can be thought, to the conclusion that God exists.

In more recent years attention has swung (especially amongst philosophers) to the first half of Chapter 3, where a number of commentators claim to find a second, logically independent, and sounder version of the Ontological Argument. This 'modal' version is supposed to proceed likewise from the alleged definition, through inferences derived from an alleged premise that *necessary* existence is a perfection, to the conclusion that God exists.

My bold claim is that all these commentators are demonstrably wrong. It is not often in philosophical theology that one is justified in using language of such finality, but in this case the matter is provable using the apparatus of modern symbolic logic. Once all the text of Chapters 2 and 3 is taken seriously and literally, it is possible to extract a series of premises and sub-conclusions which together constitute a three-stage argument for two conclusions.

The two conclusions which Anselm explicitly draws at the end of this formally valid chain of reasoning are that God 'so truly is that he cannot be thought not to be' and that God 'is something than which a greater cannot be thought'. Thus, far from this identification of God with 'such a nature' being a definition—it would be ill-formed if it were—which Anselm uses as a premise in some version of the Ontological Argument, it is demonstrably one of his conclusions. So the long tradition of interpretation which stretches from Aquinas to many contemporary commentators must be wrong. This startling result—it still surprises me—is what has led me to reappraise the character of Anselm's thought.

As I read him, Anselm begins *Proslogion* 2 with the prayer that he might be given understanding of two matters: that God is *just as* we believe, and that he is *what* we believe. He then says what we believe God to be: something-than-which-nothing-greater-can-be-thought. But since he is then struck by doubt, for the fool has said in his heart that God is not, he inquires whether there is such a nature. Chapter 2 finishes by drawing the sub-conclusion that something-than-which-a-greater-cannot-be-thought—which he does not yet understand to be God—exists in reality. That is Stage One of the overall argument. Stage Two, which occupies the first half of Chapter 3, then consists of a deduction that this same nature cannot be thought not to be. Here again God does not explicitly figure, nor is Anselm concerned with necessary existence as we might understand it.

In the second half of *Proslogion* 3 Anselm swings back into the language of address, but that does not stop him from reasoning. As I read him, he there presents two independent pieces of argumentation, both of which move him on to his two main conclusions. Together,

these comprise what I call Stage Three. The first leg of it is based on the new premise that 'if any mind could think of something better than you, the creature would rise above the creator and judge the creator, which is absurd'. The second, which is the neater and more compelling of the two, is based on the premise that 'whatever else there is, except for you alone, can be thought not to be'. In the weak form that everything that is not identical to God can be thought not to be, this is sufficient, together with his two previous sub-conclusions, to entail his two main conclusions. Read this way the entire argument emerges with a logical tightness and coherence that it is difficult to dismiss.

On this construction, the argument proper begins with Anselm's sentence 'when the fool hears what I say, "something-than-which-nothing-greater-can-be-thought", he certainly understands what he hears'. This makes the *point de départ* of the argument Anselm's use of that indefinite description in a communicative way. Understood in this fashion, Anselm's concern is whether he can continue to use with understanding the language in which he articulates his belief. His own assessment of what the argument shows is that 'no-one *understanding* what God is can *think* that he is not'.

In this regard, it seems to me to differ significantly from, for example, the Five Ways of Aquinas. The latter presents us with arguments which are supposed to be proofs in the sense that, if the arguments were sound, the conclusion that God exists would follow in a way which is thoroughly impersonal. That is, those arguments are based on certain facts about the natural world, and their cogency is in no way dependent upon what any person might say or think. In contrast, Anselm's argument crucially involves the believer who speaks of something-than-which-nothing-greater-can-be-thought, and the fool who overhears his prayer and who is able to think of such a thing. In so far as Anselm sets out from his own speech-act, an act of communication, and not from an impersonal proposition, neither is his conclusion impersonal. His entire enterprise is directed towards drawing out the implications of the language used in articulating his faith in order to determine whether it can be said with understanding.

Because that is the character of the argument, it seems to me that we should give a cautious and qualified assent to Anselm Stolz's claim that Anselm has not presented a *proof* of the existence of God,[2] even though the proposition 'God exists' is deducible validly from his premises. The purport of his argument, as I read it, is that the whole realm of discourse which admits the believer to speak of God as something-than-which-nothing-greater-can-be-thought rules out the possibility of denying with understanding the existence of God.

Yet it would be a mistake to take this assessment of the force of the argument to mean that Anselm's investigation is thoroughly internal to a closed circle of faith. The first two stages of the argument are expressed in language even the fool can understand, and they can be examined for their cogency independently of any peculiarly religious premise. Rather, I suggest that we are now in a position to see how the opposed interpretations of Anselm's approach—rationalistic or fideistic—rest on a common exegetical mistake.

If the argument did proceed from the identification of God with this nature, from the alleged definition, the methodological dispute would turn on how that 'definition' was derived. If it simply states a necessary truth, either of linguistic usage or of quasi-Platonic ideas, and if his conclusion simply were the proposition 'God exists', the argument could legitimately be classified as thoroughly rationalistic. Alternatively, if the alleged definition were either a datum of revelation or an article of faith, the entire argument would inevitably be faith-dependent. Significantly, neither of these interpretations gives Anselm's 'what I say' any logical role in the argument. And both lose their purchase once it is recognised that this identification is not a premise but a conclusion.

Nevertheless, it might be objected, does not Anselm's 'what I say' mean that what he is doing is drawing out the implications of the language of faith, so that even on my account he is a kind of fideist? To which I answer: Yes, he is drawing out the implications of the language of faith; but No, it does not follow that he is therefore a kind of fideist. This is where the role of the fool is crucial. To see this, we need in our imaginations to reconstruct the scene of the ***Proslogion,*** for the work is not to be taken for a metaphysical treatise cast in the language of prayer just for rhetorical effect. It has an implicitly narrative element which is crucial to its structure.

Anselm is praying, addressing God. He confesses the belief as to what God is, one of the beliefs he is yet to understand: 'we certainly believe that you are something than which nothing greater can be thought'. Then he is struck by doubt as he recalls the fool's denial. (It is hard to stop the mind wandering in prayer!) 'But is there any such nature?' he asks himself. To deal with this, he breaks off from the language of prayer, and switches to third-person grammar; the God he was addressing—'You'—temporarily drops out of his speech. Instead he envisages that the fool has been eavesdropping on his prayer, and has actually heard him speaking of such a nature. Since the fool does not believe that there is a God to whom prayer could ever be addressed, an analysis of God-talk would be to no avail. But—and this gets to the heart of Anselm's

methodology—the language of faith is not entirely esoteric. Believers both use distinctively religious referring expressions *and* use words which are part of the public language, shared and understood by believers and unbelievers alike. So even the fool understands what he hears when Anselm uses ordinary familiar words in speaking of such a nature. And it is those public words whose proper usage Anselm then proceeds to investigate.

Once he has established that there is such a nature, and that such a thing cannot be thought not to be, but only then, can be resume his prayer: 'And this is you, O Lord our God.' Then, continuing his prayer, he offers his two reasons for thus identifying such a nature with the God to whom he is praying. I can only think that it has been an unconscious prejudice against its being possible to think logically while one is praying which has prevented so many commentators from recognising that this is where Anselm's argument reaches its climax.

If one reads the text carefully, one can see how delicately Anselm has structured his argument through his oscillation between second- and third-person discourse. His conclusions are not impersonal factual propositions. But he arrives at them through consideration of those public words which can feature in the *oratio recta* even of the fool. Yet he shows no sign of thinking that his conclusions ought to convince, or even silence, the fool. He only adverts to the fool again in order to ask how the fool could have said what has emerged as, strictly speaking, not intelligible.

I suspect that part of our difficulty in grasping the exact character of Anselm's method is that, for complicated reasons which lie in our own intellectual history, we want justified general propositions to underpin our belief-structures. Anselm, wisely in my view, does not push his argument to that point. He is content to establish to his own satisfaction that it cannot be said that God is not. But that is not equivalent to, nor does it entail, that one should say that God is.

His same concern with what one says, with the commitments of one's discourse, can be seen in his ***Reply*** to Gaunilo, who presumed to speak *On Behalf of the Fool*. Anselm prefaces his ***Reply*** with the words:

> Since it is not the fool, against whom I spoke in my tract, who takes me up, but one who, though speaking on the fool's behalf, is not a fool and is a Catholic, it will suffice if I reply to the Catholic.

That is, Anselm insists that what is said must be 'owned'. That is the same point as I was alluding to above when I spoke of the *oratio recta* of the fool. In Anselm's view, claims must be owned; he will not indulge in idle speculation or intellectual games. Nor will a general analysis serve to compel belief. Analysis must start out from what is said, and all it can prove are the ontological commitments inherent in a domain of discourse. This, I believe, is why he said: 'I do not understand in order to believe, but I believe in order to understand.'

Notes

1. cf. my *From Belief to Understanding* (Canberra: The Australian National University, 1976).

2. 'Anselm's Theology in the Proslogion', trans. by A. C. McGill in *The Many-Faced Argument,* ed. by J. Hick and himself (London: Macmillan, 1968).

A. E. McGrath (essay date July 1981)

SOURCE: McGrath, A. E. "Rectitude: The Moral Foundation of Anselm of Canterbury's Soteriology." *Downside Review* (July 1981): 204-13.

[*In the following essay, McGrath evaluates Anselm's thought on salvation as it appears in his* Cur Deus Homo, *maintaining that Anselm's conception of justice is based on theological rather than legal foundations.*]

Anselm of Canterbury has attracted increasing scholarly attention during the past century as a major thinker standing at the dawn of the Middle Ages. His greatest intellectual achievement is generally considered to be the monograph **Cur Deus Homo,** which is of decisive importance in the history of doctrine. Its unrivalled combination of sustained argument, moral force and originality make it a landmark in the history of literature as well as of doctrine. The Reformers, as well as several of the earlier scholastics, were to take up and develop aspects of his theology, and the doctrines of justification associated with the Reformers, particularly those of Melanchthon and Calvin, are set within a theological framework which is recognizably Anselmian.[1] Anselm's interpreters, however, transferred his soteriological concepts from their original context to one considerably more juridical in outlook, with the result that his theology has generally been approached with certain preconceptions quite alien to Anselm's own time. Thus Anselm has frequently been accused of legalizing the gospel, being typical of the Latin 'impulse to carry religion into the legal sphere'.[2] His most outspoken English critic, Hastings Rashdall, dismissed his soteriology as feudal: 'Anselm appeals to justice: . . . but his notions of justice are the barbaric ideas of an ancient Lombard king, or the technicalities of a Lombard lawyer'.[3] It is a sad reflection upon the current state of English theological awareness that this misrepresentation of Anselm's soteriology is still generally accepted. Rashdall's offended liberalism, however, prevents him from grasping the theological framework of the **Cur Deus Homo.** Whilst Rashdall appreciated that Anselm 'made a serious attempt to vindicate the whole scheme (of salvation) from the point of view of justice', he failed to answer the central question posed by the Anselmian soteriology: What concept of justice is appropriate to God's dealings with men? Anselm does not employ 'ordinary ideas of justice', and his soteriology can only be understood when the concept of *iustitia* which underlies God's dealings with man is established. The present study is concerned with establishing Anselm's concept of justice. Anselm's soteriology can only be described as 'legalist' or 'juridical' if it can be demonstrated that a 'legalist' or 'juridical' concept of justice lies behind it. It is the contention of the present study that this is not the case.

God is wholly and supremely just.[4] How, then, can he, being just, spare the sinner? This is the central question with which Anselm is concerned in the **Cur Deus Homo.** How can there be justice in giving eternal life to one who deserves death?[5] In the discussion of the relation between justice and mercy in the **Proslogion,** Anselm initially locates the source of God's mercy in his *bonitas,*[6] which may be contrasted with his *iustitia.*[7] He then, however, moves on to argue that, despite the apparent contradiction between *misericordia* and *iustitia,* God's mercy must somehow be grounded in his justice. Anselm resolves this dilemma in the following manner: God is just, not because he rewards us as we deserve, but because he does what is appropriate to him, the highest good.[8] It appears that Anselm is wrestling with various concepts of justice, before finally adopting that which is most suitable for his purpose. A similar pattern emerges in the **Cur Deus Homo,** where Anselm notes various interpretations of justice: *iustitia hominis,* which obtains under law,[9] strict justice, *iustitia districta,* beyond which 'nothing more strict nor just can be imagined',[10] and supreme justice, *summa iustitia.*[11] But the final concept of justice which emerges appears to be that arrived at in the **Proslogion**—namely, justice as action directed towards the highest good. This understanding of justice has its roots in the works of St Augustine, for whom Anselm frequently professed a high regard,[12] and it is therefore to be expected that he would follow his master in this important matter.

Augustine's understanding of *iustitia* within the *civitas Dei* [13] is based on the concept of God as *iustissimus ordinator,*[13] who orders the universe in accord with his will. Thus *iustitia* can take on a wide meaning, approaching that of a physical ordering of all things, but particularly referring to the ordering of the affairs of men, and their relation to their environment.[14] For Augustine, *iustitia* is practically synonymous with the right ordering of human affairs, and that right ordering of human affairs is part of man's pilgrimage to the heavenly city.[15] Augustine's quasi-physical understanding of justice reflects his hierarchical structuring of the order of being: justice is essentially the ordering of the world according to the order of being, which is itself a reflection of the divine will.

By A.D. 396 Augustine had abandoned his previous hopes of saving or perfecting mankind through human society. This is reflected in his abandoning the concept of *lex temporalis,*[16] a human law which is derived from the eternal divine law. Augustine, becoming increasingly aware of the radical dichotomy between human *ius* and divine *ius,* rejected the former as a basis of salvation. Instead, he developed a concept of *iustitia* by which the natural order is preserved by the eternal law.[17] As God created the natural order of things, so *iustitia* is reflected in the correct order of nature. This may be illustrated by considering man's relationship with God. God created man as he ought to be—i.e., he created man in *iustitia,* the correct order of nature. But by choosing to ignore God's own ordering of his creation man stepped outside this state of *iustitia.* Man cannot save himself, as to do so involves the restoration of the correct order of things—i.e., the rectitude of the relationship between God and man. Justification is therefore a 'making right', a restoration of this relationship between God and man; it is not conceived in juridical or legalist terms. *Iustitia* reflects the ordering of the world, including the relationship of God to man, and man to his fellows, and is not a legal concept in itself.

The correct relationship between men, which is being established in the process of justification, is reflected in Augustine's understanding of social or political justice. Augustine modifies Cicero's classical definition of the *res publica*[18] by making *iustitia* an essential element of the *iuris consensus.* Where there is no true *iustitia,* there is no true *ius.*[19] For Cicero, *iustitia* is based on *ius*—i.e., justice is based on law; for Augustine, *ius* is based on *iustitia*—i.e., law is based on justice, the correct ordering of the universe, itself a manifestation of the divine will. The laws which govern the affairs of men are themselves but one aspect of the correct ordering of the entire universe—and that right ordering of things is itself justice.

In his discussion of the background to the Incarnation, Anselm appeals to the order established by God at creation; however, he reserves the term *rectitudo* to describe this basic God-given order of creation, using the term *iustitia* in a number of derivative senses, each of which can be traced back to the basic concept of rectitude. The close connection between *veritas* and *iustitia* in Anselm's thought is due to their both being

aspects of the basic concept of *rectitudo.* Thus, in general, truth is a form of rectitude, a following of the right rules.[20] In the treatise *De Veritate,* truth is defined as 'rectitude perceptible only to the mind'.[21] Elsewhere, truth can be equated with rectitude, indicating the closest of relationships between the two concepts.[22] In general, truth is regarded as *rectitudo*—anything which is as it ought to be is true, and anything which is true is as it ought to be. Thus the relationship between rectitude, justice and truth could be expressed as follows:

> *rectitudo* [conditions] *veritas* (i.e., metaphysical rectitude) [and] *iustitia* (i.e., moral rectitude).

Justice is a 'rectitude of will served for its own sake', *rectitudo voluntatis propter se servata.*[23] Anselm clearly assumes the interrelationship of the three concepts: *et quoniam de rectitudine mente sola perceptibili loquimur, invicem sese definiunt veritas et rectitudo et iustitia.*[24]

The basic meaning of *rectitudo* is the divine ordering of the universe, which has its origin in the divine will, and which is itself a reflection of the divine will. Anselm's metaphysical theory of truth considers that the truth of a cognition derives from its *rectitudo*—i.e., it is as it should be. Everything has its own particular *rectitudo;* everything is true in so far as it is what it should be according to its idea in God. Truth is the conformity of what *is* to the rule which fixes what it *should be.* As this rule is itself part of the divine nature, Anselm concludes that there is only one supreme truth, God.[25] Thus truth is basically metaphysical rectitude, conformity to the intended pattern. Of course, Anselm concedes that the notion can bear various derivative meanings—for example, the *veritas* of a proposition such as *Dies est* is evidently *secundum hanc veram eam iudicat usus communis locutionis,*[26] a non-technical notion recognised by common sense.[27] The truth of the proposition *Dies est* clearly depends upon the circumstances, and can this be said to be an extrinsic truth. But the fundamental sense of *veritas* relates to intrinsic truth, metaphysical rectitude in the sense of conformity to the divine will. Thus for Anselm, the answer to the question *Quid est veritas?*[28] requires reference to rectitude.

The concept of justice also requires reference to the fundamental notion of rectitude. Justice has, as its basic sense, the moral rectitude of the universe, the moral order established by God at creation, itself an expression of the divine will and nature. The Augustinian character of this understanding of justice will be evident. The moral ordering of the universe encompasses the relationship between God and man, between man and his fellow men, and between the various existential strata within man (on the neo-Platonic anthropological model favoured by Augustine). Just as Anselm recognized various derivative senses of the term *veritas,* so he also notes them with *iustitia.* Thus human justice is an aspect of *iustitia* in that it reflects the divine ordering of the universe. The regulation of the affairs of men by human justice is an aspect of *iustitia,* but is not identical with it. *Ius* must be based on *iustitia.* The justice which regulates the affairs of men is not equivalent to the justice which God imposed upon himself and his own dealings with man. There is a clear distinction between supreme justice (i.e., God's) and strict justice (i.e., that of man).²⁹ God's moral ordering of the created universe involves both the regulation of the affairs of men, and the self-regulation by God of his dealings with men—but it is not possible to argue that the laws governing each are the same. In its fundamental sense *iustitia* merely refers to moral rectitude—i.e., that God has imposed a moral order upon the universe. It remains to be seen what form this moral ordering takes with respect to the various aspects of creation. This point had already been made by Augustine during the course of the Pelagian controversy. Augustine is prepared to concede the validity of the Ciceronian definition of human justice as 'giving every man his due'.³⁰ Yet when Julian of Eclanum gave the same definition for *divine* justice—i.e., of giving every man what is due to him—Augustine confronted him with the parable of the labourers in the vineyard, illustrating the impropriety of applying this definition of *civil* justice to God's dealings with men.³¹ Strict justice cannot accommodate the concept of grace; supreme justice can.

Man was created in a state of *iustitia originalis,*³² which was forfeited at the Fall. Man's present state is that of *iniustitia.* It must be stressed, however, that the concept of *iustitia originalis* merely provides a convenient summary of the moral rectitude of God's created order, and does not refer to any legal status of man. Anselm states that the basic requirement of *iustitia* is that every inclination of the rational creature be subject to God³³— and this simply amounts to a statement of the place of man in the moral ordering of creation, established by God himself, and reflecting his character as *summa iustitia.* The moral ordering of the universe allots a specific place to man in creation, with a moral obligation to submit his rational nature to God, his Creator. This moral rectitude of the universe was violated by man, and not by God, at the Fall. *Iniustitia* is the privation of *iustitia,*³⁴ and the essence of original sin is the inherited lack of moral rectitude in the will of every fallen man. Before the Fall, Adam was able to submit his rational nature to the divine will; now his successors are incapable of this fundamental obligation laid upon man by God. This represents a significant departure from the Augustinian doctrine of original sin, since the stress on concupiscence is omitted. Indeed, as the es-

sential nature of injustice is that of privation, it cannot be described as a positive entity in itself, but merely the absence of a desirable quality.³⁵

Man's violation of the moral order of creation means that he is no longer capable of submitting his rational nature to God, and therefore that he is incapable of redeeming himself. If man is to be redeemed, a divine act of redemption is required. But man's violation of the moral ordering of the universe at the Fall does not permit God to violate it still further in order to redeem fallen man. God, having established the created moral order, conforms to it himself. This important point is made by Anselm at several points, particularly at that point in the **Cur Deus Homo** where the question why God cannot forgive sins by mercy alone is considered.³⁶ *Si Deus hoc vult, iustum est.*³⁷ Anselm's discussion of this proposition reveals his grave reservations concerning the concept of justice involved. God's freedom in will and in action is limited by his own nature. God is not free to do anything that violates his own nature, since that involves a contradiction. Thus what is just cannot become unjust merely because God wills it, as such an alteration would involve a radical change in the divine nature. God's character as the *summa iustitia* is expressed in the rectitude of the moral order of creation, and the free forgiveness of sins through mercy violates this moral ordering, and is therefore a contradiction of the divine nature. God's attributes are essential to his being, and are not merely accidents which he can change at will. God wills right because it is right. Anselm's important theological insight concerning the divine attributes is that they must co-exist within the limiting conditions that they impose on each other. Thus the rectitude of the established moral order requires that God redeem man in such a way that is acceptable within the limitations of the moral order established by God himself as an expression of his own nature. This is no legalism, but merely a proper insistence upon the moral character of God as *summa iustitia.*

In a very brief review of the accounts traditionally given of the Atonement, Anselm makes it clear that he is unsatisfied with their failure to understand *why* God should have willed to save man: they are merely descriptions of what happened when God *did* deliver mankind, and offer no explanations of why God should save man in the first place, nor of why he chose to save him in the particular way that he did. None of the traditional accounts can be said to be a systematic account of the nature or the necessity of the Atonement. Anselm thus presents an account of the matter based on the concept of *iustitia,* which demonstrates that:

> (1) the redemption of mankind is necessary as a matter of justice;

(2) this redemption is accomplished in a manner which does not violate the moral order of the universe, established by God himself.

We shall consider these two points separately.

If justice be understood as a *lex talionis,* or in the Ciceronian sense of 'giving each his due', it is clearly impossible to consider God's redeeming of mankind as an act of justice. This, however, is not the concept of justice employed by Anselm. For Anselm, the moral rectitude of the created order was violated by man's fall. It is therefore necessary that the moral rectitude of the created order be restored, as its present state is unjust. Because whatever is unjust contradicts God's nature, it is impossible for God to permit this state of affairs to continue. Therefore God's justice necessitates the redemption of mankind. God, as *summa iustitia,* is bound by his own nature to restore the moral rectitude of the created order, and therefore to redeem mankind. Both Augustine and Anselm's predecessor at Bec, Lanfranc, interpreted the Pauline term *iustitia Dei* as the righteousness by which God justifies believers;[38] Anselm adopts a similar interpretation, but for a different reason.

Anselm prefaces his discussion of the method by which God redeemed mankind by considering the rival theory of the 'Devil's rights'. It has often been assumed that the reason for Anselm's devoting considerable space to the refutation of this theory is its importance in the previous treatments of the question. This, however, overlooks the point that the theory made a claim to be based on justice. Anselm, whose theory depends upon a different concept of justice, must first refute the older theory. According to the 'Ransom' theory, the devil had rights over man, which God was bound to respect on account of his just nature. But this is not consonant with Anselm's concept of justice: justice relates to the moral ordering of the universe, which the devil clearly violated in his seduction of man. As the devil is part of the created order, he is subject to the same *iustitia* as that order. Himself a rational being, the devil was under the same moral obligation to submit his will to God. Only if he were outside of God's creation, and could stand aloof from its moral ordering, could this theory of the 'Devil's rights' have any credibility. By his violation of the moral order of the universe, the devil had lost any claim to *iustitia* which God was bound to respect. Anselm therefore dismisses the theory which had been current for so long: *non video quam vim habeat.*[39]

Anselm's own theory can be stated as a series of propositions, if the numerous diversions are ignored. When this is done, the centrality of the concept of justice becomes evident.

1. Man was created in a state of original justice for eternal blessedness;

2. This blessedness requires the perfect and voluntary submission of man's will to God (i.e., justice);

3. Man's present state is that of *iniustitia;*

4. Either this will result in man's being deprived of eternal blessedness, or else the situation must be rectified by an appropriate satisfaction;

5. This satisfaction must exceed the act of disobedience;

6. Man cannot offer anything to God other than the demands of *iustitia,* and on account of his present *iniustitia* he cannot even do this;

7. Therefore God's purpose in creating man has been frustrated;

8. But this is unjust, and involves a contradiction;

9. Therefore a means of redeeming the situation must exist, for justice demands it;

10. Man cannot redeem himself;

11. God could make the necessary satisfaction;

12. Since only God can, and only man ought to, make the required satisfaction, it must be made by a God-man;

13. Therefore the Incarnation is required on the grounds of justice.

The importance of justice at this stage in the argument is often overlooked. The 'syllogism' which demonstrates the necessity of the Incarnation may be stated thus:

A. Only man ought to make the offering for sin—yet he cannot;

B. Only God can make the offering for sin—yet he ought not to.

It is clear that this 'syllogism' can lead to two conclusions:

Either: Only a God-man both can and ought to make the offering for sin; *or* Only a God-man both cannot, and ought not to, make the offering for sin.

From a purely dialectical standpoint, the monograph could equally well be entitled *Cur Deus non homo.* God's justice, however, demands that the moral rectitude of the created order be restored, so that the second conclusion is to be rejected. Justice demands redemption, so a means of redemption must exist.

The weak point in Anselm's soteriology is generally considered to be his discussion of satisfaction.[40] It is not proposed to defend this in the present study. It is clear, however, that Anselm considers the payment of a satisfaction by the God-man to provide a means of satisfying the demands of moral rectitude without in any way violating the established moral order of the universe. It is quite probable that Anselm regarded the satisfaction-merit model provided by penance, and established within the church of his time, as a paradigm for divine remission of human sin which would readily be accepted by his readers as just.

The central problems faced by Anselm in formulating his soteriology were:

> 1. To demonstrate why God should wish to redeem mankind in the first place;
>
> 2. To demonstrate why God should have redeemed man in the particular manner he chose.

Anselm's answers to both these questions, and also to several subsidiary questions raised in the course of his discussion, depend upon the understanding of justice as moral rectitude. To describe Anselm's soteriology as 'legalist', 'feudal' or 'juridical' is to miss the point. It is inevitable that Anselm's concepts should be influenced by the period in which he lived; it is clear, however, that he does not use contemporary concepts of justice in his discussion of the Atonement. His concept of justice is not that of a barbaric Lombard king, but that of a theologian convinced that God created the world in rectitude, and was now acting in accordance with that rectitude to redeem it. Far from representing an unwarranted intrusion on the part of law into religion, Anselm's soteriology represents the application of the conviction that God is just to the basic article of the Christian faith—the redemption of fallen mankind through Christ.

Notes

1. For a discussion of the development of the doctrine of justification within the Western theological tradition, see my *Iustitia Dei: a History of the Doctrine of Justification,* 3 vols (to be published by James Clarke & Co, Cambridge).

2. A von Harnack, *History of Dogma,* 7 vols (London, 1894-99) vol. III, p. 310. See also G. Aulén, *Christus Victor* (London, 1934), pp. 100-09.

3. H. Rashdall, *The Idea of Atonement in Christian Theology* (London, 1920), p. 355.

4. *Proslogion,* 9; *S Anselmi Cantuarensis Archiepiscopi Opera Omnia,* edited F. S. Schmitt (Stuttgart-Bad Cannstatt, 1966) vol. I, p. 106. 18.

5. Vol. I, p. 106. 19-107. 3.

6. Vol. I, p. 107. 16-18.

7. Vol. I, p. 107. 23-6.

8. *Proslogion,* 10; vol. I, p. 109. 4-5 *ita iustus et non quia nobis reddas debitum, sed quia facis* quod decet te summe bonum.

9. *Cur Deus Homo,* I, 12; vol. II, p. 69. 22.

10. Vol. I, 23; vol. II, p. 91. 10; vol. II, p. 91. 15.

11. Vol. I, 23; vol. II, p. 91. 27-28.

12. E.g., see *Monologion,* praefatio; vol. I, p. 8. 9; *De Incarnatione Verbi,* 6; vol. II, p. 20. 14-15.

13. *De Civitate Dei,* XII, 17.

14. See E. Gilson, *History of Christian Philosophy in the Middle Ages* (London, 1978), pp. 77-81.

15. R. A. Markus, *Saeculum: History and Society in the Theology of St Augustine* (Cambridge, 1970), p. 88.

16. For its original statement, see *De Lib. Arb.,* I, vi, 15; I, v, 11.

17. See *Contra Faustum* xii, 27.

18. Cicero, *De Rep.* I, 39 *coetus multitudinis iuris consensu et utilitatis communione societatis.* See M. Testard, *Saint Augustin et Cicéron* (Paris, 1958), vol. II, pp. 39-43.

19. *De Civitate Dei,* XIX, 21.

20. D. P. Henry, *The Logic of St Anselm* (Oxford, 1967), p. 230.

21. *De Veritate,* 13; vol. I, p. 199. 19.

22. *De Veritate,* 2; vol. I, p. 178. 25; *ibid.,* 4; vol. I, p. 181. 3-9; *ibid.,* 10; vol. I, p. 189. 31.

23. *De Veritate,* 12; vol. I, p. 194. 26; *De Casu Diaboli,* 9; vol. I, p. 246. 26-30.

24. *De Veritate,* 12; vol. I, p. 192. 7-8.

25. See E. Gilson, *op. cit.,* pp. 136-9.

26. *De Veritate,* 2; vol. I, p. 179. 14-28.

27. Henry, *op. cit.,* pp. 230-1.

28. John 18, 38.

29. Anselm may have *Cod. Just.* I, 55, 6 in mind.

30. E.g., *De Lib Arb* I, xviii, 27. cf. Cicero, *Rhetoricii Libri duo qui vocantur de Inventione Rhetorica* II, 53 . . . *iustitia est habitus animi, communi utilitate conservata, suam cuique tribuens dignitatem.*

31. *Contra Iulianum,* vol. I, p. 35.

32. E.g., *De Conceptu Virginali,* 2; vol. II, p. 141. 8-11.

33. *Cur Deus Homo,* I, 11; vol. II, p. 68. 12-16.

34. *De Casu Diaboli,* 9; vol. I, p. 246. 26.

35. The influence of Anselm's doctrine of original sin appears to have been minimal until Albertus Magnus defined the formal element of original sin to be privation of justice.

36. *Cur Deus Homo,* I, 12; vol. II, p. 70. 11-30.

37. *Loc. cit.*

38. This is the general interpretation of the phrase in the patristic and scholastic eras—see my *Iustitia Dei,* vol, I for details.

39. Vol. II, p. 56. 2-3.

40. See J. McIntyre, *Anselm and His Critics* (London and Edinburgh, 1954), and especially F. Hammer, *Genugtung und Heil. Absicht, Sinn und Grenzen der Erlösungslehre Anselms von Canterbury* (Wien, 1966).

Allan Bäck (essay date 1981)

SOURCE: Bäck, Allan. "Existential Import in Anselm's Ontological Argument." *Franciscan Studies* 41 (1981): 97-109.

[*In the following essay, Bäck analyzes Anselm's ontological argument in terms of traditional logic, suggesting that criticism of it can be resolved through a consideration of the Aristotelian nature of his syllogistic reasoning.*]

The ontological argument of Saint Anselm has attracted a great deal of attention. There has been considerable discussion of whether the argument begs the question, by assuming the existence of God in the premises of the argument. But, although the theological, Augustinian context of Anselm's argument has been dealt with, and although the argument has been extensively treated in modern logical terms, little attention has been paid to how the argument fares in terms of traditional logic. In this article I shall analyze the argument of *Proslogion* 2 in traditional terms. I shall then argue that to a great extent the debate between Anselm and Gaunilon can be viewed as depending on attitudes toward the Aristotelian syllogistic.[1] In short, the standard for the validity and soundness of arguments in medieval philosophy was the syllogistic. It was apparently assumed that all terms used in the syllogistic have existential import. So Anselm's argument is suspect in that it employs a term, 'that than which nothing greater can be conceived,' which cannot be assumed to have existential import. I then shall offer a solution of this difficulty. I shall argue that the success of the argument of *Proslogion* 2 depends on the modal character of 'that than which nothing greater can be conceived.' That modal character suggests that the argument of *Proslogion* 2 is modal as well. I shall show that there are grounds in theology and in the Aristotelian modal syllogistic for rejecting the existential import assumption, and shall suggest that

Anselm does not make such an assumption, at least in the ontological argument. Rather, despite its assertoric appearance, the argument in *Proslogion* 2 is modal.

I

I shall begin by giving a syllogistic representation of the argument in *Proslogion* 2:[2]

(I) Everything that is understood (*intelligitur*) is existent in the intellect (*est in intellectu*)

That than which nothing greater can be conceived (*aliquid quo nihil maius cogitari possit*) is understood

Therefore, that than which nothing greater can be conceived in existent in the intellect

(II) If that than which nothing greater can be conceived exists in the intellect alone, then that than which nothing greater can be conceived is not that than which nothing greater can be conceived

It is not the case that that than which nothing greater can be conceived is not that than which nothing greater can be conceived

Therefore, that than which nothing greater can be conceived does not exist in the intellect alone

(III) Whatever does not exist in the intellect alone, exists in the intellect and *in re*

(IV) Therefore, that than which nothing greater can be conceived exists in the intellect and *in re*

(V) God is that than which nothing greater can be conceived

(VI) Therefore, God exists in the intellect and *in re*

I shall not be concerned with V and VI. The main problem there concerns the truth and logical form of V.

The "ontological argument" (I-IV) has two syllogistical parts. First there is a categorical syllogism, with the conclusion, "that than which nothing greater can be conceived exists in the intellect." This structure is clearly indicated by the text (". . . quia hoc cum audit intelligit, et quidquid intelligitur in intellectu est"). In the second part Anselm argues that that than which nothing greater can be conceived does not exist merely in the intellect. He shows that, if it is assumed that it did, then a contradiction follows. The form of this second argument is that of a hypothetical conditional syllogism, using *modus tollens.*[3] The third step, which is not that explicit in *Proslogion* 2, is to explain what it means for something not to exist in the intellect only, namely that it exist also *in re*. The claim that things can be arranged in a hierarchy of greatness is needed to establish the truth of the major premise of II.

This analysis of the ontological argument does not make much of the distinction between '*cogitare*' and '*intelligere*' mentioned in *Proslogion* 4 and the **Reply**

(IV and VI) to Gaunilon. However, as Anselm repeatedly says that it makes no difference what sort of understanding of 'that than which nothing greater can be conceived' the Fool has, it appears that for Anselm this distinction is not relevant to the analysis of *Proslogion* 2. Still, it may be that Gaunilon's misgivings about Anselm's indiscriminate use of '*cogitare*' and '*intelligere*' express, albeit darkly, the same problems that arise when Anselm's argument is considered with respect to the Aristotelian syllogistic.

But these remarks by Anselm need to be weighed against his use of '*cogitare*' (conceive) and '*intelligere*' (understand). In *Proslogion* 2 he uses '*intelligere*' and its noun form '*intellectus*' throughout, except when he is talking of the concept 'that than which nothing greater can be conceived' and when he says, "for if it is in the intellect alone, it can be conceived also to be *in re*" ("Si enim vel in solo intellectu est, potest cogitari esse et in re"). In *Proslogion* 3 he uses '*cogitare*' and '*cogitatio*' exclusively. In the Augustinian tradition, '*intelligere*' was commonly used only of things existing *in re*.[4] In general, what is understood to exist can be conceived not to exist, but what is conceived to exist necessarily cannot be understood not to exist. There is thus a progression from *Proslogion* 2 to 3, from proving what must be understood about 'that than which nothing greater can be conceived' to proving what must be conceived about 'that than which nothing greater can be conceived.'[5] Yet the argument in *Proslogion* 2 may still be free of the distinction between '*cogitare*' and '*intelligere*.' The existence of 'that than which nothing greater can be conceived' follows, if the ontological argument works, from the fact that that concept is understood or that it is conceived. I shall in any case ignore this distinction, in order to concentrate on a problem that I consider to be more central to the success of the ontological argument: the validity of the syllogisms there.

That problem is this: Consider the first part of Anselm's argument, the categorical syllogism (I). The minor premise is indefinite, with respect to its logical form. If it is particular or singular, then if the first syllogism is to be sound, it is asserted in the premises that that than which nothing greater can be conceived exists *in re*, just as 'being' is supposedly predicated of other terms. If the minor premise is universal, then the first syllogism yields the conclusion, 'everything that is that than which nothing greater can be conceived exists in the intellect.' But then there is difficulty with the hypothetical syllogism (II). Even if the reasoning of the second syllogism is valid, the conclusion of it will be 'everything that is that than which nothing greater can be conceived does not exist in the mind alone,' and, by III, exists *in re* as well. But then there is required the further step, to get the desired conclusion (IV), of moving from this universal affirmative proposition to its particular counterpart. I.e., from 'everything that is that than which nothing greater can be conceived exists *in re*' it has to follow that something that is that than which nothing greater can be conceived exists *in re*. But this step merely begs the question which the ontological argument was intended to answer. For, if the move from a universal to a particular proposition is allowed, it could be made in the minor premise of I, when that premise is taken universally. In traditional terms, there is a move from A to I, from III, taken universally, to IV.[6]

Now the inference from A to I was asserted in traditional logic. To justify such an inference form requires accepting a condition of existential import: each term used in the syllogistic must have at least one instantiation or member in the domain; if it is asserted that all A are B, there must exist an A and a B. What sort of existence is in question is not entirely clear. But it is clear that it is not the sort of existence something has merely by being conceived or by being logically possible. E.g., just as in modern logic, 'some unicorn has a horn' does not follow from 'every unicorn has a horn,' so, in traditional logic, given the A to I inference, it may not be asserted that every unicorn has a horn without there being some unicorn.[7] Terms in tradional logic must refer to things that exist in a stronger sense than that of being imagined. The conclusion, 'something that is that than which nothing greater can be conceived exists' is meant to assert existence *in re*, objective existence. In short, Anselm is saying that 'that than which nothing greater can be conceived' has the same sort of existence that an A has, when it is asserted that some A is B.

So we can see that, in terms of traditional logic, the use of a term that is not initially assumed to have existential import in what is claimed to be a valid and sound argument is highly suspect. It thus should not be surprising to see Gaunilon making the objection that if Anselm's argument is both valid and sound, then we can prove that anything we can imagine actually exists. Though it is not explicitly intended to make this point, Gaunilon's perfect island example fits in well here. For example, if it is asserted that a perfect island has a hamburger stand, then such an assertion is either particular or universal. If it is particular, then it asserts the existence of a perfect island. If it is universal, and if terms that are merely imagined or conceived may be used in the syllogistic, then it follows by the A to I conversion in the Aristotelian syllogistic that there is a perfect island, and a hamburger stand on it. So in either case, the proof for the existence of the perfect island is begged, since it is assumed in the initial premise.

Professor Hochberg makes the counterpart of the point that I am making about the ontological argument, in modern logical terms.[8] He claims that 'that than which nothing greater can be conceived' is a definite description. Since all definite descriptions, according to Russell, carry an existential quantifier, an assertion about a definite description carries with in the assertion that there exists a thing satisfying that description. Similarly, in traditional logic, to use a tem in a syllogistic proposition requires that that term have existential import.

The language used by Anselm leaves him open to a charge of begging the question. 'That than which nothing greater can be conceived' is a translation of *'aliquid quo maius nihil cogitari potest.'* The *'aliquid'* lends itself to be taken as indicating an existential quantifier. Then the minor premise of the categorical syllogism would be 'there is something than which nothing greater can be conceived, which is conceived.' Even *'id'* indicates a 'this,' and in the Aristotelian tradition a 'this' is a substance, an existent one. Anselm himself says, "But 'this' and 'which' are properly said only of that which is something," where 'something' clearly designates what exists *in re*.[9] So his use of *'aliquid'* and *'id'* is evidence against Anselm, that he has begged the question in the ontological argument.

II

What can be said in Anselm's defense? I shall argue that Anselm has departed from the Aristotelian tradition by not using the existential import assumption, and that his departure is justifiable, if not correct, in terms of Aristotelian modal logic. In order to make this point clear, we need to consider Anselm's views on modality.

In general, Anselm follows the modal logic of Aristotle as given by Boethius in the old logic.[10] But Anselm was especially familiar with the discussion of modality in *On Interpretation.*[11]

Henry points out that Anselm sanctions the inference from 'x can' (*'potest'*) to 'x is able' (*'est potens'*).[12] Thereby Anselm has an entry into Aristotle's distinction between potentiality (δονατόν) and actuality (ἐνεργεια).[13] For, if x is able, x has an ability or power (*potestas*). Anselm distinguishes sense of 'power':

> I know that there are two abilities: 1) an ability which is not yet *in re*, and 2) an ability which is already *in re*. (Scio duas esse potestates: unam, quae nondum est in re; alteram quam iam est in re).[14]

We may call these two senses potential and actual respectively.[15] However, not all things have abilities in both senses. The Magister goes on to dismiss the potential sense, when he talks of the world: "before it was, it was not able to be (Non ergo potuit esse, antequam esset)."[16] He still asserts that it was possible to make the world, but it was not possible for the world to come to be *per se*, on its own efforts.

Anselm is claiming that we cannot say that something has powers before it exists, because there is no thing to have these powers. So, then, 'that than which nothing greater can be conceived' cannot be said to have powers before its existence is established. But Anselm makes statements about the world before it exists; e.g., 'the world was conceived by God.' Moreover, he talks of the properties of that than which nothing greater can be conceived, presumably without assuming that it exists. How can Anselm make such assertions when he claims that before the existence of a thing is given, it has no powers, e.g., of having properties in the future?

Anselm is able to maintain this position because he holds that something may be conceived without existing *in re*. The world has no power in itself to come to be *in re*, but God, or some other external cause, has the power to make it come to be *in re*. Anselm holds that "the world was nothing before it existed";[17] 'nothing' here indicates that it was not then something *in re*. Still, if God is able to conceive what He creates, the world can be conceived without existing *in re*.

Similarly, before its existence *in re* is shown or acknowledged, that than which nothing greater can be conceived has no powers of the sort an actually existent object has, i.e., actual powers, but has those qualities or potential powers that an existent mind ascribes to it *qua* mental object, *in intellectu*. So all the being that a mental object has that does not point out something *in re* is given to it by an external cause, namely, the mind that conceives it. What has the power or possibility is not the world, but God, the being who is conceiving and will create the world. The grammatical structure is deceptive. When it is said, 'the book can be written by me,' it is not asserted that the book has a power, for, since the book does not exist yet, there does not exist a thing to have the power. Instead, I, who do exist, have the power to write the book.[18] "What is in no way, has no power" (Quod nullo modo est, nullam habet potestatem).[19]

It should be noted that Anselm's conception of possibility is what we would call physical possibility, not logical possibility.[20] For Anselm would deny that it is possible for me to write a book, before I or the book exists, but on the logical view of possibility there has always been a possible world in which I exist and where I have written that book. Again, for Anselm, I cannot fly, since I do not have that ability, even though it is logically possible for me to fly.

How is Anselm's view of possibility related to how he handles 'that than which nothing greater can be conceived'? When he argues that that than which nothing greater can be conceived is understood, Anselm does not mean to assert that there is some thing that is that than which nothing greater can be conceived, that has the power of being understood. The reason why it is understood, at least at the beginning of *Proslogion* 2, is that there is something existent, namely the mind of the Fool, and that mind has the power of conceiving things that do not exist. Even the Fool cannot doubt that he has a mind and can conceive.[21] Just as God, as a thing existing *in re,* has the power to conceive things that do not exist *in re,* so a human being has the power to conceive of things that do not exist *in re.*

Now this explanation does not account for the problem raised at the beginning of this article, with respect to the validity of the ontological argument. But it does explain why Anselm thinks that it is proper to use a term without assuming that there is something *in re* to which that term refers. Similarly, in ordinary language, though perhaps not in analytic philosophy, we make true statements about unicorns without assuming that unicorns exist, in the way that chairs and cows exist. The claim of the ontological argument (through *Proslogion* 3) is that of these imaginary concepts only that than which nothing greater can be conceived is such that included in its concept are the claims that it exist *in re* and that it cannot be conceived not to exist *in re.*

On this interpretation, 'that than which nothing greater can be conceived' would function as a singular term. For just as 'the world,' when God conceives it before Creation, refers to a single thing, which God is deciding to make, so too 'that than which nothing greater can be conceived' is a concept of an individual thing, at the beginning of *Proslogion* 2. That this is Anselm's position is seen by the fact that at the beginning of *Proslogion* 3 he refers to 'that than which nothing greater can be conceived' by a singular term ('*quod*'). Again, Anselm introduces 'that than which nothing greater can be conceived' by saying that 'you' ('God,' a singular term) are that concept. Moreover, Anselm nowhere proves that 'that than which nothing greater can be conceived' must refer to no more than a single being. The proof for this is relatively simple, but Anselm does omit this step in the *Proslogion.*[22] Now if Anselm considered the conclusion of *Proslogion* 2 to be universal in form, he would have been compelled to make this proof explicit, to rule out polytheism. That he does not give this proof strongly suggests that he views 'that than which nothing greater ca be conceived' to be a singular term.

Anselm thinks that he can use singular terms, like 'the world,' without assuming the existence of things referred to by them *in re.* We think that we can too, when we think of an individual thing with respect to a future or counterfactual context. We tend to think of terms like 'my grandson' or 'my sister' (when I have neither) as referring to things that do not exist, but

could exist, in some sense of 'could' (logical or physical possibility). But the justification for our talking of such things is that we view them as possible, since we are able to conceive them.

Anselm seems to have a similar attitude toward 'that than which nothing greater can be conceived,' in *Proslogion* 2. When he holds that that term represents a concept that is in the intellect, he suggests that that term represents something possible. Indeed, Henry claims that *Proslogion* 2 is "in the region of the Anselmian modal conplex," since if '*cogitari*' ('to be conceived') is omitted, the argument becomes obviously modal.[23] *Proslogion* 2 would then purport to prove, from assuming that that than which nothing greater can be conceived is possible, i.e., that it possibly exists, that it exists. *Proslogion* 3 then draws the further conclusion, that that than which nothing greater can be conceived necessarily exists.

These considerations, then, suggest that *Proslogion* 2, despite first appearances, is fundamentally a modal argument. And in that case the syllogisms that I have extracted from that chapter need to be reexamined with respect to their structure.

The conclusion of the first syllogism (I) is 'that than which nothing greater can be conceived is existent in the intellect.' That is, the conclusion is that anyone can understand that concept. So the mind (of the Fool) has the power of conceiving 'that than which nothing greater can be conceived,' just as God has the power of conceiving the world before it existed, since at this point in the argument it is not conceived that that than which nothing greater can be conceived is something existent, and only existent things have powers. Then Anselm argues in syllogism II that that than which nothing greater can be conceived can be conceived to exist *in re* by the mind, and indeed must be so conceived if that concept is to be thought truly. The mind has the power of conceiving that concept as existent, and is compelled to do so by the nature of that concept. That is, the mind does not have the power to conceive that that than which nothing greater can be conceived does not exist *in re* (necessary = not possible not).

In the ontological argument, unlike in Creation, the human mind does not will the concept into existence *in re.* But the mind conceives many things without creating them. I may conceive of a fish, but I do not thereby will that fish into existence, as fishermen know.

So *Proslogion* 2 concerns a singular term, the definite description, 'that than which nothing greater can be conceived.' It first is argued that the human mind has the power to conceive it. It then follows, from the meaning of the concept, that the mind has no power not to conceive it to be instantiated, to be *in re.* Anselm has not begged the question by introducing a singular term that does not exist *in re,* because he does not hold that all singular terms have existential import. He holds this position because minds have the power of conceiving what does not exist *in re.* God does not create all that he conceived, nor do men conceive only of what exists *in re.*

'Existing in the intellect' thus amounts to 'being possible.' The Fool has the power of understanding what is in his intellect, as there is nothing preventing him from understanding it. 'That than which nothing greater can be conceived is possible (possibly exists)' is true, since the Fool can think of that concept. Chimeras and unicorns are in the intellect, and, while they do not in fact exist, their existence is (logically) possible.[24] When that than which nothing greater can be conceived is asserted to be in the intellect, it has the status of the perfect island; it could exist.

The argument of *Proslogion* 2 can then be reformulated. Syllogism I will be:

> What is understood is in the intellect (is possible)
> That than which nothing greater can be conceived is
>   understood
> Therefore, that than which nothing greater can be
>   conceived is in the intellect (is possible)

The second syllogism will remain unchanged, and point out a feature of the possible object. It argues that possible existence is not the only property of existence that the concept, 'that than which nothing greater can be conceived,' has. The mind does not have the power of conceiving that concept without conceiving it to exist. (Those who claim they can either are mouthing words or are thinking of another concept). So, given that the Fool can conceive 'that than which nothing greater can be conceived,' and that when he conceives it he must conceive it to be instantiated, it follows that even the Fool has the power of knowing the existence of God. It is up to him to use this power, but he cannot deny the existence of God.

The ontological argument has the form of something like the admirable consequent.[25] From an atheist position, a theist position is deduced. As the admirable consequent was later thought to be the strongest form of proof, it is not surprising to find Anselm elated with his discovery.

So the ontological argument has this form: First Anselm argues (I) that that than which nothing greater can be conceived is possible, i.e., is possibly existent. Then (II & III) he argues that if it is possibly existent, it is actually existent.[26]

Aristotle's syllogistic needs to be changed to accommodate Anselm's new conception of possibility. In the Aristotelian modal syllogistic, all terms have existential import.[27] If 'grik' means 'blue swan,' then for Aristotle 'it is possible that griks are three-legged' assumes that there has been a blue swan. Yet Anselm holds that blue swans are possible without there having been one. That is, minds have powers of conceiving blue swans regardless of their existence in past or future. Anselm's motivation for these logical changes appears to be mostly theological: God the Creator should not be limited by the physical laws of the world that he chooses to create. Aristotle, believing that the world is eternal and uncreated, need not be concerned with preserving the freedom of a creator. . . .

So I am saying that *Proslogion* 2 gives a modal argument for the existence of God, which is quite similar to the argument that philosophers like Malcolm and Hartshorne locate in *Proslogion* 3. It has long been recognized that the argument in *Proslogion* 3 is modal. I submit that for the argument in *Proslogion* 2 to be valid, in traditional logic, the argument there must be rendered modally too.

Notes

1. I do not mean to suggest that Anselm had a complete Aristotelian syllogistic to use. However, I do claim that he had certain elements of that syllogistic at his disposal, viz., the conversion of A, E, I, and O propositions and the basic forms of Barbara, *modus ponens,* and *modus tollens.* Cf. Desmond Paul Henry, *The Logic of Saint Anselm* (London, 1967), p. 7 & pp. 240-42. In any case, my project here is simply to analyze the argument in terms of Aristotelian logic.

2. Arthur McGill, "Recent Discussions of Anselm's Argument," in *The Many-Faced Argument,* ed. Hick & McGill (New York, 1967), p. 39, speaks of syllogisms in *Proslogion* 2, but never puts the argument into syllogistic form.

   Jonathan Barnes, in *The Ontological Argument* (London, 1972), pp. 4-5, gives a syllogistical analysis for the conclusion 'God exists,' but does not emphasize the syllogistical structure with *Proslogion* 2.

   The simplicity of the formulation that I give fits in well with how Anselm views the *Proslogion:* ". . . reflecting that this (*Monologion*) was made up of a connected chain of many arguments, I began to wonder if it might perhaps be possible to find one single argument that for its proof required no other save itself . . ."; *St. Anselm's Proslogion,* trans. Charlesworth (Oxford, 1965), p. 103.

3. Henry, op. cit., p. 242, claims that Anselm uses the hypothetical *modus tollendo tollens* in *De*

Grammatico too. On my analysis of the argument cf. Anselm's *Reply:* "Now whatever can be thought and does not actually exist would not be, if it should exist, 'that-than-which-a-greater-cannot-be-thought.' If, therefore, it were 'that-than-which-a-greater-cannot-be-thought, it would not be that-than-which-a-greater-cannot-be thought,' which is completely absurd. It is, then, false, that something-than-which-a-greater-cannot-be-thought does not exist if it can merely be thought . . .," trans. Charlesworth, op. cit., pp. 170-71.

4. Cf. St. Augustine, *De Libero Arbitrio,* II.3.14; II.6.11; II.7.19; II.8.64; II.10.31.

5. Henry, op. cit., pp. 143-45; Charlesworth, op. cit., p. 62.

6. Barnes, op. cit., p. 73, makes much of this problem, and concludes that a particular form of the ontological argument is thereby invalid.

7. However, cf. *Prior Analytics* 49a23, where 'goat-stag' is used in the syllogistic, and cf. *Sophistical Refutations* 167a1.

8. Herbert Hochberg, "St. Anselm's Argument and Russell's Theory of Descriptions," *The New Scholasticism,* 33 (1959) 319-30.

9. *De Casu Diaboli* 11, trans. Hopkins, in *Truth, Freedom, and Evil* (New York, 1967).

10. Henry, op. cit., p. 135; Charlesworth, op. cit., p. 15.

11. Henry, op. cit., p. 165.

12. Ibid, pp. 134-36.

13. Cf. *On Interpretation* 21b15.

14. *De Casu Diaboli,* 12.

15. Cf. *De Anima* 412a22.

16. *De Casu Diaboli* 12.

17. Ibid.

18. Ibid.

19. Quoted in Henry, op. cit., p. 158.

20. Cf. McGill, op. cit., pp. 85-87; Henry, op. cit., pp. 140-42.

21. Cf. St. Augustine, *City of God,* XI.27.

22. Spinoza offers a proof in *Ethics* I.V & XIII; cf. *Monologion* 1.

23. Henry, op. cit., p. 146.

24. It may be that Anselm's views can be put as follows: What is in the intellect is physically possible, and what is in concept (*in cogitatione*) is logically possible. Since Anselm does not think that it makes any difference whether the Fool understands or conceives 'that than which nothing greater can be conceived,' we may assume that the lesser, logical possibility is being used here— the same possibility that describes the status of objects in the mind of the Creator before Creation.

25. Kneale & Kneale, *The Development of Logic* (London, 1962), pp. 173-74.

26. B. M. Bonansea, (in "Scotus and Anselm's Ontological Argument," in *Studia Scholastico Scotistica, Acta Congressus Scotistici Internationalis,* 1966, II, 473) has observed that Scotus offers an emendation of Anselm's proof, wherein "the possibility of a supreme conceivable being is established," and then from its possibility the actual existence of a supreme conceivable being is proved. My claim here is that Anselm himself offers, in a less explicit fashion, the same proof in syllogism I. I do not wish to denigrate the worth of Scotus' contribution; Scotus has made the argument more explicit. "*Summum cogitabile*" would seem to demand a proof of its possibility more than "*id quo nihil maius cogitari possit,*" as Anselm recognizes in the *Monologion.*

27. Ignacio Angelelli, "The Aristotelian Modal Syllogistic in Modern Modal Logic," in *Konstruktionem Versus Positionem,* ed. K. Lorenz (Berlin, 1979), pp. 181, 204.

Donald F. Duclow (essay date January 1982)

SOURCE: Duclow, Donald F. "Anselm's *Proslogion* and Nicholas of Cusa's Wall of Paradise." *Downside Review* 100, no. 338 (January 1982): 22-30.

[*In the following essay, Duclow juxtaposes Anselm's ontological argument with the symbolism of Nicholas of Cusa's "wall of paradise" in order to emphasize Anselm's use of limit or boundary thinking in his* Proslogion.]

Perhaps Gilson gave the best excuse for presenting yet another essay on Anselm's **Proslogion** when he wrote that one simply cannot resist the temptation.[1] An author does, however, need some justification for indulging his concupiscence. I would therefore make two claims for the following essay. First, it develops a new comparison between Anselm and Nicholas of Cusa. In particular, discussion of Cusanus's 'wall of paradise' discloses the implicit structure of the **Proslogion's** argument. Second, this comparison suggests a re-interpretation of the **Proslogion** in terms of phenomenology and contemporary hermeneutics. I shall first develop the textual comparison in some detail. Then, in evaluating the analogy, I shall briefly indicate its relation to contemporary thought.

I

Comparisons of Anselm and Nicholas of Cusa are appropriate for several reasons. First of all, there are clear historical connections between them. Nicholas occasionally cites Anselm by name, and in Cusanus's library there is a twelfth-century manuscript of Anselm's works.[2] While this manuscript contains several of Anselm's major works, it unfortunately has neither the **Monologion** nor the **Proslogion**. Nevertheless, there are structural similarities between Cusanus's teaching on the divine maximum and Anselm's argument in the **Proslogion,** as when Nicholas writes of the *maximum, quo nihil maius esse potest.*[3] Cusanus also echoes the **Proslogion** quite directly when he describes God as *id quo maius concipi nequit.*[4] Since Dangelmayr and Flasch have already discussed these similarities,[5] I propose a slightly different comparison between Cusanus's symbolism of the wall of paradise and Anselm's **Proslogion**.

Nicholas of Cusa's *De docta ignorantia* (1440) provoked a prolonged controversy over mystical theology.[6] During this controversy, Cusanus wrote several works, including *De visione Dei* (1453) which develops the spiritual vision appropriate to learned ignorance. Addressed to the Benedictine monks of Tegernsee, the *De visione Dei* resembles Anselm's **Proslogion** since it too is an *alloquium* or colloquy which blends intense spirituality, richly symbolic language and novel speculative analysis. Suggestive as this formal similarity may be, for this comparison I shall isolate one image from *De visione Dei,* that of the wall of paradise. Selection of this image is scarcely arbitrary, since it expresses two of Cusanus's major themes: the coincidence of opposites, and divine infinity.

Cusanus presents the wall of paradise as a gloss on the account in *Genesis* of fallen man's exile. He writes, 'I have discovered the place where You [God] are found unveiled. It is surrounded by the coincidence of opposites. This is the wall within which you dwell. . . . Therefore, You may be seen on the far side of the coincidence of opposites, but not on this side of it.'[7] In this image we find three elements: the enclosed garden where God dwells, the wall of paradise, and the exterior realm of exile. As Nicholas interprets the image, each element assumes precise meaning. Outside the wall is the region of finite distinction, where opposites are distinguished by the logic of non-contradiction. Here unity is distinct from multiplicity, beginnings from ends, etc. Reason (*ratio*) rules this realm, and with its flaming

sword bars entry to the garden. For the wall's 'door is guarded by highest . . . reason, and unless it is conquered the entrance will not be open' (*VD* 132, IX). The wall itself is the coincidence of opposites, where the power of reason gives way to intellectual insight (*intellectus*). The distinctions of reason are unified in the wall, since it is 'that coincidence where later coincides with earlier, where the end coincides with the beginning, where Alpha and Omega are the same' (*VD* 136, X). Here rational knowledge passes into learned ignorance, whose dialectic then leads to the final element in Cusanus's image: the central, enclosed garden where the infinite God dwells. 'When I see You [God] as absolute infinity . . . then I begin to see You unveiled and to enter the garden of delights. You are no such thing as can be spoken of or conceived, but are infinitely and absolutely superexalted above all such things' (*VD* 144, XII). Here Cusanus turns from the logic of coincidence to the Dionysian *via negativa.* For as utterly transcendent, this divine infinity is beyond both the distinction and the coincidence of opposites.

Nicholas further argues that all three elements of the image form a unified structure which begins and ends in the infinite God. He writes, 'Because we admit that there is an end of the finite, we necessarily admit the infinite, or the ultimate end, or the end without end. But we cannot not admit finite beings, and thus cannot not admit the infinite. Therefore, we admit the coincidence of contradictories, above which is the infinite' (*VD* 148, XIII). The full implications of the image now become clear. The 'external', finite region by its very nature has an end or limit, which the wall of paradise represents, and beyond which is divine infinity. Finitude, limit and infinity thus constitute a dialectical pattern, within which thinking is continually in motion. Cusanus uses the wall of paradise to illustrate this motion: 'I go in from creatures to You the creator, from effects to their cause; I go out from You the creator to creatures, from the cause to the effects. I go in and go out simultaneously when I see that going out is going in, and that going in is simultaneously going out' (*VD* 140, XI). Realizing this unity of going in and going out, thinking finds itself in the 'wall of coincidence, beyond which You [God] exist, utterly free from everything that can be said or thought'.[8] In sum, Cusanus's wall of paradise symbolizes the limit-situation of thinking; it is the fluid boundary where thinking oscillates between finite opposition and infinite unity. And in this oscillation, thinking discloses the common genesis of thinking and being in actual, divine infinity.

Anselm's **Proslogion** displays a similar symbolic context and speculative structure. Anselm frames the **Proslogion** between an elaborately rhetorical lament for man's fallen state (ch. I) and an ecstatic anticipation of man's restoration to God (ch. XXV-XXVI). In this way, the ***Proslogion*** shares the common Christian symbolism and devotional context of Cusanus's wall of paradise. More significant, however, is the structural similarity between Cusanus's interpretation of this symbolism and Anselm's argument. Here I shall consider Anselm's argument as extending through the entire ***Proslogion,*** rather than as confined to the *locus classicus* of chapters II-IV. In the 'Preface' Anselm claims that the ***Proslogion*** develops 'one single argument' which concerns not only God's existence, but also his supreme goodness and 'whatever we believe about the Divine Being'.⁹ The argument thus continues well beyond the early chapters' discussion of God's existence, and is complete only at the work's end. This extended context permits a full comparison with Cusanus's image, and may yield a more adequate interpretation of the *Proslogion* itself.

The structural analogy that I propose is the following: like Cusanus's wall of paradise, Anselm's *id quo maius cogitari nequit* (***Pr.*** 101, II) and its variants articulate the limit-situation of thinking. As though claiming 'Beyond this nothing can be thought', Anselm marks out the boundary between the thinkable and that which transcends thinking. Like Cusanus's wall, this boundary looks two ways: toward the region of finite distinction and contingent being, and toward God who is infinitely *maius quam cogitari possit* (***Pr.*** 112, XV) and has *maxime omnium . . . esse* (***Pr.*** 103, III). Given this double directedness, 'that than which a greater cannot be thought' is not one concept among others, but the very limit of the conceivable. Anselm underlines the distinctiveness of this limit with the negativity of each formulation of the argument: 'something than which *nothing* greater can be thought', 'that than which a greater *cannot* be thought', etc. In their negativity, these formulations lack the determinacy of a positive concept; they rather indicate the boundary of all finite conceptions and contingent being, since none of these is adequate to the God who 'dwells in inaccessible light'. As Gillian Evans remarks, for Anselm

> That which is higher than all things lies at the boundary of our understanding. So we cannot fully understand it, and we must be content to know that it is there. . . . It is therefore essential to our powers of understanding that God should be regarded as coming to meet us precisely at the limit of our understanding, and that we should recognize that where understanding ends, God is to be found.¹⁰

In the context of the ***Proslogion*** as a whole, chapters II-IV present God at the limit of thinking, and Anselm then sets himself in that limit and looks toward the garden of delights. Yet it is not a purely affective contemplation, but the very dialectic of ***Proslogion*** II-IV that effects this transition. In chapter XV Anselm says, 'Therefore, Lord, not only are You that than which a greater cannot be thought, but You are also something

greater than can be thought. For since it is possible to think that there is such a one, then, if You are not this same being, something greater than You could be thought—which cannot be.'¹¹ Here Anselm attains learned ignorance since he 'now knows why it is that God dwells in impenetrable light: God is greater than can be thought'.¹² This new awareness of divine transcendence and unknowability in ***Proslogion*** XV develops from the negative formulations of chapters II-IV in two related ways. First, the applicability of *quiddam maius quam cogitari possit* to God is deduced directly from the earlier formulations. Second, and more fundamentally, this deduction completes the self-transcending dialect of thinking. Whereas *quo maius cogitari nequit* expresses thinking at its limit, *quiddam maius quam cogitari possit* thrusts beyond that limit toward God's ultimate inconceivability. As other commentators have noted, this apophatic turn places the ***Proslogion*** within the tradition of the *via negativa*.¹³

Nor do the similarities between Cusanus and Anselm end with this description of thinking's limits and acknowledgement of divine transcendence. For both Nicholas and Anselm proceed to characterize divine being in terms of infinity. Following Augustine, Anselm correlates divine infinity with spiritual being and omnipresence:

> That is unlimited which is wholly everywhere at once; and this is true only of You alone. That, however, is limited and unlimited at the same time which, while wholly in one place, can at the same time be wholly somewhere else but not everywhere; and this is true of created spirits. For if the soul were not wholly in each of the parts of its body it would not sense wholly in each of them. You then, O Lord, are unlimited and eternal in a unique way and yet other spirits are also unlimited and eternal.¹⁴

In discussing God's eternity, Anselm also uses the language of coincidence and infinity. Commenting on the 'age of ages', he says, 'Just as an age of time contains all temporal things, so Your eternity contains also the very ages of time. Indeed, this [eternity] is an "age" because of its indivisible unity, but "ages" because of its immensity without limit.'¹⁵ Further, as Cusanus speaks of infinite simplicity beyond all opposites and contrasts, Anselm writes, 'You [God] are unity not divisible by any mind. Life and wisdom and other [attributes], then, are not parts of You, but all are one and each of them is wholly what You are and what all the others are.'¹⁶ In each of these discussions, Anselm looks beyond the contrasts of finite being and toward divine infinity. The analogy between Cusanus and Anselm is now complete: Anselm's argument parallels Cusanus's wall of paradise in overcoming finite distinctions, and in insisting on the limit of thinking and on divine infinity. Cusanus's threefold pattern of finite, limit and infinite thus expresses the implicit structure of the ***Proslogion.***

While Anselm and Cusanus share this basic pattern, each perceives it differently. Concerning the *via negativa* and divine transcendence, Cusanus claims that the divine nature is *essentially* hidden and unknowable. For Anselm, however, it is not only the excessive brilliance of God's light that renders it inaccessible, but also and primarily man's fallen state which has weakened our vision of God (***Pr.*** 111-13, XIV-XVII). Further, while Cusanus develops a systematic doctrine of divine infinity, Anselm's God is infinite in the traditional Augustinian sense of omnipresence, eternity and unity. Finally, whereas Nicholas thematizes the limit-situation in the logic of coincidence, Anselm posits it as a basic intuition which yields a different rule for thinking about God, who is 'whatever it is better to be than not to be'.[17] Even when this rule gives way to the apophatic turn of ***Proslogion*** XV, Anselm does not develop as thoroughgoing and radical a negative theology as does Cusanus. With Dangelmayr we can trace these differences to Anselm's reliance on Augustine and Cusanus's primarily Dionysian Neoplatonism.[18] Yet this contrast should obscure neither the family resemblance of Neoplatonism in its Augustinian and Dionysian forms, nor the structural similarity between Anselm's ***Proslogion*** and Cusanus's wall of paradise.

II

With our comparison complete, let us briefly examine its implications for the truth of Anselm's argument. We may begin with a critique of Gaunilo's classic discussion of ***Proslogion*** II-IV. In his ***Proslogion*** Anselm insists that Gaunilo has mis-interpreted the ***Proslogion,*** and that 'Nowhere in all that I have said will you find such an argument' as Gaunilo foists upon Anselm.[19] This conflict of interpretations is historically important because Gaunilo's critique has provided the standard reading of the 'ontological argument'. Yet the analogy with Cusanus clarifies these conflicting interpretations, and supports Anslem's response. For Gaunilo omits precisely those negative, limiting features which Anselm and Cusanus use to articulate the ontological difference between divine infinity and finite being. The contrast between Anselm and Gaunilo is evident in their very language, for Gaunilo's formulations lack the fluidity and boundary character of Anselm's language of comparison, conceivability and negation.[20] Where Anselm speaks of conceivability and its limit, Gaunilo speaks of a determinate concept. But Anselm's *quo nihil maius cogitari possit* can be neither adequately compared to Gaunilo's lost island, nor translated into his *aliquid omnibus maius,*[21] since by their determinate, positive nature these formulations set Anselm's argument within the finite domain, and hence 'outside' Cu-

sanus's wall of paradise. While Anselm correctly insists on the negativity and distinctiveness of his argument, Gaunilo consistently gives it affirmative form and views it as one concept among many. In the light of so serious a misinterpretation, it is unfortunate that Gaunilo's statement of Anselm's position has become canonical. Interpreters like Gaunilo should reject Anselm's argument, because they have failed to understand it from the beginning.

But if we consider the argument of chapters II-IV in relation to the entire ***Proslogion*** and to Cusanus, we may acknowledge its validity. For then ***Proslogion*** II-IV marks but one phase of a meditation which discloses a previously hidden presence, and the argument's truth hinges upon the success of this disclosure. The ***Proslogion's*** devotional character, its boundary language, and Anselm's doctrine of truth support this interpretation. Throughout the ***Proslogion*** Anselm seeks a progressive disclosure of God's concealed presence, as when he says,

> O supreme and inaccessible light; O whole and blessed truth, how far You are from me who am so close to You! How distant You are from my sight while I am so present to Your sight! You are wholly present everywhere and I do not see You. In You I move and in You I have my being and I cannot come near to You. You are within me and around me and I do not have any experience of You.[22]

In the ***Proslogion*** Anselm seeks to move from faith into an understanding and experience of God's presence. For these purposes, the rhetoric of persuasion and devotion is as fundamental to advancing the work's 'one single argument' as is Anselm's dialectical virtuosity. He designs both his rhetoric and dialectic so as to engage his audience and drive us to the boundaries of language and understanding, where the hidden God emerges. In the light of the comparison with Cusanus, the ***Proslogion***'s limit character here becomes crucial. Anselm uses dialectic as 'a lever whereby thought is raised above finite thinking to become insight into the reality of God, which is radically different from knowledge of the real things of the world'.[23] He also evokes God's presence in prayer, biblical allusion and all the devices of Augustinian rhetoric, which yield affective and experiential insight.

Although narrowly formal analyses of ***Proslogion*** II-IV have dominated studies of Anselm's 'ontological argument', they fail to address either the work's full scope or Anselm's conception of truth. As ***De veritate*** makes clear, Anselm's doctrine of truth includes strong normative, practical and ontological dimensions. He defines truth as rectitude, and anchors propositional truth in the truth of action and of being.[24] For these reasons, philosophical analogues for Anselm's argument may be found less in contemporary logic than in existential phenomenology, especially Jaspers's and Heidegger's explorations of the 'horizon' of thinking and Being.[25] Jaspers's central theme is the boundary situation of human experience and thinking, and Heidegger discusses truth as the disclosure or unconcealment of Being. The relevance of these themes to the *Proslogion* is evident. For rather than moving from concept to existence, Anselm's argument moves consistently *within* being, from the questing activity of thinking to its boundary and existential foundation. Because it articulates the self-transcending limit of thinking, the *Proslogion* suggests the distinctive mode of divine existence: God cannot exist as a finite object to which a concept may or may not conform, but must rather exist as an infinite unity which is 'greater than can be thought'. As Jaspers comments, 'In Anselm God is present without becoming an object'.[26] The truth of the *Proslogion* and its argument consists in their fidelity to the limit-situation of human thinking, and in their partial disclosure of the elusive God beyond that boundary.

Our inquiry cannot halt with this affirmation of the argument's truth, since we have yet to take the whole limit-situation into account. For if Cusanus's symbol and Anselm's argument point to the infinity and existence of God, they simultaneously point to the limited conditions of human reflection. The *Proslogion* and *De visione Dei* address the concerns of specific Benedictine monastic communities, and use traditional symbolism to articulate intensely personal quests for meaning. In particular, both works rely on the account in Genesis of man's fall and exile, and seek experiential, redemptive insight. This emphasis on history, belief and symbol highlights a central ambiguity in the *Proslogion.* On the one hand, Anselm starts from faith so that he may understand, and, on the other, claims for his argument a power such that 'if I did not want to *believe* that You [God] existed, I should nevertheless be unable not to *understand* it'.[27] Anselm's thinking is rooted in faith and its cultural context, yet also achieves its own autonomy. Commentators like Barth and Stolz have emphasized the former, while philosophical analyses have generally concentrated on the latter.[28] But neglect of either phase seriously distorts our interpretation of the *Proslogion,* where Anselm sustains a paradoxical tension between understanding's dependence on faith and its autonomy.

To do justice to this tension, we may turn to the hermeneutics of Paul Ricoeur. In developing his 'essentially Anselmian schema', Ricoeur restates the *Proslogion's* dialectic of faith and understanding as follows: 'The symbol gives rise to thought', which in turn begins its own inquiry into the symbol's meanings and foundations.[29] Interpretation thus requires a double vision

which both attends to the conditioned reality of history and culture, and remains open to the trans-historical truth of their symbolic and speculative creations. Only this double vision is adequate to the limit-situation, where thinking oscillates between the given, finite standpoint of the human subject, and the transcendent horizon of God. For the issues of divine infinity and transcendence emerge only within the life-world of belief, culture and tradition. In this light, the truth of Cusanus's symbolism and Anselm's argument is both necessary in virtue of the enduring structure of the limit-situation, and contingent upon the symbolic matrix of medieval Christianity and upon the personal and practical attitude of faith.

Notes

1. E. Gilson, 'Sens et nature de l'argument de Saint Anselme', *Archives d'histoire doctrinale et littéraire du moyen âge* IX (1934), p. 5.

2. Listed in J. Marx, *Verzeichnis der Handschriften-Sammlung des Hospitals zu Cues* (Trier, 1905), pp. 67-68.

3. Nicholas of Cusa, *De beryllo*, in *Philosophisch-Theologische Schriften,* ed. L. Gabriel, German trans. W. and D. Dupré (Vienna, 1964-67) III, p. 8 (ch. 7). See the classic discussion in Cusanus, *De docta ignorantia, Schriften* I, pp. 199ff. (bk I, ch. 2ff.); translated by J. Hopkins in *Nicholas of Cusa on Learned Ignorance* (Minneapolis, 1981), pp. 51ff.

4. Cusanus, *Apologia doctae ignorantiae, Schriften* I, p. 534; translated by J. Hopkins in *Nicholas of Cusa's Debate with John Wenck* (Minneapolis, 1981), p. 48. See also Cusanus, *De principio, Schriften* II, p. 242: *'quo melius cogitari nequit'*.

5. S. Dangelmayr, 'Maximum und Cogitare bei Anselm und Cusanus', *Analecta Anselmiana* IV, 1 (1975), pp. 203-10; 'Anselm und Cusanus', *Analecta Anselmiana* III (1971), pp. 112-40; and K. Flasch, *Die Metaphysik des Einen bei Nikolaus von Kues* (Leiden, 1973), pp. 161-8. J. Hopkins criticizes Flasch and denies any analogy between Cusanus and Anselm in *A Concise Introduction to the Philosophy of Nicholas of Cusa* (Minneapolis, 1978), pp., 14-15; but his critique focuses so narrowly on the issue of 'proof' that he dismisses *a priori* any fuller, thematic comparison of Anselm and Cusanus.

6. See E. Vansteenberghe, *Autour de la docte ignorance,* in *Beiträge zur Geschichte der Philosophie des Mittelalters* XV (1915). M. L. Führer discusses Cusanus's adaptation of Pseudo-Dionysius's spirituality in 'Purgation, Illumination and Perfection in Nicholas of Cusa' in *Downside Review,* vol. XCVIII (1980), pp. 169-89.

7. Cusanus, *De visione Dei, Schriften* III, p. 132 (ch. IX); hereafter cited as *'VD'* with page and chapter following. *The Vision of God* is available in an English translation by E. G. Salter (New York, 1960; reprint of 1928 ed.).

8. *VD* 140, XI. On this theme, see D. F. Duclow, 'Gregory of Nyssa and Nicholas of Cusa' in *Downside Review*, vol. XCII (1974), pp. 102-08.

9. Anselm, *Proslogion*, in *Opera omnia*, ed. F. Schmitt (Edinburgh, 1946), I, p. 93; Charlesworth, p. 103. References to the *Proslogion* will be to the Schmitt edition, cited as *'Pr'* with page and chapter following; translations will be from M. Charlesworth, *St Anselm's Proslogion* (Oxford, 1965). Concerning Anselm's *unum argumentum*, see G. Evans, *Anselm and Talking about God* (Oxford, 1978), pp. 45-48.

10. Evans, *op. cit.*, pp. 63-64.

11. *Pr* 112, XV; Charlesworth, p. 137. See Cusanus, *De venatione sapientiae, Schriften* I, p. 120 (ch. 26), where he cites Anselm, *Deus esse maius quam concipi possit*.

12. A. Pegis, 'St Anselm and the Argument of the *Proslogion*', *Mediaeval Studies* XXVIII (1966), p. 248.

13. Evdokimov, 'L'Aspect apophatique de l'argument de Saint Anselme', *Spicilegium Beccense* (Paris, 1959), pp. 233-58; M. Gogacz, 'La "Ratio Anselmi" en face du problème des relations entre métaphysique et mystique', *Analecta Anselmiana* II (1970), pp. 169-85; and J. Gracia, 'A Supremely Great Being', *New Scholasticism* XLVIII (1974), pp. 371-7.

14. *Pr* 110-11, XIII; Charlesworth, pp. 133-5. See E. Gilson, 'L'Infinité divine chez Saint Augustin' in *Augustinus Magister* (Paris, 1954) I, pp. 569-74.

15. *Pr* 116, XXI; Charlesworth, p. 143. See Cusanus, *VD* 138-40, XI.

16. *Pr* 114-15, XVIII; Charlesworth, p. 141. See Cusanus, *VD* 148-50, XIII.

17. *Pr* 104, V; Charlesworth, p. 121.

18. Dangelmayr, 'Anselm und Cusanus', p. 120. See also V. Lossky, 'Les Éléments de "théologie negative" dans la pensée de Saint Augustine' in *Augustinus Magister* I, pp. 575-81.

19. Anselm, 'Responsio editoris', *Opera omnia* I, p. 134 (V); Charlesworth, p. 179. See K. Barth, *Anselm: Fides Quaerens Intellectum*, trans. I. Robertson (Cleveland, 1962), pp. 84-89.

20. See Gracia, *art. cit.*

21. Gaunilo, 'Pro insipiente' in Anselm, *Opera omnia* I, p. 127 (IV); Anselm, 'Responsio', pp. 134-5.

22. *Pr* 112-13, XVI; Charlesworth, p. 137.

23. K. Jaspers, *Anselm and Nicholas of Cusa*, trans. R. Mannheim (New York, 1974), p. 11.

24. See K. Flasch, 'Zum Begriff der Wahrheit bei Anselm von Canterbury', *Philosophisches Jahrbuch* LXXII (1964-65), pp. 322-52; R. Pouchet, *La Rectitudo chez Saint Anselme* (Paris, 1964), especially pp. 67-83 and 225-9; and D. F. Duclow, 'Structure and Meaning in Anselm's *De veritate*'. *American Benedictine Review* XXVI (1975), pp. 406-17.

25. See, *inter alia*, K. Jaspers, *Philosophy* (Chicago, 1970); and M. Heidegger, *Discourse on Thinking* (New York, 1966).

26. Jaspers, *Anselm and Nicholas of Cusa*, p. 16.

27. *Pr* 104, IV; Charlesworth, p. 121.

28. Barth, *op. cit,;* A Stolz, 'Zur Theologie Anselms im *Proslogion*', *Catholica* II (1933), pp. 1-24; A. Stolz, 'Das *Proslogion* des Hl. Anselm', *Revue Bénédictine* XLVII (1935), pp. 331-47. A useful survey of the philosophical literature is *The Ontological Argument*, ed. A Plantinga (Garden City, N.Y., 1965).

29. P. Ricoeur, *The Symbolism of Evil*, trans. E. Buchanan (New York, 1967), pp. 347-57. Along similar lines, see W. Dupré *Religion in Primitive Cultures* (The Hague, 1975). This hermeneutical turn reaffirms Gilson's description of the *Proslogion* as *une étude de l'Ecriture Sainte sur l'intelligiblité, de la foi;* Gilson, 'Sens et nature de l'argument de Saint Anselme', p. 50. See also R. Herrera, 'St Anselm's *Proslogion*: 'A Hermeneutical Task', *Analecta Anselmiana* III (1971), pp. 141-5.

William Collinge (essay date December 1984)

SOURCE: Collinge, William. "Monastic Life as a Context for Religious Understanding in St. Anselm." *American Benedictine Review* 35, no. 4 (December 1984): 378-88.

[*In the following essay, Collinge applies a Wittgensteinian concept of "seeing-as" (in this case: viewing through the paradigm of monastic obedience) to arguments in Anselm's* Cur Deus Homo *and* Proslogion.]

Is the study of monastic life of interest to philosophers as philosophers?[1] There is much in contemporary philosophy of religion to suggest that it can be.

One of the dominant tendencies of the philosophy of the past two centuries in the West is the effort to reintegrate the realm of thought, ideas, logic, with the realm of life, existence, praxis. This is reflected preeminently in Marxism, but also (partly derivatively) in existentialism, pragmatism, and, most important in the present context, the movement of linguistic analysis that grows out of the work of Ludwig Wittgenstein.

WITTGENSTEIN ON RELIGIOUS LANGUAGE

Wittgenstein's first book, the *Tractatus Logico-Philosophicus* (1922), had taken the opposite direction. Starting from the language of mathematical logic, he had asked, in effect, "What must the world be like if your only reliable mode of analyzing it is to take this logical form?"[2] Every proposition, according to the *Tractatus,* is a concatenation of names, and each true proposition pictures, by its concatenation of names, a concatenation of objects, which constitutes a fact. Only through its capacity to picture a fact can a proposition be meaningful.

This view eventually failed to satisfy Wittgenstein, and in the notes and lectures which culminated in the *Philosophical Investigations,* published posthumously in 1953, he reacted against the *Tractatus'* "picture theory of meaning" in favor of an emphasis on the great diversity of ways in which language could be meaningful. Thus, he wrote, "For a *large* class of cases—though not for all—in which we employ the word 'meaning' it can be defined thus: the meaning of a word is its use in the language."[3] Accordingly, philosophers may not proceed by stiuplating a criterion of meaning and dismissing all language that does not conform to it. Rather, they must seek to understand the patterns of meaning, the rules distinguishing correct from incorrect usuage, that actually are at work in a language. In doing this, they will inevitably be led to consider nonlinguistic practices as well as linguistic ones, for linguistic expressions are meaningful only in the context of a shared "form of life" which comprises more than language alone. (Suppose, for instance, that you want to know what it means to call a pitched ball a "strike." This means knowing by whom and in what circumstances a strike can be called, and that in turn involves knowing a great many of the rules of baseball.)

Although he took a lifelong interest in religion and more than once seriously considered becoming a monk,[4] Wittgenstein, except for a few cryptic remarks, such as "Theology as grammar,"[5] did not write on the subject. Nonetheless, his work attracted a considerable amount of attention from theologians and philosophers of religion from the 1950s onward. The reasons for this interest were partly polemical. The logical positivists and others had claimed that religious statements are meaningless, because, at least in the case of basic doctrinal propositions such as "God exists" and "God loves us," it is impossible to specify definite sense experiences which would verify or falsify them.[6] The reply could now be made on Wittgensteinian grounds that this challenge represented an illegitimate attempt to impose on religion a standard of meaning which was appropriate to the language of science but not to that of religion. Beyond the scope of polemics, a broader aim of Wittgensteinian theologians and philosophers of religion has been to determine the standards of meaning, of appropriate and inappropriate usage, which do in fact govern religious language, and to show the relation of religious language to religious practice. Many apparent paradoxes in religious language begin to disappear when examined from this perspective.

Take, for instance, the claim, "Unless you believe, you shall not understand," which Augustine and Anselm both take over from the Septuagint version of Isaiah 7:9 and enjoin upon their readers. This can appear to be offensive and irrational—as one contemporary philosopher puts it, it is like saying, "Unless you really believe in fairies, you will never see any."[7] But, from a Wittgensteinian perspective, it makes considerable sense. Of course, before one believes, one must understand enough to know what it is that one is being asked to believe and why there is any point in believing it, but depth of personal understanding of a religious belief depends upon bringing it into relation with as much of the rest of one's life and knowledge as possible, and this is achieved by giving oneself over to a way of life which is based on and embodies what one believes. To put it in Augustine's words: "[T]here are those things which are first believed and afterwards understood. Of such a character is that which cannot be understood of divine things except by those who are pure in heart. This understanding is achieved through observing those commandments which concern virtuous living."[8] Living a Christian way of life, in other words, enables a person to recognize new significance in his or her experience and thereby to understand, in a personal way, the meaning of Christian language—to develop, in Wittgensteinian terms, distinctively Christian ways of "seeing-as."[9]

AUGUSTINIAN BACKGROUND TO ANSELM

Augustine's *De Trinitate* can and should be read in this light, particularly the second half of it, in which Augustine seeks a "more inward" understanding of the Trinity by studying the human mind as image of the Trinity, with human knowledge and love, preeminently the knowledge and love of God, as images, respectively, of the Word of God and the Holy Spirit. To come to understand our own interior life as image of the Trinity is a spiritual as well as intellectual process, one which moves from faith to understanding through "prayer, inquiry, and right living."[10] In this process we deepen our knowledge and love of God, thus becoming *more* of an image of the Trinity. In coming to be aware of this knowledge and love, we experience them *as* an image which participates in the life of the Trinity.[11] We learn, through the new significance we perceive in our experience, something of what the Christian language about the Trinity means.[12]

In Augustine, then, faith leads to understanding through a conversion in the believer's way of life, and Wittgenstein assists us in explaining how it is that conversion leads to understanding. Now Anselm professes loyalty to Augustine,[13] and Augustine's influence is pervasive in his thinking. Yet he seems to be at once a more and less promising subject than Augustine for the approach I am sketching. What makes him seem more promising is that he speaks from the background of a formally patterned way of life, life according to the monastic rule, and he has monks primarily in mind as his audience. Moreover, he took monasticism to be the most perfect form of the Christian life and was skeptical of the possibility that anyone other than a monk could be saved.[14] Augustine too envisioned a monastic form of life as his ideal for Christian living, but he wrote for a much broader audience than did Anselm, and he does not seem to take one precise form of the Christian life as normative in quite the way Anselm does.

Immediately we encounter a difficulty: While Augustine's idea of understanding clearly has the existential element characteristic of the Platonic tradition, Anselm draws upon Aristotelian dialectic for his idea of understanding. "Understanding, for Anselm, means primarily conceptual apprehension. . . ."[15] When we come to Anselm's arguments, we seem to be dealing with questions of what are the logical implications of terms and propositions—the individual who understands seems to drop out of the picture.

Actually, Aristotelian and Augustinian elements are in tension in Anselm's writings.[16] Thus, in the *Proslogion,* immediately after quoting the text, "Unless you believe, you shall not understand," Anselm presents an argument intended to convince even the "fool" who says, "There is no God," that God exists. And in *Cur Deus Homo,* reversing the order, he announces that he will "prove by rational necessity—Christ being removed from sight, as if there had never been anything known about Him—that no man can possibly be saved without Him"[17] and immediately, in the first chapter, appears to agree with Boso's statement that "right order requires that we believe the deep matters of the Christian faith before we presume to discuss them rationally."[18] Stressing one side at the expense of the other, we can arrive at a rationalistic or a fideistic Anselm; stressing both sides, at a self-contradictory Anselm. Here a Wittgen-

steinian approach can be helpful in making sense out of Anselm's work as a whole. More specifically, I suggest that the force that Anselm's arguments had for Anselm, and the force that he expects them to have for his readers, depends in part upon the background of monastic life.

I would like now to develop the approach I have been sketching by applying it to two of Anselm's central arguments. The first argument is from *Cur Deus Homo*; the second is the ontological argument of the *Proslogion.*

In *Cur Deus Homo,* Anselm offers "necessary reasons" to establish that, given the fact that man had sinned, God had to become man in order for man to be saved. Only a God-man, Anselm argues, can render satisfaction for man's sins. Why does man need to offer satisfaction for his sins? The answer to this question depends upon Anselm's conception of sin. Sin is the failure to render to God his due.[19] And what is due to God is absolute obedience: "The will of every rational creature ought to be subordinate to the will of God."[20] Man's failure to render absolute obedience violates God's honor: "Whoever does not pay to God this honor due Him dishonors Him and removes from Him what belongs to Him, and this removal, or this dishonoring, constitutes a sin."[21] This violation of God's honor demands satisfaction; if God were to forgive it without satisfaction, he would violate his own honor, which would be unjust. What is violated when God's honor is violated is "the whole complex of service and worship which the whole creation, animate and inanimate, in heaven and earth, owes to the Creator,"[22] and this in turn is equivalent to the *rectitudo* that is so important to Anselm in this and earlier dialogues—the rightness or justice which is the divine order of the universe.

MONASTIC OBEDIENCE AS PARADIGM

This set of themes—the universe as an order of service and worship, the absolute obedience which man owes to God—suggests a monastic context. Monastic obedience can in fact be seen as the underlying spiritual theme which unifies Anselm's work from *De Veritate* to the end of his life, except for those writings occasioned by external circumstances (notably *De Incarnatione Verbi* and *De Processu Spiritus Sancti*). This work centers on themes involving the will, especially freedom, sin and necessity. Willing obedience to the will of God is the rational creature's way of honoring God, its uprightness or *rectitudo,* its *veritas.* It is also the fullest realization of human freedom. *De Libertate Arbitrii* defines freedom as "the ability to keep uprightness-of-will for the sake of this uprightness itself."[23] The ability to sin is not a genuine part of freedom; rather freedom is found in complete obedience to the will of God. Disobedience, in turn, is the essence of sin. Satan's fall lay in his violation of *rectitudo* by refusing to obey the higher will of God.[24] In earthly life the closest one can come to total submission to the will of God is the perfect obedience required of a monk. Obedience is the dominant theme of Anselm's speech and writing about the monastic life. In *De Similitudinibus,* for instance, Anselm likens monks' obedience to their abbot as God's representative to a daughter's obedience to a governess appointed by her mother *(voluntas divina voluntati abbati eorum supposuit).*[25]

For Anselm, it is the monk alone who fully acknowledges his debt to God. Through his vows, the monk completely surrendered to God; through his daily life of prayer, the monk daily renews this surrender.[26] Obedience to the abbot and stability in the monastery curb self-will and actually set one free by promoting a willing obedience to God.[27] Adherence to monastic discipline down to its smallest details, Anselm says, restrains the human spirit from vice, as a dam confines water only if it is completely without breach.[28] It is to a person whose way of life is based on this sort of ideal, I think, that Anselm's argument in *Cur Deus Homo,* with its reliance on the notions of God's honor and man's debt of perfect obedience, would be removed from the realm of "pictures painted on air" and acquire a degree of "fittingness" or coherency *(convenientia)* sufficient to take on the force of a "necessary reason."[29]

The monk's obedience, for Anselm, is of greater value than the daily work of prayer and liturgy.[30] The latter, however, though not a major subject in Anselm's theological treatises, is present in the background. Anselm's definition of sin as failure to render to God his due inverts a traditional definition of worship, a definition which has roots in Cicero. A monastic life of ordered worship (which is what monastic life was in the eleventh century) would be the clearest expression of human recognition of mankind's duty to God. The transition is quite natural in the **"Meditation on Human Redemption"** when Anselm passes from a résumé of *Cur Deus Homo* to an exhortation to unite God and man in the reception of the Eucharist.

Now let us turn to the ontological argument of the *Proslogion*—a "short passage," says David Knowles, which "has been pored over and commented upon more than any other text of equal brevity in medieval philosophy."[31] Philosophers, noting that it seeks to convince the unbelieving "fool" that God exists, have tended to look upon the argument as a logical deduction, which attempts, as Kant said of later versions of the argument, "to extract from an idea the existence of an object corresponding to it."[32] Some philosophers and theologians, meanwhile, noting that the argument appears in the

context of a religious meditation whose original title was "Faith Seeking Understanding," have claimed that the argument presupposed faith. Karl Barth, for instance, contended that the argument used reason only to draw out the implications of one of the names of God which is accepted through faith. In context, the argument appears to be both a meditation within faith and a proof meant to convince an unbeliever. But how can it be both? If it presupposes faith, how can it convince an unbeliever? And if it succeeds in convincing an unbeliever, what need is there of beginning with faith?

Here again a Wittgensteinian approach can help make sense of things. In what sense can someone be said to *understand* "that than which a greater cannot be thought," which is Anselm's definition of God? A person can understand it on a purely verbal level, the way that most of my students understand "that than which a greater cannot be thought" and do not understand "*id quo maius cogitari nequit.*" But this kind of understanding is no guarantee that the referent of the term is even logically possible. I can speak of "the largest integer," and you can, after a fashion, understand what I say, even if you recognize that the very notion of "the largest integer" is self-contradictory. But if we cannot be sure that "that than which a greater cannot be thought" is even logically coherent, we certainly cannot go on to use the formula as a proof of the real existence of its referent.

Anselm himself recognizes this problem to some extent in chapter four of the *Proslogion,* where he observes:

> [T]here is not merely one sense in which something is said in one's heart, or his thought. For in one sense an object is thought when the word signifying it is thought, and in another when what the object is is understood. Thus, in the first sense but not at all in the second, God can be thought not to exist. Indeed, no one who understands what God is can think that God does not exist, even though he says these words in his heart. . . . For God is that than which a greater cannot be thought. Anyone who comprehends this, surely understands that God so exists that he cannot even conceivably not exist. Therefore, anyone who understands that this is the manner in which God exists cannot think that he does not exist.[33]

Who is it that "comprehends [*bene intelligit*] this"? Not the fool, since he denies God's existence. But then the fool lacks the sort of understanding necessary for the argument to succeed as a proof. Gaunilo makes this very point in his reply, "On Behalf of the Fool": "When I hear someone speaking of God (or of something greater than all others), I cannot have Him in my thought and understanding in the way that I might have [an] unreal man in my thought and understanding. For although I can think of a non-existent man by reference to a real thing known to me, I cannot think of God at all except only with respect to the word."[34] Against Gaunilo's claim not to understand God, Anselm rejoins, "I point to your faith and conscience as the strongest indicator of how false these inferences are."[35] If "faith and conscience" meant simply an assent to a verbal formula, Gaunilo would go unanswered. But Gaunilo is a fellow Christian and (it is assumed) a fellow monk, and "faith" for him as for Anselm would be a commitment that shapes his whole way of life.

UNDERSTANDING THROUGH SURRENDER

Who, then, "understands what God is"? Someone whose "form of life" is based on the acknowledgement that God is that than which a greater cannot be thought, who recognizes the infinite greatness of God by complete surrender and obedience, whose daily life prefers no other good to God's greatness—someone, in short, who lives up to Anselm's ideal of the monk. Only for such a person would the ontological argument have force as an argument, for in him alone would the idea of God "exist in the intellect" in such a way as to render inescapable the affirmation that God exists in reality.[36] (Perhaps it is significant that the argument occurred to Anselm "during matins," as Eadmer tells us, for it relies on that sense of the overwhelming majesty of God which is characteristic of the Psalms.)

Corroboration of the contention in the last paragraph can be found in the first part of the *Epistola de Incarnatione Verbi.* There Anselm states, "He who does not believe will not understand. For he who does not believe will not experience; and he who has not experienced will not know."[37] It is through a life of obedience, Anselm says, that this experience[38] is acquired; "For it is true that the more richly we are fed on those things in sacred scripture which nourish us through obedience, the more precisely we are carried on to those things which satisfy through understanding."[39] This is the only place known to me in Anselm's writings in which experience is explicitly said to mediate between belief and understanding. But it is not just an anomalous Augustinian holdover in Anselm. Rather, as G.R. Evans notes, this passage represents an approach to theological investigation which Anselm simply presupposed in his audience and did not need to make explicit until, as was the case with the *Epistola de Incarnatione Verbi,* he was writing for an audience composed not only of monks but also of secular dialecticians.[40]

I would like to conclude with the two suggestions as to the broader theological bearing of the line of argument I have been undertaking. First, it offers an illuminating perspective on the development of doctrine, for the language of Christian doctrine would be seen as chang-

ing in meaning, depending on the "form of life" of which it is a part. "Form of life" here would refer not only to the special forms of Christian corporate life such as liturgy and monasticism, but also to the changing patterns of Christian life in the world, as Christians live out Christian lives in a great diversity of cultures. Secondly, if it is true that Christian language is today widely felt to be meaningless, both by philosophers and by ordinary people inside and outside the churches, the cause may lie not so much in the words of Christianity as in the ways Christians live.

Notes

1. An earlier version of this paper was presented at the Benedict Sesquimillennial Symposium in Madison, Wisconsin, October, 1980.

2. William Barrett, *The Illusion of Technique* (Garden City, NY: Doubleday 1978) p. 32.

3. Ludwig Wittgenstein, *Philosophical Investigations,* trans. G. E. M. Anscombe (Oxford: Blackwell 1958) 1.43.

4. See the letter from Bertrand Russell to Lady Ottoline Morrell, December 20, 1919, quoted in Barrett, p. 31; see also W. W. Bartley III, *Wittgenstein* (Philadelphia: Lippincott 1973) p. 133, on Wittgenstein's summer at a monastery in 1926.

5. Wittgenstein, 1.373.

6. See A. J. Ayer, *Language, Truth, and Logic* (London: Victor Gollancz 1936) and Antony Flew, "Theology and Falsification," in *New Essays in Philosophical Theology,* edited by Flew and Alisdair McIntyre (London: SCM Press 1955) pp. 96-99.

7. Wallace I. Matson, *The Existence of God* (Ithaca, NY: Cornell University Press 1965) p. 28.

8. *De Diversis Quaestionibus* 83, 48, translation by David L. Mosher in *The Fathers of the Church,* vol. 70 (Washington, DC: Catholic University of America Press 1982).

9. Wittgenstein develops the idea of "seeing-as" in *Philosophical Investigations,* 2.xi.

10. *De Trinitate,* 15.27.49.

11. On love, see *De Trinitate* 8.8.

12. See William Collinge, "*De Trinitate* and the Understanding of Religious Language," *Augustinian Studies,* in press.

13. *Monologion,* preface. *S. Anselmi Cantuariensis Archiepiscopi Opera Omnia,* edited by Franciscus Salesius Schmitt (Edinburgh: Thomas Nelson

1938-61) 1.8. References to this edition in footnotes below will give the volume and page number preceded by *S.*

14. R. W. Southern, *Saint Anselm and His Biographer* (Cambridge University Press 1963) pp. 101-02.

15. John E. Smith, *The Analogy of Experience* (New York: Harper and Row 1973) p. 12.

16. On this point, see especially Dom Cyprian Vagaggini, "*La hantise des Rationes Necessariae de Saint Anselme dans la theologie des Processions Trinitaires de Saint Thomas,*" *Spicilegium Beccense* I (Paris: J. Vrin 1959) 105-06. I am indebted to one of the readers of this paper for this reference.

17. Anselm, *Cur Deus Homo* [*CDH*], preface (*S* 2.42); translation by Jasper Hopkins and Herbert Richardson in *Anselm of Canterbury* III (Toronto: Edwin Mellen Press 1976).

18. *CDH* 1.1; *S* 2.48.

19. *CDH* 1.11; *S* 2.68.

20. *Ibid.*

21. *Ibid.*

22. Southern, p. 113. See *CDH* 1.15.

23. *De Libertate Arbitrii* 3; *S* 1.212. Translation by Hopkins and Richardson in *Anselm of Canterbury*, vol. II.

24. *De Casu Diaboli* 4; *S* 1.242.

25. *De Similitudinibus* 89, quoted by R. W. Southern in a note to his edition of Eadmer, *Vita Anselmi* (Oxford: Clarendon Press 1962) p. 77.

26. Southern, *St. Anselm and His Biographer*, p. 101.

27. Anselm, *Ep.* 37, quoted by Eadmer in *Vita Anselmi* 1.20.

28. *Vita Anselmi* 1.31. See the expansion of this image in *De Similitudinibus* quoted by Southern in a note to his edition, p. 55.

29. On the impreciseness of the boundary between *convenientiae* and "necessary reasons," see *CDH* 1.10; *S* 2.67.

30. *Vita Anselmi* 2.11.

31. David Knowles, *The Evolution of Medieval Thought* (New York: Vintage Books 1959) p. 101.

32. Immanuel Kant, *Critique of Pure Reason*, trans. Norman Kemp Smith (New York: St. Martin's Press 1965) B 631.

33. *Proslogion* 4 (*S* 1.103-04); translated by Hopkins and Richardson in *Anselm of Canterbury* I (1974); this translation is used in the following, two quotations also.

34. *Reply on Behalf of the Fool,* 4 (*S* 1.127).

35. *Reply to Gaunilo,* 1 (*S* 1.130).

36. The general lines of this approach to the ontological argument were first suggested to me by Louis Dupré. See his *A Dubious Heritage* (New York: Paulist Press 1977) pp. 171-75. See also David Burrell, *Exercises in Religious Understanding* (Notre Dame: University of Notre Dame Press 1974) pp. 45-79.

37. *De Incarnatione Verbi* I (*S* 2.9); translation in Hopkins and Richardson, vol. III.

38. On the use of *experientia* by medieval monastic writers, see Jean Leclercq, *The Love of Learning and the Desire for God* (New York: Fordham University Press 1961) pp. 263-65. Leclercq notes, "This personal experience is closely linked with a whole environment; it is conditioned and promoted by the conventual experience of a community and it flourishes in the midst of a common fervor" (p. 264).

39. *De Incarnatione Verbi* I; *S* 2.8-9.

40. G. R. Evans, *Anselm and Talking about God* (Oxford: Clarendon Press 1978) pp. 118-20.

Walter Fröhlich (essay date 1984)

SOURCE: Fröhlich, Walter. "The Letters Omitted from Anselm's Collection of Letters." *Anglo-Norman Studies* 6 (1984): 58-71.

[*In the following essay, Fröhlich surveys Anselm's collected correspondence, highlighting the monk's efforts to suppress letters that could potentially damage his reputation.*]

The writing of letters and the gathering of such letters in large letter-collections is one of the striking features which distinguish intellectual life of the eleventh and twelfth centuries from those immediately preceding and following. This activity blossomed forth from the numerous schools which were attached to the monasteries and cathedrals of western Europe.

In the Middle Ages the writing of letters was closely linked to the writing of verses for teaching purposes. Both exercises were conscientiously practised; they were expressed by the same verb 'dictare' which can be rendered as either 'to write according to dictation' or 'to write poetry'. Thus, as C. Erdmann conclusively demonstrates, the writing of letters became an important and self-conscious genre of literary composition.[1] It provided a means of expression for the culture and the learning of the writers. Yet the letters themselves also have an intrinsic importance in relation to the significance and purpose of their subject matter. Many letters, therefore, acquired a twofold value derived from their form and their content.

Among the most important letter-writers were the teachers and scholars of the monastic and cathedral schools. Their learning, displayed in their writings, made them well-known so that a great number of these teachers were promoted to abbacies and episcopal sees and thus also occupied important political positions.[2]

One of these teachers and scholars was Anselm, a native of Aosta, monk, prior and abbot of Bec until 1093 and then archbishop of Canterbury until his death in 1109. In reply to a letter from Warner, a novice of Christ Church Canterbury, Anselm sent a brief piece of spiritual advice in 1104 (Anselmi Epistola, = AEp, 335). He added that if Warner wished for more profound counsel on the monastic way of life he should look up an earlier letter which he had written to a Dom Lanzo when the latter had been a novice (AEp 37). The letter to Warner was written while Anselm was spending his second exile in Lyon. The letter to Lanzo, prior of the Cluniac house of St Pancras at Lewes 1077-1107, was sent while Lanzo was still a novice at Cluny some thirty years before.

It seems unlikely that Anselm would have expected Warner to search for that particular letter among numerous miscellaneous manuscripts but rather that he would be able to find it in the library of his monastery, the cathedral priory of Christ Church Canterbury, in the codex containing the collection of Anselm's letters. For Anselm had assembled a collection of his letters which he enlarged and rearranged over a number of years.[3]

From the evidence available it appears that Anselm, in reply to enquiries and requests from various people, started collecting letters he had written from about the early 1070s. No letter written by him before 1070 has been preserved. His motive for collecting his early letters—those written while he was prior and abbot of Bec—seems to have been on account of their moral content of exhortatic and spiritual advice rather than for their literary form. Business matter and day-to-day information were almost totally excluded and entrusted to the oral report of the bearer of the letter.[4] Anselm's collection of his early letters, with a few exceptions, contains only his outgoing correspondence.[5]

Anselm's correspondence covering his archiepiscopal period comprises 328 items. It contains not only the outgoing letters but also some he received as well as some letters between third parties.[6] In those letters written while he was archbishop of Canterbury the emphasis

of the contents shows a shift from pastoral advice to political problems of church reform, Anglo-Norman statecraft and the struggle for supremacy in the 'corpus christianorum'. Thus the character of the collection changed from being a compilation of letters valued for their moral content to that of letters dealing with state affairs of the utmost political importance.

The final part of this collection seems to contain all letters bearing upon the renewed outbreak of the primatial controversy between the metropolitan sees of Canterbury and York which took place in the autumn and winter 1108 and spring and summer 1109. Thus yet again the character of the collection was changed. It acquired the character of a register of the archbishop's correspondence.

The first part of Anselm's collection of letters—those while he was prior and abbot of Bec—passed through three stages. The oldest manuscript containing the first stage is British Library, MS Cotton Nero VII (henceforth referred to as N), since it is the only manuscript that styles Anselm merely as prior and abbot of Bec. It contains 99 letters on 142 pages. Some pages are missing at the end but the letters on these lost pages can be reconstructed from London Lambeth Palace, MS 224 (M).[7] The latter is an autograph of William of Malmesbury who had copied Anselm's works and letters into this manuscript and had used N for the purpose.

The letters in N do not follow any strict chronological order, their only division being the letters written as prior and those written as abbot of Bec. This division is provided by a rubric after letter N 69 (= AEp 87) at the bottom of fol. 94r: 'Hactenus continentur epistole domni Anselmi abbatis, quas fecit donec prior Beccensis fuit. Quae vero iam deinceps sequuntur, egit postquam abbatis nomen et officium suscepit'. As this rubric is written on an erasure it must be the work of the original scribe or his immediate corrector and not that of a later copyist.[8] This points to the fact that the scribe or his corrector knew Anselm only as abbot of Bec and not yet as archbishop of Canterbury. The rubric at the beginning of the collection of Anselm's letters supports this: 'Incipit liber epistolarum domni Anselmi abbatis.' This rubric separates Anselm's letters from the letters of Lanfranc which are collected in the first part of N. Both collections appear to have been written by the same hand. This consideration is supported by the fact that two letters (AEp 30, 31) from Archbishop Lanfranc (one to Prior Anselm and one to his nephew Lanfranc at Bec) are excluded from Anselm's collection since they are already among the collection of Lanfranc's letters.

The date for the compilation of this first stage of Anselm's letter collection is provided by AEp 145 sent to Abbot Ralph of Séez congratulating him on his promotion in 1089. This letter is not to be found in N but it can be assigned to N on the evidence of M. Since the itinerary of Abbot Anselm shows no absence of the abbot of Bec from his monastery in 1089 it would seem that Anselm's first collection of his letters was assembled and written into N at Bec under Anselm's supervision and assistance.[9] The death of Archbishop Lanfranc on 26 May 1089 and the compilation of a collection of his letters could have been the incentive to do this some time in 1090. Anselm's letter to his former pupil Maurice in 1085 (AEp 104) points to the probability that Anselm had been thinking about collecting his letters for some time, for this letter closes: 'We are still waiting for our letters which Dom Maurice is supposed to have sent us'.

Barely two years later Anselm was engaged on improving the first stage of his letter collection. In autumn 1092 (AEp 147) he informs Prior Baldric and the community of Bec about the delay of his return to Bec due to King William's refusal to grant him leave to do so. He asks: 'Send me the Prayer to St Nicholas which I wrote and the letter which I had started writing against the propositions of Roscelin; and if Dom Maurice has any other letters of ours which he has not yet sent, send them as well.' It would appear that he intended using this period of enforced leisure to improve the first collection of his letters and thus required all the letters which had been collected at Bec since the compilation of N to be sent to him in England. He improved the rough chronology of N—which had only divided the letters into those of the prior and those of the abbot—by rearranging all the letters in their proper order. He also inserted in their correct order five of the letters to Maurice which had meanwhile been returned to him. Abbot Anselm's enforced stay in England took place in the wake of his third inspection tour of the English cells and estates of Bec for which he had set out on 26 August 1092.[10] Having accomplished the purpose of his journey he spent the autumn and winter 1092-1093 with his friend Abbot Gilbert Crispin at St Peter's, Westminster, waiting for the king's leave to return to Bec. Therefore the second edition of his letters was most likely executed at Westminster during this period.

The best example of this second stage of Anselm's letter collection is to be found in the first part of his collection in Cambridge, Corpus Christi College MS 135 (E_1). Having thus been gathered and compiled in two stages by Anselm himself—in 1090 at Bec and 1092/93 at Westminster—this collection of the letters of the prior and abbot of Bec developed differently in Canterbury and Bec. They are the collections of Anselm's letters to be found in London Lambeth Palace, MS 59 (= L) written at Canterbury and in Paris Bibliothèque Nationale, MS 14762 (= V) written at Bec, forming L_1 and V_1 and representing the third stage of the first part of the Anselmian letter collection. L_1 and V_1 differ from N and E_1 and from each other by the addition of further letters and in the chronological sequence of the letters which they contain. L_1 contains 132 letters while V_1 comprises 156 of which 27 are duplicates.

The earliest collection of Anselm's letters written as archbishop of Canterbury from 6 March 1093 to 21 April 1109 is to be found in the second part of L (= L_2) since all other manuscripts containing letters of the archiepiscopal period depend upon this part of L. The collection in L_2 comprises 257 letters. They were compiled by Anselm himself during another period of enforced leisure. From December 1103 to September 1106 he was banished from the Anglo-Norman realm because of the dispute about investitures between King Henry I and Pope Paschal II. Anselm spent most of this, his second exile, with his friend Archbishop Hugh of Lyon. During this time also, he directed the production of a final edition of his works and letters. Following Anselm's instructions (AEp 334, 379) this task was conscientiously and meticulously carried out by the scribe Thidricus at Christ Church Canterbury. The fruits of Thidricus' labours are the magnificent manuscripts Oxford Bodleian, Bodley 271, containing Anselm's philosophical and theological works, and London Lambeth Palace MS 59 comprising his letters. After Anselm's return to Canterbury in September 1106 his letter collection acquired the character of a registry into which new letters were copied. Soon after Anselm's death an appendix—L_a—was added to L_1 and L_2. On thirty-one pages L_a contains a miscellany of letters, tracts, poems and other documents.[11] A number of the letters in L_a are referred back to the collection of L_2 by symbols and instructions in the margin.[12] Two poems in praise of Anselm are also to be found in L_a. The second of these is introduced by the following rubric: 'Item versus de eodem praesulis Anselmi quem nuper obisse dolemus'. If 'nuper' is understood as 'recently', just as Anselm himself had used it e.g. in AEp 104, it appears that L_a was written shortly after Anselm's death on 21 April 1109, but that L_1 and L_2 were written during his lifetime.

The Bec tradition of part I of Anselm's letter collection of V_1 took over part II of the collection of L_2 in order to form V_2 without taking cognizance of possible duplications of letters or the need for inserting letters of the Bec tradition into the Canterbury tradition.

. . . . .

The final edition which Anselm made of his letters is to be found in L. It comprises 389 letters. The most recent modern edition of Anselm's works and letters by F. S. Schmitt contains 475 letters. In his edition Dom Schmitt excluded a considerable number of spurious letters which had found their way into the collection by various means during the course of centuries.[13] Indeed, had Anselm kept all the letters written to him requesting a reply, his collection would have been much larger still since in at least 120 letters he refers to some written supplication as the cause for his written reply.[14]

In all there are therefore some 206 letters—86 items from Dom Schmitt's edition and 120 items referred to—that did not find their way into L. This would amount to about 30 per cent of the items of Anselm's total correspondence or nearly 53 per cent as compared to the collection entered into L. For this reason it seems obvious that Anselm carefully selected from the mass of his correspondence and diligently compiled a collection of the letters he considered worth preserving.

Between the 389 letters of L—Anselm's final collection of his correspondence—and the 475 letters of the recent *Anselmi Opera Omnia* in which Dom Schmitt included all known items of Anselmian correspondence, there is a difference of 86 letters.[15] Why were they not included in L? Was L purely a random selection or did Anselm omit these letters because he regarded them as unworthy of preservation or unfitting for the purpose of his final collection?

A detailed examination of these omitted letters will attempt to provide clues and reasons for their omission and may point to Anselm's method and intention in compiling his collection.

The eighty-six letters not to be found in L can be split into two groups: twelve date from the period while Anselm was prior and abbot of Bec, the remaining seventy-four to the time of his archiepiscopal pontificate.

The first group of twelve letters omitted from L all date from Anselm's time as prior and abbot of Bec.[16] One is received from, and all the others are sent to, ecclesiastics—including two to Archbishop Lanfranc and two to Pope Urban. Ten of these letters deal with pastoral problems and contain advice to abbots and other monks on how to deal with excommunicated persons, with married priests or with secretly penitent priests. Anselm also intercedes with heads of monasteries on behalf of other monks and advises monks on their day-to-day problems. These letters were most likely omitted from L because of their relative unimportance, their purely local relevance, their rather lenient treatment of sinning priests which clashed with Anselm's rigorous attitude of later years, or because of some criticism Anselm may have made or demonstrated with regard to Archbishop Lanfranc.

The two letters sent to Pope Urban (AEp 126, 127) deal with Bishop Fulk of Beauvais who had been a monk of Bec. Abbot Anselm had consented to his uncanonical promotion by appointment of King Philip I of France in 1088. Having gained pardon for his uncanonical promotion from Pope Urban, and having been reinstated as Bishop of Beauvais, he was unable to administer his diocese for various reasons. In AEp 126 Anselm begs Urban's help for Fulk and in AEp 127 he implores the pope secretly to relieve Fulk of the burden of episcopal office which he is too weak to bear. He ends this letter: 'If it pleases you I wish and beg that this letter be for your eyes alone.' It seems likely that this embarrassing affair caused the exclusion of these letters from L. A third letter dealing with this problem—written when Anselm was archbishop of Canterbury—AEp 193, was also omitted from L, probably for the same reason. The positive suppression of these letters is confirmed by evidence supplied by the MS itself. There would have been enough space for both letters on fol. 54 of L. The folio between the present folios 53 and 54: that is to say, the original fol. 54 bearing these two letters has been removed, probably following Anselm's instructions. AEp 193, also omitted from L, was later added as the first item in L_a.[17]

The seventy-four letters written when Anselm was archbishop of Canterbury and which are not to be found in L, are too numerous to be examined individually. These letters can be divided into nine groups which will account for fifty-seven of them while seventeen will be left undiscussed.

1. There is a large batch of nineteen letters which were all sent to the monks of Bec as a community or to individual members of it.[18] Some were forwarded via Bec to other individuals i.e. to Bishop Gilbert of Evreux (159), Countess Ida of Boulogne (167) and Archbishop Hugh of Lyon (176). According to Dom Schmitt this is why they were preserved in V, forming the Bec tradition of Anselm's letter collection.[19] It does not, however, answer the question why they were not preserved in L at Canterbury since they were written there. Having collected his letters for some ten years up to that time and having compiled them into N of 1090 and the later E_1 in 1092/93, Anselm almost certainly kept drafts and copies of the letters he sent to his monastery following his investiture as archbishop of Canterbury on 6 March 1093.

A review of the subject matter of these letters may provide some clue to the reason for their omission from L. A few were written in reply to the widespread gossip about Anselm's cupidity for the archbishopric (156, 159, 160, 164). This gossip seems to have been common in and around Bec, in the diocese of Evreux and in the whole duchy of Normandy. Anselm saw himself repeatedly forced to protest his innocence and lack of cupidity when he travelled to England in summer 1092 and to emphasise his surprise at being made archbishop in March 1093 by King William II, by the clergy and people, the bishops and barons of the Anglo-Norman kingdom (148). In their persistent demand for him to accept the burden of archiepiscopal office he perceived the will of God which he was obliged to obey. Despite Anselm's assurances a number of the community of Bec were not convinced and refused their consent to his relinquishing the abbatial office in order to accept the archbishopric of Canterbury (150, 155). They pointed out that they were bound to him in obedience and he to them for ever. Anselm replied that his obedience to God transcended his commitment to the community but on the other hand he demanded their obedience in accepting his choice in the election of his successor. Moreover, he expected their continued obedience to him for the rest of his life, even after the election of a new abbot. In fact, the monk Boso, disregarding the authority of the new abbot, obediently followed Anselm's call to Canterbury (174, 209).

In order to assure that his nominee was elected as abbot of Bec, Anselm suggests a candidate in AEp 157 which is included in L. However two letters in which he assures the duke's consent as well as the king's protection (164) and the help of an old friend (163) for the election of his protegé are missing from L. Did he suppress these in order to conceal the extent of his interference? His demands in this connection contravene the Rule of St Benedict which does not require any bond of obedience between an abbot and members of the community after the abbot's departure from the monastery, but which postulates the free election of a new abbot by the members of the community. The long-drawn-out procedure of electing William of Beaumont as Anselm's successor, from August to October 1093, amply demonstrates the community's resentment at Anselm's intrusion in this matter.

Anselm's exclusion of these letters from L could point to the fact that he felt his image might be damaged by their publication, or the realisation that his too-frequent refutations of greed for the archbishopric might raise suspicion that he did indeed protest too much!

2. The next group of eight letters which are not preserved in L are written to Bishop Osmund of Salisbury and various members of convents in his diocese: two to Gunhilda, daughter of King Harold and nun at Wilton (168, 169), two to Abbess Eulalia of Shaftsbury (183, 337), one to the nun M., the daughter of Earl Richard of Clare (184) and three to Bishop Osmund (177, 190, 195).[20] At first sight it is surprising that these letters to nuns were not entered into L. They abound in advice and encouragement to persevere step by step towards the celestial kingdom by leading a good life as a spouse of Christ, abandoning the secular world of sin and misery. Yet Anselm's first letter to Bishop Osmund in spring 1094 might hold the reason for their exclusion.

Anselm intimates to the bishop of Salisbury that pastoral care and canon law ought to have moved him to act in regard to a certain 'filia perdita'. The lady here referred to is Eadgyth, 'filia regis Scotorum'. Eadgyth was the daughter of Malcolm, king of Scotland and Margaret, the kinswoman of Edward, of the true royal family of England, and niece of Edgar the Atheling.[21] She had possibly come to England with her aunt Christina in 1086. In 1093 both were at Wilton where Christina was a nun. King Malcolm had never intended his daughter to become a nun. In fact, since she was at the marriageable age of about fifteen she played an important part in his political plans and was to be married to Count Alan Rufus, lord of Richmond and most powerful baron in the north of England. This planned marriage came to nothing, however, since Alan Rufus became involved with the nun Gunhilda, whom he abducted from her convent in Wilton, and he died on 4 August 1093. His brother, Count Alan Niger, who succeeded him not only in his estates but also in his matrimonial plans also died soon after this.[22] The nun Gunhilda seems to have returned to Wilton as she was later remembered with honour there.[23]

The proposal of marriage with Eadgyth, then known as Mathilda, was taken up by King Henry I in 1100 as a calculated political move. In order to open the way for the planned marriage Anselm had to conduct a complicated procedure to prove that Mathilda/Eadgyth had never been a nun although she had worn the veil. For his part in the investigation Anselm was harshly criticised. Eadmer reports that many people maligned Anselm, saying that he had not kept the path of strict right in this matter.[24] After Mathilda's marriage to King Henry on 11 November 1100 Anselm became her spiritual advisor. A large number of letters bear witness to their relationship thereafter.[25]

Having referred to this lady as a 'filia perdita' in the early stages of his pontificate this letter may have been embarrassing for Anselm when he enjoyed the queen's close friendship in later years. Moreover, the inclusion of this letter and those connected with it might have stirred the sleep of dormant critics and blown about the dust of past scandals. Such considerations would explain the omission of these eight letters from L.

3. The complete collection of Anselm's letters contains fifty-four which name King Henry or Queen Mathilda as sender or recipient. Eight of these, which not only bear the names of the king or queen but also that of Pope Paschal II as sender or receiver, are omitted from L.[26]

King Henry started this correspondence in January 1101 by congratulating Pope Paschal on his promotion (215). He offered friendship, obedience and the payment of Peter's Pence as his predecessors had done. In return he expected to hold his kingdom unimpaired like his predecessors. At the end of the same year he requested the pallium for Archbishop Gerard of York from the pope (221). In reply Paschal praised Henry for the good beginning of his reign and admonished him to abstain from investitures for the sake of the liberty of the Church (224). The pope demonstrated by the authority of Holy Scripture and the Fathers that the right of investiture of bishops and abbots belonged to the Church and not to kings. He promised to grant the king whatever he asked for provided he gave up investitures (216).

In November 1103, after the failure of the four embassies to Rome in order to obtain a mitigation of the papal decrees on lay investiture and the homage of clerics, the pope resumed direct relations with the king, congratulating him on the birth of his first-born son and heir William. He once more admonished the king to abandon investitures (305). A year later Paschal assured Henry of his care for his salvation. He informed him that he was retaining his messengers until the following Lenten synod (1105) so that his queries on homage and investiture might be answered according to the will of God. He chided the king for having sent Anselm into exile once more and also for having despoiled him of his possessions. The pope praised the king, however, because the decrees of the Westminster Council of 1102 were being implemented (348). A few months later— January/February 1105—the pope admonished the king for the third time not to despise the Church, to receive Anselm back according to the papal decrees and to allow Anselm to publish them, to protect the Church in her lawful liberty and to give up his evil advisors, two of whom he was planning to excommunicate (351). At the same time the pope urged Queen Mathilda to persuade her husband to abandon investitures and to obey the will of God so that he might not lose what God had given him. He warned her about the king's evil advisors and their imminent excommunication (352). These letters represent the preserved correspondence between the king/queen and the pope. They are all omitted from L. Other letters included in L hint at even further items of this correspondence which have not yet come to light.[27]

The fact that the pope's correspondence with King Henry and Queen Mathilda is excluded from L recalls Anselm's letter to Thidricus in 1105 in which he replies to the latter's enquiry thus: 'Litteras quas quaeris regis ad papam, non tibi mitto, quia non intelligo utile esse, si serventur' (379). This letter to Thidricus seems most likely to refer to the latter's work of compiling the collection of the archbishop's letters and copying them into L. This work had been going on since about 1105. While Anselm was forced to suffer his second exile he sent these instructions to Thidricus who obediently followed them by omitting all but one of the items (323) of the correspondence between the king, the queen and Pope Paschal II from L.[28]

This correspondence was not entirely suppressed, however, since six of these eight letters are to be found in a separate integral collection of twenty-three letters from Christ Church Canterbury.[29] The pope's cautious negotiations with the king and his lenient treatment of him while Anselm was suffering the hardship of exile for having upheld the pope's decrees might well be the reason for Anselm's exclusion of this correspondence from L.

4. Also missing from L are the two letters from the pope (282) and Cardinal John (284) of December 1102. Paschal reminded Anselm of the condemnation of simony by the Council of Bari and restated his advice on married priests and deacons. Cardinal John thought it necessary to encourage Anselm to defend the right of the Church against the king and the false bishops. In view of the second exile which Anselm was suffering because of his defence of the liberty of the Church in England and the propagation of its reform these letters must have irked him somewhat, which would explain their exclusion from the main collection of his letters.[30]

5. A small batch of three very short letters representing the correspondence between Bishop Lambert of Arras and Anselm is also omitted from L. In the first of these letters Anselm asked Lambert for safe conduct for a papal cleric through his diocese (437). In reply Lambert enquired about Anselm's health and sent greetings to Dom Baldwin (438). Anselm replied very briefly that he was healthy in body but suffering from growing weakness (439).

Anselm's contacts with Flanders and Arras in particular had been intensive ever since Girard, the moneyer of Arras, and Baldwin had entered the monastery at Bec.[31] Bishop Lambert, together with the exiled Anselm, was present at the synod of Rome in 1099 when Urban pronounced sentence of excommunication on 'all lay persons who conferred investitures of churches, all persons accepting such investitures from their hands and all persons who consecrated to the office of any preferment so given'.[32] Moreover, during his stay in Rome Anselm, in the face of some opposition, had helped to secure papal promotion of John, the archdeacon of Arras, to the see of Térouane. Anselm and the bishop of Arras had become close friends as Anselm's letter of summer 1103 to Dom Conus, included in L, testifies (285).

The final expression of the intimate friendship between Anselm and Lambert can be perceived in the fact that after Anselm's death the monks of Christ Church Canterbury sent the late archbishop's personal manuscript of his works to Arras where it is still kept.[33] Despite this close connection with Arras these three short letters were omitted from L, probably because of their triviality.

6. Shortly after the Council of Westminster at Whitsun 1108 Anselm wrote to Pope Paschal requesting confirmation for the Council's decision to divide the diocese of Lincoln and to create a new bishopric of Ely (441). The see was to be established at the abbey of Ely and the monks were to assist the bishop as cathedral chapter.[34] Paschal's letters to King Henry and Archbishop Anselm granting and confirming the creation of the new see of Ely and the nomination of Hervey of Bangor as first bishop are not included in L. These four letters (457, 458, 459, 460) were all issued at Troia on 21 November 1108. Allowing at least eight weeks for a winter journey from Troia near Foggia in southern Italy to England they would not have been delivered until January or February 1109 after work on manuscript L had been completed and it was being copied in its turn. They might not even have arrived before Anselm's death in April. They were never incorporated into any copy of the Anselmian letter collection.[35]

7. Another group of five more letters is missing from L. These letters are part of the correspondence dealing with the renewed outbreak of the primatial controversy between Canterbury and York following the promotion of Thomas of Beverley to the see of York after the death of Archbishop Gerard on 27 May 1108.

The whole correspondence on this issue numbers thirteen letters, eight of which are in L.[36] Three of the missing letters are from Thomas, the elect of York, and the Chapter of York to Anselm at Canterbury. They dispute the archbishop's right to demand a profession of obedience from the elect before his consecration at the primate's hands (453, 454, 456).[37] Another letter (470) from the king to Anselm requests him to defer the consecration of the elect of York until Easter 1109 so that after his return to England he himself might settle the case between the two metropolitans.[38] Since the letters from York demonstrate the York opinion in this dispute and the king did not side wholeheartedly with the claim of Canterbury it would seem likely that the open and veiled threats to the primatial claim of the archbishop of Canterbury were the grounds for the omission of these letters from the final edition of Anselm's letters in L. Therefore it is surprising that Anselm's letter to Rannulf of Durham, representing the Canterbury point of view in this controversy (442), is also missing from the collection.[39] In this letter Anselm

states that Turgot, the elect of St Andrews in Scotland, could not be consecrated by anybody but the archbishop of Canterbury as long as Thomas, the elect of York, had not received his consecration at Canterbury.

8. Five of the thirteen letters which constitute the correspondence with Archbishop Gerard of York are omitted from L.[40] The first of these (255) was written by Gerard to Anselm after the Council of Westminster 1102. He informed Anselm that clerics were spurning the statutes of the Council and sought his help against those who evaded the canons through sophistry. He also confessed a sin of simony he had once committed. This letter demonstrated Gerard's zeal for church reform and his personal repentance.

However, after the return of Gerard and the bishops of Norwich and Chester from Rome in summer 1102 the relationship between Anselm and Gerard deteriorated considerably. The royal envoys delivered a report on their negotiations with Pope Paschal about the mitigation of the decrees forbidding lay investiture which was vehemently contradicted by Anselm's messengers. The pope refuted the bishops' report as a lie and excommunicated the royal envoys and anybody who had received investiture or had consecrated those thus invested since August 1102. Gerard caused further disagreement when, at the king's command, he was prepared to consecrate the recently invested bishops of Winchester, Hereford and Salisbury after Anselm had refused their consecration on the ground of the papal decrees of 1099, confirmed by Paschal in 1101 and 1102.[41] The letter from Paschal to Gerard in spring 1105 (354) reprimanding him for his wrongdoing and for not having been a support to Anselm is indeed included in L. Gerard's reply (362), which is not included in L, points out that the papal charge was based on false reports and that he had always favoured Anselm's cause. In summer and winter 1105/6 Gerard sent two letters to Anselm informing him that since he had found the truth he and many others would be obedient to the archbishop (363) and admitting that he now perceived the danger of lay investiture (373) he begged Anselm's prayers to assist him in his good intentions. In spring 1108 Gerard sought Anselm's help at the recommendation of Pope Paschal (440). These last four letters, demonstrating Gerard's conversion to the pope's and Anselm's position on investiture and his renewed harmony with the pope are missing from L. They and the letter of 1102 are all favourable to Gerard.

The remaining seven letters of this correspondence which are included in L create a negative image of Archbishop Gerard of York as a wicked, bickering and obstinate man. Only one letter of late 1105 somewhat mitigates this picture: in this together with other bishops, Gerard beseeched Anselm to return to England and promised him their help (386).

It would appear that Anselm omitted this correspondence with Gerard, his ecclesiastical opponent in the investiture dispute, even though it might have improved the bad impression conveyed by the other letters of Gerard's correspondence retained in L. This must support the feeling that there was method in Anselm's omissions. Was the injury inflicted by Gerard's behaviour and actions during the controversy still rankling?

9. Three more items in the list of omitted letters level harsh criticism at Anselm for his prolonged absence from the see of Canterbury and the Church of England due to his second exile from December 1103 to September 1106.[42] A member of the community of Christ Church Canterbury, possibly Prior Ernulf himself, informed the archbishop about the increase of evil caused by his long absence from England (310). He declared that Anselm's absence was unbearable and stated that his presence was essential to any improvement. He entreated him urgently to return to England to resume his duties. Another anonymous person judged the long-drawn-out quarrel between King Henry and Archbishop Anselm as nothing but the illusion of diabolic tricks and complained that it was causing the destruction of the whole Church of the English. He blamed all the misery in England on Anselm's failure to return (365). Moreover, in a long poem Gilbert Crispin, abbot of Westminster and Anselm's friend, displayed to the absent archbishop the evils which had invaded the Church of England because of the pastor's absence and beseeched Anselm to return to his flock (366). Apart from these three voices there were many people who did not understand the reason for Anselm's refusal to return to England. Even after the agreement of L'Aigle between king and archbishop on investiture and homage (21 July 1105) Anselm delayed his return because he had not yet received the pope's endorsement to the compromise agreed upon there, nor his explicit permission to absolve excommunicated persons and to associate with them, even though he was aware that the English churches were suffering cruel treatment because of his absence. In their ignorance of the dealings between the pope, the king and the archbishop, a number of Anselm's friends, his episcopal colleagues (386, 387) and many other people also criticised the absent archbishop and informed him that his absence was causing more evil than good.[43] Since in Anselm's eyes this criticism was unjustified, it would appear that he excluded these letters in order not to mar the image of himself which he wanted to convey and preserve.

This survey of letters omitted from L has thus covered the contents of sixty-nine of the missing eighty-six letters.[44] Why did Anselm omit certain letters from the final edition of his letter collection in L? Apart from those omitted for their triviality or lack of general interest, the intention of these omissions on the one hand

appears to suggest that everything was suppressed which might have caused embarrassment (criticism of Lanfranc, the case of Bishop Fulk of Beauvais, Anselm's part in arranging the king's marriage with Eadgyth/Mathilda) or revive criticism of Anselm's supposed cupidity for the wealthy archbishopric or of his long absences from England. Moreover, such letters which might have challenged Anselm's claim to be the sole advocate and protagonist for the reform and freedom of the Church (Henry, Gerard) and the mighty defender of the primatial claim of Canterbury were also omitted.

On the other hand, in the compilation of the last edition of his letters Anselm seems to have wished to supply a compendium of his thoughts on a great variety of spiritual matters as well as his ideas and the concepts underlying his disagreements with the kings of the Anglo-Norman realm on the issues of the 'usus atque leges' and lay investiture as well as church reform and the primatial claim of Canterbury over York.

More important still, the letter collection displays Anselm as a faithful monk and ardent soldier of Christ who devoted his life totally to God and His service. He appears as a zealous labourer in creating a loving and truly Christian community of monks and as an active reformer of the Church of God in unity with the pope and in agreement with papal ordinance. Thus he set the example of the impeccable Christian prelate whose faultless public conduct was to serve as a model and a precedent for others to act in the same way. The image of his behaviour was intended to create binding customs and eventually good laws. Anselm's letter collection was to be a manual of examples for his own time and for the future.

Therefore manuscript L containing this letter collection is a monument to Anselm's righteousness and firm demeanour as a churchman vigorously pursuing the demand for 'libertas et reformatio ecclesiae' and defending the Church of God resolutely in the face of threats and isolation as well as personal suffering and disadvantages. From the survey of the letters omitted from this MS it would appear that Anselm took great care to suppress any correspondence which would have damaged the picture of himself which he intended for posterity.

Notes

1. Carl Erdmann, *Studien zur Briefliteratur Deutschlands im 11. Jahrhundert,* Leipzig 1938; the same, *Briefsammlungen,* in Wilhelm Wattenbach-Robert Holtzmann, *Deutschlands Geschichtsquellen im Mittelalter, Teil II,* Darmstadt 1967, 415-22; see also *The Letters of Peter the Venerable,* ed. Giles Constable, Harvard Hist. Studies, 78, Harvard 1967, 1-12; the same, *Letters and Letter-Collections,* in *Typologie des Sources du Moyen Âge occidental,* fasc. 17, Turnhout 1976.

2. For a selection of promoted scholars see *The Letters of St Anselm,* transl. Walter Fröhlich, Kalamazoo, in the press, Introduction.

3. The following summary is based on André Wilmart, 'La destinataire de la lettre de S. Anselme sur l'état et les voeux de religion', *Revue Bénédictine (=RB)* 38, 1926, 331-4; the same, 'Une lettre adressée de Rome à S. Anselme en 1102', *RB* 40, 1928, 262-6; the same, 'La tradition des lettres de S. Anselme, lettres inédites de S. Anselme et de ses correspondants', *RB* 43, 1931, 38-54; Franciscus Salesius Schmitt, 'Zur Überlieferung der Korrespondenz Anselms von Canterbury, Neue Briefe', *RB* 43, 1931, 224-38, reprinted in *Anselmi Opera Omnia (=AOO)* ed. F. S. Schmitt, 6 vols, Edinburgh 1946-1963 and Stuttgart 1968. André Wilmart, 'Une lettre inédite de S. Anselme, à une moniale inconstante', *RB* 40, 1928, 319-32; F. S. Schmitt, 'Zur Entstehung der handschriftlichen Briefsammlungen Anselms von Canterbury', *RB* 48, 1936, 300-17 = *AOO* 154*-171*; the same, 'Die Chronologie der Briefe Anselms', *RB* 64, 1954, 176-207 = *AOO* 172*-203*; the same, 'Die unter Anselm veranstaltete Ausgabe seiner Werke und Briefe, Die Codices Bodley 271 und Lambeth 59', *Scriptorium* 9, 1955, 64-75 = *AOO* 226*-239*; Walter Fröhlich, 'Die Entstehung der Briefsammlung Anselms von Canterbury', *Historisches Jahrbuch* 100, 1980, 457-66; the same, 'The genesis of Anselm's collection of letters', *American Benedictine Review* 35, 1984. The opinion maintained in these articles is at variance to that of Richard William Southern, *Saint Anselm and his biographer,* Cambridge 1963, 67-8n, 238n.

4. See e.g. Anselmi Epistola (= AEp) 4, 5, 14, 22, 66, 68, 89, 121, 124, 126, 132.

5. Anselm sent 138 letters; he received 8 letters; one letter names Anselm neither as writer nor as addressee.

6. Anselm is the author of 234 letters, the recipient of 76 letters and neither of both in 18 letters.

7. AEp 88 = M 63; AEp 96 = M 69/70; AEp 102 = M 1; AEp 112 = M 17; AEp 113 = M 10; AEp 120 = M 79; AEp 130 = M 47; AEp 131 = M 46; AEp 132 = M 58; AEp 134 = M 57; AEp 140 = M 15; AEp 144 = M 16; AEp 145 = M 75; AEp 146 = M 74.

8. See Neil Ripley Ker, *The English Manuscripts in the Century after the Norman Conquest,* Oxford 1960, 50-1.

9. For the itinerary see Walter Fröhlich, *Die bischöflichen Kollegen Erzbischof Anselms von Canterbury,* Diss. München 1971, 191-9; now in Letters of St Anselm.

10. For Anselm's journeys to England in 1079, 1086 and 1092 see Marjorie Chibnall, 'The Relations of St Anselm with the English Dependencies of the Abbey of Bec 1079-1093', *Spicilegium Beccense,* Paris 1959, 521-30; the same, *Le domaine du Bec en Angleterre au temps d'Anselme,* Paris 1984/5.

11. L$_1$ and L$_2$ cover fol. 1r to fol. 160v, line 3 of right column. They are most carefully written with very few mistakes. L$_a$ comprises fol. 160v to 190r. It is split into two parts by nine and a half empty pages. The first part of L$_a$ consists of a letter (L 390), a tract on 'velle', a deathbed confession, a sermon on the bliss of eternal life, three tracts on 'aliquid' and 'facere', on 'de potestate' and on different modes of 'causa', two poems in praise of Anselm, the covering letter for Anselm's work 'Cur Deus Homo' to Urban II, another letter (L 391), the canons of the synods of London of 1102 and 1108 and finally seven other letters (L 392, 393, 394, 395, 396, 397, 398). The remaining folios after the gap of nine and a half empty pages contain, in a different hand, a miscellaneous collection of writings as follows: two letters (L 399, 400), two tracts on 'velle', one a repetition of those written before the gap, a repetition of the deathbed confession, another letter (L 401), a draft of a part of Anselm's tract 'De concordia', Anselm's epitaph on Hugh, a fragment of a tract on the presence of God in the Blessed Sacrament, a distich of two lines, a legal document and a repetition of the first poem in praise of Anselm. For a detailed account see Walter Fröhlich, 'The Genesis of the Collection of St Anselm's Letters', *American Benedictine Review* 1984. There are thirteen letters in L$_a$: L 390 = AEp 193; L 391 = AEp 411; L 392 = AEp 331; L 393 = AEp 212; L 394 = AEp 255; L 395 = AEp 202; L 396 = AEp 200; L 397 = AEp 440; L 398 = AEp 207; L 399 = AEp 471; L 400 = AEp 472; L 401 = AEp 469; L 402 = AEp 475. L 399, L 400 and L 401 are duplicating L 388, L 389 and L 387 which are the last entries into L before L$_a$ was added.

12. These letters are referred into L$_2$: L 390, L391, L 392, L 393, L 394, L 398.

13. F. S. Schmitt, 'Die echten und unechten Stücke der Korrespondenz Anselms von Canterbury', *RB* 65, 1955, 218-27 = *AOO* 204*-212*.

14. See e.g. AEp 4, 6, 9, 10, 11, 12, 13, 15, 17, 23, 24, 35, 36, 38, 40, 42, 43, 45, 46, 52, 53, 57, 58, 60, 61, 65, 73, 77, 80, 83, 85, 87, 88, 97, 100, 109, 113, 118, 121, 132, 138, 147; 148, 161, 162, 163, 164, 166, 173, 175, 186, 187, 191, 192, 204, 209, 218, 223, 232, 233, 246, 247, 250, 254, 262, 263, 264, 292, 293, 294, 298, 299, 300, 301, 305,

307, 315, 316, 319, 320, 322, 323, 327, 328, 329, 330, 331, 333, 334, 343, 345, 347, 348, 349, 355, 356, 357, 361, 363, 374, 375, 376, 379, 395, 399, 406, 407, 413, 415, 416, 417, 418, 419, 421, 425, 432, 433, 440, 447, 451, 457, 458, 460.

15. These are AEp 18, 26, 27, 63, 64, 65; 88, 123, 124, 126, 127, 145; 148, 150, 151, 152, 155, 159, 163, 164, 165, 166, 168, 169, 172, 173, 174, 175, 176, 177, 178, 179, 181, 183, 184, 190, 195, 204, 205, 208, 209, 215, 216, 224, 225, 226, 239, 282, 284, 304, 305, 310, 337, 348, 351, 352, 362, 363, 365, 366, 367, 373, 398, 407, 437, 438, 439, 442, 453, 454, 456, 457, 468, 459, 460, 470, 473 and the ten letters from L_a: AEp 193, 200, 202, 207, 212, 255, 331, 411, 440, 475. See footnote 11 above.

16. AEp 18, 26, 27, 63, 64, 65; 88, 123, 124, 126, 127, 145.

17. This letter fills four lines above and six lines below the margin as well as the usual writing area of two columns of 31 lines on fol. 160v and spills five lines right across into the bottom margin of fol. 161r.

18. AEp 148, 150, 151, 152, 155, 163, 165, 166, 173, 174, 178, 179, 205, 209.

19. See *AOO* 156*-162*.

20. According to F. S. Schmitt AEp 177, 183, 184, 190, 195 form a small local collection preserved on folios 67 and 68 in Cambridge, Trinity College Ms B. I. 37, see F. S. Schmitt, 'Zur Überlieferung der Korrespondenz Anselms von Canterbury', *RB* 43, 1931, 230-8; AEp 337 is in M and AEp 168 and 169 in Trier, Stadtbibliothek MS 728; see also André Wilmart, *RB* 38, 1926, 331-4, footnote 3.

21. ASC 1100.

22. See David C. Douglas, *William the Conqueror*, London 1964, 267-9, 426.

23. See 'William of Malmesbury', *Vita Wulfstani*, ed. R. R. Darlington, Camden Society, 3rd series, 40, 1928, 34.

24. Eadmer 121.

25. AEp 242, 243, 246, 288, 296, 317, 320, 321, 323, 346, 347, 384, 385, 395, 400, 406; see also F. S. Schmitt, *RB* 43, 1936, 231-4.

26. AEp 215, 216, 221, 224, 305, 348, 351, 352.

27. See e.g. AEp 315, 318, 323, 368.

28. R. W. Southern, *St Anselm and his biographer*, Cambridge 1963, 68 n is of different opinion. He holds that 'there is not the slightest reason to think

that this letter AEp 379 refers to the making of this or any other collection of letters'. In his judgement R. W. Southern merely relied on palaeographic evidence, see Walter Fröhlich, 'The Genesis of Anselm's collection of letters', see footnote 3.

29. This is British Library, MS Add. 32091; for a description of the manuscript see Walter Holtzmann, *Papsturkunden in England*, vol. 1, Berlin 1930/31, 166-7, 221-31. The letters are AEp 216 = Add. 5; AEp 224 = Add. 10; AEp 305 = Add. 16; AEp 348 = Add. 17; AEp 351 = Add. 18; AEp 352 = Add. 19; AEp 215 and 221 are preserved in *Quadripartitus,* ed. Felix Liebermann, Halle 1892, 151-2.

30. They are preserved: AEp 282 = M 83, AEp 284 = Add. 12.

31. See AEp 14, 15, 23, 96, 164; 124, 151, 223, 284, 339, 349, 367, 371, 377, 378, 390, 397, 430, 438, 462; 86, 180, 248, 249, 298.

32. Eadmer 114. Anselm sent three Paschal-letters AEp 222, 281, 353 to Lambert. These papal letters to Anselm are in accordance with the decrees of Urban's synod of 1099 and represent Paschal's hard line on investitures. Anselm included them into L as L 162, L 226 and L 287 and sent copies of them to Flanders. They were incorporated into a collection of canonical material of the bishopric of Térouane in the second half of the twelfth century being letters 11, 12 and 13 therein. Max Sdralek dealt with the material in *Wolfenbüttler Fragmente,* Münster 1891, 55-9. It seems very unlikely that Lambert received more than these three letters otherwise they would have been entered into this collection, see also *Councils and Synods,* ed. Dorothy Whitelock, Martin Brett, Christopher N. L. Brooke, Oxford 1981, vol. i, 658, 660.

33. Arras, Stadtbibliothek MS 484, catalogue nr. 805; see *AOO* 91*-94*, 213*.

34. AEp 441 = L 370.

35. They are 6210, 6211, 6212, 6213 in P. Jaffe, S. Löwenfeld, *Regesta Pontificum Romanorum,* vol. i, Leipzig 1885.

36. AEp 443 = L 367; AEp 444 = L 368; AEp 445 = L 369; AEp 455 = L 376; AEp 464 = L 382; AEp 465 = L 383; AEp 471 = L 388 and again in L_a, L 399; AEp 472 = L 389 and again in L_a, L 400.

37. They are in *Hugh the Chanter, the history of the Church of York 1066-1127,* ed. Charles Johnson, Oxford 1961, 19 = AEp 453; 20 = AEp 454; AEp 456 = Eadmer 204.

38. AEp 470 = Eadmer 205.

39. AEp 442 = M 102.

40. AEp 238, 250, 253, *255,* 256, 283, 326, 354, *362, 363, 373,* 386, *440.* Those in italics are omitted from L. They are preserved: AEp 255 = L 394; AEp 362, 363, 373, = *Quadripartitus* 155-9; AEp 440 = L 397.

41. See AEp 216, 219, 222, 224, 281.

42. AEp 310, 365, 366.

43. See Eadmer 162, 167, 171; AEp 386, 387.

44. The following letters were not dealt with: AEp 181, 200, 202, 204, 207, 208, 212, 225, 226, 239, 255, 304, 331, 367, 398, 407, 411, 473.

Hugh Feiss (essay date March 1985)

SOURCE: Feiss, Hugh. "The God of St. Anselm's Prayers." *American Benedictine Review* 36, no. 1 (March 1985): 1-22.

[*In the following essay, Feiss surveys Anselm's Trinitarian theology as it appears in his devotional writings.*]

St. Anselm was a monastic theologian, insofar as the context of his life and thought was Benedictine, and the principal aim of his thinking and praying was to seek the face of the Lord. One would, therefore, expect to find a close parallel between his thinking and his spirituality.[1]

In his faith Anselm was untroubled; in his approach to monasticism he was conservative.[2] In both his theology and his written devotions he was highly original.[3] At home in the old ways in which he had been nurtured, he brought to theological thinking new powers of thought, new ideas, and new methods which set him apart from his predecessors and also from those who came after him.[4] His prayers and meditations are suffused with feeling and subjectivity, and are forerunners of St. Bernard and St. Francis, rather than offshoots of Carolingian forebears.[5]

Anselm's favorite theological genre was a closely reasoned monograph on some theological topic of personal concern to him and his friends. In his speculative masterpieces, the *Monologion,* the *Proslogion,* and *Why God Became Man,* Anselm pondered the fundamental mysteries of God and salvation. In some of his other speculative works, such as *On the Procession of the Holy Spirit,* the *Letter on the Incarnation of the Word,* and the letters on the sacraments, Anselm was pressured by external factors to develop or defend particular doctrinal points.[6]

Sometime around the year 1100 A.D., when Hugh, the abbot of Cluny, and Anselm, formerly abbot of Bec and now the harried archbishop of Canterbury, were both old men, Anselm visited Cluny. Anselm had once thought of becoming a monk at Cluny, but at the time he thought the "severity of the order" there would have kept him from putting to use the studies he had made.[7]

Hugh and Anselm were on friendly terms. The *Dicta Anselmi* reports that the two men often talked together of heaven, of virtuous living, and of the activity of good men.[8] On this occasion, Anselm was asked to give a chapter sermon. The themes he developed in the sermon were ones he treated frequently in his discourses. So, when a monk of Cluny named William later wrote asking for the text of Anselm's remarks, Eadmer felt he could accurately write up what Anselm had said.[9]

In order to stir up in his listeners at Cluny a desire for heaven, Anselm proposed to present beatitude in bite-sized pieces, much as a big apple is cut into small slices so a child can eat it. He considered first seven bodily joys, then seven spiritual ones, and showed how heaven will be the unsurpassable perfection of all such joys. In his words about sickness and health and the joys of concord, one can sense the sufferings of the sensitive genius, in declining health, trying to cope with political issues for which he had little taste or aptitude.[10]

What one misses in the surviving versions of this discourse on beatitude is an explicit discussion of God who will be the source of all the joy of the elect. Anselm declares, "He from whom is whatever is good and who is ineffably more powerful and glorious than anything else will indwell them and watch over them";[11] they will shine like the sun because they will be the temple and dwelling place of God.[12] The blessed will stand in God's presence,[13] and seeing God face to face, they will be filled with the wisdom which is God.[14]

Beyond these general references to the mutual presence of the blessed and God, and a charming parable about God making fallen people adopted coheirs with his Son, there are few explicit references to God the Father or to Christ, and only one to the Holy Spirit.[15] This seems strange in the work of the outstanding theologian of his time, who devoted some of his greatest writing to the Trinity. Was this failure to give the Trinity a prominent place in his devotional work typical, and if so, why? Who was God for Anselm when he prayed? In seeking to answer these questions, this study will first summarize Anselm's theology of the Trinity in his speculative works. The next four sections will seek to detect in his more devotional writings what place the Trinity had in his personal religious awareness and prayer. In these sections, his *Prayers and Meditations,* the *Proslogion,* his letters, and the memorials of his familiar teaching will be examined in turn. In these sections Anselm's sense of the distance of God will come to the fore. Finally, some conclusions will be forthcoming about Anselm and the relationship of his doctrinal teaching to his personal spiritual life, and some suggestions will be made why Anselm may have prayed to God the way he did.

ANSELM'S TRINITARIAN THEOLOGY

Anselm gave a summary of his Trinitarian theology at the beginning of his work *On the Procession of the Holy Spirit,* a work in which, uncharacteristically, he wrote apologetically on a *questio* not of his own choosing. Pope Urban II had called on Anselm to present the Western position on the procession of the Holy Spirit at the Council of Bari in October, 1098.[16] In 1102, Anselm wrote this treatise, based on his remarks to the council.[17] Anselm's summary of his Trinitarian theology in the first chapter of *On the Procession of the Holy Spirit* will here be supplemented with ideas drawn from his other works, especially the *Monologion* and the *Epistle on the Incarnation of the Word.*[18]

God is one essence, unique, perfect and self-subsistent. Without parts, God is wholly whatever He is, perfect goodness, justice and holiness. God is eternal and in every time and place. The creator thinks into existence whatever else exists; and creation exists more perfectly in the mind of God than in itself or in human minds. God created everything through his Word.

God is Father, Son and Holy Spirit. Although each is the one same God, Father, Son, and Holy Spirit are plural and different from each other. The Father is one from whom another is begotten; the Son is begotten of the Father. The Holy Spirit proceeds from Father and Son. Whatever the Son is, he is from the Father; whatever the Holy Spirit is, he is from the Father and the Son. There is no Father except of the Son, nor any Son except of the Father, nor any Holy Spirit as the Spirit of anyone other than of the Father and the Son. Since the Son exists from the Father by being begotten, and the Holy Spirit exists by proceeding, by this diversity of birth and procession they are related to each other as diverse and distinct from each other. In God all are one where there is no opposition of relation.[19] The Father begets; the Son is begotten; the Spirit neither begets nor is begotten. Hence, it is fitting that the Incarnation is proper to the person of the Son.

Men cannot comprehend the ineffable truth that there are three persons in one God. Human analogies fall short, yet Christians must strive with all the powers of their minds in search of understanding of God.[20] In the human soul there is a mirror of this mystery. The human mind is one, and at the same time it is memory, intellect and will. This human soul was created to know and love the triune God, and will be eternally blessed when it remembers, knows and loves God who is Father, Son and Holy Spirit. To help clarify the mystery one may think of the analogous relationship of sun, brightness, and heat, of spring, river and pool, or of one mathematical point placed upon another.[21]

Such, in outline, is Anselm's theology of the Trinity in his more speculative works. It remains to examine the less familiar terrain of his prayers.

PRAYERS AND MEDITATIONS

Most of Anselm's prayers and meditations were early works, written before he was abbot. Although somewhat mannered and overwrought, the prayers and meditations show the theological acumen of their author. They emphasize the sinfulness and neediness of human beings, turning to God in contrition and love.[22]

In these prayers there is, besides doxologies, only one explicit Trinitarian reference. *Oratio* 3, "Before receiving the body and blood of the Lord," opens: "O Lord Jesus Christ, through the Father's arrangement and the cooperation of the Holy Spirit, by your death you freely and mercifully redeemed the world from sin and eternal death. . . ."[23] This prayer, like most of the prayers, is addressed to Christ (alone or with one of the saints). Hence, when these prayers end with a doxology, as do *Orationes* 16 and 19 and *Meditationes* I and III, the doxology takes the form: "You live and reign with the Father and the Holy Spirit." For example, the ending of the **"Meditation on Human Redemption"** reads: "[May your love] occupy me totally and possess me completely, because you are with the Father and the Holy Spirit God, alone blessed forever, Amen."[24]

The Augustinian notion of the human person as the image of the Trinity often seems to be just below the surface, but the closest it comes to explicit mention is in *Oratio* 2 which is addressed to Christ: "O most gentle one, my prayer, my memory and my meditation on your benefits tend toward this—that I may enkindle your love in me."[25] Here the mention of memory, meditation and love suggests Augustine's idea of the human being as the Trinity's image through the oneness of memory, understanding and will. The surprising thing is that Anselm doesn't invoke this idea more often. He several times mentions the divine image in the human being, but without any Trinitarian reference. For example, in *Oratio* 8 to John the Baptist, Anselm prays: "Alas for me, what I have made of myself! To think what I was, O God, and how you made me, and then how I have made myself again. . . . You reformed in me your lovable image, and I superimposed a hateful image. . . ."[26] Similarly, Anselm's refers to the sign of the cross, without mentioning the Trinity.[27]

Sometimes the prayers invoke or refer to two persons of the Trinity. For example, *Oratio* 1, addressed to God, ends by asking: "Free me from all evil, and lead me to eternal life, through the Lord." *Oratio* 4 declares: "God, the Son of God, for our sake willed to be obedient to the Father unto death."[28] Once Christ and the Holy Spirit are mentioned together: "You were once made white in the heavenly bath, given to the Holy Spirit, sworn in the Christian profession, a virgin espoused to Christ."[29] Several times Anselm prays for the love of God. At these times he seems about to ask specifically that the Holy Spirit bring this love into his heart, but he never does so.[30]

One other aspect of the prayers is germane to the Trinity. Occasionally, the prayers refer to the closeness of God or Christ to the Christian. *Oratio* 3 asks of Christ that by the sacrament of communion "I might be worthy to be incorporated into your body, which is the church, and be your member and you my head, and that I might remain in you and you in me."[31] *Meditation* III, also speaking of the Eucharist, says, "You will remain in Christ and Christ in you."[32] The same intimacy with Christ is implied by a reference to brotherhood with Christ in *Oratio* 7.[33] Finally, there is a sense of tenderness, if not closeness, in the passage on Christ as mother in *Oratio* 10.[34]

However, these passages are the exception. The usual feeling of the prayers and meditations is one of distance from God and Christ. Thus, for example, Anselm exclaims in *Oratio* 13: "O rich and happy peace, how far am I from you!"[35] Generally, the prayers envisage the Christian as serving God in a state of mind midway between hope and fear,[36] fearing Christ the just judge, hoping in his mercy. The prayers voice the sentiments of fallen humanity, yearning to return to the God who made and remade them, from whom they have turned through sin.

The prayers and meditations take up some ninety pages in Schmitt's edition of Anselm's works. Our examination has shown that in these pages there are remarkably few references to the Trinity in general or to the Holy Spirit in particular. The focus of Anselm's prayer almost always is Christ, and sometimes it is the Father. Even in contexts where one might have expected reference to the Trinity (e.g., man as God's image; the doxologies), such references are absent. God and Christ are viewed as far from the sinful supplicant who looks to them for aid.

PROSLOGION

After Anselm had written his first great treatise, the *Monologion* (1077), "it came into his mind to try to prove by one single and short argument the things which are believed and preached about God, that he is eternal, unchangeable, omnipotent, omnipresent, incomprehensible, just, righteous, merciful, true, as well as truth, goodness, justice and so on. . . ." Anselm was so taken with this effort that it cost him his appetite and his sleep, and "disturbed the attention which he ought to have paid to matins and to divine service at other times. . . . Then suddenly one night during matins the grace of God illumined his heart, the whole matter became clear to his mind, and a great joy and exultation filled his inmost being." The result was the *Proslogion,* "a volume small in size but full of weighty discourse and most subtle speculation."[37]

In the *Proslogion* Anselm's speculative powers and his intense desire to understand what he believes are brought into intimate union with prayer and devotion. The result is a sustained meditation which explores the implications of the "one argument" which Anselm struggled so hard to formulate, the heart of which is known to philosophers as the ontological argument.

Very little of the work is devoted to the Trinity as such. The first chapter recalls St. Augustine's understanding of the human being as made in the image of God: "I confess, Lord, and I give you thanks, that you have created me in your image, so that mindful of you, I can think of you and love you." Immediately, though, Anselm acknowledges that this image has been worn and darkened by sin, so it cannot do that for which it was made, "unless you renew and refashion it."[38]

Two points are noteworthy here. First, Anselm is keenly aware of the ravages of sin which have turned this life into an exile, a search for what we have lost. Secondly, in confessing that he is created in the divine image, Anselm addresses the *Lord*. For the next twenty-one chapters Anselm addresses God, the Lord our God, the Lord, or the Immense Goodness, the Inaccessible Light.

Only in Chapter 23 does Anselm change his form of address, at the very moment he introduces the topic of the Trinity: "God the Father, you are this Good; this Good is your Word, that is, your Son. In the Word you utter there can be nothing other than what you are, and nothing greater or less than you. . . . And this is the only love common to you and to your Son, that is, the Holy Spirit proceeding from both. . . . What each is himself, the whole Trinity—Father, Son and Holy Spirit—is at the same time."[39] Thus, as he turns his mind to the Trinity, Anselm addresses his prayer no longer to God or the Lord, but to God the Father.

In the remaining three chapters of the *Proslogion,* Anselm turns his mind to the enjoyment of this Supreme God, whose possession *there* in heaven contrasts with our neediness *here* below. In the climactic prayer of the final chapter Anselm addresses the Lord and God who spoke of heavenly joy through his Son. This final joy will not enter into the blessed, but they will enter into it, and then they will rejoice as much as they love and love as much as they know. Anselm prays that even *here* his love and knowledge may increase in hope, so that *there* they may be full in reality. God has advised us to seek and ask through his Son, and so Anselm does, until he will enter into the joy of his Lord who is God, one and three, blessed forever.[40]

Four things are noteworthy in this final chapter of the **Proslogion:** (1) that Anselm now explicitly, for the first time, prays through the Son; (2) that there is contrast between *here* and *there,* hope and reality; (3) that the consummation of blessedness is visualized not as an entrance of God's joy into the blessed, but of them into it; (4) that the fullness of joy comes through loving and knowing God, one and three, and thus actualizing the form of God's image within oneself.

LETTERS

St. Anselm was a prolific letter writer. Half of Schmitt's critical edition of Anselm's works is devoted to the 475 surviving letters to or by Anselm; about 400 of these are Anselm's own. The letters fall into two distinct collections: (1) those written while Anselm was at Bec (1071-93); (2) his correspondence as archbishop (1093-1109). The letters in the first collection are more personal and literary; the letters of the second group are less personal and deal primarily with church business.[41]

In his letters, Anselm followed the rhetorical conventions. He began with the *salutatio,* the form of which was dictated by the relative dignity of sender and recipient. The inferior's name was always second. Then came the *exordium* or *captatio benevolentiae* designed to gain the good will of the reader. After the *narratio* or *petitio* of the body of the letter, came some sort of *conclusio.* The opening and closing parts of the letters provided occasions for Anselm to pray for God's help and blessings. However formal the style of these prayers in the letters, they give some idea of Anselm's religious mentality.

One typical example is **"Letter 332,"** addressed to the monks of Canterbury, probably sometime before October, 1104, when Anselm was in exile in France. The salutation reads: "Archbishop Anselm [wishes] to his brothers and dear sons who are serving God in Christ Church at Canterbury, to the degree it is possible, salvation and his own and God's blessings." The body of the letter is an exhortation to the monks to be faithful to the monastic way of life during troublesome times. The letter ends with a prayer, the contents of which are characteristic of many prayers in Anselm's

letters, although this prayer is fuller than most: "May almighty God deign to cleanse you from all evils, and make you abound in all good things and exult after this life in his kingdom. May the blessing of God be upon you, and may you be granted the remission of all your sins. Amen. At present I do not know when our return to you will take place, but I hope in God that your prayer will not be in vain."[42]

There are four features of the quoted parts of this letter which are significant here and typical of Anselm's letters: (1) the salutation wishes *God's* blessing; (2) the concluding oration is addressed to *almighty God* and asks his favors in this life and the next; (3) the concluding benediction and absolution; (4) the reference to the prayers of the monks for Anselm (often Anselm will mention also his prayers for his correspondents).

Anselm employs a somewhat different style when writing to kings and popes. An example is **"Letter 378,"** written to King Henry of England around the beginning of 1106. The salutation assures the king of the archbishop's faithful service and prayers: "To Henry, his most dear lord, by the grace of God King of the English, Anselm, archbishop of Canterbury [offers] faithful service with prayers." After telling the king that he is sending the monk Gilbert of Bec to him, and defending the election of Pope Paschal, Anselm concludes: "May almighty God so make you rule over the English in this life, that you may reign among the angels in the future life."[43] This prayer, like the prayer in **"Letter 332,"** asks the favor of almighty God, and it relates and distinguishes this life and the next.

The great majority of prayers in Anselm's letters share three characteristics with these two examples: (1) they implicitly place great value on intercessory prayer; (2) they are addressed simply to (almighty) God; (3) they distinguish sharply between the transitory, pilgrim state of this life and the fullness of the life to come, which awaits those who live rightly here and now.[44]

Rarely there are hints of other emphases which are generally absent in the prayers of Anselm's letters. Some of these are as follows: (1) the indwelling presence of God in the soul[45] and in the Christian community;[46] (2) the action of the Trinity,[47] or, more specifically, the work of the Holy Spirit, who dwells in the Christian[48] and who speaks through persons he chooses,[49] and teaches, inspires, guards and warms the heart of the individual Christian,[50] or, finally, Christ, who is the Christian's leader,[51] truth,[52] and teacher,[53] the focus of Christian brotherhood and the source of good.[54]

So Anselm can on occasion situate his prayers in an explicitly Trinitarian context and speak of the indwelling of the Holy Spirit in the soul. However, almost always he prays simply to God from whom he feels himself an exile.

THE *MEMORIALS*

The *Memorials* of St. Anselm, edited by R.W. Southern and F. S. Schmitt, contain works and fragments attributed to St. Anselm and emanating from circles close to him. It is not always possible to pinpoint how closely these works represent Anselm's own ideas. However, they are of interest, since they reflect his thought, not in its speculative heights, but in the more intimate setting of his spiritual teaching and conversation in the company of his fellow monks.

The works in this category include the following: *De Humanis Moribus,* of unknown origin (perhaps notes dictated by Anselm); the **Dicta** of St. Anselm and the miracle stories, written up by Alexander, a monk of Christ Church, Canterbury, who was close to Anselm from 1100 until 1109; the *De Beatitudine,* written by Eadmer for William, a monk of Cluny; and, finally, some *Miscellanea.*[55]

In one of the miracle stories, Anselm was visiting a cell of Bec, which was under the care of the monk Tytso. Tytso told Anselm how a few days before, during Sunday lauds, the devil stole a boy, who was their donkey-keeper. During lauds the monk himself felt shaky, so as soon as the service was over, he went to their dwelling-place. Upon searching the house, he found the boy's clothes, but not the boy. That evening, when Tytso had despaired of finding the boy, he heard a lamentation in the locked barn. Tytso and his companions rushed in and found the boy hanging naked and upside down from the rafters.

When they had helped him down, the boy told them how he had heard a voice calling him, and had risen from bed and gone to the window. When ordered to, he hesitatingly put his hand out the window. He was immediately pulled out the window and whisked away. The boy protested, but the stranger assured him that he would show him wondrous things, such as how the soul is separated from the body. The boy protested: "By my faith, I do not want to see that. Let me go."

Meanwhile, they arrived at a woods. The boy saw that his abductor was a hairy, headless creature, who spoke from deep within his chest. Frightened to death, the boy began to cry: "Lord, God, help me, because I believe in you." At this his captor left him. Then an old man came along. The old man told the kidnapped boy to quit crying and go to sleep, which he immediately did. He did not wake up until evening, when the monk heard him crying in the barn. The narrator notes that this story makes one consider the mercy of God, which let the boy be tried—perhaps because he did not go to church—but kept him from perishing, on account of his piety.[56]

This story, like much of the *Memorials,* belongs to a world which seems far removed from the lofty speculations of the **Monologion** and the cultivated piety of the prayers. It is, however, a world in which Anselm was also at home; a world of homey stories, moral exhortation, and prayer for divine help.

In the *Memorials* Anselm appears as a spiritual guide who urges his listeners to live humbly and obediently according to God's will, avoiding self-will which is expressed in the desire for vain pleasure, exaltation, and knowledge.[57] Anselm's prayers are efficacious.[58] God is sometimes described in terms reminiscent of Anselm's theological works; for example, as one in whom knowledge, essence and eternity are one.[59] Most often, however, God is simply there, as God.

In much of his teaching in the *Memorials,* Anselm speaks simply of God, or prays, like the boy abducted by the devil, to the "Lord God." However, more often than in his prayers, letters and theological works, Anselm draws upon the common themes of Christian catechesis and preaching, and to a greater degree than in his other works, he explicitly refers to the Trinity.

One of the most attractive examples of this is a sermon on the dedication of a church.[60] God, who dwells everywhere, has set up a home in the world, as a special reminder of his presence and hospitality. This house of God, which is fortified against the devil, is a temple because in it sacrifice is offered: formerly the Old Testament sacrifices, now the sacrifice of Christ which they prefigured. Christ was made our brother and comrade without ceasing to be what he was before the creation of the world. He lived and taught well; persevering in justice, he was killed by evil men.

The Father could give him nothing which was not his before he became man, since with the Father and the Holy Spirit he created all things in the beginning. So his reward was distributed to his brothers and sisters. As Christ died in the flesh, so those who wish to be Christians must put to death carnal evils and desires for the love of Christ. As Christ rose from death to life, so does the Christian by means of baptism.

The celebration of the dedication of a church signifies the sanctification of each Christian soul, the union of all Christians with God, the joining of man and God in friendship. The Church and each Christian are *mothers* who teach and they are the child who is taught. The Church and each Christian soul are spouses of Christ, and both, like Christ, offer to God the sacrifice of a humbled spirit. In the Church dwell God, Christ, and the Holy Spirit. Of this temple of God, the foundation is faith, which consists above all in holding that in the divine unity there is trinity and in the trinity, unity. The church is built up in love, which cherishes all whom the Spirit makes sons, all who through the same Spirit pray "Our Father."

There are a few further Trinitarian themes in the *Memorials* which do not occur in this sermon for the dedication of a church. The Christian longs to contemplate the ineffable majesty of the undivided Trinity and Christ in glory.[61] Seeing God as He is, the blessed will become like Him.[62] Although the *Memorials* allude to sin destroying the image of God in human beings,[63] they do not make it a point to relate the triad of memory, intellect and will to the Trinity.[64] Several times, though, they refer to the seven transforming gifts of the Holy Spirit.[65]

A noteworthy accent of the *Memorials* is the emphasis they give to the intimacy which Christ has established between God and humanity. The redemption wrought by Christ was not merely a juridical achievement; it established an intimate union between God and redeemed humanity. Christians receive divine adoption;[66] they become brothers and sisters of Christ and coheirs with him.[67] They are made members of Christ's body.[68] In heaven Christ is sanctified in the blessed who rest in him.[69] So close is the friendship which Christ's grace establishes between the Christian and God[70] that it can be described in terms of marital intimacy[71] and deification.[72] In heaven God will be all in all,[73] and even now the saints are one spirit with him.[74]

CONCLUSION

There are many ideas in the *Memorials* which are not prominent in the rest of Anselm's writings, and their tone is not always typical of Anselm's other writings. In the analyses of Anselm's other devotional writings and his theological works two features stood out sharply: (1) the Trinity loomed larger in Anselm's doctrinal speculation than in his devotional writing; (2) there seemed to be a tension between the nearness and remoteness of God. The nature and origins of these two features of Anselm's thought are the subject of this conclusion.

St. Anselm's theological teaching marked the beginning of a theological renaissance, and his Trinitarian thought was not without the stamp of his genius.[75] He dealt with the Trinity extensively in the *Monologion,* and he thereafter presupposed, rather than reworked, the ideas he developed there. His later considerations on the theology of the Trinity were forced upon him by polemical situations. It was characteristic of Anselm to exhaust one theological subject and then move on to another, and so that he did not spontaneously return to a consideration of the theology of the Trinity does not necessarily imply that it was not of great interest to

him. However, that his prayers, and not just his *orationes* but also the prayers which occur elsewhere in his works, do not manifest a strongly Trinitarian devotion, does suggest that his theological interests, like his devotional life, were not as pronouncedly Trinitarian as might at first appear.

Once in his life Anselm found himself forced to defend his doctrinal orthodoxy. John, a monk of Bec, wrote him that Roscelin of Compiègne claimed that Anselm held that the Father and the Holy Spirit had become incarnate with the Son. Anselm replied to this accusation, first with several letters, then with the work *On the Incarnation of the Word.*[76] As Roscelin himself found, and Abelard was to learn in the next generation, the Trinity was a doctrine which could easily embroil one in controversy.[77] Perhaps this led Anselm to shy away from the Trinity in his theology and devotion.

Another reason why Anselm was not pronouncedly Trinitarian in his outlook was his fascination with the divine nature and attributes. In a way that may be called Platonic, he was drawn to the one "than which nothing greater can be thought,"[78] "the supremely good and supremely great."[79] That this one was triune, that the Father sent the Son to save us and give us the Spirit of adoption, Anselm believed unreservedly and devoutly. Yet in the mystery of God, it was the light of the divine nature which drew him irresistibly to itself.

When Anselm was a little boy, his mother told him that "there is one God in heaven who rules all things and comprehends all things." Reared in the mountains, little Anselm thought that God's heaven rested on their summit. One night he dreamed that he was supposed to climb the mountains to the court of God. There God greeted him affably and offered him the whitest of bread. The next day Anselm recalled to his mind's eye this visit to the one God in heaven who rules and comprehends all.[80] During his whole life his mind was drawn toward that one God.

This concentration on the oneness of God was probably reinforced by the Divine Office which he celebrated as a monk at Bec, and whenever possible during his life as archbishop and superior of the monastery of Christ Church, Canterbury.[81] Although the absence of contemporary customaries and liturgical books makes it impossible to reconstruct the liturgical life of Bec in Anselm's time, the order of the day and the arrangement of the office is not likely to have differed much from that of other observant monasteries of the time. Hence Anselm's religious life for over thirty years at Bec, and to a lesser degree afterwards at Canterbury, was nourished by the recitation of at least one hundred psalms a day, and probably many more. This was so because to the ordinary monastic *cursus,* monastic legislators and customs had added numerous accretions, most of which consisted of psalms.[82]

The God of the psalms is the one God, the *Dominus Deus,* of Abraham, Isaac and Jacob. Even when each psalm is concluded with a doxology, the cumulative impact of praying so many psalms is not likely to have contributed any Trinitarian emphasis to Anselm's religious awareness.[83]

As he grew up, Anselm attended Mass celebrated according to the liturgy of Aosta, which was influenced by the usages of Lyons. The prayers of this rite seem to have emphasized acknowledgement of sins. For example, as the faithful brought up the bread to the bishop, they prayed: "To you, Lord, my creator, I offer a sacrifice for the remission of all my sins and those of all your faithful." On the other hand, one of the prayers before communion ran: "Holy Lord, grant that I may so receive the body and blood of our Lord Jesus Christ . . . that through this I may desire . . . to be filled with your Holy Spirit."[84]

Throughout Anselm's writings, there is a similar contrast and tension between the closeness and distance of God, between being a wretched sinner and the temple of the Holy Spirit. Such a paradox is undoubtedly part of devout Christian experience, but the contrast, for example, between the sense of unworthiness in Anselm's prayers and the emphasis on God's indwelling in Chapter 20 of the *Dicta* (the sermon on the dedication of a church) seems peculiarly intense. Without implying that religious experience can be understood wholly in terms of psychological causes, or that one can pinpoint key events in Anselm's religious development, it is possible to suggest a certain parallel between Anselm's relations with God and his relations with other human beings.

Anselm's mother died when he was still young, "and then the ship of his heart had as it were lost its anchor and drifted almost entirely among the waves of the world.[85] Anselm did not get along with his father, and he soon left home. Anselm's heart seems to have not found any anchorage until he became a student under Lanfranc at Bec. For Lanfranc, Anselm's devotion was so great that if Lanfranc had said so, Anselm would have gone into the woods and spent the rest of his life there as a hermit.[86]

Only three years after Anselm became a monk at Bec, Lanfranc left to become abbot at Caen. Anselm succeeded him, and "being continually given up to God and to spiritual exercises, he attained such a height of divine speculation, that he was able by God's help to see into and unravel many obscure and previously insoluble questions about the divinity of God and about our faith."[87] As prior he was also involved in the discipline of the monastery. One very young and talented monk named Osbern was of difficult character and disliked Anselm. Anselm won him over by kindness and soon the boy began to love Anselm. Anselm, for his part, saw Osbern grow in the monastic life and, "inspired by the holy fire of charity, he loved his son more than you could believe possible." Osbern, however, soon took sick and died. Afterwards, several monks, formerly critical of Anselm, hoped "to succeed to Osbern's place" in Anselm's affection, "but he, though he thanked God for their change of heart, 'became all things to all men,' that he might save all."[88]

It seems, therefore, that to this point in his life, Anselm developed strong attachments. Each time, though, he was separated from the person he loved. Although he continued to be a kind person who attracted the affection of others, he henceforth seems to have avoided close friendships. Thereafter, Anselm was more passionately devoted to the idea of friendship, the union of wills in God, than to any friend.[89]

Perhaps his experiences of human loss and his sense of the distance of God were related. Although he believed and sometimes even felt that God was a loving Father, that Christ was his brother, and that the Spirit dwelt within him, Anselm had a deep sense of the transitoriness and incompleteness of this world and a feeling that however beautiful was the valley, God and heaven were on the top of the mountain.

Anselm thought of human beings as created in God's image, fallen into dissimilitude, redeemed objectively by Christ and subjectively by faith and baptism, and then fallen back into sin and striving for salvation.[90] The Christian life is a struggle of the sinful exile to so submit to God's grace and will that one day the Christian may be one with God again. To those struggling in this life, God seems remote; there is contact with heaven through the cross of Christ. Here below, the image of the Trinity in human beings is clouded over and worn; only in heaven will they realize fully who they are, as they forever remember, understand, and love God who is Father, Son, and Holy Spirit. Thus, when after his death Anselm appeared to a man in a dream, he could finally say: "*There* I live, where I see, rejoice and enjoy."[91]

Notes

1. I am thankful to Bro. Neil Yocom, O.S.B., who collaborated on an earlier version of this study, which was presented at the Fifteenth International Congress on Medieval Studies, Western Michigan University, May 3, 1980. This revision was

completed during a National Endowment for the Humanities seminar at The Catholic University of America in the summer of 1982. The leaders of the seminar, Professors Daniel Sheerin and Ruth Steiner, and the participants contributed much to its completion. I wish also to thank the editors of the *American Benedictine Review,* whose criticisms I have found stimulating, even when I did not agree with them.

2. St. Anselm, *Ep.* 37 (*S* 3.144-48). References to Anselm's works in the critical edition of F. S. Schmitt, *Omnia Opera,* 6 vols. (Edinburgh: Thomas Nelson 1946-61) will be indicated by an "*S*" followed by the numbers of the volume, pages and, where appropriate, the lines. Translations are my own, unless otherwise indicated. See also R. W. Southern, *St. Anselm and His Biographer* (Cambridge University Press 1963) p. 349; Benedicta Ward, *Anselm of Canterbury: A Monastic Scholar,* rev. ed. (Fairacres, Oxford: SLG Press 1977) pp. 5-7.

3. Southern, *Anselm and His Biographer,* pp. 346-47.

4. G. R. Evans, *Anselm and a New Generation* (Oxford: Clarendon 1980).

5. Southern, *Anselm and His Biographer,* pp. 42-47.

6. Anselm's works may be fitted together systematically. See John McIntyre, "Premises and Conclusions in the System of St. Anselm," *Spicilegium Beccense, I: Congrès international du IXe centenaire de l'arrivée d'Anselme au Bec* (Paris: J. Vrin 1959) pp. 95-101.

7. Eadmer, *Vita Sancti Anselmi,* ed. and trans. R. W. Southern (London: Thomas Nelson 1962) pp. 9, 121, 123. For another instance of the phrase *districtio ordinis,* see *De Humanis Moribus,* ch. 81 (*M* 71.20). As I note later, the order of the day and the divine office at Bec were probably not much different from those at Cluny. Hence, one may wonder what this *districtio ordinis* was. References to *The Memorials of Saint Anselm,* eds. R. W. Southern and F. S. Schmitt (London: Oxford University Press 1969) will be by an "*M,*" followed by numbers of pages and lines.

8. Noreen Hurt, *Cluny under St. Hugh, 1049-1109* (Notre Dame, IN: University of Notre Dame Press 1968) p. 148. *Dicta,* ch. 21 (*M* 196.10-12).

9. R. W. Southern, *Anselm and His Biographer,* pp. 362-64; *De Beatitudine Perennis Vitae* (*M* 273-91). Other versions of Anselm's remarks on this subject are found in *Dicta,* ch. 5 (*M* 127-41); *De Moribus,* chs. 48-71 (*M* 57-63); *Proslogion,* ch. 25 (*S* 1.118.12-120.20); *Miscellanea,* ch. 3 (*M* 304-05).

10. *De Beatitudine,* chs. 5, 10 (*M* 277.15-78.10, 282.23-83.22).

11. *Dicta,* ch. 5 (*M* 129.21-25).

12. *De Beatitudine* (*M* 275.20-21).

13. *Ibid., M* 280.8, 284.30.

14. *De Humanis Moribus* (*M* 60.25-28).

15. Cf. *De Beatitudine* (*M* 290.16-17).

16. Eadmer, *Vita Sancti Anselmi,* ed. and trans. R. W. Southern (London: Thomas Nelson 1962) pp. 112-13 (ch. 34); Eadmer, *History of Recent Events in England,* trans. Goeffrey Bosanquet (London: Cresset 1964) pp. 108-10.

17. G. R. Evans, *Anselm and Talking about God* (Oxford: Clarendon 1978) pp. xii, 10, 195-97; G. R. Evans, *Anselm and a New Generation,* pp. 41-59. See also Anselm, *Epp.* 239-41 (*S* 4.146-50).

18. *De Processione* (*S* 2.175-219); *Monologion* (*S* 1.13-87); *Epistola de Incarnatione Verbi* (*S* 2.1-35). On Anselm's theology of the Trinity see Helmut Kohlenberger, "*Konsequenzen und Inkonsequenzen der Trinitätslehre in Anselm's Monologion,*" *Analecta Anselmiana* V (Frankfurt/Main: Minerva 1976) 149-78; Michael Schmaus, "*Die theologiegeschichtliche Tragweite der Trinitätslehre des Anselm von Canterbury,*" *Analecta Anselmiana* IV/1 (Frankfurt/Main: Minerva 1975) 29-45; Renato Perino, *La dottrina trinitaria di Sant'Anselmo* (*Studia Anselmiana* 29) (Rome: Herder 1952); Walter Simonis, *Trinität und Vernunft* (*Frankfurter theologische Studien* 12) (Frankfurt/Main: J. Knecht 1972) pp. 5-34.

19. *De Processione Spiritus Sancti,* ch. 1 (*S* 2.180-85).

20. Evans, *Anselm on Talking about God,* p. 35; Evans, *Anselm and a New Generation,* p. 194; *Dicta,* ch. 3 (*M* 118-22); *De Incarnatione Verbi,* ch. 1 (*S* 2.3-10).

21. For discussion and references regarding these images of the Trinity in Anselm's work, see G. R. Evans, "St. Anselm's Images of the Trinity," *Journal of Theological Studies* 27 (1976) 46-57; W. Hankey, "The Place of the Psychological Image of the Trinity in the Arguments of Augustine's *De Trinitate,* Anselm's *Monologion* and Aquinas' *Summa Theologiae,*" *Dionysius* 3 (1979) 99-110; G. R. Evans, "St. Anselm and St. Bruno of Segni: The Common Ground," *Journal of Ecclesiastical History* 29 (1978) 138-40.

22. On questions of authenticity see André Wilmart, introduction to *Meditations et prières de saint Anselme,* trans. A. Castel, *Collection Pax* (Paris:

P. Lethielleux 1923) pp. i-lxii. On style and content see F. S. Schmitt, "*Des hl. Anselm von Canterbury Gebet zum hl. Benedikt. Zur Wesenart der anselmianischen Gebete und Betrachtungen,*" *Studia Benedictina* (Studia Anselmiana 18-19) (Vatican City: Libreria Vaticana 1947) pp. 295-313; René Roques, "*Structure et caractères de la prière Anselmienne,*" *Sola Ratione. Anselm-Studien für Pater Dr. h.c. Franciscus Salesianus Schmitt* (Stuttgart: Frommann 1970) pp. 119-89; Benedicta Ward, *Anselm of Canterbury,* and the introduction to her translation of the *Prayers and Meditations of St. Anselm* (Baltimore: Penguin 1973) pp. 35-75.

23. *S* 3.10.3-5.

24. *Ibid.,* 3.91.209-11.

25. *Ibid.,* 3.7.22-23.

26. *Ibid.,* 3.26.19-20, 27.30-32; also 29.82, 85. *Oratio* 14 (*S* 3.56.31-32, 59.1210; *Oratio* 17 (*S* 3.68.9).

27. *Oratio* 4 (*S* 3.11.10). In general, in the *Vita* and the *Memorials* there is little indication that the sign of the cross has Trinitarian connotations for St. Anselm.

28. *S* 3.6.16-17, 3.12,30-31. Also *Oratio* 5 (*S* 3.14.49-51); *Oratio* 13 (*S* 3.54.138-410; *Oratio* 18 (*S* 3.71.3, 7); *Meditatio* III (*S* 3.87.95 ff.).

29. *Meditatio* II (*S* 3.80.7-9).

30. *Oratio* 18 (*S* 3.72.43-46); *Oratio* 16 (*S* 3.67.79-81).

31. *S* 3.10.18-20.

32. *Ibid.,* 3.89.135-36.

33. *Ibid.,* 3.23-24.

34. *Ibid.,* 3.40-41;

35. *Ibid.,* 54.128.

36. *Oratio* 4 (*S* 3.12.47-48).

37. Eadmer, *Vita,* ch. 19, ed. Southern, pp. 29-31.

38. *S* 1.100.12-13; cf. ch. 14 (*S* 1.111.2-24).

39. *S* 1.117.6-19.

40. *Proslogion,* ch. 26 (*S* 1.120.1-122.2).

41. R. W. Southern, *St. Anselm and His Biographer,* pp.67-76. Some of the earlier letters are translated in two unpublished masters theses: Anselm Pedrizetti, *St. Anselm's Letters to Lanfranc* (Washington, DC: Catholic University 1961); Paschal Donald Honner, *Saint Anselm's Letters to the Monks of Bec* (Washington, DC: Catholic

University 1961). Some of these letters were published in Paschal D. Honnor, "Letters of St. Anselm to His Monks at Bec," *American Benedictine Review* 14 (March 1963) 138-63, and "Letters of St. Anselm to the Community of Bec, II," *American Benedictine Review* 14 (June 1963) 319-40; Anselm R. Pedrizetti, "Letters of Saint Anselm to Archbishop Lanfranc," *ABR* [*American Benedictine Review*] 12 (1961) 430-60. For the style and content of all the letters, see the doctoral dissertation of Sr. John David Loughlin, *Saint Anselm as Letter Writer* (Washington, DC: Catholic University 1967).

42. *S* 5.267.1-3, 268.25-30.

43. *Ibid.,* 5.321.1-2, 322.21-22.

44. *Ep.* 16 (*S* 3.122.21-23); *Ep.* 37 (*S* 3.147.92-148.94); *Ep.* 56 (*S* 3.171.13-14); *Ep.* 287 (*S* 4.221.37, 44-45); *Ep.* 402 (*S* 5.346.2, 11-15); *Ep.* 413 (*S* 5.358.2, 7-14, 359.25-26).

45. *Ep.* 369 (*S* 5.323.10-11).

46. *Ep.* 403 (*S* 5.347.15-16); *Ep.* 450 (*S* 5.397.9-10).

47. *Ep.* 374 (*S* 5.318.15-16).

48. *Ep.* 232 (*S* 4.139.25-26); *Ep.* 418 (*S* 5.364.22-23).

49. *Ep.* 8 (*S* 3.110.7-8).

50. *Ep.* 10 (*S* 3.114.28); *Ep.* 60 (*S* 3.175.21); *Ep.* 45 (*S* 3.159.31); *Ep.* 286 (*S* 4.206.32); *Ep.* 288 (*S* 4.208.18); *Ep.* 413 (*S* 5.358.12); *Ep.* 448 (*S* 5.395.18-19); *Ep.* 467 (*S* 5.417.17).

51. *Ep.* 2 (*S* 3.101.69-70).

52. *Ep.* 21 (*S* 3.128.20-21).

53. *Ep.* 6 (*S* 3.108.26-28).

54. *Ep.* 45 (*S* 3.158.12, 159.25-26, 36).

55. *De Humanis Moribus* (*M* 37-104); *Dicta* (*M* 107-95); *Miracula* (*M* 196-270); *De Beatitudine* (*M* 271-92); *Miscellanea* (*M* 293-360).

56. *Miracula,* ch. 51.

57. This is the explicit theme of *De Humanis Moribus,* chs. 8-46 (*M* 41-57), but it appears constantly in the teaching of the *Memorials;* e.g. *De Humanis Moribus,* chs. 127-28 (*M* 87), *Dicta,* chs. 1-2 (*M* 110-18).

58. *Dicta,* chs. 39-40, 44-45; *Miscellanea,* chs. 7-8 (*M* 306).

59. *Dicta,* ch. 9 (*M* 147.26-27).

60. *Dicta,* ch. 20 (*M* 180-94); also *Miscellanea* (*M* 310-19).

61. *Miscellanea* (*M* 358-59); cf. *De Humanis Moribus,* ch. 59 (*M* 60.25-28); *Dicta,* ch. 4 (*M* 123.17-18); *Dicta,* ch. 9 (*M* 147-49); *De Beatitudine,* ch. 8 (*M* 280.8).

62. *Miscellanea* (*M* 359.25-26).

63. *De Humanis Moribus,* ch. 119 (*M* 83.29-30); *Miscellanea* (*M* 329.8-9).

64. *Miscellanea* (*M* 306.1-5, 332.27-34).

65. *De Humanis Moribus,* chs. 131-32 (*M* 88.20-89.25); *Miscellanea* (*M* 328-29); *Dicta,* ch. 1 (*M* 110.4).

66. *Dicta,* ch. 5 (*M* 138.22-24); *Dicta,* ch. 20 (*M* 187.21); *Miscellanea* (*M* 304.32).

67. *Dicta,* ch. 5 (*M* 138.22-33); *Dicta,* ch. 20 (*M* 184.1-3; 187.22); *De Beatitudine,* ch. 12 (*M* 284.8-10); *Miscellanea* (*M* 304.33-34).

68. *Dicta,* ch. 20 (*M* 181.21-22, 191.9-10); *De Beatitudine,* ch. 10 (*M* 282.29-31, 284.10).

69. *Miscellanea* (*M* 332.4-7).

70. *Dicta,* ch. 5 (*M* 138.21; 140.15); *Dicta,* ch. 20 (*M* 185.31, 187.20-21).

71. With God: *Dicta,* ch. 20 (*M* 186.25, 187.1, 190.4 ff.); with Christ: *Dicta,* ch. 20 (*M* 186.2-3).

72. *Dicta,* ch. 5 (*M* 139.4); *Dicta,* ch. 9 (*M* 148.27-29); *De Beatitudine,* ch. 12 (*M* 284.11-13).

73. *Miscellanea* (*M* 328.27-28).

74. *Ibid.,* 332.31-32.

75. Edmund J. Fortman, *The Triune God* (Philadelphia: Westminster 1972) pp. 173-76.

76. John's letter, *Ep.* 128 (*S* 3.270-71); Anselm's reply, *Ep.* 129 (*S* 3.271-72); Anselm instructs Fulk, Bishop of Beauvais, what to say at the Council of Rheims, *Ep.* 136 (*S* 3.279-81); *Epistola de Incarnatione Verbi* (first recension: *S* 1.281-90; second recension: *S* 2.31-35); Southern, *Anselm and His Biographer,* pp. 77-81; Evans, *Anselm and Talking about God,* pp. 99-111.

77. D. E. Luscombe, *The School of Peter Abelard* (Cambridge: University Press 1969) 103-42.

78. *Proslogion,* ch. 2 (*S* 1.101.8).

79. *Monologion,* ch. 1 (*S* 1.15.12).

80. Eadmer, *Vita,* ch. 2 (ed. Southern, pp. 4-5).

81. See, for example, Eadmer, *History of Recent Events in England,* trans. Geoffrey Bosanquet (London: Cresset 1964) pp. 98-99; *Dicta,* ch. 44 (*M* 245.3-6).

82. On the horarium at Bec, see M. J. Charlesworth, *St. Anselm's Prosologion* (Oxford: Clarendon 1965) pp. 12-15; for Canterbury, see Lanfranc, *Decreta,* ed. David Knowles (*Corpus Consuetudinum Monasticarum,* 3) (Siegburg: Fr. Schmitt 1967) xvii-xxv. Cf. also Margaret Gibson, *Lanfranc of Bec* (Oxford: Clarendon 1978) pp. 27-29, 170-73.

83. *The Rule of St. Benedict,* ch. 9 and elsewhere, refers to adding "Glory be to the Father" at the end of psalms. Ironically, Anselm helped turn devotion away from exclusive concentration on the psalms. See Southern, *Anselm and His Biographer,* pp. 38-43. This suggestion that frequent use of the psalms might have reinforced Anselm's proclivity to pray to the One God implies no negative assessment of the use of the psalms in Christian prayer. Furthermore, Augustine's commentaries on the psalms and the liturgical use of the psalms both suggested a Christological understanding of the psalms to Anselm's contemporaries, just as they do to us. My point is that this particular approach to the psalms is not the one Anselm adopted, as far as one can tell from the prayers which occur in his writings.

I suspect that the roots of Anselm's sense of God are Carolingian, and I have begun studying these roots. Initial investigation of the Carolingian psalm-prayers suggests a lack of Trinitarian emphasis much like that found in Anselm. In all this I do not wish to imply that Anselm's way of relating to God in prayer is inferior or undesirable. The Spirit seems to inspire many ways of speaking to the God who discloses himself in Christ.

84. These liturgical texts are quoted in Robert Amiet, "*Saint Anselme liturgiste,*" *Analecta Anselmiana* V (Frankfurt/Main: Minerva 1976) pp. 283-95.

85. Eadmer, *Vita Anselmi,* ch. 4, pp. 6-7.

86. *Ibid.,* ch. 6, p. 11.

87. *Ibid.,* ch. 7, p. 12.

88. *Ibid.,* ch. 10, pp. 16-20.

89. Southern, *Anselm and His Biographer,* pp. 67-76; Brian Patrick McGuire, "Love, Friendship and Sex in the Eleventh Century: The Experience of Anselm," *Studia Theologica* 28 (1974) 111-52. A. Fiske, "St. Anselm and Friendship," *Studia Monastica* 3 (1961) 259-60 notes the change in Anselm's relations with his friends, but attributes it to Anselm's many responsibilities, rather than to any change in Anselm.

90. See for the various elements of this statement: *De Humanis Moribus,* ch. 37 (*M* 51), chs. 80-82 (*M* 72-74); *Dicta,* ch. 1 (*M* 110-16); *Miscellanea* (*M*

323-27); Eadmer, *Vita,* ch. 10, pp. 18-19; *Meditatio,* ch. 1 (*S* 3.76-79); Southern, *Anselm and His Biographer,* pp. 101, 109-10.

91. Eadmer, *Vita,* pp. 162-63.

Aidan Nichols (essay date July 1985)

SOURCE: Nichols, Aidan. "Anselm of Canterbury and the Language of Perfection." *Downside Review* 103, no. 352 (July 1985): 204-17.

[*In the following essay, Nichols investigates the biographical context of Anselm's* Proslogion *and defines the work's fundamental aim as the search for a "language of perfection" that would allow one to articulate the transcendent nature of God.*]

The aim of this article is to reconsider the *Proslogion* of St Anselm in its historical setting, and to suggest, in the light of recent Anselmian studies, that its basic argument is only acceptable if one shares the 'fiduciary' view of language represented, in different ways, by S. T. Coleridge and Martin Heidegger.

THE *PROSLOGION* IN CONTEXT

Anselm of Canterbury is the typical monastic philosopher, so much so that his principal contribution to the philosophical tradition is today most easily available in English dress as part of an anthology of his prayers and meditations.[1] This is as it should be. Anselm's life is unintelligible except in terms of search for transcendence, itself regarded as the heart and goal of the metaphysical enterprise by traditional philosophy in the West. At the same time, his philosophy cannot be placed until we recognize that we are dealing with a monk, a man of prayer and brotherhood. In his prayers which are formal and highly structured but nevertheless deeply felt set pieces that initiated a fresh devotional style in the Latin Church, it is characteristic of Anselm, as Professor Sir Richard Southern has pointed out, that he 'moves from inertia to a vivid apprehension of the being and love of God'.[2] This also happens to be the programme of his philosophical masterpiece, the *Proslogion,* which he wrote in a single gust of inspiration in 1078.

Anselm was fortunate in his biographer, a member of what became eventually his own monastic family at Christ Church, Canterbury.[3] Eadmer's account of the political events of Anselm's episcopate, the *Historia Novorum,* has been hailed as 'the first major Latin historical work in England since Bede and . . . one of the greatest achievements of Anglo-Norman historiography'.[4] In a more personal chronicle, the *De*

Vita et Conversatione Anselmi Archiepiscopi Cantuarensis, Eadmer gives us a childhood image of Anselm which is evidently meant to serve as a parable of the whole man. In his childhood in the Alpine foothills Anselm imagined heaven perched atop the snow-capped mountains around Aosta: once in a dream, he scaled them and was graciously received at table by God, imaged as a great king.[5] As a youth, he took the way of many Italians in the eleventh and twelfth centuries, crossing the Alps to Burgundy, France and Normandy in search of higher education. Here he would find *litterae humaniores* but also theology.[6] It is conjectured that Chartres and Fleury-sur-Loire may have been his magnets, but in time the reputation of his fellow Italian, Lanfranc, who was master of the Norman Benedictine school of Bec, drew him farther north to the area of Rouen, then governed by Normandy's most celebrated Duke, William the Conqueror.[7] Over thirty years later as abbot of Bec he would be brought to Canterbury as archbishop by the Conqueror's son William Rufus. He accepted with a reluctance which, in a monk of a house in the buoyancy of its founding generation, was probably not simulated. By this date, 1093, he had behind him his 'published' prayers, identified from an anarchic manuscript tradition by the labours of Dom André Wilmart,[8] and his philosophical writings, among which was the *Proslogion.* The later theological writings were produced in interludes of quiet in the turbulent political-ecclesiastical history that followed the struggle over the episcopate's freedom of spiritual action or 'Investiture Contest'.[9]

For the intellectual resources Anselm brought to the search for transcendence we may look to the school of Bec itself as well as to his own writings. It is known that Lanfranc had offered a generous formation in the humanities, with a particular stress on logic.[10] The researches of D. P. Henry have shown that Anselm was familiar not only with the *logica vetus,* consisting of Aristotle's *Categories, Topics* and *De Interpretatione,* but also the logical works of Boethius. The latter's logic, as expressed in his commentary on the *Isagoge* of Porphyry, and therefore, in effect, a commentary on Aristotelean logic at one remove, was much concerned with 'modal' concepts of possibility and necessity which would exercise Anselm also.[11] Anselm's theological master was undoubtedly Augustine.[12] The combination of sources is piquant and instructive. In the contemporary struggle between dialecticians and antidialecticians, Anselm was very much on the side of the former, those who saw the need for a rational exploration and systematization of the materials of revelation, against those for whom theology was simply a paraphrase of Scripture in the light of the Fathers.[13] The curious thing is that, while this is true, his proof of God's existence nonetheless issues from prayer and terminates in prayer.

The ***Proslogion*** is one of Anselm's Norman works, composed while Prior at Bec. A prior's office was essentially that of domestic administrator, far removed from the international concerns of Anselm's later period, concerns reflected in correspondence with, among others, the King of Scots and the Crusader rulers of the Latin Kingdom of Jerusalem.[14] The human background of an Anglo-Norman house of this period would be very much that described by Dom David Knowles in his *Monastic Order in England*—a highly organized conventual round of study, labour, liturgy and fraternal co-existence.[15] This background is exceedingly relevant to the presuppositions of the ***Proslogion's*** argument.

In the preface to the ***Proslogion,*** Anselm explains that, once finished with the brief treatise known as the ***Monologion,*** it occurred to him that this latter work 'consisted in a connected chain of many arguments'. He began to ask himself

> if it would be possible to find one single argument, needing no other proof than itself, to prove that God really exists, that he is the highest good, needing nothing, that it is he whom all things need for their being and well-being, and to prove whatever else we need to prove about the nature of God.[16]

After describing the mental struggle whereby at first he groped in vain for this 'unique argument' and subsequently spent his energies in keeping the problem from tyrannizing over all his waking thoughts, Anselm goes on:

> One day, when I was tired out with resisting its importunity, that which I had despaired of finding came to me, in the conflict of my thoughts, and I welcomed eagerly the very thought which I had been so anxious to reject.[17]

It is Eadmer who records that the timing of this moment was the Office of Matins in the monastic liturgy at Bec.

> Suddenly, one night during Matins, the grace of God illuminated his heart, the whole matter became clear to his mind, and a great joy and exultation filled his inmost being. Thinking therefore that others also would be glad to know what he had found, he immediately and ungrudgingly wrote it on writing tablets and gave them to one of the brethren of the monastery for safe keeping.[18]

In the light of what has been said above concerning Eadmer's integrity as an historian, this section of the *Vita* can hardly be dismissed as conventional pious ornament. The ***Proslogion*** belongs in one sense, therefore, with the devotional writings which were written largely, as Southern remarks, for Anselm's fellow-monks, though also to meet the increasingly articulate needs of lay-people with the time, inclination and (presumably) financial wherewithal to adopt the religious practices of the monastic life.[19]

Of course the word once written takes on a life of its own beyond the control or even expectations of an author. The audience which the ***Proslogion*** eventually commanded was provided by the history of philosophy, rather than a monastic *conventus*. The significance of Anselm's discovery escaped his contemporaries, apart from the immediate reply it evoked from a fellow-monk, Gaunilo of Marmoutiers,[20] and a reminiscence in the writings of Abbot Gilbert Crispin of Westminster.[21] As M. J. Charlesworth put it:

> St Anselm's ***Proslogion*** might have fallen stillborn from the scriptorium for all the influence it had upon his own intellectual milieu.[22]

The thirteenth century, however, more than made up for the twelfth's lack of acumen in Anselm's regard, and a host of writers studied his 'unique argument': William of Auxerre, the Dominican Richard Fishacre, the Franciscans Alexander of Hales and Bonaventure, through whom it became known to St Thomas. In John Duns Scotus's version it passed into the mainstream of early modern philosophy, to Descartes and Leibniz. It was this third- or fourth-hand paraphrase, it seems, which Kant attempted to refute, since when, and until fairly recent years, the argument came to be viewed as 'a quaint and naïve mediaeval conundrum'.[23] Once again, however, an Anselmian renaissance has succeeded an age of neglect, both in Continental and British writing. Its celebration is the inter-disciplinary and international collection, *Spicilegium Beccense,* published in Paris on the nine-hundredth anniversary of Anselm's arrival at Bec.[24]

PRAYER OR PHILOSOPHY?

Several of the defenders of the 'unique argument', and notably Dom Anselm Stolz, have been at pains to rescue the ***Proslogion*** from the ravages of philosophical critics by claiming that its intention is essentially spiritual or mystical.[25] It is, they say, an essay in mystical theology, in the understanding, then, of the *practice* of prayer. To discover God as necessary perfection, as Anselm does, is to offer crucial counsel on how to pray. In praying, one must never be content with one's current images of God but strive constantly to transcend them towards a reality which is of its nature *semper maior.* It is true that prayer is the vital context of the argument. Indeed, as we shall see, to sever the argument entirely from this context is to lose its strictly philosophical force. The first and last chapters of the ***Proslogion,*** in particular, are entirely characteristic Anselmian meditations. Thus for instance, from ***Proslogion*** 1:

Lord, I am not trying to make my way to your height, for my desire is in no way equal to that, but I do desire to understand a little of your truth which my heart already believes and loves. I do not seek to understand so that I may believe, but I believe so that I may understand; and what is more, I believe that unless I do believe I shall not understand.

But is it not a modern fallacy to suppose that a monastic and spiritual concern, such as Anselm's undoubtedly was, must necessarily exclude a philosophical and rational concern? We need not surrender to impaling on the horns of the dilemma which would have the *Proslogion* to be *either* spirituality *or* philosophy but on no account both. Professor E. L. Mascall has well said of Anselm in this connection:

> He believed by faith that God is supremely rational, and it therefore seemed obvious to him that, if only one could find out how to do it, it must be possible to prove the existence of this supremely rational being. He believed that God had shown him how to do this, and he could never thank him sufficiently for it. I think, therefore, that one key at least to the *Proslogion* is to be found in the fact that it could never occur to Anselm that there was anything irrational or anti-rational about faith and revelation.[26]

The relationship between faith and reason in Anselm is a complex one, partly because the question has not yet become a topic of discussion in its own right. He wished to hold *les deux bouts de la chaîne*, maintaining both that reason has a role to play prior to faith and within the realm of faith, but also that faith transcends reason, from which it follows that it cannot be on purely rational grounds alone that the mysteries of the faith are given lodging in the mind.[27]

Looking for confirmation more widely in Anselm's writing, we find him affirming in the *Soliloquies* that he accepts the teachings of Scripture in the hope that he will come more and more to understand them.[28] This is the classic sense of the Augustinian adage, *credo ut intellegam.*[29] Reason serves the life of faith by exhibiting the intelligibility of God and his decrees. In the *Cur Deus homo,* on the other hand, a novel and distinctively Anselmian note is struck. The interlocutor here is a monk who is not so much seeking reasons to confirm faith as *gaudium,* a joy that flows from one's realization that faith accords with reason, a spiritual joy of the intellect delighting in the truth.[30] And departing further still from the root Augustinian meaning of *credo ut intellegam,* the terms of the command 'Believe that you may understand' which Anselm addresses to the monk in the *Cur Deus homo* may in fact be transposed at certain points. We thus find instead: 'Understand so that you may believe'. The sceptic is challenged to understand that God exists (the *Proslogion*), that he is supremely good and just (the *Monologion*) and that he

has made provision for man's salvation in the only way possible (the *Cur Deus homo*). Jasper Hopkins warns that when we find Anselm saying that reason can never conflict with Scripture we should not take him to be asserting in doctrinaire fashion that he would not recognize any such conflict if brought to his notice.[31] Rather, he is making a prediction based, Hopkins suggests, on three factors. First, Anselm has, in fact, found himself able to resolve *prima facie* conflicts between reason and the Bible when he found them. Secondly, he recognized that adjudication in such conflicts is itself a rational undertaking. Thirdly, he believed that human reason cannot, in principle, comprehend the full mystery of the Godhead revealed in Christ. He also works on the presupposition, noted by Mascall, that a rational God cannot reveal to man anything intrinsically irrational. And so the notion that reason and revelation never conflict is a structural principle for Anselm, set to work to interpret all the data of theology. Only if the consistent interpretation of those data by that principle became too costly would it be abandoned. Anselm never found it necessary to abandon it.[32] The *Proslogion* may very well be *both* prayer and philosophy.[33]

THE LANGUAGE OF PERFECTION

The fundamental objection, or at any rate the main feeling of discomfort, shared by readers of the *Proslogion* concerns the notion that an argument to God's existence could be deduced from a mere definition—the definition of God as necessary perfection, or in Anselm's own words, 'that than which a greater cannot be thought'. It smacks of the conjuror drawing a triumphant rabbit from a top hat. But 'How did he do it?' is the response of a person who feels tricked by sleight-of-hand, rather than of the genuinely convinced enquirer. In recent years, however, it has been questioned whether this view of the treatise really corresponds to Anselm's intentions as embodied in the *Proslogion* as we have it.

At the start of the argument, Anselm attempts to identify the God *to whom he is in the course of praying* with what he calls 'something than which a greater cannot be thought'. But the point of the argument, in the first instance, is precisely to confirm this identification. As Richard Campbell has shown in his study of the *Proslogion,* the idea of necessary perfection cannot be construed as a definition playing its part in the logic of the argument as it unfolds, since it is itself one of the conclusions towards which the argument is to proceed.[34] Further, Campbell points out that the passage I have cited above from *Proslogion* 1, a passage which immediately precedes the 'unique argument', is scarcely an example of the way a man arguing from a definition of God would be likely to speak. And finally, before ending the *Proslogion,* Anselm says in so many words that he must pass beyond this characterization of God as 'that than which a greater cannot be conceived' since even this has proved inadequate to what he has found to be true in prayer.

> Lord, you are then not only that than which nothing greater can be thought; you are something greater than it is possible to think about. For since it is possible to think that this could exist, if you are not that thing, then a greater than you can be thought; and that will not do.[35]

Throughout the treatise, in fact, 'God' is a proper name, a subject of address, and proper names do not have definitions. If definitions give the meaning of terms, proper names have no meaning. Their office is to refer, and this referential function is not necessarily connected with any descriptive import that some given proper name might (as in 'Guggles Radziwill') or might not (as in 'Joe Smith') convey. And so:

> While Anselm says to God, 'You are that than which a greater cannot be thought', that assertion cannot reasonably be taken as an answer to the absurd question, 'Who or what is meant by "you"?'[36]

Years ago, Stolz had realized that the celebrated Anselmian identification is no definition but rather a conclusion. But for him, as we have noted, it was no philosophical conclusion but rather the mystical issue of the monk's prayer-life. For Stolz, Anselm simply presumes God's existence, wishing to pass over from pure believing to an experiential encounter with the ever-present God affirmed by faith.[37] But we have found already that this will not serve as an account of Anselm's view of the relationship between faith and reason. Moreover, it ignores the fact that the ***Proslogion*** is simply littered with argumentative connectives.

What then *is* the true starting-point of Anselm's thought about God's existence? The Anselmian argument is founded upon the language of perfection. In the public realm, we use and find meaning in a language about perfection. We do not regard this use of language as utterly baffling, although it may sometimes strike us as curious or provocative. At the opening of the 'unique argument', Anselm's interlocutor, the 'Fool' of the Psalter (he who 'has said in his heart: "There is no God"'), overhears Anselm praying in this language. He is speaking of that than which nothing greater can be conceived, the unconditionally perfect. The Fool

> understands what he hears, and what he understands is in his mind, even if he does not understand that it actually exists.[38]

Anselm's 'speech-act' involves limit-language that may be mysterious, but yet is not totally incomprehensible. The Fool himself makes good use of this same language

in formulating his objection to Anselm. As Ludwig Wittgenstein might comment, a person who knows how to use the language of perfection but denies that he can understand its significance does not know what he is saying.

> Just as language allows us to speak of the unspeakable, so thought allows us to think of that which, in itself, surpasses the ability of thought to comprehend.[39]

Anselm will go on from his initial speech-act to argue that the whole realm of discourse which permits one to speak of God as that than which a greater cannot be conceived rules out the possibility of intelligently denying God's existence. He claims, in effect, that the use of the language of perfection opens up a path down which all language-using and meaning-laden beings are pointed, a path leading to the mystery of God.

> In coming to understand that the Fool's challenge to faith oversteps the limits of what can be thought, in this becoming aware of the bounds of the creativity of human thought, one finds faith and reason working together to point towards the pre-containing creativity of God who transcends human thought.[40]

How then does Anselm propose to show that the Fool's construction of the language of perfection is impossible, whereas his own imposes itself? The words 'that than which a greater cannot be conceived' serve to specify an 'intentional object', what Anselm calls something 'in the mind', *in intellectu.* This object is not regarded as a mental item with some arcane autonomous existence of its own but simply as an intellectual mediation of some possibly existing reality.[41] Concepts are that by which we grasp the real, not mental impressions parallel to it. Anselm now goes on to claim that this 'that than which a greater cannot be conceived' is not only *in intellectu* but also *in re,* in existence.

> Surely that than which a greater cannot be thought cannot exist in the mind alone. For if it exists solely in the mind even, it can be thought to exist in reality also. . . .[42]

The crucial thing here is the meaning to be attached to *in re.* By *in re* Anselm means belonging to experience as a whole, which experience cannot but be informative about the realm of the real. It has become a commonplace here to drag in a cannon bearing the name of Kant with which to shoot down Anselm's enterprise. But curiously enough as Campbell has shown, Kant's *Critique of Pure Reason* may here be turned to defence of the ***Proslogion's*** argument in its authentic form. For while Kant was indeed to argue that existence is not a *determining* predicate (if it were, that which we say 'exists' would no longer be the same something as what we spoke of before we made that assertion), nevertheless he did not regard the predicative use of 'exists' as simply meaningless, mere vibration of the air. He saw it as a special kind of *relational* predicate whose task it is to locate what is thought of, or spoken of, in the context of experience at large.

> Though in my concept nothing may be lacking of the possible real content of a thing in general, something is lacking in its relation to my whole state of thought. Therefore through its existence (the object) is thought of as belonging to the context of experience as a whole.[43]

And so that than which a greater cannot be thought can be thought to exist in reality also, and this, Anselm now adds, 'is greater'. Existence is a valuational relationship, not just a brute fact. We have a preference for the actual, if only to complain of it.

> If then that than which a greater cannot be thought exists in the mind alone, this same that than which a greater *cannot* be thought is that than which a greater *can* be thought. But this is obviously impossible. Therefore, there is absolutely no doubt that something than which a greater cannot be thought exists both in the mind and in reality.[44]

Given the meaningfulness of the speech-act from which we started, it appears self-contradictory to say that that than which nothing greater can be conceived is in the understanding only. It does not make sense to deny the purchase on reality of the language of unsurpassable perfection.

But which thing, or things, answers, or answer, to this description? To secure the identification of God with such a reality, Anselm must show that there is some characteristic true of this reality which is true only of God. And this he finds to be the unthinkableness of its not existing. Whatever this thing is, it is characterized by the sheerest ontological independence. If it failed to exist, or came into existence, or passed out of it, it must be dependent on something greater still, and that is contradictory. If it exists, and Anselm has by now established to his own satisfaction, that it does, then it cannot not exist.

> And this is you, O Lord our God. You therefore so truly are, O Lord my God, that you cannot even be thought not to be. . . .[45]

The God who is the Lord of the Church is also the God of the enquiring mind.

THE FIDUCIARY APPROACH TO LANGUAGE

Since the starting-point of Anselm's argument is language-in-use, the *Proslogion* is not to be seen as an exercise in impersonal, purely logical, demonstration of the existence of God. In so far as Anselm sets out from the actual performance of a speech-act his conclusions cannot be said to be either impersonal or logically entailed. Not all exhibition of the rationality of beliefs takes the form of logical demonstration. Campbell draws an instructive parallel here with a passage from the Wittgenstein of the *Philosophical Investigations*.[46] The comparison concerns language about external objects. Since language of its very nature inhabits a shared public realm, any denial of the existence of reality beyond the self, that is, of the existence of such a public realm, is at bottom unintelligible, precisely because any such denial must itself be made in language. In saying this, it is not being claimed that the existence of external reality is logically entailed by the language we use. Nevertheless, we are showing forth the reasonableness of our belief in that external reality. Similarly, in the *Proslogion,* Anselm shows how our capacity to use the language of absolute perfection makes it unintelligible to deny that such language opens out onto the realm of the real.

Our response to Anselm will depend, accordingly, on the degree of willingness we feel to take language on trust, to accept what Doctor John Coulson has called its 'fiduciary' demands.[47] Language may have developed as it has just because of its aptness for disclosing features of reality. It always implies a commerce between the language-user and the real itself. This need not mean that every description formulated in language must necessarily describe some real thing. But it will mean that using language involves, in and of itself, a turning to the real. Thus openness to learn from what is said something of what there *is* can be commended as a rational posture. Linguistic formulae can present us with distorted pictures of the real, but in the case of the language of perfection we can come to see, through the argument of the *Proslogion,* that the formulae of *this* language, at any rate, are not systematically misleading but rather the contrary.

As Doctor G. R. Evans has shown in her recent studies of Anselm, Anselm regarded language as divine in its origins and function.[48] The self-subsistent Word, which is God himself, is the ultimate and universal 'language' from which ordinary speech is derived. In the *Monologion* Anselm proposes that all language ultimately derives from the great universal words in the divine Mind. The various languages which men use are doubtless derived from these words in complex and tortuous ways. Nonetheless, they gain their meaningfulness from their relation to the universal *verba*.[49] Such an archaic ontology of language naturally predisposes Anselm to that fiduciary view of language which thinkers as diverse as S. T. Coleridge and Martin Heidegger have embraced in very different ways. We are dealing here with a 'fundamental option' of a kind which is capable of commendation but not of coercive proof, for the very good reason that it helps to establish the conditions on which what is to count as argument will obtain. The 'option' is the view that language is in itself 'hermeneutic', revelatory of a world; that its action is comparable to that of symbol or sacrament in presenting in a concrete medium a reality otherwise inaccessible.

In Coleridge and Heidegger, the *lingua communis* grants us access to what is most fundamental in reality. In Coleridge's case, the fact of such a fiduciary approach to language is more striking than any great clarity, or even perhaps originality, in the way it is presented.[50] Heavily indebted as he was to German Romantic Idealism, Coleridge's formulations are frequently more obscure than in their original sources. In the Preface to *Aids to Reflection* he produced, nonetheless, the lapidary statement that

> Words are not THINGS but LIVING POWERS, by which the things of most importance to mankind are actuated, combined and humanized.[51]

Coleridge had already found the supreme exemplification of this idea in the verbal symbols of the Scriptures. In *The Statesman's Manual* the divinely inspired language of the biblical revelation is described as

> the living educts of the imagination; of that reconciling and mediatory power, which incorporating the reason in images of sense, and organizing (as it were) the flux of the senses by the permanence and self-circling energies of the reason, gives birth to a system of symbols, harmonious in themselves, and consubstantial with the truths of which they are conductors.[52]

But in this the divine action simply raises to a higher power the capacity of language to disclose the 'things of most importance to mankind' which Coleridge would discuss in *Aids to Reflection,* itself a manifestly philosophical rather than theological work, conceived, indeed, as a pocket version of the Coleridgean synthesis of German and English philosophy. Coleridge's theological affirmations rarely lack a philosophical correlate, or mirror-image, in just this kind of way.[53] But the point here is that for Coleridge language, as the most sensitive of all the instruments of the human mind, most fully realizes mind's basic relation to reality, which is at once projecting—and to this extent, we must be critical towards language, and yet *also* receptive—and to this extent, we must trust language to disclose the real and not to conceal it.[54]

The affinity of Coleridge with Heideggerian thought has been noted by George Steiner.[55] But Heidegger's reflections on the epiphany of being in and through speech-acts come from a writer with greater powers of prose organization. Although Heidegger's concern with language as the *logos* of being is a pervasive feature of

his work, his central discussion of a fiduciary approach to the word is that found in the essay-collection, *Unterwegs zur Sprache*.[56] Pointing out that the Prologue to the Fourth Gospel has licensed ancient Christian thinkers in speaking of the divine origin of language,[57] Heidegger develops his own account of the primacy of the *logos* over man, in conjunction with the philosophers and poets of German Romanticism and their Symbolist successors. For Heidegger, 'man succeeds in speaking only in so far as he coresponds with language'.[58] Language is the 'house of being', as Heidegger insists in his conversation 'Between a Japanese and an Enquirer'.[59] Thus the wider realm of being in which man's life is set is not subordinate to man, but quite the contrary. Man is man through his awareness of the *logos,* the language of being.

> The being of man is brought into its own by language, in such a way that it remains tributary to the very nature of language, the sound of silence. This happens in so far as language of its very nature as the sound of silence needs the speech of mortals in order to make the sound of silence audible to mortal hearing.[60]

For Heidegger, we need the poet to purify our sense of language so that we may find in it the self-disclosure of reality itself.

My fragmentary discussions of two such complex thinkers are meant only to highlight the kind of approach to language on which the argument of the **Proslogion** makes most sense. We find the 'language of perfection' in possession, in both Church and society. With the *logos* as with the law, possession must count for a very great deal. It is true that there are trivial and parasitic uses of the language of perfection in currency. For a rather gushing guest to tell his hostess that the Coupe Melba was 'absolute perfection' is of no more metaphysical interest than it would be of religious interest had he told her it was 'simply divine'. Nevertheless, the language of perfection is not wholly debased in the secular community of speech. While our world is flatter than that of the mediaevals, a *scala perfectionis* still stands. Only the rungs—sub-atomic particle, atom, molecule, cell, organism, man, society—are differently placed. And so long as the language of perfection remains a feature of our linguistic world, the Anselmian approach to God will remain of outstanding fascination.

Notes

1. B. Ward (ed.), *The Prayers and Meditations of St Anselm* (Harmondsworth, 1973).

2. R. W. Southern in, B. Ward (ed.), *op. cit.,* p. 12.

3. See R. W. Southern, *St Anselm and his Biographer* (Cambridge, 1962).

4. N. F. Cantor, *Church, Kingship and Lay Investiture in England: 1089-1135* (Princeton, 1958), p. 39.

5. Eadmer, *De Vita et Conversatione Anselmi Archiepiscopi Cantuarensis* I, 19.

6. See G. R. Evans, *Old Arts and New Theology. The Beginnings of Theology as an Academic Discipline* (Oxford, 1980).

7. M. J. Charlesworth, 'St Anselm: Life and Times' in *St Anselm's Proslogion* (Oxford, 1965), pp. 9-10.

8. A. Wilmart, o.s.b., *Auteurs spirituels et textes dévotes du moyen âge* (Paris, 1932), pp. 147-216.

9. For the problems of dating Anselm's writings, see F. S. Schmitt, o.s.b., 'Zur Chronologie des hl.Anselm von Canterbury', *Revue Bénédictine*, 44 (1932), pp. 322-50.

10. A. J. MacDonald, *Lanfranc. A Study of his Life, Work and Writing* (Oxford, 1926).

11. D. P. Henry, *The Logic of Saint Anselm* (Oxford, 1967).

12. Anselm, *Monologion* 1; cf. F. J. Thonnard, 'Caractères augustiniens de la méthode philosophique de saint Anselme', in *Spicilegium Beccense* (Paris, 1959), pp. 171-84.

13. M. J. Charlesworth, *St Anselm's Proslogion, op. cit.*, p. 25. See also A. J. MacDonald, *Authority and Reason in the Early Middle Ages* (London, 1933).

14. J. F. A. Mason, 'Saint Anselm's Relations with Laymen: Selected Letters', *Spicilegium Beccense, op. cit.*, pp. 547-60.

15. D. Knowles, o.s.b., *The Monastic Order in England* (London, 1940), ch. xxvi.

16. Anselm, *Proslogion*, preface.

17. *Ibid.*

18. R. W. Southern (ed.), *The Life of St Anselm, Archbishop of Canterbury, by Eadmer, op. cit.*, pp. 28-31.

19. R. W. Southern, in B. Ward (ed.), *op. cit.*, p. 9.

20. See Gaunilo, *A Reply on Behalf of the Fool* in M. J. Charlesworth, *op. cit.*, pp. 156-67.

21. R. W. Southern, 'St Anselm and Gilbert Crispin, Abbot of Westminster', *Mediaeval and Renaissance Studies*, III (1954), pp. 78-115.

22. M. J. Charlesworth, *op. cit.*, p. 3.

23. *Ibid.*, pp. 6-7.

24. *Spicilegium Beccense. Congrès international du IXe centenaire de l'arrivée d'Anselme au Bec* (Paris, 1959).

25. A. Stolz, o.s.b., 'Anselm's Theology in the Proslogion' in J. Hick and A. McGill (ed.), *The Many-Faced Argument* (London, 1968), pp. 183-208.

26. E. L. Mascall, *The Openness of Being* (London, 1971), p. 40.

27. Cf. M. J. Charlesworth, *op. cit.*, p. 37.

28. Anselm, *Soliloquies* II, 271, 5-8.

29. Anselm, *Proslogion* I; cf. Augustine, *De libero arbitrio* II, 2.

30. Anselm, *Cur Deus homo* II. 15; cf. *Proslogion* XXVI.

31. J. Hopkins, *A Companion to the Study of Saint Anselm* (Minneapolis, 1972), p. 43.

32. Cf. G. R. Evans, *Anselm and a New Generation* (Oxford, 1980), pp. 63-68.

33. That the *Proslogion* was really meant to be philosophy rules out Karl Barth's claim, in *Fides Quaerens Intellectum* (London, 1960), that there is no natural theology anywhere present in Anselm's work. Were Barth's claim correct, Anselm would have been at odds with the whole Augustinian tradition in his time. On the questionableness of Barth's proposal, see J. McIntyre, *St Anselm and his Critics* (Edinburgh, 1954) where reference is made particularly to the *Cur Deus homo*. The significance of the latter work for Anselm's theological project as a whole is, in this context, its recurrence to the phrase *rationes necessariae* which suggests a rationalism equally far from Anselm's intention. The phrase in his use denotes sometimes logical demonstration, but at other times, as in Cassiodorus, it means any argument attaining to truth about a thing or event by whatever means. See on this A. M. Jacquin, 'Les "rationes necessariae" de s. Anselme' in *Mélanges Mandonnet*, II (Paris, 1930), pp. 67-78.

34. See R. Campbell, *From Belief to Understanding* (Canberra, 1976), to which my treatment of the *Proslogion* is much indebted.

35. Anselm, *Proslogion* XV.

36. R. Campbell, *op. cit.*, p. 27.

37. A. Stolz, o.s.b., *art. cit.*

38. Anselm, *Proslogion* II.

39. R. Campbell, *op. cit.*, p. 37.

40. *Ibid.*, p. 203.

41. See P. Michaud-Quentin, 'Notes sur le vocabulaire psychologique de saint Anselme', *Spicilegium Beccense op. cit.*, pp. 23-30.

42. Anselm, *Proslogion* II.

43. I. Kant, *Critique of Pure Reason* B 628/9. Alternatively, one may espouse M. J. Charlesworth's formulation in *St Anselm's Proslogion, op. cit.,* p. 67: 'To function as a subject of predication in a real realm of discourse is greater than to function as a subject of predication in a functional or imaginary or conceptual realm of discourse'. This 'translation' makes it clear that 'exists' is not being used as a predicate in the ordinary sense, but that nevertheless some distinction and some comparison is being made between real and conceptual existence.

44. Anselm, *Proslogion* II.

45. *Ibid.,* III.

46. R. Campbell, *op. cit.,* pp. 177-8; cf. L. Wittgenstein, *Philosophical Investigations* (Oxford, 1953), especially 243-370.

47. J. Coulson, *Newman and the Common Tradition. A Study in the Language of Church and Society* (Oxford, 1970), pp. 3-13.

48. G. R. Evans, *Anselm and Talking about God* (Oxford, 1978), p. 49.

49. G. R. Evans, *Anselm and a New Generation* (Oxford, 1980), p. 86.

50. See N. Fruman, *Coleridge, The Damaged Archangel* (London, 1971).

51. S. T. Coleridge, *Aids to Reflection* (London, 1825; Edinburgh, 1905), p. xvii.

52. S. T. Coleridge, *The Statesman's Manual* (London, 1816), in W. G. T. Shedd, *The Works of S. T. Coleridge* (New York, 1853), I, p. 436.

53. The ground for this has been located in Coleridge's debts to German Romantic Idealism. As G. Hough wrote, 'The aim of all Coleridge's religious writing is to show that all the central doctrines of Christianity . . . are deducible, with the aid of revelation, from the structure of the human mind itself', 'Coleridge and the Victorians', *The English Mind* (Cambridge, 1964). It is difficult not to see in this a fundamental affinity with the later philosophy of Schelling, or even with Hegel's *Phenomenology.*

54. For Coleridge's account of the relation between mind and extra-mental reality, see S. Prickett, *Coleridge and Wordsworth. The Poetry of Growth* (Cambridge, 1970).

55. G. Steiner, 'The House of Being', *The Times Literary Supplement* (9th October 1981), p. 1143.

56. M. Heidegger, *Unterwegs zur Sprache* (Tübingen, 1959).

57. *Ibid.,* pp. 14-15.

58. *Ibid.,* pp. 85-155. Heidegger had already spoken in similar tones in the *Brief über den Humanismus* (Frankfurt, 1949), p. 5.

59. *Unterwegs zur Sprache,* p. 30.

60. One might consult further here the article 'Language' by F. Mayr in *Sacramentum Mundi* (London, 1968); for the period between the Early Middle Ages and the Romantics see K. O. Apel, *Die Idee der Sprache in der Tradition des Humanismus von Dante bis Vico* (Bonn, 1963).

Thomas A. Losoncy (essay date 1985)

SOURCE: Losoncy, Thomas A. "Language and Saint Anselm's *Proslogion* Argument." In *Acta Conventus Neo-Latini Bononiensis: Proceedings of the Fourth International Congress on Neo-Latin Studies,* edited by R. J. Schoeck, pp. 284-291. Binghamton, N. Y.: Medieval & Renaissance Texts & Studies, 1985.

[*In the following essay, Losoncy claims that critical appraisals of the* Proslogion *have generally failed to recognize and understand Anselm's particular use of language, thus reaching misleading conclusions.*]

In the over nine hundred years since Saint Anselm wrote the *Proslogion* steadfast disagreement over what he meant, and sometimes over what he said, functions as an unbroken principle of interpretation among its readers and commentators alike. How to explain this phenomenon has proven equally controversial. However, two explanations of the long embattled history of the *Proslogion* are feasible.

One is that access to the complete *Proslogion* was impossible for many of Anselm's successors, including such renowned reviewers of the work as Aquinas, Scotus, and the noted modern critic of the ontological argument, Immanuel Kant. A second, applying more to recent times, appears to be a failure to exercise due regard for the language of the work.[1] This is further evidenced by a tendency to concentrate only on part of the *Proslogion,* principally chapters two-four.[2]

Certainly earlier interpreters and commentators might pose conflicting views of the *Proslogion* argument as a result of sketchy familiarity with the work. Whether, for a fact, this was a factor in producing their differing assessments is a matter for the historians to determine. More recently, however, one cannot explain conflicting views of this work as arising from the lack of a suitable text, even a critical text. On the other hand, if the source of disagreement among interpreters is a neglect of the language employed this would seem scandalous in an age where philosophical analysis of language is the proclaimed *forte* of the philosophical scene.

This paper endeavors to show that any study of Saint Anselm's *Proslogion* argument depends upon an analysis of the Saint's precisely selected terminology. Procedurely this will involve studying his formulation of the problem and examining the argument to see whether or not it conforms to the guidelines stated in posing the problem. This examination of Anselm's consistency with the problem initially posed will be extended to the entire *Proslogion* as a means of discerning how its language is central to developing key notions of the argument. Finally the very basis for the argument will be studied briefly for its use of language and to illustrate a consistency in Anselm's reasoning both in the *Proslogion* and in related works.

Discussion and studies of the *Proslogion* argument usually focus on Saint Anselm's expression, ". . . aliquid quo nihil maius cogitari possit."[3] This phrase occurs after Anselm's request for God's assistance that he may understand God to be as he believes. The phrase is translated as saying we believe that God is "something than which no greater can be thought."[4] What is essential in treating this expression is the meaning of this *thinking* about God. Generally it is taken to mean that somehow one has obtained an idea of God. Anselm is thought to be formulating the first premise of an ontological argument, that is, he is claiming to have an "idea" of a being than which no greater can be thought.[5] Such an understanding of Anselm's phrase reflects later formulations of the ontological argument, especially Descartes',[6] rather than the carefully controlled argument Anselm is structuring. One must turn to chapter one of the *Proslogion* and its precise language to discover the thinking about God Anselm intends in this work.

In chapter one, Anselm establishes the problem, as he sees it, by inquiring "how" and "where" one is to look for and seek after God. His adverbial queries are obvious in such questions as the following:

> . . . doce cor meum ubi et quomodo te quaerat, ubi et quomodo te inveniat. Domine, si hic non es, ubi te quaeram absentem? Si autem ubique es, cur non video praesentem?[7]

These questions have a threefold significance. First Anselm is indicating that God's existence is not self-evident. Second, he is affirming his purpose to try to know God's existence. Third, he deploys definite

guidelines on how one is to gain knowledge of God's existence. The attainment of such knowledge is to be "modal" in character. The way in which God exists rather than who or what God is acts as the key to one's grasp of God's existence.

Anselm's modal approach to one's knowledge of God's existence is explicit when he states that he desires only to know God "in some measure" or "a little bit" (*aliquatenus*).[8] One might well wonder what a knowledge of God "in some measure" might be. But one thing is clear. This knowledge is of a modal sort rather than a knowledge of God's very quiddity or substance. Thus, when Anselm selects the phrase, "something than which no greater can be thought," he is citing a modal knowledge of God that is not to consist of a knowledge of who or what God is, as through an idea of the highest being. This is rather an indication of the way in which God exists, the highest way of any being.

Chapter three employs this modal sense in observing that God exists so truly that his non-existence is unthinkable. This superlative manner of existing is then contrasted with all other modes of existing when Anselm notes, "Indeed, except for you alone, whatever else exists can be thought not to exist."[9] The contrast is definitely modal. One way of existing is said to be open to non-existence and the other to exclude the possibility of non-existence. And Anselm's reasoning is that beings open to non-existence in any manner whatsoever necessitate a being not so disposed.

Two issues must be engaged at this point. Their resolution is crucial to understanding Anselm's claim at the end of chapter four that "he now so understands God's existence that even if he did not believe it to be true he could not help but understand it to be true."[10] First one must investigate whether or not Anselm's understanding remains true to the guidelines of his quest in chapter one, that is, to seek to understand God in some measure. Second, one must ask what is the basis of the understanding reached, if it is not simply the unfolding of the content of an idea. In both instances, Anselm is obliging in the remainder of the *Proslogion* and elsewhere in his writings.

In chapter five of the *Proslogion* Anselm proceeds to elaborate on his newly achieved understanding by entertaining a question about God that is clearly not modal. This suggests a break with the earlier rubrics of chapter one. Anselm asks, "What, then are You, Lord God, than whom nothing greater can be thought?" (*quid igitur, es, Domine deus, quo nil maius valet cogitari*?)[11] The response, however, evades the precise question asked because Anselm's reply shifts into the modal pattern he initiated in chapter one. He responds that God is, "the highest of all beings, existing through himself alone, who made all things from nothing."[12] In fact, then, Anselm tells the reader that God is justice itself, mercy itself, life itself, unlimited, eternal, truth and mercy but always to the highest degree.

Chapter fourteen, as a result of the efforts of chapters five-thirteen, reminds the reader that one has both truly seen God in recognizing the way in which he must exist and yet has never known God directly as he is. He is consistent with the avowed purpose of chapter one when Anselm observes, "Or is it that it (the intellect) saw both the truth and the light, and yet it did not see You because it saw You only in some measure (*aliquatenus*) but did not see You as You are?"[13]

Chapter fifteen, then, recasts Anselm's original formula to reflect precisely man's modal knowledge of God. God is found to exist in the highest manner of any being. This manner of existing, however, is knowable to man only somewhat. Thus Anselm writes, "Lord, not only are You that than which a greater cannot be thought, but You are also something greater than can be thought."[14] Again the influence of chapter one is manifest. Man cannot know what God is because God's way of being exceeds the capacity of human comprehension. Only the manner of existing falls within the range of human knowing in this life.

Chapters eighteen to twenty-two further scrutinize the way in which God exists as that than which no greater can be thought. Yet when Anselm concludes this detailed analysis he realizes that he still does not know who or what God is but rather only the manner in which such an absolute being exists.

In chapters twenty-four to twenty-six of the *Proslogion,* Anselm launches a last appeal to man's experience of the goods of this life for insight into the nature of God.[15] And, once again, he is led to concede that such a knowledge is not forthcoming in this world. Man can only hope to progress and grow in the knowledge of God in this life, (knowledge in some measure) a knowledge that will only be made complete in the next life.[16]

Clearly the *Proslogion* reflects, in its totality, Anselm's avowed desire and full compliance with his original goal, to know God in some measure. This small measure of knowledge goes only so far as to show the necessity of a supreme being possessing a supreme mode of existing. The modal nature of this "measure of knowledge" is reflected elsewhere in his *Rejoinder to Gaunilo* and in the *Monologion.* In both cases, the language chosen is deliberate and rigorous.

In the *Rejoinder,* section eight, Anselm insists, *contra* Gaunilo's claims, that there is a way to gain some measure of knowledge of God. The knowing activity he cites each time[17] is a matter of "puzzling out" or "conjecturing to" a superlative manner of being. The word employed is *conicere* and its usage is consistent with his approach in the *Proslogion,* namely, that one cannot achieve an idea of God's nature.[18] This limited knowledge of God is likened to the kind of knowing one experiences when endeavoring to grasp something not completely comprehensible or understandable. In section nine of his *Rejoinder,* Anselm contends that this type of knowing is appropriate for an object that is ineffable to man.[19] He reasons similarly in the *Monologion,* chapter sixty-five, when he concludes that:

> the word "wisdom" does not suffice for disclosing to me this Being through which all things were created from nothing and are kept from (falling away into) nothing. Nor can the word "being" express that (reality) which is far removed from all things by virtue of its own nature. So, then, this Nature is ineffable because words cannot at all express it as it is; and yet, if under the instruction of reason we can apprehend something about it obliquely, as in a dark manner (this apprehension) is not false.[20]

The language of the *Proslogion* reveals that man's knowledge of God is limited and not of God's essence as such. The knowledge to be obtained is of the highest way of being, a way of being that remains ineffable to man. This knowledge in some measure, is further explained and argued for in Anselm's *Rejoinder to Gaunilo* and reflects the earlier *Monologion.*

It is appropriate, at this point, to consider the second issue mentioned, the basis of such a modal knowledge of God. Anselm elaborates on the basis he selects for man's knowledge of God in section eight of his *Rejoinder to Gaunilo.* He enlists a Platonic metaphysics of participation. This does not exclude, however, certain adjustments to bring the metaphysical enterprise into allignment with the Christian notion of a supreme being.

Anselm indicates that reason may proceed from lesser goods to a highest good beyond which there is no other. Likewise he contends that reason may consider various modes or levels of being until it reaches a highest beyond which there can exist no greater. The focal point of the argument hearkens back to Parmenides' own questioning of being. If being is, then one must ask, Was it always? Or did it come from nothing? Anselm adjusts this question to the context of his own world view and asks himself: If beings are do they come from nothing? From others like themselves? Or from some supreme being beyond which there is no greater? He argued for the last alternative in the *Monologion.*[21] He succinctly repeats the same preference in the latter part of the *Proslogion.*

In chapters eighteen to twenty-two of the *Proslogion,* Anselm contrasts the supreme way of being (absolute being) with all other ways of being witnessed in the universe. Ultimately the contrast he points out is as follows:

> And what began (to exist) from non-existence, and can be thought not to exist, and returns to non-existence unless it subsists through some other; and what has had a past existence but does not now exist, and a future existence but does not yet exist—such a thing does not exist in strict and absolute sense.[22]

Taking lesser beings as his starting point Anselm has two alternatives, either they originate from nothing (an alternative he rules out in Parmenidean fashion) or they come from a being beyond which no greater can be thought, namely, a being that has none of these limiting features. His choice is the latter option.

In claiming that all beings originate from a being beyond which no greater can be thought Anselm both reflects the contrast he had argued for in chapter three of the **Proslogion** and breaks with the Platonic metaphysics of participation. The highest or supreme nature, in this case, is totally unlike the beings which participate in being. Their being is one of dependence upon the highest being and yet they do not affect its nature at all because it is utterly simple and unchangeable.[23] Thus the basis for Anselm's argument is the world of beings of experience. The directing of reason to God (to a knowledge in some measure) is a matter of proceeding from differing modes of existence, none of which is wholly simple, complete and unchanging, to the highest mode of being.

In assessing the language of the **Proslogion,** one finds the following: 1) an argument that there exists a supreme way of being necessitated by and knowable from the mode of existence exercised by beings in this world; 2) a modal approach to being that relies upon a Platonic metaphysics of participation with a modification in the case of the supreme instance of being; and 3) a selective language prevailing throughout the **Proslogion** (and other writings) that is tailored to meet the demands of no. 1 and no. 2 above. In short, such an analysis renders the "ontological interpretation" of Saint Anselm's **Proslogion** unacceptable. A positive evaluation of Anselm's work, that recognizes its use of language, would view the **Proslogion** as an introspective pronouncement upon the knowledge of God attainable by man from the world of experience.

Notes

1. Two recent discussions of the *Proslogion* deserve notice in this regard. Professor G. R. Evans, *Anselm and Talking about God* (Oxford: Clarendon Press, 1978), devotes more time to talking about the interpretation a large tradition has placed upon the *Proslogion* argument than to an analysis of the argument's language as such. See, especially, chapters two and three, pp. 39-75. On the other hand, Professor Gregory Schufreider's study, "The Identity of Anselm's Argument," *The Modern Schoolman,* LIV (1977), pp. 345-61, breaks genuinely new ground in its search for the argument in Anselm's *Proslogion* instead of a new search for confirmation of an old rendition. In arguing that Saint Anselm has a single argument in the *Proslogion* Schufreider provides a careful analysis of Anselm's use of "*vere esse*" in chapter eleven's heading and chapter three's text (pp. 349-52); of "*absolute*" in chapters twenty-two and twenty-eight of the *Monologion* (pp. 353-58) and the modal quality of the *Proslogion's* "*vere esse*" (p. 360). The conclusion Schufreider reaches reinforces the argument of this paper from a different perspective.

2. The "snippet collections" of the numerous *Readings in Philosophy* available today, as well as some *Histories of Philosophy,* have had much to do with fixing this approach to the *Proslogion.* It would be nearly impossible to enumerate such instances here.

3. *Proslogion,* caput II; in *S. Anselmi Opera Omnia,* ed. F. S. Schmitt, vol. I (Edinburgh, 1946), p. 101. All page references to Saint Anselm (and Gaunilo) will be to this volume.

4. See, for instance, M. J. Charlesworth. *Saint Anselm's Proslogion* (Oxford: Clarendon Press, 1965), p. 117; and more recently *Anselm of Canterbury,* ed. and tr. by Jasper Hopkins and Herbert W. Richardson (Toronto & New York: The Edwin Mellen Press), 1974; vol. I. p. 93. English translations are my own but their indebtedness to the translations of others and the helpful comments of others are gratefully acknowledged.

5. See E. Gilson, *History of Christian Philosophy in the Middle Ages* (New York: Random House, 1955), pp. 133-34, for the traditional interpretation. Also Jasper Hopkins in his, *A Companion to the Study of Saint Anselm* (Minneapolis, Minn.: University of Minnesota Press, 1972), chapter III, p. 71, outlines what has been called the "First" (traditional) Ontological Argument and presents the so-called "Second" in the same chapter, pp. 78-89. For a rebuttal of this latter approach see, especially, Gregory Schufreider's article, *supra,* n. 1.

6. *Meditation V.*

7. *Proslogion,* cap. I, p. 98.

8. ". . . sed desidero *aliquatenus* intelligere veritatem tuam . . .," ibid., p. 100. Italics mine.

9. "Et quidem quidquid est aliud praeter te solum, potest cogitari non esse." Ibid., cap. III, p. 103.

10. ". . . iam sic intelligo te illuminante, ut si te esse nolim credere, non possim non intelligere." Ibid., cap. IV, p. 104.

11. Ibid., cap. V, pa. 104.

12. ". . . id quid summum omnium solum existens per seipsum, omnia alia fecit de nihilo?" Ibid.

13. "An et veritas et lux est quod vidit, et tamen non-dum te vidit, quia vidit te *aliquatenus,* sed non vidit te sicuti es?" Ibid., cap. XIV, p. 111. Italics mine.

14. "Ergo domine, non solum es quo maius cogitari nequit, sed es quiddam maius quam cogitari possit." Ibid., cap. XV, p. 112.

15. The opening lines of the three chapters are striking on this point: "Excita nunc, anima mea, et erige totum intellectum tuum et cogita quantum potes, quale et quantum sit illud bonum. Si enim singula bona delectabilia sunt, cogita intente quam delectabile sit illud bonum, quod continet iucunditatem omnium bonorum; et non qualem in rebus creatis sumus experti, sed tanto differentem quanto differt creator a creatura." Ibid., cap. XXIV, pp. 117-18. "O qui hoc bono fruetur: quid illi erit, et quid illi non erit! . . . Ibi quippe erunt bona corporis et animae, qualia 'nec oculus vidit nec auris audivit nec cor hominis' cogitavit." Ibid., cap. XXV, p. 118. "Deus meus et dominus meus, spes mea et gaudium cordis mei, dic animae meae, si hoc est gaudium de quo nobis dicis per filium tuum: 'petite et accipietis, ut gaudium vestrum sit plenum.'" Ibid., cap. XXVI, p. 120.

16. "Oro, deus, cognoscam te, amem te, ut gaudiam de te. Et si non possum in hac vita ad plenum, vel proficiam in dies usque dum veniat illud ad plenum. Proficiat hic in me notitia tui, et ibi fiat plena; crescat amor tuus, et ibi sit plenus: ut hic gaudium meum sit in spe magnum, et ibi sit in re plenum." Ibid., cap. XXVI, p. 121.

17. Five times Anselm states sentences and phrases which affirm a knowledge of God in some way and the series is worth noting: ". . . nec eam ex alia simili potes *conicere:* palam est rem aliter sese habere." *Responsio Editoris,* VIII, p. 137. "Quoniam namque omne minus bonum in tantum est simile maiori bono inquantum est bonum: patet cuilibet rationabili menti, quia de bonis minoribus ad maiora conscendendo ex iis quibus aliquid maius cogitari potest, multum possumus *conicere* illud quo nihil potest maius cogitari." Ibid. "Aut non est hoc ex iis quibus maius cogitari valet,

conicere id quo maius cogitari nequit? Est igitur unde possit *conici,* 'quo maius cogitari nequeat.' Sic itaque facile refelli potest insipiens qui sacram auctoritatem non recipit, si negat 'quo maius cogitari non valet' ex aliis rebus *conici* posse." Ibid. Italics mine.

18. It is interesting to note how this important notion has fared in two recent translations. The Charlesworth translation, *supra* n. 4, renders *conicere* as "to conjecture about" only once in section VIII of the *Rejoinder.* In the remaining four instances *conicere* is rendered as "forming an idea of something" (p. 187). Apart from a lack of consistency in translating the latter rendition is not faithful to Anselm's intent and language. The Hopkins and Richardson translation also, *supra* n. 4, renders *conicere* as "to conceive" throughout their translation of this passage (pp. 132-33). In this second case adherence to the view that Anselm offers an "ontological argument" obviously is controlling the translation.

19. "Sicut enim nil prohibet dici 'ineffabile,' licet illud dici non possit quod 'ineffabile' dicitur; et quemadmodum cogitari potest 'non cogitabile,' quamvis illud cogitari non possit cui convenit 'non cogitabile' dici: ita cum dicitur 'quo nil maius valet cogitari', procul dubio quod auditur cogitari et intelligi potest, etiam si res illa cogitari non valeat aut intelligi qua maius cogitari nequit." *Responsio,* IX, p. 138.

20. ". . . nec nomen sapientiae mihi sufficit ostendere illud, per quod omnia facta sunt de nihilo et servantur a nihilo; nec nomen essentiae mihi valet exprimere illud, quod per singularem altitudinem longe est supra omnia et per naturalem proprietatem valde est extra omnia. Sic igitur illa natura et ineffabilis est, quia per verba sicuti est nullatenus valet intimari; et falsum non est, si quid de illa ratione docente per aliud velut in aenigmate potest aestimari." *Monologion,* cap. LXV, pp. 76-77.

21. *Monologion,* cap. III, pp. 15-16.

22. "Et quod incepit a non esse et potest cogitari non esse, et nisi per aliud subsistat redit in non esse; et quod habet fuisse quod iam non est, et futurum esse quod nondum est: id non est proprie et absolute." *Proslogion,* cap. XXII, p. 116.

23. "Et quidem quidquid est aliud praeter te solum, potest cogitari non esse. Solus igitur verissime omnium, et ideo maxime omnium habes esse: quia quidquid aliud est non sic vere, et idcirco minus habet esse." Ibid., cap. III, p. 103.

William L. Craig (essay date February 1986)

SOURCE: Craig, William L. "St. Anselm on Divine Foreknowledge and Future Contingency." *Laval théologique et philosophique* 42, no. 1 (February 1986): 93-104.

[*In the following essay, Craig assesses Anselm's arguments against theological fatalism and his ideas regarding free will.*]

Contemporary discussions of foreknowledge and future contingency have all but completely overlooked the contributions of Anselm of Canterbury on this score, despite that fact that his treatise. ***De concordia praescientiae praedestinationis et gratiae Dei cum libero arbitrio*** (1107/08) contains a very interesting and illuminating discussion of the problem of theological fatalism. That work is divided into three sections, dealing respectively with the harmony of foreknowledge, of predestination, and of grace with human freedom of the will. In the first section, which will be the focus of our interest, Anselm draws upon the analyses of both Augustine and Boethius to present a multi-faceted solution to the alleged incompatibility of God's foreknowledge and man's free choice.

COMPATIBILITY OF FOREKNOWLEDGE AND FREEDOM

Admittedly, he begins, these two do seem to be incompatible: "for it is necessary that the things foreknown by God be going to occur, whereas the things done by free choice occur without any necessity."[1] Anselm's procedure therefore is to assume that both are the case and to try to derive therefrom an impossibility. This, he thinks, cannot be done:

> Now, on the assumption that some action is going to occur without necessity, God foreknows this, since He foreknows all future events. And that which is foreknown by God is, necessarily, going to occur, as is foreknown. Therefore, it is necessary that something is going to occur without necessity. Hence, the foreknowledge from which necessity follows and the freedom of choice from which necessity is absent are here seen (for one who rightly understands it) to be not at all incompatible.[2]

Anselm's reasoning obviously derives from Augustine. He does not yet clearly distinguish, as he will, between precedent and subsequent necessity. The point is rather that God's foreknowledge makes it necessary that a contingent event occur. Therefore, God's foreknowledge actually secures man's freedom rather than annuls it.[3]

But someone will object that God foreknows that I shall sin or He foreknows that I shall not sin. So if I sin, it is necessary that I sin, and if I do not, then it is necessary

that I do not. Again the Augustinian context of the problem is apparent.[4] Anselm replies that his opponent should have said, "God foreknows that it is without necessity that I shall sin" or "God foreknows that it is without necessity that I shall not sin." It follows that whether one sins or not, he does so without necessity. Thus, the necessity which accompanies foreknowledge is not incompatible with freedom of choice, whereby many actions are performed without necessity.

But the objector may persist: if it is necessary that I sin willingly (*ex voluntate*), then, since necessity implies either coercion (*coactio*) or restraint (*prohibitio*), I am compelled by some hidden power to sin; and if I do not sin, then I am restrained from willing to sin. So if I sin, I do so by necessity, and if I do not, it is also by necessity. This objection seems obviously aimed at the Augustinian account of free will and necessity, according to which free choice and compulsion are incompatible. The objector is a sort of compatibilist who thinks that my sinning voluntarily and under hidden compulsion are not incompatible. Augustine in *De libero arbitrio* would have rejected the idea that a decision of the will could be voluntary and yet somehow compelled. Indeed, the will cannot be compelled to do anything. Anselm agrees.[5] Both men reject the inference from "It is necessary that I sin willingly" to "I am secretly compelled to sin willingly." Clearly, therefore, Anselm must be interpreting the necessity wrought by God's foreknowledge of a future contingent as something other than coercion or restraint. This is in fact the case.[6] According to Anselm, something may be necessary without compulsion's being involved. For example, when we say, "It is necessary for God to be immortal" we do not mean something compels God to be immortal. Rather we mean nothing can cause Him not to be immortal. Anselm elsewhere explains further the distinction between a necessity which compels and a necessity which does not compel.[7] When we say in God's case that something is necessary, we mean that in all other things there is a necessity which prevents them from doing—and compels them not to do—anything contrary to that which is being said of God. "For example, when we say 'It is necessary that God always speak the truth' and 'It is necessary that God never tell a lie,' nothing else is meant except that in God the steadfastness for maintaining the truth is so great that it is necessary that no thing can cause Him not to speak the truth or can cause Him to tell a lie."[8] The point is reminiscent of Augustine's distinction in *De civitate Dei* 5.10, except that Anselm seems to interpret the necessity of essential predication in terms of a sort of inverse causal impossibility; that is to say, when a property belongs necessarily to some substance, this is taken to mean that nothing can cause that substance to lack that property. Now applied to the problem of theological fatalism, this means that when I say "It is necessary that you will sin voluntarily," this does not imply that something prevents the act of will to not-sin or compels the act of will to sin.[9] God foreknows that the act of will is neither compelled nor prevented by anything. Hence, Anselm concludes, what is done voluntarily is done freely.

This account, while clearly non-compatibilist, does not, however, explain much. On the above analysis, "It is necessary that you will sin voluntarily" would seem to be equivalent to "Nothing can cause you not to sin voluntarily." That is to say, letting *p* stand for "You will sin voluntarily," [not] *p* = nothing can bring it about that *p*. The problem is, this still appears to be fatalistic. For it seems obvious that something could bring it about that *p;* for example, I could kill you prior to your willing to sin. In saying that if God foreknows p, then nothing can cause *p* to be the case, Anselm does not, therefore, seem to have escaped fatalism. Perhaps, however, this is pressing Anselm's analogy too far. It may be only that Anselm wished to assert that the notion of necessity does not always involve compulsion and that the necessity of essential predication is an example of this. Similarly, the necessity wrought by foreknowledge involves neither compulsion nor restraint; but Anselm may not thereby mean that the same analysis in terms of inverse causal impossibility may be applied to it.

PRECEDENT AND SUBSEQUENT NECESSITY

DISTINCTION BETWEEN PRECEDENT AND SUBSEQUENT NECESSITY

Indeed, he proceeds to provide a rather Boethian analysis of the necessity involved in God's foreknowledge in terms of precedent and subsequent necessity.[10] He writes,

> Indeed, (if someone properly considers the word), by the very fact that something is said to be *foreknown,* it is declared to be going to occur. For only what is going to occur is foreknown, since knowledge is only of the truth. Therefore, when I say "If God foreknows something, it is necessary that this thing be going to occur," it is as if I were to say: "If this thing will occur, of necessity it will occur." But this necessity neither compels nor prevents a thing's existence or nonexistence . . . For when I say "If it will occur, of necessity it will occur," here the necessity follows, rather than precedes, the presumed existence of the thing. The sense is the same if we say "What will be, of necessity will be." For this necessity signifies nothing other than that what will occur will not be able not to occur at the same time.[11]

On this analysis the proposition "If God foreknows something, necessarily this thing will occur" is logically equivalent to the proposition "If this thing will occur, necessarily it will occur." Anselm thereby reduces the problem of theological fatalism to the original logical problem of fatalism. Equally important, he insists that the necessity here operative involves no compulsion or restraint, but ultimately reduces to logical necessity. For when we say that if an event will occur then necessarily it will occur, we do not mean that its opposite is unconditionally impossible; rather granted that it will occur, it is then impossible for its opposite to happen, since two contradictory states of affairs cannot obtain in reality at the same time. For example, it is not the same thing, he claims, for a thing to be white as for a white thing to be white. A staff is not necessarily white, since before it was white it could be non-white, and after it is white it is able to become non-white. But it is necessary that a white thing always be white. For it cannot happen that a white thing is at the same time not-white. Similarly, it is not necessary that a thing be temporally present; but it is necessary that a present thing be always present, since a present thing is not able at the same time to be not-present. Hence, the proposition "If the event will occur, of necessity it will occur" is logically equivalent to "What will be, of necessity will be," which in Anselm's analysis means that it is an analytic and hence necessary truth that "What will be will be." Anselm thereby implies that the future cannot be changed, for by definition the future is what will be. This is not fatalistic because the necessity of this statement is that of a tautology.[12] Necessarily, what will be will be; but this involves no precedent necessity which determines the content of what will be.

Elsewhere Anselm analyzes the notion of precedent necessity in terms of causal necessity.[13] A true prophecy, he states, does not make the predicted event happen. The proposition "It was necessary that the event happen because the prophecy about it was true" is logically equivalent to "It was necessary that the event happen in this manner because it was going to happen in this manner." Anselm explains that this kind of necessity does not compel a thing to be; rather the being of the thing makes (*facit*) the necessity to be. There is a necessity which precedes and is the cause of a thing's being the case; but there is also a necessity which succeeds and which is made by the thing. An example of the former is the necessity which efficiently causes the heavens to revolve. An example of the latter is the necessity involved in saying "Because you are speaking, you are of necessity speaking"—here the necessity does not cause anything but is rather itself made. "For when I make this statement, I signify that nothing can cause it to be the case that while you are speaking you are not speaking; I do not signify that anything is compelling you to speak."[14] Now wherever there is precedent necessity, there is subsequent necessity; but the converse does not hold. For example, we may assert, "Because the heavens are revolving, necessarily they are revolving," but we may not say, "You are speaking because it is necessary for you to speak." On Anselm's analysis, then, precedent necessity seems to be unconditional causal necessity, while subsequent necessity is conditional, logical necessity. It is, however, interesting that he seems to reintroduce his analysis of subsequent necessity in terms of inverse causation: in "Because you are speaking, necessarily you are speaking," the necessity is said to mean that nothing can cause the consequent to be false if the antecedent is true, for then the law of contradiction would be violated. This understanding does not entail the fatalism that his earlier implied formulation did. At the same time, it is evident how foreign such an analysis of necessity is to modern logical theory.[15]

Now subsequent necessity furnishes the key to unlock the problem of fatalism posed by Aristotle:

> Subsequent necessity applies to all tenses, in the following manner: Whatever has been, necessarily has been; whatever is, necessarily is and necessarily was going to be. This is the necessity which (when Aristotle deals with singular and future propositions) seems to deny that there are real alternatives and to affirm that all things occur of necessity. Since the faith (or the prophecy) concerning Christ was true faith (or true prophecy) *because* He was going to die of His own will and not by necessity: it was necessary—in terms of the necessity which is subsequent and which does not efficiently cause anything—that His death would occur voluntarily . . . for because these things were going to occur, necessarily they did occur; and because they occurred, necessarily they were going to occur; and because they occurred, necessarily they occurred.[16]

Here Anselm explicitly breaks with Aristotle (and Boethius) in affirming that future contingent singular propositions are true or false.[17] For he states not only that "Whatever is, necessarily is," but also "Whatever is, necessarily was going to be," which Aristotle could not admit. These statements are not fatalistic because the necessity follows from the fact that the thing in question will in fact be, but there is no precedent necessity which compels the thing to be. Here Anselm supplements the Augustinian analysis of "It is necessary that *x* do *y* voluntarily": the necessity here operative is now revealed to be subsequent necessity. Thus, because Christ would die voluntarily, necessarily He would die voluntarily. This changes the Augustinian solution entirely, for now the necessity is conditional. *If* Christ will die voluntarily, necessarily He will die voluntarily. But the antecedent of this hypothetical is not causally determined, indeed it cannot be, given Anselm's understanding of "voluntary." Therefore, the consequent is not unconditionally necessary either; it is necessary only if the antecedent is true, and nothing compels the antecedent to be true.[18] Hence, both of the following statements are true:[19]

> 1. Something did exist and does exist and will exist, but not out of necessity.

> 2. All that was, necessarily was; all that is, necessarily is; and all that will be, necessarily will be.

This is so because (1) speaks of precedent and (2) of subsequent necessity.

CONTRAST OF THE PAST AND THE FUTURE

Anselm provides on this basis an interesting analysis of the necessity of the past and the future:

> In the same way, some event—e.g., an action—is going to occur without necessity, because before the action occurs, it can happen that it not be going to occur. On the other hand, it is necessary that a future event be future, because what is future is not able at the same time to be not future. Of the past it is similarly true (1) that some event is not necessarily past, because before it occurred, there was the possibility of its not occurring, and (2) that, necessarily, what is past is always past, since it is not able at the same time not to be past. Now a past event has a characteristic which a present event or a future event does not have. For it is never possible for a past event to become not-past, as a present event is able to become not-present and as an event which is not necessarily going to happen has the possibility of not happening in the future. Thus, when we say of what is going to happen that it is going to happen, this statement must be true, because it is never the case that what is going to happen is not going to happen. (Similarly, whenever we predicate something of itself, [the statement is true]. For when we say "Every man is a man," or "If he is a man, he is a man," or "Every white thing is white" or "If it is a white thing it is white"; these statements must be true because something cannot both be and not be the case at the same time.) Indeed, if it were not necessary that everything which is going to happen were going to happen, then something which is going to happen would not be going to happen—a contradiction. Therefore, *necessarily,* everything which is going to happen is going to happen, and if it is going to happen, it is going to happen. (For we are saying of what is going to happen that it is going to happen.) But ["necessarily" here signifies] subsequent necessity, which does not compel anything to be.[20]

In two respects the past and the future are on a modal par: events in the past and in the future alike may be causally contingent, and neither the past nor the future can be changed, for it is tautologously true that what has been has been and what will be will be. Nonetheless, Anselm struggles to elucidate a sense in which the past is different from the future or the present. A past event is always past, while a present event may become non-present, presumably by receding into the past.[21] On this parallel one would expect him to say that a future event may become non-future, by becoming present. Instead, he says that a future contingent event (*res quae non necessitate futura est*) can either be or not be in the future. But in terms of precedent necessity, the parallel is true of past events, as we have seen; and in terms of subsequent necessity it is contradictory to say a future contingent event will not be future.[22] I think that what Anselm is attempting to express is that the past is somehow actual in a sense in which the future is not. The events of the past *were* open to occurring or not, but are so no longer; but the possibility remains open whether any event or its opposite will occur in the future. Thus in terms of precedent necessity the future is open, while the past is not. Thus, on Anselm's analysis neither the past nor the future can be changed, for this would land one in self-contradiction. But the necessity that characterized past and future alike is merely subsequent necessity: if a thing has been, necessarily it has been; and if a thing will be, necessarily it will be. On the other hand, while the past is now causally isolated (denial of backward causation), nevertheless the future is causally open. The implication is that though the future is as unchangeable as the past, fatalism does not follow because we freely determine what it is that will be future.

APPLICATION TO FATALISM

Anselm proceeds to underline the fact that though an event is going to occur, it is not always the case that it occurs by (causal) necessity.[23] For example, the proposition "Tomorrow there will be an insurrection among the people" may be true, but it is not the case that the insurrection occurs by necessity. "For before it occurs, it is *possible* that it not occur even if it *is* going to occur."[24] Sometimes a future event will occur by necessity; for example, that there be a sunrise tomorrow. The insurrection which is going to occur tomorrow is, necessarily, going to occur, but the sunrise which is going to occur tomorrow is going to occur by necessity.

> For if the insurrection is going to occur tomorrow, then—necessarily—it is going to occur. On the other hand, the sunrise is understood to be going to occur with two necessities: (1) with a preceding necessity, which causes the event to occur (for the event will occur because it is necessary that it occur), and (2) with a subsequent necessity, which does not compel anything to occur (for because the sunrise is going to occur, it is—necessarily—going to occur).[25]

To draw the application to the problem at hand, when we say of an event foreknown by God that it is necessary that it be going to occur, we do not mean that it will occur by necessity; rather we mean that an event which is going to occur is, necessarily, going to occur. When God foreknows future events, He foreknows that some of these things will happen contingently, for example, the free decisions of men. It is not necessary that these events take place, but if they are going to take place then God foreknows this, and, necessarily, they will take place.

SUMMARY

Thus, on Anselm's view neither God's foreknowledge nor the antecedent truth of future contingent singular proposition entails fatalism. Theological fatalism reduces to the problem of the antecedent truth of such propositions. But such propositions are true only if the events in question will occur. Whether they will occur is causally indeterminate; either the event or its opposite may possibly eventuate. One of the opposites will occur and that future-tense proposition corresponding to it is true. It is not, however, necessarily true, since its contradictory could have been true. Granted that it is true, then necessarily the event described will happen. This necessity is, however, conditional; it depends on which of the contingent events will be realized, and that is up to the free wills of the persons involved. Therefore, the antecedent truth of a future contingent singular proposition does not entail fatalism. Similarly, whatever God foreknows will, necessarily, come to pass; but it is not necessary that God foreknow that any given contingent event come to pass. For since the event is causally indeterminate, either it or its opposite may eventuate, depending on the free decision involved. Some decision will be taken, and God foreknows what it will be; therefore, necessarily, that decision will be taken. But this necessity is entirely dependent on which decision will be freely taken, and it is still possible for either decision to be taken.

GOD'S KNOWLEDGE AND ETERNITY

Anselm emphasizes that this solution is not dependent upon whether one ascribes to God timeless eternity or merely everlasting temporal duration.[26] Drawing once more upon Augustine, he warns that if God's knowledge or foreknowledge imposes necessity upon everything He knows or foreknows, then, since He knows what He wills and causes and He foreknows what He shall will and cause, He does not freely will or cause anything—rather He wills and causes everything by necessity, which, Anselm snaps, is absurd. Hence, we must say for any given future contingent both that it is not compelled to occur by any necessity and that, necessarily, it will occur (because it is going to occur).

Although the notion of God's eternity does not, as we have seen, play a part in Anselm's initial foray against theological fatalism, when the relationship between foreknowledge and predestination arises, he does turn to the concept of God's timelessness in order to frame his discussion.[27] According to Anselm, many people were lamenting because they believed that free choice was of no avail for salvation or condemnation, but that as a result of God's foreknowledge only necessity determined one's salvation or damnation.[28] Anselm wants to hold to both free choice and predestination. He argues that what is immutable in God's timeless eternity is changeable in time prior to its occurrence, by a free act of the will. In Anselm's understanding God transcends both space and time, so that it may be said of Him that He exists in no place at no time.[29] God does not experience temporal succession and therefore has neither past nor future. "Does none of Your eternity pass by so that it no longer is, and is none of it going to become what, so to speak, it not yet is?" asks Anselm: "Then in no case *were* You yesterday or *will* You *be* tomorrow; instead, yesterday, today, and tomorrow You *are*. Or better, You simply *are*—existing beyond all time."[30] God has only a present. But, Anselm cautions, this is not a temporal present, but an eternal present in which the whole of time is contained.[31] He explains that what transcends space and time is not restricted by the law of space and time, namely, that whatever is in space and time is subject to division into parts, for example, past, present, and future.[32] Since God is not so temporally restricted, He is not prevented from being present as a whole to all times.

> Therefore, since an inescapable necessity demands that the Supreme Being be present as a whole in every place and at every time, and since no law of space or time prohibits the Supreme Being from being present as a whole in every place at once or from being present as a whole at every time at once, the Supreme Being must be present as a whole in every different place at once and present as a whole at every different time at once. Its being present at one place or time does not prevent it from being simultaneously and similarly present at another place or time.[33]

God is, strictly speaking, not, therefore, *in* every place and time, but is *with* every place and time. Therefore, God's acts of foreknowing, predestining, calling, and justifying men at different points in time and space take place in His timeless eternity.[34] For Anselm this presence of God to all times seems to be not merely epistemic, but real; that is to say, it is not just that God in His timeless eternity knows the content of the entire temporal process, but that that process as a whole— past, present, and future—is itself present to God:

> . . . I am not saying that my action of tomorrow at no time exists; I am merely denying that it exists today, even though it always exists in eternity. And when we deny that something which is past or future in the temporal order is past or future in eternity, we do not maintain that that which is past or future does not in any way exist in eternity; instead, we are simply saying that what exists there unceasingly in its eternal-present mode does not exist there in the past or future mode . . . [In eternity] there is no time before it exists or after it exists; instead it exists unceasingly, because in eternity nothing exists temporally.[35]

Although Anselm's statements concerning the flow of time appear to be inconsistent with this view, we seem to have here a remarkable anticipation of the widely held modern theory of the universe as a "block" of space-time itself subsisting timelessly as a whole. Future events do not yet exist in the sense that they do not exist at the present time; but they do exist at their own times, and all events exist timelessly in eternity, where God beholds them. While from our perspective within the temporal series, a future event is mutable because it is determined by our freely chosen actions, still from God's timeless perspective everything within the temporal series is static and immutable.[36] From our point of view, it appears that God foreknows and predestines men's future choices, but from His vantage point, He simply knows what the men in the temporal series are choosing and His "predestination" consists simply in leaving the will to its own power and concurring in its choice.[37] Therefore, just as *fore*knowledge is not properly found in God, neither is *pre*destination. Thus, once again foreknowledge is seen not to be inconsistent with free choice.

Anselm, then, has at least two arguments against theological fatalism. First, the subsequent necessity which results from God's foreknowing the future is in no sense incompatible with contingency and free choice. Second, because God exists timelessly and is therefore present to all times, He strictly speaking does not foreknow anything, but simply knows what men freely choose.

RELATION OF GOD'S KNOWLEDGE TO THE OBJECT KNOWN

There is, however, one final aspect of Anselm's thought that would seem to be nettlesome for the theological libertarian.[38] This is the issue of the relation between God's knowledge and the objects of God's knowledge. Boethius expressed misgivings with the Origenist view that the objects of knowledge determine the content of what God knows. Now Anselm considers "whether His knowledge derives from things or whether things derive their existence from His knowledge."[39] He is confronted with the dilemma:

> . . . if God derives His knowledge from things, it follows that they exist prior to His knowledge and hence do not derive their existence from Him; for they can only exist from Him in accordance with His knowledge. On the other hand, if all existing things derive their existence from God's knowledge, God is the Creator and the author of evil works and hence is unjust in punishing evil creatures—a view we do not accept.[40]

Anselm's problem with the view that God's knowledge derives from things is that the things would thereby become ontologically independent of God. This seems exceedingly odd, for the priority of such objects to God's knowledge is not metaphysical, but epistemic. He knows them to be as they are because they in fact are as they are. But Anselm seems to think this casts doubt on God's creative activity. For things are as they are because God created them as they are. But if God created them as they are apart from His knowledge of them, then His creation was blind and unknowing, which is impossible. Since God creates in accordance with His knowledge, to say that God's knowledge derives from the object is to imply that the object was uncreated by God. At least this may have been Anselm's fear; his comments are too terse to be certain. Therefore, he thinks that in some unexplained sense, God's knowledge of objects itself *causes* those objects to exist. Now he rightly sees that this causes difficulty concerning the origin of evil; but perhaps he does not fully appreciate how fatalistic this must also appear. For now God's foreknowledge causally determines the future and the temporal series is caused by His timeless knowledge. Hence, even if Anselm's escape from the dilemma, in terms of the Augustinian view of evil as a privation and hence something not caused by God, is successful, it is still not clear that he has escaped fatalism, or more correctly, determinism. For the good acts of will are determined to be what they are because God causes them to be that way, by knowing them into existence, so to speak. This difficulty was to elicit a great deal of thought on the part of Thomas Aquinas and helped to spawn the debate between subsequent generations of Thomists and Molinists over the notion of divine "middle knowledge" (*scientia media*).

Notes

1. Anselm, *De concordia praescientiæ et praedestinationis et gratiae Dei cum libero arbitrio* 1.1 (All citations of Anselm's works are from the Hopkins and Richardson translation, *Anselm of Canterbury,* 4 vols. (New York: 1947). ". . . quoniam ea quae deus praescit, necesse est esse futura, et quae per liberum arbitrium fiunt, nulla necessitate proveniunt." The text used throughout is that of Franciscus Salesius Schmitt, ed. *S. Anselmi Opera omnia,* 6 vols. (Stuttgart-Bad Cannstatt: Friedrich Fromman Verlag, 1968).

2. *Ibid.* 1.1.

   Sed si aliquid est futurum sine necessitate, hoc ipsum praescit deus, qui praescit omnia futura. Quod autem praescit deus, necessitate futurum est, sicut praescitur. Necesse est igitur aliquid esse futurum sine necessitate. Nequaquam ergo recte intelligenti hic repugnare videntur praescientia quam sequitur necessitas, et libertas arbitrii a qua removetur necessitas . . .

3. Anselm's solution seems misunderstood by Paul A. Streveler, "Anselm on Future Contingencies: A Critical Analysis of the Argument of the *De concordia*," *Anselm Studies* 1 (1983): 170, who mistakenly infers that "I will sin freely at *t*,"

means "I will sin at *t*, or I will not sin at *t*," which is tautologically true.

4. This is interesting because Anselm denied that freedom of choice is the ability to sin and not to sin. For then neither God nor the elect angels would have free choice. But we must have a concept of freedom that is univocal for God and creatures. That concept is the ability to keep uprightness of will for its own sake. Thus, Satan and Adam both sinned by their own choice, which was free; but neither sinned by means of that in virtue of which his choice was free. Moreover, after the Fall, man still has this ability, though he is a slave of sin. For although he never has the ability to possess uprightness when he does not have it, it remains true of fallen man that when he does have uprightness, he has the ability to keep it. Just as when the sun is behind a cloud we say that a man has the ability to see the sun, so when uprightness of will is absent we may say that man is able to keep uprightness of will for its own sake. For a man has the eyes to see the sun when it is present, and he has understanding and will by which he may keep uprightness when he has it. (Anselm, *De libertate arbitrii*.) This peculiar concept of freedom, however, plays little role in Anselm's discussion of foreknowledge and human freedom. See also Anselm, *De concordia* 3.3-5.

5. Anselm, *De libertate arbitrii* 5-8.

6. Anselm, *De concordia* 1.2. For a brief discussion of Anselm's modalities see Desmond Paul Henry, *The Logic of Saint Anselm* (Oxford: Clarendon, 1967), pp. 172-9.

7. Anselm, *Cur Deus homo* 2.17; cf. *Philosophical Fragments* 24.16-25.

8. Anselm, *Cur Deus homo* 2.17. "Nam cum dicimus quia necesse est deum semper verum dicere, et necesse est eum numquam mentiri, non dicitur aliud nisi quia tanta est in illo constantia servandi veritatem, ut necesse sit nullam rem facere posse, ut verum non dicat aut ut mentiatur."

9. Anselm, *De concordia* 1.2.

10. On the Boethian antecedents, see Henry, *Logic of Anselm,* pp. 177-8; for a critical discussion see Streveler, "Anselm on Future Contingencies," pp. 166-7.

11. Anselm, *De concordia* 1.2.

    Denique si quis intellectum verbi proprie considerat: hoc ipso quod praesciri aliquid dicitur, futurum esse pronuntiatur. Non enim nisi quod futurum est praescitur, quia scientia non est nisi veritatis. Quare cum dico quia si praescit deus aliquid, necesse est illud esse futurum: idem est ac si dicam: Si erit, ex necessitate erit. Sed haec necessitas nec cogit nec prohibet aliquid esse aut non esse . . . Nam cum dico: si erit, ex necessitate erit: hic sequitur necessitas rei positionem, non praecedit. Idem valet, si sic pronuntietur: Quod erit, ex necessitate erit. Non enim aliud significat haec necessitas, nisi quia quod erit non poterit simul non esse.

12. On this see Léon Baudry, "La prescience divine chez S. Anselme," *Archives d'histoire doctrinale et littéraire du Moyen-Âge* 13 (1940-2): 228.

13. Anselm, *Cur Deus homo* 2.17.—Not, as Henry states, physical necessity, since for Anselm causes may be non-physical. (Henry, *Logic of Anselm,* p. 173.)

14. *Ibid.* "Cum enim hoc dico, significo nihil facere posse, ut dum loqueris non loquaris, non quod aliquid ti cogat ad loquendum."

15. See comments by Henry, *Logic of Anselm,* p. 179, who nevertheless overlooks Anselm's curious analysis of subsequent necessity in terms of inverse causal impossibility. Streveler remarks, "It seems curious to me that Anselm should define subsequent necessity in terms of the lack of any power able to bring about the denial of the sentence said to be subsequently necessary. For, it seems quite superfluous to note that, in addition to not-P being self contradictory, there exists no power able to bring it about that it is true." (Streveler, "Anselm on Future Contingencies," pp. 166-7)

16. *Ibid.*

Ista sequens necessitas currit per omnia tempora hoc modo: Quidquid fuit, necesse est fuisse. Quidquid est, necesse est esse et necesse est futurum fuisse. Quidquid futurum est, necesse est futurum esse. Haec est illa necessitas quae, ubi tractat ARISTOTELES de propositionibus singularibus et futuris, videtur utrumblibet distruere et omnia esse ex necessitate astruere. Hac sequenti et nihil efficienti necessitate, quoniam vera fuit fides vel prophetia de Christo, quia ex voluntate non ex necessitate moriturus erat, necesse fuit ut sic esset . . . Ideo enim necessitate fuerunt, quia futura erant; et futura erant, quia fuerunt; et fuerunt, quia fuerunt.

17. Cf. Anselm, *Monologion* 10; *idem, De veritate* 10; see also Baudry, "Prescience," pp. 233-6.

18. We would today say that the modal operator governs the *dictum* as a whole; but Anselm does not appear to see this. For him the consequent is necessary, but only conditionally so, in a tautolo-

gous and hence vacuous way. As Henry notes, later medievals would doubtless understand his distinction as that between *necessitas consequentiae* and *necessitas consequentis.* (Henry, *Logic of Anselm,* p. 179; so also Streveler, "Anselm on future contingencies," pp. 165-171.)

19. Anselm, *De concordia* 1.2.

20. *Ibid.*

Eodem modo res aliqua—ut quaedam actio—non necessitate futura est, quia priusquam sit, fieri potest ut non sit futura; rem vero futuram necesse est esse futuram, quoniam futurum nequit esse simul non futurum. De praeterito autem similiter verum est quia res aliqua non est necessitate praeterita, quoniam antequam esset, potuit fieri ut non esset; et quia praeteritum semper necesse est praeteritum esse; quoniam non potest simul non esse praeteritum. Sed in re praeterita est quiddam, quod non est in re praesenti vel futura. Numquam enim fieri potest, ut res quae praeterita est fiat non praeterita; sicut res quaedam quae praesens est potest fieri non praesens, et aliqua res quae non necessitate futura est potest fieru, ut non sit futura. Itaque cum dicitur futurum de futuro, necesse est esse quod dicitur, quia futurum numquam est non futurum, sicut quotiens idem dicimus de eodem. Cum enim dicimus quia omnis homo est homo; aut si est homo, homo est; aut omne album est album; et si est album, album est; necesse est esse quod dicitur, quia non potest aliquid simul esse et non esse. Quippe si non est necesse omne futurum esse futurum, quoddam futurum non est futurum, quod est impossibile. Necessitate ergo omne futurum futurum est; et si est futurum, futurum est, cum futurum dicitur de futuro; sed necessitate sequente, quae nihil esse cogit.

21. Cf. *ibid.* 1.5: ". . . temporally past things are never able not to be past. But all temporally present things which pass away do become not-present." (". . . temporis praeterita non valent umquam praeterita non esse, praesentia vero tempore omnia quae transeunt fiunt non praesentia.")

22. The difficulty here is also spotted by Streveler, "Anselm on future contingencies," pp. 167-9, though his remarks on p. 168 strike me as an obscure and inaccurate interpretation of Anselm.

23. Anselm, *De concordia* 1.3.

24. *Ibid.* "Potest enim fieri antequam sit, ut non fiat, etiam si est futura."

25. *Ibid.*

Si enim cras futura est, necessitate futura est. Ortus vero solis duabus necessitatibus futurus intelligitur, scilicet et praecedenti quae facit rem esse—ideo enim erit, quia necesse est ut sit—, et sequenti quae nihil cogit esse, quoniam idcirco necessitate futurus est, quia futurus est.

26. *Ibid.* 1.4.

27. *Ibid.* 1.5.

28. *Ibid.* 1.6.

29. Anselm, *Monologion* 21-2; *idem Proslogion* 19.

30. Anselm, *Prologion* 19. "An de aeternitate tua nihil praeterit ut iam non sit, nec aliquid futurum est quasi nondum sit? Non ergo fuisti heri aut eris cras, sed heri et hodie et cras es. Immo nec heri nec hodie nec cras es, sed simpliciter es extra omne tempus."

31. Anselm, *De concordia* 1.5.

32. Anselm, *Monologion* 22.

33. *Ibid.*

> Quare quoniam summam essentiam totam et inevitabilis necessitas exigit nulli loco vel tempori deesse, et nulla ratio loci aut temporis prohibet omni loco vel tempori simul totam adesse: necesse est eam simul totam omnibus et singulis locis et temporibus praesentem esse. Non enim quia huic loco vel tempori praesens est, idcirco prohibitur illi vel illi loco aut tempori simul et similiter praesens esse.

34. Anselm, *De concordia* 1.5.

35. *Ibid.*

> Non enim dico actionem meam crastinam nullo tempore esse, sed hodie tantum nego eam esse, quae tamen semper est in aeternitate. Et quando negamus fuisse vel futurum ibi esse aliquid, quod in tempore fuit aut erit, non asserimus id quod fuit aut erit nullo modo ibi esse; sed tantum praeterito vel futuro modo dicimus non ibi esse, quod ibi indesinenter est suo praesenti modo . . . non antequam sit vel postquam est, sed indesinenter, quia nihil est ibi secundum tempus.

36. This serves to resolve the inconsistency alleged by Streveler, "Anselm on future contingencies," pp. 169-70. Since the entire time-line of the univers subsists finelessly with God and temporal becoming is mind-dependant, God may know timelessly and immutably events which on the time-line are temporal and mutable. To say that an event is mutable in the eternal present means that on the time line it is causally contingent vis à vis its proximate causes and, therefore, were these to act differently, some other event would be eternally present. Modern defenders of the B-theory of time have, I think, successfully rebutted charges of determinism or fatalism.

37. Anselm, *De concordia* 2.3.

38. See the struggles of Baudry, "Prescience," pp. 229-31; also STREVELER, "Anselm on future contingencies," p. 170, though once we understand Anselm as a B-theorist, his difficulties concerning priority in the eternal present vanish, since this is a causal, not a temporal priority.

39. *Ibid.* 1.7. "utrum eius scientia sit a rebus, an res habeant esse ab eides scientia."

40. *Ibid.*

> Nam si deus a rebus habet scientiam, sequitur quod illae prius sint quam eius scientia, et sic a deo non sint, a quo nequeunt esse nisi per eius scientiam. Si vero quaecumque sunt a scientia dei sumunt essentiam, deus est factor et auctor malorum operum, et ideo non iuste punit malos; quod non suscipimus.

Drew E. Hinderer (essay date spring 1986)

SOURCE: Hinderer, Drew E. "Anselm's Ontological Argument: What's in the Fool's Understanding?" *Michigan Academician* 18, no. 2 (spring 1986): 271-77.

[*In the following essay, Hinderer contends that Anselm's ontological argument for the existence of God fails because its premise that "God exists in the understanding" is problematic and false.*]

Anselm's ontological arguments have been the subject of very sustained philosophical interest from his own day through the present. The vast majority of those who have written about the arguments have treated them as proofs, i.e., as efforts to persuade unbelievers that the very nature of God's being is such as to make His nonexistence (in this universe) impossible, and hence that He not only exists, but is as Christians believe Him to be, a being than which no greater can be conceived, a being lacking no perfection. Philosophical attention has predominantly rested on the logical mechanics of Anselm's arguments, and, at least since Kant, on questions concerning the status of existence: whether existence is a "predicate," whether it is a "perfection" or "great making property," whether the idea of necessary existence is coherent, etc. These concerns are understandable only if we assume that readers are trying to decide, with Gaunilon, whether they are rationally justified, or even compelled, to believe in God on the basis of the ontological argument construed as an effort to establish God's existence "by the force of reason alone."[1]

It is surely fair to say that most of Anselm's philosophical critics have denied that the argument is a fully successful proof of the existence of God, though they have not all agreed as to why it fails. Many, if not most, have either followed Kant in locating the failure in the problem of proving existence by reason alone, or in finding fault with the logical apparatus of "necessary existence." I accept the consensus that the proof as a proof does not work, but locate the problem elsewhere.

In the following pages, I shall argue that the failure of the ontological argument as a proof stems from Anselm's rightful insistence on the transcendence of God, that God is "the being than which no greater can be conceived,"[2] together with the unfortunate result that, if God is such a being, then it will be false that, as Anselm says, "This Very fool, when he hears of this being of which I speak—a being than which no greater can be conceived—understands what he hears, and what he understands is in his understanding; although he does not understand it to exist."[3] If God is not in the fool's understanding, then God does not, so far at least, exist "both in the understanding and in reality,"[4] nor would Anselm's conclusion be "so evident, to a rational mind, that (God) does exist in the highest degree of all."[5] Put more simply, my point is that on Anselm's terms, the argument's initial premise, that "God exists in the understanding,"[6] is false.

Spelling out Anselm's arguments in such a way as to make clear their logical structure is a complicated task. At least since Norman Malcolm's influential article it has been customary to differentiate two such arguments.[7] The first, which appears in Chapter II, is an indirect proof which derives a contradiction from the supposition that the being than which nothing greater can be conceived exists in the understanding alone. The second, sometimes called the "modal version," derives God's existence in reality from God's necessary existence in the understanding. Among Anselm's current supporters, it has been the second version of the ontological argument which has recently received the most persuasive defenses.[8]

However, both versions of Anselm's argument unavoidably involve the premise that God exists in the understanding (*in intellectu*), so that if my argument is correct, it applies equally to each formulation. Therefore, I have not taken pains in this paper to preserve the distinction between the indirect proof and modal versions of the ontological arguments, and refer to Anselm's work as a single proof.

Anselm defines "God" as "a being than which nothing greater can be conceived."[9] This definition, which is interesting for many reasons, is consistent with Anselm's assertions that "I have never seen thee, O Lord, my God; I do not know thy form,"[10] and that "I do not endeavor, O Lord, to penetrate thy sublimity, for in no wise do I compare my understanding with that,"[11] because it does not define God's sublimity in terms of human imagination at all. Instead, Anselm's definition is a criterion by which to determine that inadequate conceptions of God are not conceptions of God at all, but at best of something inferior.

Suppose the fool believes that God is the greatest being that he (the fool) can imagine, and that this being is one who is faster than a speeding bullet, more powerful than a locomotive, able to leap tall buildings at a single bound, but nothing more. Such a fool, Anselm might say, mistakenly thinks he is thinking of God, but in fact he is using the expression "God" uncomprehendingly, without adequate attention to its true signification. To prove that the fool is not thinking of God, the fool need only ask himself whether he can imagine a being greater than the one which is faster than a speeding bullet, and so on, and of course he can: a being faster than a bolt of lightning, more powerful than an earthquake, and just barely able to leap Mt. Everest at a single bound (but nothing more) would be greater. But since God is the being than which nothing greater can be conceived, the first being (call him "Superman") cannot be God. But is the second imagined being God? To answer that question, Anselm counsels, the fool must ask himself whether he can imagine a being greater than "Even More Superman," and again, he certainly can; a being that is all that Even More Superman is, but who can leap Mt. Everest by a margin as high as the tallest building in Metropolis would be greater than Even More Superman.

Now suppose that the fool continues his imaginings up to the limit of his ability to imagine, so that he is now imagining the Most Superman Imaginable by the Fool. Again, Anselm would presumably suggest that if anyone, say the greatest human imaginer, could conceive of a being greater than that imagined by the fool, the Most Superman Imaginable by the Fool would not be God. But would the greatest being imaginable by the greatest human imaginer be God?

Anselm's criterion will not decide this question, for it defines God as the being than which nothing greater can be conceived, not the being than which nothing greater can be conceived within the limits of human imagination. But there is also independent reason to suppose that Anselm would deny that God could be conceived, even by the greatest human imaginer. This is because sin prevents us. As Anselm says of himself, "I am bowed down and can only look downward. . . . My iniquities have gone over my head . . . and, like a heavy load, they weight me down . . . Lord, I acknowledge and I thank thee that thou hast made me in this thine image . . . but that image has been so consumed and wasted away by vices, and obscured by the smoke of wrongdoing. . . ." Indeed, even if "thou renew it, and create it anew," the best that can be hoped for is "to understand in some degree thy truth."[12] Again, Anselm asks,

> What, O most high Lord, shall this man do, an exile far from thee? What shall thy servant do, anxious in his love of thee, and cast out afar from thy face? He pants to see thee, and thy face is too far from him. . . . He desires to seek thee, and does not know thy face. Lord, thou art my God, and thou art my Lord, and never have I seen thee. It is thou that hast made me, and hast made me anew, and hast bestowed upon me all the blessing I enjoy; and not yet do I know thee.[13]

Thus does Anselm deny that he can adequately conceive God, for sin blinds him. But Anselm's definitional insight is that being unable to conceive adequately what God is does not render Anselm or man generally unable to determine what God is not. Anselm's definition, that God is the being than which nothing greater can be conceived, provides a conclusive test by which to eliminate inadequate conceptions, but it is entirely independent of particular people's abilities to imagine.

In light of all this, what does Anselm mean when he asserts that "this very fool, when he hears of this being of which I speak—a being than which nothing greater can be conceived—understands what he hears, and what he understands is in his understanding; although he does not understand it to exist"?

Anselm offers two accounts of what it is to have something in one's understanding. These I shall refer to as the "linguistic account" and the "artistic account." It is unclear precisely what the relation is between these accounts, in that whatever Anselm may have intended, the latter artistic account may or may not be an elaboration or explanation of the former linguistic account. Because of this ambiguity, I shall treat each separately.

Anselm's linguistic account runs as follows.

> But at any rate, this very fool, when he hears of this being of which I speak—a being than which nothing greater can be conceived—understands what he hears, and what he understands is in his understanding; although he does not understand it to exist. . . . Hence, even the fool is convinced that something exists in the understanding, at least than which nothing greater can be conceived. For, when he hears of this, he understands it. And whatever is understood exists in the understanding.[14]

Subsequently in Section IV, Anselm elaborates this linguistic account to suggest that it is only if what the fool says in his heart is said either "without any, or with some foreign signification"[15] that saying that "(Christians believe) God exists" does not entail "God exists." So long as the expression "God exists" is used meaningfully, then, "he who thoroughly understands

this, assuredly understands that this being so truly exists, that not even in concept can it be nonexistent."[16] (For the sake of this paper, I shall assume that Anselm's expression "he who thoroughly understands" means "he who has used the expression in question meaningfully.")

Here, Anselm may be alluding to a difference he employs elsewhere between the colloquial use of words (*usus loquendi*), in which a speaker might make the mere "breath of an utterance" (*flatis vocis*) without relevantly connecting an expression with its mental or physical referent, and the use of words with strict attention to their significance (*significatio per se*).[17] Thus the fool's initial inability to see that "(Christians believe) God exists" entails "God exists" might be due to the fool's "breathing an utterance" without giving it any signification, or perhaps, as Anselm says, a "foreign" one.

While Anselm's exact theory of meaning is a much disputed question, it does seem likely that he insists upon an objective referent for words used meaningfully, according to which, once he thoroughly understands what he says in his heart, the fool must link his utterance to the "being than which nothing greater can be conceived." But what would such an objective referent be?

There seem to be only two plausible possibilities. One is that "God" refers to God, and that in order to use the expression "God" meaningfully, the fool must relevantly connect his utterance of the sound "God" with God. This, however, requires that the fool somehow already know God with sufficient accuracy and vividness that the referent to which he links his utterance cannot be confused with something else, say Superman. For if the fool lacks such knowledge, if, for example, he is unable to distinguish between God and Superman, then his use of the term "God" does not strictly mean God, but rather "a being indistinguishable from Superman." In this case, if the fool lacks such knowledge, what the fool has in his understanding is not God, but the being indistinguishable from Superman.

Moreover, it is doubtful, in light of Anselm's earlier remarks, that the fool would be able to see God's face or know God any more successfully than Anselm, since the fool, like Anselm, is in sin, and his sin must blind him as effectively as Anselm's. I therefore conclude that when the fool utters "there is no God," he does not have God in his understanding, and that on this interpretation, Anselm's premise is false.

The other natural explanation is that the referent of "God" is a kind of mental image of God, and that Anselm's artistic account is his explanation of the linguistic account. The artistic account runs as follows.

> When a painter first conceives of what he will after-wards perform, he has it in his understanding, but he does not yet understand it to be because he has not yet performed it. But after he has made the painting, he both has it in his understanding, and he understands that it exists, because he has made it.[18]

(That Anselm is here assuming a procedure of artistic creation that is extremely implausible need not concern us here.)[19]

But Anselm cannot consistently suppose that the fool has or could have vividly in his understanding the sort of mental image of God which Anselm here compares to the image had by a painter who imagines his unpainted picture to himself. As we have already seen, Anselm thinks sin obscures the divine image, so that man cannot see God's face nor know God. But also, Anselm, like Plato in the *Seventh Letter,* must recognize that to have an image of God in one's understanding, however vivid, is a very different thing from having God in one's understanding, and that insofar as it is an image, it is a falsification of God's true nature and an obstacle to knowing God Himself, quite apart from the inadequacies of the foolish imagination.[20] As Plato says,

> For everything that exists there are three classes of objects through which knowledge about it must come, the knowledge itself is a fourth, and we must put as a fifth entity the actual object of knowledge which is the true reality. We have then, first, a name, second a description, third, an image, and fourth a knowledge of the object. . . . Furthermore these four do as much to illustrate the particular quality of any object as they do to illustrate its essential reality.[21]

This, of course, is an expression of a common problem in mystical epistemology, namely how one penetrates through language, descriptions, images, and knowledge itself to a direct apprehension of God. The fact that it confronts Anselm has led scholars such as Frederick Sontag to try to rescue the ontological argument by denying that it is, or was intended to be, a proof, claiming instead that "Anselm's central point (is only that) 'that being than which no greater can be conceived' is not such a simple phrase as you might at first expect, and that, the longer you consider it and what it involves, the more you will be led to change both the disarm-ingly simple wording of the phrase and your own first feeling of easy optimism over your ability to understand it."[22] While I cannot pursue the issue further here, I think a fairer assessment is only that, as a proof, Anselm's argument fails.

But suppose Anselm replies to the foregoing objections as follows. Granted that the being than which nothing greater can be conceived cannot be conceived, either in the understanding of the fool or in the understanding of the (sinful) believer, still even the fool must realize that

God must be a being that exists (or exists necessarily) because anything less would not be the greatest being that can be conceived, much less a greater being still. Even if man's sinbound powers of conception cannot provide him with a fully adequate mental picture of God, a more adequate mental picture of God than the one often foolishly entertained is sufficient to entail that God must exist.

Unfortunately, however, this fallback position is unavailable to Anselm. This is because, according to Anselm's criteria for meaningful language use, if the expression "the being than which nothing greater can be conceived" cannot be used meaningfully, neither can "the being greater than the greatest being that can be conceived by sinful man," nor even "the greatest conceivable being" (except by the greatest human imaginer), which, in any case, Anselm would certainly reject as an adequate conception of God. Moreover, and perhaps more importantly for Anselm's argument, the greatest being conceivable by the fool may or may not include existence in reality as a perfection (still less "necessary existence" if the fool can imagine this) because ideal but unactual perfections may be greater than mere existence in this universe.

I conclude, then, that if we wish to give Anselm the credit he may deserve for anticipating in his definition of God the limits of human imagination, we must recognize that, by either criterion Anselm offers, it will be false that "even the fool is convinced that something exists in the understanding, at least, than which nothing greater can be conceived." But if this premise is false, the proof, as a proof, fails.

Notes

1. St. Anselm, in *St. Anselm, Basic Writings, Proslogium, Monologium, Cur Deus Homo* and *Gaunilon's In Behalf of the Fool,* trans. S. N. Deane. (La Salle, IL: Open Court, 1962) p. 38.

2. St. Anselm, *Proslogium*, p. 7.

3. Ibid., p. 7.

4. Ibid., p. 8.

5. Ibid., p 9.

6. See William L. Rowe, "The Ontological Argu-ment," in *Reason and Responsibility,* ed. Feinberg. (Belmont, CA: Dickenson Publishing Co., 1965) p. 8.

7. Norman Malcolm, "Anselm's Ontological Argu-ments," *Philosophical Review* 69 (1960).

8. See Alvin Plantinga, *God, Freedom, and Evil* (New York: Harper and Row, Publishers, 1974).

9. St. Anselm, *Proslogium,* p. 7.

10. Ibid., p. 4.

11. Ibid., pp. 6-7.

12. Ibid., pp. 6-7.

13. Ibid., p. 4.

14. Ibid., pp. 7-8.

15. Ibid., p. 10.

16. Ibid., p. 10.

17. St. Anselm, *The De Grammatico of Saint Anselm: The Theory of Paronymy,* Latin and English text with discussion, D. P. Henry (South Bend, IN: Notre Dame, 1964).

18. St. Anselm, *Proslogium,* p. 7.

19. For an extended discussion of Anselm's assumption, see E. H. Gombrich, *Art and Illusion* (Princeton, NJ: Princeton University Press, 1960).

20. Plato, *The Collected Dialogues,* ed. Hamilton and Cairns (Princeton, NJ: Princeton University Press, 1961), Letters VII, 342a9ff. By citing Plato as the author of the *Seventh Letter,* I do not wish to commit myself to asserting his authorship; I merely use "Plato" to refer to the author of the *Seventh Letter.*

21. Plato, *Seventh Letter,* 342a9 ff.

22. Frederick Sontag, "The Meaning of 'Argument' in Anselm's Ontological 'Proof,'" *The Journal of Philosophy;* LXIV (15) (August 10, 1967):474.

Thomas H. Bestul (essay date 1988)

SOURCE: Bestul, Thomas H. "St. Augustine and the *Orationes sive Meditationes* of St. Anselm." *Anselm Studies* 2 (1988): 597-606.

[*In the following essay, Bestul elucidates the stylistic influence of St. Augustine's work on Anselm's devotional writing.*]

St. Anselm composed most of his nineteen prayers and three meditations between the years 1060 and 1078, while he was a monk at Bec. As scholars have frequently observed, those *Orationes sive Meditationes* mark a turning point in the devotional literature of the Western Church. Composed in an effusive, exclamatory, highly personal style, making use of lengthy balanced periods and carefully balanced cadences, his writings are characterized by an intense, emotional intimacy that is quite unlike anything known before his time. In seeking to identify the sources of Anselm's devotional writing, most scholars have rightly identified three contributing influences: the Psalms, the liturgy, and the earlier, mainly Carolingian, tradition of private prayer.[1] Yet these influences, important as they are, do not adequately account for his achievement. I believe that Anselm's devotional writings can be better understood if they are examined in the light of the works of St. Augustine, particularly the *Soliloquia,* the *Confessiones,* and the *De trinitate.* While it is true that there are no quotations or direct borrowings from any of these three works in the **Orationes sive Meditationes,** I will argue for a general influence that is nonetheless profound and fundamental.

The **Orationes sive Meditationes** were written in a period of Anselm's life when he had given himself to an intense study of St. Augustine, especially the *De trinitate,* as preparation for the composition of the **Monologion,** as we know from Anselm's own account in a letter to Lanfranc and from the Prologue to the **Monologion.**[2] Apart from the theology, Anselm seems to have been especially interested in the form Augustine used for this treatise. The *De trinitate* is a theological discussion combined with meditative passages drawn from personal experience. The work seems the record of a personal, inward voice speaking in the presence of God. This form was essentially Augustine's invention. He had used a variation of it in his early work, the *Soliloquia,* where the narrator conducts an interior dialogue on the nature of the Deity with Reason, who is identified as an aspect of his own being. The dialogue, of course, was well established as an appropriate form for the conduct of philosophical or theological discussion: it is the interior character of the conversation which makes Augustine's usage of the form so novel. Augustine himself sensed this in coining a new word to give title to his *Soliloquia.* He speaks to Reason as follows:

> It is ridiculous if you are ashamed, as if it were not for this very reason that we have chosen this mode of discourse, which since we are talking with ourselves alone, I wish to be called and inscribed *Soliloquies*—a new name, it is true, and perhaps a grating one—but not ill-suited for setting forth the fact.[3]

Anselm no doubt has Augustine in mind when in the Prologue to the **Proslogion** he gives the title of his first work as *Monologion, id est Soliloquim.*[4] Anselm found in Augustine's works well-developed examples of the interior dialogue dealing with theological or devotional matter, often in combination. Anselm's prayers are really inner conversations between the speaker and his soul, or the speaker and his sins, conducted in the presence of God or of the saint to whom the prayer is addressed. In the **Meditatio redemptionis humanae** and in the *Proslogion* Anselm treats theological issues in a meditative form, much in the formal and stylistic manner of Augustine in the *De trinitate* and the *Soliloquia.*

The soliloquy form as originated by Augustine was one that greatly interested Anselm and his age. Isidore's *Synonyma* is a devotional and philosophical dialogue following Augustine's model, and is sometimes called *Soliloquia* in the many eleventh- and twelfth-century manuscripts of the work.[5] In a thirteenth-century manuscript of Anselm's *Proslogion* that work is described in the colophon as an *opusculum Soliloquiorum more compositum.*[6] Certain commentaries on the Psalms describe them as soliloquies, and Augustine in the *Enarrationes in Psalmos* distinguishes in Psalm 37 two different speakers—Christ as Head and Christ as Body—who yet are a single entity, in the manner of his own *Soliloquia.*[7] In the twelfth and thirteenth centuries the soliloquy form became widely used and the title was applied to a range of works, but Anselm, I think, was perhaps the first after Isidore to imitate the prototype of Augustine and to adapt its spirit to his own purposes.[8]

Anselm's use of a cadenced, carefully balanced prose style is certainly a reflection of contemporary literary tastes, but its use in the *Orationes sive Meditationes* could well have been inspired by the example of Augustine's *Soliloquia.* An extract of that work, beginning *Deus universitatis conditor,* had circulated independently as a prayer since Carolingian times, and could have given Anselm a stylistic pattern to imitate.[9] Augustine's *Soliloquia* indeed were recognized in the later Middle Ages as a particularly fine example of a cadenced prose style. John of Garland, writing in his *Poetria* of the mid-thirteenth century, describes what he calls the Isidorian style as having clauses not balanced by equality of length but by rhyming cadences, as are found in Augustine's *Soliloquia.*[10]

Yet in reading the treatise one is struck by the cold formality of those balanced periods, which contrast so strongly with the personal ardor permeating almost all of Anselm's *Orationes sive Meditationes.* It is, finally, to Augustine's *Confessiones* that one must turn to discover perhaps the genesis of Anselm's style and method. In the first place, Anselm would have found in the *Confessiones* the detailed record of spiritual strife which had similarities to his own, provided we accept, as seems reasonable, that the first two of his meditations contain at least a core of biographical truth. He would have seen in Augustine another great sinner (and fellow fornicator), who had struggled to control his passions, finally attaining inner peace in the duties of pastor and teacher. We may be certain that Anselm was familiar with the *Confessiones,* even though he does not quote from nor allude to the book. The twelfth-century

catalogue of the library of Bec lists a copy, and there is precedent for using extracts from it for devotional purposes as early as the Carolingian age.[11] From the *Confessiones* Anselm could have acquired the traits of his fervent personal style, in particular the extensive use of exclamation and of the successions of agitated questions, directed in part to oneself, in part to God, through which an attempt is made to probe the depths of private religious experience. Like Anselm, Augustine describes his own inability even to begin to approach God in prayer because the burden of sin is so deeply felt. As Augustine laments:

> How shall I call upon my God for aid, when the call I make is for my God to come to myself? What place is there in me to which my God can come, what place that can receive the God who made heaven and earth? Does this mean, O Lord my God, that there is something in me fit to contain you? Can even heaven and earth, which you made and in which you made me, contain you?[12]

Anselm's predicament in his *Oratio ad Christum* is similarly expressed:

> What shall I say? What shall I do? Where shall I go? Where shall I seek him? Where or when shall I find him? Whom shall I ask? Who will tell my beloved that I languish for love?[13]

Anselm might also have found in the *Confessiones* many instances of the sinner's fervent address to the soul, usually in the form of a series of questions and answers:

> Barren soul, what do you do? Why do you lie still, sinful soul? The day of judgment approaches.[14]

Anselm's first and second meditations often use this device in ways reminiscent of Augustine. The narrative complexities of Anselm's devotional works, with their speeches addressed to different aspects of one's interior existence seem to reflect the subtleties of the *Confessiones.*

As well as providing possible stylistic models, the *Confessiones* offers an articulate apologia for literary explorations of the inner spiritual life, showing their utility for a Christian reading public. Throughout his career Anselm seems to have had a sense of himself as a teacher and spiritual guide, combined with a literary self-consciousness of a kind that is unexpected in his age and that in some ways resembles Augustine's. One of the most remarkable characteristics of Anselm's *Orationes sive Meditationes* is the fact that they circulated in their own time as an integral collection under the name of their author. There are few precedents for the circulation of devotional work in this manner between the patristic age and Anselm's own time. Isidore's *Syn-*

onyma may be an exception; Carolingian prayers are usually found anonymously in compendious anthologies attached to psalters, and when they have attributions, they usually belong to the fathers, especially Augustine and Gregory.[15] We may well ask what Anselm's intention was in allowing so personal and intimate a collection to be spread abroad with his authorship clearly inscribed, and with a preface instructing the reader how it is to be used. In the *Confessiones* Augustine justifies the dissemination to the public of spiritual autobiography in words that apply to Anselm's own practice in his devotional writing. Augustine notes:

> But when others read of those past sins of mine, or hear about them, their hearts are stirred so that they no longer lie listless in despair crying "I cannot." Instead their hearts are roused by the love of your mercy and the joy of your grace by which each one of us, weak though he be, is made strong, since by it he is made conscious of his own weakness.[16]

As is Augustine, Anselm is keenly aware of the emotional impact his writing would have, and was meant to have, on others. Indeed in his Prologue he states that the chief purpose of the prayers and meditations that follow is "to stir up the mind of the reader to the love, or fear of God, or to self examination."[17]

A letter to Anselm from Durand, Abbot of La Chaise-Dieu, describes in almost Augustinian terms the effect that the reading of Anselm's *Meditatio ad concitandum timorem* had on his community:

> When we read these words, your pious tears were before us, drawing the same from us, so that we marvelled in every way, both that such a dew of blessing should overflow from your heart, and that from thence without a murmur such a stream should descend into our hearts. For this is in fact what happened. The goodness of the prayers you have written stirs this up in us, loving this in you, or rather you in them, and above them and through them loving God and you.[18]

This truly remarkable letter reproduces the rationale developed by Augustine for publishing the record of an individual's most intimate encounters with the deity: it is given to the world not so much for personal glory or publicity, nor even for purposes of biography, but so that persons reading and contemplating such written records may be stirred to similar emotions of fear, remorse, and love, and be inspired to seek God.

Finally, I would like to suggest that a profound understanding on the part of Anselm of Augustine's celebrated discussion of memory in *Confessiones* X could have formed the theoretical basis for the methodology used in Anselm's fervid personal meditations. In speaking of human memory Augustine observes:

> Out of the same storehouse, with these past impressions, I can construct now this, now that image of things that I have experienced or believed on the basis of experience—and from these I can further construct future actions, events, and hopes; and I can meditate on all these things as if they were present.[19]

Augustine then offers an application of this technique of meditation as he probes his memory, seeking to recall the history of his search for God. Memory is crucial in Anselm's *Orationes sive Meditationes*—the prayers derive much of their efficacy from our vivid awareness of Anselm's sinful past, as it is marshalled before his memory with lively horror and regret. The same faculty can construct images which evoke the past historical events of Christ's passion or suggest the future terrors of the Last Judgment. The *Oratio ad Christum* well illustrates the method:

> To this, most merciful Lord, tends this my prayer, this remembrance and meditation of your kindnesses, that I may enkindle in myself your love . . . Thus not as I ought but as I am able, I remember your passion, remember your buffeting, remember the scourging, remember the cross, remember the wounds, remember how you were slain for me.[20]

The first two meditations of Anselm especially hinge upon the recollection of past sin and the formation of powerful images which summon before the mind the dreadful day of judgment:

> What is this, O God, what is this that I perceive in the land of miseries and darkness? Horror! Horror! What is this that I see, where they dwell with no order, but everlasting horror? Alas, the confusion of wailing, the tumult of those gnashing their teeth, an inordinate multitude of sighs. Woe, woe; again and again and again woe, woe! The sulphurous fire, the hell-like flame, the gloomy whirlings, how I see you swirling with terrific roaring![21]

Of course the language of this passage surpasses any standards of stylistic decorum that Augustine would have recognized, but the importance of the memory as a well of tangible images of things not seen (*invisibilia*) is surely evident. This is a technique of meditation and contemplation which realized its full potential in the centuries following Anselm's death, but we can find its beginnings in his works.

The structure of Anselm's *Orationes sive Meditationes* may well owe much to the patristic doctrine of compunction as expressed most notably in Gregory's *Moralia,* as has been noted.[22] Compunction is defined as abasement of the mind with tears arising from the remembrance of sin and the terror of judgment, and the sources of emotion associated with it are the remembrance of past sins, the calling to mind of future punishments, and the desire for the heavenly home.[23] Yet, at the same time, Anselm's force of utterance, his emotionalism, and the intimacy of his diction, all find their nearest analogues in Augustine's *Confessiones*

What part Augustine played in the formation and development of Anselm's *Orationes sive Meditationes* can never be identified with complete certainty and assurance. As R. W. Southern has noted, it is not characteristic of Anselm to use quotations or to identify sources.[24] But just as his reading of the *De trinitate* suffused the **Monologion** with an Augustinian spirit and perhaps gave the impetus to the **Proslogion,** so it seems likely to suppose that Anselm found in Augustine examples to follow and models to imitate, a mode of expression eminently congenial to him as he committed to writing his prayers and meditations in a time of his life when the work of Augustine was much with him.

Notes

1. See R. W. Southern, *Saint Anselm and His Biographer* (Cambridge: Univ. Press, 1963), pp. 34-47; *The Prayers and Meditations of St. Anselm,* trans. B. Ward (Harmondsworth: Penguin, 1973), pp. 27-46.

2. *Epistola 77:* Schmitt III,199-200; *Monologion,* prologus: Schmitt I,7-8. On the relation of Anselm to Augustine, see Southern, pp. 31-33.

3. *Soliloquia* II,14: *PL* XXXII,891: Ridiculum est si te pudet, quasi non ob idipsum eligerimus huiusmodi sermocinationes: quae quoniam cum solis nobis loquimur, Soliloquia vocari et inscribi volo: novo quidem et fortasse duro nomine, sed ad rem demonstrandam satis idoneo; trans. C. C. Starbuck, in Philip Schaf, ed., A Select Library of Nicene and Post Nicene Fathers, Vol. VII (New York: Christian Literature Company, 1908), p. 551.

4. *Proslogion,* Prooemium: Schmitt I,94.

5. See *Synonyma: PL* LXXXIII,825-68; on the manuscripts, see M. Oberleitner, et al., *Die handschriftliche Überlieferung der Werke des Heiligen Augustinus: Sitzungsberichte der Österreichische Akademie der Wissenschaften, philosophisch-historische Klasse,* 263, 267, 276, 281, 289, 292 (Vienna: Böhlau in Komm., 1969-74).

6. *Proslogion* XXVI: Schmitt I,122, ad notas.

7. For the Psalm commentaries, see A. J. Minnis, *Medieval Theory of Authorship* (London: Scolar, 1984), p. 44; *Enarrationes in psalmos* XXXVII,6: *PL* XXXVI,400.

8. See Hugh of St. Victor, *Soliloquium de arrha animae: PL* CLXXVI,951-70; William of St. Thierry's *De contemplando deo* was also often given the title *Soliloquium:* see *On Contemplating God,* trans. Sister Penelope, Cistercian Fathers Series, No. 3 (Kalamazoo: Cistercian Publications, 1977), p. 34.

9. It is found, for example, in the *Officia per ferias* attributed to Alcuin, and in a ninth-century prayerbook from Fleury; see, respectively, *PL* CI,580 and *PL* CI,1397.

10. See C. S. Baldwin, *Medieval Rhetoric and Poetic* (1928; rpt. Gloucester, MA: Peter Smith, 1959), p. 194.

11. See R. Constantinescu, "Alcuin et les 'Libelli Precum' de l'époque carolingienne," *Revue d'histoire de la spiritualité* 50 (1974), 17-56. For the influence of the *Confessiones* on the devotional writing of Anselm's fellow Norman and near contemporary, John of Fécamp (d. 1078), see A. Wilmart, *Auteurs spirituels et textes dévots du moyen âge latin* (1932; rpt. Paris: Etudes augustiniennes, 1971), p. 135. For the copy in the Bec library catalogue, see G. Becker, *Catalogi bibliothecarum antiqui* (Bonn: Fr. Cohen, 1885), p. 258.

12. *Confessiones* I,ii,2: *PL* XXXII,661: Et quomodo invocabo deum meum, deum et dominum meum? Quoniam utique in me ipsum eum vocabo, cum invocabo eum. Et quis locus est in me quo veniat in me deus meus? quo deus veniat in me, deus qui fecit coelum et terram? Itane, domine deus meus, est quidquam in me quod capiat te? An vero coelum et terra quae fecisti, et in quibus me fecisti, capiunt te?—trans. R. S. Pine-Coffin (Harmondsworth: Penguin, 1961), p. 22.

13. *Oratio II:* Schmitt III,9: Quid dicam? Quid faciam? Quo vadam? Ubi eum quaeram? Ubi vel quando inveniam? Quem rogabo? Quis nuntiabit dilecto quia amore langueo?—translations of Anselm are my own unless otherwise indicated.

14. *Meditatio I:* Schmitt III,77: Anima sterilis, quid agis? Quid torpes, anima peccatrix? Dies iudicii venit.

15. See the prayerbooks edited by A. Wilmart, *Precum libelli quattuor aevi Karolini* (Rome: Ephemerides Liturgicae, 1940); two Anglo-Irish prayerbooks from the eighth or ninth centuries contain a few prayers attributed to contemporaries; see *The Prayer Book of Aedeluald the Bishop, Commonly Called the Book of Cerne,* ed. A. B. Kuypers (Cambridge: Univ. Press, 1902), pp. 143-44, 155, 207, 219.

16. *Confessiones* X,iii,4: *PL* XXXII,780-81: Nam confessiones praeteritorum malorum meorum, quae remisisti et texisti ut beares me in te, mutans animam meam fide et sacramento tuo, cum leguntur et audiuntur, excitant cor ne dormiat in desperatione et dicat, Non possum; sed evigilet in amore

misericordiae tuae et dulcedine gratiae tuae, qua potens est omnis infirmus, qui sibi per ipsam fit conscius infirmitatis suae; trans. Pine-Coffin, p. 208.

17. *Orationes sive meditationes,* Prologus: Schmitt III,3; see also *Epistola 10:* Schmitt III,113, and *Epistola 28:* Schmitt III,135.

18. *Epistola 70:* Schmitt III,190: Deinde: 'terret me vita mea, namque diligenter discussa,' cum eo quod sequitur, scriptum hoc et praeter hoc alia piissime de contrito spiritu tuo et de pietate contriti tui cordis edita et scripta: pias praestant nobis lacrimas tuas legere, nostras edere, ita ut utrumque miremur: et in corde tuo redundare tantae rorem benedictionis, et sine susurro inde descendere rivum in cordibus nostris. Nam ita est vere. Pietas scriptae tuae orationis excitat in nobis pietatem sopitae compunctionis, adeo ut quasi mente prosiliendo congaudeamus, ea diligendo in te, vel potius in eis te, super ea et per ea deum et te; trans. Ward, p. 70.

19. *Confessiones* X,viii,14: *PL* XXXII,785: Ex eadem copia etiam similitudines rerum vel expertarum, vel ex eis quas expertus sum creditarum, alias atque alias et ipse contexo praeteritis, atque ex his etiam futuras actiones et eventa et spes, et haec omnia rursus quasi praesentia meditor; trans. in *Confessions and Enchiridion,* ed. A. C. Oulter, The Library of Christian Classics, No. 7 (London: Westminster Press, 1955), p. 209.

20. *Oratio 2:* Schmitt III,7: Ad hoc, clementissime, tendit haec oratio mea, haec memoria et meditatio beneficiorum tuorum, ut accendam in me tuum amorem . . . sic et ego non quantum debeo, sed quantum queo, memor passionis tuae, memor alaparum tuarum, memor flagellorum, memor crucis, memor vulnerum tuorum, memor qualiter pro me occisus es.

21. *Meditatio 2:* Schmitt III,82: Quid est, deus, quid est quod animadverto in terra miseriae et tenebrarum? Horror, horror! Quid est quod intueor, ubi nullus ordo, sed semptiternus horror inhabitans? Heu confusio ululatuum, tumultus dentibus stridentium, inordinata multitudo gemituum. Vae, vae; quot et quot et quot vae, vae! Ignis sulphureus, flamma tartarea, caliginosa volumina, quam terrifico rugitu video vos rotari!

22. See *The Prayers and Meditations,* trans. Ward, pp. 53-56.

23. Gregory, *Moralia* XXIII; Gregory's teaching on compunction is summarized in Isidore of Seville, *Sententiae* II,12: *PL* LXXXIII,613.

24. Southern, *Saint Anselm,* pp. 31-32.

Frederick Van Fleteren (essay date 1991)

SOURCE: Van Fleteren, Frederick. "Augustine and Anselm: Faith and Reason." In *Faith Seeking Understanding: Learning and the Catholic Tradition,* edited by George C. Berthold, pp. 57-66. Manchester, N.H.: Saint Anselm College Press, 1991.

[*In the following essay, Van Fleteren highlights some features of the theological relationship between Anselm and St. Augustine.*]

It would be but an elaboration of the obvious to prove that the thought of Anselm was greatly influenced by Augustine. Anselm's own description of his thought, *fides quaerens intellectum,* owes much to the *credo ut intelligam* of Augustine and indeed is an excellent description of Augustine's project in the *De trinitate.* The similarities between Augustine and Anselm are partially explainable by the fact that, from Augustine's own time to Anselm's and in large part until the present day, Augustine has defined the mainstream of Christian, and indeed Catholic, thinking. Augustine was not *in* the mainstream; he defined the mainstream.[1] Further, a fund of philosophical *cum* theological teaching, common to all thinkers, existed. This common fund stemmed ultimately from Pythagoras and was enhanced greatly through the Academy of Plato. Augustine, and others, made significant contributions to it until the time of Anselm. Many of the teachings found in both Anselm and Augustine are part of this common fund. That Augustine influenced Anselm at least in these ways is beyond dispute.

Contemporary scholars would, however, like to go beyond a mere noting of common theme. Ideally, they would like to establish a direct literary dependence of Anselm upon Augustine and determine what works of Augustine Anselm had read. And it is precisely here that difficulties begin to arise. Anselm, like many other authors of late antiquity and the early medieval period, only infrequently acknowledges direct positive dependence on an earlier author. The use of other authors was deemed a compliment both to the earlier author and to the reader. Acknowledgement was not necessary.[2] Further, Anselm did not directly borrow entire literary passages from Augustine or other authors whereby direct philological parallelism could be established. Rather, he had imbibed the thought of his master, interpreted it, and made it his own. What then is the contemporary scholar, enamored of nineteenth-century historical principles, to do?

One recent attempt to show the influence of the Augustinian corpus on Anselm has concentrated on thematic development. Professor Klaus Kienzler has shown the similarity in themes in the *Confessiones* and the *Soliloquia,* on the one hand, and the ***Proslogion*** on the other.[3] It is likely that the same could be done for other works. Another avenue of approach has been to establish the list of Augustinian works which were present in the monastic library in Bec.[4] Such independent evidence would be at least confirmatory of what internal evidence would lead us to suspect. Nevertheless, the results of these investigations have been relatively meager.

Direct references to Augustine in Anselm's corpus are sparse but instructive in establishing dependence. Augustine's name appears eight times in six passages in the works of Anselm. All of the references are to the *De trinitate* and concern the ***Monologion*** or ***Proslogion.*** In the prologue to the former, Anselm writes:

> Reviewing this work often, I could not find that I said anything in it which was not in harmony with the writings of the catholic fathers and especially St. Augustine. Wherefore, if it seems to anyone that I have published anything in this small work which either is too new or is not true, I ask that he not immediately cry out that I am a presumer of novelties or an asserter of falsehood, but that he first read diligently the books of the famous teacher Augustine *De trinitate,* and then judge my small work according to them.[5]

This is not the only time that Anselm refers to Augustine in connection with the ***Monologion.*** Indeed, Anselm seems to have viewed the work as a brief summation of some arguments found in the *De trinitate.* Often Anselm turns to Augustine to support his use of Trinitarian terminology or to show the differences between the Greeks and Latins on this matter. Augustine's name would of course have been enough to end any dispute.

How closely Anselm's intellectual project in the ***Monologion*** and ***Proslogion,*** *fides quaerens intellectum,* follows Augustine's *credo ut intelligam* needs little demonstration. Anselm's remark that he was attempting to follow the thought of Augustine in his intellectual project is by and large justifiable.[6] Both Augustine and Anselm are trying to achieve an understanding of the mysteries of faith through philosophy. Both use the philosophical *cum* theological tradition as it has come down to them to achieve this understanding. In several passages, both Augustine and Anselm use the identical text from the book of Isaiah, *Nisi credideritis, non intelligetis* as the scriptural basis for their project.[7] In particular, it is the *De trinitate* which provides the background against which we should judge Anselm's views on faith and reason. Anselm's descriptive title of the ***Monologion*** as *Exemplum meditandi de ratione fidei* and the ***Proslogion*** as *Fides quaerens intellectum* would both be apt descriptive titles for the *De trinitate.*

Augustine's over-all project does not change that much over the years. From the beginning in Cassiciacum, it

was the role of philosophy to give understanding to the Christian mysteries. A much studied passage from the *Contra Academicos* points this out:

> No one doubts that we are led to learning by the twin weight of authority and reason. I am certain never to depart from the authority of Christ for I do not find a stronger. What must be pursued by the most subtle reasoning—I have been so affected that I desire with impatience to grasp what is true not only by belief but also by understanding—I am confident provisionally that I shall find it with the Platonists, a project that is not repugnant to our sacred writings.[8]

Augustine is but a Christian neophyte at this time. Yet his project is clear. He wishes to understand the mysteries of faith, a project which is in accord with the scriptures. Faith was to provide the subject matter, philosophy the understanding. This project remains fundamentally the same in the *De trinitate.* A classic statement of it occurs in *De trinitate IX:*

> An intention of one seeking is most prudent until that is apprehended toward which we tend and are extended. But that intention is right which sets out from faith. A certain faith in some way is the beginning of knowledge; a certain knowledge is only perfected after this life when we shall see face to face (1 Cor. 12:12). Therefore, let us be so wise that we may know that the disposition to seek the truth is safer than to presume unknown things as if they were known. Therefore let us seek as one who will find; and thus let us find as one who will seek. For when man has been consummated, then he begins (Sir. 18:6). Concerning things to be believed let us not doubt with infidelity; concerning things to be understood, let us not affirm with rashness; in the former authority is to be held; in the latter truth is to be sought.[9]

The scriptural foundation for this project, as in many other fathers of the church, is Matthew 7:7: *Quaerite et invenietis.*[10] Faith provides the matter of the search; reason provides the understanding. *Fides quaerit; intellectus invenit.*

If these were the only similarities of methodology between Augustine and Anselm, there would be little point in establishing a relationship. Although Augustine may have been the first to attempt on a large scale an understanding of the faith, any Christian intellectual could be said to be attempting an *intellectus fidei.* Augustine's synthesis, if such it might be called, stands out since it was the outstanding attempt at an understanding of the faith through the use of philosophy until the thirteenth century. However, there is much more to the relationship between Augustine and Anselm. An important text for understanding the methodology of Anselm and its relation to that of Augustine occurs in the *Epistola de incarnatione verbi:*

> That God is one, unique, individual, and simple nature and three persons has been argued by the unshakeable reasons of the holy fathers and especially St. Augustine

after the apostles and the evangelists. If anyone would deign to read my two small works, namely the **Monologion** and **Proslogion,** which were done especially for this purpose, that what we hold by faith concerning the divine nature and its persons outside of the incarnation, is able to be proved by necessary reasons without the authority of scripture; if anyone, I say, wishes to read these works, I think that he will find there concerning this matter what he can not disapprove or wish to condemn. If in these works I have placed something which either I have not read somewhere else or I have not remembered that I have read—not as if by teaching what our teachers did not know or correcting what they did not say well, but perhaps by saying what they were silent about, which nevertheless is not out of harmony with it or is comfortable to it—in order to respond in behalf of our faith against those who, unwilling to believe what they do not understand ridicule those who believe, or to help the religious desire of those who humbly seek to understand what they firmly believe, I do not think that I ought to be reproved for this.[11]

In this passage, two aspects of Anselm's *intellectus fidei* are relevant to a discussion of his relationship to Augustine. The first is that Anselm views his work in the **Monologion** and **Proslogion** as providing an understanding of the nature and persons of God outside of the incarnation by necessary reasons without the authority of Scripture. Olivier duRoy has maintained that such methodology is peculiarly Augustinian.[12] In the *Confessiones VII,* when Augustine describes his intellectual conversion after the reading the *libri Platonicorum,* he tells us that he found there a teaching on the Trinity, but no teaching on the incarnation.[13] Augustine understood God becoming man against the Neoplatonic, and especially Porphyrian, background of a way of salvation. Nevertheless, an understanding of the Trinitarian Godhead he was to take from Neoplatonism, the understanding of the incarnation as a way of salvation from the scriptures. And, in duRoy's view, this methodological point of Augustine's intellectual conversion was to have a major effect on his early works and was to remain with him the remainder of his life, so that even in the *De trinitate,* the incarnation does not provide an understanding of the Trinity. And, in duRoy's view, this methodology has had an enormous impact on later theology so that in Anselm and Aquinas, for example, the incarnation does not provide a means to the understanding of the Trinity. And, again in duRoy's view, this influence was not necessarily for the good.

I am not so sure that duRoy's view is entirely correct. First of all, I believe that Augustine read the Neoplatonists through the prism of Christianity. Certainly the preaching of Ambrose, the ambiance of the so-called Milanese Circle, and perhaps the religious teaching of Monica brought Augustine a perspective from which he viewed the Platonists. And I am sure that duRoy would

agree with this. It is certainly true that in the *Confessiones* and Augustine's early works, his triadic, if not to say Trinitarian, thought is based upon ancient philosophy, primarily Neo-platonism, understood through the prism of Christianity. It is further true that he viewed the incarnation as a way of salvation and at times tends to see Christianity as Platonism for the masses. Nevertheless, I do not think that it is wholly accurate to say that in the *De trinitate* Augustine's understanding of the Trinity is entirely devoid of scriptural and incarnational understanding. Indeed, the *locus classicus* for finding Augustine's teaching on the incarnation is in fact the *De trinitate.* It is true, however, that in his search for images of the Trinity in creation Augustine is more dependent on ancient philosophy than on the Scriptures. It is even possible that this is as it should be. In any event there is no doubt that this tendency in Augustine becomes a methodology in Anselm.

The second point of this passage in the **Epistola de incarnatione verbi** which I should like to discuss is Anselm's search for "necessary reasons." This is not the only time this or a like phrase is used in his works.[14] *Rationes necessariae* and other like phrases are also found in his treatment of the incarnation. Anselm tried to prove the necessity of the incarnation on the part of God for man's salvation, *remoto Christo* as Anselm himself puts it.[15] But, in the **Epistola de incarnatione verbi** the phrase is connected with the **Monologion** and the **Proslogion** and the discussions of the existence and nature of God found there. Here the words "necessary reasons" seem equivalent to "without the authority of Scripture." In those works, both the unity and the trinity of the Godhead are mentioned.[16]

Anselm is much more optimistic than his mentor in the *De trinitate* about man's ability to reach knowledge of God in this life. In this work—and Anselm is aware of it—Augustine maintains repeatedly that knowledge of God is available to man in this life only *per speculum et in aenigmate.* Augustine explains this Pauline phrase in terms of the figures of speech of classical Latin with which he, as a rhetor, was familiar.

> This is one entire phrase which is said: *Videmus nunc per speculum et in aenigmate.* Next, insofar as it seems to me, just as he wished image to be understood by the word mirror, so he wished by the word aenigma a similitude, albeit an obscure one, difficult to perceive, to be understood. . . . Therefore by the words mirror and aenigma some similitudes signified by the Apostle can be understood which are accommodated to understanding God in the way that he can be. . . ."[17]

Augustine came to be rather pessimistic concerning man's ability to reach any knowledge of the triune God in this life, though, of course, he did not reject the human possibility of such knowledge entirely. This pessimism is perhaps the principal reason why the writing of the *De trinitate* took some twenty years.

Such pessimism was not always the case with Augustine. From the time of his conversion in 386 until well into the next decade, Augustine maintained that man could attain, with the help of God, a direct vision of God in this life.[18] Augustine was influenced in this direction by his reading of Plotinus' *Ennead on Beauty* and Porphyry's *De regressu animae*. And when man would attain this vision, he would also attain a full understanding of the Christian mysteries.[19] At this time, although Augustine saw major differences between Platonism and Christianity on the possibility of the incarnation, he was optimistic concerning their similarities. During the middle of the last decade of the fourth century, Augustine was called upon to examine and explain Paul's *Epistle to the Romans* and *Epistle to the Galatians* in detail. The themes of salvation through grace attainable fully only in the next life are of paramount importance in each of these Epistles. During this period Augustine came decisively to realize that man could attain the vision of God only in the next life and that salvation was attainable only through the grace of God. Of course, Augustine was still interested in the degree of knowledge that man could attain concerning God in this life. Augustine's—and might we say man's—final answer to this question is contained in the *De trinitate*.

The use of the term "necessary reasons" by Anselm still bothers us. The term has been traced back to Marius Victorinus. Anselm's optimism concerning finding these "necessary reasons" is more reminiscent of the early Augustine than the older bishop. If I am correct that the *De trinitate*, and not the earlier works, forms the Augustinian background to Anselm's thought, then Anselm's project bespeaks a greater optimism than that of his master. It is even possible that Anselm did not realize the difference between the early and late Augustine on this point.

In the *Cur deus homo* and elsewhere, Anselm argues to the necessity of the incarnation from its suitability.[20] He argues many times that, because the incarnation was the most suitable means for God to justify man, it was necessary that it happen. Not that Anselm is unaware of the problem which necessity works on the Godhead. He is well aware that necessity would place a limitation on God and this he does not want to do. In the course of the *Cur deus homo* Anselm distinguishes an absolute necessity from a conditioned necessity and tries to show that it is under this second type of necessity that God is necessitated.[21] A complete discussion of necessity in Anselm's works would take us too far afield. Yet, enough has been said to show in what area a problem exists.

Anselm's mindset in the *Cur Deus homo* concerning necessary reasons is not so far different from the *Proslogion* argument for the existence of God. In the latter, Anselm argues from the idea of God to his real existence. While this argument obviously owes something to the argument from eternal truth in *De libero arbitrio* II, iii, 7-xv, 40, it is significantly different from it. Whereas Augustine argues for an immutable ground for eternal truths, Anselm argues from the idea of God to his real existence. Nevertheless, Anselm's reasoning from suitability to real existence is not far removed from a kind of ontological argument for the truths of faith. This mindset almost bespeaks a kind of meliorism by which a good God would be necessitated to act in the most fitting manner. Although Augustine argues the suitability of the incarnation for man's salvation in *De trinitate* XIII, such reasoning is not Augustine's. It would take another two centuries of thought after Anselm to distinguish more clearly between *debet* and *decet*. And it would take the reaction to the *Aufklärung* to show us more clearly that optimism introduced an unwelcome necessity into the Godhead.

What can account for the differences between Anselm and Augustine in these matters? We can speculate about the Dark Ages and the lack of genuine theological genius until Anselm during that period. We can further speculate concerning the monastic life of reflection and meditation to which Augustine had aspired most of his life, and had realized for various short periods, but which Anselm possessed for over thirty years. Augustine's speculations came out of a rugged experience in his own life and the life around him. Anselm's came out of monastic reflection, the life of the spirit. The rise of the monastic school also played a part in this difference. Theology, if it could be distinguished from philosophy, was beginning to be treated as a formalized scientific pursuit in the time of Anselm. While Augustine laid down the first program for the Christian use of the liberal arts and the *De doctrina christiana* remains the charter for the Christian intellectual, his thought, steeped in the ancient tradition of rhetoric and occasioned by contemporary problems in the African Church, was a far cry from the contemplative atmosphere of a monastic school. However, *his dictis*, we must also allow for the difference of individual genius. A thinker is not the mere product of his influences. If *Quellenforschung* has taught us one thing, it is that the thought of a man is not the sum total of the influences upon him. And so it is with Augustine and Anselm. Though they are in the same stream and one has exerted a powerful influence on the other, their thought remains different.

Both of these intellectual giants offer us food for thought on the matter of faith and reason for the contemporary world. In a world which is so highly specialized that one science finds it difficult to speak to another, that even two scientists within the same field find communication difficult, Augustine and Anselm speak to us concerning the unity of truth. In a time when a kind of Cartesian split between philosophy and theology, between faith and reason, has occurred even on Catholic campuses, Augustine and Anselm speak to us concerning the ultimate unity of the theological and philosophical enterprise. In a world grown increasingly interested in the quantitative and the rational, Augustine and Anselm speak to us of the spiritual and the intuitive. And finally in a world which has become increasingly embarrassed in speaking of God, Augustine and Anselm point out that God—and not man—is at the center of the universe. On this, the hundredth anniversary of a school under the aegis of Anselm and his followers, it is well for us to reflect on these truths.

Notes

1. For this reason, the Catholic Church has been reluctant to condemn even the more extreme predestinationist views of Augustine, given their final formulation in the heat of the Pelagian controversy.

2. Even the scriptures are many times alluded to without direct citation. Both the scriptures and the tradition were so much a part of many writers that direct citation was neither necessary nor indeed possible.

3. K. Kienzler, "Zur philosophisch-theologischen Denkform bei Augustinus und bei Anselm von Canterbury," *Anselm Studies 2,* ed. J. Schnaubelt and F. Van Fleteren (New York: Kraus International Publications, 1988):353-387.

4. The existence of such a list was suggested to me by my colleague Professor Thomas Losoncy, of Villanova University and the Augustinian Historical Institute.

5. *Monologion,* prologue: Schmitt 1,8: Quam ego saepe retractans nihil potui invenire me in ea dixisse, quod non catholicorum patrum et maxime beati AUGUSTINI scriptis cohaereat. Quapropter si cui videbitur, quod in eodem opusculo aliquid protulerim, quod aut nimis novum sit aut a veritate dissentiat: rogo, ne statim me aut praesumptorem novitatum aut falsitatis assertorem exclamet, sed prius libros praefati doctoris AUGUSTINI De trinitate diligenter perspiciat, deinde secundum eos opusculum meum diiudicet.

6. See note above.

7. Isaiah 7:9. Both Augustine and Anselm use an old Latin form of this text not found in the Vulgate.

8. *Contra Academicos* III,xx,43: Green 71: Nulli autem dubium est gemino pondere nos impelli ad discendum, auctoritatis atque rationis. Mihi autem

certum est nusquam prorsus a Christi auctoritate: non enim reperio ualentiorem. Quod autem subtilissima ratione persequendum est, ita enim jam sum affectus, ut quid sit verum, non credendo solum, sed etiam intelligendo apprehendere impatienter desiderem, apud Platonicos me interim quod sacris nostris non repugnet reperturum esse confido.

9. *De trinitate* IX,i,1: PL XLII, 961: Tutissima est enim quaerentis intentio, donec apprehendere illud quo tendimus et quo extendimur. Sed ea recta intentio est, quae proficiscitur a fide. Certa enim fides utcumque inchoat cognitonem: cognitio vero certa non perficietur, nisi post hanc vitam, cum videbimus facie ad faciem. Hoc ergo sapiamus, ut noverimus tutiorem esse affectum vera quaerendi, quam incognita pro cognitis praesumendi. Sic ergo quaeramus tamquam inventuri: et sic inveniamus tamquam quaesituri. Cum enim consummaverit homo, tunc incipit (Si 18:6). De credendis nulla infidelitate dubitemus, de intelligendis nulla temeritate affirmemus: In illis auctoritas tenenda est, in his veritas exquirenda.

10. J. Danié*lou,* "Recherche et Tradition chez les Peres", *Studia Patristica,* XII, 1:3-13.

11. *Epistula de incarnatione verbi* VI: Schmitt II, 20-21: Quod utique deus una et sola et individua et simplex sit natura et tres personae, sanctorum patrum et maxime beati AUGUSTINI post apostolos et evangelistas inexpugnabilibus rationibus disputatum est. Sed et si quis legere dignabitur duo parva mea opuscula, Monologion scilicet et Proslogion, quae ad hoc maxime facta sunt, ut quod fide tenemus de divina natura et eius personis praeter incarnationem, necessariis rationibus sine scripturae auctoritate probar: possit; si inquam aliquis ea legere voluerit, puto quia et ibi de hoc inveniet quod nec improbare poterit nec contemnere volet. In quibus si aliquid quod alibi aut non legi aut memini me legisse—non quasi docendo quod doctores nostri nescierunt aut corrigendo quod non bene dixerunt, sed dicendo forsitan quod tacuerunt, quod tamen ab illorum dictis non discordet sed illis cohaereat—posui ad respondendum pro fide nostra contra eos, qui nolentes credere quod non intelligunt derident credentes, sive ad adiuvandum religiosum studium eorum qui humiliter quaerunt intelligere quod firmissime credunt: nequaquam ab hoc me redarguendum existimo.

12. duRoy, *L'intelligence de la foi en la trinité selon saint Augustin* (Paris: Etudes Augustiniennes, 1966), 458ff.; see also his article in the *New Catholic Encyclopedia,* "Augustine", vol 2, s.v.

13. *Confessiones* VII,ix,13: BA 13,608; xxi,27: BA 13, 638-42.

14. Many similar phrases are found, such as *oportet esse* and *necesse est,* throughout the works of Anselm.

15. See *Cur deus homo, praefatio:* Schmitt 1, 42. The proof of the reasonableness of the incarnation is the theme of the entire *Cur deus homo.*

16. For the existence of one God see *Monologion* I-VI, *Proslogion* I-IV. For the existence of a triune God, see *Monologion* XXXVIII-LXI, *Proslogion* XXIII.

17. *De trinitate* XV,ix,16: PL XLII,1069: Una est enim cum tota sic dicitur, Videmus nunc per speculum et in aenigmate; Proinde, quantum mihi videtur, sicut nomine speculi imagine voluit intelligi; ita nomine aenigmatis quamvis similitudinem, tamen obscurum, et ad perspiciendum difficilem . . . igitur speculi et aenigmatis nomine quaecumque similitudines ab Apostolo significatae intelligi possint, quae accommodatae sunt ad intelligendum Deum, eo modo quo potest.

18. The texts in Augustine are numerous on this point. See for example, *Contra Academicos* II,ii,4; III, xix,42; *De ordine* I,viii,23ff., II,v,15; xix,51; *Retractationes* I,iii,2-4; *De moribus ecclesiae catholicae* XXXI,66; *De quantitate aniae* XXXII,76; *De vera religione* XII,24; *De sermone domini in monte* I,4,12; *Contra Adimantum Manichaeum* IX,1. See F. Van Fleteren, "Augustine and the Possibility of the Vision of God in this life", *Studies in Medieval Culture,* XI, 9-16.

19. See *De ordine* II, v, 15; ix, 27; xix, 51.

20. See *Cur deus homo, passim,* but especially 1, 25; II, 6.

21. See *Cur deus homo* II, 17.

Richard Law (essay date 1991)

SOURCE: Law, Richard. "The *Proslogion* and Saint Anselm's Audience." In *Faith Seeking Understanding: Learning and the Catholic Tradition,* edited by George C. Berthold, pp. 219-26. Manchester, N.H.: Saint Anselm College Press, 1991.

[*In the following essay, Law summarizes the rhetorical effects of the* Proslogion *while observing that the work was probably originally drafted simply to bring joy to its first intended audience, the monks of Bec.*]

The epigraph for this talk is from Sir Richard Southern's notable book first published twenty-five years ago, *Saint Anselm and His Biographer* (1963): the **Proslogion**

"was written in a state of philosophical excitement which (it is probably safe to say) had never before been experienced so intensely in any Benedictine monastery, and was probably never again to be repeated in Benedictine history."[1] Taken literally, this historical generalization is no less disputable than any other containing the phrases, "never before" and "never again," but undoubtedly it reflects Professor Southern's keen appreciation of the spirit of Saint Anselm's famous treatise. The state of philosophical excitement mentioned by Professor Southern pervades the **Proslogion** beginning with its very first words. The title of Chapter I is, "A Rousing of the mind to the contemplation of God," and Saint Anselm's rhetoric therein is vibrant with short directive phrases and energetic predications, as in the first paragraph: *fly* from your affairs, *escape* from the tumult, *abandon* yourself to God, *shut out* everything else. There are series of questions in rapid succession that denote urgency—as in the second paragraph on page 2: "What have I undertaken? What have I actually done? Where was I going? Where have I come to? To what was I aspiring? For what do I yearn?" Chapter I, in which Anselm addresses God and also reflects on himself—"Come now, insignificant man," he writes—exhibits an ardent dramatic style that registers the emotions of Saint Anselm anxious to find the single proof that God really exists. My thesis is that the **Proslogion,** the vehicle for the imperishable ontological argument, is a vivid and lively document that conveys Saint Anselm's profound personal experience with an expressive power that is sufficient to evoke corresponding feelings from the audience. Sir Richard Southern's enthusiastic response, cited above, serves as prime evidence.

My approach to the **Proslogion** is rhetorical, not philosophical. It does not aim to dissect or interpret the ontological argument *per se,* or to take sides in the centuries-long debate that began with the exchange between Saint Anselm and the first doubter of his proof, Gaunilo of Marmoutier. Saint Anselm's argument or derived versions of it have been defended, rejected, or modified by major figures including Saint Bonaventure and Saint Thomas Aquinas, Duns Scotus, Descartes, Immanuel Kant, Hegel, Royce, Santayana, and Karl Barth. During the last thirty years, several books and important articles in philosophical journals have examined the proof, paralogism, or conundrum some more.

In a compact review of the history and the current state of the debate, Arthur C. McGill states that "the traditional view, that the argument simply analyzes a subjective concept, has fallen out of favor, but no broadly accepted alternative has been found."[2] Professor McGill cites Paul Evdokimov, who likens the ontological argument to "one of those inns in Spain to which each person brings his own food and drink.'"[3] This wry analogy implies that among the variety of views or impressions in the unending debate, none is elite. From his survey of Christian scholars, among whom there is no consensus on interpretation and evaluation, Professor Anthony Nemetz concludes: "Judgments concerning the validity of [Anselm's] argument are as varied as the interpreters."[4] This is not surprising to those of us who would agree with the learned literary historian, Rene Wellek, that criticism is personal but it aims to discover a "structure of determination" in the text itself.[5] The esteemed M. H. Abrams pronounces as follows on the subjectivity of interpretation: a critical essay reflects or is informed by a critical theory, i.e., "a type of theoretical perspective to which the critic is committed, whether explicitly or implicitly, and whether deliberately or as a matter of habit."[6]

By sustaining the disputation over Saint Anselm's proof for hundreds of years, the philosophers comprise the audience that have been the most instrumental in perpetuating it. I would call them the dialectic audience. Engaged in philosophical discussion and debate, understandably they minimize or disregard the emotiveness of Saint Anselm's presentation in order to concentrate on semantic, grammatical, and logical elements. Regardless of how they perceive or reformulate the argument in the *Proslogion,* the dialectic audience characteristically would aim for dispassionate understanding and reasoning.

Notwithstanding the historic significance of the philosophical debate, my disciplinary interest is in the *Proslogion* and the readers that one could call the sensitive audience, an audience which includes Sir Richard Southern, Professor G. R. Evans, and other persons of note who put a premium on the personal appeal that the treatise exerts by virtue of Saint Anselm's eloquent, imaginative verbal expression. Professor Southern associates the manner of the *Proslogion* with that of Saint Anselm's devotional pieces written a little earlier, including the prayers, which are praiseworthy as "the work of a man with great literary gifts."[7] Professor Southern calls attention to the abundant imagery, figures of speech, and emotional pitch that the prayers display. It is his brief commentary on the prayers that furnished the impetus for me to highlight figurative and dramatic elements in the *Proslogion* which make the text so affective. The ontological argument is contained in a rhetorical discourse that affects or influences the disposition of the sensitive audience.

To appreciate the dramatic imagination of Saint Anselm as he recalls how he felt at the time he was occupied with the ontological argument, let us peruse just the middle of the first paragraph of the preface. Therein he discloses that his diligent search for the argument was frustrating. Sometimes he "almost reached what [he] was seeking"; sometimes it "eluded [him] completely." "Finally, in desperation," Anselm writes, he was about to quit the search, the idea seeming to be "something impossible to find."

But in lines 17-22, the hide-and-seek becomes a personal encounter that includes three reversals in quick succession:

1. "In spite of [his] resistance to it," the idea, which had been tantalizing and eluding Anselm, now on the contrary, "began to force itself upon [him] more and more pressingly."

2. Instead of yielding to or embracing the idea, Anselm got "quite worn out with resisting" it and endured mental conflict, despair, and distraction.

3. For the third reversal, the idea, which had previously been an elusive quarry, finally overcame Anselm's resistance, and he "eagerly grasped the notion which [he] had been rejecting."

Saint Anselm's occupation with the irrepressible idea is depicted as though it were a match or contest between him and a percipient agent. According to his preface, it was forceful; it eluded, importuned, and enlightened Anselm. The figurative overtones which I have stressed augment the vivid dramatic impression of Saint Anselm's perturbing experience trying to formulate the argument. Extremely important, furthermore, is the connection between the idea personified as an active agent and the Creator that it represents. Turning now to the *Proslogion* proper, please observe how the second paragraph of Chapter I begins: "Come then, Lord my God, teach my heart where and how to seek You . . . and find You." This prayer or petition supports, I trust, my impression that the shifting reactions of Saint Anselm and the idea correspond to the spiritual engagement between Saint Anselm and God, in which Anselm struggled almost to the point of despair, and then was divinely inspired.

Another metaphorical function of this prayer, "Lord my God, teach my heart," is worth pursuing, too. Obviously, the search for the single argument or proof that God really exists is work for a powerful mind. Yet Saint Anselm beseeches God to teach his heart. Also, the first paragraph ends as Saint Anselm directs his "whole heart" to speak to God. And in Chapter IV (in the middle of page 3), he rebukes the Fool for saying "in his heart what he could not think." Indeed, the first assumption in this paragraph is, "to say in one's heart and to think are the same." Here I would suggest that the image of saying in one's heart, which Saint Anselm appropriates from the Psalms, functions as synecdoche. That is, the heart signifies all aspects of human comprehension; it is not the alternative to reasoning. In combining the metaphorical heart with thought or the process of thinking, Saint Anselm is linking faith and reason and is professing that his philosophical quest is not exclusively intellectual or cerebral, but actually engages a person's whole disposition, which inherently involves the emotions. (Early in this century, T. S. Eliot explained that during the Age of Reason poets were impaired by "dissociation of sensibility." Mr. Eliot's famous term surely does not pertain to Saint Anselm.)

Chapter I is predominantly a supplication to God, whose presence is so utterly certain that searching for proof of his real being is an unequivocal demonstration of Saint Anselm's faith. Please observe lines 18-23 in Chapter I (near the bottom of the first page). "What shall your servant do?" Saint Anselm asks, and then describes himself as "tormented by love" of God, yearning to see God, desiring to come close to God, and longing to find God. The predication here signifies that for Saint Anselm this is a personal mission—as distinct from a theoretical exercise. That it is not abstract, but substantial, is signified by another image from the Psalms that Anselm reiterates: "I seek your countenance," he pleads; "I do not know your face"; I am "cast off from your face." Over on page 2, the third paragraph pursues a lament comprised of phrases from the Psalms: "O Lord, how long, how long will you turn your countenance from us? When will you look upon us?" and so on.

The forlorn tone is intensified by Saint Anselm's naming himself "this exile" and grieving over the sad condition of humanity since the Fall. Anselm states that he was made in order to see God, but cannot do so. The next paragraph focuses on all mankind, and the first sentence exclaims that everyone has lost what he was made for. Thus Saint Anselm individually and man collectively or universally suffers the same anguish, being unable to see God. (Parenthetically, I should acknowledge here Father Anselm Stolz's cogent thesis [published in 1933] that the *Proslogion* "is essentially a piece of mystical theology," "a quest by faith for a vision of God.")[8]

The imagery in the first paragraph on page 2 is striking, and the rhythmic series of antithetical clauses and phrases is arresting. "Once man ate the bread of angels; now he eats the bread of sorrow," and so on. In the couplet, "He groaned with fullness; we sigh with hunger," just as the concepts of well-being and misery are contrasted, so also are the tonal impressions. To groan is to utter a low or deep sound of strain, perhaps indicative here of Adam's reaction to the incredible immensity of his blessings; whereas to sigh is to breathe somewhat audibly, a faint sound indicative here of weakness and depression. The paragraph is replete with tell-and-show expressions, such as "[Adam] was prosperous; we go begging." The rhetorical questions in

lines 9-11 underscore how unbelievable it seems that Adam lost Paradise. "Why," Saint Anselm asks, "since it was easy for him, did he not keep for us that which we lack so much?"

The first sentence in the second paragraph on page 2 completes the bond between the anguished speaker, Saint Anselm, and all "the miserable children of Eve." Then comes the series of rapid rhetorical questions that convey his sense of dismay, perhaps even incomprehension, that he is possessed of this desire to see God. Lines 15ff. contain a list of stark reversals for Anselm. His endeavors have resulted in confusion, not goodness; tribulation, not peace; sobbing, not happiness; sighs, not gladness. Following the paragraphs depicting his and all humanity's exile and anguish, and also the frustration or futility of his immediate strivings, the final paragraphs of Chapter I emphasize Saint Anselm's reliance on God. With this faith he proceeds into Chapter II, beginning with the friendly greeting, "Well then, Lord," and expresses confidence that God will grant him the understanding for which he yearns.

In the brief context of the ontological argument, Saint Anselm borrows from the Psalms the familiar figure of the Fool who said in his heart, there is no God. Anselm then posits the Fool as the individual who must be convinced by the proof. He uses the Fool to stress the point that obviously any sensible or intelligent person would acknowledge the validity of the proof. "Even the Fool, then, is forced to agree," Anselm declares in line 18 (near the bottom of page 2). Over on page 3, Saint Anselm concludes Chapter III by separating the Fool from anyone with a "rational mind"—thus implying that the Fool is irrational. Then he dismisses the Fool by means of a rhetorical question containing a redundancy that is at once amusing and decisive: Why did the Fool deny God's existence? is the question. "Why indeed, unless because he was stupid and a fool?" The Fool functions as the atheist *via* the scriptural allusion and also as a straw man whose position is confuted with such ease that no reasonable person ought to consider it seriously. Apparently, the monk Gaunilo appreciated Saint Anselm's tactic, for his criticism of Anselm's proof is entitled, "A Reply by a Certain Writer on Behalf of the Fool."

It is most likely that Saint Anselm's first audience, the monks at Bec (that Professor Southern names "eager pupils")[9] were especially edified by the *Proslogion* because they knew it was a true account of their Prior's recent endeavor and achievement. The ontological argument proper occupies Chapters II, III, and part of IV. Chapter I and most of the text after Chapter IV comprise a devotional context for the argument which enhances its appeal to the faithful. By and large, the *Proslogion* is a profound meditation rife with biblical allusions and also a recollection capable of eliciting the fervent response of the faithful and fostering their personal involvement in meditating God.

At the beginning of the second paragraph in the preface (on the first page again), Saint Anselm reveals that he wrote the *Proslogion* because he judged "that what had given [him] such joy to discover would afford pleasure . . . to anyone who might read it." Professor G. R. Evans comments on this objective as follows: "A little Wordsworth, [Anselm] wanted to be able to recollect emotion in tranquillity, to be able, in times of meditation, to feel that first sensation again. . . . He [also] tries to help the reader by a shorter route into that state of preparedness which he himself had had to reach before the argument became clear to him."[10]

For its first audience at Bec, the *Proslogion* afforded the pleasure that Saint Anselm intended, no doubt, just as it has done for so many readers since then, especially those with religious inclination. That pleasure derives, not only from the proof whose discovery gave him such joy, but also from his account of his search, discovery, and exaltation, and because it is written so expressively. The words *joy* and *happiness* occur often in the later chapters of the work. Naturally this is so because these are Saint Anselm's feelings while he continually thanks God and celebrates His divine attributes. The gratitude and praise begin as soon as the compact proof is completed, that is, with the vigorous one-sentence paragraph that concludes Chapter IV: "I give thanks, good Lord, I give thanks to You," and so on. The joy that Anselm got through discovering the proof outweighs the despondence he felt beforehand. Chapter V exhibits the spirit that prevails through the succeeding twenty-one chapters. It is noteworthy that among the first attributes of the Supreme Being, Saint Anselm designates happiness. He tells God, "You are . . . whatever it is better to be than not to be," and this includes being "happy rather than unhappy." Small wonder that the *Proslogion* still gratifies the minds and hearts of Saint Anselm's audience.

Notes

All citations of the *Proslogion* are to the reprinted edition by M. J. Charlesworth (Notre Dame: University of Notre Dame Press, 1979).

1. R. W. Southern, *Saint Anselm and His Biographer* (Cambridge: Cambridge University Press, 1963), 57.

2. Arthur C. McGill, "Recent Discussions of Anselm's Argument," in *The Many-Faced Argument*, ed. John Hick and Arthur C. McGill (New York: The Macmillan Co., 1967), 104.

3. Paul Evdokimov, *Spicilegium Beccense*, 234, cited in McGill, n. 230, 104.

4. Anthony Nemetz, "Ontological Argument," *New Catholic Encyclopedia*, 10 (New York: McGraw-Hill Book Co., 1967), 701.

5. Rene Wellek, *A History of Modern Criticism: 1750-1950*, (New Haven: Yale University Press, 1986), 76:296.

6. M. H. Abrams, "What's the Use of Theorizing about the Arts?" in *In Search of Literary Theory*, ed. Morton W. Bloomfield (Ithaca, N.Y.: Cornell University Press, 1972), 37.

7. Southern, 46.

8. Anselm Stolz, "Anselm's Theology in the *Proslogion*," in *The Many-Faced Argument*, 183-206.

9. Southern, 51.

10. G. R. Evans, *Anselm and Talking About God* (Oxford: Clarendon Press, 1978), 41.

Paschal Baumstein (essay date March 1992)

SOURCE: Baumstein, Paschal. "Benedictine Education: Principles of Anselm's Patronage." *American Benedictine Review* 43, no. 1 (March 1992): 3-11.

[*In the following essay, Baumstein outlines the influence of Anselm's character and ideals on the fundamental principles of Benedictine education.*]

When creating the Benedictine college in Rome in 1687, Innocent XI promulgated the Apostolic Constitution *Inscrutabili*. That decretal invested Anselm of Bec (1033-1109) as the athenaeum's titular. It also lent him empire, ordaining that his thought, his perspective, should be embraced as the topos of all Benedictine education. The school's faculty was bound to vigilant fidelity to Anselm's teaching, while academics throughout the Order were to reflect the genius and consequence of his thought.

The present study considers the standards an Anselmian temper should lend to Benedictine education. Anselm wrote no educational treatise. Principles used here are drawn primarily from the design and categories of his thought, an endeavor made practicable by the consistency of his critical and evaluative reason. A challenging model results, a vision of Benedictine education that is based on character rather than behavior.

CHARACTER OF THE IDEAL

In Anselm, Innocent prescribed an anomalous example for the Benedictines. Despite the brilliance of his intellect and the elegance of his reason, Anselm's mind does not exemplify rigorous scholarship or academic attainment—at least not according to the modern, heavily footnoted motif. Rather than a scholar, Anselm is a man of original thought. He finds reason more engaging than memory. Logic affords a beauty, an eloquence, that research cannot supply. In his works, thought and reflection act as sovereign (*sola cogitatione*) instruments for penetrating truth[1] and revealing its necessary inferences (*necessariis rationibus*).[2] Those necessary lessons install the format of order.

Truth, according to Anselm, is being "as it ought to be."[3] In that, it is an absolute predication of reality, the rightness of alignment with good order as designed by God. That order is one of truth's necessary inferences. It is a profound quality, too, since truth is an attribute of God.[4]

This placement of truth within divinity contributes the essential coloring of Anselm's educational vision. Reality leans on God for its truth. To lead a mind to absolute reality is to lead to truth, is to lead to God. Anselm's reasoning may be posited:

> 1. *God is Absolute Truth.*[5] Whatever is called "true" must in some way reflect his Absolute Truth.[6]
>
> 2. *All that is true participates in God.*[7] Indeed, "nothing is true except by participating in [God's] truth."[8]
>
> 3. Therefore, *the perception of truth is necessarily and rightly aligned with the perception of the divine.* There is a sense in which a student's search for truth is, in reality, a search for God.

Truth is not just the focus of education; it is its wealth. Truth alerts the mind, raising vision rather than satisfying it. It stirs the soul and incites the intellect toward the motion Anselm terms "faith seeking understanding."[9] Under that postulate, Anselm proposes the dynamic of education: Faith sparks the mind, demanding more than knowledge; it seeks the depth and intellectual substance of genuine understanding.

This emphasis on understanding rather than knowledge is significant in Anselm. Reason requires understanding for its satisfaction. Knowledge is a prelude, creating the repository on which the mind will draw. That does not belittle knowledge; indeed, its provisions must be substantial, for Anselm says that a man of "little learning" will be unequal to the discernments required of him.[10]

THE EDUCATOR

Although he does not discuss the classroom, Anselm does present his depiction of the ideal educator. For this he does not cite the example of his own scholarly master, Lanfranc of Pavia (c. 1010-89), nor does he adopt Benedict's call for a paternal abbot[11] or a wise and pastoral master of novices.[12] Instead, Anselm proposes the ideal educator under the form of a saint: the model teacher is Benedict himself, a man who has 1) known truth, and 2) responded to it.

There is great beauty in the image Anselm creates. He displays a confident acceptance of the natural allure that the attributes of God—citing truth and goodness in particular—exercise over humanity.[13] By demanding a master (Benedict) who manifests these attractive qualities, Anselm suggests the urgency that the practical means of education—namely teaching—can satisfy. He remembers the education he derived from knowledge of Benedict, being "drawn to [Benedict's] blessedness, wondering at [that saint's] life, [being] stirred by [his] kind admonition, [and] instructed by [his] gentle doctrine."[14] Anselm also admires the active dimension: Benedict's followers become disciples,[15] not merely "knowers." This master lives truth as well as teaches it; he demonstrates that understanding elicits a response. This is as it should be: Benedict responds to truth, understanding that it is not merely some mental exercise; instead, it is the character of reality, an attribute of the Divine. It would be absurd to know God, to understand him, then choose not to pursue him.[16]

The response to truth is rectitude (*rectitudo*),[17] an alignment of mind and will with reality, with truth. This ordering is not manifested as a conversion, but as an embrace. Anselm describes it as the commitment of one's "entire ability and will to [the end of] remembering, understanding, and loving the Supreme [Being]."[18] According to Anselm's vision, rectitude concretizes truth: it makes reality as it ought to be; it effects the alignment of creation with providential design.

Whether in the context of a monastery or of a school, truth demands a response: rectitude. Yet rectitude must assume the proper character. It is not merely to be practiced; instead, it must be a state, a condition. The properly educated person should understand the necessity of living truth, of living in rectitude. With education, at least as Anselm proposes it, one learns to recognize truth; then that recognition—met by understanding—informs the will for a life of rectitude. Rectitude is a state of conformity with rightness, with truth, i.e., with being as it ought to be.

THE "HONOR" OF GOD

Anselm uses the feudal concept of "honor" to characterize this state of rectitude or of right order in life.[19] By "honor," he indicates the full dimension of what is properly due to a greater being. For a secular ruler, this might refer to land, service, or deference due him. The immensity of God, however, raises "honor" to a more expansive element; moreover, it contributes and demands a more absolute character: "I owe my entire self to [God],"[20] says Anselm; an upright, uncompromised gift of self "is the sole and complete honor which we owe to God and which God demands from us."[21] It "preserves the beauty [of God's design]."[22]

Anselm uses "honor," in its feudal composition, to erect the necessity of addressing perceived truth with willed rectitude. There is an eloquent symmetry to the design that results: From perceiving truth, and understanding it, one is moved to live it. This results in rectitude, ordering of mind, will, and creation that is the "honor" of God.

Eadmer of Canterbury (c. 1060-c. 1128) has preserved a story[23] from around 1070 that illustrates Anselm's use of the "honor" of God as an educational principle. The incident concerns a rude and obstreperous youth named Osbern. Anselm says this young monk possessed "keenness of mind" and "good promise," but his lack of due order left him "disfigured," outside his right place and thus offensive to the "honor" of God.

The Rule allowed Anselm to address Osbern with the rod.[24] That course was deemed inappropriate, however, for it might win submission to the law, without either ensuring understanding or exposing truth as the path to rectitude. According to Eadmer, Anselm was aware of the lesson he needed to impart: the restoration of right order, rectitude and truth. Anselm sought "to bring [Osbern's] character into conformity with the brightness of his intellect."

So Anselm teaches Osbern through the *modus vivendi* he sees in Benedict, rather than the *modus operandi* he reads in the Rule. He draws from Benedict's life the means for exposing Osbern to truth. First, he displays God's attribute of goodness, revealing it through his own conduct and response. When Osbern responds, Anselm draws him in. He adds discipline, and finally (and gradually) imparts an understanding of the truth or rightness of good order. Thus Anselm educates Osbern for a life of rectitude. Education follows on the student's exposure to and recognition to the truth of God. In this case, the "being as it ought to be" is the virtue of goodness, as seen in gentleness.

This story shows Anselmian education as a process of ordering, of lending right order, truth. He educates for the "honor" of God. Education brings about alignment with truth. It invokes rectitude: God (truth) is exposed; Divinity exerts an appeal that invigorates the will, inciting a response. The result is rectitude, preserving the unimpugned "honor" of God.

To achieve its end, education is required by Anselm to equip an intellect "to distinguish what is just from what is unjust, what is true from what is not true, what is

good from what is not good."[25] This demands that perception be sensitized to God, to the confluence of Divinity and truth. For Benedictine education, this is an essential product. Indeed, Anselm describes the Benedictine patrimony under the rubric of a "continual turning to God."[26] Benedict proposes, and Anselm concurs, that human faculties, properly ordered, can focus mind and will so that they are continually alert and sensitive to God and his truth.[27]

BENEDICTINE CHARACTER

There may seem to be nothing specifically Benedictine in this vision of education. Anselm's clear focus on truth, that is really a focus on God, is not exclusively Benedictine. Neither does it relate to the traditional understanding of Benedictine life, that amalgamation of common liturgy, silence, the discipline of the clausura, the hospitality, stability, the reverence of the oratory, abbatial rule, and countless others observances.

Anselm, however, finds character in essence, not in accidents. Each of the observances mentioned above is an accident; it follows, in an Anselmian schema, on the real character of Benedictinism. Benedict's patrimony is not found in these observances, but in the charism that informs them. It would confuse the brilliance of Benedict's insight to focus on behavior over character.

This is a very important distinction for Anselm. The Rule in his system, is not the focal point of the monk's life. The Rule provides means; it does not embody the end. After all, no one enters the monastery for the sake of the Rule; one enters for the sake of God.[28] So God, in an Anselmian appraisal, is the essential element of the Benedictine life. The life is directed toward God; the Rule facilitates that, but without supplanting the primacy of divinity.

This hinges on a crucial figure in Anselmian reason. Anselm demands that the focus be on the end, not the means—in this case, on God rather than on the Rule itself. For if one does something (like pursuing God), he must indeed do it for God. If, however, he does it out of a desire to satisfy something else (like the Rule), even if that something else is itself oriented toward the proper end, then the person has really endeavored to satisfy that other thing (the Rule), not the true goal (God).[29]

This standard means that the Benedictine should not cite his observances as the mark of his Benedictinism. Instead, the mark of the Benedictine is the resolute and intense entanglement of his being with God's. No one observance or even set of observances will do justice to this concept. The observances follow on the character; they do not state its nature or enshrine its essence.

Anselm's theory filters life through Benedict's principle "ut in omnibus glorificetur Deus."[30] It erects the primacy of God and insists that it mark Benedictinism and feed its behavior (the observances).

In applying this character to education, the Benedictine school should impart habits of mind and normative values that secure the primacy of God in every aspect of life. Under the patronage of Anselm, the character of a Benedictine school would be more properly understood in terms of the motto "that in all things God may be glorified" than in terms of any particular "monastic" practices.

The Benedictine is educated and sensitized to know God. The Benedictine school cannot properly be distanced from that ideal. If Anselm reasons correctly, an understanding of the divine will urge reason and will to respond. The rectitude that results will promote the honor of God.

BENEDICTINE EDUCATION

The patronage of Anselm of Bec lends Benedictine education a nobility more than a schema. There is no philosophy of the classroom, no system of instruction, no job description for the teacher, no graduation inventory for the student. Instead, Anselm roots education in the belief

1. that faith seeks understanding,

2. that understanding demands truth,

3. that truth (which is an attribute of God) reveals matters as they ought to be (in conformity with the design and providence of God),

4. so that the person who pursues truth is really pursuing God.

Anselm finds education to be enlivened and ennobled by the imperative derived from truth, for truth carries "necessary inferences"; it demands a response. That response results in rectitude, an ordering of life in conformity with truth (with God). And this rectitude ensures the honor of God.

So education, according to an Anselmian appraisal, is far more practical than it may at first appear, for it would affect more than mind and behavior. It educates character, as well. If marked by a true Benedictine character, "a continual turning to God," it strives to secure that state where "in all things God may be glorified." In that, it responds to truth well and properly—"as it ought to be." It effects rectitude, truth, and "honor."

Thus, we may postulate:

1. *Benedictine Education solicits understanding* and thus sensitizes the rational faculties for the perception of truth. Since God is truth, this fulfills the basic tenet of Benedictinism, the "continual turning to God."

2. *It exposes truth's legitimate demand for a response.* Properly embraced, that response is an ordering of life toward conformity with truth.

3. *Therefore, Benedictine education alters both the mind and will for the embrace of Absolute Reality,* of God, of truth. This effects and endorses the honor of God.

This model of education established, as does the Rule, a life in pursuit of God. It erects the same ambition. Benedictine education should impart this habit of mind, these normative values, securing God's primacy before the workings of reason and of will.

A school cannot bear the label "Benedictine" nor boast subscription to Anselm's patronage while denying or diffusing the essential aspects proposed in those names. The primacy of God is not a merely pious aspiration for Benedictine education. To the contrary, it is the elemental figure in its identity. Without that, there would be no pertinence to Benedict, no appeal to Anselm. With that primacy, however, if it functions according to Anselm's vision, the Benedictine school enlists in the "honor" of God. Mind, will and creation are ordered with Divinity. "Honor" is the fruit of a sound education in which truth (God) is exposed, embraced, and pursued.

Notes

1. Anselm of Bec, *Monologion,* preface. Unless otherwise noted, translations of Anselm's works are taken from *Anselm of Canterbury,* 4 vols, ed. and trans. by Jasper Hopkins and Herbert Richardson (Toronto: Mellon 1974-76).

2. *Monologion,* ch. 64.

3. Anselm of Bec, *De Veritate,* ch. 13.

4. *Ibid.,* ch. 1.

5. *Monologion,* ch. 16.

6. *De Veritate,* ch. 2.

7. *Ibid.,* ch. 13.

8. *Ibid.,* ch. 2.

9. Anselm of Bec, *Proslogion,* preface.

10. Eadmer of Canterbury, *Vita Anselmi,* ch. 11, translation from Eadmer, *The Life of Saint Anselm,* ed. and trans. by R. W. Southern (Oxford: Clarendon 1962).

11. RB 2.

12. RB 58.6.

13. *Monologion,* ch. 1.

14. Anselm of Bec, "Prayer to Saint Benedict," lines 6-10, translation from *The Prayers and Meditations of Saint Anselm,* trans. by Benedicta Ward (New York: Penguin 1973) pp. 196-200.

15. *Ibid.,* line 121.

16. *Proslogion,* ch. 1.

17. *De Veritate,* ch. 11.

18. *Monologion,* ch. 68.

19. Anselm of Bec, *Cur Deus Homo,* I.13 *et seq.*

20. Anselm of Bec, "A Meditation on Human Redemption."

21. *Cur Deus Homo,* I.11.

22. *Ibid.,* I.15.

23. Eadmer, *Vita Anselmi,* ch. 10.

24. RB 30.3.

25. *Monologion,* ch. 68.

26. "Prayer to Benedict," line 21.

27. *Proslogion,* ch. 14.

28. RB 58.7.

29. *Cur Deus Homo,* II.1.

30. RB 57.9.

C. J. Mews (essay date 1992)

SOURCE: Mews, C. J. "St. Anselm and Roscelin: Some Texts and Their Implications." *Archives d'histoire doctrinale et littéraire du moyen age* 58 (1992): 55-98.

[*In the following excerpt, Mews concentrates on the text and arguments of Anselm's* Epistola de Incarnatione Verbi, *a polemical treatise aimed against Roscelin of Compiègne's conception of the Trinity.*]

The solid reputation of St Anselm as thinker and saint could scarcely be more different from the few hazy details commonly remembered about Roscelin of Compiègne.[1] Was not St Anselm a deeply spiritual monk determined to explain his religious faith in terms of reason rather than of written authority? The contrast is often drawn between a saint who was also a sophisticated intellectual and a secular minded logician like Roscelin of Compiègne, whose attempt to apply secular reasoning to the doctrine of the Trinity resulted in nothing short of heresy. Was he not, as St Anselm implied, a leading exponent of the nominalist heresy that there were no eternal realities beyond the evanescent categories of human language? In any history of philosophy in which he is mentioned, Roscelin is remembered as someone who challenged philosophical and religious authority, but without anywhere near the success of his most famous pupil, Peter Abaelard.

These stereotypes owe much to the way St Anselm was able to commit his reflections on language and theology to writing and become quickly recognized as the outstanding intellectual of the Latin Church in the late eleventh and early twelfth century. He had the ear of the Pope when he wrote a treatise *De incarnatione uerbi,* condemning the absurd and dangerous argument of Roscelin of Compiègne, who was reported to maintain that the Father, Son and Holy Spirit had to be three separate things if the Father did not become incarnate with the Son in the person of Jesus Christ. Anselm reminded the Pope that as a logician Roscelin held the equally absurd belief that universal substances were in Roscelin's view no more than "the puff of an utterance"—*flatum uocis.* Anselm's rhetoric has been all the more persuasive given that Roscelin seems to have left us no major treatise to put his side of the argument. The only document so far successfully attributed to him is a letter to Peter Abaelard, accusing his former pupil in no uncertain terms not just of despicable ingratitude towards his master, but of heresy in the exposition of Christian doctrine.[2]

Despite an occasional attempt to re-evaluate the very scant and almost uniformly hostile surviving testimony about Roscelin as a thinker, no historian has been able to escape the opacity of the historical record with regard not just to Roscelin but to intellectual life in the late eleventh century in general. Anselm of Bec has been the only figure of the period to have a mind and feelings which we can explore with a degree of intimacy.[3] Much of our problem has to do with the stubborn anonymity of texts which may be significant, but which have hitherto eluded efforts at firm identification of their author and specific milieu. In the studies which follow we shall present some new or relatively little studied texts relating to intellectual life in the late eleventh century, making suggestions as to their provenance and authorship, in the hope that they may deepen our understanding of a period of dramatic intellectual ferment. We shall begin by looking more closely at Anselm's treatise against Roscelin, the *Epistola de incarnatione uerbi,* addressed to Pope Urban II.

1. THE *EPISTOLA DE INCARNATIONE UERBI AD URBANUM PAPAM.*

Anselm's *De incarnatione uerbi* has never attracted the same critical attention as some of his more famous writings. Philosophers have long been fascinated by those chapters of the *Proslogion* which seem to offer a proof for the existence of God, while theologians have admired the *Cur deus homo* for its exposition of the redemption in terms of reason alone. Anselm is generally remembered as a calm, meditative thinker whose natural environment was that of the cloister, rather than as a disputatious polemicist of the schools like Roscelin of Compiègne or Peter Abaelard. Among Anselm's writings the small treatise is often seen as marking a short uncomfortable moment between the philosophical tranquillity of over thirty years at Bec (1059-1092) and the firm intellectual authority of his time as archbishop of Canterbury (1093-1109). The polemical tone of the *De incarnatione uerbi,* first drafted in his last years at Bec and then rewritten shortly after he had been appointed archbishop, fits awkwardly into an image of Anselm as a progressive and meditative thinker. Roscelin must have been a singularly unattractive figure to merit such condemnation from a philosophical saint.

Anselm was, however, profoundly troubled by the ideas that he thought Roscelin represented. As a result of the pioneering work of Dom André Wilmart and Dom Franciscus Schmitt, we have learnt that five different versions survive of the *De incarnatione uerbi.*[4] The earliest *(DIV¹)* Anselm drafted sometime between 1090 and 1092 while he was still abbot of Bec, in response to a report that Roscelin was arguing that the three persons of the Trinity had to be distinguished as three things. Apparently he claimed that if the divine persons were not three separate *res,* the Father must have become incarnate with the Son—and that Anselm would concede this in debate. The abbot of Bec initially prepared an open letter (known through only a single copy: London, Lambeth Palace 224, ff. 121ᵛ-124ᵛ *[W]*) for a forthcoming council at Soissons, where Roscelin was obliged to abjure all heretical views on the Trinity.[5] Soon after being appointed archbishop of Canterbury (6 March 1093) Anselm transformed and greatly lengthened his earlier text into a letter to Pope Urban II *(DIV²),* countering ideas that Roscelin was continuing to propagate after supposedly abjuring heresy at this council, or so he explains in its revised introduction.[6]

Schmitt also argued intermediate recensions were preserved in three other manuscripts, all twelfth-century.[7] The Hereford Cathedral MS P.1.i, ff. 154ᵛ-155ᵛ *(H)* comprised in his view three fragments of the *De incarnatione uerbi:* the first two were of its introduction (the first closer to that of *DIV¹* as printed in 1, 281.3-283.25, the second identical to that in *DIV²* in 2, 7.5-9.11, almost identical to 1, 283.26-284.29), the third a preliminary version of chapters 8-10 in *DIV²* (2, 22.22-28.3). *DIV¹* had extended only as far as the beginning of ch. 6 in *DIV².*[8] He also found a complete text of *DIV²* in Vatican, Reg. lat. 452, ff. 131ʳ-141ʳ *(V)* and Paris, Bibl. nat. lat. 2479, ff. 1ʳ-10ʳ *(P)* slightly earlier than the most widely disseminated version, and which may have been the one originally sent to Urban II.[9]

Schmitt did not notice another recension of chapters 10-11 of the *De incarnatione uerbi,* occurring in three other manuscripts (none of which he notes in his 1968 list of manuscripts surveyed):[10]

A Paris, Bibliothèque de l'Arsenal 269, ff. 107ʳ-108ʳ (s. xii), introduced with the rubric *Anselmus. Quod magis conuenit filio incarnatio quam patri uel spiritui sancto.*

B London, British Library, Royal 5 E xiv, ff. 81ʳᵇ-82ᵛᵃ (s. xiii), untitled, but within a collection of the works of St Anselm.

C Cambridge, U.L. Dd. 1.21, f. 147ʳᵇ-147ᵛᵇ (s. xiv), untitled, but within a collection of the works of St Anselm.

The text begins in the same way as ch. 10 of *DIV²* (apart from an *autem* added after *Cur* in all three recensions): "Cur deus magis assumpserit hominem in unitatem persone filii, quam in unitatem alicuius aliarum personarum?" However, while the second sentence in *CDM* (as we shall subsequently call the text, after its incipit) begins with a factual response, "I think this reasoning should be given: (Hanc reddendam rationem existimo:)", Anselm begins the equivalent sentence in *DIV²* with an apology for digressing from the subject matter of the treatise. He explains that another question had come to mind: "Quamvis in hac epistola nostrum hoc non fuerit propositum, tamen quoniam huius rei mentio se obtulit, aliquam reddendam rationem existimo." The remaining first half of *CDM* is identical to the text of ch. 10, as found in the Hereford MS, a passage radically revised in *VP* and then touched up slightly in the final version. The remaining part of *CDM,* although touching the same subject matter as ch. 11 in *VP* and the final version, is significantly different from Schmitt's published text of the chapter. Is *CDM* a disciple's modification of this part of the *De incarnatione uerbi,* or an authentic draft of chapters 10-11 by its author?

Before answering this question, we need to examine Schmitt's analysis of different recensions of the work. He thought that the scribe of *H* had copied out in continuous form fragments of three originally separate recensions, which he titled Rec. I, 2, Rec. II (indeterminate recension) and Rec. II, 1. respectively.[11] The second fragment he was inclined to think had been extracted from a complete text of *DIV²,* even though the third fragment certainly contained a preliminary version of chs. 8-10. He did not explain why the copyist should wish to make such an apparently arbitrary selection from three different copies of *DIV.* Such an analysis seems unnecessarily complicated. For our discussion it is simpler to consider all three fragments in *H* as part of a single recension, transitional between *DIV¹* and *DIV²,* and a sketch for a future revision rather than a series of extracts from separate, larger wholes.

Taken on its own, the text of *CDM* reads as a separate essay on why God assumed manhood in the person of the Son rather than of any other divine person. There would be too many "inconveniences" if it were otherwise, compromising the evident equality of the three persons. *CDM* has no direct invective against the absurdity of Roscelin's trinitarian argument, as in ch. 9 of *DIV*². In *H* this essay about the rationale for the incarnation in the Son occurs within a longer, although still incomplete text of the *De incarnatione uerbi*. Anselm is obliged to include an apology for diverting from the main subject matter of the treatise "because it had come to mind". Only at the end of ch. 11 in *DIV*²—to which there is no parallel in *CDM*—does Anselm abruptly return to Roscelin: "As to the writings of him to whom I am replying in this letter, I was not able to see anything beyond what I have mentioned above [i.e. the argument reported to him]".[12] In chapters 12-16, found only in *VP* and the final version, Anselm continues his earlier assault against any attempt to identify plural substances within the divine nature.

The second part of *CDM* continues with a version of ch. 11 quite different from that found in either *VP* or the final form of *DIV*². It opens with an apology of touching honesty, for which there is no equivalent in other versions of *DIV:*

> "Why however or by what beautiful and necessary reason or rational necessity did the supreme majesty—since he is capable of everything by will alone—assume our nature with our weakness and mortality without sin to conquer the devil and to free man? If I included this—which many are asking—within this letter, the digression would be too long. Sometime however, if divine grace gives any effect to my will, because it has deigned to show this to me, I want to write on this, driven by the prayers of the many who have heard this from me."[13]

The voice echoes closely that of Anselm in the opening chapter of the *Cur deus homo*.[14] The author of *CDM* broaches an issue that he is anxious to talk about—why should God have assumed mortal nature—but realises that this is not the subject matter of the letter which he is writing. The reference to the present text as an *epistola* within *CDM* is as clear an indication as any that it is written as a draft for the *Epistola de incarnatione uerbi*. Having voiced this thought on a subject about which many people ask, the author of *CDM* then continues with another question about the incarnation—the adequacy of Boethius's refutation of the Nestorian argument that there were two persons in Christ.

If we compare the subsequent text of *CDM* with that of ch. 11 in the second recension in *VP* (not significantly modified in the final form), we see that much fairly tortuous technical questioning in *CDM* has been radically abbreviated when incorporated within the larger work. . . .

CDM is not the work of a less sophisticated disciple amplifying the thought of Anselm, even though stylisti-cally *DIV*² is clearly the superior text. A wordy, but thoughtful preamble about a possible question about Christ's nature "against our faith" needing to be dissolved rationally is reduced in *DIV*² to a terse: "it seems not without use to me to say something". The author of *CDM* explicitly criticises the adequacy of Boethius' reasoning in the *Contra Nestorium et Euticen*: "Although Boethius argues against Nestorius that Christ does not exist out of two persons, he does not seem to me to destroy the reason by which he [Nestorius] asserts that there are two persons in Christ." In *DIV*² this is turned into an unintimidating "Certain people say". While such explicit critical citation of a traditional authority is unusual in Anselm's published writing, it is complicated to argue that someone else has here made explicit the complex tissue of authorities to whom Anselm alludes so indirectly in the *De incarnatione uerbi*. *CDM* makes more clear what is only indirectly evident in the final text, namely that Anselm glimpsed an indirect parallel between the argument of Nestorius about Christ and that of Roscelin on the Trinity. His preferred solution went beyond that of Boethius by focussing on common semantic problems of unity and plurality.

2. The Making of the *De incarnatione uerbi.*

The relationship of *CDM* to Anselm's treatise is so complex that it must be an authentic draft of ch. 10-11 of the *De incarnatione uerbi*. (While the numbering of chapters in *DIV* is Schmitt's device, they do correspond to authentic dividing marks in the manuscript tradition.) In this draft Anselm explicitly identifies the common ground of any discussion about unity and plurality as philosophical definition of an individual (in fact from Porphyry) as that which is distinct in its collection of properties: "Philosophi utique diffiniunt esse indi-uiduum, cuius proprietatum collectio non est in alio eadem, id est non dicitur de alio."[15] Although the definition of an individual might suggest that as the properties of God are different from those of man, there have to be two individuals in Christ, there is such a connection of God and man in Christ that one cannot say that God and man are two individual things. One can only say of a tongue that it makes speech and of a hand that it makes writing (and not a tongue writing or a hand speech), even though only one person is involved. Apparently contradictory statements about Peter being buried in Rome and being in Paradise can both be true if one distinguishes whether each signifies *secundum spiritum* or *secundum se*. Anselm's argument in *CDM* relied on a strict application of the semantic principles articulated in the *De grammatico*. It was not so far removed from the argument Roscelin claimed to have heard Anselm use, that the three divine persons were predicated of God in the same way as *albus, iustus* and *grammaticus* were predicated of an individual man.[16]

In *DIV²* Anselm summarizes a rather long argument into a single brief paragraph. He also leaves out the reference to *philosophi* as the source of the definition of an individual as that which has a distinct collection of properties, perhaps as being too 'academic' in tone. He prefers instead to begin with a more concrete illustration that the proper name "Jesus" like "this man" or "that man" referred to a particular collection of properties. Only at the end of the paragraph does he conclude with a definition, seemingly his own but in fact based on Porphyry: "Diversarum vero personarum impossibile est eandem esse proprietatum collectionem, aut de invicem eas praedicari." As with so many Augustinian ideas, Anselm took a traditional thought (in this case of Porphyry), and presented it in his own words as a reflection evident to reason. Even though there is more explicitly philosophical semantic discussion in *CDM,* the revised form of ch. 11 in *DIV²* still stresses as an underlying theme that one must pay attention to the particular mode of signification of a phrase like "Son of God", different from that of "Son of Man", albeit expressed in more compact form. The smooth, deceptively simple philosophical style of Anselm did not spring automatically from his pen. It emerged only from careful pruning of initially elaborate and complicated reflections generated by a sophisticated and subtle mind.

If the draft *CDM* was incorporated into the longer text of *DIV* in the Hereford MS, why is the latter recension still so manifestly incomplete? Its text is too incomplete to make sense as another draft of a projected revision. In *H* Anselm sketches out a revised introduction, modifying or leaving out certain phrases. Thus instead of saying "I have recently been informed by a letter that . . .", he writes "It is known to many that . . ." His earlier admission that "I knew this man [Roscelin] because he is my friend", he left out altogether as too compromising.[17] Anselm did not include the remaining part of *DIV¹* in his draft *H,* because he was reasonably satisfied with its substance. Only technical details would be modified in the writing out of *VP.* Chapters 8-10 in *H* are written to bridge what he had already written in *DIV¹* to the new ideas sketched out in *CDM,* introducing the idea that it was quite possible for one divine person to be in man, and the other not in man.[18] That part of *CDM* which Anselm felt still needed revision (equivalent to ch. 11), he did not copy out into *H.* Only with the writing out of *VP,* very likely the recension sent to Urban II, did Anselm knit together a text based on *H* (introductory), *DIV¹* (ch. 2-6.2-10), *H* (ch. 8-10) and *CDM* (ch. 10-11), simplifying ch. 11 significantly.[19]

He also added a new section to where *DIV¹* left off (= ch. 6.10) recommending a reader who wished to understand by "necessary reasons" without scriptural authority how God was both a single nature and three person—a doctrine firmly taught by the Fathers and above all by Augustine—to consult his *Monologion* and *Proslogion.* Insisting that in those works—"neither teaching what our doctors did not know, nor correcting what they did not say well, but saying perhaps what they were silent about, which, far from disagreeing with their propositions, coheres with them"—he was only countering those who "deride believers". He wished to help those who "humbly seek to understand what they firmly believe". For those who did not want to trouble themselves with reading further, he then supplied a short summary of the ideas mapped out in those earlier works.[20] When writing out the complete text in *VP* Anselm also greatly simplified the subtle argument of *CDM's* version of c. 11. He left out its criticism of Boethius' *Contra Euticen et Nestorium,* and then added chs. 12-16 to the text of *H.* Anselm's major new argument in this final part, was in fact adapted from an analogy suggested by Augustine in a relatively minor work, the *De fide et symbolo,* although he presented it as his own: that of the Trinity as like a spring from which flowed a river, which then became a lake. All might be called "the Nile", even though each was also something separate. Anselm emphasised the philosophical aspect of Augustine's analogy, not making any direct identification of one person with the spring or the river, rather making a point about predication, that things could be different while being the same. Only in one sentence did he extend Augustine's image to the Incarnation, in comparing the channel through which the water flowed from its source to the lake to the incarnate Son.[21] These new passages in the first complete text of the treatise *(VP)* give the impression of being written in a hurry. He concluded his rather brief discussion of how the Son was born of the Father and the Holy Spirit proceeded from both, as he had begun the section tagged onto *DIV¹,* by appealing to the authority of Augustine, whose *De trinitate* could be supplemented by what he had himself said in the *Monologion.*

Perhaps the most significant change which Anselm made in writing out the letter was to re-address it to Pope Urban II, submitting it for censure and correction if anything was to be found therein contrary to the catholic faith.[22] In no earlier treatise had Anselm offered such a dedication to the Pope. Neither Lanfranc nor any other writer against heretical opinions had ever before made such a direct appeal to papal authority, allowing a work to be corrected.[23] This act of personal submission needs to be seen in the light of another change in tone in the introduction, emphasizing the orthodoxy of his position. In *VP* Anselm deleted his reference to Roscelin's specific charges against himself of doctrinal unorthodoxy (repeated in *H*), instead emphasising that everything he had said in the *Monologion* and *Proslo-*

gion conformed totally to what Augustine taught. He avoided any hint that he (or Lanfranc for that matter) might ever have sympathised with any aspect of Roscelin's teaching. By appealing directly to the Pope Anselm was presenting himself as a totally loyal son of the Church, defending the catholic faith from a pernicious intellectual, one of a breed of "modern pseudo-logicians or rather heretics of dialectic, who do not think universal substances to be anything but the breath of an utterance, say they understand a colour as nothing other than a body, nor wisdom of man as anything other than the soul who had to be excluded from discussion of all spiritual questions".[24] In rhetorical language Anselm repeated such claims of a radical gulf between himself and Roscelin (never named explicitly except as "a certain cleric in France") to an audience which now included the Pope.

When he came to writing out this new version of the *De incarnatione uerbi,* Anselm had no further knowledge of why or how Roscelin had arrived at his conclusion about the three divine persons as three *res.*[25] He still thought that it must be a consequence of inflated intellectual self-esteem and spiritual blindness. He was particularly upset by Roscelin's apparent failure to recognize that the word "thing" had a different meaning dependent on its context. The only extra information Anselm admits to (not present in *H,* but found in *VP*) is that after he had been captured for the episcopate he had heard "the author of the aforesaid novelty, persevering in his opinion, say that he had only abjured what he used to say because he feared being killed by the people". Roscelin apparently justified his approach by saying that "the pagans defend their Law, the Jews defend their own Law; therefore we Christians ought to defend our faith."[26] Yet, as the isolated promise in *CDM* to write a work about the reason for the Incarnation makes clear, Anselm was already thinking about bigger issues than Roscelin's argument when he wrote out the complete text of *DIV*[2]. His heart was set on the theme of why God should have become man, an issue that touched on the very essence of the human condition, not just on the language one should use about God.

Anselm touched up his letter to Urban II only slightly after finishing the version *VP* (very likely that sent to the Pope). The biggest change was the title. Only in this modified version, the one most widely diffused in the manuscript tradition, is the subject matter of the letter to the Pope defined as *De incarnatione uerbi.*[27] The letter in fact says relatively little about the incarnation of the Word, as Roscelin's argument concerned the nature of the Trinity. As late as 1097-98, perhaps four years after its redaction, Malchus, bishop of Waterford, asked Anselm for that book "composed about the Holy Trinity and commended by apostolic authority."[28] One reason why Anselm gave the title *De incarnatione uerbi*

to the revised final version is suggested by the draft *CDM.* Here he was concerned with a question raised indirectly by Roscelin's argument: why did God assume man in the Son rather than in any other person? Roscelin had maintained that it was logically necessary to distinguish the three persons as three things; otherwise the incarnation would have involved the whole Trinity.[29] After rejecting Roscelin's conclusion in *DIV*[1] as palpably absurd, Anselm then tried in the draft *CDM* to explain why God became incarnate in the Son and not in the other persons. We see in its second part that he was here groping towards a way of explaining how God and man could co-exist in the Son, going beyond the arguments of Boethius in the *Contra Euticen et Nestorium.* As the apology added to the beginning of *CDM* in *H* makes clear, Anselm was aware that this was not the proper subject of the letter. Only in *CDM* does Anselm promise to write sometime in the future about the "beautiful and necessary reason and rational necessity" as to why God should have assumed human nature with its weakness and mortality. The promise confirms Southern's argument—based on comparison of passages in *DIV*[2] with Gilbert Crispin's *Disputatio Iudei et Christiani*—that Anselm was already starting to think about the reasons why God became man in the winter of 1092/93, spent in England prior to being appointed archbishop of Canterbury 6 March 1093.[30] After he had been consecrated archbishop (4 December 1093), he sent for Boso, his disciple at Bec since 1090, to come to Canterbury. Boso's stimulation was instrumental in writing the *Cur Deus homo,* a work he says he began in England at a time "of great tribulation of heart".[31] Anselm completed it in 1098 at Sclavia (modern day Liberi), in southern Italy, while staying at a mountain-top manor belonging to John, abbot of Telese, the Roman cleric and former monk of Bec who first informed Anselm about the dangerous opinions of Roscelin of Compiègne.[32]

Notes

1. I am indebted to the Institut de Recherche et d'Histoire des Textes, whose fichier led me to the British Library manuscript with which this study is largely concerned, to the Institute for Advanced Study (Princeton) for enabling me to research and write this paper, and particularly to Giles Constable for his prudent comments. I am also grateful to Irène Rosier for checking my transcription of the Arsenal manuscript *in situ.*

2. The letter was discovered by J. A. Schmeller in the Bavarian State Library, Munich Clm 4643, ff. 93v-99r (s. xii) and published with arguments for its authenticity in the *Abhandlungen der philosophisch-philologischen Klasse der königlichen bayerischen Akademie der Wissenschaften,* 5 Bd. 3 Abt. (Munich, 1849), 187-210; it was re-

edited by J. Reiners as an appendix to his study, *Der Nominalismus in der Frühscholastik. Ein Beitrag zur Geschichte der Universalienfrage im Mittelalter,* Beiträge zur Geschichte der Philosophie [und der Theologie] des Mittelalters, Bd 8.5 (Münster, 1910), pp. 62-80.

3. By far the most important attempt to bring together the known testimony as it stood in 1911 was that of François Picavet, whose *Roscelin, philosophe et théologien d'après la légende et d'après l'histoire* (2nd revd ed. Paris, 1911) was a much enlarged version of a study of the same title published in Paris in 1896. The few other studies that have been produced since then rely on the same limited evidence and have been very lacking in historical context: cf. Heinrich Christian Meier, *Macht und Wahnwitz der Begriffe. Der Ketzer Roscellinus* (Aalen, 1974); Eike-Henner W. Kluge, "Roscelin and the Medieval Problem of Universals", *Journal of the History of Philosophy* 14 (1976), 405-14. Medieval nominalism has its own not inconsiderable literature; for most recent views, see Calvin G. Normore, "The Tradition of Medieval Nominalism", in *Studies in Medieval Philosophy,* ed. John F. Wippel, Studies in the Philosophy and the History of Philosophy 17 (Washington, 1987) and William J. Courtenay's "*Nominales* and Nominalism in the Twelfth Century" to appear a volume being published by Vrin in honour of Paul Vignaux. I am indebted to Courtenay for allowing me to see this article in typescript, as for the same reason to Yukio Iwakuma, who is preparing an article on "*Vocales,* or early nominalists".

4. André Wilmart edited the hitherto unknown initial version in "Le premier ouvrage de saint Anselme contre le trithéisme de Roscelin", *Recherches de théologie ancienne et médiévale* 3 (1931), 20-36. Franciscus Salesius Schmitt edited both this text and the final version (DIV^1 and DIV^2, as the two major recensions will subsequently be referred to) quite independently in the same year along with other relevant documents in *S. Anselmi Epistola de incarnatione verbi; accedit prior eiusdem opusculi recensio nunc primum edita,* Florilegium Patristicum 28 (Bonn, 1931). He edited the two recensions again in *S. Anselmi Opera* vol. 1 (Seckau, 1938), pp. 281-90 and vol. 2 (Rome, 1940), pp. 1-17, volumes reprinted as the first two of a six volume series of the *Opera* (Edinburgh, 1946-61), reprinted again with an important *Prolegomena seu Ratio Editionis* and corrections in *S. Anselmi Opera* (Stuttgart-Bad Canstatt, 1968), 2 vols. Schmitt's editions of DIV^1 and DIV^2 have been photographically reproduced with accompa-

nying notes and translation into French by Alain Galonnier in *L'œuvre de S. Anselme de Cantorbéry,* vol. 3 (Paris, 1988), pp. 171-193 and 195-275 respectively. References to Anselm's writing will be to the volume, page and line of the 1946-61 edition, retained in the 1968 reprint.

5. The council is not specifically mentioned in DIV^1, but we know that in *Ep.* 136 (2, 279-81) he asked Fulco, bishop of Beauvais, asking to carry *has autem litteras* to the forthcoming council, as much as anything to disassociate himself from any opinion attributed to him by Roscelin. In the Lambeth MS (of which f. 122^r is reproduced by Schmitt facing 1, 282) the treatise is untitled, but addressed as an open letter "Dominis et patribus et fratribus omnibus catholicae et apostolicae cultoribus, qui hanc legere dignabuntur epistolam" (1, 282.3-4)

6. DIV^2 2, 4.5-5.6.

7. "Cinq recensions de l'*Epistola de incarnatione verbi* de s. Anselme de Cantobéry", *Revue bénédictine* 51 (1939), 20-36, substantially unchanged as "Die verschiedenen Rezensionen der *Epistola de Incarnatione Verbi*", in the 1968 *Opera* 1, 78*-89*.

8. Schmitt learnt about the Hereford MS from Richard Southern after having prepared the 1938 Seckau edition of DIV^1; consequently the variants to its text in *H* are to be found in the apparatus to DIV^2 in vol. 2 (Rome, 1940). On *H,* see A. T. Bannister, *A Descriptive Catalogue of the Manuscripts in the Hereford Cathedral Library* (Hereford, 1927), pp. 96-98. Rodney M. Thomson is preparing a new catalogue of the Hereford Cathedral Library. In none of the MSS of the *De incarnatione uerbi* are chapter divisions identified by number. Schmitt's numerical divisions are however based on dividing signs within the MS tradition, and consequently will be used for convenience; cf. his notes to *Opera* 1, 281 and 2, 3.

9. *V* is our oldest copy (c. 1100, of unknown provenance) of DIV^2 (f. 133^v illustrated facing *Opera* 2, 12). The Greek associations of its contents lend weight to Schmitt's thought that this was the copy sent to the Pope, who used the work in his debate with the Greeks at Bari in 1108 according to Eadmer, *Historia novorum,* ed. Martin Rule, Rolls Series (London, 1884), p. 105. *V* also contains the *Liber Prognosticon* of Julian, the *Vita Johannis Eleemosynarii* of Leontius and the *Historia Lausiaca* of Palladius. *P* is from the first half of the 12th century, probably from Canterbury. In both *V* and *P DIV^2* is followed by Augus-

tine's *De doctrina christiana; Catalogue général des manuscrits latins de la Bibliothèque nationale* 2 (Paris, 1940), pp. 479-480.

10. Schmitt lists the manuscripts he used in his edition in the 1968 Prolegomena to *Opera* 1, 213*-225*. For description and bibliography of these three manuscripts, see below, pp. 68-81.

11. "Die verschiedenen Rezensionen", pp. 79*-86* (see note 4).

12. *DIV²* (2.30): "De scriptis illius cui respondeo in hac epistola, nihil potui videre praeter illud quod supra posui; sed puto sic rei patere veritatem ex eis quae dixi, ut nulli lateat intelligenti nihil quod contra illam dicitur vim veritatis tenere."

13. *A* f. 107ᵛ-108ʳ, *B* f. 81ᵛᵇ-82ʳᵃ, *C* f. 147ᵛᵃ: "Cur autem uel quam pulchra et necessaria ratione siue rationabili necessitate summa maiestas cum omnia sola uoluntate possit, nostram naturam cum infirmitate et mortalitate nostra absque peccato ad uincendum diabolum et liberandum hominem assumpserit, quod utique multi querunt, si huic epistole insererem, nimis longa esset digressio. Aliquando tamen si diuina gratia effectum uoluntati mee tribuerit, quod inde michi dignata est ostendere multorum qui hoc a me audierunt precibus compulsus, scribere desidero."

14. *Cur deus homo* I, 1 (2, 47.5-7): "Saepe et studiosissime a multis rogatus sum et verbis et litteris, quatenus cuiusdam de fide nostra quaestionis rationes, quas soleo respondere quaerentibus, memoriae scribendo commendem. . . . (47.11-48.3) Quam quaestionem solent et infideles nobis simplicitatem Christianam quasi fatuam deridentes obicere, et fideles multi in corde versare: qua videlicet ratione vel necessitate Deus homo factus sit, et morte sua, sicut credimus et confitemur, mundo vitam reddiderit, cum hoc aut per aliam personam, sive angelicam sive humanam, aut sola voluntate facere potuerit. De qua quaestione non solum litterati sed etiam illitterati multi quaerunt et rationem eius desiderant."

15. *Isagoge* 7.21, transl. Boethii, ed. Laurenzo Minio-Paluello, *Aristoteles Latinus* 1, 6-7 (Bruges, Paris, 1966), pp. 13.24-14.2: "Individua ergo dicuntur huiusmodi quoniam ex proprietatibus consistit unumquodque eorum quorum collectio numquam in alio eadem erit."

16. *DIV¹* (282.10-15): "Dictum quoque mihi prius fuerat similiter, quia Francigena quidam—hunc autem novi, quia amicus meus est—assereret se a me audisse ita de Deo dici patrem et filium et procedentem a patre et filio spiritum, quomodo albus et iustus et grammaticus et similia de quodam in-

dividuo homine." In translating this passage Galonnier considered that *Francigena* was the name of a friend different from that of Roscelin, in *L'œuvre de S. Anselme* 3 (see n. 1), pp. 175 and 193. The reading of this passage in *H* (omitting *Francigena . . . meus est,* as indicated in the apparatus on p. 202 of the Schmitt-Galonnier edition-translation) makes clear that the *Francigena* is identical to the *quodam clerico in Francia,* as Richard W. Southern pointed out in *Saint Anselm and his Biographer* (Cambridge, 1963), p. 80 n. 1.

17. *DIV¹* (1, 281.4, 11-12; cf. apparatus on 2, 6).

18. *DIV²* (2, 24.1-2).

19. This construction of the text also explains Schmitt's observation that certain phrases in *VP* replicate those in *DIV¹* (see his apparatus to 2, 12.8-11, 14.21, 16.16, 17.7).

20. *DIV¹* (20.11-21.10).

21. *DIV²* (2, 31.2-33.8), alluding to Augustine's *De fide et symbolo* c. 8.17 (*CSEL* [*Corpus Scriptorum Ecclasiosticorum Latinorum*] 41, p. 18).

22. *DIV²* (2, 3.2-4.4).

23. G.B. Flahiff, "The Censorship of Books in the Twelfth Century", *Mediaeval Studies* 4 (1942), 1-22 did not notice this example of voluntary pre-censorship in *DIV²*. He thought that the earliest known example of a writer to seek approval directly from the Pope (as distinct from any other patron) was Gerhoch of Reichersberg, who asked c. 1150 for Eugenius III to correct his commentary on the Psalms, as well as the archbishop of Salzburg and Otto of Freising (*PL* 193, 491); three others were Godfrey of Viterbo, Herbert of Bosham and Ralph Niger. Nonetheless such examples of voluntary pre-censorship are extremely rare, prior to the mid twelfth-century. The one earlier example Flahiff thought to be provided by the reason for Abaelard's condemnation at Soissons in 1121, as explained in the *Historia calamitatum* 11. 848-854, ed. Jacques MONFRIN (Paris, 1978), p. 87: "Dicebant [*scil.* emuli mei] enim ad dampnationem libelli [*scil. de unitate et trinitate divina*] satis hoc esse debere quod nec romani pontificis nec Ecclesie auctoritate eum commendatum legere publice presumpseram, atque ad transcribendum jam pluribus eum ipse prestitissem; et hoc perutile futurum fidei christiane, si exemplo mei multorum similis presumptio preveniretur." Flahiff assumed this passage to mean that "the legate was persuaded to condemn the book . . . solely, it is said, because he had taught this book publically and allowed copies to be made

without its being approved by the Pope or by the Church" (*art. cit.*, p. 4 and n. 16). Flahiff's interpretation was cited by Hubert Silvestre as evidence against the authenticity of the *Hist. cal.* ("L'idylle d'Abélard et Héloïse: la part du roman", Académie royale de Belgique. *Bulletin de la classe des lettres et des sciences morales et politiques*, 5ᵉ sér., 71 [1985-5] 183, following John Benton's assumption in the Cluny volume *Pierre Abélard-Pierre le Vénérable. Les courants philosophiques, littéraires et artistiques en Occident au milieu du* XIIᵉ *siècle* [Paris, 1975], p. 484). In "Abelard's Mockery of St Anselm", *Journal of Ecclesiastical History* 41 (1990), 1-23, Michael Clanchy has followed the same assumption that Abaelard's failure to pre-censure his book provided sufficient grounds for its condemnation, arguing that his accusers cited this passage in Anselm's *DIV²* to persuade the legate. Yet the Latin of *Hist. cal.* 1.849 says that his critics thought his failure *ought* to be sufficient, not that it *was* sufficient. The charge made at Soissons which prompted the archbishop's sentence was that Abaelard had said only God the Father was omnipotent (*Hist. cal.* ll. 871-4). Flahiff's reading of *Hist. cal.* is undermined by his much more important general observation (ignored by Clanchy) that such rare examples as survive from the twelfth-century of submission to papal censorship are all *voluntary* and not legal obligations. Alberic may have thought pre-censorship should be accepted practice and have admired Anselm's precedent in *DIV²*, but this was not the grounds of the actual condemnation at Soissons.

24. *DIV²* (2, 9.21-10.1): "illi utique nostri temporis dialectici, immo dialecticae haeretici, qui non nisi flatum vocis putant universales esse substantias, et qui colorem non aliud queunt intelligere quam corpus, nec sapientiam hominis aliud quam animam, prorsus a spiritualium quaestionum disputatione sunt exsufflandi." The passage is taken over from *DIV¹* (1, 285.4-7) with the addition in *H* and *DIV²* of *nostri temporis* and *immo dialecticae haeretici.*

25. *DIV²* (2, 30.7-9).

26. *DIV²* (2, 10.19-21): "Dicit, sicut audio, ille qui tres personas dicitur asserere esse velut tres angelos aut tres animas: "Pagani defendunt legem suam, Iudaei defendunt legem suam. Ergo et nos Christiani debemus defendere fidem nostram."

27. Schmitt notes (apparatus to 2, 3.1) that in *P* the treatise is just known as an *epistola* to Pope Urban II; no titles occur in *W, H* or *P*. Only one MS (Munich, Clm 21248, from Ulm; early twelfth

century) adds to the title "contra blasphemias Ruzelini Compendiensis". The title *De fide trinitatis*, retained by Migne in *PL* 158, 259-84, was first given by Gerberon in his 1675 edition without any manuscript foundation.

28. *Epist.* 207 among the letters of Anselm (2, 101-2).

29. John, *Ep.* 128 (270.8-271.11); *DIV¹* (282.5-7), *DIV²* (2, 4.6-9).

30. Shown by Richard Southern through comparison of the *De incarnatione uerbi* (for which he used *H*) and Gilbert Crispin's *Disputatio*, "St Anselm and Gilbert Crispin, Abbot of Westminster", *Mediaeval and Renaissance Studies* 3 (1954), 78-115.

31. *De conceptu virginali et de originali peccato* (2, 139.5): "quem ut ederem tu maxime inter alios me impulisti"; *Vita Bosonis, PL* 150, 725D.

32. *Cur deus homo*, Pref. (2, 42.6-9); Eadmer, *Vita Anselmi* c. 30, ed. Richard W. Southern, *The Life of Saint Anselm* (Oxford, 1962, reprinted with corrections 1979), p. 107. While the traditional date for Anselm's beginning *CDH*, first suggested by Gerberon, has been 1094, René Roques thinks that it was begun closer to the first exile of Anselm from England in late October 1097; *Pourquoi Dieu s'est fait homme*, Sources chrétiennes 91 (Paris, 1963), p. 65. The period February 1095 - May 1097 was a relatively peaceful one for Anselm; cf. Sally N. Vaughn, *Anselm of Bec and Robert of Meulan. The Innocence of the Dove and the Wisdom of the Serpent* (Berkeley, 1987), pp. 185-203. Schmitt is open on the question 1, 59*-60*. Eadmer tells us more about John in his *Historia novorum*, ed. Martin Rule, Rolls Series (London, 1884), p. 96. From Pope Urban II's first known letter to Anselm (*Ep.* 125 in the collection, 3, 265-6) we learn that John was a Roman cleric who came to France to study under Anselm, became a monk and priest at Bec (incurring some controversy in Rome), returned to Rome at the Pope's behest, but was released to France at the request of Fulco, bishop of Beauvais, to serve as his secretary for a year. John subsequently became abbot of Telese, cardinal-bishop of Tusculum by around 1100, and papal legate to England in 1101; Southern, *Vita Anselmi*, p. 106 n. 1.

J. F. Worthen (essay date 1993)

SOURCE: Worthen, J. F. "Augustine's *De trinitate* and Anselm's *Proslogion*: 'Exercere Lectorum.'" In *Collectanea Augustiniana*, edited by Joseph T. Lienhard, Earl C. Muller, and Roland J. Teske, pp. 517-29. New York: Peter Lang, 1993.

[*In the following essay, Worthen asserts that St. Augustine in his* De trinitate *and Anselm in his* Proslogion *engage in a narrative process of leading readers toward an understanding of God, and compares the methods used by both writers to achieve this goal.*]

I

The power of speech, Socrates says in the *Phaedrus,* consists in ψυχαγωγία, which we might translate as "the leading of souls."[1] Plato as an author is interested in discourse not as a neutral medium for the communication of information but as a way of leading—of shaping, transforming—the souls of his readers. Augustine and Anselm are similarly concerned to create texts that will not only transfer knowledge but engage their readers in the process of coming to know, that will not only inform but rather reform the careful reader. Like Plato, they see the power of discourse in its capacity to mould the mind. This claim could be discussed from many perspectives and with attention to many works, but today I wish to focus exclusively on two particular texts: Augustine's *De trinitate* and Anselm's **Proslogion.**[2] The following paper will attempt to outline the ψυχαγωγία, the soul-leading, suggested by each work and to trace the continuity between them.[3] For Anselm was indebted to Augustine as much for a vision of theological reading and writing as for any individual item of theological dogma.

II

Volentes in rebus quae factae sunt ad cognoscendum eum a quo factae sunt exercere lectorem:[4] these are the opening words of the fifteenth book of the *De trinitate.* Reviewing the project in which he has been enmeshed since Book VIII, Augustine sees in it a sustained attempt to exercise the reader, *exercere lectorem.*[5] Note that Augustine distinguishes Books VIII-XIV from the earlier, exegetical part of the *De trinitate* not only by their method—proceeding from created things rather than from the text of Scripture as such—but also by their relationship with the reader. Unlike the first part of the work, the purpose of these books is not so much to inform the reader as to elicit his participation in a journey whose culmination is signalled by the second part of the sentence just quoted: *iam peruenimus ad eius imaginem.*[6]

How do these later books of the *De trinitate* exercise the reader in a way that finds no parallel in Books I-VII and indeed, I would argue, in theological literature generally? Augustine's own verb, *peruenimus,* supplies an initial clue. It is a verb of travelling, and Augustine here and elsewhere is at pains to emphasize the character of these books as a movement, as a journey, both through using the language of travel and quest and through reflecting on the ground that has been traversed and now past.[7] And to describe a journey is to tell a story; that is, it is to construct a narrative.

Now, to begin with, narrative texts make demands on their readers—exercise their readers—in ways that non-narrative texts do not.[8] The later books of the *De trinitate,* however, not only develop a narrative but develop a narrative of a very particular kind—a narrative of internal events. The elements of this story do not concern physical movements or encounters but rather mental operations. Perception, love, mind, memory, intellect, will—these provide the structure of Augustine's interior narrative. And although some of these mental operations have an external aspect either necessarily or potentially, it is their internal aspect that interests Augustine; indeed, the dynamic of the narrative derives from a progressive concentration on the internal aspect of each individual operation and then on the more internally oriented of the operations until in Book XIV we arrive at the pure interiority of *memoria sui, intellectus sui* and *amor sui* which is the *imago dei.*[9] Hence Augustine's mixing of his spatial metaphors in the attempt to describe the journey: *ascendentibus itaque introrsus.*[10] The narrative moves not over space but across the mind and not towards any physical point but towards the point of utter self-consciousness.

Reading such an interior narrative is different from reading a narrative of external events in certain crucial respects. First, as a narrative focusing on the purely interior as the universal and inalienable *imago dei* in humanity it is a narrative about everyone—about every reader. By contrast, for instance, with the *Confessiones* the narrative is as much the reader's as it is the author's, for all external references that might identify it as the author's peculiar property are progressively eliminated.[11] The narrative lies open to the reader for his or her possession. Furthermore, the fact that this narrative is a narrative of the self positively invites the reader's participation, in that the narrative requires an inner self to be about, and the only interiority to which readers have direct access, the only self which for them can be the narrative's subject, is their own.[12]

For Augustine, speech about intellectual truths refers to that which is always present to the mind of the speaker, whereas speech about physical objects refers to that which is always at a distance from it;[13] hence any reader may experience this narrative of universal interiority. But if his or her reading is an attentive reading then the narrative must be undergone, because to conceive of an inner condition is already to be experiencing it.[14] It is not simply that the later books of the *De trinitate* present a spiritual itinerary which the reader has the option of following or ignoring once the book has been replaced on the shelf. For the stages in this narrative are inevitably enacted by the reader *as he or she reads.* Augustine himself makes this clear. He comments explicitly, for example, on the role of memory and will in reading.[15] We cannot read about remembering and willing without ourselves engaging our own memory and will. Similarly, Augustine analyzes the interaction of physical perception and wholly internal reason in the act of reading:[16] as we peruse the page we are necessarily exercising both the outermost and the innermost trinities of this narrative. But the reader's enactment of the represented narrative has a further, more dynamic dimension. If the inward ascent consists in turning our attention progressively away from the mind's external operations towards the simple interiority at its centre, then are we not necessarily engaged in that ascent as we turn over the pages of the *De trinitate,* as we focus ever more inwardly on the functioning of our own mind? "However much the mind extends itself towards that which is eternal, to that degree it is then shaped according to the image of God."[17] In reading Augustine's interior narrative we are enacting it, and in enacting it we are realizing in ourselves the divine trinitarian image through which we may best perceive the everlasting Trinity of God.

The ψυχαγωγία of Books VIII-XIV of the *De trinitate,* then, proceeds by inviting the reader to enact a narrative of the self whose enactment will end in self-reformation and theological knowledge.

III

What Augustine's *De trinitate* contains implicitly, Anselm's *Proslogion* displays openly. The kind of interior narrative that underlies the later books of the *De trinitate* constitutes the immediate form of the *Proslogion.* The *Proslogion* is, and does not merely suggest, a meditation. It presents itself as the script of a self alone before its creator, a text written "in the person of someone striving to raise his mind to contemplate God," as Anselm phrases it.[18] The speaker of the *De trinitate* is evidently Augustine, with his magisterial *nos,* and its explicit addressee is its human audience. The *Proslogion* is addressed to no one but God and the speaker's self, while its speaker is a nameless and singular "I." What we have identified as the hidden structure of Books VIII—XIV of the *De trinitate* therefore becomes the overt structure of the *Proslogion:* a narrative about the self, any self, alone with itself before God. How does this affect the ψυχαγωγία developed by St. Anselm?

Augustine's interior narrative exercises the reader in that it both invites him and in a certain sense compels him to undergo the narrative himself. The mechanism of invitation is the absence of the author: the narrative of the *De trinitate* is not about Augustine specifically, does not belong to Augustine rather than to anyone else and in that sense creates a certain community of equality between author and reader.[19] The author as special authority absents himself so that the reader can become present within the narrative through his own interpretative activity. But Anselm is absent from his narrative in a more palpable sense than Augustine. Augustine's interior narrative appears within a text whose overall form is an authoritative exposition by an identifiable historical figure. This expository context, in which the reader would be excluded from interpretative activity, is discarded in the *Proslogion.* The only voice in the text is a voice that we know in advance to be a fiction, dissociated from the abbot of Bec,[20] and a voice moreover which represents itself as ignorant and sinful, incapable of grasping let alone of imparting truth. The text is then necessarily narrative, in that it is bound to recount the successive states of this mind over time, and necessarily open to the reader's participation: the reader may identify his own self with the self of the text, because that self is never anyone definably other and never presents itself as an author/authority. The author is absent not only from the hidden structure but from the overt structure of the text. The invitation to experience the textual narrative is so much the more unavoidable.

But if the way in which the *Proslogion* lies open to the reader's participation is closely parallel to the strategy of the *De trinitate,* it does not demand the reader's participation in quite the same way. Augustine's method of ψυχαγωγία derived from the fact that his narrative was primarily *about* mental operations, and that both the mental operations described and also their successively inward ordering were enacted by the reader precisely by virtue of his or her reading. The *Proslogion* is not primarily about mental operations but about the being and nature of God, and therefore the necessity of enactment that we found in Augustine cannot apply straightforwardly here. Yet that does not mean that it does not apply at all. For example, the so-called ontological argument could be considered as a case of the same essential method transposed into a different key. We are reading not about a general mental operation—willing, remembering, understanding—but about a very specific mental act: the denial that God is.[21] But, as in the *De trinitate,* in reading about this mental event we are necessarily re-presenting it: we echo the speaker's denial of God's existence, just as the speaker—here himself a reader[22]—is echoing the denial of the fool. And Anselm, like Augustine, will use that echo to create in the reader's self a knowledge of theological truth. For he will show that the presence, within the echoed denial, of the name of God has already committed the speaker and in turn the reader to acknowledging the truth of God's existence. The mental event of conceiving God—even in conceiving his non-existence—contains in itself a knowledge that God is, just as the mental event of remembering, understanding and loving oneself contains in itself a knowledge of the Trinity. In both cases, the reader's own performance of a mental event described in the "script" becomes the fulcrum of theological understanding. The ontological argument can then be seen as another example of Anselm moving to the surface of the text a reader strategy implicit in the *De trinitate*.[23]

In Book XIV of the *De trinitate* Augustine discusses the need for some external force to provoke us to an awareness of the self-knowledge we have always possessed. The initial example of such an external force is an interlocutor, but Augustine then continues:

> the same effect is achieved by letters written about those things which the reader finds to be true with reason as his guide, not which he believes to be true on the authority of the person who wrote them in the manner that history is read, but which he himself finds to be true either in himself or in that very truth that is the mind's guide.[24]

Is not this in essence the ψυχαγωγία of both the *De trinitate* and the **Proslogion,** that the external text provokes a knowledge of the inner self, which in itself contains an understanding of God? In their use of textual narrative to construct interiority, and in their confidence that God can always be found within the interiority so constructed, the bishop of Hippo and the abbot of Bec are one.

IV

Before concluding this paper, however, I want to consider in a little more detail Anselm's refusal to follow directly the route mapped out in the *De trinitate* as the road to God—the route that traces the trinitarian structures of the mind.[25] Towards the end of the first chapter of the **Proslogion** the speaker says:

> I confess, Lord, and I give thanks, that you have created in me this image of you, so that remembering you I may think of you, I may love you. But it is so destroyed by the wearing down caused by my vices, it is so darkened by the smoke of my sins, that it cannot do that for which it was made, unless you renew and reform it.[26]

Now, there is nothing here to contradict the letter of the Augustinian doctrine of the *imago Dei* delineated in the *De trinitate*. Yet it is not, I think, insignificant that this is the only indisputable reference to that doctrine in the **Proslogion:**[27] placed at the end of the programmatic opening section, it constitutes something of a *recusatio*. Anselm is not going to invite the reader to approach the knowledge of God by exploring the trinitarian structures of his own mind. Rather, the possibility of exploring that road has been radically jeopardized by sin, by the speaker's overwhelming sense of an unbreachable chasm between himself and the divinity.[28] Whereas for the Augustine of the *De trinitate* self-knowledge is the certain way to God, for the speaker of the **Proslogion** self-discovery soon precipitates a collapse in confidence that threatens to submerge the whole theological project:

> I was reaching towards God, and I struck against myself. I was seeking rest in my solitude, and I 'found trouble and sorrow' in my innermost parts.[29]

The interior journey instigated in the first few sentences of the text leads not to illumination and understanding but to crippling despair.

It may seem—and indeed it seems to the speaker himself[30]—that this despair is lifted in chapters 2-13, as we steadily advance towards a comprehensive grasp of the divine existence and attributes. But the **Proslogion** does not end with chapter 13.[31] Chapter 14 opens with the self-addressed question, *an invenisti, anima mea, quod quaerebas?*[32] And the clear answer is a perhaps surprising negative. The speaker does not yet perceive God, he does not yet see God.[33] His eye is overcast by too much shadow, while God himself is shrouded in the most blinding light. The idea of God's inaccessible light prompts more constructive reflection in chapters 15-17, but chapter 18 restates the sense of failure with such force that we might be back at chapter one: "And again, see how confusion, see how again sorrow and grief stand in the way of the one who is seeking joy and happiness!"[34] *Iterum . . . iterum,* again and again. We are back at chapter 1—back with the awareness of separation and alienation that tempts us to despair but yet contains the seed of desire. And it is that desire that forces the voice of the text to go on, forbidding it to rest either in despair or in hope.[35]

This continual deferral of satisfaction is a fundamental—perhaps the fundamental—aspect of Anselm's ψυχαγωγία in the **Proslogion.** Even in those passages where it would appear that the speaker does achieve some kind of satisfaction there is always an element of deferral. For instance, in seeking to understand the divine mercy, the speaker is forced to acknowledge that *et videtur unde sis misericors, et non pervidetur.*[36] Similarly, although he thinks he may have grasped why God should save the wicked, he has to admit his inability to penetrate the mystery of why some wicked people should be saved and others should not.[37] Coming to understand, however successfully, some truths about the divine being also opens up vistas of inscrutable shadow. And at the end of the text, where the speaker finally seems to find the joy he has always been seeking,[38] he only finds it in his contemplation of that which of necessity he does not possess: heaven. What satisfaction is here attained inevitably includes the non-satisfaction of being confined to earth. Contemplation of the ultimate eschatological deferral of happiness is the only happiness we can hope to find. But if happiness can only be found in the embrace of hope and desire, it must always carry in itself the marks of absence and exile. Enacting Anselm's narrative, submitting to his ψυχαγωγία, means abandoning rest for a restless journey.

V

I have so far been presuming that the element of deferral in Anselm's ψυχαγωγία is something that differentiates him from Augustine. Yet perhaps that is to state the matter too simply. Perhaps Anselm is, again, placing on the surface of his text a motif that lies implicitly in Augustine, transposing that same motif from the hidden structure to the overt structure.

We might note, for example, Augustine's concern to stress the provisionality of all that he writes in the *De trinitate*. In the opening chapters of Book I he defines his role not as instructing his readers in what he definitively knows but as disclosing to them simply *quantum eiusdem uiae peregerim.*[39] Similarly, the prologues to Books II and III insist on the need for the reader himself to be questioning and searching: if author and reader are truly on the same road, then not only must the author be humble but the reader must be his active partner. And as the narrative of the later books unfolds, it becomes ever more evident that this road stretches on without limit in this life, that neither writing nor reading the *De trinitate* will permit us to abandon the arduous pilgrimage towards truth: "so let us seek as those who are going to find, and let us find as those who are going to seek."[40] Perfection in this life is nothing but a forgetting of what is past and a reaching out to what lies ahead: it is quest, journey, narrative. Complete knowledge, like complete joy for Anselm, is ineluctably deferred to the time of eternity.[41] Even when some glimpse of the eternal is given to us, this vision of something outside the structure of journey and narrative in which we are bound to live does not absorb but rather is absorbed by our journey, our narrative: *et fit rei non transitoriae transitoria cogitatio.*[42]

The theme of movement without arrival also finds expression at the level of form. For although we described the later books of the *De trinitate* as containing a narrative, it might be more accurate to say that they contain several, or at least the same narrative told twice. Books VIII-X, for instance, represent one telling of the story: from the trinity of outward love (Book VIII), to the psychological trinity of *mens-verbum-amor* (IX), to the purely mental trinity that is the image of God, *memoria-intelligentia-voluntas* (X). With the conclusion of Book X, we reach the end of the journey; but then we do not, for the journey commences again, from a different point of departure, the mechanism of perception, in Book XI, to arrive at the same mental trinity in Book XIV. In other words, this is not a journey that can be undertaken, a narrative that can be experienced, once and for all. It must be continually undertaken, continually experienced.

Book XV begins to make more sense as the culmination of the *De trinitate* when seen from this perspective.

It might seem somewhat careless of Augustine to have ended his great work with a long series of rather disconnected essays, the burden of which appears to be to play down the immense theological achievements of Books VIII-XIV. And yet if Augustine's ψυχαγωγία includes a systematic thwarting of the reader's desire to have read enough, to have done enough, then surely this lack of an ending is the perfect ending. Augustine does not leave us with the sense of achievement and closure to which we might have been tempted if he had ended the *De trinitate* with Book XIV. He leaves us rather with a sense of having hardly begun, or perhaps of needing to begin again, and again. And he leaves us in the end not with exposition but with a solitary address to his solitary self, weak and sinful,[43] and with a prayer that his desire may be kindled with ever increasing intensity.[44] *Exercere,* we should perhaps remember, means not only to exercise but also to vex, to provoke, to disturb. Augustine ends the *De trinitate* by bringing the reader to a point where she must confront her own sin, her own exile and her own desire. It is the point at which Anselm will begin the **Proslogion,** some seven centuries later.

Notes

1. *Phaedrus* 271C-D.

2. For a very brief attempt to describe the *De trinitate* in terms of such a project of soul-leading, see P. Hadot, "Exercises spirituels," *École pratique des hautes études: Vᵉ section—sciences religieuses* 84 (1976-77) 67-68. Augustine "veut faire expérimenter l'âme, par un retour sur elle-même, le fait qu'elle est l'image de la Trinité" (p. 68). The article argues that ancient philosophical texts in general need to be read from the point of view of the ψυχαγωγία contain, although Hadot himself does not use this term (pp. 59-70).

3. The idea of relating the two works in the title was suggested by Anselm himself, who tells us that his *Monologion* was based on Augustine's *De trinitate* and that the *Monologion* in turn served as the point of departure for the *Proslogion*. Anselm asserts the dependency of the *Monologion* on the *De trinitate* in *Epistola* 77: III,199,13-26, and in the prologue to the work itself (*Monologion,prologus:* I,8,8-14). For the origin of the *Proslogion* in Anselm's desire to rework the basic themes of the *Monologion,* see his prologue to the *Proslogion* (*Proslogion,prooemium:* I,93,2-10). All references to Anselm's works include the volume, page, and lines in *S. Anselmi Cantuariensis Episcopi opera omnia,* ed. F. S. Schmitt, 6 vols. (Seckau, 1938; repr. Edinburgh: Thomas Nelson, 1946-61).

4. *De trinitate* XV,i,1: *CC* L/A,460: "Wanting to exercise the reader in the things that were made in

order to know him by whom they were made." All translations are my own.

5. *De trinitate* XI,i,1: *CC* L,333-34 sets out the methodology of "exercising" ourselves in the sensible so that we may come to a comprehension of the spiritual. The verb *exercere*, however, does not appear here. It recurs several times in Book XV: *ut . . . distinctius in ea lectoris exerceretur intentio,* where Augustine is referring specifically to Book XI (XV,iii,5: *CC* L/A,466); *exercitata in inferioribus intellegentia,* speaking of the whole of Books IX-XIV (XV,vi,10: *CC* L/A,473); and finally, in a passage concerning the obscurities of Scripture rather than Augustine's own methodology, *ut autem nos exerceret sermo diuinus* (XV,xvii,27: *CC* L/A,501). The Bible also has its ψυχαγωγία in Augustine's eyes.

6. "Now we have arrived at his image."

7. E.g. *De trinitate* X,xii,19: *CC* L,332; XII,xv,25: *CC* L, 379-80; XIV,viii,11: *CC* L/A,435-38; XV,iii,4-5: *CC* L/A,462-67; XV,vi,10: *CC* L/A,472-74.

8. To construe a series of statements as a narrative—as related along a temporal rather than a logical or otherwise static axis—requires a special effort of the imagination, in which the referents of those statements are perceived to possess a coherence that cannot always be reduced to simple implication. Their happening, one after another, is sufficient basis for the validity of the narrative form whether or not they are causally related. Yet to read a text as a narrative is inevitably to seek some relation other than that of brute consecutivity between the events portrayed. Reading a narrative commits us to a search for coherence, while the narrative form—we might say the fact of the temporal axis itself—denies the possibility of ever reducing those events to a simple and static unity and therefore denies that search any straightforward closure. The narrativity of the texts under consideration already contains in itself, then, the tension between projection towards and postponement of closure that is discussed in sections IV and V of the paper.

9. *De trinitate* XIV,viii,11: *CC* L/A,436: *Ecce ergo mens meminit sui, intellegit se, diligit se. Hoc si cernimus, cernimus trinitatem, nondum quidem deum sed iam imaginem dei.*

10. *De trinitate* XII,viii,13: *CC* L,368: "To those thus ascending inwards"; see *De trinitate* XII,xv,25: *CC* L,379: *introrsum ascendere* and *De trinitate* XIV,iii,5: *CC* L/A,426: *ab inferioribus ad superiora ascendentes uel ab exterioribus ad interiora ingredientes.*

11. The specifically "autobiographical" passages that do occur in the *De trinitate* are found at the early stages of the narrative, where the topic is the more externally oriented operations such as perception; so in the analysis of remembering perception Augustine uses the example of an arch he had seen at Carthage; see *De trinitate* IX,vi,11: *CC* L,302-3.

12. *De trinitate* VIII,vi,9: *CC* L,280: *Animum igitur cuiuslibet ex nostro nouimus, et ex nostro credimus quem non nouimus.* Compare Georges Poulet on the experience of reading generally: "as soon as something is presented as thought, there has to be a thinking subject with whom, at least for the time being, I identify, forgetting myself, alienated from myself" ("Phenomenology of reading," *New Literary History* 1 [1969] 56-57). The use of interior narrative by Augustine and Anselm might then be seen as a textual strategy which foregrounds the process of identification and alienation implied in every act of reading.

13. *De trinitate* VIII,vi,9: *CC* L,279-84.

14. Cf. *De trinitate* IX,ix,14: *CC* L,305-6, where Augustine argues that in spiritual things simply to conceive of and to will something is to possess it.

15. *De trinitate* XI,viii,15: *CC* L,352.

16. *De trinitate* XIII,i,4: *CC* L/A,383-85.

17. *De trinitate* XII,vii,10: *CC* L,365: *Quantumcumque se extenderit in id quod aeternum est tanto magis inde formatur ad imaginem dei.*

18. *Proslogion, prooemium:* I,93,21-94,1: *Sub persona conantis erigere mentem suam ad contemplandum deum.*

19. The preface to Book III of the *De trinitate* reveals Augustine's awareness of this community: he wants his readers to be actively critical and not merely passively receptive in their reading, while his own writing is as much a way of learning for himself as of instructing others (III,*prooemium: CC* L,127-130).

20. In saying this I am contradicting most of the modern commentators on the *Proslogion*, who unquestioningly consider it to be the transcript of Anselm's personal struggle for theological understanding mentioned in the prologue (*Proslogion,prooemium:* I,93,2-19). This is to ignore the fact that the only connection made by Anselm himself between that experience and the text he is presenting is the inspiration for its central idea, while he explicitly asserts that the work is written *sub persona* (n. 18 above). He therefore equates the status of the text with that of the *Monologion*, which he also describes as writ-

ten *sub persona* (*Monologion,prologus:* I,8,18-19), and which is patently not autobiographical. For the assumption of autobiography, see for example K. Barth, *Anselm: Fides quaerens intellectum,* tr. W. Robertson (Cleveland and New York: World Publishing, 1962), p. 168; H. de Lubac, "Sur le chapitre XIVᵉ du Proslogion," *Spicilegium Beccense* 1 (1959) 297; and most recently Y. Cattin, "La prière de S. Anselme dans le Proslogion," *Revue des sciences philosophiques et théologiques* 72 (1988) 375-76.

21. It was Barth who especially stressed the crucial role of the cognitive dimension of the argument, a dimension written into the very definition of God as *id quo maius cogitari nequit* (e.g. *Proslogion* II: I,101,15-16), and who saw in Gaunilo's neglect of that dimension the root of the argument's subsequent misunderstanding; see *Fides quaerens intellectum,* pp. 84-89.

22. The discussion of God's existence in chapters 2-4 is occasioned by the speaker's recollection of a text from Scripture: *dixit insipiens in corde suo: non est deus* (*Proslogion* II: I,101,6-7). These are the opening words of Psalms 13 and 52.

23. That Anselm was both aware of the self-enacting aspect of the *De trinitate* and consciously transposing it to perform the specific function of theological proof is suggested by the *Monologion,* a work which is far more obviously modelled on the *De trinitate.* For the speaker—and therefore by implication the reader—of the *Monologion* by reflecting on his own mental operations performed in the text both discovers and validates the trinitarian nature of God (chapters 29-68). See especially *Monologion* XXXIX: I,51,7-18, where the speaker's own activity of rational reflection becomes a key premise in an argument about the eternity of the Word. Anselm has already departed from Augustine in the *Monologion* by constructing a proof about the nature of God from the mind's reflection on its own textual activity, a road he will pursue to its conclusion in chapters 2-4 of the *Proslogion.*

24. *De trinitate* XIV,vii,9: *CC* L/A,434: *Id agunt et litterae quae de his rebus conscriptae sunt, quas res duce ratione ueras esse inuenit lector, non quas ueras esse credit ei qui scripsit sicut legitur historia, sed quas ueras esse etiam ipse inuenit siue apud se siue in ipsa mentis duce ueritate.*

25. To the objection that Anselm neglects this route because his search for understanding encompasses more than just the Trinity, it might be pointed out that he has little use for Augustine's route even when the speaker does finally consider the three persons of the Godhead in chapter 23.

26. *Proslogion* I: I,100,12-15: *Fateor, domine, et gratias ago, quia creasti in me hanc imaginem tuam, ut tui memor te cogitem, te amem. Sed sic est abolita attritione uitiorum, sic est offuscata fumo peccatorum, ut non possit facere ad quod facta est, nisi tu renoves et reformes eam.*

27. Cf. *Proslogion* XXVI: I,121,14-17, where intellect and love are coupled and contrasted: *cognoscam te, amem te. . . . Proficiat hic in me notitia tui . . . crescat amor tuus.* But no third term is added to these two.

28. This mood is firmly established throughout the whole of the opening chapter, from the question of *Proslogion* I: I,98,2-3 onwards: *ubi te quaeram absentem?*

29. *Proslogion* I: I,99,10-12: *Tendebam in deum, et offendi in me ipsum. Requiem quaerebam in secreto meo, et "tribulationem et dolorem inveni" in intimis meis.*

30. E.g. *Proslogion* IV: I,104,5-7.

31. This point was brilliantly expounded by De Lubac, in "Sur le chapitre XIVᵉ du *Proslogion,*" *Spicilegium Beccense* 1 (1959) 295-312.

32. *Proslogion* XIV: I,111,8: "Have you found, my soul, what you were seeking?"

33. We might compare Anselm's third meditation, where a successful intellectual exploration of the doctrine of the incarnation similarly fails to satisfy the speaker's desire to know and experience its reality: *Fac precor, domine, me gustare per amorem quod gusto per cognitionem. Sentiam per affectum quod sentio per intellectum* (*Meditatio* III: III,91,196-97).

34. *Proslogion* XVIII: I,113,18-19: *Et iterum ecce turbatio, ecce iterum obviat maeror et luctus quaerenti gaudium et laetitiam!*

35. Cattin considers desire to be the unifying force in the *Proslogion;* see "La prière de S. Anselme dans le Proslogion" 394-95. In the light of this reading of the whole text of the *Proslogion* it is clear that Barth's denial of crisis or anxiety in Anselm's theology is unacceptable (*Fides quaerens intellectum,* pp. 26 and 151).

36. *Proslogion* IX: I,107,14-15: "And it is seen whence you are merciful, and it is not seen clearly." My translation does not do justice to the force of the prefix *per* in this context; that *pervidetur* is here to be understood as something like "is seen through" becomes evident from both the sense and the parallel structure of the next sentence in the text (*Cernitur unde flumen manat,*

et non perspicitur fons unde nascatur: Proslogion IX: I,107,15-16). For a similar use of *pervidere,* though not one with which Anselm was necessarily familiar, see Lucretius, *De rerum natura* I,1114-17.

37. *Proslogion* XI: I,109,21-24.

38. *Proslogion* XXVI: I,120,25-121,1: *Inveni namque gaudium quoddam plenum, et plus quam plenum.*

39. *De trinitate* I,v,8: *CC* L,37: "How much of the same road I have traversed."

40. *De trinitate* IX,i,1: *CC* L,293: *Sic ergo quaeramus tanquam inuenturi, et sic inueniamus tamquam quaesituri.*

41. *De trinitate* IX,i,1: *CC* L,293. This is a theme to which Augustine will return again and again, echoing the words of St. Paul that the only knowledge available to us now is *per speculum in aenigmate* (*De trinitate* XIV,xix,25: *CC* L/A,456-57; XV,ix,16: *CC* L/A,482-83). Trinitarian theology is no different from the rest of Christian experience in its ineradicable resistance to completion and to closure.

42. *De trinitate* XII,xiv,23: *CC* L,376: "And a transitory act of thought about a thing that is not transitory takes place."

43. *De trinitate* XV,xxvii,50: *CC* L/A,531-33.

44. *De trinitate* XV,xxviii,51: *CC* L/A,533-35.

Montague Brown (essay date 1994)

SOURCE: Brown, Montague. "Anselm's Argument for the Necessity of Incarnation." *Proceedings of the PMR Conference* (1994): 39-52.

[*In the following essay, Brown evaluates and ultimately rejects Anselm's rational claims in his* Cur deus homo *regarding the necessity of God's Incarnation as Christ in order to save humanity.*]

In *Cur deus homo,* Anselm presents a rational argument for the necessity of the Incarnation, an argument suitable for convincing nonbelievers that the Incarnation is not only possible (that is, it does not involve a contradiction), but can be shown, by natural reason alone, to be necessary. Since there are many (believers as well as unbelievers) who do not think that reason can even prove the existence of God, such a claim as Anselm's is rather surprising. Is Anselm's claim credible? In our present inquiry, four subjects are involved—

(1) Anselm's overall project.

(2) The principles of Anselm's method in *Cur deus homo.*

(3) The outline of Anselm's argument for the necessity of the Incarnation. This argument involves two distinct proofs: that human beings require salvation, and that salvation could only come through God becoming man, suffering, and dying for us. (I shall touch on this second point briefly, but my focus will be on the first proof).

(4) Evaluation of Anselm's success in demonstrating the necessity of God becoming man.

I

What is Anselm's general project in *Cur deus homo*? In the short preface, Anselm indicates his intention to answer the objections of nonbelievers to the Incarnation, suffering, and death of Christ as God's way of saving us. Their main objection is that attributing such activities to God is an injustice and a dishonor to him.[1] If one says that this is the only way God could save us, one seems to be denying God's omnipotence.[2] If one will not deny his omnipotence and admits that God could have saved us another way, then one must deny his wisdom, for to go through all this suffering when a simple act of will would have been enough does not seem like a wise decision.[3] If one says that he manifests his love for us by suffering and dying in such a manner, one must explain the appropriateness of these works.[4] And finally, if one claims that God saves us by condemning an innocent man to death, it seems that God is not just and therefore not good.[5] Asserting that "the will of God is never irrational,"[6] Anselm believes that all these objections can be given reasonable answers without denying God's omnipotence, wisdom, or justice. Although Anselm himself, through his faith, is ready to accept the wisdom of God's actions, he does not think that a nonbeliever is without justification in asking such questions. So confident is Anselm in the reasonableness of Christ's Incarnation, Death, and Resurrection that he claims reasons sufficient to convince a nonbeliever that he should become a Christian. In short, his project is to show "how the death of the Son can be proved reasonable and necessary."[7]

Anselm's arguments are founded on natural reason, without reference to Christ. The boldness of the project is striking. For how can natural reason prove something that is a free act of grace by the Creator? After all, Anselm admits that God can do things beyond our comprehending.[8] Is it not misguided or even blasphemous to try to answer the questions of nonbelievers? Not necessarily! There is nothing wrong with asking questions; indeed, it is natural to be inquisitive. Questions cannot be evaded! If we suspect that God's actions cannot be defended, but continue to have faith in such a God, then we are in danger of blasphemy and idolatry. For to worship a being whom we suspect might not be all-powerful, all-wise and all-good is to worship an idol—a thing we must never do. To believe beyond all reason, simply because it is absurd, is to open up the possibility of pledging oneself to a being who may be of *limited* strength (and hence unable to save us), of *limited* wisdom (again unable to save us) or evil (then certainly not going to save us). Faith in God may reach beyond what we comprehend, but it must not contradict what we hold to be really wise and good; if it does, we are intentionally choosing ignorance and evil, and such a choice can never be justified.

Anselm himself is well aware of the dangers inherent in his project. He says in the preface that he only began the work because others entreated him so persistently, and that he had to finish it more quickly than he would have liked, in order to ensure that what has been copied and distributed would not be misunderstood. Beyond this he places his work under the jurisdiction of higher authorities.[9] Anselm was not condemned for heresy. On the contrary, he was made saint and doctor of the Church. But is his argument for this central doctrine of the faith cogent?

II

Toward the middle of the first book Anselm lays out the basic principles of his intellectual method. As he is addressing the arguments of those who think that Christianity is unreasonable, Anselm presents the following principles not as theological guides but as the very stuff of natural reason.

> I wish to have it understood between us that we do not admit anything in the least unbecoming to the Deity, and that we do not reject the smallest reason if it be not opposed by a greater. For as it is impossible to attribute anything in the least unbecoming to God; so any reason, however small, if not overbalanced by a greater, has the force of necessity.[10]

The first principle assumes that there is a God and that we know something about Him, at least what would be inappropriate to say about him. The second principle is a more general one about the nature of reason and demonstration.

Since the project of the *Cur deus homo* is to provide reasons for God becoming man, what are the reasons for believing that God exists? Anselm presents his demonstrations for God's existence in *Monologion* and *Proslogion*. In *Monologion,* Anselm traces out a basically Platonic argument for the existence of God.[11] Thus we are confronted in our experience with a hierarchy of good things. But things are said to be more or less good by being compared to something which is the highest good. Therefore, there is a highest good, which is the cause of goodness in all things, and which is good in itself.[12] Unlike Plato, however, Anselm goes on to attribute to this greatest being the status of creator.

Therefore, not only are all good things such through something that is one and the same, and all great things such through something that is one and the same; but whatever is, apparently exists through something that is one and the same.[13]

Thus, through our awareness of a variety of things at different levels of perfection, we come to know that there is a perfectly good being who is the source of everything else.

The argument in *Proslogion* is founded on the same insight into the hierarchy of actually existing things as the argument in *Monologion.* Recall the formulation of the first premise of the argument: "we believe that thou art a being than which nothing greater can be conceived."[14] The very possibility of our understanding the term "greater" lies with our having an experience of things that vary in greatness. The idea of our having this notion a priori is doubtful. If I begin with myself alone, with no other object with which to compare myself, I shall not come up with a notion of "greater" on which I could base an argument such as Anselm's. And in the chapter following the formulation of the argument, Anselm says: "To thee alone, therefore, it belongs to exist more truly than all other beings, and hence in a higher degree than all others."[15] In short, it is prerequisite to saying that there is a "being than which none greater can be conceived" that one has recognized that there are other beings ranking in an order of perfection (greater and lesser) that one has conceived. And what more immediate storehouse is there than our experience of the things of this world? To quote Anselm from *Monologion:* "Since there are goods so innumerable, whose great diversity we experience by the bodily senses, and discern by our mental faculties, must we not believe that there is some one thing, through which all goods whatever are good?"[16] Thus, we know of God that he exists as the perfectly good creator of all things. Reason has shown us this, and if we would be true to reason, we must not say anything that would be incompatible with there being a good creator.

When we turn to the second basic principle of Anselm's method, we are presented with a statement that overflows with confidence in reason: "Any reason, however small, if not overbalanced by a greater, has the force of necessity."[17] Elsewhere, Anselm goes so far as to speak of "infallible reason."[18] But why such unbounded confidence? Has Anselm not heard of all the reasons why we should doubt reason? Anselm's response to this aspect of the modern critical spirit would be to turn the question around and ask why the modern lack of confidence in reason? For, of course, there cannot be any good reasons to doubt reason. If reason is defective, then my propositions which say as much must also be called into question, for they are propositions of reason. Thus, exhaustion, or fear, or some other malaise—not rigorous thinking—gives rise to modern methodic doubt.

There are, as Anselm would certainly agree, grounds for caution in reasoning procedures. If, for example, we begin with the wrong facts through some defect in the senses, such as color-blindness, or if our capacity of reasoning is disrupted by some chemical imbalance in the brain or a blow to the head, then certainly we cannot accept as certain the conclusions of our reason. And of course passions can interrupt or skew our reasoning, as can also laziness or weariness. But it is reason that tells us that these are problems. They are not problems with reason itself, but with things getting in the way of reason.

Anselm would have no problem agreeing that our reason is not comprehensive. In speaking of the Incarnation, he writes: "Who, then, will dare to think that the human mind can discover how wisely, how wonderfully, so incomprehensible a work has been accomplished."[19] And later he says: "God can certainly do what human reason cannot grasp."[20] But again, it is reason itself which tells us this. Reason tells us that God is the infinite source of all truth and that he is our creator. No creature can be infinite. Thus, the comprehensiveness of any creature's knowledge will of necessity be limited. But to say that human reason cannot comprehend all that is intelligible is not the same thing as saying that reason is defective. Recognizing that there really do not seem to be good reasons to doubt the faculty of reason itself, we can better understand the enthusiasm Anselm has for what he calls "infallible reason."

Granted that reason on its own terms is infallible, there are many who would say that some of the conclusions of reason are merely fitting arguments while others are demonstrations. Typically, the division would be drawn between arguments which claim to prove the essential dogmas of the faith, such as the Trinity and the Incarnation (these are called fitting arguments), and those which claim to prove things that are not unique to the faith, such as mathematical proofs or metaphysical proofs of the existence of God or the immortality of the human soul (these are called demonstrations). Now it is quite obvious that Anselm does not draw the distinction between arguments of fittingness and demonstrations along the lines of what can be known about the faith and what can be known about the natural world. However, he does make a distinction between fitting arguments, which he says are just pictures, metaphors, "painting upon a cloud,"[21] and rational arguments where reasons are given. The former are not sufficient to command our assent since they are not derived by logical analysis from evidence; but the latter, which are derived by logical analysis from evidence, should command our

assent so long as there is no weightier evidence to the contrary. The challenge presented by Boso and the nonbelievers and taken up by Anselm is to provide a foundation in demonstration for the many beautiful pictures, and "harmonious proportions" of the faith.

> Therefore, the rational existence of the truth must be shown, I mean, the necessity, which proves that God ought to or could have condescended to those things which we affirm. Afterwards, to make the body of the truth, so to speak, shine forth more clearly, these harmonious proportions, like pictures of the body, must be described.[22]

The arguments he presents are not, to his mind, arguments of fittingness—but demonstrations. But are they philosophically respectable?

III

Laying out his argument shortly after the enunciation of his two principles, Anselm states: "Be it agreed between us that man was made for happiness, which cannot be attained in this life, and that no being can ever arrive at happiness, save by freedom from sin, and that no man passes this life without sin."[23] Here Anselm makes two points: (1) man was created for happiness and (2) because of sin man cannot attain such beatitude. These assumptions are the premises of his argument which concludes by saying that the Incarnation, suffering, death and Resurrection of Christ were necessary. While Anselm puts off the discussion of the first premise (that man was made for happiness) until Book II, it is appropriate to look at the philosophical justification of this premise first since it is the major premise in the argument.

Anselm begins with the observable fact that human beings seek what is true and good. This is obvious, and to say such a thing does not seem too surprising. However, Anselm goes on to say that since we seek the true and the good, we shall find the ultimate truth and the ultimate good,[24] or at least some of us will.[25] A rational desire to know the good does not end until it reaches the ultimate good, for if a good is recognized as being a means to another good, we want the other good, or if a good is only a partial good, then we want the whole good. Now the good that is good in itself and wholly good is God. Therefore, we desire to know and love God.

Accepting this conclusion, nevertheless we must ask why, given our natural desire for God, we should achieve the object of our desire. Anselm's argument is curiously reminiscent of Aristotle's argument in *De caelo* where Aristotle says that nature does nothing in vain.[26] The difference is that Anselm, as might be expected since he believes in a creator and designer of nature, says that God (not nature) does nothing in vain. Why does Anselm say this? Surely, God is not under any compulsion at all to create anything, nor to bring things to fulfillment. While Anselm will grant this,[27] he does not think that there is any reason to believe that God will not bring his creatures to fulfillment, and he thinks that there are good reasons to believe that he will, based on the natures he has created. In fact, it is precisely because God creates under no compulsion, and precisely because his will is all-powerful, and his wisdom infinite, that human nature will achieve happiness. There is nothing in God's creation that takes him by surprise. One cannot even say that God is surprised by our sin. Thus, if he freely created us to be what we find ourselves to be, i.e., creatures who desire happiness which, for a rational creature, is to be in God's presence, there is no reason to believe that he will not fulfill his design. Nothing can stop him, not even our sin, and since he is perfectly wise and good, we have no reason to doubt that he wills the perfection of what he has made. In Anselm's own words:

> It would not be proper for him to fail in his good design, because wanting nothing in himself he began it for our sake and not his own. For what man was about to do was not hidden from God at his creation; and yet by freely creating man, God as it were bound himself to complete the good which he had begun.[28]

We turn now to sin, and the relation between sin and God's will and ability to save us (as Anselm puts it, the "necessity" of God saving us). Having established the fact that the human being was made for happiness, Anselm goes on to show that, because of sin, happiness is presently unavailable to the human being. Anselm does not attempt to answer the question "Do we sin?" probably because he takes this as immediately evident. No one always does what he knows he should. Anselm defines sin as "not to render to God his due."[29] And what is due to God? Anselm answers that we owe everything to God. Since all that exists is created by God, everything is his. It is not that God needs anything, or that we hurt him in sinning. Perfect in himself and first cause of everything, God is not affected by his creatures. To sin is to hurt oneself. Anselm avers that the only thing we take from God is the good he had planned for us,[30] that is, our happiness.

While our sin does not hurt God, sin is nonetheless a disorder in creation, and it is unsuitable that God (who is perfect) should allow any disorder to exist in what he has made.[31] Therefore, either restoration must be made, or man is to be eternally punished. Otherwise, God cannot be just, nor man happy.[32] The trouble is, the enormity of the sin (judged by the object sinned against, i.e., God) is infinite, and man cannot give God anything which is not already due to God, let alone something infinitely valuable.

Since man cannot pay, one might object that he is not unjust in not paying, for one is only obliged to do something which one can do. To this objection, Anselm answers that it is man's own fault that he cannot pay. Thus, he is doubly unjust, first, because he violated the good will that God had given him, and secondly, because he cannot repay his debt: "By his own fault [he] disabled himself, so that he can neither escape his previous obligation not to sin, nor pay the debt which he has incurred by sin."[33] If we say that God could just forgive man's iniquity without repayment, we are suggesting that God is either unable to obtain payment (since man cannot pay) in which case we impugn his omnipotence, or we are suggesting that he is not just, since God would be making man happy on account of his sin.

Having said that man was made for happiness, but due to his own fault has made his achievement of that end impossible, Anselm asks who it is that could pay the debt and restore man to happiness. Anselm's answer is, of course, the God-man. Only the one who owes the debt *ought* to make the payment, and only someone who could give something to God *could* make the payment.[34] The payment must be infinite, since the affront of sin is infinite, and only God is infinite. To make a gift of satisfaction to God, one must have something to give, that is, something that is not already God's by justice. But all creatures are God's. The only thing that is not God's is God himself. Hence God must make the payment as man: "No man but this one ever gave to God what he was not obliged to lose, or paid a debt he did not owe."[35] What Christ gave to God was obedience, perfect obedience unto death. It is not that God required death, but that he required the man Jesus to be good. Jesus was perfectly good, and he was killed for it. In his divinity—that is, the perfect power, wisdom, and goodness of God—Christ's humanity was made perfect, even in the jaws of death. Christ did not offer himself by necessity; as God he was not constrained to obedience. Rather, he offered himself for his own honor. As Anselm says, he gave "his humanity to his divinity."[36] In this act all humanity is given the divine grace of forgiveness.

IV

Has Anselm succeeded in showing the necessity of God becoming man? At best, Anselm has only partially succeeded in his task. Granted that humanity must be saved, Anselm's arguments for the Incarnation as the way of salvation are persuasive. However, there are two good reasons not to grant the necessity of our salvation. First, the evidences in favor of our salvation are only ones of formal and final causality based on human nature, and not of efficient causality based on direct knowledge of the divine will. Second, there is the deeper problem of sin.

The reasons Anselm gives for the necessity of our salvation are based on the natural end of the human being, which is to achieve perfect happiness in knowing the true and the good. The reasons are not based on a necessity placed on God's will, for as first cause, he is not under any higher cause. Anselm's argument is that, since God made man for man's own sake (for if God is perfect, then he does not create to perfect himself), and since God is omniscient and omnipotent such that he knew man would sin and yet sin could not defeat God's plan for man, God is necessitated by his own will to save this jewel of his creation. In Anselm's own words, there is no "antecedent" necessity for God to save man, but a "subsequent" necessity based on God's free choice to create such a creature.[37] Antecedent necessity would be in the realm of efficient causality, subsequent necessity in the realm of formal and final causality. God's will is not coerced, but there are reasons, based on the formal structure and dynamism of the intellectual creature which God freely chose to create, to believe that human beings are made for happiness.

As far as they go, these arguments based on subsequent necessity are strong arguments, but they are insufficient to prove that God must save. For, God's intention in creating, which we do not know, is prior to the formal and final requirements of human nature. It is not that we find any evidence that God will not fulfill what human nature requires, just that we do not know all that he wills. In a way, Anselm is right to leave the question of God's secret intentions out and include only what we know of the natural scheme of things, for we cannot know what those intentions are, while we can know about human nature. However, we do know that God has intentions and that we cannot comprehend them. Thus, this objection is one of caution, not of contrary evidence.

Contrary evidence does come into play with the consideration of sin. Anselm himself uses the fact of sin in the second premise of his argument to explain why human beings could not have saved themselves and so needed a savior in the form of the God-Man; but the fact of sin also counts against the first premise, which holds that God made man for happiness. The problem is not so much that God could not in his mercy save us from sin. God who is omnipotent can bring good out of evil. The problem comes in with judging when God is necessitated to do this. Why is it that God must save us from our sin when evidently he did not have to prevent us from sinning? For certainly God could have prevented us from sinning just as easily as he could save us after we had sinned. He did not have to let us sin any more than he had to let us wallow in sin for eternity.

The formal and final exigencies of human nature were the same before the fall as they are after the fall. If anything, the advent of evil in human choices provides an additional reason for God not to save us, since in justice we who have sinned do not deserve to be forgiven and saved. If one answers that God allowed us to sin so that he could bring good out of evil, why not apply the same principle to the loss of human nature as a whole? Perhaps God could bring good out of this, as well. Granted that there are good reasons, based in human nature's ordering to infinite happiness, for God to complete his evident intention in creating such a nature, these good reasons were also operative before the fall. It is not evident to us through natural reason why God should allow evil in one place and irradicate it in another. Or granted that there are no good reasons to believe that God would allow his creation of human nature to perish, it is also true that there are no good reasons, if one means by "reasons" evidences which we can understand by natural reason, for God to allow human beings to sin when he could easily have prevented it. Since sin is clearly bad for us, such a permissive act on God's part is not a clear manifestation of his loving nature.

Anselm's own answer to why God did not prevent us from sinning is decidedly weak. He claims it was "because it was neither possible nor right for anyone of them [angels or our first parents] to be the same with God, as we say that man was."[38] But there is no reason why there could not be creatures, in their limited natures unequal to God, who did not sin. As to why there was no Incarnation before man sinned, Anselm says it is "because reason did not demand any such thing then, but wholly forbade it, for God does nothing without reason."[39] But neither did reason demand that we sin (do evil) so that we may be saved (good may come). Anselm is not necessarily to be faulted for not having good answers to these questions, since there are none. Such issues are mysteries at the heart of the Christian faith. They cannot be proved to be absurd, but neither can they be shown to be necessary conclusions of natural reason.

CONCLUSION

In conclusion, Anselm is right to have great confidence in reason, and right to think that there is evidence, open to natural reason, which indicates that God would save us; but there is evidence, again open to natural reason, which counts against his argument. As noted earlier, there can be no good reasons not to have confidence in reason. And placing our confidence in reason, we do find that there are arguments, based on God's free creation of a creature whose nature is only fulfilled by perfect happiness, which indicate that God would save us. God did not need to create, but did so for the good of his creatures. In his perfect wisdom and power, nothing could prevent him from bringing his plan to fruition. However, there are two reasons not to accept

Anselm's claim that God must save us. In the first place, there is no external necessity on God to act nor any way for us to know directly what God's providence is. In the second place, there is the problem of why God will not allow us to remain under sin yet permits us to sin in the first place, since sin is certainly not good for us. These are the key reasons for rejecting the overall sweep of Anselm's claim to prove the necessity of the Incarnation. Anselm has meditated deeply and fruitfully on the requirements implied in the formal and final characteristics of human nature. But it is those mysterious shadows which we meet when we attempt to spell out the hidden meaning of God's providence, or understand the darkness of sin, that keep us in wonder at the salvific mercy of the Incarnate God, a mercy beyond what the heart or mind of man could ever have guessed or hoped for.[40] And it is these shadows which diminish Anselm's claim to have proved by necessary reasons that God had to become man.

Notes

1. *Cur deus homo* I,3. All references are to the works of Anselm as they appear in S. Anselmi Opera Omnia, ed. F. S. Schmitt (Stuttgart-Bad Cannstatt: Friedrich Frommann Verlag, 1968) Volume I: *Monologion* and *Proslogion,* Volume II: *Cur deus homo.* Latin texts will also be from this work.

2. Ibid. I,6; I,8.

3. Ibid. I,6; I,8.

4. Ibid. I,6.

5. Ibid. I,8.

6. "Voluntas namque dei numquam est irrationabilis." *Cur deus homo* I,8 (p. 59). The translation is from St. Anselm: Basic Writings, trans. S. N. Deane Lasalle, Illinois,: Open Court Publishing Company, 1962, p. 190. All translations will be from Deane.

7. ". . . qualiter mors illa rationabilis et necessaria monstrari possit." Ibid. I,10 (p. 66); Deane, p. 200.

8. Ibid. II,17.

9. "But I wish all that I say to be received with this understanding, that, if I shall have said anything which higher authority does not corroborate, though I appear to demonstrate it by argument, yet it is not to be received with any further confidence, than as so appearing to me for the time, until God in some way make a clearer revelation to me." (. . . sed eo pacto quo omnia quae dico volo accipi: Videlicet ut, si quid dixero quod maior non confirmet auctoritas—quamvis illud ratione probare videar—non alia certitudine accipiatur, nisi quia interim ita mihi videtur, donec deus mihi melius aliquo modo revelet.) Ibid. I,2 (p. 50); Deane, 181.

10. ". . . volo tecum pacisci, ut nullum vel minimum inconveniens in deo a nobis accipiatur, et nulla vel minima ratio, si maior non repugnat, reiciatur. Sicut enim in deo quamlibet parvum inconveniens sequitur impossibilitas, ita quamlibet parvam rationem, si maiori non vincitur, comitatur necessitas." Ibid. I,10 (p. 67); Deane, p. 200.

11. Cf. *De trinitate* VIII,ii,3ff. Anselm himself tells us that he wanted to do no more in *Monologion* than present a precis of what he found in *De trinitate.* See Frederick Van Fleteren, "The Influence of Augustine's *De trinitate* on Anselm's *Monologion,*" to appear in *Proceedings of the Anselm Conference,* Paris 1991.

12. *Monologion* I. It should be noted that Aquinas's Fourth Way is much like this argument.

13. "Denique non solum omnia bona per idem aliquid sunt bona, et omnia magna per idem aliquid sunt magna, sed quidquid est, per unum aliquid videtur esse." Ibid. III (p. 15); Deane, p. 41.

14. ". . . credimus te esse aliquid quo nihil maius cogitari possit." *Proslogion* 2, (p. 101); Deane, p. 7.

15. "Solus igitur verissime omnium, et ideo maxime omnium habes esse. . . ." Ibid. 3 (p. 103); Deane, p. 9.

16. ". . . Cum tam innumerabilia bona sint, quorum tam multam diversitatem et sensibus corporeis experimur et ratione mentis discernimus: estne credendum esse unum aliquid, per quod unum sint bona quaecumque bona sunt, an sunt bona alia per aliud?" *Monologion* 1 (p. 14); Deane, p. 38.

17. ". . . quamlibet parvam rationem, si maiori non vincitur, comitatur necessitas." *Cur deua homo* I,10 (p. 67); Deane, p. 201.

18. "ratio inevitabilis," ibid. II,9 (pp. 105-06); Deane, p. 251. Also, "immutabilis ratio," ibid. II,21 (p. 132); Deane, p. 287.

19. "Quis ergo praesumat vel cogitare quod humanus intellectus valeat penetrare, quam sapienter, quam mirabiliter tam inscrutabile opus factum sit?" Ibid. II,16 (p. 117); Deane, p. 266.

20. ". . . deus facere potest, quod hominis ratio comprehendere non potest." Ibid. II,17 (p. 126); Deane, p. 278.

21. "super nubem pingere," ibid. I,4 (p. 52); Deane, p. 184.

22. "Monstranda ergo prius est veritatis soliditas rationabilis, id est necessitas quae probet deum ad ea
quae praedicamus debuisse aut potuisse humiliari;
deinde ut ipsum quasi corpus veritatis plus niteat,
istae convenientiae quasi picturae corporis sunt
exponendae." Ibid. I,4 (p. 52); Deane, p. 184.

23. ". . . constet inter nos hominem esse factum ad
beatitudinem, quae in hac vita haberi non potest,
nec ad illam posse pervenire quemquam nisi di-
missis peccatis, nec ullum hominem hanc vitam
transire sine peccato, . . ." Ibid. I,10 (p. 67);
Deane, p. 201.

24. Ibid. II,1.

25. Ibid. II,16. Anselm wants to avoid saying that all
will be saved since this is not implied by Scripture.
However, it is difficult to see how he can avoid
saying this on his principles since his reasons for
saying that some will be saved should equally
imply universal salvation, for every human being
has an intellect with a dynamism toward perfect
happiness, and no individual human being is
reducible to being merely part of the species.
Anselm's argument does not provide a suitable
answer to this problem.

26. Aristotle, *De caelo* II, 2 (291b14).

27. *Cur deus homo* II,5.

28. ". . . non deceat eum a bono incepto deficere
. . . quia hoc propter nos, non propter se nullius
egens incepit. Non enim illum latuit quid homo
facturus est, cum illum fecit, et tamen bonitate sua
illum creando sponte se ut perficeret inceptum
bonum quasi obligavit." Ibid. II,5 (p. 100); Deane,
p. 244.

29. ". . . non reddere deo debitum." Ibid. I,11 (p. 68);
Deane, p. 202.

30. "Did not man take from God whatever He had
purposed to do for human nature? (Nonne abstulit
deo, quidquid de humana natura facere
proposuerat?) Ibid. I,23 (p. 91); Deane p. 232.

31. Ibid. I,20.

32. Ibid. I,19.

33. ". . . sua culpa deiecit se in hanc impotentiam, ut
nec illud possit solvere quod debebat ante pecca-
tum, id est ne peccaret, nec hoc quod debet, quia
peccavit, inexcusabilis est." Ibid. I,24 (p. 92);
Deane, p. 234.

34. Ibid. II,6.

35. "Nullus umquam homo moriendo praeter illum
deo dedit quod aliquando necessitate periturus
non erat, aut solvit quod non debebat." Ibid. II,18
(p. 127); Deane, p. 280.

36. "humanitatem suam divinitati suae," ibid. II,18 (p.
129); Deane, p. 283.

37. "praecedens, sequens," ibid. II,17 (p. 125); Deane,
p. 276.

38. "Quoniam nec debuit nec potuit fieri, ut unus-
quisque illorum esset idem ipse qui deus, sicut de
homine isto dicimus." Ibid. II,10 (p. 108); Deane,
p. 255.

39. ". . . quia ratio tunc fieri nullatenus hoc exigebat,
sed omnino, quia deus nihil sine ratione tacit, pro-
hibebat." Ibid. II,10 (p. 108); Deane, p. 255.

40. Along these lines there is a kind of explanation
(clearly not a necessary demonstration) that can
be given for God's permitting and forgiving our
sin. For if God created us for our own sake, and it
is good for us to know the fountain of all truth
and goodness, i.e., God, then it can be said that, in
the mystery of sin and redemption, we learn that
God is unfathomable love. For it is a love beyond
what we could imagine or hope which not only
gives us existence through creation when we do
not deserve it, but gives us a share in the divine
life through redemption when we deserve eternal
death.

Ryan Topping (essay date February 2002)

SOURCE: Topping, Ryan. "Transformation of the Will
in St. Anselm's *Proslogion*: A Response to Augustine's
Articulation of the Problem of Human Evil." *European
Legacy* 7, no. 1 (February 2002): 33-43.

[*In the following essay, Topping explores Anselm's
response to St. Augustine's formulation of human will
as the root cause of evil, seeing Anselm's solution to
this problem in the transformation of man's will through
the contemplation of God.*]

1. INTRODUCTION

Anselm wrote the ***Proslogion*** between 1077 and 1078
while abbot of the Benedictine monastery at Bec, in
Normandy. While little is known of his youth, much is
known about his latter years. He entered Bec in 1060,
and held the post of Prior for almost 15 years before
becoming abbot. Bec was a well known monastery in
the 11th century and, because of his brilliance and wise
counsel Anselm was in 1089 ordained Archbishop of
Canterbury. He was later exiled by King William Rufus
of England for refusing to acquiesce certain rights of
the Church to the imprudent ruler. As abbot and as
Bishop, then, did Anselm conduct his copious study
amidst the turmoil of 11th century feudalism.[1] His writ-

ings were not taken up until the next century at the University of Paris, but from that time forward one requires only a superficial knowledge of the subsequent history of European thought to recognize Anselm's perennial influence.[2]

In this essay I attempt to outline the historical progression of one aspect of metaphysical doctrine from Augustine to Anselm. I argue that Anselm's emphasis on the transformation of the will through philosophical reflection on God in the *Proslogion* is a significant development in the history of the Latin tradition. My argument has two main parts. In the following section, I argue that Augustine's interpretation of the *Genesis* narrative places emphasis on the will as the *cause* of the introduction of evil into creation. I look chiefly at the *City of God* as Augustine's final statement on the relation of human will to the problem of evil. This is justified as the work is Augustine's last significant statement on the subject. In Section 3 I begin by introducing the *Proslogion* text through an examination of the relationship between faith and reason in Anselm. Next, I look at chapters II and III of the *Proslogion* argument as key texts, from which I will argue that the whole of the *Proslogion* must be considered in order to grasp its pedagogical purposes. Finally, I show how Anselm's emphasis on the *transformation of the will* through philosophical reflection in the *Proslogion* is a development of Augustine's earlier treatment of the will. No doubt Anselm wrote from within the tradition defined by Augustine's articulation of human nature. However, what I intend to demonstrate is how that tradition was furthered by Anselm's positive emphasis on the transformative aspect of the will in the reparation of the soul before God. We begin by looking at Augustine's account of the will in his interpretation of the Genesis narrative.

2. THE AUGUSTINIAN INTERPRETATION OF GENESIS ON EVIL AND THE NATURE OF SIN

The Genesis account is fundamental to the medieval conception of human nature. The text argues that because humanity transgressed God's moral Law in the Garden, all creation, including human nature since that time, has been subject to decay and the presence of evil in the world.[3] In turning to St. Augustine's interpretation of the Genesis narrative we will have two questions in view: what is the nature of evil, and from where does it come?

In Book XII of *The City of God* Augustine discusses the nature of evil. Here Augustine tells us that evil, in fact, should not be thought to be something existing in itself. He reasons that since the Creator God (cause) is good, everything that has being (effect) must also be good. Accordingly evil can only be thought of as a cor-

ruption of a good nature.[4] Evil is not a *thing* but a perversion of something good. It is the absence of good. In the 12th century Christian understanding it is God which alone possesses supreme existence since he is the cause of all that is. Consequently, there is a proper relationship between Being and beings in creation. There exists a proper order for the angelic powers, and within the human soul itself. The mind is to be fixed upon God as He is the only Good (and the common Good) which will bring to us happiness.[5] This proper order, the mind in contemplation and the will directed in devotion to God, describes the original state which we have fallen from, and even in this life must seek to return to. Thus evil is understood to be *a turning away from the Being and Will of Supreme Existence towards a lesser existence.* Where does evil come from then? In the sixth chapter Augustine discusses the cause of the wicked angels' misery, and says that their misery is the result of their "turning away from Him who supremely is, and their turning towards themselves, who do not exist to that supreme degree."[6] And as such, the source of evil is in the will of a rational creature. To illustrate this Augustine offers an example of two like-minded men who view the same woman, one holding fast to his chastity, the second being stirred to enjoy her body unlawfully.[7] The questioned posed is this: what is the cause of the evil choice in the one man and not the other? Augustine argues that it could have been neither the woman's body, nor the minds of the men, since each saw the same flesh and were assumed to be similar in disposition. The only answer possible is that the one consented in his will to lust while the other did not.[8] More exactly, the source of evil is in the turning of the will towards a lesser existence. The beginning of an evil will is to "defect from him who is the Supreme Existence, to something of less reality."[9] Recalling Genesis III, we may say that when the serpent, representing human will tempted Eve with the knowledge that would enable them to "be as gods" she turned away from the supreme good to a lesser good, and it was the very act of turning the will towards the lower existence (i.e. her own self) which was the evil act. Hence, the fall of humanity was caused by the desiring of an inferior thing in a perverted manner.[10]

What may we conclude from our survey of Augustine's teaching on evil? First, we have seen that evil does not exist in or of itself. Since God (Cause) is good, all of creation (effect) is also good. Evil can only be said to *exist* in a qualified sense, as a decay of a good nature which already exists. It is an absence of a good that ought to be there. Second, and more importantly, the source of evil is in the *will* of rational creatures. Humans and angels choose to do evil out of their own free will. Further, evil itself consists in the turning of one's will from a higher good to a lower good which is against nature and the created order in the sense of God's original and good design for the universe. Speaking of Adam and Eve, Augustine writes that their "defection [away from God's will towards their own] is evil in itself, as a defection from Him who supremely exists to something of a lower degree of reality; and this is contrary to the order of nature."[11] Later, in Book XIV Augustine asks: what is pride except a longing for a perverse kind of exaltation? He continues, "it is a perverse kind of exaltation to abandon the basis on which the mind should be firmly fixed, and to become, as it were, based on oneself, and so remain."[12] In short, since the fall of humanity this is exactly the position which we find ourselves in: where human will, as the cause of evil, is misdirected towards lesser goods, leading the human soul away from its intended destiny. And it is in the awareness of this distorted condition of the human will that Anselm provides his answer to Augustine's articulation of the problem of evil.

3. St. Anselm's *Proslogion*

3.1. Faith Seeking Understanding in the Proslogion

In the *Proslogion* St. Anselm is engaged in the act of turning his mind towards God. The text is written as though directed to God, and within it we find the language of lament and despair, and finally of hope in the future beatific vision of God.

From Anselm's own preface we find that the *Proslogion* was written after an earlier tract entitled the *Monologion*. The *Monologion* is described as a meditation on the meaning of faith from the perspective of one "seeking, through silent reasoning within himself, things he knows not." After completing this work, the author is said to have wondered whether it was possible to find one single argument "that for its proof required no other save itself, and that by itself would suffice to prove that God really exists, that He is the supreme good needing no other and is He whom all things have need of for their being and well-being, and also to prove whatever we believe about the Divine Being." To paraphrase, Anselm has set for his argument three main tasks: (a) to establish the existence and then (b) to establish something about the nature of that-than-which-nothing-greater-can-be-thought and finally, (c) to prove that this being is in fact the God of the Christian faith.[13]

What is the meaning of the *Proslogion* subtitle? Anselm's original title for the work was "faith seeking understanding," which later became the subtitle.[14] The given subtitle was taken from an earlier Neoplatonic/Augustinian tradition of interpretation of the relationship between faith and rational argument.[15] A detailed exploration into the nature of both Augustine's and Anselm's belief about the relationship between faith and reason would be necessary to fully appreciate the given subtitle. As this task is beyond the scope of the present essay, I will nevertheless offer a few necessary introductory comments on Anselm's understanding of the place of faith and reason in the relationship to our knowledge of God. We will look to both the *Cur Deus Homo* as well as *The Author's Reply to Gaunilo* for insights into Anselm's own position.

Anselm asserts the primacy of reason. In his writings Anselm argues that knowledge of Christian doctrine is possible through purely rational demonstration. To illustrate, we find in the *Cur Deus Homo* Anselm discussing with Boso, who assumes the role of an unbeliever, the necessity of certain Christian dogmas and that they are discoverable to any rational intellect, independent of faith. In the preface Anselm makes clear his intent to prove in Book 1 "by necessary reasoning that (Christ being left out of the question as though nothing were known of Him) it is impossible for any man to be saved without Him." In Book 2: "as if nothing were known of Christ" to show by reasoning that human nature has been constituted for the end of knowing immortality which could only be effected by means of a God-man.[16] Throughout the work Anselm commits himself to Boso's request to offer reasons for the necessity of believing the Christian doctrine of Christ,[17] as though Boso himself were an unbeliever, and therefore without appealing to special revelation (such as the Tradition of interpretation embodied in the Church, or the Holy Scriptures).[18] Further, at the end of *Cur Deus Homo* Boso concludes that Anselm's rational proofs "would satisfy, by reason alone, not only Jews, but even [the] Pagan" that God necessarily become man.[19]

In the same way we find in the discussion between Anselm and the monk Gaunilo, that Anselm answers the objections raised as if the argument presented in the *Proslogion* were to be accepted by any rational mind. For example, Gaunilo in his reply purely on behalf of the fool treats Anselm's argument as if it were meant to be accepted on rational grounds. In this way he concludes his objection to Anselm's assertion that "that which is greater than everything truly exists in reality" by stating that: "It must first of all be proved to me then that this same greater than everything truly exists in reality somewhere, and then only will the fact that it is greater than everything make it clear that it also subsists in itself."[20] We must conclude, then, that Anslem has accepted Gaunilo's interpretation of his work since his reply offers no reasons from Scripture or Tradition in support of his original argument. Further, Anselm takes up Gaunilo's challenge and answers as though he were speaking to the Fool of the eighth Psalm who has no belief in the existence of God.[21]

Therefore, in both the *Cur Deus Homo* and Anselm's *Reply* to Gaunilo, Anselm believes reason is able to show to the unbeliever that the truths of Christianity are discoverable through rational argument alone. Anselm's rationalism, however, does not stand in isolation. We find a second equally prominent element within his thought about faith and reason, which stands along side the first.

In his philosophical speculations Anselm asserts the primacy of faith. There is a profound sense of humility which Anselm ascribes to our ability to know God by reason. Although all things may conceivable be known rationally, not all things can be known exhaustively. For example, he believes that our knowledge of God will never be complete: "whatever a man can say or write on the subject, the deeper reasons for so great a truth still remain concealed."[22] It is in the recognition of our humble state, therefore, that Anselm believes there to be a proper order of inquiry for the believer. He writes as if proper reasoning about theology depended upon God's grace—that His unmerited favor were necessary in all of our reasoning about divine matters. For instance, in the second chapter of **Cur Deus Homo** Boso begins by saying that it is the right order of investigation to first believe the deep things of the Christian faith before presuming to discuss them by reason. The way in which Anselm frames the entire dialogue, in fact, embodies his understanding of the way in which "faith seeking understanding" is to be practiced. That is, within the structure of the dialogue we find the principle that faith should precede the search for reasons to be embodied. Boso clearly testifies at the outset of their discussion that he holds

> [the] faith respecting our redemption so firmly that even if I could not comprehend what I believe by any process of reasoning, there is nothing which could tear me away from its firm basis.

In the same sentence Boso continues by adding that it would be

> a sign of negligence if after we have been confirmed in the faith we are not eager to understand what we believe.[23]

In other words, it would only be a weakness of will and of faith which would cause Boso to doubt that which has been received from God by revelation. In this way we realize the significance of understanding faith in terms of the theological virtue of reason. Reason accepts on the authority of God those things which it could not have discerned on its own. Reason is in no way contrary to the theological virtue of faith, but finds its completion and proper end within it. Before Anselm agrees to continue Boso's rational method of inquiry into the necessity of Christ's Incarnation two things occur. First, he is exhorted by Boso to remain courageous (i.e. the virtue of the will) in his attempt to explain his ideas because God often makes clear what was once

concealed to those who are looking into these matters.[24] And secondly, Anselm himself insists that if he speaks anything which "a higher authority does not confirm, although I seem to prove it by reason, it be not received as a certainty, but only as what in the meanwhile seems true to me" until God in some way gives me a clearer revelation (i.e. the virtue of reason knowing that it is perfected by faith in the authority of God's word).[25] Here again we see the proper relationship between reason and the will being articulated. One must continue in the courage of believing that which reason has recognized to be given from God. For Anselm, clearly, reason is not an autonomous power of the mind, wholly sufficient to articulate divine truth.

What may we conclude, then, about Anselm's belief about the nature of faith in relation to reason, and subsequently the meaning of the **Proslogion** subtitle "faith seeking understanding?" First, that some of the defining truths of Anselm's Christianity such as the existence of God and that a mediator was required to bring about the redemption of man, are such that they may be rationally proved to be necessary. We see this in Anselm's acceptance of both Gaunilo's interpretation of the **Proslogion** argument as being a completely sufficient proof for God's existence, and further, from his own outlined purposes for the **Cur Deus Homo** argument to prove the logical necessity of the Incarnation.

Second, and more importantly for our purposes, we saw that there exists a proper order of inquiry for the believer. Reason itself is not a wholly sufficient power of the mind. It is therefore most rational that human reason should acknowledge its own limitations and believe in the words of a higher authority. Reason, then, is to be submitted before the authority of Christian revelation, and exercised alongside prayer in humility before God's great and unknowable essence. In the **Proslogion** Anselm is in fact attempting to do much more than offer a purely rational *a priori* argument for God's existence. When one considers the entirety of the text we see that faith seeking understanding encompasses more than a logical demonstration, *but an act of the will turning the rational power of the soul towards God*. Before engaging the text as a whole, we will turn to the opening argument itself where Anselm defends his famous definition. For the purposes of clarification I have numbered the logical sequence by which the argument proceeds.

3.2. ANSELM'S ONTOLOGICAL ARGUMENT

In chapter II we find Anselm's definition of God as "that than which nothing greater can be thought." After petitioning God to grant understanding, Anselm offers the above definition of God and then immediately asks how it is that the Fool (spoken of in Psalm 14) may say in his heart that there is no God? He first (1) distinguishes existence in the mind from existence in reality and cites as an example of this distinction a painter who plans out a picture in his mind before executing it. By analogy he argues that once the Fool hears this definition, necessarily, it is logical to agree that God (that than which nothing greater can be thought) exists at least in the mind—since whatever is understood must be in the mind. Next, (2) Anselm infers that we are compelled to believe that-than-which-nothing-greater-can-be-thought cannot exist in the mind alone. Since (2a) if we admit that that-than-which-nothing-greater-can-be-thought exists in the mind, than (we should all recognize that) "God" can further be thought of as existing in both mind and reality. Hence, as it is *greater* to exist in both the mind and in reality, then (3) that-than-which-a-greater-*cannot*-be-thought (God existing in both the mind and reality) is the same thing as that-than-which-a-greater-*can*-be-thought: and this would be a contradiction of terms. Therefore, (4) Anselm concludes that "there is no doubt that something that than which nothing greater can be thought exists both in the mind and in reality."

Nowhere within this text does Anselm offer a justification for his belief that actual existence is greater than potential existence, which is key to his argument. This should not be seen as an oversight, however, but understood in relation to Anselm's knowledge of earlier (and in his estimation) proven foundations which were well argued by Neoplatonists. We may recall, for instance, St. Augustine's proof in the *Confessions* demonstrating the reasons why evil must be thought of as an absence of goodness rather than as a substance in itself (*Conf.* VII, xii, 18). Building upon Augustine's argument about the nature of evil as the *absence* of goodness it is clear how it is that some beings possess greater or lesser amounts of goodness. Thus, a virtuous woman possesses more goodness than a morally deficient woman. And as possession of goodness is a constitutive characteristic necessary for fulfilling the *telos* of human nature, the good person can rightly be said to possess existence to a greater degree than an evil person. Instead of imagining existence to be an attribute which a thing either does or does not possess, then, reflection upon the nature of evil allows us to see how existence is something which beings possess in varying degrees.

Next, we turn to Anselm's "second proof" found in the third chapter. Although Anselm believed chapter III to be a supporting and complimentary argument to the preceding chapter, some commentators have thought this second argument to make the first redundant.[26] Whether this is so is not our concern here. It is clear, however, that both chapters II and III employ the same common definition of God as that-than-which-nothing-

greater-can-be-thought. Anselm opens the chapter: "certainly this being so truly exists that it cannot be even thought not to exist. For something can be thought to exist that cannot be thought not to exist, and this is greater than that which can be thought not to exist."

The argument's premise may be simplified thus: since we can think of something that necessarily exists (*x*)—and that which does not necessarily exist (*y*) is lesser—given the above definition of God as that which nothing greater can be thought, it follows that God necessarily exists. Further, since everything else can be thought not to exist except for God, He alone is the one who may be said to possess "existence to the highest degree." It is from this last premise that Anselm will later deduce divine attributes such as omnipotence and His infinity (see chapters VII and XIII).[27] In short, following La Croix's summation of the two chapters, we may say that these two chapters represent one move in a larger effort to establish: (i) whatever must be believed about God; (ii) that that-than-which-a-greater-cannot-be-thought *exists;* and, more importantly (iii) that this being of which nothing greater can be thought bears all the properties identified with the Christian God.[28]

It has not been my intention to evaluate the content of the *Proslogion* argument for the existence of God. Rather through reproducing the structure of the key text within Anselm's work, I hope to illustrate the pedagogical nature of the whole of the *Proslogion* argument in the final section of our discussion.

3.3. TRANSFORMATION AND THE WILL IN THE ASCENT OF THE SOUL: ANSWERING AUGUSTINE

How does our earlier understanding of faith seeking understanding apply to the key chapters of the text, in the light of the larger *Proslogion* argument? That is, what is Anselm himself doing by turning his reason, by an act of his will, to the consideration of the existence and properties of God? This turn is clearly what Anselm invites us to take part in from the opening sentences of the book, and again as echoed in the 24th chapter:

> Come now, insignificant man, fly for a moment from your affairs, escape for a little while from the tumult of your thoughts. Put aside your weighty cares and leave your wearisome toils. Abandon yourself for a little while to God and rest for a little in Him . . . Come then, Lord my God, teach my heart where and how to seek You, where and how to find You.
>
> Now, my soul, rouse and lift up your whole understanding and think as much as you can on what kind and how great this good is.

From the first chapter onward the *Proslogion* is written in the language of prayer directed towards God. In the opening chapter and throughout Anselm's prayer is often a bitter lament to God for the wretched, and fallen condition which we find ourselves in. In Eden we were able to see God, but now we are blinded by the smoke of sin and our utter darkness. Anselm is painfully aware of his own neediness and lack before God, and echoing the language of the Psalmist he cries out in his opening chapter: "Give yourself to us that it may be well with us, for without You it goes so ill for us. Have pity upon our efforts and our strivings towards You, for we can avail nothing without you" (see for example Ps 90, 130). Anselm invokes the presence of God to uphold and educate his soul's striving towards Him. Continuing in the opening chapter he prays, "Teach me to seek you, and reveal yourself to me as I seek, because I can neither seek you if you do not teach me how, nor find you unless you reveal yourself."[29]

Though he has roused his intellect by an act of the will, still he does not experience what he knows he has found.[30] In his striving towards knowledge of God he finds that he cannot attain what his will has set out to do. The more he realizes he does not know, the more he is brought to despair at his separation from God. His will moves his reason to apprehend God, but he finds that he is thrown back to the darkness from which he first ascended.[31]

How are we to reconcile these two modes of speech within the *Proslogion*? The one is highly technical, as illustrated in our discussion of *Proslogion* II and III. The other is highly personal and at all times moving between the language of praise and lament. Sometimes he is elated, while at other times Anselm is brought to despair because he (partially) fails in his efforts to gain knowledge of the Creator.[32] The two parts of speech are accounted for once we see that they are intended to be part of a single effort aimed at the reparation of the human soul. Anselm has engaged in the act of turning his mind towards God, yet he experiences despair in this seeking with his will, because he cannot find God who is hidden and unknown to him.[33] Through whatever mode of speech employed in the *Proslogion* Anselm is participating in the reparation and the proper ordering of his soul through reflection upon the existence and nature of Deity.

Anselm engages in the act of rousing his mind to the contemplation of God, in an act of the will aided by divine assistance. Philosophically, what is going on during the *Proslogion* to the monk's soul? Anselm, and those who accept his invitation, engage in a pedagogical exercise through which *the effects of the fall are reversed by a reparation of the power of the will.* In short, through the movement of his will towards God he is participating with God's grace in the restoration of his soul to its proper order and harmony.

In conclusion, we can now return to complete our original task, which is to show how it is that Anselm's emphasis on the transformation of the will is an answer to Augustine's formulation of the problem of human evil. To summarize our findings: first, we recall that Augustine identified the human will as the cause of evil, and the means by which humans turn away from contemplation of God in his philosophical interpretation of the *Genesis* narrative. Second, we looked at Anselm's understanding of the relationship between faith and reason. In this we discovered that for Anselm reason properly ordered exists along side the habit of faith, and one consequence of this relationship is that rational speculation is to take place within the context of prayer. That is, the intellect for Anselm is logically dependent upon divine assistance. Third, we looked at *Proslogion* II and III as our primary textual example of the *Proslogion* argument. In this we concluded that the whole of the *Proslogion* text must be considered as part as a single argument, which itself is intended for certain pedagogical purposes.

Finally, in relation to Augustine's articulation of the relationship between the human will and the cause of evil we see that Anselm has provided an answer to the earlier problem as set out in the *City of God*. Anselm's emphasis on the transformative aspect of the human will in the role of the contemplation of God responds to Augustine's earlier statement on the defective results which came about because of human will. Now, in Anselm we find within the *Proslogion* that it is through the faculty of the human will, always aided by God through prayer, that the effects of the first transgression are to be partially repaired by returning the mind's contemplation, once again, toward the Supreme Good.

Notes

1. For a good general introduction to Anselm's life and times see M.J. Charlesworth's introduction in *St. Anselm's Proslogion* (Oxford: Oxford University Press, 1965), 8-21.

2. In the 13th century both Aquinas (cf. *Summa Contra Gentiles,* I, chs 10-11) and Bonaventure (cf. *Quaestiones disputatae de mysterio Trinitatis,* q. 1, a. 1) were influenced by Anselm's *Proslogion* argument in some form. In the modern period Descartes, Kant, and Leibniz each responded to various aspects of Anselm's thought. For some contemporary responses see John Hick and Arthur C. McGill, *The Many Faced Argument* (New York: The Macmillan Co., 1967).

3. See Book XIV.3, 513. Note: All references to St. Augustine's work, *Concerning The City of God Against the Pagans,* are taken from the edition by David Knowles, translated by Henry Bettenson (Great Britain: Penguin Books, 1972).

4. "Therefore it is not by nature but by a perversion that the rebellious creation differs from the good, which adheres to God; yet even this perversion shows how great and honorable is the nature itself. For if we are right to condemn the perversion, that shows without doubt that the nature is honorable, since what justifies the condemnation of the perversion is that the perversion disgraces a nature which deserves honor." Book XII.1, 472.

5. Book XII.1, 471.

6. Book XII.6, 477.

7. Book XII.6, 478.

8. Further, he asks: "How can a nature which is good, however changeable, before it has an evil will, be the cause of any evil, the cause, that is, of that evil will itself?" To this Augustine answers that we must not look for any efficient cause of the evil act of the will. A wrong choice "is not a matter of efficiency, but of deficiency; the evil will itself is not effective but defective . . . To try to discover the causes of such defection . . . is like trying to see darkness or to her silence." Book XII.6-7, 478-9.

9. Book XII.7, 479.

10. "How, I repeat, can good be the cause of evil? For when the will leaves the higher and turns to the lower, it becomes bad not because the thing to which it turns is bad, but because the turning itself is perverse. It follows that it is not the inferior thing (the lower, created nature whatever that may be) which causes the evil choice; it is the will itself, because it is created, that desires the inferior thing in a perverted and inordinate manner." Book XII.7, 478.

11. Book XII.8, 480.

12. Book XIV.13, 571.

13. I am here following Richard La Croix's determination of the structure of the *Proslogion* text by which he argues that chapters II and III are interconnected components of a single argument (*Proslogion II and III*) especially see 3, 17. This interpretation is against Charlesworth (*Proslogion*), 77ff.

14. Etienne Gilson, *History of Christian Philosophy in the Middle Ages* (London: Sheed and Ward, 1955), 132.

15. For a concise summary of the uses of faith (*pistos*) in the New Testament see Thomas Oden, *Systematic Theology Vol. 1: The Living God* (New York: Harper San Francisco, 1987). Also, see a discussion on faith and reason in St. Augustine in relation to St. Anselm in *St. Anselm's Proslogion,* translated with an introduction and philosophical commentary by M.J. Charlesworth (Oxford: Clarendon Press, 1965), 26-30.

16. All quotations from *Cur Deus Homo* are taken from Edward S. Prout's translation (London: The Religious Tract Society).

17. That is, the doctrine that only a mediator participating fully in both the human and divine nature could effect the atoning sacrifice which was made possible through Christ's vicarious death. See the *New Bible Dictionary,* eds J.D. Douglas, F.F. Bruce *et al.* s.v. "Atonement," (Illinois: Intervarsity Press, 1996), by L.L. Morris.

18. Book 1.2, 137.

19. Book 2.22, 176.

20. Charlesworth, *A Reply on Behalf of the Fool,* ch. 5, 163.

21. From the opening of Anselm's reply "*Since it is not the Fool . . .* but one who, though speaking on the Fool's behalf, is an orthodox Christian and no fool, it will suffice if I reply to the Christian" (emphasis mine) a question arises: would Anselm have chosen not to defend his argument if it were objected to by a fool? As G.R. Evans points out in her work *Philosophy and Theology in the Middle Ages* (New York: Routledge, 1993), 51-2, Anselm's purpose in the *Proslogion* is to "heighten faith, and ground it in intellectual apprehension, not to win to faith recalcitrant or slow minds." We should keep in view that Anselm's meditation is in the language of prayer primarily directed towards God, and that he is not in the first instance engaged in a polemic with unbelievers. As such, Anselm's purposes in the *Proslogion* "proof" of the 11th century cannot be legitimately compared to the situation which confronted the 18th and 19th century apologists who were writing against persons who actually needed to be convinced of God's existence.

22. Ibid., 37. Similarly, Anselm comfortably holds both the sufficiency of our rationality and its necessary humility in discerning truths about God in tension: "The will of God ought to be a sufficient reason for us when He does anything, though we may not see why He so wills it, for the will of God is never unreasonable." Book 1.8, 48. On this point Anselm echoes St. Paul's dictum in I Corinthians 13.12 that while we live on earth we shall only ever know in part, seeing "as through a glass darkly."

23. *Cur Deus Homo,* Book 1.2, 34.

24. Ibid., 35.

25. Ibid., 37.

26. M.J. Charlesworth takes this view in *St. Anselm's Proslogion,* 73. Contrarily, Richard R. La Croix argues that chapters II and III are logically interrelated parts of the *Proslogion's* single argument, *Proslogion II and III: A Third Interpretation of Anselm's Argument* (Leiden, Netherlands: E.J. Brill), 11-7.

27. This connection is pointed out by F.C. Copleston, *A History of Medieval Philosophy* (Great Britain: Harper and Row Publishers, 1972), 75.

28. I have here followed La Croix's determination of the relation between *Proslogion II and III.* La Croix argues that his "analysis revealed that Anselm does not purport to establish the existence of God in either *Pros.* II or *Pros.* III, but rather, that he purports to establish there the existence and something about the existence of the being than-which-a-greater-cannot-be-thought." Ibid., 77.

29. *Proslogion,* ch. 1, 115.

30. "Have you found, O my soul, what you were seeking? You were seeking God, and you found Him to be something which is the highest of all . . . But if you have found [Him], why is it that you do not experience what you have found? Why O Lord God, does my soul not experience You if it has found You." Ibid, ch. 14, 135.

31. "Behold, once more confusion, once more sorrow and grief stand in my way as I seek joy and happiness! Even now my soul hoped for fulfillment, and, lo, once again it is overwhelmed by neediness! . . . I strove to ascend to God's light and I have fallen back into my own darkness." Ibid., ch. 18, 139.

32. The place of human desire in Anselm's intellectual ascent is highlighted in Marilyn McCord Adam's essay "Romancing the Good: God and the Self According to St. Anselm of Canterbury," in *The Augustinian Tradition,* ed. Gareth B. Matthews (Berkeley: University of California Press, 1999).

33. Ermanno Bencivenga gives an insightful commentary on the differing results when contrasting Anselm's philosophical project, as a believer, and the consequences of 20th century theoretical "play" which is undergone within a fragmented and secular social order: "Without the internal balancing factor that religious reverence provided, players-scientists . . . will [force] the political and administrative powers to constantly rewrite directions for a landscape that keeps changing before their very eyes" (109). See his fascinating work *Logic and Other Nonsense: The Case of Anselm and His God* (Princeton: Princeton University Press, 1993), 108-1.

FURTHER READING

Criticism

Bäck, Allan. "Anselm on Perfect Islands." *Franciscan Studies* 43 (1983): 188-204.

Schematizes Anselm's counterargument to Gaunilo regarding that critic's objection to his lost, perfect island line of reasoning originally laid out in the *Proslogion.*

Bestul, Thomas H. "St. Anselm, the Monastic Community at Canterbury, and Devotional Writing in Late Anglo-Saxon England." *Anselm Studies: An Occasional Journal* 1 (1983): 186-98.

Reviews the manuscript tradition of Anselm's collected prayers and meditations *Orationes sive meditationes.*

Bourke, Vernon J. "A Millennium of Christian Platonism: Augustine, Anselm, and Ficino." *Proceedings of the PMR Conference* 10 (1985): 1-22.

Briefly encapsulates Anselm's philosophical thought, calling it "Theocentric Platonism," as part of a combined survey of developments in Christian Platonism from the fifth to the fifteenth century.

Colish, Marcia L. "Anselm: The Definition of the Word." In *The Mirror of Language: A Study in the Medieval Theory of Knowledge,* pp. 55-109. Lincoln: University of Nebraska Press, 1983.

Detailed exposition of the proofs for the existence of God found in Anselm's *Monologion, Proslogion* and *Contra Gaunilonem,* studied within the context of his collected theological writings.

Evans, Gillian R. "*Sententiola ad Aedificationem*: The *Dicta* of St. Anselm and St. Bernard." *Revue Bénédictine* 92, no. 1-2 (1982): 159-71.

Concentrates on the didactic sayings, parables, and *exempla* of Saints Anselm and Bernard as significant indicators of their pedagogical and theological methods frequently dismissed by modern editors and commentators.

Fröhlich, Walter. "The Genesis of the Collections of St. Anselm's Letters." *American Benedictine Review* 35, no. 3 (September 1984): 249-66.

Endeavors to reconstruct the manner and timeframe within which Anselm created his collection of personal correspondence.

Gollnick, James. "Jungian Reflections on Transformation in St. Anselm's Theology." *American Benedictine Review* 36, no. 4 (December 1985): 353-71.

Draws parallels between the theories of human transformation expressed by Anselm in his theological writings and those of psychologist Carl Jung.

Olds, Marshall. "Note on Mallarmé and Anselm." *French Literature Series* 6 (1979): 131-34.

Suggests the influence of Anselm on Stéphane Mallarmé by highlighting affinities between the *Proslogion* and the French writer's "Prose pour des Esseintes."

Pegis, Anton C. "St. Anselm and the Argument of the *Proslogion*." *Mediaeval Studies* 28 (1966): 248-51.

Summarizes and explains Anselm's principal arguments for the existence of God in the early chapters of the *Proslogion*.

Pranger, M. B. "Masters of Suspense: Argumentation and Imagination in Anselm, Bernard, and Calvin." *Assays: Critical Approaches to Medieval and Renaissance Texts* 1 (1981): 15-33.

Contrasts the diverse linguistic strategies and methods of argumentation used by Anselm, Bernard

of Clairvaux, and John Calvin in their approaches to understanding identity.

Rasmussen, Carl J. "Karl Barth on St. Anselm: A Theological Response to the Dilemma of Liberal Theory." *Graven Images: A Journal of Culture, Law, and the Sacred* 1 (1994): 37-51.

Argues that Karl Barth's 1931 study *Anselm: Fides Quarens Intellectum: Anselm's Proof of the Existence of God in the Context of His Theological Scheme* offers valuable insights toward the resolution of disputes in contemporary liberal philosophical theory.

Seifert, Josef. "*Si Deus Est Deus, Deus Est*: Reflections on St. Bonaventure's Interpretation of St. Anselm's Ontological Argument." *Franciscan Studies* 52 (1992): 215-31.

Defends St. Bonaventure's ideas in regard to the ontological argument of Anselm.

Weaver, J. Denny. "Violence in Christian Theology." *CrossCurrents* 51, no. 2 (summer 2001): 150-76.

Invokes Anselm's theological theory of satisfaction atonement (articulated in *Cur Deus Homo* and involving the universal ameliorative effect of the death of Jesus on human sin) in order to explore the paradoxical role of violence in Christian theology.

Additional coverage of Anselm's life and career is contained in the following source published by the Gale Group: *Dictionary of Literary Biography*, Vol. 115.

Eilhart von Oberge
fl. late twelfth century

German poet.

INTRODUCTION

A seminal figure among German courtly poets, Eilhart von Oberge is the author of the oldest complete version of the medieval romance of Tristan and Isolde (or, Tristant and Isalde, in Eilhart's orthography). In his *Tristant* (c. 1170) Eilhart relates the tale of a tragic love affair between the eponymous Cornish hero and an Irish princess wedded to his uncle. Featuring a protagonist controlled by his predetermined fate, Eilhart's *Tristant* is viewed by contemporary scholars as an homage to the already declining feudal social order and epic literary style of the medieval period. Because the work is presumed to be the closest among many versions to the narrative of the lost French prose archetype, scholars tend to value Eilhart's rendering of the tale particularly highly. *Tristant* is frequently studied in conjunction with other adaptations of the same material, including those by the French poet Béroul and the Anglo-Norman bard Thomas of Britain. In addition, the poem is important for its considerable influence on later versions of the story, including Gottfried von Strassburg's *Tristan* (c. 1210) and its subsequent variations.

BIOGRAPHICAL INFORMATION

Almost nothing is known about the life of Eilhart aside from his composition of the *Tristant*. Extant documentary evidence from the court of Braunschweig, including nearby Oberg, suggests that Eilhart may have been a vassal to Duke Heinrich the Lion. Some scholars speculate that he may have been commissioned to write the poem by Heinrich's second wife, Mathilde, but no conclusive proof exists to support this claim. While the majority opinion holds that Eilhart was born at Oberg and lived his life there, it is also possible that he may have composed his famous work elsewhere, or under the direction of another patron. In addition to the paucity of evidence concerning his life and career, no existing records authenticate the time or place of Eilhart's death.

TEXTUAL HISTORY

Scholars generally regard Eilhart's version of the Tristan story as the most faithful to the original French prose *Tristan* (speculatively dated between 1150 and 1160), which is now lost. Probably composed in about 1170, Eilhart's poem may have been written as late as 1190, according to some theories. Its survival into the contemporary period relies on a number of sources, including three fragmentary twelfth- to thirteenth-century manuscripts, three redactions from the fifteenth century (all complete), and a late-fourteenth-century Czech translation that includes added material to compensate for missing scenes from Eilhart's version. An extant medieval chapbook also offers a rendering of Eilhart's story in prose outline. Contemporary translations of the *Tristant* include one in French verse and an English prose adaptation by J. W. Thomas.

MAJOR WORKS

Eilhart's sole work, the *Tristant,* depicts the life of the noble warrior Tristant, a peerless knight in service of his uncle, King Mark of Cornwall. Stoic and brave, Tristant brings high honor upon himself by successfully winning battle after battle. His main adversary off the battlefield, King Mark, is usually considered to be a rather conventional villain figure (although some critics have questioned this simplification of his character). The singular object of Tristant's desire, Isalde the Fair, returns the hero's love passionately, but remains unattainable to him because she is married to Mark. For her, love is a form of exquisite suffering, and life without Tristant is inconsequential. In an early encounter in the story, Tristant challenges the Irish duke Morolt, who has unjustly demanded that Cornwall pay him tribute. Engaging in single combat on a small island, Tristant emerges victorious after delivering Morolt a mortal wound to the head. He later learns, however, that Morolt has poisoned him during the battle. Now Tristant must visit Morolt's sister, Queen Isalde of Ireland, in order to acquire an antidote. Healed by the Queen, Tristant subsequently slays a dragon that has been terrorizing the kingdom of Ireland. In return he secures the Queen's daughter, Isalde the Fair, as a bride for King Mark. On the return trip to Cornwall, Tristant mistakenly drinks a love potion prepared by the Irish Queen for her daughter and King Mark and instantly falls in love with the young maiden. After the marriage of Isalde and Mark, the secret affair between Tristant and Isalde becomes the central feature of the tale, as Mark and other jealous noblemen of the Cornish court attempt to catch Tristant and Isalde in adultery. Meanwhile, the King engages a cunning dwarf to set traps for the lovers and gather evidence of their deceit. Eventually, Mark discovers Tristant and Isalde after they have run off to the forest together. Clothed and sleeping, they lie separated by Tristant's sword. Quietly, Mark exchanges the sword for his own (an act they will be certain to notice when they awake) and departs. Afterwards, Tristant is exiled and years pass. The hero marries another woman, but cannot forget his love for Isalde. When it becomes clear that he will never again be with his beloved, he loses his will to live and dies. Shortly thereafter, Isalde arrives to join the mourners of his death. Lying beside his motionless body, she dies as well. In a symbolic denouement, two trees spring up from their graves, their limbs intertwined. In addition to the main action described above, the poem also features several Arthurian interludes, including a visit to the court of King Arthur, a stag hunt, and appearances by other noteworthy knights of the tradition. Scholars perceive the poem only peripherally as a work of Arthurian legend, insisting that such sketches in Eilhart's *Tristant* occur only briefly, serving to juxtapose an established epic setting with the closer and more problematic court of King Mark. Thematically, Eilhart's *Tristant* has been viewed as a depiction of heroic valor subverted by reckless passion. The inexorable progress of fate looms large in the poem, demonstrating that nothing can be done to change its path once certain events have transpired, even if seemingly by pure chance. Overall, the poem's theme is thought to hinge on its blending of heroic honor, fate, and passionate love.

CRITICAL RECEPTION

Scholars have traditionally analyzed Eilhart's *Tristant* alongside other versions of the Tristan legend from roughly the same period, including those by the French poet Béroul, the Anglo-Norman Thomas, and the German Gottfried von Strassburg. Through such comparisons, Eilhart's work has been found generally lacking, whether it be in terms of exposition, character delineation, or thematic development. Thus scholars have variously deemed Béroul's version (with its emphasis on passionate love and high adventure), or Thomas's and Gottfried's more psychological renderings of the Tristan legend as superior to Eilhart's somewhat informal and stylistically simplified verse narrative. Additionally, a number of scholars believe that Eilhart may have omitted some original scenes from the story (later included by subsequent authors) for the sake of clarity or brevity. Such omissions are thought to have contributed to Eilhart's avoidance of psychological depth or motivation in his characterizations, a quality often thought to mar the *Tristant*. Others have questioned Eilhart's use, or misuse, of narrative motivation in the work. Many commentators have acknowledged a lack of traditional narrative plausibility in Eilhart's *Tristant*, arguing that the inexplicable and supernatural forces of fate and chance condition and carry the action of the poem. Still others have observed that Eilhart's narrative was perhaps intended primarily as a defense of the feudal social order and its ideology. The author's focus on the inexorable power of destiny, in contrast to his characters' actions or desires, frees Tristant, Isalde, and Mark from guilt or complicity and externalizes the concerns in the story, making it an exemplum of deterministic fate and providential order in action. In this sense, scholars have noted, the poem validates the status quo of feudal hegemony, rather than analyzing the individual merits of its protagonist or other principal figures. Despite all of these objections, a contemporary trend in critical thought on the *Tristant* has been to question the received view of the poem, and instead to study the work on its own artistic merits. Recalling elements that made the poem popular in a bygone era, late twentieth-century commentators have begun to admire the dynamic qualities of Eilhart's storytelling technique, including his exploitation of narrative intervention to carry the tale, his robust style unimpeded by the demands of psychological motivation, as well as his use of low, whimsical, and almost mock-heroic humor—features almost universally lacking in contemporaneous versions of the story. Minor elements, such as Eilhart's clever use of epithets in delineating character and foreshadowing action, have also been noted. Putting aside discussion of its similarities to or departures from other versions of the tale, commentators on Eilhart's *Tristant* have instead concentrated on its skilled blend of romantic and epic forms, and have admired its artistic integrity as it traces the heroic arc of Tristant's life and the events culminating in his tragic demise.

PRINCIPAL WORKS

Tristant (poetry) c. 1170

Principal English Translations

Eilhart von Oberge's Tristant (translated by J. W. Thomas) 1978

CRITICISM

Frederick Whitehead (essay date 1959)

SOURCE: Whitehead, Frederick. "The Early Tristan Poems." In *Arthurian Literature in the Middle Ages: A Collaborative History,* edited by Roger Sherman Loomis, pp. 134-44. London: Oxford University Press, 1959.

[*In the following excerpt, Whitehead contrasts versions of the Tristan legend by Eilhart and Béroul, claiming that Eilhart's German poem suffers in comparison because of its narrative abridgement and occasional psychological implausibility.*]

THE ARCHETYPE

Nineteenth-century scholars agreed in regarding the [*Tristan*] poems of Eilhart and Béroul as essentially a single version (*version commune* or *version des jongleurs*) and in contrasting it with that of Thomas and his derivatives (*version courtoise*). Bédier, having demonstrated that the three poems and the Prose *Tristan* were derived from a common source,[1] showed that Eilhart and Béroul reproduced this archetype with great fidelity,[2] whereas Thomas made considerable changes. This was also the opinion of Gertrude Schoepperle.[3] But Bédier believed[4] that Eilhart and Béroul had departed from the archetype in limiting the effect of the potion to three or four years, and since this deviation could not have been made independently, he postulated an intermediate common source, which he called *y*.

The duration of the spell is bound up with the problem presented by Tristan's voluntarily abandoning Isolt and starting a new life in Brittany. According to Bédier,[5] the separation took place in the original as a result of a sudden awakening of the lovers' conscience, and the limitation of the potion in *y* was an attempt by this later redactor to explain something that his source had left unexplained. Thomas and the Prose *Tristan*[6] recast this account in order to avoid making the lovers' separation proceed from a sense of sin. But Bédier's hypothesis does not remove the fundamental incompatibility between the theme of the lovers' repentance and the idea that they are bound for ever by a spell whose chains they cannot break. A weakening of the potion seems the only way to give surface plausibility to a *motif* that is out of keeping with the fundamental assumptions of the story. It thus seems unnecessary to postulate an intermediate source *y*.

The archetype has been variously dated: Bédier put it not long after the Norman Conquest,[7] Gertrude Schoepperle after Chrétien de Troyes.[8] A date around 1150 or 1160 seems the most probable. Bédier treated the work as a story of love which, because it is unlawful, can only have a tragic end.[9] According to him, the plan is based on the theme of the lovers' sufferings, which grow in intensity as the story unfolds: from shame and remorse to social degradation and then on to physical separation and the quarrel between them, with death as the final refuge. Later criticism[10] has insisted on the disparity between the two halves of the story; the second half, from the separation of the lovers onward, showing a courtly inspiration which is absent from the first. Yet it cannot be denied that the theme of the potion, i.e. the theme of love as inordinate desire, which is the source of tragic suffering, gives unity to the work, however disparate the elements it contains.

EILHART AND BÉROUL

Eilhart seems to have preserved more or less faithfully the substance of the archetypal narrative. He gives us, however, the bare facts of the story without much elaboration. Moreover, his work is not just a servile translation. He has probably omitted some episodes—for example, those of the ambiguous oath[11] and of the mysterious stranger who abducts Isolt[12]—and may have added others.[13] The narrative is in places drastically abridged, and it is usually passages of great psychological interest that suffer most.[14] That Eilhart is capable of freely remodelling the details of his narrative is shown by a comparison of all four versions in the tryst under the tree and the flour on the floor episodes.

In the former episode, Béroul and Thomas agree in making the lovers' behaviour extremely guileful. Isolt declares that she has always been faithful to him who had her maidenhood. Both lovers try to dissipate the suspicion that attaches to so compromising a meeting, asserting that Tristan has sought the interview only because he hopes that Isolt will work for a reconciliation between him and Mark or, if this fails, that she will provide him with means to leave the country. The same treatment is found in the version of the Prose *Tristan* (B.N. fr. 756-7)[15] which contains the episode. In Eilhart, however, Isolt displays hostility to the hero, refusing to help him because he has brought shame on her, and ending the interview by hoping that he will never make his peace with Mark. Since Isolt would obviously not consent to a compromising interview merely in order to overwhelm the hero with reproaches and to have the satisfaction of refusing his pleas for assistance, Eilhart's treatment is lacking in plausibility.

The real weakness of Eilhart's handling comes out in the subsequent scene, where Mark requires the queen to give an account of what happened between her and Tristan in the garden. The very form of the request should reveal to Isolt that Mark has learned of the interview. Nevertheless, she denies having seen Tristan and expresses the wish never to see him again. Mark is not disturbed by the lie, but merely says that he saw what happened in the garden and asks for Isolt's help in order to get Tristan back to court. Isolt still feigns anger, upon which Mark promises, if she will only persuade Tristan to stay, to allow them to see as much of each other as they wish. It is difficult to see the purpose of Isolt's lie, difficult also to understand Mark's attitude, seeing that he assumes that Isolt is at one and the same time an enemy of Tristan and on a footing of the closest intimacy with him. In Béroul, Mark asks Isolt if she has seen Tristan recently, and this gives her an opportunity to relate everything that passed between them.

Equally close agreement between Béroul and Thomas against Eilhart is found in the scene of the flour on the floor. In Eilhart the dwarf outlines his plot to sprinkle flour on the floor in order to have traces of Tristan's footprints when he goes to Isolt's bed, but at the same time seems to anticipate the situation that arises after its breakdown—Mark is to be roused when the lovers have come together and watchers are to be posted to prevent the hero's escape. In Béroul and Thomas the king is absent when Tristan goes to Isolt and so does not catch the lovers *in flagrante delicto*.

The substance of Béroul's narrative down to the return from the forest is found in Eilhart. Béroul's account of the forest life contains, however, four additional episodes—the slaying of the dwarf by Mark, the training of the dog Husdain to hunt silently, the death of the 'riche baron' at the hands of Governal, and the invention of the bow that never fails. As Eilhart's account of the forest life is abridged, all four may go back to the original poem. One—the training of Husdain—certainly does.[16]

Although the two versions have the same general subject-matter,[17] the details of the narrative are completely different. Where the evidence of the other versions is not available, we may suspect that Eilhart has altered his original, without necessarily assuming that Béroul's account is authentic. Take the treatment of the discovery of the lovers in the forest. While Béroul stresses Mark's grief and anger as he rides to avenge his wrongs, and then brings out his revulsion of feeling when he spies the separating sword, the German poet

Depiction of Tristan kidnapping Isolde, from a 15th-century illuminated manuscript.

makes nothing of this and seems to regard Mark's leaving the sword in the place of Tristan's as more important than the reasons that prompted the act. Eilhart's account, with its complete lack of psychological motivation, cannot be attributed to the original author. On the other hand, Béroul's motivation is excellent, but just as Eilhart's account is a simplification, so this may be an elaboration. Nevertheless, it is clear that a feature in Béroul cannot be condemned just because it is absent from Eilhart or appears there in a different form.

We should be better able to appreciate Béroul's originality if we were in a position to compare his style with that of his source. At once archaic and advanced, it has epic features, while at the same time the treatment of the octo-syllabic couplet is based on that of Chrétien de Troyes.[18] Whether Béroul has simply modernized the versification of an original the technique of which had affinities with that of the epic or whether the style is completely his own cannot be determined. The emotional vigour of Béroul's account are consequent upon the style that he has adopted. Mergell[19] contrasts the coarse realism, the inclination towards violence, and the harshness of tone that mark Béroul's version with Eilhart's more placid narrative methods. These characteristics may be bound up with Béroul's own method of presentation, but the tendency towards realism and violence already existed in his source, as is shown by the presence there of an episode such as that of the lepers[20] or that of the blades at the bed, with its strange mixture of chivalric elements and what Bédier calls 'une barbarie joyeuse et superbe'. At most, therefore, Béroul has developed the story along lines laid down by his predecessor; he has not reinterpreted it in a new way.

Béroul and Eilhart differ in their attitude towards the lovers' guilt, but what we have in Béroul is again not a reinterpretation but at most the development of an idea which was implicit in the original account. Eilhart, in the scene where Brangain is substituted for Isolt, attributes Tristan's treacherous action to the influence of 'der vil unsêlige trang' (the most unhallowed drink). Béroul, on the other hand, tries to vindicate the lovers' conduct in terms of feudal law. What matters is not whether Tristan and Isolt are guilty but whether they can be proved to be so by the standards of feudal justice. Tristan behaves correctly in submitting to the king, refrains from violence against the barons who demand punishment, and he has therefore the right to trial by battle. In refusing this right, Mark becomes in a sense the offender and hence God rescues Tristan by a miracle (the leap from the chapel).[21] When negotiating the return of Isolt to Mark Tristan likewise insists that their innocence can be proved by a judicial battle. This interpretation arises too naturally out of the events of the story to be dismissed as foreign to the original poet's intentions.[22]

The episodes in Béroul that follow the separation of the lovers offer special problems. The ambiguous oath episode occurs in Thomas in a different form, but there it fits awkwardly into its context,[23] since it presupposes a situation in which the lovers are either permanently or temporarily separated. In Béroul, it seems to come at the right place—before Tristan has left Cornwall but after he has given Isolt back to Mark. It may therefore have occurred in the original at this point.[24] The noteworthy feature of the episode is its inordinate length. It branches out into a number of sub-episodes and contains an extraordinary wealth of detail, more appropriate to an episodic poem than to a chapter in a long romance. It contains farcical incidents[25] but also chivalric scenes, treated in a broadly popular style.[26] The following episode, which relates the death of the two barons, Denoalen and Godoïne, at the hands of Tristan, is introduced somewhat abruptly into the story, very much as if it were an independent *conte*. Nevertheless, it carries on the theme of vengeance over Tristan's enemies which is so prominent a feature of the first part. The absence of this episode from the archetype

and the fact that the ambiguous oath episode is so much out of scale indicates a change in Béroul's original plan, if not a change of author.[27]

Notes

1. Bédier, ii. 168-87; W. Golther in *Tristan und Isolde in den Dichtungen des Mittelalters und der neuen Zeit* (Leipzig, 1907), pp. 30-97, put forward a similar theory, deriving all extant versions from a lost Ur-Tristan. Likewise Miss Schoepperle, op. cit. i. 5-10, derived all versions except the Prose *Tristan* from an *estoire*, substantially represented by Eilhart's poem. In vol. ii, pp. 439 f., she ascribed the death of Tristan at the hands of Mark as related in the Prose *Tristan* to a source different from and perhaps earlier than the *estoire*. Most later scholars have accepted the existence of one main source for Béroul, Eilhart, and Thomas, though B. Panvini, *La Leggenda di Tristano e Isotta, Biblioteca dell' Archivum Romanicum*, xxxii (1951), proposes a much more complicated scheme of descent.

2. This is clear from his reconstruction of the archetype, op. cit. ii. 194-306.

3. G. Schoepperle, *Tristan and Isolt* (Frankfurt, London, 1913), p. 8.

4. Bédier, ii. 236-9, 306-9.

5. Ibid., pp. 88, 258.

6. According to Thomas, Mark recalled the lovers from the forest when he had been convinced of their innocence by the separating sword, but was again disillusioned by finding them together in a garden, and Tristan escaped and left the country. According to the Prose *Tristan* (Bédier, ii. 362-4), Mark carried Isolt back to his castle by force, and Tristan, wounded, went off to Brittany to be healed by Isolt of the White Hands.

7. Bédier, ii. 313.

8. Schoepperle, op. cit. i. 182 f. This, of course, is impossible if Eilhart wrote about 1170.

9. Bédier, ii. 175-8.

10. Schoepperle, op. cit. ii. 448-54; F. Ranke, *Tristan und Isold* (Munich, 1925), pp. 8-39; A. Witte in *ZDA*, lxx (1933), 177-9. According to these writers the difference implies two separate stages in the growth of the story.

11. Found in both Thomas and Béroul.

12. Found in Thomas, the Prose *Tristan* (Bédier, ii. 346), and in the Berne *Folie Tristan* (the allusion to Gamarien, vss. 378-93), therefore presumably in Béroul.

13. The visit of Tristan and Gurvenal to Cornwall, disguised as *jongleurs,* rouses suspicion since it breaks into the Kaherdin-Gargeolain story in an awkward way, and the names Haupt and Plot are obviously of Eilhart's invention.

14. For example, the first visit to the hermit Ogrin and the marriage with Isolt of the White Hands.

15. Bédier, ii. 347-53.

16. It is mentioned in the Oxford *Folie Tristan* (vss. 873 f.) and in the Prose *Tristan* (Bédier, ii. 362). Eilhart seems to have known this feature since he described the escape of Husdain (vss. 4368-490) and later asserted that Tristan was the first man to train dogs (vss. 4541-5). The verbal similarity between Eilhart's vss. 4457-65 and Béroul's vss. 1694-6 suggests that Eilhart knew the 'riche baron' episode. On the possibly Celtic origin of the story of Mark's ears see Schoepperle, op. cit. ii. 269-71; Foulon in *Bulletin Philologique et Historique,* 1951-2; and above, p. 128.

17. An important difference is that while in Béroul the spell of the potion is broken completely after three years (vss. 2133-46), in Eilhart it is weakened but not destroyed after four (vss. 2279-3000).

18. On Béroul's style see Muret's edition, *SATF* (1903), pp. xxv, lxvi.

19. Mergell, *Tristan und Isolde* (Mainz, 1949), pp. 34 f.

20. See Chap. 12, p. 124, n. 1.

21. Ibid.

22. In a very fine study, 'La Légende de Tristan vue par Béroul et Thomas', *RP,* vii (1953), 111-29, Le Gentil takes the view that Béroul's treatment is independent of the archetype.

23. Bédier, ii. 260.

24. Bédier suspected (ii. 265) that the ambiguous oath episode was not in the *estoire,* but was a parasitic growth attached to it.

25. The behaviour of Tristan at the Mal Pas (vss. 3697-878).

26. The threats of Arthur's knights against the three barons and the jousts in which Tristan is disguised as the Noir de la Montaigne.

27. Muret in his edition of Béroul for the *SATF,* pp. i-xiv, suggested that the second half of the poem (vss. 2765-4485) was due to a continuator, but abandoned this view in his 1928 edition, pp. vi-viii. See above, p. 134, n. 1.

Ann Trindade (essay date 1974)

SOURCE: Trindade, Ann. "The Enemies of Tristan." *Medium Aevum* 63, no. 1 (1974): 6-21.

[*In the following essay, Trindade discusses the narrative structure of the Tristan legend as it exists in poetic versions by Eilhart and others, placing particular emphasis on the function of antagonists in the story.*]

The enemies of Tristan are many and varied in what are usually called the 'primary' versions of the legend. Their number and degree of individualization varies, and while the principal editions and studies of Tristan texts have included comments on individual variants as they occur, there has been, as far as I am aware, no study devoted entirely to this group of characters alone. I propose to show that there are important advantages to be gained from studying them as a group and in terms of their narrative function.

First, while a number of influential Arthurian scholars have maintained that the study of origins is less important than the application of traditional literary criteria to the texts themselves,[1] nevertheless the fact that we refer so frequently to the 'legend', or 'story', or Tristan independently of the Tristan versions indicates that the processes of transmission and development will always be a legitimate object of study. The Arthurian field is not unique in possessing a number of traditional themes and characters which persist throughout several centuries in the oral and written literature of widely divergent cultural groups, but these characteristics make it a particularly appropriate choice of field for the comparative and the historical approach. Scholars will continue to try to trace the evolution of the Tristan legend, or to assess the contribution of the Continental adaptors to the Celtic deposit. They will ask whether the enemies of Tristan, singly or collectively, figured in the earliest forms of the story, whether the variation in names and distribution of rôles is derived from the independent cognate versions. Students of comparative literature will ask whether the main narrative devices employed in the creation and distribution of rôles can be seen to relate to any universal or at least widely distributed forms with which they may be familiar, and perhaps use this material as the basis for further comparative study.

Secondly, a survey of the enemies as a group enables us to confine our attention to a limited but important area. Logically, the category of enemies might be very widely drawn, to include any character who fulfils a hostile function from the point of view of Tristan and Isolt. This would include, for instance, the kidnapping merchants and the Morholt of the first section of the story as well as the adversaries encountered by Tristan and Kaherdin in the final part, the jealous husband whom Tristan helps Kaherdin to outwit, Riole von Nantis and the other foes against whom Tristan takes up arms on his friend's behalf and even Isolt of the White-hands, his wife. Though I shall have more to say about some of these later, it is primarily with the more restricted group of Tristan's enemies at court that I am here concerned. These are the opponents whose function is part of the intrigue surrounding the triangular relationship between Tristan, Mark and Isolt. I shall first list them briefly for convenience, with some reference to their activities, before attempting to consider them as a group.

Perhaps the most prominent among these and the one whose portrayal comes closest to modern ideas of characterization is Andret, who appears in Eilhart and Béroul (and in the Prose version, with which I am not here concerned, as Sandret), though not in Thomas. He appears chiefly in the following episodes in Eilhart: The Chips on the Stream (3250-3702); the Flour between the Beds (3765-3975); the subsequent banishment of Tristan (4203-4242); Tristan's Second and Third Visits to Cornwall (7445-7714 and 8028-8548); and finally, in a preliminary skirmish with the disguised Tristan just before Tristan enters Mark's court as the Fool (8695-8786). He also appears in Béroul, though in a considerably reduced rôle. In Eilhart's version he has certain distinguishing characteristics—he is usually represented as acting in connection with other enemies, the dwarf or the hostile counts and dukes, he is the guardian who attends the Queen and he is, like Tristan, a nephew of Mark by his sister. Ewert has argued, convincingly, that Béroul's version displays knowledge of these traditional attributes, since Andret is represented there as accompanying the Queen; though in one reference he is made to speak on Tristan's behalf and in another he is killed by Tristan, this could be the residue of an account in which he was at once a close companion and a rival of Tristan.[2] There is no suggestion in Béroul's text that Andret is a nephew of the king, unless we accept that the 'nevo' in line 2869 refers forward to 'Andrez, qui fu nez de Nicole', and not to Tristan, as is generally held.[3]

It is interesting in passing to note that all the references to Andret—or Audret—occur in the part of the poem which Raynaud de Lage,[4] Rita Lejeune[5] and T. B. W. Reid[6] would assign to 'Béroul II', yet it is also the first part in which we find the closest correspondence between Béroul and Eilhart. If, as some advocates of the theory of dual authorship maintain, the author of 'Béroul II' was working from different sources from those represented in the 'version commune', then the appearance in this part of Béroul of Andret—with all the inconsistencies alluded to by Ewert—may lend weight to the idea that he might be in some sense the

'original' enemy. Most commentators have been quick to recognize the similar pattern which links Mark, Tristan and Andret with Arthur, Gauvain and Modret.[7] Attention has also been drawn to the widespread distribution of nephews in the *Chansons de geste* and in the courtly romances.[8] The Arthur-Gauvain-Modred pattern is of course connected with the persistent motif of a Celtic abduction story seen in the abductions of Guenievre, and echoed here in the Harp and Rote episode.[9]

Closely connected with Andret in Eilhart's version in the early incidents at Mark's court is the dwarf, who is named as 'Frocine' in Béroul and perhaps Melot in Thomas, if Gottfried is to be followed.[10] In all these versions the dwarf acts as the agent of the hostile faction in plotting to trap the lovers in two consecutive episodes, the Chips on the Stream and the Flour between the Beds. Béroul alone attributes occult powers to him, but Ewert considers that this is an invention. In Béroul alone too, we hear of the dwarf's death at the hands of the king in the curious little tale of the Horse's Ears,[11] while in the other poems we find his banishment and reinstatement at the court. In the latter part of both the Eilhart and the Thomas versions there is no trace of the dwarf, although various minor figures appear in the same intermediate role in the episodic returns of Tristan. There is another 'nain' who appears in the final section of Eilhart, the 'nain Bedenis', for whose story, which was certainly known to him, Thomas substitutes the watered-down story of Tristan le Nain. Dwarfs of course, like nephews, abound in medieval epics and romances, and there is no reason to imagine any elaborate symbolism in such a choice of name, even though Thomas presents him in such a way as to enhance by contrast the reputation of 'Tristan l'amerus'.

Thomas's version is interesting in that the loosely coordinated groups of enemies in the versions of Eilhart and Béroul are replaced by one figure, the steward Meriadoc.[12] It is he who assumes Andret's rôle in the episodes of the Chips on the Stream and the Flour between the Beds, and appears in a number of loosely constructed incidents preceding these, the purpose of which seems to be to explain and motivate the growth of hostility between Meriadoc and Tristan, his former friend and confidant. As Bédier and more recent scholars such as Frappier[13] have shown, this procedure is characteristic of Thomas, and it is an interesting reminder of some of the factors involved in any attempt to formulate a theory of mediæval poetics. On the one hand, we see the difference between modern notions of individuality and originality and the mediæval respect for tradition, oral and written, on the other, the relative sophistication of poets like Thomas, Marie de France and Chrétien in their interest in motivation and ideology. It is therefore difficult to say whether the reduction of all the enemies to one (presupposing that Thomas was working from sources, written or in part oral, which included groups of enemies) is another instance of editorial procedure, or whether it represents a tradition inherited by Thomas. As we know from studies of oral narrative and mythological material and its interaction with written forms, fission of characters and its opposite, fusion, occur with the same frequency. Both are manifestations of the transference of function rather than individual identity in traditional literature.[14]

The choice of name is not particularly revealing. It is intended to be Breton and characters with this name or one of its variants occur in other Arthurian texts.[15] Like the dwarf, Meriadoc plays no part in the closing section of the story. Another knight, described as 'uns riches cuns de grant alo',[16] brings the news of the ill-fated marriage to the Queen. He subsequently provokes the anger of Brengain by taunting her for having slept with a coward. Thomas has him killed by Kaherdin in revenge during Tristan's second return to Cornwall. This knight is described as a long-time admirer of Queen Isolt, and again, appears only in Thomas. In keeping with the '*fin' amors*' ideology[17] which seems to have influenced Thomas's presentation of the famous love-story, he is cast in the mould of the Provencal '*losengier*', whose concern is to denigrate Tristan in the eyes of the Queen, rather than to reveal their association to the jealous husband. As one of the versions derived from Thomas gives Mariadokk here, it might be tempting to assume that the Meriadoc of the first part is the same as the Cariado of the Fragments; Bédier maintains that both may be inventions of the poet and this may well be so.

I turn now to a quite different group of enemies, the three barons of Béroul's version, named as Guenelon, Godoine and Denoalen.[18] They are introduced abruptly in the extant part of Béroul's narrative and there is some confusion about their final destiny. In the early part of the story, where the versions of Eilhart, Béroul and Thomas follow a similar pattern (roughly from the Tryst under the tree to the banishment of the lovers to the forest) the rôle of the three barons corresponds to that of Andret and Meriadoc respectively. After the return from the forest, their rôle is less clearly defined, further confusion being engendered by the killing of one of them by Governal[19] and the reappearance of all three later. Two minor points have attracted some discussion, why the barons should be three in number and whether their names have any significance. The fact is that not until line 1711 when one of them is killed, and 3138-19, when they are named, are they distinguished one from the other. Ewert's explanation of this seems an unnecessary rationalization.[20] Even less impressive is Vàrvaro's[21] attempt to detect something approaching characterization here—in a way reminiscent of Bédier's remarks about characterization.[22] In fact the

weakness of Bédier's ground here, owing no doubt to his anxious desire to underscore the unique literary nature of his 'archetype', is surely emphasized by the fact that even the most ardent Bédierists have never attempted to defend his position by using this particular argument. On the contrary, the existence of three closely-related characters who seem to share an identical function is no strange phenomenon to be explained away by editorial confusion or '*una certa misteriosa ossessione, che avrà certamente un senso che a noi sfugge della triplicità dei baroni*'.[23] Irish tradition as reflected in the major tale cycles abounds with such instances; two immediate examples are the three identical foster brothers of Conaire in *Togail Bruidne da Derga*,[24] and the three sons of Uisliu in *Longes mac n-Uislenn*,[25] and there are a host of others, Irish and Welsh.[26] This preference for threes is also reflected in certain formal and stylistic arrangements, the Irish and Welsh Triads, for instance, and groups of stories such as the *Trí Truaighe na Sgéalaigheachta*[27]—though in this case the grouping in three may be the work of a late, i.e. fifteenth or sixteenth century, author. Mrs. Bromwich links these literary conventions with the mythological systems of the early Celts,[28] and Georges Dumézil has devoted a life-time of study to this fundamental question.[29]

The Romance field offers, in the Continental *matière de Bretagne,* an unmistakable echo of this predilection for tripling, as indeed for animal transformations, multiple personality patterns and so on. It would not then be unreasonable to imagine that Béroul's three barons may derive from a Celtic original, just as do the three brothers of Gauvain.[30]

The names of the three are discussed by Bédier,[31] Lot[32] and Ewert.[33] Godoine and Guenelon are typical names of traitors, virtually symbolic in their context no doubt, and Ewert accepts Lot's conclusion that Denoalen may also have been a Breton traitor of note, though unfortunately there is no obvious candidate at hand.[34] The choice of three such names reminds us immediately of Marie de France's habit of using bilingual titles from time to time and may be said to be some indication of a multilingual milieu for which the poems were destined.

It is possible that Eilhart also knew of a version in which the three barons played a larger rôle than that implied in his vague references to groups of four or seven counts or dukes. The section which occurs at the end of Béroul's text in its extant form, which describes Tristan's revenge and the death of two of the barons, has been described by Ewert as standing 'entirely apart from all other versions'. There are, however, some slight resemblances between this section and the much shorter section in Eilhart, lines 8931-9032. In this episode, which follows immediately upon the Folie Tristan episode, Tristan and Isolt are meeting secretly at night, after the king has agreed that the Fool shall remain at court. Some of Tristan's enemies, alerted by spies—cf. Béroul 4273—plot to surprise the lovers but are prevented by a show of force from Tristan. The difference in length, which might well have been even greater had Béroul's poem not been interrupted, is not important, as we know from the development of folktale research that 'the length of a variant is a completely irrelevant aspect as to the structure'.[35] The number of the enemies here is also interesting, five in all, two spies who report to a group of three.

These resemblances are rather general but there are also clues in the context of both extracts. In Eilhart the discomfiture of the evil chamberlains follows, as we have seen, the episode of Tristan disguised as a fool at Mark's court, and provides the necessary release mechanism for Tristan to leave Isolt and return to Brittany. In Béroul, the episode in question follows upon a sequence of incidents, the Tryst at the Mal Pas, when the disguised Tristan answers questions in much the same way as he does in the versions of the Folie Tristan episode, the ambiguous oath and the vindication of Isolt, which ends with the establishment of a temporary equilibrium (4262-6). Ewert thinks, with Schoepperle, and apparently also with Mrs. Bromwich,[36] that the original poem, and probably too Béroul's version, ended after this with Tristan's death at the hands of King Mark, or one of his agents. In Eilhart, despite the fact that the location changes to Brittany, the new sequence which opens from the state of temporary equilibrium established by the preceding section involves the wounding and death of Tristan at the hands of another foe. On the other hand, there are in both texts indications that these sections may have belonged to an autonomous episodic unit of a type which we shall see is very familiar. Ewert has drawn attention to the fact that in Béroul's version this section contains several inconsistencies and obscurities, though the poet has attempted in places to link it with what went before. In Eilhart, the appropriate section is tacked on to the end of an earlier and complete section, the Folie Tristan episode. Logically it is superfluous except that it provides the occasion for the lovers to part. It is, however, by a more detailed examination of the narrative structure of this whole section that this becomes clearer. As this examination will provide the basis for subsequent discussion, a short digression is in order.

G. Schoepperle divided Eilhart's narrative into roughly equal sections for the purpose of summary, a division based partly on content and partly on the manuscript rubrics in Lichtenstein's edition. More recently C. A. Robson[37] has subjected these divisions to a closer examination and has demonstrated how each segment of narrative was expanded symmetrically from its original nucleus of oral narrative substance. Applying these methods to the final set of segments in Schoepperle's list, we see that the recurrent unit is a section of roughly 68-74 lines in the Lichtenstein text, each of which corresponds to a single movement of the tale in the chain which constitutes the narrative sequence. Thus stylistic and linguistic criteria, manuscript indications, sometimes metrical arrangement, confirm at the textual level what the mental perception of the reader or hearer apprehends as a discrete segment of content, and perhaps goes on to identify, through the existence of paradigmatic inventories like the Aarne-Thompson[38] and Thompson[39] indices, as part of a universal repertoire of story telling. Lines 6106-804 in Eilhart are a good instance of this. Section 'p', on the other hand, where this section in question occurs, is far more chaotic in its order. The opening segments seem to follow a pattern established previously, but the pattern changes with the presentation of the Folie Tristan episode, which Eilhart seems to have arranged in a rather different way,[40] and finally there is this abortive attempt to trap the lovers, which does not follow the preceding section very logically, as we have seen. This short section falls into three clearly defined parts, each of which is roughly half the 'average' length alluded to above. It looks very much as if they belong to a context from which they have been displaced, or if some kind of conflation has taken place. The conclusion then towards which this points is that the three barons, named or originally anonymous, may belong to a tradition known to Eilhart as much as to Béroul.

I have discussed the principal—named—enemies of Tristan, but there are also various minor characters or intermediaries of a hostile kind; the forester in Béroul, the leper band and their leader, as well as other characters with whom Tristan comes into conflict in other parts of the story, the cowardly seneschal of Ireland, the ancestral enemies of this homeland and the enemies of Kaherdin and his father.

These, then, are the principal enemies of Tristan. Despite the fact that most Tristan studies since the turn of the century have been more or less exclusively concerned with origins, scholars have been unable to say which of the enemies belong to which stages in the evolution of the legend, or whether individual choices throw any light on the earliest forms of the story. Schoepperle concluded that the different groups of enemies were introduced into the story by different redactors and *remanieurs* and that the poet of the *estoire* 'made no effort to connect them with each other'.[41] These and similar conclusions have been drawn from a study of each individual enemy taken separately. What happens when we consider them as a group, and in terms of their narrative function? One of the most profitable aspects of the modern structuralist approach to literature[42] has been the renewed emphasis on what we might call the immanent aspect of literature. This concept of a literary work as a system of signs, a structured set of codes, which is clearly influenced by modern linguistics, is by no means revolutionary, but is in many ways a restatement of Aristotle and 'the old methods of classical rhetoric, poetics or metrics'.[43] In the mediæval field, no doubt because of the numerous problems of transmission, oral and written, the different concept of authorship, the physical condition of texts and all the consequences of what Paul Zumthor in a challenging new book[44] calls 'l'éloignement du moyen âge, la distance irrécupérable qui nous en sèpare', this approach has not been over-favoured. None the less, it is possible to apply to the study of Arthurian texts some of the methods used by scholars who are not in the first instance mediævalists, because of the close connection between the mediæval Arthurian romances and Celtic narrative tradition and because of the enormous influence of oral tradition on both Celtic and 'neo-Celtic' literature.

Apart from the researches of Celticists and scientific folklorists, the most valuable development has been the productive effect of Propp's *Morphology of the Folktale*.[45] Commentaries, discussions, further contributions extending the range of interest from the original (Aarne-Thompson 300-749) fairy stories discussed by Propp to the whole field of narrative in general have been carried on by scholars like Bremond,[46] Greimas,[47] Pop,[48] Meletinski,[49] Dundes[50] and Köngäs-Maranda[51] and the reviews *Poétique, Poetica, Semiotica, Communications* and *Fabula,* as well as the orthodox folklore journals, and occasional articles in literary or linguistic periodicals. Some of the terminology, which is still largely experimental, will be borrowed for the purposes of this discussion.

It is immediately obvious that the Tristan story, as represented in its primary versions, displays two patterns of overall narrative arrangement, one a cyclic, repetitive pattern, the other a kind of overarching pattern which approximates more closely to a complete Tale Type. Both patterns are visible in all primary versions despite the fragmentary nature of the texts. The second pattern coincides with what has long been felt by scholars to be a natural division of the story into three parts; the boyhood deeds of Tristan, the love story, and the exile, marriage and death. Mrs. Bromwich[52] has shown how these divisions are the product of the different stages through which the story passed and the different sources from which it developed. The existence of these independent sections is confirmed by an attempt to analyse the whole story in terms of Propp's list of functions. The first section, birth and boyhood deeds, down to the vindication of the triumphant dragon-slayer, follows Propp's outline with almost no variation. This is no doubt because the type known

internationally as the Dragon-Slayer is very well-defined and widely distributed.[53] The other two divisions are less easy to analyse along the same lines, but their independence is confirmed in the first case by the existence of a formal system of classification for Irish tales,[54] and in the last instance by the existence of parallel versions of the Man with Two Wives, which corresponds in part to a type or subtype in the Aarne-Thompson inventory.[55]

The other pattern, with which we are more immediately concerned, appears to be at first one of narrative technique, since it reappears in all the versions and in the narration of the three major sections alike. It is seen most clearly in the episodic returns of Tristan to Cornwall after his exile in Brittany, but it is also illustrated in similar sequences in the middle section where the separation of the lovers is more psychological than physical, but where an identical procedure of ruse, counterruse and solution is employed. This pattern is closely linked with the arrangement of those recurrent units noted earlier in Eilhart. We notice if we analyse each example that an enemy or enemies appears in a more or less fixed place in each instance. The sequences in question, the Chips on the Stream, Flour between the Beds, and the various returns of Tristan, two in Thomas, four in Eilhart, show a basic succession of moves (and doubtless there are others, Thomas' Harp and Rote, Blades at the Bed (Eilhart), Life in the Forest, which follow a similar pattern but are excluded as the enemies do not figure significantly in them). These could be summarized as follows:

> Tristan and Isolt are separated, either by physical or mental obstacles.
> They attempt to reunite. An enemy plans to frustrate them.
> Tristan by counter-trickery foils the adversary.
> Isolt either delays the pursuer or allays the King's suspicions.
> Tristan escapes or is restored to court, at any rate establishes a temporary advantage.

It is almost as if the poet were operating a simple formula. But is it the result of a personal predilection on the part of one of the many *remanieurs* through whose hands the story passed?

Some of Propp's interpreters, notably Bremond and Dundes, have pointed out that his remarks about the order and linking of functions[56] ought to be modified. Some of them, for example, as Propp himself was aware, seem to be in complementary distribution and others seem to be binary pairs, or again, within the succession of functions there appear groupings of two or three in a closer or more dependent relationship. Dundes has shown that North American Indian tales in particular (which are purely oral tales with a relatively simple structure) do not possess anything like all the thirty-one functions noted by Propp, but consist usually of the short sequence 'Lack' to 'Lack liquidated'.[57] By contrast the structure of most European folktales is far more complicated. In short, though we cannot expect the schemes worked out by Propp on the basis of one particular corpus to apply exactly, nevertheless, as he himself foresaw, since the origins and development of many mediæval *romans de chevalerie* are closely linked to folktales we should expect vestiges of the same structure to appear.

This is true of the narrative segments we have isolated in the Tristan versions. The rough schema preceding can be further reduced and it will be seen that the pattern conforms fairly closely to the important group of functions which Propp calls basic to all forms of the fairy tale, and which Bremond has tried to apply to all types of narrative in general.

Separation:	Lack. (Propp VIII a)
Initiative:	Lack made known, Hero accepts action, Hero departs. (Propp IX-XI)
Counter ruse:	Hero under attack. (Propp XII)
Foiling of enemy:	Reaction of (hostile) Hero to donor, (XIII 8 or 9)
Establishment of advantage:	Lack Liquidated. (Propp XIX)

It is noticeable that 6 functions are missing from Propp's list. This is not particularly important, since Propp and his successors themselves pointed out that even in those fully developed tales which conform most closely to the abstract model not all the functions will always be present. What we have here is a much simpler model than the one drawn up by Propp, one which seems to be particularly suited to oral composition, delivery and transmission and which could only be incorporated in a longer, more complex and partly written version by repetition.[58] This is the simplest type of linking and though the individual poets of the extant versions, Thomas, and to a lesser extent Eilhart and Béroul, have introduced some degree of overall motivation, the repetitive nature of the pattern is still obvious.

It seems clear that the earliest forms of the story were in fact separate ones about Drust the Dragon-Slayer, Drystan, Essyllt and March, and perhaps versions of the Dragon-Slayer in a Breton setting.[59] Does it then follow that of the two types of narrative structure we have noticed, the 'overarching' or more complex type is the earlier or more basic form, and the simpler arrangement, the concatenation *bout à bout* of identical sequences differing only in content is a feature of the poetic technique of individual poets or redactors?

This seems highly unlikely, since we possess an obvious example of this latter type in Triad 26 of the Welsh Triads,[60] which Mrs. Bromwich has said 'belongs to the oldest stratum of Arthurian tradition in Wales'. Bédier dismissed this triad as part of a vague and amorphous body of tradition which preceded the formation of the poem by a man of genius who was certainly a Frenchman. Even now, some scholars have attempted to minimize the importance of the Celtic contribution, not only just to the substance of the story but also to its shaping. On the contrary, the relation between Triad 26 and the extant versions is a most interesting one, since it suggests that Triad 26 provides the model for the later versions and confirms very strongly Mrs. Bromwich's belief that it was in S. Wales that the celebrated love story was first composed. This early Welsh Tristan story, in versions partly or wholly oral, was almost certainly not as lengthy as our present versions. But if this narrative sequence involving separation, attempts at reunion, frustration by an enemy, counter ruse of the hero and ultimate success represents the original nucleus of the story, then it is clear that the various enemies are a product of the process of repetition and expansion.

This implies, in turn, that there is somehow one basic enemy. To examine this implication, we must look at the second aspect of Propp's study of the folktale, the distribution of *dramatis personae*. Propp said that the tale could be defined in terms of two axes, its functions (or predicates) and its performers (or subjects) which in the case of the Russian fairy tale he found to be equally constant in number, seven to be exact. Rather less work has been done here by Propp's followers, and in this area the work of A. J. Greimas is probably unique. The mixed reception accorded to his work on semiology should not obscure the fact that his comments on Propp are more readily appreciated despite the use of jargon to which some of his English-speaking reviewers have taken exception.[61] Valuable work has also been done by Köngäs and Maranda. Such studies have broken down Propp's distinction between functions and performers, and highlighted that which sometimes appears between rôles and actors. Basic to all forms of narrative is a hero or centre of interest; Köngäs and Maranda have labelled this the 'first term' and advocate the startlingly simple method of statistical assessment to answer the question who is the hero of a given story. The hero is simply the one mentioned the greatest number of times. This is not so naïve as it may seem: in other words, the term has meaning only at the level of discourse, his mode of existence is purely linguistic. Having established the hero, 'most European folktales add an opponent . . . plus . . . a number of actors who bring into relief, or make possible, the actions of the hero (and the opponent) and who can become helpers or adversaries. But they are as a rule undefined, because the motivation of their actions rests with the hero's fate, not with their own selves. Thus we are inclined to see two "fronts" in a folktale and a host of actors who can become allies of one or the other.'[62] Here we see the difference between actors and rôles discussed by Greimas and it is interesting to consider in this light the relationship which exists in the Tristan texts between the two groups of go-betweens, the helpers and the enemies.

Assuming this process, the addition of intermediaries attaching themselves to either of two 'fronts', to be visible in the diachronic process—the 'history' of the evolution of the legend—, the obvious figure on to whom all the other enemies can be mapped is King Mark himself. The sympathy and pathos of his relationship with Tristan in the French versions and in Gottfried is irrelevant here. In the various Irish analogues, disregarding for a moment the question of derivation, the husband is depicted in active pursuit of the hero. Indeed it is this very point which leads Carney[63] to maintain that the Irish analogues are based on a lost original British *Tristan,* and not *vice versa;* he contrasts the remorseless, treacherous Conchobor of *Longes mac n-Uislenn* with the paternal figure of the Ulster cycle, and points out that Finn too, in the *Tóraigheacht Dhiarmada agus Ghráinne,* is at variance with his usual portrayal. The second Isolt, according to Carney, did not belong to the early British Tristan, since the third party who in most of the Irish stories misinterprets the sign and thus brings about the tragic ending is a man. 'This points also to the part played by Isolde, the wife, having been played by Mark in the primitive story.'[64] Had Carney been using the terminology of Greimas, he might have said that the '*acteur*' Isolt of the Whitehands was here filling the slot, or rôle, of the '*actant*' enemy, originally lexicalized by Mark! (It should be noted, however, that the structural study of narrative form practised by Greimas and others is resolutely synchronic and avoids identifying the notion of hierarchy in the grouping of elements with any chronological stage in the development of a form. This would be one of the main differences between Dundes and the so-called 'Finnish' or 'historicogeographical' school of folklorists, of which Stith Thompson is the chief American representative.)

At the crucial Welsh stage in the formation of the legend, then, there may well have been many current versions of a simple story involving March, Essyllt and Drystan of which Triad 26 is a reminder and an example. In a manner closely reminiscent of a modern cultural equivalent, the radio, T.V. or comic strip serial, the story tellers who wished to extend the story or revive an old favourite for frequent recitation had recourse to one of the commonest of narrative procedures, repetition, doubling and tripling. The mediæval Continental poets who adapted the Welsh or Breton material may have been responsible for incorporating these concatenated sequences into the more complex structure of the biographical outline as we know it. It is

at this point, one is inclined to think, that the 'lexicalization' of the rôle of enemy took place. Although some of the individual enemies show, as we saw earlier, characteristics which are consistent with a Celtic milieu, or at least one in which Irish and Welsh stories and traditions were not just a fossilized deposit—a rival nephew closely connected with the Queen, three hostile figures sharing virtually one identical function—the growth of a tradition concerning the enemies of Tristan is much more likely to have been a consequence of the evolution of the rôle of King Mark. At the level of structure, as the quotation from Köngäs and Maranda points out, the process of development from simple oral narrative forms in which the hero is balanced by an enemy[65] gives rise in more complex versions of the tale to the use of intermediaries who act out in a concrete way the hostile relationship between the two principals. At the level of content, the situation in which a monarch is portrayed as dependent upon the counsels of his advisers and subject to a detailed system of rules of procedure is somewhat more reminiscent of the literary presentation of feudalism familiar to us from the *chansons de geste* as from the romances. As Idris Foster points out,[66] the Arthur of *Culhwch* is far closer to the shadowy but powerful 'dux bellorum' hinted at in the few precious references in early Welsh tradition than to the 'roi fainéant' of the romances.

It is not possible to say at what precise stage in the progress of the legend these changes took place. Frappier[67] has argued with a good deal of sense that Bédier's theory of a fully developed written narrative immediately preceding our present versions must be modified, and it is likely that most Tristan scholars today would agree that such a rigid distinction should not be drawn between oral and written forms. But we are probably entitled to assume that the original enemy of Tristan was Mark himself, and that the earliest versions of the story of their hostility were Welsh and consisted already of concatenated sequences based upon the model given in Triad 26, in which first Mark, then Tristan gained the advantage. It is not unlikely, though purely conjectural, that some intermediaries appeared in the versions at that stage as indeed Triad 26 itself suggests.[68] As the story was used by different *conteurs* with different skills and in different cultural contexts the enemy was 'lexicalized' in different ways, but his basic function, his place in the narrative sequence, remained unchanged. Having introduced them or inherited them, however, the poets had to get rid of them and it is here that the uniform structure breaks down, with the clumsy attempts at harmonization by Béroul, the sudden fade-out of Andret in Eilhart and so on.

These observations are made on the basis of a study of the narrative structure of the existing versions and a comparison between them. The methods used by Propp and so on coincide here in part with some of those favoured by modern structuralist critics like Barthes and Todorov and, in this field, Zumthor. In so far as such methods fall within the sphere of well-established disciplines like stylistics and poetics, they are hardly revolutionary; their value lies in the attempt to broaden the base of such studies to include not merely the textual or surface aspects of a narrative—its 'style' as one might have said—but also what Köngäs and Maranda have called, using an analogy from contemporary linguistics, its 'deep structure'. From such studies is emerging an interest in the characteristic shape and properties of narrative in general, as a legitimately autonomous area of literary discourse.[69]

Notes

1. Helaine Newstead 'Recent Perspectives on Arthurian Literature' *Mélanges Frappier* (Paris 1971) II, 877-83.

2. A. Ewert ed. *The Romance of Tristran* by Béroul (Oxford 1970) II, 120.

3. Unfortunately the context is ambiguous. The line itself is an example of the transitional, almost formulaic lines with which the poet proceeds from one narrative movement to the next, and so could refer either to the preceding section, as a kind of summary statement or to the following one. On the other hand, the words *nevo, nies* are used frequently throughout the entire poem, often in direct exchanges between Tristan and Mark. It is therefore probable that Ewert is right and that this reference is to Tristan.

4. G. Raynaud de Lage 'Faut-il attribuer à Béroul tout le *Tristan*?' *Le Moyen Age* LXIV (1958) 249-70 and LXVII (1961) 167-8.

5. Rita Lejeune 'Les "influences contemporaines" dans les romans français de Tristan au XIIe. siècle' *Le Moyen Age* LXVI (1960) 143-62.

6. T. B. W. Reid 'The Tristan of Béroul: One Author or Two?' *Modern Language Review* LX (1965) 352-8. See also A. Vàrvaro *Il Roman de Tristan di Béroul* (Napoli 1966) pp. 9-22 and Ewert op. cit. pp. 1-3.

7. Ewert op. cit. p. 218.

8. See R. Bezzola 'Les neveux' in *Mélanges Frappier* II 88-111. Bezzola's article concludes with a long list of nephews found in both *chansons de geste* and romances. He is of course seriously mistaken when he refers to 'les mythologies germaniques et celtiques, òu, à notre savoir, les neveux ne jouent jamais un rôle de premier plan'. One has only to cite a few examples: Cú Chulainn

nephew of Conchobor (and referred to in the *Táin* as 'the king's sister's son'—*mac sethar ind ríg*), Diarmaid nephew of Finn, Gwern nephew of Bran (*Branwen verch Lyr*), Gilfaethwy and Gwydion nephews of Math (*Math*), Lleu Llaw Gyffes nephew of Gwydion (*Math*), and of course we learn at the start of *Culhwch* that Arthur and Culhwch were fellow-nephews, evidently a relationship of some importance. See Rachel Bromwich *Trioedd Ynys Prydein* (Cardiff 1961) p. 371 and T. M. Charles-Edwards 'Some Celtic Kinship Terms' *Bulletin of the Board of Celtic Studies* XXIV (1971) 105-21.

9. Helaine Newstead 'The Harp and the Rote, an episode in the Tristan legend and its Literary History' *Romance Philology* XXII (1969) 463-70.

10. M. Delbouille 'Le nom du nain Frocin(e)' *Mélanges Istvan Frank* (Univ. des Saarlandes 1957) pp. 191-203.

11. J. Bédier *Le roman de Tristan de Thomas* (Paris 1902-5) II 250; Ewert op. cit. pp. 160-2.

12. Bédier op. cit. pp. 245, 247.

13. J. Frappier 'Sens et structure du Tristan; version commune, version courtoise' *Cahiers de Civilisation Médiévale* VI (1963) 255-80 and 441-54.

14. R. S. Loomis *Arthurian Tradition and Chrétien de Troyes* (New York 1949); A. Olrik 'Epic Laws of Folk Narrative' in A. Dundes ed. *The Study of Folklore* (Englewood Cliffs 1965) pp. 131-41 (originally appeared in *Zeitschrift für deutsches Altertum* LI (1909) 1-12). See also K. Krohn *Folklore Methodology* (Texas 1971) pp. 78-98, and V. J. Propp 'Transformations des contes merveilleux' first published 1928 translated in *Morphologie du Conte* (Paris 1970).

15. The name appears in Geoffrey of Monmouth, as Conanus Meriadocus. See also M. Roques ed. *Erec* (Paris 1955) lines 2076ff. and J. Rychner ed. *Lais de Marie de France* (Paris 1966) *Guigemar* (index). See also R. S. Loomis ed. *Arthurian Literature in the Middle Ages* (Oxford 1959) pp. 379ff., 472ff.

16. B. H. Wind ed. *Les Fragments du Roman de Tristan* (Paris-Geneva 1960) Fr. Sneyd 1, line 796.

17. Moshe Lazar *Amour courtois et 'fin amors' dans la littérature du XIIe. siècle* (Paris 1963).

18. Ewert op. cit. p. 119.

19. Ibid. lines 1656-1750.

20. Supra n. 18.

21. Varvaro op. cit. p. 150.

22. Bédier op. cit. II 175ff.

23. Vàrvaro op. cit. p. 150.

24. E. Knott ed. *Togail Bruidne da Derga* (Dublin 1963).

25. Vernam Hull ed. *Longes mac n-Uislenn* (New York 1949).

26. Three sons of Tuirill Bicred or of Nechta Scéne, and the various groups of triple deities like the Trí Dé Donand (*Book of Leinster* ed. Bergin and Best (Dublin 1954) I 124). See further Bromwich op. cit. p. 155.

27. Myles Dillon *Early Irish Literature* (Chicago 1949) p. 62.

28. Op. cit. p. lxiiiff.

29. For bibliographical information see C. Scott Littleton *The New Comparative Mythology* (Berkeley and L.A. 1966).

30. Loomis *Arthurian Tradition* p. 487.

31. Bédier op. cit. II 125.

32. *Romania* XXXV (1906) 605-7.

33. Op. cit. pp. 222-3.

34. The name itself is well-attested. The *Cartulaire de Redon* ed. Courson gives several instances of variations on the form Donoalus, Donuuallonus etc. (pp. 74, 86, 261, 243, 299, 129, 333). Later instances from the *Cartulaire de Quimperlé* see J. Loth *Chrestomathie Bretonne* p. 202. For the probable etymology see Ellis Evans *Gaulish Personal Names* (Oxford 1967) pp. 196-7 and Fleuriot *Grammaire du vieux breton* pp. 41, 1135.

35. E. Köngäs and P. Maranda *Structural Models in Folklore and Transformational Essays* (Hague 1971) p. 73.

36. In her review of Binchy's edition of *Scéla Cano Meic Gartnáin* (Dublin 1963), in *Studia Celtica* I (1966) 152-5.

37. C. A. Robson 'The Technique of symmetrical composition in medieval narrative poetry' *Ewert Miscellany* (Oxford 1961) pp. 26-75.

38. A. Aarne and Stith Thompson *The Types of the Folktale* (Helsinki 1961).

39. Stith Thompson *Motif Index of Folk Literature* (Copenhagen 1955-8).

40. The section in question is divided clearly into three segments, clearly indicated by the switch of attention from one actor to another and by formulaic lines—8787, 8845 and 8887. These seg-ments are slightly shorter than the average narrative unit of 68-74 lines. A similar treatment involving an initial, pivotal and conclusive section is found in Eilhart lines 5700-6105, a description of a battle. This is slightly more complicated though as we might expect from Eilhart's taste for battle scenes, each of the three main stages is divided into two subsections.

41. Gertrude Schoepperle *Tristan and Isolt* (Frankfurt 1913) I 252.

42. The literature on Structuralism is unfortunately increasing copiously and in a manner which, due to the diffuse nature of the subject, makes bibliographical reference difficult. See M. Lane ed. *Structuralism, a Reader* (London 1970) and T. Todorov et al. eds. *Qûest-ce que le structuralisme* (Paris 1968).

43. R. Wellek and A. Warren *Theory of Literature* (London 1963) p. 139.

44. P. Zumthor *Essai de poétique médiévale* (Paris 1972).

45. V. J. Propp *Morfologija skazki* (Leningrad 1928) translated as the *Morphology of the Folktale* (Indiana 1958) and new translation (Austin 1968), and *Morfologia della Fiaba* (Torino 1966) second Russian edition 1969 translated into French 1971, see n. 14. Of the two English editions the second is preferable, since it contains an excellent introduction by Alan Dundes. The Italian version adds a Comment by Lévi-Strauss, also available in the *International Journal of Slavic Poetics and Linguistics* III (1960) 122-49, plus Propp's reply which is not found there. All references are to the French version unless otherwise stated.

46. C. Bremond 'Le message narratif' *Communications* IV (1964) 4-32; 'La logique des possibles narratifs' ibid. VIII (1966) 60-76; 'Postérité américaine de Propp' ibid. XI (1968) 148-56; 'Morphology of the French Folktale' *Semiotica* II (1970) 247-76.

47. A. J. Greimas *Sémantique structurale* (Paris 1966) pp. 172ff. 'La structure des actants du récit' *Word* XXXIII (1967) 221-38; *Du Sens* (Paris 1970) pp. 185-230; 'Narrative Grammar; Units and Levels' *Modern Language Notes* LXXVI (1971) 793-806.

48. M. Pop 'Aspects actuels des recherches sur la structure des contes' *Fabula* IX (1967) 70-7; 'La poétique du conte populaire' *Semiotica* II (1970) 117-27.

49. E. M. Meletinski 'Problèmes de la morphologie historique du conte populaire' *Semiotica* II (1970) 128-34 and see the extremely useful synthesis

'L'étude structurale et typologique du conte' appended to the French translation of Propp, pp. 201-54.

50. A. Dundes 'From Etic to Emic Units in the Structural Study of Folktales' *Journal of American Folklore* LXXV (1962) 95-105.

51. See note 35.

52. R. Bromwich 'Some remarks on the Celtic Sources of Tristan' *Transactions of the Hon. Society of Cymmrodorion* (1953) pp. 32-60.

53. Aarne-Thompson op. cit. pp. 88ff.

54. R. Thurneysen *Die Irische Helden- und Königsage bis zum 17ten Jahrhundert* (Halle 1921) p. 21ff.

55. Aarne-Thompson op. cit. pp. 128ff.

56. There is a problem of terminology here. Propp's 'function' is defined thus: 'function must be taken as an act of dramatis personae which is defined from the point of view of its significance for the course of action of a tale as a whole' (first English ed. p. 20). The confusion is compounded by the fact that, for instance, Greimas' 'syntagme narratif', Propp's 'sequence', Dundes' 'motifeme', and others such as Dorfman's 'narreme' (*The narreme in the Medieval Romance Epic* (Toronto & Manchester 1969)) do not always correspond exactly. See Köngäs-Maranda op. cit. p. 21.

57. A. Dundes *The Morphology of North American Indian Folktales* (Helsinki 1964).

58. Propp op. cit. 112, attempts to distinguish between a 'Conte qui peut se composer de plusieurs séquences' and a text which contains more than one *conte* juxtaposed. By any criteria advanced by Propp what we have here is not an example of the latter case.

59. A. Witte 'Der Aufbau der ältesten Tristandichtungen' *Zeitschrift für deutsches Altertum* LXX (1933) 161-95 and R. Bromwich art. cit. p. 59.

60. *Trioedd Ynys Prydein* p. 45.

61. See for instance Ullmann in *Lingua* XVIII (1967) 296-303.

62. Op. cit. p. 33. The intrusion of Isolt does not really prove an exception here as she can legitimately be regarded as Tristan's *alter ego,* see on this J. Campbell *The Hero with a Thousand Faces* (New York 1949) p. 342.

63. J. Carney *Studies in Irish Literature and History* (Dublin 1955) vi 'The Irish Affinities of Tristan'.

64. Ibid. p. 204.

65. Cf. Olrik op. cit. p. 135, the Law of two to a scene, and p. 139 Concentration on a leading character. As Dundes points out in his editorial note, p. 135, it is interesting to see how some of Lévi-Strauss's structuralist ideas have been anticipated here. In fact this little-quoted essay by an eminent Danish folklorist of the past merits more attention, since it anticipates in non-technical language many of the findings of contemporary structuralists and folklorists.

66. In *Arthurian Literature in the Middle Ages* pp. 31-9 at p. 33.

67. See n. 13.

68. The other two important pieces of evidence in Welsh, the late but almost certainly independent *Ystoria Trystan* and the problematic fragments in the *Black Book of Carmarthen,* do not in any way alter this. The former involves the polarization of Tristan and Mark, and the presence of intermediaries, and appears to repeat the familiar sequence of threat, counter-ruse and so on; the fragments would appear at very least to hint at enmity between the two principals, the presence of intermediaries and possibly a specific reference to one of the early incidents in the story. See R. Bromwich art. cit. p. 58.

69. See above n. 47 for the number of *MLN* devoted to Comparative Literature.

J. W. Thomas (essay date 1978)

SOURCE: Thomas, J. W. Introduction to *Eilhart von Oberge's* Tristrant, translated by J. W. Thomas, pp. 1-46. Lincoln: University of Nebraska Press, 1978.

[*In the following excerpt, Thomas encapsulates the manuscript tradition of Eilhart's* Tristant *and summarizes what is known of the poet's life. The critic continues by examining structure, style, narrative technique, and the theme of fate in the poem.*]

Author and Text

Composed some time between 1170 and 1190, the ***Tristrant*** of Eilhart von Oberge is the earliest complete account of the tragic love story of Tristan and Isolde and the version which, according to many scholars, most closely resembles the lost original.[1] As such, it is an invaluable reference point for all studies of the medieval Tristan material: its origins, as well as its widespread literary exploitation during the twelfth and thirteenth centuries. However, Eilhart's epic poem is also important in its own right and was popular in Germany for some five hundred years, inspiring various works of plastic arts as well as of literature.

We know *Tristrant* through three early manuscripts, three late ones, a Czech translation, and a chapbook. The early manuscripts are from the end of the twelfth or the beginning of the thirteenth century and are fragmentary, containing in all only 1,075 (85 overlapping) verses, or slightly more than one-tenth of the complete work. The later manuscripts, the translation, and the chapbook are all of the fifteenth century, although based on much earlier, presumably thirteenth-century, sources. Two of the later manuscripts are complete, while the third uses Eilhart's version only to fill out the unfinished portion of that of his younger contemporary, Gottfried von Strassburg. The Czech translation appears in almost identical form in two manuscripts and is complete, although three sections (making up almost half) follow Gottfried and a redaction by Heinrich von Freiberg rather than Eilhart. The chapbook gives the story in prose. All variants of *Tristrant,* including the early ones, are corrupted to the extent that it is impossible to reproduce the exact language of the original, but at the same time there is close agreement with regard to plot, general spirit, and style. One can therefore gain a reliable general acquaintance with the story as Eilhart told it, even though minor details may have been altered.[2]

The threads which connect the author of *Tristrant* with a historical person are few and tenuous: one of the fifteenth-century manuscripts cites a "von Hobergin her Eylhart" as the poet; ten documents (1189-1207) contain the name of an "Eilardus de Oberge" as a witness and indicate that he was a vassal of Duke Heinrich the Lion; and the manuscripts contain traces of Low German, such as was spoken at the court of Braunschweig and at Oberg, some ten miles to the west. The scholars who identify the author with the Braunschweig nobleman remind us that Heinrich's second wife, Mathilde, was the daughter of Henry II of England and that famous patron of the arts, Eleanore of Aquitaine. They suggest that Mathilde may have brought a French version of the Tristan story with her when she came to Braunschweig and commissioned Eilhart to put it into German verse, or that Eilhart may have accompanied the duke to England, when he was banished, and learned the story there. Other scholars do not accept the Eilardus of the documents as the poet, for various reasons, chief of which is their feeling that the first courtly epic in German must have been composed at a well-known literary center, such as the Wartburg, in Thuringia, and certain courts of the Middle and Lower Rhine area. It has also been suggested that the Eilhart of the manuscript was not the original German poet at all, but a redactor of the early thirteenth century. The majority of scholars, however, believes the Eilhart of the manuscript to be the original poet and identical with the Eilhart of the documents. Nevertheless, some of this group do maintain that, although he may have been born at Oberg and served on occasion at Heinrich's court, he composed *Tristrant* somewhere else. The language of the manuscripts, even the early ones, is of little help in resolving the controversy as to where the poet lived because of their linguistic corruption and because he may have composed in a normalized Middle German or High German rather than in a specific dialect.[3]

Scholarly opinion is as divided about the date of composition of *Tristrant* as about the identity of the author and the place where it was written. Those who judge strictly by internal evidence—in this case the most reliable method—point to characteristics of pre-courtly style and the frequent use of assonance instead of pure rhyme and agree on a date of about 1170. Another and smaller group prefers a later date and gives one or more of the following reasons: the Eilhart of the documents first appears with his father, which indicates that he was a young man at the time (1189); Chrétien de Troyes refers repeatedly to Tristan and Isolde in his *Erec,* but Hartmann von Aue in his redaction of the work (about 1190) does not, which means that Hartmann did not know any Tristan story when he was writing it; the monologue of Isalde in *Tristrant* when she has just drunk the love potion resembles one of Lavina's in heinrich von der Veldeke's *Eneit* (completed about 1185) and must have been borrowed from it. Of these grounds for giving *Tristrant* a later date (1185-90), only that dealing with the Isalde monologue deserves serious consideration, which it has frequently received.[4] Unfortunately, however, the many discussions have only shown how difficult it is to determine who was the borrower and who the lender when the relative chronology is unknown. The dispute has thus far produced not two, but five different conclusions: (1) *Eneit* is the older work, and Eilhart borrowed from it; (2) *Tristrant* was written first, but a later redactor interpolated an adaptation of passages from *Eneit;* (3) *Tristrant* was written first and influenced Lavina's monologue; (4) there was no borrowing or lending between *Tristrant* and *Eneit,* for the similarities result from an exchange between Eilhart's unknown source and the *Roman d'Enéas,* which was Heinrich's model; (5) there was no exchange on any level, and resemblances between the monologues can be explained by the similarity in the situations of the two heroines and by the prevailing poetic language of love.

The chronological relationship between *Tristrant* and *Eneit* is of considerable significance with respect to the position of the former work in medieval German literature. If Eilhart wrote before Veldeke—which, all things considered, is most likely—he was an innovator in style, language, and manners, as well as in subject matter. If he wrote after Veldeke, he was outside the mainstream of literary development, presenting his new material in archaic dress. In any event, one can hardly consider a date of composition for *Tristrant* of later than 1190 because both language and script of the early manuscripts are characteristic of the twelfth century.

Eilhart mentions no authors or works by name in his epic, but he does exhibit characteristics of style which resemble those of a number of earlier German writings—*Annolied, Kaiserchronik, Rolandslied,* and Lamprecht's *Alexanderlied*—and it is assumed that he was influenced by them in a general way. His chief source, however, appears to have been a lost French work which some scholars believe was the earliest written account of the Tristan story and others say was a redaction of this original. The author may have been Chrétien; an otherwise unknown trouvère called La Chèvre; or a third, completely anonymous poet.[5] It is generally held that Eilhart's source, if not the original work, was very similar to it.

THEME

The account of the most famous lovers of the medieval period has lent itself to greatly differing literary treatments. Even the three earliest versions use the material in quite distinctive and dissimilar ways. Thomas concentrates on the erotic passion itself and the psychological reactions to it of educated and sophisticated members of courtly society. Béroul, on the other hand, tells an uncomplicated adventure story which turns about a feud between Tristan and certain noblemen of the court and employs the love affair primarily as a device to expose the former to danger and intrigue. Eilhart presents a classic tale of a hero's struggle against his fate, always emphasizing the desperate, though sometimes comic, situation of a strong and resourceful man confronted by an enigmatic force which seems bent on his destruction. Where Thomas is careful to motivate the action and reveal the underlying reasons for emotions and behavior, Eilhart just as consciously points to the irrational or at least inexplicable nature of existence, the working of what might be called either destiny or pure chance. Where Béroul's antagonists are well defined and thoroughly evil, those in *Tristrant* change from episode to episode, and the hero is as likely to be endangered by his friends as by his enemies. Eilhart's version is usually considered the most primitive, which in many respects it is, however its basic assumption—that the course of human events is intrinsically inscrutable—is sufficiently modern to have permeated much of contemporary literature.

Eilhart develops his theme of Tristrant and fate by means of a variety of devices: the repeated use of certain irrational forces to direct the action; frequent references to luck, chance, and destiny; the exploitation of highly paradoxical and ironical situations; and the employment of quite unlikely, but still possible, coincidence. These devices at first produce something of a fairy-tale atmosphere and later perhaps a feeling that the author is manipulating his plot in a rather capricious manner. However, the reader is soon aware that what seemed arbitrary and whimsical is in fact the working of a fate whose intervention in Tristrant's affairs becomes more and more consistent, if not predictable.

The two chief instruments of fate are the sea and the love potion, which are also used as symbols: the sea as the outer, the potion as the inner necessity which determines the hero's destiny. Tristrant was born aboard ship, or rather, it was there that he was cut from his dead mother's womb. In his characteristically terse manner Eilhart does not give the exact cause of death, but does imply that the sea was to blame: perhaps with motion sickness inducing premature labor. The Caesarian birth, of course, presages great deeds; that it should occur aboard ship foreshadows the important role the sea was to play in his life. The death of Blankeflur anticipates the seasickness of Isalde, which eventually led also to her death. Tristrant's second voyage—the journey from his homeland of Lohenois to Cornwall—is uneventful, but significant, for it marks the beginning of the heroic life prophesied by the abnormal birth.

The first great exploit is the battle with Morolt, which evokes the first three of many allusions to what may be translated as chance, luck, or fate (*heil, unheil, gelucke, ungelucke*). When Kurneval tries to dissuade Tristrant from the undertaking, the latter says, "We could be lucky and win both wealth and honor;" later a Cornish nobleman tells the hero that Morolt will certainly defeat whoever opposes him, and the youth replies, "I'll leave that to chance;" finally Mark's council accepts him as their champion, thinking "that they would leave the victory to fate." It is clear that Tristrant associates chance or fate with the sea, for when he arrives on the small island which is to be the battleground, he at once pushes Morolt's boat away from shore. This symbolic act proves prophetic because soon afterwards Morolt dies of his wounds at sea. The defeat of the huge and powerful veteran by the totally inexperienced youth is clearly an intervention of a supernatural force and was foreshadowed by the references to luck, chance, and fate.

When it becomes apparent that Tristrant's own wound will not heal, he has himself placed in a small boat, which drifts out into the sea, rudderless and completely at the mercy of wind and wave. This picture of a man and his destiny was a literary commonplace in the Middle Ages, and it is obvious that Tristrant is consciously placing himself in the hands of fate. The winds blow him to Ireland, a place of great danger for him as the slayer of its national hero, but also the only place where he can be cured. One begins to wonder whether it is the intent of fate to destroy Tristrant, who after all escapes through his own shrewdness, or save him. And the question as to the nature of this intervening force—malign, benevolent, or indifferent—is never fully resolved. After three voyages, Tristrant returns to Cornwall at the end of exactly a year, the very day on which Kurneval, according to his lord's orders, was to cease waiting for him and go back to Lohenois. Since winds and waves—the primary factors in determining the length of his absence—have already affected the course of the story in a decisive manner, this "coincidence" reinforces the concept of the sea as a symbol of fate.

Not long afterward Mark sees two swallows fight and let fall a long, beautiful strand of woman's hair. The birds are readily seen as additional instruments of fate, just as in retrospect their struggle appears to be a foreshadowing of the conflict of Mark and Tristrant over Isalde. Mark declares that he will marry only the owner of the hair, and his nephew sets out to find her. This time he is in good health, has a full crew and a rich cargo, and is accompanied by a hundred knights. Still, although determined to avoid Ireland at any cost, he is driven to the very spot at which he had arrived as a helpless invalid, where once more both danger and success wait. The symbolism of the sea as fate is further strengthened, and the conflict between Tristrant and his destiny comes into the open, for, at least on a superficial level, it is his own heroic deed, the killing of the dragon, which saves his life, makes his search successful, and postpones catastrophe. The episode of the beautiful hair and the random search has exposed Eilhart to criticism from his own day to the present for what some have considered a wanton disregard for probability, but unjustly so.[6] For it is neither carelessness nor naïveté, but the deliberate construction of a metaphysical framework which gives universality to the situation of the hero.

The most important effect of the sea on the story takes place during the return voyage, while Tristrant is bringing Isalde to Cornwall to be Mark's bride. When she gets seasick and the journey is interrupted so that she may recuperate in a harbor, a fatal chain of events is initiated. Brangene goes for a walk along the shore, leaving the love potion unguarded when Tristrant comes to Isalde's cabin to ask if she is ready to continue the journey. It is a hot day, and he asks that wine be brought for him and Isalde. A girl brings the potion, they drink, and destiny in a new form takes control of their lives. Distressed by his sudden passion, Tristrant leaves abruptly, and the confused and frightened Isalde pours forth a lengthy and eloquent protest to a personified Lady Love for having so violently taken possession of her. This monologue is the focal point of the entire work, not because it is a love story—which, of course, it is—but because Lady Love herself is merely a representative of the destiny which is formed by inner compulsions. It is both interesting and effective that Eilhart should place his lament against an inexorable fate at the point where the tragic situation emerges, rather than at its final resolution, and that he should put it in the mouth of the heroine, rather than that of the narrator. Brangene knows Tristrant and Isalde will die if they do not become lovers and enlists the aid of Kurneval to bring this about. "I'll leave it all to fate," she says. Outer fate has caused them to become subject to an inner fate in a manner quite consistent with modern determinism. From now on the sea, though retaining its symbolic quality, is less of a directing force, and the potion takes over. Its power is such that for four years hero and heroine must remain together or die, and after that period they will still love each other for the rest of their lives.

Most of the episodes which follow are accounts of Tristrant's struggles for life. He knows the power of the potion is irresistible, accepts this fact completely, and is not troubled by feelings of guilt at deceiving Mark. The narrator is also not concerned with the deception—he is no moralist—and his frequent condemnations of the potion are essentially a refrain, a reminder that his hero is caught up in a battle with fate. The potion, like the sea, is ambiguous. Although it is a constant and consistent threat to Tristrant's life, it is also his chief source of happiness. He cannot withstand it directly, but can only make every effort to extricate himself from the perilous situations into which it draws him. He succeeds at times by cleverness, boldness, and the help of friends, at times by the intervention of an opposing and more favorable fortune. His wit saves him in the humorous scene by the linden, and his great strength and daring enable him to leap safely from the chapel, but it is purely by chance (1. 4161: *von geschichte*)[7] that he then encounters Kurneval with his horse and sword. The narrator does not know why Tristrant placed his bare sword between Isalde and himself while they slept in the wilderness, but it proved very fortunate for him (1.4593: *quam im doch zu heile*). When his coat tears at the athletic contest and compromises his disguise, it is only luck that preserves him (1. 7834; *von gelucke he abir genas*), as was the case when a piece of the spear Antret throws at him serves as the means of his escape (1. 8306: *daz was ouch sîn gelucke*), and he would not have evaded the nationwide search that followed if he hadn't been lucky (1. 8677: *wen daz es gelucke wîlt*).

Other intrusions of an irrational or superhuman power are suggested by the pronounced irony of certain episodes. One is that in which Tinas, one of Tristrant's best friends, brings the dwarf, him most dangerous enemy, back to the court, where he almost causes the hero's execution. Another occurs at the end of the second war against Count Riole, when Tristrant, the shrewd and skillful general, is permanently disfigured and nearly killed because, quite inexplicably, he neglects to put on his helmet in a minor attack on a tower and is felled by a stone. And much of Tristrant's last adventure is pervaded by a fateful irony, which is seen especially in the fact that the hero receives his mortal wound neither in a great struggle against a national enemy such as Morolt, the dragon, or Count Riole's army, nor as a result of his overwhelming passion for Isalde, but merely as a helper in a petty and transient affair which is essentially a parody of his own deep and lasting love. Fortune turns against him in a series of seemingly chance events: Kehenis's hat blows into Nampetenis's moat; Tristrant forgets the telltale darts in the wall; and the two exhaust their horses in an accidental encounter with a deer which, as bad luck would have it, they couldn't catch (11. 9118-19: *von gelucke ez muste geschîn, daz sie ez nicht enmochtin vân*).

In the skirmish which follows, Kehenis is killed and Tristrant is again wounded by a poisoned spear. When the ship bringing Isalde to heal him is sighted, he asks his wife the color of the sail. She says it is black—meaning that Isalde is not coming—and in despair he lies back and dies. Her words came not from malice or jealousy, it was simply a foolish lie which she instantly regretted, an inexplicable instrument of an inscrutable fate. Eilhart has been censured for not having the falsehood spring from jealousy as Thomas does, but such criticism ignores the fundamental differences between their works.

The final, devastating revelation of the enigmatic nature of the forces which determine Tristrant's destiny is contained in the lament of King Mark at the death of the lovers. "I would gladly have treated Queen Isalde and my nephew kindly, so that the knight would have stayed with me always," he says sadly, "It was very foolish of them not to tell me that they had drunk the fatal potion." So it was, and their stratagems, sorrow, heroism, and deaths were all unnecessary, but quite believable, for that's how life is. However, the author does not end his story there. Cautiously, even somewhat dubiously, he adds: "I don't know if I should repeat this to you, but I heard say that the king had a rosebush planted over the woman and a fine grapevine over the man and that the two grew so tightly together that they could not be separated without being broken. Indeed, I also heard it said that this was due to the power of the potion." It is just possible, he thus suggests, that there is meaning and even benevolence after all behind that which appears as pure chance. And not just for his hero and heroine, for they now have been generalized to man and woman.

STRUCTURE

Fate provides not only a theme for Tristrant, but also a structure, since the story falls readily into three main parts which coincide with three divisions in the life of the hero with respect to the forces which determine his destiny: the period of the predominant influence of outer fate (symbolized by the sea) and the two periods of the predominant influence of inner fate (symbolized by the potion). These are preceded by an introduction that includes the Rivalin-Blankeflur tale and the hero's birth and followed by a conclusion which tells of the Kehenis-Gariole affair and the hero's death. Although the work as a whole has an episodic quality, it is by no means formless. Structural unity is achieved primarily by the use of parallel situations and events, arranged in symmetrical patterns which show similarity, contrast, and continuity. In addition to this geometrical harmony, there is a certain amount of progression from one episode to another, although, in an account of a man and the irrational or superrational forces which act on him, the author must use restraint in having one incident develop from another by simple logic. When Gottfried tells of the two journeys to Ireland, the hero sails there the first time because Morolt had said that only the Irish princess could cure him. Tristan learns to know and admire her, recommends her to Mark as a bride when he returns to Cornwall, and later sets out again for Ireland to win her for his uncle. A story of an enigmatic fate cannot connect events so simply, even though it too must have unity.

The introduction not only supplies the first intimation of Eilhart's theme, but is also a significant structural element. The Rivalin-Blankeflur-Mark situation in which Rivalin comes to Mark's aid, wins his sister, and takes her away with him is duplicated in the main narrative when Rivalin's son comes to Mark's aid and wins his wife, who finally leaves him to join her dying lover. The highly romantic love of Rivalin and Blankeflur thus serves as a thematic prelude to the Tristrant and Isalde story and contrasts to the Kehenis-Gariole affair in the conclusion, a rather cynically portrayed episode in which Kehenis for years delays the satisfying of his desire, needs the assistance of a clever friend to attain his lady, and is betrayed by the object of his affection. The development is from a simple account of true love, to a story of irresistible and faithful, though adulterous passion, to a tale of casual adultery, with moderate desire and limited loyalty, and then back to the central love story. Tristrant's birth at sea prepares the audience for the voyages of part one, however unmotivated they might be, and finds a certain parallel in the events of the conclusion, when he dies by the sea and his body is transported over it to Cornwall.

The events of part one lead, by means of the potion, to those of part two and are paralleled by those of part three. Sections one and three are filled with journeys. Two of the earlier voyages resemble most of the later voyages in that their goal is Isalde, although Tristrant is not aware of this at the time. However, the two series of voyages are also dissimilar. Those of part one are connected with the service of Mark—the hero goes to Cornwall to serve its king, sails to Ireland as a result of having fought for him, and sails there again to find a bride for him—while the journeys of part three result in Mark's humiliation. There is also some correspondence with respect to the role the traveler plays. He comes to Cornwall as an anonymous nobleman, to Ireland once as a minstrel-merchant, and a second time simply as a merchant. In the later journeys, he arrives in Cornwall first as an Arthurian knight, with the entire court of Arthur, next in secret but under his own name and accompanied by a king's son and two attendants, a third time with Kurneval as a pilgrim, a fourth time with Kurneval as a homeless squire, and finally, all alone, as a fool. The first sequence may show a downward progression, the second one definitely does. It is true that the leper disguise does not fit into the pattern, but this was only an impromptu expedient, the purpose of which was not so much to conceal Tristrant's identity as to convince Isalde of his boundless devotion and remind her of her rescue from the lepers.

The most unusual parallel situations of parts one and three have to do with the two Isaldes: the one of Ireland, who twice saves Tristrant's life, and the less beautiful, less passionate, less clever one of Karahes, who unintentionally causes his death. Tristrant consummates his love to Isalde of Ireland without marrying her and almost is killed as a result. He marries the other but for a long time does not consummate the marriage, which also nearly costs him his life. Since the hero is reunited with the first Isalde after his death, his relation to the second does not establish a downward trend such as that indicated by the disguises.

The central part of the story, part two, consists of the four years of greater force of the potion, the period during which the lovers must be together or die. It is set in Cornwall, first in the royal castle at Tintanjol and later in a desolate wasteland in a remote area of the kingdom. The two settings provide the contrasts and similarities which give form to the work. At the castle the lovers are constantly threatened by the plots of their enemies, and Tristrant shows his cleverness in foiling them while when in the wilderness the lovers are endangered by hunger and cold the hero displays his ingenuity in meeting these perils. At the castle Mark is deceived as to Isalde's virginity by the substitution of Brangene; in the wilderness he is deceived as to her loyalty by the bare sword lying between her and Tristrant.

When the power of the potion decreases, the sojourn in Cornwall comes to an end, and part three of the story begins. This parallels all that has happened to Tristrant since leaving Lohenois. He travels to a land which desperately needs his help, saves it from its enemies, wins the love of a beautiful Isalde, who has a close relationship to the country's king, and establishes an intimate and permanent connection with her. Tristrant could have been happy and content, but, just as the sea had formerly twice carried him off to the Irish Isalde, so now does the might of the potion repeatedly draw him away to her. However, this last period does not merely duplicate what has gone before, for there is also a clear development toward the concluding episode. The visits to Cornwall become progressively longer, the intervals between them also longer (the last journey after an absence of three years), and the meetings between the lovers increasingly intimate, until at last even Brangene and Kurneval are gone and Tristrant and Isalde are all alone. These trends, together with that suggested by the disguises, point toward an end to the Tristrant-Isalde relationship and toward the concluding events.

The Kehenis-Gariole episode reflects the basic situation of the Tristrant and Isalde story in that it presents a tale of adultery and stresses the clever means by which the lovers circumvent the precautions of the jealous husband. It therefore might have been used as a sardonic commentary on the preceding narrative and thus have reduced it to the level of an amusing anecdote. But the death for love of the Irish Isalde contrasts so sharply with Gariole's weakness in danger that the intent of the author becomes quite obvious: to emphasize that the love story of Tristrant and Isalde, although containing humorous passages and situations, is not merely an adultery *Schwank* (short, comic narrative), but a thing of dignity and beauty. Tristrant's end is tragic in the classic sense, for he has fought nobly against his fate and bravely succumbed to it.

The fundamental structure of Tristrant consists of three major parts with an introduction and a conclusion. These are unified by a system of parallel events and situations which pair introduction and conclusion, parts one and three, and part two with itself, so that the second half of the work is carefully foreshadowed by the first. At the same time, events of one part lead thematically to those of the following. The same technique is used, but less consistently, to connect individual episodes within the primary units. The author also employs a variety of other linking devices which tie together events that have no causative relationship. When Isalde hurries to save the life of the injured Morolt, it is obvious that she will be the one to cure the wound of his antagonist, so that the audience is prepared for Tristrant to land in Ireland even though he is driven there by chance winds.

And, on the second voyage, Tristrant's warning to his crew to avoid Ireland is an adequate hint of their destination. Soon afterwards Isalde's discovery that the notch in Tristrant's sword matches the splinter she took from Morolt's skull joins all three adventures: the Morolt battle and the first and second voyages. In like manner, the warning given by Isalde's mother to Brangene to guard the potion well so that none but Mark and his bride drink it anticipates the fatal error of hero and heroine, thus connecting the second voyage to the following events.

Several of the subsequent episodes are connected and given a sense of continuity by having them share distinctive settings and secondary characters. Four of the more noteworthy occurrences—the aborted murder of Brangene, the deception of Mark at the linden, the delivery of the priest's letter, and the penultimate meeting of hero and heroine—take place in an orchard with a brook which was right beside the palace at Tintanjol. In the case of two of these events, the orchard also serves as a thematic link, for when Tristrant comes by night to bring Mark the letter telling of his renunciation of Isalde, the sad and defeated hero recalls the many happy nights he had spent there with his loved one and ties his horse to the tree in which Mark was hiding on one of those occasions. Another specific setting is the clump of thorn bushes near the deer stand by the road leading from Tintanjol to Blankenland. Two successive adventures in part three begin at these thorn bushes where, in contrast to the intimate meetings under the linden, the lovers can communicate only at a distance. The best example of incidents being related to each other by a secondary character is the use of Aquitain, the dwarf, who unexpectedly appears to set the trap by the linden and the one in the king's bedroom, and then drops from the story. Other examples are the two campaigns which Tristrant leads against the same rebel, Count Riole, and the fact that the knight who captured Kehenis in the first campaign is the Nampetenis who kills him in Tristrant's last battle.

Many of the events of part three reveal, in addition to oblique linking devices, direct causal relationships. As a result of the "bold water" episode, Tristrant is forced to take Kehenis to Cornwall to prove that the first Isalde loves him more than does the second. Kehenis lies on this occasion, saying that Tristrant refused a challenge even though it was made in the name of the queen, and Isalde therefore causes her lover to be beaten. Because of her subsequent remorse at this deed, she sends a message begging the hero to come to her so that she can atone for her offense. He does so and, on the way back to his ship, is forced against his better judgment to take part in an athletic contest because he is challenged to do so in Isalde's name: he has to prove that he is incapable of being so unfaithful as Kehenis had said.

The causal link between Tristrant's return to Lohenois and his fourth visit to Cornwall is that he is about to lose the service of Kurneval (who is to govern Lohenois for him) and is afraid he could never again manage to see Isalde without the aid of his friend. The connection between the second campaign against Count Riole and Tristrant's last voyage to Cornwall during his lifetime is simply that he became so disfigured by the falling stone that he has a perfect disguise for the undertaking.

It is clear that the relationship of specific episodes to each other is not nearly as refined as is their connection to the general framework of the story; *Tristrant* does not have a closely knit plot. At the same time, the sequence of events is neither capricious nor awkward, the transitions from one to another are not too abrupt, and there is sufficient anticipation and retrospection to provide at least a minimal sense of unity. In short, the arrangement gives the impression of conscious artistry. Indeed, some studies have maintained that *Tristrant* was constructed according to an intricate system of numerical composition in which each verse is a part of a mathematically exact, symmetrical structure of verse, verse-groups, group-blocks, and main divisions which is based on both language and plot.[8] Because of the corruption of the texts this thesis can be neither proven nor disproven. What has been established is that Eilhart, like many other medieval poets, had a strong sense of form and symmetry.

MOTIFS

Certain motifs contribute to the structural unity of *Tristrant* and, since they also reveal something of the nature of fate, to the thematic unity as well. The most pervasive motif is that of the journey, with which the majority of the adventures begin and end. By putting them into a similar framework, consistency is added to the work as a whole, and, since the hero usually travels by sea, the audience is constantly reminded of the role of fate in his life. A similar unifying effect is exerted by the joy-grief motif, which the narrator stresses in his opening remarks and Isalde expounds upon in her monologue. It reveals itself graphically in the physical pain the hero experiences in his attempts to reach his source of happiness, Isalde; in the anguish both feel when they cannot be together; and in the deprivation they experience in the wilderness when they can be with each other all of the time. The motif is prefigured even before the drinking of the potion by the poisoned wound and the dragon's burns which the hero must endure before his first two contacts with Isalde, and it makes a series of later appearances: Tristrant's leap over the flour to Isalde's bed is so strenuous that old wounds break open and both he and she are covered with blood; for their constant companionship in the wilderness they have to pay with hunger and cold; they share their love on the night after King Arthur's hunting party only after the hero cuts himself on Mark's trap and bleeds "like a stuck pig"; their meeting during the fool episode is made possible by Tristrant's long sickness and disfigurement; and they are not permanently united until one dies of poison and disappointment and the other of a broken heart. All of this suffering, as well as the constant danger which surrounds them, has a significance beyond the particular circumstances, indeed beyond their individual fates. For it is a reminder that this is the nature of human destiny, that everyone must inevitably pay for joy with sorrow and pain.

A like conclusion can be drawn from the substitute motif, the first three appearances of which center on Isalde. The Irish steward announces that he killed the dragon and attempts to take the place of its real slayer as the husband of the princess. The king learns the truth and awards his daughter to Tristrant who, however, proposes Mark as a substitute. However, on his wedding night, Mark goes to bed with Brangene, who has been prevailed upon to fill in for her mistress. Soon afterwards a dog is killed instead of Brangene and its liver brought to Isalde as that of her lady-in-waiting. When the lovers flee to the wilderness, Mark notices Tristrant's dog and orders that it be hanged in his place. Two years later, Tristrant helps Havelin defeat his enemies and marries his daughter only because her name is Isalde. To show Kehenis why the marriage with his sister was not consummated, the hero takes him to Cornwall, where the latter can see how fondly Isalde caresses Tristrant's dog in his stead. In the following journey to Cornwall, Tristrant and Kurneval are seen and escape only after two errant squires take their places. In one instance, the substitute motif is comic— when Kehenis sleeps with a magic pillow instead of with Gymele—but in the other cases the substitution is a very serious matter. Brangene protests bitterly at being obliged to take Isalde's place, Isalde is grief-stricken at the presumed murder of her friend, the squire is so sympathetic with Tristrant's dog that he risks severe punishment to set it free, Tristrant's marriage to Havelin's daughter and Isalde's demonstration of affection for Tristrant's dog both spring from their deep love for each other, and Tristrant's life depends on the success of the decoys. A constant factor in the motif is that in all seven instances something of lesser value is substituted for something of greater value. The implication is that this is life. Just as one must always pay dearly for happiness, one must often accept less than that for which one has paid.

From the time at which Mark first becomes suspicious of Tristrant to the end of the story the dominant motif is that of the hunt. It first appears when Mark arranges a large hunting party in order to see if Tristrant will visit Isalde during his supposed absence. It recurs several times while the lovers are in the wilderness: Kurneval, after having become separated from Tristrant and Isalde, uses Tristrant's dog to track him down; Tristrant shoots game to supplement their meager diet of roots and herbs; Mark is hunting when he finds the lovers. Later, as a guest in Britain, Tristrant helps Gawain drive a deer from King Arthur's lodge to Tintanjol so that he may circumvent Mark and see Isalde. She initiates hunting parties on two further occasions with the same goal in mind. And just before their deaths, Kehenis and Tristrant so exhaust their horses chasing a deer that they themselves are easily overtaken by Nampetenis when he returns from his daily hunt. Sometimes Tristrant is the hunter, but when Mark watches him from the linden, when Utant follows his scent, when Mark finds him in the wilderness, when Mark (during another hunt) almost rides into the thorn bushes where he is hiding, and when Nampetenis catches up with him, he is the hunted, "a beast which was tame" (1. 4489: *eime wilde, daz was zam*). Except in the chase with Kehenis, whenever Tristrant does the hunting or Isalde arranges the hunt, the sport is only a means to an end, for what the hero actually pursues is happiness with his loved one. The hunt motif, therefore, repeatedly calls attention to Tristrant's situation as the persistent hunter of love's joys and the prey of forces determined to destroy him because of this pursuit.

The last motif to be discussed is that of death. It appears at the hero's birth with the tragic demise of Blankeflur and does not recur until Tristrant kills Morolt, an event which, however welcome in Cornwall, brings widespread grief to Ireland. Eight or nine years later, the faithful Brangene dies, and then—at ever-decreasing intervals—Rivalin, Havelin, Kehenis, Tristrant, and (only an hour or so afterwards) Isalde. In almost every instance the deaths are individually significant to the story: that of Blankeflur provides it with a mood and an omen; the exigencies of the plot require the deaths of Morolt and Kehenis, and those of Brangene and Rivalin serve (in the former case directly, in the latter indirectly) to isolate hero and heroine from their closest companions. However, the death of Havelin, since it is in itself unnecessary, indicates that the author intended to exploit the deaths of the secondary characters for an additional purpose: the establishment of a motif which should point in the most direct manner toward the final catastrophe. At the end, only Tristrant's wife and Isalde's husband remain to mourn and bury the dead.

One may see other motifs in Tristrant, but those mentioned are the most important. They help to tie the episodes together and thus contribute to the structural unity of the work. At the same time, the motifs raise questions about the nature of fate which continually reinforce Eilhart's basic theme.

STYLE

Although the use of motifs is surprisingly consistent, the style in general is highly informal and casual, sometimes repetitive, often deficient in explanatory material, and quite careless with respect to details. The tone and manner of composition are set by a narrator who frequently interrupts his tale with exclamations and comments to his audience and always takes a lively, personal interest in the events. He is not as didactic and digressive as the genial storyteller of Wirnt von Grafenberg's *Wigalois,* nor as ironic and humorous as the irrepressible narrator of *Parzival.* Nevertheless, he has his share of these qualities, and they blend with others to form a distinct personality which, of course, colors the entire account. We make the acquaintance of our reporter at the very beginning when he assails with mock bitterness those who don't want to hear and threatens to have them ejected. Having thus unified his listeners behind him against possible troublemakers, he soon develops a chatty, bantering rapport with them: frequently assuring them of the accuracy of his account, inviting their concurrence with his sentiments, and even asking their opinions as to how situations can be resolved. It is true that most of the narrator's asides to the audience consist of a single line and thus serve as convenient rhyme fillers, but they also create an intimate atmosphere of dramatic immediacy and establish a specific and consistent outlook.

The narrator's attitude toward his sources varies. Although he often insists on the exact truth of his account, at other times he hedges, saying only, that was what he heard, or, that was what the book said. Sometimes he pretends to be surprised himself at what has happened, and occasionally he allows several of his listeners to express their beliefs as to what took place. All this naturally has nothing to do with the author and his sources, but is one of many devices to produce verisimilitude. The narrator's attitude toward his hero is always the same. He admits that it looked bad for Tristrant to sleep with Isalde on her wedding night, but it did not really show disloyalty to Mark since he could not help it. It was also very stupid for the hero to attempt to go to Isalde when he saw the flour on the floor, but this too was due to the potion. Otherwise he was smart enough to have refrained. However, there are surprisingly few justifications of Tristrant's actions, just as there is little speculation as to the motives of others. The narrator is interested primarily in what happened and how it happened, not why. Perhaps this explains the small number of didactic digressions. For, with the exception of a somewhat lengthy attack on the evil of

jealousy and a brief discussion of the futility of keeping watch over one's wife, he has little advice to give his listeners.

The narrator's occasional admission of ignorance as to fact and motives is related to a stylistic device—the controlled or restricted point of view—which is used quite skillfully in *Tristrant* when one considers that this use of point of view was not perfected until the nineteenth century. Usually the effect is to emphasize the role the hero is playing at a particular time or to stress the impression he makes on a certain group. As soon as the young Tristrant arrives incognito at Mark's court, the narrator ceases to refer to him by name, but, except when he is alone with Kurneval, calls him only *daz kind* (the boy) until shortly before he is knighted. This, of course, is how the court thinks of him. A similar procedure is followed during Tristrant's second journey to Ireland. When he goes to find the dragon, he is described according to the impression he made on the lord high steward and his men as the one who rode up with spear and shield like a great storm. Later when Isalde and Brangene are seeking the unknown knight who killed the dragon, the narrator does not mention Tristrant's name until he regains consciousness. Then the point of view is shifted from that of the ladies to that of the hero, and he once more becomes Tristrant. There are other examples of this technique, the most consistent of which are seen during Tristrant's last two journeys from Karahes to Cornwall. As soon as he and Kurneval decide to disguise themselves as errant squires, the narrator begins to refer to them with designations which fit their role: *jungelinge, garzune, gesellen,* all words for youths. But when they arrive with Tinas and Isalde and reveal their identities to them, the hero is spoken of as Tristrant. Eilhart apparently learned with practice, for the last use of the controlled point of view is the most successful. The hero becomes "the fool" as soon as he arrives in Cornwall so disguised and retains this designation until he reveals himself to Isalde. Thus the narrator sees him only as does the court at Cornwall.

Eilhart's restricted point of view is a development of his use of epithets. However, his epithet is not intended to limit knowledge concerning a person, but only to stress a specific aspect of a character as revealed in a particular situation. Eilhart's epithets, like his asides, frequently serve as rhyme fillers, but they are always appropriate to the individual and his condition. Those referring to Tristrant have a function similar to that of background music in that they help to interpret the successive roles he plays, telling the listeners just how they are to view him at a particular moment and sometimes even giving them a glimpse into the future. An account of the epithets which describe the hero during his early adventures will illustrate their use in general.

As has been said, when Tristrant first comes to Mark's court, he is referred to only as "the boy." However, when he offers to fight Morolt, he becomes "the noble warrior," which is a glance ahead since he has never yet been in a battle. In order to prove himself worthy of facing such an opponent, the hero has to reveal his relationship to the king and is thereafter repeatedly called "Mark's nephew." This emphasizes both the king's reluctance to let him take so great a risk and the hero's loyalty to his uncle. Just before the battle, while Mark is placing his own armor on Tristrant, the narrator speaks of the latter once more as "the boy" in order to remind the listeners of his disadvantage in size, strength, and experience, after which he confers the epithets "Mark's nephew," "the hero," and "the bold warrior, Tristrant." However, when Morolt sees him, he addresses Tristrant as "handsome and brave boy," so that the disparity between the combatants is again stressed. The fight begins, and the narrator calls the hero "the steady warrior" and "the very bold Tristrant." The epithets given to Morolt throughout the episode—"the strong," "the large," "the bold"—are of a nature to emphasize the danger and bravery of Tristrant. After winning the struggle, the latter becomes sick from the poisoned spear and is called "the sick one" or "the poor sick one" until Isalde's medicine cures him. At the end of the first sojourn in Ireland, the Irish king asks his advice with regard to the famine, and the narrator designates him as "the clever Tristrant," which is again an anticipation, for the hero has as yet done nothing wise or shrewd.

So it is that the hero is accompanied throughout the work by a large number of frequently repeated epithets which, if merely listed by themselves, would almost give a sort of resumé of Tristrant's story. Not only he and Morolt, but also the other prominent characters have their epithets, which are more likely to indicate temporary than permanent attributes. This is especially apparent when Isalde, after planning the murder of Brangene, is called "the treacherous lady." On the other hand, the designation, "the clever Tristrant," is used so often that it becomes a sort of leitmotif, which describes the type of story Eilhart is telling, as well as its hero. The epithets interpret for the listeners and do so much more concisely than would be possible with phrases and clauses, thus contributing to the brevity that characterizes much of Eilhart's expression.

Many elements of Eilhart's style are connected with his passion for brevity. The almost total lack of psychological motivation fits the theme of an almighty, perhaps capricious, fate and also has a telescoping effect. So does the author's spotlighting technique with which he focuses on the primary actors and situations and does not bring others into the field of vision until or unless they are required. This is seen particularly in the case of Kurneval, who, except for the first voyage to Ireland, is constantly with his lord from Tristrant's childhood almost to his death. Yet at times the squire goes unmentioned for hundreds of verses, during the entire stay at Arthur's court, for example. When he is needed, he steps into the spotlight, and we see that he has been there all along. This method produces some surprises, as during the journey of the hero and Kehenis to Cornwall. They go by ship, hide in the thorn thicket, spend the night with Isalde in Blankenland, and only when they have started for home do we learn that they have been accompanied by Kurneval and Kehenis's squire, who appear because they are needed for the Pleherin incident.

The application of this technique to situations has the effect of putting the entire contents of the work into a single chronological sequence of simple events. This arrangement is seen most graphically in the prevalence of the word "then" (*dô*), which appears almost a thousand times in *Tristrant,* and in a marked inclination to use verbs in a perfective sense.[9] The latter characteristic causes some problems when the author attempts to describe simultaneous actions, for the reader is likely to assume momentarily that they occurred in sequence. The spotlighting method works best when it contributes to clear-cut situations with symbolic or dramatic impacts. Two incidents will serve as examples, one in the introduction, the other in the conclusion. When Rivalin is in Cornwall, he wins the favor of Blankeflur "with a painful wound" and lies with her. If Eilhart had gone into details as to how he was wounded and how he happened to lie with Blankeflur—as Gottfried does in some 200 verses—the symbolic and prophetic implications for Tristrant would have been obscured. It is enough to say that he won her as a hero, as Tristrant was to win Isalde. A similar and praiseworthy restraint can be seen when Nampetenis, after giving Tristrant a mortal wound, predicts his own death at the hands of the hero's and Kehenis's friends. It is necessary, of course, that Tristrant be avenged, but an account of the battle and the slaying of Nampetenis certainly would have detracted from the crowning event of the story, the final reunion of hero and heroine.

Eilhart does not always condense: the Isalde monologue is about 200 verses long, the account of the first battle against Riole takes some 250 verses (almost twice the number Gottfried uses), and the description of the gala procession past the thorn thicket requires over 100 verses. But these are all dramatic scenes, and the author lets them develop without intrusion or comment to the point where a maximum impact is produced. Then he hurries on to the next scene. His strong interest in dramatic effects is seen especially in the propensity for letting the characters communicate directly to the audience in monologues and dialogues. *Tristrant* contains many monologues (ranging in length from a single verse to two hundred), although not appreciably more than other narrative works of the same general period. Although the nature of the Eilhart monologue is not particularly unique, his dialogues are quite distinctive, primarily for two reasons. The first is the pronounced tendency to pass without warning from indirect to direct discourse, usually after 1 or 2 verses, almost always after 4 or 5.[10] The second is the highly staccato quality of the dialogue in direct discourse, in which the speaker often changes after each verse and sometimes after each half verse. This clipped, rapid-fire exchange, frequently continuing for some time, is perhaps Eilhart's most unusual stylistic feature. It would be interesting to know the extent to which the reader dramatized the work for medieval audiences. Since over one-third of *Tristrant* is in dialogue and even minor characters have speaking roles, it could have been quite a performance.

Another marked trait of Eilhart's style is the frequent foreshadowing of coming events. Sometimes this amounts only to a short, two-line summary of what immediately follows; often it is a brief glimpse into a more remote future.[11] The summaries can be effective introductions to new episodes, but occasionally they are a little distracting, for they interrupt the chronological sequence of incidents, and Eilhart does not always do this smoothly. For example, when the priest learned that the hero was willing to give up Isalde, "he quickly wrote a letter to the king and sent it by Tristrant, since he had no other messenger." One might expect the next statement to tell the king's reaction, but it does not. We hear an account of what was written, how Tristrant started out, and something of his trip to the castle. The duel with Riole is another case in which the audience is likely to mistake the summary for the action itself: "Tristrant rode at him and struck him down, then rode back to him and used force to make him yield." This is followed by a more detailed description of the combat. The short references to occurrences in a more distant future—a common characteristic of medieval heroic narratives—are well done. They help tie the episodes together and stimulate the anticipation of the listeners. As soon as Tristrant is wounded in the battle with Morolt, they are warned that he will be sick a long time because of it. When a piece of his sword remains in his opponent's skull, they are told that later it will be found, and the potion no sooner enters the story than the narrator hints at a fatal mishap to come. Such foreshadowings continue through the work and become more frequent toward the end. The narrator reminds his audience that Kehenis has the keys to Nampetenis's castle and adds that both he and Tristrant suffered later because of this. Tristrant's skill at throwing darts in the castle evokes the comment that it will bring him into mortal danger, and the lie of Tristrant's wife is followed immediately by the observation that she greatly regret-

ted it afterwards. All these comments are to make us apprehensive about the safety of the hero; however, there is one whose purpose is to allay our fears. When, after the stay in the wilderness, Isalde returns to King Mark, who previously had condemned her to death, we are assured that "he kept her fondly for many years."

A final noteworthy characteristic of the style of *Tristrant* is its simple, unadorned language, with few foreign words, similes, metaphors, and poetic exaggerations. Similes like "the king began to glow like a coal" are apt but rare, as are such metaphors as "Brangene brought her a potion she liked" (news that Tristrant was coming), or the designation of Nampetenis's castle as a hermitage because of his wife's confinement there. With respect to poetic exaggeration, one must admit that in the battle against Riole the blood ran unbelievably deep, but the number of combattants was well within the range one might expect of such a rebellion. As for exaggeration of feeling, Eilhart shows commendable restraint. The grief of King Rivalin and his retinue at the death of Blankeflur is briefly and unpretentiously expressed and does not obscure the tragedy itself. The same is true of the account of the deaths of Tristrant and Isalde: the sorrow of the hero's wife, King Mark, and the people of Karahes is described, but not at great length and without the commiseration of the narrator.

Notes

1. Among these are Friedrich Vogt, *Geschichte der mittelhochdeutschen Literatur,* 3d. ed., Grundriss der deutschen Literatur, no. 2 (Berlin: de Gruyter, 1922), 1: 117; Arthur Witte, "Der Aufbau der ältesten Tristandichtungen," *Zeitschrift für deutsches Altertum* 70 (1933): 162; Maurice Delbouille, "Le premier *Roman de Tristan,*" *Cahiers de Civilisation Médiévale* 5 (1962): 286; Karl Otto Brogsitter, *Artusepik,* Sammlung Metzler, no. 38 (Stuttgart: Metzler, 1965), p. 99; Gerhard Schindele, *Tristan: Metamorphose und Tradition,* Studien zur Poetik und Geschichte der Literatur, no. 12 (Stuttgart: Kohlhammer, 1971), p. 13; and especially Gertrude Schoepperle, *Tristan and Isolt: A Study of the Sources of the Romance,* 2d ed. (New York: Franklin, 1960), 1:8. A smaller number of scholars believes either the version of Thomas or that of Béroul to be closer to the original.

2. Most Eilhart research has dealt with the relationships and reliability of the various texts. The latest work to describe and evaluate the texts is Hadumod Bussmann's *Eilhart von Oberg: Tristrant: Synoptischer Druck der ergänzten Fragmenten mit der gesamten Parallelüberlieferung,* Altdeutsche Textbibliothek, no. 70 (Tübingen: Niemeyer, 1969), which also presents in parallel columns the texts of the old fragments and the corresponding

sections of the later manuscripts. One can readily see that there are few significant differences in content.

3. The various attempts to identify the original language of *Tristrant* have been summarized by Gerhard Cordes, *Zur Sprache Eilhards von Oberg,* Hansische Forschungen: Arbeiten zur germanischen Philologie, no. 1 (Hamburg: Wachholtz, 1939). About half of the scholars believe it was written in Middle Franconian; others assume it was a normalized Middle or High German. Cordes thinks the language was basically Thuringian.

4. Careful analyses of the Eilhart-Veldeke relationship and surveys of the preceding scholarship on the subject are found in Jan van Dam, *Zur Vorgeschichte des höfischen Epos: Lamprecht, Eilhart, Veldeke,* Rheinische Beiträge und Hülfsbücher zur germanischen Philologie und Volkskunde, no. 7 (Bonn and Leipzig: Schroeder, 1923), and Hadumod Bussmann, "Der Liebesmonolog im frühhöfischen Epos. Versuch einer Typbestimmung am Beispiel von Eilharts Isalde-Monolog," *Werk-Typ-Situation: Studien zu poetologischen Bedingungen in der älteren deutschen Literatur,* ed. Ingeborg Glier et al. (Stuttgart: Metzler, 1969), pp. 45-63.

5. Delbouille, "Le premier *Roman de Tristan,*" p. 434, believes that Eilhart's source was that of all the Tristan versions. Schoepperle, *Tristan and Isolt,* 1:8, 108, thinks it the source of all versions except the continuation of Béroul and the French prose romance, but the majority of scholars maintain that Eilhart's source was one step removed from that of Thomas. The fifteenth-century verse redactions mention a book from which the author got his story, but the references are supported neither by the early fragments nor by the chapbook and may have been only a literary device. Bodo Mergel, *Tristan und Isolde: Ursprung und Entwicklung der Tristansage des Mittelalters* (Mainz: Kirchheim, 1949), p. 70, suggests that Eilhart's source was the lost Tristan story which Chrétien at the beginning of *Cligès* mentions as one of his first works. Other scholars are inclined to accept the trouvère with the amusing pseudonym, La Chèvre, who is mentioned in a miracle play as the author of a Tristan work, as Eilhart's immediate, though perhaps not ultimate source. Kurt Wagner, "Wirklichkeit und Schicksal im Epos des Eilhart von Oberg," *Archiv für das Studium der neueren Sprachen* 170 (1936): 182-83, theorizes that Eilhart's source was written by a cleric of northern France. Roger Sherman Loomis, "Bleheris and the Tristan Story," *Modern Language Notes* 39 (1924): 321, and "Problems of the Tristan Legend," *Romania* 53 (1927): 102, says that Eilhart's chief source, although perhaps

not his immediate one, was a French-speaking Welshman named Bleheris. An extensive review of the scholarship on this question is found in Rosemary Picozzi, *A History of Tristan Scholarship,* Canadian Studies in German Language and Literature, no. 5 (Berne and Frankfurt: Lang, 1971), pp. 11-59.

6. Gottfried ridicules such coincidences in the old story (probably referring to Eilhart's account) in his *Tristan und Isold,* 14th ed., edited by Friedrich Ranke (Dublin and Zurich: Weidmann, 1969), lines 8601-28.

7. All line references are to Franz Lichtenstein, ed., *Eilhart von Oberge,* Quellen und Forschungen zur Sprach- und Culturgeschichte der germanischen Völker, no. 19 (Strassburg: Trübner, 1877).

8. Hans Eggers, "Der Liebesmonolog in Eilharts *Tristrant,*" *Euphorion* 45 (1950): 275-304, and "Vom Formenbau mittelhochdeutscher Epen," *Der Deutschunterricht* 11 (1959): 81-97; C. A. Robson, "The Technique of Symmetrical Composition in Medieval Narrative Poetry," *Studies in Medieval French: Presented to Alfred Ewert in Honour of his Seventieth Birthday* (Oxford: Clarendon, 1961), pp. 53-64; Danielle Buschinger, "La Structure du *Tristrant* d'Eilhart von Oberg," *Études Germaniques* 27 (1972): 1-26, and "La Composition numerique du *Tristrant* d'Eilhart von Oberg," *Cahiers de Civilisation Médiévale* 16 (1973): 287-94.

9. Daniel-Hermann Schorn, "Die Zeit in den Tristandichtungen Eilharts und Gotfrids: Studie zur Wirklichkeitsauffassungen in mittelalterlichen Dichtungen" (Ph. D. diss., University of Cologne, 1952), pp. 124-25.

10. The shift from indirect to direct discourse in the middle of a statement appeared in German literature with the "Hildebrandslied," but by the time the courtly novel developed it was somewhat rare.

11. Heinz Stollte, *Eilhart und Gottfried: Studie über Motivreim und Aufbaustil,* Sprache, Volkstum, Stil: Forschungen zur deutschen Literaturgeschichte und Volkskunde, no. 1 (Halle: Niemeyer, 1941), p. 33, includes the summaries in his concept of *Motivreim.*

Friederike Wiesmann-Wiedemann (essay date 1980)

SOURCE: Wiesmann-Wiedemann, Friederike. "From Victim to Villain: King Mark." In *The Expansion and Transformations of Courtly Literature,* edited by Nathaniel B. Smith and Joseph T. Snow, pp. 49-68. Athens: University of Georgia Press, 1980.

[*In the following essay, Wiesmann-Wiedemann compares versions of the Tristan story by Eilhart, Thomas, and Gottfried with the prose French narrative source, argu-*

ing that Eilhart's work privileges the feudal order, while the other writers take elements of psychology, love, and action (respectively) as their main components.]

In her study of the Tristan story, Joan Ferrante compares corresponding episodes in different versions of the legend, but she treats characters only insofar as they figure within these episodes.[1] This article follows one character, Mark, in order to show how the ethos of different versions and the effect that each work as a whole has on its readers influenced the portrayal of the cuckolded king. Four texts lend themselves to a comparison because they are meant to tell the whole story, even if we lack the complete versions. These are Eilhart, with his feudal point of view; Thomas, with his interest in unhappy love; Gottfried, with his elevation of love to a religious level; and the French *Prose Tristan,* with its simplistic ideology.[2] I concentrate on three points of special importance for assessing Mark's role: his relationship to the lovers, his relationship to King Arthur (who in all versions sides with worldly love), and his relationship to God. In the conclusion, I show to what extent the change in Mark's character is a function of the development in the narrative genre.

In Eilhart's rendition of the legend, at first a strong friendship binds Mark to Tristan, who serves him so well that the king decides not to marry and to leave his kingdom to his nephew. Tristan destroys this tie when he deceives Mark. The first deception takes place on the wedding night, when Tristan invents the supposed Irish custom of the dark bridal chamber in order to substitute Brangaene for Isolt. Eilhart underlines Tristan's duplicity by commenting that "Tristrant spoke shrewdly to his dear lord" (vv. 2808-9, p. 80) and that "this was the greatest deceit of which Tristrant was ever guilty" (vv. 2838-39, p. 80), for at the same time he lies with Isolt. Tristan is, however, completely excused, for he is a victim of the potion.

From this point on, Mark is shown in a new light. He loses his love and his generosity. It is true that he does not believe the first reports concerning the unlawful love affair, but when he finds the lovers embracing he exclaims: "That is evil love. How can I keep my honor [wereltlîchen êre] . . . ? Since no one should have either joy or sorrow with another's wife, I wouldn't believe it when they told me so often" (vv. 3261-63, 3266-69, p. 85). He is jealous not of Isolt's love but of his honor, of the order of his court and his country.

At the scene of the tryst under the tree, he vacillates. He believes what he sees because he wants to; therefore he appears as a weak character. He restores all Tristan's former privileges, only to let himself be talked into setting another trap; and when he catches his prey his wrath knows no end. His eyes are opened; those he had

protected were faithless rebels, disregarding him and everything he stood for as a king. At this moment he sees vengeance as the only solution. Once again his motive is not jealousy but honor. Tristan is to be broken on the wheel and Isolt is to be burned at the stake. Once Tristan has disappeared, thanks to his lucky jump from the chapel, Mark wants to vent his wrath on his wife (vv. 4246-47, p. 96), and he is only too glad to turn her over to the lepers. Here he shows the same lack of moderation that Tristan and Isolt have shown, but unlike the lovers the king is held fully responsible for his actions. Eilhart, through the voice of the people, blames him: "Many people in the country spoke ill of him" (vv. 4298-99, p. 97).

If Mark reacts as a man at this point, his next action is in the role of king and overlord. Finding Tristan and Isolt sleeping in the forest, he places his sword next to his nephew and his glove on his wife. Eilhart does not explain the action, but the tokens Mark leaves are significant. As Jean Marx points out with reference to Béroul's version, the sword and glove represent Tristan's and Isolt's vassalage.[3] Eilhart's poem does not seem to admit any other interpretation, for when Mark lays the glove on Isolt he does not do so to protect her from the sun as in most other versions. His action means not that he forgives her but that he insists on his own rights.

When Mark agrees to resume his married life with Isolt, he tells his counselors that there had been no physical love between Tristan and Isolt, only an exaggerated sentiment of kindness. He feels so threatened by this supposedly innocent love, however, that he refuses to let Tristan live at the court. Does he really believe what he says? Or is his motive purely diplomatic? Why else would he set the wolf trap in a later episode? A king whose wife has been unfaithful loses his dignity; so he does better to pretend that nothing has happened than to repudiate his wife and become the subject of bawdy stories. Mark's lie is motivated not by a personal reason but by *raison d'état.* More than at any other moment in the story, Mark serves the community by removing the only obstacle to its well-being. In opposition to his earlier exaggerated wrath, moderation now characterizes his action. As Eilhart excuses Tristan's and Isolt's deceptions because of the love drink, so Mark's lie may also be excused, for it results from the same desire to keep appearances and it too is caused, in the last analysis, by the potion.

The king's prime concern from this point forth will be to try to prevent Tristan from seeing Isolt. The first time Tristan comes back to Cornwall, in the company of the Arthurian knights, Mark sets the wolf trap. His personality is clearly opposed to that of Arthur: Mark is a king who makes the rules; Arthur is a pawn of his knights.

Gawain prolongs the hunt so that Arthur is forced to ask Mark for hospitality; Kay has the idea that all the knights should cut themselves in order to protect Tristan from detection; all that is left for Arthur to do is to look at his limping knights and to explain pitifully to Mark that "they do this all the time" (v. 5440, p. 109).

Again and again Mark pursues Tristan, who keeps coming back to Cornwall, but never is Mark forced to admit his shame publicly. Joan Ferrante explains the lack of the ordeal scene in Eilhart's text by saying: "The absence of God is an indication of Eilhart's antipathy for the love; he alone, of the poets, has no desire to show God's sympathy to the lovers in any way."[4] On the contrary, God is on Mark's side. Ogrin, the representative of God on earth, sends Tristan and Isolt back to Mark, and the king says that if he let Tristan come back to the court, "God would have to despise me" (v. 4932).[5] It is Mark who represents everything that is good and proper. He does not doubt; he does not need the help of an ordeal; he knows and he directs—until the final blow when Isolt leaves her husband and her country, her treasure and her royal robes, all she ever had, and, most of all, her royal honor (vv. 9327-29, 9339, pp. 153-54). But this is also the time when Mark learns about the potion, when he realizes that he has lost not against base faithless feelings but against fate: "It was very foolish of them not to tell me that they had drunk of the fatal [unsêligen] potion and, against their will, were forced to love each other so. Oh, noble queen and dear nephew, Tristrant! I would give you my whole kingdom, people and land, forever for your own if this could bring you back to life" (vv. 9486-97, p. 155). In this final scene Mark is the generous being we had met at the beginning of the poem; more than that, he is a man who knows life, who fights relentlessly for what is right, but who is also aware of human limitations and the power of fate.

Much more than Tristan and Isolt, it is Mark who embodies the human condition, who blindly combats fate, who believes he can order life only to recognize in the end that his struggle had always been hopeless. He surpasses the human condition, however, by humbly acknowledging his limitations and by honoring those who, on a human level, wronged him. That Tristan and Isolt do not reach these heights, that they gave in to fate even though they knew that their behavior was immoral, that they are therefore guilty in spite of their innocence, is symbolized by the intertwining plants on their graves, for as Eilhart tells us "this was due to the power of the potion" (v. 9521, p. 155). Mark, who undergoes a sentimental and political education, becomes a tragic and heroic figure. He is the true victim of the potion, while Tristan and Isolt are but its instruments. Mark, then, is the true hero of Eilhart's poem.

In no other version of the story is the position of the king so exalted. It would appear that Eilhart wrote his poem for an audience less interested in the power of love than in the preservation of the feudal order. By the same token, Eilhart, it seems, did not feel compelled to justify this ethos. There is no discussion of the characters' motives; they act as they must. Thus the poem affects our intellect less than our emotions.

Thomas composed his story for a different audience, "that it may please lovers, and that, here and there, they may find some things to take to heart. May they derive great comfort from it, in the face of fickleness and injury, in the face of hardship and grief, in the face of all the wiles of Love" (fragment Sneyd[2], vv. 833-39, p. 353). The poet is concerned not so much with the feudal ethos as with the ideology of love. Mark is less a king than a lover and, like all the lovers depicted by Thomas, Mark is unhappy.

We understand the power of this love when we learn that Mark empties the vial containing the fatal potion,[6] and later when the poet tells us how Tristan, the two Isolts, and Mark suffer for love: "I do not know what to say here as to which of the four was in greater torment . . . ; let lovers pass their judgement as to who was best placed in love, or who, lacking it, had most sorrow" (fragment of Turin[1], vv. 144-45, 149-51, p. 317).

That his love for Isolt and not his social position motivates Mark's actions becomes clear in the forest scene, where he lays his glove on Isolt's cheek in order to protect her from the sun but does not exchange swords, even though he recognizes the weapon lying between Tristan and Isolt as the one he had once given to his nephew.[7] He depends completely on Isolt and so gives up his liberty. He is a weak, even a ridiculous character. In the orchard scene he catches Tristan and Isolt *in flagrante delicto,* but afraid of assuming his responsibility, it seems, he runs out to find witnesses, giving Tristan enough time to flee. When Brangaene comes to see him in an attempt to spite Isolt, she tells him: "You are dishonored when you consent to all her [Isolt's] wishes and suffer her lover about her. . . . I am well aware why you are dissembling: because you have not the courage to let her see what you know" (fragment Douce, vv. 392-94, 399-402, p. 330).[8] Mark loses his honor, not the worldly honor Eilhart's king claimed but the honor of a lover.

The true hero of Thomas's story is Tristan. This explains perhaps why we do not learn how Mark reacts to the death of Tristan and Isolt. The last scene is the touching one of the dying Isolt clinging to the body of the only man she has ever loved. No plants intertwine on their graves, for their love was not a fate thrust upon them but a passion they willingly share.

Presumably because Tristan is the heroic figure in this romance, Thomas does not compare Mark directly to Arthur. The poet suggests that Mark plays Arthur's role, for in this version Mark is king of all England, but it is Tristan who is shaped in the image of Arthur. It is Tristan who fights the enormous nephew of Orgillos, the giant whom Arthur himself had slain. Tristan no longer needs Arthur's help, as he does in Eilhart's poem, but equals him, assuming his heritage in his roles of ideal protector and lover.

God is on the lovers' side, and so Thomas suppresses the figure of Ogrin. In the ordeal scene Isolt safely carries the red-hot iron, "and God in his gentle mercy granted her sweet vindication and reconciliation and concord with the king, her lord and husband, with abundant love, honor, and esteem."[9] Thus, God protects Tristan and Isolt and justifies the laws of their worldly love.

Friedrich Naumann explains courtly culture in these words: "Man bejaht die Welt, die man eigentlich nicht bejahen sollte. Man bejaht die Welt mit einer Schambewegung. Diese gezähmte, zögernde, verhüllte Weltbejahung des Mittelalters nennen wir höfische Kultur."[10] Thomas's lovers belong to the courtly world. Mark's legal rights are of no value when compared to those of reciprocal love. And so he appears as a weak, pathetic figure, a nonentity who suffers and causes others to suffer. He is merely an obstacle to the fulfillment of Tristan's and Isolt's love, a catalyst causing their death.

Thomas's work clearly belongs within the ranks of courtly literature. It exalts love, presents love's psychology, and is directed to lovers. These two key words, love and psychology, make clear that Thomas addresses himself as much to the emotion as to the intellect of his audience.

Gottfried von Strassburg does not write for all lovers; he writes only for the *edelen herzen* (noble hearts, v. 47, p. 42), those who strive to reach the very essence of love which Gottfried describes in the well-known formula "I have another world in mind which together in one heart bears its bitter-sweet, its dear sorrow, its heart's joy, its love's pain, its dear life, its sorrowful death, its dear death, its sorrowful life" (vv. 58-63, p. 42).

Tristan and Isolt find their way to the world of the *edelen herzen* when they drink the love potion. In opposition to courtly lovers who look for personal satisfaction only—in this version the concept of courtliness thus carries with it a negative connotation—Tristan and Isolt serve Love. It is here that a religious element enters the romance. One might say that the love potion is for Tristan and Isolt what grace is for the Christian saint.[11]

Eilhart's *unsêlig trang* (cursed drink, v. 9489[12]) has become a blessed drink. Mark does not take part in this world of the noble hearts, and therefore he cannot partake of the love potion.[13]

Immediately after Tristan and Isolt have acknowledged their love and accepted it as constituting their true being by surrendering to one another, the poet inserts a "discourse on Love" (vv. 12187-361, pp. 202-4), where he interprets Tristan's and Isolt's reciprocal feeling, opposing it to the love of the world, the pursuit of happiness. He lets us understand that for Tristan and Isolt physical love is the expression of their deep feeling, religiously speaking, a sacrament.[14] For Mark, the courtly lover, physical love is not a means but an end. He does not recognize the truth Isolt embodies. Lying with Brangaene and Isolt, "he found gold and brass in either" (vv. 12674-75, p. 208). He therefore is not willing to fight for his wife. When Gandin insists on taking Isolt with him, Mark looks for someone to defend her. Because of Gandin's strength, nobody volunteers, "nor was Mark willing to fight for Isolde in person" (vv. 13253-54, p. 216).[15] What Mark looks for in love is possession not devotion.

Thus he cannot decide whether he should believe Isolt innocent or guilty. He submits to the counsel of his courtiers and tries to force his wife into betraying herself. But he is convinced of the love between Tristan and Isolt not through any of the tricks his counselors devise, but through his own observation: he sees their love in Isolt's eyes—not Tristan's—another indication of the courtly, possessive character of his love. "It was death to his reason that his darling Isolde should love any man but himself" (vv. 16521-24, p. 258). His love turns to jealousy and anger, and he bans Tristan and Isolt. How courtly his love is, in the positive sense of the word, becomes clear when we hear him say that he loves them too much to want to take vengeance: "Take each other by the hand and leave my court and country. If I am to be wronged by you I wish neither to see nor hear it" (vv. 16607-10, p. 259), and so he grants Tristan and Isolt the happiest time of their lives. His generosity, however, cannot be compared to that of the king at the end of Eilhart's poem, for he is blind to the truth and is moved by self-pity. This is why Gottfried's Mark appears less tragic than pathetic.

In the love-cave scene Tristan and Isolt reach union with the summum bonum. It is a realm closed off, where Mark can find no entrance. Through the window he sees Isolt—he scarcely looks at Tristan—and her beauty makes his passion return with the same intensity as before. As in Thomas's version of the story, he wants to protect her from the sun, but he does not use his glove, the sign of her dependence on him within courtly society: if she returns to him it will be because she wants to not because she has to. Blocking out the sun, Mark takes honor away from the lovers, for Gottfried had told us earlier that the sun represented "that blessed radiance, Honour, dearest of all luminaries" (vv. 17071-72, p. 265), the honor of divine love, not that of courtly society. On the contrary, Mark restores worldly honor to the lovers when he calls them back. Gottfried underlines the precariousness of Mark's relationship with Isolt by saying: "Mark was happy once more. For his happiness he again had in his wife Isolde all that his heart desired—not in honour, but materially" (vv. 17727-31, pp. 274-75), and he shows his contempt for such a love in his long digression on jealous husbands.

It is in fact Mark's jealous suspicion that makes him surprise Tristan and Isolt and causes his agony. The final judgment of Mark is pronounced, ironically, by his counselors: "You hate your honour and your wife, but most of all yourself" (vv. 18389-90, p. 282). Since Mark's situation springs from his concern for himself, it is diametrically opposed to that of Tristan.

But what might have become of this hatred after Tristan's and Isolt's death? Learning that they had died for one another, would Mark not have recognized that he would not have been capable of giving up his life for his wife's sake? Would he not have realized that Tristan and Isolt were drawn together by a feeling much stronger than his love had ever been? Would he not have acknowledged the truth known to the *edelen herzen*? Such an ending seems possible when we consider Mark's words at the banishment scene: "Since I can read it in the pair of you that, in defiance of my will, you love and have loved each other more than me, then be with one another as you please" (vv. 16596-601, p. 259). De Boor's interpretation takes the same direction. He compares Mark to the pagan king of the saint legend who causes the martyr's death only to recognize his own mistake and to convert to the true religion.[16]

Such an ending would be comparable to that of Eilhart's poem insofar as Mark understands that he has fought against a power superior to his own, but it would be different from that of Eilhart, because it would not be tragic. All through the story Mark is clearly at fault for not recognizing what he sees. He is not a victim of fate but of his self-centered outlook on life. At best he is a pathetic figure, at worst a villain intent on destroying the truth.

Arthur is mentioned only once in this text. Gottfried sets the *Minnegrotte* apart from the Round Table: "Their company of two was so ample a crowd for this pair that good King Arthur never held a feast in any of his palaces that gave keener pleasure or delight" (vv. 16863-67, p. 263). Tristan is not Arthur's heir, but

surpasses his splendor. Mark, on the other hand, does not reach Arthur's glory. Arthur outdoes him then, but on a material level, not on a spiritual one.

The role of God has troubled many scholars.[17] In the ordeal scene Gottfried says: "Thus it was made manifest and confirmed to all the world that Christ in His great virtue is pliant as a windblown sleeve" (vv. 15737-40, p. 248). But what does this passage mean if not that Gottfried mocks the attitudes of the church? After all, it is the ecclesiastical establishment that devises the ordeal; and not God but courtly society is deceived by the wording of the oath. Gottfried never lets us know where God stands, perhaps because in his work love takes God's place.[18]

Like Thomas's poem, Gottfried's *Tristan* affects the reader's emotions and demands that he reflect on its content. It requires, however, a more sophisticated audience capable of grasping new concepts and recognizing subtleties of which Thomas never dreamed. In other words, Gottfried's poem is written for an elite courtly public.

The French prose romance, on the other hand, aims at entertaining the bourgeoisie as well as the nobility. The prologue states that the Tristan legend "would be a thing that poor and rich alike would very much enjoy, as long as they were willing to hear and listen to the beautiful adventures that are so very pleasing" (p. 1). Speaking of the various episodes Eugène Vinaver states: "Leur intérêt n'est plus dans les idées qu'ils illustrent; il réside dans les intrigues et les événements qu'ils racontent."[19] Psychological intricacies are not in the foreground of the story, but this does not mean that there is no moral judgment; it is just an extremely simple one. Basically, the court of Arthur is good, and Mark, Andret, and most of the Cornish are bad (Tristan and Dinas are laudable exceptions). Dinadan, a brave Arthurian knight whom we respect for his independent and logical thought, says about Arthur's court: "The good who come there leave better, but whoever comes there bad and evil . . . and of wicked birth and wicked nature, cannot in any way change his being, just as copper cannot become gold or lead silver" (p. 113).[20] But "King Mark . . . would have appeared a worthy man and a valiant and wise prince, if he did not have a villainous face" (pp. 123-24).

The reader knows immediately what to think of Mark, whose first noteworthy deed in the romance is to kill his brother for no other reason than a well-deserved rebuke. The king uses Tristan when he needs a strong knight, as in the Morolt episode (interestingly enough, Morolt is a knight of the Round Table), but tries to destroy him at all other times. This is the only version where the animosity between uncle and nephew is established before Isolt is mentioned. Thus, Mark sends Tristan to Ireland not so much to fetch Isolt as in the hope that the Irish will kill the young knight. The king is as subject to his love for Isolt as in the versions by Thomas and Gottfried, but because of his unworthiness he does not earn our sympathy. Nor will the reader take his side when, obviously afraid of meeting his nephew face to face, he abducts Isolt twice from the protection of Tristan, who happens to be absent.

Mark's vilest deed is to ban Tristan from Cornwall, for this injustice toward his nephew contributes to the demise of Arthur's reign, a catastrophe for which Tristan acts as a catalyst since he undermines the Arthurian moral system by bringing out the worst in Arthur's knights. Gawain's first dishonorable deed is to threaten a damsel with death unless she tells him who her companion is, and that companion is Tristan.[21] Lancelot rewards Tristan's service with his friendship, but he is debased by it. For Lancelot, who had treated the affair with Guenevere with the utmost secrecy (cf. p. 79), now is linked to Tristan, who openly rebels against Mark, his king, and carries on a flagrant affair with Isolt, his queen. Under such circumstances, how can the knights of the Round Table hope to defend a moral system that is based on trust? How can they reach the Grail when their foremost representative is Lancelot?

But Mark influences the fate of Arthur's court directly as well. Twice he comes to Logres. The first time, he wants to kill Tristan. He splits the head of one of his own knights who does not agree with his plan and then successfully defends himself in single combat, taking advantage of his position as king (which exempts him from the obligation of swearing an oath on his innocence). He thereby all but destroys the moral system Arthur had constructed.

Mark returns, now intent on killing King Arthur, whose best knights are on the Grail quest. He succeeds in wounding Arthur dangerously, but he is defeated by Galahad, a representative not of Arthur's worldly kingdom but of God's spiritual reign. The Arthurian system has lost its balance. Arthur's knights, among them Tristan, the emissary of Mark, fail to attain the values Galahad serves and cannot even defend their king. There is nothing to fill this void. Mark has given the death blow to the Arthurian dream. It is no coincidence that Arthur at the same time learns of the disastrous outcome of the Grail quest and Tristan's death.

Tristan is not granted a heroic death but is killed by a poisoned lance that Mark, the vilest of all persons, treacherously thrusts at him. It is true that Mark later repents of this murder, but this repentance only underscores the despicability of his action.[22]

Without Mark's actions, Tristan could have been an exemplary knight, better even than Lancelot. As it is, Mark's lack of honor debases Tristan and contributes to the destruction of Arthur's kingdom. He is a villain who ruins all.

In conclusion, Eilhart's poem glorifies feudal law and order. The story line is simple. Outside of the potion no motive is explained in detail. The text addresses itself to our emotions. Mark is a servant of God; morally he surpasses Arthur. He is good, a victim of fate and a hero in facing reality.

Thomas concerns himself with the suffering of unhappy lovers. The plot does not oppose right and wrong but instead presents the effects of love on unhappy lovers in different situations. The poem tells not only what happened but why. It addresses itself to our emotions as well as to our understanding. Mark does not understand God's will; he equals Arthur, but only in his feudal position. He is an unhappy lover who would like to do what is right, but who is too weak to accomplish anything. He loses himself, a victim of his longing for a love that cannot be.

Gottfried introduces a new concept by opposing generous to selfish love. He lets us know not only what happened and why but also what it means. The text speaks to our emotions, our understanding, and our judgment. Mark opposes love, which in this poem takes the place of God; he is inferior to Arthur, even on a material level. He is a selfish lover, a victim of his egoism. If indeed Gottfried meant to end the romance as we have suggested, the king would recognize his flaw, and thus go through the same learning process as the reader.

The author of the *Prose Tristan* is less concerned with ethos or psychology than with interlacing the various story lines. The characters are defined just enough to make their conduct believable. The text addresses itself primarily to our sense of plausibility. Mark opposes God's spiritual reign as well as Arthur's worldly kingdom. He is a villain.

The uncourtly versions of Eilhart and the *Prose Tristan* present a relatively simple form of ethos, of reader manipulation, and of character portrayal. It is the courtly versions of Thomas and Gottfried that really define the ethos, address the whole psychological being of their reader, and that present complex characters who are neither good nor bad but fundamentally human. Might the confluence of these three qualities be one of the properties of courtly narrative literature?

Notes

1. Joan Ferrante, *The Conflict of Love and Honor: The Medieval Tristan Legend in France, Germany and Italy,* De Proprietatibus Litterarum, Series Practica, no. 78 (The Hague: Mouton, 1973).

2. Franz Lichtenstein, ed., *Eilhart von Oberge,* Quellen und Forschungen zur Sprach- und Kulturgeschichte der germanischen Völker, no. 19 (Strassburg: Karl J. Trübner, 1877); Thomas, *Les Fragments du Roman de Tristan,* ed. Bartina H. Wind, Textes Littéraires Français, no. 92 (Geneva: Droz, 1960); Gottfried von Strassburg, *Tristan,* ed. Reinhold Bechstein, 5th ed. (Leipzig: Brockhaus, 1930); E. Löseth, ed., *Le Roman de Tristan, Le Roman de Palamède et La Compilation de Rusticien de Pise: Analyse critique d'après les manuscrits de Paris* (Paris, 1891; rpt. New York: Burt Franklin, 1970).

For Eilhart's text, I quote *Eilhart von Oberge's Tristrant,* trans. J. W. Thomas (Lincoln: University of Nebraska Press, 1978). For the texts of Thomas and Gottfried, I quote Gottfried von Strassburg, *Tristan with the Tristan of Thomas,* trans. A. T. Hatto (Baltimore: Penguin, 1960). All other translations are mine. Each quotation is followed by a verse reference to the original text or a page reference for the *Prose Tristan* and, for Eilhart, Thomas, and Gottfried, a page reference to the respective translation.

3. Jean Marx, "Observations sur un épisode de la légende de Tristan," in *Recueil de travaux offert à M. Clovis Brunel* (Paris: Société de l'Ecole des Chartes, 1955), pp. 265-73. See as well Eugène Vinaver's answer to Marx in *A La Recherche d'une poétique médiévale* (Paris: Nizet, 1970), pp. 92-94.

4. Ferrante, p. 51.

5. This is my understanding of "sô muste mich got hônen." J. W. Thomas translates the verse as "may God scorn me" (p. 103).

6. Because Thomas's version of this scene is not extant, I am basing my observations on Brother Robert's translation of his text. The passage alluded to can be found in *The Saga of Tristan and Isönd,* trans. Paul Schach (Lincoln: University of Nebraska Press, 1973), p. 72.

7. Ibid., p. 103.

8. I have altered Hatto's translation of "Huntage avenir vus en deit / Quant tuz ses bons li cunsentez" (vv. 392-93), which he renders as "dishonour is bound to overtake you if you consent to all her wishes." In her edition, Bartina H. Wind translates "Que fere li osissez senblant" (v. 402) as "de lui montrer ce que vous pensez d'elle" (to show her what you think of her; p. 102n).

9. Schach translation, p. 94.

10. Friedrich Naumann, "Hohe Minne," *Zeitschrift für Deutschkunde* 39 (1925): 81-91, at p. 81. (One assents to the world, to which one should actually not assent. One assents to the world with some embarrassment. This medieval assent to the world, restrained, hesitant, covert, is what we call courtly culture.)

11. This interpretation differs fundamentally from that of W. T. H. Jackson, "Gottfried von Straussburg," in *Arthurian Literature in the Middle Ages: A Collaborative History,* ed. Roger Sherman Loomis (Oxford: Clarendon Press, 1959), pp. 145-56, who believes that the potion "hands them [Tristan and Isolt] over to the tyranny of the senses, and this tyranny is so powerful that it brushes from its path all considerations of honour and loyalty. . . . So strong is it, indeed, that the ultimate sin is committed in its name, when the oath before God is reduced to a mockery by a crude piece of deception" (p. 153).

12. J. W. Thomas translates the adjective as "fatal" (p. 155).

13. Gottfried underlines this difference from Thomas: "No, none of that philtre remained. Brangane had thrown it into the sea" (vv. 12659-60, p. 208).

14. Again, this interpretation differs from that of W. T. H. Jackson: "The love of Tristan and Isolt is a mystic love in human terms. Its purer aspects were subjected through drinking the potion to the devil of sensual passion. Only by death can their love be freed from this snare and the 'love-death' means that the lovers can be reunited in mystic love, freed from all grossness and carnal attraction" (p. 154).

15. It is Tristan who brings her back. Joan Ferrante claims that "the point is to diminish Mark's legal, and therefore to some extent, his moral claims to Isolt, and so strengthen Tristan's in contrast" (p. 45). However, since Mark and Tristan operate on two different levels, Isolt belongs to Tristan and there is no need for him to strengthen his position. Tristan's saving Isolt is an effect of the truth they both represent, not an attempt to establish that truth. On the other hand, Mark's action does not mean that because of his cowardice he no longer has a legal right to his wife. By the same reasoning he would have lost his claim to his kingdom by not doing battle with the Morolt.

16. Helmut de Boor, "Die Grundauffassung von Gottfrieds Tristan," *Deutsche Vierteljahresschrift* 18 (1940): 262-306; rpt. in *Gottfried von Strassburg,* ed. Alois Wolf, Wege der Forschung, no. 320 (Darmstadt: Wissenschaftliche Buchgesellschaft, 1973), pp. 25-73, at p. 68.

17. For a bibliography, see Ferrante, pp. 52-53n.

18. Cf. de Boor, pp. 68-73, where he analyzes the reasons for the "organic mistake" in Gottfried's poem.

19. Eugène Vinaver, *Etudes sur le Tristan en Prose* (Paris: Champion, 1925), p. 13. (Their interest no longer lies in the ideas they exemplify but in the intrigues and events they recount.)

20. For an assessment of Dinadan's character and role in the *Prose Tristan,* see Vinaver, *Etudes,* pp. 91-98.

21. Only once before is there an allusion to Gawain's worthless character. Significantly, it is Tristan who makes the remark (p. 28).

22. Emmanuèle Baumgartner, *Le "Tristan en Prose": Essai d'interprétation d'un roman médiéval,* Publications Romanes et Françaises, no. 133 (Geneva: Droz, 1975), comments: "Sincèrement épris d'Iseut, par moments accessible à la pitié et au repentir, Marc reste, en dépit de tout l'odieux de sa conduite, un être humain et non un traître de mêlodrame" (p. 230). (Sincerely in love with Isolt, at times capable of pity and repentance, Mark remains, in spite of his detestable conduct, a human being and not a traitor of melodrama.)

James A. Schultz (essay date June 1987)

SOURCE: Schultz, James A. "Why Does Mark Marry Isolde? And Why Do We Care? An Essay on Narrative Motivation." *Deutsche Vierteljahrs Schrift für Literaturwissenschaft und Geistesgeschichte* 61, no. 2 (June 1987): 206-22.

[*In the following essay, Schultz studies the differing forms of narrative motivation employed by Eilhart and Gottfried in their versions of the Tristan legend.*]

Although narrative motivation has only recently become a theoretical concern of literary scholars, it has always been a practical concern of storytellers, for anyone who tells a story must give some attention to the causal connections that join the events being recounted. It is not surprising then that storytellers who are inclined to reflect on their own activity will occasionally offer us their thoughts on the subject nor that Gottfried von Straßburg, surely one of the most self-conscious of medieval vernacular writers, should introduce such reflections into his *Tristan*. These reflections are formulated as an attack on another "Tristan" with which he assumes his audience is familiar and which closely resembles the somewhat earlier *Tristrant* of Eilhart von Oberg. At issue is the motivation of a crucial event in the story, Mark's marriage to Isolde.

Eilhart and Gottfried begin their accounts of Mark's marriage from the same premise: Mark has made his nephew, Tristan, his heir and has vowed to remain single; but the members of Mark's family and court, consumed by fear and envy of the young hero, begin to exert strong pressure on the king to go back on his word and take a wife. In both accounts Mark responds to this pressure with a ruse by which he thinks he can outwit his courtiers and keep his promise to Tristan. According to Eilhart, just when Mark has promised to respond to the courtiers, two swallows fly in the window and drop a strand of hair in front of him; Mark picks up the hair and swears that he will only marry the woman to whom it belongs—assuming, along with his courtiers, that she will never be found (ETr 1370-95, 1424-25).[1] According to Gottfried, Mark recalls the hatred that the king of Ireland bears him and vows that he will only marry the king's daughter, Isolde—assuming, quite reasonably, that the king's hatred will thwart any proposed marriage (GTr 8478-88, 8517-22).[2] Yet in both cases Mark's assumptions are mistaken, and the ruse by which he hoped to preclude marriage becomes instead a promise to marry Isolde. For Tristan accepts the challenge implied in the ruse, sets out, and returns with Isolde, the specified bride.

It is just as Tristan sets sail for Ireland that Gottfried's narrator interrupts his account of the story to attack that other "Tristan" for the ways in which its motivation differs from his own. Who ever heard of a Cornish swallow flying to Ireland for nesting materials? he asks (GTr 8601-13). And what king would be so foolish as to send the members of his council off in search for the source of a strand of hair? (GTr 8616-28). A story that depends on such reasons is talking nonsense (GTr 8614-15). Gottfried's narrator attacks such motivation because he finds it unrealistic (swallows don't behave that way and neither do kings) and because, he feels, such implausible motivation makes a story incoherent (it talks nonsense). In making these objections he raises two important issues regarding narrative motivation: first, the relation of narrative motivation to everyday standards of probability, and, second, the relation of narrative motivation to narrative coherence.

Of course the word "motivation" is not part of Gottfried's vocabulary but of ours. It was introduced into critical discourse by the Russian formalists and taken up later by the French structuralists.[3] Since then it has been considered, usually more or less in passing, by a number of writers on narrative;[4] but, as anyone who studies the literature will see at once, those who use the term have very different ideas of what it means. Before turning to the issues raised by Gottfried's polemic, therefore, it will be necessary to consider briefly the various kinds of narrative motivation. Then it will be possible to consider the questions raised by Gottfried's narrator concerning the relation between motivation and coherence, both within texts and beyond. First, in other words, I will consider the kinds of answers that can be given to the question, Why does Mark marry Isolde? Then I will turn to the more general question, Why do we care?

As seems almost obligatory in such matters, I begin with Propp, who states quite clearly: "by motivations are meant both the reasons and the aims of personages which cause them to commit various acts."[5] Motivations, according to Propp, are what cause personages to commit acts. If one attends to Propp's examples, however, it becomes clear that acts can be motivated not only by an actor's reasons and aims, but also by that actor's nature—by the "greedy, evil, envious, suspicious character of the villain," for instance (p. 76). Later we learn that various props and other external stimuli can also function as motivations: a feather, a portrait, another actor, and so forth (pp. 76-77). The kinds of motivation mentioned by Propp are all constituent parts of the story itself: the aims of the personages are stated, the nature of the villain is specified, the appearance of the feather is noted. Because such motivational elements are actually part of the story, I will refer to this type of motivation as *story motivation.*

Story motivation is the most obvious sort of narrative motivation, and examples are correspondingly easy to find. The arrival of the strand of Isolde's hair, for instance, a motivational device to which Propp himself refers (p. 78n1), is explicitly written into Eilhart's plot: after the swallows flew into the hall and began to fight, *"do empfiel in ain hăr"* (ETr 1385). The consequences are also made explicit in the text: after the strand of hair fell to the floor, *"deß wart der herr gewar . . . do nam der kúng den gedanck . . . 'hie mit will ich weren mich'"* (ETr 1383-92). Both the agents and the causal relations they engender are demonstrably part of the story: one can cite the words of the text by way of illustration, as I have just done. Thus story motivation not only motivates the story, it constitutes the story at the same time.

Story motivation not only constitutes that stretch of the story where it occurs; it also contributes to the constitution of a fictional world defined in part by the causal relations it implies. The fictional world of Eilhart's *Tristrant* is one in which it is natural for swallows to travel overseas and return with a strand of hair. This fictional causality can be held up to our everyday causal assumptions and, if one is so inclined, taken to task for its deviations. That, of course, is what Gottfried's narrator does, thereby illustrating Tomashevsky's dictum that new literary schools always attack their predecessors for their unrealistic motivation.[6] But within Eilhart's world international swallows are perfectly natural;

indeed, by their behavior they help define what *is* natural in that world.

The story is motivated not only by the elements that constitute it but also by the narrator as he tells it. Gérard Genette notes the way in which narrators will offer a "justification of the particular fact by a general law, assumed to be unknown or perhaps forgotten by the reader and of which the narrator must inform or remind him or her."[7] Genette draws particular attention to the function of these "general laws" in disguising the arbitrariness of the narrative (p. 85): if the events of a story, in themselves perhaps quite improbable, can be shown to proceed according to laws valid not only within the story but in the world at large, then these events seem less improbable. It is not important whether or not such "general laws" are in fact generally valid; their function is only to appear so and thus to motivate the particular actions they pretend to explain. They constitute what Genette calls an "artificial verisimilitude" (p. 79). Because this motivation is not actually part of the story but is added by the narrator in telling it, I will distinguish it from story motivation by calling it *narrator motivation.*

Gottfried offers an example of narrator motivation at the very beginning of the episode in which the barons urge Mark to marry. Tristan has returned from his first trip to Ireland and is said to have the king and the court at his service—presumably this includes the barons (GTr 8316-17). But in the very next line the barons suddenly fall victim to *"der verwazene nit, der selten iemer gelit"* (GTr 8319-20); this causes them to turn against Tristan, to accuse him of sorcery, and to seek his death. At first glance the narrator's observation that envy never rests seems quite gratuitous: the barons could have been motivated by envy even if it had roused itself specially for their sakes after a long slumber. But in fact the observation is not gratuitous at all: it is one of those "general laws" that, by asserting a constitutive quality of envy, thus move the motivation out of the particulars of the story into the realm of common knowledge, a knowledge that claims validity outside of the narrative in the world at large. By invoking a "general law," the narrator masks the improbable suddenness of the barons' change of attitude towards Tristan: if envy is always at work everywhere, then it is quite natural that the barons should succumb to its power. That there are many human relationships in which envy *does* rest is irrelevant; in the fictional world of *Tristan* is does not—by definition.

The narrator gives reasons not only for the events of the story he tells but also for his own behavior as storyteller. Gottfried's narrator explains that he has busied himself for the sake of the world of noble hearts, those who acknowledge both joy and suffering, that they might have partial relief from the sorrows of love (GTr 45-76, 97-100); he explains his activity in part with the "general truth" that lovers love tales of love (GTr 121-22). Later he tells us that stories about medicine are not suitable for courtly ears (GTr 7942-54) and that lots of talk about love is tedious to courtly sensibilities (GTr 12183-84). With maxims such as these he explains and justifies his choice of the story he tells as well as the way he tells it. It is no accident that the narrator relies so heavily on "general truths" in motivating his own behavior, for he stands closer than the hero to the extratextual world from which these truths are supposed to derive: on the one hand, he is the mediator between story and audience; on the other, he is the representative within the text of two real-world figures, the author and the performer. Thus the narrator has recourse to "general truths" to motivate two different stories: the one he is telling and the one of which he is a part.

Although story motivation and narrator motivation are both expressed in the words of the text, there are other kinds of narrative motivation that are not. Umberto Eco gives an illustration of such extratextual motivation with reference to a scene from a short story that takes place in a brothel. At a certain point in the story one of the staff is said to pick up a sheet and wrap it around her head—but, Eco points out, there is no explanation of where she got the sheet. This oversight, however, poses no particular threat to the coherence of the story since the reader "is furnished with a *common frame:* in brothels there are rooms, these rooms have beds, these beds have sheets. According to the previous frame 'sleeping in a brothel,' whoever sleeps in such places sleeps on a bed, and so on." Anticipating our objections, Eco protests: "I am not playing a Byzantine game. That is exactly what a reader *is supposed* to do in order to actualize the surface intensional level."[8] The text does not have to supply this kind of information because it is perfectly obvious to us that there are sheets in brothels, and that which is "perfectly obvious" need not be stated: once the common frame has been activated, its contents need not be specially enumerated. At some point all narratives rely on common knowledge about the world, on shared assumptions about what acts are natural in a given situation, and on our ability to supply the "obvious" reasons for those "natural" actions that are not explicitly motivated. Since all recipients must be potential motivators of the story in order to understand it at all, I will call their (potential) activity *recipient motivation.*

The manuscript history of Eilhart's **Tristrant** offers a useful example of how recipient motivation can function. Of the two extant manuscripts that contain the scene with the swallows, one states merely that two swallows started to bite each other in Mark's hall and then a strand of hair fell to the ground (ETr ms. D 1381-82, 1386). The other reports the same but adds that the swallows flew in through a window (ETr ms. H. 1381-82b, 1385). When Gottfried's narrator refers to this scene he ignores the window but adds that the swallows (he gets by with only one) had been to Ireland to collect nesting material (GTr 8602-07). Obviously it is not particularly important how the birds get into Mark's hall or why they had been abroad: as long as they drop Isolde's hair in front of the king the story can proceed. And yet we do not find any of the additional information surprising: we know that birds enter buildings through windows and that they carry nesting materials, perhaps strands of hair, in their beaks. In adding this information, the more elaborate versions have merely recorded the "obvious" reasons that we or any other recipient might automatically supply for any action that we regard as "natural" in a given situation. Because the reasons for "natural" actions are always "obvious," they need not be mentioned explicitly; indeed, no narrative could possibly give reasons for every detail it contains— why did the swallows need nesting materials? why do swallows need nests? why do swallows lay eggs? why is there life on earth?

If, however, no reason is given in the text and we cannot supply an "obvious reason" on our own, then the narrative seems incoherent. This is the reaction of Gottfried's narrator when he confronts Eilhart's swallows. Posing as a recipient of the earlier version, he recognizes the context and sets about explaining the appearance of a swallow with a strand of Isolde's hair. He invokes a common frame for birds and concludes that the swallow has the strand of hair in its beak because it was collecting nesting materials (GTr 8604-05). Not content with this he wonders why it had a strand of *Isolde's* hair and concludes that it must have been collecting nesting material in Ireland (GTr 8602). According to the everyday common frame the narrator has activated, this is impossible: Cornish swallows do not fly to Ireland in search of nesting supplies (GTr 8608-15). By not explaining how the swallows got Isolde's hair Eilhart implies that the reason is obvious, that it can be supplied by reference to a common frame. But Gottfried's narrator finds that this is not possible and concludes therefore that the story is incoherent.[9]

Although there are many ways the recipient is involved in motivating narrative, there is also a sense in which narrative motivates itself automatically. As Peter Brooks explains: "plot starts (or must give the illusion of starting) from that moment at which story, or 'life,' is stimulated from quiescence into a state of narratability, into a tension, a kind of irritation, which demands narration. . . . The ensuing narrative . . . is maintained in a state of tension, as a prolonged deviance from the quiescence of the 'normal'—which is to say, the unnarratable - until it reaches the terminal quiescence of the end."[10] As long as the state of tension is maintained, however, the story *must* continue.[11] In other words, an action that generates disequilibrium, narrative tension, *must* be followed by another, it is not so important precisely which other, until some sort of equilibrium has been attained. Thus one action can motivate another simply because it, like most actions, generates disequilibrium rather than the reverse. Because this kind of motivation inheres in actions as such, I call it *actional motivation.*

One can illustrate the way this works by trying to imagine a "Tristan" essentially the same as Eilhart's or Gottfried's except that it stops just after the courtiers urge Mark to marry. For example: Tristan enjoyed such renown at court that Mark decided to remain single and make Tristan his heir; this so upset the courtiers that they pressured the king in every way they could think of to take a wife; then they all lived happily ever after. This is impossible: the courtiers' pressure on Mark requires a response from him; disequilibrium requires resolution. As it turns out, Mark's response only generates more disequilibrium: he agrees to marry but the bride he specifies is hard to find or dangerous to approach. Thus one action will lead to another until some sort of equilibrium has been achieved. Not only does one action lead to another, but we tend to assume, from the mere fact of their sequential arrangement, that there must be some causal connection between them. After Tristan returns from his first trip to Ireland, for instance, Eilhart tells us that he acquired great renown for his valor at tournaments and in battle (ETr 1332-36b). This is followed at once by news of Mark's decision not to marry: "*der kúng waß im so hold, daß er durch sinen willen wolt nicht elichß wib pflegen. er daucht, daß er den tegen wolt zů ainem sun hon, und daß er im unterton sin rich wölt machen*" (ETr 1337-43). We automatically assume that Tristan's prowess and renown are somehow the cause of Mark's decision to make Tristan his heir—although the text does not say this and other explanations are surely possible.[12] We make this assumption because we tend in general to assume that subsequent events are caused by prior ones. According to Roland Barthes, "Everything suggests . . . that the mainspring of narrative is precisely the confusion of consecution and consequence, what comes *after* being read in narrative as what is *caused by.*"[13]

Our expectation that disequilibrium will be followed by something as well as our assumption that consecutive events are causally related are attitudes we bring to narrative from everyday life. If I trip going through a door you expect something to follow: I will regain my balance or, more likely, fall on my face. If Lybia invades Egypt we again expect something will follow: Lybia will withdraw or, more likely there will be a war.

Conversely, if you see me sprawled on the ground in front of my door you assume something has caused me to fall: perhaps I tripped going through the door. And if two nations are at war, we assume something caused them to start fighting: perhaps one of them invaded the other. Although philosophers question such logic, we ordinarily assume that most everyday events have causes and consequences[14]—and we assume the same of events in narrative. Actional motivation, then, does not describe a property of narrative actions themselves but rather a property they have because of the expectations and assumptions we bring to them; because we expect them to proceed causally one from the other and assume they will cohere, we think that they do. Actional motivation is, then, a sort of recipient motivation, but a very general and basic sort.

Both recipient motivation and actional motivation engage us in a kind of complicity with the narrative, for in both cases we supply reasons or assume connections where the text is silent. We motivate it where it does not motivate itself. In the case of recipient motivation we supply a prior cause of which a given event is the effect, while in the case of actional motivation we assume a subsequent action for which the given event is the cause. Recipient motivation engages us in a retrospective complicity, actional motivation in a prospective complicity. Both coincide in the extreme case in which we posit the coherence of the narrative absolutely: the swallows arrive with a strand of hair because that's the way the story goes. In such cases our complicity reaches its maximum (we merely assert the sequence of events) while our motivational involvement reaches its minimum (we no longer trouble about causes).

The four varieties of narrative motivation represent four different ways of explaining narrative events: they differ according to their site (textual or extratextual) and their nature (story element or commentary). Story motivation and narrator motivation are situated in the words of the text: they are ways a narrative motivates itself. Recipient motivation and actional motivation are brought to bear on the text from outside: they are ways we motivate narrative. Story motivation and actional motivation explain narrative events in terms of other story elements: they generate story. Narrator motivation and recipient motivation offer reasons for narrative events: they generate commentary. Each kind of motivation represents a different combination of site and nature and thus a different way of explaining the existence of a given narrative event.

Those familiar with the scholarship on narrative motivation will recognize that my understanding of the term is, in important respects, more inclusive than others that have been advanced. There is a long tradition, stretching from the Russian formalists down to the present, that considers motivation to be merely a disguise. The real "motivation" for the order of the elements of narrative is held to be artistic and therefore arbitrary; explicit motivation hides this arbitrariness behind more or less credible everyday explanations. To study motivation from this perspective one must first come to some understanding of the artistic order—what Propp calls the "functions or connectives," Tomashevsky "the laws of plot construction," Genette "le *pour quoi?*," and Sternberg "the functional requirements of art."[15] Then one considers the quasi-mimetic ruses by which this artful order is made to seem plausible and natural—"the feelings and intentions" attributed to the "dramatis personae," "realistic material," "le *parce que*," "referential processes and linkages analogized to life."[16] These ruses are said to motivate (that is, disguise by providing realistic motivation for) the essentially arbitrary order of the artistic text.

This approach is unneccessarily restrictive in two ways. First, it relies on an untenable and exclusionary distinction between the artistic order and its motivation. Mark's marriage to Isolde, for instance, follows a widespread narrative pattern, the bride quest or *Brautwerbungsschema,* that has helped many fictional princes to find their brides; Mark's agreement to marry is a conventional element of this traditional scheme. If one assumes that the *Brautwerbungsschema* is responsible for the (arbitrary, artistic) order of events in this portion of the Tristan story, then one can ask how any of the (conventional) constituent elements of the scheme—like the prince's agreement to marry—is motivated in a given instance—in Eilhart, say, or Gottfried. But one must not forget that Mark's agreement to marry is not only an element in need of motivation but also itself a motivating element: it causes Tristan to depart for Ireland. To assume that any element is either an arbitrary element or a motivating element is to ignore the double functionality of most narrative events: Mark's agreement to marry is both story and motivation.

This common understanding of motivation is unnecessarily restrictive in a second way as well, for it cannot accommodate those motivational elements that are unrelated to the task of disguising the arbitrariness of art. Take, for instance, the appearance of the swallows in Mark's hall. Is the manuscript version of Eilhart's *Tristrant* in which they are said to fly in through the window somehow less arbitrary than the one in which no explanation is given for their entry? It hardly seems so. The swallows' entry through the window is representative of a large number of motivational explanations, present everywhere but especially important in realist

narrative, that seem to be introduced for their own sakes, not to disguise the artificial functionality of a particular plot element.[17]

My own definition of narrative motivation attempts to overcome the restrictiveness of the traditional one by emphasizing description rather than purpose. It embraces all causal explanations for narrative events, regardless of whether they happen to disguise traditional structures, to create new artistic patterns, or to generate the "effect of the real"—even, as is often the case, when they seem quite gratuitous. Only with such a definition is it possible to describe the motivation of narrative as a phenomenon in its own right.

There is, however, a second tradition in the scholarship on motivation in comparison with which my use of the term is considerably narrower. This tradition, which also stretches back to the Russian formalists, includes in the category of motivation all those procedures by which we, as recipients, explain nonmimetic features of literary texts to ourselves. Confronted with the improbable appearance of Isolde's hair in Mark's court, for instance, a reader might recall that in certain genres, like folktale and romance, unmotivated coincidences are quite natural. Another reader might decide that Isolde's hair is a synecdoche for Isolde and conclude that its appearance actually increases the meaningful coherence of the text. One might go further and argue that the hair represents the woman, absent and present, distant and desired, who is known only from hearsay or other traces and that the strand of hair thus symbolizes the distinctive long-distance love that inspires the bride quest in so many medieval narratives.[18] Finally one might invoke the author and conclude that Eilhart was "motivated" to introduce the strand hair by his respect for tradition, his love of tropes, or his desire to generate meaning. If these can all be called motivation, then the term embraces virtually any kind of explanation for any kind of textual phenomenon.

And yet, although these kinds of explanation are advanced by the recipient, they are clearly different from the examples of recipient motivation given earlier. One of those earlier examples was provided by Gottfried's narrator when he assumes the role of recipient of Eilhart's story and tries to explain the appearance of Isolde's hair at Mark's court. To do so he invokes an everyday common frame about birds—birds collect nesting material, of which the hair is an example—and concludes that the swallow must have been to Ireland picking up building supplies. When, on the other hand, we explain the hair as a synecdoche, or a symbol, or as the product of Eilhart's intentions we invoke different sorts of common frames, specifically literary ones that allow us to identify tropes, to explain symbols, to elicit meaning, and to speculate on the intentions of the author. There is a great difference between the first explanation, which relies on the familiar nesting habits of birds, and the others, which have recourse to the special properties of literary texts and the presumed behavior their authors. The first represents a naive complicity with the narrative—the relatively automatic provision of obvious reasons for the actions of a story that is essential for ordinary reading; the others represent a sentimental complicity—the self-conscious provision of literary reasons that enables critical "readings." The former is essential if one wants to make any sense out of narrative texts; the latter are essential if one wants to determine "the sense" of a narrative text.

I would restrict the term motivation to the former, the naive activation of an everyday causal common frame. And this for three reasons. First, there is no value to a category so broad that it includes everything: if the nesting habits of birds, the introduction of tropes, and the symbolic intentions of the author are all instances of narrative motivation, then the category is so imprecise as to be meaningless. Second, my restricted usage is closer to the ordinary one: we can say of a real-life swallow, just as Gottfried's narrator assumes for Eilhart's fictional one, that its need of nesting material "motivates" it to pick up strands of hair. Third, this definition of motivation insures that the categories of extratextual (recipient, actional) motivation remain equivalent to those of textual (story, narrator) motivation: Eilhart *might* have motivated the appearance of the hair with the explicit notice that the swallows had been to Ireland in search of nesting material (story motivation), just as Gottfried's narrator supposes (recipient motivation); but Eilhart would never have justified the appearance of the hair by labeling it a synecdoche for Isolde.

My definition of narrative motivation attempts to overcome the protean vagueness of the traditional one by insisting on the analogy to everyday causality. Needless to say, the two are not identical: only in Eilhart do swallows fly overseas to collect nesting materials; only in romance does the same knight win every battle. But these are merely modifications to regular causality and remain analogous to it; and they contribute to the constitution of the fictional world precisely because of this analogy. To call the strand of hair a synecdoche or a symbol, however, is to proffer a kind of explanation that we would neither find within the text nor advance in our everyday life. While to say that Eilhart was "motivated" by this or that intention is to turn the composition of the narrative into a story and to speculate on the motivation of its hero, the author. Such explanatory procedures do not contribute to the constitution of a fictional causality proper to the narrative text and should therefore be called something other than motivation—naturalization or recuperation, perhaps

even biography or interpretation.[19] If we would describe the motivation of Eilhart's *Tristrant,* however, then we must limit ourselves to what is possible within its fictional world: nesting swallows, storms, jealousy, love potions, and the like.

Narrative motivation is fictional causality. As a category, motivation comprises all causal explanations for narrative events, whether they are part of the text, assumed or implied by the text, or supplied in the reception of the text. It assumes that the fictional world is a model of the real world, that narrative events are more or less analogous to real-life events, and that the explanations of the former (motivation) will be similar in kind to the explanations of the latter (causality). Such a definition of motivation enables one to study two important related phenomena: first, the role of causal explanations in constituting the narrative; second, the role of causal explanations in generating narrative coherence.

To study the role of causal explanations in constituting the narrative one can begin by following the method of Propp or Genette mentioned above. Such an approach takes the story as given—in practice it is usually a particular story event—and then searches backwards to discover what caused it: given an arbitrary event, Mark's decision to marry, how is it motivated? One discovers the courtiers' campaign and is content. This retrospective operation of critical reading is analogous to a continuous operation of ordinary reading. As E. M. Forster puts it: over the plot, "as it unfolds, will hover the memory of the reader (that dull glow of the mind of which intelligence is the bright advancing edge) and will constantly rearrange and reconsider, seeing new clues, new chains of cause and effect."[20] As we read from one moment in the story to the next, each new element is our momentary point of reference, our "given": when we come to Mark's decision we put it in relation to what we already know and realize that it is the consequence of the courtiers' campaign.[21] The analytic reading of Propp and Genette and the common-sense reading of Forster have this in common: the search for the cause follows the recognition and isolation of its effect. Or, in other words, the discovery of the cause is temporally subsequent to and logically subordinate to the existence of the effect.

Yet this formulation contradicts our ordinary understanding of cause and effect, for ordinarily we assume that causes precede their effects and are independent of them. The "general law" that envy never rests must exist *prior* to the envy of Mark's courtiers if it is to motivate that envy. And the courtiers' envy must precede their campaign to have Mark marry, if the envy is the cause of the campaign—just as this campaign, if it in fact motivates Mark's decision to marry, must necessarily precede that decision. Again there is an analogue in the way we read. When the courtiers urge Mark to marry we wonder what will happen next: will he follow their advice? will he marry one of their daughters? will he have them all burned at the stake? In anticipating and speculating we assume that the courtiers' exertions will be the cause of *something:* any moment of disequilibrium must lead somewhere. We *want* it to lead somewhere, for, to cite Forster again, "we are all like Scheherazade's husband, in that we want to know what happens next" (p. 27). According to our ordinary understanding and according to the anticipatory aspect of reading, the expectation of an effect follows the isolation of a (potential) cause; the effect is temporally subsequent to and logically subordinate to the cause.

Well then, which is it? Are we to begin with the effect and then inquire after its cause, like Propp? Or are we to begin with the cause and anticipate its effect, like Scheherazade's husband? Is narrative motivation retrospective or prospective? It is, in fact, either—or, more accurately, both. In the series of narrative events, Mark's decision to marry is subsequent to his courtiers' campaign and prior to Tristan's departure for Ireland. *As effect* it is dependent on the courtiers' campaign for its very existence: Mark would not have decided to marry had he not been pressured. But Mark's decision is also dependent on Tristan's departure. Not for its existence: Mark will have made his decision whether Tristan leaves for Ireland or not; but for its status *as cause:* if there is no departure, Mark's decision can hardly be the cause of it.[22] Thus Mark's decision is both cause and effect; as such it is dependent on what precedes and on what follows—although in different ways. Of course it was necessary to begin somewhere, so we began by taking Mark's decision to marry as "given" and rummaged about until we found its motivation. But what we took as *given* is in fact entirely *dependent*—as effect on what precedes, and as cause on what follows.

That Mark's decision is both cause and effect is another way of saying what we noted above, that story motivation motivates the story at the same time it constitutes the story. But the same is true of the other sorts of motivation as well. The observation that envy never rests (narrator motivation) motivates the actions of Mark's courtiers at the same time it constitutes part of the narration of the story. Our understanding that swallows seek nesting material (recipient motivation) motivates the story at the same time it helps constitute our reception of the story. And the same can be said of our assumption that the pressure exerted by the courtiers on Mark must be followed by some consequent action (actional motivation). Thus story motivation and narrator motivation not only motivate the story but at the same time constitute the narrative as text. While recipi-

ent motivation and actional motivation not only motivate the story but at the same time constitute the narrative in its reception. All forms of motivation are then both cause and effect, both means and end.

If narrative motivation is prospective and retrospective, if each motivational element is both cause and effect, then motivation not only constitutes the narrative as a network of causal relations but, precisely because of these relations, it fosters the coherence of narrative. Sometimes the causal coherence of the narrative events among themselves will be expressly noted by the narrator in telling the story—as when Gottfried's narrator informs us that the enmity of the courtiers grew so obvious "*daz er* [Tristan] *ervorhte den mort*" (GTr 8374); the subordinating conjunction makes the causal connection explicit. But many of these connections are not made explicit: neither Eilhart nor Gottfried, for instance, says outright that Mark's decision to marry is caused by the courtiers' campaign. Yet we are sure that it is. First, we are accustomed to assume a relation between adjacent events: we know that disequilibrium entails something; and we like to believe that what follows is caused by what precedes. This is that aspect of our complicity with the narrative that I have associated with actional motivation. Second, we observe that there is something in common between the campaign and the decision: the courtiers want *Mark to marry;* what follows are discussions between Mark, Tristan, and the courtiers on the subject of *Mark's marriage;* then comes the decision of *Mark to marry.* This is the usual sort of story motivation, and few of us require any more explicit statement of causal connection than it offers. The necessity that disequilibrium be followed by something; our assumption that consecutive events are causally related; the causal relations of story elements, whether these relations are expressed by the narrator or merely "obvious" to the recipients: all these conspire to link story events, to establish the causal connexity of narrative events among themselves. They generate what might be called diegetic coherence.

But there is another, equally important sort of coherence fostered by narrative motivation. When Gottfried's narrator explains that Mark's courtiers are motivated by envy, he explains this motivation in terms of a "general truth": envy never rests. Such a "truth" is, ostensibly, valid in the world at large; and by stating it the narrator asserts the congruence of his narrative with such extra-textual "truths." In doing so he also provides an example for the recipient, who is expected to do the same. As recipients we are constantly engaged in motivating the events of the narrative from our stock of everyday causal explanations: yes, of course birds carry nesting materials in their beaks, we see it every spring. This is the aspect of our complicity with the narrative that I have associated with recipient motivation. In addition, we are constantly engaged, often without being consciously aware of it, in monitoring the adequacy of the story motivation with regard to received opinions about the world: we recognize that it is quite natural for kings to act on the advice of their courtiers. The explicit assertion that the narrative is motivated according to "general truths"; our complicit eagerness to supply explanations for narrative events from our everyday supply of motivational reasons, as well as our more passive complicity in monitoring the everyday plausibility of the explicit motivations in the text: these conspire to establish the congruence of the narrative with received opinions about the world. They generate what might be called mimetic coherence.

It is for inadequate mimetic coherence that Gottfried's narrator attacks Eilhart's motivation: Cornish swallows do not fly to Ireland; kings do not send embassies off in search for the source of a strand of hair. Since these things do not occur in everyday life, the narrator implies, they have no place in narrative. Needless to say, this is an impossible standard. Improbable events abound in narrative, even Gottfried's own: it seems unlikely, for example, that Gottfried believed real-world lovers could really nourish themselves on love alone—the personal testimony of the narrator notwithstanding (GTr 16807-40, 16909-22). As noted above, we have various ways of explaining such troublesome events, as well as various reasons for delighting in them. Nevertheless, such instances of narrative "incoherence," even when we welcome them, cannot disguise the very powerful investment we have in the coherence of narrative, both diegetic and mimetic. As Eco wrote years ago: "It is only natural that life is more like *Ulysses* than *The Three Musketeers:* nevertheless we are all more likely to think about it in the categories of *The Three Musketeers* than in those of *Ulysses:* or better, I can only remember life and evaluate it when I consider it as a traditional novel."[23] Narrative, as others have pointed out, is an important way we make sense out of the world. It can only serve this function if it seems to make sense itself, and it will seem to make sense only if it conforms to the standards of what Eco calls the "traditional novel"; only, in my terms, if it manifests a certain degree of diegetic and mimetic coherence. Narrative motivation is one of the most powerful ways in which this coherence is generated—in the text and in the reception of the text.

The standards for making coherent narratives, of course, are no more absolute than those for making sense out of the world: they vary from one person to another, from one text to another, from one genre to another, from one generation to another, and so forth. They differ, as the example of Eilhart and Gottfried shows, from one author to another, even when they claim to tell the same story in the same language only a few decades

apart.[24] The tracing of these differences is a largely untouched but potentially very fruitful field of inquiry: it can tell us of the historical variations in the ways we have explained events to ourselves, in the ways we have made events into coherent narratives, in other words, in the ways we have made sense out of the world.[25]

Why then does Mark marry Isolde? According to Eilhart because of his relatives and some swallows and a strand of hair; according to Gottfried because of his courtiers and Tristan and his previous knowledge of Isolde. And why do we care? Because we want the story to continue and because we want it to continue in a coherent way. Why does Mark marry Isolde? So that the story will continue in a coherent and plausible way. And why do we care? Because we want narratives to make sense; because we want the world, as we tell it to ourselves, to make sense.[26]

Notes

1. Eilhart von Oberg, *Tristrant: Edition diplomatique des manuscrits et traduction en français moderne,* ed. Danielle Buschinger, Göppinger Arbeiten zur Germanistik, 202 (1976). References to Eilhart will be given in parentheses in the text and distinguished by the abbreviation: ETr. Unless otherwise noted, I cite from ms. H.

2. Gottfried von Straßburg, *Tristan und Isold,* ed. Friedrich Ranke, 15th ed. (1978). References to Gottfried will be given in parentheses in the text and distinguished by the abbreviation: GTr.

3. Besides those texts cited in notes 5, 6, and 7, see: Viktor Schklowskij, "Das Sujet im Kinematographen," in Viktor Schklowskij, *Schriften zum Film* (1966), pp. 17-25; Victor Shklovsky, "Sterne's *Tristram Shandy:* Stylistic Commentary," in *Russian Formalist Criticism: Four Essays,* ed. Lee T. Lemon and Marion J. Reis (1965), pp. 25-57; *Russischer Formalismus: Texte zur allgemeinen Literaturtheorie und zur Theorie der Prosa,* ed. Jurij Striedter (1969, 1971) [includes the Šklovskij essay just cited, unter the title "Der parodistische Roman: Sternes 'Tristram Shandy,'" pp. 245-99; see also under "Motivierung" in the index]; Oswald Ducrot and Tzvetan Todorov, *Encyclopedic Dictionary of the Sciences of Language,* trans. Catherine Porter (1979), p. 262-63.

4. Besides the substantial treatment by Culler cited in note 19, see: Seymour Chatman, *Story and Discourse: Narrative Structure in Fiction and Film* (1978), pp. 51-52; Shlomith Rimmon-Kenan, *Narrative Fiction: Contemporary Poetics* (1983), pp. 123-29, 142; Mieke Bal, *Narratology: Introduction to the Theory of Narrative* (1985), pp. 130-

32. The most important recent discussion of the issues is Meir Sternberg, "Mimesis and Motivation: The Two Faces of Fictional Coherence," in *Literary Criticism and Philosophy,* ed. Joseph P. Strelka, Yearbook of Comparative Criticism, 10 (1983), 145-88.

5. Vladímir Propp, *Morphology of the Folktale,* trans. Laurence Scott, 2nd. rev. ed. Louis A. Wagner (1968), p. 75. Subsequent references will be given in parentheses in the text.

6. Boris Tomashevsky, "Thematics," in *Russian Formalist Criticism: Four Essays,* ed. Lee T. Lemon and Marion J. Reis (1965), pp. 61-95, here p. 82.

7. ". . . la justification du fait particulier par une loi générale supposée inconnue, ou peut-être oubliée du lecteur et que le narrateur doit lui enseigner ou lui rappeler" (Gérard Genette, "Vraisemblance et motivation," in *Figures II* [1969], pp. 71-99, here p. 80). Subsequent references will be given in parentheses in the text; the translations are my own. For a feminist elaboration of Genette's essay see Nancy K. Miller, "Emphasis Added: Plots and Plausibilities in Women's Fiction," in *The New Feminist Criticism: Essays on Women, Literature, and Theory,* ed. Elaine Showalter (1985), pp. 339-60, here pp. 340, 343-44. For a critique of Genette see Sternberg (note 4), pp. 160-62.

8. Umberto Eco, *The Role of the Reader: Explorations in the Semiotics of Texts* (1979), p. 36.

9. In Genette's terms, because Gottfried's narrator cannot supply a "maxim" to explain the swallows' behavior, he regards Eilhart's narrative as a "récit *arbitraire*" rather than a "récit *vraisemblable*" (Genette [note 7], pp. 98-99; see also pp. 71-78, 92-99).

10. Peter Brooks, *Reading for the Plot: Design and Intention in Narrative* (1984), p. 103.

11. This may have been what Propp had in mind when he wrote that "the majority of characters' acts in the middle of a tale are *naturally* motivated by the course of the action" (Propp [note 5], p. 75, my italics).

12. In connection with Gottfried's version, for example, Rüdiger Krohn has suggested the possibility that Mark is motivated by sexual attraction for Tristan (Rüdiger Krohn, "Erotik und Tabu in Gottfrieds 'Tristan': König Marke," in *Stauferzeit: Geschichte, Literatur, Kunst,* ed. Rüdiger Krohn, Bernd Thum, Peter Wapnewski, Karlsruher kulturwissenschaftliche Arbeiten, 1 [1979], pp. 362-76). I do not find Krohn's argument convincing, but it does give some idea of the range of alternative explanations that would be possible.

13. Roland Barthes, "Introduction to the Structural Analysis of Narratives," in *Image, Music, Text,* trans. Stephen Heath (1977), pp. 79-124, here p. 94. Frank Kermode puts the same idea more simply: "Sequence goes nowhere without his doppelgänger or shadow, causality" (Frank Kermode, "Secrets and Narrative Sequence," *Critical Inquiry* 7 [1980], 83-101, here p. 84).

14. "The universality of causation [the assertion that no change ever occurs without some cause] has throughout the history of philosophy, until very recent times, usually been regarded as very obvious, sometimes even self-evident. . . . [But] what was once considered quite obvious is now at least controversial." "No one, for example, has ever shown experimentally that all the simple voluntary actions of men are caused or that similar such actions always have similar causes, and the opinions of philosophers are, in fact, divided on these questions" (Richard Taylor, "Causation," in *The Encyclopedia of Philosophy,* ed. Paul Edward [1967], 2: 57, 60).

15. Propp (note 5), p. 75; Tomashevsky (note 6), p. 81; Genette (note 7), p. 97; Sternberg (note 4), p. 167.

16. Propp (note 5), p. 78; Tomashevsky (note 6), p. 83; Genette (note 7), p. 97; Sternberg (note 4), p. 167.

17. I assume here a causal aspect to Barthes's "effect of the real": the generous provision of causal explanations merely to create the illusion that the story is well motivated—as we assume reality is (Roland Barthes, "L'effet de réel," *Communications* 11 [1968], 84-89).

18. Here I paraphrase Gerhard Schindele, *Tristan: Metamorphose und Tradition,* Studien zur Poetik und Geschichte der Literatur, 12 (1971), p. 23.

19. Naturalization and recuperation are words sometimes used interchangeably with motivation but which are more properly differentiated from it. See the important discussion in Jonathan Culler, *Structuralist Poetics: Structuralism, Linguistics, and the Study of Literature* (1975), pp. 131-60 as well as Sternberg's critique (note 4), pp. 163-65.

20. E. M. Forster, *Aspects of the Novel* (1955), p. 88. Subsequent references will be given in parentheses in the text.

21. For a very brief (nevertheless, so far as I know, the only) consideration of how we construct causal connections as we read see Tzvetan Todorov, "Reading as Construction," in *The Reader in the Text: Essays on Audience and Interpretation,* ed. Susan R. Suleiman, Inge Crosman (1980), pp. 74-75.

22. Here I have parodied Aquinas's commentary on Aristotle's *Metaphysics,* 1013a29-36. Aquinas writes: "The efficient cause is related to the final cause because the efficient cause is the starting point of motion and the final cause is its terminus. . . . Hence the efficient cause is the cause of the final cause, and the final cause is the cause of the efficient cause. The efficient cause is the cause of the final cause inasmuch as it makes the final cause be, because by causing motion the efficient cause brings about the final cause. But the final cause is the cause of the efficient cause, not in the sense that it makes it be, but inasmuch as it is the reason for the causality of the efficient cause. For an efficient cause is a cause inasmuch as it acts, and it acts only because of the final cause. Hence the efficient cause derives its causality from the final cause" (Thomas Aquinas, *Commentary on the Metaphysics of Aristotle,* trans. John P. Rowan [1961], 1: 308 [Book 5, Lesson 2, Section 775]).

23. I give here my own English version from the German translation: Umberto Eco, *Das offene Kunstwerk,* trans. G. Memmert (1973), p. 202.

24. I have tried to work out the differences between Eilhart and Gottfried in a related article: James A. Schultz, "Why Do Tristan and Isolde Leave for the Woods? Narrative Motivation and Narrative Coherence in Eilhart von Oberg and Gottfried von Straßburg," to appear in *MLN,* 102 (1987).

25. It is motivation thus broadly conceived that has engaged Kenneth Burke in *A Grammar of Motives* (1969).

26. The impetus for this essay grew out of a seminar on narrative theory that I taught with David Wellbery at Stanford University in the spring of 1985. I would like to express my gratitude to Professor Wellbery for that extremely rewarding collaboration as well as to Professor Theodore M. Andersson for arranging my visit to Stanford. For their helpful comments on earlier versions of this essay I would also like to thank Professors Efraín Barradas of the University of Massachusetts-Boston, Matilda Tomaryn Bruckner of Boston College, and Ingeborg Glier of Yale University.

William C. McDonald (essay date 1988)

SOURCE: McDonald, William C. "The Fool-Stick: Concerning Tristan's Club in the German Eilhart Tradition." *Euphorion: Zeitschrift für Literaturgeschichte* 82, no. 2 (1988): 127-49.

[*In the following essay, McDonald interprets the symbolic significance of Tristan's club in* Tristan *and in later adaptations of the legend the followed Eilhart.*]

Although critics have examined the *Tristan* poems of Eilhart von Oberge (fl. ca. 1170) and his followers through a wide variety of methodologies and critical approaches, a pervasive motif has largely gone unexplored: the large stick carried by the protagonist when he is dressed as a fool is placed in high relief. The function of Tristan's club engages our attention here, not least for its contribution to reception theory. Eilhart, whose poem affords very early access to the episode of Tristan's folly[1], introduces the club as the hero's distinguishing feature for his final adventure of love. Tristan, in exile, wishes to see Isolde again and feigns madness to enter Mark's court. After a battle in support of Kehenis (Kaherdin), from which he receives a head wound, Tristan has a long period of convalescence. He is shorn of hair and scarred, so disfigured that he need not fear discovery when assuming the role of Isolde's rescuing devotee in Cornwall. Tristan's nephew advises him to go to court alone, acting foolish and dressed in a hooded coat; in his present state the courtiers will believe he is a genuine fool (8698ff.)

After Tristan has donned the fool's costume, he searches out a great club:

> *allain gieng der kün man,*
> *deß in nicht verdroß.*
> *ain kolb gar groß* [*einen kolben lang und groß* MS. B]
> *trůg er gar sicherlich.*
>
> (8720-22a)[2]

Because of his fool's apparel and erratic behavior (boasting, insulting), Tristan is indeed thought to be a fool and accorded admittance to Mark's court. One characteristic gesture of Tristan in the disguise of a fool is the flourishing of his club:

> *de rait der küng uff den hoff.*
> *der tor lieff im nach.*
> *sin kolben er hoch trůg.*
> *allfenwÿß begieng er gnůg*
> *und manig torlich spil.*
>
> (8787-91)

Holding the cudgel high is thus an accompaniment to foolish behavior and enhances the comic aspect of the spectacle. It is not exclusively a burlesque or comic gesture, however.

That Eilhart views the club from another perspective is immediately apparent. Tristan takes it in hand when visiting Isolde's private quarters—as protection from meddlesome spies (8967)—, and in this scene the former symbol of his identity as fool becomes a side arm, not a badge of folly. Upon parting from Isolde, the bold hero again holds his club high (8998), but now the former laughing-stock brandishes a potentially deadly weapon. He plans to kill anyone who would seize him:

sin kolben trog er hoch,
alß ob er da mit wölt schlachen,
ob sie in wölten bestan,
die sin gewartet hatten.

(8998-9001)

The club has the desired effect, frightening off Tristan's enemies. He effects his safe departure through the threat of violence—by means of his club—and leaves his shamed tormentors blaming one another for his escape.

When Ulrich von Türheim (ca. 1235), whose *Tristan* is greatly indebted to Eilhart, relates the episode of Tristan as fool, he not only takes up the motif of the club, but richly orchestrates it. The scene begins with Isolde's summons: Tristan is to come to his lady wearing a fool's cowl and carrying a cudgel made from a tree[3]. The hero does as he is bidden. The narrator mentions the stick again, this time in the rhetoric of personification: the club is his traveling companion (*sîn geverte* 2512). Next a key transition is registered that challenges Eilhart's notion of the object, a change setting the pattern for subsequent mediations. Ulrich converts the fool-stick from an instrument of intimidation into an actual weapon; he therefore explores the interplay between the cudgel as the mark of the fool and as the means of working Tristan's will. When Antret, Mark's courtier and Tristan's most implacable and dangerous foe, attempts to have the hero removed from Isolde's presence, Tristan bloodies his head with a blow from his club:

Antret quam dar gegân
und wolte in dan gezogen hân.
dem sluoger einen slac,
daz er unversunnen lac.

(2547-50)

With the club, Tristan puts out the eye of the spying dwarf Melot (2653) and so terrorizes the court that no-one dares approach him:

Tristan gie durh die stat.
swâ im diu strâze was versat,
mit den kolben, den er truoc,
machet er si wît genuoc.

(2733-6)

The mace, it soon becomes clear, is no mere fool's attribute, but the predominant aspect of his persona, a multivalent object and ever-recurring motif. It is a means of declaring his natural superiority, physical freedom and the right to act like a wild man. Considered mad (see 2575 and 2644), Tristan achieves a rule of terror with a single piece of wood. The court accords him autonomy out of fear of his "dementia" and his club.

As can be seen, Ulrich significantly alters the nature of Eilhart's motif, taking an object that functions symbolically as a potential agent of harm, and creating from it

a more authentic instrument rivaling courtly weapons. The narrative path is thus from Eilhart's threat to Ulrich's realization of the potential of the cudgel. In Ulrich's account the club manifests itself as a kind of leitmotif, for instance, when Tristan the fool is surprised by Antret in Isolde's arms and when his crime is publicly announced. Tristan wields the club to ensure his safe passage from the place to avoid death by burning (2733-6). But Ulrich has more in mind than Tristan's mere brandishing the club, as in Eilhart, in order to make his escape. The protagonist soon comes upon King Mark in the woods, takes up his cudgel and beats him with it. This weapon has replaced the sword of the traditional knightly encounter in the woods; with it he defeats Mark, forcing him to take flight (2755).

The club (*der kolbe* 2765) becomes Tristan's rudder, as he paddles a boat to make good his escape.[4] And now comes a death scene, for which the frequent, and ever more violent uses of the club have prepared the reader. Ulrich tells how Mark's vassal, Pleherin, challenges the hero, urging him to return to court for Isolde's sake. Tristan replies out of an explicit sense of *menlich ellen* (2778) that he'd rather perish for the sake of his beloved than to flee. Without fear, he rushes up to Pleherin and kills him with his club:

âne vorhte er an in lief.
mit dem kolben er in sluoc,
daz ers iemer hât genuoc:
er lac tôt von sîner hant.

(2780-3)

The murder of Pleherin exposes the conceptual structure of those poems in the Eilhart tradition: bravery and brute force, with the club as the chief instrument for accomplishing the sovereignty of the fool. In Ulrich's poem, violence with the cudgel has the further function of unveiling Mark's court as open to attack. The king has already fled before Tristan's club and now finds it has left him bereft of his beloved courtier. Mark's reaction is rage (he wishes to burn both Tristan and Isolde), but he is powerless to bring the hero to justice. Tristan has no fear of Mark's court (2812), the club providing a visual metaphor for his contempt for the king. Mark concedes that the death of Pleherin signals the loss of honor, of face (2820-1), the club emblematizing his inability to control his wife and his nephew, as well as his impotence in protecting himself and his vassals. The wild man, a law unto himself and Isolde, is victorious.

When Heinrich von Freiberg sets down his *Tristan* (1260-90), he stresses in even greater degree than his predecessors the heroic qualities of his protagonist. Tristan is a bold, model knight and full subscriber to the chivalric ethos. Heinrich's hero is almost anachronistic in his invincibility and imperviousness to fear; he is mightier than even the best of the knights of the Round Table (1986-2009). *rechte manheit* (2007ff.) is his essential quality, adventure his chief occupation, and honor his goal. Heinrich again takes up the motif of Tristan's unwillingness to flee: facing the warrior Nampete̅r̅i̅ ̅ ̅ was, the reader is informed, not accustomed ̅ ̅ ̅ ̅ ̅ ̅ ht (6256).

crucial means of exhibiting Tristan's valor and devo-͵on to Isolde is his assumption of the role of the fool with a cudgel. It is the only costume that the hero dons in the poem, and the narrative is so constructed as to make it a partial disguise only. For, following Eilhart, Tristan has entered the scene with wounds so disfiguring that he is unrecognizable. To his confidants he looks the fool and thus can easily pass for one (5100ff.). Persuaded that he can visit Isolde with success, Tristan puts on a fool's cloak and carries a cudgel:

> *und nam eynen kolben gros*
> *und stark genůg in sine hant*
>
> (5142-3)

The cudgel that this *degen balt* (5140) brings with him is soon shown to be an instrument charged with the potential for outward violence. Upon his arrival at court, Tristan brandishes the club to force the gaping spectators to take flight. Heinrich therefore neatly turns Eilhart's threat of blows at Tristan's departure into an immediate threat upon arrival: the club is consistently a weapon meant to deter enemies and to inflict punishment upon them.

Heinrich's self-assured hero proves his status by a significant alteration of detail concerning the club. Whereas Isolde, in Ulrich's poem, orders Tristan to take revenge on his enemies by coming to court dressed as a fool with a club in his hand (2480ff.), Tantrisel, Tristan's nephew in Heinrich's romance, suggests that Tristan play the fool. The hero himself decides to take a large, strong club with him (5142-3).

It is soon apparent what Tristan's equipment is meant to achieve. Radically altering Ulrich's scene at court with Antret, Heinrich has Mark seize the fool by the ears because of his insulting behavior before Isolde (5202ff.). Tristan raises his club with both hands and swings it at no less than the king himself:

> *der dor sinen kolben zoch*
> *uff mit beiden henden hoch,*
> *na dem kunyge er so slug.*
>
> (5207-9)

Antret wards off the mighty blow intended for Mark, but pays dearly for his intervention. The hero knocks him senseless with a blow from the club that is so force-

ful, the narrative drolly reports, that Antret was paid back for every offense he had committed since childhood (5216-8). Expanding on the episode, Heinrich adds a blow causing deafness and pain in every bodily member of Antret (5234-5). Owing to Tristan's torrent of blows with the club, the entire court flees from him:

> *er liez mit slegen umbe gan.*
> *sie vluhen alle von im dan;*
> *der kunic und die kunegin,*
> *eines her, daz ander hin,*
> *ritter und juncherren,*
> *die minren und die meren;*
> *vrowen und juncvrowen,*
> *die mochte man da schowen*
> *uber ein ander vallen.*
>
> (5219-27, MS. F)

The club causes chaos, as the courtiers hurry to effect their escape (Cf. Ulrich, 2550-4); and Tristan, possessor of enormous strength, is able to proclaim the ironic words: *nů si frede!* (5236). The fool induces anarchy, showing himself to be the true sovereign.

The peace he has in mind is effected by the cudgel. Recognizing that the club is not his natural armament, the narrator says, in an aside, that Tristan is more used to destroying lances (5242ff.). Nevertheless, the club controls the attitudes of contending forces as much as a lance can, even as it reveals the court incapable of taking effective action against the hero and fearful of violence. Those courtiers challenging Tristan openly succumb to the club, as the homicide episode with Pleherin demonstrates. Eilhart allows his protagonist to flee and to refuse Pleherin's challenge (6844ff.); Ulrich, as we have seen, portrays a brief scene where Mark's vassal is murdered by the club; but Heinrich offers an imaginative new version. His appetite for pageantry animates a vivid and dramatic encounter granting further centrality to the club.

Heinrich depicts a lengthy scene of over 200 verses, which begins with Mark's hunting journey and continues through Tristan's saving leap and discovery of his identity by Pleherin. The latter rides after the hero, challenging him to a duel for the sake of Isolde. In some 40 lines Heinrich allows the reader to savor Tristan's decision to stand his ground armed only with a club, while his opponent has a sword and shield. Reversing the leitmotif of fleeing in Eilhart, Heinrich now has Pleherin, not Tristan, wish to run away (5587). Tristan fells his adversary's horse with a stroke from his club; next, he wards off Pleherin's attack with his cudgel; and then he smites him with such a blow that Pleherin falls dead, his sword and shield in a heap (5607-11). Again, as in Ulrich's story, the club serves as Tristan's knightly equipment, proving itself to be superior to conventional weapons. Through its agency, the fool (and wild man) subdues his enemies and gains his freedom.

Another reversal closes Heinrich's episodes featuring Tristan with the club. After the precipitous arrival of King Mark at the duel of Pleherin and his nephew, the king pauses to admire the strength and daring of the fool (5644). Even though Tristan escapes courtly justice, using the club as a rudder for his get-away vessel, Mark allows his advisors to persuade him that the fool was in fact not Tristan and that his wife has not deceived him. The monarch, rendered incapable of taking action because of his gullibility and love for Isolde, persuades himself that all is well. Ironically, it would seem, Tristan's violent actions with the club have served to drive Mark closer to his queen; they live together henceforth in peace and harmony (5716-8). This is not to state, however, that the club works at cross purposes with the love of Tristan and Isolde. The cudgel, an emblem of Tristan's essential autonomy, is both the instrument of the hero's escape and of Isolde's salvation. The lovers are separate from one another, but, still in all, they have outwitted the court.

Next, we consider the so-called *Czech Tristan,* a poem from the late 14th century (preserved in two manuscripts from the fifteenth century), which is ascribed to two nameless authors, probably clerics. This *Tristan* is an amalgam of German sources—Eilhart, Gottfried von Strassburg and Heinrich von Freiberg. A close adaptation in many places, the poem also betrays significant departures, most clearly in the use of motifs (= Isolde's near scuffle with Isolde of the White Hands; Brangene has herself sealed in the lovers' tomb; the miracle of the rosebush and grapevine is absent). One adaptation of note is the fool's club, which, although showing significant points of contact with Heinrich's account, is imaginatively rendered.

In conception, the figure of Tristan is here clearly modelled on the version of Heinrich von Freiberg. He is a knight errant and lover-knight at home in adventure and combat. The Czech redactors follow Heinrich in constructing the fool-episode: Tantrisel, Tristan's nephew, recognizes that the hero's deformity will easily allow him to be designated a fool and thus permit a rendezvous with Isolde (7337ff.). But suddenly a marked textual emendation appears: the giant club is absent from the description of Tristan's costume. The reader only learns that the hero puts on a cowl so that everyone will think him a fool (7385-7).

The cudgel is also missing from the scene in which the fool arrives at Mark's court. Tristan does not enter the stage as a threatening figure, ominously raising his club to make the onlookers flee, but rather performs amusing deeds to the delight and amazement of the crowd (7393ff.). Since there has been no mention of the club, even as the fool's scepter, its sudden and destructive appearance catches the reader—and Mark's court—off guard. For Tristan menaces the king with an overt challenge unique to this poetic version:

> *Ich rate dir, Königlein, tritt hier vor mich*
> *und sei nunmehr mein Diener,*
> *sonst gebe ich dir mit der Keule einen Schlag,*
> *daß du von der Königin zur Seite fällst!*
>
> (7424-7)

Tristan's *dérision de la royauté* is here an expansion of Heinrich's comic words at court, *phy! sal der ein kunyg sin? / er were kome eyn kunygelin / bi mir, als ich ein kunyg bin* (5183-5), with substantial differences. In the *Czech Tristan* the fool speaks to the king in a hostile manner (7419), he predicts that Isolde will leave Mark's side, and he provokes the ruler with his club.[5]

The court laughs, unaware that this is no veiled threat, but rather a prophesy of an assault on King Mark, which soon comes to pass. Limned in greater detail, and with more attention given to the club, the episode contains a new, aggressive and heroic speech by Tristan. After Mark abuses him, Tristan reacts violently:

> *Der Narr zog seine Keule heraus und empor*
> *und sprach: "Ich stürbe hundertmal leichter,*
> *eh' daß ich dies jemandem nicht heimzahlte,*
> *lieber würde ich das Leben verlieren."*
> *Und er schlug nach dem Könige mit der Keule*
> *und sprach: "Hier waschen wir uns ohne Lauge!"*
> *Antret, um dem Könige gefällig zu sein,*
> *verhielt (bzw. 'stellte') sich sehr kühn:*
> *er deckte den König mit seinem Leibe.*
> *Der Narr gab ihm einen Schlag, daß er stürzte*
> *und von dem Schlage betäubt ('stumm') wurde.*
>
> (7458-68)

The scene becomes even more drastic and pictorial, as the club is said to reach the skullbone of Antret and to cause blood to stream in all directions (7469-70).

Commenting on Tristan's second blow to Antret, the narrator states: *Den betäubte er so mit der Keule- / ein Wunder, daß er ihm das Leben ließ!* (7484-5). The Czech version also augments Tristan's motivation for exacting revenge on Antret, explaining that he sought satisfaction for treason and evil that Antret had earlier visited on him (7471-3). Whatever his motivation and his deeds, Mark pardons the fool, claiming that he acted in a fashion consistent with his office: *"Wer geschlagen wurde,"* Mark concludes, *"muß es auf sich nehmen."* (7493). Here the club assumes still another function, namely the exposure of Mark's world of delusion. The object thus serves to focus on the king's self-deception and foreshadows his assertion—unique to the Czech version—after the escape of the fool/Tristan that he fully accepts Isolde's state of innocence:

> *Ich glaube euch, daß sie nicht in solches*
> *Gerede gekommen ist,*
> *und will sie nun in Gnaden aufnehmen,*
> *ohne einen Argwohn ihr gegenüber zu hegen.*
>
> (7931-3)

The club has purchased Tristan's freedom from Antret, who is now deaf (Melot is blind). But the hero—as fool—still fears treason when he lies in bed with Isolde. As protection against assassination, he takes the club under his arm as soon as he rises. Tristan makes very clear what the cudgel can do:

> *Wenn etwas geschieht, werde ich mich solange vertei-*
> *digen,*
> *so lange ich nur vermag,*
> *auch werde ich jemanden mit dieser Keule hauen*
> *und ihm am Leibe solche Schrunde (bzw. 'Beule')*
> *zufügen,*
> *daß ihm die Gedärme heraustreten.*
>
> (7635-9)

Tristan's intimidating gestures with his club even extend to women, as when, playing the fool, he says to Isolde:

> *Laßt mich, ich muß singen.*
> *Allein, wenn ihr mich nicht lassen wollt,*
> *kann es so [weit] kommen mit mir ('mir solche Sache*
> *k.'),*
> *daß ich einer mit der Keule einen Schlag gebe,*
> *daß sie von mir (weg) auf die Seite fällt.*
>
> (7647-51)

(These last words are an echo of Tristan's earlier challenge to King Mark in Isolde's presence, when he says the king will receive such a blow that he will fall from the queen's side, 7424-7.) The threat just cited hints at the twist the Czech authors give the traditional scene in which Tristan holds the cudgel as Isolde's doorkeeper. He guards her chamber, following her with his weapon in hand (Heinrich: 5462ff.).

All of the power symbolized by the club, which until now has been a warning and a weapon striking only Antret, comes to bear in the duel with Pleherin. The Czech redactors follow the outlines of Heinrich's episode but are at pains to explore the layers of complexity in Tristan's club as both a defensive and offensive weapon. They flesh out the episode with fresh details, most prominently involving the club, which Tristan seizes as soon as he hears Isolde's name in Pleherin's challenge (7774-5).

The hero, who casts evil glances at his opponent, has in mind murder of both beast and rider. In the Czech ver-

sion the horse is not merely dazed by the club, but killed in a grotesque manner:

> *. . . und er schlug das Pferd, daß er die Keule fast*
> *hineinjagte,*
> *sodaß er vom Haupt bis zum Schenkel*
> *das Fleisch mit der Haut heraustrieb (bzw. '-riß').*
>
> (7786-8)

Tristan's method prefigures the death of Pleherin himself, who suffers a blow on his head from the club so forceful that his brains come forth (7807-8). As if these grotesque descriptions of brutal slaying were not enough, a chorus of courtiers' voices tells King Mark how Pleherin perished:

> *"Lieber König, bewahre ruhigen ('guten') Sinn;*
> *denn als du jagtest, gerade in der Zeit*
> *hat er den Narren immer mit Haß verfolgt;*
> *drum hat er ihn mit der Keule geschlagen*
> *und ihm mit der Keule einen Schlag aufs Haupt gege-*
> *ben,*
> *daß das Blut wie aus einem Eber lief.*
> *Da fand er von dem Schlage denn auch sein Ende."*
>
> (7824-30)

Throughout the duel, the narrator stresses Pleherin's courtly excellence and knightly armaments, even observing that the mighty blows rained on Tristan remove fragments from the cudgel (7799). But the hero parries each thrust with his club and succeeds in knocking away Pleherin's sword. Indicative of the almost magical power of Tristan's weapon is the narrative observation that the club wreaks more havoc than even a sword could (7809). Here the club shows itself—by authorial intervention—to surpass knightly equipment; the club is mightier than the sword.

The avowal that Tristan's cudgel is superior to conventional weapons must attract our attention, especially when linked to the courtiers' comparison of the hero with an avenging animal:

> *. . . so rächte er sich wie ein Bär,*
> *schwang seine Keule empor*
> *und verwandte darauf seine ganze Kraft,*
> *daß er den so zugerichtet hat,*
> *der ihn geschlagen oder an den Ohren gezogen.*
>
> (7918-22)

Whether the Czech adapters are here offering criticism of the courtly world through the sovereignty that the feral fool effects, living as he does in a primitive state and armed only with a natural object, is not easy to discern. Without doubt, the *Czech Tristan* exploits and underscores features of the club as a superior agent of revenge. The echo of Eilhart in the Czech account is unmistakable (*schwang seine Keule empor,* 7919); but now the club is only a faint echo of the parent version. Earlier threats have become blows and murder, while a rude club has achieved a status superior to knightly sword and shield.

Authors in the Eilhart tradition impose on his text a pattern saturated with violence by means of the club, as we have seen. The scenes with the cudgel increase incrementally in dramatic intensity from Eilhart's version to the final treatment of the Tristan subject matter in the German Middle Ages, Hans Sachs' play *Tragedia von der strengen lieb herr Tristrant mit der schönen königin Isalden* (1553). Eilhart himself, as observed, was content to make Tristan's club a dark prop and to hint at its ominous possibilities. In this he is followed by the anonymous German *Prose Tristan* of 1484, which refers to the club several times (4700-11; 4733-4 and 4824-6), assigning to it the Eilhartian functions of diversion, protection and intimidation.[6] Seeking escape from court, Tristan holds his club [*kolben*] high, *als ob er sy all erschlahen* [190!9002] *wolte.* (4850-1). Since his enemies among the courtiers fear for their lives in the presence of the club, *schwigen all still. vnd getorst auch keiner ruren. noch sich melden. vnd liessen in mit gutem frid hinweg geen* (4852-4). He therefore returns home as a direct consequence of the menace that the club portends. In spite of this close reception of Eilhart from the late period, it is important to establish that the German medieval Tristan poems do not conclude with threatening gestures, but rather with the club serving violent ends.

Hans Sachs (d. 1576), whom Eli Sobel characterizes well as a "master shoemaker and master singer of Nürnberg," wrote both songs and a play based on the Tristan legend, clearly drawing on the prose romance of 1484 in chapbook form (= version of 1550).[7] Sachs devotes one song to *her dristrant in dem narren klaid* (No. V of 1551), verses in which a by now familiar picture of the club emerges. Tristan learns that spies are aware of his liason with Isolde and seek to capture him:

> *Vnd als tristrant merckt dise ding*
> *zuckt er sein kolben schwere*
> *in alle Hoch, nach heldes muet,*
> *ging zu seiner kungin.****
> *Keiner angrieff den kunen helt.*

(V, 3,5-9)

Once again the club is a weapon frightening away Tristan's enemies, its power suggested by the actual weight of the cudgel. Just as important, Sachs establishes a clear link between the club and heroism: the object and Tristan's state of mind are inseparable. The club is symbolic of heroic valor, self-confidence and fidelity, and, as such, defines the man. No matter that Sachs ultimately looks askance at the adulterous love of

Tristan and Isolde, suggesting that such affection is truly *le folie d'amour.* In the costume of the fool Tristan is a hero, and his heroism is one with his club.

We have suggested that the incremental ferocity which the German Tristan exhibits with his club, turning intimidation into violent deeds, has defining undercurrents in the conception of Tristan as an intrepid hero. Sachs caps off this tendency in his *Tristan* play, which gives conceptual clarity to the motif traced. Antret challenges the fool openly at court, calling him a rogue who must be caught and hung on the gallows. The stage direction then reads: *Herr Tristrant reist sich von ihn, schlecht mit dem kolben unter sie, biß sie alle entlauffen, unnd Tristrant spricht . . .* (VI, p. 180, 21-2) His words are a farewell to Isolde and to her kingdom, brief words followed by the hero's departure with club in hand. Antret closes the act with this speech:

> *Alle drey sind wir worden geschlagen.*
> *Doch dürff wir Tristrant nit verklagen.*
> *Man würd uns halten für verzagt,*
> *Das uns ein narr all drey hat jagt.*
> *Wir wöllen sagen nichts darvon,*
> *Sonder wöllen gleich alle thon,*
> *Samb uns gebissen hab der hon.*

(VI, p. 180, 27-33)

Violence and heroism allow Tristan to escape, his natural superiority intact. The club, essential to the maintenance of Tristan's reputation in the episode, is both his companion and the souvenir of his victory.

Notes

1. There is controversy about the dating of Eilhart's *Tristrant*, which is transmitted in three fragmentary manuscripts from the 12th and 13th centuries and three 15th-century manuscripts. Of the two possible dates for composition, ca. 1170 and ca. 1190, scholars incline toward the first. On the place of Eilhart's poem in the "Folly Story," see Duncan Robertson, *Toward an Aesthetic of the Conteur: The 'Folie Tristan'*, Tristania, 2 (1977), 4-5. See also Merritt R. Blakeslee, *Mouvance and Revisionism in the Transmission of Thomas of Britain's 'Tristan': The Episode of the Interwining Trees*, Arthurian Literature, 6 (1986), 140ff.

2. For the reader's convenience I list in one place the editions from which references in this paper appear:

   * Eilhart von Olberg, *Tristrant*, ed. D. Buschinger, Göppingen, 1976. Quotations following Cod. Pal. germ. 346 (Heidelberg), unless otherwise indicated.

   * Ulrich von Türheim, *Tristan*, ed. T. Kerth, Tübingen, 1979.

* Heinrich von Freiberg, *Tristan,* ed. D. Buschinger, Göppingen, 1982. Quotations following W*f087 (Cologne), unless otherwise indicated.

* *Das altčechische Tristan-Epos,* ed. U. Bamborschke, Wiesbaden, 1968, II. Quotations given in the modern German version by Bamborschke.

* *Tristrant und Isalde: Prosaroman,* ed. A. Brandstetter, Tübingen, 1966.

* Eli Sobel, ed., *The Tristan Romance in the Meisterlieder of Hans Sachs,* Berkeley and Los Angeles, 1963.

* *Hans Sachs,* ed. A. von Keller, 1879; rpt. Hildesheim, 1964, XII, 142-86.

Regarding the term "Kolbe"/"Kolben" Jacob and Wilhelm Grimm observe in their *Wörterbuch* (ed. Hildebrand): *Wegen der Verwandschaft denkt man zunächst an "Keule," das im Begriffe fast oder ganz gleich ist; denn wie "Keule" bezeichnet "Kolbe" einen Knüttel mit dickem Ende, und wie dort fällt auch hier das Hauptgewicht des Begriffs auf das dicke, kugelige 'kolbige' Ende, das eben selbst "Kolbe" heißt (wie "Keule").* (Cited in vol. V=11, 1602).

3. Isolde says, in Ulrich's account: *heiz in komen in tôren wîs: / zehanden tragen ein kolbenrîs* (2479-80). About this club, Grimm states it is *offenbar noch ein einfacher Knüttel vom Baume* (V=11, 1604). The so-called *Munich Tristan* (Staatsbibl. Cgm. 51), a manuscript containing Ulrich's poem, includes depictions from about the year 1300 of Tristan's deeds as a fool. See Roger S. Loomis, *Arthurian Legends in Medieval Art,* New York, 1938, pp. 132-4.

The contemporary conception of Tristan's club as an awesome weapon is clearly visible from the miniatures. Loomis describes them thusly: "[The] illustrator sets forth with neat deftness Tristram's escape in the garb of a fool, when he clubbed his way from Ysolt's room,—his encounters with Mark and Pleherin, whom, in the third row, he strikes down with the club, and with the same club paddles away" (pp. 133-4). See also Tony Hunt, *The Tristan Illustrations in MS London, BL Add. 11619,* in *Rewards and Punishments in the Arthurian Romances and Lyric Poetry of Mediaeval France,* ed. P. V. Davies and A. J. Kennedy, Cambridge, Eng., 1987, esp. pp. 51-2.

4. D. J. Gifford, in *Iconographical Notes towards a Definition of the Medieval Fool,* in *The Fool and the Trickster: Studies in Honour of Enid Welsford,* Cambridge, Eng., 1979, p. 20, notes that the fool's club or stick in the manuscript tradition "can look rather like a canoe paddle."

5. There are in Tristan's gestures an echo of the tradition of the "mock king" as described by William Willeford in *The Fool and His Scepter: A Study in Clowns and Jesters and Their Audience,* Evanston, Ill., 1969, pp. 158ff. Willeford's book contains a plate depicting jesters' baubles (p. 37).

6. The German *Prose Tristan* (= *Tristrant und Isalde,* ed. Brandstetter), printed by Anton Sorg in Augsburg in 1484, contains woodcuts, among which is Tristan disguised as a fool in the presence of Mark and Isolde. The difference in pictorial illustration of Tristan as fool in the *Munich Tristan* and in the German *Prose Tristan* is so striking that Loomis, in *Arthurian Legends in Medieval Art,* p. 141, describes the protagonist in the latter as a "jester." Tristan is garbed as a late-medieval fool with no trace of the earlier conception, according to which he seems to be a figure in disguise.

7. Eli Sobel, "The Earliest Allegories and Imagery of Hans Sachs: An Introductory Essay," *Yale French Studies,* 47 (1972), 212. See also Sobel's study, *The Tristan Romance in Hans Sachs' Meisterlieder,* in *Festschrift for John G. Kunstmann,* Chapel Hill, 1959, 108-117.

Raymond J. Cormier (essay date 1990)

SOURCE: Cormier, Raymond J. "Eilhart's Seminal Tower of Pleasure." *Fifteenth-Century Studies* 17 (1990): 57-63.

[*In the following essay, Cormier comments on Eilhart's innovative retelling of the story-within-a-story of Gariole and Kehenis in his* Tristant.]

Eilhart von Oberg postpones the *dénouement* of his tragic *Tristan* love story by inserting a cameo that mirrors the sad destiny of his main characters.[1] This observation refers to the tale of Gariole and Kehenis, who find themselves deeply in love but thwarted by an evil, jealous husband.

In the words of Eilhart (as translated by J. W. Thomas, 137-38): "Not far from Karahes lived a mighty lord named Nampetenis. . . ." This warrior, having retired from high, knightly deeds and pursuits, now spends all his time at the hunt shooting game or stays busy watching over his beautiful wife whom he keeps guarded in complete custody, grimly even and dishonorably. That is, he has very high castle walls built and three moats dug around the structure. Nampetenis himself carries the keys to the castle; he is the gatekeeper and allows no males young or old, bondsmen or nobles, to remain within whenever he rides out to hunt. Only women can stay to watch over and keep the company of the sorely vexed Lady Gariole.

Now Gariole, before her marriage, had promised Kehenis secretly that she would receive him if he came to visit. When Nampetenis heard of this, he had the watch doubled, but nevertheless, since both Kehenis and Gariole were filled with thoughts of love for each other, Kehenis succeeded and came in secret to visit one day when Nampetenis was off hunting.

On this quiet, windless day, Gariole up above the gated wall, sees and welcomes her lover. Kehenis reminds her of her promise of pleasure before the hateful marriage. The lady is perfectly willing, but recalls her state—locked up so that no one can reach her. "'You have surely heard,' she calls out, 'how my lord guards me, but my heart is so inclined toward you that I shall do your will if you can get in here to me'" (138). To help his brother-in-law (Kehenis is, of course, Isolde of the White Hands's brother) solve this logistical problem, Tristrant the consultant in adultery advises Kehenis to have a wax impression of the castle keys made so that another set can be cast from the imprint.

Eilhart interrupts this suspenseful episode with the unexpected news of Tristrant's father's death. The hero must leave Kehenis, but will return soon. Once Kehenis has the keys and Nampetenis goes off to his daily hunt, the youth, along with his companion Tristrant, goes to tryst with Lady Gariole. But Nampetenis, upon his return, because of the visitors' foolishness and brazen carelessness, realizes that both Tristrant and Kehenis must have entered the castle tower.

The jealous, enraged husband enters the chamber, draws his sword, then threatens Gariole with death unless she tell the truth (151):

> Nampetenis: "'What did he do to you?'"
> Gariole: "'He kissed me.'"
> —"'Did you make love to him?'"
> —"'No, I didn't.'"
> —"'You're lying.'"
> —"'Lord, I am.'"
> —"'It did come to that.'"
> —"'It came to what?'"
> —"'He pulled me down under him against my will.'"
> —"'How did he get in?'"
> —"'Lord, I don't know. He did it without my help.'"

Thereupon, Nampetenis rides off with eight armed knights to chase his enemies—for vengeance. Kehenis and Tristrant are obliged to take a desperate stand, and try to save themselves, but to no avail. Kehenis is slain and Tristrant mortally wounded by Nampetenis's poisoned lance—a wound that only Isolde the Blond can heal.

The Kehenis and Gariole mini-love story of adultery and its tragic consequences stands inside of the Tristrant and Isolde frame so that it echoes and enhances the imagery. It is not unlike a "narrative illusion," a pun on the story of Tristran and Isolde. The character of Nampetenis will culminate in Molière's Arnolphe, an individual obsessed with maintaining order and control over his life. Such obsessed monomaniacs refuse to accept that the universe has its own design, its own ineluctable and often irrational structure.

To come directly now to our topic, towers of love and towers of pleasure, which are so common in medieval literature, it seems that the antecedents may lie first of all in the Carthaginian cave of adultery into which Dido and Aeneas withdraw from a storm in Virgil's Book IV (and perhaps this was fused to the Elysian Fields notion in Book VI of the *Aeneid*). Numerous stories of love in Ovid's *Metamorphoses* feature a lookout post or watchtower for the maiden. But the image may also arise from some confusion regarding two key words in medieval Latin: *arx, arcis,* a Classical Latin form meaning "castle, citadel, fortress," which appears concurrently with *turris, turris,* "tower." Over and above this, one finds also *arca, arcae,* a chest, box coffin, and of course, *the* ark, i.e., both of the Covenant and of Noah (there are about 200 references in the Old Testament). These two terms became confused as early as the 4th century A.D., when Servius used them together toward the beginning of his commentary on the *Aeneid* (*ad* I.262).[2]

Closer in time to Eilhart, one thinks of the historically novel wooden forts (donjons or "keeps") brought to England by William the Conqueror in 1066. The essentials were transported across the Channel in prefabricated form and erected at Hastings beachhead for the battle. The fort consisted of a raised mound of earth (*motte*), with a flattened top, which was then surrounded by a barbican or palisade, within which a tall tower of light timber (not heavy stone) was constructed, then further encircled by a bailey or ward, i.e., a ditch, the earth from which was thrown inward to form a bank behind which stood the wooden spiked palisade.[3]

Moreover, there are a number of romances dating from the third quarter of the 12th century that incorporate a pleasure dome of some kind. One thinks immediately of the tower of Lavinia in the *Roman d'Eneas*, so admired and so irresistible to the hero's longing stare. Lavinia in the tower is the image with which Eneas falls in love, for he never speaks to her face-to-face (*Roman d'Eneas*, ed. Salverda de Grave, vv. 8903-8907; 8661-9099; 9236-9252). The *mal mariée* in Marie de France's *Guigemar* is imprisoned in a tower-garden; Chrétien's *Erec et Enide* also come to mind with its intriguing *Joie de la Cort* episode. In Chrétien's *Cligés*, the hero has a secret underground dwelling designed for his beloved Fénice, mindful of both the Cave of Lovers and the Hall of Statues in the courtly *Tristan* tradition.

I should like to review these texts now to focus on the constructs in question. Because of its semiotic position in the **Tristrant** story of Eilhard, the tower-garden prison of his Lady Gariole seems to me significant and seminal.

For Marie de France's Guigemar, salvation is paradoxically found in an old fortified place, the capital of the kingdom (*Lais*, ed. J. Rychner, vv. 200 ff.). Like Nampetenis, the jealous lord's lovely spouse is of "high birth, noble, courtly, beautiful and wise." He had her locked up in a garden, at the foot of a donjon or tower, where the enclosure was surrounded by a high green marble wall. The single exit was under guard night and day. On the far side, the sea blocked any passage and no one could reach his wife—except by boat. Enter Guigemar hopelessly in love, by boat of course!

In Chrétien's *Erec et Enide,* at Brandigan castle, a self-contained and impregnable fort, the hero willingly undertakes a dangerous and fearful adventure (ed. Roques, vv. 5340 ff.). At a nearby orchard, he finds no palisade, only a magical wall of air that encloses the place. Within are varied and exotic fruits that cannot be brought outside because one cannot leave with them, unless they wither. The singing birds, the sweet spices and herbs all suggest to Erec a foretaste of Paradise.

Within this vale of life and death, Erec sees a silver bed, covered with gold-embroidered sheets: in the shadow of a sycamore, there reclines a maiden fair, lovely and noble. Her knight champion (named later: Mabonagrain) threatens the hero because he came near the maiden; a battle ensues (vv. 5890-5990) and Mabonagrain is defeated. Now he explains the situation; their enthralling passion led him to accept a rash boon from his beloved—pronounced once he became a knight: the lady ". . . ordered him forthwith to keep his word," and made him swear "never to leave [from the orchard] until an armed knight should come who could submit [him] to his power" (vv. 6028-6030; 6250 ff.).

This is why Mabonagrain must stay—or break his word. The lady, because of her immoderate love, thought to keep him there a long time, in prison with her—dominated and outside of the social order. By liberating Mabonagrain from this frightful bind, Erec brings joy to the whole court and countryside.

In Fourquet's interesting explication (as Burgess reports), this episode functions at two levels, courtly and mythical or non-courtly. In the latter view, a series of young men arrive at an enchanted world that is governed by a fairy princess; the entrance is protected by a fierce guardian, whom the predestined hero defeats and thereby can take possession of the enchanted kingdom. The wall of air, the permanent springtime atmosphere, the stakes with impaled heads and helmets, the vacant pike, Mabonagrain's size, the magic horn that will announce the call to joy—all belong here. On the chivalric level, one should stress Mabonagrain's overdeveloped sense of honor and his adolescent infatuation with the damsel. He actually becomes a "prisoner of words" (Burgess, 88), and submission to the damsel's wishes means "slavery." "Defeat for him means liberation. He wanted to be beaten, provided that his honor was safeguarded."[4]

In Chrétien's *Cligés,* the architect/engineer Jehanz (Jean) leads the hero to a secret dwelling, never seen by any human, and proposes it as a safe location for Fénice, *la fausse morte.* It is Jean's workshop, where he paints and sculpts (ed. A. Micha, vv. 5840 ff.). He designed this isolated dwelling in the tower with great art and painted the interior with lovely illuminated images. Cligés visits the whole place, realizes it is commodious, beautiful, and appropriate for his beloved.

Jean assures Cligés no one will find her there since ingenious and cunning hiding places exist within. Featuring a well-stocked larder and hidden stone doorway, the tower is ever more fair and comfortable, vast in its underground flooring (vv. 5531 ff.). Jean then leans against a polished and colorfully painted door that magically opens to a spiral stairway, leading to Jean's solitary workshop. For Cligés and his *amie,* there are bedrooms, bathrooms, and hot, running water in the bathtubs.

This labyrinth-like retreat—vaguely mindful of Vonnegut's pleasuredome on Trafalmador—almost seems like an objectification of the human brain. Perhaps Chrétien is hinting here at the "hall of statues" found in the Tristan tradition. The tower-basement, a structure whose design wins freedom for Cligés' engineer/vassal is, according to the critic Lucie Polak, an "artificial paradise, a world of illusion, as well as of death."[5]

Deep inside and below the tower, Fénice revives and is nursed from her false death and wounds by Thessala and by Cligés' love (vv. 5570 ff.; 6079ff.). There she spends some fifteen long, dark months, until spring arrives. Hearing the nightingale, she wishes to go outside (vv. 6259 ff.). Jean leads them through another magical door to a delightful, sun-drenched orchard (v. 6305). In its midst rises a huge leafy tree in full bloom, shaped like a cradle (perhaps a weeping willow?), its branches hanging down to the ground. Like a latter-day Tristan and Iseut in Beroul's Morois forest—who recline for rest and pleasure in a leafy bower—Fénice and Cligés make their bed under the shady, blossoming tree, whose thick branches had been artfully pruned by Jean so that the sun could never penetrate the intimacy of their flowery bower (but see vv. 6342 ff., for the interruption that leads to the *dénouement*).

In the so-called courtly version, Thomas d'Angleterre (i.e., Thomas of Britain) and Gottfried von Strassburg's *Tristan* describe two different hideaways, the Lovers' Cave (Hatto, 261 ff.) and the Hall of Statues. In flight from the King, Tristan, Isolde, and Curvenal hasten through the forest and find an abandoned cavern in the wilderness, on a tree-covered mountainside. The cave, hewn in heathen times by giants, is a high, snow-white, round, and broad grotto that features a bronze door. Like a cathedral for love, the vault boasts tiny, high windows for light and, on the keystone, an engraved crown of gold-encrusted jewels with a pavement of smooth, green marble. In the center sits a high crystal bed, dedicated to Venus. Three lime trees shade the entrance, and nearby a brook flows "clear as the sun." The flowers, a green glade, singing birds and breezes all complement this pagan *locus amoenus* (263). Here was the lovers' court of love, like heaven on earth, and as if in a company of courtiers, Tristan and Isolde enjoyed the green limes, the sunshine, the shade, stream and flowers (264).

Later in the story tradition, by defeating a huge giant and accepting his homage, the Tristan of Thomas d'Angleterre orders the loser and his skilled minions "to make a hall in a cavern, then to fashion lifelike statues of Queen Ysolt and Brengvein" (315). Ysolt is represented with a sceptre on the tip of which a bird is perched that beats its wings. In her left hand she holds a ring with an inscription, the words she uttered at the lovers' parting.

At her feet cringes the image of the Dwarf-Traitor, and the dog Petitcreu rests next to her; as it shook its head, bells would jingle. Brengvein's statue holds forth a vial containing the potion. Whenever Tristan could, he would visit and kiss and embrace the image. Here in this Hall of Statues, all his emotions can be expressed: he talks to them, weeps, and laments . . . (316).

Brother Robert's *Saga* (Schach, 101) reiterates the depiction of the underground vault in the forest built by heathens. The fragrant herbs, the beautiful, tall shade tree, and running brook are lovely indeed, but the star-crossed hero must keep busy with hunting (for food, not just simple amusement). Subsequently, Tristan fights and defeats an African giant, who then constructs for him a vaulted edifice, "Hewn and carved with the greatest skill" (16 ff., 118). Situated near Mont St. Michel, it can be entered only at ebbtide. Here within, the giant's craftsmen set up in secret carved and veneered figures— wooden carving colored and gilt. These lifelike and artistic images cunningly exhaled a fragrance from their mouths. It was Tristan who devised the idea of placing tubes down the mouth into a hidden container of sweet-smelling herbs. Brother Robert follows the courtly tradition in most details, but adds to the entry-way a huge statue of the giant (it recalls the villein in *Yvain*). A lion guards the other side of the entrance and its tail lashes around another statue, that of the traitorous steward. Tristan visits Isolde's statue for consolation and recalls their former happiness and joy. (122).

A study that would analyze in more depth than time or space allowed here could doubtless show how crucial and original Eilhart's Lady Gariole episode is. But the image of the tower and its inverted form, the underground dwelling, remain fascinating icons in a broad selection of medieval narrative texts. More study and more examples of the image—from the Tower of Babel on—will doubtless bear out Hanning's observation (*Individual;* cit. Noble 45) regarding the tower in *Cligés,* namely that it represents in visual and palpable terms the imprisoning effect of the lovers' enthralling affair, which, ironically, is supposed to liberate them, especially Fénice.[6]

Both the enclosed underground basement or tower-dungeon, the isolated and abondoned cavern to which the lovers retreat, and the high tower-prison, all suggest a positive and a negative interpretation. On the one hand, the *mal mariée* is a prisoner of love, forcibly confined and guarded by a jealous, aged husband. On the other, the tower is an enclosed refuge for the lovers, a sacred locus cut off from the profane. From the frequency of the rich and creative image of the tower of pleasure in the twelfth-century it may be inferred that we are dealing with yet another unique innovation arisen from a fusion of a distant antique model and an indistinct Christian doctrine.

Notes

1. This study was the object of a short presentation at the Tristan Studies Symposium, 21st International Congress of Medieval Studies, Western Michigan University, Kalamazoo, May 1986. I am grateful for the useful remarks made by respondents, especially for those by Professor Merritt R. Blakeslee.

2. Professor Blakeslee recalled also, along these lines, the ambiguity of the Vulgar Latin phrase *in montem* ("into, in").

3. "Engineering, Military." *Encyclopaedia Britannica* III, Vol. 6.

4. G. Burgess, *Chrétien de Troyes: Erec et Enide,* pp. 89-93. Burgess hints at the paradox inherent in all this. Sara Sturm-Maddox presents cogent arguments in favor of seeing the Sparrowhawk episode and the winning of Enide by Erec (plus the *récréance* theme evoked in Laluth) as a foreshadowing of the Joie de la Cort episode—with Erec's defeat of Mabonagrain.

5. L. Polak, *Chrétien de Troyes: Cligés,* pp. 66-67.

6. Noble, *Love and Marriage,* p. 45, refers to R. Hanning, *The Individual in Twelfth Century Romance* (169).

References

Bedier, Joseph. *Le Roman de Tristan par Thomas.* 2 vols. SATF. Paris: Didot, 1902-1905.

Beroul, *Romance of Tristan.* Ed. Alfred Ewert. 2 vols. Oxford: B. Blackwell, 1939, 1967, 1970.

Burgess, Glyn S. *Chrétien de Troyes: Erec et Enide. Critical Guides.* London: Grant & Cutler, 1984.

Buschinger, Danielle. *Le 'Tristrant' d'Eilhard von Obert.* Lille: Université de Lille III/Service de reproduction des thèses, 1974.

Chrétien de Troyes, *Cligés.* Ed. A. Micha. Paris: Champion, 1957.

Cormier, Raymond J. "Bédier, Brother Robert and the *Roman de Tristan.*" Pp. 69-75 in *Etudes de Philogie romane et d'Histoire Littéraire offertes à Jules Horrent.* Ed. J. M. D'Heur and N. Cherubini. Liège: Université de Liège, 1980.

———. "Frappier, Eilhart, and the *Roman de Tristan.*" Forthcoming.

———. "Open Contrast: Tristan and Diarmaid." *Speculum* 51 (1976):589-601.

———. "Remarks on 'The Tale of Deirdriu and Noísiu' and the Tristan Legend." *Etudes celtiques* 15 (1977):303-315.

———. "Tristan and the Noble Lie." *Studies in the Humanties* 4 (1974):10-14.

Delage, M. J. "Quelques notes sur Chrétien de Troyes et le Roman de *Tristan.*" Pp. 211-19 in *Mélanges Jonin. Aix-en-Provence:* Senefiance 7/Publications du CUER MA, 1979.

Eilhart von Obert, *Tristrant.* Ed., trans. Danielle Buschinger. Göppinger Arbeiten zur Germanistik, 202. Göppingen: Kümmerle, 1976.

———. Trans. J. W. Thomas. Lincoln, NE and London: University of Nebraska Press, 1978.

Frappier, Jean. "Structure et sens du *Tristan:* Version commune, version courtoise." *CCM [Cahiers de Civisation Medievale]* 6 (1963):255-80; 441-54.

Friar, Robert. *The Saga of Tristram and Isönd.* Trans. Paul Schach. Lincoln: University of Nebraska Press, 1973.

Gottfried von Strasburg. *Tristan.* Trans. A. T. Hatto. Harmondsworth: Penguin, 1960, 1967.

Marie de France. *Les Lais.* Ed. J. Rychner. Paris: Champion.

Noble, Peter S. *Love and Marriage in Chrétien de Troyes.* Cardiff: University of Wales Press, 1982.

Patch, H. R. *The Literature of the Other World According to Descriptions in Medieval Literature.* Cambridge, MA: Harvard University Press, 1950.

Polak, Lucie. *Chrétien de Troyes: Cligés. Critical guides.* London: Grant & Cutler, 1982.

Schach, Paul. "The *Saga of Tristram de Isodd:* Summary or Satire?" *Modern Language Quarterly* 21 (1960):336-352.

Schoepperle, Gertrude. *Tristan and Isolt: A Study of the Sources of the Romance.* 2 vols. 2nd ed. New York: Burt Franklin, 1963. [RP Frankfurt a. Main, 1913.]

Shirt, David J. *The Old French Tristan Poems.* Research Bibliographies and Checklists, 28. London: Grant & Cutler, 1980.

Sturm-Maddox, Sara. "*Hortus non conclusus:* Critics and the *Joie de la Cort,*" in *Oeuvres et Critiques* (ed. R. Cormier), 5,2 (1980-81):61-71.

Mary Brockington (essay date April 1998)

SOURCE: Brockington, Mary. "Tristran and Amelius: False and True Repentance." *Modern Language Review* 93, no. 2 (April 1998): 305-20.

[*In the following essay, Brockington explicates a scene from the Tristan legend in which King Mark discovers the sleeping lovers in the forest, exploring the different approaches to the episode taken by Eilhart, Béroul, and Thomas.*]

The scene in the Morrois forest, where the wronged husband, King Marc, sees Tristran and Yseut, the fugitive lovers, asleep, decides not to kill them, and retires silently, leaving tokens of his presence, is one of the most important in the whole *Tristran* tradition.[1] The verse redactors, particularly Beroul, present it in highly dramatic form, and it appears in manuscript and textile illustrations of the story. In terms of plot, it is pivotal; it closes one series of episodes (blood on the sheets, capture, escape) allowing Yseut's eventual return to Marc, and prepares the way for the next series (Tristran's exile, returns, and eventual death). The French prose redactor discarded it, as its softening of Marc's harsh attitude was inconsistent with his reworking, and instead has Marc discover Yseut alone and recapture her; yet he discarded Beroul's version with reluctance, retaining details for use in other scenes (appropriate or not).[2] The earlier form of the scene was not lost, however. An Italian who adapted the *Prose* version reincorporated a variant, probably derived from Thomas, at a different point in his *Tavola Ritonda* (Chapters 66-67), and the redactor of a late passage in the *Suite du Merlin* used Beroul's version in the story of Pelleas, Gawain, and Arcade, later to be adapted by Malory.[3] In terms of narrative technique, too, the role of this scene is pivotal. That the sword symbolic of chastity should be deceptive represents an innovation in the history of the Separating Sword motif, an innovation that adds a third element to an already bivalent sexual symbol: henceforth the sword (in addition to representing concepts of military activity, authority, and punishment) can symbolize sexuality, chastity, and also adultery.[4] The general sense of the episode is clear enough, but paradoxically the detailed interpretation of this crucial scene has proved contentious. Scholars have made numerous attempts to explain its meaning, but none has succeeded in resolving all the problems. In previous articles I have examined the sources of the scene's individual components;[5] in this final part of the trilogy, I offer a further set of suggestions towards an understanding of the scene as a whole.

Chief among the difficulties raised by the discovery scene are not so much the nature of the tokens exchanged as first, the question why Marc should become convinced of the lovers' innocence, and secondly, the function of the scene in the whole narrative. Jean Marx called attention to the incongruity of the King's gesture in using his glove to shield Yseut's face from the sun, calling it 'un raffinement de délicatesse un peu étonnant, malgré tout, chez un monarque qui, quelques mois avant, livrait sans scrupule la reine au bûcher, puis aux lépreux'.[6] The last speech Marc had addressed to Tristran was unequivocal:

> 'Trop par a ci veraie enseigne;
> Provez estes', ce dist li rois,
> 'Vostre escondit n'i vaut un pois.
> Certes, Tristran, demain, ce quit,
> Soiez certains d'estre destruit.'
>
> (l. 778)

He knows beyond all doubt that the lovers have been conducting an adulterous relationship. Is Beroul really trying to tell us that he now believes them to be innocent? The fugitives' clothing, and the sword that separates them, it is true, both proclaim that they have not had intercourse immediately before falling asleep, but otherwise their attitude suggests the exact opposite of a chaste relationship:

> Oez com il se sont couchiez:
> Desoz le col Tristran a mis
> Son braz, et l'autre, ce m'est vis,
> Li out par dedesus geté;

> Estroitement l'ot acolé,
> Et il la rot de ses braz çainte;
> Lor amistié ne fu pas fainte.
> Les bouches furent pres asises,
> Et neporquant si ot devises
> Que n'asenbloient pas ensenble.
>
> (l. 1816)

Beroul has gone out of his way to describe such a close embrace that it is hard to see where the Separating Sword could have fitted in, and the similarity to the conventional lovers' pose as portrayed by Chrétien de Troyes is striking: 'Boche a boche antre braz gisoient, Come cil qui mout s'antramoient' (*Erec*, ll. 2477-78; trans. p. 33) and

> Ensi jurent tote la nuit,
> Li uns lez l'autre, bouche a bouche,
> Juisqu'al main que li jors aproche.
> Tant li fist la nuit de solas
> Que bouche a boche, bras a bras,
> Dormirent tant qu'il ajorna
>
> (*Perceval*, l. 2064; trans. p. 402)

The behaviour of Tristran and Yseut is clearly intended to be ambiguous, if not utterly compromising, and it is hard to credit even Marc with such gullibility. As for the function of the scene, commentators have been puzzled by what Gertrude Schoepperle harshly condemned as its 'grotesque inconsequence'.[7] In the Thomas-based versions Marc is moved by his discovery to recall the lovers to court.[8] In Beroul, the King returns covertly to his apartments and, in Schoepperle's words, 'seems to forget the incident immediately and completely. The redactor fails signally to utilize it for the subsequent narrative'.[9] Eilhart's version is similar to Beroul's, though he does make his King refer to the discovery when the fugitives ask for reconciliation.[10] Beroul, however, is above all a skilled and careful narrator. His material is not thrown together. It is an artistically organized construction, with (as far as can be judged from the extant fragment) a minimum of narrative loose ends, and serious anomalies are given thoughtful attention by a poet who kept the requirements of his later episodes in mind. For instance, for Husdent to function as a love-token (as he does in Eilhart's version, and he has no other narrative function in either poem), he must be given to Yseut before the return to court; therefore he must be with the lovers in the Morrois, but he cannot realistically leave Lancien with them; therefore he must escape later and be taught to keep silence so as not to betray the lovers. Similarly, the whole ambiguous oath episode is totally implausible, considered from the rational point of view (an important ceremony sited across a bog, and a queen—a queen on trial—whose escort crosses safely but leaves her to fend for herself, so that she feels forced to mount, of all creatures, a leper). Beroul distracts his audience's attention from this improbable story-line by the sheer exuberance of his elaborate descriptions and salacious comedy. In both episodes, narrative necessity has been not merely accommodated, narrative weakness not merely disguised; they have been used positively to create respectively an emotive and a comic triumph. It is inconceivable that the same author should have expended so much effort on the discovery scene if it had no function in his plot. If that function is not apparent to us, perhaps it is we who are at fault, not Beroul, and we should look at his work in some different way.

The many previous interpretations have been of varying plausibility. Jean Markale, for instance, adducing the personal nature of a knight's equipment, suggested that Marc removes his nephew's sword so that Tristran will be forced to give back Yseut in order to redeem his weapon: that the gesture represents 'une invitation à échanger la reine'.[11] This fanciful hypothesis merits little consideration. Beroul portrays Marc as credulous, but not as a complete nincompoop. Nowhere in the whole *Tristran* tradition is its hero portrayed as capable of such baseness, nor is any other character made to think him so capable. Also flawed is Alain Corbellari's attempt to relate the three tokens of Marc's presence (sword, glove, and ring) to Dumézil's three functions.[12] Such a schema is of course possible only if all three tokens are original to the *Tristran* plot, but the exchange of rings is unique to Beroul and almost certainly introduced by him, much too late in the chain of transmission for this interpretation to be valid.

The interpretation that has found most general acceptance is that of Jean Marx, who relates the tokens to ceremonies of feudal investiture, and sees the episode as Marc reasserting his rightful authority over his wife and his vassal.[13] This careful study has much to commend it, and the significances Marx attaches to the tokens may have influenced the original author's selection, particularly in the case of the gloves (curious objects to choose just as a sun-shade). It does not, however, address either of the main problems (Marc's excessive gullibility, and his failure to act upon his discovery of the lovers' apparent innocence). More important still, Marc's presentation and removal of the tokens surely operates in the wrong direction, not convincingly explained away by the concept of *saisine.* I shall discuss this point more fully later.

Alberto Vàrvaro, commenting on Marx's views in a sensitive study of the episode, asserts:

> The juridical element takes a subordinate place in [Beroul's] poetic treatment and that the human and affective aspects of the tale are for him considerably more important than the social aspects. It might well be true that in the minds of the narrator and his audience, at-

tuned to the customs of their time, the sword, the glove and the rings did have some feudal significance. But first and foremost they are emblems of a human relationship.

He sees the exchange of rings and the placing of the gloves as signs of affection and tenderness, and the exchange of swords as a gesture of friendship, concluding: 'The act of exchanging rings and swords is a symbol in Beroul, but not (or not only) of a feudal relationship: it is chiefly the sad and moving symbol of an indissolubility of bonds, of a tragic and unresolvable emotional situation.'[14] Perceptive and appealing though this interpretation is, it still does not answer the basic problems of improbability and inconsequence.

Various other possible interpretations of the tokens also seem to lead up a blind alley. The gloves might be thought to represent a challenge, as a glove does when Tristran fights the Morholt, and also in the Anglo-Norman version of *Amicus et Amelius,* which is roughly contemporary with Beroul,[15] though this suggestion would carry more weight if the gloves were left on Tristran's face, not on Yseut's. In support of it is the fact that a sword also can represent a kind of challenge: in *Beowulf* (ll. 1142-44), the son of Hunlaf rouses Hengest to action with the 'accustomed remedy', a sword placed across Hengest's knees. Such an interpretation, however, accords ill with both Marc's declared non-hostile intent and Tristran's reaction. The knight would no doubt have felt obliged to accept a challenge, rather than flee in terror as he does.

Conversely, the giving up of a sword is a well-established act of surrender, offered for instance by Owein to Gwalchmai ('The Lady of the Fountain', p. 172), but still in use in the twentieth century: in the Second World War, fought as it was with the most modern of weapons, the British and Japanese commanders in turn used a sword as a token of their submission. More pertinently, in the episode in a late part of the *Suite du Merlin* mentioned earlier, the love-lorn Pelleas discovers that Gawain has betrayed his trust, and leaves his sword, in a gesture remodelled from Beroul, as an indication that he has discovered the sleeping couple and had them in his power. Malory's Pelleas similarly resists the urge to act dishonourably himself by killing the couple in their sleep, but leaves his sword in a more threatening gesture 'overthwarte bothe their throtis'. In both cases the discovery is one of guilt, not of apparent innocence, and Pelleas is inhibited from taking vengeance only by his own *courtoisie.* He has no further need for his sword, as he intends to take to his bed and die of grief, so his gesture in leaving it behind can be seen to include an aspect of surrender; he is admitting defeat and withdrawing from the battle for his mistress's affection. That the sword functions simultaneously as a phallic symbol adds a further dimension to its significance, which may well also be a factor in the *Tristran,* and explains why the sword is the only one of Beroul's three tokens that has been retained for use in the Pelleas story. This interpretation would explain Marc's failure to follow up his discovery, but he can hardly be surrendering his marital sexual rights to Tristran if he believes that the fugitives are living a life of innocent chastity, and Tristran and Yseut certainly do not interpret his gestures in this way. Since any attempt to explain the scene based on an analysis of the individual tokens seems unable to answer the two main problems (Marc's excessive gullibility and the lack of a clear function for the scene), a different approach is called for. Let us examine the scene as a whole, from the point of view of Beroul the master-narrator.

The stories told by Beroul, Eilhart, and Thomas, superficially so similar, are sharply differentiated by each author's approach: so much is obvious, but the differences of style extend beyond expression to narrative technique, and give valuable clues to each author's conception of his story. Thomas seems to have indicated his characters' thoughts and emotions by means of lengthy, refined explorations of the issues involved. Accordingly (at least as represented by Gottfried's adaptation), Marc's deception results from a cynical plan carefully thought out by the lovers beforehand. Eilhart's terse, vigorous style relied heavily on interaction between narrator and audience (the role of the performer and the nature of the expected audience in these orally based works should not be neglected). His work is characterized by a vein of humour that is sardonic, often coarse and salacious, and sometimes expressed in mock-serious terms. In the discovery scene we can imagine the exaggeratedly innocent facial expression, the knowing winks, the pregnant pauses and mock-modest hesitations with which the narrator assured his barrack-room listeners that each night in the forest Tristran and Yseut did no more than talk before sleeping. The skill with which Eilhart builds up to his climax is better conveyed in this instance by Danielle Buschinger's verse rendering than by J. W. Thomas's English prose:

> lorsqu'ils s'étaient couchés
> et avaient parlé ensemble
> jusqu'à ce que cela leur parût assez,
> il tirait son épée du fourreau
> et la posait entre elle et lui;
> le héros ne voulait y renoncer
> pour rien au monde:
> chaque fois qu'ils devaient dormir,
> l'épée était entre eux.
> C'était une étrange preuve d'esprit guerrier.

(l. 4583)

Properly performed, the timing of these lines, with the responsive sniggers culminating in a guffaw at the 'fremder manneß sin' (the 'strange custom for a man') would do credit to any music-hall stand-up comic. Eilhart does not mean that he does not understand the meaning of the Separating Sword symbol inherited from his source: he means that he understands it only too well, but considers it inappropriate, incongruous, indeed unbelievable in the circumstances. He knows, as well as Marc does, that Tristran and Yseut are lovers. He presents the sword motif as a dirty joke.

Beroul's technique is less polarized than those of either Eilhart or Thomas, but just as distinctive. His sword is as deceptive in its effect as Thomas's, and as inappropriate in its intent as Eilhart's, but its accidental presence is viewed as an act of Providence. Like Eilhart, he gives his audience action, not analysis. Like Thomas, though, he is interested in conveying emotion, but he does so chiefly by indirect narrative means, not by discursive monologues; he uses associations of ideas to implant suggestions in the minds of his characters and his audience. Parallelism of structure is important to Beroul: his narrative contains a number of doublets, and often one has a positive aspect, one a negative, such as the two visits to the hermit Ogrin. As a good *conteur,* he knows a wide variety of stories and component motifs, drawing on them at will but adapting them to suit his own narrative purposes. What is more, he expects his audience to know these stories too, at least in outline. The comic effect of Marc's deception by Yseut's ambiguous oath is emphasized by Beroul's importation of King Arthur to oversee the ceremony and lecture Marc on his behaviour. The ironic effect of this scene is considerably enhanced if the audience sees Arthur simultaneously as the type of justice and chivalry, and also as the great cuckold. Dual symbolism, irony, and ambiguity of this kind characterize Beroul's work, but are most effective if, as in the ambiguous oath episode, understanding of the bivalent role can be assumed, and does not have to be explained in heavy-handed detail.[16] Finally, Beroul has a sharp eye for inconsistencies and anomalies, distracting attention from implausible details in his narrative where he cannot avoid them, but in either case making constructive use of the necessity. . . .

Notes

1. Except in direct quotations, I have standardized on the forms *Marc, Tristran, Yseut, Morholt,* and *Beroul* throughout this article, although a wide variety of spellings is found in the texts. Use of the name Beroul is simply a convenient shorthand, implying nothing more dogmatic about authorship than 'the person who first put together this particular episode as it is preserved in the version

now known as Beroul's'. For a number of recent editions of Beroul's text, and details of other texts cited, see the list at the end of the article: references in this article are to Ewert's edition.

2. In Beroul, Marc is too courtly to kill Tristran when he has him at his mercy; in the *Prose* the positions are reversed, and it is a sign of courtliness in Tristran that he refuses to take advantage of the uncourtly Marc when he stands over the King, sword raised ready to strike. Later, the lovers are discovered in bed together (in words that echo Beroul, lines 1807-10, 1995-2000) 'en braies et en chemise'. The clothing is here quite inappropriate (this is the discovery for which they are condemned to death), yet nothing more is made of it; text, ii, 118, §514 and ii, 142, §543; translation, pp. 129 and 154.

3. Sommer, pp. 33-34; Malory, i, 170; for commentary on both episodes, see F. Whitehead, 'On Certain Episodes in the Fourth Book of Malory's "Morte Darthur"', *Medium Aevum*, 2 (1933), 199-216 (especially p. 205) and Malory, iii, 1361-62.

4. I have in preparation a study of the origin and development of the Separating Sword motif (Thompson T 351).

5. 'The Separating Sword in the *Tristran* Romances: Possible Celtic Analogues Re-Examined', *MLR*, [*Modern Language Review,*] 91 (1996), 281-300, and 'Discovery in the Morrois: Antecedents and Analogues', *MLR* 93 (1998), 1-15.

6. 'La surprise des amants par Marc', in Jean Marx, *Nouvelles recherches sur la littérature arthurienne* (Paris: Klincksieck, 1965), pp. 288-97 (p. 294), first published as 'Observations sur un épisode de la légende de Tristan', in *Recueil de travaux offert à M. Clovis Brunel*, 2 vols (Paris: Société de l'École des Chartes, 1955), ii, 265-73.

7. *Tristan and Isolt: A Study of the Sources of the Romance,* 2 vols (Frankfurt a.M.: Baer, 1913; 2nd edn, New York: Franklin, 1960), i, 262.

8. *Saga,* trans. by Schach, p. 104. Gottfried, trans. by Hatto, p. 274. *Sir Tristrem*, ll. 2562-69.

9. Beroul, ll. 2055-62; Schoepperle, *Tristan and Isolt* I, 262.

10. Trans. by J. W. Thomas, p. 102.

11. *La femme celte: mythe et sociologie* (Paris: Payot, 1972), p. 298. Markale's other suggestion, that 'Mark *ne peut pas tuer* Tristan parce qu'une des particularités de Tristan était "que quiconque lui tirait du sang mourait, que quiconque à qui il tirait du sang mourait aussi". Par conséquent, Mark, s'il

avait frappé Tristan, même pendant le sommeil de celui-ci, apparemment en toute sécurité, était quand même voué à la mort' is equally flawed. There is no justification for reading this motif back from the Welsh *Ystorya Trystan* into the twelfth-century continental poems, even if we assume that the sixteenth-century manuscript version of the *Ystorya* records a long-established tradition, which is by no means certain.

12. 'La légende tristanienne et la mythologie indo-européenne: à propos du *Gant de verre* de Philippe Walter', *Vox Romanica,* 52 (1993), 133-46 (pp. 137-41). It is unfortunate that Corbellari does not appear to know Jean Batany's work on the 'ganz de voirre' in his article, 'Le manuscrit de Béroul: un texte difficile et un univers mental qui nous dérange', in *La légende de Tristan au Moyen Age,* ed. by Danielle Buschinger (Göppingen: Kümmerle, 1982), pp. 35-48; it would have been instructive to see his comments.

13. See n. 6 above.

14. *Beroul's 'Romance of Tristran'* (Manchester: Manchester University Press, 1972), pp. 115-16, trans. by John C. Barnes from *Il 'Roman de Tristran' di Béroul* (Turin: Bottega d'Erasmo, 1963). For the presentation of a sword as a gesture of friendship, see *Roland, laisse* 48, but compare *laisses* 49-50, where a helmet and jewels are similarly presented; all three gestures are gifts given for their material value rather than their significance as abstract symbols.

15. *Saga,* trans. by Schach, p. 41; Gottfried, trans. by Hatto, p. 128; *Amys e Amillyoun,* ed. by Fukui, ll. 385-88, trans. by Weiss, p. 165.

16. This presumably implies a post-Chrétien date for that part of the Beroul text, if not for the whole, but for evidence of an irreverent view of Arthur in early Welsh material, see Brynley F. Roberts, '*Culhwch ac Olwen,* the Triads, Saints' Lives', in *The Arthur of the Welsh,* ed. by Rachel Bromwich, A. O. H. Jarman and Brynley F. Roberts (Cardiff: University of Wales Press, 1991), pp. 73-95 (pp. 81-84), and Rachel Bromwich, 'The *Tristan* of the Welsh', in *The Arthur of the Welsh,* pp. 209-28 (pp. 214-15).

FURTHER READING

Criticism

Haug, Walter. "Reinterpreting the Tristan Romances of Thomas and Gotfrid: Implications of a Recent Discovery." *Arthuriana* 7, no. 3 (fall 1997): 45-59.

Argues that the discovery of the so-called Carlisle Fragment of Thomas of Britain's poem *Tristan* calls for a scholarly reappraisal of the relationship between the principal post-Eilhart versions of the Tristan story.

Henning, John. "Irish Saints in Early German Literature." *Speculum: A Journal of Mediaeval Studies* 22, no. 3 (July 1947): 358-74.

Considers the Tristan tradition as it highlights developments in continental European perceptions of Ireland during the medieval period.

McDonald, William C. "Character Portrayal in Eilhart's *Tristant.*" *Tristania* 9, no 1–2 (autumn-spring 1983–84): 25–39.

Seeks to evaluate *Tristant* on its own merits, examining the poem's style, genre, and characterization.

———. "King Mark, the Holy Penitent: On a Neglected Motif in the Eilhart Literary Tradition." *Zeitschrift für Deutsches Altertum and Deutsche Literatur* 120 (1991): 393–418.

Discusses King Mark as a complex figure, arguing that Eilhart's subtle characterization prevents him from coming across as a stereotypical villain.

Schoepperle, Gertrude. *Tristan and Isolt: A Study of the Sources of the Romances,* New York: Burt Franklin, 1960, 266 p.

Influential study of sources and the manuscript tradition. Includes a detailed prose outline of Eilhart's *Tristant.*

Schultz, James A. "Why Do Tristan and Isolde Leave for the Woods? Narrative Motivation and Narrative Coherence in Eilhart von Oberg and Gottfried von Strassburg." *MLN* 102, no. 3 (April 1987): 586-607.

Contrasts techniques of narrative motivation employed in Eilhart's *Tristant* and Gottfried's *Tristan,* characterizing the former as generally "reticent, actional, and open," the latter as "abundant, durative, and closed."

Thomas, Neil. "The *Minnegrotte*: Shrine of Love or Fools' Paradise? Thomas, Gottfried and the European Development of The Tristan Legend." *Trivium* 23 (summer 1988): 89-106.

Discusses the possible use of Eilhart's *Tristant* and other sources by the subsequent major authors of the Tristan tradition, Thomas and Gottfried.

Additional coverage of Eilhart's life and career is contained in the following source published by the Gale Group: *Dictionary of Literary Biography,* **Vol. 148.**

Laxdaela Saga

Thirteenth-century Icelandic poem.

INTRODUCTION

The *Laxdaela Saga,* a story of the men and women of the Salmon River valley, is an Icelandic family saga believed to have been composed in the middle of the thirteenth century. The author of the work is unknown. It relates the history of some five or six generations of prominent individuals descended from emigrant Norwegian chieftains, tracing the tragic sweep of many lives during the early Icelandic Commonwealth period. These years were a time of settlement, Christianization, and national independence prior to Iceland's annexation by Norway in 1262. The saga begins with two branches of the family: those of Unn the Deep-Minded and Bjorn the Easterner, whose lines respectively produce the heroic Kjartan and fiery Gudrun. An amalgam of historical fact, myth, epic, romance, anachronism, and literary invention, the *Laxdaela Saga* is, in essence, a dramatization of the circumstances surrounding a blood-feud between two sides of a great dynasty; in its second and decisive portion, it treats a love triangle that re-ignites the feud and its adjoining intrigues. Principal among its unique narrative features is the central role of women, especially that of its main protagonist, Gudrun. The story itself, though filled with myriad episodes and vignettes from the lives of dozens of characters, is carried forward by the mysterious workings of fate, symbolized by the prophetic dreams of Gudrun. Noted for its detached narrative style and ornately-patterned structure, the *Laxdaela Saga* remains a highly influential work of Scandinavian literature and is considered an outstanding example of medieval prose romance.

TEXTUAL HISTORY

Extant manuscripts of the *Laxdaela Saga* include six complete or partial parchment editions dating from around the fourteenth century and numerous older, fragmentary manuscripts, including one dated approximately 1250, which some believe to be the archetype text. Historical dating of events in these texts can be traced from about 892, the arrival of Unn in Iceland, through the death of Saint Olaf in 1030, and to the time of the saga's actual composition, sometime after 1228. Modern versions of the *Laxdaela Saga* include the 1826 Copenhagen edition, a standard text that was used by Thorstein Veblen for his English translation of the saga a century later. His adaptation

Manuscript page of the Laxdaela Saga, *from the* Modruvallabok, *c. 1350.*

was preceded by that of the Muriel Press, whose complete translation, the first in English, appeared in 1899 and has been frequently revised and reprinted. Additional English editions were published in the 1960s, including A. Margaret Arent's 1964 standard, and a more popularly-oriented adaptation published by Magnus Magnussen and Hermann Pálsson in 1969. The work also inspired English poet William Morris's 1869 "The Lovers of Gudrun," a loose adaptation in verse of the prose original, and the first partial translation into English.

PLOT AND MAJOR CHARACTERS

Scholars generally separate the *Laxdaela Saga* into two chronological parts. The first half centers on the sons and daughters of the Norwegian chieftain Ketill Flatneff (Flatnose) and their offspring as they settle the valley of the Salmon (Lax) River in western Iceland beginning in the late ninth century. The first portion of the narrative is comprised of a somewhat episodic account of the ensuing century in Iceland, and features the commanding presence of family matriarch Unn the Deep-Minded. As generations pass, Unn's descendants consolidate possession of Laxdale under her great-grandson Hoskuld Dala-Kollsson. Hoskuld marries Jorunn, but later takes a young concubine, Melkorka, whom we subsequently learn is an Irish princess. Hoskuld and Melkorka have a child, Olaf Peacock. As time passes, squabbles break out regarding the rightful possession of lands among the various scions of the expanding family line. Before his death, however, Hoskuld manages to secure much of his land for Olaf. Upon reaching adulthood, the wise and moderate Olaf marries and sires Kjartan Olaffson, a man of matchless valor and physical beauty who will become the central male heroic figure in the main portion of the saga. In addition to Kjartan, the primary focus of the saga's second half is on Gudrun Osvifsdottir, great-great-granddaughter of Bjorn the Easterner (son of Ketill). Extremely vain, beautiful, and proud, Gudrun experiences four dreams in the winter of her fifteenth year, later explained to her by the prophetic wise woman Gest Oddleifsson, who tells her she will have four husbands. Gudrun's first two marriages, to Thorvald and later Thord, are unhappy and relatively brief. Later, she discovers Kjartan and a third pivotal figure, Bolli Thorleiksson, whose strength and heroic prowess the narrator tells us are unsurpassed, save by Kjartan himself. Both of these men, Bolli and Kjartan, come into possession of preternatural weapons; Bolli's sword, Leg-biter, is said to be cursed, while Kjartan wears the majestic blade Konungsnaut, which carries a charm of protection. According to the seer Gest, Leg-biter will play a pivotal role in the death of Kjartan, although the young men, as yet, remain unaware of this portent. Half-brothers Kjartan and Bolli are close but later become rivals for the attention of Gudrun. As their desire for her matures, Kjartan's father, Olaf, senses approaching doom and warns his headstrong son. Ignoring his counsel, Kjartan continues his affair with Gudrun and rivalry with Bolli. The half-brothers then travel together to Norway, but Kjartan is delayed, ostensibly to marry into Norwegian royalty. Bolli returns to Iceland first, and delivers this news to Gudrun. Disappointed, she accepts Bolli's marriage proposal to become her third husband. Having converted to Christianity, Kjartan returns to Iceland shortly thereafter, still unmarried. The conflict within the family deepens. Meanwhile, Kjartan chooses the demure Hrefna as his bride—a woman unlike Gudrun in temperament but matching her in beauty. Soon the feud between families, spurred by Gudrun's hatred and jealousy, ignites. As acts of aggression on both sides escalate, Gudrun finally urges Bolli to kill Kjartan. Bolli agrees and devises a cowardly plan to outnumber and surprise his former friend. As Bolli attacks him, Kjartan drops his sword, refusing to fight his kinsmen. Bolli advances nonetheless, killing him with Leg-biter, thus fulfilling Gest's prophecy. Upon Bolli's return, Gudrun delights in the death of Kjartan, but only briefly. Meanwhile the slain hero's brothers set a trap for Bolli and avenge Kjartan's death, making him pay with his life. While plotting further revenge, Gudrun marries Thorkel, a mighty war chieftain, and gives birth to Bolli Bollason. Her plans to retaliate for the death of the elder Bolli, however, are thwarted and, in a final closing movement, Bolli's son asks his mother Gudrun whom she loved the best of all the men in her life. She replies, "I was worst to the one I loved the most."

MAJOR THEMES

As a multigenerational family romance with historical elements and an epic story inspired by mythological tradition, the *Laxdaela Saga* combines thematic material from many genres. On an ethno-historical level, it depicts the circumstances of Icelandic settlement in the Commonwealth period, detailing individual and social adaptation to new circumstances of life, the amassing of property, and the grounding of a new society in transition from the pagan Viking Age to the early Christian epoch in Scandinavia. In this sense, its principal theme centers on disputes over lands, marriages, divorce settlements, and inheritances that culminate in a violent blood-feud. Some, like Olaf the Peacock, recognize the senselessness of the feud and its destructiveness to the community. Others, particularly Gudrun, place their personal codes of honor and lust for revenge far above communal bonds. From this perspective, the *Laxdaela Saga* can be categorized as the tragedy of a passing way of life and of a shifting moral and social order. Critics also view Gudrun as central to the saga's epic themes, which privilege dreams, prophecy, curses, visions, and the deterministic path of fate. To varying degrees, Gudrun personifies the proud pagan spirit. Her character is thought to resemble the mythological Brynhild of the Nibelungen cycle, a figure who jealously urges the death of her heroic lover Sigurd, following his plot, which tricks her into marrying another man. Other significant characters in the story have also been examined as symbols of competing worldviews in a society positioned between Christian and pagan ideals of community and justice. Thus, the saga narrator uses Kjartan as a symbol of medieval Christianity, a pious and faultless warrior-saint, while Gudrun's son, Bolli Bollason, is thought to embody the chivalric and courtly ideals of the high Middle Ages as a synthesis of antique honor and Christian virtue. While most critics hesitate to completely reduce these and other characters to symbolic signifiers, they also suggest that the *Laxdaela Saga* is principally concerned with rendering patterns and developments in social life on a very broad scale, rather than with the minutia of individualized psychological analysis.

CRITICAL RECEPTION

Conventional critical assessment of the *Laxdaela Saga* has tended to compare the work with other outstanding pieces of medieval Scandinavian literature, admiring it for its complex depiction of life in the early Commonwealth period, while also praising its evocation of romantic beauty. Over the years, however, considerably more measured estimations have been offered by some, including early-twentieth-century translator Thorstein Veblen, who called the *Laxdaela Saga* "a somewhat prosy narrative, cumbered with many tawdry embellishments and affections of style and occasional intrusive passages of devout bombast." Veblen identified these contrivances as the additions of the work's thirteenth-century author-editor and denounced the insertion of Christian piety into what he viewed as an essentially pagan and romantic narrative. While Veblen's opinions continue to reflect a minority view, tensions within the mixed thematic character of the *Laxdaela Saga* have largely informed scholarly evaluation of the work in the modern period. Most scholars recognize the saga as a valuable historical document concerning the Scandinavian peoples in social transition between the pagan Viking age and early Christian eras. Commentators interested in the literary qualities of the work, however, have often remarked on its epic substructure. In 1908 W. P. Ker was the first to describe the *Laxdaela Saga* as the prose actualization of heroic epic, stripped of supernatural elements in order to better convey the conditions and events of everyday life. Observing affinities between the saga and the tragedy of the Nibelungen, the critic noted the manner in which mythological figures like Sigurd and Brynhild were sublimated by the *Laxdaela* author into those of Kjartan and Gudrun. A number of contemporary critics have also been drawn to the overarching design of the saga and have analyzed its characteristic rhetorical and structural patterns, including its sophisticated use of parallelism, repetition, balance, and contrast. Additional areas of scholarly interest include the work's elaborate compositional patterns and narrative techniques which elegantly combine epic metaphor with the speech rhythms of ordinary life. Having thus begun the process of analyzing the saga's underlying structure, contemporary scholarship has generally aligned in support of A. Margaret Arent Madelung's appraisal of the *Laxdaela Saga* as "one of the most remarkable and brilliant prose works of the medieval period."

PRINCIPAL WORKS

Principal English Translations

Laxdale Saga (translated by Muriel A. C. Press) 1899
Laxdaela Saga (translated by Thorstein Veblen) 1925
Laxdoela Saga (translated by A. Margaret Arent) 1964
Laxdaela Saga (translated by Magnus Magnussen and Hermann Pálsson) 1969

CRITICISM

W. P. Ker (essay date 1908)

SOURCE: Ker, W. P. "Tragic Imagination." In *Epic and Romance: Essays on Medieval Literature,* pp. 207-24. New York: Dover Publications, 1908.

[*In the following essay, Ker describes the tragic quality of Icelandic sagas, with particular reference to the* Laxdaela Saga *as a historical and epic romance.*]

In their definite tragical situations and problems, the Sagas are akin to the older poetry of the Teutonic race. The tragical cases of the earlier heroic age are found repeated, with variations, in the Sagas. Some of the chief of these resemblances have been found and discussed by the editors of *Corpus Poeticum Boreale.* Also in many places where there is no need to look for any close resemblance in detail, there is to be seen the same mode of comprehending the tragical stress and contradiction as is manifested in the remains of the poetry. As in the older Germanic stories, so in the Sagas, the plot is often more than mere contest or adventure. As in *Finnesburh* and *Waldere,* so in *Gísla Saga* and *Njála* and many other Icelandic stories, the action turns upon a debate between opposite motives of loyalty, friendship, kindred. Gisli kills his sister's husband; it is his sister who begins the pursuit of Gisli, his sister who, after Gisli's death, tries to avenge him. Njal has to stand by his sons, who have killed his friend. Gunnlaug and Hrafn, Kjartan and Bolli, are friends estranged by "Fate and their own transgression," like Walter and Hagena.

The Sagas, being prose and having an historical tradition to take care of, are unable to reach the same intensity of passion as some of the heroic poems, the poems of *Helgi* and of *Sigurd.* They are all the more epic, perhaps, on that account; more equable in their course, with this compensation for their quieter manner, that they have more room and more variety than the passionate heroic poems. These histories have also, as a rule, to do without the fantasies of such poetry as *Hervor and Angantyr,* or *Helgi and Sigrun.* The vision of the Queens of the Air, the return of Helgi from the dead, the chantings of Hervor "between the worlds," are too much for the plain texture of the Sagas. Though, as has already been seen in *Grettir* and *Gisli,* this element of fantastic beauty is not wholly absent; the less substantial graces of mythical romance, "fainter and flightier" than those of epic, are sometimes to be found even in the historical prose; the historical tragedies have their accompaniment of mystery. More particularly, the story of the *Death of Thidrandi whom the Goddesses slew,* is a prose counterpart to the poetry of Sigrun and Hervor.[1]

There are many other incidents in the Sagas which have the look of romance about them. But of a number of these the distinction holds good that has been already put forward in the case of *Beowulf:* they are not such wonders as lie outside the bounds of common experience, according to the estimate of those for whom the stories were told. Besides some wonderful passages that still retain the visionary and fantastic charm of myth and mythical romance, there are others in which the wonders are more gross and nearer to common life. Such is the story of the hauntings at Froda, in *Eyrbyggja;* the drowned man and his companions coming home night after night and sitting in their wet clothes till daybreak; such is the ghastly story of the funeral of Viga-Styrr in *Heiðarvíga Saga.* Things of that sort are no exceptions to common experience, according to the Icelandic judgment, and do not stand out from the history as something different in kind; they do not belong to the same order as the dream-poetry of Gisli or the vision of Thidrandi.

The self-denial of the Icelandic authors in regard to myth and pure romance has secured for them, in exchange, everything that is essential to strong dramatic stories, independent of mythological or romantic attractions.

Some of the Sagas are a reduction of heroic fable to the temper and conditions of modern prose. *Laxdœla* is an heroic epic, rewritten as a prose history under the conditions of actual life, and without the help of any supernatural "machinery." It is a modern prose version of the Niblung tragedy, with the personages chosen from the life of Iceland in the heroic age, and from the Icelandic family traditions. It is not the only work that has reduced the Niblung story to terms of matter of fact. The story of Sigurd and Brynhild has been presented as a drama by Ibsen in his *Warriors in Helgeland,* with the names changed, with new circumstances, and with nothing remaining of the mythical and legend-

ary lights that play about the fortunes of Sigurd in the Northern poems. The play relies on the characters, without the mysteries of Odin and the Valkyria. An experiment of the same sort had been made long before. In **Laxdœla,** Kjartan stands for Sigurd: Gudrun daughter of Osvifr, wife of Bolli, is in the place of Brynhild wife of Gunnar, driving her husband to avenge her on her old lover. That the authors of the Sagas were conscious at least in some cases of their relation to the poems is proved by affinities in the details of their language. In *Gísla Saga,* Thordis, sister of Gisli, has to endure the same sorrow as the wife of Sigurd in the poems; her husband, like Sigurd, is killed by her brother. One of the verses put in the mouth of Gisli in the story contrasts her with Gudrun, daughter of Giuki, who killed her husband (Attila) to avenge her brothers; whereas Thordis was waking up the pursuers of her brother Gisli to avenge her husband. With this verse in his head, it is impossible that the writer of the Saga can have overlooked the resemblance which is no less striking than the contrast between the two cases.

The relation of the Sagas to the older poetry may be expressed in this way, perhaps, that they are the last stage in a progress from the earliest mythical imagination, and the earliest dirges and encomiums of the great men of a tribe, to a consistent and orderly form of narrative literature, attained by the direction of a critical faculty which kept out absurdities, without impairing the dramatic energy of the story. The Sagas are the great victory of the Humanities in the North, at the end of a long process of education. The Northern nations, like others, had to come to an understanding with themselves about their inherited myths, their traditional literary forms. One age after another helped in different ways to modify their beliefs, to change their literary taste. Practically, they had to find out what they were to think of the gods; poetically, what they were to put into their songs and stories. With problems of this sort, when a beginning has once been made, anything is possible, and there is no one kind of success. Every nation that has ever come to anything has had to go to school in this way. None has ever been successful right through; while, on the other hand, success does not mean the attainment of any definite end. There is a success for every stage in the progress, and one nation or literature differs from another, not by reason of an ultimate victory or defeat, but in the number of prizes taken by the way.

As far as can be made out, the people of the Northern tongue got the better of the Western Teutons, in making far more than they out of the store of primeval fancies about the gods and the worlds, and in giving to their heroic poems both an intenser passion of expression and a more mysterious grace and charm. The Western Teutons in their heroic poetry seem, on the other hand, to have been steadier and less flighty. They took earlier to the line of reasonable and dignified narrative, reducing the lyrical element, perhaps increasing the gnomic or reflective proportions of their work. So they succeeded in their own way, with whatever success belongs to *Beowulf, Waldere, Byrhtnoth,* not to speak of the new essays they made with themes taken from the Church, in the poems of *Andreas, Judith,* and all the rest. Meanwhile the Northerners were having their own difficulties and getting over them, or out of them. They knew far more about the gods, and made poems about them. They had no patience, so that they could not dilute and expand their stories in the Western way. They saw no good in the leisurely methods; they must have everything emphatic, everything full of poetical meaning; hence no large poetry, but a number of short poems with no slackness in them. With these they had good reason to be content, as a good day's work in their day. . . .

[In *Laxdæla*] . . . the elements of grace and strength, of gentleness and terror, are combined in a variety of ways, and in such a way as to leave no preponderance to any one exclusively. Sometimes the story may seem to fall into the exemplary vein of the "antique poet historicall"; sometimes the portrait of Kjartan may look as if it were designed, like the portrait of Amadis or Tirant the White, "to fashion a gentleman or noble person in vertuous and gentle discipline." Sometimes the story is involved in the ordinary business of Icelandic life, and Kjartan and Bolli, the Sigurd and Gunnar of the tragedy, are seen engaged in common affairs, such as make the alloy of heroic narrative in the *Odyssey.* The hero is put to the proof in this way, and made to adapt himself to various circumstances. Sometimes the story touches on the barbarism and cruelty, which were part of the reality familiar to the whole of Iceland in the age of the Sturlungs, of which there is more in the authentic history of the Sturlungs than in the freer and more imaginative story of Kjartan. At one time the story uses the broad and fluent form of narrative, leaving scene after scene to speak for itself; at other times it allows itself to be condensed into a significant phrase. Of these emphatic phrases there are two especially, both of them speeches of Gudrun, and the one is the complement of the other: the one in the tone of irony, Gudrun's comment on the death of Kjartan, a repetition of Brynhild's phrase on the death of Sigurd;[2] the other Gudrun's confession to her son at the end of the whole matter.

> Gudrun meets her husband coming back, and says: "A good day's work and a notable; I have spun twelve ells of yarn, and you have slain Kjartan Olaf's son."
>
> Bolli answers: "That mischance would abide with me, without thy speaking of it."
>
> Said Gudrun: "I reckon not that among mischances; it seemed to me thou hadst greater renown that winter

Kjartan was in Norway, than when he came back to Iceland and trampled thee under foot. But the last is best, that Hrefna will not go laughing to bed this night."

> Then said Bolli in great wrath: "I know not whether she will look paler at this news than thou, and I doubt thou mightest have taken it no worse if we had been left lying where we fought, and Kjartan had come to tell of it."
>
> Gudrun saw that Bolli was angry, and said: "Nay, no need of words like these; for this work I thank thee; there is an earnest in it that thou wilt not thwart me after."

This is one of the crises of the story, in which the meaning of Gudrun is brought out in a short passage of dialogue, at the close of a section of narrative full of adventure and incident. In all that precedes, in the relations of Gudrun to Kjartan before and after her marriage with Bolli, as after the marriage of Kjartan and Hrefna, the motives are generally left to be inferred from the events and actions. Here it was time that Gudrun should speak her mind, or at least the half of her mind.

Her speech at the end of her life is equally required, and the two speeches are the complement of one another. Bolli her son comes to see her and sits with her.

> The story tells that one day Bolli came to Helgafell; for Gudrun was always glad when he came to see her. Bolli sat long with his mother, and there was much talk between them. At last Bolli said: "Mother, will you tell me one thing? It has been in my mind to ask you, who was the man you loved best?"
>
> Gudrun answers: "Thorkell was a great man and a lordly; and no man was goodlier than Bolli, nor of gentler breeding; Thord Ingwin's son was the most discreet of them all, a wise man in the law. Of Thorvald I make no reckoning."
>
> Then says Bolli: "All this is clear, all the condition of your husbands as you have told; but it has not yet been told whom you loved best. You must not keep it secret from me longer."
>
> Gudrun answers: "You put me hard to it, my son; but if I am to tell any one, I will rather tell you than another."
>
> Bolli besought her again to tell him. Then said Gudrun: "I did the worst to him, the man that I loved the most."
>
> "Now may we believe," says Bolli, "that there is no more to say."
>
> He said that she had done right in telling him what he asked.
>
> Gudrun became an old woman, and it is said that she lost her sight. She died at Helgafell, and there she rests.

This is one of the passages which it is easy to quote, and also dangerous. The confession of Gudrun loses incalculably when detached from the whole story, as also her earlier answer fails, by itself, to represent the meaning and the art of the Saga. They are the two keys that the author has given; neither is of any use by itself, and both together are of service only in relation to the whole story and all its fabric of incident and situation and changing views of life.

Notes

1. It is summarised in Dasent's *Njal,* i. p. xx., and translated in Sephton's *Olaf Tryggvason* (1895), pp. 339-341.

2. Then Brynhild laughed till the walls rang again: "Good luck to your hands and swords that have felled the goodly prince" (*Brot Sgkv.* 10; cf. p. 103 above).

Thorstein Veblen (essay date 1925)

SOURCE: Veblen, Thorstein. Introduction to *The Laxdaela Saga,* translated by Thorstein Veblen, pp. v-xv. New York: B. W. Huebsch, Inc., 1925.

[*In the following introduction to his English translation of the* Laxdaela Saga, *Veblen enumerates the underlying characteristics of the work, including its depiction of a blood feud, its rendering of a society situated between paganism and Christianity, and its idiomatic status as the product of thirteenth-century Iceland.*]

It has been something of a convention among those who interest themselves in Icelandic literature to speak well of the *Laxdæla Saga* as a thing of poetic beauty and of high literary merit. So, characteristically and with the weight of authority, Gudbrand Vigfusson has this to say of the *Laxdæla,* in the Prolegomena to his edition of the *Sturlunga Saga:* "This, the second only in size of the Icelandic Sagas, is perhaps also the second in beauty. It is the most romantic of all, full of pathetic sentiment, which, like that of Euripides, is almost modern, and brings it closer to the thoughts and feelings of our day than any other story of Icelandic life."

Further, as regards the tale which it has to tell: "Besides the customary but always interesting introduction, the story falls into two parts. First the early love of Kjartan and Gudrun, the hero and heroine, and the poet's career in Norway. The second part goes on with the story after Kjartan's return to Iceland, relating his death at his rival Bolli's hand, Bolli's death no long while after, and the vengeance taken for both."

As in other sagas whose incidents date from the same period (tenth and early eleventh centuries) so also in the *Laxdæla,* it is the paramount exigencies of the blood-feud that shape the outlines of the narrative and create the critical situations of the plot and give rise to the main outstanding incidents and episodes. Such are the classic sagas which have come down from the saga period. The blood-feud was then a matter of course and of common sense, about the merits of which no question was entertained—no more than the merits of national patriotism are questioned in our time. It is only in late and spurious tales, dating from after the infiltration of the mediæval chivalric romances into the Scandinavian countries, that other interests or principles of conduct have come to supplant the blood-feud as the finally dominant note. And in its class, doubtless, the *Laxdæla* rightly takes rank among the foremost, as a tragic tale of intrigue and adventure driven by the imperative call of the blood-feud. Other factors and motives come into the tale, in some profusion indeed, and they find adequate expression, but this is what may be called the axis of its structure.

But all the while the *Laxdæla* remains also an ethnological document of a high order; perhaps standing in this respect at the head of the list. So that it is of prime significance for any understanding of that peculiar phase of culture that makes up its setting; that is to say the period which comprises the close of the Viking Age, so called, and the advent of the Christian Faith in Iceland and in northern Europe more at large. More intimately and more naïvely than any other, this saga reflects the homely conditions of workday life in its time, together with the range of commonplace sentiments and convictions which animated this workday life. So that it is fairly to be taken as a competent though perhaps accentuated record of late-Pagan and early-Christian manners, customs, convictions and ideals among the Germanic peoples at large, but more particularly touching the Scandinavian and the English-speaking peoples at the point of their induction into their feudal and ecclesiastical status in early-Christian times.

By force of what may be called historical accident the Scandinavian peoples, and the Icelandic community in particular, underwent the conversion to mediævalism, civil and religious, at a relatively late date and with a relatively swift transition; so late that it falls wholly within the scope of recorded history, and so late also that it comes at a time when the feudal system of civil life as well as the feudalistic Church had already attained their majority, had reached maturity and finished certitude as an intrinsic order of things, or perhaps had even entered on an incipient stage of decay.

These peoples came somewhat abruptly out of a footloose paganism which comprised neither Church nor State, properly speaking; neither feudalism nor ecclesiasticism. Both in the secular and in the spiritual respect their paganism was already infirm and insecure.

And they fell somewhat precipitately and uncritically into the coils of the new Faith and that new status of servile allegiance that made up the universal bond of mediæval society, civil and ecclesiastical. Both of these institutional innovations alike rested their case on an assumed congenital unworthiness of the common man; the two pillars of the new institutional edifice being Sin and Servility. And both of these concepts are in principle alien to the spirit of the pagan past. The sagas of the classical period reflect that state of experience, spiritual and temporal, which prepared the way for these new canons of right and honest living; canons according to which the common man has in the nature of things no claims which his God or his masters are bound to respect. They are at the same time the canons which have since then continued to rule the life of these Christian peoples in Church and State.

The conversion of these peoples to the ritual and superstitions of the new Faith was swift, facile, thorough and comprehensive, both in the temporal and in the spiritual phase of it, but more notably so in the latter respect. Indeed the gospel of Sin and Redemption was accepted by them with such alacrity and abandon as would argue that they had already been bent into a suitable frame of mind by protracted and exacting experience of a suitable kind. And on the side of the temporal reorganization, as concerned the revolutionary change in their civil institutions, they made the transition in only less headlong fashion. And in both respects the submission of these peoples to this new order of allegiance was notably abject.

This new gospel of abnegation, spiritual and temporal, was substantially alien to the more ancient principles of that pagan dispensation out of which the North-European peoples had come; but the event goes to show that in principle the new gospel of abnegation was consonant with their later acquired habits of thought; that their more recent experience of life had induced in these peoples such a frame of mind as would incline them to a conviction of sin and an unquestioning subjection to mastery. The discipline of life in the Viking Age appears to have been greatly conducive to such an outcome. And the *Laxdæla* reflects that state of society and that prevalent frame of mind which led the Scandinavian peoples over from the Viking Age to the Mediæval Church and State.

Here it is necessary to note that while the Viking Age prepared the ground for the Christian Faith and the Feudal State, there were at the same time also certain institutional hold-overs carried over out of remoter pagan antiquity into the Christian Era; hold-overs which also had their part in the new dispensation. Chief among these was the blood-feud; which appears to have suffered no impairment under the conditions of life in the

Viking Age. At the same time it appears that in principle, and indeed in the concrete details of its working-out, the habits of thought which underlie the blood-feud were not obnoxious to the interests of Holy Church or to the Propaganda of the Faith. Familiarity with its underlying principles and its logic would rather appear to have facilitated conversion to the fundamentals of the new Faith. The logic of the blood-feud, with its standardized routine of outlawry and its compounding of felonies, lends itself without substantial change of terms to the preachment of Sin and Redemption; perhaps in an especially happy degree to the preachment of Vicarious Atonement. So that this ancient and ingrained familiarity with the logic of the blood-feud may even be said to have served as an instrument of Grace. And as might fairly have been expected, the institution continued in good vigor for some centuries after the conversion to Christianity. In a certain sense, at least permissively, it even enjoyed the benefit of clergy; and it eventually fell into decay under the impact of secular rather than religious exigencies.

The Viking Age had prepared the ground for the new Faith and for the new, feudal order of Society. The Viking Age had run for some five or six centuries, and the discipline of habituation which was brought to bear through these centuries by that peculiar institution which has given its name to that era was exacting and consistent in an exemplary degree; rising steadily in point of stress and legitimation through the greater part of the period; until, in the end, the depleted resources of the Viking enterprise were taken over by the feudal State and the ecclesiastical establishment, and its pirate captains were supplanted by the princes and prelates of the new dispensation.

That occupation which gave its name and its character to the Viking Age was an enterprise in piracy and slavetrade, which grew steadily more businesslike and more implacable as time went on. It was an enterprise in getting something for nothing by force and fraud at the cost of the party of the second part; much the same, in principle, as the national politics pursued by the statesmen of the present time.

Unavoidably though doubtless unintentionally this business quite consistently yielded a cumulative net average deficit at large and resulted in a cumulative privation and servility on the part of the underlying population. Increasingly as time passed, the ethics of the strong arm came to prevail among these peoples and to dominate men's ideals and convictions of right and wrong. Insecurity of life and livelihood grew gradually more pronounced and more habitual, until in the course of centuries of rapine, homicide and desolation it became a settled matter of course and of common sense that the underlying population had no rights which the captains of the strong arm were bound to respect. And like any other business enterprise that is of a competitive nature this traffic in piracy was forever driven by its quest of profits to "trade on a thinner equity," to draw more unsparingly on its resources of man-power and appliances, and so cut into the margin of its reserves, to charge increasingly more than the traffic would bear. Until, between increasing squalor and privation on the material side and an ever increasing habituation to insecurity, fear and servility on the spiritual side, this population was in a frame of mind to believe that this world is a vale of tears and that they all were miserable sinners prostrate and naked in the presence of an unreasoning and unsparing God and his bailiffs. So this standardized routine of larceny and homicide ran through its available resources and fell insensibly into decay, and the State and Holy Church came in and took over the usufruct of the human residue that was left. It is the inchoate phase of this taking-over, specifically as it is to be seen in Iceland, that is reflected in the **Laxdæla.**

The subsequent share of Holy Church and its clerics in the ulterior degradation of the Scandinavian peoples, including Iceland, was something incredibly shameful and shabby; and the share which the State had in that unholy job was scarcely less so. But these things come into the case of the Icelandic community only at a later date, and can not be pursued here. The mediæval Church in Iceland stands out on the current of events as a corporation of bigoted adventurers for the capitalizing of graft and blackmail and the profitable compounding of felonious crimes and vices. It is of course not intended to question that this mediæval Church all this while remained a faithful daughter of Rome and doubtless holy as usual; nor is it to be questioned that more genial traits and more humane persons and motives entered into the case in a sporadic way. It is only that the visible net gain was substantially as set forth. In abatement it should also be noted, of course, that there is no telling what else and possibly shabbier things might have come to pass under the given circumstances in the conceivable absence of Holy Church and its clerics.

But this fuller blossoming of the Faith in Iceland, and its eventual going to seed, comes on in the decades which follow the period covered by the **Laxdæla;** which reflects only the more genial inchoate phase of the new dispensation. So also the further growth and fruition of that system of Boss Rule that made up the working constitution of the Icelandic Commonwealth likewise comes gradually to a head at a later date; and this too is shown only in its genial beginnings in the Laxdæla. Yet the elements, civil and ecclesiastical, which eventually entered into that teamwork of intrigue and desolation that brought the Commonwealth to its end in grief and shame are to be seen here. For a nearer view of that tangle of corrosive infelicities there are an abundance of documents available; such, e. g., as the *Saga of Gudmund the Good* and the *Islendinga Saga,* together with the rest of what is included in Vigfusson's *Sturlunga Saga;* while for the Norwegian community at home the *Heimskringla,* together with certain detached sagas of the later kings of Norway, will show how the fortunes of that people, from the advent of Christianity onward, swiftly tapered off into a twilight-zone of squalor, malice and servility, with benefit of Clergy.

The action of the saga runs over the period from the last quarter of the ninth to the first quarter of the eleventh century, coming to a head in the first decade of the eleventh.

For this translation use has been made of the Copenhagen edition of 1826, with some reference to later and more critical editions of the text. Later editions, as, e. g., that of Kaalund, are doubtless preferable in point of textual precision; but except for textual, essentially clerical, variations, there is no notable divergence between one edition and another or between one and another of the manuscript copies of the Laxdæla. The translation has also had the benefit of comparison with those made by Mrs. Press (Dent, London 1899) and Rudolf Meissner (Jena 1913), both of which are excellently well done, perhaps especially the German rendering. The German language appears to offer a more facile medium for a rendering of the Icelandic; its idioms appear to run more nearly parallel with those of the original.

As is true of the general run of Icelandic sagas, the language of the **Laxdæla** is the language of colloquial speech in its time; the speech of practiced storytellers, idiomatic in an extreme degree and with a pronounced bent for aphoristic diction. Consequently the difficulties in the way of a faithful translation are very appreciable. Necessarily, the idiomatic speech of that time runs on metaphor and analogy drawn from the familiar usage and custom of its own time and setting; such as would be pointed, sententious, and suggestive to the hearers who were familiar with that range of usage and custom. The language of the Saga, therefore, conveys in its own substance and structure that range of sentiments, convictions, ideals, knowledge and belief which is embodied in the action of the story. But it follows that the spirit of its action is not readily, or indeed at all adequately, to be carried over into another language which articulates with the usage current in a different time and place, and the run of whose idiom therefore is, by so much, substantially alien to that of the original.

The idiomatic speech of any given time and place springs from and reflects the workday experience and preconceptions of men in that given time and place.

And much water has run under the bridge since the days when the lives of those men and women took shape in the idiomatic speech of the Saga. The run of idiom in the English language as now current is as widely out of touch with that of the Icelandic saga as the current run of custom, knowledge and belief among the English-speaking peoples is now out of touch with the arts of life in that archaic phase of their culture. Under these circumstances translation becomes in good part a work of makeshift and adumbration, in which any consistently literal rendering of the text is out of the question.

By comparison with the common run of sagas, the received text of the **Laxdæla** is a somewhat prosy narrative, cumbered with many tawdry embellishments and affectations of style and occasional intrusive passages of devout bombast. The indications are fairly clear that the version of the text which has come down to the present has come through the hands of a painstaking editor-author whose qualifications were of a clerkly order rather than anything in the way of literary sense, and whose penchant for fine writing would not allow him to let well enough alone. Coupled with an unctuous sanctimony and a full run of puerile superstitions, such as were current in the late thirteenth century, this clerkly animus of the editor-author has at the same time overlaid the chief characters of the story with an ecclesiastical whitewash of meretricious abnegation, quite alien to the action in which these characters are engaged. So that, e. g., Kjartan Olafson comes to be depicted as a sanctimonious acolyte given to prayer, fasting, and pious verbiage; instead of being a wilful spoiled child, vain and sulky, of a romantic temper and endowed with exceptional physical beauty, such as the run of the story proclaims him. Whereas Gudrun, a beautiful vixen, passionate, headstrong, self-seeking and mendacious, is dutifully crowned with the distinction of having been the first nun and anchorite in Iceland and having meritoriously carried penance and abnegation to the outer limit of endurance. Yet, doubtless, all this glamour of sanctimony which the clerkly editor-author has dutifully thrown over the chief persons of the story is true to life, in the sense that such was the color of Icelandic life and sentiment in his own time, in the seedy times of the Icelandic community's decline and decomposition. Also it will be true to life in the sense that such will have been the consummation to which the drift of things under the new order converged from its beginning in the decades in which the action of the story is laid.

It may be in place to add that this translation follows the Copenhagen edition of the text also in the respect that it includes the chapters at the end (LXXIX-LXXXIII) devoted to the exploits of the younger Bolli, as well as the short story of Gunnar Thidrandabani,

which is appended to that edition. This story of the younger Bolli is commonly accounted spurious, doubtless rightly so; as being a late and mythical fabric of the mediæval romancer's art, designed to make Bolli illustrious in the eyes of his descendants. Similarly spurious are the passages in the body of the saga which detail the earlier doings of Bolli the younger. So, e. g., his share as well as the share of his brother Thorleik in the killing of Helgi Hardbeinson and in the negotiations which preceded and followed that exploit are known to be altogether fanciful; Helgi having been disposed of at a date when the two brothers were no more than two and six years old. Indeed, apart from the notice of his birth and his marriage, all that is here told of Bolli the younger is without known foundation.

A. Margaret Arent (essay date 1964)

SOURCE: Arent, A. Margaret. Introduction to *The Laxdoela Saga,* translated by A. Margaret Arent, pp. xv-xlii. Seattle: University of Washington Press, 1964.

[*In the following excerpt from her introduction to her English translation of the* Laxdaela Saga, *Arent probes the work's literary contexts, authorship, manuscript history, and sources, then concludes by providing an overview of its plot, structure, and style.*]

LITERARY BACKGROUND

With the Christianization of Iceland (A.D. 1000), a new era in the life and letters of the nation can be said to have begun, although the conversion was not marked by any great upheaval, politically or culturally. The old shaded off into the new and blended imperceptibly with it. The Church, which gradually brought the culture of southern Europe to Iceland, established schools, and taught the art of writing, did not squelch indigenous traditions, but rather served as the stimulus under which Icelandic letters developed to their height in the thirteenth century.

In this classical period, literary creativity burgeoned in Iceland, preserving poetic forms of the past and developing a new literary genre, the saga. The political scene, however, would seem to preclude this propitious endeavor, for Iceland at that time was in the throes of vindictive feuds and power struggles which sapped the nation's vitality and led to the forfeiture of independence. An age notorious for savageries and depravities of every sort thus also fostered Iceland's finest cultural achievement. The Sagas of Icelanders which were produced in this atmosphere depict the heyday of the Commonwealth, the days when Iceland enjoyed political autonomy and lived under a code of honor based on personal dignity and worth. It is perhaps not so puzzling that in the midst of moral and social disintegration there were those for whom the past loomed large in nostalgic reminiscence. On the one hand, as a kind of tribute to the heroic age of greatness, the sagas revitalized the past. On the other hand they combined the essential substance of the bygone days with the experience of contemporary developments. In this discrepancy between the cultural reference and the cultural context lies some of the fascination and enigma of the saga literature.

Iceland was settled late in the ninth century. The emigration from Norway, undertaken by many of the chieftains and petty kings to escape the domination of King Harald Fairhair, marked the last of the major movements of the Viking period. Iceland enjoyed home rule until 1262 when it fell under the Norwegian Crown. In the founding days, the sovereign power lay in the hands of the *goðar*, chieftain-priests who fulfilled both political and religious functions. A *goði*'s authority (pl. *goðar*) extended over those who paid dues and worshiped at his temple. In exchange for this privilege and the *goði*'s protection, these followers pledged him their allegiance and support. These quite naturally were the farmers and neighbors in his immediate vicinity. The number of *goðar* was limited, and the title was generally hereditary. The farmers reserved the right to choose the *goði* whom they wished to follow, but loyalty to a certain one usually became more or less habitual. The relationship was thus one of mutual trust and agreement—the old Germanic code of loyalty between chieftain and followers.

The years of the Commonwealth saw the establishment of the Althing (A.D. 930), a democratic parliament with a strong aristocratic base. The *goðar* automatically became members of the ruling bodies of parliament (the legislature and the judicature), and a Lawspeaker was elected to recite the laws at the meeting of the Althing which took place once a year on the plains of Thingvellir in the southwest of the country. As time went on, the *goði*'s obligations became more political than religious, his power territorial. There was no centralized authority over and above the *goðar*—a weakness in the political structure which left much leeway for internal feuds and later led to power politics and personal aggrandizement.

The old moral order had rested on a sense of personal dignity, honor, and loyalty, and on obligations of kinship. Any injury to one's honor or that of one's kin demanded payment, in blood or money. Theoretically justice was a meting out in kind, like for like, wergild for wergild, one killing for another. In the weighing and balancing of just deserts, a man's worth and station were taken into account. The equalizing of damages, compensation, arbitration, and mutual agreement were self-imposed codes, respected and carried out with a sense of responsibility. The fact that the courts were not empowered to carry out sentence was another inherent weakness, however, which not only condoned but encouraged the taking of the law into one's own hands. Outlawry, fines, and settlements had to be enforced by the plaintiff.

The petty slights and insults to one's honor which occasioned bloody revenge and internecine feuds seem exaggerated and pathetic by present-day standards, yet these were the codes by which men lived, passionately at times, and violently. Justice did not necessarily presuppose killings; there were peaceable men who strove to settle differences in a way that would do both sides honor without the spilling of blood. But it is the other alternative that most captivated the minds of the saga authors, and it is no wonder that they readily saw a parallel in the contemporary scene where vendettas and indiscriminate bloodshed were the order of the day. The honorable code of justice had recoiled upon itself, like the snake swallowing its own tail.

The Icelanders, as their Scandinavian forebears, were polytheistic, although worship of the gods was rather haphazard and had been on the wane throughout the tenth century. The individual therefore was more apt to rely on himself, placing his trust in his own weapons and strength (chapter 40). Superstitious belief in portents, omens, dreams, fetches, and visions of second sight, however, found widespread acceptance. Along with this, the conviction prevailed that life was ruled by an inscrutable destiny, a fatalism that manifested itself in the fortune or misfortunes of individual lives, but which ultimately pervaded all life as a nemesis and sickness at the core, a doomsday from which there was no escape. Christianity could do little to eradicate these deep-seated convictions. Substituting one God for a plurality in whom the people had little faith to begin with is minor compared with any unseating of these more diffuse beliefs which are part of the soul of the folk. It is understandable, too, that this fatalistic belief was readily amalgamated with the Biblical conception of the end of the world and apocryphal omens (cf. the "Vǫluspá" in the *Edda*). Thangbrand, after an unsuccessful attempt to convert the Icelanders, returned to Norway and reported to what a sorry pass his mission had come, saying that "to his mind Christianity would never take root in Iceland" (chapter 41).

To some of the more perceptive authors of the day, the fateful destiny toward which the nation was headed in the thirteenth century must also have presented a visible parallel to the age-old belief in fate. In some ways it must have seemed like a fulfillment of a chain of causes begun in the past, a snowballing of the consequences of an ethical system that demanded equal revenge, linking disaster to disaster. What had been present from the beginning in germ was now coming to fruition.

At the beginning of the Christian period, Iceland came under the diocese of Bremen, and the influence of the Church was limited. Native Icelanders traveled and were educated abroad; many became bishops in the new church at home. The great distance from Rome, the loose ties with Bremen, and the independent spirit of the Icelanders hampered any real domination by the Church. Men of high rank, the *goðar* and their sons, reinforced their authority and titles by serving the Church as priests and clerics. The bishops held seats in parliament; celibacy was never successfully enforced among the clergy. Thus here again in the early days of the Church there was no sharp demarcation between ecclesiastical and secular functions. Those schooled under Holy Church were men of the world, secular in outlook and interests. They learned to write under monastic guidance, but what they wrote reflected their own life and culture, their nation's spirit, and their national language.

The Commonwealth was a way of life which had deep roots in the past. It was conservative, even reactionary, tenaciously clinging to the values, traditions, and language of the homeland—a trait not uncommon to a people that has emigrated. They had brought with them a heritage of poetry—mythological and heroic lays that lived on in oral tradition and were later collected and written down in the *Edda* (*ca.* 1270). They had particularly gifted poets, the scalds, whose verses have been preserved in many of the sagas; and they no doubt brought along with them the innate desire and ability for storytelling, common to remote and primitive peoples in the preliterate stage.

The craft of writing is usually first exercised on the applied arts, and this too was the case in Iceland. The recording of the laws, translations of didactic religious works, the lives of saints, and the like paved the way for proficiency in narrative expression. A predilection for secular topics, however, apart from the laws, early made itself apparent. There had always been a lively interest in heritage and genealogy since most of the families in Iceland could trace their origin back to kingships and the nobility in Norway. Thus the Icelanders in the eleventh and twelfth centuries committed to parchment works concerning their ancestors, the Settlement of Iceland, and accounts of its Christianization. From the beginning they seemed to have had a sense for history and their place in it. Among some of these early works there is Sæmundr the Wise's *History of the Kings of Norway,* Ari Thorgilsson's *Íslendingabók,* and the *Landnámabók* (The Book of the Settlement, a compilation of the names of the first settlers, their ancestors and descendants, with brief biographical sketches).

When one considers that the most popular and striking figure of the day, King Óláf Haraldsson (died 1030), was both king and saint, the transition from writing saints' lives to Kings' Sagas is quite understandable. The so-called *First Saga of Saint Óláf* was probably written around 1180. About ten years later, Oddr Snorrason wrote a saga about King Óláf Tryggvason, the king who Christianized Norway and Iceland. (Both of these kings figure as prominent characters in the ***Laxdoela saga,*** cf. chapters 40 and 73.) Both Sæmundr and Oddr wrote their works in Latin, but they were so soon translated into the vernacular that we know them only in that form.

In 1190 the diocese under whose jurisdiction Iceland fell was changed from Bremen to Trondheim. Iceland was thus drawn into the religious and political orbit of Norway. At this time it was decreed that no *goðar* could be ordained unless they renounced their secular title. Although this brought about a clearer separation of Church and State, along with it came tighter control by the Church and closer ties with the Crown in Norway. Bonds with the mother country had never been entirely broken—Icelandic scalds had long been court favorites and there had always been those who sought honor abroad. Now, however, increasing numbers of prominent Icelanders became liegemen to the king, relinquishing more and more their national independence for personal gain.

By this time, however, writers and clerics had become sufficiently exercised in written expression that a lay literature could develop independently of the Church. The Kings' Sagas gradually shed their hagiographic tinge. Snorri Sturluson, who put his stamp on the age of the Sturlungs (1200-62), had not learned Latin. In his *Heimskringla* (Orb of the World), he recast the Kings' Sagas into a lively and realistic narrative. With contemporary events drawing Iceland into ever closer relationship with Norway, it was natural that authors should turn to recording these connections and tracing the continuity with the mother country. Snorri, and in all likelihood many of the anonymous contemporary writers, was not a mere observer but an active participant in the events of his time.

Like the Kings' Sagas, the Sagas of Icelanders (or Family Sagas) also reflect the genealogical and historical interest of those times. In presentation and form they resemble the Kings' Sagas; in subject matter they too draw on historical material—primarily the lives of Icelanders during the days of the Settlement, but also on the common cultural heritage, legal and religious customs. But these sagas were composed with something else in mind than chronicles, family histories, or documentation, and they rely to varying degrees on historical facts. The authors have formed and organized their material into something more than esthetically pleasing history. The best of them are unified wholes, their structures ordered toward symbolizing an idea in esthetic form. The apex of the period brought forth among others *Egils saga, Eyrbyggja saga,* **Laxdoela saga,** and *Njáls saga.* Despite a certain solidarity of style and similarity of theme and handling, each one will be found unique. Though anonymous, the perceptiveness and predilection of individual authors can usually be detected. They use common themes and devices to suit their own ends, exhibit varying degrees of mastery over their material, and handle their historical sources with greater or less freedom. At such an early stage in the history of European literatures, these sagas boast a narrative style that rings surprisingly modern in contrast to the courtly romances and epic verse forms of contemporary medieval Europe.

MANUSCRIPTS, DATE, AND AUTHORSHIP

The **Laxdoela saga** is a fine representative of the saga genre created in Iceland in the thirteenth century. The English equivalent of its title would read: *The Saga of the Laxdalers.* It is both a regional and a family saga. The Laxdalers were the settlers and inhabitants of the Laxárdal, a valley on the western coast of Iceland in the district Dalasýsla at the head of the Hvammsfjord.

Two classes of manuscripts are extant from which we know the story. We are indeed fortunate in having the text whole or in part on six vellums, for in general a vellum is to be preferred over paper copies. The Y-class vellums include a sequel to the story, the *Bolla þáttr.* There are two complete Y-class vellums that are independent of one another and thus serve as excellent control for editions made from this class. The most famous manuscript of this class is the *Möðruvallabók.* It is a parchment of two hundred leaves from the first half of the fourteenth century and contains eleven sagas, of which **Laxdoela** is the tenth in the series.

The Z-class MSS are older and would be preferred, except for the fact that they are all fragmentary. The oldest of these (D2) has been dated *ca.* 1250. Thus the saga must be at least that old, and some think it likely that this fragment (luckily salvaged from a bookbinding) may even be the archetype of the text.

Internal evidence corroborates this dating of the saga. The genealogies in the saga lead both backward and forward. The latter frequently include the names of bishops and priests who lived beyond the frame of the story and take us into the time of composition. The dates of many of these personages are known from church records. A *terminus a quo* can be derived from the mention of Thorvald Snorrason who died in 1228 (chapter 31). The arrival of Unn in Iceland can be set fairly close to the date 892. (The first permanent settler arrived in 874.) Saint Óláf's death (1030) is mentioned shortly before the end of the saga. The events of the story proper cover then a period of approximately one hundred and fifty years from the ninth into the eleventh century (*ca.* 892-1030). Roughly one hundred and eighty to two hundred years had thus elapsed between the last events described in the saga (1030) and the composition of the work (sometime after 1228). One might naturally expect that scribes tended to interpolate names bringing the story up to their own time, but there is sufficient evidence that this has not been the case in **Laxdoela.**

The consciousness of the time discrepancy is evident in the author's expressions contrasting the "then" and "now." The mention of the ordeal of "going-under-the-sod" (chapter 18)—which was taken just as seriously by the heathen as "Christian men do *now* [italics mine] when such ordeals are performed"—leads to external evidence that helps narrow down the possible date of the saga. Ordeals were abolished by Cardinal William of Sabena in Norway in 1247, and mention is made in the Icelandic annals of such a change in ordinance in 1248.

Anachronisms in the text such as insignia on shields, the use of courtly words (*riddari,* "knight"; *glaðel,* "lance"; *kurteisi,* "courtoisie"), and the obvious fascination of the author with ostentation and dress point to the influence of the southern romances in the author's own day. Translations of them had begun with Friar Robert's *Tristans saga* in Norway in 1226, and these romances with their courtly ideals began filtrating into Iceland around 1240-50.

Echoes of contemporary accounts found in the *Sturlunga saga* (a composite of many sagas and *þættir* [shorter tales] composed in the thirteenth century about contemporary events and taken to be reliable accounts) have been noted in **Laxdoela** by Rolf Heller and others.[1] Two events in particular aid in dating **Laxdoela.** The *Deildartungumál* (a famous legal case mentioned in the *Sturlu saga* in the *Sturlunga saga*) concerns the succession to inheritance in a family that perished in a single shipwreck about 1178. The drowning of Thorstein Surt (**Laxdoela,** chapter 18) seems to be patterned after the contemporary event. There is not even a hint in the *Landnámabók* or other sources that Thorstein drowned at all. Either **Laxdoela**'s author has assimilated material still within memory of his day or actually knew the *Sturlu saga,* and this is not at all inconceivable since it was probably written early in the thirteenth century and in the same district as **Laxdoela.**

Another incident from contemporary times which the saga author likely incorported occurs in *Þórðar saga kakala* in the *Sturlunga saga:* "Then his wife Vigdís

Markúsdóttir came up. Ásbjorn dried his bloody sword on her clothes."[2] In 1244 Ásbjorn Gudmundarson went with some men to Húnavatnssýsla on this mission. If the author has indeed utilized this episode in the passage where Helgi Hardbeinsson wipes his bloody spear on Gudrún's fine attire (*Laxdoela,* chapter 55)—suiting the deed to be sure to his own purpose—then *Laxdoela* must have been written after 1244 and rather soon after.

Laxdoela saga is mentioned by name in other sagas, the earliest reference being in the *Eyrbyggja saga,* which has been dated around 1250. Thus it is reasonable to assume that *Laxdoela* was composed between 1228 and 1250, and likely between 1244 and 1248.

Conjectures about the author and place of composition continue to occupy the imagination of many. It has been assumed from geographic orientations within the saga that the place of composition must have been in the local district around the Hvammsfjord, and the favored localities are the two prominent settlements at Helgafell and Hjardarholt. It is probable that the author was a cleric, but all attempts to ascertain his name have been futile.

Sources and Origins

As for the substance of the narrative, we are undeniably presented with echoes from the *Landnámabók,*[3] from the poetic *Edda,*[4] from other sagas, and from contemporary accounts found in the *Sturlunga saga.* Thus we find an amazing amalgamation of material old and new. Evidence of these influences and interdependencies throws light on the author's acquaintance with both the oral and written traditions of his time, but the parallels can by no means be called slavish borrowings. Many of the motifs are so common that proof of actual influence from one saga to another cannot be established with any certainty. And in those cases where the parallels seem obvious and striking, the author of *Laxdoela* has made something entirely his own out of them.

It has long been a debatable issue how much of the substance of the Family Sagas has come down from oral tradition. What sort of tales were told in the preliterate period we can only guess; how much of them went into the Family Sagas will forever remain unknown. Naturally an indigenous facility in oral story-telling precedes any literate age of poetry, and although reflexes of the former oral techniques are without a doubt discernible in the transitional literature of an early lettered age, these oral devices will continue to be drawn upon only as long as they serve the purposes of the new medium, where they have become, properly speaking, *literary* devices. It must be remembered, too, that a real connection between oral presentation and written literature did exist at the time of the composition of the sagas, for they were meant to be read aloud.

There are many indications that point to a teller-to-audience directive: "Now let us return to Iceland and see what has been going on there since Thorkel went away" (chapter 58), or the perfunctory announcement of a newcomer to the saga: "There was a man by the name of. . . ." Oral clichés such as "people say," "that is the talk of people," and so forth are found on nearly every page. It is not surprising that a written story should now properly seem to be a told story. But there are signs that the techniques are already on the verge of becoming hackneyed and outworn. The important thing, as far as the author's sources are concerned, is that oral technique be distinguished from the handing down of the content of the story. The author has drawn on all of his experience—the literature he knew, the historical material available to him, a form of presentation accepted and familiar in his day, episodes from contemporary events—and transformed them in his own creative imagination to suit his master design.

Historical Reliability

Coupled with the issue of the oral saga is the problem of historical reliability. The Free-prosaists, as the advocates of an oral origin are called, assert not only that oral sagas preceded the written works as a substratum but that these sagas were passed down from the time of the events and were thus reliable accounts even to the individual dialogues. This theory has persisted with modifications and concessions down to the present century.[5] In 1949 Sigurdur Nordal dealt a devastating blow to this theory with his *Hrafnkatla,*[6] in which he demonstrated conclusively that the characters and story of *Hrafnkels saga* are fictitious and that realistic prose can in fact present a semblance of reality so convincing that it has taken scholarship centuries to recognize the genius of the saga authors. The Free-prosaists had always been hard pressed in their argument for an oral folk tradition in free prose that could transmit through centuries historically accurate accounts. The mental arabesques and exceptions required to make the theory plausible have had to yield to more cogent arguments. Several factors contributed to the almost fanatic desire on part of the older generation of scholars and laymen in general to salvage the venerable age and truthfulness of the sagas: (1) The saga literature was discovered at the beginning of the seventeenth century, a time when national interests in Scandinavia ran high. Each nation vied with the other in obtaining the valuable codices, and each sought to find in them proof of a past grandeur. Even the mythological sagas were taken as bona fide history, and the Kings' Sagas and Family Sagas were naturally taken at face value. Some of this "belief" in the sagas continues to the present day. (2) Especially in the case of the Family Sagas it seemed obvious that the accounts were reliable—most of the characters could be attested and were known to have lived; the genealogies in the main were accurate; the time and setting were real; the farmsteads stand today in their original places with the names of their owners of a thousand years ago. (3) Since the Family Sagas went back to the time of the events, they were felt to have preceded the composition of the Kings' Sagas. Nordal has argued for a reversal of the chronology—the Family Sagas begin with biographical sagas of scalds who were court poets in Norway. These sagas then are a transition from the Kings' Sagas, both in content and form. The Kings' Sagas made use of scaldic verses as sources for the facts and episodes about the kings, and the verses were incorporated into the sagas. In sagas about scalds, their verses were naturally part of the narrative. Thus it came to be assumed that verses in a saga indicated authenticity of the content. In the Family Sagas these could then very well be invented to give the appearance of valid tradition and verification. From time immemorial the poet has captured his audience by appealing to the credibility of his tale. It is therefore not to be wondered at that the saga authors would want their stories to seem true. The devices they used to create the illusion are discussed below, pp. xxxviii-xxxix. (4) The direct narrative prose and dialogue were naïvely taken at face value as discursive language and oral recounting. Critics failed to consider the possibility of artistic semblance and the poetic use of language, especially in free prose.

According to the various conjectures concerning the oral origin of the sagas, they were deemed more or less historical. Some Free-prosaists assumed that the sagas were amalgamations of separate parts—the *þættir* theory. These *þættir* were collected and put together by a redactor or scribe. The more a saga exhibited a unity of structure, the more changes it had undergone, the more it deviated in other words from its original purity and genuineness. Thus unity of composition came to be a decisive factor in the arguments of oral *vs.* written, of fact *vs.* fiction.

The Book-prosaists, as the opposition school is called, place greater emphasis on the artistic nature of the sagas and assign them to the literate period—they are written works of artistic merit, composed by individual authors, who succeeded to varying degrees in unifying their subject matter. The Book-prosaists argued that unity could only be attributable to an author who could view his work as a whole, and that the masterful handling of the materials pointed to a written tradition. Paradoxically, the most radical of the Free-prosaists insisted that the oral tradition could account for everything, both historical reliability and artistic excellence—the earliest sagas, closest to the oral tradition, were the most perfect as compositions, and also the most accurate.

National and romantic interests, wishful thinking, and disregard for adjacent disciplines prevented more objec-

tive discrimination. Nordal has shown that the literary endeavors in Iceland do indeed follow an ascending gradient—the best compositions are the latest—and that there are many inaccuracies and deviations from strict historical fact. Scholars are now beginning to ferret out the relationships between sagas, the influences from the thirteenth-century *Sturlunga saga,* and see the Family Sagas as compositions of individual writers. All of these findings would seem to indicate that the Bookprosaists have won the day. Even the Kings' Sagas can no longer satisfy the requirements of the historical disciplines. It is thus reasonable to concede that the Family Sagas are primarily works of art and belong to the literary discipline, which does not deny that they have a basis in real life, real persons, and events. Yet what the author has made of the cultural and historical material is not history.

In the case of the **Laxdoela saga** specifically, it has been sufficiently demonstrated that the author has created some fictitious characters and scenes, that the chronology cannot bear too close scrutiny, and that the position of Icelanders abroad is obviously enhanced beyond strict fact. As examples of the cases in point, I might just mention that the genealogy of Óláf the White is confused, that Thorbjorn Skrjúp and his son Lambi are otherwise unattested, that the Mýrkjartan and Melkorka episodes seem to have been invented for the purpose of the story, and that the Helgi Hardbeinsson scene has no historical basis. The main disruption of historical time occurs when young Bolli Bollason appears in the story as a lad of twelve years (chapter 59). No reader who is participating in the illusion of the story, however, would even be aware that a chronological shift, measured by historical time outside the story, had occurred. It is the author's poetic end that justifies the manipulation. The superlative descriptions of the reception of Icelanders abroad in their stereotyped formulations are obvious exaggerations. That Bolli Bollason was the first to be in the Varangian Guard is chronologically impossible (chapter 76).

While comparisons with historical facts, correlation with real time outside the story, sifting of fact from fiction, ferreting out influences and origins are interesting in themselves, such studies do little to illuminate the author's intent in creating the work. Analyses extraneous to the work can only succeed in diverting attention from the work as a whole and as it stands before us. Recent investigations into the sources and materials used by the author rather give the impression of a patching together of fragments from here and there—not much different from the piecing together of *ættir,* only that now the pieces are from written literature rather than oral traditions. Reducing the end product to all its elements cannot satisfactorily explain its art form and organic unity, for it is more than the sum of its parts.

Whatever the origin of technique and substance, whatever prompted the conception in the author's mind, all of it has been rewoven in the author's formative imagination, emerging as a totally new and felicitous creation.

Summary of the Plot

According to the story, Ketil Flatnose, a chieftain in Norway, together with his children and kinsmen, set sail from the homeland in the latter decades of the ninth century. Ketil settled in Scotland, his daughter Unn the Deep-minded in the Breidafjord Dales in Iceland. She claimed all the lands around the head of the Hvammsfjord, including the Laxárdal (literally meaning the "Salmon River Valley," cf. map). Her brother Bjorn the Eastman also settled in Iceland in the Breidafjord District. The saga sets forth an account of the generations descending from Unn and Bjorn.

The story falls into three interlocking parts. The first or prelude (chapters 1-31) takes up almost half of the book, and the saga has often been criticized for its lengthy introduction. There is such a multiplication of characters and episodes that the reader may feel he is getting nowhere with the plot. These many colorful characters and unforgettable episodes are like vignettes that can be enjoyed in themselves. But upon closer reading, each of these scenes will be found to be subordinate to the whole design, slowly but surely laying the foundation for what is to come, injecting an element that forms the node for the next link in the chain of action.

It is by no means easy to give a straightforward account of the plot in this first section, for although a thread follows the succeeding generations and leads to a culmination, the reader is constantly called upon to relate back and forth, picking up threads that have been temporarily dropped, comparing and substantiating what he has heard before. The movement is not strictly cumulative, gaining momentum to the end. The sweeping dramatic impulse, once begun, is offset by a leisurely epic pace. The action halts at intervals, introducing yet another character and episode, reflecting back, rounding out what has been prepared and hinted.

Generation after generation of Unn's side of the house marches past, each successive one perhaps a bit more illustrious than the former. There are quarrels, disagreements, and battles among the kinsmen, but all with their temporary assuaging of ill feelings. The characters and situations prepare the reader for the same types of themes in the central action, laying before him a mural of the saga world and accustoming him to the social and moral ordering of that world. The characters we meet have some of the stuff in them that makes the main characters what they are—Óláf Feilan, Hoskuld,

Óláf Peacock—all have in them something of a Kjartan, the hero of the story. Unn, Jórunn, Vigdís, Melkorka are not so much different from Gudrún, the heroine of the main theme.

It might perhaps be useful to the reader to give some glimpses in preview so that the rambling and diversified introduction may take on continuity with the main theme. Unn, the matriarch of the family, sets the tone for the story, planning wise marriages, generously parceling out her land claim, and keeping her dignity to the end. The plot moves forward with the birth of Hoskuld, Unn's great-great-grandson, one of the most illustrious figures in the saga. He journeys abroad and purchases a concubine. With a few masterful strokes, the author sets before us the brightly colored tent of Gilli with the twelve concubines behind the curtain, Hoskuld's transactions with Gilli, and the weighing of the purse. Then we catch a glimpse of this rare beauty whom Hoskuld has bought for three times the price of an ordinary bondwoman. It turns out that she is the daughter of the Irish King Mýrkjartan. She gives birth to a son by Hoskuld, who is Óláf Peacock, the father of Kjartan.

Before Óláf's career is launched with the claiming of his royal pedigree and the wooing of his bride, the saga takes time to introduce us to the neighbors of Hoskuld. The story of Hrapp, his haunted farm, and ghost walkings holds our interest through many chapters. Other neighbors of Hrapp and Hoskuld are Thórd Goddi and Vigdís. The two of them get involved in the sheltering of an outlaw, as a result of which Vigdís divorces Thórd, who is then forced to give over all his property to Hoskuld and to foster Hoskuld's son Óláf. After Hoskuld's death Óláf and his half brothers Thorleik and Bárd divide the paternal inheritance in thirds, much to the discontent of Thorleik. The argument between Óláf and Thorleik is settled when Óláf offers to foster Thorleik's son Bolli (Thorleiksson), by which time Óláf's own son Kjartan has been born to him out of his marriage with Thorgerd Egilsdóttir. The coming together of the foster brothers Kjartan and Bolli brings the generations to a culmination. With the extraordinary prowess and accomplishments of these brilliant and gallant lads the prelude comes to a happy close.

The main theme (chapters 32-56) is sounded with the entrance of the other side of Ketil's house into the saga—Gudrún and her father Ósvíf, the descendants of Bjorn the Eastman. Essentially this main theme relates a tragedy in the personal lives of Kjartan, Bolli, and Gudrún, who are bound together in love and friendship, but for whom fate has preordained hatred and killings. It is a tale of a love triangle with all its subterfuges, vicious insinuations, retaliations, and heartaches, presented with the detachment and subtle discernment so typical of the sagas.

Chapters 32-33 serve as an interlude, setting the stage for all the subsequent action. In these two chapters the prophetic statements of Gest (the prophet-seer par excellence in the saga) follow one upon the other in rapid succession. From here on the plot is easy to follow for it is a denouement of what has been predicted. Kjartan's life and death hang by two swords that come into the family—the one, Footbite, owned first by the scoundrel Geirmund and later by Bolli, has a curse on it that will be the death of that member in the family hardest to lose. The sword Konungsnaut, a gift of the king to Kjartan, carries with it a protective blessing. Through the curse and the blessing the two swords are juxtaposed, their powers pitted one against the other. Gest predicts that Bolli will "stand over Kjartan's crown and thereby reap his own death." The antagonism between the foster brothers arises over their love for Gudrún.

Gudrún Ósvífsdóttir—high-spirited, strikingly beautiful, sharp-tongued, witty, proud, vain, ambitious, fiercely jealous, calculating, and unrelenting in venting her hurt pride—directly and indirectly instigates the death of her two lovers. Her life is laid before her in four dreams, foretelling her four marriages. Lifted from the context all these previews of the lives of Kjartan, Bolli, and Gudrún provide the scaffolding for the remainder of the saga. Subordinate premonitions and hints throughout the narrative substantiate and strengthen the inevitability of their fates. The suspense is not based on ignorance, but on the incompletion of a foreknown completion. What is so fascinating about the story is thus to watch and see how the natural involvements of the characters and the demands of the moral code of revenge play hand in hand with what fate has already predicted.

After the fulfillment of Gudrún's first two marriages, which are full of exciting and amusing episodes, we are told of the friendship between the house of Óláf and the house of Ósvíf—a bond which is strengthened by the close friendship of the three young people. It is here that the fates of Kjartan and Bolli become intertwined with that of Gudrún in the fulfillment of her third dream.

Óláf, prescient and cautious, has premonitions of the impending breach between the two families. But Kjartan, unheedful of his father's foreboding, continues to frequent the hot spring at Laugar where he and Gudrún can enjoy each other's company. Bolli always goes along, and it is not hard to guess that he may secretly be nurturing an affection for Gudrún, despite the fact that the author has camouflaged it under the foster brothers' habit of always being together—"no matter where they went."

Kjartan—impetuous, gallant, eager for fame and glory—hastily decides to journey abroad, leaving Gudrún behind. Kjartan and Bolli, their friendship unimpaired, journey together to Norway, where the rivalry between them first flares to the surface. The ruffled feelings and undercurrent of envy on Bolli's part remain subdued and controlled while attention is turned to another problem. The king of Norway has been exerting pressure on the heathen to accept the new religion. During the altercations in the Christianizing of Iceland, Kjartan is held hostage, whereas Bolli is permitted to sail for home.

Upon his arrival, Bolli loses no time in paying court to Gudrún and wins her hand, much to the dismay of his foster father Óláf. Snatching the bride is the feather in his cap that bolsters his pride. The motives are nowhere made explicit; Bolli himself would be the first to deny that he deliberately acted against his foster brother.

Upon Kjartan's return, the interplay of emotions, the fury of passion and resentment are at first restrained, only to break through periodically in whiplash insinuations or be repressed in poignant silences. But the pent-up emotions cannot be contained for long. Three festive parties harbor the seeds of hatred and revenge. At the first one Kjartan refuses Bolli's gift of a stud of horses. Subsequently he marries the sweet and gentle Hrefna, the very opposite in temperament to Gudrún. At the next party, Gudrún, who can scarcely suppress her jealousy, inveigles Hrefna into letting her see the fabulous headdress which Kjartan had brought from Norway and which had been meant for her, Gudrún, as a wedding gift. It is touching to see how the guileless Hrefna obliges Gudrún, taking her to the storehouse where it is safely kept in a chest. Slowly unfolding it, Gudrún has not a word to say—her reticence expresses more than any words could. When the party ends, the sword Konungsnaut is stolen by Gudrún's brothers. It is recovered, but without its scabbard, so that Kjartan never carries it again. The protective sword will thus not be ready when Kjartan needs it most.

At the third party, Hrefna's expensive headdress disappears, never to be found again. Now the breach is irreparable; hostilities and spiteful acts ensue until Gudrún finally eggs Bolli on into killing Kjartan. Bolli regretfully draws the sword Footbite and the first part of Gest's prophecy is fulfilled.

After the peaceful Óláf dies, Kjartan's mother and brothers take up the revenge. They make a raid on Bolli in a dairy hut, where he fights a lone defense against fearful odds. Helgi Hardbeinsson deals Bolli a fatal wound and predicts that the child Gudrún is then carrying in her womb will be the death of him, Helgi. With this the main theme comes to a close—Gudrún's third dream and all of Gest's prophecies concerning the fates of Kjartan and Bolli have come to completion.

The postlude (chapters 57-end) is a working out of all the remaining prophecies—revenge for Bolli and Gudrún's fourth dream. Gudrún's friend and mentor, Snorri Godi, cunningly plans out both, securing for Gudrún the death of Helgi Hardbeinsson (just as Helgi had predicted) and a great chieftain as a fourth husband (just as her dream indicated). Gudrún lives out her life in remorse and mourning, confessing to her son Bolli Bollason which man she loved most: "To him I was worst whom I loved most." The saga has come full circle, the passions of hatred have been spent; the reader's expectations have all been fulfilled.

UNITY OF COMPOSITION, TECHNIQUE, AND STYLE

Prophecy and fulfillment as an enactment of destiny set the pattern for the structure of the narrative. Popular belief in portents, curses, dreams, visions of second sight and the like are all utilized as a convenient literary convention in which to couch the oracles of fate. Their presence is neither fanciful nor artificial, but part of real life. With a fine sensitivity for human nature, the author cloaks these sudden flashes of insight in the ambiguity and uncertainty that human beings are wont to ascribe to premonitions, and they are so subtly imbedded in the natural circumstances that they are even likely to be overlooked. Thus the characters are able to shrug them off as something inexplicable, and the reader is left in some apprehension and doubt whether it will actually come true, how it will happen, and when.

Fate never operates as a *deus ex machina.* Very deftly the author has amalgamated the natural and the supernatural causes. The characters follow the dictates of their own hearts and the demands of the moral law, neither flinching before what is ordained nor attempting to avert the inevitable. The involvements of the characters are always precisely what the plot demands, and the plot allows only those characteristics to predominate which further the action and suit the design. Plot and character are thus reflections of one another.

The structure of the plot rests on preparation and subsequent fulfillment, just as destiny is the coming to completion of what was present in embryo from the beginning. In the light of this, one can also better assess the function of the prelude. Every thread of the narrative is knotted and tied. The author never forgets, and if the reader does, he will be reminded. The little phrase occurring with such frequency in the saga: "You would not have brought this up, if you did not know where it was to land," admirably sums up the author's working method. He never "brings something up" without reason, and he always knows where it is leading, "where it will come down."

This structure is carried out in miniature in the subordinate episodes and scenes, each minor hunch ultimately finding, sometimes over great spans, its complementary statement of fulfillment. The phrases "if I don't miss my guess," "it will come as no surprise to me," and so forth reappear with such consistency that the reader may take them as a cue to heed well what is said, to look for a consequence later.

In addition to outright prophetic statements the author employs other devices to carry through the same formal concept of anticipation and completion. The characters are introduced by perfunctory adjectives; later in the action they act out in word and deed these traits assigned to them. The reader then knows beforehand what to expect of them. Since character and plot are so mutually dependent, the characters are apt to appear as types. Strikingly many are those who are "unfair" and "hard to deal with," or tagged as "a big man and strong," "a paragon among men (women)." And not only are we prepared for the types of characters, but also for the characters themselves through their inconspicuous inclusion in genealogical listings long before they enter the stage of action. Snorri Godi, for instance, is mentioned in a genealogy as early as chapter 7 but does not take part in the story until chapter 36; Gudrún's family branch is included in chapter 2 and is not picked up again until chapter 32; and the list of such examples could be greatly enlarged. Thus it has not been found prudent to leave these seemingly superfluous genealogical listings out of the translation and relegate them to footnotes, as some translators have done.

Until now the genealogies have been the last stronghold of appeal in the argument for the chronicle nature of the sagas (the modicum of historicity left to them undisputedly); their integral function in enhancing the esthetic design has been overlooked. For the modern reader, less interested perhaps in genealogy and unacquainted with the characters from other sagas (the sagas are often complementary—the light focusing on certain characters in one saga, who then fade into background figures in another), genealogical charts have been inserted in this edition at those places where the reader is most likely to get lost in the maze, or where a refresher is needed to bring new characters into relationship with the family lineages already mentioned.

Another important means by which the author facilitates relating back and forth and carrying through the strands of narrative is through repetition in the lexical items. The author does not need to state explicitly, as he so often does, that a prophecy has now run its course, or that "now" it was the same "as before"—this he also does by re-using the linguistic pattern. Furthermore the same device is effectively employed to evoke comparisons between themes, scenes, and characters. Despite the wealth of episodes and characters, a basic structural pattern is thus brought into focus. Indeed, it is only by the linguistic components that many of the relationships and juxtapositions can be recognized. As a guide for the fuller enjoyment of the saga, I shall illustrate a few of them:

Vigdís rewards the slave Ásgaut with the money ill-gotten by her husband Thórd saying: "Now the money has fallen into better hands" (chapter 16). Subsequently Thórd turns over all his property to Hoskuld and Óláf to safeguard it from Vigdís who has divorced him and would like to get half his property in settlement. Thórd on this occasion says to Hoskuld: ". . . now the money has fallen into better hands" *(ibid.).* Repetition of the phrase evens out their play, tit for tat.

The Irish are intimidated by the appearance of Óláf's warlike vessel and "a murmur of discontent" runs through their group (chapter 21). Upon seeing the cavalry of the Irish king Mýrkjartan, "a murmur of discontent" over the odds passes through Óláf's ranks, thus neatly equalizing through the repeated phrase the two sides in their fear and strength.

Geirmund owned a trusty sword, which he always carried with him: "This sword he called Footbite, and he never let it very far out of his sight" (chapter 29). At the party at Hjardarholt, where Kjartan's sword is stolen, it is said: "Kjartan had not been carrying his sword Konungsnaut around with him while going about these duties, although he was rarely in the habit of letting it very far out of his sight" (chapter 46). The reader already knows the roles assigned to each of the swords, and the lexical repetition in describing them is no accident on the part of the author. It underscores their juxtaposition.

Throughout the saga the lexical repetitions are a guide to the structure of the saga and the intent of the author. They are not brought in arbitrarily, nor are they evidence of lack of imagination—a rote parroting of formulae. The number of parallels and pairs is astonishing, and they serve a deliberate function: Kjartan and Bolli Thorleiksson are characterized in similar phrases, yet are also counterparts; Kjartan has his match in Bolli Bollason; Gudrún hers in Thorgerd, and her counterpart in Hrefna. These relationships are always indicated by parallel and contrasting phrases. Two brothers of opposite temperaments are a regular theme in the saga, and parallels of all sorts abound. These repeated themes with their similar phrases either may point up a fulfillment of the expected or may set up equalities of matching and counterbalancing.

Another type of repetition in the saga which exceeds twofold occurrence I call recurrence, for the phrases become stereotyped and formulaic, running on indefi-

nitely. One might possibly see in them crystallizations of oral clichés that have now been used in the new medium. The whole technique of repetition as a literary device no doubt derives from similar techniques known to oral traditional poetry. The recurring phrases are particularly noticeable in the activities in the round of existence—birth and marriage proposals, careers abroad, and deathbed scenes. Again the reader is placed in a known and closed world, just as he was with the prophecies. There are no essential surprises. The element of chance is all but eliminated, just as destiny cancels chance. And this limited and foreknown world is reflected in the language of the saga—we know what to expect even as to the lexical choices.

Since the author has integrated the supernatural sphere (fate) with the moral realm (code of honor and revenge)—the one being the reflection of the other—the structural devices of repetition and recurrence symbolize the formal aspects of both. Repetition is a type of apparition of destiny, in that it underscores the fulfillment. On the other hand it balances the score, in a like-for-like compensating that mirrors the code of justice in its equal retaliation aspect. Recurrence enhances the sense of a predetermined and calculated world—life caught in its own mesh of formulae—inescapable, unalterable. On the other hand recurrence represents the run-on chain of endless revenge killings, the other aspect of the moral order.

The author also works with units of three, thereby reinforcing the tripartite division of the saga and the dominance of three main characters. There are, for example, three parties, each one patterned after the other; three goadings; three drownings, and three land sales, each with their reappearing motifs.

It would be tempting to multiply the examples of the author's technique, lest the subtleties be missed, for this overruling design permeates every level of the saga. But it would go beyond the purpose of this introduction to enumerate them further.[7] Suffice it to say that the reader's attention should be drawn to these repetitions and parallels, which I hope have survived in the translation.

If an analogy were to be given, I suppose the bargaining process itself, the evening of sides and meting out of justice would serve as the most apt image to express what the saga is about. There is a marked preference for weighing of evens and odds, of equalities and inequalities in every sort of dealing—be it comparison of men and their worth, wergild compensations, land sales, skirmishes, horse trades, or marriage contracts. The pulling back and forth, evening the trade, sizing up the odds, considering that a neighbor has "much land and little cattle," or "little land and much cattle" are all conspicuous elements throughout the saga.

The up-down, back-forth movement related to the weighing and balancing process sets up a counter-rhythm to the dramatic sweep of destiny that carries the action forward—it is a measured step and counterstep. The primacy of the natural sequence of prelude, central theme, and postlude (the chronological progression of "before," "now," and "after"—historical time) is thereby somewhat weakened—a good indication that the story moves in virtual time not practical time. But enough of the semblance of real time is retained in the succession of the generations to insure the likeness to historical account.

Something remains to be said of the over-all tone and style. Here again the author works with contrasts and alternations. There is a certain discrepancy between the restrained and precise form and the violence of the content—a fact which lends an ironic cast to the whole. This quality is especially conspicuous in the ambiguity in idioms, the tension between the apparent meaning and the significant meaning. Also part of the ironic tinge lies in the anonymity and impartiality of the author-creator who sees everything from above, something like fate operating from behind the scenes. To observe not so much *what* is being said, but *how* it is being said is one of the most interesting features in reading the saga.

The general splendor and formulaic superlative expressions also stand in contrast to the restrained presentation—hyperbole alternating with litotes. The background of ennobled reality heightens the tragic happenings. It is the most illustrious of the race that are doomed for a tragic end. Likewise there is a contrast between periods of relative calm and stormy violence. The saga rarely affords us descriptive passages, but the following reference to the weather sums up this type of alternation admirably: "The weather was squally, gusting to a sharp gale when the showers came on, but with scarcely any breeze between times" (chapter 18). Sunshine and gaiety almost always harbor a thundercloud that grows increasingly more menacing, turning the casual into the inevitable. We are plunged from hope to despair, from merriment to apprehension, where the first is almost the prerequisite for the second. The comic and tragic often stand side by side.

Although the central theme is basically tragic, the postlude ends on an upbeat. The genealogies continue, the life process begins anew, balance is restored. This is essentially the comic rhythm, and it is probably for this reason that some of the tragic impact is lost. Perhaps the formal structure is too mechanical, too pat, the detachment too great for us to become really involved with the characters. Be that as it may, the author has combined the comic and tragic elements to enhance his basic notion. Destiny and the moral code are brilliantly displayed in the precision of his form which reflects the rigidity and mechanical quality of this conception of life. Although its romantic theme sets it apart from most of the other sagas, and although Gudrún is one of the most well-drawn characters in saga literature, *Laxdoela* is not primarily a story of character development. It is more than a tragedy of human beings; it is the tragedy of a way of life.

Out of his "givens" and within the framework of his all-pervasive design, the author has created a vivid illusion of historical actuality. With a sureness of touch he has woven his pattern, arranging his material from the past and present. The historical material, the occasional but deliberate appeal to authority (by using Ari Thorgilsson's name [the founder of Icelandic historical discipline] and including poems), the lavish use of proper names and proper settings all contribute to the illusion of actuality. We are in a real place, in a real time, and with real persons. It is the arrangement of these factors in a pattern that lifts the work outside of history and gives it symbolic significance beyond its discursive content. The author's awareness of the irretractable demands of wounded honor, of the lust for revenge and the greed for power, his perception of an unavoidable destiny, his dark consciousness of the inescapable entanglements of life "then" and "now" made it possible for him to conceive a work that embraces the spirit of the Commonwealth as well as the spirit of the Sturlunga Age. It can delight the twentieth-century reader with its freshness and unstilted idiom, its sensitivity to human nature, its cool detachment, and tautness of structure.

Notes

1. Parallels between the *Sturlunga saga* and *Laxdoela saga* were first noted by Kr. Kålund, *Aarbøger for nordisk oldkyndighed* (1901), p. 387; by Guðbrandur Vigfússon, *Origines Islandicae,* II (1905), 137; by Finnur Jónsson, *Litteratur historie* (2nd ed.; København, 1920-24) II, 551; by Andreas Heusler, *Deutsche Litteraturzeit* (1932), p. 2469. Einar Ó. Sveinsson, in his introduction to the *Laxdoela saga* (*Íslenzk fornrit* [Reykjavík, 1934], V, xxxii-xxxiv) discusses those passages in *Laxdoela* that indicate the influence of *Sturlunga saga* and aid in dating the *Laxdoela*. Cf. also Einar Ó. Sveinsson, *Dating the Icelandic Sagas* (Viking Society for Northern Research, Vol. III; London: University College, 1958), p. 73. Rolf Heller has recently gathered together all the passages from the *Sturlunga saga* which exhibit striking parallels with *Laxdoela* and which must have influenced the author. Cf. Rolf Heller, "Laxdoela saga und Sturlunga saga," *Arkiv för nordisk filologi,* LXXVI (1961), 112-33.

2. Cf. *Þórðar saga kakala* in the *Sturlunga saga,* edited by Jón Jóhannesson, Magnús Finnbogason, and Kristján Eldjárn (Reykjavík, 1946), II, chapter clxxxiv (supplementary fragment), 283.

3. Cf. the article by Björn M. Ólsen, "Landnámabók und Laxdæla," *Aarbøger for nordisk oldkyndighed* (1908), pp. 151-232. The version used by the author of *Laxdoela* seems to have been an earlier redaction than the extant one of *Landnámabók.*

4. *Laxdoela* shows evidence that the author has been influenced by the Eddic poems, especially in the characters of the women—Melkorka, Thorgerd, and Gudrún. There are also many thematic parallels (in some cases even in the very wording) between Brynhilde and Sigurd on the one hand and Gudrún and Kjartan on the other. But the Gudrún of the saga also reflects the *Edda* Gudrún as well as Brynhilde. Association was probably made through the sameness of the names. This is also no doubt the case where the saga Gudrún has attracted the author to the Gudrún in *Guðmundar saga dýra* (in the *Sturlunga saga*), from which he assimilated some themes. Some of the more striking passages for comparison are: *Edda,* "Guðrúnarkviða I" (verses 9 and 10), and *Laxdoela* chapter 13, where Melkorka has been forced to serve the master and mistress of the house in the shoes and stockings episode, and in the master's (Hoskuld's) relationship to the servant; *Edda,* "Grípisspá" (verse 53), and *Laxdoela* chapter 33, where Gudrún mentions that Gest could have given fairer prophecies if the dreams had so warranted; *Edda,* "Guðrúnarkviða II" (verse 30), and *Laxdoela* chapter 42, where Bolli says that Gudrún may be sitting some years husbandless; *Edda,* "Guðrúnarhv_ot" (verse 2), and *Laxdoela* chapter 48, where Gudrún eggs her brothers on to attack Kjartan; *Edda,* "Sigurðarkviða in skamma" (verse 30), and *Laxdoela* chapter 49, where Gudrún gloats over Hrefna's grief that she won't be going to bed laughing that night; *Edda,* "Sigurðarkviða in skamma" (verses 31 and 32), and *Laxdoela* chapter 49, where Bolli tells Gudrún that she wouldn't have turned less pale at the news that he (Bolli) had been killed instead of Kjartan; *Edda,* "Guðrúnarkviða I" (verse 1 and the refrain lines in verses 2, 5, and 11), and *Laxdoela* chapter 50, where it is stated that Hrefna died of a broken heart; *Edda,* "Brot Sigurðkviða" (verses 8 and 10), and *Laxdoela* chapter 55, where Thorgerd praises Steinthór for the "work of his hands" in killing Bolli.

5. A work as recent as Marco Scovazzi's *La Saga di Hrafnkell e il problema delle saghe islandesi* (Editrice Libreria Paideia, 1960) takes issue with Nordal's *Hrafnkatla* and reasserts the oral and historical origin of this saga.

6. Sigurður Nordal, *Hrafnkatla, Íslenzk fræði 7* (Reykjavík, 1949). An English translation by R. George Thomas (Cardiff, 1958) has appeared under the title: *Hrafnkel's Saga Freysgoða: A Study.*

7. I refer the reader to my forthcoming publication, *The Structural and Formal Elements of the Laxdoela saga,* Vol. XL of *Islandica* (Cornell University Press).

Peter Foote (essay date 1964)

SOURCE: Foote, Peter. Introduction to *The Laxdale Saga,* translated by Muriel Press, pp. v-xvi. London: J. M. Dent & Sons Ltd, 1964.

[*In the following excerpt from his introduction to a revised edition of Muriel Press's 1899 translation of the* Laxdaela Saga, *Foote discusses the epic subtext of the poem, its idealized characters, and its generally clear, unassuming style.*]

Laxdæla saga, the saga of the men of Salmon-river-dale, was written in Iceland about A.D. 1250. The author was at home in the Dales, the inner districts of Breiðifjörðr, the scene of most of the action of the story.

The saga is the work of a mature and sophisticated artist. After the unique *Egils saga Skalla-Grímssonar,* written perhaps some twenty-five years earlier, it is the second of the sagas of Icelanders to be conceived and executed on a grand scale. In so far as it is permissible to speak of the development of these sagas as a *genre,* irrespective of the idiosyncrasies and merits of individual authors, the ***Laxdæla saga*** may be said to mark a culmination and a turning-point. Before it lay a period of about sixty years of practice in the composition of sagas of this kind. In that time the saga-writers established a style and method of narration and achieved freedom and flexibility in their treatment of the stories they chose to tell about Icelandic heroes of the so-called Saga Age, the century from about A.D. 930 to 1030. The conventions thus existed for the author of the ***Laxdæla saga*** to follow or adapt, and there was nothing to deter his imagination from shaping as it would the great heroic and romantic drama that lies at the heart of his story. After it was written there followed another period of something over half a century in which many more sagas were written. They include the nearly flawless *Hrafnkels saga* and the majestic *Njáls saga,* but in general this period is one of decline. It is not so much a decline in literary competence, however, for in some ways the writers become more and more fluent and adept in handling literary artifice, to the extent that effects of excitement or suspense or pathos often seem bought on the cheap, but the falling-off lies rather in an unwillingness to treat serious themes in a sustainedly serious way. The *Laxdæla saga* was a deservedly popular and influential work, but to some extent it foreshadows the decline to come, not least in a certain preference its author shows for ornament above substance in the presentation of masculine character. As may be expected, it was easier to imitate the weaknesses of its author than to emulate his great achievements.

A saga like *Laxdæla saga* may be described by a paraphrase of a well-known definition of epic: it is a long story with history in it. The chief people in it were real Icelanders of the tenth and early eleventh centuries. The family relationship described, for example, and things such as Gudrun's four marriages, or Kjartan's stay as a hostage at the court of King Olaf Tryggvason while the conversion of Iceland to Christianity was in the balance, or his death in a feud against the sons of Osvif—these are historical facts. Some of the historical framework must have been common knowledge in the author's day, some he could learn from books. Most important among the latter was a twelfth-century work, now lost, on the settlement of Iceland, probably chiefly compiled by Ari Thorgilson, the 'Deep-in-lore', who lived from 1067 to 1148 (cf. pp. 6, 269).[1] From the critical point of view of the modern historian, the interest of the *Laxdæla saga* as a source must depend almost exclusively on the author's borrowing of genealogical and chronological information from this early work.

The author was familiar with other written stories, and he refers to two of them by name (pp. 235, 239). He also knew many family and local traditions, and he had heard many stories, of all kinds, that were passed around by word of mouth. What he may have learnt from these in the way of matter and technique is naturally hard to investigate. Even if we are able to decide with some degree of probability what is drawn from local tradition and what is the product of the author's imagination, we are still faced with the virtually insoluble problem as to how far any tradition generally current in the author's day was faithful to the historical facts. Sometimes, as in the story of the execution of the family of Kotkell the wizard, for example, or the story of Harri the ox (pp. 121, 124, 95), a connection is made with place-names, and the author may well be repeating local tales, however little or much truth there may be in them. But the combination of such anecdotes with other matters that have an important bearing on the general progress of the narrative is clearly the result of the author's imaginative ordering. Although it may be thus difficult to distinguish between traditional and imaginative elements, we may certainly admire the author's skill in introducing what is intrinsically interesting and exciting, some of it certainly from traditional tales, in such a way as to serve the larger purposes of his story-telling.

It can also be seen that the author's imagination was prompted by accounts, written and oral, of occurrences in Iceland in his own lifetime and in that of the preceding generation. Perhaps the most striking instance of this is to be found in the parallel between the following event, which occurred in 1244, and the description of the action of Helgi Hardbeinson when he meets Gudrun after the death of Bolli (p. 197):

> A party of men under the leadership of Ásbjörn Guðmundarson and Björn Dufgusson set on a man called Magni, a supporter of the enemies of the Sturlungs. Björn gave him a wound which appeared mortal—'At that Ásbjörn came up and asked why he did not kill him. Björn said he had done as much as he was going to. Asbjörn then went to Magni and cut off his head. Then Vígdís Markúsdóttir, Magni's wife, came up. Ásbjörn dried the blood off his sword on her clothes; and she called down many curses on them and prayed God to be quick to avenge on them their crime.'[2]

Helgi's similar action in wiping his spear on the end of Gudrun's shawl is barbaric enough, but the author has turned Ásbjörn's piece of raw savagery to artistic account. The characters of Helgi himself, of Gudrun and of Halldor are deepened by the episode, and the whole narrative gains by the link forged with the future: we looked forward to the birth of the younger Bolli and the vengeance to be taken on Helgi.

Out of materials such as these, fused and moulded by the working of a powerful imagination, the author has made an ample family chronicle, which in its middle part is raised to the level of the tragic heroic. This is the part which makes *Laxdæla saga* the famous work it is, and on this the memory dwells. The story of Kjartan, Bolli and Gudrun is the story of two men and a woman, and the woman loves the man who is not her husband. This is a common theme in the story-telling of any age, and it was popular in Iceland, where a number of early sagas show the same basic situation. It must however seem a rare twist to this well-tried tale, when we find that the wife urges her husband to bring about the death of the man she truly loves. This is what happens in the legend of Sigurd the dragon-slayer, preserved in antique form in some of the poems of the *Edda*.[3] Sigurd ought to be the husband of Brynhild, he is the *nonpareil* to whom she can fittingly give herself, but instead, by a deceit, she is married to Gunnar, his friend. Sigurd is married to Gudrun, Gunnar's sister. When Brynhild discovers the deceit and after quarrelling with Gudrun, she incites Gunnar to kill Sigurd, and he is an accomplice in his murder. Brynhild's motive is double-edged, in keeping with the hard heroic outlook of this early poetry. On the one hand her integrity demands that the mind-disturber, the temptation, should be removed; on the other hand her pride cannot be content with the second best she knows her husband to be. The death of Sigurd removes the cause of her conflicting loyalties, and after his death her husband would achieve the pre-eminence that satisfies her pride. Her feelings toward Sigurd are never those of hatred, but she is glad that his death means he can be no longer enjoyed by his wife, Gudrun, for whom she feels rankling jealousy and swollen malice. Sigurd falls as a sacrifice that must cause terrible hurt to Brynhild, but her hatred of Gudrun is satisfied and her self-respect is whole, finally fulfilled by self-inflicted death, joining Sigurd on his funeral pyre.

There is here an essential key to the understanding of Gudrun's conduct in the *Laxdæla saga.* It is only necessary to replace the names of Brynhild and Sigurd, Gunnar and Gudrun, by those of Gudrun and Kjartan, Bolli and Hrefna, and the illumination is given. But it cannot of course be the whole story, partly because the author has to transpose this ancient legend in terms that suit an aristocratic farming society against a familiar Icelandic background of time and place, and partly because he is writing within a convention that imposes its own requirements on the form of the narrative. An essential part of the attitude and technique of the saga-writers depends on the fact that, although they themselves create the personalities of their characters, they yet choose to know those characters imperfectly, as if they were witnesses of their conduct and not the manipulators of it. They only go part way in imposing the characters of their story on the reader, who is given the illusion that he too is a witness, hearing and observing side by side with the writer. The author guides our imagination by describing, at certain selected moments only, the action and speech of the people, but the exploration of the possibilities inherent in their characters is left largely to our own creative curiosity. The author of the *Laxdæla saga* thus does not overtly attempt to work out the implications of the relationships between Gudrun, Bolli and Kjartan. Insight into Gudrun's mind is given on several occasions, into Kjartan's almost never. No attempt is made to convey Bolli's feelings, the conflict, the ignominy and affliction of his mind both before and after the death of Kjartan, but just once, when it can make its most devastating impact, Bolli's words give us our deepest glimpse into the seething passions that lie just below the surface of this 'volcanic saga'. This is in the exchange between Gudrun and Bolli after his return from the slaying of Kjartan:

> Then spake Gudrun, 'Harm spurs on to hard deeds; I have spun yarn for twelve ells of homespun, and you

have killed Kjartan.' Bolli replied, 'That unhappy deed might well go late from my mind even if you did not remind me of it.' Gudrun said, 'Such things I do not count among mishaps. It seemed to me you stood in higher station during the year Kjartan was in Norway than now, when he trod you under foot when he came back to Iceland. But I count that last which to me is dearest, that Hrefna will not go laughing to her bed tonight.' Then Bolli said, and right wroth he was, 'I think it is quite uncertain that she will turn paler at these tidings than you do; and I have my doubts as to whether you would not have been less startled if I had been lying behind on the field of battle, and Kjartan had told the tidings.'

Nothing could be more vitally concentrated or more ambiguously revealing.

The movement of the narrative in the first part of the book is easy paced. Each episode is told as if for its own sake, but they all bring development to the story of Hoskuld and of Olaf the Peacock, his son. The *tempo* quickens when we arrive at the generation which is to play out the tragic central story, and episode follows episode in which the future is foreshadowed: the curse on the sword Foot-biter, Olaf's dream after the slaughtering of Harri the ox, Gest Oddleifson's interpretation of Gudrun's dreams and his dark forebodings about Kjartan and Bolli—and there are many other minor notes of premonition. The story of Kjartan and Bolli in Norway, essential for the construction of the whole, is made into a rounded episode, but in Iceland events move swiftly and naturally on to the slaying of Kjartan, the vengeance on Bolli, and in time to the death of Helgi Hardbeinson. Thereafter a gentler pace is resumed, interest dies away, family chronicle returns, though now the story is not much of the men of Herdholt but more of Gudrun's sons by Bolli and of her last husband, Thorkell Eyjolfson. Only at the end does the author, with a consummate sense of timing, lead us back to the great riddle and the real reason why the story was told, when Gudrun, pressed by her son's questioning, says: 'To him I was worst whom I loved best.'

Of the characters in the saga it is the women who have outstanding vitality and naturalness. There is a whole series of striking portraits, Unn, Vigdis the wife of Thord Goddi, Jorunn, Thorgerd, Breeches-Aud, Thordis Olaf's daughter, and, of course, Gudrun herself. It is appropriate that the saga begins and ends with pictures of two old women, who after imperious and momentous careers are now described with small authentic touches that firmly anchor them in our own sort of reality: Unn the matriarch, who did not like to be asked about her health, and Gudrun, given to solitude and piety but devoted to her granddaughter and glad when her son came to visit her. By contrast the chief men, Olaf, Kjartan and Bolli Bollison, appear still more wooden. The last of these never becomes real at all, while Olaf makes a more natural impression as the solicitous peace-loving father of grown-up sons than he does as the glorified young prince seeking his royal grandfather in Ireland, and Kjartan becomes somewhat more human when he takes his petty and effective revenge on the men of Laugar. But in general the author gives them small scope to persuade us of their outstanding abilities, and they win the high esteem of mighty men far too cheaply. In Kjartan's case an intentional resemblance to the flawless Sigurd of heroic legend may have been sought, but the idealization of these characters must also be partly due to the influence of the lifeless and hyperbolic perfection of the heroes of southern romance, literature that was becoming fashionable in Scandinavia in the lifetime of the author of *Laxdæla saga.* Influence from the same source may also be detected in the author's taste for the courtly and stately, his love of clothes and colours, the magnificent and the vaguely beautiful. In his description of individuals, he is usually content with brief, stereotyped and rather more than life-size phrases—a more elaborate portrait of Kjartan (pp. 86-7) is an idealized picture of virile beauty, not of any single man. The great exception to this general rule is found in the description he gives of the men who are to attack Helgi Hardbeinsson (pp. 220-3), although here much attention is also paid to their clothes and trappings. It is a patent literary device, this episode, and one of venerable antecedents, but few of us would be willing to lose this fascinating series of rapid sketches, where we see real Icelandic faces, spoilt only by the description of young Bolli as 'aged [literally, swollen] with grief'.

The style of the author has an unassuming ease and propriety, it is smooth yet powerful, an impression not seriously affected by an occasional emptiness of phrase. The story moves on naturally and inevitably, and the whole book must be counted a masterpiece of construction when we consider the great range of the materials to be welded together. The self-effacing manner of the writing concentrates our attention on the progress of the narrative, but the author often surprises us with some quick and unexpected observation of human nature or of a life-like scene—Thord's generous appreciation of Aud's conduct in attacking him (p. 111), the bondswoman's description of Stigandi, the evil outcast, her lover, '—and in my eyes very handsome' (p. 123), the picture of Kjartan 'slipping on a red tunic' as he overhears the talk of which woman should have precedence at the feast (p. 161). There are many other moments, great and small, when we recognize the author's mastery, a mastery which reaches its height in his profound realization of the tragic theme at the saga's centre.

Notes

1. On Ari, cf. the Introduction to Snorri Sturluson, *Heimskringla* (Everyman's Library, No. 847, 1961); G. Turville-Petre, *Origins of Icelandic Literature* (Oxford, 1953), pp. 88 ff., especially pp. 102-8.

2. Guðbrandur Vigfússon, *Sturlunga saga* (Oxford, 1878), ii. 38.

3. The saga shows closest connections with the very ancient fragmentary poem called *Brot of Sigurðarkviðu* and the much younger *Sigurðarkviða in skamma.*

Magnus Magnussen (essay date 1969)

SOURCE: Magnussen, Magnus. Introduction to *Laxdaela Saga,* translated by Magnus Magnussen and Hermann Pálsson, pp. 9-44. Harmondsworth, England: Penguin Books, 1969.

[*In the following excerpt, Magnussen summarizes the plot, theme, style, and historical and literary contexts of the* Laxdaela Saga.]

Of all the major Icelandic sagas, *Laxdæla Saga* has always stirred the European imagination the most profoundly. More than any other of the classical prose sagas of medieval Iceland it is essentially a romantic work; romantic in style, romantic in taste, romantic in theme, culminating in that most enduring and timeless of human relationships in story-telling, the love-triangle. Gudrun Osvif's-daughter, the imperious beauty who married her lover's best friend against her will and then, in a rage of jealousy, forced her husband to kill her former lover and forfeit his own life thereby, is enshrined for all time in the gallery of great tragi-romantic heroines in world literature.

It was written by an unknown author around the year 1245, as nearly as can be deduced, at a time when the Age of Chivalry was at its fullest flower in continental Europe, when knights were dedicated to the service of the Church against the infidel, and tournaments and courtly love were the standard pastimes of the feudal aristocracy. *Laxdæla Saga* reflects a European outlook and attitude more than any of the other major sagas of the thirteenth century; and yet it is also one of the most essentially Icelandic of all the sagas, the truest of the Family Sagas proper, a dynastic chronicle that sweeps from generation to generation for 150 years from the Settlement of Iceland by the Norsemen late in the ninth century. In this sense, in the care with which the dawn of Iceland's history is recorded and interpreted in saga terms, *Laxdæla Saga* is also something of a national epic, giving to this young nation's past a dignity and grandeur which it seemed to lack in comparison with older and more powerful neighbour-states.

Although *Laxdæla Saga* is best known for the love-story of Gudrun Osvif's-daughter, it is a much more complex saga than that; indeed, the 'Gudrun episode' comes relatively late in the saga (Chapter 32 onwards), and the pattern of the saga in the earlier chapters is not immediately apparent to the modern reader—particularly one who is waiting impatiently for Gudrun to take the stage. And yet it is vitally important to discern and understand this saga pattern, as thirteenth-century audiences would have had no difficulty in doing; the early episodes not only set the scene for the Gudrun tragedy but also give it more texture and meaning, for Gudrun and the men who loved her are caught up in an extraordinary web of conflicting kinships and loyalties. Far from being a series of disconnected episodes, the early action of the saga has an intense bearing on what follows; for *Laxdæla Saga* is a saga of property as well as passion, a story of lands as well as loves, and the great diversity of character and incidents in the early stages are all designed to show how the wealth and property inherited by Gudrun's lover, Kjartan Olafsson, were amassed by his ancestors. It is only when Kjartan's standing is established that the author turns to another branch of the Laxriverdale family, and the two family streams meet in fatal confluence.

It is not easy to find a meaningful analogy for this particular form of saga pattern. Perhaps it could be compared to the course of a long river, starting in a slow trickle and splitting into two streams, but gradually increasing in volume and power as new tributaries swell its waters; these tributaries give the saga-pattern a herring-bone effect in places, for the author often jumps from the main flow to trace a tributary right from its source. When the two major streams converge again the river develops an irresistible current that sweeps everything along with it; the central tragedy forms currents which the characters are helpless to avoid, and which only the strongest can survive. Finally, the saga flows into broader, calmer waters, a serene estuary as the survivors of the tragedy drift tranquilly to their old age and quiet deaths.

Throughout its course, the saga changes in texture in the same way as the nature of a river is determined by the terrain through which it flows. *Laxdæla Saga* begins in the remote past, in a different land, with different customs and different problems; Iceland is then virgin territory, and the river drives its own path where it will as it comes pouring down from the mountains of the pagan, rather mysterious hinterlands of history. With it, it brings the glacial debris of its past, the boulders and

silt that it sweeps down into the lusher reaches to create hidden currents and rapids as it moves through a deceptively lyrical, Christianized lowland landscape. Indeed, one of the most memorable aspects of *Laxdæla Saga* is the way in which the style and nature of the story alter subtly as the generations succeed one another.

The saga opens in Norway with a fleeting glimpse of the heroic period of Scandinavia. As King Harald Fine-Hair of Norway consolidates the power of his throne in the second half of the ninth century, the more independent-minded chieftains decide to emigrate. One of them is Ketil Flat-Nose (does his nickname suggest a Lappish origin?); he himself decides to settle in Scotland, but his sons emigrate to newly-discovered Iceland, and it is to Iceland, too, that his strong-willed daughter, Unn the Deep-Minded, eventually comes after some hazardous adventures in Scotland (Chapters 1-5). It is from one of Ketil's sons, Bjorn the Easterner, and from his daughter, Unn the Deep-Minded, that the two main streams of this family chronicle are descended.

In the first section of the saga (Chapters 1-31) the main narrative follows the fortunes of Unn's descendants. Unn is the archetypal pioneer, a forceful matriarch who establishes dynasties in Scotland, Orkney and the Faroe Islands by marrying off her grand-daughters to carefully-chosen suitors. When she comes to Iceland she lays claim to an enormous area of land in the virgin territory of Breidafjord, on the west coast, which she parcels out to her followers with due regard to their social standing, lineage and intrinsic merit (Chapter 6).

To her grandson, Olaf Feilan, she leaves her own estate of Hvamm (Chapter 7); Olaf Feilan fades from the saga immediately, but three generations later his family line is destined to emerge into the saga again, for his great-grandson, Thorkel Eyjolfsson, becomes the fourth husband of Gudrun Osvif's-daughter (Chapter 68).

It is the family line of another of Unn's grandchildren, Thorgerd, that the saga now follows; for when Thorgerd marries Dala-Koll her dowry is the whole of Laxriverdale (Chapter 5), and it is with the fortunes of the Laxriverdale dynasty, the 'Laxdalers' of the title, that *Laxdæla Saga* is most concerned. Every incident that now follows is seen to have a bearing on the eventual appearance of one of the most illustrious figures in that family, Olaf the Peacock, the father of Kjartan Olafsson.

Dala-Koll is succeeded by his son, Hoskuld Dala-Kollsson (Chapter 7), who quickly establishes himself as a forceful and ambitious chieftain. His widowed mother, Thorgerd, restlessly emigrates to Norway where she marries again and has a son, Hrut Herjolfsson, who is Hoskuld's half-brother (Chapter 8). When she dies,

Hoskuld takes possession of her whole estate, and clearly has no intention of allowing his half-brother to claim his rightful share.

Hoskuld, ever anxious to improve his position, looks for a marriage alliance that will add to his wealth and power, and marries the daughter of a wealthy farmer up north (Chapter 9). But his bride, Jorunn, turns out to be a hard woman, steely-tempered and wasp-tongued, and the marriage, despite a litter of children, is loveless. Two sons are introduced—Thorleik Hoskuldsson, who takes after his mother's side of the family, and Bard Hoskuldsson, who is his exact opposite, sweet-natured and generous-hearted.

At this point the saga abruptly turns aside to explore the first of the 'herring-bone' tributaries. A man called Hrapp of Hrappstead is briefly introduced, a disagreeable Hebridean (like so many other stock villains in this and other sagas) who is excessively brutal to his neighbours (Chapter 10). He is one of Hoskuld's neighbours in Laxriverdale; but his significance in the saga-pattern is not fully apparent until after his death (Chapters 17-18); for Hrapp's ghost haunts the farm at Hrappstead so viciously that the people flee from it. When Hrapp's brother-in-law, Thorstein Black the Wise, attempts to settle there he and all his immediate family are drowned as they are sailing across Breidafjord; and the disaster is attended by an enormous seal with human eyes. . . . Thus, through Hrapp's baleful supernatural activities, the Hrappstead lands remain deserted and ownership falls into the hands of a farmer in another district, Thorkel Fringe, who has no desire to farm them himself (Chapter 18). This is an important sub-theme in the saga; but its significance does not emerge until some time later, when the Hrappstead lands are bought by Olaf the Peacock (Chapter 24). So it is on this haunted estate, its name changed to Hjardarholt but still shadowed by the malignant shade of Hrapp, that Kjartan Olafsson grows up.

Immediately after Hrapp of Hrappstead is first introduced another important sub-theme is begun, with the entry of another of Hoskuld Dala-Kollsson's neighbours, Thord Goddi (Chapter 11). This is an even more tortuous tributary, but it, too, leads towards Olaf the Peacock, as follows: Thord Goddi is married to a mettlesome woman called Vigdis Ingjald's-daughter (a granddaughter of Olaf Feilan, incidentally, cf. Genealogical Table No. 5); the two of them become involved in giving shelter to a penniless outlaw, Thorolf, who had killed the brother of a powerful local chieftain, Ingjald Saudisle-Priest (Chapter 14). When Ingjald comes to kill the outlaw, Vigdis and her craven husband fall out; Vigdis routs the visitors and divorces her husband for his cowardice. Then Vigdis tries to claim half the marital estate in a divorce settlement; but to prevent her

getting her hands on any of his money, Thord Goddi goes to Hoskuld Dala-Kollsson and makes over all his wealth to him in trust for Hoskuld's son, Olaf the Peacock, whom he now takes into fosterage, being childless himself (Chapter 16).

But we have over-run the story in following these two meandering tributaries to the point where they flow into the main narrative stream; for they are digressions from the story of Hoskuld Dala-Kollsson, whom we left in Chapter 9 newly married to Jorunn. Hoskuld now decides to go abroad to fetch timber from Norway with which to build himself a home suited to his stature in the community (Chapter 11). But timber is not, apparently, his only aim, for while he is abroad he buys himself a beautiful young concubine (Chapter 12). Jorunn of the steely temper is little pleased when he brings this domestic acquisition back to Iceland; but her jealousy is only really aroused when it is revealed that the concubine is no mere slave-girl but a lady of impeccable aristocratic birth—Melkorka, the daughter of an Irish king (Chapter 13). Hoskuld, however, is delighted with this revelation, for he always laid great store by wealth and breeding; and now he gives all his love and devotion to the illegitimate son his concubine had borne him—Olaf the Peacock.

When Hoskuld's half-brother, Hrut Herjolfsson, comes to Iceland and claims his share of their mother's estate Hoskuld refuses to hand it over, and a bitter quarrel between the brothers ensues; but the quarrel is settled just short of fratricide (Chapter 19). Hoskuld is now mellowing into old age, and our attention turns to the growing brilliance and renown of Olaf the Peacock, the apple of his father's eye. His mother, Melkorka, is anxious that he should go to Ireland to vindicate his noble lineage, and to provide him with the necessary capital (and to spite Hoskuld) she marries a local farmer, Thorbjorn the Feeble (Chapter 20). Olaf sets off on a triumphant progress abroad, and meets his grandfather in Ireland (Chapter 21). King Myrkjartan fêtes him and flatters him, and even offers him the succession to the throne, but Olaf politely declines and returns to Iceland in a blaze of glory (Chapter 22). Back in Iceland, Hoskuld plans for Olaf an ambitious dynastic marriage into the family of the great warrior-poet, Egil Skalla-Grimsson of Borg. The daughter, Thorgerd, at first refuses to marry a mere concubine's son, but is dazzled and swept off her feet when Olaf turns up to woo her in person (Chapter 23). Olaf now buys the deserted lands of Hrappstead, as was mentioned earlier, and builds himself a handsome manor there, renaming it Hjardarholt (Chapter 23).

In contrast, Olaf's half-brother, Thorleik Hoskuldsson, lives up to the mean strain in his mother's ancestry, and gets involved in a brief flare-up of trouble with his uncle, Hrut Herjolfsson (Chapter 25).

Now Hoskuld Dala-Kollsson dies; on his death-bed, intent to the last on enhancing Olaf's standing, he manages to bequeath a third of the estate to Olaf by a trick—much to the displeasure of Hoskuld's disgruntled legitimate son, Thorleik (Chapter 26). In order to staunch the ill-feeling between them, Olaf magnanimously offers to foster Thorleik's son, Bolli (Chapter 27); so now Bolli Thorleiksson goes to stay at Hjardarholt, where he is brought up with his cousin and foster-brother, Olaf's eldest son, Kjartan Olafsson (Chapter 28).

Now the stage is set for the next generation to take over. Under the benign influence of Olaf the Peacock, Kjartan and Bolli grow up together absolutely devoted to one another, two young men of outstanding prowess and accomplishments; yet of the two, Kjartan always has the edge on Bolli, and Bolli grows up in the shadow of his more brilliant cousin (Chapter 28). With these two, the House of Hoskuld has reached its fullest flower; but two small episodes now cast a shadow of apprehension over this lyrical mood. Olaf the Peacock has a very disagreeable dream, ominously portending that he will see his favourite son drenched in blood one day (Chapter 31); and his daughter, Thurid, marries a rogue Norwegian, Geirmund the Noisy, whom Olaf had reluctantly brought back to Iceland from a voyage abroad (Chapter 29). When that marriage disintegrates, a sword with a curse on it comes into Olaf's family—the sword 'Leg-Biter', which is fated to cause the death of the most brilliant scion of the family; and the sword is given by Thurid to her cousin, Bolli Thorleiksson (Chapter 31). And with these fleeting shivers on the clear, sunlit waters of the river, the first section of the saga ends.

The second section, the core of the whole saga (Chapters 32-56), opens with the entry of the other main dynastic line from Ketil Flat-Nose—the descendants of Bjorn the Easterner: Osvif Helgason of Sælingsdale and his daughter Gudrun. In the same breath we hear of a minor property transaction in which Osvif buys some upland grazing in Sælingsdale on which to pasture his livestock in summer; and that shieling is to be the scene of tragedy later (Chapter 32).

And now one crucial chapter clenches the whole story together, through the medium of a sage, Gest Oddleifsson, who can foretell the future. In the course of one day he utters three prophecies that are to shape the rest of the saga narrative (Chapter 33).

He meets Gudrun, his kinswoman, a beautiful, self-confident young girl of only fourteen or fifteen, who tells him about four strange dreams she has had and asks him to interpret them. In one stroke her whole destiny is laid bare to us (as it was already known to the saga audience) when Gest Oddleifsson predicts that she will have four husbands. Later that day he comes to Hjardarholt at Olaf the Peacock's invitation; Gest has never seen the two cousins, Kjartan and Bolli, before, but now as he watches them swimming with some friends he prophesies with tears in his eyes that one day Bolli will stand over Kjartan's body, and earn his own death thereby. In a third, minor prediction, Gest prophesies that one day he himself and Osvif Helgason will be much closer neighbours (this comes true in Chapter 66, when they are buried in the same grave at Helgafell).

In this pivotal chapter the destinies of Gudrun and Kjartan (who have not yet met) are juxtaposed; and from now on, the saga narrative flows strong and clear as these prophecies are worked out.

Gudrun marries her first husband, much against her will, at the age of fifteen; he is a wealthy but pusillanimous man called Thorvald Halldorsson, whom she divorces after two years (Chapter 34).

Next she marries a man called Thord Ingunnarson; Thord is already married to a fierce-tempered woman called Aud, whom he divorces in order to marry Gudrun (at the cost of a vengeful sword-thrust that mutilates his chest and arm). The marriage between Thord and Gudrun is very happy; but now Thord tangles with a family of evil Hebridean sorcerers (Kotkel and his family), and is drowned by their spells (Chapter 35). Kotkel and his family are eventually wiped out, but not before they have embroiled the luckless Thorleik Hoskuldsson in yet another violent quarrel with his uncle, Hrut Herjolfsson (Chapter 37). The outcome of this is that Thorleik goes abroad for ever, leaving his son Bolli with Olaf the Peacock at Hjardarholt (Chapter 38).

And now Gudrun, with her second marriage over, meets Kjartan Olafsson, who starts making frequent visits to see her at the natural hot-spring baths in Sælingsdale. There is close friendship between their parents, Olaf and Osvif; but Olaf is obscurely uneasy at the growing love between Kjartan and Gudrun (Chapter 39). And always the faithful Bolli tags along with Kjartan, the inseparable companion who always comes second.

Kjartan is eager to seek fame and fortune abroad. He decides rather abruptly to go to Norway, and asks Gudrun to wait three years for him as his betrothed. Gudrun is put out by the suddenness of his decision and refuses, and they part rather huffily. Kjartan sails off to Norway, accompanied as always by Bolli (Chapter 40). They sail straight into trouble, for the King of Norway, Olaf Tryggvason, is putting tremendous political pressure on Iceland to accept Christianity. Kjartan's almost superhuman accomplishments are readily appreciated by King Olaf, and for the first time Bolli's submerged resentment of his more brilliant cousin breaks to the surface. They and their companions eventually are baptized, but Iceland is still proving stubborn; so King Olaf keeps Kjartan and three other Icelanders hostage in Norway in an attempt to exert more pressure on the leading chieftains of Iceland. Bolli is not held, however; and in the year 1000 (the third year of Kjartan's absence) Bolli returns to Iceland, leaving Kjartan with King Olaf enjoying the favour of the king's sister, Ingibjorg.

The first thing Bolli tells Gudrun when he returns to Iceland is that Kjartan looks as if he intends to settle in Norway, especially in the light of his intimate friendship with Ingibjorg. Then he proposes to Gudrun himself, and eventually Gudrun, grieved by Kjartan's apparent perfidy but much against her will none the less, is pressurized by her father and brothers into marrying Bolli (Chapter 43).

The following year, Kjartan Olafsson returns. News that Iceland had accepted Christianity reached Norway in the spring of the year 1001, and the moment that Kjartan is released by King Olaf he hurries to Iceland, brusquely breaking off his affair with Princess Ingibjorg—who nevertheless shows her regality by giving him an immensely valuable gold-woven head-dress as a wedding-present for Gudrun; and King Olaf gives him a sword which has the power of making him immune to all other weapons for as long as he carries it (Chapter 43). When Kjartan discovers that Gudrun is already married to his foster-brother he shows no outward signs of emotion; and soon he is persuaded to get married himself. His choice falls, casually enough, on Hrefna Asgeir's-daughter (sister of his former partner abroad, Kalf Asgeirsson), a girl as demure and sweet as Gudrun is ambitious and imperious; and to Hrefna he gives the coveted head-dress (Chapter 45).

The fierce jealousies and resentments inherent in this tense situation soon break out, despite Olaf the Peacock's constant efforts to keep the peace. Kjartan rudely snubs a generous gift offered by Bolli; in revenge, Gudrun's brothers steal Kjartan's sword, the sword that would have kept him safe from all weapons. And at a feast, Hrefna's priceless head-dress is also stolen mysteriously. Kjartan gives vent to his fury by humiliating Bolli and Gudrun and her family, by besieging their home for three days and denying them access to the outdoor privy (Chapter 47).

There is now open enmity between the two houses; and after some further spiteful exchanges, Gudrun at last goads Bolli and her brothers into making an attempt on Kjartan's life. They ambush him as he rides home down Svinadale with only two companions. Kjartan fights

them off while the reluctant Bolli stands aloof; but when Bolli at last joins in the battle, Kjartan throws down his weapons rather than fight his own foster-brother, and Bolli grimly and silently strikes him dead—with the sword 'Leg-Biter' (Chapter 49).

In a chilling passage, Gudrun gloats over Kjartan's death, and the grief it will cause Hrefna. But Bolli, deeply repenting what he has done, knows her better, and recognizes the frustrated love that has inspired the jealous rage in her breast. Hrefna moves north to her family home, where she dies of a broken heart (Chapter 50).

Olaf the Peacock strives desperately to heal the awful breach that has opened in his family; for three years, until his own death, he manages to secure an uneasy peace. But when his moderating influence is gone, Kjartan's brothers, goaded on by their mother Thorgerd (no less fierce and unforgiving than Gudrun herself), plan their revenge on Bolli. Helped by their uncle, Melkorka's son Lambi Thorbjornsson, and a warrior called Helgi Hardbeinsson, the Olafssons set upon Bolli in the summer shieling that Osvif had once bought, and kill him there (Chapter 55). Gudrun is pregnant at the time; and when one of the killers, Helgi Hardbeinsson, meets her and wipes his bloody spear on her sash, he prophesies that her unborn son will eventually cause his own death in revenge. The following spring, Gudrun gives birth to Bolli Bollason (Chapter 56).

The last section of the saga (Chapters 57-78) tells of the long and complex plans that Gudrun laid to avenge her husband Bolli, and of the final fulfilment of the prophecies. Once again, the author introduces two men in juxtaposition who are going to have a marked effect on Gudrun's destiny—Thorgils Holluson and Thorkel Eyjolfsson (Chapter 57). And now the complexities of kinship become very dense, for Thorgils is himself a descendant of Bjorn the Easterner, and as such is related to Gudrun, as well as to her dead husband, Bolli Thorleiksson, and her dead lover, Kjartan Olafsson; and he is also related, distantly, to Thorkel Eyjolfsson, through Ketil Flat-Nose.

Gudrun has by now moved from Sælingsdale to Helgafell, by exchanging homes with her great friend and mentor Snorri the Priest (Chapter 56). And now Thorgils Holluson begins to pay court to her assiduously. Gudrun is more concerned to have her late husband avenged, and will not even think of remarrying until that is achieved—and certainly not marrying Thorgils Holluson. But when her son, Bolli Bollason, is twelve years old and ready to fulfil his destiny as his father's avenger, Snorri the Priest thinks up an ingenious scheme whereby Thorgils Holluson can be used to further Gudrun's ends. Gudrun makes him an ambiguous promise of marriage on condition that he leads a punitive expedition against one of Bolli's killers, Helgi Hardbeinsson (Chapter 60). Bolli Bollason goes with him, and after a fierce defence Helgi is killed—by Bolli (Chapter 64). Gudrun now explains to Thorgils the ambiguity in her promise of marriage—she had only promised to marry no other man in the land than him, and Thorkel Eyjolfsson, whom Snorri the Priest had already decided should be her fourth husband, was abroad at the time. Thorgils leaves in a rage, and soon Snorri engineers his death to leave the way completely clear for Thorkel Eyjolfsson (Chapter 67).

Gudrun now marries Thorkel, who becomes a great chieftain (Chapter 68). Soon, however, Thorkel goes abroad to fetch timber for a church he intends to build at Helgafell; in Norway the king chides him for arrogance and forecasts that the timber will never be used for church-building (Chapter 74). That prediction comes true when Thorkel is drowned in Breidafjord, after taking part in an abortive attempt to purchase Hjardarholt (the property theme is never long absent in this saga). And so Gest Oddleifsson's four-fold prophecy about Gudrun's marriages is finally fulfilled (Chapter 77).

And now the survivors of this complex dynastic tragedy live out their lives. Bolli Bollason becomes a man of great pomp and magnificence, living in a blaze of chivalric courtliness; he marries Snorri's daughter, Thordis, and inherits his estate in Sælingsdale, the estate that Gudrun and Bolli had once owned. Gudrun's son by her fourth marriage, Gellir Thorkelsson, becomes a man of great influence and piety, and dies on his way home from a pilgrimage to Rome.

And Gudrun herself, after her passion-racked life, becomes a nun and Iceland's first anchoress; when she dies she is very old, and blind, and she is buried at Helgafell.

But before she dies, her son Bolli Bollason comes to see her. He is curious to know one thing about his mother's life: he asks her, 'Which man did you love the most?'

The old widow answers evasively at first, and merely gives a perfunctory catalogue of the qualities of her four *husbands*. But Bolli is insistent, and asks again, 'Which man did you love the most?' And now Gudrun answers, 'I was worst to the one I loved the most.'

It is the final, enigmatic confession of a woman seeking serenity and expiation after a cruelly passionate life; and Bolli is satisfied by it.

'And there this saga ends.'

Such is the bare outline of the 'plot' of the saga, the sequence of events that make up its narrative framework. Summarized in this way, it implies a certain historicity; but the concept of historicity has to be approached rather carefully in the Icelandic sagas. In the past, they have sometimes been treated as literal historical truth, because they could be shown to fit, more or less accurately, into the general context of the known early history of Iceland.

As far as *Laxdæla Saga* is concerned, most of the major characters are undoubtedly historical personages, and many of the major landmarks in their lives are corroborated by other historical sources. The *Icelandic Annals,* for instance, which briefly chronicle outstanding events year by year, record some of the main points of reference:

> 963 birth of Snorri the Priest (Gudrun's friend)
> 979 birth of Thorkel Eyjolfsson (Gudrun's fourth husband)
> 997 King Olaf Tryggvason sends Thangbrand to Iceland
> 1000 Christianity adopted in Iceland
> 1003 Kjartan Olafsson killed (Gudrun's lover)
> 1007 Bolli Thorleiksson killed (Gudrun's third husband)
> 1026 Thorkel Eyjolfsson drowned
> 1031 death of Snorri the Priest
> 1073 death of Gellir Thorkelsson, aged sixty-four (Gudrun's son by her fourth husband)

In addition, *Landnámabók* (Book of Settlements) makes sporadic references to Gudrun's husbands, which corroborate the fact that she was married four times—the central theme of the whole saga:

> 'The sons of Osvif were outlawed for the killing of Kjartan Olafsson. Osvif's daughter was Gudrun, the mother of Thorleik (Bollason), Bolli (Bollason), and Gellir (Thorkelsson).'

> '. . . Thorvald Halldorsson, who married Gudrun Osvif's-daughter.' (Gudrun's first husband, Chapter 34.)

> '. . . Thord Ingunnarson, who married Gudrun Osvif's-daughter.' (Gudrun's second husband, Chapter 35.)

> '. . . Bolli Thorleiksson, who married Gudrun Osvif's-daughter.' (Gudrun's third husband, Chapter 43.)

> '. . . Bolli Thorleiksson, who married Gudrun Osvif's-daughter. They had six children. . . . Gudrun had previously been married to Thord Ingunnarson. Her last husband was Thorkel Eyjolfsson.' (Gudrun's fourth husband, Chapter 68.)

It's not really surprising that *Laxdæla Saga* should be so well informed about Gudrun Osvif's-daughter, for Gudrun was the great-grandmother of Iceland's first vernacular historian, Ari Thorgilsson the Learned; and it is hard to avoid the conclusion that Ari the Learned (1068-1148) was a major source for Gudrun's life-story. The only extant historical work which can be ascribed to Ari with absolute certainty is *Íslendingabók* (or *Libellus Islandorum,* the Book of Icelanders), which he wrote around the year 1127; but he was in all probability one of the compilers of the original version of *Landnámabók* (Book of Settlements) in the first half of the twelfth century, and it is also thought by some scholars that he was the prime source of information for the entries in the *Icelandic Annals.*

On two occasions in **Laxdæla Saga,** Ari the Learned is specifically cited as a historical source (Chapters 4, 78); but such appeals to historical authority are not unusual in other sagas, and give no indication of the special importance of the family connexion between Gudrun and Ari the Learned for the creation of **Laxdæla Saga.** Gellir Thorkelsson, Gudrun's son by her fourth husband, was the father of Thorkel Gellison, who was Ari's uncle (Chapter 78); and in *Íslendingabók* and *Landnámabók,* Thorkel Gellison is cited more than once as a significant source of information, particularly for Ari's account in *Íslendingabók* about the Icelandic colonists in Greenland (cf. *The Vinland Sagas,* Penguin Classics, 1960, p. 26):

> Erik the Red went out to colonize Greenland fourteen or fifteen years before Christianity came to Iceland, according to what Thorkel Gellison was told in Greenland by a man who had himself gone there with Eirik the Red.

Elsewhere in *Íslendingabók,* Ari refers to him as 'my uncle Thorkel Gellison, who could remember far back'.

. . . . .

There are several . . . echoes of contemporary events in **Laxdæla Saga** which point to a deliberate manipulation of material for artistic ends, especially the rather complicated succession to the inheritance in the family of Thorstein Black the Wise when they all drowned in a single shipwreck (Chapter 18); there was a very similar legal wrangle in 1178, recorded in *Sturlunga Saga*—and the suspicion that the author of **Laxdæla Saga** may have borrowed this theme is strengthened by the fact that there is no suggestion in any other extant source that Thorstein Black the Wise, or any of his family, died by drowning. The story seems to have been invented in order to explain how the deserted lands of Hrappstead came into the possession of Thorkel Fringe.

Similarly, the many dreams and prophecies which the author uses to tauten the material of his narrative are essentially literary devices that cannot by definition be historically true—whether he himself invented them, or whether some of them had already accreted to various episodes of the story before he worked his material into its present literary form.

Indeed, it sometimes seems as if the more vivid, the more 'real', the more compellingly visualized a scene in an Icelandic Saga is, the less likely it is to be historically 'true'. The only valid 'historicity' in the sagas is not so much what it tells us about the history of Iceland as what it tells us about thirteenth-century attitudes to the history of Iceland. The saga-writers were not trying to write history in our sense of the term; they were trying to create an acceptable image of the past. And like great composers, they took themes, the written or unwritten folk-tunes of the nation's past, so to speak, and orchestrated them with their own literary skill and intellectual interpretations. To understand the historical value of the sagas, we have to understand what history meant to a saga-writer and his thirteenth-century audience.

Laxdæla Saga is strung between two historical poles, the two most significant events in the early history of Iceland—the Settlement, from about 870 onwards, and the Conversion to Christianity in the year 1000. These two major national events form the background of the whole saga age, and permeate most of the major sagas. In *Laxdæla Saga* they form a twin polarity, for the physical demands of the Age of Settlement and the intellectual demands of the Age of Christianity affected the motivation of people in markedly different ways. They thicken the texture of the narrative and give extra meaning to it. In some sagas, like *Njal's Saga,* for instance, the Conversion is the more important of the two events; the events leading to the Conversion are described at considerable length, and the impact of Christianity on the major characters has a decisive effect on the course and the meaning of the narrative. In *Laxdæla Saga* the Conversion has one decisive effect on the plot, because it is the year that Kjartan Olafsson spends in Norway as a hostage while King Olaf Tryggvason was putting political pressure on Iceland that cost him the chance to win Gudrun's hand in marriage; but apart from that, the impact of the Age of Christianity is not explored so subtly as in *Njal's Saga.* In *Laxdæla Saga* the Age of Settlement is the more meaningful.

We know a great deal about the Age of Settlement as a whole, chiefly from *Landnámabók,* whose extant versions record the names and families of some 400 of the original settlers and brief anecdotes about them. This and other accounts of the Settlement may not be entirely reliable; but this was how the Icelandic antiquarians saw the birth of their nation, and, to them, remembering the past was not an idle pastime, but a matter of extreme importance.

In the first place, it had a functional importance. It was necessary to remember how much land was claimed by each settler, and how the land was claimed. Future land-claims would always relate back, through the memory of witnesses, to the various stages of ownership that the land had passed through—who had inherited from whom, how extensive the land was, where the boundaries lay; in *Laxdæla Saga* there is an example of the kind of trouble that could arise over a forgotten or disputed boundary title, when Hrut Herjolfsson inadvertently settled a freed slave on land that actually belonged to his neighbour (Chapter 25). This kind of necessary remembering helped to create a detailed tapestry of the physical landscape of the early settlements, which was further picked out with vivid folk etymologies of how places got their names—this is where Unn the Deep-Minded lost her comb, which is why it is called Kambsness, and this is the headland where she had her breakfast one morning long, long ago, and that is why it is called Dogurdarness (Chapter 5). Such anecdotes tell us nothing about the real life of the early Icelandic pioneers, but they throw an interesting light on the devoted interest that Icelanders of the twelfth and thirteenth centuries took in their ancestors.

Their purpose, like that of so many historians, was to justify the present in terms of the past. This is argued quite explicitly in *Landnámabók*:

> It is often said that writing about the Settlements is irrelevant learning, but we think we can all the better meet the criticisms of foreigners when they accuse us of being descended from slaves or scoundrels, if we know for certain the truth about our ancestry. And for those who want to know ancient lore and be able to trace genealogies, it is better to start at the beginning than to come in at the middle. And indeed, all civilized nations want to know about the origins of their own society, and the beginnings of their own race.

In precisely the same frame of mind, Geoffrey of Monmouth concocted a totally fictitious *History of the Kings of Britain* [Geoffrey of Monmouth, *The History of the Kings of Britain*, translated by Lewis Thorpe, Penguin Books, 1966.] in *c.* 1136 (the same period as the early Icelandic historians were documenting their own past), inventing for Britain a respectable past by promoting an obscure British war-leader of the early sixth century called Arthur to the status of a Christian Emperor of Europe descended from Rome. No one wants to be accused of being 'descended from slaves or scoundrels', and all nations tend to idealize their past. In *Laxdæla Saga* this idealization is positively romantic; the kings of Norway are wheeled on to the stage merely to fête and to flatter the illustrious Icelanders who visit them—Hoskuld Dala-Kollsson, Hrut Herjolfsson, Olaf the Peacock, Kjartan Olafsson, Bolli Bollason. Nobility of lineage is given excessive importance and colours the whole narrative; the saga constantly emphasizes the splendour and style in which the tenth-century men of Laxriverdale lived, and how they were accepted as men

of high importance in the royal courts of Scandinavia. The author's admiration for aristocratic genealogy knows no bounds, particularly in the case of Olaf the Peacock; the revelation that Olaf's mother Melkorka is in reality an Irish princess of the blood royal and not merely a slave concubine is crucial to the family's history. Olaf's sumptuous acceptance by his grandfather, King Myrkjartan of the Irish (Chapter 21), is a triumphant refutation of the lurking sneer about his birth that breaks to the surface every now and again—from Hoskuld's wife, Jorunn ('That concubine's son certainly has the wealth to ensure that his name is long remembered', Chapter 24); from the girl Olaf wanted to marry, Thorgerd Egil's-daughter ('. . . if you want to marry me to a concubine's son, no matter how handsome and flashily dressed he is', Chapter 23); from the princess Ingibjorg of Norway ('I want the women of Iceland to see that the woman whose company you have been keeping in Norway isn't descended from slaves', Chapter 43). What is really poignant about the author's attitude is that he was depicting these tenth-century Icelanders as the intimates, if not quite the equals, of kings at a time when thirteenth-century Iceland was being relentlessly crushed of its independence by the power-politics of the kings of Norway.

The harsh reality of Iceland's dwindling political independence in the thirteenth century (Iceland was eventually annexed by the crown of Norway in 1262), and the decades of savage internal strife that contributed to it, lent a desperate nostalgia to the image of the pioneering Age of Settlement. Relatively speaking, the birth of the Icelandic nation was very recent. To the twelfth-century historians, the Pagan Age was only three generations away (and easily bridged by reliable memory), and another three generations would take them right back to the beginnings. And these beginnings had been extraordinarily traumatic.

The Age of Settlement stands out in stark contrast to the Viking Age out of which it was born. Elsewhere the Scandinavian intrusions had been brutally disruptive, but in Iceland there had been nothing to disrupt, no long-established civilization to plunder or take over; the country was uninhabited except for a few Celtic monks who had come there in search of solitude, and who fled when the first Norsemen arrived. The newcomers did not even have to face up to the hostility of indigenous natives as their descendants had to do a century later, when they tried to colonize North America and were repulsed by the Red Indians. They were free to carve up the virgin island as they thought fit; and from out of the chaos of the Viking Age behind them, they had the opportunity of establishing a new system of order without interference from other states. They had come for a variety of reasons. Many, like Ketil Flat-Nose and his family (Chapter 2), seem to have believed they were escaping from the tyranny of King Harald Fine-Hair in Norway, and this may well be true—blended perhaps with the hope of being able to make a better livelihood in Iceland ('for they . . . heard . . . there was excellent land there . . . for the taking', Chapter 2). Others were outlaws, forced to leave Norway 'because of some killings', like Eirik the Red and his father (*The Vinland Sagas*).

Whatever their motives for coming, they were a disparate collection of people. Most of them were pagan, but some were already Christian, or had come into close contact with Christianity in the British Isles. Most were of Scandinavian blood, but some were Celtic or of mixed Norse and Celtic blood, first-generation Norsemen from the Scottish islands and Ireland. No one can be sure precisely where they came from, or precisely how mixed a population it was. But the mere fact of not having a common adversary to resist them must have made the problem of organizing the settlers politically into a coherent state all the more difficult. It has been suggested (by the late Barði Guðmundsson) that one reason why the new nation settled down so quickly into an organized state may have been because the bulk of the original settlers perhaps belonged to one particular tribe in Scandinavia (the Heruli?) whose community identity had not been completely lost by the time Iceland was discovered. This tribe would have had distinctive customs that marked them out from other Norwegians and would account for some of the distinctive, non-Norwegian features that have puzzled scholars about the new Icelanders—people who buried their dead instead of cremating them, people with a system of voluntary allegiance to priest-chieftains that was anti-monarchist in spirit, people with a tradition of esoteric 'court-poetry' that was almost exclusively composed by Icelanders, either in Iceland or in royal courts abroad. Such a tribe would have been more reluctant than most to tolerate the increasing centralization of political power in Norway when King Harald Fine-Hair was strengthening his authority over the whole country (cf. Chapter 2). It is certainly a striking theory, but it can be no more than a speculation that attempts to explain the astonishing feat of organization that the early pioneers brought about—a feat that the twelfth- and thirteenth-century antiquarians looked back on with amazement and awe.

As soon as the country was fully settled, despite the fact that it was larger than Ireland, with primitive communications and no village communities and no royal court to provide a focus, a common law was accepted for the whole country. The foundation of the Althing, the General Assembly, in A.D. 930, was a remarkable achievement to come out of that raw, impactual period; what characterized pagan Iceland and early Christian Iceland above anything else, setting it quite apart from any other medieval European country, was a dynamic veneration for law and order. The early Icelanders owed no allegiance to king or earl; their allegiance was primarily to the concept of law—and it is worth noting that *law*-breakers were sentenced not to death or imprisonment, but to out*law*ry. To be a member of society was at once a privilege and an obligation, and anyone who violated the law of society forfeited his right to remain within that law, within that society; they were banished from Iceland. That was how Iceland protected itself against disruptive elements.

The major flaw in this system was that the state had no executive power to enforce its punishment; that was left to society at large, which in most cases meant in effect the aggrieved party, if it was strong enough. The sagas constantly deal with themes of violence; this was not, as is often assumed, from any admiration for killings and vengeance, but arose from a deep concern about the seriousness of violent action, of taking the law into one's own hands. The saga-writers were interested in exploring these effects; they were more concerned with the motivation and consequences of violence than with the violence itself; death was only important in the effect it had on the people who caused it, and the people who suffered from its consequences.

In the sagas, crime is seen as a crime against society, rather than a crime against individuals; and more often than not it is the outcome of irregular relationships, a crime against the natural order of things. There are a remarkable number of irregular relationships in **Laxdæla Saga,** all of which lead to trouble; failures to 'observe . . . kinship properly'—like Hoskuld and Hrut (Chapter 19), and Olaf and Thorleik (Chapter 27); flawed marriages—like that of Thurid and Geirmund which introduces the fatal sword 'Leg-Biter' (Chapter 30), of Hoskuld and Jorunn which introduces Melkorka (Chapter 12), and above all the flawed marriage of Gudrun and Bolli which Gest had prophesied (Chapter 33). The most important moral and ethical concept in early Icelandic society was *drengskapr,* the idea of fairness of conduct; a crime like Bolli's in killing his fosterbrother could only come about when he lost—even though only momentarily—his sense of fairness, his sense of propriety of conduct. Anyone who takes up the wrong sort of challenge in the sagas, as a result of responding to the goadings of others, always comes out the loser in the end.

In the sagas it is not the great warriors who are the heroes, the men who could kill most people with fewest strokes; it is the sages, the men of moderation, the men like Njal of Bergthorsknoll or Olaf the Peacock who understand the awful futility of violence and devote their lives to combating it. There is less real admiration for Kjartan Olafsson, the peerless, than for his father,

Olaf the Peacock, the man of peace, the man of wisdom and responsibility who constantly thinks in terms of the good of the whole community: 'He was extremely well-liked, for whenever he intervened in other people's affairs he did it in such a way that everyone was satisfied' (Chapter 24). To him, vengeance was a purely negative attitude—'Bolli's death would not bring back my son', (Chapter 49)—and it was only after his death that the bitter anti-social hatreds he had striven to keep in check erupted again.

This idealization of the concept of law and order was in some ways no doubt a reflection of the nostalgia of thirteenth-century Icelanders, beset as they were by violence and political treachery on a scale undreamed of in the tenth century. They saw their hard-won freedom, their independent political institutions, being destroyed before their eyes; so it is little wonder that they thought of the tenth century as being more secure, more stable. And the most stabilizing influence, to them, seemed to be the chieftains, many of whom are heavily idealized. Unn the Deep-Minded sets the pattern in *Laxdæla Saga,* a standard of large-mindedness and concern for the community; it was the role of chieftains to protect, to supervise, to give cohesion to society—a role from which the thirteenth-century chieftains had abdicated so disastrously. And so, in retrospect, the thirteenth-century Christian writers in Iceland seldom felt or expressed rancour towards paganism; indeed, the author of *Laxdæla Saga* goes out of his way to do the opposite—'Pagans felt their responsibilities no less keenly when performing such ceremonies than Christians do now when ordeals are decreed', (Chapter 18).

But this tolerant attitude towards paganism, and even approval of the society which practised it, does not conceal the fact that the thirteenth-century authors were keenly aware of the barrier between themselves and the past—the barrier of Christianity. In so far as they were writing 'history', it was a very stylized history, a stylized image of the past that was being held up as a guiding light for later generations; and the very antiquarianism so evident in *Laxdæla Saga* is a measure of this. The thirteenth-century Christian man of learning, as our author undoubtedly was, could know something about the external phenomena of paganism, but he could not know the attitudes, the ethics; he could know details of ritual worship—but he could not know the real relationship between priest and worshipper, for instance, or fully understand the relationship between priest and gods.

Nor, surely, could he know about the emotions and motivations of people who had lived and died two centuries or more earlier. Emotions are ephemeral; the events remain, but they are interpreted in retrospect, subjectively, according to the experience of the individual. And one of the striking aspects of *Laxdæla Saga* which sets it a little apart from the other classical sagas is the extent to which the author describes the actual emotions felt by his characters.

The success of these thirteenth-century interpretations depended to a large extent on the intellectual and emotional capacity of the individual authors, and their own observations of human nature. The saga-writers were highly articulate authors whose intention was to create an atmosphere of actuality, and sagas are judged nowadays by the success with which they achieved this; they are praised for their objectivity, the cool impartiality with which they present events, whether good or bad. In some measure, this objectivity was natural to the learned medieval mind, which saw men not as good or evil but as a sum of actions, a synthesis of many elements both good and bad. Theology classified actions, rather than people; in the sagas, the only thoroughly evil people, the scoundrels like Hrapp and Kotkel, are symbols rather than characters; the others are a compound of both good and bad, of noble impulses and base motives, of fine and wicked deeds. Here, the book-learning of the thirteenth century helped to broaden the author's natural talents; and *Laxdæla Saga* is above all the product of a sophisticated, keenly-trained European mind.

Mercifully, the Icelandic Sagas have now lost most of their old Germanic glamour. They are now being treated at last as serious medieval literature, shorn of the spurious romanticism so dear to the nineteenth century. Past generations of scholars have often tended to see the sagas as products of the Noble Savage mind, as tribal expressions that realized tribal dreams; others have regarded them as great artistic achievements of the Native Genius, their authors being untutored and uninfluenced by current European ideals and tastes. *Laxdæla Saga* is certainly a home-grown product, sprung from Icelandic soil; but it also has its roots in European civilization, in the civilized medieval mentality of Europe—and one of its purposes, it could be argued, was to Europeanize Iceland's image, to give Iceland a European context.

This can be seen most clearly in the Gudrun-Kjartan-Bolli situation, where three distinct European cultures meet. Gudrun, partly at least, is a product of the heroic Germanic spirit; Kjartan, more complex, is a product of the Celtic medieval Christian spirit—but more than that, he is a composite of conflicting cultures and attitudes, of saint and warrior and knight combined; while Bolli, and more particularly his son Bolli Bollason, represents the European Age of Chivalry (it is only when Bolli finally breaks away from Kjartan in Norway and ceases to play second fiddle to him that he emerges as a character in his own right).

Take Gudrun first. In the native literature, there is a clear model for Gudrun. In the *Edda,* a collection of heroic and mythological poetry, the Nibelungen cycle tells the powerful and tragic story of Brynhild and her lovers. Brynhild, the Valkyrie, loves the peerless hero Sigurd Fafni's-Slayer, but is tricked into marrying the second-best, Sigurd's sworn-brother, Gunnar, while Sigurd marries Gunnar's sister, Gudrun. Like the Gudrun of *Laxdœla Saga,* Brynhild becomes fiercely jealous when she realizes how she has been tricked, and goads her husband Gunnar into having Sigurd killed (unlike Bolli, he has scruples about actually killing his sworn-brother himself). Brynhild commits suicide after Sigurd's death, and Sigurd's widow now marries Brynhild's brother, Atli, and Atli later kills Gunnar.

The *Edda* situation is obviously rather more intricate than the *Laxdœla Saga* situation, but the core of it is undoubtedly very similar; and there are also some suggestive verbal echoes between the two. The author clearly knew the *Edda* poems; indeed, it would be surprising if he had not known them, for this pagan legacy of heroic poetry was greatly treasured in thirteenth-century Iceland—vellum manuscripts of them were being copied out during that period, particularly the great *Codex Regius;* and Snorri Sturluson, the historian, was working on his *Prose Edda,* in which he retold some of these poems, not long before *Laxdœla Saga* itself was written. But one should beware of making too much of the parallels; our author was bound by historic facts to a certain extent (he could not, for instance, allow Gudrun to commit suicide over Kjartan's death); there were few gaps in the historic framework to give him any room to manoeuvre. We are more concerned with the literary affinities which influenced his interpretation of the emotions involved in the situation. Gudrun's reactions are in essentially the same spirit as those of her pagan ancestress.

Kjartan's career, on the other hand, seems to be envisaged as a Christian victory; and here there are some fascinating parallels with Celtic literature, quite apart from the overtly Christian aspects of his life—the conversion to Christianity by King Olaf Tryggvason in Norway, the strict observance of fasts, and so on. There are some really striking similarities between the death of Kjartan and the death of a sixth-century Irish saint, St Cellach of Killala. Both of them observed a very strict fast throughout Lent (people came from miles around just to look at Kjartan, Chapter 45); both are killed a few days after Easter, by a former friend and kinsman; in both there is an ominous dream on the Wednesday night after Easter (An Brushwood-Belly's dream at Hol, Chapter 48); Cellach is described as being 'poor and feeble' from fasting, and there is a strong

suggestion that Kjartan, too, was recuperating from the rigours of a long fast ('He was only slightly wounded, but very weak with exhaustion', Chapter 49).

The parallels seem too close to be mere coincidence, and certainly the manner of Kjartan's death has a flavour of Christian martyrdom about it, for Kjartan achieves the ideal, flawless art of dying a Christian death. But despite the attempt to make him a Christian hero ('He was a man of great humility, and so popular that everyone, man or child, loved him', Chapter 28), Kjartan's actions fell far short of any Christian ideals and sprang rather from a pagan ethic—pride and self-reliance, a fierce concern for his 'honour' if it meant losing face, a capacity for brutal and coarse retaliation against Bolli and Gudrun.

This Christian wash on Kjartan's portrait is by no means the only echo from Celtic literature in the saga. For instance, Hrapp the Hebridean asks to be buried standing upright in his grave under the threshold of his house, 'So that I can keep an even better watch over my house', (Chapter 17); and St Cellach's father, the King of Connacht, had himself buried in just the same way, with his face to the north confronting his enemies, who were unable to attack his kingdom until they had disinterred him and buried him again in Sligo with his face turned downwards. Similarly, Hrut Herjolfsson's foray against Hoskuld Dala-Kollsson's livestock in pursuit of his claim to his mother's estate (Chapter 19), is nothing more nor less than a classic Irish cattle-raid (*táin bó*)—one of the very few cattle-raids in the Icelandic sagas. And even the colouring of the four horses that Bolli tries to give to Kjartan (Chapter 45)— white, with red ears and red forelock—is a curiously unnatural colour for a horse; but it is a common colouring motif for cows in Irish legends, particularly magic cows. In a saga as deeply concerned with Ireland as *Laxdœla Saga* is, where a major theme is Kjartan's descent from King Myrkjartan of the Irish, it is hard to think of these echoes as merely accidental, although it would be a mistake to try to define these influences too strictly in terms of specific literary borrowings. They should be seen rather in spatial terms (they could have been brought to Iceland from various sources long before the saga was written) illustrating the author's literary eclecticism.

The third major literary strand is the flavour of courtly chivalry, which is represented at its most thorough in the portrait of Bolli Bollason. These influences were making themselves felt very strongly in Norway and Iceland from the second quarter of the thirteenth century onwards, starting with the translation of *Tristram's Saga* from French into Norse by one Brother Robert (presumably an Englishman?) in 1226 at the behest of King Hakon Hakonsson of Norway (*d.* 1263). A stream of translations followed—*Charlemagne's Saga,* the *Chanson de Roland, Le Mantel Mautaillé, Elie de Saint Gille, Floire et Blanceflor,* Chrêtien de Troyes' *Conte del Graal,* and the *lais* of Marie de France; all these and many others quickly circulated throughout Iceland, and soon inspired a vast number of translations, adaptations, and new compositions in the vernacular, a great torrent of popular literature that continued to be written for several centuries.

All these literary tastes and styles meet in the composition of *Laxdæla Saga*—the clerical religious learning, the courtly literature of chivalry, the antiquarian feeling for history, the sympathy for the old heroic poetry. But there is nothing freakish about the fact that such an author should live and write in thirteenth-century Iceland, combining native traditions and European learning so brilliantly; for thirteenth-century Iceland seemed capable of producing authors of this kind and calibre almost at will. It was a society where opposition between laity and clergy was never sharp, where the same man could be abbot, saga-writer, historian, and Law-Speaker of the Althing (like Styrmir the Learned, who died in 1245), where many of the leading personalities, whether priests or chieftains, belonged to the same great families. Snorri Sturluson, the poet, saga-author, historian and politician (cf. *King Harald's Saga,* Penguin Classics, 1966, Introduction), was brought up in a church school at Oddi, and his foster-brother was a bishop. Ari the Learned was a priest, a chieftain and a historian. Sæmund the Learned, who wrote the first history of Iceland in Latin (now lost), was also a priest, chieftain and historian.

Many Icelanders studied abroad; Sæmund the Learned studied in Paris; Snorri Sturluson's foster-brother studied in England. Medieval Christianity was the great intellectual uniter, and the monasteries were the great repositories of European learning (it is recorded that soon after the monastery of Helgafell was established in 1184, it had a library of no fewer than 120 books).

There was constant traffic and interchange. In the eleventh century alone, there were six foreign bishops in Iceland, one of whom was Irish (Bishop Jon the Irishman); the others were English or German. In the twelfth century there were priests in Iceland with distinctly English names; and the monastery of Thykkvaby had a number of foreign monks on its strength. There were numerous foreign books available, in original or translation. Geoffrey of Monmouth's works, both the *History of the Kings of Britain* and the *Prophecies of Merlin,* were translated into Icelandic by the early thirteenth century, as was a Latin narrative about the destruction of Troy. Abbot Brand Jonsson (*d.* 1264), of the monastery of Thykkvaby, translated into noble Icelandic prose the celebrated twelfth-century

poem *Alexandreis* by the Frenchman Phillipe Gautier de Chatillon. In the middle of the twelfth century, round about 1155, an Icelandic priest called Nikulas Bergsson, abbot of the Benedictine monastery of Thverriver, in Eyjafjord, composed a guide-book for Icelanders visiting Rome and the Holy Land, basing it on his own four-year pilgrimage throughout Europe.

Such was the literary background against which *Laxdæla Saga* was written, with full awareness of European literary and intellectual traditions. Interestingly enough, this awareness is reflected, subconsciously perhaps, in the actual narrative of the saga; it is remarkable how often the impact of foreign culture and foreign attitudes are shown to have a disruptive effect on early Icelandic society. Bolli Bollason says (Chapter 72), 'I have always wanted to travel to southern lands one day, for a man is thought to grow ignorant if he doesn't ever travel beyond this country of Iceland'; but every journey abroad in *Laxdæla Saga* has a momentous effect, in one way or another—it is Kjartan's absence in Norway, for instance, that loses him both Gudrun and his life. Consider what the saga characters bring back with them—new ideas and new styles, certainly, like Olaf the Peacock and Kjartan Olafsson and Bolli Bollason; cosmopolitan tastes in clothes and weapons; timber for building mansions and churches. But sometimes the weapons have a baleful effect, like the sword 'Leg-Biter', or the kingly gifts turn sour, like the gold-woven head-dress, and inspire only jealousy and hatred. Sometimes the timber is ill-fated, like the timber that Thorkel Eyjolfsson brought back to build a new church at Helgafell. Sometimes the people who are brought back play a crucial part in the lives of the characters, like Hoskuld's Melkorka, or Olaf's Geirmund the Noisy. It is almost as if the author, knowing the impact that Norway was having on Iceland's internal politics in the thirteenth century, counterpoints his literary Europeanism with an uneasy recognition of the dangerously dynamic effect that foreign influence can have on a small, self-reliant community—the small, idealized, vulnerable society of early Iceland which he evoked so nostalgically.

We have talked throughout of 'the author' of *Laxdæla Saga,* with the familiarity of long acquaintance. And yet he is totally unknown. No one can even guess who he might have been, although it seems inevitable from the evidence of the saga itself that he must have been a Breidafjord man, a descendant, no doubt, of the Laxriverdale dynasty; and that he must have been intimately connected either with Hjardarholt, the estate that plays so important a part in the early sections of the saga, or Helgafell, which came to have such an important place in Iceland's religious history (Chapter 66). The closest we can come to him, in fact, is a little scrap of manuscript, known as D2, which was salvaged from a bookbinding; this fragment, one worn and somewhat damaged leaf of vellum, which covers Kjartan's return to Iceland after his stay in Norway (Chapters 43-4), has been dated *c.* 1250—much the oldest of the surviving manuscripts, and therefore very close indeed to the original manuscript of our anonymous author.

Apart from this, we know nothing of him—except that he existed, and that he stamped his genius unmistakably and distinctively on his work. *Laxdœla Saga* is not, to our minds, so rich and profound a work as *Njal's Saga;* but it is great and remarkable none the less, a magnificent achievement in the great body of Icelandic literature of which he was so clearly aware. The grand design of the saga is astonishingly dense yet supple, using all the sophisticated literary techniques of saga-writing to impose a masterly coherence on his sprawling material. The whole structure of the saga is constantly tautened by the use of dreams and prophecies and supernatural portents that haunt the reader's memory while they await their fulfilment; and the generations are punctuated by careful descriptions of betrothals and marriages and funerary feasts (indeed love and marriage play an extraordinarily pervasive and multifaceted part throughout the whole saga).

There is about it the air of a pageant—a style that luxuriates in descriptions of ornate occasions, an emphasis on emotion that is akin to mime rather than method acting, a certain repetitiveness of phrasing, a surface glitter. There are any number of superbly visualized scenes, tableaux almost: Melkorka talking to her baby son on a sunlit morning (Chapter 13), Gest Oddleifsson watching the innocent swimmers who are to become central figures in the family tragedy (Chapter 33), the shepherd describing to Helgi Hardbeinsson the circle of men eating breakfast before coming to kill him (Chapter 63). There is a sense of grandeur, of the grandiose, almost, that grows stronger as generation succeeds generation and gives the climacteric tragedy of Gudrun-Kjartan-Bolli a horror and a pity that such brilliance and beauty and prowess should be so cruelly destroyed.

Sometimes one feels the portraits to be overdrawn—Bolli Bollason, in particular, seems to be only a glittering but empty husk of a character (but then, he is never really allowed the chance to come alive); but the superlatives are a distinctive feature of the author's style, and the air of lyricism contrasts effectively with the grim tensions gathering below the surface. And at the end of the saga we are left with the memory of an unforgettable gallery of varied and intensely individual people, the men and women who lived and died in Laxriverdale, both stupid and clever, noble and base, aggressive and peaceful, humble and arrogant, brave and cowardly, generous and mean, obstinate and compliant.

But dominating them all is Gudrun Osvif's-daughter, lovely and imperious, as fierce in hatred as in love, proud, vain, jealous, and infinitely desirable. Like all great women, she remained an enigma all her life; and long after her death we can still argue about her, and admire her, and care about her; and wonder still who it was she really loved the most.

A. Margaret Arent Madelung (essay date 1972)

SOURCE: Madelung, A. Margaret Arent. "Literary Perspectives." In The Laxdoela Saga: *Its Structural Patterns,* pp. 147-96. Chapel Hill: University of North Carolina Press, 1972.

[*In the following excerpt, Madelung presents a detailed structural analysis of the* Laxdaela Saga, *emphasizing such features as balance, symmetry, recurrence, comparison, and temporal patterning in various elements of the work.*]

THE SOCIAL AND MORAL ORDER

Although knowledge of the historical, social, and cultural background of a literary work often contributes appreciably to the better understanding of it, an artistic interpretation may, conversely, illuminate with even greater penetration the vitality of the age which produced it. *Laxdœla* presents the cultural ethos prevailing in Iceland from the time of Settlement to the author's own day. In creating so very real a world in which the characters move and act, the author has set before us the familiar events of that world: births, deaths, wooings, marriage feasts, journeys abroad, business deals and bargainings, ghosts, divinations, dreams, and above all killings and feuds. All the social and moral enactments have been selected in consonance with the saga's overall purpose and design and put into a form that brings out that design most advantageously. Against the backdrop of social conventions, figures move across the landscape in multi-colored array, weapons and shields brightly shining. In spite of its splendor, fate and doom hang over this world; in spite of its variety, the activities contain no real surprises. Everything is caught in a round of formulae, stereotyped scenes, and recurrent phrases. The formulaic character of the language and the predictable patterns in which life in the saga world is depicted mirror the inflexibility of that world.

In the moral order is found the same kind of rigidity and inescapableness as characterizes the social sphere. Here again is formula. Comparison of men and their worth underpins the moral code. Disparities are weighed and counterbalanced; in combat and contests skill is pitted against skill. Snorri Godi recognizes the disparity between Lambi and Bolli in the compensating of one life with another. In the competitions at Ásbjarnarnes Kjartan is matched against the strongest and best; and at court, talk apparently often runs to the comparison of men (*mannjafnaður:* xix, 44). When king Óláf and Kjartan are measured by the yardstick, they are found to be equally tall: "Þat sgðu menn, at þeir hafi *jafnmiklir menn* verit, þá er þeir gengu undir mál, Óláfr konungr ok Kjartan" (xli, 124-125). Doubtless the physical comparison is meant to suggest a sizing-up of their worth as well. Equalizing is basic to the meting out of justice, to the settling of arbitrations, to the paying of indemnities. But perfect atonement, an evened score, can never be attained, for the demands of wounded honor carry the killings onward: "'It may well be that we cannot even the score exactly with these Laxdalers,' Gudrún says, 'but now someone must pay dearly, no matter from what dale he comes.'" A retaliatory system of point counterpoint sets up a measured rhythm within the run-on chain reaction of retribution, from which there is no respite. To be sure, disputes could always be settled peaceably, in a way that would do both sides honor, but efforts in this direction are abortive, even though they stand out as an admirable alternative, an unattainable ideal that is reluctantly relinquished. The aesthetic analysis has shown how the author neatly symbolized this two-edged sword of justice: through Repetition and Comparison, the like-for-like and compensating of likes and unlikes respectively; through Recurrence, the eternal chain.

From the concept of equalization and comparison the saga derives its vital form. Aside from the killings, other activities have been purposely selected to point up the same underlying idea: division of inheritances, marriage contracts, divorce settlements, sharing a catch of fish, making equal trades of horses and land. Bargaining stands out as a particular preoccupation in the saga. Much of the substance of the narrative relates to this equivalent and compensatory aspect of the moral law, as do the lexical, syntactical, and rhetorical preferences.

The round-of-life activities with their repeated patterns lend emphasis to the notion that the enactments of the social code, like those in the moral order, can develop into a vicious cycle. The formal organization of the linguistic materials tells us that this is so. As the tendency toward mutliple repetition presents itself in the triplets and quadruplets, where the balance is preserved, however precariously, through resolution into pairs in varying combinations, so the Recurrent linguistic formulations strive for equilibrium in a sort of

check and balance system between negatives and positives. The delicate balance is on the verge of being upset at any moment.

The reappearance of the lexical combinations throughout the saga transmits a sense of necessity and predeterminism. The inner world of the saga is *always* (*jafnan*) the same world, one inextricably caught in its own entanglement, one ethically as well as metaphysically prescribed.

Destiny

The irretractable demand of the code of honor is expressed in the lives of the agents as unavoidable entanglements which lead to misfortune and, ultimately, to death. What is called misfortune by the individual is really part of a larger mysterious doom which pervades life itself; for all things there is an ill-fated destiny. Fate works behind the scenes, yet is manifested primarily in and through the characters. The course of events is determined not only by the will of the characters—and their will is motivated by the ethical code—but also by the will of this inscrutable force. Free and self-determined though the characters may seem to be, there is a power at the core of life itself which motivates both the agents and through them the action. The element of chance is thus all but eliminated. By amalgamating an apparition of destiny with the moral order of things, the author has created a compendious impulse that sets off the dramatic tension.

To represent this supernatural force, the author has made use of the convenient folk belief in dreams, portents, curses, premonitions, and revelations of second sight. These "natural" phenomena, belonging in one sense to the "real" world, were also manifestations of the preternatural. They offered a ready-made device by which a preview of events could be given. But so skillfully has the author couched the will of destiny in the language of dreams and the like—a language characteristically ambiguous—that both agents and audience are left in doubt whether what is suggested will really happen. Ambiguity permits the agents to shrug off prophecies or portents as something puzzling or inexplicable. In any case they pay them no heed, and warnings are deliberately ignored (Án Brushwood Belly's dream, Thorstein's admonishment to Thorkel, for instance), a fact which is again motivated by the characters' own will and stubbornness. Fate is actualized through the agents; it is not a *deus ex machina*. The audience, if alert and atuned to the subtleties of the text, may bear all the long-termed prophetic statements in mind, but somehow also retains doubt concerning the probability of realization. Apprehension aroused increases dramatic anticipation. It is a case of "agents having heard, that still do not hear" and of an "audience having heard, that knows but still plans and hopes." Alternations between fear and hope heighten the excitement. An evil sword comes into the family; but soon a protective one is acquired, an antidote. Hopes are raised, then dampened when the good sword is stolen, raised again when it is found, and again disappointed when it is put aside in a chest. Similarly, we hope that Kjartan will heed Aud's warning, but he refuses to take her brothers along; they go at her insistence, only to turn back before the crucial moment. Finally, the shepherd "by chance" sees the ambush and wishes to head Kjartan off. But the shepherd is overruled by his master, who, along with Thorhalla Chatterbox, is one of the malicious characters in the saga who delights in the misfortunes of others. Thus, Kjartan's destiny overrides all obstacles and takes its course. From the outset it is clear what the end will be.

In addition to vatic pronouncements of various kinds, other elements in the saga contribute to the establishing of a known result. The seemingly perfunctory adjectives used in introducing a character sum up his temperament before it is revealed in the action. Genealogies introduce even the agents themselves long before they come into the story. Ambiguities and rhetorical devices of different kinds aid in transmitting hints ironically veiled by the context, but transparent to the audience "in the know."

Although what the characters experience appears to happen naturally or as chance would have it, the underlying concept is not chance but destiny, a predeterminism which fulfills all that is implicit from the beginning. The inflexibility of fate corresponds associatively and structurally with the inflexibility in the ethical order. In the saga, these two spheres, the ethical and metaphysical (represented by the preternatural), are for all practical purposes amalgamated, and the formal aspects in the saga reflect both. Lexical repetitions set opposing sides against one another in balanced strength and power, either as parallels or antitheses, and hence present a symmetry of their own that has the semblance of an evened score. Furthermore, any given item reappearing underscores the inevitability of what has been intimated or once said and so produces a semblance of function fulfilled. Enactment of the moral law and fulfillment of fate are in each instance binding and necessary. The precision with which the formal elements (i.e. the lexical components and the formalized patterns) reappear shows them to be necessary rather than arbitrary. The whole saga is executed according to a preconceived plan. The author, omniscient and behind the scenes, manipulates his puppets and the actions on stage, much as fate has determined all from the beginning.

THE CHARACTERS

The foregoing investigation has shown that the *Laxdœla* author worked with a selected number of personality traits and attributive phrases. The character types are not infinitely varied nor are the events and situations of unlimited kinds. Both have been chosen to illustrate a formal concept—either balance and compensation or serial happenings. Both agents and events are subordinate to that function. The inner and outer worlds are thus brought into closest correspondence. The agents in general show those qualities that can best motivate the action and set the ethos in motion—stubborn, hard to deal with, prideful, vain, ready to retaliate when honor is at stake. But despite the patterning, the psychological inner workings of the characters are conveyed by the author with remarkable sensitivity. Here he is a master, somehow capable of working with the stereotyped and with the distinctively individual, the true to life, blending them together.

If any one character can be said to dominate the action, it is Gudrún. She arrests our attention from the moment she appears. High-spirited, beautiful, proud, ambitious, fiercely jealous, quick-witted, sharp-tongued, calculating, and insatiable in vengeance, she of all the characters is the most carefully drawn. We observe her in all four of her marriages: spoiled and petulant in the first; mischievous and self-assured in the second; accepting the third one in spite and ill-humor; and agreeing to the fourth as a means toward gaining revenge. How and when she is moved to remorse or begins to see clearly that the flaws in her third marriage initiated the tragedy is hard to say, for we never look into her heart, except for once and even then briefly. The last words she is represented as speaking suggest that ultimately she has come to see her life for what it was: "To him I was worst whom I loved most." The forces of passion have spent themselves; blind and weary and old she finishes her days as a nun and hermitess. But the fate that is hers has not been imposed upon her by an alien spirit; it has been there inside her all along, forming and shaping her life and finally recoiling upon her. Rather, Christian humility and contrition are the alien elements here; just as medieval gallantry and pageantry comprise, as it were, a light wash over the world depicted in the saga, so, too, Christianity runs thin. The old world order and the fateful conception of life retain their efficacy.

The other women in the saga have something of Gudrún in them: Unn, Jórunn, Melkorka, Vigdís, and of course Thorgerd,—all except the sweet and gentle Hrefna, who is of an entirely different cast and in every respect a foil to Gudrún. Here again the author has brought a contrast into the series, just as a negative element suddenly offsets a preponderance of positives.

The male characters all have something of Kjartan in them: Óláf Feilan, Hoskuld, Óláf Peacock, Bolli Thorleiksson, and Bolli Bollason. Kjartan, as Gudrún's lover, plays the leading male role. He is gallant, self-confident, impetuous, eager for fame and glory, capable in weapons and sports, a born leader, and an extrovert. He comes close to the ideal hero type. When events begin to turn against him, he maintains self-assurance, first through restraint, then by over-compensation, taking especial care to appear gay, flaunting his prowess and authority wherever he can. He is cocky and throws caution to the winds to sport with death. But he, too, has become infected somewhat by Christian ethics: he keeps the fast and Holy Days and in the fight for his life finds it better to receive death than to deal it.[1] Both he and Bolli Bollason with their pomp and weapons and clothes betray the influence of medieval knighthood on the heroic tradition. Nonetheless, both Kjartan and Gudrún are tragic heroes and, like those of old, carry in themselves their fate. In this sense they are like their Eddic counterparts or the classical Greek heroes who are doom-eager. Fate is internalized.

Although Bolli Thorleiksson is said to be closest to Kjartan in prowess and accomplishments, he, like Hrefna, is of a different stamp. What makes the breach between Bolli and Kjartan the more charged with tension is the initial fondness they had for one another. Bolli's passive and introspective nature, his silent, brooding sullenness stand in contrast to Kjartan's outgoing assurance and active retaliation. The first overt act and triumph of Bolli's life, the snatching of the bride, is not enough to bolster his ego; it only brings him inner pain; and his second, the slaying of Kjartan, ultimately is his undoing.

However deft the *Laxdæla* author is in portraying accurately reactions true to life and in suggesting and inferring through the subtlest of means and rhetorical devices psychological truths, his main aim is not character study. Foremost is his achievement in cleverly controlling his verbal units to bring balance, symmetry, and symbolic imagery to his composition. It is through the mixing and correlating of the patterned phrases that most of the characters are "mixed characters" rather than black-and-white types. Even the events surrounding their lives, we have seen, represent an amalgam from various sources. The mixing and matching of the verbal components was particularly evident among the pairs of inimical brothers. When the characters appear, what they say, what is said about them are totally subordinate to the arrangement of linguistic units with which the author is ultimately concerned. For it is this arrangement that forms an abstract pattern that conveys in itself the notions of comparison, of predetermined

necessity, and of a repetitive progression, and these meanings coincide with the structural concepts inherent in the two aspects of the moral code and in a fateful destiny.

Many of the elements appear stereotyped and crystallized even before the *Laxdæla* author employed them, phrases like *mikill maðr ok sterkr;* many others become stereotyped within the saga by virtue of the author's repetitious use of them. However true it may be that the author had precedents for his phraseology or that he used merely ordinary Icelandic idiom or common storyteller's devices, he has nonetheless so organized, concentrated, and repeated them that they have become stereotyped patterns for the first time in *Laxdæla.* Within the overall patterning occasioned by the repeated verbal units, there are thematic patterns or groupings into a complex of specific motifs like the whettings, the drownings, the hero's accoutrements. Characters, too, are modelled after one another. Thorgerd, for instance, represents the stereotype of the prodding woman much more than does Gudrún; Bolli Bollason approaches the stereotype of the gallant much more than does Kjartan. What is intriguing is the author's ability to individualize the elements he has made into stereotypes in the first place, enabling him to conceal his patterns. And here again the author holds the balance.

THE EPIC BASE

The recounting of events in a chronological progression from one generation to the next gives the saga epic scope. The introductory section in particular lays a broader epic base for the central action. The narrative is slow in getting started, halting at intervals to introduce yet another character or episode, looking backward to pick up threads that have been temporarily dropped, rounding out what has been prepared. Chronicling of births, deaths, wooings, marriages, careers, feudings, traffickings between farms, tales of ghosts, gossips and hired hands provide a broader picture of time and place, and supplies, as it were, an epic setting. The terrain and landscape around the Breidafjord Dales, the skerries and channels in the sound, the relationship of the farmsteads to one another and geographical directions, too, set a definite stage, familiar to epic narration. Recurrence, aside from creating the greater tragic aspect of the ethical code through its serial patterning, supplies through its content an epic backdrop for the more dramatic happenings in the foreground.

Many of the trappings and rhetorical devices associated with epic form are also present: backtracking of the action and the use of flash-backs; exaggerations and magnification, a glorification of agents and events. Typical of epic retardation are the incidents prior to the assault on Helgi's hut: the shepherd's account of the band in the woods with the details of dress and appearance; the eating of the *dagverðr* (main meal) by the group of attackers, as if they were in no hurry to get on with the business; the appearance of the comic Víga-Hrapp on the scene. Again epic delay is apparent in the leave-taking scene between Ingibjorg and Kjartan. Pause is taken to describe the expensive headdress, the little chest in which she keeps it, and its velvet case. This scene affords opportunity, too, to convey between the lines what Ingibjorg's feelings are by the fact that she prolongs these moments while in Kjartan is eagerness and expectancy pressing for departure.

Some few descriptions arrest one's attention like vignettes, masterfully presented with a few strokes that catch the eye: Thórólf standing at the landing stage with halberd ready as Hall comes rowing in to shore in high spirits; Vigdís flinging the purse into Ingjald's face, dealing him a bloody nose; Melkorka sitting on a sunny slope talking to her little son; Jórunn lashing Melkorka about the head with a pair of stockings; Óláf all dressed up in battle array striding forward to the prow of his vessel, which is manned from stem to stern, shields and spears studding the gunwales; Óláf again in all his finery marching off to Egil's booth at the heels of his father; Thorstein and Thorkel in the home meadow at Hjardarholt, nudging so close to Halldór that they are sitting on his cloak, while Beinir stands over them with poised axe. In addition, every now and then some small detail of weaponry or clothes is mentioned: shields embossed in gold with a lion, cross, or knight; or Gudrún's bodice and fancy sash of foreign mode. But there is little time to dwell on any of these in the saga. The descriptions are suggested in a minimum of words that form instantaneous pictures.

Although the story is mainly told through dialogue and indirect discourse and through the actions and deeds of the agents, lending an immediate presence to the action, some awareness that the story moves in the memory of bygone days is preserved. Epic time is past time, whereas dramatic time is an imminent future. *Laxdœla* participates in both.

THE DRAMATIC PRESENTATION

All the essential elements of drama are present in the saga: actors, motives turned into action, dialogue, and a limited setting made broader through suggestion. The characters act out their parts, and their words and deeds unfold the plot. But the dramatic quality of the saga runs much deeper than such ordinary histrionic devices. The scene before our eyes is suspended as a theatrical present between the past and the future. What has gone on before is the necessary prerequisite for the present moment, and the present action is, in turn, charged with implication for the future. Herein lies the essence of the dramatic conception of tragedy. The saga is essentially a dramatic presentation in epic form. The central action present before our eyes is always moving against a backdrop of past action.

The prophecies and portents, although more internalized than the oracle or chorus in classical Greek drama, boom forth their doom and disaster and intensify the necessity that is already present as moral obligation. Fate and the code of ethics offered the author ready-made dramatic material in the broadest sense. Both work together toward the same end, and the action fulfills all that was implicit from the beginning.

Tragedy dominates the central theme, and destiny brings the saga to its close. All passions have been spent; the forces of doom have run themselves out; all prophecies have been executed; the demands of justice satisfied. Yet, the saga ends on a different note. The generations continue; the life process goes on. Balance and compensation have been attained momentarily; and so the saga ends on a sort of up-beat. Such a rhythm belongs actually to comedy.[2] Our interest in the story has in a way also remained somewhat disengaged, not because emotions have not been presented, but because they have, without our knowing it, been harnessed in a pattern. Because of this conformity to a mechanical system on all levels in the saga, the tragic impact is not overwhelming. The feeling, however, remains that the closing scenes could easily be as implicitly portentous as the innocent relationships with which the saga opened. It is as if the whole could repeat itself like the round-of-life cycle under Recurrence. The end has run into the beginning. The epic and the dramatic, the comic and the tragic are played off against one another in this two-levelled saga.

STYLE AND TONE

In view of the fact that the structural components, especially Foreknowledge and Repetition and Comparison, are generally so well camouflaged that it requires some sleuthing to detect them, something more should be said about the method of camouflage and the overall style and tone of the saga. The tension produced within the plot through the incompletion of a foreknown conclusion postulates a double audience consisting of some that "hearing shall hear and shall not understand" and others that "when more is meant than meets the ear, [are] aware both of that more and of the outsider's incomprehension."[3] This double treatment penetrates the saga to its core. It is first of all most noticeable in the unawareness of the agents and the omniscience of author and audience. The similarity between the plot structure of *Laxdœla saga* and the dramatic irony of classical Greek drama is obvious. The agents in the saga remain in the dark about the dreams and portents.

They accept them on one level, the audience on another, if the latter is "in the know" and can interpret the signs. The language of dreams is by nature ambiguous; and the other vatic statements (in the broader and narrower sense) are likewise veiled through poetic and rhetorical devices such as litotes, euphemism, idioms and expressions of all kinds that show a discrepancy between surface meaning and significant meaning, between specific reference and general reference, between the literal and the figurative meanings (e. g. *kátr; kyrrt; at drepa skeggi; spenna um þngulshfuð; snarisk í bragð; loka hurðir*).

Omniscience is also evident in the attributing to the agents knowledge which has been previously heard only by the audience. Statements made by the author or by other characters are often picked up by one of the agents without their having been transmitted. The audience is again "in the know"; the agents, to all intents and purposes, "in the dark." These passages offer good evidence for the author's method and aim. He, being omniscient, has manipulated his phrases and repetitions, letting them fall at just the right places in the narrative to awaken the sense of necessity and fulfilled function. Some of them (e. g. *siti kyrrir ok í friði; framarla til*) are so pertinent to the situation that the speaker conceivably could have arrived at the idea independently, by chance, so to speak, under the given circumstance. This veils their invented origin and the author's deliberate purpose. Other of these repetitions by omniscience (e. g. *eigi er váttum bundit; Þórhllusonu, er þeir eru sendir til Helgafells; gaman ok skemmtan af viðskiptum þeira*) are too good a surmise on the part of the speaker to be coincidental. Rather than resort to pragmatic explanations like neighborhood gossip, which would lead away from the text and outside the poetic illusion, to explain the transmission by real life situations, it is more fitting to see in them part of the total scheme of the author to create structural parallels. Only in some places he has not veiled his method as well as in others. Balanced form and necessary connection are his primary concerns and govern the choice of words and where they occur. He would like to make it all seem as if by chance. Recognition of the reuse of precisely the same words, whether transmitted or untransmitted, discloses their contrivance. The latter type does so more readily since the plausibility for the reappearance of the same words has not been produced.

The irony of the presentation as seen in the double audience also comes out in the contrast between the precise form and the passion and intensity of the events described, causing some disengagement on the part of the reader. Related to this is the objectivity for which the Icelandic sagas have frequently been praised, a generality that needs some qualification. In **Laxdœla,** objectivity consists in a deliberate literary approach where the author disappears behind the scenes, his planning, selecting, contriving, fabricating all so skillfully concealed that the whole action seems to happen through natural motivation and of itself. But the author, like fate, is doing the directing, whether the audience realizes it or not. Again we meet with double treatment and with camouflage.

Camouflage, duplicity, and ambiguity are the keys to much of the substance of the narrative and to the means of its presentation. Snorri Godi's scheming and the play on the word *samlendr* immediately come to mind. But the technique runs much deeper. The author has favored those events, those agents, and those lexical, and syntactical arrangements, those rhetorical and stylistic devices that would play hand in hand with his central concept. Events such as bargainings and their counterpart, impasses; antithetical agents (e. g. inimical brothers; Gudrún-Hefna); parallel agents (e. g. Kjartan-Bolli Bollason; Gudrún-Thorgerd) abound. In the larger and smaller units of the narrative the author has played with all possible arrangements of such architectonics as chiasmus: parallels with opposite actions and effects (e. g. *lendur góðar / minna lausafé; fá lnd / fjlða fjár;* Án the Black's two dreams) and opposites with same action and effect (e. g. Bolli Thorleiksson and Thorleik Bollason where the chiasmal transposition of the names sets up a kind of opposition but results in their having identical roles; or the two Bolli's despite the same name having opposite roles); or negative reversals (e. g. *jafnræði / eigi jafnræði;* good marriages and bad marriages; smooth sea crossings and difficult sea crossings; *með mikilli blíðu / með engri blíðu*); or antitheses set up through substitution of antonyms (e. g. *kært / þústr; vináttu / kærleik; ekki efni / gott efni*). He also works with parallel comparatives (e. g. *firr / nær; hvergi betr / nkkuru fleiri; vel / miklu betri*), as well as with sentences constructed on the basis of parallel syntax (e. g. the sentence about the brothers Ingjald and Hall). Correlatives and duplicates of all kinds abound. Alternations as between the hope and fear discussed above, contrasts between the calm (*kyrrt*) and the storm, between preparatory gaiety and ensuing tragedy, are used by the author to derive the greatest possible effects. So the major enmities grow from incidents which occur at three festive occasions, and an ominous cloud throws its shadow into the jesting and jostling at Hól before Kjartan's fateful ride into Svíndadal, where the comic and the tragic are also juxtaposed. The tension of the tragedy imminent there in the valley is relieved briefly by the pretense of joking when his companions drag Bolli down the slope by his heels. The puny and ludicrous Víga-Hrapp appears on the scene before the attack on Helgi's hut. Likewise the splendor and ennoblement of the social backdrop complements the disastrous events; the most illustrious of the family are doomed to tragic end. Love and hate, a good sword and an evil sword—such contrastive pairs could be enumerated with many more.

One might gather from these remarks that the prose of this saga could easily verge on the trite, almost the euphuistic. But the author has employed his devices so cleverly, making them one with the content, that the trick is well concealed. Besides, the artistic devices are not mere ornaments but are themselves turned into poetic imagery, hence are bearers of meaning. The embellishment of the accoutrements of the hero, helmet, sword, shield, with golden adornments (usually *gullrekit* and the like) is on the formal level also an embellishment (i. e. amplification) of the pattern. Substitution of antonyms also mirrors the content—a turn in the situation described, for instance; or parallel syntax as used about Hrapp dead or alive parallels the discursive idea.

The relationships and comparisons which the repetitions among the verbal units set up are not explicitly or discursively stated, they are implied. Only once in a while does the author himself intrude to give hint of his intent, as with the *þótti mjk á hafa hrinit* in the case of two lesser prophecies or with his *sem fyrr* that makes a reference direct. These phrases cue the reader as to what the saga is about: the necessary fulfillment of what has been suggested before; a return of the same situation as obtained before, or, most importantly, the reuse of verbal configurations. The audience must be alert not only to what has been said before but also to how it has been worded.

The repetitions and correlations are first of all masked through integration with the content. Any one phrase can be interpreted at face value within the context where it appears; as soon as its counterpart is found, the co-relationship carries the significance beyond the contextual meaning. Through the arrangement, the language itself becomes an event rather than a medium or vehicle. An abstract pattern emerges that conveys the ideas of necessity, fulfillment, compensatory balance, comparison, reiteration, recurrence.

Another way in which the verbal repetitions are concealed from the casual observer is through subtle variations in the wording itself: e. g. the pair *áttu þau Guðrún þar mikit traust / þau Ósvífr eiga allt traust;* or the statement referring to Gudrún's remembering exactly what men were in on the raid against Bolli and the corresponding statement that Gudrún's sons hadn't forgotten what men were in on the raid; or the fact that the *at klæðum ok vápnum* phrase is applied to Bolli's men, not specifically to Bolli. These substitutions are practically synonymous, and in every case mutually inclusive by inference so that the correspondence in pattern remains.

Use of vague terms, plurals, or generalities often conceals the specific implication: (e. g. the plurals *nkkura, svívirðingarorð;* the vague *af inum versti manni;* or the future of probability *mun auðit verða;* the generality *spenna um þngulshfuð*). Substitution of synonyms into the same pattern also disguises the parallelism or comparison intended (e. g. *hlutgjarn / framgjarn; sómamaðr / vaskr maðr*). Increment embellishment serves the same purpose of making the similarities fuzzier (e. g. "hafim *gaman af leik þeira*" / "gerði sér af *gaman ok skemmtan af viðskiptum þeira*"; "þessir menn *siti um kyrrt* allir" / "Óláfssynir *siti kyrrir ok í friði*"; "jafnan *til trausts*" / "*tils halds og* [sic] *trausts*"; "sitr Óláfr nú *í búi sínu*" / "Óláfr sat nú *í búi sínu með miklum sóma*"; "hafði *sverð í hendi*" / "hafði *í hendi sverð gullrekit*").

In the thematic patterns made up of a concatenation of motifs, the camouflaging is also achieved through variation and substitution, and through rearrangement somewhat of the sequence of the motifs. But above all, camouflaging is accomplished through imbedding the same forms, whether single phrases or whole patterns, in entirely new contexts. Halldór, for instance, is said to take the lead among his brothers ("hann var mjk fyrir þeim brœðrum"). The confirmation of the statement is put in a new setting: Thorgerd, in goading her sons to take action, says to Halldór: "'Þú þykkisk mest fyrir yðr brœðrum'" ("'You consider yourself leader among you brothers'"), which adds a shift of viewpoint to the blanket narrative statement. Despite slight variations and new contexts the designs are never obliterated. The individual motifs in the patterns of the parties, goadings, killings, and drownings offer the best examples of rearrangement and substitution of new substance each time into the same molds. There is no doubt that the author has mastered fully the use of patterns, recognizing established ones, creating new ones.

Many of the themes and well turned phrases can be found elsewhere in saga literature, but their specific and unique form and function in **Laxdæla** make them wholly pertinent to the literary work regardless of their provenance. What has the author done with the materials of his language? He has created formulae out of normal phrases; he has repeated them in accordance with his own structural idea, turning them to new function. He has created patterns and formulae that have become so for the first time within **Laxdæla** alone. Whether any of them are solidified patterns taken over bodily from tradition outside the saga or from other sources, requires further investigation. The hero accoutrements pattern attracts particular attention in this regard.[4] Since with the patterns under Recurrence, as with those in triplicate, not every motif occurs in each repetition of the theme, the archetype of the pattern can only be obtained by building a composite from the specific instances. . . . These nucleus patterns must have been the basis for the composition, whether newly invented or borrowed. It is as though the author, visualizing the whole structure, worked, so to speak, from these germinating centers outward, just as the saga is more fully developed in the middle, ripples of its main themes spreading to the periphery as preparation or recapitulation. Indeed, only if one has recognized the patterns, seen the saga as a whole, can one—in retrospect—detect the fact that Hoskuld's not riding to meet Hrút, for instance, is a negative reversal of the expected; or that Bolli's not having on a coat of mail contradicts the pattern, or that Hrút's accoutrements and the descriptive details about them are but iterations of a thematic complex. The chronological order of the saga as preparation, central theme, recapitulation must be distinguished from the sequence of the creative process. The critical analysis has perhaps given us some clues as to the nature of that formative process. The reader (or audience), like the author, must keep the patterns in mind in order to anticipate and recall and thus read the saga from the center outwards. The effect of the patterns and formulae is a cumulative one since ever more elements are introduced and repeated as the saga progresses—which accounts for the concentration of formulae in the last part of the saga. One has the impression toward the end that everything has already been said somewhere, sometime before. The author's method has become all too patent.

The patterns under the round-of-life category are the most readily recognized. Rather than being concealed, they act as distractors and do the concealing, especially in those cases where the more or less stereotyped recurrent phrases take on individual and qualified function (e.g. *ráðakostr,* which is used innocuously enough in the career-abroad offers and then with special intent and double meaning to hint of marriage with Ingibjorg; or the *unni mest,* which is a running theme but also strengthens comparative bonds among the agents: Hoskuld-Óláf, Óláf-Kjartan, Hoskuld-Bard, Gudrún-Bolli B.). Many motifs receive this double treatment. The agents and events of the main action, it must be remembered, also participate in those events which belong to the background; thus some of the motifs are bound to show a twofold application, i.e. as Recurrence and as Repetition or Comparison. That both Kjartan and Bolli B. are *kurteisligr* or *mikit afbragð annarra manna,* for instance, would not by itself be enough to establish any meaningful comparison between them. Seen against all the other parallels, these attributes become part of the foreground schematism, being lifted momentarily from the chain, so to speak, to act as comparatives, which accords them greater significance.

The author's schemes (patterns of words) are thus themselves a scheme. This "bragð" of his is equal to any of Snorri Godi's. Without doubt he would hope that his patterns and formulae might be recognized, for his architectonics of matching prophecy and fulfillment, of equalizing events and agents, of comparing and setting up antithetical relationships, of duplicating and doubling are the key to understanding what the saga is really about. But the repeated phrases, like all the veiled hints in the saga, are subtle and apparent only to the knowledgeable reader or audience, whose position must become analogous to that of the author to see through the subterfuge.

After the foregoing analysis and this discussion it is all but a foregone conclusion to say that **Laxdœla** is composed to a great extent, despite the historical frame, of fabricated situations, fabricated dialogues, and when necessary for the composition, of fabricated characters, and that it is a literary work of contrived design. The author has capitalized on a technique, using rhetorical devices, patterns, and formulaic phraseology to set forth his idea complex, whatever their ultimate derivation proves to be. The saga is almost what one could call a self-parody. For after the author produced his patterns and formulae, he reshuffled and recombined them, so that they became unique again, individualized, and thereby camouflaged. His ingenuity is hence twofold. He succeeded so well in his endeavor that his highly stylized composition appears natural and uncontrived to all but the initiated, the ideal audience that has caught on to the tricks involved.

Such self-parody can be witty, consciously or unconsciously, e.g. such as we meet in Gudrún's playing with the term *samlendr* almost to the point of divulging the secret. The author's *sem fyrr, sem ván var* also come close to this type of wit when read with the whole aesthetic design in mind. In the flash-back reminder about the events in Iceland while Thorkel is abroad (lviii, 176; lxviii, 199), the author's repeating of his own sentences would in itself function as a correlative between referent and antecedent apart from the literary convention used. Is the author's allowing Gudrún to turn the excuses of her sons to her own advantage (a kind of antistrophon) deliberate or the result of the system of repetitions, the witticism being incidental or concomitant? Irony is indeed the distinctive quality of this prose.

RHYTHM AND TIME

Circumstances prevalent in thirteenth-century Iceland, when saga writing was at its height, no doubt encouraged interest in the Age of Settlement and the heyday of the Commonwealth. Rise of power politics had brought with it a breaking down of the traditional moral order; political and material aggrandizement superceded personal honor and prestige based on integrity. This century witnessed the outbreak of feuds, vendettas, intrigues, and savageries on a scale hitherto unknown. Times were undeniably crucial.

The turning to historical subjects probably reflects a consciousness that history was in the making. The relentless step by step movement toward relinquishment of freedom and the end of the Commonwealth must have seemed to some, at least, like the machinations of an inscrutable destiny propelling the country toward disaster. *Laxdæla saga* is judged to have been composed about 1250; the Commonwealth came under Norwegian control in 1262. Contemporary events in many ways must have appeared like the disastrous result of the code of vengeance and the fulfillment of a fateful destiny. In a sense it was a turning point where past and future met, a time of precarious balance in the life of the nation.

Laxdæla saga reveals this continuity between time past and time present first of all through the genealogies, some of which follow the names back to a time before the story, while others project the names forward to persons beyond the frame of events in the saga but contemporary with the time of the author and his writing. The author's intrusion into the narrative is minimal and difficult to detect. The few places where he does reveal himself point to his consciousness of the discrepancy between the time of the events he is writing about and the time of the composition, and to the fact that he is writing about the past from the perspective of the present.[5] Some of the anachronisms also show that he is comparing the present with the past. The obvious one concerning the fact that "heathen men *then* had no less at stake than Christian men do *now* when ordeals are performed" (xviii, 42-43), which has already been discussed in another connection,[6] explicitly draws the comparison between time "then" and time "now." Two other statements where the author's comment reveals his mediating position between former times and contemporary times carry the comparison implicitly. Halldór is described as wearing a cloak with a clasp that was the fashion *at that time:* "Halldórr hafði yfir sér samða skikkju ok á nist lng, *sem þá var títt*" (lxxv, 219). The author herewith gives us a fact about mode of dress in saga times, a small detail that shows an attempt at historical accuracy, keeping his characters appropriate to their times. More importantly, the *þá* tells us that that time and the author's are not the same time. It shows the perspective. But we have met with a similar phrase before, and consideration of the author's general method makes it likely that an association is intended between these two, as is the case with any of the repetitions in the saga. It will be recalled that Bolli Bollason carried a lance "as is the custom in foreign lands": "hann hafði glaðel í hendi, *sem títt er í útlndum*" (lxxvii, 225). In contrast to the appropriate-

ness of the clasp to the times about which the author is writing, this reference tells us that a contemporary mode of dress has been superimposed on that past time. The one points to time past, the other to time present; and particularly to be noticed, the one is in past tense, the other in present tense. The similarity of the phrases lexically (*títt* is used only in these two places in the saga), the similarity of the contexts with their references to fashions then and now indicate that a juxtaposition and comparison is being subtly suggested by the author. The natural contexts in which the phrases occur camouflage again the underlying meaning. What the author is hinting is that the fashion is to talk about the present in terms of the past. These inadvertent (I'd rather call them advertent) "slips" on the author's part[7] tell us on the discursive level that there is a time discrepancy, and on the formal level that the two times represented are to be compared and contrasted. What structural peculiarities in the saga would further substantiate such a supposition?

We have had many occasions to note that the rhythm in the saga is one of a back-and-forth relating of cause and resultant, of antecedent and referent. Recognition of prophecy and associating it with its fulfillment, or correlating a repeated phrase with its forerunner produce the effect of anticipation and recollection. There is a constant back-and-forth comparing going on within the saga by virtue of its formal structure. The same structural rhythm was found in the bargainings, in the handing of the decision back and forth between father and daughter in the betrothals, in the living alternately first in one place and then in another, in the sea crossings, in the forward-looking and backward-looking genealogies, and in the compositional flash-backs.

The narrative itself, we have noted, shows a mingling and a superimposing of the epic and the dramatic mode of presentation. Epic handling would indicate the remembering of things past and giving an account of them, whereas the dramatic handling renders these past events present and actual. This feeling is transmitted throughout the narrative. The events the author is describing are supposed to be of a by-gone time, yet the action is always vividly present. Time past and time present are merged and blended. The dramatic presentation itself consists in compacting into the present moment the culmination of all that was implicit from the beginning and all that is portentous for the future. Past and future meet in the present moment. The visually present action of the saga, suspended between past and future, is completely analogous to the point in history where Iceland stood in the thirteenth century at the time the saga was composed.

The structure and plot of *Laxdæla saga* are based on a formal conception—that of destiny and dramatic tragedy. The plot is executed through the analogously structured form of the ethical code as necessity and inevitability. The prophecies and the presupposition of rigid fulfillment of the code of honor with its equal retaliations represent that omniscient force in the background which shapes and forms the main action of the drama, action that seemingly takes place naturally and of itself before our eyes. The social order of things, as recognized under Recurrence, serves as the epic backdrop in front of which the drama, the action of the saga, moves as before a screen. This drama itself is also conceived by the author as part of that round-of-existence, part of the whole, the bigger tragedy. Here we discovered the point of contact between the epic mode and the dramatic mode, between the background and the foreground. They are mutually inclusive. And we have seen, too, how on the formal level Repetition and Comparison (used most for the main action) also in places participate in Recurrence. The analogy the author wishes to draw could not be more obvious. The whole saga world, so to speak, was the epic background for the events of the drama taking place in mid thirteenth-century Iceland. Seen against the by-gone days of the Commonwealth as the epic backdrop, the drama of the present represented a culmination of what had been set in motion in Iceland's past and a turning point for the future. What was implicit from the beginning (the social order, the demands of a retaliatory system of justice) was working itself out fatefully in the author's own day. Again we see the author's use of camouflage and pattern. The events of his day supply the new context for the old forms. The background world of the saga represents the same world as that of the thirteenth century—the same social order is implied, the same two-edged sword of justice. Yet the *Laxdæla saga* holds itself up like a mirror to the thirteenth century, in the sense that it gives a positive reflection of the negative contemporary happenings.

The discussion of the *títt* phrases and of the epic and dramatic handling has incidentally also touched upon another closely related problem—that of tenses. The realization that Iceland's historical past has been made actual and the present converted into a semblance of the past throws further light on the mixture of past and present verb forms in the narrative, something which has occasioned much puzzlement in saga research. Use of historical present to enliven action is a well-known storyteller's device. It does not, however, explain the mingling of grammatical tenses found in some sagas, and particularly in *Laxdæla,*[8] a practice which has generally been dubbed as primitive, inept, or a meaningless enigma. Such mixing apparently has an aesthetic function which has evaded critics.[9] The reader is never disoriented in respect to the time of the action; it is always immediately present before his eyes. And, indeed, the shift in tenses is so unobtrusive that it generally passes unnoticed. This in itself should tell us that

the author has prepared for us another "bragð." The juxtaposing of the two tenses, past and present, even within the same sentence does not signify that the action in the present tense is the resultant of the action in the past tense in any specific instance—a literary device used by some poets. In *Laxdæla saga* the mingling has broader implication: all the virtually present actions in the saga are the result of those in the past, and by analogy all the present-day events of the author's time, disastrous and portentous as those in the saga, are the culmination and consequence of Iceland's past and the cultural ethos that generated that history. The mixture of tenses is appropriate to the first level—the saga understood as a closed aesthetic unit in which both epic and dramatic handling are inherent to the structure. And the mixture is a clue to the relationship of the saga as a whole to its cultural context—mid-thirteenth-century Iceland. By mixing his tenses the author has confounded the critics and concealed the fact that he was not only writing about the past, but about and for the present. The interspersing and distributing of the two grammatical tenses, like the mixing, distributing and reordering of the patterned phrases and motifs in the saga, camouflage their existence and their function. Like the prophecies and other hints, like the repeated phrases, the tense shifts, too, go by practically unnoticed. The use of tenses, their specific function already indicated in the *títt* phrases, is another camouflaged hint.

We thus see that the saga can be read on two levels. To test this out, one only need apply the categories derived from the aesthetic analysis to the analoguous situation of the thirteenth century. The saga functions as Foreknowledge, the preparation for the events of the author's time. Everything that has happened later is present *in nuce,* as prophecy. The saga events form a Comparison with later times. The author's own day is a Repetition, a parallel to the earlier period of history. But it is also a contrast, for in the saga Repetition and Comparison received the main focus, whereas in the author's day Recurrence is the aspect which has come to the fore. Thus the author's time comprises a negative reversal, a reversed image. The saga as a mirror for the contemporary age gives the positive image. The one historical period is the reversed reflection of the other. Since the analogy the author is drawing is one of formal principles, namely the idea behind the events, it is clear why he attached so much importance to building the formal relationships in the saga. It was through abstract pattern that the analogy could best be conveyed without stating either the function of the pattern or the analogy that he intended.

This supposition can be tested and explored further. The recurrence of the cycle implied at the close of the saga turns out indeed to be the more disastrous one, for the repeat performance in the thirteenth century illustrates the adverse aspect. The structural analysis of the saga showed how the formal aspects tended constantly toward establishing a balance, even when the repetitions threatened to multiply into triplets and quadruplets. The chain reaction itself, illustrated under Recurrence, tended toward setting up its own checks and balances. By contrast, the thirteenth century was not headed toward balance. The concatenation of events had clearly got out of hand; there were no more checks and balances in the system; the nation was headed for disaster. The saga presented an ideal and through it a warning.

The virtual and essential time rhythm of the saga as a comparing back and forth within the saga and between the saga and its contemporary context has also been camouflaged through a semblance of real time and historical progression. The events depicted carry a semblance of history, and with it a semblance of real time. The natural progression of the generations produces a forward movement. The impression is given of a sequence of before, now, and after, corresponding to the three main divisions of the saga; there is a time before the main action, the main action itself, and its sequel. Increment and increase, embellishment and enhancement also accompany the generations. Qualitatively the enhancement stands in contrast to the analogy the author is drawing with his own times. The purpose of what we have called epic magnification, of the grandeur and idealization of saga times becomes apparent. As a contrast with contemporary times, those times appeared as ideal. Quantitatively the series repetitions under Recurrence and the cumulative effect of the patterning toward the end of the saga represent a parallel with the author's times. Increase and increment of the patterns is not only a natural result of all that has been presented and gone before, on the second level it is also meaningful. For the author's own day shows the cumulative effect of all that has gone before, the increased tragedy. Recurrence in the saga represented this larger aspect of the ethical code—there it was the background. For the author's own day, this background has become the foreground. The quantity of the feuds and retaliations has increased, whereas the quality—the honorable reasons for performing the deeds, the ethical demands of equalization and compensation that would do both sides honor (Repetition and Comparison)—has faded into the background.

There is another aspect to this comparing of the present time with the past time. If the agents and situations in the saga are analogous, as has been demonstrated through the repeated patterns and comparisons, the relationship between the "before" in the story, the "now," and the "after" are also for all practical purposes annulled. What is happening now has happened before, and will happen again, or at least so it seems, and it is this seeming that counts. Past and present are one and the same, can therefore be superimposed on each other. Just as one generation is patterned after the former, so the author's generation is derived from the preceding generations and his times are like those times in the saga. But if everything is really like everything else, despite new contexts, substitutions, and negative counterparts, then in effect the happenings are lifted into a time which is like every other time, and hence indefinite in reference to everything except the depicted action. The references to the fall of Óláf the Saint, like mention of Ari, put the saga in a historical frame and help create the illusion of historical reality, whereas actually the saga contains a philosophy of history that is related to the syncretic thinking of the Middle Ages. The events in the saga are merely relative to one another, as the time designations in the story will show. The author is purposely working in poetic time, and that time is a virtual present or eternal time in which repetitive instances can be said to take place "at the same time." The instances in the saga and the analogously repeated instance of the thirteenth century can be interpreted as reenactments of the ethical code, of the pattern of destiny that was common to both. History was therefore envisioned by this poet-author as repetitions of a preestablished pattern—in the history of his country this pattern was based on the cultural ethos, that vital center from which all else sprang. The events of then or now the author saw as taking place *in illo tempore,* in that eternal time of reenactment, synchronic time. The sequence of historical time is thus erased. The likenesses which have been set up within the saga, and the analogy intended with his own time indicate that this is the case. The pattern, this abstraction of the formative principle behind the course of history, was the central nucleus from which all else could be derived. The author employed the same method in miniature with each one of his patterns in the saga: for the goadings, the killings, the drownings, the hero's accoutrements a nucleus pattern could be established from which the specific examples had emanated, in the creative process, as from a center. Substitution of new content in the same forms, displaying of the negative counterpart, the opposites, does not invalidate or obliterate the pattern. Is it any wonder that the ***Laxdœla*** author was so interested in patterns, repetitions of patterns, and their contrastive aspects? Here the spheres of art and history are brought into closest relationship.

The structural analysis has shown the bigger pattern with which the author was ultimately concerned. The agents and events within the saga are analogous to one another, and these in turn are analogous to those of times before the saga and times after the saga—the happenings of those times and the author's time follow the same pattern, hence can be superimposed on one another. The happenings within the saga and those of the analogy outside the saga can also be drawn together in a simultaneous vision; all and both are immediately present. Indeed, one of the favored expressions in the saga is *mjk jafnskjótt,* which indicates that two actions are coincident. The expression is a loaded one and carries several connotations relevant to basic notions in the saga: On the one hand, two events may be taking place concomitantly: "Nú setr Þorkell fram ferjuna ok hlóð. Þorsteinn bar *jafnskjótt* af útan sem Þorkell hlóð ok þeir frunautar hans" (lxxvi, 221-222: "Now Thorkel launched the ferry and started loading. Thorstein carried the timber off just as fast as Thorkel and his comrades loaded it"). On the other hand, two events may converge at the same time: "Eptir þetta ræðr sá til, er skírsluna skyldi af hndum inna, ok *jafnskjótt* sem hann var kominn undir jarðarmenit, hlaupask þessir menn at mót með vápnum, sem til þess váru settir" (xviii, 43: "Now the one who was to carry out the ordeal gets started, and just at the moment when he had come under the sod, the men who had been put up to this rush at each other with their weapons"). This situation is, of course, contrived and the audience is aware of the manipulation. Other such incidents in the saga are also "arranged," but the author would like it to seem as if "by coincidence," as for example when Hoskuld and his housecarls arrive home at the same time: "Þat var *mjk jafnskjótt,* at húskarlar hans koma heim" (xix, 46); or when Óláf Peacock moves to Hjardarholt: "Þat var *mjk jafnskjótt,* at húskarlar hfðu ofan tekit klyfjar af hrossum, ok þá reið Óláfr í garð" (xxiv, 68: "Just as the housecarls had got the packs down from the horses, Óláf rode into the farmyard"). The same precision attends the meeting of Gudrún and Snorri: "Þat er í Lœkjarskógs landi; í þeim stað hafði Gudrún á kveðit, at þau Snorri skyldu finnask. Þau kómu þar *mjk jafnsnimma*" (lix, 176: "That is on land belonging to Lœkjarskóg and at this place Gudrún had arranged to meet with Snorri. They arrived there just at the same time"). This simultaneity is everywhere manipulated by the omniscient author; it is related to the exactness and symmetry of the saga; it is like a contrivance of destiny. Indeed, the fact that Thórólf and Ásgaut escape across the river is attributed to fate, and in this scene significantly the *jafnskjótt* also appears:

> Ok með því at menn váru hraustir, ok þeim varð lengra lífs auðit, þá komask þeir yfir ána ok upp á hfuðísinn ðrum megin. Þat er *mjk jafnskjótt,* er þeir eru komnir yfir ána, at Ingjaldr kemr at ðrum megin at ánni ok frunautar hans (xv, 34: And seeing that they were sturdy men and fated to live longer, they got across the river and up onto the pack ice on the other side. Just at the time when they had got across the river, Ingjald and his companions reached the other side of the river).

Much as Halldór expected the men from other farms to arrive just when the sale of the Hjardarholt lands should have been closed, and which they in fact did, the author, too, has neatly prearranged everything. Contemporary time is parallel to saga time, simultaneous with it and also predestined. *Jafnskjótt* is a coded word to be read first on the normal discursive level within the context, second as a clue to the meaning of the time relationships between the events within the saga (what happens in Hoskuld's day can happen in Óláf's day, in Kjartan's day, in Bolli B.'s day), and third as a key to the meaning of the time comparisons the author has contrived with his superimposed images of time present and time past. It reveals also his view of history.

The flash-backs in the saga repeat this structural form. They, too, relate of events in the saga that are taking place simultaneously and produce a back-and-forth comparing. From this new aspect, the whole saga can be said to be a flash-back from the author's time to saga time, a comparing of events "then" and "now" which emphasizes their simultaneity, their parallelism, and their contrast.

Since the present time (thirteenth century) is superimposed on the past time of the saga and simultaneous with it, the saga can be read like a coded message. That is, the structural categories and stylistic devices, the abstracted forms, have double reference. Why the regular occurrence of *bæði . . . ok* and its negative counterpart *hvárki . . . né,* why are there always *tveir kostir,* why is *jafnan* a loaded word? The saga is *both* what it seems to be *and* something more; it is also *neither* the one *nor* the other: neither saga time nor contemporary time. The thirteenth century is not wholly analogous to the positive world of the saga; it is the negative counterpart. We have noted, for example, that the positive forms quantitatively outnumbered the negative formulations in the saga, but that the negative reversal in a pattern always carried more than face-value significance. Any one pair of inimical brothers, too, was found not to be a completely opposite pair: Bárd and Thorleik Hoskuldsson overlap in regard to some points, as do Kjartan and Bolli Th., as do Thorleik and Bolli B. The eleventh century and the thirteenth century are the same, yet antithetical. The further import of images in reverse also becomes apparent, as in the betrothals where the pattern is consistently one of presentation of the woman's qualifications to the man and of the man's to the woman; or as in the sea voyages and receptions back and forth in Norway and in Iceland, the one a mirrored image of the other. Then there are reversed images, that is, negative contrasts to a predominantly positive pattern: a bad marriage, a poor sea voyage, a cool reception, an incomplete hero. Án's two dreams are also reversed images of one another, the one negative, the other positive.

It is *always* the same world that is being suggested— the world of the saga shows within itself a repetitive sameness, but beyond this is implied that the Heroic

Age is like the Age of the Commonwealth, is like the Age of the Sturlungs, yet the latter also contrasted with the former ones—Parallels and Contrasts are always implied in Comparison. So there are *two* choices for the reader: the one level or the other. The game could go on.

The nonsense riddle of the cloak tells of Snorri's "bragð," and it also explains the riddle of the saga:

> Wet it hangs on the wall,
> Wot the cloak a trick,
> Ne'er more dry after this,
> Nor deny I, it knows of two.

The saga contains one trick—the concealed formal elements; the cloak knows of another, the analogy with contemporary times. The saga is not dry, but wet (filled with significance and knowledge). There seems no limit to the author's ingenuity and to the camouflages that can be unveiled. The language of the saga is ironic beyond anyone's expectation. Its layers are actually threefold. Here is then confirmation of the significance of the structural components based on two and three. The first layer, the normal discursive one, is a camouflage, a coded message, for the second layer, the abstract formal layer that the aesthetic analysis revealed. This layer in turn is the key for the third layer, the analogy with the thirteenth century. The first must be decoded to find the second, and the second to find the third. The one hinges on the other. By veiling his patterns, the author has hidden the internal structure, hence the analogy remains concealed, both are hidden by the cloak. And what better image could the author have selected than a hooded cloak for concealment? Could it be that the indictment of his own age he could not state directly and openly, so he spoke in parables much as, for example, Brueghel the Elder dared not speak out against the atrocities, the tragedy of his times but feigning innocence depicted them symbolically through analogy with the remoter times of Biblical happenings? It has taken critics long enough to see through *Laxdœla*'s tricks, something with which we have been confronted all along in this analysis, but which only opened up to myself at the very end. And that is as it had to be, for only after the conclusion of the aesthetic analysis could the next level be unfolded, and that is what has taken place as the sections on Style and Tone and Rhythm and Time were conceived. The saga becomes extremely witty, once the parable is recognized, indeed a self-parody. Some of this wit comes through even if one is not fully "aware." Did the contemporary audience see through it? The saga gives us the author's surmise: Gudrún thinks Thorgils will see through Snorri's first trick: "'Sjámun hann.'" Snorri answers: "'Sjá mun hann víst eigi'"; and this is confirmed: "ok sér hann ekki í þetta." If the first trick is not discovered, the second

will forever remain a secret. The author is telling us throughout the saga what it is all about, but the audience has not been wily enough for this "second Snorri."

The anonymous *Laxdœla* author can be credited with having produced one of the most remarkable and brilliant prose works of the medieval period. His was a genius of extraordinary power and perception. Significant as literature, significant as a commentary on the age that fostered it, *Laxdœla saga* represents a *tour de force* that few could duplicate. With a sensitivity to the workings of human beings and of history, with a sureness of touch, and with a consciousness of the symbolic import behind the happenings he has selected to depict, the author created not just an account of them on the discursive level, but on the formal level through organization of his linguistic materials a virtual and conceptual image of what he observed. Acutely aware of the irrepressible demands of wounded honor, of the lust for retaliation, of commitments that ever led to further involvement, he perceived a destiny behind the inescapable entanglements of life whether the time was that of the Settlement and the Commonwealth or of the Age of the Sturlungs. In this merging of the cultural reference with the cultural context rests the secret of the saga. If *Laxdœla saga* is a tragedy, it is not one of the human beings but rather of a cultural ethos which had ceased to be constructive. By reason of the selection, arrangement, and organization of all the materials that went into the composition of the saga, it must be conceded that it is a literary monument of the highest order. It stands as a witness to the age that produced it and as a symbol that conveys the meaning of that age more forcibly than any chronicle.

Notes

1. Heller [*Literarisches Schaffen in der* Laxdaela Saga. Halle, Germany, 1960] compares these words of Kjartan to those of Earl Tostis in Chap. 117 of the *Mork.* (erroneously cited as Chap. 35 in his *Laxdœla Saga und Königssagas*, p. 9). Kjartan's casting away of the weapon he compares with King Óláf Haraldsson's similar act in *Óláfs saga helga*, Chap. 228 (*ibid.*, p. 11).

2. Cf. Susanne Langer, *Feeling and Form* (New York: Charles Scribner & Sons, 1953), pp. 326-350.

3. H. W. Fowler, *A Dictionary of Modern English Usage* (Oxford, 1958), (*sv.* Irony) pp. 295-296.

4. See my article in the forthcoming Hollander Festschrift.

5. The author's consciousness of the difference between conditions obtaining at the time of the saga's events and the time of writing comes to the

fore in such passages as: "Ok sér þar tóptina, sem hann lét gera hrófit" (xiii, 26: "And one can see there traces of where he had the shed built"); or where he gives explanation for the men being able to conceal themselves in a woods where in his day there was no longer one: "Skógr þykkr var í dalnum í þann tíð" (lv, 165: "There was a thick woods in the valley at that time"); or in "þar sem Kaupstaðrinn í Bjrgvin er síðan" (xi, 22).

6. For the previous discussion of the passage in connection with the understatement about Thorkel's concern, see above, Chap. I, p. 40. For the help this passage gives in dating the saga, see below [A. Margaret Arent Madelung, The Laxdoela Saga: Its Structural Patterns, Chapel Hill: Universtiy of North Carolina Press, 1972], p. 190.

7. What at first might seem like inadvertant slips or nodding on the part of the author may in fact be deliberate cues for his audience. In any case, it is in these places that we can best detect the trick: e. g. repetitions that appear too pat without a motivating circumstance; seemingly inappropriate uses of *sem fyrr;* misplacement of expected elements in a pattern, like *at skilnaði;* and of course the anachronisms.

8. How far do other authors or other sagas go in verb-mixing? To answer this the following points will have to be considered first, abbreviations in the MSS and normalizing of editions. Each saga will have to be studied for these aspects individually.

9. See in this connection the articles by M. C. van den Toorn, "Zeit und Tempus in der Saga," *Arkiv,* LXXVI (1961), 134-152; and by Carl C. Rokkjær, "Om tempusblandningen i islandsk prosa indtil 1250," *Arkiv,* LXXVIII (1963), 197-216.

Arnold R. Taylor (essay date 1974)

SOURCE: Taylor, Arnold R. "*Laxdaela Saga* and Author Involvement in the Icelandic Sagas." *Leeds Studies in English* 7 n.s. (1974): 13-21.

[*In the following essay, Taylor investigates the subtle use of authorial intrusion in the* Laxdaela Saga, *focusing principally on the author's characterization of Gudrun through the use of her prophetic dreams.*]

Laxdœla saga has recently attracted detailed consideration by many eminent scholars who have concerned themselves either with the date of composition or the name of its author.[1] What I have to say will also relate to the author, though I am not concerned with his name

nor with the rival claims of Sturla Þórðarson or any other writer for so proud a position. My interest lies more in what motivated him and made him write in the way he did. Njörður Njarðvík, in a perceptive and sensitive article, has touched on the same subject but from a different point of view. He concentrates more on the saga author's interest in contemporary events and the relevance of what he had to say on the social life of his times; I am more concerned with his interest in the past.

Let us look first at the problem of the author's involvement or lack of involvement in the finished product.[2] Usually it has been said that the Icelandic saga author keeps himself in the background, that he refrains from comment upon the actions of his characters, that he prefers to give a cinematographic, eye-witness account of the action, and leaves his readers to draw their own conclusions on the characteristics and motives of his people. I believe such statements to be substantially true if we confine ourselves to explicit comment on the author's part and are prepared to admit that this seeming lack of involvement is secondary and only real as a deliberate, and remarkably effective, literary device. As is well known, there are a few general exceptions to this avoidance of intrusion on the part of the author. It has often been pointed out that when a person who plays any considerable part in the story is first introduced a short description is normally given of his or her characteristics, both physical and moral. We may perhaps add that this is the basis upon which the saga author builds and that his subsequent portrayal of the character is but an amplification, an explication, a colouring-in of this introductory portrait. A typical example of this is the picture given of the chieftain Hrafnkel in *Hrafnkels saga freysgoða*.[3] Occasionally also the author will intrude an opinion of his own in the guise of popular or public comment. Sometimes this is explicit enough: the author will say in comment on an action that something or other *mæltist* or *taldist illa fyrir;* sometimes the comment is partly veiled, e.g. in *Hákonar saga góða,* after the fall of Egill ullserkr in the battle at Fræðaberg, one chapter ends with the words *Hávir bautasteinar standa hjá haugi Egils ullserks* (Tall memorial stones stand beside the burial mound of Egill ullserkr).[4] Snorri Sturluson not rarely permits himself such an aside in order to give his own opinion of an action. The author of *Njáls saga* is very fond of this device: in his account of the death of Gunnar he is able to say *ok sgðu þat allir menn at hann brygði sér hvártki við sár né við bana* (but everyone is agreed that he flinched neither at wounds nor death itself); he makes Rannveig comment *Illa ferr þér ok mun þín skmm lengi uppi* (You are an evil woman and your shame will long be remembered); and he finally lets Gissur sum up the whole action with *Mikinn ldung hfu vér nú at velli lagit, ok hefir oss erfitt veitt, ok mun hans vrn uppi, meðan *landit er byggt* (We have felled a great champion, and we have not found it easy. His last defence will be remembered as long as this land is lived in).[5] But it is unnecessary to enumerate further examples; you must all have come across many of them. In a very interesting and informative article on this subject of intrusion Paul Schach, in addition to noting the opinions of commentators in the past, suggests five ways in which the saga author commonly shows his own involvement, and in case we may feel that his evidence is slight he rightly adds the useful caution that further evidence of author involvement may well have been removed from our surviving texts by subsequent scribes and copyists who notoriously did not always treat their exemplar with the respect which later generations might have preferred.

I have suggested above that the seeming lack of intrusion is really nothing but a literary device. All of us are aware both of the author's presence and of the reality of his involvement. Every writer or artist must reflect his times, not only in his choice of material but also in his techniques. One might therefore ask both why the saga author generally preferred to adopt the technique of the "outside observer" and also where he got it from. These are big questions and merit detailed consideration, and hence an investigation of them is far beyond the scope of this paper. But clearly the choice is partly dictated by the fact that the thirteenth-century Icelandic author is employing techniques which he inherited from the oral storyteller. Unlike the modern author, who can make his confidential appeal to a single reader, he is addressing not one person but many. In medieval times, whether we are thinking of the homilist, the saga writer or the composer of heroic story in verse, the audience of one was rare, and it was the storyteller's duty to involve not so much himself as his audience in what was happening. And so, by seeming withdrawal, the saga writer was aiming at a definite effect; by his seeming non-intervention the author is bound to abrogate the necessity for judgment and moral comment upon his characters, but equally he is bound to hand over the responsibility for judgment, both moral and aesthetic, to his audience.

Such a device is by no means rare in other medieval authors, for it is in effect one facet of a characteristic common to most extant Old English and Old Icelandic literary remains. In the Old English poem *Beowulf,* for example, we are early left in no doubt as to the outcome of the story, that tragedy lies ahead. We know that although the hall of King Hrothgar will be cleansed by Beowulf, his efforts will be in vain, for the hall, like the farm at Bergþórshváll, will go up in flames and the dynasty of the Scyldings—the Skjldungar—will be destroyed. In the same way it is clear in the late Old English poem *The Battle of Maldon* that the English cause is lost long before Byrhtnoth, their leader, falls,

and that success in the material sense will not be achieved by his followers, though their greatness of heart and heroism may compensate somewhat for their tragic failure.

Now it may well be that this literary device, so common in Old English and Old Icelandic literature, of hinting at the outcome of the story is the direct result of the fact that the content of the story was often already known to the audience, so that there could be no virtue—as in a modern production such as the detective novel—in deliberately hiding the outcome in order to build up tension and excitement; this last could be better done by constantly reminding the listener that he already knew the tragic points of the impending disaster. Under medieval circumstances it was useless for the storyteller to put himself forward as the omniscient power behind the narrative who grudgingly, yet cunningly, hands out carefully calculated snippets of information until such time as all is revealed. He must rather create the excitement in another way, involve his audience and make the listener the creator of excitement and tension by forcing him to call to mind the varied small details of the story to come. This he does by hinting at the future, sometimes even by prefiguring the whole story in some way, as for example in Gunnlaugs saga. To sum up then, I believe that this literary device although generally described as "lack of author intrusion," might equally well, if not better, be thought of as a device aimed at "audience participation."

But it is now time to return to **Laxdæla saga.** Dreams are commonly used in saga writing both to prefigure the story and to build up tension; examples immediately spring to mind in *Gunnlaugs saga, Gísla saga, Droplaugarsona saga* and many others. But perhaps nowhere are they employed more prolifically or more successfully than by the author of **Laxdæla.** There are in all nine dreams used in the story, some much more aptly than others. There is the dream of Ólafr about Harri the ox which, as has often been pointed out, serves as a keystone in the build-up of tension before the death of Kjartan.[6] There are the two dreams of Án hrísmagi, one before and one after the battle in Svínadalr; they are used as a sort of emphasizing bracketing of the most important episode in the story. There is the dream of Þorkell Eyjólfsson which is variously interpreted by himself and by his wife Guðrún, and the dream of Herdís Bolladóttir about the disturbance at the chapel at Helgafell. In addition there are the four dreams which prefigure the marriages of Guðrún.

Professor Foote has pointed out that there are different stages in the development of **Laxdæla:** that it begins and remains down to chapter thirty-two a family chronicle, that after chapter thirty-two Guðrún takes over and it is the story of her loves and marriages, and the consequences of them, that we remember.[7] Professor Foote implies that there is a later return to the family chronicle once the pre-ordained marriages have taken place; though that there is a return to the family chronicle is only partially true, since for the modern reader at any rate—and I suspect for the thirteenth-century Icelander—the whole of the story, after her introduction, is dominated by Guðrún.

Nevertheless such a structure is natural enough and has precedent in an earlier saga, that of Egill Skallagrímsson. There, also at first, the family chronicle prevails, for we are not told of the birth of Egill before chapter thirty-one. Thereafter Egill dominates the story, though it would probably be true to say that the co-ordination in *Egils saga* is stronger, since it is at least his family that the first thirty chapters concern. Unlike those of Guðrún, Egill's adventures take place for the most part abroad, but late in the saga he too returns to his family and lives out his life to old age. It is interesting to note the fact that the old age of the "heroic" Egill and of the "heroic" Guðrún are by no means secondary elements in the sagas but are dwelt upon at some length, and it is equally interesting that both authors add another factor, one that would seem likely to destroy completely the early image of a heroic character, namely, blindness. I think it is a noteworthy achievement in both authors that they manage to keep our interest in heroic figures in decay and to maintain to the very end the outstanding, gigantic nature of their main characters. The resemblance in structure between the two sagas is so striking that, although I have no wish to enter on the controversy of the literary influences on **Laxdæla saga,** there seems to me little doubt that its author, at some time in his life, must have read *Eigla* or listened to a reading of it.

It is only natural that the saga author of the earlier half of the thirteenth century—and his successors in the latter half—should use the family chronicle form; it was imposed upon him by tradition, by the love of genealogy in the nation, by the historical precedent of the Lives of the Norwegian kings but above all by the temper of the times, which would make any saga inadequate if it lacked at least mention of the *Landnáma* forebears of its hero. The commonwealth needed its heroic founders to maintain its prestige and standing in troublous times, and though the modern reader may feel such a lengthy treatment to be a tedious and unnecessary preliminary it was in their day an essential part of the story. But the authors of both these sagas were particularly attracted to the single heroic figure, the author of *Eigla* as a result of his interests in continental monarchy and court poetry, and the author of **Laxdæla** because of the earlier heroic verse of the *Elder Edda.*

As everyone has realized, the love of Guðrún Ósvífrsdóttir for Kjartan is intended to parallel that of Brynhildr for Sigurðr; as W. P. Ker has said, the old story was modernized in the aristocratic rural society of western Iceland.[8] Guðrún herself is a composite of Brynhildr, who died glorifying in and grieving at the vengeance she had achieved, and of her namesake Guðrún Gjúkadóttir, who demanded and attained so ruthless a vengeance for her family on her husband Atli and on her son-in-law Jrmunrekr. Our author must indeed have been greatly attracted to this story, for in making it the basis of his saga he subordinates almost everything, including his family chronicle introduction, to its theme. Kjartan is developed into a new tragic Sigurðr and Bolli into a Gunnar, but not, I would suggest, for their own sake but to the greater glory of the woman Guðrún.

That this was the author's intention is made clear by the introduction and positioning of Guðrún's dreams, which are told within a page or so of her first introduction and which could be regarded not only as motivating elements in the development of the story but also as the first climax of the tale. Professor Andersson, in accordance with his scheme, would make Kjartan's death the climax of the story, and in one sense, of course, he is right.[9] But it is not the only climax; there are a whole series of them in this saga, the slaying of Bolli, Guðrún's final confession and the earlier chapter in which the four dreams are interpreted. At this point a peak has been reached in the story which turns out to be the beginning of a plateau, dominated perhaps but not overshadowed by those later peaks of tragedy and revenge. The author prepares very carefully for this chapter, in a way in which another man less personally involved in the story of Guðrún might not have done: he subordinates the earlier part of his story to it and indeed uses the latter part of his chronicle element as a threatening prelude. The scene has been set on the male side by the fostering together of Kjartan and Bolli, the instrument of slaughter is provided by the baleful acquisition of the sword Fótbítr, innocently given to her cousin by Kjartan's sister, and a direct threat against Kjartan is presaged by the introduction of the first dream—of Harri the ox. Ólafr's dream is deliberately mysterious. Who is this woman who threatens him? The very question suggests the only possible answer—a figure of folktale brought in, not too elegantly but with perfect timing, to bring to fulfilment the necessary build-up of tension before the entry of the female protagonist.

The single chapter which follows brings the whole story into focus, for Gestr Oddleifsson, the sage, is able to foretell her four marriages from her dreams and later also the tragedy which Ólafr will have to face in the loss of his son at the hands of his foster brother.

The four dreams are fulfilled—in outcome at least, but not as literally as one may expect. Normally in the sagas the details of a prophetic dream are carefully observed and the event mirrors its interpretation. One might say that this is true of the first three of Guðrún's dreams, for from them we learn of her attitude towards and estimate of her first three husbands; and one might therefore have expected the fourth to follow suit. But either our author is too expert to account for every detail and by so doing to make a monotonous reality of an exciting, suggestive prophecy, or else we have here an instance of the character actually taking over from the author who cannot bring himself to permit the reality of Gestr's interpretation:

> Sá er inn fjórði draumr þinn, at þú þóttisk hafa hjálm á hfði af gulli ok settan gimsteinum, ok varð þér þung-bærr; þar munt þú eiga inn fjórða bonda. Sá mun vera mestr hfðingi ok mun bera heldr œgishjálm yfir þer . . .[10]

> In your fourth dream you dreamed that you were wearing on your head a helmet of gold set with precious stones, and you found it heavy to bear; this means you will have a fourth husband. He will be the greatest chieftain of them all, and he will dominate you completely . . .

It may be, of course, that at this stage in the writing of his story the author intended to show Guðrún in her fourth marriage as a woman overawed by so great a chieftain. But if so, it is evident that he changed his mind. He later finds that he cannot allow his heroic female figure, whom he so much admired, to be belittled by any man, for on the very day of her wedding-feast he deliberately retails the story of her defiance of this husband over the affair of Gunnar Þiðrandabani. On this occasion it is Snorri goði who points out what an exceptional woman Guðrún is: *Máttu sjá, hversu mikill skrungr Guðrún er, ef hon berr okkr báða ráðum* (You can see for yourself what an exceptional woman Guðrún is, when she gets the better of both of us);[11] and her superiority is cleverly emphasized by a further dream. Þorkell dreams that his beard covers the whole of Breiðifjrðr and interprets the dream to his own advantage by suggesting that it means he will be overlord of the whole district; but Guðrún remembers—and recalls to the reader after the passage of so many years and so many pages—her own dream, which like the rest of the dreams spells tragedy, and we know that Þorkell will drown.

This leaves one final dream upon which to comment, and it is important for our purpose. It is the dream of Herdís Bolladóttir that her grandmother, Guðrún, now in her Christian character of a nun and in her old age, is still powerful enough to disturb and overcome the powers of paganism and evil in the form of a sorceress buried under the floor of the church at Helgafell.[12] Like the dream of Ólafr after the killing of Harri the ox, this dream is pure folktale, but it is used by the author to good, though very different, purpose. For at this stage in his story he is nearing the end. Þorkell, Guðrún's fourth husband, is dead and her prophesied destinies fulfilled, and something is now needed to bolster up the anticlimax before the final scene where Guðrún at last admits the love which has motivated so many of her actions and a great deal of the story. It is not sufficient for our author to see her, as he had formerly seen Kjartan, as a protagonist for Christianity, though he had this point at heart too, as had many another saga author of the thirteenth century. He must also show her as successful in this new role, in order that her stature should remain high and be remembered before the memorable scene when she makes confession to her son.

My reading today of our author's purpose has been based upon his use of dreams, and in summing up I should like to stress my two main points. Whether the author was Sturla Þórðarson or some other of the Sturlung clan we shall probably never know, but we know him to have been a good Christian, a man of his own age, of thirteenth-century Iceland, yet one who also welcomed the new world typified by romance;[13] his saga also tells us that he still found no necessity to reject that old world of heroism which he found so attractive in the poems of the *Elder Edda*. It is interesting, indeed, to note that for the modern reader it is this element in his story which still appeals; it is this element which remains timeless. Secondly, may I revert to my first thesis of author involvement. Too often when the expression "writer intrusion or the lack of it" is used it does not seem to be appreciated that the Icelandic author of the thirteenth century is as involved in his material as any modern storyteller, that the device of withdrawal, real though it is, does not reflect the attitude of the author towards his subject-matter but is a literary artifice to enable him to put across his story to a multiple audience in the most effective way he knows. Professor Schach in his article made clear that he was talking of explicit "author intrusion,"[14] but Professor Lönnroth was equally right to stress the implicit involvement of the saga writer.[15] It has been demonstrated that the author of *Laxdæla* was greatly concerned with the questions of his day, but let us not forget that the saga writer's main purpose was to tell a good story, and in order to do this he had to become involved with his characters. The author of *Laxdæla* showed this in Guðrún. He became himself so involved in this story of a woman—as no other saga writer ever did—that once she was on the stage he was unable to leave her, and nearly every incident is introduced to colour and enliven her portrait. In so doing he proved himself to be one of the most interesting and self-revealing authors of thirteenth-century Iceland.

Notes

1. (a) Various articles by R. Heller, mainly concerned with the connection of the saga with other Icelandic sagas, in *ANF* [*Arkiv foer Nordisk Filologi*] (1960, 1961, 1962, 1965).

(b) R. Heller, *Laxdæla saga und Königssagas* (Halle, 1961); "Neue Wege zur Verfasserbestimmung," *Forschung und Fortschritte,* 41 (1967), 239 ff.; "Das Alter der Laxdæla saga," *ZDA* [*Zeitschrift fuer Deutsches Altertum und Deutsche Literatur*] (1968), 134-155.

(c) P. Hallberg, "Ólafr Þórðarson hvítaskáld, Knytlinga saga och Laxdæla saga," *Studia Íslandica,* 22 (1963).

(d) M. Mundt, *Sturla Þóðarson und die Laxdæla saga* (Oslo, 1969).

(e) N. P. Njarðvík, "*Laxdæla* saga—en tidskritik?," *ANF,* 86 (1971), 72-81.

All references to *Laxdæla saga* are to the edition by E. Ó. Sveinsson in *Íslenzk Fornrit,* V (Reykjavík, 1934). Translations from *Laxdæla saga* are from *Laxdæla Saga,* trans. Magnusson and Pálsson (London, 1969). Translations from *Njáls saga* are from the same translators' *Njal's Saga* (London, 1960).

2. See (a) Paul Schach, "Some forms of writer intrusion in the Íslendingasögur," *Scand. Stud.,* 42 (1970), 128-156 and (b) Lars Lönnroth, "Rhetorical Persuasion in the Sagas," *Scand. Stud.,* 42 (1970), 157-189.

3. *Hrafnkels saga freysgoða,* ch. 2, ed. Jón Jóhannesson, *Íslenzk Fornrit,* XI (Reykjavík, 1950).

4. *Hákonar saga góða,* ch. 27, ed. Bjarni Aðalbjarnarson in "Heimskringla I," *Íslenzk Fornrit,* XXVI (Reykajavík, 1951).

5. *Brennu-Njáls saga,* ch. 77, ed. E. Ó. Sveinsson, *Íslenzk Fornrit,* XII (Reykjavík, 1954).

6. *Laxd. s.,* ch. 31.

7. *The Laxdale Saga* (London, 1964), pp. ix ff.

8. W. P. Ker, *Epic and Romance* (London, 1897), p. 209.

9. T. M. Andersson, *The Icelandic Family Saga* (Cambridge, Mass., 1967), pp. 163-74.

10. *Laxd. s.,* ch. 33.

11. *Laxd. s.,* ch. 69.

12. *Laxd. s.,* ch. 76.

13. This point is clearly demonstrated by E. Ó. Sveinsson in the introduction to his edition. See especially pp. v-xxiii.

14. See articles listed in note 2 above.

15. See articles listed in note 2 above.

Florence S. Boos (essay date 1983)

SOURCE: Boos, Florence S. "Morris' Radical Revisions to the *Laxdaela Saga*." *Victorian Poetry* 21 (1983): 415-20.

[*In the following essay, Boos details Morris's reworking of the second half of the* Laxdaela Saga *into his poem "The Lovers of Gudrun," calling it the transformation of "a feud-narrative of property negotiations and family rivalries into an exemplum of doomed friendship and heterosexual love."*]

"The Lovers of Gudrun" provides one of the most interesting examples of Morris' reworking of an earlier narrative, for both the *Laxdaela Saga* and "The Lovers of Gudrun" are in their divergent ways impressive literary works. "The Lovers of Gudrun," published in December, 1869, was Morris' first poetic narrative based on an Icelandic saga, and its dramatic qualities may seem to reflect his temperamental identification with medieval Norse literature. In fact, no *Earthly Paradise* tale shows more fidelity to the historical letter of its original, and few more infidelity to its spirit.[1] Essentially, Morris rewrote a feud-narrative of property negotiations and family rivalries into an exemplum of doomed friendship and heterosexual love.

Morris once advocated the following use of narrative source material: "Read it through, then shut the book and write in your own way."[2] As he matured, he began more and more consistently to "write in [his] own way" and came to consider one of the central virtues of his narrative method the emotional transformation of classical and medieval legend. It is no accident that the "idle singer" of *The Earthly Paradise* bases his apology on the claim to present a historical palimpsest of human passions: the deeper Morris' feeling for an existing tale, the more radical his changes; and, with few exceptions, the better the result.

The changes in the *Laxdaela Saga* were in fact very deep and may be taken as a prototype of his most independent narrative practice. Morris retains only vestigial elements of the central preoccupation with interfamilial negotiation and the establishment of law in the *Saga.* Kjartan and Guðrun are the most dramatic characters of the *Saga,* but Kjartan's father, Olaf

Peacock, is its central figure. His prophecies, counsels of forbearance, and strategic alliances are carefully detailed both in the Kjartan-Bolli-Guðrun subplot and in many parallel episodes (after Olaf's death, Snorri the Priest fulfills a similar function). The *Laxdaela Saga* is essentially a celebration of its principal families' rise to dynastic power.

In particular, the *Saga* is not about the pain of spurned love or the conflict of friends who love the same woman. Some residual inconsistencies of motivation and action in "The Lovers of Gudrun" show the strains of Morris' efforts to graft onto this psychologically stark and penurious framework intricate ambiguities of sexual conflict and emotion. The intense friendship of Morris' male principals Bodli and Kiartan becomes more convincing than its placement in the context of tribal feuds. Morris was an internal realist, however, and here, as elsewhere, was able to make inconsistent behavior follow plausible psychological patterns. Gudrun, Bodli, and Kiartan (Guðrun, Bolli, and Kjartan in the *Saga*), the three principal characters of "The Lovers of Gudrun," are all faithful to their deepest and most "fateful" passions. Gudrun is least scrupulous and suffers least, and Bodli is assigned the worst crime and the most pitiable fate, but Morris maintains roughly equal sympathy for all three. This parity of flaws and virtues recalls the detachment of *The Defence of Guenevere,* but the suffering and guilt are here more complexly shared. Again, the "heroic" plot, not the characters' convoluted psychological anguish, seems peripheral to Morris' poem.

This interpretation seems consistent, at least, with Morris' remark in the 1887 essay, "The Early Literature of the North," that The Lax-dalers' story contains a "very touching and beautiful tale, but it is not done justice to by the detail of the story."[3] As he revised the "beautiful tale," for example, Morris essentially obliterated Guðrun's chief passions: family pride and greed. Guðrun greatly enjoys the wealth of her unloved first husband Thorvald: "In all the Westfjords there were no jewels so costly that Guðrun did not consider them her due, and she repaid Thorvald with animosity if he failed to buy them, however expensive they might be" (p. 124).[4] She divorces him after only two years and retains half his estate. Morris gives Gudrun the more sensitive motive of revulsion at Thorvald's physical violence.

Morris also made major changes in the motives of Bodli and Kiartan. The immediate motive of the clash between the *Saga*'s Bolli and Kjartan is a property dispute: Kjartan has extorted the sale of an estate which Guðrun and Bolli had arranged to buy, and *this* is the "humiliation" which most seems to rankle Guðrun, when she rebukes Bolli:

Kjartan has given you a harsher choice than he offered Thorarin: either that you leave this district with little honour, or else that you confront him and prove yourself rather less fainthearted than you have been hitherto.

(p. 169)

[Y]ou don't have the luck to be able to please everybody; and if you refuse this journey, it will be the end of our marriage.

(p. 172)

Morris also omitted completely the earlier account in the *Saga* of Guðrun's ruthless revenge of her second husband, Thord. In the *Saga,* it is Guðrun who conceives the plan to ambush Kjartan, not her loutish brother Ospak. Indeed, she berates the reluctant Ospak: "'Men like you have the memory of hogs. . . . You just sit at home pretending to be men, and there are always too many of you about'" (p. 172). Morris' Gudrun, by contrast, expresses her (inconsistent) distaste for "those murderous men."

In the *Saga,* Guðrun later plots for twelve years her revenge of Bolli's murder, promises marriage to a potential avenger, and demands that her still-adolescent sons participate in the ambush. Her brief love for Kjartan is simply the most self-defeating of her several struggles for personal and dynastic preeminence.

Other omissions also help sharpen the focus of Morris' tale. In the *Saga* Kjartan is fully satisfied with his wife, who bears him a son, Asgeir. Guðrun eventually has four sons, one by Thord, two by Bolli, and a fourth by her last husband, Thorkel (she also casually relinquishes her eldest son for adoption, another aspect of her character which might blur the image Morris creates).

On the other hand, Morris also represses one of Guðrun's more admirable traits: her physical bravery. As Kjartan's relatives come to murder Bolli, he and Guðrun are alone in a shed:

Bolli recognized Halldor by his voice, and several of his companions. He told [the pregnant] Guðrun to go away from the shieling, saying that this was not an encounter she would be likely to enjoy. Guðrun said she thought that nothing would happen there which she should not be allowed to watch, and added that it could do Bolli no harm to have her by his side. Bolli insisted on having his own way, however, and so Guðrun left.

(p.186)

This Guðrun would have been unlikely to throw herself weeping on her bed to lament "Bodli's" departure to murder "Kiartan."

Kjartan and Bolli are also more straightforward and less reflective than their Morrisean counterparts. Kiartan's refusal of Gudrun's offer to accompany him to Norway is relatively wistful and "romantic":

So fought love in him with the craving vain
The love of all the wondering world to gain.

    thou a word or twain of me shalt hear
    E'en if the birds must bear them o'er the sea.

                  (III, pp. 284, 280)

In contrast, Kjartan remarks mundanely that "'That's out of the question . . . Your brothers haven't settled down yet and your father is an old man, and they wouldn't have anyone to look after them if you leave the country. So wait for me instead for three years'" (p. 142).

Nor does Kjartan send any message to Guðrun to accompany Bolli's return to Iceland, as does Kiartan in Morris' tale. While they are in Norway, the more hotheaded and ill-tempered Kjartan had also plotted to burn the King's house but was narrowly dissuaded by the more temperate Bolli. Kjartan's later marriage in Iceland to Hrefna (Refna in Morris) is motivated not by pity but by her father's standing as one of the leading landowners of northern Iceland.

The **Saga** Bolli is less handsome and admired than Kjartan, but he is "courteous and very warrior-like" for all that and has a "taste for the ornate" (p. 110). He is also a calm and essentially consistent man, who acts for the most part to defend his interests. When he chooses to leave Norway, he does not, unlike Bodli, propose immediately to Guðrun on his return. Nor is his offer diffident and self-effacing, as is Bodli's. Bolli does not attack Kjartan before the final fight, and when he is accused of theft, he addresses Kjartan with dignity: "'We are not guilty of the charges you make against us, Kjartan. We would have expected anything of you but to accuse us of theft'" (p. 166). Ultimately, Bolli does not attack Kjartan to placate Guðrun but because he takes seriously a warning by Gudrun's father, Oswif, that Kjartan will have to take revenge on Bolli as Ospak's relative.

In the **Saga,** neither Kjartan nor Bolli mentions Guðrun during their final combat, and Kjartan surrenders from physical fatigue, not despair. In "The Lovers of Gudrun," by contrast, the emotionally charged confrontation between Kiartan and Bodli becomes virtually a suicide pact. The **Saga**'s Bolli is bitterly angry when he returns:

"This luckless deed will live long enough in my mind without you reminding me of it."

"I do not think it luckless," said Guðrun. "It seems to me that you had more prestige the year that Kjartan was in Norway than now when he has ridden roughshod over you since he came back to Iceland. But last of all, what I like best is that Hrefna will not go laughing to bed tonight."

Then Bolli said, in sudden fury, "I doubt if she will turn any paler at the news than you, and I suspect you would have been less shocked if I had been left lying on the field of battle and Kjartan had lived to tell the tale."

                  (p. 176)

In Morris' tale, *Gudrun* berates *Bodli*. The **Saga**'s Guðrun is actually intimidated by Bolli's rage:

Don't say such things, for I am deeply grateful to you for what you have done.

                  (p. 176)

Bolli's death in the **Saga** is one of Morris' more pointed omissions. After a brave effort at self-defense, Bolli is both eviscerated and decapitated:

Bolli said, "It's safe now for you brothers to come a little closer than you have done so far." And he said he did not think his defence would last very long now.

It was Thorgerd who answered him, and said there was no need to shrink from dealing with Bolli thoroughly; she told them to finish off their work. Bolli was still standing up against the wall of the shieling, clutching his tunic tightly to stop his entrails falling out. Steinthor Olaffson now sprang at him and swung a great axe at his neck just above the shoulders, and the head flew off at once.

"May your hands prosper," said Thorgerd, and added that Guðrun would now have some red hairs to comb for Bolli.

With that they left the shieling.

                  (pp. 187-188)

In summary, the Bolli of the **Laxdaela Saga** is a sturdy farmer, who calmly protects his pregnant wife and stoically confronts his sordid death.

In "The Lovers of Gudrun," the initial dichotomy of character between Kiartan and Bodli actually diminishes as Morris' tale progresses. In the end, the two friends are complementary figures in a kind of intricate rite of immolation. Bodli, the most affectionate of the three protagonists, is the one most blamed for harming the others. Morris' intricate casuistry creates sympathy for his greater suffering and remorse, and Bodli assumes he will resume his friendship with Kiartan in heaven (he is noticeably less certain of his relationship there with Gudrun). Kiartan, the man of action, is the most "heroic" and least comprehensible of the three.

Rossetti particularly praised this tale, and biographical parallels to the complex rivalry between Morris and Rossetti can readily be adduced;[5] several of Bodli's expressions of helpless longing seem to reach beyond conventional poetic expressions of frustrated desire. Nevertheless, the "biographical" motif of fidelity-in-rejection had always been an attractive one to Morris: it appears in *The Defence of Guenevere,* the early prose romances, and even his juvenilia. In 1856, Morris wrote a "Nordic" prose romance, "Gertha's Lovers," about two men who love the same woman. The introspective, dark-haired Leuchnar expiates one brief flash of envy for his light-haired friend King Olaf with a lifetime of devotion and serves Olaf's Queen after his friend's death. In effect, "The Lovers of Gudrun" superimposes such motifs on the revenge plot of the *Laxdaela Saga.* In both "Gertha's Lovers" and "The Lovers of Gudrun," the friendship suggests division within a single composite character, but the plot of the *Laxdaela Saga* sharpens the division to one in which each half mortally wounds the other and thus itself.

In conclusion, then, "The Lovers of Gudrun," the most successful tragedy of *The Earthly Paradise,* does *not* derive its brooding power from darkly tragic qualities of a Nordic original. The ominous conflicts and psychological complexities of the tale are Morris' own creation, and its bleak insights sometimes work against the harsher but more straightforward grain of the *Laxdaela Saga.* Here, too, as in others of his twice-told tales, Morris created a thoroughly individual catharsis of pity, fear, and respect for his characters' emotions.

Notes

1. Those familiar with the original have differed over whether Morris improved or distorted the *Laxdaela Saga.* There have been two good discussions of Morris' alterations: Oscar Mauer's "William Morris and *Laxdaela Saga,*" *TSLL* [*Texas Studies in Literature and Language*], 5 (1963), 422-437, dwells more on the *Saga* text but finds more favor with Morris' choices. Ralph Bellas' "William Morris' Treatment of Sources in *The Earthly Paradise,*" Diss. Univ. of Kansas, 1960, pp. 283-302, insightfully analyzes Morris' revisions but seems to prefer the *Saga;* he deprecates Bodli's lament over the dead Kiartan with the remark that "there is nothing in Morris' tale that carries so little of the spirit of the Icelandic original as the piteous mutterings of Bodli over the dead Kiartan" (p. 298). I would agree with the contrast but not the evaluation. Less useful is Dorothy Hoare's *The Works of Morris and Yeats in Relation to Early Saga Literature* (Cambridge Univ. Press, 1937); she finds Morris' *Earthly Paradise* a work filled with "cloying sentiment" and "vague and confused" emotion (p. 41).

2. *Collected Works,* ed. May Morris (London, 1910-15), III, xxii.

3. Eugene LeMire, ed., *Unpublished Lectures of William Morris* (Wayne State Univ. Press, 1969), p. 197.

4. Translations are taken from *Laxdaela Saga,* trans. with intro. by Magnus Magnusson and Hermann Pálsson (Harmondsworth, 1969), and will be identified by page number.

5. See, for example, Mauer, pp. 435-437.

Paul Schach (essay date 1984)

SOURCE: Schach, Paul. "Major Sagas about Icelanders." In *Icelandic Sagas,* pp. 97-130. Boston: Twayne Publishers, 1984.

[*In the following essay, Schach offers a brief overview of the subject, story, and artistry of the* Laxdaela Saga.]

LAXDÆLA SAGA

Like *Egils saga,* the "story of the people of the Laxárdal" begins at the time when Harald Fairhair is extending his dominion over the whole of Norway, and the picture of the king is similar in both sagas. The introduction is equally long in both works, although considerably more intricate in *Laxdæla.* Greed for money and power, which motivated most of Egil's deeds and misdeeds, is also a major theme in this work. Otherwise the two stories are very dissimilar. *Laxdæla* relates the story of a family, the descendants of Ketil flatnef, for several generations. Whereas Snorri derived much of his information from skaldic poetry and *konungasögur,* the anonymous author of *Laxdæla* derived his inspiration from Eddic lays, from a wide variety of sagas and chronicles, and from current events.[1]

The nucleus of the story is the love triangle involving Kjartan Ólafsson, his cousin and foster brother Bolli Thorleiksson, and Gudrún Ósvifrsdóttir, all of them descendants of Ketil. W. P. Ker characterized this story as "a modern prose version of the Niblung tragedy, with the personages chosen from the life of Iceland in the heroic age, and from the Icelandic traditions."[2] The question that formerly occupied students of this saga is to what degree the author was indebted to Eddic poetry on the one hand and to oral traditions on the other. Einar Ólafur Sveinsson represented what might be called the older conservative view. According to him, the nucleus of the story existed as a coherent oral tale, and "the events as they occurred were seen in the light of the heroic lays."[3] What little information we have about the historical personages whose names are borne by the saga characters suggests, however, that many of the crucial events of the story could not have happened as there described. A. Margaret A. Madelung demonstrated in her literary analysis of *Laxdæla* that the work is "of one piece." Heinrich Beck has recently shown that the Niflung tragedy provided a design that embraces not just the nucleus but the entire saga. And Rolf Heller has furnished cogent evidence that **Laxdæla** is an artistic creation of the thirteenth century."[4]

On a trading voyage to Norway, Kjartan's grandfather Höskuld buys a slave named Melkorka, who pretends to be mute. One day Höskuld overhears her speaking to their son Ólaf pái ("Peacock") in Irish. She now reveals that she is an Irish princess and some years later sends Ólaf to visit her father Mýrkjartan. Off the coast of Ireland, the ship runs aground, and a band of hostile natives approach and demand ship and cargo as stranded goods. At this point, the author describes the young hero. "Ólaf walked forward to the prow, and he was dressed thus. He wore a coat of mail and had a gilded helmet on his head. He was girded with a sword, and the guard and pommel were adorned with gold, and in his hand he carried a barbed spear, chased and finely inlaid. He held a red shield before him, on which a lion was traced in gold" (chap. 21).

Mýrkjartan chooses Ólaf over his own sons to succeed him, but Ólaf wisely declines the honor, declaring it better to have "brief honor than lasting shame." In Norway he is welcomed warmly by King Harald gráfeld and even more warmly by Gunnhild, who offer him any office he wishes if he will remain at the Norwegian court. But Ólaf insists he must return to his "noble kinsmen" in Iceland, and in parting the king gives him a merchant ship. Upon his return to Iceland with precious gifts from two kings, Ólaf marries Thorgerd Egilsdóttir, to whom, according to *Egils saga*, we are indebted for the poem *Sonatorrek*. Their son is Kjartan, the central figure of the story. On his deathbed Höskuld tricks his legitimate sons into agreeing to a large inheritance for Ólaf. In order to placate his enraged brother Thorleik, Ólaf offers to foster Thorleik's son Bolli. Thus Kjartan and Bolli grow up together and become inseparable companions. Both are tall, handsome, strong, and dexterous, but Bolli is described as "second only to Kjartan in all skills and accomplishments" (chap. 28).

Like other saga writers, the "**Laxdæla** artist" (Heusler) employed foreshadowing to strengthen the cohesion of his story, to maintain suspense, and to create the illusion that the fate of the major characters was inevitable. When still unmarried Gudrún has four dreams, which the sage Gest interprets as predictions of her four marriages. Gest further foretells the slaying of Kjartan by Bolli and the death and burial of himself and his friend Ósvíf. When Kjartan begins to visit Gudrún at her home at Laugar, Ólaf has forebodings that their friendship will not bring good luck to them or their families. Kjartan does not share his father's pessimism. "Kjartan continued his visits in his usual way, and Bolli went with him" (chap. 39).

Before going abroad, Kjartan asks Gudrún to remain unmarried for three years, but Gudrún refuses, declaring that his decision to leave the country is rash. In Norway Kjartan competes with Ólaf Tryggvason in an aquatic contest, which the king barely wins. The role played and the lines spoken by Hallfred vandræðaskáld in Odd's biography (chap. 40) are here assigned to Bolli (chap. 39). The king, depicted in this story as benign and benevolent, patiently persuades Kjartan to submit to baptism (after he has threatened to burn Ólaf in his hall), and Bolli and the crew follow his example. When the ban on sailing to Iceland pending acceptance of Christianity by the General Assembly is lifted, Bolli returns home, but Kjartan remains for another year at the Norwegian court. Bolli convinces Gudrún that Kjartan plans to marry the king's sister Ingibjörg and with the support of her kinsman persuades her to marry him. This episode seems to have been influenced by *Bjarnar saga*.

Upon returning to Norway, Kjartan marries a woman named Hrefna. Gudrún's love for him turns to jealousy and hatred. Ólaf's forebodings are fulfilled. Insults are exchanged between the two families. Kjartan bluntly refuses Bolli's gift of a stud of beautiful horses. At Gudrún's instigation, Kjartan's sword, the gift of Mýrkjartan, and Hrefna's precious headdress, a gift from Ingibjörg originally intended for Gudrún, are stolen. Kjartan retaliates by forcing the cancellation of a land sale to Bolli and by besieging the house at Laugar for three days to prevent the inhabitants from using the outdoor privies.

Like Brynhild in the Niflung tragedy and Sigríd the Haughty in *Óláfs saga Tryggvasonar*, Gudrún now demands that her husband kill her former lover or else lose her favor. Bolli reluctantly accompanies Gudrún's brothers to ambush Kjartan but remains aloof from the fighting as long as possible. When Bolli finally makes his attack, Kjartan throws away his sword with the crushing words, "It is truly a dastardly deed, kinsman, that you are about to do, but I think it far better to receive death from you, kinsman, than to give it to you" (chap. 49). Without speaking a word, Bolli deals Kjartan his death blow, and he holds him in his arms as he dies.

When Bolli arrived at Laugar, Gudrún asked him what time it was, and Bolli replied that it was about three o'clock (*nón*).

> Then Gudrún said, "Morning tasks are of different kinds. I have spun yarn for twelve ells of cloth, and you have killed Kjartan."

> Bolli replied, "That luckless deed would not soon leave my mind even if you did not remind me of it."

Gudrún said, "I don't regard that as a luckless deed. It seemed to me that you enjoyed greater esteem the winter Kjartan was in Norway than now, when he has trodden you underfoot since he returned to Iceland. But last but not least, what seems best to me is that Hrefna will not be laughing when she goes to bed tonight."

Then Bolli said, and he was very angry, "I think it unlikely that she will pale more than you at this news. And I suspect that you would have been less shocked if we were lying dead on the field and Kjartan had brought you the news."

Gudrún now saw how angry Bolli was and said, "Don't say such things, for I am very grateful to you for the deed. I feel certain now that you will not do anything to displease me."

(chap. 49)

Ólaf protected Bolli as long as he lived, but after his death Bolli was killed. In due course, countervengeance was taken by his son Bolli Bollason, so named because he was born after his father's death. Gudrún became a nun, and when she was quite old, her son Bolli asked her which man she had loved the most. Gudrún tried to evade the question by listing the good qualities of three of her former husbands but at last had to admit, "I was worst to him I loved the most." This classical quotation from the sagas is "a paradoxically pointed formulation of tragic human experience."[5]

Turville-Petre characterized *Laxdœla saga* as "in some ways, the richest" of all the *Islendinga sögur,* and Andersson commented on the "generosity" of both narrative and personal dimension.[6] The language is fuller than that of many sagas, and the author took pains to describe and explain emotions. He made skillful use of antithesis and parallelism. Until recently, strong lexical and stylistic influence from the *riddarasögur* has been assumed, but Rolf Heller has demonstrated that earlier *konungasögur* were the chief models for *Laxdœla.* Although we find no demonic, superhuman vikings here, the characters are larger than life, and they stride majestically through the pages of the book. The men characters are somewhat overdrawn in that their descriptions sometimes are more impressive than their deeds. The women characters, however, are superb, from the matriarchal Unn (Aud) the Deep-minded to Gudrún. Enigmatic, imperious, passionate, Gudrún is one of the most fascinating women in saga literature.

More than any other saga writer, the *Laxdœla* artist had an eye for visual beauty, for pomp and pageantry. His description of Bolli Bollason upon his return from Constantinople, where he had served in the emperor's bodyguard, may serve as one example for many:

He was dressed in clothing made of silk wrought with gold, which the king of Miklagard [Constantinople] had given him, and over this he had a scarlet cloak with a hood. He was girded with the sword Fótbít ["Leg-biter"], of which the guard and pommel were inlaid with gold and the hilt bound with gold. He wore a gilded helmet on his head, and at his side he carried a red shield adorned with a knight inlaid in gold. In his hand he carried a lance of a kind that is popular abroad, and wherever he and his followers took lodging, the women paid heed to nothing else but to gaze at Bolli and at the finery of himself and his men. With such courtly splendor Bolli rode through the countryside with his retinue until he came to Helgafell. Gudrún was very happy to see her son Bolli.

(chap. 77)

Laxdœla has been ascribed to various men including Sturla Thórdarson, Ólaf Thórdarson, and Snorri Sturluson.[7] Snorri must be eliminated on lexical and stylistic grounds. Whoever the author was, it is certain that he was a member or a close acquaintance of the Sturlung family.[8]

Notes

1. The sources of *Laxdœla* are thoroughly discussed by Heller in his monograph *Die Laxdœla saga. Die literarische Schöpfung eines Isländers des 13. Jahrhunderts* (Berlin: Akademie-Verlag, 1976).

2. W. P. Ker, *Epic and Romance. Essays on Medieval Literature,* 2d rev. ed. (New York: Macmillan & Co., 1908), p. 209.

3. Einar Ól. Sveinsson, ed., *Laxdœla saga,* Îfslenzk fornrit, vol. 5 (Reykjavík: Hið íslenzka fornritafélag, 1934), p. lxvii.

4. See A. Margaret A. Madelung, *The Laxdœla Saga: Its Structural Patterns* (Chapel Hill: University of North Carolina Press, 1972), p. 13; Heinrich Beck, "Brynhilddichtung und Laxdæla Saga," in *Festgabe für Otto Höfler,* ed. Helmut Birkhan (Vienna: W. Braumüller, 1976), pp. 1-14; Rolf Heller, *Die Laxdœla Saga* (Berlin, 1976), pp. 150-52.

5. Hallberg, *The Icelandic Saga,* p. 137.

6. Turville-Petre, *Origins,* p. 246; Andersson, *The Icelandic Saga,* p. 171.

7. See Marina Mundt, *Sturla Þórðarson und die Laxdæla saga* (Bergen-Oslo-Tromsö: Universitetsforlaget, 1969); Hallberg, *Óláfr Þórðarson hvítaskáld;* A. Margaret A. Madelung, "Snorri Sturluson and *Laxdœla:* The Hero's Accoutrements," in *Saga og språk: Studies in Language and Literature,* ed. John M. Weinstock (Austin, Texas, 1972), pp. 45-92.

8. See Heller, *Die Laxdœla Saga,* pp. 151-52.

Jonna Louis-Jensen (essay date 2002)

SOURCE: Louis-Jensen, Jonna. "A Good Day's Work: *Laxdaela Saga,* ch. 49." In *Cold Counsel: Women in Old Norse Literature and Mythology,* edited by Sarah M. Anderson, pp. 189-99. New York: Routledge, 2002.

[*In the following essay, Louis-Jensen attempts to correct possible textual corruptions in* Laxdaela Saga *chapter 49 in order to unveil a subtle, ironic reading of Gudrun's character in her response to Kjartan's death.*]

I

A notable feature of the "saga style" is the emphatic phrase (apophthegm, laconism), which marks the dramatic peak of a dialogue, and thereby of a scene. Well-known examples are the heroic understatements "Hneit þar," "Þau tíðkask nú en breiðu spjótin," "Vel hefir konungrinn alit oss, feitt er mér enn of hjartarœtr". With its "slow, measured dialogues" (Clover 1974:65), *Laxdæla saga* may be atypical in this respect, but even *Laxdæla* contains at least two phrases that have been assigned to this category. It is perhaps no coincidence that both are spoken by Guðrún Ósvífrsdóttir, the *primadonna assoluta* of the saga, who is not only "kvenna vænst" but also "bezt orði farin". One of them is of course the aging heroine's enigmatic confession: "Þeim var ek verst er ek unna mest". The other is more difficult to quote, for it has been badly bungled in the manuscript tradition of *Laxdæla saga,* and critics have disagreed as to how it should be emended.

The textual history of *Laxdæla* was treated by Kristian Kålund a century ago in his edition of the saga (*Laxdæla* 1889-91). Kålund established two main classes of manuscripts, y and z, but his edition only sporadically goes beyond constituting the text of the y-class, and no editor has as yet coped with the task of editing the z-class, which is represented by fragments and late paper manuscripts only.[1]

The passage under discussion here reads thus in Möðruvallabók, the main text of Kålund's edition:

> Þá mælti Guðrún: "Mikil verða hermdarverk, ek hefi spunnit tólf álna garn, en þú hefir vegit Kjartan".

The word "hermdarverk" is a hapax legomenon in Old Norse, and its precise sense accordingly difficult to establish, although it has been used in later Icelandic in the sense "act of terrorism; sabotage" (Sverrir Hólmarsson *et al.* 1989:184). It is, however, questionable whether the word has been in continuous use in the language; it might conceivably be a revival, based on the above passage as it reads in the older editions of *Laxdæla.* Einar Ól. Sveinsson, in his edition of the saga for *Íslenzk fornrit* (henceforth, ÍF), rejected the Möðruvallabók reading "Mikil verða hermdarverk" and replaced it with a variant reading found in a paper manuscript of the z-class: "Misjfn verða morgunverkin". This is most likely a pessimistic twist of the maxim "Drjúg eru morgunverkin," (cf. Ólafur Halldórsson 1973) and probably means something like "it varies how much work one gets done in the morning," although most translators of the saga have understood it differently. Jónas Kristjánsson (1984) gives a comprehensive survey of translations of this passage, but omits the snappy, if unorthodox "Morning tasks are often mixed" (*Laxdæla* 1969:176). As demonstrated convincingly by Ólafur Halldórsson (1973), however, the basis of the reading "Misjfn verða morgunverkin" in the manuscript tradition of *Laxdæla* is so slender that there is in fact no chance of its being original; Jónas Kristjánsson (1984), notwithstanding, puts up a gallant defence of the ÍF text.

Ólafur Halldórsson goes on to suggest that the reading "hermdarverk" in Möðruvallabók with its variants *hernaðar-* and *hefndarverk* could be due to corruptions of an original reading "hér váðaverk", which he sees as a pun on the double meaning of *váð(a)verk,* "accidental damage" and "cloth-making". Even if we accept the somewhat strained homonymy between *váðaverk* and *váðverk,* other objections suggest themselves: Guðrún has been spinning, not weaving, and the word *váðverk* seems to denote the latter only, also, as Guðrún has occasion to remember, the killing of Kjartan was far from accidental.

Although I cannot accept his solution in its entirety, I do think Ólafur Halldórsson has put the discussion on the right track: *hermdar* and *hernaðar* are both likely to be corruptions of the adverb *hér* + a sequence of graphs bearing some resemblance to "mdar," and the same can be said to apply to *hefndar,* since this reading could well have been copied from *hem(n)dar* in an exemplar.

At this point I should like to draw attention to a translation of our passage not included in Jónas Kristjánsson's survey. This is W. P. Ker's rendering of central passages in *Laxdæla saga* (Ker 1908:223). Ker translated the passage as follows:

> "A good day's work and a notable; I have spun twelve ells of yarn, and you have slain Kjartan Olaf's son".

This translation seems to be based on inspired guesswork rather than on any printed or unprinted text of the saga that could have been available to Ker. Whether independently of Ker or not, at least two other translators render the passage in a similar way:

> Da sa Gudrun: "Store blir dagsverkene nu; jeg har spundet garn til 12 alen tøi, og du har fædt Kjartan".
>
> (*Laxdæla* 1924:147)

Då sade Gudrun: "Goda dagsverk ha vi gjort. Jag har spunnit garn till tolv alnar, och du har dräpt Kjartan".

(***Laxdæla*** 1935:313)

My intuitive reaction to these translations of Guðrún's words is that they are much more satisfactory than the others on the market; it seems a pity that they translate a reading that is not found in any manuscript of ***Laxdæla.*** On reflection, however, I see it as a distinct possibility that the word "hermdarverk" with its variants "hernadarverk" and "hefndarverk" could be a corruption of a phrase that meant more or less what these translators guessed that it should mean. I also believe that this hypothesis can be supported by paleographical and orthographical evidence.

Laxdæla saga is thought to have been written around the middle of the thirteenth century, perhaps a little later (Heller 1968:135 ff.). In Icelandic manuscripts from this period (and later), a common type of the letter "x" was one that looked like minuscule "r" with an extra hook below the line.[2] It sometimes happens that the hook is quite detached from the descender, in which case the letter is easy to confuse with an "r".[3] The element "dar" in "hermdar", "hernadar", "hefndar" could thus very plausibly be a corruption of "dax", which is how the genitive of *dagr* is written in some early Icelandic manuscripts, e.g. AM 645 4to A (early thirteenth century) (Larsson 1891:46); similar examples of the cluster "gs" being written "x", even when it spans a morpheme boundary, can be found in manuscripts from the second half of the thirteenth century, e.g. "lax menn" in Grágás (Gks 1157 fol., c. 1300; Grágás 1852, II:166,10). Following Ólafur Halldórsson as far as the element "her" is concerned, I would suggest to emend the passage to "Mikil verða hér nú dagsverkin". The sequence "her nu dax" is equally amenable to being misread as "hermdar," "hernadar," and "hemndar", and the sentence has an authentic ring, for which compare "Skammt verðr hér nú illra verka í milli ok stórra" in *Gísla saga Súrssonar,* the S redaction (*Íslendinga sögur* 1985, I:924).[4]

II

One of the difficulties about the reading "Misjfn verða morgunverkin" is that it is hard to understand why Guðrún at three o'clock in the afternoon talks about her morning tasks as though they represent all the work she has done that day. This difficulty is neatly glossed over in the English translation, where *nón* is taken to mean "noon," which of course marks the end of the "morning" in the modern English sense (***Laxdæla*** 1969:176). In Old Icelandic, and no doubt well into the modern period, the morning did not extend beyond *dagmál* (9 a.m.), as may be inferred, e.g., from the refrain: "Stuttir eru morgnar í Möðrudal, því eru dagmál þá dagar". The

difficulty disappears if "morgunverk" is changed into "dagsverk". Even if Guðrún's spinning were discontinued when her brothers came home to report the killing of Kjartan, this must have been considerably later than 9 a.m., judging from the activities that take place during the day: Kjartan starts out from Hóll "early in the morning," and on his way to Hafragil, a distance of some 20 km, he stops at Hvítidalr to perform an errand. The fight at Hafragil must be assumed to take at least an hour, after which the brothers ride back to Laugar, a distance of about 7 km. All in all, it is not likely that the news reaches Laugar much before 1 p.m., which gives Guðrún at least four or five hours of spinning, most of which it would clearly be unidiomatic to refer to as "morgunverk".

If we emend Guðrún's words to "Mikil verða hér nú dagsverkin", we moreover get closer to understanding why the author of the saga opens the scene between the couple in such a strange way:

> Síðan reið Bolli heim til Lauga. Guðrún gekk í móti honum ok spurði hversu framorðit væri; Bolli kvað þá vera nær nóni.[5] Þá mælti Guðrún: "Mikil verða hér nú dagsverkin[6] . . ."

Guðrún presumably knows as well as Bolli what time it is; what she wants from him is not the time of day, but the cue for her obviously well-prepared speech. She is staging the scene as a kind of elaborate metaphor, pretending that the couple are merely exchanging domestic commonplaces suitable for the end of a working day or shift.

Although the sources are very reticent on this point, a working day on an Icelandic farm in the eleventh or thirteenth century was no doubt organised much as in later times in Scandinavia and the Atlantic islands, i.e. divided into four or five shifts of approximately three hours each, interspersed with meals (Ejder 1969:423 ff.). One word for such a shift which seems to have been used in all the Nordic languages was *eykt* (older *eykð*) (Jansson 1958:393).[7] We also know that *nón* marked the end of one such *eykt*; Ivar Aasen's Norwegian dictionary gives the following entry (Aasen 1918:539):

> Nonsøykt (-ykt), f. den tredie Arbeidsstund paa Dagen, Tiden imellem Dagverd og Non.

In Iceland, too, *nón* must have meant time for a break between two shifts, or on a Saturday or the eve of a feast-day, the beginning of the weekend or feast (*nónheilagt*), and the opening lines of the dialogue between Guðrún and Bolli could have been spoken by any industrious farming couple, making a preliminary assessment of the day's work towards the end of the third *eykt*.

A closer look at the composition of this and the preceding chapter reveals that the scene of Bolli's return parallels that of his departure earlier in the day; both scenes are staged by Guðrún in much the same manner, using everyday situations as her frame of reference. It is expressly stated in the saga that the day on which Kjartan was killed was Thursday in Easter week. In medieval Iceland this was the first workday after four holidays (Grágás 1852, I:29), and Guðrún stages it emphatically as a workday by getting up at sunrise, waking up her brothers and asking them about their plans for the day. Except for the unusual casting of the lady of the house as supervisor of the work, this is an everyday situation in a large Icelandic farmhouse, as can be seen from a comparison with ch. 55 in *Laxdæla*: "Bolli hafði verit snemma á fótum um morgininn ok skipat til vinnu" and ch. 13 in *Eyrbyggja*: "Þóroddr bóndi stóð upp snimma um morguninn ok skipaði til verks". Guðrún's brothers, still half asleep, react to the immediate content of her question and answer that they will be having a quiet day—"for there isn't much work to be done just now" ("ok er nú fátt til verknaðar"). This answer launches Guðrún on her famous *Hetzrede*, in which she reproaches her brothers in terms suitable for scolding lazy farmhands: instead of doing their work, they are acting like farmers' daughters, who do neither good nor harm (but presumably lead pampered lives), they sleep and play, sit at home and talk big ("láta vænlega"), and there are always too many of them about—the eternal complaint of women in a society with a clear division of labour between the sexes. In the course of the speech it becomes quite clear that Guðrún is in fact goading her brothers to undertake a revenge expedition against Kjartan, and several of the rhetorical elements in her speech are also well-known ingredients in the goading speeches delivered by women in Old Norse literature: charges of effeminacy (daughters rather than sons), somnolence, forgetfulness (Hermann Pálsson 1986:31-37), but the ambiguity of both the situation and the speech is exceptional. In her two speeches, Guðrún can thus be said to use the gender-determined division of labour as a metaphor for the different roles and duties of men and women in connexion with blood revenge.

When Guðrún pretends that Bolli's killing of Kjartan is all in a day's work and so belongs to the same sphere as her own spinning, she is no doubt being ironical about Bolli's deed and refusing to see it in a heroic light.[8] But the equation works both ways: either both achievements are trivial or both are fateful. At a higher level of the text, the level of composition, Guðrún's spinning acquires a mythical dimension; the distaff is not only the emblem of women's work, but also the attribute of the Fates. Ólafur Halldórsson (1990:274) calls attention to the provision in Grágás, that twelve ells is

the price of a burial-place: "Tólf álnum skal kaupa leg undir mann," and suggests that the author of *Laxdæla* by letting Guðrún spin—or at least boast of having spun—"tólf álna garn" may have intended to designate her as the spinner of a fatal web, Kjartan's destiny.

This ingenious suggestion presupposes that the meaning of "tólf álna garn" is "twelve ells' worth of yarn" and not "twelve ells of yarn", as W. P. Ker translates it. Jónas Kristjánsson (1984) advocates the latter, "minimalist" interpretation, and imagines that Guðrún is too restless to spin at an even pace while she is waiting for news of the outcome of the fight between Bolli and Kjartan. It seems to me that there is a strong linguistic argument against the translation "twelve ells of yarn": the Icelandic equivalent of this phrase surely would be "tólf álnir garns," not "tólf álna garn". Moreover, twelve ells of yarn is an incredibly poor outcome of four or five hours of spinning (and of course incompatible with the reading "Mikil verða hér nú dagsverkin"). On the other hand, "yarn or warp for twelve ells of cloth" is an unrealistically large quantity to spin in half a working day: according to Jónas Kristjánsson's calculations, warp for twelve ells of standard *vaðmál* amounts to 3,600 metres of yarn, or the equivalent of twenty-four hours' spinning on a nineteenth-century spinning-wheel. However, as Ólafur Halldórsson (1990:274) reminds us, an old suggestion by Brynjólfur Jónsson frá Minna-Núpi (1892) is that "tólf álna garn" could mean "twelve ells' worth of linen thread". This seems linguistically possible, but as far as I know nobody has made calculations of how much linen thread one can spin in less than a day; "twelve ells' worth" still sounds like rather a lot. Perhaps the old explanation, that "tólf álna garn" means "yarn or warp for twelve ells of cloth", should not be dismissed out of hand. It would, of course, be a mistake to imagine Guðrún spinning all alone in a room by herself. More likely, we are meant to visualize her together with other female members of the household, all occupied with different aspects of cloth-making, as is the case in the hall at Bjarg in *Grettis saga*, ch. 14: "konur unnu þar tó á daginn". When Guðrún says that she has spun warp for twelve ells of cloth, she may be referring to the joint efforts of the women of Laugar, for which she, the mistress of the house, is responsible.

Guðrún's statement, although not necessarily unrealistic, is certainly not without ambiguity. I do not want to argue that Guðrún herself is aware of the symbolic value of twelve ells' worth of yarn; it has already been suggested that this construction belongs to the compositional level of the saga. As I understand the dialogue, Guðrún's irony is aimed at Bolli; by reducing his killing of Kjartan to something trivial she means to hurt and humiliate him (and to provoke him to hit back); she may, however, be driving home an additional point.

Having been informed by her brothers about the fight in Svínadalr, Guðrún knows that Kjartan died not in single combat but fighting alone against five. Perhaps the impossibly large quantity of yarn she alleges to have spun is a sly hint that the killing of Kjartan was no more of a singlehanded achievement than her own spinning.

III

In *Epic and Romance,* W. P. Ker characterizes *Laxdæla* in the following way:

> Some of the Sagas are a reduction of heroic fable to the temper and conditions of modern prose. *Laxdæla* is an heroic epic, rewritten as a prose history under the conditions of actual life, and without the help of any supernatural "machinery". It is a modern prose version of the Niblung tragedy with the personages chosen from the life of Iceland in the heroic age, and from the Icelandic family traditions . . . In *Laxdæla,* Kjartan stands for Sigurd: Gudrun daughter of Osvifr, wife of Bolli, is in the place of Brynhild wife of Gunnar, driving her husband to avenge her on her old lover.

> (Ker 1908:209)

Ker views *Laxdæla*—or at least the story of Guðrún and her lovers—as a literary experiment of the same order as Ibsen's *Hærmændene paa Helgeland,* a conscious remodelling of the Eddic story of Brynhild and Sigurd, to meet the demands of a very different genre. In addition to the more general similarities between the saga and the Brynhild lays of the Edda, the dialogue between Guðrún and Bolli after Kjartan's death shows a specific and detailed agreement with *Sigurðarkviða en skamma,* an agreement that was analysed by Bouman (1962, see Further Reading) in terms of literary borrowing. Bouman proves his point, but there might be other aspects of the literary affinity between the two texts worth exploring. It is an interesting dissimilarity between the poem and the saga that the behaviour of the saga heroes is very restrained when compared to that of their poetical prototypes, a fact that is largely due to generic differences; the sagas are at least as fond of litotes as the Edda of hyperbole. Brynhild laughs "af llum hug" on hearing the "gjallan grát" of her rival who is mourning her dead husband, whereas Guðrún coolly and collectedly remarks that to her the most important aspect of Kjartan's death is that his widow will not go laughing to bed that night. Both heroines, however, betray their true feelings by changing colour, but while Brynhild flushes, Guðrún characteristically turns pale. Throughout the saga Guðrún exercises remarkable self-control; the only reaction she shows to a particularly harsh treatment by the man who has just killed her husband is a smile (it is up to the reader to imagine what kind of smile). If saga-readers have generally not regarded Guðrún as an unfeeling monster, but rather as a woman who conceals strong passions under a cool and controlled surface, part of the reason might be the saga's intertext with the Brynhild legend.

The transformation of the heroic epic into a prose saga under what Ker calls "the conditions of actual life" or "the ordinary business of Icelandic life' is for the most part successful, but at least in one scene it seems to me that the Icelandic paint has been applied too thinly to cover the foreign colouring. This is in ch. 46, where Guðrún is made to cede her time-honoured right to the high-seat at Hjarðarholt to Kjartan's new wife. This scene is, as shown by Marina Mundt (1973), modelled on the quarrel between Brynhild and Grimhild "in the version we otherwise know from *Þiðriks saga*". Both queens have a certain claim to the throne—Brynhild by virtue of her marriage to Gunnar, and Grimhild by virtue of her royal birth; Icelandic women, on the other hand, never occupied the high-seat, either in their own homes or as visitors, if we are to believe the evidence of the sagas apart from this one instance. Guðrún herself, at the wedding-feast celebrating her fourth marriage, sits on the bridal bench "innar á þverpalli", while the bridegroom takes the seat of honour.

A comparison between chs. 48-49 in *Laxdæla* and the chapter in *Þiðreks saga* in which Sigurd's death is related, shows quite striking similarities, which as far as I know have hitherto gone unnoticed. At the same time it illuminates the technique of transforming the paraphernalia of kings and queens into the ordinary business of Icelandic farm life. In *Þiðreks saga* the killing of Sigurd is placed in the context of a hunting expedition, which is initiated by the royal brothers Gunnar and Hgni having an early breakfast ("árdegis," cf. Guðrún's getting up early, "snemma . . . þegar er sólu var ofrat," on the day of Kjartan's death). In both texts, this apparently unusual behaviour elicits a question from one of the unsuspecting participants in the impending drama. Sigurd asks Gunnar, as Guðrún's brother Óspakr asks his sister: "Why are you up so early?" The answers are: "Because we are going hunting" and "Because I want you to get some work done," respectively, but in both cases an innocent pursuit is used as a cover for a sinister intent: "Because we are going to kill you" / "Because I want you to kill Kjartan". Out in the forest, Hgni stabs Sigurd to death, and the brothers subsequently refer to his dead body as "the bison ox" ("visundr"). On their return to the castle with the body, they are met by Brynhild who acts and speaks in a manner remarkably similar to her Icelandic counterpart, except that she draws her metaphor from the pastimes of princes rather than "the ordinary business of Icelandic life":

Drottning Brynhildr . . . gengr ór borginni móti þeim ok mæti at þeir hafi veitt allra manna heilastir".

(Þiðriks saga, II, 267, my normalization)

Guðrún gekk í móti honum ok spurði hversu framorðit væri . . . þá mæti Guðrún: "Mikil verða hér nú dags-verkin".

(z-text, emended)

Along with the similarities, we find equally interesting dissimilarities. In Þiðreks saga, the hunting metaphor is employed by several of the characters (Gunnar, Hgni, Brynhild), who apparently have no purpose of their own in employing it. The "dagsverk" metaphor in **Laxdæla** is the exclusive property of Guðrún, who uses it as a weapon of manipulation and sarcasm. This observation would seem to lend additional support to Ker's view of the central plot in **Laxdæla,** the story of Guðrún, as mainly a literary experiment, a reworking of the Brynhild legend in the language of the Íslendingasögur. The inspiration to have Guðrún refer to Bolli's killing of Kjartan as a "dagsverk" could have come to the saga author from some version of the Niflung story, possibly Þiðreks saga itself,[9] where Sigurd's Waldtod was placed in the context of a hunt and where the parties involved used hunting terms as a metaphor for manslaughter. Adapting this circumlocution to "Icelandic conditions" implied a complete change of both scenario and style, a change that would have been, I think, eminently successful, if an unlucky scribe had not accidentally destroyed the meaning of a whole phrase by confusing an "x" and an "r".

Notes

1. An edition of the z-text is now in preparation at the Arnamagnæan Institute in Copenhagen.

2. A good example can be seen in the fragment AM 655 X 4to, fol. 1r, l. 3 in the word "rex" (Hreinn Benediktsson 1965, pl. 65). The fragment is dated to the second half of the thirteenth century.

3. An "x" of this type is e.g. found in AM 519a 4to (*Alexanders saga*) (Hreinn Benediktsson 1965: pl. 77, line 6). The word in question, the name Oxatreus, was in fact read as "Oratreus" in Árni Böðvarsson 1974:23.

4. The unpublished concordance to *Íslendinga sögur* 1985 has this one occurrence of the sequence "hér nú", as Örnólfur Thorsson kindly informs me.

5. Thus the z-text; Möðruvallabók adds "þess dags".

6. "-verkin", thus the z-text; "-verk" Möðruvallabók.

7. The word *eykt* is thought to derive from Proto-Germanic *jaukiþō, cognate with English *yoke*. Its original meaning seems to have been "the act of yoking (harnessing) a draught animal", but

presumably also "the time between one yoking and the next" (Ejder 1969:107, with references). This assumption rests on the Old Norse evidence, since ON *eykt* meant both "temporal unit (shift) of three hours" and "point of time demarcating three-hour shift". (The specialized sense of ON *eykt:* "three o'clock [or half past three] in the afternoon [= *nón*]" does not concern us here).

8. Helga Kress (1980:104-05) adopts Ólafur Halldórsson's conjecture (*váðaverkin*) and reads bitterness and sarcasm into Guðrún's words. According to her interpretation Guðrún stresses the contrast rather than the complementarity between the male and female fields of activity, thus expressing her frustration at being kept away from the centre of events (i.e., the battlefield).

9. On the question of the sources of Þiðreks saga, see most recently Andersson 1986.

Works Cited

EDITIONS AND TRANSLATIONS:

Gísla saga Súrssonar 1985: = *Íslendinga sögur* 1985, 1:899-953.

Grágás 1852: = *Grágás. Islændernes Lovbog i Fristatens Tid.* Ed. Vilhjálmur Finsen. Copenhagen.

Íslendinga sögur 1985: = *Íslendinga sögur 1-2.* Eds. Jón Torfason, Sverrir Tómasson, Örnólfur Thorsson. Reykjavík.

Laxdala 1889-91: - *Laxdæla Saga.* Ed. Kr. Kålund. STUAGNL vol. 19. Copenhagen.

Laxdæla 1924: = *Laksdøla Saga.* Oversat av Fr. Bie. Kristiania.

Laxdæla 1934: = *Laxdæla saga. Halldórs þættir Snorrasonar. Stúfs þáttr.* Ed. Einar Ól. Sveinsson. *Íslenzk fornrit* V. Reykjavík.

Laxdæla 1935: = *Isländska Sagor. Eyrbyggarnas Saga. Laxdalingarnas Saga.* Översatta och utgivna av Hjalmar Alving. Repr. [1979]. Stockholm.

Laxdæla 1969: = *Laxdæla saga.* Translated with an Introduction by Magnus Magnusson and Hermann Pálsson. Harmondsworth.

Þiðriks saga 1905-11: - *Þiðriks saga af Bern 1-2.* Ed. Henrik Bertelsen. STUAGNL vol. 34. Copenhagen.

SECONDARY LITERATURE:

Aasen, Ivar. 1918. *Norsk Ordbog.* Fjerde uforandrede Udgave. Kristiania.

Andersson, Theodore M. 1986. "An Interpretation of Þiðreks saga". *Structure and Meaning in Old Norse Literature.* Eds. John Lindow, Lars Lönnroth, Gerd Wolfgang Weber. Odense, pp. 347-77.

Árni Böðvarsson. 1974. *Handritalestur & gotneskt letur.* Reykjavík.

Bouman, A.C. 1962. *Patterns in Old English and Old Icelandic Literature.* Leiden.

Clover, Carol J. 1974. "Scene in Saga Composition". *Arkiv för nordisk filologi* 89:57-83.

Ejder, Bertil. 1969. *Dagens tider och måltider.* Lund.

Helga Kress. 1980. "'Mjk mun þér samstaft þykkja'—Um sagnahefð og kvenlega reynslu í Laxdæla sögu". *Konur skrifa til heiðurs Önnu Sigurðardóttur.* Reykjavík:97-109.

Heller, Rolf. 1968. "Das Alter der Laxdæla saga". *Zeitschrift für deutsches Altertum und deutsche Literatur* XCVII:135-55.

Hermann Pálsson. 1986. *Leyndarmál Laxdælu.* Reykjavík.

Hreinn Benediktsson. 1965. *Early Icelandic Script: Íslenzk handrit.* Ser. in folio. Vol. II. Reykjavík.

Jansson, Sam Owen. 1958. "Dygn (och dess indelning)". *Kulturhistorisk leksikon for nordisk middelalder* 3. København:389-94.

Jónas Kristjánsson. 1984. "Tólf álna garn." *Festskrift til Ludvig Holm-Olsen.* Øvre Ervik:207-14.

Ker, W. P. 1908. *Epic and Romance.* New York. Repr. 1957.

Larsson, Ludvig. 1891. *Ordförrådet i de älsta isländska handskrifterna.* Lund.

Mundt, Marina. 1973. "Observations on the Influence of Þiðriks saga on Icelandic Saga Writing". *The First International Saga Conference, Edinburgh 1971, Proceedings,* London: 335-59.

Ólafur Halldórsson. 1973. "Morgunverk Guðrúnar Ósvífursdóttur". *Skírnir* 147. Reykjavík:125-8.

Ólafur Halldórsson. 1990. "Morgunverk Guðrúnar Ósvífursdóttur". *Grettisfærsla. Safn ritgerða eftir Ólaf Halldórsson gefið út á sjötugsafmæli hans.* Reykjavík: 271-4.

Sverrir Hólmarsson, Christopher Sanders, John Tucker. 1989. *Íslensk-ensk orðabók.* Reykjavík.

FURTHER READING

Criticism

Beck, Heinrich. "*Laxdaela Saga*—A Structural Approach." *Icelandic Journal* (1974): 383–402.

> Focuses on the structure of the *Laxdaela Saga,* stressing its discontinuity between narrative and objective time, repetition of narrative elements, and thematic patterning of narrative sequences.

Bouman, A. C. "Patterns in the *Laxdaela Saga.*" In *Patterns in Old English and Icelandic Literature,* pp. 107–32. Leiden: University of Leiden, 1962.

> Studies structural patterning, character portrayal, and the motif of prophetic dreams in the *Laxdaela Saga.*

Julian, Linda. "*Laxdaela Saga* and 'The Lovers of Gudrun': Morris' Poetic Vision." *Victorian Poetry* 34, no. 3 (autumn 1996): 355-71.

> Comments on William Morris's poetic adaptation of the *Laxdaela Saga* as "The Lovers of Gudrun," noting his simplifications of plot and omission of various original elements in favor of psychologically delineated characters, and heightened realism and clarity in the story.

Maurer, Oscar. "William Morris and *Laxdaela Saga.*" *Texas Studies in Literature and Language* 5 (1963): 422–37.

> Analyzes Morris's partial verse adaptation of the *Laxdaela Saga* entitled "The Lovers of Gudrun," comparing it to the original in terms of its structure and characterization.

Sappho
fl. c. 6th century B.C.

Greek poet.

The following entry contains recent criticism on Sappho's poetry. For additional information on Sappho's life and works, see *CMLC,* Vol. 3.

INTRODUCTION

Acknowledged as the greatest female poet of the classical world, Sappho is renowned for her intensely personal verse, only a fragmentary portion of which has survived into the contemporary era. Considered the most accomplished and influential lyric poet of antique Greece, she composed poems that continue to be admired and respected for their characteristic passion, lucid simplicity, and evocative imagery. As a literary figure surrounded by legend, Sappho has also been the subject of much critical controversy and speculation and has been linked with both female homoeroticism and the grounding myths of poetic discourse. A fascinating subject for successive generations of poets, novelists, playwrights, and biographers, Sappho of Lesbos remains a figure whose elusive thoughts writers have attempted to reconstruct. In addition to her lyric works, Sappho also wrote a variety of occasional poems, in particular a number of epithalamia, or marriage songs, for which she became famous during her own lifetime. Her compositions in other poetic forms, including narrative and elegiac verse, have largely been lost.

TEXTUAL HISTORY

While tradition holds that Sappho composed enough poetry to fill nine volumes, collected in Alexandria during the third century B.C., only a minute portion of her poetry survives. Her writings are thought to have endured into the early medieval period before being lost or destroyed by about the ninth century. Since that time, her poetry has, for the most part, only been accessible through quotations in a variety of secondary sources. An 1898 discovery of several Egyptian papyri containing additional verse fragments added somewhat to the Sapphic manuscript tradition, which includes only one poem in its entirety. Beginning in the eighteenth century efforts were made by German classicists to translate her literary remains into Latin, an important source for later

translators. This process continued into the twentieth century as new texts containing bits of Sapphic verse were unearthed. Though English translations of individual poems by Sappho appeared in the seventeenth century, the first complete English translation of the Sapphic fragments was not completed until 1885 and the publication of Henry Thornton Wharton's *Sappho: Selected Renderings, and a Literal Translation,* which made extensive use of German scholar Theodor Bergk's 1882 Latin edition. In the contemporary era the most well-regarded version of Sapphic verse in English has been Mary Barnard's *Sappho: A New Translation* (1958). Edgar Lobel and Denys Page's *Poetarum Lesbiorum Fragmenta* ranks as the definitive Greek edition of Sappho's work.

BIOGRAPHICAL INFORMATION

Little is known about Sappho's life and the information that is available cannot be viewed as trustworthy because accounts of the poet's life have become thoroughly interwoven with legend and myth. The only standard, but unreliable, source of information about Sappho's life is the *Suda,* a Greek lexicon compiled about the end of the tenth century. It records that Sappho was a native of Lesbos, an island in Asia Minor, and that she was probably born in either Eresus or Mytilene. Her father's name is given as Scamandrony-mus, and her mother's as Cleis. Evidence also suggests that Sappho had three brothers, and that her family belonged to the upper class. She is believed to have married a wealthy man named Cercylas—they had a daughter named Cleis together. Sappho apparently spent the majority of her life in the city of Mytilene, and most of her time there was occupied in organizing and running a *thiasos,* or academy for unmarried young women. As was the custom of the age, wealthy families from Lesbos and neighboring states would send their daughters to live for a period of time in these informal institutions in order to be instructed in the proper social graces, as well as in composition, singing, and the recitation of poetry. Ancient commentary attests to the fact that Sappho's *thiasos* ranked as one of the best and most prestigious in that part of Greece, and as its dedicated teacher and spiritual leader, she enjoyed great renown. Some legends of Sappho's life indicate that she lived to old age, but several others contend that she fell hopelessly in love with a young boatman, Phaon, and, disappointed by their failed love affair, leaped to her death from a high cliff—a story made famous by the Roman poet Ovid in his *Heroides,* but one which has been largely discredited by scholars.

MAJOR WORKS

Sappho wrote her poetry in the Lesbian-Aeolic dialect, her native Greek vernacular. Though she used a less refined language than that of the formal Ionian literary mode employed in Homeric epic, Sappho's poetry is said to demonstrate an innate verbal elegance that closely mirrors the rhythms of natural speech. Her standard metrical form, designated as the Sapphic meter by scholars, consists of four lines: three with eleven syllables each and a fourth line of five syllables. Characteristically mellifluous, Sappho's verse also exhibits her trademark directness, whether she is writing about nature, the gods, or the voluptuous physique of one of her pupils. Most of Sappho's poems are monodies, songs composed for the single voice and intended to be sung to the accompaniment of the lyre. Much of her verse was also occasional, usually meant to commemorate some event taking place in her *thiasos,* but she also composed narrative poetry, religious hymns, and epithalamia, or wedding songs. Sappho's lyrics are first and foremost personal, conveying deeply felt emotion in a simple, lucid style. The speaker in her poems (generally assumed to be Sappho herself) spontaneously exhibits an unusually wide range of emotional responses: tender protectiveness and friend-ship; erotic longing and jealousy; playful chiding of her

pupils; extreme anger toward those who have proven disloyal; and outright vilification of the headmistress of a rival *thiasos.* Probably her most famous piece (the only poem she composed to have survived intact), the "Hymn to Aphrodite" is something of an incantation or a prayer to the Greek goddess of love, patron of Sap-pho's circle. Twenty-eight lines in its entirety, the "Hymn" calls on Aphrodite to soothe the speaker, pos-sibly in her suffering from unrequited love. Internal anguish also figures prominently in the epithalamion referred to as "Phainetai moi," which captures Sappho's jealousy and distress upon seeing a young woman she loves with her new husband. Other works features folk or mythological motifs, such as that of "The Wedding Reception of Hektor and Andromache."

CRITICAL RECEPTION

Sappho's works have been admired for their stylistic brilliance since antiquity. In a famous epigram, Plato named her the tenth Muse, and praise of such a superla-tive nature has been common through the centuries. Scholars believe that Sappho's epithalamia raised the ancient folk tradition of the marriage song to a new level of artistic excellence, and her lyrics, fragmentary as they are, have been nearly universally considered outstanding poetic achievements. However, while her literary reputation has remained high into the contempo-rary period, Sappho's personal reputation has been controversial, sometimes even to the point of overshad-owing her status as a poet. The dispute over her reputa-tion seems to have begun two or three centuries after her death, and consists of mostly unfounded accusations of immorality, including contentions that she was the lover of Alcaeus, and that she instructed her pupils in homosexual practices. By the twentieth century Sap-pho's name had become synonymous with lesbianism in both popular and scholarly parlance. Though many contemporary critics have emphasized Sappho's skilled versification, exploring her themes, imagery, and influ-ence, discussion of her school and sexual preference has been renewed in the era of feminist literary studies and academic interest in the dynamics of erotic desire. The true purpose of Sappho's *thiasos* also remains something of a mystery: was it mainly a religious as-sociation dedicated to the worship of Aphrodite; was it primarily a sort of finishing school intended to prepare young women for marriage; or was it a female retreat where maidens were instructed in lesbian practices? Scholars have posited theories across the spectrum. As the critical speculation surrounding Sappho's poetry continues, so does the admiration and appreciation of it. Commentators have unanimously praised her sincerity and intensity, as well as her remarkably simple, yet ef-fective style. She has also been lauded for her ability to establish an intimate relationship with the reader. Contemporary critics, meanwhile, have continued in the established traditions associated with this powerfully enigmatic figure, endeavoring to unveil the poetic subtleties and intensities of her fragmentary work, drawn from aged and corrupted texts. Her influence on various poets, from her contemporary Alcaeus to writers as diverse as Catullus, John Donne, Lord Tennyson, Algernon Charles Swinburne, and Hilda Doolittle, has been studied. Above all, in the late modern period scholars have sought to redefine Sappho as the overarching symbol of feminine discourse, portraying her as the original, finest, and most defiantly personal female poet of all time.

PRINCIPAL WORKS

Principal Editions

Poetarum Lesbiorum Fragmenta (edited by Edgar Lobel and Denys Page) 1955

Principal English Translations

The Odes, Fragments, and Epigrams of Sappho; With the Original Greek Plac'd Opposite to the Translation (translated by John Addison in his *The Works of Anacreon*) 1735

"Sapphic Fragments" (translated by Dante Gabriel Rossetti in his *Poems*) 1870

Sappho: Selected Renderings, and a Literal Translation (translated by Henry Thornton Wharton) 1885

Sappho: One Hundred Lyrics (translated by Bliss Carman) 1907

The Poems of Sappho (translated by Edwin Marion Cox) 1924

The Songs of Sappho (translated by Marion Mills Miller and David M. Robinson) 1925

Sappho: The Poems and Fragments (translated by C. R. Haines) 1926

Sappho: A New Translation (translated by Mary Barnard) 1958

Sappho: Lyrics in the Original Greek with Translations (translated by Willis Barnstone) 1965

Sappho: Poems and Fragments (translated by Guy Davenport) 1965

Sappho: Love Songs (translated by Paul Roche) 1966

The Poems of Sappho (translated by Suzy Q. Groden) 1967

"Sappho" (translated by Guy Davenport in his *Archilochos, Sappho, Alkman: Three Lyric Poets of the Late Greek Bronze Age*) 1980

Sappho: Poems and Fragments (translated by Josephine Balmer) 1992

Sappho: A Garland, the Poems and Fragments of Sappho (translated by Jim Powell) 1993

Sappho: Poems (translated by Sasha Newborn) 1993

Love Songs of Sappho (translated by Paul Roche) 1998

CRITICISM

Eileen Gregory (essay date winter 1986)

SOURCE: Gregory, Eileen. "Rose Cut in Rock: Sappho and H. D.'s *Sea Garden*." *Contemporary Literature* 27, no. 4 (winter 1986): 525-52.

[*In the following essay, Gregory explores the poetry of Sappho in terms of its influence on Hilda Doolittle, characterizing the Greek poet's work as "the timeless matter of ephemeral feeling."*]

If we accept Sappho as a great erotic poet, Paul Friedrich suggests, "then her body becomes an icon for a myth of the inner life" (113). What are the contours of the myth seen through this female "body" of language? What is that interior landscape of Lesbos, and how is it present in H.D.'s *Sea Garden?* I would like to evoke Sappho herself, as her poetry—in translation—can render her presence, and to evoke as well H.D.'s Sappho. H.D.'s specific meditation on the Greek poet, recently published as "The Wise Sappho," has great resonance in the world of *Sea Garden*.[1] Here H.D. shows keen awareness of Sappho's poetry, and at the same time sees the Greek poet through the lens of her own alienation from the island and her longing as lover and poet for such a place.

Perhaps the most remarkable quality of Sappho's imagined Lesbos is the "liminality," the threshold quality, of its central mysteries, all of which reflect the goddess Aphrodite whom Sappho both serves and embodies in song.[2] Aphrodite's theophany occurs within mood, in the state of *aphrodite,* an interiorized quality of feeling indistinguishable from the numinous presence of the goddess herself (Friedrich 97, 124). Aphrodite dissolves boundaries between inner and outer, between self and other. In the same way the central values of Sappho's world are at once deeply subjective and radically impersonal (god-given); they represent a deep interiority infusing an outward shape or motion, making it vibrant and golden. The quality of grace, or *charis,* which the goddess and the poet cultivate, is a refined excellence at the center of life, a revelation, through one's whole presence—in movement, speech, action—that one shares in the life of the gods (Friedrich 106-7). A similar quality of exquisiteness (*habrosune*) is the very texture of aphroditic/sapphic vision (Friedrich 122-23). Sappho says in one fragment (Lobel and Page no. **"58"**), "But I love [the exquisite], . . . this, and yearning for the sun has won me Brightness and Beauty" (trans. Nagy 176). This delicacy and refinement, like the quality of grace, is present both in the outward richness of the other and in the vision that endows it with beauty. Aphrodite stands within and between seer and seen, speaker and spoken, giver and given. And the poet through the liminal rite of the poem makes the moment of her theophany a communal event.

One Sapphic fragment especially points to the nature of Aphrodite and to some of the images surrounding her. In fragment **"LP 2,"** Sappho summons Aphrodite to come to a sacred grove and participate in ritual festivities in her honor:[3]

> You know the place: then
>
> Leave Crete and come to us
> waiting where the grove is
> pleasantest, by precincts
>
> sacred to you; incense
> smokes on the altar, cold
> streams murmur through the
>
> apple branches, a young
> rose thicket shades the ground
> and quivering leaves pour
>
> down deep sleep; in meadows
> where horses have grown sleek
> among spring flowers, dill
>
> scents the air. Queen! Cyprian!
> Fill our gold cups with love
> stirred into clear nectar

Sappho invokes the goddess to leave her island and come to this intimate place; but the sensuous, incantatory poem itself manifests her presence. For both Aphrodite and poetry have each the power of *thelxis*, enchantment, manifest in bodily response (Segal 144). In the erotic charm of the poet's language, Aphrodite enters the body and soul, awakening the motions of desire. The rich and dense fragrance of frankincense mingles with the delicate odors of flowers, and the murmur of cold water through graceful trees blends with the exquisite shadowing of roses. This complex heightening of senses is climaxed, when from quivering leaves—kindled and alive, as are body and vision too—a *koma*, an enchanted sleep, descends. The spell complete, the entranced eyes open to the larger animation of burgeoning spring, to feeding horses, to a

meadow of blossoms, through which move refreshing breezes. When Sappho calls, finally, "Queen! Cyprian! / Fill our gold cups with love / stirred into clear nectar," the goddess is with these words no longer latent but suddenly manifest. Having already awakened the suppliant to the fresh yet erotically charged life within her presence, she crowns the moment as Divine Queen. As if among the imperishable gods, she pours out into gold cups immortal nectar mingled with the lucid joy of this consummated mortal rite.

What is this rite, and where does it take place? An altar has been prepared, and perhaps a feast as well, but no one is present; nothing is present except the longing voice of Sappho and the images by which she gives body to longing. This sacred place where the goddess enters is intimate and interior: it is, Thomas McEvilley suggests, "the imagination of the poet, the grove of transformations in which visions are seen and the breaches in reality are healed." Moreover, the "sacred grove" is the poem itself, creating in the reader through the speech of the poet "the trance of paradise" in which the goddess is entertained ("Fragment Two" 332-33).

This poem also suggests a set of images that are central to Sappho's world. One of these is the spatial image of a "private space." Lesbos itself—or Sappho's *thiasos* or group of young girls—is such an insular space, a liminal "island" set apart from ordinary life, within which a ritual passage is experienced.[4] But there are still other distinct spaces within the daily life of the *thiasos*, Eva Stehle Stigers says, such as the "invisible bond or . . . single enclosure, impenetrable by others" wherein two women are united in intimacy. The private space in Sappho's poetry "is a metaphor for emotional openness in a psychological setting apart . . . from everything experienced by a woman in the ordinary course of life" ("Private World" 56-57). These spaces often enclose one another within imagination and memory, as in **"LP 96,"** when Sappho in an intimate moment with Atthis comforts her for the loss of a friend, creating the space of the remembered *thiasos* as well as the imagined solitary moment when her separated friend in Lydia now longs for her. Likewise in **"LP 2,"** the space of the grove is interiorized to become the space of the longing body and the innermost shrine of the goddess. Through the poems, however, this private space is communal space, the very matter of intimacy celebrated within the *thiasos*.

This "emotional openness" so necessary to the growth of the young woman is also at the basis of two other mysteries: the figure of the bride or *nymphe*, and the image of the flower. These recurring presences point to the paradoxical, threshold quality of Sapphic eroticism, both virginal (cold streams through apple branches, the meadow of spring flowers, fresh breezes) and sensually charged (smoking incense, shadows of roses, quivering leaves, the gold cup waiting to be filled).

The young women on Lesbos are virgins being prepared for marriage. The nuptial moment is a threshold state, and the bride is a figure of passage. For the Greeks, the bride or *nymphe* denotes a woman at the moment of transition from maiden to wife and mother. Aphrodite, who is herself a Bride, guides these women in the refinement of their grace and in the cultivation of desire. The threshold of the bridal moment, sacred to the goddess, represents then a moment of fullness in beauty, of openness to the demands of Eros. That very openness carries intense potency; mythically the bride or nymph is associated with an ambiguous, aphroditic state of delicate yet awesome erotic potential.[5] The name of nymph is also given to the goddesses who inhabit the wild regions of nature. They too are elusive and liminal figures, being, like aspects of elemental nature itself, both inviolate and erotically suggestive.

The flower is a natural image for the young girls of Sappho's Lesbos, for the delicacy and beauty of youth coming to distinct perfection at the moment of opening. The brief time of the opened flower is another liminal moment; and it is the major image attending descriptions of the community of girls surrounding the poet. But in Sappho's poetry—contrasting markedly, as Stigers shows, with a male poet's use of the image—the flower does not represent an incomplete process of development, but rather a specific kind of fullness possible in the *thiasos,* wherein a "maiden's delicate charm" and her "youthful, self-celebrating erotic drive could find expression without compromise of . . . her emotional freshness" ("Retreat from the Male" 92).

That flower and maiden are at the center of Sappho's world points to an obvious lyric preoccupation: loving and witnessing to the ephemeral. These two images represent "that brief moment when the beautiful shines out brilliantly and assumes, for all its perishability, the stature of an eternal condition in the spirit if not in the body" (McEvilley, "Sapphic Imagery" 269). Because they represent the gracious time of the union of souls in beauty, flowers carry the remembrance of the bonds within the *thiasos* of maidens. In one fragment (**"LP 94"**) Sappho recalls her parting words to a woman: "'If you forget me, think / of our gifts to Aphrodite / and all the loveliness that we shared / all the violet tiaras, / braided rosebuds'" (trans. Barnard no. **"42"**). The garlands of flowers are woven times of the animated body, woven graces. Sappho's poems, recalling that unfading beauty in the heart, are themselves such moments, such woven roses (McEvilley, "Sapphic Imagery" 269).

Though H.D. understands fully her distance from this religious and mythic world of Lesbos, she nevertheless claims it in her way. She drew at least as much guidance from her study of Greek lyric poetry as from any contemporary influence or immediate tradition. That she absorbed aspects of craft and conception from these sources seems evident in her early poetry, in the choric voice, in rhythms associated with dance and erotic enchantment; in the figure of the nymph and the image of the flower; and in the image of the marginal space of erotic intimacy. Furthermore, like Sappho's lyrics, the early poems are forcefully ritualistic and liminal, demanding that the reader surrender ordinary orientation and participate in the erotic ordering of the poem. Jean Kammer has seen H.D.'s early poems as resting in a certain poetic mode which, unlike other forms of metaphor, does not move from concrete to abstract, but which rests in juxtaposition and suspension of concrete poetic elements in a configuration. Kammer says that the "absence of a named feeling . . . force[s] us to search for other, less rational entries into the poem." This form of speech turns the metaphoric activity inward, so that "the reader is forced *through* the singular experience of the poem" (158).

H.D.'s poetic affinities with Sappho, however, are more fundamental than any external influences. They rest ultimately, one might say, in the kind of "goddess" they each imagine serving, and in the kind of lyric necessities that service entails. Sappho has Aphrodite at the center, and H.D. a more complex, syncretic figure drawing together qualities of Aphrodite, Artemis, and Athene. It is not so important to name this figure as to recognize her powerful, shaping presence. She insists upon the primacy of Eros as a ground of value and vision, and thus upon the worth of the animated mortal body. She promises within the experience of passion not only suffering but grace and loveliness, and a certain kind of purity and wisdom. This figure compels an ever deepening interiority as the matter of poetic exploration, so that a moment of mood comes to reveal its lucid truth, and the ephemeral becomes the god-given, oracular substance upon which the poetess works. Finally, this goddess by her liminal nature, her movement under and between cultural fixities, bequeaths to the lyricist her paradoxical role as a threshold figure, pointing inward to the truth of intimacy and suggesting withdrawal, while at the same time inviting public celebration.

H.D. in her essay "The Wise Sappho" might be describing this veiled and complex figure who gives sanction and potency to her lyric song. She calls upon the memory of Sappho's creation in a meditation upon the question of poetic and psychic survival. H.D. opens her reflection with the remark of Meleager of Gadara about the poems of Sappho that he gathered in his *Garland:* "'Little, but all roses'" (*Notes* 57). Her whole meditation plays upon this phrase. H.D. at first negates, then qualifies and turns, then finally returns at the end of the essay to affirm his statement. But what accounts for her continuous metamorphic word play? *Not* roses, not *all* roses, not roses *at all;* not flowers—but rocks, island, country, spirit, song (*Notes* 57-58). This rhetorical process is necessary in order for H.D. to articulate the network of association defining for her the nature of Sappho's immortality. In this essay the Greek poet serves as a guide to her in working through what is essentially her own puzzle: what is the durable matter of fragile lyric song, what is the principle of durability within one's openness to the suffering of Eros? In other words, how does the rose survive, how is the rose a rock? One thing is certain: upon Sappho's endurance as the image of woman/poet/lover somehow depends her own.

In "The Wise Sappho" H.D. places herself implicitly in the position of Hellenistic Meleager, who lived, like the modern poet, in a mongrel and graceless age. In the proem to his *Garland,* Meleager says that he has gathered "flowers" from the ancient poets, adding his own, to weave a "garland" for his friends, though "the sweet-speaking garland of the Muses is common possession of all the initiated" (*Palantine Anthology* 4.1 [Paton 1]; my translation). In her work H.D., too, in a sense, gathers those flowers, the woven roses of Sappho and others, transmuted into her own severe poems; and they too are for an implied audience of friends and *mystai,* those within the mysteries of Eros.

But H.D. in this essay seems also to identify herself with Sappho—like the ancient poet she fashions roses with stubborn endurance in time. In that transmission/ transmutation of Sappho into a new time, H.D. would not choose roses as the sign of Sapphic power and beauty: "I would bring orange blossoms, implacable flowerings made to seduce the sense when every other means has failed, poignard that glints, fresh sharpened steel: after the red heart, red lilies, impassioned roses are dead" (*Notes* 57). H.D. here reveals her literary place in relation to Sappho: after the "impassioned roses" are dead—after the living poems are lost, after the passionate life they represent is inaccessible—she would offer through her poetry what Sappho's fragments also seem to offer—other "implacable flowerings" that would "seduce the sense," almost through violence, within the extreme numbness of modern life.

Though little remains of Sappho's work, H.D. reflects, it is durable matter: her fragmentary, "broken" poems are not lush roses, not flowers of any color, but rocks, within which "flowers by some chance may grow but which endure when the staunch blossoms have perished." The fragments, in other words, are a ground, an enduring subtext, for imagination. More durable than individual poems is this rock-world: "Not roses, but an island, a country, a continent, a planet, a world of emo-

tion, differing entirely from any present day imaginable world of emotion" (*Notes* 58).

What are the qualities of Sappho's Lesbos that flourish in imagination? H.D. remembers it in terms of its grace, its ample loveliness. Yet more than this she emphasizes the deep bitterness, "the bitterness of the sweat of Eros," within which Sappho suffered (*Notes* 59-62). That suffering is essential to Sappho's "wisdom"—which H.D. understands not as an abstract, Platonic wisdom, not Greek *sophrosyne* or Christian constancy, but one gained within the nets of devastating feeling (*Notes* 63-64). The wisdom of Sappho's poetry, H.D. suggests, came from "the wind from Asia, heavy with ardent myrrh," but tempered with a Western wind, "bearing in its strength and salt sting" the image of Athene (*Notes* 63). It is, in other words, characterized by its sensuous immediacy, but also by its questing spirit, its penetrating consciousness, its clarity and control. Sappho was "emotionally wise," capable in her simplicity of seeing within the momentary awkward gesture of a girl "the undying spirit of goddess, muse or sacred being." Sappho's wisdom is a concrete, human love which merges "muse and goddess and . . . human woman" in the perception of grace and beauty (*Notes* 64-65).

"Sappho has become for us a name." As a cultural and artistic figure, H.D. finally implies, she is one with her poems and one with the power of her poems: she is "a pseudonym for poignant human feeling, she is indeed rocks set in a blue sea, she is the sea itself, breaking and tortured and torturing, but never broken." She is an island "where the lover of ancient beauty (shipwrecked in the modern world) may yet find foothold and take breath and gain courage" (*Notes* 67). For this reason the puzzle of Sappho's mortal durability is significant—her poetry, rose/rock/island/sea, is the timeless *matter* of ephemeral feeling and ephemeral speech at the basis of lyric expression. In this sense—that Sappho *is* feeling, *is* a rocky island retreat for the lover of beauty—she *is,* I suggest, H.D.'s "sea garden." She is the mythic figure at the ground of H.D.'s world of fragile sea- and rock-roses. She is the goddess who guards it, the sea that washes it, and the spirit informing the poet who suffers her ecstasies within it.

Notes

1. The manuscript from which "The Wise Sappho" was taken is not precisely dated. I do not claim, then, that H.D.'s essay directly informs *Sea Garden*—the case may indeed be the reverse—but that both come from the same imagination of the island experience, of which Lesbos was a configuration.

2. My understanding of Aphrodite and of the liminal qualities of Sappho's world has been greatly shaped by Friedrich, especially chs. 5 and 6.

3. In the major points of my interpretation of this poem I am indebted to McEvilley, "Sappho, Fragment Two."

Because of its grace, and not because of its literal accuracy, I quote here the version of Barnard. Here is my own literal rendering of the fragment: Come from Crete, for my sake, to this holy temple, where is the lovely grove of apple-trees, and where altars are smoking with frankincense; therein cold water murmurs through apple branches, and the space is all shaded over with roses, and from quivering leaves an enchanted sleep descends; therein a meadow where horses feed has blossomed with spring flowers, and soothing breezes blow . . . there . . . Cypris, pour gracefully in golden cups nectar mingled with these festivities.

4. For a discussion of rites of passage see Turner 94ff.

5. Two important elaborations of the significance of the *nymphe* are those of Winkler 77-78; and Detienne 102-3.

Works Cited

Detienne, Marcel. "The Myth of 'Honeyed Orpheus.'" *Myth, Religion and Society: Structuralist Essays by M. Detienne, L. Gernet, J.-P. Vernant and P. Vidal-Naquet.* Ed. R. L. Gordon. Cambridge: Cambridge UP; Paris: Editions de la maison des sciences de l'homme, 1981. 95-109.

Doolittle, Hilda (H.D.). *Notes on Thought and Vision & The Wise Sappho.* San Francisco: City Lights Books, 1982.

Friedrich, Paul. *The Meaning of Aphrodite.* Chicago: U of Chicago P, 1978.

Kammer, Jean. "The Art of Silence and the Forms of Women's Poetry." *Shakespeare's Sisters: Feminist Essays on Women Poets.* Ed. Sandra M. Gilbert and Susan Gubar. Bloomington: Indiana UP, 1979. 153-64.

Lobel, Edgar, and Denys Page, eds. *Poetarum Lesbiorum Fragmenta.* 1955. Oxford: Clarendon-Oxford UP, 1968.

McEvilley, Thomas. "Sapphic Imagery and Fragment 96." *Hermes* 101 (1973): 257-78.

———. "Sappho, Fragment Two." *Phoenix* 26 (1972): 323-33.

Nagy, Gregory. "Phaethon, Sappho's Phaon, and the White Rock of Leukas." *Harvard Studies in Classical Philology* 77 (1973): 137-77.

Paton, W. R., ed. *The Greek Anthology.* 5 vols. 1916. Loeb Classical Library. Cambridge, Mass.: Harvard UP; London: William Heinemann, 1969.

Sappho. Trans. Mary Barnard. Berkeley: U of California P, 1958.

Segal, Charles. "Eros and Incantation: Sappho and Oral Poetry." *Arethusa* 7.2 (1974): 139-60.

Stigers, Eva Stehle. "Retreat from the Male: Catullus 62 and Sappho's Erotic Flowers." *Ramus* 6.2 (1977): 83-102.

———. "Sappho's Private World." *Reflections of Women in Antiquity.* Ed. Helene P. Foley. New York: Gordon and Breach Science, 1981. 45-61.

Turner, Victor. *The Ritual Process: Structure and Anti-Structure.* 1969. Symbol, Myth, and Ritual Series. Ithaca, N.Y.: Cornell Paperbacks-Cornell UP, 1977.

Winkler, Jack. "Gardens of Nymphs: Public and Private in Sappho's Lyrics." *Reflections of Women in Antiquity.* Ed. Helene P. Foley. New York: Gordon and Breach Science, 1981. 63-89.

David Sider (essay date 1986)

SOURCE: Sider, David. "Sappho 168B Voight: Δέδχε μεν α Σελαννα." *Eranos* 84 (1986): 57-68.

[*In the following essay, Sider discusses multiple poetic meanings of the term "ôra" in the Sapphic fragment designated as 168B Voight.*]

> Δέδυχε μὲν ἀ Σελάννα
> χαὶ Πληῖαδες· μέσαι δὲ
> νύχτες, παρὰ δ' ἔρχετ' ὤρα,
> ἔγω δὲ μόνα χατεύδω.[1]

Recent discussion of this poem has concentrated on the meaning of *ôra*, scholars as usual arguing for only one of the possible meanings the word may have: (*i*) *hour* of the night, i.e., the night itself ("nottata");[2] (*ii*) fixed time (for meeting one's lover);[3] (*iii*) indefinite period of time, i.e., "time passes;"[4] (*iv*) ἤβη, *flos aetatis*, referring to Sappho's own life;[5] (*v*) φυλαϰή, a watch in the night.[6] Rather surprisingly, nobody has argued for the word's basic meaning, *season* of the year (*hôra* is cognate with year/Jahr), although, as I shall show, two learned poets have so interpreted the poem (see below, n. 13). The approach to the problem has been a somewhat circular one: to survey Greek (and other) literature for situations said to be parallel to the one described here in order to determine which meaning is most appropriate.[7] But all that has been demonstrated by this discussion and disagreement is that no meaning is obviously inapplicable or inappropriate. My approach will differ from earlier ones in that I shall begin with the poem itself, noting its development clause by clause, in order to show that it is the poem itself rather than the rest of Greek literature that determines the range of meanings connoted by *ôra*.

In the first line we learn that the moon has set for the night; with the next two words we also learn that "the Pleiades have set." But the latter phrase, in one form or another, appears frequently in the sense that the Pleiades have had their cosmical setting in November, hereby marking the end of the sailing season and the onset of winter.[8] This sense is so prevalent that we are very artfully led by this syllepsis to feel that the Pleiades have both set for the night and set for the season. An ancient reader would know immediately that it was midwinter,[9] for as the time of the Pleiades' setting below the horizon before sunrise occurs earlier and earlier every day after the cosmical setting, it will not be before late January or early February that Sappho can say at midnight that the Pleiades have set, in both senses.

From the first two and a half lines, therefore, we learn that the sky is dark[10] and that the night is cold. Surely this weather report cannot be entirely objective: Sappho's remarks upon the external darkness and cold must derive from and reflect a feeling of a more subjective gloom. Some proof that this is indeed the case may be found both in the use of δύω, which often appears as a metaphor for human life,[11] and in the fact that it is female deities who are said to have passed from their position of glory in the sky.[12]

From these three senses of δέδυχε derive three equivalent senses of *ôra*: (*a*) the time of the night (δ. with Selanna), (*b*) the season of the year (δ. with Pleiades),[13] and (*c*) the passing of Sappho's life (the metaphorical sense of δ.). It is *ôra* in this last sense in fact that both crystallizes the inchoate personal feelings underlying the first three lines and acts as a glide between the astronomical description of the poem's beginning and its intensely personal last line. After some (few?) nights of sleeping alone, Sapho sees her life passing; perhaps, given μέσαι δὲ νύκτες, having passed its midpoint.[14]

I conclude, therefore, that all three meanings discussed here are called forth in the poem.

Notes

1. Fr. 94 Diehl = fr. 52 Bergk. Although I regard the poem as Sappho's, whether it was in fact written by her is not of concern here, and hardly (see below, n. 10) affects the argument. For a review of the controversy over authorship, see M. Treu, *Sappho* (Munich 1968) 211 f.; D. Clay, "Fragmentum Adespotum 976," *TAPA* 101 (1970) 119-129; B. Marzullo, *Gnomon* 50 (1978) 711 f. Lobel and Page did not admit it into *Poetarum Lesbiorum Fragmenta* (cf. Page *JHS* 78 [1958] 84 f.), but they seem to have made few converts; the poem has since appeared in E.-M. Voight, *Sappho et Alcaeus* (Amsterdam 1971).

2. P. Luňák, "De Sapphus Fragm. 52 Commentariolum," *WS* 40 (1918) 97-102 (whose sense of the poem is destroyed by his insertion of οὐ before Χατεύδω); B. Marzullo, *Studi di poesia eolica* (Florence 1958) 41 ff.; P. Berrettoni, "Per una lettura linguistica di un frammento di poesia eolica," *SCO* 19-20 (1970) 254-269 (who cannot decide between this meaning and (*iii*) below); Clay 128.

3. V. Longo, "Aristofane e un'interpretazione di Saffo," *Maia* 6 (1953) 220-223; H. Hoffmann-Loss, "Die Bedeutung von ὤρα in Δέδυχε μὲν ἀ σελάννα," *Mnemosyne* 21 (1968) 347-356.

4. L. Massa Positano, *Saffo* (Naples 1967) 164 f.

5. B. Lavagnini, *Nuova antologia dei frammenti della lirica greca* (Torino 1932) 184 ff.

6. P. Maas, "Zum griechischen Wortschatz," *Mélanges Émile Boisacq* 2 = *AIPhO* 6 (1938) 131 f., identifies the word as ὤρα (A) in LSJ, a variant of the stem found in οὖρος = φύλαξ; cf. EM 117, 18. Treu translates as *Warten*, but argues in his commentary as though for (*ii*) above in the sense of Χαιρός—a lack of clarity he admits *apud* Hoffmann-Loss 350 n. 2.

7. E.g., Longo argues for "appointed time" largely on the basis of the similarity to Sappho 168B of *A.P.* 5.150 (Asclepiades X Gow-Page): Niko promised to come this night but has not, φυλαχὴ δὲ παροίχεται.

8. A constellation is said to set when it is seen to set for the first time that year at sunrise; cf. M. L. West, *Hesiod. Works and Days* (Oxford 1978) 379 f. The Pleiades "rise" in mid-May, marking the beginning of the sailing season. That the dates of their rising and setting were known to all hardly calls for demonstration; I refer only to Hes. *Op.* 383 f., with West's notes ad loc.

9. See the last note, and compare the way in which Theocritus implies the season of the year at 7.52 ff. (with Gow's note). Berrettoni 256 infers from the poem's beginning that "la notte è serena" (in contrast to the last line, where "l'animo è turbato"), but it should be noted that the setting of the Pleiades was traditionally associated with rain and wintry storms; cf. Hes. *Op.* 319 ff., Democr. B 14.3 (*VS* 2.143), Antipater Thess. XXXVII Gow-Page (*A.P.* 11.31).

10. If the moon set not long before midnight, the night would have been illuminated by only a half moon—a fact worth noting also because thrice among Sappho's exiguous remains beautiful girls are likened to the full moon: (*i*) fr. 34 σελάννα . . . ὄππota πλήθοισα, (*ii*) fr. 154 πλήρης . . . ἀ σελάννα, and (*iii*) fr. 96.6 ff.

νῦν δὲ Λύδαισιν ἐμπρέπεται γυναί-
χεσσν ὥς ποτ' ἀελίω
δύντος ἀ βροδοδάχτυλος σελάννα [Schubart μήνα
ms.]
πάντα περρέχοισ' ἄστραέ,

where the moon seen first at sunset is a full moon, which also helps to explain the ποτε that has puzzled the commentators looking for a nightly occurrence. For an explanation of the moon's reddish appearance when first rising, see. I. Waern, "Flora Sapphica," *Eranos* 70 (1972) 4.

Note the converse to Sappho 168B: Housman, *Last Poems* 26, "The half-moon westers low, my love," entails that the time of speaking is approximately midnight.

11. Aesch. *Ag.* 1123 βίου δύντος αὐγαῖς, Arist. *Poet.* 1457b25 τὸ γῆρας ἑσπέραν βίου ἢ δυσμὰς βίου, Pl. *Laws* 770a, 781c, Callim. *Ep.* 20.1-2.

12. *Selanna* with article presents fewer problems in Aeolic if it is regarded as a proper noun, as Aeolic permits this construction elsewhere: Sappho fr. 168, Alcaeus fr. 338, 349; cf. E. Lobel, Ἀλχαίου Μέλη (Oxford 1927) lxxxvii f.; T. Clay 123 f; McEvilley, "Sapphic Imagery and Fr. 96," *Hermes* 101 (1973) 262. Note that in one of his renderings of this poem, Housman, *More Poems* 11, introduces the male Orion: "The rainy Pleiads wester, / Orion plunges prone, / The stroke of midnight ceases, / And I lie down alone." For the Pleiades and Orion's setting signalling the onset of winter's storms, cf. Hes *Op.* 619-21 (cf. above, n. 9).

13. This seems to have been understood not only by Housman (see last note) but also by Asclepiades XLII Gow-Page (*A.P.* 5.189) νὺξ μαχρῆχαὶ χεῖμα, †μέσην δ' ἐπὶ Πλειάδα δύνει (χεῖμα μέσον, Πλειὰς δὲ δέδυχεν Ludwig *Gnomon* 38 [1966] 23; Ludwig recognizes that this line implies that "es is um Mitternacht").

14. Thus we can answer Treu's question (212), warum soll die [sc. Jugendblüte] gerade nach Mitternacht schwinden? Similarly, Marzullo 35 f., who objects to Lavagnini's interpretation on the grounds that a mere description of the heavens would not lead to ὥρα = ἥβη, and who wants to see the first sign of personal concern in ἔγω.

Joan DeJean (essay date summer 1987)

SOURCE: DeJean, Joan. "Fictions of Sappho." *Critical Inquiry* 13, no. 4 (summer 1987): 787-805.

[*In the following essay, DeJean probes Ovid's fictionalization of Sappho in his* Heroides *as an abandoned woman who kills herself because of unrequited love.*]

. . . [In] the *Heroides*, . . . Ovid recounts tale after tale of women abandoned by unfaithful lovers. Ovid's fiction is a prime example of the complicity between female humiliation and canonical positioning . . . for the *Heroides* concludes with a vignette that makes plain the bond between physical abandonment and critical appropriation. Ovid transfigures the original woman writer, Sappho, into the archetypal abandoned woman. He portrays Sappho's physical humiliation as both a necessary prelude to her acceptance into the canon of great writers and as the action that empowers him to speak in her name. I would like to suggest the possibility that Ovid fabricated a legend of Sappho in response to what were for him the threatening aspects of the vision of poetic creation she presented, in the hope of making her poetry work, as it were, against its author, to discredit both her person and her poetic authority. Before I discuss the process through which Ovid transformed literary mother into abandoned woman, I would like to review briefly the aspects of Sappho's biography and of her literary production that could have set this transfiguration in motion.

Sappho's commentators have responded in particular to her presentation of the context of poetic creation. Sappho consistently portrays both the composition and the performance of her verse as an exchange among women, as the product of a female community whose members were united by bonds both personal and professional. Her oeuvre is most famous and most notorious because of its celebration of a type of female friendship that commentators try to understand through reference to the biographical scenario they promote for Sappho. Commentators thus most often consider Sapphic friendship solely in terms of what they believe to be its sexual content and react to the subject with moral condemnation, or sympathetic defense, or even attempts to deny the sexual content of her poetry. Yet this female bond can be considered in purely literary terms as an attempt to bypass male literary authority and to deny men any primary role in the process of poetic creation. Sappho presents poetic creation as a gift handed down from woman to woman, as literature written by women for other women. In this poetic universe, males are relegated to a peripheral, if not an intrusive, role. Most strikingly—and this, I contend, constitutes the central threat of Sappho's creation for canonic critics such as Ovid—the Sapphic narrator, a woman, assumes what is generally a male prerogative. She is the desiring subject and controls the gaze that objectifies the beloved woman, thereby giving the poem its visual focus and creating its geometry of desire.

Let us consider briefly what is perhaps Sappho's most celebrated poem, the ode widely known in English by the apocryphal title **"To a Beloved Girl"** (and in French as **"A l'aimée"**). Here is the poem in a recent French translation by Edith Mora. (I will provide only French translations of Sappho because the feminine forms essential to my argument are retained in French.)

Il égale les dieux je crois
l'homme qui devant toi vient s'asseoir
et qui tout près de toi entend
ta voix tendre

et ton rire enchanteur qui a, je le jure,
affolé mon coeur dans ma poitrine
Car si je te vois un instant je ne peux
plus rien dire

ma langue est brisée, sous ma peau
un feu subtil soudain se glisse
mes yeux ne voient plus, mes oreilles sont
bourdonnantes

une sueur glacée me couvre et un tremblement
me prend toute et je suis plus verte
que l'herbe, tout près de mourir
il me semble . . .

Mais il faut tout oser car même abandonnée . . .[1]

The poem recounts what appears at first to be a rather banal story: the narrator is a voyeur, observing from a distance the woman who is the object of desire while this woman demonstrates her love for a man. For today's reader and for readers at least as early as Ovid's day, however, there is something "wrong" with the scene of love reciprocal and frustrated that is staged in the poem. The triangle of desire inscribed there is unlike either of those formations that literary portrayals of love have schooled the reader to expect. The narrator's femininity is not immediately stressed, so that the presence of a feminine adjective ("je suis plus verte") in the poem's second half can come as a shock, an invasion. This woman is a usurper, for she has displaced the male from his role as viewer in the most common literary love triangle in which a man sees the woman he loves in the arms of *another* man. However, the triangle configured after this displacement can in no way be confused with what has become the stereotypical literary love triangle composed by two women and one man, in which one woman laments her abandonment for the *other* woman.

To judge from responses to her poetry over the centuries, Sappho's (re)configuration of the plot of love, the triangle of desire that she proposes, was the source of the threat she has so often constituted for canonic critics. Sappho usurps for her female narrator the control over the gaze that is normally a male domain. I realize that it is impossible to reconstitute the original "horizon of expectations" for erotic poetry and that her poetry may well predate the stereotypes I have in mind, yet the axiom Luce Irigaray posits, that "the prevalance of the

gaze" has always been "particularly foreign to female eroticism," in all likelihood predates those stereotypes as well.[2] When Sappho put a woman in the place reserved for the male poet-lover, she initiated a pattern in the economy of desire that many "strong" male writers have tried to overturn. Poets like Catullus (in his Ode 51) and Ronsard (in his 'Je suis un demy-dieu") propose a masculine reconfiguration of Sappho's erotic geometry in which a male narrator controls the gaze and has regained control over the beloved woman. Poets like Ovid . . . elect instead the fictionalization of Sappho, a process by which they make Sappho's poetry of desire a tool in the displacement of the desiring female subject from a position of control.

The complicated process by which Sappho became an exemplar of rejected female passion was initiated in antiquity. The legends about Sappho's life that were then formulated time and again took a recurrent form: biographers imagined that a series of mythical (or in some cases dubiously historical) figures could be seen as doubles for Sappho. The least troubling of these doubling fictions are those in which the Sappho character is something like a line-by-line copy of the original. Thus Philostratus cites the example of a "clever woman" Damophyla who "was said to have had girl companions like Sappho, and to have composed love-poems just as she did." More intriguing are the doubles who bear Sappho's name generally without sharing either her poetic gift or her sexual preferences. The doubles in this category are either courtesans or, in Lipking's terms, abandoned women, in this case, women betrayed by their *male* lovers. Aelian, for example, alleges the presence in Lesbos in Sappho's day of another woman named Sappho, a courtesan. To these legends of the courtesan double should be linked the sources from antiquity accusing Sappho herself of having been a prostitute.[3] Those who do not make Sappho a lover of many men rather than of many women describe her double as wild with love for one man, a male lover whose betrayal drives her to commit suicide by leaping from a cliff. Witness the account in the ancient lexicon, the Suda, of this other Sappho: "a Lesbian of Mytilene, a lyre player. She threw herself from the Leucadian Cliff for love of Phaon the Mytilenaean. Some authorities say that she, too, was a lyric poetess."

All early attempts to forge a biography for Sappho are troubling because of the recurrent tendency to replace the original woman writer with a pair of Sapphos. This doubling makes it possible to distinguish, for example, between a female sexuality judged unorthodox, even disreputable, and a respectable female sexuality, or even between female sexuality and poetic genius. This splitting, though it may originally have been inspired by a desire to separate a sexually disreputable Sappho from the poet and thereby protect the poet from criticism, provided nevertheless the basis for subsequent fictions of Sappho in which the desire to domesticate both woman and writer is evident. The repeated disjuncture between the female desiring subject and the female poetic subject can always therefore be seen as a more or less articulate response to the dual threat of sapphism and of Sappho's subversive poetic genius.

Let us examine just one example of the fictionalization of Sappho in order to reconfigure the triangle of desire created by her poetry, a process Mora has referred to as "remodeling the erotic face" of Sappho's poetry.[4] Many scholars today believe that, in some poem or poems now lost to us, Sappho must have evoked a certain Phaon. They believe that she was naming not an actual individual but perhaps a mythical figure, the ferryman Phaon who was said to have transported an old woman without remuneration. The old woman revealed herself to be Aphrodite and, to thank Phaon for his generosity, transformed him into a perfectly handsome young man. The goddess then proceeded to fall so madly in love with Phaon that she tried to hide him to keep him from other women. It is probable, however, that Sappho used the name Phaon simply as a symbol, to designate the name's root meaning, the light. Phaon, as Gregory Nagy has demonstrated, is another name, a doublet, for Phaethon.[5] In this context, let me reiterate part of Lipking's argument: he contrasts the female fear of abandonment with "masculine fantasies and myths [that] compulsively reenact the rise and fall of Phaethon, his premature ambition and precipitate plunge." You will remember that, anxious to be recognized as a legitimate son of Phoebus, Phaethon begs his father to let him drive the chariot of the sun for a day. But he is unable to dominate the horses, and they veer wildly out of control. In order to protect the earth from conflagration, Zeus is obliged to hit Phaethon with a thunderbolt, and he plummets to his death. Lipking does not specify the "masculine fantasies" he has in mind, but the desire of the son to put himself in Phoebus' place and his failure to carry out his father's role could figure a male fear of sexual inadequacy—a fear that the young man's sexual rite of passage will not be successfully accomplished, that the son will not live up to his father's example.

We can only guess at the explanation of Sappho's invocation of Phaon/Phaethon. Howard Jacobson sums up the prudent stance on this issue: "It is generally believed that Sappho alluded to the mythical Phaon in some such way that later readers were able to misinterpret it (willfully?) as a personal relationship."[6] I will break with critical prudence and allow myself a moment of speculation in an attempt to account for the violence prominent in subsequent fictions of the archetypal woman writer that center on her involvement with Phaon. Given all surviving examples of Sappho's poetry, it seems unlikely that Phaon figured as part of

one scenario of female abandonment consistently stressed by canonic critics, the plot in which, as in the ferryman-Aphrodite legend that supports Lipking's theory, the young man deserts the older woman. It is possible that Sappho's biographers from antiquity (willfully?) read a more personal reference to Phaon/Phaethon into a reference to the luminosity at the root of these names. They could have decided that Sappho had introduced Phaon/Phaethon to suggest the limits of male hubris. The persistent attempt to humiliate Sappho could therefore have been a response to the specter of male (literary) inadequacy her poetry was thought to represent. The Sapphic narrator, after all, displaces male desire by dominating the erotic gaze. Furthermore, Sappho herself was viewed as a primal voice of personal passion, a literary force that deprived male writers of preeminence in a domain crucial to erotic poetry and later to prose fiction. The male author who makes the actual Sappho rather than her double, the lyre player from Mytilene, commit suicide for love of a man named Phaon triply reassures his male audience: the desiring woman rejects her love for women; the woman writer loses her poetic gift; and Phaon/Phaethon is triumphant and completes his sexual rite of passage, while the older woman is hurled into the sea in his place. I would like now to examine several fictions of Sappho, notably Ovid's canonical fiction, to present the way in which male writers take revenge on Sappho in the name of Phaon/Phaethon. I imitate the focus of these canonic critics and will therefore limit my consideration of Sappho's poetry to the triangle of desire central to her poem "A l'aimée" and my consideration of Sappho's biography to what has been alleged to be its final scene, her leap from the White Rock of Leukas.[7]

. . . . .

Ovid's *Heroides* is a collection of fictive epistles addressed by women to men, for the most part to men who have betrayed their love and abandoned them for other women. With this collection, Ovid, like his heirs Richardson and Rousseau, established both a model for epistolarity and a model for women's writing. The mark of his craft is his apparent lack of control. The female style as he defines it is instinctive. In the *Heroides,* Ovid maintains a complicated stance with respect to the heroines whose voices he re-creates. He reverses the narrative focus of traditional accounts, where attention is centered on the male as a nexus of continued adventures, to allow women previously condemned to silence to present their sides of well-known tales. Yet they are given a voice only to try to win back unfaithful lovers and to complain of their solitary pain. Ovid establishes a model for canonic critics by standardizing and simplifying the plot of female passion. Women write, in Ovid's model, only in abandonment, only spontaneous cries from the heart, uncontrolled outpourings of unrequited passion. Thus the shepherdess

Oenone blames Paris because he has deserted her for Helen, and Ariadne condemns Theseus for having left her alone in her "abandoned bed."[8]

Ovid brings together the most famous abandoned women of classical literature and legend. To this collection, he introduces a single historical figure, Sappho, whose epistle to Phaon brings the work to a close.[9] For his portrait of the archetypal woman writer, Ovid consolidates biographical information from a variety of sources and creates a "Sappho" whose life conforms to the plots of the mythical heroines whose epistles precede hers. Yet nowhere in Sappho's passionate cry from the heart as Ovid imagines it does he draw the line between fact and fiction; nowhere does he indicate that, in her case alone of all the characters in the *Heroides,* is he dealing with a historical rather than a legendary figure. In short, Ovid never discloses that he is presenting a fiction of Sappho, enshrining the original woman writer as a male myth.[10]

"My name is already sung abroad in all the earth. . . . I am slight in stature, yet I have a name that fills every land; the measure of my name is my real height" (*H* 15.28, 33-34). When Ovid has Sappho thus proclaim the rewards of genius, his canonization of the woman writer is only granted in exchange for the debasement of Sappho first as woman and then as writer. Ovid's "Sappho" is a fiction remarkable above all for its taming of deviant female sexuality and its erasure of the female bond that was the inspiration for Sapphic poetic creation. Ovid has Sappho renounce what he presents as a youthful transgression—"my eyes joy not in Atthis as once they did, nor in the hundred other maids I have loved *to my reproach*" ("non sine crimine," "not without blame or wrongdoing") (*H* 15.18-20, my emphasis). His heroine has realized that one man is preferable to a multitude of women, to the female community celebrated by Sappho in her poetry: "the love that belonged to many maids you alone possess." Furthermore, her acceptance of the superiority of an *ars amatoria* that resembles Ovid's own over that which she herself formerly preached has brought about her public humiliation. Ovid's Sappho is a madwoman (see *H* 15.139), consumed with a desire for a man who has betrayed her, a desire so strong that it "embarrasses" her, a desire that, like her lover, constantly betrays her: "Modesty and love are not at one. There was no one who did not see me; yet I rent my robe and laid bare my breast" (*H* 15.121-22).

For his allegedly "heroic" presentation of Sappho, Ovid portrays her *not* in full possession of her literary powers but at a time when her genius has been interrupted and her towering stature diminished: "My former power in song will not respond to the call; . . . mute for grief is my lyre" (*H* 15.197-98). Because she realizes that her writing is no longer recognizably hers, Sappho has recourse to what Foucault terms a *nom d'auteur* to authenticate this outpouring: "unless you had read their author's name, Sappho, would you have known whence these brief words come?" (*H* 15.1-4). In his vision of Sappho, Ovid poses her on top of the White Rock of Leukas, poised for the suicidal leap that she hopes will bring her much desired oblivion, the ability to forget the beautiful young man, Phaon, for whom she had abandoned her sapphism, and whose subsequent betrayal had silenced her poetic gift. Sappho's flagrant debasement is a form of expiation: Ovid uses Phaon to make her atone for the interrelated sins of having preferred many women to one man and of having achieved formidable literary status for her celebration of a feminocentric world. He grants her a signature, an author's name ("auctoris nomina Sapphus"), but only once she has lost control over herself and her passion.

In the final image of this inaugural fiction of the woman poet, Sappho declares that, unless her letter provokes a quick response from her unfaithful lover, she will "seek [her] fate in the Leucadian wave" (*H* 15.220). In the *Amores,* Ovid alludes to a possible reply from Phaon, but such a letter, like the responses invented in the seventeenth century to the letters of the Portuguese nun, is an impossible fiction: Sappho can win no stay of execution. In his account of the White Rock of Leukas, Ovid's contemporary, Strabo, mentions both Sappho's alleged suicide and an ancient cult practice associated with the cliff: "Every year, . . . some criminal was cast down from the white rock into the sea below for the sake of averting evil."[11] This ritual sacrifice followed a model, as René Girard has analyzed, frequently chosen in antiquity for scapegoats.[12] Sappho's leap into water is the crucial moment in Ovid's rewriting of her biography, for it completes the exorcism of her inadmissible sexuality. His fictional Sappho functions as a scapegoat since her suicidal leap guarantees the continuing orderly functioning of life inside the literary city. This gesture purifies her and serves as a necessary prelude to her acceptance as a canonical author. By lending his authority to the fiction of Sappho's suicide, Ovid completed her baptism as "mascula Sappho," a phrase coined by his contemporary Horace in his first epistle (composed during the same period as one of the most influential canon-forming texts of antiquity, his *Ars poetica*). The adjective has been seen as a commentary on Sappho's authoritative prosody,[13] but it can also signify the discrediting of her sexuality and the severing of her ties to a female tradition. "Masculine" or "manlike" Sappho: Sappho domesticated (made to follow a "normal" sexual scenario); Sappho naturalized (portrayed as a great author according to a male literary model).

Furthermore, Ovid's fiction of Sappho illustrates perfectly the process to which I alluded earlier by which

Sappho's poetry of desire is used to displace the female subject from a position of control. Both Jacobson and Mora uncover numerous Sapphic echoes and actual citations from Sappho's poems in Ovid's fictive epistle.[14] Most notable is the passage (*H* 15.110-13) based on the celebrated images from **"To a Beloved Girl"** that evoke the physical power of the narrator's desire for another woman: here they are used to convey the extent of the humiliation suffered by the woman when the man who had at last taught her the full force of desire abandons her. When Ovid makes the object of Sappho's passion a man, he simultaneously recovers for men the right to make women suffer in love, and recovers for the male writer the right to portray the force and torments of female desire. Ovid's vision proved so attractive—so useful, I am tempted to say—that it successfully dominated public opinion of Sappho for nearly nineteen centuries, to such an extent that only recently have scholars attempted to set the record straight.[15]

Notes

1. Edith Mora, *Sappho: Histoire d'un poete et traduction integrale de l'oeuvre* (Paris, 1966), p. 371.

2. Luce Irigaray, "This Sex Which Is Not One," trans. Claudia Reeder, in *New French Feminisms,* ed. Elaine Marks and Isabelle de Courtivron (New York, 1980), p. 101.

3. On classical references to Sappho, see Mora's informative study *Sappho,* esp. pp. 16, 129. The Philostratus quotation is from his *Life of Apollonius of Tyana,* the Aelian reference from his *Historical Miscellanies.*

4. Mora, *Sappho,* p. 137; my translation.

5. See Gregory Nagy, "Phaethon, Sappho's Phaon, and the White Rock of Leukas," *Harvard Studies in Classical Philology* 77 (1973).

6. Howard Jacobson, *Ovid's "Heroides"* (Princeton, N.J., 1974), p. 281 n. 22. Marguerite Yourcenar offers a reconstruction of the process by which Phaon could have been identified with Sappho in *La Couronne et la lyre* (Paris, 1979), p. 72.

7. On the basis of the surviving examples of the Greek literary motif of falling from a white rock, Nagy concludes that "falling from the white rock is parallel to falling into a swoon—be it from intoxication or from making love" ("Phaethon," p. 142). Even the place chosen for Sappho's suicide could therefore be viewed as an attempt to use her poetry against her: her leap from the White Rock of Leukas would be a fitting revenge against the poet who inaugurated the evocation of the *physical* power of love, the poet who made the swoon of love the central image of "A l'aimée."

8. Ovid *Heroides* (Loeb Classical Library, trans. Grant Showerman), 10.14; all further references to this work, abbreviated *H,* will be included in the text. On occasion, I modify Showerman's translation.

9. I follow Jacobson's practice of considering the first fifteen epistles independently from the six "double letters" usually printed with them. The authenticity of the Sappho herois was for a long time the subject of dispute. Jacobson, who like most recent commentators considers the poem genuine, rehearses the arguments made by both sides in the debate over its authenticity (see *Ovid's "Heroides,"* p. 277).

10. The critical economy of this essay forces me to set aside discussion of two questions that merit continued debate, the alleged feminism of Ovid's position in the *Heroides* and what I see as a related issue, his wit in this work. On the latter point, see especially Florence Verducci, *Ovid's Toyshop of the Heart: Epistulae Herodium* (Princeton, N.J., 1985). In general I feel that criticism focused on Ovid's wit distracts from the complexity of Ovid's involvement with Sappho. I do not intend my reading as confirmation of Ovid's hostility to women or to unconventional sexuality. Critics have long been sensitive to the exceptional quality of the voice Ovid adopts in the Sappho herois (see Jacobson, *Ovid's "Heroides,"* p. 286). I would argue—although to do so adequately would necessitate an extensive excursion into Ovid's work—that Ovid lent his authority to the most extreme fiction of Sappho because of his own alarming proximity to his female precursor. Ovid becomes Sappho for the space of the fifteenth herois—and he uses Sappho's leap to exorcise the transvested ventriloquism that threatens to usurp his own literary authority.

11. Nagy, "Phaethon," p. 141.

12. See René Girard, "Generative Violence and the Extinction of Social Order," *Salmagundi* 63-64 (Spring/Summer 1984): 216.

13. See Marie-Jo Bonnet, *Un Choix sans équivoque: recherches historiques sur les relations amoreuses entre les femmes, XVIe-XXe siècle* (Paris, 1981), p. 28.

14. See Jacobson, *Ovid's "Heroides,"* pp. 280-85; Mora, *Sappho,* p. 83.

15. In addition to Marguerite Yourcenar's and Edith Mora's studies, see also Bonnet, *Un Choix sans équivoque,* and Mary R. Lefkowitz, *The Lives of the Ancient Poets* (Baltimore, 1981).

Joan DeJean (essay date September 1987)

SOURCE: DeJean, Joan. "Female Voyeurism: Sappho and Lafayette." *Rivista di Letterature moderne e comparate* 40, no. 3 (September 1987): 201-15.

[*In the following essay, DeJean concentrates on Sappho's resistance to the objectifying male erotic gaze in favor of a poetic vision that reflects feminine desire.*]

«Within [the logic that has dominated the West since the time of the Greeks], the gaze is particularly foreign to female eroticism [. . .]. [Womans] entry into a dominant scopic economy signifies [. . .] her consignment to passivity: she is to be the beautiful object of contemplation» (25-6). In *This Sex Which is Not One,* Luce Irigaray offers this categorical denunciation of an erotic economy dominated by the gaze. It could be objected that she follows too closely the logic that, from the time of the Greeks, has decreed that, since desire operates through the eyes, Woman should not be allowed to look directly on the male. However, Irigaray offers a challenge to this axiom dictating acceptable female behavior. She argues that «Woman's desire [does not] speak the same language as man's», that «Woman takes pleasure more from touching than from looking» (25-6). According to her theory, there is no need to forbid the gaze to women, for women do not speak their desire through the eyes.

And why would they want to? The gaze, Irigaray argues, is the instrument of a pleasure that is as restricted as it is restricting. «Can pleasure be measured, bounded, triangulated, or not?» (10), she queries. Behind her question is a never explicitly formulated attack on the concept articulated by René Girard, the triangulation of desire. In Girard's theory, male desire—in Girard's model, the desiring subject is always a man or a woman, like Emma Bovary, created by a man—is never original, but is inspired by the desire of a male rival. Both the functioning of the gaze as Irigaray presents it and the triangulation of desire act to objectif Woman, to deny her an active role in the economy of desire.

It seems logical to assume as Irigaray does that «Woman's desire does not speak the same language as a man's». However, what seems missing from Irigaray's reformulation of the language of desire is a reading of representations by women writers of the creation of a female erotic language. The gaze has been forbidden to women, but that does not mean that they have not used it. It may be that readers have not been sensitive to Woman's invasion of «the dominant scopic economy» because the female erotic gaze does not function according to the model that male representations have schooled us to expect. I would like to examine texts that contradict both Irigaray's description of

Woman's relation to the gaze and her implicit critique of Woman's role in triangular desire. These are two of the founding texts of an erotic literature in which women authors portray a female desiring subject in the process of expressing her desire. These texts run counter to the logic Irigaray develops, according to which Woman situates herself outside the erotic geometry constructed with the gaze, for they depict Woman openly speaking her desire through the eyes. Furthermore, they suggest that there may also be a female variant or variants of the triangulation of desire: in both these texts, female desire expresses itself voyeuristically, through a gaze that is mediated, although in ways that are not recognizable on the basis of male-oriented discussions of the triangulation of desire.

The women's texts I have in mind also refute the rare portrayals by male authors of women who take an active role in «the dominant scopic economy». Let us begin to measure the originality of female representations by briefly considering Woman's fate in male texts. Without exception, male depictions of a female desiring subject who looks openly upon the object of her desire reveal that Woman adopts what is assumed to be a male language at her own risk.

Let me inaugurate the precarious historical balance I will maintain throughout this discussion by illustrating the male presentation of the female desiring subject with two examples, one classic (Greek) and one French neo-classic. In Greek tragedy, Woman is a dangerous speaking subject because she comes to language in order to speak about sexual desire. Nowhere is this more strikingly illustrated than in the work of Euripides, frequent inspiration for the French poet of Woman's passion, Racine. Recently, critics have begun to speak of Euripidean feminism to refer to his staging, especially in the character of Phaedra but also with his Medea and his other women wronged, of the discourse of female desire. However, that characterization is perhaps hasty, as is evident from the example of Euripedes' heir, Racine. No one expresses with more complexity the power of Woman's *prise de parole* and its threat to the social order than Racine. Racine establishes female desire as a dangerous force that must be annihilated when he portrays the desiring woman as active subject controlling the gaze, and when he allows her to propose a novel triangulation of desire, in which the object of desire is doubled, rather than the desiring subject.

Such early commentators on French neo-classical tragedy as Germaine de Staël's protégé Schlegel considered Euripides' rendering of Phaedra's tragedy superior to Racine's because of its more restrained portrayal of the heroine's expression of her desire. The most striking illustrations of what Schlegel terms the «shameful degradation» of Racine's Phèdre are the famous double scenes of Phèdre's avowal of her forbidden love for Hippolyte (I, 3, II, 5). In both instances, Racine pointedly inscribes the functioning of desire through the eyes—«je le vis, je rougis, je pâlis à sa vue»; «tel que je vous vois» (lines 273, 640). Phèdre is «shameful» because she refuses the founding classical dictate of female modesty which forbids her to look directly at a man. However, her degradation is even more complete in the second scene because, when she turns her desiring gaze on Hippolyte, she enriches the erotic present by conflating it with the erotic past. In addition, Phèdre triangulates her desire incestuously when she fractures the functioning of genealogy to see not the son's resemblance to his father but the father's resemblance to the son. She objectifies Hippolyte as the beautiful object of her contemplation, then endows him with her memories of his father's past: «[Thésée] avait votre port, vos yeux, votre langage, / [. . .] Lorsque de notre Crète il traversa les flots» (lines 641, 643). It is this memorialization through and of the gaze, this use of the gaze to create an erotic scene in which past and present function simultaneously, that constitutes Racine's greatest insight into the gaze of the female desiring subject and into Woman's invasion of the «dominant scopic economy».

During the scene in which Phèdre uses her memorializing gaze to combine the seductive traits of father and son, displacing thereby both the legendary womanizer Thésée and the aspiring warrior Hippolyte from the male's customary place as organizer of love's geometry, she is still unaware of Hippolyte's love for Aricie. She therefore does not yet know that she has been assigned a place in a traditional love triangle, in which she plays the conventional role of older woman abandoned for younger woman. While Phèdre still believes that she has the power to rearrange the geometry of desire, Racine has her give voice to that desire on several occasions by borrowing from the original voice of women's erotic literature, Sappho. Most notably, for the moment at which Phèdre, brought low by her passion, memorializes her initiation into the transgressive role of desiring/gazing female—«je le vis», etc.—Racine's heroine speaks not with her own Racinian voice but with a virtual citation from what has been since Racine's day Sappho's most famous ode, the ode traditionally referred to by the French tradition as **«A l'aimée»**. Racine's one major transformation of Sappho's original, his translation of Sappho's present tense into a past tense, may signal his recognition of memory's central place in Sappho's poetry of desire. The punishment Racine reserves for Phèdre, her suicide under the spectator's gaze, a flagrant violation of 17th-century theatrical practice, may also be an act of authorial revenge against Sappho, the female poet indecent enough to have dared both to appropriate the gaze for a desiring woman and to invent a female triangulation of desire.

Sappho's commentators through the ages have responded in particular to two characteristics of her work, her presentation of the context of poetic creation and her configuration of the plot of female passion. Sappho portrays both the composition and the performance of her verse as an exchange among women, as the product of a female community whose members are united by bonds both personal and professional. Her *oeuvre* is most famous and most notorious because of its celebration of a type of female friendship that commentators try to understand through reference to the biographical scenario they promote for Sappho. Commentators thus most often consider Sapphic friendship solely in terms of what they believe to be its sexual content and react to the subject with moral condemnation, or sympathetic defense, or even attempts to deny the sexual content of her poetry. Yet this female bond can also be considered in purely literary terms as an attempt to bypass male literary authority and to deny men any primary role in the process of poetic creation. Sappho presents poetic creation as literature written by women for other women and about other women. In this poetic universe, males are relegated to a peripheral, if not an intrusive, role. Most strikingly—and this, I contend, constitutes the central threat of Sappho's creation for male writers—the Sapphic narrator, a woman, assumes what is generally a male prerogative. She is the desiring subject. Because the object of her desire is also a woman, she is in control of the gaze that objectifies the beloved woman, thereby giving the poem its visual focus and creating its geometry of desire.

Let us consider the transgressive qualities of Sappho's use of the gaze in the poem cited by Racine, the ode **«A l'aimée»**. Here is that scandalous ode in a recent, fairly literal French translation by Edith Mora. (I provide only a French translation because the feminine forms are retained in French).

> Il égale les dieux je crois
> l'homme qui devant toi vient s'asseoir
> et qui tout près de toi entend
> ta voix tendre
>
> et ton rire enchanteur qui a, je le jure,
> affolé mon coeur dans ma poitrine
> Car si je te vois un instant je ne peux
> plus rien dire
>
> ma langue est brisée, sous ma peau
> un feu subtil soudain se glisse
> mes yeux ne voient plus, mes oreilles sont
> bourdonnantes
> une sueur glacée me couvre et un tremblement
>
> me prend toute et je suis plus verte
> que l'herbe, tout près de mourir

il me semble . . .

Mais il faut tout oser car même abandonnée . . .

The poem recounts what appears at first to be a conventional tale of the triangulation of desire: the narrator is a voyeur, observing from a distance the woman who is the object of desire while this woman is demonstrating her love for a man. However, for today's reader and for readers at least as early as the time of the first translator to remodel Sappho's erotic geometry, Catullus, there is something «wrong» with the scene of love reciprocal and frustrated that is staged in the poem. The triangle of desire inscribed there is unlike either of those formations that literary portrayals of love have schooled the reader to expect. The narrator's femininity is not immediately stressed so that the appearance of a feminine adjective («je suis plus verte») in the poem's second half can come as a shock, an invasion. The reader suddenly realizes that the poem is not what it first appears to be. The narrator is a usurper, for she has displaced the male from his role as viewer in the most common literary love triangle in which a man sees the woman he loves in the arms of another man. However, the triangle configured after this displacement can in no way be confused with what has become the stereotypical literary love triangle composed by two women and one man, in which one woman laments her abandonment for the other woman.

To judge from responses to her poetry over the centuries, Sappho's (re)configuration of the plot of love, the triangle of desire that she proposes, was the source of the threat she has so often constituted for male writers. Sappho usurps for her female narrator the control over the gaze that is normally a male domain. I realize that it is impossible to reconstitute the original «horizon of expectations» for erotic poety and that her poetry may well predate the stereotypes I have in mind, yet the axiom Irigaray posits, «the prevalence of the gaze» has always been «particularly foreign to female eroticism» in all likelihood predates those stereotypes as well. When Sappho put a woman in the place usually occupied by the male poet-lover, she initiated a pattern in the economy of desire that many «strong» male writers have tried to overturn. Poets like Catullus (in his ode 51) and Ronsard (in his «Je suis un demi-dieu») propose a masculine reconfiguration of Sappho's erotic geometry in which a male narrator controls the gaze and has regained control over the beloved woman.

For their so-called «translations» of **«A l'aimée»,** both Catullus and Ronsard revise Sappho's geometry of desire. In «Ille mi par esse deo videtur», Catullus puts a man in the place of Sappho's female narrator. As a result of this substitution, he sets up triangular desire zero degree: a man desires a woman when he sees her in the arms of another man. Ronsard is more radical than his Latin precursor: he eliminates both the transgressive desiring woman and her scandalously innovative triangulation. In «Je suis un demy-dieu, quand, assis vis-à-vis / de Toy», the male poet («je») has assumed the double control over the gaze Sappho and Catullus divided between the narrator and the man seated next to the beloved woman. While in Catullus all attention is focused on the exchange between men from which both desire and poetry are born, Ronsard's poem is constructed around a single gaze, through which the male objectifies the beloved woman.

Critics and commentators are unable to erase Sappho's transgression as easily as her poet-translators. Since they are obliged to accept the erotic triangle she proposes, they attempt instead to account for the Sapphic gaze in a manner that alleviates the threat of its uncanny functioning in the poem. Witness the efforts of the man who is arguably the most influential Sappho commentator of our century, Denys Page. In his still authoritative *Sappho and Alcaeus* Page devotes a disproportionately long section of his extensive commentary on Sappho **"31"** to an attempt to reposition the reader's vision of Sappho's vision. Page views the poem as an interpretive option: «We have to choose . . . whether the emphasis falls on *love of the girl* or on *jealousy of the man*» (22). Page turns this choice between «love» and «jealousy» into a decision between two types of triangulation. He seeks above all to persuade us of the absolute centrality of the first member of the triangle to be introduced, the anonymous man presented only as «he», a pronominal interloper in the intimacy shared by «I» and «you». «The greatest obstacle to our understanding of the whole is indeed our ignorance of the relation of this man to the girl and to Sappho . . . : But we must not forget that the *man* was the principal subject of the whole of the first stanza; and we shall not be content with any explanation of this poem which gives no satisfactory account of his presence and his prominence in it» (28).

By centering his account on the man and on Sappho's jealousy of him, Page makes the poem function according to a standard masculine triangular scenario. Echoing Freud's conclusion about female homosexuality (in «The Psychogenesis of a Case of Homosexuality in a Woman»), Page thereby also makes Sappho's female narrator desire a woman *as a man*. The commentator who promotes jealousy as the narrator's primary emotional response to the scene and reinforces the man's «prominence» argues by implication that the narrator is involved with greatest intensity in the process by which the gaze is used to objectify the girl who is the object of masculine desire. To see the process of objectification as the primary function of the gaze in Sappho **"31"** is to imply that this poem inscribes the origin of Sapphic desire, to view that desire as existing primarily in the present, and finally to suggest that the narrator's silent interlocutor, the girl she addresses as «you», plays only an incidental role in the generation of her desire.

This triple implication of Page's reading denies the specificity of Sappho's vision of the erotic moment. Like Racine, Sappho stages the gaze as an act of memorialization. Unlike the male vision of female desire, however, Sappho's female desiring subject immortalizes the memory of an erotic gaze in order to comment on the creation of female desire, rather than, as in Phèdre's case, in order to build a monument to the young male's physical beauty and heroic prowess. Sappho's use of the present tense is her canniest poetic strategy. She appears to be grounding her gaze in the moment of its generation—«si je te vois un instant»—as if to invite comparison with the focus on the moment of sexual desire that is a commonplace of male erotic poetry. But to read Sappho **"31"** as a standard use of the present tense is to fall into the oldest misreading of the poem's erotic situation in which the poem becomes both the archetypal vision of Woman, transported by the frenzy of untamed physical desire, writing in the heat of the moment, and the archetypal model of women's writing as the spontaneous, uncontrolled outpouring of personal passion. It is against this traditional vision of the poem, prominent for centuries and dominant in Racine's day, when Sappho was rediscovered for modern literature, that Page and other recent commentators insist, with an overbearing sense of superiority, that Sappho **"31"** must above all be seen as a tribute to Sappho's artistic *control:* Page stresses «the uncommon objectivity» of her attitude toward her emotions, the «accurate definition» of symptoms, the «precision» of expression, the «exactitude» of portrayal, all the while leading up to what was surely in its original formulation a bold conclusion: «There is certainly no lack of control in the expression, whatever there may have been in the experience» (27).

However, this recent refocusing of the critical viewing angle from Sappho's spontaneity to Sappho's control simply reverses the coin, without attempting either to explain the specific nature of Sapphic poetic control or to account for the role played in the poem by the appearance of spontaneity. In Sappho's erotic vision, the gaze does not function as a unique occurrence, as the lightning-bolt vision of love/desire at first sight. The Sapphic gaze is doubly repetitive, both an action that takes place again and an original action that is recreated in memory. Catullus projects the multiple gaze onto the man who, sitting «opposite» the beloved, «gazes at her again and again [*identidem*]», and he uses this recurrence to spark the narrator's jealous desire. Sappho's repetition is both less predictable and more complex.

The man does not *look* at the beloved girl; he is shown *listening* to «her voice and her laughter». The female poet alone turns the gaze on the object of desire, in a use of «see» that has troubled translators for centuries. Here are a few of the attempts to render its complexity: «while I gazed» (Ambrose Philips, Sappho's first English translator, 1711), «should I but see thee a little moment» (Symonds, 1883), «when I see thee but a little» (Wharton 1885), «si je te vois un instant» (Mora, 1966). By adding temporal constraints to the present, or by making it conditional («if», «should»), Sappho's translators attempt to render the evocative plenitude of the present tense in which the female erotic gaze is displayed. Sappho's use of the present stretches the boundaries of that tense: she packs into «I see» both a present of repetition—«each time that I see you»—and a present of memorialization—«the minute I catch a glimpse of you my desire comes back to me in full force». Sappho uses the gaze to evoke not the instant of desire but both the recreation of an erotic association that no longer exists, and the duration, the past stability of that relationship. This duration, this endurance, returns in the fragment that sounds what must remain for us the poem's end: «I must dare all, for even abandoned . . . ».

Instead of a standard scenario of the birth of desire, in Sappho **"31"** we find a model for the regeneration of desire. The gaze acts to keep desire alive, to give the poet the potential for a renewed and ongoing erotic experience, even in the face of abandonment. Sappho's controlled recreation of the function of the gaze displays her female narrator desiring a woman not as a man, as Freud would have it, but as a woman. In the model for the operation of the gaze in female eroticism that she establishes, Woman gazes in a present that renews the past and reaffirms the bond that is at the origin of the renewable erotic trance, the controlled and spontaneous outpouring of female desire.

Rosanna Warren (essay date 1989)

SOURCE: Warren, Rosanna. "Sappho: Translation as Elegy." In *The Art of Translation: Voices from the Field*, edited by Rosanna Warren, pp. 199-216. Boston: Northeastern University Press, 1989.

[*In the following essay, Warren details the influence of translated Sapphic poetry on such writers as Catullus, Charles Baudelaire, and Algernon Charles Swinburne, with a principal focus on Sappho's poem known as "Phainetai moi."*]

Our dreams pursue our dead.

Swinburne, *Ave atque Vale*

Ille mi par . . .

He's like a god, that man; he seems
(if this can be) to shine beyond
the gods, who nestling near you sees
    you and hears you

laughing low in your throat. It tears me
apart. For when I glimpse you,
Lesbia, look—I'm helpless:
    tongue a frozen

lump, and palest fire
pouring through all my limbs; my ears
deafened in ringing; each eye
    shuttered in night. . . .

You're wasting your time, Catullus,
laying waste to your life. You love it.
Whole kingdoms and blissful cities
    have wasted away, like you.

I seem to have given a misleading title, for the poem I present is not by Sappho, but by Catullus. And I revise further by pointing out that it is not "by" Catullus either, but "by" me. There may seem to be no little immodesty and downright foolishness in putting forward my own translation of Catullus' famous translation of Sappho's famous poem **"Phainetai moi."**

My translation of Catullus' *"Ille mi par . . ."* occurs, with another Catullus poem in the Sapphic meter, in a volume of my own poems. But these possessive phrases become obtrusive, as indeed they ought in matters of authorship. The purpose in focusing on a translation of a translation is not to claim that the world *needs* yet another version of this perennially retranslated poem; nor is it to demonstrate that I have outpaced all my predecessors and found a perfect English equivalent for Catullus. Rather, I should like to offer it, impersonally, as a small instance of lyric lineage, a type or model for poetry's perpetual re-engendering of itself. It is to argue that poetry is, finally, a family matter, involving the strains of birth, love, power, death, and inheritance; and that, given such strains (in every sense), one is never "by oneself" however isolated the act of writing may appear. The so-called original poems in my book are, in their own way, translations of several lyric traditions into personal experience and idiom, and are possible only because of strenuous acts of reading, one form of which we know, conventionally, as translation. I am concerned here with the way in which the individual poet inherits poetry, or, in Eliot's formulation, is catalyzed by it; and I take translation as a specific and especially focused instance of the reception and transformation of literary tradition.

I was drawn to Catullus 51 (*"Ille mi par . . ."*) not only because it has haunted me since adolescence, not only because I am more at home in Latin than in Greek,

but precisely because I was touched by the pathos of its being a translation and not "the real thing." In Catullus' forging of a new poetry from his still rather primitive native traditions and Greek models, I recognized the situation of any poet in the strain of self-creation through confrontation with the foreign and the past, the choosing of a parentage. And that situation may be seen as an analogy for the self-creation of a whole literature which develops by exposure to the "other," as English literature, also fairly barbaric in its early stages, has done in burst after burst, and as American literature, given its colonial inception, could not avoid doing.

The word "inheritance" implies death, grief, contest, and riches. In presenting the literary genre of elegy as a model for translation, I shall be relying on Peter Sacks's *The English Elegy* (The Johns Hopkins University Press, 1985). This book traces the work of mourning from its anthropological origins on into complex literary codification. In elegy, with its association with the ritual death and rebirth of a fertility god, I see a figure for the work of translation, which involves the death, dismemberment, and (one hopes!) rebirth of a text, with relative consolation for the mourners, or readers.

Sacks's work is essential in restoring our sense of the primitive vigor, I could almost say sacred power, at the source of our inherited rituals of mourning, of elegiac writing, and, I will argue, of all writing. In recalling the rites of sacrifice and cannibalism associated with early cults of Dionysus, and the survival of such rites symbolically in ancient Greek and later funerary practice, Sacks reveals the terror and *virtú* latent in such an apparently artificial form as English pastoral elegy. He shows how individual loss may be integrated within larger rhythmic structures dramatized by the poem, and he provides a vision of literature as a communion perpetually renewed in the light of death. In considering Sappho and some of her progeny, I am trying to recover that visceral sense of the rite of poetry: that sense in which, as Auden said of Yeats, "the words of the dead / Are modified in the guts of the living," and in which Pound, also translating a translation, envisioned Odysseus summoning the dead in canto 1 of the *Cantos:* ". . . A sheep to Tiresias only, black and a bellsheep. / Dark blood flowed in the fosse, / Souls out of Erebus. . . ."

The term "elegy" requires more than a little elucidation. The word is a rather mysterious one, with veiled origins, and auspicious dual associations with death and with love. The original Greek elegiac couplets were not necessarily associated with funerals, but were used for a wide variety of exhortation and reflection.[1] But Hellenistic grammarians derived *elegos,* in an imaginative etymology, from "*e e legein*" (to cry 'woe, woe').[2] In Euripides it is used as a song of mourning associated with the *aulos,* a flute whose tone was considered woeful as opposed to the *barbitos,* the lyre associated with lyric. In *Heroides* 15, Ovid has Sappho say, in elegiac couplets, *"Flendus amor meus est—elegiae flebile carmen; / non facit ad lacrimas barbitos ulla meas"* (ll. 7-8: My love is lamentable—a weeping song of elegy; no lyre suits my tears). "Elegy," in that passage, is doubly anachronistic: in Ovid's time the term was used for witty amatory complaint, and in Sappho's sixth century B.C. the elegiac meter had no necessarily doleful connotation. However, there is a strong possibility that the *elegos* was at an earlier period specifically associated with ritual grief.[3] Sacks describes the evolution of elegy through Latin love poetry into the English pastoral elegy, which reclaims some of the primitive features such as structures of repetition, myth of a vegetation god, bursts of anger and cursing, procession of mourners, detachment from the deceased, and consolation through symbolic substitution.[4] For my purposes, which are to define a private ritual figure for translation, the perhaps fictive origin of elegy as the art associated with funerals, and thus with the death and resurrection of vegetation gods and the rechanneling of eros into song, serves beautifully. We are considering the death and resurrection of texts in a myth of literary metamorphosis whose deities are those grieving poet-lovers whose nymphs turn into the tools—or emblems—of the trade: Pan's Syrinx into the panpipes, Apollo's Daphne into the laurel. Its other deities are those vegetation figures Dionysus, Adonis, Hyacinth, who survive sacrifice to reemerge as myths of eternal song.[5] It becomes apparent then that two senses of elegy, love and loss, can only rarely be disentangled.

We shall find our way back to Sappho through *Lycidas.* The death of Edward King provided Milton with an occasion to negotiate with grief—in this case a rather ceremonial grief—and, more pointedly, with the inherited genre of pastoral elegy and his own ambition and fear of death. His apparent heartlessness, or at least jauntiness, in the twitch of the mantle blue and the turn from pastoral to epic has often been noted. A poet's elegy for another poet is somehow a translation of that poet or at least of a tradition, and involves some kind of transfer of powers, perhaps aggressively asserted by the survivor. In any case, the underlying question is not that of personal survival, but of the survival of poetry. If all real poetry is, as I believe, writing in the light of death, elegy is the genre which performs most consciously in that light.

In *Lycidas* Milton's grief, anger, and fear crystallize appropriately around the figure of Orpheus, in classical mythology the mystic singer whose death by dismemberment could be read either as the failure of art or as its resurrection and purification.[6] Orpheus' *sparagmos* and drowning in the Hebrus not only suit the fate of Edward King, but fit within Milton's cosmic pattern of drownings and ascensions of stars and the sun. Such a pattern is hinted at early in the poem when the shepherds sing undisturbed by the passage of time ("Oft till the star that rose at evening bright / Toward Heaven's descent had sloped his westering wheel"); the pattern is fulfilled at the end, in a Christian design: "So sinks the day-star in the ocean bed / And yet anon repairs his drooping head." The final couplet astonishingly detaches the surviving poet, the uncouth swain, from the natural cycle to which the dead poet has been assimilated; yet the solar association haunts the conclusion in the ambiguous pronoun "he": "And now the sun had stretched out all the hills, / And now was dropped into the western bay; / At last he rose, and twitched his mantle blue: / Tomorrow to fresh woods and pastures new."[7]

In a crucial turn *Lycidas* associates Orpheus with Sappho:

> What could the Muse herself that Orpheus bore,
> The Muse herself, for her inchanting son
> Whom universal Nature did lament,
> When by the rout that made the hideous roar,
> His gory visage down the stream was sent,
> Down the swift Hebrus to the Lesbian Shore?
>
> (ll. 59-63)

The classical Orpheus envisaged in his humiliation emphasizes the death of Lycidas, in this phase, as horror. This Orpheus serves as anti-type to, and will give way before, "the dear might of him that walked the waves"; cut off from Christian revelation, he is an inadequate figure for resurrection. Even at this nadir, however, when the "hideous roar" of the Thracian women seems to overwhelm the "inchanting" powers of music, Milton hints at the resurrection of those powers by imagining the current of the Hebrus flowing south over a hundred miles along the coast of Asia Minor to wash Orpheus' head to the shores of Sappho's island. That "supreme head of song," as Swinburne called her, and the possibilities of poetry she represents, are immediately challenged in *Lycidas* by the speaker's questions and the visions of the blind Fury. In Milton's poem Sappho remains a faint allusion. It is significant, however, that she should be glimpsed here in the context of the drowned poet who will be raised, like the "daystar," into the morning sky, and into a familiar mythology of resurrected divinities. Sappho, too, is said to have drowned, disappointed in love, by leaping from the Leucadian Rock; as Gregory Nagy has shown,[8] she rises, in her legend if not in *Lycidas,* into a similar myth of solar resurrection as Sappho/Aphrodite pursuing Phaon/Phaethon.

But why Sappho? I have been considering her as a legend, not as a poet. Indeed, it is partly as legend that she presides over the family matters I want to trace, in translation, through Catullus, Baudelaire, and Swinburne. Nagy's argument linking her to Aphrodite/Istar/Eos and a solar myth of recurrent death and rebirth—an argument so intricate as to deserve Sappho's own epithet for Aphrodite, *doloplokos,* weaver of wiles—derives to some degree from Sappho's invocations to the goddess, but for the most part from a fragment of Menander's *Leukadia* preserved by Strabo, from Ovid's *Heroides* 15, and from a bristling array of mythological sources. Through Menander and Ovid and earlier comic traditions, Sappho entered the Western imagination as a priestess of song and of illicit love who died by flinging herself off the white cliff at Cape Leukas for the love of the handsome ferryman Phaon. Satirically viewed in various plays of Middle Comedy, the story is one of the insufficiency of poetry, and perhaps also of the just come-uppance meted out to a woman who has spurned too long the love of men. Even the burlesque plays and Ovid's arch diagnosis, however, veil a glorious Sappho linked to ancient cults at Cape Leukas. Through "Longinus," that is, through the treatise "*De Sublimitate*" to which we owe the preservation of **"Phainetai moi,"** Sappho has imposed herself as the exemplary sublime poet, with a halo of primacy for the lyric akin to that of Homer for epic. She was known in the Palatine Anthology as the Tenth Muse, and comes down to us as a kind of mother goddess of poetry, of whom Swinburne said, "Judging even from the mutilated fragments fallen within our reach from the broken altar of her sacrifice of song, I for one have always agreed with all Grecian tradition in thinking Sappho to be beyond all question and comparison the very greatest poet that ever lived."[9]

But again, why Sappho? Why such a legend? Why should she seem to have engendered the Western lyric, not once, but over and over again, as we see in the twentieth century's rapture over the Oxyrhynchan fragments and their shaping touch on Aldington, Pound, HD, Guy Davenport . . . ? We must turn to these fragments, to the poems. If the legendary Sappho rising from the sea as the evening star gives us an emblem of the translation and survival of song, the actual survival of her texts in quoted snippets and in the papyri of grave wrappings is all the more eloquent. In the idea of elegy, with its dual allusions to love and death, we can sense something of the power of these mutilated poems stripped from mummies but still casting erotic spells.[10]

The enchantment resides, however, not in an idea, but in her "visible song," as Swinburne so rightly understood; supremely, in the Sapphic stanza, which burned its shape into Catullus' brain five centuries after Sappho's death, and which has shaped our desire ever since. If we consider Sappho as a myth, it must be as a myth not of love, but of form.

Phainetai moi keinos isos theoisin
emmen oner ottis enantios toi
izanei kai plasion adu phoneisas upakouei

kai gelaisas imeroen, to m'ei man
kardian en stethesin eptoasen;
os gar es t'ido, broke', os me phonas
ouden et' ikei

all' akan men glossa eage, lepton
d'autika kroi pur upadedromaken,
oppatessi d'oud' en oreimm', epirrom-
beisi d'akouai,

kad de m'idros psukros ekei, tromos de
paisan agrei, klorotera de poias
emmi, tethnakein d'oligo pideueis
phainomai . . .

It is a haunting shape. In Sappho's hands it plays release against restraint with unrivaled cunning: the poem runs from stanza to stanza like water pouring from basin to basin down a trout stream, twisting and flashing, unfurled and checked. As Charles Segal has observed, its very motion is the erotic persuasion, *peitho,* of which Sappho so often writes. Within each hendecasyllabic line the opening trochaic feet give way to the impulse which throbs forward in the choriamb, to be teasingly checked by the concluding bacchiac. . . . The halt teases because more often than not the sentence's propulsion launches us into the next line, sometimes through enjambment within a word: *phonei-/sas* (ll. 3-4), *epirrom-/beisi* (ll. 11-12). After three such hendecasyllables the adonic seems to dam up the current with its wedgelike, truncated shape and final pair of long syllables; but Sappho admits no such resolution, and spills her poem over barrier after barrier. Within this flow, the eddies of assonance and consonance complete the work of hypnotic enchantment. In its expansions and contractions this is a stanza fatally gauged to register the pulse of desire.

Can a living stream be translated? One of Sappho's finest interpreters, Swinburne, has testified:

To translate the two odes and the remaining fragments of Sappho is the one impossible task; and as witness of this I will call up one of the greatest among poets. Catullus "translated"—or as his countrymen would now say "traduced"—the ode of Anactoria—"*Eis Eromenan*"; a more beautiful translation there never was and will be; but compared with the Greek, it is colorless and bloodless, puffed out by additions and enfeebled by alterations. . . . Where Catullus failed, I could not hope to succeed.[11]

Swinburne is here mourning the death of the original. To pursue the elegiac analogy, he has brought himself to that stage of grief which recognizes irreplaceable loss. But just as the work of mourning proceeds by rehearsal of the trauma and ritual self-mutilation to detachment from the deceased and acceptance of a symbolic substitute, so the work of translation repeats the destruction of the original, dismembers and ingests it as in the Thracian sacrifice of Orpheus or the rites of Dionysus, and finally offers its transubstantiated version as consolation for, and recognition of, loss. In the passage just quoted Swinburne was defending his free translation of Sappho in his poem "Anactoria":

> "That is not Sappho," a friend once said to me. I could only reply, "It is as near as I can come; and no man can come close to her. . . . I have striven to cast my spirit into the mould of hers, to express and represent not the poem but the poet. . . . Here and there, I need not say, I have rendered into English the very words of Sappho. I have tried also to work into words of my own some expression of the effect: to bear witness how, more than any other's, her verses strike and sting the memory in lonely places, or at sea, among all loftier sights and grounds—how they seem akin to fire and air, being themselves "all air and fire"; other element there is none in them."[12]

We shall presently consider the fruits of such devotion; before that, we need to turn to her first translator, Catullus.

SAPPHO AND CATULLUS

51

Ille mi par esse deo videtur,
ille, si fas est, superare divos,
qui sedens adversus identidem te
    spectat et audit

dulce ridentem, misero quod omnis
eripit sensus mihi: nam simul te,
Lesbia, aspexi, nihil est super mi . . .

lingua sed torpet, tenuis sub artus
flamma demanat, sonitu suopte
tintinant aures, gemina teguntur
    lumina nocte.

otium, Catulle, tibi molestum est:
otio exsultas nimiumque gestis:
otium et reges prius et beatas
    perdidit urbes.

Though Catullus seems to have written only two poems in the Sapphic meter, the extent of his debt to the poet of Lesbos may be judged from the name he gave to the woman he loved: Lesbia. The two Catullan Sapphic poems record stages in that affair. The translation of **"Phainetai moi"** can be seen either as celebrating an early, happy phase, substituting erotic rapture for Sappho's distress,[13] or, as had been plausibly argued, as commenting ironically on the destructiveness of his love for Lesbia through allusion to supposed marriage

elements in Sappho's poem.[14] "*Furi et Aureli*," Catullus' other Sapphic poem (Catullus 11), is a savage and lyrical farewell to the unworthy lover. However Lesbia is seen by Catullus in these poems, it is through a Sapphic lens which emphasizes, by contrast, Lesbia's Roman corruption.

This is not the occasion to pore, syllable by syllable, over the transposition from Greek to Latin; a few details will have to suggest the enterprise. Most tellingly, however, we can observe right from the start that Catullus has "lost it" (to use current parlance) with the very first word. *Phainetai,* from *phaino* (to appear), shares a root with *phaos* (light), and with the verb *phao* (to give light, to shine). The "appearance" Sappho indicates is no mere seeming or being seen, but something more on the order of our "epiphany," an English cognate of *phaino.* It is used of the apparitions of deities. The man in Sappho's poem, *keinos,* that one, whoever he is who sits next to the beloved girl, blazes in the first stanza with a radiance reflected from Aphrodite, through the girl. It is an epiphany of Love, working upon the man and, beyond him, upon Sappho observing. We are confronted here not simply with a relative poverty in Latin and English verbs of seeming, but with an entirely different conception of the manifestation of the divine.

Another detail: Sappho's *imeroen* (l. 5). A long-drawn-out, caressing neuter adjective used adverbially ("and listens to you laughing *enticingly*"), it contains the words *eros,* and is charged with desire, with the dread and sacred power of love, to a degree that annihilates most dippy English substitutes and far outstrips Catullus' merely sensory *dulce* (sweetly). As if *imeroen* had not sufficient voltage, Sappho renews the charge in a phonetic echo, completing the line *kai gelaisas imeroen, to m'ei man,* whose sensuous alliteration and assonance can be savored even by the Greekless reader. A few final points: Catullus inserts a legalistic clause into line 2: *si fas est, superare divos* (if it is permitted, [he seems] to surpass the gods). It testifies to a peculiarly Roman attitude about men and gods, but it also slows up the poem, and a good deal is lost in line 6 in the replacement of Sappho's heart shuddering in her breast by the abstract *sensus* (general powers of apprehension).

What has Catullus salvaged? First and foremost, the stanza form, through which he knowingly pours his own poem. It was Catullus' muscular twining of sentences through lines and stanzas that mesmerized me years ago when I did not know the Greek. He has taken over, likewise, something of Sappho's vowel and consonant play, though his seems more programmatic and symmetrical: "*flamma demanat, sonitu suopte*" (l. 9). Where Sappho was entirely flexible, Catullus moves toward practices which will be codified in Horatian Sapphics, often making the fourth syllable of the hendecasyllable long, and ending a word after the fifth syllable. He does not have Sappho's radiance, but he grasps the simplicity with which she lists the medical symptoms of love, symptoms taken over from Homeric descriptions of shock and fear, the drama of war imported to the love chamber, epic into lyric. Where Sappho emphasized intimacy in stanza 1, Catullus insists on the recurrent nature of the scene with the rare adverb *identidem* (again and again) which appears in his other Sapphic poem, "*Furi et Aureli,*" in an obscene context. He misses the ring structure in her poem that linked the apparition (*phainetai*) of the rival man in line 1 through the sundering of her own body to a reunification of self in the strongly enjambed verb "to be" (*emmi,* l. 15) and felt apparition of self "I seem" (*phainomai,* l. 16). Where her poem went at this juncture is a wild surmise. Catullus seems to have omitted her remarkable fourth stanza, and his poem may or may not have ended with the famous *otium* stanza. If the *otium* lines did close his poem, as I sense they did, they set Catullus' passion in the typically Roman context of politics and empire at odds with private erotic life, and glance out again in the direction of epic.

That epic glance is given more scope in the "*Furi et Aureli*" poem. There Catullus addresses his two enemies as his "companions," and charges them, in a torrent of bombast mimicking imperial rhetoric, with a simple message of farewell to his "girl." After that calculated understatement, "*non bona dicta*" (not good words), explodes a stanza of obscene abuse which gives way to one of the most delicate of all Latin lyrics, the stanza recalling Sappho's cut flower:[15]

> But she'd better not look, like last time, for my
> love reviving. It's her fault it's fallen,
> a flower at the rim of the meadow, touched
>   by the plow passing.

Not surprisingly, the anatomy of love, and perhaps jealousy, in **"Phainetai moi"** has never lost its grip on the Western imagination. But the history of Sappho in English is by and large a sorry one. It is the story of the awkward adaptation of classical quantitative prosody to the English accentual-syllabic system.[16] The faint presence of stress in Latin meter only complicates the problem further. John Hall, translating **"Phainetai moi"** in 1652, sensibly opts for a loose stress equivalent to Sappho's quantities, and gives tetrameters with a dimeter for the adonic. The poor man can muster almost no other poetic resources beyond his common sense, however: his instinct for the rhyming couplet wars with the shape of the stanza, his meter thuds, his vocabulary is trite; to top it all off he has misunderstood (wilfully perhaps) the gender relations in the poem, rendering stanza 2:

> How did his pleasing glances dart
> Sweet languors to my ravish'd heart
> At the first sight though so prevailed
>   That my voice fail'd.[17]

E. M. Cox's 1925 version exemplifies the mess that results when a quantitative system is clamped arbitrarily onto English. One line will suffice. The conflict between natural word stress and fictive quantity results in verse which, if pronounced according to its own system, sounds downright idiotic: "Peér of the góds ¦ the hăppiĕśt ¦ măn Í seém."[18] J. A. Symonds in 1887 was more successful in aligning English stress with the requirements of length; his version is hardly felicitous syntactically ("Nothing see mine eyes, and a noise of roaring / Waves in my ear sounds"), but his first line at least shows how an accommodation might plausibly be reached: "Peér of góds hé ¦ seémĕth to mé, ¦ the blíssfúl. . . ."[19] For an approach which ignores the Sapphic stanza but tries to approximate its simplicity and concision, we can turn to Mary Barnard's 1958 version:

> He is more than a hero
>
> He is a god in my eyes—
> the man who is allowed
> to sit beside you—he . . .[20]

Hers has the virtue of cleanliness, but it lacks the rhythm of expansion and contraction which sustains life in Sappho's form.

The twentieth century has in fact been rich in appropriations of Sappho's poem. In "Three Letters to Anaktoria" from *Imitations* (1958), Robert Lowell supplies in hyperbole, exaggerated assonance and alliteration, extraneous similes, and sheer gusto what he lacks in subtlety: the man sits next to the girl "like a cardplayer"; "refining fire," filched from Dante's Arnaut Daniel, perhaps by way of Eliot, purifies the speaker's flesh in a discordantly Christian way; and Sappho's pale grass becomes blindingly verdant: "I am greener than the greenest green grass." Basil Bunting, working freely from Catullus in 1965, turns the poem back to Sappho by imitating her ring structure: "O, it is godlike to sit selfpossessed / When her chin rises and she turns to smile," he begins, and concludes the last stanza: ". . . I dissolve / When her chin rises and she turns to smile. / O, it is godlike!"[21]

Examples could proliferate endlessly. I indulge myself in one final instance. John Hollander's canny "After an Old Text"[22] uses the fact of its being a translation and revision of Sappho as a figure for the speaker's nostalgia for, hence re-vision of, an old lover, with the pronoun "you" conflating Sappho and his own lost love. The final stanza runs:

> This revision of you sucks out the sound of
> Words from my mouth, my tongue collapses, my legs

Flag, my ears roar, my eyes are blinded with flame;
 my
        Head is in hell then.

I would like to close, not by nagging at the innumerable translations of **"Phainetai moi"** in English, but by penciling briefly a larger sketch of translation as an elegiac genealogy. I spoke of poetry as a family matter; a record of translations is a family tree. I want now to trace, through a series of elegies, a perpetuated acknowledgment of Sappho as lyric mother, and therefore of her progeny as siblings. At issue is the enduring life of poetry. The poems to bear in mind are Catullus' elegy for his real brother ("*Multas per gentes,*" poem 101), Baudelaire's Sapphic poems, Swinburne's "Sapphics," and his elegy for Baudelaire "*Ave Atque Vale.*" Through these elegies, I suggest, we can sense Sappho, the lyric impulse, rising again and again like Hesperus from the waters of language, and perpetually lost; and we will sense translation in action as the blood pulse of our continuing, shared literary life, keeping time with the larger cycles of nature. I freely confess it: this is a myth. A working myth for a poet and translator.

Baudelaire and Swinburne

Baudelaire studied Greek as well as Latin in the *lyçée,* and was surely familiar with Sappho's **"Phainetai moi."** But the Sappho reincarnated in Baudelaire is not a metrical essence, as she was in part for Swinburne. Rather, Baudelaire is haunted by the myth of Sapphic sexuality. In a number of poems, two of which were excluded from *Les Fleurs du Mal* by the censor in 1857, he celebrates an eros which has nothing to do with the Greek Sappho's frank and splendid pleasure. Baudelaire's lesbian love is consecrated, not as joy, but as deviance. Set in the ghoulish context of Christian damnation on the one hand, and of "natural," socially useful, reproductive mating on the other, his lesbians are artists and outcasts in their pure search for beauty and sensation. "*O vierges, o démons, o monstres, o martyres, / De la réalité grands esprits contempteurs, / Chercheuses d'infini . . .*" ("O virgins, O demons, O monsters, O martyrs, great spirits contemptuous of reality, seekers of infinity . . ." from "*Femmes Damnées*"). Theirs is the true spirituality in, and against, a materialistic world, and, not surprisingly, they are associated with Baudelaire's cherished images of infinity: the abyss and the gulf, and their corollary, death: "—*Descendez, descendez, lamentables victimes, / Descendez le chemin de l'enfer éternel! / Plongez au plus profond du gouffre, où tous les crimes . . .*" ("Descend, descend, sad victims, descend the path of eternal hell! Dive to the depths of the gulf, where all crimes . . ." from "*Femmes Damnées: Delphine et Hippolyte*"). This *gouffre* has its analogies in Baudelaire's sense of Sappho's poetry: the

nearest he comes to describing her verse is his evocation, in "Lesbos," of the lesbian embraces where the imaginary cascade behaves rather like a Sapphic stanza:

Lesbos, where the kisses, like cascades
teeming and turbulent yet secret, deep,
plunge undaunted into unplumbed gulfs
and gather there, gurgling and sobbing till
they overflow in ever-new cascades![23]

At issue for Baudelaire is not the survival of Sappho's poetry. His Sapphic poems suggest something of the hell created in French nineteenth-century society for homosexual lovers, but his true absorption is with his own deflected eroticism as a figure for art. For him, art is and must be profoundly anti-natural; it joins in holy alliance with a sterile eros and with death, with infinity and the soul, in opposition to the squalid claims of nature and literal fact.

Though he claims to be Sappho's sentinel keeping vigil on the Leucadian cliff, Baudelaire takes us far afield from Sappho's hyacinths and the "dew on the riverside gleaming."[24] With Swinburne the inheritance is much more complex because it is expressed "genetically"— that is, in meter and stanza form. Sappho's strain is crossed, however, with the strong influences of Baudelaire and, at his worst, the Marquis de Sade. Before considering the fraternal relationship between Swinburne and Baudelaire, I want to address the matter of Sappho's more direct incarnation in Swinburne's poetry.

First, the meter. Swinburne's Greek was excellent and, more than excellent, it was passionate, so that he writes the Sapphic stanza naturally, translating long and short syllables to stress with an ease scarcely ever matched in English. I will now make a risky claim: that Sappho lives in English, not in any word-by-word reproduction of her texts, but in Swinburne's poems "Sapphics" and "Hendecasyllabics." I would claim in addition that Sappho's rigor and subtlety saved Swinburne from his own worst propensities toward prosodic exaggeration, and that his finest poems, to which we do not sufficiently confess our gratitude,[25] are those disciplined by Greek. In "Sapphics" Swinburne has allowed himself to be possessed by Sappho's "visible song," and his poem, in places, surges and pauses as delicately as hers down its streamed, its vowels and consonants as cunningly in play:

. . . and I too,
Full of the vision,

Sáw thĕ whíte ím̃plácăblĕ Áphrodíté,
Saw the hair unbound and the feet unsandalled
Shine as fire of sunset on western waters;
  Saw the reluctant
Feet, the straining plumes of the doves that drew her
  . . .

                                              (ll. 7-13)

I scan one line to show with what grace the stress corresponds to the Greek's requirements for length. In "Anactoria" the rhyming pentameter couplets make for a cruder versification. Here, however, actual translation of Sappho rises out of hyperbolic Sadean rhetoric, and so filially imbued is Swinburne with her spirit that those fragments from the "Hymn to Aphrodite" seem intrinsic to his own poem:

> Saw Love, as burning flame from crown to feet,
> Imperishable, upon her storied seat;
> Clear eyelids lifted toward the north and south,
> A mind of many colors, and a mouth
> Of many tunes and kisses; and she bowed,
> With all her subtle face laughing aloud,
> Bowed down upon me, saying "Who doth thee wrong,
> Sappho?"
>
> (ll. 67-74)

Swinburne is straining to render the first lines of the ode "*poikilothron athanat' Aphrodite / pai Dios doloploke*"; literally, "Richly (dappled, intricate, with various colors) enthroned immortal Aphrodite, child of Zeus, weaver of wiles." Swinburne has at least made incantatory what in Barnard seems blunt and curt, though clean ("Dapple-throned Aphrodite / eternal daughter of God, / Snareknitter!"), and in Davenport rococo ("God's stunning daughter deathless Aphródita / A whittled perplexity your bright abstruse chair . . .").

Swinburne has taken from **"Phainetai moi"** the conceit of love as a pathology, "Yea, all thy beauty sickens me with love" (l. 56); he has grossly exaggerated it with Sadean extrapolation that shies not from cannibalism: "Ah that my mouth for Muses' milk were fed / On the sweet blood thy sweet small wounds had bled!" (ll. 107-8). For a modern reader such a passage can only be comic; nor is there much to be said in defense of the workaday verse. I pause for a moment, however, on the theme of cannibalism. For all its hysteria, the passage points back to primitive rites of communion associated with funerals, and may recall my elegiac emblem of translation for which Sacks provided the model. The erotic communion Swinburne solicits, an invitation to rather than a defense against death, is itself merely a figure for the poet's real communion with the spirit of Sappho, and, as such, is an elegiac act. At the end of "Anactoria" the poetic eros does fend off death, for it allows Sappho, resurrected through Swinburne, to assert the immortality of song:

> I Sappho will be one with all these things,
> With all high things forever; and my face
> Seen once, my songs heard in a strange place,
> Cleave to men's lives . . .
>
> (ll. 276-79)

Communion with a ghost from antiquity is one thing; acceptance of the death of an immediate poetic forebear is quite another and more shocking matter. The loss felt is more urgent, as is the threat to one's own life and voice. The death of Baudelaire was, for Swinburne, such a shock, and one that elicited from him one of the majestic pastoral elegies in English, "*Ave Atque Vale.*" The title conjures up Catullus' farewell in elegiac couplets to his brother, and proclaims a fraternity between Sappho's lyric offspring: Catullus, Baudelaire, and himself.

Sappho, the mother, is immediately invoked in stanza 2:

> Thine ears knew all the wandering watery sighs
> Where the sea sobs round Lesbian promontories,
> The barren kiss of piteous wave to wave
> That knows not where is that Leucadian grave
> Which hides too deep the supreme head of song.

Peter Sacks has charted this poem with exemplary intelligence and learning. For my purposes, it will suffice to emphasize the way in which an elegy involves translation. In rejecting the traditional garland "rose or rue or laurel," in favor of "Half-faded, fiery blossoms, pale with heat," Swinburne is translating "Lycidas" into *Les Fleurs du Mal.* The poem proceeds to "translate" Baudelaire's own "translation" of Sappho: "Fierce loves and lovely leaf-buds poisonous . . ." (l. 25). Facing the death and, worse still, the silence of his brother poet, Swinburne is led to question whether poetry itself survives: "Thou art far too far for wings of words to follow / Far too far off for thought or any prayer" (ll. 89-90); note the lack of caesuras streamlining the distance. In this crisis, the poem attempts to assert poetic communion as the symbolic consolation proffered in traditional elegy: ". . . and not death estranges / My spirit from communion with thy song" (ll. 103-4); the whole lyric tradition appears as one long, shared lament: "Or through mine ears a mourning musical / Of many mourners rolled" (ll. 109-10). But this death and the impotence of Apollo and Aphrodite, poetry and love, seem to blight consolation: ". . . not all our songs, O friend, / Will make death clear or make life durable" (ll. 171-72). After much synaesthesia, the elegy seems to end in silence; the dead poet is not to rise as day-star or genius of any shore, and the figure of Sappho has blended into that of a more tragic mother: "And chill the solemn earth, a fatal mother, / With sadder than the Niobean womb . . ." (ll. 191-92).

The dead poet seems beyond the reach of poetry. This crisis corresponds to the moment in Moschus' lament for Bion in which "Bion is dead, and with him dead is music, and gone with him likewise the Dorian poesy."[26] The work of mourning, that is, would be completely blocked, were it not for the *translation* of Catullus that opens the final stanza, and in its very nature as translation belies the silence of death which it asserts. As long as Catullus speaks through Swinburne, he is neither dead nor silent, and neither, in some sense, is Baudelaire: "For thee, O now a silent soul, my brother, / Take at my hands this garland, and farewell" (ll. 188-89). Besides being one of the noblest versions of the Catullus we are likely to get, Swinburne's closing echo ensures that Hesperus will once again rise from Okeanos, that Sappho lives on, transmuted, in her children, and that poetry will continue to voice us to ourselves.

Notes

1. D. A. Campbell, *Greek Lyric Poetry: A Selection* (MacMillan/St. Martin's Press, 1967), xxv.

2. Georg Luck, *The Latin Love Elegy* (Methuen, 1969), 26.

3. Peter Sacks, *The English Elegy* (The Johns Hopkins University Press, 1985), 3.

4. Ibid., 2.

5. Sacks, 26ff.

6. In the fourth Georgic, Virgil sets the defeat of Orpheus against the life-giving success of the peasant Aristaeus. Thanks to the narration of Proteus, Aristaeus is able to appease the vexed spirit of Orpheus and bring life out of death, reviving his beehive:

   > When from the bellies, over the rotten flesh
   > Of the corpses, bees buzz out from caved-in flanks,
   > Swarm in heavy clouds to treetops, group,
   > And hang in clusters down from the pliant boughs.

   (Virgil, *The Georgics,* tr. S. P. Bovie (University of Chicago Press, 1956, 4: 555-58).

7. For an elegant and clear-sighted reading of the passage, with particular attention to the anaphora "And now" and the ambiguous "he," see Sacks, 116.

8. Gregory Nagy, "Phaethon, Sappho's Phaon," *Harvard Studies in Classical Philology* 77 (1973): 173-75.

9. H. T. Wharton, *Sappho* (John Lave, 1898, 4th ed.; repr. Libera, Amsterdam, 1974), 168.

10. Charles Segal, "Eros and Incantation," *Arethusa* 7 (1974): 139-160.

11. Wharton, 34.

12. Ibid., 36.

13. C. J. Fordyce, *Catullus, A Commentary* (Oxford University Press, 1961), 218ff.

14. T. P. Wiseman, *Catullus and His World: A Reappraisal* (Cambridge University Press, 1985), 152-54. I am not convinced that we need accept Wiseamowitz's theory of a marriage ceremony as occasion for Sappho's poem in order to sense that poem bitterly invoked by Catullus. The elemental drama of *Phainetai moi,* a happy couple excluding the former lover, suffices in my mind to charge Catullus' address to Lesbia with retrospective anguish. Yes, the symptoms he enumerates appear to be those of passion, not jealousy, since *"ille"* (ll. 1, 2: that man, any man is not as definite and particular as Sappho's *"keinos . . . aner"* (that man). In both poems, I think, attention focuses more on the painful mystery of love itself rather than on an interloper; and Catullus could be seen as recalling his own innocent, early passion only to underscore his disillusion by reference to Sappho's distress as well as to the destruction of whole kingdoms in the *otium* stanza. For further discussion, see Denys Page, *Sappho and Alcaeus* (Oxford University Press, 1955), 20, 21, and Anne Pippin Burnett, *Three Archaic Poets* (Harvard University Press, 1983), 229-43.

15. Wiseman, 146.

16. For a learned and lucid account of such efforts, see John Hollander's *Vision and Resonance* (Yale University Press, 1975; 1985), 59-70. It is an indispensable book.

17. E. M. Cox, *The Poems of Sappho* (Charles Scribners Sons, 1925), 34.

18. Ibid., 70.

19. Ibid., 72.

20. Mary Barnard, *Sappho* (University of California Press, 1958), 39.

21. Basil Bunting, *Collected Poems* (Oxford University Press, 1978), 119.

22. John Hollander, *Spectral Emanations* (Atheneum, 1978), 57. John Hollander, a rare *doctus poeta,* has written Sapphics with splendid ease throughout his career. The form has been for him a rich inheritance, allowing him serious spoofs of the modern relationship to Antiquity ("Making It" and "Epilogue: the loss of smyrna" in *Town and Country Matters* (Yale University Press, 1958), as well as a severely graceful meditation on love and representation, "The Lady of the Castle," over which Sappho, the poet of Aphrodite, presides through the evocatory power of her stanza (*Spectral Emanations,* 54, 55). Sappho's form affords Hollander more than thematic resonance; he uses Sapphic enjambment, so often avoided by her translators, to the hilt: "My desire, my memory was so intelli- / gently caressing" ("A Thing So Small," *Harp Lake* (Knopf, 1988), 80.

23. Charles Baudelaire, "Lesbos," stanza 2, tr. Richard Howard, *Les Fleurs du Mal* (Godine, 1982), 123.

24. Guy Davenport, *Archilochus, Sappho, Alkman* (University of California Press, 1980), 93, a translation of fragment 42. Guy Davenport has brought the Poundian imperative of clarity to bear in his long and honorable engagement with archaic Greek poetry.

25. A notable exception is Jerome McGann, whose sprightly *Swinburne: An Experiment in Criticism* (University of Chicago Press, 1972) begins to repair the wrong.

26. J. M. Edmonds, *The Greek Bucolic Poets* (Harvard University Press, 1938; 1950; 1960), 445.

Joyce Zonana (essay date spring 1990)

SOURCE: Zonana, Joyce. "Swinburne's Sappho: The Muse as Sister-Goddess." *Victorian Poetry* 28, no. 1 (spring 1990): 39-50.

[*In the following essay, Zonana highlights poet Algernon Charles Swinburne's identification with Sappho and her apotheosis as the "Tenth Muse."*]

In an important early poem, "Sapphics" (1:333-335),[1] Swinburne introduces a theme that was to dominate both his poetry and prose: Sappho's apotheosis as the tenth Muse, a poet whose "visible song" soars as "a bird soars." By identifying Sappho as a Muse—and ultimately, as we shall see, as the Muse, not only for him, but for all poets—Swinburne radically redefines the nature of poetic inspiration and the role of a female principle in art produced by men; by elevating a mortal woman into the place normally reserved for immortal goddesses, he expresses his special notion of the relation between humanity and divinity while simultaneously revising the inherited Christian notion of an exclusively male deity. Neither femme fatale nor chaste virgin nor nourishing spiritual mother, Swinburne's Muse is a human sister who manifests "ineffable glory and grace as of present godhead" ("The Poems of Dante Gabriel Rossetti," 15:33). Her inspiration is neither dangerous temptation nor transcendent revelation, but a steady celebration of humanity, a celebration that makes "each glad limb" of the human body a "note of rapture in the tune of life" ("The Last Pilgrimage," *Tristram of Lyonesse*, 4:144).

Throughout nineteenth-century British poetry, one finds a persistent dissatisfaction with inherited notions of the Muse. From Wordsworth's search for a Muse "greater" than Milton's Urania, through Keats's exploration of various female inspirers, to Arnold's choice of a "Muse of Righteousness," both Romantic and Victorian poets express a longing for a Muse that would firmly connect life and art, art and religion, joining earthly and heavenly sources of inspiration in a new and stable synthesis. Barbara Fass, in her perceptive study, *La Belle Dame sans Merci and the Aesthetics of Romanticism* (Detroit, 1974), has carefully explored the Romantic vision of the Muse as an enchanting and enchanted figure who represents an art that simultaneously transforms and transfixes the poet seeking an ideal not present on earth and only questionably present in heaven. Yet Fass stops short of an examination of nineteenth-century poets' attempts to escape from the paralyzing notion of art as seductive siren. She fails to consider these poets' efforts to locate an earthly Muse who could properly replace Milton's heavenly Urania. Even in the work of Swinburne, who in "A Nympholept" would exclaim that "Heaven is as earth, and as heaven to me / Earth" (6:81), Fass sees only another instance of a failed quest for a union of spirit and sense, "Christian" and "pagan" objects of worship and sources of art.

Yet within the context of nineteenth-century poetry, Swinburne's relationship to his Muse-figure is peculiarly untormented. For Swinburne the goddess of poetry is neither elusive nor seductive, neither pure spirit nor pure sense. As he writes in his study of Victor Hugo's *L'Année Terrible*, the Muse is "omnipresent and eternal, and forsakes neither Athens nor Jerusalem, Camelot nor Troy, Argonaut nor Crusader, to dwell as she does with equal goodwill among modern appliances in London and New York" (13:249). In "Ave Atque Vale," he is careful to stress that the "most high Muses" bend "usward" (3:49) in their concern for and engagement with human life. Similarly, his Apollo, in "The Last Oracle," is drawn "Down from heaven" by the "song within the silent soul" (3:2-3). Unlike Arnold's "scornful" and "implacable" young god, Swinburne's Apollo is fit to sing on either Etna or Parnassus. Because Swinburne defines his Muse as an unmistakably human figure who has achieved divinity through her full experience of humanity, he can embrace his art with an unambivalent passion, trusting that it will demonstrate the indissoluble union between "spiritual truth" and "bodily beauty," expressing "the sweet and sovereign unity of perfect spirit and sense, of fleshly form and intellectual fire" ("The Poems of Dante Gabriel Rossetti," 15:13). Not incidentally, he is also able to use his Muse to unify pagan and Christian symbol systems.[2]

Swinburne develops his myth of the Muse in a group of poems—"Sapphics," "Anactoria," and "On the Cliffs"—that revolve around the figure of Sappho, long honored as a figurative "tenth Muse" by poets and critics since Plato, but never before literally perceived and used as such.[3] In these poems Swinburne incorporates Sappho's language, translating and interweaving fragments of her work; her voice, like a Muse's, "enters" his. Even more significantly, Swinburne addresses and invokes Sappho here in a manner previously reserved only for sources of inspiration imagined to be genuinely divine—the maids of Helicon for Hesiod and Homer, Jesus for the earliest Christian poets, Urania for Milton, the "dread Power" for Wordsworth, Psyche and Autumn for Keats. Finding in Sappho the "subtle breath and bloom of very heaven itself, that dignity of divinity which informs the most passionate and piteous notes" ("The Poems of Dante Gabriel Rossetti," 15:33), Swinburne appropriates her as a new goddess who teaches, like his beloved Victor Hugo, that "the vibration of earthly emotion" is the surest means to achieve "a note of divine tenderness" ("L'Homme Qui Rit," 13:215).

Sappho as Muse challenges tradition not simply in her humanity; she also directly confronts the Western (male) poetic imagination through her fully sexual femaleness. Ever since Hesiod and Homer, the Muse has typically been conceived as a female divinity, although post-Classical writers have been able to accept her as such only after a careful spiritualization and/or disembodiment.[4] Thus, though Milton's Muse is indeed characterized as feminine, she is divorced from all association with the actual female body. The English poet is not free, as the Greeks had been, to praise the Muses' "tender bodies," "soft feet," or "violet" hair.[5] The Christian Muse is an incorporeal Virgin Mother; and the spiritualization of the ancient Muses is so much a part of the English tradition that Matthew Arnold, in *Culture and Anarchy,* sees them, with the Madonna and chivalry, as but another instance of the "feminine ideal" invented by "the delicate and apprehensive genius of the Indo-European race."[6]

When nineteenth-century men began their attempts to imagine the Muses once again as physical creatures, they were haunted by fears of sexual seduction by a female whose "earthliness" threatened to consume their own uncertain "heavenliness"; because God and Woman are irrevocably divorced in Christian tradition, the female gender (as much as the pagan origin) of the Muse proved a constant embarrassment to the male writer seeking a divine sanction for his art.[7] Thus Swinburne's Muse, a mortal woman who unabashedly celebrates her own sexuality, choosing, through her homoeroticism, to accept and love the female body so distrusted by Christian misogyny, poses a unique challenge to the Western artist afraid that the Muse might be an unholy seduction from his chaste worship of a male god. Indeed, the failure of even the most sympathetic critics to perceive Swinburne's redefinition of the Muse suggests how radical is his view of the relationship between woman and god, art and religion. Only

recent feminist criticism of the Christian religious tradition enables us to appreciate the implications of Swinburne's "post-Christian" transformation of a divine female source of poetry.[8]

Long recognized as a studied reversal of its original, Sappho's celebrated **"Ode to Aphrodite,"** Swinburne's "Sapphics" functions as an initiation for both poet and reader into the writer's startling new worship of a human Muse.[9] Whereas in her own poem, Sappho had appealed for the aid of an Olympian Goddess, Aphrodite, imploring her to descend from heaven to Lesbos, in Swinburne's inversion the Goddess is on earth, pleading with the poet to look at and listen to her. And while in the original poem Aphrodite had promptly responded to Sappho's plea, in the Swinburne poem the mortal refuses the Goddess: Sappho has eyes only for "her chosen, / Fairer than all men," and for her "newly fledged, . . . visible song" (1:334-335). Aphrodite flees in horror, even as her doves longingly look "Back to Lesbos, back to the hills whereunder / Shone Mitylene" (1:333).

When she rejects Aphrodite, Swinburne's Sappho also implicitly rejects the "crowned nine Muses," who, with Apollo, are "sick with anguish," "stricken at heart," to hear her independent song—"Ah the tenth, the Lesbian!" (1:334-335, 334). The Muses wax pale to hear Sappho because they know not the "wonderful things," "full of thunders" (1:334, 335) of which Sappho sings: she feels, loves, and composes as only a mortal can. Similarly, Aphrodite knows not the glory of song—nor the nature of Sappho's love for women. Though Sappho herself had invoked both the Muses and Aphrodite, Swinburne suggests that each alone is inadequate to define fully or account for the choices and achievements of her life and her art. Because she fuses their separate spheres, Sappho rivals and surpasses the very goddesses to whom she is devoted: song and love are inextricably entwined in her work "Made of perfect sound and exceeding passion" (1:335); she is, as Swinburne would later define her, both "Love's" and "Song's" priestess ("On the Cliffs," 3:310). The gods flee her presence because she is greater than they; she figures precisely as Christ does in the banishing of the pagan gods and the silencing of the oracles. Yet, unlike the victory of the Galilean as it is portrayed by Swinburne in "The Last Oracle," Sappho's triumph is an affirmation rather than a denial of human power and song.

In "Anactoria," Swinburne uses many of the same fragments he incorporated into "Sapphics," though here they enter into a first-person cry of love and longing, rather than a distanced and controlled third-person account of poetic fulfillment. The poem begins with Sappho's account of her vision of Aphrodite—the same vision that forms the context for "Sapphics"—but the poetic persona breaks off in the midst of her recitation to exclaim to her beloved Anactoria:

> but thou—thy body is the song,
> Thy mouth the music; thou art more than I,
> Though my voice die not till the whole world die.
>
> (1:192)

Apparently Sappho is distracted from her vision of Aphrodite into an exploration of art; her equation of Anactoria's body with song does not, however, imply that sexuality replaces creativity, but rather that consideration of one necessarily leads to consideration of the other.[10]

Sappho cannot think of Aphrodite or Anactoria without thinking of the Muses, as she reveals again a few lines later:

> Ah that my lips were tuneless lips, but pressed
> To the bruised blossom of thy scourged white breast!
> Ah that my mouth for Muses' milk were fed
> On the sweet blood thy sweet small wounds had bled!
>
> (1:193)

Here Swinburne's Sappho utterly violates the received notion of the Olympian Muses, suggesting that violent (and literally consuming) sexual passion might give the poet access to "Muses' milk." And though Sappho is willing to allow her own lips to be temporarily "tuneless," she cannot live (or love) without song, wishing as she does to

> Strike pang from pang as note is struck from note,
> Catch the sob's middle music in thy throat,
> Take thy limbs living, and new-mould with these
> A lyre of many faultless agonies.
>
> (1:194)

Anactoria's body is to become a lyre, her blood Muses' milk; this does not so much represent a renunciation of art as a transformation of both song and the body. In desiring Anactoria, Sappho does not abandon her desire for the lyre, though she chooses a lyre with a difference, a lyre constructed from the skin of the flayed Marsyas. Her Muse is a Chthonian Muse of flesh, deeply bound to the joy and pain of love; and the product of such inspiration is poetry that shares the concreteness and vitality of its source: "one with all . . . things," it "Cleave[s] to men's lives and waste[s] the days thereof / With gladness and much sadness and long love" (1:198).

While "Sapphics" portrays Sappho as a tenth Muse, and "Anactoria" explores the corporeal nature of her inspiration, neither poem places Sappho in specific relation to Swinburne, as his Muse, much less as the Muse of all poets. The explicit fulfillment of this identification does not appear until 1879, in "On the Cliffs" (3:304-317).

Although Swinburne does not use the term "muse" in the poem, it is in its entirety an elaborate and self-conscious muse-invocation, echoing the language of Milton's appeals to Urania, as well as Wordsworth's calls to the wind and Keats's pursuit of the nightingale. Like his precursors, Swinburne uses the extended invocation to define carefully the nature of his Muse; like them as well, he places her within the context of both Christian and pagan concepts of divinity and poetry.

Alone in a barren seascape characterized by incompleteness and partiality, the poet opens his invocation with a request for a fulfilling word, one that will make both landscape and speaker whole. Calling at first on the wind, he asks what message it carries from the sea. Suddenly hearing a nightingale, he begins to address it instead, "For but one word . . . / Is blown up usward ever from the sea" (3:306). The sea's word is a sad one, evoking the pain, loss, and death that haunt human memory; it cannot fulfill the poet's request. But the nightingale takes no "shadow of sadness" on its song (3:307). "With throat of gold and spirit of the sun," it is identified with the Olympian Apollo, living and singing in an atmosphere above the human realm of passion and pain. Like Keats's (but unlike Arnold's) nightingale, this bird is "not marked for sorrow" (3:308), but neither is it marked "for joy." For a moment, Swinburne allies himself with this Olympian singer; calling it "sister," he suggests that it has provided him with the word he has been seeking.

Yet as David G. Riede has pointed out,[11] the poet immediately recognizes that such a vision of self and song is incomplete. To be "above" human pain is not to resolve the problem that it poses, but simply to ignore it, and Swinburne, like Arnold and Keats before him, cannot rest with such an easy avoidance. Thus, immediately after his paean to the bird's freedom from human limitation, he plummets, in a movement comparable to Keats's in the "Nightingale" ode, to a passionate recognition of pain: "*But me, for me* (how hadst thou heart to hear?) / *Remains a sundering with the two-edged spear*" (3:308). Cassandra's cry leads Swinburne towards Sappho, a poet whose pain, unlike that of the prophetess, has been embodied in significant form, and hence "heard."

And suddenly Swinburne is addressing Sappho, demanding and expecting a word of her—"Because I have known thee always who thou art" (3:311). This Sappho is, like the bird, a "sister" to Swinburne; also like the bird, she burns with Apollo's eternal fire:

> As brother and sister were we, child and bird,
> Since thy first Lesbian word
> Flamed on me, and I knew not whence I knew

This was the song that struck my whole soul through,
Pierced my keen spirit of sense with edge more keen,
Even when I knew not,—even ere sooth was seen,—
When thou wast but the tawny sweet winged thing
Whose cry was but of spring.

(3:311)

Though originally perceived as a nightingale or a god, Sappho is far more: she is a "soul triune, woman and god and bird" (3:315), representing a principle of poetry more inclusive than that embodied by either the bird or the god alone. And, as in "Sapphics," Swinburne once again demonstrates the triumph of this mortal singer over the immortal gods of song:

The singing soul that moves thee, and that moved
When thou wast woman, and their songs divine
Who mixed for Grecian mouths heaven's lyric wine
Fell dumb, fell down reproved
Before one sovereign Lesbian song of thine.

(3:313)

Sappho's "ruling song," the speaker now recognizes, is present, has always been present, even in his barren northern landscape, making "all the night one ear / One ear fulfilled and mad with music" (3:313).[12] All "earth and heaven and sea" are "molten" in this music "made of thee [Sappho]" (3:316). The phrase "of thee" suggests not merely that the music is made by Sappho, but also that it is composed from her own substance which has entered into the substance of the landscape, just as she had longed, in Swinburne's "Anactoria," to be "molten" into the body of her lover (1:194). As in the earlier poem, Sappho's self and song are one with all things; even more significantly, they make all things one. Sappho is the unifying, "fulfilling" force in the landscape: she cannot be separated from her song, and her song cannot be separated from the landscape, now held together in a new harmony. And it is this "ruling song" that teaches Swinburne his own "song, and the secrets of it"—the secret being simply that "knowing not love nor change nor wrath nor wrong / No more we knew of song" (3:317).

Thus Swinburne completes his identification of Sappho, not merely as his Muse, but as the Muse of all poets and readers of poetry. Sappho, through her uniquely passionate song of pain and joy, makes the souls of all who hear her "sublime"; she is heard by anyone "whose heart was ever set to song"—"even Aeschylus as I" (3:315). Yet she is a Muse who functions quite differently from any encountered earlier in the Western tradition. Like the classical Muses, she is a daughter of Memory, "mother of all songs made" (3:317); unlike them, however, her function is not to erase human memory but to intensify it, not to release her listeners from their cares but to make them more conscious of

all their experiences, both pleasurable and painful. Because she has accepted its limitations, time does not touch her; because she has not struggled against them, her loves survive in her songs.

Further, a poet need not invoke her in order to experience or benefit from her; she is continuously present and always accessible, "in the notes of the nightingales, . . . in the presence of the glory of the sky."[13] The poet does not have to seek special inspiration from either the gods or nature; Sappho's song is part of the very substance of the universe. But this cosmic song is not identical to the music of the spheres that Milton had so longed to hear; it is, as Riede points out, akin to Wordsworth's "still sad music of humanity," or what we might call instead the "music of the elements"—air, earth, and water, fused by fire.[14] To hear this music one need not purify oneself by the study of god or nature, as Milton had suggested; all one need do is live passionately and fully, swim exultingly in the sea of life and death. Such immersion in experience enables one not merely to hear or to sing but to be song, at one with Sappho, at one with nature, at one with divinity.

Sappho, Swinburne tells us repeatedly in "On the Cliffs"—both explicitly and through his carefully worked images of fusion—is "woman and god and bird," an indissoluble "soul triune." Thus he transforms the pagan-Christian dialectic that had informed most post-classical approaches to the Muse. Swinburne defines Sappho, an unquestionably pagan poet, as a trinity that transcends—even as it mimics—the Christian mystery of the Triune God. While Milton had to specify that he called on Urania's "meaning, not the name," and Arnold had to discover a "Muse of Righteousness" identified with the Holy Spirit, Swinburne is free to address his Muse "inly, by thine only name, / Sappho" (3:311). Ignoring the difficulties of the pagan-Christian debate, Swinburne defines his Muse using both Christian and pagan terminology: the "god" who is one with Sappho is God the Father and "Father" Apollo; the "bird" simultaneously Christian Dove of the Holy Spirit and pagan nightingale whose name in Greek is "synonymous with poetry itself and the poet."[15] And, as a human embodiment of the divine, Sappho evokes both the Christian Incarnation and pagan anthropomorphic deities. Yet for Swinburne, Christ is but the type of Sappho—his incarnation of divinity less complete than her achievement of it, his fusion of man and god less thorough than hers. For as Swinburne makes clear in his comment on Blake's belief that "God only Acts and Is in beings or Men": "It must be remarked and remembered that the very root or kernel of this creed is not the assumed humanity of God, but the achieved divinity of Man; not incarnation from without, but development from within; not a miraculous passage into flesh, but a natural growth into godhead" (*William*

Blake, 16:259).[16] Thus Swinburne suggests that his new myth transcends—even as it incorporates—those that preceded it.

While Swinburne's trinity differs from the Christian one in its greater emphasis on the human achievement of divinity rather than the divine descent into man, it also introduces an even more radical change: the substitution of "woman" for "man." Sappho, in clear counterpoint to Christ the son of God, is female, the sister of men. Of course such a choice makes her identification as a Muse more natural; the Muses have almost always been represented as women and sisters (to one another, if not to mortal men). Yet it is precisely this "femaleness" of the Muses that caused such problems for Christian writers, who, despite the example of the Virgin, found it difficult to imagine woman except in connection with sin and deception. Even Milton could not entirely divorce the Muses from the Sirens, and, particularly in Victorian poetry, the Muses were constantly in danger of slipping over into their more sinister relatives. Western writers have sought continually to bring their art into accord with their theology; but if the source of art is imagined to be a female goddess (or, worse, a set of female goddesses), while the focus of religion is a male (or at best sexless) god, then the writer who wishes to maintain allegiance to both art and religion must develop a vision of the female that escapes Christian limits, or a notion of divinity that includes the feminine.

The ability to imagine a female divinity—as well as to perceive the "godliness" of mortal women—may well be dependent, as Mary Daly has argued, on abandoning the belief in a transcendent deity; since Swinburne's "post-Christian" god is nothing if not immanent, the incorporation of woman into the godhead poses no logical problems for him; indeed, it helps to enforce the recognition of god's immanence. And because god and woman are not at odds, Swinburne can love his Muse unambivalently, no longer afraid of an art whose female source might be a worldly temptation or a false divinity.

Yet, although female, Sappho is also "strange," a "man-like maiden" who fuses qualities typically considered contradictory, and who bears little resemblance to the traditional Western image of woman. Swinburne calls her "maiden" even though she is known to have married and borne a child; deeply identified with women, she is nevertheless termed "manlike," perhaps for the strength and clarity of her passion and her song (for it is doubtful whether Swinburne, who insisted that "qualities called virtues and vices depend on time, climate, and temperament" [*Letters,* 1:138], would have branded her "manlike" on the basis of her homoeroticism). But what is this woman whom Swinburne identifies as a

god, this Muse who loves women and is neither virgin nor whore, neither good nor bad mother, neither all spirit nor all flesh—in a category of her own that seems to escape the traditional Western dualism of spirit and flesh, male and female, good and evil?

The answer must be Swinburne's own: Sappho is a "sister," a literally kindred spirit born of the same mother and father—Memory and Apollo—as the poet. Surprisingly, the aspect of woman as man's sister has generally been overlooked by male poets in their conceptions of the female Muse. For this is a female not inherently "other" from the male, evoking neither sexual attraction and fear, nor filial love and terror. She is, indeed, something quite different from the "Swinburnean woman" who has so often been the focus of Swinburne studies,[17] and who so much resembles the anima figure identified by Jungians as the presumed matrix from which the Muse image has emerged. Though Swinburne has rightly been noted for his bold exploration of the nature of woman as "other"—mother and lover, destroyer and healer, femme fatale and grand ideal—what critics have failed to see is that his Muse is not part of this complex. Sappho, though female and god, is not other to Swinburne, male and mortal: her femaleness does not stand in opposition to his maleness, nor her divinity to his humanity. She is not an anima figure, not Hertha, or Dolores, or Proserpine, or the sea—she is, quite simply, his sister, a woman with whom he can unproblematically identify himself.

And it is this that is Swinburne's distinctive contribution to the history of the female Muse: he is the first male poet to imagine her not as other but as image of his own self, a reflecting sister who can be known and loved unambivalently. As god she is not distinct from humans; as woman she is not apart from men. Swinburne does not, however, define his relationship with the Muse as sexual. By choosing Sappho, whose desire was directed towards omen, and by defining her as sister, Swinburne avoids the implication that this human Muse and her poet might themselves engage in a sexual relationship. Yet by celebrating a Muse whom he defines as having found inspiration in her own sexuality, Swinburne suggests a new model for creativity, and a new vision of personal and artistic integration. Male and female, "spirit" and "sense," are fused, and the artist need not seek outside him (or her) human self for inspiration. Swinburne's vision of the Muse makes room for (is in fact dependent upon) both female creativity and female sexuality. His identification of Sappho as Muse thus offers a unique resolution to the dilemma of the Victorian artist; recognizing that woman and art need not be other to man or god (or the moral life), Swinburne suggests that only through recognition of the sister-Muse can the brother (or sister) poet recognize and fully express his or her own "present godhead."

Poetry written under the inspiration of such a Muse neither escapes nor transforms the human condition; rather, it reflects and celebrates it for what it is: "the sweet and sovereign unity of perfect spirit and sense, of fleshly form and intellectual fire" ("The Poems of Dante Gabriel Rossetti," 15:13).

Notes

1. All citations from Swinburne's poetry and prose are taken from the twenty-volume Bonchurch edition, *The Complete Works of Algernon Charles Swinburne,* ed. Sir Edmund Gosse and Thomas J. Wise (London, 1925). Volume and page number are given parenthetically in the text. The edition of the letters, also cited parenthetically, is Cecil Y. Lang, ed. *The Swinburne Letters,* 6 vols. (New Haven, 1959-62).

2. In this achievement, Swinburne to some extent echoes Keats, who, as Helen Vendler has shown in *The Odes of John Keats* (Cambridge, 1983), creates a thoroughly human, thoroughly divine goddess of nature and art in "To Autumn." Swinburne's Muse, however, unlike Keats's was a historically real mortal woman before becoming an "immortal."

3. In "Sapphistries," *Signs* 10 (1984):43-62, Susan Gubar explores women writers' uses of Sappho as a figurative, if not literal Muse. Gubar's article is groundbreaking, though she is on familiar territory when she censures Swinburne for creating a "passionately depraved" Sappho who functions as a "lesbian femme fatale" (p. 49). As I hope to demonstrate, Swinburne's myth of Sappho as Muse defuses the myth of the femme fatale that had entrapped many of his fellow nineteenth-century poets.

4. For an instructive analysis of the early Christian response to women, a response that can also be traced in early Christian treatments of the Muse, see Rosemary Radford Ruether, "Misogynism and Virginal Feminism in the Fathers of the Church," in her *Religion and Sexism: Images of Woman in the Jewish and Christian Traditions* (New York, 1974), pp. 150-183. See also Elaine Pagels' recent study, *Adam, Eve, and the Serpent* (New York, 1988) for a careful analysis of the early Christian perception of women and their relations to divinity.

5. See, e.g. Hesiod's *Theogony,* in Richmond Lattimore, trans., *Hesiod* (Ann Arbor, 1959), p. 123. See also Pindar's *Pythia* 1 in *The Odes of Pindar,* ed. Lattimore (Chicago, 1947), p. 43.

6. Matthew Arnold, *The Complete Prose Works,* ed. R. H. Super (Ann Arbor, 1960-78), 5:208. See also my "Matthew Arnold and the Muse: The Limits of the Olympian Ideal," *VP* [*Victorian Poetry*] 23 (1985): 59-74.

7. Ernst Curtius, in *European Literature and the Latin Middle Ages,* trans. W. R. Trask (New York, 1953), has carefully traced the development of what he calls the *topos* "Contrast between Pagan and Christian poetry" (p. 235); studies of English Renaissance poetry, most notably John M. Steadman's *Milton's Biblical and Classical Imagery* (Pittsburgh, 1984) have applied Curtius' analysis to a developing English tradition. Certainly, the "pagan-Christian" dichotomy is significant, even within the nineteenth century. Yet the terms of the opposition may obscure an even more fundamental conflict: pagan gods were both male and female, while for the Christian, there is only one God, and He is a male Father, Son, and Holy Spirit. The consequences of this opposition—between female and male concepts of divinity—have only begun to be explored.

8. See, e.g., Mary Daly, *Pure Lust: Elemental Feminist Philosophy* (Boston, 1984). It is worth noting that in *Pure Lust,* as well as in her most recent work, *Websters' First New Intergalactic Wickedary of the English Language* (Boston, 1987), Daly makes abundant references to the Muses, whom she sees as essential images enabling women's renewed "participation in Powers of Be-ing" (*Pure Lust,* p. 148).

9. See Jerome J. McGann, *Swinburne: An Experiment in Criticism* (Chicago, 1972), pp. 112-116. McGann's reading of "Sapphics" is similar to my own, though he does not emphasize the significance of Swinburne's decision to make Sappho a Muse. For other observations on Swinburne's aesthetics, as embodied in this poem and others, I am indebted to Robert L. Peters, *The Crowns of Apollo: Swinburne's Principles of Literature and Art, A Study in Victorian Criticism and Aesthetics* (Detroit, 1965); Meredith B. Raymond "Swinburne Among the Nightingales," *VP* 6 (1968): 125-142, and her *Swinburne's Poetics: Theory and Practice* (The Hague, 1971); and, especially, David G. Riede, *Swinburne: A Study of Romantic Mythmaking* (Charlottesville, 1978).

10. David A. Cook, "The Content and Meaning of Swinburne's 'Anactoria,'" *VP* 9 (1971): 77-93, has argued that the poem shows that "for Sappho, art is a mere bauble in the presence of sex," and that the progress of the poem demonstrates that art is possible for Sappho (and, presumably for Swinburne) only when sexuality is renounced (p. 86). As Thaïs E. Morgan has observed, in "Swin-

burne's Dramatic Monologues: Sex and Ideology," *VP* 22 (1984): 175-195, Cook's is the consensus view of the poem. Morgan, as I, finds instead that "Anactoria" expresses Swinburne's view of the possible—and desired—conjunction of art and sexuality.

11. David G. Riede, *A Study of Romantic Mythmaking,* pp. 131-132.

12. Swinburne's language here specifically echoes Keats's Mnemosyne speaking to Apollo in *Hyperion: A Fragment.* Indeed, much of Swinburne's characterization of Sappho as Muse recalls Keats's attempts to define a humanized divinity who will function as a source and subject of poetry—Psyche in "Ode to Psyche," Apollo and Saturn in *Hyperion: A Fragment,* Moneta and Mnemosyne in *The Fall of Hyperion,* Autumn in "To Autumn." Each of these figures in Keats functions in ways comparable to Swinburne's Sappho, mixing pleasure and pain, love and song, mortal and immortal. Yet the important difference is that Keats's figures are drawn from the realm of myth rather than human history, and thus their "apotheosis" is neither as dramatic nor as transformative as Sappho's.

13. "Dedicatory Epistle," *The Poems of Algernon Charles Swinburne,* 6 vols. (London, 1904), 1:11.

14. For another view of Swinburne's relation to Milton, see William Wilson's excellent discussion in "Algernon Agonistes: 'Thalassius,' Visionary Strength, and Swinburne's Critique of Arnold's 'Sweetness and Light,'" *VP* 19 (1981): 381-395.

15. H. W. Garrod, "The Nightingale in Poetry," in his *The Profession of Poetry and Other Lectures* (Oxford, 1929), p. 134.

16. These lines came to my attention as cited by McGann, pp. 299-300.

17. See, e.g., Antony H. Harrison's categorization in "The Swinburnean Woman," *PQ* [*Poetry Quarterly*] 58 (1979): 90-102. Interestingly, Harrison fails to include Sappho among Swinburne's women.

Dolores O'Higgins (essay date 1990)

SOURCE: O'Higgins, Dolores. "Sappho's Splintered Tongue: Silence in Sappho 31 and Catullus 51." *American Journal of Philology* 111 (1990): 156-67.

[*In the following essay, O'Higgins explicates the Sappho poem referred to as "Phainetai moi" (fragment no. "31") in the context of a verse response by Catullus.*]

Sappho[1] "31" concerns poetry as much as love or jealousy, like Catullus' "response" in 51, a poem which addresses Sappho's poetic claims and poetic stance at least as much as Lesbia's beauty.[2] This study considers the impact of the beloved on each of the two poets, focusing especially on the disturbing and memorable image of the "broken" tongue in Sappho's poem, and the relative seriousness of Sappho's "fracture" and Catullus' sluggish tongue.

The Greek poem's first line introduces what appears to be a highly charged emotional situation, whose "literary" implications appear only later. Sappho (as I shall designate the speaker) supposes a man who sits—or any man who might sit—opposite the girl she loves.[3]

φαίνεταί μοι χῆνοσ ἴσοσ θέοισιν

Before she identifies the subject of the verb *phainetai,* Sappho introduces the pronoun *moi,* the indirect object of the verb and perceiver or interpreter of the scene. The line might translate "It seems to me that he is like the gods. . . ."[4] The verb reappears at line 16, where Sappho "seems to *herself.*" Thus, most of the extant poem is contained within a framework or "ring" of authorial memory, perception, imagination or opinion. Although the poet dramatizes herself as an alien figure, looking wistfully at the unattainable, she is not altogether an outsider. **"Phainetai moi"** marks the boundary of a world contained within Sappho. By contrast, Catullus begins his poem, *and* its second line, with the third person pronoun *ille,* a change which shifts the emphasis from perceiver to perceived. Catullus' naming of his beloved—Lesbia—also grants her a specific identify and a more substantial independent existence than Sappho's anonymous girl.

Lesbia's audience responds to both her visual and her verbal charm; the man watches and listens to (*spectat et audit* 4) the seductress, who laughs sweetly. In Sappho the man only listens (*hupakouei* 4), but the girl's aural charms are double; she speaks sweetly (*hadu phoneisas* 3-4) and laughs caressingly (*gelaisas himeroen* 5). Thus in Sappho's opening scene the girl's seductiveness is emphatically vocal. The subsequent expression "whenever I see you—even for a short time . . ." in 7 may suggest that the girl's beauty was such that it could be felt in the briefest glimpse, yet the passage seems at least as concerned with Sappho's extraordinary susceptibility to her beloved's presence as with the girl's appearance.

> This thing makes the heart in my breast tremble.
> For when I see you even for a short time
> I can no longer speak . . .
>
> (7-8)

The poet's heart is shaken by "this thing,"[5] i.e., by the girl's voice, the man's reaction to the girl, her own sense of mortality, in fact by the complete "moment and its beauty and anguish" as Ralph Johnson has put it.[6] The verb *eptoaisen* ("causes to tremble"), describing the scene's shattering effect on Sappho, connotes more than a *frisson* of sexual excitement; she feels the debilitating fear that precedes lethal encounters on the battlefield.[7] The poem gradually unravels the signs and implications of her terror/excitement.

The man faces the girl, listening closely, and seems "like the gods" in his felicity or perhaps his hardihood.[8] Although the immediate context allows either reading, the tone and imagery of the remainder of the poem point in the direction of hardihood. The man, in his divine invulnerability, may dally in the girl's destructive *ambiance,* but Sappho fears even a momentary and relatively long range encounter.

Sappho is a battered "veteran," whose previous encounters with the girl have always had the same outcome.[9] First she is struck dumb. Then a subtle fever (9-10) is succeeded by blindness, humming in her ears, cold sweat, a grass-like pallor—and finally (15-16), "I seem to myself to be little short of dying." It has been observed that details of this disintegration echo Homeric descriptions of dying or mortally threatened warriors—for example the pallor, blindness (or faintness) and sweat.[10] I wish to focus on another aspect of Sappho's reaction, however.

Symptoms that do *not* characterize the beleaguered warrior include the humming, fever and silence.[11] Of these the silence—the first in Sappho's catalog—is perhaps the most interesting. Silence does not generally afflict Homeric warriors, even desperate ones. More significantly, it does *not* afflict the one Homeric poet who is threatened with mortal danger. Phemius pleads eloquently—and successfully—for his life at *Odyssey* 22.344-53. Yet, just as Sappho evokes the girl with a double description of her voice—speaking and laughing—so Sappho's reaction begins with a double account of the poet's own voicelessness, a double wound to correspond to the double blow. Sappho is no longer permitted to say anything; instead, her tongue has been shattered into silence.

ἀλλ' ἄχαν μὲν γλῶσσα † ἔαγε † . . .

(9)

The hiatus in line 9 has placed the reading *eage* in doubt. I believe with Nagy, however, that it is deliberate, intended audially to reproduce the "catch" in the poet's voice; Sappho dramatically represents herself as being almost at the point she describes—losing her voice altogether.[12] It is a critical loss for an oral poet, and a paradoxical and dramatic beginning to the poet's response.

I do not maintain that Sappho was an oral poet in the sense that Homer has been described by Parry and Lord, but, as Ruth Finnegan has shown, oral and written literature form a continuum rather than entirely separate traditions.[13] Sappho inherits an ancient lyric tradition which sees and describes itself as essentially performative, and communicated, if not created, with the voice.[14] Pindar for example uses the word *glossa* (tongue) and its compounds—"straight tongued," "tongueless"—to describe poets and poetry.[15] Although she was almost certainly literate, Sappho's references to tongue and voice reflect a lingering concept of poetry as an oral medium.[16]

By contrast, in the aftermath of the Hellenistic revolution, Catullus occupies a point nearer the other extreme of the oral/literary spectrum. Thus for Catullus, being "tongue-tied" does not to the same extent threaten his ability to create or communicate his poetry. His poetry is a *libellus,* separable from himself and transmitted as a gift to a friend. For Catullus, poetry exists on paper or tablets, and indeed, destruction of the material may mean the end of the poem. At 68.45-46 the paper containing Catullus' poems is imagined as an old woman, transmitting its message:

sed dicam vobis [i.e., Musis, deis], vos porro dicite multis
milibus et facite haec charta loquatur anus.

Poem 36 opens and closes with the famous reference to the *cacata charta* of Volusius' *Annales*. This poem also includes a drama between Catullus and his beloved, who has been injured by angry iambics. She wants to burn the poems, but Catullus deliberately misinterprets and consigns Volusius to the flames instead. Burning may be a symbolic gesture of destruction, but in the case of a single copy, burning will end the poems' existence.

In Catullus poetry may be lost, burnt, stolen, but it is not necessarily imperilled by a silenced poet. Poems are comically—but significantly—endowed with independent life and moral responsibility; "little verses" may be wicked while their creator is still unsullied in 16. They are newborn infants in 65. Poems take part as third characters in the little dramas taking place between himself and their recipients; hendecasyllables are sent out to dun for missing tablets in 42. Their effect may be felt in the absence of their creator. In 35, merely *reading* Caecilius' poem on the Magna Mater has caused a girl (who is described as more learned than Sappho's Muse) to fall passionately in love with him.

For Sappho, however, the poet's voice is the instrument of seduction. Sappho's verb *eage* ("shattered" 9) describing her tongue metaphorically associates this "symptom" also with a warrior's death on the battlefield. Just as the Homeric warrior defines, defends and justifies himself with a sword, so the poet with a tongue. Sappho is disarmed, her voice a splintered weapon, like the sword or spear of a doomed warrior who has encountered an immortal or immortally aided foe. After only a glimpse, *before* she can engage in "combat," Sappho's weapon—the tongue—is destroyed. One might compare *Iliad* 16.786ff., where Apollo knocks off Patroclus' helmet and destroys his corslet and spear directly before Patroclus is killed by Hector.

At the end of the fourth stanza Sappho marks a break with what precedes with a repetition of the verb *phainom*' ("I seem to myself") in 16, which completes the "ring" of the perceptual, imaginary world of the poem's first four stanzas and begins a new phase in the drama. It is followed by a one line fragment of what I take to be the poem's final stanza, as the poem—hitherto an account of the narrator as vulnerable audience—turns to consider its own audience.

ἀλλὰ πὰν τόλματον ἐπεὶ † χαὶ πωνητα †

The expression *pan tolmaton* is not simply an exhortation to endure, although connotations of endurance are present.[17] In this martial context *pan tolmaton* may be translated "all can be dared." It is a call to arms providing a dramatic *peripeteia* within the poem itself. The poem which ironically records the poet's own near death, repeated in the past and again imminent, now reveals itself as a lethal weapon. Whether it was the girl's voice or appearance (or both) that seduced Sappho, it is her own voice with which she plans to attack in her turn, uncannily recreating her fractured weapon. The rout will become a duel, indeed perhaps an upset victory. In fact *pan tolmaton* marks a "counter-offensive" *already* launched—a song, divinely seductive as the Sirens'. Sappho seduces in her turn, by daring to approach her audience and perform it. The poem's various audiences—including the girl—experience the dangerous felicity of listening and coming under its spell.

Sappho probably concluded her poem with a gnomic statement of fortune's reversal. "Even the poor man may become rich—and the rich man poor."[18] Martin West cites as parallel Theognis 657, which exhorts the addressee to maintain a calm spirit in good fortune and adversity—for reversals of fortune are commonplace. I agree with West that Sappho here speaks of fortune's reversal—for good and ill. It does not follow, however, that she takes the same attitude as Theognis, seeing fortune's vagaries as uncontrollable, simply to be endured. As her Hymn to Aphrodite suggests, a reversal in the fortunes of love can be deliberately achieved: by the lover who enlists the help of Aphrodite. This poem

(1 L.P.) consists of a prayer—and a corresponding promise from the goddess—not, as we might expect, to unite Sappho in bliss with her beloved—but to reverse the situation, to inflict on the girl who has wounded Sappho an equal agony. She will give presents instead of receiving them: she will chase instead of fleeing.

It has long been recognized that Sappho's **"Hymn to Aphrodite"** resembles in tone and diction the lethally vengeful prayer of Diomedes to Athena at *Iliad* 5.115-20.[19] Sappho's "borrowing" of the Homeric situation establishes a complex, reciprocal literary relationship, many of whose ironies have been well discussed.[20]

Homer's battlefield afforded little opportunity for relationships between enemies (the exchange between Glaukos and Diomedes in *Iliad* 6 being a famous exception). The only permanence or stability lay in the shared *kleos* of death, the poetic fame that united victor and vanquished, incorporating the victim into his conqueror's song of triumph. Similarly on Love's battlefield in the **"Hymn to Aphrodite"** a reciprocal relationship seems impossible; there is only unequal battle: pursuit or flight.[21] For the speaker of Sappho **"31"** also, Love's battleground seems tense, unstable and lethal, with the additional threat of oblivion, since love's imperilled "warrior" is also the singer. This "warrior's" death, far from earning an expensive glory for the hero from the poet or poetic tradition, will necessarily silence the singer.

Sappho's "myriad-mindedness" makes her battlefield less bleak than Homer's, however. Whereas in Homer the victor and victim seem to be clearly distinguished from one another, Sappho incorporates both roles in herself within her poem as she moves from victim of love to conqueror/seducer. Further, for all the grimness of these metaphorical battles, there is also a sense of the generative excitement of the lethal dialogue between lover and beloved, a sense of irony, delight, and of exhilarating—and divine—energy. The expression "paler than grass," for example, even as it evokes unconsciousness and death, also suggests tender growth and life.[22] Moreover, Sappho in a sense achieves the enviable divinity that she attributes to another. It is not merely a question of survival, of enduring recurrent brushes with death or approaches to death; as far as the poem is concerned, death is a threat that is never fully realized. But the terrible silence, which threatens both the poet's existence as a poet, and the existence of this or any poem of Sappho, actually and repeatedly assails her. The act of *poiesis* resists the obliteration that passion threatens, and the existence of the *poema* proclaims a permanent triumph over the recurrent threat of poetic non-being. Indeed, to an extent, the act of making a poem *replaces* the passion, just as epic may be said to replace the mortal organism with a divine artifact.[23]

Sappho's poem, in its final stanza, dramatically wills itself into existence despite the silencing nature of its subject. Catullus' final stanza, however, shifts in a different direction. His poem details a disintegration both similar to and subtly different from Sappho's. Sappho records a heart-stopping fear or shock, which she then explains in terms of a recurrent series of past catastrophic symptoms, beginning with loss of her voice and ending in a state near death. Catullus summarizes his entire reaction at the outset. He does not, like Sappho, explain a present sense of fear with reference to repeated past experience; this particular (vicariously experienced) encounter with Lesbia affects him precisely as all other encounters. All of his senses are snatched away ("misero quod omnis / eripit sensus mihi . . ." 5-6). Whereas Sappho's poem may be located in the moment of fear between the vision of her beloved and the physical breakdown which usually results from such an encounter, Catullus leaves no distance between his vision of Lesbia and his reaction. He sees her and loses all his senses. Catullus' anticipatory summary has the effect of placing on an equal footing all of the symptoms he subsequently lists. Loss of all the senses is unconsciousness, of which loss of speech is merely one aspect. The following catalog of individual symptoms only spells out what has already been said.

Catullus' "lingua sed torpet" achieves roughly the same sense as *glossa eage,* but lacks the hiatus, the violence and the military connotations of Sappho's expression.[24] A slender flame (*tenuis . . . flamma*) answers Sappho's *lepton pur;* the humming in the ears also reappears. But in Catullus unconsciousness ("gemina teguntur / lumina nocte" 11-12) apparently interrupts the poet before he himself can describe his own approach to the edge of death. Catullus depends on his audience's familiarity with the Sapphic poem to create this sense of interruption. His poem enacts the final unconsciousness of which Sappho stops short before he moves to an entirely different plane of reality, stepping abruptly aside from the obvious impossibility of saying anything further within his current dramatic framework.

In place of Sappho's reversing "resolution" (*pan tolmaton*), Catullus' final stanza moves to self reproach. The disputed meaning of *otium* in Catullus' final stanza lies at the heart of the poem's notorious interpretative difficulties.[25] My treatment is very brief, its purpose merely to suggest how I feel Catullus' final stanza may comment on Sappho's poem and on the question of orality/literariness and the poet's silence.

For the Roman Neoteric poets *otium* was a symbol—the antithesis of *negotium,* a responsible citizen's official "activity," forensic, military, mercantile, or political. It was an attitude as much as the state of leisure, and could be considered the very soil which nourished elaborate, personal poetry.[26] Catullus 50, for example, records a day in which Catullus and a friend composed verse "in a leisurely way" (*otiosi*). Significantly he uses the word *scribens* (writing) to describe this process; even though each man had a ready audience in the other, they apparently required *tabellae* to facilitate the process of composition and exchange. Even the most light-hearted and casual symposium requires writing implements. In poem 50 *otium* facilitates the leisured process of *writing* poetry.

In poem 51 the effect of *otium* on Catullus himself apparently is analogous to its destructive effect on "kings" and "wealthy . . . cities."[27] *Otium* can mean a state of peace, in contrast to the rigors of war, a state which allows the growth of moral degeneration, and renders cities vulnerable to attack.[28] By this reading, the word *otium* responds to Sappho's military imagery of love. Catullus has not been "fighting" in Love's wars, and his idleness has made him unfit for close "combat" with Lesbia—the sort of literary/amatory "confrontation" that Sappho's poem seems to indicate.[29]

Yet although Catullus seems to rebuke himself for succumbing to *otium,* he does *not* indicate that he intends to abandon or resist it. It is significant that, unlike Sappho (with her *pan tolmaton*), Catullus does not express intention or desires for the future, although it is possible to *infer* that the poem develops out of the poet's resistance to *otium.* Thus, to a greater extent than Sappho's, Catullus' poem presents itself as rooted in the poet's present, which is colored by persistent indulgence in *otium.* I suggest that *otium* is not inactivity—literary or amatory—so much as a reluctance or failure to *confront* in one or more areas of life.[30] Poems are created and love is expressed—in private. *Otium,* which I define as a withdrawn and leisurely indulgence in a lover's sensibilities, forms the background of Catullus' poem. The poem can address Lesbia in the absence of its creator, who can thus reproach himself for his *otium*—a "disengagement" both literary and emotional.

In conclusion, Catullus depicts total breakdown as the direct and immediate result of his vision of Lesbia. He narrates his collapse as an accomplished thing rather than a threatening possibility. Thus his peom does not, like Sappho's, claim to be situated in a terrifying moment of suspense and anticipation. His narrative of disintegration, rather like Horace's ironic description of his own transformation into a swan in *Odes* II 20, bespeaks a certain detachment. Thus Catullus clearly establishes the poem's existence as separate from the dramatic situation that it describes and independent of the precarious articulateness of its poet. Catullus' final stanza, with its thrice intoned *otium,* formalizes this emotional and literary distance between himself and his subject.

Sappho's poem, in contrast, appears delicately balanced between the inspiring/destructive girl, and Sappho's daring/enduring response, and between the anticipatory fear or excitement produced by this particular "occasion" and the familiar series of debilitating reactions which such an encounter generally produces. Her fear or tension exists because she expects these reactions, but although they are imminent, they are not yet fully realized. The poem breathlessly describes such an imminent breakdown, beginning with a critical failure of her tongue, the instrument of self-expression. Her tongue "breaks" and seems to doom her, as a fractured spear often dooms a warrior in Homer—before he can harm his opponent.

Sappho's poem is conditioned by the oral culture in which it was created. It is not only a vividly enacted drama of seduction; the poem actually dramatizes its dependence on the vulnerable living organism who must perform it. Of course, as has often been observed, its very existence testifies to a considerable degree of emotional and literary control, but the poem *presents itself* as suspended in a state of tension between past silences and a future, imminent silence. The song exists in the threat of its own extinction, a threat which is formally confronted and triumphantly survived only at the end, where, in a dramatic *peripeteia,* Sappho reveals that she has replied to unanswerable enchantment with her own song of seduction. Ultimately Aphrodite proves to be the mother of Persuasion and not the death of the poet.[31]

Notes

1. For bibliography on this and other poems of Sappho, see D. E. Gerber, *Studies in Greek Lyric Poetry: 1967-1975* (special edition of *CW* [*Classical World*] Vol. 70 #2 [1976]) 105-14; *Studies in Greek Lyric Poetry: 1975-85* (part 1) *CW* Vol. 81 #2 (1987) 132-44. For bibliography on Catullus 51, see James P. Holoka, *Gaius Valerius Catullus. A Systematic Bibliography* (New York 1985) 195-97. For summary of earlier treatments of the poem's *cruces* and insightful comment, see G. M. Kirkwood, *Early Greek Monody. The History of a Poetic Type* (Cornell Studies in Classical Philology Vol. 37 [Ithaca 1974]) 120-23, 255-60.

2. Himerius, *Orations* 28.2 significantly says that Sappho made a girl's beauty and graces a pretext (πρόφασις) for her songs. M. R. Lefkowitz, "Critical Stereotypes and the Poetry of Sappho," *GRBS* [*Greek, Roman, and Byzantine Studies*] 14 (1973) 113-23, shows how Sappho's work has been seen as the artless outpouring of a woman whose emotional energies have been diverted from the "normal" channel—i.e., child-raising. For the artistry of Sappho 31, see C. Segal, "*Eros* and

Incantation. Sappho and Oral Poetry," *Arethusa* 7 (1974) 139-60. This issue of rationality and poetic control is related to the question of poetic *persona*. My position resembles that of W. R. Johnson in *The Idea of Lyric* (Berkeley 1982) 40-41. The singer is "partly herself perhaps, the woman Sappho; partly an ideal, universal fiction: their fusion in imagination. . . ."

3. I agree with J. Winkler, "Public and Private in Sappho's Lyrics" in H. Foley, ed., *Reflections of Women in Antiquity* (New York 1981) 63-89 (74) that the expression "that man whosoever" is "a rhetorical cliché, not an actor in the imagined scene."

4. The verb is not used impersonally at this early date—but my translation preserves the order in which the pronouns appear. Catullus' poem reverses that order.

5. The antecedent of *to* has been the subject of much debate. For recent discussion and bibliography, see E. Robbins, "Every Time I Look at You . . . Sappho Thirty-One," *TAPA* [*Transactions of the American Philological Association*] 110 (1980) 255-61. Whether or not the ambiguity of the relative pronoun in line 5 is deliberate, it cannot be argued into clarity; *to* glances cursorily back at all that precedes it—the entire series of images, impressions and opinions.

6. W. R. Johnson (note 1 above) 39.

7. For discussion of the meaning of *ptoieo,* see L. Rissman, *Love as War: Homeric Allusion in the Poetry of Sappho* (Königstein 1983) 110, note 22. For comparable uses of the verb in an amatory context, see Mimn. 5.1-3 W; Alcaeus 283.3-4; Anacr. 60.11-12. G. Wills, "Sappho 31 and Catullus 51," *GRBS* 8 (1967) 167-97 (186-87) takes *eptoaisen* as hypothetical (*ken* being understood) but the aorist makes better sense, and the indicative mood is accepted by most scholars (see G. L. Koniaris, "On Sappho, Fr. 31 (L.-P.)," *Philologus* 112 (1968) 173-86 [184-85]).

8. E. Robbins (note 4 above) 260 takes the expression as capable of referring both to strength and happiness; I also prefer an inclusive reading. See Koniaris (note 6 above) 181-82 for discussions of *isos theoisin.*

9. See M. Markovich, "Sappho Fr. 31: Anxiety Attack or Love Declaration?" *CQ* [*Classical Quarterly*] N.S. 22 (1972) 19-32 (21), who notes—citing Kühner-Gerth ii 449—that the subjunctive *ido* in line 7 "denotes the repetition of this chain reaction." See also Wills (note 6 above) 170 and Koniaris (note 6 above) 184.

10. See L. Rissman (note 6 above) 72-90. Rissman studies the expressions *eptoaisen, tromos . . . agrei, khlorotera . . . poias, isos theoisin* etc. in the context of certain Homeric passages. See also J. Svenbro, "La tragédie de l'amour. Modèle de la guerre et théorie de l'amour dans la poésie de Sappho," *QS [Quaderni di Storia]* 19 (1984) 57-79 (66-72). Svenbro remarks that several of Sappho's "symptoms"—trembling, blindness, sweat, pallor—resemble those of wounded, struggling or fearful warriors.

11. See Svenbro (note 9 above) 69 for discussion of the humming and fever, both of which are without parallel in Homer. See also D. Page, *Sappho and Alcaeus. An Introduction to the Study of Ancient Lesbian Poetry* (Oxford 1955) 29 for (rare) parallels of these erotic symptoms in Greek and Roman poets. Page cites several Homeric passages where silence afflicts someone who is shocked or afraid. Antilochus' inability to speak at his discovery of Patroclus' death (*Iliad* 17.695-96) is not, as Svenbro claims, a symptom comparable to the trembling, sweat etc. of an embattled warrior. As in the case of Eurylochus (*Odyssey* 10.244-46), Antilochus is temporarily too shocked to communicate terrible news.

12. See D. Page (note 10 above) 24-25. G. Nagy, *Comparative Studies in Greek and Indic Meter* (Harvard 1974) 45 defends the hiatus as Sappho's conscious effort to reproduce the sense in the sound. See also M. L. West, "Burning Sappho," *Maia* 22 (1970) 307-30 (311). West also defends the MS reading, which seems to have been the one with which Lucretius was familiar (*infringi linguam* at *DRN* 3, 155 seems also to have been a unique metaphorical use).

13. See R. Finnegan, *Oral Poetry. Its nature, significance and social context* (Cambridge 1977) 272. Finnegan rejects Lord's definition of oral poetry as too narrow. On p. 22 she observes, "If a piece is orally performed—still more if it is mainly known to people through actualization in performance—it must be regarded as in that sense an 'oral poem.'"

14. See Segal (note 1 above) for the importance of the oral tradition for understanding Sappho's work. See also R. Merkelbach, "Sappho und ihr Kreis," *Philologus* 101 (1957) 1-29.

15. See *P.* 2.86 where Pindar talks about the *euthuglossos* man and his responsibility to speak out within various political systems. The passage immediately succeeds one in which Pindar speaks of himself and his own function as a poet in society. *Aglossos* (tongueless) at *N.* 8.24 signifies (amongst

other things) the man who lacks a poet to speak for him. The word *glossa* is used of the poet's tongue, and the process of poetry making at *O.* 6.82, *O.* 9.42, *O.* 11.9, *O.* 13.12, *P.* 1.86, *P.* 3.2, *N.* 4.8, *N.* 4.86, *N.* 7.72, *I.* 5.47, *Pa.* 6.59.

16. For other references by Sappho to the voice and its seductive power see fragments 118, 153, 185 L.P. Of course, like all ancient poets, Sappho is known to us only through the printed page. Athenaeus 13.596cd quotes Posidippus:

> Σατφωαι δὲ μένουσι φίλης ἔτι χαὶ μενέουσιν
> ᾠδῆς αἱ λευχαὶ φθεγγομέναι σελίδες.

Frag. 157D, an epigram probably of Hellenistic date, ascribed to Sappho, announces that even though she is *aphonos* she will speak, because she has a tireless voice (*phonan akamatan*) set at her feet—i.e., a stone inscription.

17. H. Fränkel, *Dichtung und Philosophie des frühen Griechentums*² (Munich 1963) 199, n. 16 draws a distinction between the endings *-tos* and *-teos* in the verbal adjective. *-tos* (the ending of *tolmaton* in line 17 of Sappho's poem) indicates possibility, not necessity. See Smyth 358. I differ from Fränkel and those who translate "may be *endured*." See P. Pucci, *Odysseus Polutropos, Intertextual Readings in the Odyssey and Iliad* (Ithaca 1987) 47 where he remarks with reference to *Iliad* 10.231 that the verb *tolman* (as distinct from its cognate, *tlenai*) usually means to dare rather than to endure, and that is does not appear to be used in the sense of "endure" in the *Iliad*. Given the martial tone of Sappho 31, valor, rather than endurance, seems particularly appropriate.

18. See M. L. West (note 11 above) 312-13.

19. See Svenbro (note 9 above) 57-63 and Page (note 10 above) 17.

20. See especially J. Winkler (note 2 above) 65-71. For example, Winkler shows how, in the Hymn to Aphrodite, Sappho encompasses within herself *both* the role of expelled female (like Aphrodite in *Iliad* 5) *and* that of aggressive male who seeks the help of a female goddess (Diomedes and Athena in *Iliad* 5). Thus Sappho shows how she responds, as a subtle and many-minded female reader, to the "male" text of the *Iliad*. Far from being excluded from the warrior's world, like Homer's Aphrodite, she contains many aspects of it within her single *persona*.

21. But E. Stehle Stigers, "Sappho's Private World" in *Reflections of Women in Antiquity* (note 2 above) 45-61 argues that Sappho's description of love exhibits a mutuality characteristic of women, rather than the desire for domination more typical of men. Stigers does not discuss this poem.

22. For *khloros* see Eleanor Irwin, *Colour Terms in Greek Poetry* (Toronto 1974) 31-78.

23. See G. Nagy, *The Best of the Achaeans. Concepts of the Hero in Archaic Greek Poetry* (Baltimore 1979) 144ff. for this question of the living organism replaced by or opposed to inorganic *kleos.*

24. The final lines of Catullus 11 show a similar "softening" of a Sapphic image; his love is like a flower which has been brushed by the plough and falls. It is not—as K. Quinn points out in his commentary *ad loc.*—actually ploughed under, merely fatally bruised. Sappho frag. 105 c L.P. depicts a hyacinth trampled underfoot by shepherds.

25. For *otium* in Latin literature, see J. M. André, *L'Otium dans la vie morale et intellectuelle romaine, des origines à l'époque augustéene* (Paris 1966); W. A. Laidlaw, "Otium," *G&R.* [*Greece & Rome*] Ser. 2, 15 (1968) 42-52.

26. For discussion of the elegiac poets on *otium,* see André (note 24 above) 403ff.; Laidlaw (note 24 above) 47-48; L. Alfonsi, *Otium e vita d'amore negli elegiaci Augustei.* Studi in onore di A. Calderini e R. Paribeni, I (Milan 1956).

27. R. Lattimore, "Sappho 2 and Catullus 51," *CP* [*Classical Philology*] 39 (1944) 184-87 cites similar lines in Theognis 1103-4, where *hubris* is said to have destroyed famous cities like Colophon and Smyrna. Troy also comes to mind, with its proverbial wealth, the luxurious peace shattered by the Greek expedition. A. Passerini, *SIFC* [*Studi Italiani di Filologia Classica*] 11 (1934) 52ff. links Catullus' *otium* with *truphe.*

28. For *otium* as peace as opposed to war, see for example, Sall. *Cat.* 10.1; *Jug.* 41.1; Livy 1.19.4; 1.22.2; 6.36.1; Sen. *Ep.* 51.6.

29. For discussion of the final stanza of Catullus' poem, and its possible relationship with the Sapphic poem, see G. Wills (note 6 above). Wills argues (196) that Catullus is talking about "a lover's code—one that embraces suffering and condemns desertion under trial. . . . Love is his *negotium,* and he must be fit for all its encounters." Wills' interpretation of *otium* is persuasive, although there is no "must," no exhortation to abandon *otium*—which constitutes a major difference between Catullus' poem and Sappho's.

30. C. Segal, "Catullan *Otiosi:* The Lover and the Poet," *G&R* 17 (1970) 25-31 argues that, for Catullus in poems 50 and 51, the concept of *otium* links love and the writing of poetry. "50 deals primarily with the literary or "poetic" side of *otium;* 51 with the amatory side; but the two

strands of *otium* are intertwined" (31). I agree that there is a literary and an amatory aspect to *otium,* but I prefer not to divide its twin aspects between the two poems. Recently J. B. Itzkowitz, "On the Last Stanza of Catullus 51," *Latomus* 42 (1983) 129-34 also argued that *otium* has twin aspects—*otium-amor* and *otium-poesis.*

31. Frag. 200 L.P. (a scholiast on the *Works and Days*) says that Sappho made Aphrodite the mother of Peitho.

Diane J. Rayor (essay date 1990)

SOURCE: Rayor, Diane J. "Translating Fragments." *Translation Review,* no. 32-33 (1990): 15-18.

[*In the following essay, Rayor explores some of the difficulties associated with translating Sappho's fragmentary poetic texts.*]

Since ancient poetry so often survives only in fragments, it would seem to present the translator with special problems not shared by those who translate complete texts. But although some of the problems are unique, the methods used to "solve" them are much the same. Yet focusing on the translation of fragments makes it easier to see the additions, subtractions, and changes that occur in all translations. The awkward loss of text exaggerates the ever-present temptation to "fix" a text rather than represent the poet's words—and the gaps between those words—accurately. Incomplete texts illuminate the criteria, strategies, tactics, and alternatives available for any rendering.

Quotations and papyri provide our only sources of ancient Greek lyric poetry. The quotations generally are very brief excerpts of one or two lines isolated from their original context within longer poems; occasionally a whole poem is quoted. Egyptian papyri containing poetry turn up in various stages of disintegration or in pieces. Indeed, many recent finds of poetry are on strips of papyrus wrapping mummies. Thus poems found on papyrus often are missing the right or left side; sometimes entire lines or scattered words have been erased by time.

The poetry of Sappho (seventh century BCE) demonstrates both the possibilities of translation and the necessity for establishing consistent principles of translation. Of the nine books of her poetry (some five hundred poems) collected in the Hellenistic period, only one definitely complete poem remains. The rest are fragments. The combination of the distance in time, the physical state of the manuscripts, the lack of reliable biographical information, and the poet's gender have led to the constant creation of new Sapphos by translators.[1]

Fragments clarify strategies of reading and translating poetry because their absences expose our necessary interaction with the text. They also expose where the translator distorts the text by interacting too much, thus not allowing the readers a chance to experience the potential of the poem. Translations work best when they fully exploit the connection and activity of the reader with the text. Letting the absences show in the translation leaves room for the reader to determine meaning and make connections.

Fragments implicitly remind us of their physical inscription and call into question the illusion of self-contained, "whole" texts. The holes in the text are not left empty in the reading process. As we read, we fill in, "read between the lines." While we do this in all reading, fragments tempt us to guess authorial intention, to imagine what the poet originally wrote that is now missing.

Reading a translation of Greek poetry should be as close to the experience of reading the Greek text as possible. Yet the reader can discover the possibilities of the Greek text only through the eyes of the translator. Optimally, the translation recreates as much of the potential meaning of the Greek as possible—opening up rather than narrowing the range of possible interpretations. It is a delicate business to provide enough information without over-determining the meaning of the poem.

To recreate the experience of reading Sappho, for instance, the translation needs to show the reader where the Greek text breaks off. Most available translations of Greek lyric give no indication of fragmentation, where one thought does not immediately follow the last. Translators generally opt for expanding or condensing the text by adding or subtracting phrases. Peter Newmark's terms of over- and under-translation[2] have special meaning for fragments.

Over-translation and under-translation erase evidence of physical gaps. "Completing" the poem by filling in gaps overly privileges the translator's interpretation, and fragmentary lines left out through condensing often contain vital information. Both practices simplify the poetry and mislead the reader. While the translator's interpretation of the text always informs the translation, she should resist the temptation to add or subtract text itself.

Over-translation was once common because the editors of Greek texts used to add the Greek they guessed the author originally had written. Some additions to fragmented texts certainly are acceptable, and it would be a disservice not to include them. The standard Greek editions include generally accepted supplements based on quotations in other ancient authors, probable readings of papyri, information from ancient marginalia, and the sense of the texts themselves. The translator accepts or rejects these supplements on a individual basis according to probability and necessity. It is not over-translation to accept a suggested word that is likely paleographically and needed for an intelligible reading.

On the other hand, early editions of the Greek, such as Edmonds'[3] Sappho, contain large-scale reconstruction. Edmonds fills in whole passages missing in the extant texts of Sappho; he even composes entire poems from a few fragments. More recent editions of Sappho, by Lobel and Page[4] and Voigt,[5] provide texts free from these restorations. Translations based on poorer editions, therefore, are an additional stage removed from the Greek. Translations not based on the latest findings or the most accurate scholarship are mistranslations rather than over-translations.

The justification given for over-translation is that fragmentary poetry should be completed by the translator to provide the reader with the closest possible experience of the original. The problem, of course, is that the translator cannot know what the poet originally wrote, and that translators always interpret through their own biases. For example, in Sappho ["16"],[6] lines 13-14 are missing:

> She had no
> memory of her child or dear parents,
> since she was led astray
> [by Aphrodite] . . .
>
> . . . lightly
> . . . reminding me now of Anaktoria
> being gone,
>
> I would rather see her lovely step
> and the radiant sparkle of her face
> than all the war-chariots in Lydia
> and soldiers battling in shining bronze.

Richmond Lattimore's[7] translation adds this for the missing lines:

> Since young brides have hearts that can be persuaded
> easily, light things, palpitant to passion/as I am.

This addition completely transforms the tone and purpose of the poem. Sappho's poem argues that "whatever one loves" (line 4)—the paraphernalia of war or an individual person—appears most desirable, not that women are particularly excitable and irrational. The lines Lattimore adds to to fill the gap are symptomatic of changes throughout his translations of Sappho; earlier in ["16"] he changes the neuter "whatever one loves" to "she whom one loves best."

While over-translated poems second-guess the author, under-translated poems tend to leave out even more text than is available in their fragmentary form. Should the translator trim more off a poem already pruned by time? Mary Barnard's[8] translation of Sappho ["**95**"] provides an example of three strategies: under-translation (1) by leaving out the first three partially visible lines, and (2) by pretending the poem is unbroken, and (3) over-translation by adding an explanation to the name of Hermes:

> Hermes, Lord, you
> who lead the ghosts
> home:
> But this time
> I am not happy; I
> want to die, to see
> the moist lotus open
> along Acheron.

Omission of the woman's name, "Gongyla," from the first extant line removes the suggestion that perhaps the "longing" to die is based on erotic longing for another woman:

> Gongyla . . .
> Surely a sign . . .
> especially . . .
> [Hermes] came into . . .
>
> I said: O Lord . . .
> By the blessed [goddess]
> I take no pleasure on [earth]
>
> but longing to die holds me,
> to see the dewy lotus-
> shaded banks of Acheron . . .

Translators need to be particularly aware of their biases or assumptions when translating women's poetry to avoid distorting the message, or closing off interpretive possibilities available in the source text.[9] Over-translations, such as Lattimore's of Sappho ["**16**"], fill in the fragment gaps with inappropriate or trivializing phrases. While fragments lend themselves to that sort of misrepresentation, whole poems also are subject to distorted or censored renderings. Obvious examples include translations that switch pronouns or even the subject from female to male. Nineteenth-century translations of Sappho ["**1**"] changed from female to male the object of the (female) speaker's desire:

> For if she flees, soon she'll pursue,
> she doesn't accept gifts, but she'll give,
> if not now loving, soon she'll love
> even against her will.

Fragments that are excerpts from lost longer poems frequently lack a context for interpretation. In these short fragments, it is sometimes difficult to determine the gender from the Greek verb. For example, in ["**15**."4] the Greek could be "he came" or "she came":

> . . . Kypris,
> may she find you very bitter
> and may Doricha not boast, saying
> how she came the second time
> to longed-for love.

Nothing in the poem suggests a masculine pronoun, since the only person mentioned is female. Yet the poem generally has been translated "he came," which shifts the focus of the poem to an unidentified man. This has been justified by an unreliable biographical tradition that associates Doricha with a prostitute with whom Sappho's brother fell in love. Even if we accept that the rest of the poem dealt with that story, nothing hinders Doricha from being portrayed as the active one. Poems that have an erotic element are especially apt to be reconstructed according to the individual translator and prevalent attitudes. Whether words or context are missing, fragments illustrate the need to be sensitive to tone and potential meaning of the poetry translated.

Yet without "completing" the poem, how does one make a wounded poem live in the new language? Gaps in poems can be bridged by loosely linking sense or images, so that the poem reads well, without being deceptive. The translator's job is to make the absences work as part of the poetry without being distracting: to evoke connections, enticing the reader to bridge the gap.

Fragments can engage the reader's imagination by actually using the breaks. Poems of recollection or memory have inherent possibilities. In Sappho ["**94**"] the speaker tells of how she reminded a friend who was leaving of their past days spent together. Throughout the second half of the poem, scattered words are missing:

> "I simply wish to die."
> Weeping she left me
> and said this too:
> "We've suffered terribly
> Sappho I leave you against my will."
> I answered, go happily
> and remember me,
> you know how we cared for you,
> if not, let me remind you
> . . . the lovely times we shared.
>
> Many crowns of violets,
> roses and crocuses
> . . . together you set before me
> and many scented wreaths
> made from blossoms
> around your soft throat . . .
> . . . with pure, sweet oil
> . . . you anointed me,
> and on a soft, gentle bed . . .
> you quenched your desire . . .
> . . . no holy site . . .
> we left uncovered,
> no grove . . . dance
> . . . sound

The recollection in the second part might read as if the speaker's voice drifts off into silent memory.

Word selection is crucial to tantalize the reader and evoke the sensuality of the poem. Lines 21-22 demonstrate the double meaning exploited by the translation. The phrase, taken with the following lines, implies that the women visited every temple, and that they participated in the rituals of Aphrodite, goddess of love. But the eroticism of earlier lines, particularly line 20, is enhanced by the second meaning of covering every "holy site" of the body.

No images are left out, none are added. Each word is given its full impact through word choice and position, each line building on the images and sounds of the previous lines. The need for and effect of devices used in translating all poetry are exaggerated by the fragmentation of the text.

Poems with more radical breaks, such as those with the right side missing as in ["**95**"] (above), are more difficult to work with. The translator can make the most of the extant text by indicating missing parts through line breaks and punctuation. Some translations can even imitate the physical texture of the papyrus by showing where the lines were torn. But recording very fragmentary pieces containing an interesting myth or image is sometimes more a matter of preserving it than creating viable poetry. One example is an eighteen-line fragment ["**58**"] missing the left-hand margin, which tells the myth of Tithonos in the context of the speaker's aging:

> . . . rosy-armed Dawn
> . . . taking (Tithonos) to the ends of earth.

A second example, a two-line poem, tells an alternative story to the traditional one in which Zeus, in the form of a swan, rapes Leda and fathers Helen. Sappho ["**166**"] perhaps suggests that there was no rape and that Leda found an egg containing Helen:

> They say that once Leda found
> an egg hidden in the hyacinth.

Small fragments like ["**166**"] have inspired modern poems; H.D. has a series of poems based on Sappho fragments. One can admire the pieces, as one does broken statues or shards of pottery.

To offset gaps or lack of context, the translator needs to employ many different strategies to make the poem work on as many levels as possible. Effective strategies include sound and tempo effects, and even grouping the poems thematically. Sounds with a similar effect, although not usually the same sound, as the source language develop the potential of whole poems and fragments. Translations of Sappho ["**2**"] and a poem by another seventh-century-BCE writer, Alkman, both work with sound, especially with repeated vowels, to echo the hypnotic effect of the Greek:

Sappho ["**2**"]

> cold water ripples through apple
> branches, the whole place shadowed
> in roses, from the murmuring leaves
> deep sleep descends.

and

Alkman [89][10]

> All asleep: mountain peaks and chasms,
> ridges and cutting streams,
> the reptile tribes that black earth feeds,
> mountain beasts and race of bees,
> monsters deep in the purple sea,
> and tribes of long-winged birds all sleep.

Sappho ["**140**"] emphasizes the ritualistic aspect of the festival in honor of Aphrodite's (i.e., Kytheria's) lover Adonis, through alliteration in Greek: two words begin with a "t" sound, two with an "ah," and the rest with a "k" sound. The translation echoes the effects:

> Delicate Adonis is dying, Kytheria—what should we
>   do?
> Beat your breasts, daughters, and rend your dresses.

Since an attempt to reproduce the Greek meter would work clumsily in English, one can compensate for this by recreating the vivid and direct effects of the Greek sound.

Placing short poems together will also help recreate a context through association. Grouping Sappho's short fragments according to such themes as friendship, rivalry, or epithalamia (marriage songs) builds meaning by accumulation. It is an interpretive move, for instance, to place Sappho ["**51**"] "I don't know what I should do—I'm of two minds," with erotic poems or with poems about writing poetry ("do" can mean "set down" in writing.)

By paying particular attention to the words on each side of the gap, by word choice and use of sound, and by the grouping together of short excerpts, the translator can develop the available text, the remaining words, in ways conducive to the reader's activity. As in translating non-fragmentary poetry, the translator abides by certain criteria that remain flexible enough to solve the individual problems posed by every poem. Tactics shift for individual poems, but the underlying approach should be consistent. The translator tries to incorporate as many facets of the source poem as possible, compensating for what is lost either from the fragmentary source text or in the transmission from source to target language. Fragments can make us more aware of how we "complete" texts as readers and interpreters. Then we are more likely to find the balance between over- and under-translation, finding the elusive fine line that is "just right."

Notes

1. See J. DeJean, *Fictions of Sappho, 1546-1937,* Chicago: 1989.

2. P. Newmark, *Approaches to Translation,* Oxford: 1981.

3. J. M. Edmonds, *Lyra Graeca,* vol. 1, Cambridge: 1928.

4. E. Lobel and D. Page, *Poetarum Lesbiorum Fragmenta,* Oxford: 1955.

5. E.-M. Voigt, *Sappho et Alcaeus Fragmenta,* Amsterdam: 1971.

6. All of the translations not otherwise identified are my own from *Sappho's Lyre: Archaic Lyric and Women Poets of Ancient Greece,* Berkeley and Los Angeles: forthcoming 1991; I use Voigt's edition and numbering.

7. R. Lattimore, *Greek Lyrics,* Chicago: 1960.

8. M. Barnard, *Sappho,* Berkeley and Los Angeles: 1958.

9. See M. Díaz-Diocaretz, *Translating Poetic Discourse: Questions on Feminist Strategies in Adrienne Rich,* Amsterdam: 1985.

10. See note 6; I used the edition and numbering of D. Page, *Poetae Melici Graeci,* Oxford: 1962.

David Bevington (essay date 1991)

SOURCE: Bevington, David. "Introduction to *Sappho and Phao.*" In *John Lyly:* Campaspe *and* Sappho and Phao, edited by G. K. Hunter and David Bevington, pp. 141-96. Manchester: Manchester University Press, 1991.

[*In the following excerpt, Bevington explores Elizabethan dramatist John Lyly's version of the Sappho myth—derived from Ovid—in his 1584 play* Sappho and Phao.]

[John Lyly, in his drama *Sappho and Phao,*] seems unaware of, or uninterested in, much of the historical information that we possess today about Sappho. *The Oxford Companion to Classical Literature* and the *Dictionary of Greek and Roman Biography and Mythogra-*

phy[1] report that she was born at Mitylene, or perhaps Eressos, on the island of Lesbos in the eastern Aegean, probably in the seventh century B.C. She was of good parentage, and was a contemporary of the poet Alcaeus. Forced to leave Lesbos, perhaps because of political difficulties, she may have gone to Sicily and died there. Apparently she married and had a daughter, Cleis. Among her brothers was Charaxus, whom she reproached for his involvement with an Egyptian courtesan named Doricha or Rhodopis. Sappho gathered together a group of women dedicated to music and poetry, or perhaps to the worship of Aphrodite. Her own literary production included nine books of odes, epithalamia, elegies and hymns, of which one complete ode and various fragments survive. They are in a variety of metres, including the so-called Sapphic. Some appear to celebrate a passionate love for other women. Virtually none of this information makes its way into Lyly's play.

About Sappho's supposed 'Lesbianism' or 'Sapphism' in the homosexual sense, references are indeed hard to find not only in Lyly but in most writers before A. C. Swinburne and others in the late nineteenth century. The *O.E.D.*'s earliest citation for 'Lesbian' or 'Sapphism' in the homosexual sense is in 1890. If Lyly was aware of the allegation, as he probably was in view of Ovid's reference to Sappho's attraction for young women '*non sine crimine*' (*Heroides,* xv.19) and of John Donne's 'Sapho to Philaenis' (written of course after Lyly's play), he seems to have chosen to overlook the matter as entirely unsuited to his project of flattering Queen Elizabeth.

His reticence on the subject of Sappho as a poetess is perhaps more surprising. Elizabeth, like her father, Henry VIII, nurtured her self-image as a monarch with a flair for literary pursuits, and so Lyly might have been expected to capitalise on the flattering analogy. Possibly he preferred to think of rulers as patrons rather than as dabblers, as his portrait of Alexander with Apelles suggests. But the larger answer may be simply that Lyly was not interested in what he could have learned about the historical figure of Sappho. Even for the historical association of Sappho with Sicily he seems to have been indebted to a suggestion in Ovid. Lyly was primarily attracted to the Sappho of legend and poetry.

Paradoxically, one legendary source to which he turned does not actually link Sappho and Phao, though it does give information about both. Phaon or Phao is instead linked with Aphrodite or Venus. This legend may have been influenced in turn by the story of Aphrodite and Adonis; indeed, Karl Otfried Müller argues that 'Phaon' or 'Phaethon' is simply another name for Adonis.[2] At any rate, Lyly found the story of the encounter between Venus and Phaon in the *Varia Historia* of Aelian or

Claudius Aelianus (fl. *c.* A.D. 200). This author of *De Natura Animalium,* to whom Lyly often turned, as he did to Pliny, for abstruse lore in natural history, put together in his *Varia Historia* a compendium of broad but uncritical learning about political, literary and legendary celebrities of the classical world. Included in it is the following account of Phaon (XII.18):

> That Phaon was of a fair complexion.

> Phaon, a proper youth, excelling all other in favour and comeliness, was hidden of Venus among long lettuce [original text: lettisse] which sprung up and grew very rankly. Some hold opinion that this Phaon was a ferryman, and that he used that trade of life and exercise. So it fortuned that Venus had occasion to pass over the water, whom he, not so readily as willingly, took by the hand and received into his wherry and carried her over with as great diligence as he could for his life, not knowing all this while what she was. For which dutiful service at that instant exhibited, Venus bestowed upon him an alabaster box full of ointment for her ferryage [ferrage in Q1], wherewith Phaon, washing and scouring his skin, had not his fellow in fairness of favour and beautiful complexion alive, insomuch that the women of Mitylene were inflamed with the love of Phaon, his comeliness did so kindle their affections.[3]

Aelian adds that Phaon was afterwards taken in adultery and killed. The account makes no mention of Sappho, but is set in Mitylene. Aelian reports in his next paragraph of Sappho:

> Plato, the son of Aristo, numbereth Sappho, the versifier, and daughter of Scamandronymus, among such as were wise, learned and skilful. I hear also that there was another Sappho in Lesbos, which was a strong whore and an arrant strumpet.[4]

Aelian's reference to two Sapphos, one a poetess and one a whore, may reflect a male Athenian difficulty in coming to terms with the frankness of Sappho's lyric poetry; in many later writers, Sappho the poet is represented as a courtesan. Aelian here makes no explicit connection between his accounts of Phaon and Sappho, but he does present them in such a way that Lyly would have found them in adjacent paragraphs, both figures associated with Mitylene and Lesbos.

Lyly could have encountered this story of Phao and Venus connected with that of Phao and Sappho in Palaephatus' *De fabulosis narrationibus* (*Peri Apistōn* in Greek), a widely used compilation of Greek mythography that was surely available to him.[5] As Bond says (I.157), one occasionally wonders if Lyly may not have used the succinct accounts provided by this and other convenient reference works, though he is very likely to have known Aelian and of course Ovid as well.

The legend of Sappho's love for Phao or Phaon seems to have appeared first in several lost Attic comedies,[6] but it is not until Epistle XV of Ovid's *Heroides,* 'Sappho to Phaon', that the story becomes available to Lyly in literary form. Here Lyly not only could learn the narrative details of the legendary connection between Sappho and Phao, but, more importantly, could also read an impassioned fictional account of the heroine's suffering. As is his manner, Ovid allows the woman to speak directly of her lost hopes, her fallen fortune, her fatal infatuation for a man who no longer cares for her. To avoid Sappho's love, Phaon has fled to Sicily and Mount Etna. The speaker, consumed in more than Etna's fires, takes no consolation in music or in her own poetry. No more is she moved by guilty love of the Lesbian dames as of yore. She sees herself as greater than Daphne or Ariadne in that they were not lyric poets; she believes herself worthy of comparison with her fellow islander Alcaeus, of world-wide fame, and yet has been deserted by the man she loves. She concedes her inferior stature and beauty, but pleads with Venus to help. Her life has had many sadnesses—the early loss of her parents, a brother, an infant daughter—but none so great as the loss of Phaon. Warning the maidens of Sicily to beware of the tempter now in their midst, she resolves to throw herself off the cliff at Leucadia (off the coast of Epirus). She will die while careless Phaon stays.

It was apparently common to read ll. 51-2 of this Epistle as indicating that Sappho followed Phaon to Sicily, although by no means obligatory in the text itself. Ovid's poem was translated by George Turberville in 1567, although Lyly surely must have known the original. In any event, the combination of Aelian's and Ovid's narrations gave Lyly many of the essentials of his dramatic situation: a high-born and cultivated woman protagonist torn by an unhappy love, the suggestion of a setting in Sicily (though it is Phaon alone who certainly goes there in Ovid), Venus' gift of extraordinary beauty to a ferryman with whom she has taken passage, the infatuation of other women besides Sappho with Phaon and the lack of romantic completion in the love relationship.

Lyly's changes are no less compelling. Sappho is a queen, no poetess. There is no mention of guilty love for other women. Phao is far below Sappho in station; the difference in rank between ruler and subject, a plausible deduction from Phaon's position in Aelian as ferryman used to a 'trade of life and exercise', is much emphasised in the play. Phao is not only beloved, as in the classical sources, but is himself in love, with no suggestion of the insolent masculine carelessness so characteristic of Ovid's deserting men. As a consequence, Lyly's Sappho must learn to master her own affection for a willing Phao instead of suffering the pangs of rejection.

The symbolic contest between Sappho and Venus for the control of passionate feeling in love is new in the play; Ovid and Aelian introduce Venus in a conventional role only as the goddess of love and provider of physical beauty. Venus' motive in bestowing beauty on Phao as a means of entrapping Sappho in amorous longing is an invention of Lyly's. So is the inclusion of Cupid, of Vulcan and of the Cyclopes. Lyly adds philosophers and courtiers to the court of Sappho so that they may debate issues already aired in *Campaspe,* and in turn parodies their debate with the pert badinage of servants. Sappho's ladies-in-waiting are perhaps hinted at in Aelian's women of Mitylene and their infatuation with Phaon, but fill an expanded role in a discussion of court manners and feminine experiences in love. The ancient Sibylla to whom Phao turns for advice is derived from Ovid's *Metamorphoses* (XIV.130ff.) and perhaps from Virgil's *Aeneid* (VI.8ff.), but the inclusion of her in the present story is new, while her role as an adviser in love is indebted to medieval traditions of the court of love.[7]

Notes

1. Sir Paul Harvey, ed., *The Oxford Companion to Classical Literature* (Oxford, 1937), pp. 381-2, and Sir William Smith, ed., *Dictionary of Greek and Roman Biography and Mythography,* 3 vols. (London, 1890), III.707-11.

2. Karl Otfried Müller, *A History of the Literature of Ancient Greece,* 3 vols. (rpt. Port Washington, N. Y., 1958), I.231.

3. The translation, here modernised, is that of Abraham Fleming, *A Register of Histories, Containing Martial Exploits of Worthy Warriors . . . Written in Greek by Aelianus, a Roman, and Delivered in English . . . by Abraham Fleming* (London, 1576), pp. 125-6.

4. Trans. Abraham Fleming (1576), p. 126.

5. Palaephatus, *De fabulosis narrationibus,* published with the *Fabularum Liber* attributed to C. Julius Hyginus (Basel, 1535), ed. Stephen Orgel (New York, 1976). For the Greek text see *Peri Apistōn, Mythographi Graeci,* III, fasc. 2, ed. Nicolaus Festa, Leipzig, 1902), p. 69.

6. Müller, *A History of the Literature of Ancient Greece,* I.231.

7. See William Allan Neilson, *The Origins and Sources of the Court of Love* (Boston, 1899); rpt. (New York, 1967), pp. 31, 33, and 134-5.

Kai Heikkilä (essay date 1992)

SOURCE: Heikkilä, Kai. "Sappho Fragment 2 L.-P: Some Homeric Readings." *Arctos* 26 (1992): 39-53.

[*In the following essay, Heikkilä traces Homeric parallels—sometimes recast in erotic contexts—in Sappho's second fragment.*]

INTRODUCTION

The relationship of Sappho's poems to Homer has been studied several times.[1] Fairly recently four fragments of Sappho, namely frs. **"1," "16," "31,"** and **"44"** L.-P. have been studied by Leah Rissman as to their Homeric allusions.[2] Rissman's methodological approach to Homeric allusions in Sappho deserves attention as a model with which to highlight the purposes and method of this study. Rissman assigns the types of Homeric allusions in three general categories: repetition of a word or expression, adaptation thereof and similarity of situation. The effect of the allusions is produced if the audience thinks of Homer in the first place.[3] She rightly notes that this approach involves several difficulties: epicisms in archaic poetry can be coincidental, lyric formulae may arise from an independent tradition, and what seem to be allusions to epic poetry may in fact be allusions to other poems.[4]

The present study sets out to compare certain key themes of Sappho's fragment **"2"** L.-P. to similar themes in Homer. Although certain lexical and thematic parallels will suggest that Sappho has constructed her poem with similar Homeric themes in mind, certainty is often impossible, and the corrupt state of parts of fr. **"2"** further complicates establishing exact Homeric borrowings. Yet even if direct Homeric influence could not be demonstrated, it can be safely assumed that Sappho and Homer work in the same tradition and make use of it for their own purposes. It should also be noted that most of Greek lyric poetry has a close relationship to Homer and the dominance of Homer in Greek culture and literature will have made it the most suggestive field of reference for the poets and their audience. Furthermore, the only surviving literary context, apart from some other lyric poetry, that is contemporaneous with Sappho or precedes her literary output is the epic tradition of Homer and Hesiod. Thus a comparison of Sappho to Homer is a matter of necessity dictated by the chance of survival. The purpose of this study is also to show that contrasting Sappho with the Homeric tradition will make the unique character of her work appear more clearly. Moreover, the Homeric parallels or allusions that can be plausibly identified often create a system of reference that Sappho uses to introduce different shades of meaning for a word, expression or image. How this system of reference emerges in fragment **"2"** and how it enhances the understanding of the meaning and artistry of the poem will be the main concern of this study.

FRAGMENT "2 L.-P" : THE FIRST STANZA

The basic structure of fr. **"2"** has been indicated in several studies.[5] The first stanza contains the address to a deity that is not mentioned, a plea that the deity come to a temple with a grove and an altar. The two following stanzas describe the grove in detail, and the fourth names the goddess Aphrodite and by asking her to perform a libation returns to the cletic and cultic setting of the first stanza. This establishes a tripartite structure for the poem (or the part of it that has been preserved) as well as the principle of ring-composition without lexical pointers which are often used to announce the ring.[6]

The wish that the deity would appear is expressed by δεῦρυ without the verb, if the word is not missing in the fragmentary first line.[7] The call upon the deity is followed by a short description of the locality: it is a holy temple (ναῦον ἄγνον)[8] where Aphrodite (as identified later in the fourth stanza) would find a pleasant grove (χάριεν ἄλσος) of apples with altars which have been perfumed with incense (βῶμοι τεθυμιάμενοι [λι]βανώτῳ). The key words temple, altar and grove have all been defined with adjectives and the grove with an additional μαλί[αν]. These words not only describe the place but also indicate by the addition of perfumed altars that a cult is being practised. These notions of locality and activity anticipate the following stanzas so that an introduction is created which already indicates the structure and the basic ideas of the poem. A thorough analysis of the first stanza is therefore essential for a proper understanding of the poem as a whole.

The aspect of cult of the first stanza of fr. "2" finds its Homeric parallel in the formulaic expression ἔνθα τέ οἱ τέμενος βωμός τε θυήεις, found several times in diffesent contexts.[9] In Od. 8. 362f. Aphrodite moves from Olympus to her shrine (τέμενος) in Paphos where a fragrant altar (βῶμος θυήεις) awaits her and where the Charites will wash and anoint her body. The movement of the goddess from one place to another, the fact that she comes to her shrine and the fragrant altars there suggest strong similarity in theme and organization, the lexical connection being provided in the image of the fragrant altars. Both accounts move gradually deeper into the shrine to suggest the movement of the goddess, and the movement takes the same course in both: 1. Paphos - δεῦρυ, 2. τέμενος-ναῦος, 3. βῶμος - βῶμοι. Sappho gives a further lexical connection by describing the grove of the precinct as χάριεν (l. 2). In the Homeric passages describing Aphrodite's arrival at her temple she is assisted by Charites, who as personifications of erotic attraction are associated only with her.[10] Here Sappho seems to invite comparison between her poem and Aphrodite's advent scenes in Homer, although the goddess is not named by her until in the fourth stanza.

Despite the evident similarities, Sappho's first stanza is substantially different from its Homeric parallels. Already the function of Sappho's poem as a cletic hymn demands a different and more personal approach which is reflected in the cletic δεῦρυ and the use of the second person (τοι) when the goddess is addressed instead of the Homeric third person in οἱ.[11] The narrative purpose of Homer emphasizes the action and contains little of the descriptive and picturesque detail that decorate Sappho's account. Sappho's poem emerges as a curious mixture of personal address and generalizing omissions: although the locality is elaborately described by Sappho the place of the shrine is not mentioned and the name of the deity addressed remains unknown for the time being. This creates two important effects that separate Sappho's poem from the Homeric account and the conventional form of a cletic hymn. The omission of the name of the deity creates suspense that is not released until in the last stanza, which gives Sappho's poem a forward impetus quite different from the Homeric linear narrative.[12] Moreover, the mention of the godhead's name is essential for a cletic hymn or invocation. The connection between the mortal and the god can be fully established through identification, as Sappho duly does in fr. "1" L.-P., which mentions Aphrodite in the first line with a characteristic epithet.[13] Thus the omissions of proper names for the locality and the godhead summoned can be regarded as a programmatic statement to indicate that Sappho's intentions are different than those of Homer and the hymnic genre.

The basic elements of Aphrodite's advent that appear in Sappho's poem were already present in the Homeric account: the holy precinct (τέμενος) and the fragrant altars. Sappho, however, developes the notion of holiness by adding the temple (ναῦον), describing it holy (ἄγνον) and giving the whole scene the dimension of nature with the addition of the pleasant grove of apples (χάριεν ἄλσος μαλί[αν]).

Ναός or ναῦος is usually a temple with the cult image, whereas τέμενος suggests the holy precinct in general.[14] By ναῦος Sappho brings us to the center of the cult where the existence of the temple suggests a permanent establishment for cult rather than just a holy precinct. The word ναῦος also indicates the connection between the goddess and mortals who have built the temple and perform the sacrifices. Whereas in Homer Aphrodite was attended by the Charites, in Sappho humans await her arrival. The adjective ἄγνον is an interesting choice to describe the temple. In Homer ἄγνός is used of places and things dedicated to gods and the word even otherwise always refers to what is particular to the sacred.[15] But it is also the special epithet of virgin goddesses, especially of Artemis. Homer never uses the adjective of Aphrodite.[16] Burkert in fact thinks that the word means sacred and pure as opposed to things defiled (μιαρά), although this is a matter of some controversy.[17] Parker regards the term ἄγνός as too vague to mean pure or chaste without qualification from its context.[18] According to Williger the term when applied to gods conveys rather a notion of respect than purity.[19] Doubtlessly the term ἄγνον when it in Sappho's poem describes the temple conveys a sense of separation, holiness and awe, but the possibility of associating the adjective with Artemis and therefore the connotation of sexual purity and virginity cannot be ruled out since Artemis is the ἀγνή goddess *par excellence,* and she and her cult are especially connected with groves and meadows.[20]

In the first stanza the eroticism is represented by the presence of χάρις in the landscape, and those associated with the grove become part of that χάρις.[21] Yet the erotic potentiality inherent in the Sapphic grove (χάριεν ἄλσος) first becomes real and tangible through the Homeric reference to Aphrodite (later confirmed in the fourth stanza) assisted by her Charites. Aphrodite brings in the notion of sensual love and by their association with Aphrodite the Charites suggest erotic attraction and sexual maturity.[22] The participants of the cultic celebration of Aphrodite who have perfumed Aphrodite's altar and in the fourth stanza invite her to pour the libation take in Sappho's poem the place of the Homeric Charites as the attendants of Aphrodite. Thus the Homeric reference not only activates the landscape, it also places those present there in their function and status.

Aphrodite's role as the goddess of physical sexuality and her suggested presence in the first stanza seem quite incompatible with the idea of purity and virginity also prominent in the stanza. It is also important to note that sexuality in general was banned from places of cult, which makes the Sappho's combination of eroticism and worship original and striking.[23] So even if the interpretation of ἄγνον as implying sexual purity here could not be regarded as conclusive, the contrast between sexuality and the sacred still persists. Such flowery meadows as the one in Sappho fr. "2." could of course include sexuality, even invite its violation, but what has usually escaped the scholars' attention is that in Sappho fr. "2" the meadow is a hallowed temple with all the trappings of cult and sacrifice and not merely described as "inviolate" (ἀκήρατος).[24] This Sapphic innovation to combine purity, sexuality and the sacred points out her original genius, but creates problems for the interpretation of the passage. Therefore the following similarity that reconciles the concept of ἄγνος with both Homeric passages describing Aphrodite's advent and the aspect of sexuality in Sappho's poem should be considered.

Aphrodite's arrival at Paphos in Cyprus in the Odyssey is part of one of the most famous and original stories in the poem, the song of Demodocus.[25] The story is a parody of passion, adultery and punishment, where the adulterous couple Aphrodite, the wife of Hephaestus, and Ares are trapped *in flagranti* by the suspecting husband. Without further going into the details of the story, it suffices here to note that the main point of the story is sexuality, namely illicit sexuality, and the shame and ridicule that follows it.[26] What is important here is the fact that she leaves Olympus and Ares (who heads to Thrace), the scene and partner of her adulterous affair, to bathe in her shrine. Her departure from Olympus can be understood not only spatially but also as a symbolic separation from the sexual status of an adulteress she had put herself in during the affair.

Since Aphrodite's bathing happens in a holy precinct a comparison with ritual baths suggests itself. Ritual baths were a regulated ceremony before entering holy places and precede sacrifice and mysteries. In them a symbolic separation from the world outside and a transformation into different status or capacity took place.[27] Even here it could be suggested that Aphrodite's bath purifies her from the stain of her adultery and marks her transition to a new status, which also is sexual as can be seen from the rest of the Homeric passage: at 366 her clothes are described as captivatingly beautiful (ἐπήρατα) and a wonder to behold (θαῦμα ἰδέσθαι). What makes Aphrodite *acquiring* this status similar to a worshipper approaching ἄγνόν, is that in both cases purity and separation are the key elements. The bath itself shows that purity is not a concept incompatible with Aphrodite, yet Aphrodite's bath does not purify her absolutely, but marks her new sexual status. Similarly in the Homeric hymn to Aphrodite 61 the goddess is bathed by the Charites when she wants to seduce Anchises.[28] Here again the bath marks the preparation and the beginning of her new sexual mood and purpose. Of course Aphrodite's purity is by no means virgin purity, but for the interpretation of the Sappho 2 it is essential to note that the allusion to these Homeric passages brings in the idea of purity as a marker of an active sexual status and a limiting factor as regards other sexual statuses. The allusion colors the place of cult and the term ἄγνον by showing that the sexual purity they both imply here can be understood not as a sort of anti-sexuality but as an erotic mood.[29] Therefore the purity in this context need not be inconsistent with the sexuality that Aphrodite and χάρις imply, but rather a reflection of the Sapphic idea of the type of love connected with the grove. The virginity and purity suggest that the maiden, like the unmarried priestesses of Artemis,[30] was supposed to have no sexual contact with men. If we assume that the love celebrated in Sappho's temple of Aphrodite was strictly between women, the ἄγνον quality of the temple would not have been compromised.[31]

The idea of purity and sexuality combined can be further strenghtened by considering the apple-grove which is the center of activity. The symbolism and function of the apple-grove become fully clear only in the second and third stanzas, but the image has here suggestive power by itself. Apple-trees in the Odyssey in a garden setting with other trees represent abundance, wealth and the high position of their owners. This is clear in the way Alcinous' orchards in Od. 7.114f. stand for his wealth and the splendour of his court. Apples also figure among the gifts of nature Tantalus is denied as punishment (Od. 11.588ff.). The presence of apples in a holy grove of Aphrodite with its erotic implications and suggestions of purity obviously connects the apple to a different symbolic structure than was the case in Homer. Burnett has noted that the ambiguity of the grove is paralleled by apples which represent both virginity and its loss.[32] The connection of apples and ἔρως is made clear by Ibycus in fr. 6d where the sensually beautiful garden setting bears a striking resemblance to Sappho's fr. **"2."**

The problem that the apple presents is again the same as with the advent of Aphrodite to a setting that suggests virginity and sexual purity, a landscape that would be more suitable for Artemis, the pure (ἀγνή) goddess who loves to haunt meadows and groves.[33] Burnett notes that Aphrodite was associated with groves as well, but this might represent later tradition. Also her idea that virginity existed only to be lost seems forced in this context.[34] Rather if we assume, as suggested above, that the advent of Aphrodite and the eroticism of the landscape do not pose a threat to virginity, the goddess of love can enter with impunity a precinct that also exhibits attributes of Artemis. The fact that the name of the goddess is not mentioned leaves the reader/listener free to associate the scene with both Artemis and Aphrodite and to accomodate the oblique Homeric reference to Athena (Od. 6. 291, see above note 20). The virgin Artemis who only associates herself with women and Aphrodite the goddess of sexual love thus enter the scene to create a setting with a decidedly homoerotic flavor. The ambiguity of the apple is transformed in this grove to a coherence of sexuality and virginity, an ἔρως of distinctly Sapphic character, with suggestions of purity, holiness and Artemis controlling the loss of virginity associated with the apple.

STANZAS 2-4 OF "FR. 2": EXPANSION AND
CONCLUSION

The image of the apple-grove of the first stanza is elaborated and expanded in the second and third stanzas. The flow of the cool water through apple branches, the shadows of roses, rustling leaves that create deep slumber and a flowery meadow with gentle breezes create a paradise-like atmosphere. This idea of a paradise is indebted or related to some Homeric passages, most notably the amorous encounter between Zeus and Hera in Il. 14.347-51, the description of the scenery around

Calypso's cave in Od. 5.63ff. and the grove where Odysseus waits before he follows Nausicaa to the city (Od. 6.291ff.). In Calypso's abode trees, flowers, meadows and water are all present and an image of this kind is echoed in Sappho. Sappho's grove in fr. 2, however, has important additions and implications that form what Burnett has called a landscape of female sexuality.[35] Burnett further notes that Aphrodite's "best known attributes and parts are rendered by bits of landscape . . . to specify and reinforce the aspect of the divinity that the worshipper would meet."[36] It was suggested above that the Aphrodite worshipped in this garden represented the union of sexuality and purity. How do the details of the landscape agree with this?

The first feature of the grove that Sappho gives is the purling of cold water through the apple-branches. In Homer the only instance when water is called ψυχρὸν is when it comes from a spring in a garden of Nymphs (Od. 17. 205f.). Also the verb κελάδειν that in Sappho's poem describes the purling of the water is used in Homer of rivers (Il. 18.576). It is therefore plausible to assume that Sappho is describing a spring or a creek. Some of the apple-branches could have fallen into the water or could be long enough to reach it. As the above examples show, water in Homer is an integral part of a pleasant natural setting. But in fact the word ὕδωρ in Homer is most often associated with purification, especially the washing of hands (χέρνιψ). In the Iliad purification with water takes place in connection with oaths (3. 270), prayers (9. 171f.) and reception of guests.[37] Water thus purifies to prepare men for a contact with gods and marks the transition of the stranger into the status of guest. Nilsson notes that water was the most usual means of purification in several Greek cults.[38] The implications of purity, purification and virginity were already suggested for the first stanza. The sounding water in the second stanza can consequently be seen both as the limit between the holy and the profane and as a means of the purification that gives entry to the area marked pure and holy (ἀγνον) in the first stanza. On the whole the connection of the word ὕδωρ here to Homer shows how Sappho uses the epic parallel to create awareness of the expression she uses, but it also indicates the skill of Sappho to unite the most important aspects of the image in the parallels to a personal and effective synthesis.

In Sappho's poem the flow of water is intimately connected with apple-branches. Whereas water here can be seen to represent the purity and holiness of the grove, apples stand for virginity and sexuality. In the first stanza Sappho had tried to dissolve the inherent contradiction in the symbolism of the apple. In the second stanza Sappho emphatically returns to her interpretation of apple as an erotic symbol. The water that flows among the apple branches cleanses them of the residues of their ambiguous message (especially the loss of virginity) and brings them in line with the definition of their sexual symbolism already formulated in the first stanza.[39] This is in keeping with the Homeric qualities of water as a purifier but also as a means and marker of transformation. Moreover, the verb κελάδει can be seen as an oblique reference to Artemis, whose special epithet in Homer is κελαδενή (sounding).[40] This lexical connection to Artemis again points out the particular virgin quality of the purity inherent in the landscape and in the image of flowing water (as well as expected of those entering the holy precinct), which was more vaguely expressed in the first stanza.[41]

The roses that cast their shadow on earth recall with their erotic implication[42]—which also other flowers can have—the scene in Il. 14. 347f. where lotus, crocus and hyacinth spring up under Zeus and Hera as they make love. The floral imagery reappears coupled with sweet breezes in the third stanza, but because of textual corruption the exact nature of these flowers remains unknown.[43] As it is the horse-rearing meadow expands on the rosy earth of the previous stanza. Even if it cannot be attested whether Sappho modelled her account on the famous Homeric passage, the fact that this passage is the only epic occurrence of extensive floral imagery in an erotic setting suggests the parallel.[44] The Homeric parallel makes it evident where Sappho's originality lies: roses do not occur in Homer except in the adjective ῥοδοδάκτυλον,[45] and the idea of the shadow is also alien to Homer apart from the formulaic description of how the dusk falls.[46] Sappho's garden of love preserves the already Homeric idea of the flowery meadow of love but gives it a distinctly new colouring to mark the difference between her concept of pure and virgin love and the Homeric sexual union of the two gods.

The κῶμα, i. e. the state of total relaxation comes in Sappho's poem from the quivering leaves. Because of its association with the paradise-like garden of love, the Sapphic κῶμα is easily identified with the pleasant state of slumber (Il. 14.359) that covers Zeus after he has made love to Hera. The passage in the Odyssey where Athena covers Penelope with κῶμα (18. 201) also has erotic implications: Penelope is made more appealing to the suitors in her slumber. The positive connotation of the word seems to be retained in Sappho's poem: indeed Burnett has suggested that κῶμα suggests the consummation of love in Sappho's garden.[47] Since κῶμα in the Iliad follows Zeus' lovemaking and can be ultimately traced back to Aphrodite, it seems plausible to suggest that the κῶμα in Sappho's poem has an erotic flavor and is connected to Aphrodite. But κῶμα can be a negative occurrence as well. Wiesmann has suggested that the threatening side of κῶμα is already present in the verb καλύπτω which in Homer describes the onset

of κῶμα but also the coming of death.[48] Hesiod (Theog. 798) speaks about a bad κῶμα that seizes the god who breaks his or her oath on Styx. The god can be revived from this state of paralysis only by nectar.

The link between κῶμα and nectar brings us to the last stanza of Sappho's fr. "2." Aphrodite is finally addressed, named, and asked to gently pour nectar with her golden cups among the festivities. Just as the gods in Hesiod could be awakened from coma and Hector's corpse in the Iliad 19.379 saved from putrefaction with nectar, it could be suggested that Aphrodite in Sappho's poem pours out nectar to ward off the possible bad effects of κῶμα. We need not take the nectar as an antidote against κῶμα itself,[49] whose pleasant nature is suggested by the setting and the parallel in the Iliad and from which no rescue is needed. Rather we can see Aphrodite using the nectar against the wrong kind of κῶμα, which might even result from a flawed sexual union,[50] but also to bring the notion of the divine, immortal and eternally young among the festivities. Nectar belongs to the gods, and this notion of divine is further confirmed by the presence of the golden cups with which Aphrodite pours the nectar. The golden quality which is associated with Aphrodite's dwellings in Olympus in Sappho fr. "1."8 is in Homer often connected to other gods as well, as Page's note on the passage shows.[51] Thus Sappho makes it explicit that the participants of the ritual in the holy grove would by association acquire godlike qualities. These qualities were already suggested in the first stanza and elaborated in the second and third by paralleling the landscape of love to which initiated mortals can gain entry with that of Zeus and Hera in the Iliad. Here the theme grows into a vivid image of the consummation of the ritual which culminates in the realization of the godlike qualities in the beneficiaries of the Sapphic garden of love.

Notes

1. Generally, M. Treu, *Von Homer zur Lyrik* (Zetemata 12), 1955, 136ff. passim. On the use of formulae E. Risch, MH 3, 1946 and more recently, F. Ferrari, "Formule saffiche e formule omeriche", *Ann. Scu. Norm. Sup. di Pisa* XVI, 1986, 441-447. For an excellent study on a Homeric expression in Sappho fr. 2, see P. Wiesman, "Was heisst koma?", in *MH [Mediaevalia et Humanistica]* 29, 1972.

2. L. Rissman, *Love as War: Homeric Allusion in the Poetry of Sappho* (Beiträge zur klassischen Philologie 157), 1983.

3. Rissman 1983, 15.

4. Ibid. 14.

5. I have followed the text established by D. Page, *Sappho and Alcaeus. An Introduction to the Study of Ancient Lesbian Poetry*, 1955, 34. For older

literature (mostly dealing with textual problems), see his notes at 35, for structural analysis, 39ff. Page's text is followed closely by D. Campbell, *Greek Lyric Poetry,* 1982, repr. 1990, 41-42. For further textual problems reference has also been made to the detailed study of the poem by G. Lanata in *Studi italiani di filologia classica* 1960, 64-90, to the edition by Eva-Maria Voigt (*Sappho et Alcaeus,* 1971, 33-35) and to the article by C. Gallavotti (L'ode saffica dell'ostracon, *Bolletino dei Classici* ser. 3, fasc. 1, 1980, 3ff.). On questions of completeness and the identification of the genre, T. McEvilley, "Sappho Fragment Two," *Phoenix* 26, 1972, 323ff. Further H. Saake, *Sappho Studien,* 1972, 62ff. The poem has been studied relatively little recently. The latest major account by A. P. Burnett, *Three Archaic Poets: Archilochus, Alcaeus, Sappho,* 1983, 259ff. is indispensable for textual problems, interpretation and bibliography.

6. Whether the fragmentary line (numbered 1a by Voigt 1971, 33) that begins the text of the ostracon actually belongs to the poem is a vexed question. Page 1955, 35 points out that the text as it stands cannot belong to the ending of a Sapphic stanza, although the copyist is careless to the extent that it is difficult to assume anything on the basis of the metrical distortion. Burnett 1983, 261, note 86 evaluates earlier solutions rightly emphasizing the inconclusive nature of the evidence. The solutions to the problem ranging from the rather ambitious attempt to reconstruct a complete first stanza by Theiler and von der Mühll (Das Sapphogedicht auf der Scherbe, *MH* 3, 1946, 22ff.) to the complete rejection of line 1a Voigt (e.g. McEvilley 1972) have to remain tentative. At any rate the problems of metre and dialect that line 1a presents make it likely that it does not belong to the poem and that line 1 indeed represents the beginning. See further M. West, *Maia* 22, 1970, 315ff. and A. Rivier *MH* 5, 1948, 227ff.

7. Apart from δεῦρυ the interpretation of the first line is extremely uncertain. Most scholars have contended that the line contains a mention of Crete or Cretans (e.g. Page 1955, 36), but this has been contested. See Burnett 1983, 262, note 87 and Gallavotti 1980, p. 5f. for different theories. Gallavotti proposes a solution that would turn the word +κρητεσι+ (this reading by Lanata 1960) into a third person of the verb κρετημι = κρατέω and consequently would do away with the cletic element of the first line. This solution seems hardly tenable, however, in view of the fact that it presupposes the existence of an atematic κρετημι, not conclusively proven by the existence of the

aorist infinitive κρετησαι in Sappho fr. 20, and for the extremely corrupt state of the text here that makes emendations more or less conjectural. Moreover, if we indeed assume that this line begins the poem, we would except a call of some sort upon Aphrodite, whose identity is subsequently revealed in the fourth stanza.

8. Here the form ναῦον adopted by Page 1955, 34 and Voigt 1971, 33 seems to be preferable to the word ἐναῦλον proposed by Gallavotti 1980, 5, note 4, since the latter needs a heavier and more controversial emendation, especially the addition of the beginning epsilon of which there is hardly any trace on the ostracon.

9. Aphrodite's arrival at her precinct in Paphos in *Od.* 8. 362-6 and *H. Ven.* 59-63, the advent of Zeus at his shrine in Ida in *Il.* 8. 47-48 and the description of the shrine of the river god Spercheus in Il. 23. 148 (with ὅθι τοι).

10. The association of Charites and sexual love is more clearly developed in Hesiod than in Homer, and is likely to have sprung from their intimate association with Aphrodite. See Hes. *Theog.* 907ff., with comments in M. West's commentary (Hesiod, *Theogony,* 1966). For the coupling of Aphrodite and Charis, Hes *Op.* 65f: καὶ χάριν ἀμφιχέαι κεφαλῆ χρυσῆν Ἀφροδίτην / καὶ πόθον ἀργαλέον καὶ γυιοβόρους μελεδῶνας.

11. Second person address appears in Homer with the formula in *Il.* 23. 148 when Achilles addresses the river god. As for Sappho it should be noted that τοι is added in the lacuna by Page 1955, followed by Campbell 1982, 41, omitted by Voigt 1971 and Lanata 1960. Perhaps the existence of τοι in the Homeric formula gives some authority to Page's emendation, although it is unlikely that Sappho makes reference to Achilles' address to the river god.

12. Probably the educated reader will have been able to supply Aphrodite's name by reference to the Homeric parallel, but Sappho still leaves room for ambiguity, which is not dissolved until in the last stanza. The reasons for this will be discussed below.

13. Cf. Alc. 34a L.-P., where Castor and Polydeuces are invoked with a mention of their name, common haunt and genealogy.

14. On ναός see W. Burkert, *Greek Religion,* 1985, 88f.

15. *Od.* 21. 258-9 (ἑορτὴ τοῖο θεοῖο ἀγνή); H. *Merc.* 187 (ἄλσος). Cf. Pindar *Pyth.* 4. 204 (τέμενος), Aisch. *Suppl.* 223 (ἐν ἀγνῷ) "on holy ground".

16. Artemis is often styled ἀγνή, e.g. *Od.* 5. 123; 18. 202; 20. 71, Persephone and Demeter less frequently: *Od.* 11. 386, H. Cer. 337 (Persephone), H. Cer. 203; 439 (Demeter). What Demeter's virginity consisted of is harder to assess. Perhaps she could be seen as a defender of Persephone's virginity, as she in the Homeric Hymn to Demeter tries to save her from Hades, who by abducting her when she is still a maiden threatens (and finally conquers) her virginity.

17. Burkert 1985, 270f. with bibliography.

18. R. Parker, *Miasma, Pollution and Purification in Early Greek Religion,* 1983, 147.

19. E. Williger, *Hagios, Religionsgeschichtliche Versuche und Vorarbeiten* 19.1, 1922, 37ff. This is also the opinion of B. Gentili, *Poesia e Pubblico nella Grecia antica da Omero al V secolo,* 1984, 287f. He argues that the sense "ritually pure" develops for ἀγνός only after the archaic period, but his evidence is inconclusive. For instance it is very hard to assess whether in the passage of Simonides (fr. 577a P) that he cites the prevalent notion of lustral water is that of reverence or purity. In fact both aspects seem to be equally present.

20. Burkert 1985, 150, with bibliography. On Artemis' special relation with nature and growth see e.g. the ample evidence collected by K. Wernicke in *RE* (*Revue d'Esthetique*] 2, 1342f. (Artemis). In Homer ἄλσος is favored especially by the nymphs, so that the notion is already attached to the expression (e.g. Il. 20.8) Compare Athena's ἄλσος in Od. 6. 291, which in its structure is close enough to have served as a possible model for Sappho's description of the grove. Athena's ἄλσος contains a spring (κρήνη, cf. the second stanza in Sappho fr. 2), a meadow, a holy precinct (τέμενος) and lush vegetation, i.e. the elements of a hallowed *locus amoenus* that make up Sappho's garden. Athena's grove suggest virginity and Treu 1955, 213 in fact thinks that the inclusion of sexuality by the description of a holy grove as χάριεν seems to be a Sapphic innovation. See the chapter below on this question.

21. Saake 1972, 63: "Diese Erweiterung gipfelt einerseits in der Wahrnehmung der Charis des ganzen Menschen, anderseits in dem Wiederfinden eben dieser Eigenschaft in den natural objects in der Landschaft und Pflanzenwelt".

22. Ibycus 7 calls the beloved Eurualos Χαρίτων θάλος. Furthermore χάρις is according to Page 1955, 36 used by the Lesbian poets only of personal charm. If this indeed was so, Sappho's use of the word to describe nature must have sounded striking and given the grove an immediate ambivalence between nature and man. The grove could indeed be understood to refer not in the first place to nature but symbolically to human physis and emotion. Burnett 1982, 263-4, note 90, in fact emphasizes that the natural scene in fr. 2 is not natural at all with roses blooming and apples maturing at the same time. This can be seen as a confirmation of the symbolic character of the landscape and as a way to show that this is no ordinary garden but rather divine place where the rotation of seasons is no object.

23. Evidence on the exclusion of sexuality from cult is collected and interpreted by Parker 1983, 74ff.

24. Evidence on meadows and love has been gathered in the monumental work by A. Motte, *Prairies et Jardins de la Grèce antique* (Academie Royale de Belgie, Mém. Classe des Lettres, 61.5, 1973), see especially 147ff. For a more succinct treatment and evidence on the theme meadows and sexuality, see now J. M. Bremer, "The Meadow of Love and Two Passages in Euripides' *Hippolytus*," *Mnemosyne* 28, 1975, 268ff, especially 271 that compares Sappho 2, "Ibycus" 5 and Eur. *Hipp.* 73ff. without noticing, however, how different the Sapphic ναῦον ἄγνον is from what Ibycus and Euripides describe only with the adjective ἀκήρατος.

25. The bibliography to the song of Demodocus (*Od.* 8. 266-369) is very large. For older literature see W. Burkert, "Das Lied von Ares und Aphrodite," *RM* [*Rhenische Museum*] 103, 130ff. and for a recent commentary and additional literature, see now J.B. Hainsworth's commentary (Omero, Odissea, vol. II, 1987, 269ff.).

26. Hephaestus calls the adulterous affair at 307 ἔργα γελατὰ καὶ οὐκ ἐπιεικτὰ, ridiculous and intolerable deeds, which neatly summarizes the tenor of Demodocus' song.

27. Parker 1983, 19 aptly states that "Without purification there is no access to the sacred". His account following this statement (in fact all of the first chapter [Purification: a Science of Division] of his book) well demonstrates the centrality of lustrations before dealing with the sacred and how purification was a liminal marker between the sacred and the profane. Older evidence is presented by M. P. Nilsson, *Geschichte der Griechischen Religion* I, 1951, 102, with more detail in L. Moulinier, *Le pur et l'impur dans la pensée des Grecs d'Homère à Aristote,* 1952, 71ff. For an expert study on bathing, see now R. Ginouvès, *Balaneutiké, recherches sur le bain dans l'antiquité grecque,* 1968.

28. Note also that Aphrodite at 82 approaches Anchises in the guise of a virgin maiden. Thus the idea of purification and virginity is already suggested in the hymn.

29. This is a striking modification by Sappho of the usual purpose of purification before cult and sacrifice. Normally the celebrant would exclude sexuality altogether while practising the cult and symbolize the exclusion by ritual washing, but in Sappho sexuality in a form defined by purity is an integral element of the cult.

30. A comparison between the celebrants of Aphrodite and priestesses seems justified since Sappho's grove is clearly a place for cult. Virgin priestesses are best attested for Artemis, see E. Fehrle, *Die kultische Keuschheit im Altertum* (Religionsgeschichtliche Versuche und Vorarbeiten 6), 98ff. More in Burkert 1985, 150 and Parker 1983, 90f. who finds the evidence on virgin priests and priestesses (especially for those of Demeter) difficult to interpret and stresses the idea that the abstinence from sex in cult was more often occasional than absolute.

31. This mood is again contrasted to other forms of erotic self-expression, as the idea of separation inherent in the term ἄγνον and expressed in the Homeric passages describing Aphrodite's bath shows. Therefore it does not seem plausible to see Sappho allowing any broad spectrum of eroticism in her poem, but instead a restricted form of sexuality. Compare Sappho fr. 94 L.-P.where the locality of the past (homosexual) love seems to have included something holy (25: ἴρον) and a grove (27: ἄλσος), that is, the basic setting of eroticism present in fr. 2 as well.

32. Burnett 1982, 266ff. By not considering the Homeric parallels she nevertheless misses the subtle way Sappho already in the first stanza creates and dissolves the ambiguity by a masterly play with the Homeric passages.

33. Burkert 1985, 150f. He notes that Artemis' virginity is not asexuality, but the evidence he has gathered pertains more to her following than to the goddess herself. At any rate even her followers always fall victim to rape rather than have erotic adventures out of their own will. No such sexual intrusions can be found in Sappho 2. Nevertheless Burkert's idea of Artemis and sexuality is interesting in this context, as Sappho could be seen in her way to make good of such potential when she combines purity and sexuality. But the fact that the ἄγνον quality of the temple is respected excludes sexual excesses such as rape and abduction.

34. Burnett 1982, 269.

35. Burnett, 1982, 266.

36. Burnett 1982, 263. Saake 1972, 62ff. thinks that the topographical Ekphrasis replaces the Aretalogie that would have been at place in a cletic hymn. For more on this type of Ἀφροδίτη ἐν κήποις in art, see E. Langlotz, *Aphrodite in den Gärten*, 1954.

37. For more, see Nilsson 1951, 90.

38. Nilsson 1951, 102. Nilsson emphasizes that only water in motion is suitable. This makes one think of the verb κελάδει in Sappho's poem.

39. Sappho fr. 105a provides an interesting parallel. The apple on the bough-top is not accessible to pickers and can be only seen. In fr.2 the apple is not only accessible but also defined by its association with the image of purity. The contrast between the actively pursuing apple-pickers in 105a and the passive reception of love in fr. 2 is also notable: love, the gift of Aphrodite, comes when it is mature and the setting is suitable for its enjoyment. J. Winkler, *The Constraints of Desire: The Anthropology of Sex and Gender in Ancient Greece,* 1990, 183f. thinks the apple in fr. 105a is an image of the secure and unattainable nature of female sexuality which men cannot fully know or understand. Winkler's notion of the exclusivity and special nature of female sexuality in fr. 105a goes well with the general tone of fr. 2, although in fr. 105a the image of the apple ripening represents existing but not fully ready sexuality, whereas in fr. 2 sexuality is an active presence in an erotic landscape.

40. Artemis is styled κελαδεινή in Il. 16, 183; 20, 70; 21, 510; H. Ven. 16; 118; H. Diana 27. The scholiasts suggested that the name suggested the barking of his dogs, but neglected the connection of the term to images of nature and landscape.

41. The virgin quality of the landscape need again not be understood to exclude all but virgins, but should rather be seen to point out the female exclusivity of the sexual landscape. The water that flows through the apple-branches is not only a boundary between the pure and the stained, but also an active purifier that can create a sexual status suitable for the Sapphic temple and garden of Aphrodite.

42. Burnett 1982, 263, n. 89.

43. See further Page 1955, 38.

44. See E. S. Forster, 'Trees and Plants in Homer', *CR* [*Classical Review*] 50, 1936, 100. Cf. D. A. Campbell, *The Golden Lyre,* 1983, 3.

45. Forster 1936, 100.

46. Treu 1955, 213ff.

47. Burnett 1982, 272f.

48. Wiesmann 1972, 3ff.

49. Burnett 1982, 274 thinks that nectar revives the participants of the ritual from their coma.

50. In *Il.* 14.216f. Hera prepares to trick Zeus into bed with her so she can work freely while Zeus slumbers. It should be noted that most of Sappho's Homeric parallels serve to define the concept of love and sexuality peculiar to fragment 2.

51. Page 1955 7 n. 8. Rissman 1983, 2 notes that the adjective χρυσέη is applied to Aphrodite ten times in Homer.

Paul Allen Miller (essay date spring 1993)

SOURCE: Miller, Paul Allen. "Sappho 31 and Catullus 51: The Dialogism of Lyric." *Arethusa*, 26, no. 2 (spring 1993): 183-99.

[*In the following essay, Miller applies a Bakhtinian theory of lyric dialogism to Sappho's fragment number "31" and Catullus's translation of this poem, in order to suggest that the two works reflect radically different genres of composition.*]

Mikhail Bakhtin, in "Discourse in the Novel," formulates what seems an ironclad distinction between poetic and novelistic discourse. Poetry, he argues, is essentially "monologic" and strives for a unity of discourse, "so that the finished work may rise as unitary speech, one co-extensive with its object." The novel, on the other hand, is "dialogic," representing a multiplicity of voices, not only through its characters, but also in its style, ideology, and representation of society.[1] This distinction, while provisionally useful for establishing what is unique to novelistic discourse, offers an ultimately unsatisfying account of dialogism's role in literature as a whole, and poetry in particular. To remedy this problem and thereby deploy the considerable power of Bakhtin's theoretical insights for a more satisfying account of the poetic as well as the novelistic, this paper will propose that a further distinction be made between primary and secondary dialogism. Such a distinction, as Caryl Emerson and Gary Saul Morson have pointed out, is implicit in Bakhtin from the beginning, though never made explicit.[2] This failure on Bakhtin's part to distinguish between the various but related ways in which he uses the terms *dialogue, dialogism,* and *dialogic* has, in turn, become the source of no small amount of confusion.

From this perspective, the term *primary dialogism* refers to that interplay of voices and concepts which is found in realist fiction and daily life. It designates that set of relations which governs the exchange of complete "utterances" between individuals, social groups, and/or their fictional representatives: the utterance being, as Bakhtin defines it, the basic unit of speech, delimited not by the sentence, the proposition or the paragraph, but by the completion of one speech act by one speaker and the beginning of a second by another.[3] Primary dialogism, thus, represents that font of social and linguistic interaction from which the larger and more abstract phenomenon of secondary dialogism springs.

This latter phenomenon, which results from the speaker's simultaneous response to past and anticipation of future utterances, every time (s)he speaks, represents that more subtle level of dialogical interaction which occurs not only within utterances, but even within individual words. For every word we use carries with it the sights, sounds, and smells, the social and rhetorical contexts of its previous uses.[4] Thus as Bakhtin points out in his Dostoevsky book, even soliloquies are in essence dialogic. Clearly, this latter form of dialogism can be found in poetry as well as prose.[5] Indeed, Bakhtin admits as much in a later essay, "The Problem of the Text in Linguistics, Philology, and the Human Sciences":

> Is not any writer (even the pure lyricist) always a "dramaturge" in the sense that he directs all words to others' voices, including to the image of the author (and to other authorial masks)? Perhaps any literal, single-voiced word is naive and unsuitable for authentic creativity. Any truly creative voice can only be the *second* voice in the discourse. Only the second voice— *pure relationship*—can be completely objectless and not cast a figural shadow.[6]

My argument is that we can use this concept of secondary dialogism to help clarify the differences between a lyric designed for oral performance and a lyric of the book, that the concept of dialogism in its broadest form can make us see that these are in fact two very different genres of composition. To illustrate this thesis I will examine the work of two representative poets, Sappho and Catullus, and will take as a basis of comparison Sappho **"31"** and its translation, Catullus 51. By looking at these two poems, which are in some ways practically identical but were produced in and for radically different dialogical situations, I hope to demonstrate the validity of this distinction between the two forms of dialogism and its usefulness in making generic discriminations. The crucial determinant in this investigation will be the establishment of the radically different contexts of utterance which characterize these two texts.

We can begin by imagining the setting for which Sappho's poetry was first intended. It is now widely accepted that the primary mode of diffusion, if not composition, for Sappho's poetry was oral performance, inasmuch as there was virtually no book trade in Greece until the late fifth century.[7] Such performances imply, in turn, a certain anticipation of how the poem's addressees would have received it. For utterances are always other-directed, and this is particularly so in the case of public artistic performances where the audience is immediately present. Such poems are of necessity communal events, rather than closeted confessions. Each new performance is a separate utterance, indissolubly linked to the moment of enunciation and so forever reinforcing the radically occasional nature of archaic lyric.[8]

Moreover, as Bakhtin points out, the ways these anticipations of an audience's response structure a text, and ultimately its interpretation, constitute the dialogic situation staged by that text and serve to distinguish one literary genre from another.[9] Thus, to understand a poem such as Sappho "31," the reader must begin by asking what sort of performative context would have been required for such a work to have had a public meaning on the island of Lesbos; that is to say, on what sort of occasion could such a poem have been appropriately sung to a public which was well acquainted with the poet, and indeed constituted her friends, neighbors, and potential political allies and enemies in this small island community?[10] This is very different from the question posed by the traditional romantic understanding of lyric: what is the poet trying to express? In a dialogic analysis, it is the relation of "responsive understanding" between poet and public which is foregrounded.[11]

The most obvious performative context which comes to mind for Sappho "31" is a song performed for a wedding, since it is difficult to imagine many other occasions when a man and woman would be publicly seated together in close converse, in Lesbos' sexually segregated society. Indeed "31" is the sole text in Sappho's corpus to show a woman and a man in an intimate conversation.[12] This interpretation of the poem was, of course, standard up until the mid-fifties, having been first advanced by Wilamowitz and later vigorously defended by Snell.[13] In 1955, it was to many people's minds decisively refuted by Page, who termed it a "theory . . . based on nothing but a preconceived notion about Sappho's moral character." Kirkwood, thus, refers to Page's having "demolished" a view which could only appeal to the "sentimentally inclined," and which was designed to repress Sappho's homoeroticism.[14] Yet such an indictment is little more than an *ad hominem* attack, and in this reader's case it is applicable neither on the count of sentimentality nor of homophobia. More importantly, McEvilley has persuasively shown that both Snell's and Wilamowitz's major theses

were more correct than even they realized. He makes three major points: first, the term *anêr* ("man") in Sappho always refers to a husband; second, the direct comparison with a god only occurs in marriage poems; and third, Lesbos in all the surviving literature would appear to have been so sexually segregated as not to have allowed the sort of public interaction between a man and woman portrayed in the poem, except in the context of marriage.[15] Ruth Neuberger-Donath has also demonstrated, by using comparative evidence gathered from the Homeric poems, that any time a man and woman are shown to be sitting *enantios* to one another, they are necessarily *philos* to one another. It can thus be assumed, she concludes, that the couple celebrated in Sappho's poem were in fact man and wife, and probably recently so.[16]

This reading is also a tempting solution because Sappho wrote numerous epithalamia and, as Judith Hallet has noted, the social function of her verse would appear to have been that of preparing the young women of Lesbos for their communally sanctioned roles.[17] Likewise Gregory Nagy has recently argued that Sappho's role as a singer was that of a *khoregos,* a publicly sanctioned poet/educator comparable to Alcman in his "Partheneia":

> To say that Sappho is an "educator" is a prosaic way of saying that her assumed role, through her lyric poetry, is that of *khoregos,* "chorus leader," speaking both to and about members of an aggregate of female characters who are bound together by ties that correspond to the ties that bind a chorus together.

Her expression and probable practice of homoerotic love was thus, like that of her male counterparts, a form of *paideia,* not the public expression of a private desire.[18]

It is, of course, impossible to prove whether this poem was actually sung at a wedding(s) or not, but the attempt to formulate a response to the question of the poem's performative context goes a long way towards elucidating the concrete nature of its dialogical situation. For it makes clear the radically different nature of Sappho's poetry from the vastly more privatized verse which is read and written today. Moreover, as of yet, there have been no other satisfactory performative contexts envisioned, and those who have opposed this interpretation have generally chosen to ignore the question altogether, leading to anachronistic interpretations in which Sappho is read more as an author composing books of poetry, than as an archaic singer performing orally before her peers.[19]

At all events, the poem can hardly have been intended to be heard by the citizens of Lesbos as a purely personal confession. Its focus is not the *moi,* but the *toi* and the *kenos.*[20] The initial naming complex concentrates not on the speaking voice's ego, but on that of the addressees: "This man seems equal to the gods, that sits opposite you and listens close by to your sweet voice." Likewise the feelings of the speaking subject are only present to the extent that they can be directly expressed in an objectified and externalizing catalogue of symptoms.[21] In fact the poetic ego, through its enactment of a universalizing symptomology, functions as an analogue to the central mythic section of a Pindaric ode. It renders public and understandable a unique experience which otherwise would be purely personal and thus meaningless to the public at large. As Kirkwood says, "Sappho used herself as the illustrative equivalent of a simile or myth."[22] We find out next to nothing about the poet herself, or the persona she wishes to project; instead, we are invited to marvel at the devastating effect of the woman's beauty, even as this unnamed, godlike man sits before her, seemingly unfazed. What we have is a poem of praise, directed in the first instance to the young woman and in the second to the man sitting across from her.[23]

If, however, we examine Catullus' translation of this same poem, the dialogical relation has changed. First, Catullus no longer thinks in terms of communal occasions, but in terms of private readers or intimate friends.[24] Second, the poem now not only gains its meaning from its relation to its audience, but also from its relation to other poems in the corpus. These poems provide the primary context in which the individual poem is to be understood. Our vision of Lesbia and Catullus is unalterably modified by our knowledge of these other poems, and thus the poem itself is in constant dialogue not only with its readers, but with the other poems of the collection. It is, in fact, this intertextual quality of Catullus' work that gives it that sense of intimacy which all readers perceive. We seem ever to be eaves-dropping on the poet in dialogue with himself, but that dialogue is infinite because it is always being reshaped and remodelled by our own reading of the corpus.[25]

Aside from the final stanza of Catullus 51, it and its Sapphic model appear to be substantially alike, except for the seemingly minor difference that Catullus names his addressee Lesbia.[26] Now, there is no great mystery as to whom the name Lesbia referred. Apuleius tells us (*Apology* 10) that it was a woman named Clodia, who is generally thought to have been either Clodia Metelli or one of her sisters. A more important question, though, is: what is the poetic significance of this particular pseudonym? The answer is twofold. First, and most obviously, *Lesbia* is the metrical equivalent of *Clodia,* so that if Catullus chose to circulate a private manuscript, the actual name could have been easily substituted. Second, and more important for our purposes, *Lesbia* is also the Latin adjective denoting a woman

from Lesbos, in this context obviously Sappho.[27] In Sappho's original, however, she is the one who is tongue-tied. Likewise she is the singer of the poem, not its recipient. Yet in Catullus' version, the woman named with an adjective which alludes to Sappho is in the opposite position. She is now the object, not the subject. She is the woman sung about, not the singer.[28] There has been an inversion of roles, which as we shall see will have reverberations throughout the collection, and which necessarily calls the poet's double relation to both his reading public and his predecessors into question. For each of these relations is now mediated by the other and can only be understood from within the other's perspective. The poem is neither a simple presentation of an event to the reading public, nor a univocal reproduction of Sappho's original, but a complex mixture of both, situated within the larger context of Catullus' portrayal of the affair as a whole.

The point is a somewhat obvious one, though it has yet to be fully considered. For, in the very act of self-consciousness this alteration supposes, Catullus' poem comes to transcend the moment of its enunciation and enters into a new and more complex series of dialogic relations which ultimately center around the multi-voiced and often conflicting intentions of the Catullan poetic ego as they are revealed in poem 51's relations with the other poems in the collection.[29] There is, then, in this one name, *Lesbia,* a measure of conscious reflexivity, which is utterly alien to Sappho's original. This seemingly innocent substitution of *Lesbia* for *Clodia* opens a whole range of questions about artistic intent and self-conscious intertextuality which would be unimaginable in Sappho's predominantly oral culture.

Are we for example to assume, given the use of the name *Lesbia* in the context of a poem by Sappho, that there is a reciprocity of symptoms between Catullus and his beloved, so that not only Catullus is Sappho, but also the woman who bears the Sapphic epithet? Or has there been a mere inversion of roles? From the beginning we are in a quandary as to what precise roles Catullus and Lesbia/Clodia/Sappho are going to play, and as to what levels of conscious intent the triple-faceted object of Catullus' desire corresponds. Moreover, what does it mean to send Lesbia/Sappho a reinscription of her own poem into another language, another alphabet, especially when this Lesbia/Sappho is only Sappho and not Clodia through a trick of orthography, through a private code made possible by writing? No simple answers can be supplied to these questions. But what is interesting is the fact that we have now entered into a new genre of poetry whose radically different context of enunciation makes those questions not only possible, but necessary. For they show we are now in a complex and sophisticated world of literary allusions, artistic self-consciousness, and psychological ambiguity, a cosmopolitan and Hellenistic world alien to the predominantly oral culture of archaic Lesbos.

Nonetheless, this reading of 51 has only scratched the surface of the complexities and circuitous routes of responsive understanding this poem contains. For, in this same alteration of Sappho's original can also be seen still another motif of Catullus' poetry, which can be tracked throughout the collection, and which constitutes one of the primary thematic elements organizing it as a whole: that of sex-role reversal.[30] A precise parallel to Catullus' intertextual alteration of expected sex-roles in 51 can thus also be seen in poem 70's relation to its original, Callimachus' eleventh epigram, wherein the passive and active roles played by Catullus and Lesbia respectively in 70 are reversed in Callimachus' original.[31] There the man, Callignotis, is active, and the girl, Ionis, is passive. Likewise, in poem 68, Catullus compares his own need to overlook Lesbia's infidelities with that of Juno's ignoring the *omnivoli plurima furta Jovis*.[32] And this thematic element of the collection, in turn, can be seen as adding yet another ironic level to Catullus' use of the name Lesbia for Clodia, inasmuch as it was widely thought in antiquity (probably correctly) that Sappho was a Lesbian in both senses of the word. As such, she could have easily been thought of as usurping the masculine role (did not Horace refer to her as *mascula Saffo*?), and hence within the binary logic of conventional Roman sexual relations: if Catullus was on the receiving end of Lesbia's infidelities, he would thus naturally be in the woman's or at least the effeminate position.[33]

Given the recurrent nature of this motif of sex-role reversal in the Catullan collection, it is perhaps not accidental that another important example of this same phenomenon can be found in the final strophe of poem 11, the only other poem in the collection written in Sapphic stanzas: "And let her not look for my love which has perished through her blame, just as a flower at the edge of the meadow when touched by the passing plough." And, as it turns out, the particular sex-role reversal found in the poem appears to be a direct imitation of still another fragment attributed to Sappho (105c), thus seeming to confirm the thesis that 11 and 51 are to be read as a diptych.[34] Yet there is more to this stanza than a simple imitation of Sappho, or another example of sex-role reversal. Indeed, by means of its brutal imagery, the reader gains admittance into a realm of associations, which lead him or her into the darkest and least conscious depths of the Catullan poetic ego, into images of mutilation and disease such as Attis' self-castration in 63, or 76's reference to the Lesbia affair as a *pernicies pestis*.[35] At the same time, however, through this double image of the flower destroyed by the plough, the collection demands still another even more complex reading, linking all these poems in a

further set of associations which ultimately produce an image of artistic self-consciousness and deliberate inter- and intratextuality unimaginable in an oral context; with the result that the reader has simultaneously a sense of being let into the secret reaches of the Catullan soul, even as (s)he recognizes that it is through that soul's conscious will to artistry that this very insight is possible.

The plough of poem 11's final stanza was of course a common symbol in ancient literature for the masculine phallus while the flower often signified an unmarried woman. Thus in Catullus' first epithalamium, for example, the bride is referred to as *flos* or *floridus* four separate times. Hence Catullus, in at least a figurative sense, portrays himself here as deflowered by the phallus of *mascula Lesbia*. Moreover, this same conjunction of images, the flower and the plough, is also found in Catullus' second epithalamium, where it is made unmistakably clear that the flower represents the still virgin bride-to-be, and the plough the ravishing male.[36] In addition, it will also be recalled that Sappho's poem "31," the original for Catullus 51, was itself probably created for a wedding, so that if Catullus could count on his readers recognizing the wedding background of Sappho's original, then the creation of an ironic contrast between 51 and 11, as poems of marriage and divorce, would have been evident. Thus Sappho herself, through her poetry and its various erotic themes, becomes the unifying subtext, uniting what have often been read as the first and last poems of the affair into a complex dialogical unity in which each poem's meaning is relativized by the reading of the other and by the way in which both of these poems are read by other texts in the collection, such as the epithalamia, the Attis, and poem 76's reflections on the affair as a *pernicies pestis*.[37] Yet the ironic relation obtaining between 11 and 51 is raised to an even higher power when it is seen that poem 11's imitation of Sappho (105c), which in 62 functions as a symbol of intact virginity, here is transformed into an image of Lesbia's insatiable lust.[38] Taken as a totality, this set of poems (11, 51, 61, 62, 63, 76) and their Sapphic recollections allude to the full range of Catullus' emotions, ranging from dumbstruck awe, to fear, loathing, and obsessive images of defloration and castration.

This complex set of both inter- and intratextual dialogical relations, in which Catullus 51 necessarily becomes embedded because of its role within the Catullan collection, would be unimaginable for its Sapphic original. Rather than illustrating the linear temporal movement of a performance which must first and foremost be construed in its immediate communal and cultural context, the Catullan poem becomes part of a complex dialogue which moves forward and backward within the Catullan collection itself, as well as back and forth between its literary sources. It is only from within this complex textual network that the individual poem then starts to refer to the larger world of Roman and Hellenistic culture in which it was produced. Each individual moment of the Catullan ego as presented within the collection becomes a dialogical nexus which communicates with all the others. In the Catullan corpus, the reader always participates in a multifaceted dialogue constituted first by the poems themselves and only secondarily by its reading public. Yet the limits of that dialogue can never be fully mapped, never completely exhausted. The process of rereading and interpretation within its bounds is ultimately infinite.[39] For a poetry of oral performance the process of interpretation is also, properly speaking, infinite, but the hermeneutic circle it describes is not in the first instance the internal dialogue of the poet, but his or her dialogue with both the (oral) poetic tradition and the collective ideological and social world in which it is performed.

Bakhtin's work, then, allows us to understand the difference between orally performed and written lyric more completely than previous theories have. For the concept of dialogism allows us to see that the primary focus of a work is its relation to its context, both performative and textual, and that written and orally performed texts must necessarily conceive of their contexts in radically different ways. Moreover, by distinguishing between primary and secondary dialogism, we have been able to maintain Bakhtin's concept of the unique nature of novelistic discourse—as allowing multiple, separate linguistic consciousnesses to come together in an ongoing, serious but relativizing play—while at the same time making use of Bakhtin's broader theoretical insights into the inherently dialogical nature of all language, genres, and consciousness, without being forced to see these phenomena as precursors of the novel.[40] Consequently, the concept of secondary dialogism allows the full range of Bakhtin's theoretical insights to be applied to ancient texts, rather than seeing them as primarily useful for the study of prose from Rabelais and the sixteenth century onward. Finally, this reading has shown that not only *can* we apply Bakhtin's concepts to ancient literature, but through them we are also able to make fine distinctions which allow us to see those texts in a new light. Therefore works which on the surface may appear to be closely related can be shown to pertain to radically different dialogical situations and thus to be different types of utterances. Hence, through the concept of secondary dialogism, we have been able to show that the poems of Sappho and Catullus, even when their semantic contents are all but identical, represent two quite separate genres of composition.

Notes

1. Bakhtin 1981.278, 284-88, 296-98, 300, 325-31. The importance of this distinction as well as its controversial nature have been pointed out by more than one critic. See Morson and Emerson 1989.53-54; de Man 1989.111; Roberts 1989.133 and Todorov 1984.64-67.

2. Morson and Emerson 1989.52-53. For Morson and Emerson's attempt to separate out the different senses of dialogism, from a different point of view, see 1990.49-62.

3. Bakhtin 1981.274-76, 282, 326, 332-33 and Morson and Emerson 1989.53. On the utterance as a complete verbal performance by one speaker which expects a reply from another, see Bakhtin 1986a.71-73, 82, 92-93; Todorov 1984.x and 43-44 and Volosinov 1986.94-96.

There is still considerable dispute over whether the texts originally published under the names of Volosinov and Medvedev were: a) in reality written by Bakhtin; b) heavily influenced by him; or c) rejoinders in a dialogue in which he was influenced by the others as much as he influenced them. All commentators agree, however, that there are numerous and striking similarities between the works of the members of the Bakhtin circle. The main areas in which there remain disputes about the compatibility of the theoretical positions elaborated in these works are: whether Bakhtin shared the latter two's Marxism; and whether Medvedev and Volosinov can be said to think in terms of closed, binary oppositions, while Bakhtin can be said to prefer open dialogized pairs. Neither of these problems has a direct bearing on my argument. Thus I shall consider the various works of the Bakhtin circle as all part of the same discourse, even if they were not all written by the same author. In my citations, I use the names under which the texts were published in English. For more views on this debate, see Morson and Emerson 1990.11, 77, 102, 104, 106-07, 111, 118-19, 124-25, 161-62, 479 ns. 6-7; Holquist 1990.8; Todorov 1984.11; Bakhtin/Medvedev 1985.vii and ix.

4. Bakhtin 1981.276-77, 279-80, 282, 293; 1984.73; Todorov 1984.48-49 and Volosinov 1986.19, 23. On the internal dialogism of individual words, see Bakhtin 1981.279 and Morson and Emerson 1990.138-39.

5. Bakhtin 1984.120; 1986a.93; Morson and Emerson 1990.49, 131, 143, 146.

6. Bakhtin 1986b.110. On the importance of this passage, see Roberts 1989.133-34 and Todorov 1984.68. On Bakhtin's wavering on the possibility of dialogism in lyric, see Morson and Emerson 1989.6 and 54-55. Tavis 1988.75 and 77 has

argued that Bakhtin in his early work "Toward a Philosophy of the Act," employs a dialogic method in his analysis of Pushkin's "For the Shores of Your Distant Country." Thus at the beginning and at the end of his career Bakhtin was more liberal in his granting of dialogic status to poetry than he was in the middle period of his work. Bakhtin's reading of the Pushkin poem can be found in 1990.208-31.

7. See Snyder 1989.17; Griffith 1989.60; Gentili 1985.3, 41, 75, 204-05; Hallet 1979.461-64; Segal 1974.139-40, 153; Russo 1973/74.709; Havelock 1982.17-20, 189; 1963.37-39, 43. On the lack of a substantial book trade in the sixth and seventh centuries, thus eliminating the only alternative mode by which Sappho's poetry could have been widely diffused, see Harris 1989.92-93, as well as 84-87.

8. Gentili 1985.52; Zumthor 1983.48, 56, 234; Winkler 1981.65; Finnegan 1977.129; Adkins 1972.5; Havelock 1963.46, 121, 182-83. On the unrepeatability of utterances, see Bakhtin 1986b.108 and Morson and Emerson 1990.126.

9. Bakhtin 1986a.60-65, 95-96; Bakhtin/Medvedev 1985.11, 130-31; Morson and Emerson 1990.129, 290; Todorov 1984.82.

10. Lasserre 1989.147. On Sappho's possible political problems, see the reference to her exile during the reign of the tyrant Pittacus, *Marm. Par.* Ep. 36 (p. 12 Jacoby), reprinted in Campbell 1982.8-9; on oral poetry's audience as a small, relatively homogeneous social group, see Zumthor 1983.40.

11. Bakhtin 1986a.95-96, 1984.87-88; Morson and Emerson 1990.129-30.

12. Griffith 1989.59. Race's statement (1989.31) that the situation presented at the beginning of 31 is "ordinary" is anachronistic in its assumption of routinized commerce between unrelated members of the opposite sex.

13. Wilamowitz 1966/1913.5; Snell 1931.71-90.

14. Page 1955.30-33; Kirkwood 1974.121-22; see also Snyder 1989.20.

15. McEvilley 1978.1-9. Lasserre 1989.150-51, argues persuasively against McEvilley's suggestion that the wedding scene evoked by the poem might be imaginary.

16. Neuberger-Donath 1977.199-200. Wiseman (1985.153) also accepts the Wilamowitz thesis, finding support for it in Catullus. For further corroborating views, see Griffith 1989.59-61; Lasserre 1989.149-52; Winkler 1981.73; Fränkel 1975.176 and Treu 1954.178-79.

17. Hallet 1979.450, 456, and 461-64. See also Gentili 1985.102-08; Calame 1977.396 and Segal 1974.141 and 153.

18. Nagy 1990.435 and 370-71, especially: "It should be clear that I understand the monodic form not to be antithetical to the choral but rather predicated on it. A figure like Sappho speaks as a choral personality, even though elements of dancing and the very presence of a choral group are evidently missing from her compositions. Still, these compositions presuppose or represent an interaction, offstage, as it were with a choral aggregate." This is another way of saying the performance implies an immediate and formalized dialogic relationship with the listening public. For more on Sappho's relation to Alcman and *paideia,* see Calame 1977.88, 126-27, 369, 421-34; Hallet 1979.463-64; Dover 1978.181; Lefkowitz 1981.51-52; Stigers 1981.45.

19. Thus Race 1983.92-93 argues that while Wilamowitz's wedding hypothesis solves the historical problem of the performative context it "creates a literary one," since the word *marriage* is never mentioned. But the dichotomy is false. Literary problems are always simultaneously historical ones, inasmuch as works of literature are profoundly dialogized utterances which presume a relation of responsive understanding between themselves and their audiences or reading publics. Literary questions are thus inevitably social and historical questions as well.

20. Snell 1953.52.

21. Page 1955.26-27; Fränkel 1975.176.

22. Kirkwood 1974.122; West 1970.314-15.

23. Burnett 1983.236; Lasserre 1989.157.

24. Wiseman 1982.38-39.

25. There remains disagreement over how much of Catullus' corpus was arranged by the author himself. Although there is more and more reason to believe Catullus arranged the collection as a whole, there is at minimum widespread belief that he arranged at least poems 1-51. My argument does not depend upon accepting any one schema of arrangement, but rather on the notion that we read the poems in terms of one another, and that the numerous cross-references between the poems and the use of repeated motifs show that they were meant to be read as a group, whether they were originally placed in the order we now have them or not.

On the consensus, that at least part of the present collection was arranged by the author, see Skinner 1988.337. Among those who believe the collection as a whole is the work of the poet are: Ellis 1979/1889.1-5, with some minor rearranging of 61-68; Wiseman 1985.136-37, 1969.30; Quinn 1972.9-20 and 38-50; Skinner 1988.338, n. 2, where she revises her claim (in 1981.passim) that only 1-51 were arranged by the author; Ferguson 1986.2; Minyard 1988.343-53; Dettmer 1988.371-81 and Arkins 1987.847-48.

26. For a recent discussion of the close relations between the two texts, see Vine 1992.251-58 and Wiseman 1985.152-53.

27. Fredricksmeyer 1983.69.

28. Skinner 1981.88.

29. Thus Fredricksmeyer (1983.66-68) has noted Catullus' use of the word *identidem* ("again and again, habitually") as one of the parallels linking poems 11 and 51. It has no analogue in Sappho's original and changes what was a particular occasion in the original into a constantly recurring one. Professor Charles Platter has pointed out to me that this adverb may also be making reference to the common recurrence of the adverb *deute* in archaic lyric. See Kirkwood 1974.112, 249, n. 23 and Sappho 1.

Note also Commager's interesting observation (1965.87): "Where [Sappho 31] has two verbs to describe the action of the girl and one for the spectator, Catullus reverses the emphasis, also adding the adjective *misero*. The alterations, admittedly minor, suggest that the poem will be even more self-centered than Sappho's."

30. Rubino 1975.294.

31. Page 1975.93.

32. For a fuller examination of these issues see Miller 1988.127-32.

33. *Epistles* 1.19.28, see also Porphyrio's commentary on this passage, reprinted in Campbell 1982.18-19. On the binary logic of conventional Roman sexual relations, see Wiseman 1985.10-14.

34. Quinn 1972.163; Duclos 1976.86.

35. For 76 as "a sort of summary and model for the entire elegiac and erotic segment of the Catullan oeuvre," including specific reminiscences of poem 51, see Rubino 1975.289; see also Wiseman 1985.170-71; Quinn 1972.102 and Commager 1965.97-98.

36. Ferguson 1985.44; Fredricksmeyer 1983.73; Putnam 1974.79-80. Poem 62.39-47: *Ut flos in saeptis secretus nascitur hortis,/ ignotus pecori, nullo convolsus aratro, / . . . sic virgo, dum intacta manet, dum cara suis est; / cum castum amisit polluto corpore florem,/ nec pueris iucunda manet, nec cara puellis.* ("As a solitary flower which has been born in a walled garden, unnoticed by the herd, and yet to be plucked by the plough . . . so the young maid, while she remains untouched, is dear to her family; yet once she has lost the chaste flower and her body is befouled, she remains neither a joy to the boys, nor dear to the girls.")

37. Ferguson 1988.14; Wiseman 1985.153; Duclos 1976.78; Quinn 1972.56.

38. Quinn 1972.162.

39. For an excellent reading of the temporal complexity of Catullus' poetry and how each new reading both builds on and surpasses all past readings, with particular reference to poem 11, see Sweet 1987.514, 522-23, and 526. Rereading is of course something only available in a literate poetic tradition.

40. Morson and Emerson 1990.9, 131, 155, 236-40, 307, 319-25, 328-30; Bakhtin 1984.87-88.

Bibliography

Adkins, A. H. W. 1972. "Truth, χόσμος, and ἀρετή in the Homeric Poems," *CQ* [*Classical Quarterly*] 22.5-18.

Arkins, Brian. 1987. "Callimachus and *Catulli Veronensis Liber,*" *Latomus* 46.847-48.

Bakhtin, M. M. 1981. "Discourse in the Novel," *The Dialogic Imagination: Four Essays by M. M. Bakhtin,* trans. Caryl Emerson and Michael Holquist, ed. Michael Holquist, pp. 258-422. Austin.

———1984. *Problems of Dostoevsky's Poetics,* ed. and trans. Caryl Emerson. Theory and History of Literature, vol. 8. Minneapolis.

———1986a. "The Problem of Speech Genres," *Speech Genres and Other Late Essays,* trans. Vern W. McGee, edd. Caryl Emerson and Michael Holquist, pp. 60-102. Austin.

———1986b. "The Problem of the Text in Linguistics, Philology, and the Human Sciences: An Experiment in Philosophical Analysis," *Speech Genres and Other Late Essays,* trans. Vern W. McGee, edd. Caryl Emerson and Michael Holquist, pp. 103-31. Austin.

———1990. *Art and Answerability: Early Philosophical Essays by M. M. Bakhtin,* trans. Vadim Lupanov and Kenneth Brostrom, edd. Lupanov and Michael Holquist. Austin.

Bakhtin, M. M./P. M. Medvedev. 1985. *The Formal Method in Literary Scholarship: A Critical Introduction to Sociological Poetics,* trans. Albert J. Wehrle. Cambridge, Mass.

Burnett, Anne Pippin. 1983. *Three Archaic Poets.* Cambridge, Mass.

Calame, Claude. 1977. *Les choeurs de jeunes filles en Grèce archaïque,* vol. 1. Rome.

Campbell, D. A. 1982. *Greek Lyric,* vol. I. Loeb Classical Library. Cambridge, Mass.

Commager, Steele. 1965. "Notes on Some Poems of Catullus," *HSCP* [*Harvard Studies in Classical Philology*] 70.83-110.

De Man, Paul. 1989. "Dialogue and Dialogism," in Morson and Emerson 1989, pp. 105-14.

Dettmer, Helena. 1988. "Design in the Catullan Corpus: A Preliminary Study," *CW* [*Classical World*] 81.5.371-81.

Dover, K. J. 1978. *Greek Homosexuality.* London.

Duclos, G. S. 1976. "Catullus 11: *Atque in perpetuum, Lesbia, ave atque vale,*" *Arethusa* 9.77-89.

Ellis, Robinson. 1979/1889. *A Commentary on Catullus.* New York.

Ferguson, John. 1985. *Catullus.* Lawrence, Kansas.

———1986. "The arrangement of Catullus' poems," *LCM* [*Liverpool Classical Monthly*] 11.1.2.

———1988. *Catullus. Greece and Rome: New Surveys in the Classics,* no. 20. Oxford.

Finnegan, Ruth. 1977. *Oral Poetry: Its Nature, Significance, and Social Context.* Cambridge.

Fränkel, Hermann. 1975. *Early Greek Poetry and Philosophy: A History of Greek Epic, Lyric, and Prose to the Middle of the Fifth Century,* trans. Moses Hadas and James Willis. Oxford.

Fredricksmeyer, E. A. 1983. "The Beginning and End of Catullus' *Longus Amor,*" *Symbolae Osloenses,* 58.63-88.

Gentili, Bruno. 1985. *Poesia e Pubblico nella Grecia Antica: Da Homero al V Secolo.* Rome.

Griffith, R. Drew. 1989. "In Praise of the Bride: Sappho Fr. 105(A) L-P, Voigt," *TAPA* [*Transactions of the American Philological Association*] 119.55-61.

Hallet, Judith P. 1979. "Sappho and her Social Context: Sense and Sensuality," *Signs* 4.447-64.

Harris, William V. 1989. *Ancient Literacy.* Cambridge, Mass.

Havelock, E. A. 1963. *Preface to Plato.* Cambridge, Mass.

———1982. *The Literate Revolution in Greece and Its Cultural Consequences.* Princeton.

Holquist, Michael. 1990. *Dialogism: Bakhtin and His World.* London.

Johnson, W. R. 1982. *The Idea of Lyric: Lyric Modes in Ancient and Modern Poetry.* Berkeley.

Kirkwood, G. M. 1974. *Early Greek Monody: The History of a Poetic Type.* Ithaca.

Lasserre, François. 1989. *Sappho: Une Autre Lecture.* Padua.

Lefkowitz, Mary. 1981. *Heroines and Hysterics.* New York.

McEvilley, Thomas. 1978. "Sappho, Fragment Thirty-One: The Face Behind the Mask," *Phoenix* 32.1-18.

Miller, Paul Allen. 1988. "Catullus, *C.* 70: A Poem and Its Hypothesis," *Helios* 15.127-32.

Minyard, John Douglas. 1988. "The Source of the *Catulli Veronensis Liber,*" *CW* 81.5.343-53.

Morson, Gary Saul and Caryl Emerson. 1989. "Introduction," *Rethinking Bakhtin: Extensions and Challenges,* pp. 1-60. Evanston, Illinois.

———1990. *Mikhail Bakhtin: Creation of a Prosaics.* Stanford.

Nagy, Gregory. 1990. *Pindar's Homer: The Lyric Possession of the Epic Past.* Baltimore.

Neuberger-Donath, Ruth. 1977. "Sappho 31.2s . . . ὄττις ἐνάντιός τοι / ἰσδάνει," *Acta Classica* 20.199-200.

Page, Denys. 1955. *Sappho and Alcaeus.* Oxford.

———1975. *Epigrammata Graeca.* Oxford.

Putnam, Michael C. J. 1974. "Catullus 11: The Ironies of Integrity," *Ramus* 3.70-86.

Quinn, Kenneth. 1972. *Catullus: An Interpretation.* London.

Race, William H. 1983. "'That Man' in Sappho Fr. 31 L-P," *CA* [*Classical Antiquity*] 2.92-101.

———1989. "Sappho, *FR.* 16 L-P. and Alkaios, *FR.* 42 L-P.: Romantic and Classical Strains in Lesbian Lyric," *CJ* [*Classical Journal*] 85.16-33.

Roberts, Mathew. 1989. "Poetics Hermeneutics Dialogics: Bakhtin and Paul de Man," in Morson and Emerson 1989, pp. 115-34.

Rubino, Carl A. 1975. "The Erotic World of Catullus," *CW* 68.289-98.

Russo, Joseph. 1973/74. "Reading the Greek Lyric Poets (Monodists)," *Arion* n.s. 1.707-30.

Segal, Charles. 1974. "Eros and Incantation: Sappho and Oral Poetry," *Arethusa* 7.139-60.

Skinner, Marilyn. 1981. *Catullus' Passer: The Arrangement of the Polymetric Poems.* Salem, New Hampshire.

————1988. "Aesthetic Patterning in Catullus: Textual Structures, Systems of Imagery and Book Arrangements, Introduction," *CW* 81.337-40.

Snell, Bruno. 1931. "Sapphos Gedicht φαίνεταί μοι χῆνος," *Hermes* 66.71-90.

————1953. *The Discovery of the Mind: The Greek Origins of European Thought,* trans. T. G. Rosenmeyer. New York.

Snyder, Jane McIntosh. 1989. *The Woman and the Lyre: Women Writers in Classical Greece and Rome.* Carbondale, Ill.

Stigers, Eva Stehle. 1981. "Sappho's Private World," *Reflections of Women in Antiquity,* ed. Helene P. Foley, pp. 45-61. New York.

Sweet, David R. 1987. "Catullus 11: A Study in Perspective," *Latomus* 46.510-26.

Tavis, Anna A. 1988. "Early 'Pushkinizm' as a Critical Dialogue: Bakhtin's and Zhirmunsky's Reading of Pushkin's 'For the Shores of Your Distant Country,'" *The Contexts of Alexander Pushkin,* edd. Peter I. Barta and Ulrich Goebel, pp. 67-83. Studies in Russian and German, no. 1. Lewiston.

Todorov, Tzvetan. 1984. *Mikhail Bakhtin: The Dialogical Principle,* trans. Wlad Godzich. Theory and History of Literature, vol. 13. Minneapolis.

Treu, Max. 1954. *Sappho.* Munich.

Vine, Brent. 1992. "On the 'Missing' Fourth Stanza of Catullus 51," *HSCP* 96.251-58.

Volosinov, V. N. 1986. *Marxism and the Philosophy of Language,* trans. Ladislav Matejka and I. R. Titunik. Cambridge, Mass.

West, M. L. 1970. "Burning Sappho," *Maia* 22.307-30.

Wilamowitz-Moellendorff, U. von. 1966/1913. *Sappho und Simonides.* Berlin.

Winkler, Jack. 1981. "Gardens of Nymphs: Public and Private in Sappho's Lyrics," *Reflections of Women in Antiquity,* ed. Helene P. Foley, pp. 63-89. New York.

Wiseman, T. P. 1969. *Catullan Questions.* Leicester.

————1982. "*Pete Nobiles Amicos:* Poets and Patrons in Late Republican Rome," *Literary and Artistic Patronage in Ancient Rome,* ed. Barbara K. Gold, pp. 28-49. Austin.

————1985. *Catullus and His World: A Reappraisal.* Cambridge.

Zumthor, Paul. 1983. *Introduction à la Poésie Orale.* Collection Poétique. Paris.

Linda H. Peterson (essay date spring 1994)

SOURCE: Peterson, Linda H. "Sappho and the Making of Tennysonian Lyric." *ELH* 61, no. 1 (spring 1994): 121-37.

[*In the following essay, Peterson notes the literary influence of Sappho's poetry on Alfred, Lord Tennyson and, more broadly, on the "feminine" tradition in nineteenth-century English lyric verse.*]

In 1830, on a summer tour in southern France and the Pyrenees, Alfred Tennyson wrote the poem now known as "Mariana in the South." When Arthur Henry Hallam, Tennyson's travelling companion on that tour, sent a copy of the poem to their mutual friend W. B. Donne, he included a paragraph of critical commentary that has since become part of Tennyson studies—although, as I shall argue, in a strangely half-acknowledged way. Hallam noted that the poem was a "pendant to his [Tennyson's] former poem of Mariana, the idea of both being the expression of desolate loneliness"; that the southern Mariana required "a greater lingering on the outward circumstances, and a less palpable transition of the poet into Mariana's feelings"; that this lingering on the external was appropriate, for "when the object of poetic power happens to be an object of sensuous perception it is the business of the poetic language to paint"; and that Tennyson's technique was sanctioned by "the mighty models of art, left for the worship of ages by the Greeks, & those too rare specimens of Roman production which breathe a Greek spirit." Hallam's commentary ends with a comparison of Tennyson's poetry to "the fragments of Sappho, in which I see much congeniality to Alfred's peculiar power."[1]

What has come down in critical studies—as, for example, in the great Ricks edition of Tennyson's poetry—is the association of "Mariana in the South" with Sappho's fragment **"1."**

> The Moon has set
> And the Pleiades
> It is midnight
> The time is going by
> And I sleep alone.[2]
>
> Δέδυκε μὲν ἀ σελάννα
> καὶ πληΐαδες, μέσαι δέ
> νύκτες, πάρα δ' ἔρχετ' ὤρα,
> ἔγω δὲ μόνα κατεύδω.

This certainly was, for the nineteenth century, the great Sapphic fragment of "desolate loneliness" and unquestionably an influence on Tennyson's lyric. But, following Hallam's lead, I want to associate Sappho's fragments not only with "Mariana in the South," but also with the original "Mariana" and, more generally, with

Tennyson's early lyrics. I pursue this association not so much to trace Tennyson's debt to Sappho or his interest in archaic Greek poetry, though these are important matters, but rather to suggest how a conception of Sappho and Greek lyric poetry—a conception Tennyson shared and worked out with Hallam—helped him understand his role as a poet and his place in the English poetic tradition.

Tennyson's interest in Sappho began early in his career and lasted long. In the 1827 volume, *Poems by Two Brothers,* he quoted a line from the Ovidian ode, "Sappho to the absent Phaon"—"Te somnia nostra reducunt [You my dreams bring back to me]"—as an epigraph to his own lyric, "And ask ye why these sad tears stream." Very late in his career, in the 1886 *Locksley Hall Sixty Years After,* Tennyson referred to Sappho simply (and supremely) as "the poet," alluding to her fragment on Hesperus, "Έσπερε, πάντα φέρων, ὅσα φαίνολις ἔσκέδασ' αὖως, / φέρεις οέν, φέρεσ αέγα, φέρεισ ἄπυ ματέρι παῖδα," in the line "Hesper, whom the poet call'd the Bringer home of all good things" (185). And, throughout his work, he regularly quoted or praised Sappho—as, for example, in *The Princess,* where Lady Psyche cites Sappho as one who "vied with any man" in "arts of grace" (2.147-48), or in the *Idylls of the King,* where Elaine's lament echoes the bitter-sweet antithesis of Sappho's fragment, "Έροσ δαὖτέ μ' ὁ λυσιμελης δόνει, / γλυκύπικρον ἀμάχανον ὄρπετον": "Love, art thou sweet? Then bitter death must be: / Love, thou art bitter; sweet is death to me."[3]

Tennyson seems also to have had a lifelong obsession with the technicalities of Greek poetry, including Saphics and Anacreontics. In December, 1863, William Allingham witnessed a dinner conversation, continued for three nights running, in which Tennyson discoursed on "Classic Metres." ("Mrs. T.," Allingham reports, "confessed herself tired of hearing" about the subject).[4] Another friend, Mrs. Montagu Butler, recorded in her 1892 diary that Tennyson had told her that the Sapphics of Horace were "uninteresting and monotonous," whereas "the metre was beautiful under [Sappho's] treatment"; "the discovery for which he always hoped the most," Mrs. Butler added, "was of some further writings of Sappho."[5]

It was in the early 1830s, however, during his time at Cambridge and his friendship with Hallam, that Tennyson showed the most concentrated interest in Sappho's poetry, and this interest marks the short lyrics of his 1830 *Poems Chiefly Lyrical* and the 1832 *Poems.* In the 1830 volume Tennyson paraphrases (and disagrees with) Sappho's fragment on Hesperus in his "Leonine Elegiacs":

> The ancient poetess singeth, that Hesperus all things
>   bringeth,

> Smoothing the wearied mind: bring me my love, Rosalind.
> Thou comest morning or even; she cometh not morning or even.
> False-eyed Hesper, unkind, where is my sweet Rosalind?

(13-16)

He repossesses and augments Sappho's fragment "**1**" in "Mariana" and again, in the 1832 *Poems,* in "Mariana in the South." Moreover, as Stephen C. Allen has recently argued, another of Sappho's fragments—"Sweet mother, I cannot weave my web, broken as I am by longing for a boy, at soft Aphrodite's will"—influenced Tennyson's conception of "The Lady of Shalott," in which a female artist, like Sappho's speaker, is overcome by the onset of Love.[6] Finally, in the 1832 *Poems,* Tennyson includes two adaptations of the famous Sapphic ode "φαίνεταί μοι κῆνος ἴσος θέοισιν / ἔμμεν ὤνηρ [Peer of the gods he seems to me]": an extensive translation-adaptation in "Eleanore" (122-44) and a partial borrowing in "Fatima" (15-19). Indeed, when Tennyson published "Fatima" in 1832, he did so without a title and with only an epigraph repeating the opening words of Sappho's ode: "φαίνεταί μοι κῆνος ἴσος θέοισιν / ἔμμεν ὤνηρ."[7]

Admittedly, the 1830 and 1832 *Poems* contain many other allusions, classical and modern, a point to which I shall return. Even so, the density of the allusions to Sappho in 1830-1832 marks her profound influence and presence in these early volumes of Tennyson's poetry. Given this presence, we may surmise that Sappho—both the poet and her poetry—provided Tennyson with a means for pursuing his own poetic agenda and locating his place among English poets. Nineteenth-century myths of Sappho also, I believe, allowed Tennyson to work out a model of influence that enabled poetic production—and that enables us to revise our current discourse about poets and their literary relations, particularly in the early Victorian period.

(RE)POSSESSING SAPPHO: SOME USES OF SAPPHIC LYRIC

That Tennyson used Sappho as a vehicle for self-definition is not, of course, unprecedented in literary history. As Joan deJean has argued for French literature, male poets have frequently used Sappho's poetry as an initiatory vehicle or an object of exchange. In *Fictions of Sappho,* deJean posits a triangulation of desire in which young male poets compete for recognition and priority by translating Sappho's lyrics and thus taking possession of her voice.[8] Typically, the site of this competition is Sappho's second ode, in French known familiarly as "**A l'aimee,**" what we know in English (thanks to Swinburne) as the "Ode to Anactoria," what Tennyson translated partially in "Eleanore" and "Fatima":

Just like a god he seems to me
That man who sits
Across from you so closely
Attentive to your sweet words.

Φαίνεταί μοι κῆνος ἴσος θέοισιν
ἔμμεν ὄνηρ, ὄστις ἐναντίος τοι
ἰζάνει, καὶ πλυσίον ὗδυ φωνεύσας ὑπακούει.⁹

In this male competition, a poem of sapphic desire—a female speaker gazing at a man gazing at her beloved—gets translated into a heterosexual triangle of desire—a male speaker gazing at another man gazing at his beloved. The woman, whether the woman in the poem or the female poet Sappho, becomes the object of homosocial exchange between men.

Although we might apply deJean's model directly to Tennyson's case, perhaps by viewing Sappho as his means for circumventing Romantic influence and gaining priority over his immediate poetic predecessors, I believe that the Tennyson-Sappho relationship operates on slightly different terms. For one thing, as Hallam suggests and as the 1830 volume bears witness, it was not Sappho's odes but the shorter fragments that were seminal to Tennyson's development. Today we refer to all Sappho's lyrics as fragments, but in the nineteenth century it was customary to refer to the two odes—the "Ode to Aphrodite" and the "Ode to Anactoria"—and to the rest as fragments.¹⁰ In eighteenth- and nineteenth-century editions, fragment **"1"** was "Δέδυκε μὲν ἀ σελάννα," the lyric that inspired "Mariana" and "Mariana in the South"; fragment **"3"** was "Γλύκεια μᾶτερ," the fragment relevant to "The Lady of Shalott."¹¹ It was the fragmentary nature of Sappho's poetry, the sense of lyric possibilities limned but not fulfilled, that attracted Tennyson. Frederick Tennyson, the poet's brother, expressed a simple version of this attraction in his own expansion of Sappho's lyrics, *The Isles of Greece* (1890): comparing Sappho's fragments to "muscatel grapes shaken from the vine"—"they leave such a delicious flavour on the tongue, that we long to pluck, if possible, the entire bunches from which they have fallen"—he noted the irresistible urge to manufacture what could not be gathered: "What is a Poet to do under these circumstances, but imagine what they might have been when full-orbed perfect compositions?"¹²

Alfred Tennyson's attraction to Sappho's poetry was more complex, less a desire to complete the fragments themselves than to fulfill the lyric tradition Sappho had begun. Whereas the epic tradition of Homer had been adapted and expanded by multiple successors (Virgil, Spenser, Milton, to name only the most obvious), the lyric tradition had seen no successors to Sappho—at least not as Hallam and Tennyson interpreted that tradition. When Hallam tried to give W. B. Donne examples of other lyrics "which breathe a Greek spirit," he could

think of only two: "the divine passage about the sacrifice of Iphigenia in Lucretius" and "the desolation of Ariadne in Catullus"; he did not even consider English poems as possible candidates.¹³ According to Hallam, however, Tennyson possessed a "peculiar power" that made him heir to an ancient, original lyric voice. We know that Tennyson was frustrated by the lack of space available in the epic tradition: "Why should any man / Remodel models?" the poet Everard Hall asks in "The Epic"; the result can only be "faint Homeric echoes." Given the fragmentary state of Sappho's *oeuvre,* he had ample space to develop a lyric strain.

It was not simply the fragmentariness of Sappho's poetry, but its particular techniques and its place in literary history that must also have fascinated Tennyson. Tennyson's development of the lyric depended on his sensitivity to "impressions of sense" and on his reading of Sappho as a poet of sensation, of "sensuous perception" (the phrases are Hallam's). Archaic Greek poetry was generally believed to concentrate on the particular, the concrete, and the sensual. Sappho's lyrics in particular were viewed as emerging at a historical moment when the ancient Greek lyricists, only having recently learned to distinguish outside phenomena from inner perceptions and reactions, "busied themselves with studying this relationship of inner and outer, and were led naturally to a preoccupation with the particular feeling or experience."¹⁴ We can see the focus on the particular, concrete, and sensual in Sapphic fragments like these:

> (1) Thus at times with tender feet the Cretan women dance in measure round the fair altar, trampling the fine soft bloom of the grass.
>
> (2) A broidered strap of fair Lydian work covered her feet.
>
> (3) Come, goddess of Cyprus, and in golden cups serve nectar delicately mixed with delights.
>
> (4) Now Eros shakes my soul, a wind on the mountain falling on the oaks.
>
> (5) And round about the [breeze] murmurs cool through the apple-boughs, and slumber streams through quivering leaves.¹⁵

In such verses the natural world serves not as symbol but provides objects of and occasions for "sensuous perception." The Sapphic preoccupation with the relation between inner feelings and outer phenomena is especially evident in the final two fragments, as well as in the fragment that inspired the Mariana poems—"The Moon has set, and the Pleiades; it is midnight, the time is going by, and I sleep alone"—in which the loneliness of the speaker heightens (or is heightened by) her sensitivity to external phenomena. This relationship—

between outer object and inner perception, between sensation and consciousness—was Tennyson's forte; he, like Sappho, was to be the leading "poet of sensation" of his age.

Sappho's historical and generic relation to epic poetry provided Tennyson, moreover, with a means of comprehending (perhaps rationalizing) his own ambivalent relation to the epic tradition. Frank M. Turner has shown that the Victorians regularly and rigorously compared themselves to the Greeks.[16] The general view of classical Greek poetry held that a Lyric Age had succeeded the Epic Age, that Homer (his *Iliad*, his *Odyssey*, plus other now-lost epic poetry) was followed by lyricists like Alcaeus and Sappho, and in that succession came a shift in poetic interest. The epic age was "the age of heroism, aristocracy, and the equation of external appearance with reality," whereas the lyric age focused on "the world of the individual, the πόλις [city-state], and the discovery of inner life and emotions."[17] This critical view became even more dominant after the discovery of Sappho's fragment **"16"**:

> Some say that an army of cavalry
> Others that infantry
> And others that a fleet of ships
> Is what is most desirable
> On this dark earth
> But for me it is whatever
> Inspires one's passionate love.[18]

> οἰ μὲν ἰππήων στρότον, οἰ δὲ πέσδων
> οἰ δὲ νάων φαῖσ᾽ ἐπὶ γᾶν μέλαιναν
> ἔμμεναι κάλλιστον, ἔγω δὲ κῆν ὄτ-
> τω τις ἔραται.

Although in 1830 Tennyson could not have known this poem of stark contrast between war and love, epic conquest and lyric passion, he would have shared with Hallam and his contemporaries a historical sense of lyric developing after and out of epic.[19] And, by comparing himself with Sappho, he would have located his place in the progress of literature.

"The age in which we live comes late in our national progress," Hallam wrote in his 1831 review of Tennyson's *Poems Chiefly Lyrical* in the *Englishman's Magazine*. In modern criticism, that lateness has routinely been associated with "belatedness," with coming at the end of an exhausted poetic tradition, when "that first raciness, and juvenile vigour of literature . . . is gone, never to return."[20] In Hallam's scheme of literary history, however, coming late meant something more. The historical distance between Homer and Sappho (the eighth century BCE to the sixth century BCE) was roughly the same as the distance between the English Renaissance epicists and Tennyson—a comparison which meant that Tennyson must acknowledge historical

context in imagining his poetic career.[21] Hallam's view of literary history explains, in part, his comment in the 1831 review that "the French Revolution may be a finer theme than the war of Troy; but it does not so evidently follow that Homer is to find his superior."[22] Hallam's point is not simply that Homer represents the golden age of epic, but rather that poets must know their place in a "national progress" and work accordingly.

(RE)IMAGINING SAPPHO: SOME VERSIONS OF INFLUENCE

Thus far I have been arguing that Tennyson's relation to Sappho operates in terms different from those developed by Joan deJean, that Sappho helped Tennyson comprehend his lyric sensibility and his place in poetic history. I want also to acknowledge the relevance of deJean's model to Tennyson's early lyrics, however, even as I modify her notions of poetic influence. Consonant with deJean's model, Tennyson did turn a sapphic triangle of desire into a heterosexual triangle, and he did finally use Sappho's second ode as a means of expressing male (poetic) desire. It is of course the case that all English versions of Sappho prior to Swinburne's depict heterosexual (not sapphic) love—whether the translations by Ambrose Philips (1711), John Addison (1735), and Thomas Moore (1800), or the fictions of Sappho by Mary Robinson (1796), John Nott (1803), and Letitia Elizabeth Landon (1824).[23] Tennyson could hardly have done otherwise, given the biographical information and the state of the editions available to him.[24] Thus, in translating and adapting Sappho's second ode in "Eleänore," he turns a lyric of female passion into one of male desire:

> But when I see thee roam, with tresses unconfined,
> While the amorous, odorous wind
>   Breathes low between the sunset and the moon;
>   Or, in a shadowy saloon,
> On silken cushions half reclined;
>   I watch thy grace; and in its place
>   My heart a charmèd slumber keeps,
>   While I muse upon thy face;
>   And a languid fire creeps
>   Through my veins to all my frame,
> Dissolvingly and slowly: soon
>   From thy rose-red lips MY name
> Floweth; and then, as in a swoon,
>   With dinning sound my ears are rife,
>   My tremulous tongue faltereth,
>   I lose my color, I lose my breath,
>   I drink the cup of a costly death,
> Brimmed with delirious draughts of warmest life.
>   I die with my delight.

> (122-40)

Here it is a male poet who feels physical ravishment, while the female beloved is scarcely allowed to speak, allowed only to utter the poet's name, an utterance that causes her (temporary) silence but ultimately produces his (immortal) lyric. In this heterosexual version of Sappho, Tennyson inscribes common nineteenth-century gender dichotomies: female muse/male poet, female silence/male voice, female erotic object/male gaze. We might even add that in "Eleänore," perhaps the last of Tennyson's youthful Sapphic borrowings, Sappho becomes the object of exchange between men—not the object of competition between male poets, but the object of bonding between Tennyson and Hallam, the poet and the critic who had shared her lyrics during 1830 and 1831.

That bonding may, as the deJean-Sedgwick model implies, have homosocial elements—in that Tennyson transforms a homoerotic desire for Hallam into a socially-acceptable form of love via his public, heterosexual translations of Sappho's poetry and Hallam's official, public discussions of Shelley and Keats, not the dangerous Sappho, as the dominant poetic influences. Indeed, if we follow Richard Dellamora's line of argument in *Masculine Desire,* we might see the homoerotic interest of Tennyson and (or for) Hallam implied by their mutual interest in Sappho and then by Tennyson's decision to "normalize" that interest into poetic versions of heterosexual love. That Hallam discussed Tennyson's affinities with Sappho in a private letter to a mutual friend, but not in his public 1831 review in the *Englishman's Magazine,* might further support this interpretation.[25]

Despite these possibilities, it may be more useful critically to replace the competitive "masculine" model that deJean posits with an alternative "feminine" model of influence that Sappho offered to Romantic and Victorian poets. Many eighteenth- and nineteenth-century accounts of the Greek poetess emphasized her educative function, the role of her academy in Greek culture and her personal role as an intellectual exemplar for Lesbian women. In her 1796 *Sappho and Phaon,* for example, the poet Mary Robinson viewed Sappho as an original and originating figure, one who fulfilled the criteria for Romantic artistry yet added the specifically female features of nurture and community to the myths of becoming a poet: "Sappho undertook to inspire the Lesbian women with a taste for literature; many of them received instructions from her, and foreign women increased the number of her disciples." The amateur classicist John Nott similarly imagined scenes of intellectual and pedagogical exchange in his prose fiction, *Sappho, After a Greek Romance* (1803), which depicts the lovelorn Sappho living in Sicily among a community of philosophers, poets, and critics; within this community, she composes and recites her two great odes.[26]

Nott's vision of artistic community and poetic influence varies from Robinson's on one significant point: for Nott, Sappho becomes part of an already-existing male community of philosophers and littérateurs, one which invites her participation because she so evidently possesses genius; for Robinson, Sappho represents the founder of an exclusively female community, one which educates and produces other female poets and readers. For Nott, Sappho is an anomaly, a gifted woman living among men; for Robinson, Sappho is the supreme poet but still representative of other women writers. In both cases, however, the function of the artistic community is the same: to nurture poetic production, to provide what we might designate "feminine" support.

There is good historical evidence to suggest, in other words, that Tennyson and Hallam conceived of influence (or, at least, *some* poetic influence) as following this more gentle, encouraging, educative Sapphic mode—a mode that would have been emotionally as well as intellectually important to Tennyson who, in the 1830's, was known to be sensitive to negative criticism.[27] Current critical models tend to emphasize the competitive element, the "anxiety of influence" articulated so forcefully by Harold Bloom: the "battle between strong equals, father and son as mighty opposites, Laius and Oedipus at the crossroads."[28] In a recent essay on *Maud,* however, Leslie Brisman provides a basis for analyzing Tennysonian influences more subtly and accurately. Differentiating between Byronic and Keatsian influence in Tennyson, Brisman suggests that the former be associated with "masculine" terms like "force, aggression, explosiveness, acquisitiveness, and institution," the latter with "feminine" terms like "balance, responsiveness, perseverance, the accumulative, and community." According to Brisman, Tennyson conceived of his relation to Byron and Keats differently and thus treated their poetic texts differently: "Tennyson turned to Keats as a woman writer turns to a woman writer."[29]

What Sappho—the poet and her poetry—enables us to see is that Tennyson not only invoked a feminine model in his relation to Keats, but that he learned this mode of poetic influence from a woman writer, one the ancients considered the tenth Muse, the 19th-century the greatest lyricist of all time. If we have come, in the late twentieth century, to associate a feminine mode of influence with Keats, Tennyson's immediate predecessor, it is because we have forgotten Sappho and her heirs. But our association derives as much from critical myth as it does from literary history. Privately, in the letter to W. B. Donne, Hallam noted Tennyson's affinities with and inheritance from Sappho; publicly, in the 1831 review in the *Englishman's Magazine,* he linked Tennyson only to the male poets of the prior generation, Keats and Shelley. Whatever the reason for this discrepancy between private and public, whether happenstance or rhetorical moderation (it was, after all, audacious to compare a young poet with the great Sappho, known to the ancients as "*the* poetess," "κατ'ἐξοχήν, ἡ ποιήτρια" just as Homer was known as "*the* poet") or even a desire to keep shared intellectual pleasures secret, the fact is that Hallam's public omission of Sappho began an all-too-successful critical tradition of denying women writers' influence and recognizing only Tennyson's male predecessors.[30]

This tradition has become most forceful in the criticism surrounding "Mariana," Tennyson's greatest poem written under Sappho's influence. The Victorian critic John Churton Collins noted, in his now notorious *Illustrations of Tennyson* (1891), that, despite Tennyson's intimation of his debt to Shakespeare, the more ancient debt was to Sappho: "Probably the four exquisite lines in which Sappho appears to be describing some Mariana of antiquity were not without their influence on him." Collins then quoted the fragment "Δέδυκε μὲν ἀ σελάννα" as Tennyson's primary source.[31] Perhaps because no critic wants to be associated with a man whom Tennyson called "a louse on the locks of literature," Collins's critical knowledge has been virtually ignored.[32] Modern criticism of "Mariana" recognizes allusions to Homer and Euripides (Kincaid), Virgil (Bloom), Samuel Rogers (Ricks), Wordsworth (Thomson), Keats (Hollander, Bloom, Tucker), Shelley (Bloom), and obviously Shakespeare—but except for Robert Pattison's wide-ranging *Tennyson and Tradition,* it ignores Sappho.[33]

(RE)POSSESSING SAPPHO: TENNYSONIAN VERSIONS

If Hallam's critical writings—and our own—fit the model of masculine competition and domination that deJean posits, Tennyson's poetic borrowings fit less readily. "Eleänore," the single poem in which a male speaker assumes Sappho's words and voice, is unusual among Tennyson's adaptations, for in most he gives voice to female desire. Tennyson's Sapphic lyrics tend not to silence the female voice as do the French translations that deJean cites. Unlike his male counterparts, who typically use Sappho's words to express male desire for the female sex and male competition for female objects, Tennyson's poems most frequently choose female speakers: Mariana cries "He cometh not," the southern Mariana bemoans that she must "live forgotten, and love forlorn," and Fatima assumes Sappho's voice:

> Last night, when some one spoke his name,
> From my swift blood that went and came
> A thousand little shafts of flame
> Were shivered in my narrow frame.
>
> (15-18)

Such adaptations of Sappho represent a new strain in the English lyric. Whereas other poets made the lyric voice essentially masculine, Tennyson experimented with a feminine voice and developed a tradition more ancient and original than did any other English poet, including Shelley and Keats, under whose influence he allegedly languished.[34]

That Tennyson meant to explore a feminine lyric tradition is demonstrated further, I believe, by the many other, non-Sapphic allusions in the 1830 and 1832 volumes, especially in the "lady" poems. These allusions—to Spenser's Claribel, Shakespeare's Mariana and Isabel, Keats's Madeline, Irving's Anacaona—all suggest a poet looking for hiatuses in the masculine traditions of epic and drama, searching for unexplored territory in a literary tradition "late," as Hallam put it, "in our national progress." If, in classical scholarship, Sappho had been called "κατ'ἐξοχήν, ἡ ποιήτρια" and her supremacy in the lyric domain unquestioned, in the 1830's Tennyson seems to have been eager to explore that feminine domain, willing to question or abandon the masculine.[35]

And yet, to give the argument one more twist, it may be that Tennyson's exploration of the Sapphic strain represents the most devastating attempt to subsume the female voice in English literary history. It may be that his exploration became the exploitation I have been attempting to deny. Prior to Tennyson, at least in England, only female poets had assumed Sappho's persona or used her words to develop a specifically feminine lyric. In the first decades of the nineteenth-century, Sappho became the inspiration for a self-consciously feminine literary agenda, with women writers in England and on the continent modeling their professional lives on hers. Mary Robinson's *Sappho and Phaon* used Sappho to lament her own lost loves, as well as to further her literary career and legitimize her poetry (*In a Series of Legitimate Sonnets,* as her subtitle puts it).[36] For Robinson, Sappho represented "the unrivalled poetess of her time," a "lively example of the human mind, enlightened by the most exquisite talents," and thus a model for a Romantic poetess like Robinson who wished to assert her genius and superior literary taste. Sappho was also, Robinson noted, an inspiration to "my illustrious country-women," who, "unpatronized by courts, and unprotected by the powerful, persevere in the paths of literature."[37]

Two such countrywomen were the second-generation Romantic writers Letitia Elizabeth Landon and Felicia Hemans, both of whom used Sappho, in combination with Madame de Staël's fictional Corinne, as a model for their professional careers. As Angela Leighton has shown, Landon enacted the Sappho-Corinne myth in her life and art.[38] Known to readers as L.E.L., Landon made her name writing verses about slighted and unrequited love, wearing her hair *à la Sappho,* as young Disraeli described it, and making the heroine of her widely-popular *The Improvisatrice* (1824) a modern Sapphic artist.[39] *The Improvisatrice* begins with its poetess-heroine singing "a last song of Sappho" and ends with her Sappho-like death of unrequited love. Landon's later poem "Sappho" depicts a successful poetess, "upon whose brow the laurel crown is placed," falling desperately in love with Phaon and learning that "genius, riches, fame, / May not soothe a slighted love."[40]

Hemans also developed a series of lyricizing women who, like most English Sapphos, lament their losses in love and life. Hemans's "Last Song of Sappho" (1828) is representative, as Lawrence Lipking has argued, of the Romantic tendency to depict Sappho in "isolation from any human or natural community": "The Romantic Sappho stands *alone*."[41] Such isolation, as Angela Leighton has further noted, is the feminine consequence of the Romantic male quest: "The man aspires, but the woman mourns; he scales the heights, but she longs for home."[42] Tennyson develops this feminine perspective, introduced by Hemans and Landon, when he creates such Sapphic figures as Eleänore, Fatima, and the two Marianas who, obsessed by heterosexual passion, live in isolation and seem oblivious to—indeed, seem to exist without—families or friends.

Tennyson's contemporaries recognized the link between Greek and contemporary women writers. When in 1833 Father Prout contributed his sketch of Landon to the "Gallery of Literary Characters" in *Fraser's Magazine,* he compared Landon's poetry to Sappho's. Defending Landon against critics who thought she wrote too much (and too exclusively) about love, he argued that her choice had good feminine precedent:

> How, Squaretoes, can there be too much of love in a young lady's writings? Is she to write of politics, or political economy, or pugilism, or punch? Certainly not. . . . We think Miss L.E.L. has chosen the better part. She shews every now and then that she is possessed of information, feeling, and genius, to enable her to shine in other departments of poetry; but she does right in thinking that Sappho knew what she was about when she chose the tender passion as a theme for woman.[43]

Even classical scholars made this sort of connection. In an 1832 article for the *Edinburgh Review,* the classicist D. K. Sandford surveyed the achievements of "Greek Authoresses," beginning with Sappho and regularly comparing Greek with modern female poets. His introduction, for instance, draws the line of female genius "from Miriam the prophetess to Mrs Hemans," "from the days of out-poured inspiration to those of hot-pressed twelves"; he calls the Greek poetess Erinna, who achieved fame "when scarcely more than a year past seventeen," "the Fanny Kemble of ancient days";

and he explains the rivalry of Pindar and Corinna (and Corinna's victory) by comparing these Greek poets to Robert Burns and Letitia Landon:

> Partly, says Pausanias, her beauty, and partly her Æolian dialect, made her successful with an audience, whose eyes and ears were thus alike regaled. We can believe him. Burns, in his most inspired mood, would have had little chance with a southern tribunal, beside the English strains of L.E.L.[44]

For Sandford, such comparisons come naturally, presumably because he had learned them from contemporary female poets who self-consciously presented themselves as Sappho's heirs.

One might argue, then, that Tennyson, by developing his Sapphic affinities, took over the strain that Robinson and her female successors, Hemans and Landon, meant to claim. By creating and speaking for his abandoned women, his Marianas, Fatimas, and Oenones, Tennyson entered the domain of contemporary women poets and assumed their poetic voices. That takeover launched him to preeminence as a lyricist, allowing him to create poetry that consciously developed and counterpointed feminine and masculine strains. It allowed him to mix his "lady" poems with more masculine subjects like "The Poet," "The Mystic," or the philosophical "Supposed Confessions of a Second-Rate Sensitive Mind" in the *Poems* of 1830 or with the Homeric epic monologues "Ulysses" and "The Lotos-Eaters" in the *Poems* of 1832. Later, it allowed the mixing of masculine narrative and feminine lyric in *The Princess* (1847) and of masculine and feminine speakers in *In Memoriam* (1850). But it also gave to a male poet what female poets might have achieved for themselves—that is, if literary history had remembered the Sapphic tradition of which they and he were a part.

Notes

1. Letter to William Bodham Donne (13 February 1831), in *The Letters of Arthur Henry Hallam,* ed. Jack Kolb (Columbus: Ohio State Univ. Press, 1981), 401-2.

2. *The Poems of Tennyson,* ed. Christopher Ricks (London: Longman, 1969), 362. Subsequent references to Tennyson's poetry are to this edition; line numbers cited parenthetically in text. Biographers like Robert Bernard Martin (*Tennyson: The Unquiet Heart* [Oxford: Clarendon Press, 1980], 120) have expanded the literary associations to include the geographical, suggesting that "the Pyrenees provided [Tennyson] with a local habitation for the classical myth and poetry which he had loved since childhood, and which were to suggest much of his best work. The miles of uninhab-

ited mountains, little changed in the generations that they had been known, stood in for those of Italy and ancient Greece."

Classicists no longer attribute this fragment to Sappho, but its influence on Tennyson's Marianas is still relevant since in the nineteenth century it would have been considered authentic. Throughout this essay I have used Henry Thornton Wharton's *Sappho: Memoir, Text, Selected Renderings, and a Literal Translation,* 4th ed. (London: John Lane, 1898) for texts and translations, except where noted. Although Tennyson could not have known this edition till late in his life (it was first published in 1885), Wharton's is the best nineteenth-century English edition available and includes the Sapphic poems commonly known to Victorians.

3. "Lancelot and Elaine" (note 2), 1003-4. Wharton (note 2) translates this Sapphic fragment (no. 40): "Now Love masters my limbs and shakes me, fatal creature, bittersweet." The Sapphic allusions I cite were first noted by Wharton, John Churton Collins in his *Illustrations of Tennyson* (London: Chatto & Windus, 1891), or David M. Robinson in *Sappho and Her Influence* (Boston: Marshall Jones, 1924).

4. William Allingham, *A Diary,* ed. H. Allingham and D. Radford (London: Macmillan, 1907), 93-95.

5. H. Montagu Butler, "Recollections of Tennyson," in *Tennyson and His Friends,* ed. Hallam Tennyson (London: Macmillan, 1911), 216.

6. "Γλύκεια μᾶτερ, οὔτοι δύναμαι κρέκην τὸν ἴστον, / πόθῳ δάμεισα παῖδος βραδίναν δι' Αφρόδιταν." See Stephen C. Allen's "Tennyson, Sappho, and 'The Lady of Shallot,'" *Tennyson Research Bulletin* 2 (1975): 171-72.

7. Collins noted many of these allusions in his *Illustrations of Tennyson* (note 3), including those in "Mariana," "Eleänore," and "Fatima." Ricks includes most in his notes to *The Poems of Tennyson* (note 2), but not the important use of fragment 1 in "Mariana"—perhaps, as I shall argue below, because Tennyson so vehemently objected to Collins's commentary on that poem.

8. Joan deJean, *Fictions of Sappho, 1546-1937* (Chicago: Univ. of Chicago Press, 1989), esp. the introduction, 1-28. See also Lawrence Lipking, "Sappho Descending," in *Abandoned Women and Poetic Tradition* (Chicago: Univ. of Chicago Press, 1988), 57-126, for a more varied survey of the figure and poetry of Sappho in the Western literary tradition.

9. Translation by Terence DuQuesne in *Sappho of Lesbos: The Poems* (Thame, Oxon: Darengo, 1990), 38. Following the definitive Lobel and Page edition, de Jean refers to this poem as "fragment 31." I follow nineteenth-century practice here in referring to it as Sappho's second ode, the first being the "Ode to Aphrodite."

10. See, for example, the preface to Arthur Henry Hallam's *Remains,* new ed. (London: John Murray, 1869), xxxvi, in which a memoirist refers to Hallam's interest in "the short poems and fragments of Sappho," and Swinburne's 1866 "Notes on *Poems and Reviews,*" in *Swinburne: Poems and Ballads,* ed. Morse Peckham (New York: Bobbs-Merrill, 1970), 328, in which Swinburne refers to "the two odes and the remaining fragments of Sappho."

11. The numbering of the fragments was not consistent, although fragment 1 was usually "Δέδυκε μὲν ἀ σελάννα." I follow here the numbering in John Addison's *Works of Anacreon, Translated into English Verse* (London: John Watts, 1735), which included, in addition to the two odes, six fragments of Sappho: (1) "Δέδυκε μὲν ἀ σελάννα," (2) "κατθάνοισα δὲ κείσεαι πότα," (3) "Γλύκεια μᾶτερ," (4) "Εροσ δαῦτέ μ' ὁ λυσιμελης δόνει" combined with "ἄτθι, σοὶ δ' ἔμεθέν μεν ἀπήχθετο / φροντίσδην," (5) "Εἰ τοῖσ ἄνθεσιν ἤθελεν ὁ Ζοῦσ οπιθεῖναι Βασιλέα" (from Achilles Tatius, now not attributed to Sappho), and (6) "ἔλθε, Κύπρι, χρυσίαισιν ἐν κυλίκεσσιν ἄβρως."

12. Frederick Tennyson, *The Isles of Greece: Sappho and Alcaeus* (London: Macmillan, 1890), v. In the preface, Frederick Tennyson notes that his poems were inspired by his reading of an 1825 French edition of Sappho's fragments. Although he gives no sense of when he first read the volume, it may have been as early as the 1830 tour of France and the Pyrenees, on which Frederick accompanied his brother and Hallam. A new English edition of Sappho's poetry, *Scriptores Graeci Minores, quorum reliquias, fere omnium melioris notae, ex editionibus variis excerpsit,* ed. J[ohn] A[llen] Giles (Oxford: D. A. Talboys, 1831), was published while Tennyson and Hallam were at Cambridge.

13. Kolb (note 1), 401.

14. I have used a modern summary of this view from R. L. Fowler's *The Nature of Early Greek Lyric: Three Preliminary Studies* (Toronto: Univ. of Toronto Press, 1987), 54-57. The view Fowler summarizes was articulated, if with less sophistication, in the nineteenth as well as twentieth century; quoting Longinus, an anonymous writer [D. K.

Sandford] on "Greek Authoresses" for *The Edinburgh Review* 55 (1832): 198, notes that Sappho gives "strictly a *physical* picture" of love in the second ode—"no play of the fancy—no fairy frost-work."

15. All quotations come from Wharton's *Sappho* (note 2), where they are fragments 54, 19, 5, 42, and 4, respectively.

16. Frank M. Turner, *The Greek Heritage in Victorian Britain* (New Haven: Yale Univ. Press, 1981), 1-14.

17. Fowler (note 14), 4.

18. Trans. by DuQuesne (note 9), 30.

19. The poem was first published in the 20th century, too late to fulfill Tennyson's dream of another discovery of Sappho's verse. It is fragment 16 in *Poetarum Lesbiorum Fragmenta,* ed. Edgar Lobel and Denys Page (Oxford: Clarendon Press, 1955), 14.

20. The words are Hallam's (see *Tennyson: The Critical Heritage,* ed. John D. Jump [London: Routledge & Kegan Paul, 1967], 40), but the concept of "belatedness" derives in modern criticism from Harold Bloom, beginning with his *Anxiety of Influence: A Theory of Poetics* (New York: Oxford Univ. Press, 1973).

21. Tennyson did, of course, finally write epic, and his mastery of both the lyric and epic traditions suggests his desire to subsume and exceed his poetic predecessors—much as Browning's desire to be both "subjective" and "objective" poet suggests another version of poetic mastery.

22. Jump (note 20), 41.

23. Mary Robinson, *Sappho and Phaon, In a Series of Legitimate Sonnets, with Thoughts on Poetical Subjects, and Anecdotes of the Grecian Poetess,* new ed. (London: Minerva Press, 1813); [John Nott], *Sappho, After a Greek Romance* (London: Cuthell and Martin, 1803); "Sappho," in *The Poetical Works of Letitia Elizabeth Landon* (Philadelphia: Jas. B. Smith, 1859), 367-70.

24. Although Sappho's sexual ambivalences were discussed by some scholars, it is simply not the case, as Swinburne suggests in his "Notes on *Poems and Reviews*" (note 10), that every schoolboy "compelled under penalties to learn, to construe, and to repeat" Sappho's "imperishable and incomparable verses" would have recognized her desire as anything but heterosexual. During the eighteenth and nineteenth centuries it was standard to alter certain feminine endings

(especially in the ode, "Peer of the gods") and thus "regularize" Sappho's desire. See deJean (note 8).

25. See Richard Dellamora, *Masculine Desire: The Sexual Politics of Victorian Aestheticism* (Chapel Hill: Univ. of North Carolina Press, 1990), 16-41.

26. Robinson (note 23), 28; Nott (note 23), esp. 2:viii-ix and 3:iv, "The Table-Dispute," "The Afternoon Hours," and "Poetry," 187-217, 250-60. Robinson is citing the biographical sketch of Sappho by the Abbé Barthelemy.

27. Indeed, in *Tennyson: The Unquiet Heart,* Martin devotes a separate entry in his index to "criticism, sensitivity to" ([note 1], 636).

28. The phrases come from Sandra M. Gilbert and Susan Gubar, *The Madwoman in the Attic: The Woman Writer and the Nineteenth-Century Literary Imagination* (New Haven: Yale Univ. Press, 1979), 6, and refer to Harold Bloom's *The Anxiety of Influence* (note 20).

29. Leslie Brisman, "*Maud:* The Feminine as the Crux of Influence," *Studies in Romanticism* 31 (1992): 23, 26. Brisman is here modifying terms from Michael Cooke's *Acts of Inclusion: Studies Bearing on an Elementary Theory of Romanticism* (New Haven: Yale Univ. Press, 1979).

30. David M. Robinson (note 3), 5-6, for a discussion of the epithets for Sappho and Homer.

31. Collins (note 3), 27.

32. Anthony Kearney has recently resuscitated Collins's criticism in "Making Tennyson a Classic: Churton Collins' *Illustrations of Tennyson* in Context," *Victorian Poetry* 30 (1992): 75-82.

33. James R. Kincaid, *Tennyson's Major Poems: The Comic and Ironic Patterns* (New Haven: Yale Univ. Press, 1975), 23; Harold Bloom, "Tennyson: In the Shadow of Keats," in *Poetry and Repression* (New Haven: Yale Univ. Press, 1976), 149-52; Ricks (note 2), 187; Alastair W. Thomson, *The Poetry of Tennyson* (London: Routledge and Kegan Paul, 1986), 31-32; John Hollander, "Tennyson's Melody," *Georgia Review* 29 (1975): 683; and Herbert F. Tucker, *Tennyson and the Doom of Romanticism* (Cambridge: Harvard Univ. Press, 1988), 76-77. In *Tennyson and Tradition* (Cambridge: Harvard Univ. Press, 1979), Robert Pattison discusses several classical influences, including the Sapphic lyric, which Tennyson used not simply "because he liked it, but because it provided an appropriate lyric context upon which he could dilate" (11).

34. The Bloomian reading of Tennyson's early poems, one that has dominated the past two decades of

criticism, is that they fall "in the shadow of Keats." Bloom's discussion of "Mariana" acknowledges the presence of Virgil behind Keats, but it does not recognize Sappho, whose presence is far more fundamental and powerful than that of any other classical or English poet. See "Tennyson: In the Shadow of Keats" (note 33), 149-52, as well as "Tennyson, Hallam, and Romantic Tradition," in *The Ringers in the Tower: Studies in Romantic Tradition* (Chicago: Univ. of Chicago Press, 1971). Following this line of criticism, but with greater interest in the cultural work of Tennyson's poetry, is Tucker's chapter "Emergencies," in *Tennyson and the Doom of Romanticism* (note 33), 93-174.

35. As in "Anacaona," where a feminine speaker exposes the violence of masculine (epic) colonialism.

36. Some readers interpret *Sappho and Phaon* as a sonnet sequence *à clef* about her affair with the Prince of Wales, others about the end of her long relationship with Colonel Tarleton. See Lawrence Lipking (note 8), 82-83, and Stuart Curran, "Mary Robinson's *Lyrical Tales* in Context," in *Revisioning Romanticism: British Women Writers, 1776-1837* (Philadelphia: Univ. of Pennsylvania Press, forthcoming), 6 in ms.

37. Robinson (note 23), 16-18. Robinson called herself "the English Sappho."

38. Angela Leighton, *Victorian Women Poets: Writing Against the Heart* (London: Harvester Wheatsheaf, 1992), chap. 2, 45-77.

39. Letter from Disraeli to his sisters, quoted in D. E. Enfield, *L.E.L.: A Mystery of the Thirties* (London: Hogarth Press, 1928), 74; L.E.L., *The Improvisatrice; and Other Poems* (Boston: Munroe and Francis, 1825), 71-72.

40. L.E.L. (note 39), 367-70. The crowning of Sappho derives from book 2 of *Corinne*, where the Italian poetess is publically celebrated and crowned with laurel. The name Corinne comes from Corinna, the female poet-teacher of Pindar.

41. Felicia Hemans, "Records of Woman" and "Last Song of Sappho," in *The Poetical Works of Mrs. Felicia Hemans* (Philadelphia: Grigg and Elliot, 1845), 200-26, 391-92; Lipking (note 8), 83-84.

42. Leighton (note 38), 24.

43. [Father Prout], *Fraser's Magazine* 8 (October 1833): 433. Accompanying this article is the famous engraving of Landon wearing her hair *à la Sappho* and holding a rose, the flower thought dear to Sappho.

44. [D. K. Sandford] (note 14), 183, 199, 200.

André Lardinois (essay date 1994)

SOURCE: Lardinois, André. "Subject and Circumstance in Sappho's Poetry." *Transactions of the American Philological Association* 124 (1994): 57-84.

[*In the following essay, Lardinois questions modern historical reconstructions of Sappho as either a schoolmistress or a symposiast, claiming instead that the historical evidence is most consistent with her occupation as an "instructor of young women's choruses."*]

Holt Parker, in a provocative article in [*Transactions of the American Philological Association*] 123 (1993) 309-51, has questioned one hundred eighty years of classical scholarship on the relationship of Sappho to her addressees, if we take Friedrich Welcker's little monograph *Sappho von einem herrschenden Vorurteil befreyt* as the beginning of modern scholarship on the subject.[1] Parker argues that there is no credible evidence that Sappho's audience consisted of young, unmarried girls (316), and instead proposes that she sang at banquets about her love for other adult women (324, 346).[2] The positive aspect of Parker's paper is that it forces us to reexamine the evidence and question some of the scholarly traditions about Sappho, which, as Parker rightly points out (312), were often born in ignorance, sometimes coupled with sexism and homophobia.[3] It is my conclusion, after a review of the evidence, that Parker is correct in rejecting the 'Sappho school-mistress' paradigm as a plausible reconstruction of the performance circumstances of her poetry, but that the subject of her poetry is, nevertheless, young women or girls,[4] and its occasion has to be sought in public performances rather than private banquets. Like Parker, I will first discuss the testimonia, then the fragments and the external evidence. I will finally measure this evidence against Parker's reconstruction of Sappho as a symposiast and against the other modern images of Sappho: teacher at a school, leader of a *thiasos,* and instructor of a chorus.

1. THE TESTIMONIA

Parker, to his credit, inserts a whole section on "the evidence" (316-25). By his own account there are seven testimonia that "present some sort of picture of Sappho consorting with 'girls'" (321),[5] but he forgets four: the Suda Σ 107 (=test. 2) and Themistius *Or.* 13.170d-171a (=test. 52) speak respectively about Sappho's "pupils" (μαθήτριαι) and her *paidika,* while Philostratus *Im.* 2.1.1-3 (=test. 120 Gallavotti) is reminded of Sappho when he sees a picture of a female chorister (διδάσκαλος) leading a band of girls (κόραι) and Himerius *Or.* 9.4 (=fr. 194), similarly, portrays her as heading a group of young women (παρθένους) in what appears to be a musical procession. What can we do with this information? It has been a long time since scholars uncritically accepted what the ancients report about the archaic Greek poets. Welcker's treatise on the modern prejudices about Sappho was actually one of the first to contain a critical examination of the *testimonia* of an archaic Greek poet. He argued that Athenian comedy was responsible for most of our information about Sappho's life, including her alleged homosexuality.[6] More recently, Lefkowitz has concluded that "virtually all the material in all the lives is fiction" and "the ancient biographers took most of their information about poets from the poets themselves" (1981: viii). They, as Parker puts it, were "turning poetry into biography" (321). Does this mean that "[a]s evidence the testimonia are valueless" (idem)?

The Greeks or Romans in subsequent ages probably knew little more than we do about events on Lesbos in the sixth century B.C. They had, however, one distinct advantage over us: they still possessed Sappho's poetry in fairly complete form.[7] Therefore, whenever they mention a fact which could stem from her poetry, it has to be treated as at least possibly valuable information. A case in point is their frequent portrayal of Sappho consorting with young women. This is something they could have gathered from her poetry. Christopher Brown has recently concluded on the basis of the diction in fr. 16.18 that Anactoria, who is the subject of this poem, must have been a young woman, and when Ovid (test. 19) and Maximus of Tyre (test. 20) come to the same conclusion, they may have done so on similar grounds.[8]

Parker argues, however, that the composers of our testimonia misread Sappho's poetry and practiced "something quite familiar to feminists: the wholesale restructuring of female sexuality and society on the model of male sexuality and society" (321). More specifically, they would have changed any reference to same-aged and power-free lesbian relationships in Sappho's poetry into a pederastic relationship between an older woman and a young girl (322). We have become much more aware than, for example, Welcker that all our testimonia are written by men who could have easily misunderstood, or deliberately distorted, expressions of female desire.[9] The question is whether this is also the case with their interpretation of the age of the women in Sappho's poetry.

Parker adduces as parallels for the way in which the ancient commentators would have misread Sappho's lesbianism the virile portrayal of *tribades* in Roman literature (Hallett 1989, cited by Parker 321 n.24) and Lucian's similar representation of a homosexual woman from Lesbos in *Dialogues of the Courtesans* 5 (referred to by Parker top, p. 322). These portrayals of lesbian women are actually our best evidence *against* the supposition that the ancient commentators misconstrued the age of the subjects in Sappho's poetry. If Sappho indeed spoke about adult women in her poetry, as Parker assumes, there is no reason why Roman or Hellenistic poets and scholars had to change them into girls: as Lucian shows, they were perfectly well capable of imagining a woman from Lesbos in hot pursuit of other adult women.

If our sources collectively invented the notion that Sappho spoke about young women, it was not based "on the model of male sexuality" in their own society, where pederasty had become less acceptable than in the archaic Greek period,[10] but by comparison with the male poets from that same period, who often sing about their love for boys in language very similar to Sappho's.[11] One testimonium explicitly states that Sappho praises her "paidika" the same way Anacreon did, and there may be something to this comparison.[12] As Parker points out (340), the ancients likened in particular Sappho's love poetry to that of the male (pederastic) poets.

There remains the problem that these commentators may be turning a poetic fiction into a biographical fact. Anactoria, who in fr. **"16"** is cited as an example of something the "I"-person loves (fr. 16.4), is turned by Ovid into one of the girls whom Sappho loved (*Her.* 15.18-19=test. 19). We do not know if the sentiments which Sappho in fr. 16 expresses for Anactoria are genuine.[13] We do not even know if Sappho herself is the speaker. The ancient commentators were notorious in trying to identify every speaker with the poet/composer himself, which, as Karl Ottfried Müller already observed, is also the most likely origin of the story about Sappho's love for Phaon.[14] There are several impersonations of characters in Sappho's poetry,[15] and in some of the fragments now attributed to Sappho they may be speaking rather than the poetess herself.

In the case of Sappho we are faced with the additional problem that we know that she composed choral poetry as well as what appear to be monodic songs.[16] Page had argued that the two sets of songs were easily distinguishable and that "[t]here is nothing to contradict the natural supposition that, with this one small exception [i.e. marriage songs], all or almost all of her poems were recited by herself" (119), but his most important argument, the linguistic evidence, has in the mean time been questioned.[17] There is no clear, metrical division between Sappho's choral and monodic poetry either, since we possess wedding songs (frs. **"27"** and **"30"**) as well as supposedly monodic songs (fr. **"1"**) in the same Sapphic stanza.[18] This means that of most fragments it is impossible to say whether the speaker is a chorus or a soloist, who may or may not be Sappho.[19] In all these cases the testimonia would contend that Sappho is the speaker.[20] In some fragments Sappho is mentioned by name (frs. **"1," "65," "94," "133"**), in which case we can at least identify her as the speaker (not necessarily the performer), but such clarity is exceptional. I hope to argue elsewhere that most of Sappho's poetry was choral, i.e. sung and danced to by a chorus (cp. Philostratus *Im.* 2.1.1-3=test. 120 Gallavotti) or performed by a soloist who accompanies a dancing chorus (cp. *Anth. Pal.* 9.189=test. 59).[21] In both cases Sappho can still be the narrator in the poem, but she need not be.

In fact, we do not even know for certain if Sappho as a person ever existed. An increasing number of archaic Greek poets (Homer, Hesiod, Archilochus, Theognis) are believed by some to have been poetic *personae,* who may at some time have lived but soon became stock characters in the poetic tradition they were supposed to represent.[22] Herodotus is the first author to declare that Sappho and her brother Charaxus lived in Mytilene at one time (Hdt. 2.135.6), but he historicized many mythical figures, including Heracles (Hdt. 2.44), Europa (1.2), the heroes of the Trojan War (1.3, 2.112f.), as well as Homer and Hesiod (2.53),[23] and the fact that Alcaeus addressed Sappho in his poetry and spelled her name differently from the way it is spelled in the poetry preserved in her name, could possibly be an indication that she was a poetic construct rather than a real life figure in sixth-century Lesbos.[24] But even if we accept that Sappho really existed and composed all the poetry preserved in her name, we do not know if she was the speaker and/or performer in, for example, fr. **"16"** or if she meant it when she said that she would rather see Anactoria's lovely walk and the bright sparkle of her face than the Lydians' chariots and armed infantry.[25] One thing we can, however, be reasonably certain of, as a result of Brown's analysis and the plausible assessment of Ovid and Maximus of Tyre: Anactoria was a young woman. I will from here on concentrate on the subject and possible audience of Sappho's poetry, while assuming that, outside of the wedding songs, she is in most cases the speaker, although not necessarily the performer.[26]

Besides objecting that the testimonia about Sappho's involvement with young women are male-biased and turn poetry into biography, Parker adds that they are chronologically late ("the earliest witness, Horace, is 600 years after Sappho").[27] The lateness of these testimonia is indeed problematic and should prepare us for possible anachronisms in their portrayal of Sappho's relationship with her subjects and addressees. A case in point are the testimonia that refer to Sappho as a teacher of young women (test. 2, 20, 21, 49, fr. **"214B"** fr. **"1"**). As far as we know, there existed no schools for women in archaic Greece, and it is dangerous to assume on the basis of these testimonia alone that Sappho's Lesbos was somehow an exception.[28] The only "education" girls received outside of the house in archaic Greece was in choruses where they were taught

songs and dances and, at least in Sparta, some gymnastics (Marrou: 57, Calame 1977: 1.385-420). From the fifth century onwards, we find representations of women who teach girls how to dance or to play an instrument, and there are some indications of girls being instructed in reading and writing (Beck 155-62 with plates 78-88). Women teachers are attested for Roman Egypt (Cribiore).

One can easily imagine that ancient commentators, anxious to explain Sappho's familiarity with a number of girls in her poetry, took as their model the women teachers they found in their own society. (Welcker and Wilamowitz basically did the same.) The long-time association of pederasty with the education of young boys must have helped connect Sappho's homoerotic poetry with her supposed rôle as a teacher, as e.g. Maximus of Tyre shows (=test. 20).[29] At the same time, it is possible that in all these references to Sappho as a teacher there is a memory preserved of Sappho's involvement with the setting up of young women's choirs. This is certainly suggested by Philostratus *VA.* 1.30 (=test. 21), who claims that a certain Damophyla, "like Sappho, had gathered around her young women disciples and composed love-poems and hymns" (τὸν Σαπφοῦς τρόπον παρθένους θ' ὁμιλητρίας κτήσασθαι ποιήματά τε ξυνθεῖναι τὰ μὲν ἐρωτικά, τὰ δ' ὕμνους). The only problematic, because anachronistic, term in this description is ὁμιλητρίας.

We may conclude that there is much distortion and misinformation in the testimonia, but that we do not have to reject them entirely. They are based on Sappho's poetry, so that any plausible information they provide, which may have come from Sappho's poems, must be taken seriously. One such piece of plausible information is their identification of the subject of Sappho's poetry as young, adolescent women.[30] With regard to their assessment of the speaker of Sappho's poems we have to be much more careful. Not only is there a tendency in all the ancient testimonia to attribute every sentence to the poet/composer himself, but they also tend to read them as personal revelations. Finally, the repeated portrayal of Sappho as a teacher in the testimonia could be an anachronistic interpretation of her involvement with young women's choruses.

2. THE FRAGMENTS

The most important evidence about Sappho is of course the poetry itself. All attempts to reconstruct a life of Sappho and a performance situation are ultimately intended to understand this poetry, and the best reconstruction is the one that takes account of most of the fragments and explains them consistently. In the following paragraphs I will ask again two questions: who are the subjects of Sappho's poetry, and what possibly was Sappho's relationship to these subjects? Parker (323) lists six references to the age of the women to whom or about whom she is singing, outside the wedding songs, biographical or mythological fragments.[31] First there is fr. **"140a:"** κατθνάσκει, Κυθέρη', ἄβρος Ἄδωνις· τί κε θεῖμεν; / καττύπτεσθε, κόραι, καὶ κατερείκεσθε κίθωνας ("Delicate Adonis is dying, Cythera, what are we to do?"; "Beat your breasts, girls, and tear your clothes"). Parker rejects the idea that κόραι in this fragment means "girls," because "the Adonia was everywhere that we know of a festival of adult women" (323). This statement is incorrect, and Winkler, to whom Parker refers (323 n. 26), does not support Parker's claim. Winkler remarks (about the Athenian Adonis-festival) that "[t]he celebrants, it seems, were not organized according to any city-wide rule but simply consisted of neighbors and friends . . ." (1990: 189). Winkler does not say that girls were excluded from these festivities because he knew better: on p. 191, he cites the opening of Menander's *Samia,* in which a young man tells how he got a young girl pregnant while she was present at the celebration of the Adonis festival in her neighbor's house.[32] Parker (323 n. 26) further mentions "the same use" of the word κόραι in Telesilla fr. 717 Page/Campbell (an address to the goddess Artemis), but the context here does not specify what is meant by the term any more than in Sappho. However, given the universal use of the term for young women in archaic and classical Greek (and the close connection of Sappho and Artemis with young, adolescent women), Campbell's translation of the term with "girls," both in Sappho and the Telesilla fragment, seems reasonably secure (1982: 155; 1992: 79).

The next question is: to whom does this word refer? Parker says that "[i]t would, in any case, presumably apply to the poet as well" (323 n.26). This is actually highly unlikely. As Page remarks (119 n.1), the dialogue form of the fragment "could be used as evidence for choral recitation" (cp. fr. 114: a wedding song), and, as in Sappho's wedding songs, the I-person (actually a "we"—person) does not include the poetess but consists precisely of young women.[33] If Sappho participated at all in the performance of this song, she may have played the part of Aphrodite, telling her chorus (the κόραι) to beat their breasts and tear their clothes.[34] This fragment confirms Sappho's composition of songs for girls' choruses outside the wedding songs. The composition of such a song would have entailed the training of the girls and probably the participation in the performance as a singer and/or the accompanist (see below).

In some of the other fragments Sappho speaks *about* young women. In fr. **"17."**14 (a hymn to Hera), "the reference is not necessarily to the celebrants" (Parker 323), but given the fact that Sappho's maiden choruses were involved in the performance of other hymns to the gods (fr. **"140a"**), it certainly could be.[35] In fr. 49, Atthis is mentioned as one of Sappho's beloved (**"49."**1) and perhaps she is identified as being a *pais* at that moment (**"49."**2),[36] while in fr. **"96"** this same Atthis is described as having performed a song-dance (μόλπαι, line 5) in which a woman who is now in Lydia took much delight.[37] These are two very important fragments because they explicitly connect one of Sappho's beloved with musical activity. Of course, we do not know for certain that Atthis performed her "song-dance" in one of Sappho's choirs, but it is a distinct possibility.[38] Frs. **"153"** and **"56"** speak, respectively, about a "sweet-voiced girl" (πάρθενον ἀδύφωνον) and a girl (πάρθενον) with much skill (σοφίαν), "probably poetic" (Campbell 1982: 91 n.1). Parker is right that the context of these poems is unknown, but given Sappho's involvement with the setting up of choruses of, precisely, *parthenoi,* it is not too far-fetched to assume that these two fragments somehow relate to the girls whom she dealt with in her choruses. Finally, Parker mentions that the *pais* who is described in fr. **"122,"** "may well be mythological" (323), but according to Athenaeus, who preserved the fragment, Sappho (read: the speaker in the fragment) had said that she saw the child herself (καὶ Σαπφώ φησιν ἰδεῖν· ἄνθε' ἀμέργοισαν παῖδ' †ἄγαν† ἀπάλαν, Athen. 12.554b).

There are two more fragments (frs. **"58"** and **"93"** Voigt) that mention *parthenoi* and *paides,* outside the wedding songs, biographical or mythological fragments. Of these two fragments, fr. **"58"** looks most promising.[39] Line 11 mentions *paides* with beautiful gifts, either of the deep or violet-bosomed Muses.[40] The speaker (a woman) says that she is overcome by old age and no longer able to do like the young fawns (probably to dance[41]). A similar-looking poem is preserved among Alcman's fragments. Here the speaker (according to Antigonus, who preserved the fragment, Alcman himself) addresses a group of "honey-tongued, holy-voiced girls," telling them that "his limbs no longer can carry" him.[42] I submit that Sappho in this fragment invokes the same image and that the *paides* of line 11 make up the chorus which is dancing while she is singing.[43] There thus seems to be ample proof in the fragments that Sappho not only composed songs for young women's choruses, both in and outside of her wedding songs, but also spoke about girls and sometimes addressed them directly.[44]

Parker opposes to this evidence five fragments which, he argues, show "Sappho surrounded by age-mates" (323). The first one is fr. **"49."**1, ἠράμαν μὲν ἔγω σέθεν, Ἄτθι, πάλαι ποτά ("I loved you once, Atthis, long ago"), which he interprets as pertaining to Sappho's love for Atthis while *both* of them were still young. Parker bases this interpretation on a remark by Terentianus Maurus, who recast this fragment as: cordi

quando fuisse sibi canit Atthida / parvam, florea virginitas sua cum floret ("when she sang that she loved little
Atthis when her virginity was in flower").[45] Parker
concludes that "the *virginitas sua* is Sappho's" (323),
but I am not so certain about this. The possessive
pronoun *suus* can refer to other persons besides the
subject of a sentence, particularly in late Latin and in
subordinate clauses.[46] This could well be the case here,
since "parvam" (qualifying Atthida) announces the
content of the subordinate clause and by enjambment
draws Atthis, the last mentioned topic, into the same
line.[47]

Of two of the other four fragments (frs. **"23"** and
"24a"), Parker says: "The speaker may not be Sappho,
though I am assuming that she probably is, and it is not
impossible that these two, like **"27"** and **"30,"** are *epithalamia*" (324 n.28). If, however, these fragments are
wedding songs, like **"27"** and **"30,"** they were probably
not spoken by Sappho but by age-mates of the bride, as
Parker himself admits on p. 332. He assigns fr. **"23"** to
a same-age addressee because one of the two *comparandae* is Helen (the other is Hermione), and "[n]o male
lyric poet compares his *pais* with the adult male gods
or heroes" (324). For the same reason Atthis and the
woman in Lydia would be adults in fr. **"96"** (because
they are compared to goddesses) and Leto and Niobe,
who are called dear companions (φίλαι . . . ἔταιραι)
in fr. **"142,"** the *comparandae* of two same-aged
friends. Parker wisely adds "lyric" to poet, because
otherwise he would have had to admit that Phoenix
already compares his pupil Achilles to the married hero
Meleager in Book Nine of the *Iliad*. His statement is
not even true for lyric poetry, however, since the boy
victory in Pindar *Ol.* 10, to whom Parker refers in note
29, is not only compared to Ganymede but also to Patroclus (*Ol.* 10.19). This passage, which compares Patroclus and Achilles to, respectively, the boy victor and
his trainer, demonstrates that age plays no determining
rôle in mythological *comparanda,* while Alcman's
partheneia show that girls can be compared to adult
gods and goddesses (fr. **"1."**41, **"71,"** **"96f."**).[48] Of all
five fragments Parker adduces, not one is proof that
Sappho in her poetry spoke about same-age women.
Contrast this with the eight fragments about κόραι,
παρθένοι or παῖδες (frs. **"17."**14, **"49."**2, **"56,"** **"58,"**
"93," **"122,"** **"140a,"** **"153;"** outside the wedding
songs, the biographical or mythological allusions), and
the different poems addressed to women whom the testimonia identify as girls (Anactoria, fr. 16, cp. test. 2?,
19, 20; Gongyla, frs. 22, 95, cp. test. 2, fr. 213; Megara,
fr. 68a, cp. test. 2; Atthis, frs. 49.1, 96.17, 131, cp. test.
2, 19 and 20), and the verdict is clear: young women
are in all likelihood the subject of most of Sappho's
poetry.[49]

The question next becomes: what relationship(s) did
Sappho have with these young women? The minimum
we can say is that she composed songs for them to
perform, like the wedding songs, the Adonis hymn, and
fr. **"58."** From fragments like fr. **"1,"** as well as the testimonia, we can further deduce that Sappho expressed
desire for some of them in her poetry, although we do
not know for sure if her young lovers were also part of
her choruses: the only tenuous piece of evidence are the
fragments that speak about Atthis as both her lover (fr.
"49."1) and a performer (**"96."**5). The crucial fragment
is, in my opinion, fragment **"94."** In this fragment Sappho inserts her own name (ψάπφ', 5), so the persona
of the narrator is beyond doubt. Sappho speaks to a
woman who is leaving her (ἄ με . . . κατελίμπανεν,
2) and reminds her of all the pleasant things they did
together: stringing flower-wreaths (12f.), putting on
garlands (15f.), wearing perfumes (18f.), going to holy
places (25, 27) and possibly performing there.[50] Parker
is right in resisting any attempt to read "a course
description" (315) into these words, but the activities
are compatible with those of a chorus and one can even
read a linear progression into them, starting with the
preparations and leading up to musical performances at
temples and in other places. Sappho would be reminding a girl of previous performances perhaps at the very
moment that she and her choir, of which the girl no
longer was part, were performing again a song-dance.[51]
In the middle of all this (between the perfume and the
holy shrine) we read the words: "and on soft beds,
tender . . . you would satisfy your longing . . ."[52] If
these words indeed refer to sexual longing, which Sappho had satisfied,[53] they would show that the girl was
not only once a member of Sappho's chorus, but that
she at the same time had a homoerotic relationship with
Sappho.

· · · · ·

CONCLUSION

We may conclude that there is no reason to doubt that
Sappho talked about young, adolescent women in her
poetry. This is confirmed by eleven testimonia which,
although late, could have easily inferred this from her
poetry. Parker's hypothesis that our classical sources
misread Sappho's poetry in this respect, changing adult
women into girls, lacks positive proof and is actually
contradicted by other representations of homosexual
women in the Roman period. The fragments also speak
overwhelmingly about *paides* and *parthenoi* and, in one
or two cases, address them directly (frs. **"58"** and
"140a"). There are, furthermore, among her poetry at
least two types of songs, the wedding songs and the
hymns, which must have involved her in the setting up
of young women's choruses.

Reviewing the different modern reconstructions of Sappho, one has to reject both the schoolmistress' model as

basically anachronistic and Parker's reconstruction of Sappho as a singer at banquets because it lacks proof and is contradicted by too many fragments and testimonia. The reading of Sappho as a leader of a *thiasos* is either too vague or unhistorical. The model which can best be reconciled with the fragments, the historical period and the testimonia, is that of Sappho as an instructor of young women's choruses. I would therefore suggest that we continue speaking of Sappho's "circle" (which is at least reminiscent of the Greek terminology of choruses: Calame 1977: 1.77-79) or, indeed, of her choruses, which probably included her young lovers.[54]

Notes

1. Göttingen 1816, reprinted with a "Nachtrag" in *Kleine Schriften, Vol. II: Zur griechischen Litteraturgeschichte,* Bonn 1845, 80-144. Also referred to by Parker (310 n.4, 313). For even earlier representations of Sappho, see DeJean.

2. Parker's article brings to its logical conclusion a trend in modern Sappho studies to refer to the subjects of her poetry as "women," without specifying that they were probably young, adolescent women: Winkler 1981/1990, Stehle 1990, Snyder 1991. These studies, however, unlike Parker's, do not explicitly deny that these women were adolescent (cp. Stigers [Stehle] 1981: 45).

3. Calder and DeJean (207-09, 217-19) had already made this argument where Welcker's and Wilamowitz's interpretation of Sappho as a chaste schoolmistress is concerned.

4. By young women or girls, I mean women who in our sources, including Sappho's poetry, are referred to as κόραι, παρθένοι and sometimes παῖδες. They denote the age-group between puberty and marriage (roughly twelve to eighteen year olds): see Calame 1977: 1.63-64.

5. Horace *Carm.* 2.13.24-25 (=test. 18), Ovid *Her.* 15.15-20 (=test. 19), *Tr.* 2.365 (=test. 49), Maximus of Tyre 18.9 (=test. 20), Philostratus *VA* 1.30 (=test. 21), Himerius *Or.* 28.2 (=test. 50), SLG 261A (=fr. 214B fr.1). All fragments and testimonia of Sappho are cited from D. A. Campbell's edition in the Loeb Classical Library, Cambridge MA 1982, unless noted otherwise.

6. Welcker 1816/1845: 105-14; cp. Calder: 141-42. There were in Welcker's time two explicit testimonia about Sappho's love for (young) women: Ovid *Her.* 15.15-20 and 201-202 (=test. 19) and the Suda (=test. 2). In the beginning of the twentieth century, a papyrus was found which refers to rumors about Sappho being a "woman-lover" (γυναικεράστρια, test. 1). The weakness

of Welcker's argument was that, as far as we know, Sappho was not portrayed as a lesbian on the Athenian stage, but, on the contrary, as an extreme heterosexual: test. 8; cp. Lardinois 1989: 22-25.

7. The Alexandrians had made a collection of Sappho's poems in nine books, which, as the many papyrus fragments show, survived through most of the Hellenistic and Roman period. Parts of her poetry were still directly known in Byzantium in the twelfth century: see Garzya 1971, cited by Campbell 1982: 51 n.1, and more recently Garzya 1991.

8. The name Anagora, who is mentioned as one of Sappho's pupils (μαθήτριαι) in the Suda (test. 2), is probably also derived from references to Anactoria in Sappho's poetry (Lefkowitz 1981: 64).

9. Anne Le Fèvre Dacier in her famous "Vie de Sapho," first published in Paris in 1681, already suggested that jealousy for a woman, "who not only surpassed all other women . . . but soared far and above the very best male poets," produced "the calumnies with which they attempted to blacken her" (1681/1716: 235; cp. DeJean: 57). She used the male bias of our sources to discredit any reports that Sappho was a lesbian, while Parker uses it to strengthen them.

10. Flacelière 1960/1962: 197, Foucault 189-232. The Romans explicitly forbade pederasty with free boys in the so-called *lex Sca(n)tinia,* a law dating from before Cicero's time: see Bremmer (1980: 288 with notes) and Cantarella (1988/1992: 106-19) for the evidence.

11. See Lanata, Lasserre 1974, Giacomelli [Carson], Cavallini 1986: 17-67.

12. Themistius *Or.* 13.170d (=test. 52). Parker dismisses this testimonium as another example of Sappho "being assimilated as much as possible to the male, in order to neutralize her" (322), but otherwise he encourages a direct comparison of Sappho to the male poets, arguing that she was a woman who "shares concerns and subject matter with Alcaeus and the other lyric poets" (346). Parker 318 himself compares Anacreon fr. 357 (about a boy who does not love him back) and Theognis 250-54 or 1299-1304 (about Cyrnus) to Sappho fr. 1, when arguing that the woman she sings about was not necessarily part of a circle.

13. Here, as Parker puts it, "[t]he question of 'sincerity' raises its pointless head" (333 n. 59). This is not a pointless question, but a very important one, which arises precisely when one starts questioning the move from poetic to bio-

graphical fact. Parker's objection that "no one has ever claimed that Alcaeus or Theognis was forced into writing homosexual poetry by convention" (334 n.59) is incorrect. Welcker (1826: Introd. 77-78) already suggested that Cyrnus, Theognis' addressee, is not a real person but a foil for the audience, to which Nagy (1985: 33-34) has added that the figure of Theognis himself is probably a *persona*. All this does not bode well for the sincerity of Theognis' expressions of affection. In his review of Schneidewin's edition of Ibycus in 1834, Welcker further suggested that Ibycus' love lyrics should be read as public praise rather than private longing (cited by Kurke: 86, who herself points to the conventionality of Pindar's expression of love for Thrasyboulus in *Pythian* 6). See also Von der Mühll, and Lasserre 1974.

14. Müller 1858: 231, cp. Bowra: 212-14, Nagy 1973/ 1990: 228-29, Lardinois 1989: 23. Phaon was a mythological figure who, just like Adonis, ranked among Aphrodite's lovers. We know that Sappho composed songs about the love of Aphrodite for Phaon and Adonis (fr. 211) and in one of the songs about Adonis (fr. 140a) the goddess is made to speak. It is very well possible that Sappho put into the mouth of the goddess a similar profession of love for Phaon, which was later misread as being her own.

15. E.g. frs. 1.18-24, 140a.2 (Aphrodite), fr. 102 (a girl speaking to her mother), fr. 137 (a dialogue between a man and a woman). For more examples, see Tsagarakis 77-81.

16. The only explicit reference to Sappho's monodic songs is in the Suda (test. 2), which places her μονῳδίαι, however, outside of her nine books of lyric songs. There are, on the other hand, many references to her choral compositions: e.g. *Anth. Pal.* 9.189 (=test. 59), Demetrius *Eloc.* 132 (=test. 111 Gallavotti), Himerius *Or.* 9.4 (=test. 194), Philostratus *Im.* 2.1.1-3 (=test 120 Gallavotti). It is further worth noting that when the third century B.C. poet Nossis wants to send a message to Sappho, she sends it to "Mitylene with the beautiful choruses" (καλλίχορον Μιτυλήναν, *A.P.* 7.718.1=Nossis, *Epigram* 11.1 Gow & Page).

17. Page followed Lobel in his assessment that Sappho wrote in her Lesbian vernacular, "uncontaminated by alien or artificial forms and features," with the exception of some "abnormal" poems, to which most of the wedding songs (though not all: frs. 27 and 30) belonged (327). This distinction has been successfully challenged by Hooker, and Bowie 1981. It appears that all of Sappho's poetry is a complicated mix of old Aeolic, epic, and her

local dialect, not unlike Alcman's (choral) poetry (on which see Calame 1983: xxiv-xxxiv).

18. Not all of Sappho's wedding songs were assigned to Book Nine in the Alexandrine collection of her poems. Most of the other eight books were arranged by meter, and if the wedding songs fitted the meter of one of the other eight books, they were apparently assigned a place there. Such is the case with frs. 27 and 30, which, together with other poems in the Sapphic stanza, were included in Book One (Page 125). Sappho also used the dactylic hexameter for wedding songs (frs. 105, 106, 143) and for such a song as fragment 142, believed to be the opening line of one of her amorous songs (Campbell 1982: 157).

19. The speaker in Sappho's poetry alludes a couple of times to songs which other women, whom the testimonia identify as her young companions, sing about each other (frs. 21, 22; in fr. 96.4 the person in Lydia is said to have compared Atthis once to a goddess and it is not unlikely that she did so in a song). Were these their own compositions or did Sappho compose these songs for them, the same way she composed the marriage songs?

20. E.g. Demetrius *Eloc.* 167 (=fr. 110b) on Sappho fr. 110a (a wedding song); Servius in Verg. *G.* 1.31 on Sappho fr. 116: Sappho, quae in libro qui inscribitur Ἐπιθαλάμια ait χαῖρε, νύμφα, χαῖρε, τίμιε γάμβρε, κτλ . . .

21. Lardinois 1995. Hermann Fränkel already noted that "among the Lesbians too, then, there were songs fairly close to choral lyric" (1962/1975: 186 n.45), like Sappho fragment 16, "which meditates and argues like choral poetry" (172). More recently, Claude Calame (1977: 1.127, 368-69) has suggested that Sappho's circle was organized as a young women's choir which sang or danced to songs composed by Sappho, and Judith Hallett declared that "many of Sappho's fragments thought to be personal, autobiographical statements might in fact be part of public, if not marriage, hymns sung by other females" (1979: 463).

22. See in particular Nagy 1979: 296-300 (on Homer and Hesiod), 1982/1990: 47-48, 71 (on Hesiod), 1985: 33-34 (on Theognis), 1990: 79, 363-65 (on Archilochus), but, for example, also Lamberton: 23 (on Hesiod), who draws a parallel with the relationship of Anacreon to the *Anacreonta*. Orpheus is a good example of a legendary figure whose name was attached to a particular kind of poetry in the archaic Greek period, and who was historicized by the end of the fifth century B.C. (fr. 1A5 D.-K.)

23. Hdt. 2.134 (=test. 9) places Sappho and Charaxus together with the courtesan Rhodopis, whom Charaxus was supposed to have courted (=Sappho's Doricha?: frs. 7.1?, 15.12; Strabo 17.1.33 = fr. 202b), in the time of the Egyptian pharaoh Amasis (568-526 B.C.), which is actually later than the Parian Marble (test. 5) or most scholars want to date her: e.g. Lesky 1971: 167, Campbell 1982: xi, 1985/1989: 162 (floruit around 600 B.C.).

24. Σάπφοι, Alc. fr. 384, cp. ψάπφοι, Sappho fr. 65.5, 133b; ψάπφ', Sappho fr. 1.20, 94.5. The meter prohibits emending Alcaeus' Σάπφοι to ψάπφοι. The existence of such metrical variants is typical of names which belong to an oral poetic tradition: cp. Ἀχιλλεύς/ Ἀχιλεύς, Ὀδυσσεύς / Ὀδυσεύς.

25. Fr. 16.17-20. Sappho's preference for the personal (what she loves) over cavalry and ships is matched by the composer of the Apatouria song, which in the *Vita Herodotea* is ascribed to Homer (lines 426-27 Allen p. 211=*Ep.* 12 Markwald): ἵπποι δ' ἐν πέδιῳ κόσμος, νῆες δὲ θαλάσσης, / χρήματα δ' αὔξει οἶκον.

26. On fr. 16 as possibly performed by a chorus, see Fränkel 1962/1975: 172, 186, Hallett 1979: 463 and Lardinois 1995. Stern's objection that the priamel is voiced too personally for choral poetry is answered by Bundy 6 n.19, if Pindar's epinikia are choral (on which see most recently, and sensibly, Morgan 1993).

27. Parker 321. One of the readers pointed out to me that the reference to Sappho, "teaching the noblest women not only from the local families but also from families in Ionia" (παιδεύουσα τὰς ἀρίστας οὐ μόνον τῶν ἐγχωρίων ἀλλὰ καὶ τῶν ἀπ' Ἰωνίας), preserved in a fragment of a second century A.D. Sappho commentary (SLG 261A=fr. 214B), may actually be older, since its author cites the Hellenistic scholar Callias of Mytilene (lines 14-15), although not necessarily for the part about Sappho's teaching: cp. Gronewald 114.

28. This is basically the position that Marrou (71) adopts. Parker correctly notes that "nowhere in any poem does Sappho teach, or speak about teaching, anything to anyone" (314), in the sense of any formal education. Sappho does sometimes provide gnomic advice to her internal addressees (frs. 81, 150), but not very often and not more than, for example, Archilochus or Alcaeus.

29. Maximus compares Sappho's amorous relationship with Gyrinna, Atthis, and Anactoria to those of Socrates with Alcibiades, Charmides, and Phae-drus. About all three women, whom I believe to be girls, some erotic-sounding fragments are preserved: Gyrinna (=Gyrinno?): fr. 82a; Atthis: 49.1, 96, 131, cp. test. 2 and 19; Anactoria: frs. 16, cp. test. 19.

30. Although Parker rejects the testimonia as late, male distortions of female relationships, he still feels the need to question our understanding of them. He notes that Ovid (*Tr.* 2.365=test. 49, *Her.* 15.15=test. 19) and Horace (*Carm.* 2.13.24f.=test. 18) speak of Sappho as in love with *puellae* but that, "*puella,* of course, is used equally of girls, mature women, and goddesses, especially as objects of love" (321). This is true, but the context in Ovid *Tr.* 2.365 (=test. 49), where we are told that Sappho "taught" (*docuit*) her *puellas* to love, as well as the other testimonia, strongly suggest that in this case *puellae* does refer to young girls.

31. These are frs. 17, 49.2, 56, 122, 140a and 153. Add frs. 58 and 93 Voigt. Parker further mentions frs. 27, 30, 105, 107, 113, 114 and 194, "where the youth and the virginity of the bride are mentioned" (add fr. 112.2: bride is a παρθένος). In fr. 132 παῖς refers to Sappho's daughter, Cleïs (see Hallett 1982, Lardinois 1989: 22), in fr. 104a.2 to an unspecified child of a mother, in fr. 155 to "the daughter of the house of Polyanax" (Gorgo or Andromeda: her "rivals"), in frs. 1.2, 16.10, 103.3 Voigt, and 164 ("perhaps Eros," Campbell [1982] ad loc.) to mythological figures.

32. The girl is referred to as κόρη, 36 and παῖς, 49 Sandbach. Winkler, in his footnote 2, mentions Pausanias' report about the women of Argos not as evidence that the Adonia were celebrated by adult women, as Parker suggests, but to show that "in other times and places" the festival may have had a more public character. This may have been the case on Lesbos as well, and fr. 140a was probably performed in public (Page 119, Campbell 1982: xiii, 1985/1989: 162).

33. Compare fr. 30.9 "let us see" ([ἴ]δωμεν) to which the word παρθένοι in the nominative in line 1 is probably related, and 27.8: σ]τείχομεν γὰρ ἐς γάμον. On the performance of Sappho's wedding songs by age-mates of the bride, see Page 120, Calame 1977: 1.161 n.230 and Contiades-Tsitsoni 40-41, 100. Parker agrees: 331-32.

34. Bowra 212, otherwise, suggested that the part of Aphrodite was played by a priestess.

35. Compare fr. 30.1 (a wedding song) for a similar self-reference: παρθένοι. Fränkel 1962/1975: 181 already suggested that this poem, which has been variously interpreted as an unspecified hymn to

Hera (Page 61-62) or a *propemptikon* (Merkelbach 23-25), may have been sung by a chorus.

36. I agree with Parker 323 that these two lines do not necessarily belong together.

37. The "you" of line 4 and 5 probably has to be identified with Atthis, whose name is mentioned in line 16: Page 92, Saake 1971: 172. Atthis is also identified as one of Sappho's "companions or girlfriends" in test. 2, 19 and 20.

38. The Suda (test. 2) in fact distinguishes between Sappho's pupils (μαθήτριαι) and her "three companions and friends [including Atthis], through whom she got a bad name for impure friendship" (ἑταῖραι δὲ αὐτῆς καὶ φίλαι γεγόνασι τρεῖς, Ἀτθίς, Τελεσίππα, Μεγάρα, πρὸς ἃς καὶ διαβολὴν ἔσχεν αἰσχρᾶς φιλίας), but this probably represents an attempt by the Suda or its source to account for the two Hellenistic traditions about Sappho: Sappho as teacher and Sappho as tribade. One may compare Aelian *V.H.* 12.19 (=test. 4), who claims that there were two Sapphos of Lesbos: one a poet and the other a prostitute.

39. Fr. 93 Voigt (not included in Campbell 1982) preserves a first person singular verb in line 4 (ἔχω) and the word *parthenoi,* seemingly in the genitive plural, in line 5 (παρθένωω): no further details.

40. Di Benedetto 147-48. It is not unlikely that this line constitutes the actual beginning of the poem (idem: 147, Gallavotti 1962: 113). Page (129) also begins the poem in this line.

41. ὄρχ]ησση': Edmonds' conjecture in line 16, cited by Voigt and Campbell ad loc.

42. οὔ μ' ἔτι, παρσενικαὶ μελιγάρυες ἰαρόφωνοι, / γυῖα φέρην δύναται, Alcm. fr. 26.1-2a Page/ Davies. Compare Sappho fr. 58.15: γόνα δ' [ο]ὐ φέροισι. Antigonus (cited by Davies [1991] ad loc.) further specifies that Alcman speaks this poem, "being weak from old age and unable to whirl about with the choirs and the girls' dancing" (φησὶν γὰρ ἀσθενὴς ὢν διὰ τὸ γῆρας καὶ τοῖς χοροῖς οὐ δυνάμενος συμπεριφέρεσθαι οὐδὲ τῆι τῶν παρθένων ὀρχήσει). Calame 1983: 474 already noted the similarity between this poem and Sappho fr. 58.

43. Sappho fr. 21 describes a similar situation (χρόα γῆρας ἤδη, 21.6b=58.13b), and here it is clear that we are dealing with some kind of an exchange, for in line 11-12 the speaker calls on another woman (λάβοισα, line 11, cp. Fr. 22.9-11) to "sing about the violet-robed one" (according to

Campbell 1982: 73 n.3 Aphrodite, otherwise perhaps a bride: cp. fr. 30.5). According to Di Benedetto (148-49), line fr. 58.11 opened with an invitation to the chorus to sing (e.g. γεραίρετε) and line 12 contained the instruction to "take up the song-loving, clear-sounding lyre (. . . λάβοισαι] φιλάοιδον λιγύραν χελύνναν). Calame 1977: 1.127, 369, citing *Anth. Pal.* 9.189 (=test. 59), already suggested that Sappho may have sung some of her poetry in public while her chorus danced. One may compare for this type of musical performance Demodocus' song about Ares and Aphrodite, which is sung by Demodocus and danced to by a group of young Phaeacian men (*Od.* 8.262-64), the wedding song in *Od.* 4.17-19, or the execution of the Linos song in *Il.* 18.569f. For some applications of this type of performance to other archaic Greek poetry, see Davies 1988: 62-63.

44. One should add the many names of persons whom the testimonia identify as girls: Anactoria (fr. 16, cp. test. 2?, 19, 20), Gongyla (fr. 22, 95, cp. test. 2, fr. 213), Megara (fr. 68a, cp. test. 2), Atthis (frs. 49.1, 96.17, 131, cp. test. 2, 19 and 20).

45. Ter. Maur. 2154-55 = 6.390.4-5 Klein, quoted by Parker 323.

46. Leuman, Hofmann & Szantyr: 2. 175; Klenin 115: "Despite occasional claims to the contrary, there is no subject condition on Latin reflexivization, although antecedents are often also subjects; apparently the basis of their eligibility to trigger reflexivization involves empathy relations as described by Kuno and Kaburaki ["Empathy and Syntax," *Linguistic Inquiry* 8.4, 1977, 627-72]." I owe this reference to Brent Vine.

47. Of course, even if Terentianus Maurus meant Sappho's virginity with "sua virginitas," we cannot be certain that he understood the poem correctly and, for example, did not confuse the speaker, who may not have been Sappho but one or more of Atthis' companions (cp. frs. 21, 22). It is interesting in this respect that we are told in fr. 96.4 that Atthis once was praised, probably in a song, by a woman who now dances in Lydia (one of her former companions?).

48. σιειδής in Alcman fr. 1.71 closely resembles θέαι σ' ἰκέλαν in Sappho fr. 96.4 and the comparison of the woman in Lydia with Selanna (Sappho fr. 96.8) matches that of Agido and the sun (Alcman fr. 1.41). Even if fr. 142 (about Leto and Niobe) refers to two same-aged companions, we would still not know whether they were pictured as two adult or two young women at the time. Athenaeus (13.571d) adduces the fragment in order to show

that "free women *as well as girls* call their intimate and dear friends companions" (καλοῦέι γοῦν καὶ αἱ ἐλεύθεραι γυναῖκες ἔτι καὶ νῦν καὶ αἱ παρθένοι τὰς συνήθεις καὶ φίλας ἑταίρας, ὡς ἡ Σαπφώ . . .). Parker's suggestion that the commentary preserved as fr. 90.10a (=90d Voigt) would somehow reveal that Sappho compared herself and Atthis to these two mythological figures (339 n.78), is highly speculative at best. The fragment does not mention the names of Sappho or Niobe. It preserves Atthis' name in line 15 and the letters]λατωσ in line 3 without there being even the slightest suggestion that the two are somehow connected. Fr. 23 not only compares the addressee to Helen but also to Hermione, Helen's daughter. The comparison is cumulative (you are as beautiful as Hermione, no as Helen herself) and, I would argue, suits a young woman just as well, if not better, than an adult. It may be that this fragment is derived from a wedding song (cp. Parker 324 n.28), in which case it would probably refer to the bride: Lucian (*Symp.* 41) in a wedding song also compares the bride to Helen. It is, furthermore, not unlikely that Helen in fr. 16 is the *comparanda* both for the speaker and Anactoria (Macleod 217-19, Carey 368-69, Dane 192 *contra* Parker 324 n. 28), who has been positively identified as a young woman (Brown; cp. test. 19 and 20).

49. There are, of course, other types of songs as well: marriage songs, hymns, satires about "rivals" and girls who threatened to leave her, songs about her daughter Cleïs and her brothers Charaxus and Larichus, and mythological tales: see Lardinois 1989: 16-17.

50. At the end of line 28 the word ψόφος ("sound") is preserved and Theander proposed reading κροτάλων] ψόφος here (cp. fr. 44.25: see Voigt ad loc.). The end of line 27 may contain the word χόρος, but this is uncertain (Voigt ad loc.). The "we" in "we took care of you" (πεδήπομεν, 8) could indicate that Sappho and the woman were not alone; Page (78): "If the plural is strictly interpreted, the implication will be that Sappho is speaking on behalf of her companions," or at least others besides herself (cp. Burnett 312 on the first person plural in fr. 96.21). The "we" in "we were absent (from no shrine)" (ἄμ]μες ἀπέσκομεν, 26) may also include these "others," who with Sappho and the addressee could have been the chorus of line 27.

51. We find a similar situation in fr. 96 where the speaker also reminds the addressee of her previous performances (5, 26f.?) and of a dance which it imagines to go on right now in Lydia (on ἐμπρέπεται in line 6 as suggestive of dancing, see Calame 1977: 1.91). Fragment 94 has been identified as a "farewell song," which invokes memories of previously shared experiences: most recently, Rauk 1989.

52. καὶ στρώμν[αν ἐ]πὶ μολθάκαν / ἀπάλαν πα.[] . . . ων / ἐξίης πόθο[ν].νίδων, fr. 94.21-23. From the structure of the preceding strophes we can determine that these words belong together. Every strophe seems to contain one pleasant thing Sappho and the girl did together.

53. See Burnett (298 n.56) for some other suggestions. To her examples of πόθος expressing sexual desire in Sappho (frs. 36 and 48), add frs. 22.11 and 102. ἀπάλαν (either a feminine genitive plural or singular accusative) could refer to a person (cp. frs. 82a, 122, 126); fr. 126 is particularly relevant in this regard: δαύοις ἀπάλας ἑταίρας ἐν στήθεσιν. On the other hand, one can already in Homer experience desire (ἔρος) or longing (πόθος) for other things besides sex. Since the expression ἐξίημι πόθον means "to get rid of a longing by indulging in it" (Page 79) and the woman lies in a bed (στρωμνή), the best alternative seems to be that the girl is taking a nap: cp. *Il.* 13.636f.: ὕπνου κτλ . . . τῶν πέρ τις καὶ μᾶλλον ἐέλδεται ἐξ ἔρον εέναι / ἢ πολέμου. (This was also the reading of Wilamowitz: 50.) Lasserre's recent suggestion (1989: 136-37, 140) that the girl is playing with dolls (reading παρ[α πλ]αγ[γ]όνων in line 22), has to be rejected: see Liberman 234-35, Rösler 1990: 197-98. Even if this fragment is inconclusive, there is in my opinion enough other evidence (particularly fr. 1) to suggest that Sappho presented herself as having homoerotic relationships with some of the young women she sang about in her poetry.

54. The term circle, although not original by him (cp. Schadewaldt 1950: 11), was first made popular by Merkelbach's 1957 article: "Sappho und ihre Kreis."

Works Cited

Fragments and testimonia of Sappho are cited from D. A. Campbell's edition in the Loeb Classical Library, Cambridge MA 1982, unless noted otherwise.

Allen, T. W. 1946. *Homeri Opera,* vol. 5, Revised Edition, Oxford [First published in 1930].

Arthur, M. B. 1973/1984. "Early Greece: The Origins of the Western Attitude toward Women," *Arethusa* 6 (1973) 7-58, repr. in J. Peradotto & J. P. Sullivan (eds.), *Women in the Ancient World: The Arethusa Papers,* Buffalo 1984, 7-58.

Beck, F. A. G. 1975. *Album of Greek Education: The Greeks at School and at Play,* Sydney.

Bonnafé, A and M. Casevitz. 1991. "Review: François Lasserre, *Sappho. Une autre lecture,*" AC [*Archaeologia Classica*] 60: 323-25.

Bowie, A. M. 1981. *The Poetic Dialect of Sappho and Alcaeus,* New York.

———. 1983. "Review of W. Rösler, *Dichter und Gruppe,*" JHS [*Journal of Hellenic Studies*] 103: 183-85.

Bowra, C. M. 1961. *Greek Lyric Poetry from Alcman to Simonides,* Second Revised Edition, Oxford.

Bremmer, J. N. 1980. "An Enigmatic Indo-European Rite: Paederasty," *Arethusa* 13: 279-83.

———. 1989. "Greek Pederasty and Modern Homosexuality," in J. N. Bremmer (ed.), *From Sappho to de Sade: Moments in the History of Sexuality,* London, 1-14 (The second edition, New York 1991, contains some slight revisions and updates).

———. 1990. "Adolescents, *Symposion,* and Pederasty," in O. Murray (ed.), *Sympotica: A Symposium on the Symposion,* Oxford, 135-48.

Brown, C. 1989. "Anactoria and the Χαρίτων ἀμαρύγματα: Sappho fr. 16.18 Voigt," QUCC [*Quaderni Urbinati di Cultura Classsica*] 61: 7-15.

Buffière, F. 1980. *Eros adolescent: la pédérastie dans la Grèce antique,* Paris.

Bundy, E. L. 1962/1986. *Studia Pindarica,* Berkeley. [First published as Vol. 18 nos. 1 and 2 of the University of California Publications in Classical Philology.]

Burnett, A. P. 1983. *Three Archaic Poets: Archilochus, Alcaeus, Sappho,* Cambridge MA.

Calame, C. 1977. *Les choeurs de jeunes filles en Grèce archaïque,* 2 vols., Rome.

———. 1983. *Alcman Fragmenta,* Rome.

Calder III, W. M. 1986. "Welcker's Sapphobild and its Reception in Wilamowitz," in W. M. Calder III etc. (eds.), *Friedrich Gottlieb Welcker. Werk und Wirkung,* Hermes Einzelschriften 49, Stuttgart, 131-56.

Campbell, D. A. 1967. *Greek Lyric Poetry: A Selection of Early Greek Lyric, Elegiac and Iambic Poetry,* New York (A new edition with corrections, additional bibliography and new appendix of additional fragments was published by Bristol Classical Press, 1982).

———. 1982. *Greek Lyric I,* Loeb Classical Library, Cambridge MA.

———. 1985/1989. "Sappho," in P. E. Easterling & B. M. W. Knox (eds.), *Cambridge History of Classical Literature,* Vol. 1 Part 1, Revised Edition, Cambridge, 162-68.

———. 1988. *Greek Lyric II,* Loeb Classical Library, Cambridge MA.

———. 1992. *Greek Lyric IV,* Loeb Classical Library, Cambridge MA.

Cantarella, E. 1981/1987. *Pandora's Daughters: The Role and Status of Women in Greek and Roman Antiquity,* Baltimore. Trans. by M. B. Fant of *L' ambiguo malanno. Condizione e immagine della donna nell' antichità greca e romana,* Rome 1981.

———. 1988/1992. *Bisexuality in the Ancient World,* New Haven. Trans. by C. Ó Cuilleanáin of *Secondo natura: La bisessualità nel mondo antico,* Rome 1988.

Carey, C. 1978. "Sappho Fr. 96 LP," CQ [*Classical Quarterly*] 28: 366-71.

Cavallini, E. 1986. *Presenza di Saffo e Alceo nella poesia greca fino ad Aristofane,* Ferrara.

———. 1991. "Review François Lasserre, *Sappho. Une autre lecture,*" Gnomon 63: 673-80.

Contiades-Tsitsoni, E. 1990. *Hymenaios und Epithalamion: Das Hochzeitslied in der frühgrichischen Lyrik,* Stuttgart.

Cribiore, R. 1993. "Women Teachers in Roman Egypt," *APA Abstracts of the One Hundred and Twenty Fifth Annual Meeting,* 85.

Dane, J. A. 1981. "Sappho Fr. 16: An Analysis," *Eos* 69: 185-92.

Davies, M. 1988. "Monody, Choral Lyric, and the Tyranny of the Hand-Book," *CQ* 38: 52-64.

———. 1991. *Poetarum Melicorum Graecorum Fragmenta,* post D. L. Page, vol. I: *Alcman, Stesichorus, Ibycus,* Oxford.

DeJean, J. 1989. *Fictions of Sappho, 1546-1937,* Chicago.

Devereux, G. 1967. "Greek Pseudo-Homosexuality and the 'Greek Miracle'," SO [*Studia Orientalia*] 42: 69-92.

———. 1970. "The Nature of Sappho's Seizure in Fr. 31 LP as Evidence of her Inversion," *CQ* 20: 17-31.

Di Benedetto, V. 1985. "Il tema della vecchiaia e il fr. 58 di Saffo," *QUCC* NS 19: 145-63.

Diels, H. 1896. "Alkmans Partheneion," *Hermes* 31: 339-74.

Dodds, E. R. 1960. *Euripides. Bacchae,* Second Edition, Oxford.

Dover, K. J. 1978. *Greek Homosexuality,* Oxford. (Reprinted in 1989 with a postscript).

Everard, M. 1984. "De liefde van Lesbos in Nederland: Sappho in de nederlandse letteren van 19de en begin 20ste eeuw," *Tijdschrift voor vrouwenstudies* 5: 333-50.

Flacelière, R. 1960/1962. *Love in Ancient Greece,* London. Trans. by J. Cleugh from *L'Amour en Grèce* (Paris 1960).

———. 1962. *Histoire littéraire de la Grèce,* Paris. [Engl. trans. by D. Garman, *A Literary History of Greece,* London 1964.]

Foucault, M. 1984/1986. *The History of Sexuality, Vol. 3: The Care of the Self,* New York. Trans. by R. Hurley of *Histoire de la sexualité, Vol. 3: Le Souci de soi* (Paris 1984).

Fränkel, H. 1968 [1924]. "Eine Stileigenheit der frühgriechischen Literatur," in *Wege und Forme frühgriechischen Denkens,* Third Edition, Munich, 40-96.

———. 1962/1975. *Early Greek Poetry and Philosophie,* New York. Trans. by Moses Hadas and James Willis of *Dichtung und Philosophie des frühen Griechentums* (Munich 1962).

Gallavotti, C. 1962. *Saffo e Alceo, Testimonianze e frammenti, Vol. 1: Saffo,* Third Revised Edition, Napels.

———. 1978. "Alcmane, Teocrito, e un' iscrizione laconica," *QUCC* 27: 183-94.

Garzya, A. 1971. "Per la fortuna di Saffo a Bisanzio," *Jahrbuch der Österreichischen Byzantistik* 20: 1-5.

———. 1991. "Ancora Saffo a Bisanzio?," in *Studi di filologia classica in onore di Giusto Monaco, Vol. 4: Linguistica, mitologia, medio evo, umanesimo,* Palermo, 1441-42.

Gentili, B. 1966. "La veneranda Saffo," *QUCC* 2: 37-62.

———. 1985/1988. *Poetry and its Public in Ancient Greece: From Homer to the Fifth Century,* Baltimore. Trans. by A. Thomas Cole of *Poesia e publica nella grecia antica* (Rome 1985).

Gerber, D. E. 1970. *Euterpe: An Anthology of Early Greek Lyric, Elegiac and Iambic Poetry,* Amsterdam.

Giacomelli [Carson], A. 1980. "The Justice of Aphrodite in Sappho Fr. 1," *TAPA* [*Transactions of the American Philological Association*] 110: 135-42.

Governi, A. 1981. "Su alcuni elementi propemptici in Saffo e in Omero," *SIFC* [*Studi Italiani di Filologia Classica*] 53: 270-71.

Gow, A. S. F. & D. L. Page. 1965. *The Greek Anthology: Hellenistic Epigrams,* 2 vols., Cambridge.

Gronewald, M. 1974. "Fragmente aus einem Sapphokommentar: Pap. Colon. inv. 5860," *ZPE* [*Zeischrift fuer Papyrologie und Epigraphik*] 14: 114-20.

Hallett, J. P. 1979. "Sappho and her Social Context: Sense and Sensuality," *Signs* 3: 447-64.

———. 1982. "Beloved Cleïs," *QUCC* NS 10: 21-31.

———. 1989. "Female Homoeroticism and the Denial of Roman Reality in Latin Literature," *Yale Journal of Criticism* 3: 209-27.

Hamm [Voigt], E.-M. 1957. *Grammatik zu Sappho und Alkaios,* Berlin.

Hooker, J. T. 1977. *The Language and Text of the Lesbian Poets,* Innsbruck.

Howie, J. G. 1977. "Sappho Fr. 16 (LP): Self-Consolation and Encomium," in F. Cairns (ed.), *Papers of the Liverpool Latin Seminar,* vol. 1, Liverpool, 207-35.

Keil, H. 1874. *Grammatici Latini, Vol. VI: Scriptores Artis Metricae,* Leipzig.

Klenin, E. 1975. "Medieval Latin Empathy and Discourse Structure," *Harvard Studies in Syntax and Semantics* 1: 113-25.

Kranz, W. 1958. *Geschichte der griechischen Literatur,* Third Revised Edition, Bremen.

Kurke, L. 1990. "Pindar's Sixth *Pythian* and the Tradition of Advice Poetry," *TAPA* 120: 85-107.

Lanata, G. 1966. "Sul linguaggio amoroso di Saffo," *QUCC* 2: 63-79.

Lamberton, R. 1988. *Hesiod,* New Haven.

Lardinois, A. 1989. "Lesbian Sappho and Sappho of Lesbos," in J. N. Bremmer (ed.), *From Sappho to de Sade: Moments in the History of Sexuality,* London, 15-35 (The second edition, New York 1991, contains some slight revisions and updates).

———. 1995. "Who Sang Sappho's Songs?," in E. Greene (ed.), *Rereading Sappho: A Collection of Critical Essays,* Berkeley, forthcoming.

Lasserre, F. 1974. "Ornements érotiques dans la poésie lyrique archaïque," in J. L. Heller and J. K. Newman (eds.), *Serta Turyniana: Studies in Greek Literature and Palaeography in honor of Alexander Turyn,* Urbana 1974, 1-33.

———. 1989. *Sappho: Une autre lecture,* Padua.

Le Fèvre Dacier, A. 1681/1716. *Les Poésies d' Anacréon et de Sapho, traduites en François avec des remarques,* Revised Edition, Amsterdam 1716 [First published in Paris 1681].

Lefkowitz, M. 1973/1981. "Critical Stereotypes and the Poetry of Sappho," *GRBS* [*Greek, Roman, and Byzantine Studies*] 14 (1973) 113-23; reprinted in *Heroines and Hysterics,* New York 1981, 59-68.

———. 1981. *The Lives of the Greek Poets,* London.

Lesky, A. *Geschichte der griechischen Literatur,* Bern, 1st ed. 1957/58, 2nd rev. ed. 1963 (Engl. trans. by J. Willis and C. de Heer, New York 1966), 3rd rev. ed. 1971.

Leuman, M., Hofmann, J. B. & A. Szantyr. 1972. *Lateinische Grammatik, Vol. 2: Syntax und Stilistik,* Revised Edition, Munich.

Liberman, G. 1989. "A propos de Sappho." *Revue de Philologie* 63: 229-37. [Review of Lasserre 1989.]

Macleod, C. W. 1974. "Two Comparisons in Sappho," *ZPE* 15: 217-20.

Maehler, H. 1989. *Pindari carmina cum fragmentis, Pars II: Fragmenta. Indices,* ed. H. Maehler, Leipzig.

Markwald, G. 1986. *Die Homerische Epigramme: Sprachliche und inhaltliche Untersuchungen,* König-stein.

Marrou, H.-I. 1965. *Histoire de l'éducation dans l'antiquité,* Sixth Edition, Paris.

Merkelbach, R. 1957. "Sappho und ihre Kreis," *Philologus* 101: 1-29.

Morgan, K. A. 1993. "Pindar The Professional and the Rhetoric of the ΚΩΜΟΣ," *CP* [*Classical Philology*] 88: 1-15.

Most, G. W. 1982. "Greek Lyric Poets," in T. J. Luce (ed.), *Ancient Writers. Greece and Rome: Vol. 1: Homer to Caesar,* New York, 75-98.

Müller, K. O. 1858. *A History of the Literature of Ancient Greece,* 3 vols., translated from the manuscript and continued by J. W. Donaldson, London. [The first German edition appeared in 1841.]

Nagy, G. 1973/1990. "Phaethon, Sappho's Phaon and the White Rock of Leucas," in *Greek Mythology and Poetics,* Ithaca NY, 223-62. [An earlier version of this article was published in *HSCP* [*Harvard Studies in Classical Philology*] 77 (1973) 137-77.]

———. 1979. *The Best of the Achaeans: Concepts of the Hero in Archaic Greek Poetry,* Baltimore.

———. 1982/1990. "Hesiod and the Poetics of Pan-Hellenism," in *Greek Mythology and Poetics,* Ithaca NY, 36-82 [An earlier version of this chapter was published under "Hesiod" in T. J. Luce (ed.), *Ancient Writers: Greece and Rome, Vol. 1: Homer to Caesar,* New York 1982, 43-73].

———. 1985. "Theognis and Megara: A Poet's Vision of His City," in T. J. Figueira and G. Nagy (eds.), *Theognis of Megara: Poetry and the Polis,* Baltimore.

———. 1990. *Pindar's Homer: The Lyric Possession of an Epic Past,* Baltimore.

Page, D. L. 1955. *Sappho and Alcaeus: An Introduction to the Study of Ancient Lesbian Poetry,* Oxford.

Parker, H. 1993. "Sappho Schoolmistress," *TAPA* 123: 309-51.

Podlecki, A. J. 1984. *The Early Greek Poets and Their Times,* Vancouver.

Pomeroy, S. B. 1975. *Goddesses, Whores, Wives and Slaves. Women in Classical Antiquity,* New York.

Poulsen, F. 1947. *I Det Gaestfrie Europa: Liv og Rejser indtil Første Verdenskrig,* Copenhagen.

Rauk, J. 1989. "Erinna's *Distaff* and Sappho Fr. 94," *GRBS* 30: 101-16.

Rivier, A. 1967. "Observations sur Sappho, 1,19 sq.," *REG* [*Revue de Etudes Greques*] 80: 84-92.

Rösler, W. 1980. *Dichter und Gruppe: eine Untersuchung zu den Bedingungen und zur historischen Funktion früher griechischer Lyriker am Beispiel Alkaios,* Munich.

———. 1992. "Review of François Lasserre, *Sappho: une autre lecture,*" *AAHG* [*Anzeiger fuer die Alterumswissenschaft*] 45: 197-99.

Saake, H. 1971. *Zur Kunst Sapphos: Motiv-analytische und kompositionstechnische Interpretationen,* Munich.

———. 1972. *Sapphostudien: Forschungsgeschichtliche, biographische und literarästhetische Untersuchungen,* Munich.

Sandbach, F. H. 1990. *Menandri Reliquiae Selectae,* Revised Edition, Oxford.

Schadewaldt, W. 1950. *Sappho. Welt und Dichtung. Dasein in der Liebe,* Potsdam.

Sergent, B. 1986. *L'Homosexualité initiatique dans l'Europe ancienne,* Paris.

Skinner, M. B. 1993, "Women and Language in Archaic Greece, or, Why is Sappho a Woman?," in N. S. Rabinowitz and A. Richlin (eds.), *Feminist Theory and the Classics,* New York, 125-44.

Snyder, J. M. 1989. *The Women and the Lyre: Women Writers in Classical Greece and Rome,* Carbondale IL.

———. 1991. "Public Occasion and Private Passion in the Lyrics of Sappho of Lesbos," in S. B. Pomeroy (ed.), *Women's History and Ancient History,* Chapel Hill, 1-19.

Stehle, E. 1990. "Sappho's Gaze: Fantasies of a Goddess and Young Man," *differences* 2.1: 88-125.

Stern, E. M. 1970. "Sappho Fr. 16 L.P.: Zur strukturellen Einheit ihrer Lyrik," *Mnemosyne* Ser. 4, Vol. 13: 348-61.

Stigers [Stehle], E. 1979. "Romantic Sensuality, Poetic Sense: A Response to Hallett on Sappho," *Signs* 4: 465-71.

———. 1981. "Sappho's Private World," in H. Foley (ed.), *Reflections of Women in Antiquity,* London, 45-61.

Tsagarakis, O. 1977. *Self-Expression in Early Greek Lyric, Elegiac and Iambic Poetry,* Wiesbaden.

van Erp Taalman Kip, A. M. 1980. "Enige interpretatie-problemen in Sappho," *Lampas* 13: 336-54 (with a brief summary in English).

———. 1983. "Review of W. Rösler, *Dichter und Gruppe,*" *Mnemosyne* 36: 397-401.

Versnel, H. S. 1990. *Inconsistencies in Greek and Roman Religion, Part 1: Ter Unus: Isis, Dionysos, Hermes. Three Studies in Henotheism,* Leiden.

Voigt, E.-M. 1971. *Sappho et Alcaeus. Fragmenta,* Amsterdam.

Von der Mühll, P. 1964. "Weitere pindarische Notizen," *MH* [*Mediaevalia et Humanistica*] 21: 168-72.

Welcker, F. G. 1816/1845. *Sappho von einem herrschenden Vorurteil befreyt,* reprinted with a "Nachtrag" in *Kleine Schriften,* vol. 2, Bonn, 80-144. [Originally published as a monograph in Göttingen 1816.]

———. 1826. *Theognidis Reliquiae,* Frankfurt.

———. 1834. "Ibykos." *RhM* [*Rhenisches Museum fuer Philologie*] 2: 211-44. [A revised version is included in *Kleine Schriften,* Vol. I, Bonn 1844, 220-50.]

Wilamowitz-Moellendorff, U. von. 1913. *Sappho und Simonides: Untersuchungen über griechische Lyriker,* Berlin.

Winkler, J. J. 1981/1990. "Double Consciousness in Sappho's Lyrics," in Winkler 1990, 162-87. [An earlier version of this chapter was published in H. Foley (ed.), *Reflections of Women in Antiquity,* New York 1981.]

———. 1990. *The Constraints of Desire: The Anthropology of Sex and Gender,* New York.

Page Dubois (essay date 1995)

SOURCE: Dubois, Page. "Sappho's Body-in-Pieces." In *Sappho Is Burning,* pp. 55-76. Chicago: University of Chicago Press, 1995.

[*In the following excerpt from her monograph containing feminist, materialist, and historicist approaches to Sappho, Dubois uses the example of Sappho's fragmentary poem no. "31" to suggest the central importance of fragmentation and dismemberment to our modern, theoretical understanding and reconstruction of the antique past.*]

One of Walter Benjamin's theses on the philosophy of history expresses scorn for a certain view of historicism. He wrote: "Historicism gives the 'eternal' image of the past; historical materialism supplies a unique experience with the past. The historical materialist leaves it to others to be drained by the whore called 'Once upon a time' in historicism's bordello. He remains in control of his powers, man enough to blast open the continuum of history."[1] Benjamin here argues, in scandalously sexist terms, against a kind of historicism called by Fredric Jameson "existential historicism," that aesthetic contemplation of an immutable past called "once upon a time," "the experience . . . by which *historicity* as such is manifested, by means of the contact between the historian's mind in the present and a given synchronic cultural complex from the past."[2] I argue here for a historical materialist historicism, one that is not content merely to contemplate the past from the point of view of an autonomous subject in the present, who comes into contact with the collective past, but that rather engages with the past in order to generate some vision of a utopian future. And if Benjamin, in his vision of the aestheticizing, contemplative version of historicism, uses the image of the whore in historicism's bordello, feminism needs not only to reject such degrading imagery but also to consider a dialectical materialist theory of history, to use Marxism, to see difference, to put into question contemporary assumptions about such concepts as gender, sex, sexual difference and to struggle for change.

We may need a counter to what I see as feminism's continuing and sometimes exclusive emphasis on the present, a circumstance in which even an "existential" historicism might have much to offer. If we focus on the nineteenth and twentieth centuries, see only contemporary women writers, reflect only on what is to be done in the next few months, the next few years, we limit ourselves radically in speculation, in strategies and tactics, in the invention of new realities. It seems important to reinsert the possibility of utopian thinking into feminist work, and to argue that historicism, a certain variety of historicism, can expand the vocabulary of possibilities for all work on gender. This [essay] is not only an argument for feminists to adopt a theory of history but also perhaps a regression to a pre-postmodernist vision of history and progress. I realize that such a line is out of fashion, that postmodernity has erased history, rendering all of our experience flat and one-dimensional, that the concepts of past and future, of linear time, evoke unfortunate associations with master narratives, with the humanist trajectory of patriarchy. But to refuse any model of historical difference and change limits us inevitably to a purely aleatory experience of time, without the possibility of political and intellectual change and practice, and will restrict us to a passive observation of the machine of the world as it displays itself and us. I argue for a Marxist-feminist historicism, one that includes not only a narrative about the past but a vision of equality and emancipation in the future not only for women but for everyone.

Historicism will allow us to claim other histories for our political and intellectual work, allow us to see other peoples, other ideas of gendering, power, and sexual difference that help us see beyond the horizons of our own culture's essentializing notions of gender and difference. The ancient Greeks are, for me, a particularly suggestive example for historicist work, in part because we often name them as our origin, in part because they are in fact radically different from us. And fragmentation can stand as a figure for a difference in approach from the traditional classicist drive for wholeness and integrity, origins and continuity rather than recognition of difference.

Before reading Sappho's poem **"31,"** let me recall some ways in which fragments figure in ancient culture, and undo from the first any possible confidence concerning the integrity and stability of this distant place and time. Ancient Dionysiac ritual included reference to a *sparagmos,* the ritual dismemberment and devouring of animals in Bacchic celebration. Sophocles' heroine Antigone is haunted by the figure of her brother's broken and unburied body. The Athenians buried the broken bodies of the *korai,* the cult statues of Athena, after the Persian invasion at the beginning of the fifth century; they used broken pieces of statuary and masonry to refashion the wall that protected the city. The various Greek tribes saw themselves and their settlements as fragmentary, disseminated bits, broken off into individual cities from original unitary founding ancestors' families, saw their colonies as similarly dispersed fragments of an original whole.

What is the political meaning for Athenians both of tribal dispersion after the death of their founder Ion, and of the dissemination of citizens in colonization? What are the discourses in historical texts on dialects, what are the political attempts to establish leagues, to reconstitute wholeness? The Athenians, in their imaginary integrity and homogeneity, descended from a single ancestor, or sprouted from the earth, lived surrounded by refugees, slaves and foreigners, the metics, broken away from their places of origin. The Athenians in particular seem to have seen their existence as a community as haunted by a dialectic between integrity and dissemination. How did they think about democracy— the dispersed, heterogeneous votes, scattered bits of broken shells, ostraka, pebbles broken from rocks, shards once part of whole bodies of vases—transformed through the vote into a single unified voice of the majority, of the polis as a new whole?

And what is writing itself, the inscription on the ostraka that led to ostracism? Writing is the scattered letters, lots, seeds, like the dragon's teeth of Thebes, the gift of Kadmos, like the fragmented bodies of Actaeon and Pentheus, sons of his house, like the stones of the wall of Thebes, moved by the singing of Amphion and Zethus, like the severed, singing head of Orpheus, dismembered by maenads. Can we consider the imaginary opposition between Thebes and Athens in terms of this slippage, this oscillation between fragmentation and integrity, Thebes as the site of dispersion and dismemberment, Athens the city of remembering, recollection, democracy which is the unification of the once dispersed and scattered?[3]

The period of the earliest democracy and of the Persian Wars, the latter part of the sixth century B.C.E. and the early part of the fifth, exhibit the Greek's own fascination with fragments. An *ostrakon* is an oyster shell. The term came to be applied to broken bits of pottery. The ceramic vases of the Greeks, when broken, provided myriad shards. Vases came to bear the names of potter and painter, of donor, of the recipient of the gift, epigraphs naming the figures in paintings; they bore writing on them, random letters at first, when the painter wanted to demonstrate his ability to write, then parts of words, names, whole words, whole names, even sentences. Was it these inscribed words, painted and fired into the surfaces of the rounded vases and then split off from their former sites, that led the Athenians to see these broken pieces of vases as proper surfaces for the names of those who were becoming too prominent, who threatened to unbalance the democracy and who thus had to be exiled? The word *ostrakon* has an interesting history, moving as it does from the split leaves of the oyster, the two sides of the bivalve, to an extended meaning, the broken-up bits of the vases, which might have vaguely recalled oyster shells. The mound of Testaccio in Rome, a hill of waste, of shell and broken pieces of pottery, still looms as a considerable elevation in the modern city. Archaeologists excavating in the modern city of Athens discovered a cache of 190 ostraka, all bearing the name of Themistokles written in just a few hands. They conjecture that Themistokles' political opponents were plotting to have him ostracized, and planned to distribute these potsherds either to the illiterate or to supporters who would be organized to vote against their enemy.

In a significant parallel to the Athenian practice of using pottery fragments for the most important type of voting, the casting out of a prominent man from among the citizens, the citizens of Syracuse in Sicily, a Corinthian foundation, engaged in a political ritual called *petalismos,* after the *petala,* or olive leaves, used in voting. Homer, in a famous passage, likens the generations of human beings to leaves on a tree:

As is the generation of leaves, so is that of humanity
The wind scatters the leaves on the ground, but the
   live timber
burgeons with leaves again in the season of spring
   returning.
So one generation of men will grow while another
   dies.[4]

Olive leaves were a convenient and available source of writing material in the Mediterranean, but it is nonetheless significant that this act of scapegoating and expelling a member of the ancient community of Syracuse would use the medium of leaves, the once living and then fallen parts of the olive tree.[5] These practices of expulsion take up fragmentary elements of ordinary life, use them to mark someone and to expel him, in order to reconstitute the integrity of the city. The fragments are the instruments of the construction of a new whole, one renewed and strengthened by the breaking off of one of its parts, one of the citizen members of the polity.

Voting in the assembly of Athens took place by a show of hands and does not exhibit the characteristics of the casting of names into a pool for ostracism. However, voting by juries in legal trials was done by secret ballot, and thus has affinities with ostracism; it is remarkable that these two kinds of activity fall into the same field because of the Greeks' physical practices of voting with objects. Questions concerning individuals (*ep'andri*) were decided with secret ballot (*psēphisma,* from *psēphos,* voting-stone, voting-pebble), even in the assembly, and the decisions of juries on individuals similarly used pebbles dropped into an urn, a black stone for conviction or a white one for acquittal. These deliberations, pointed at an individual member of the community, required a secret ballot, one conducted by means of these fragments, *ostraka,* potsherds, and pebbles, when what was at stake was the punishment or removal of one element of the polity. It is as if all these practices were understood as efforts at cleansing and repair, the reestablishing of balance after a moment of fragmentation and harm brought on the group by the efforts of a single person on his own behalf. The selfish acts of conspirators, criminals, and potential tyrants split the community; the fragments used to name such actors, or to condemn them, served to renegotiate the bonds of community and to create a new whole, one no longer split and fragmented by the actions of the culprit. So both the ostracism and the jury system of Athens might be said to exhibit similarities to the process of historiography, the recognition of fragmentation, the use of fragments to negotiate some change, and the provisional, temporary, establishing of coherence.

The metaphorics of the discourses and practices of the Athenians, in some sense our ancestors, in some sense descendants of Greeks of the archaic age, like Sappho,

themselves exhibit a sense of fragmentation, dismemberment. The Greek words that derive from *speirō,* "sow," interestingly combine the metaphorics of dissemination with those of fragmentation and dismemberment. It is as if the ear of grain, the source of seeds, is seen as a whole from which parts are stripped, in a move that transfers that act of separation from the *sparagmos,* which is in fact derived from *spaō,* "draw, tear, rend," rather than from the verb for sowing. In a typically unscientific but interesting ancient etymology, there is a confusion between these two verbs and their derivatives which makes both of them partake of the connotations of the other, sowing becoming rending, rending becoming sowing, the Sown Men, the Spartoi of Thebes, the ancestors of the dismembered members of the house of Thebes, Dionysos, Aktaion, and Pentheus.[6] All these etymological nets and metaphors, although applied to the city of Thebes, are known from Athenian tragedy, from Athenian accounts of the history of that state.

The semantic complex associated with sowing and rending connects the practices of agriculture, which functioned to unite the community, with myths and rituals of dismemberment. In the *Bacchae,* for example, a messenger describes the ripping apart, the *sparagmos* of the ruler of Thebes, Pentheus:

> Ignoring his cries of pity,
> she seized his left arm at the wrist; then, planting
> her foot upon his chest, she pulled, wrenching away
>   [*apesparaxen*]
> the arm at the shoulder. . . .
> Ino, meanwhile, on the other wide, was scratching off
> his flesh. Then Autonoe and the whole horde
> of Bacchae swarmed upon him. Shouts everywhere,
> he screaming with what little breath was left,
> they shrieking in triumph. One tore off an arm,
> another a foot still warm in its shoe. His ribs
> were clawed clean of flesh [*sparagmois*] and every
>   hand
> was smeared with blood as they played ball [*diesphai-
>   rizde*] with scraps of Pentheus' body.
>   The pitiful remains lie scattered,
> one piece among the sharp rocks, others
> lying lost among the leaves in the depths
> of the forest. His mother, picking up his head,
> impaled it on her wand. She seems to think it is
> some mountain lion's head which she carries in tri-
>   umph.[7]

The passage has some of the baroque strangeness of the scene of Creousa's melting flesh in the *Medea;* Euripides links by a half-pun the dismemberment and playing ball. The sundered shoulder recalls the body of Pelops, partially consumed at the feast of Atreus and Thyestes, although his shoulder was replaced by one of ivory, and he lived on. While this Bacchic scene is hardly agricultural, it does associate the choruses, the dancing groups of bacchants, with the chorus of the theater, performing before that assembly of the city of Athens that unifies them in the act of watching and seeing. Although this tragedy was supposedly written in Macedonia during Euripides' exile there, it was performed in Athens.

Other relevant scenes of tearing apart, ripping apart, include the image of the city at the time of the Peloponnesian War, when parties struggled against one another and when people turned against each other in fear of Sparta. The ancient historian Thucydides writes about the rebuilding of the walls of the city of Athens after the Persians sacked and burned the city's akropolis. They built broken pieces of the old wall into the new, constructing a fabric consisting partly of stones, the "bones of the mother," and partly of fragments of earlier man-made structures. Although these elements of the visual culture of Athens may seem distant, these classical Athenian texts to have little to do with the archaic Lesbian Sappho, they demonstrate a cultural preoccupation with the fragmentary that goes beyond the fact that the Greeks of the archaic and classical ages were widely dispersed across a great geographical territory. They saw themselves as scattered parts of a former whole, and the tribes, then dispersions of peoples, then colonization as dialectically related phenomena.

This essay considers the figure of fragmentation of the body in relation to the world of the ancient Greeks and to our own naturalized notions about the body. I am concerned with postmodernity's focus on contemporary culture and with the concomitant loss of a perspective on past and future that might enable other visions of bodies, sexualities, genders. Our lack of relationship to the past, our refusal of its fragmentedness, may depend on a psychological resistance to the fragmented body, a resistance that Jacques Lacan's work can perhaps help us to understand. Our fear of coming to terms with the fragmented historical past leads us to re-member its dismemberment, often to falsify that past. Such misrecognitions have implications not only for how we read the past and its fragments but also for how we read the world and women's place in it. Sappho's poems, their form and the ways in which we receive them, can exemplify an alternative aesthetic. Seeing the possibilities of this alternative—recognizing and accepting our own fragmentation and the inevitably fragmented past— has implications for how we treat bodies of poetry, bodies in poetry, and bodies in the world.

In a recent book called *Rethinking Art History,* Donald Preziosi characterizes his discipline in terms that cast light on classics as a field. He argues that "the discipline . . . serves to project or to validate a certain kind of viewing Subject: ideally, passive consumers, and, in more contemporary contexts, educated and discerning cryptographers—but receivers of messages all the same." He points out further that the discipline actually "shares with other humanistic disciplines . . . a highly complex and self-perpetuating analytic theater of power and knowledge, a discourse always written in the third person singular."[8] I am especially concerned here with the ways in which the field of classics projects and validates a similar Subject, "the classicist," who is at once consumer, cryptographer, and receiver of messages, but who has rarely acknowledged rhetorically his own power and presence in the act of interpretation of the fragments of antiquity, assuming rather a transparency, an unmediated access to the remnants of the past.

My question here is: How do classicists come to terms with ancient culture? What sort of subject does ancient culture produce, in the person of the classicist? And how can contemporary theory, especially psychoanalysis, help us think the relationship we have to antiquity?

Classicists receive antiquity in pieces, as fragments. There are various attempts to come to terms with the material of the past, both to break it up further, into more manageable entities, and to recover an imagined lost unity. Paradoxically, both those attempts to reunite lost parts and to break down the past can deter readers from the act of interpretation, from considering what the past means for us, what it makes of us. One way of responding to this recognition is to pursue a dream of wholeness, transparency, perfect access to what we desire to know through such scholarly practices as "conjectures," imagining the word that might have once been where there is now a gap. Another is to try to manage the instability of our relationship to the past by reducing it to atoms accessible to philological science, through the production of a scholarly apparatus and commentary, through the perusal of lexicons, catalogs of all the words, fixing them into alphabetic lists. Another is to accept the partiality of our experience, to seek, even as we yearn for more—more fact, more words and artifacts, more lines of Sappho, more poems of Sappho—to read what we have in light of who we are now.

Speaking of those ancient writers whose work "counted for something," in praise of Horace, Nietzsche said:

> This mosaic of words, in which every unit spreads its power to the left and to the right over the whole, by its sound, by its place in the sentence, and by its meaning, this *minimum* in the compass and number of the signs, and the *maximum* of energy in the signs which is thereby achieved—all this is Roman, and, if you will believe me, noble *par excellence.*[9]

Nietzsche's appreciation of Horace does not concern the fragment, nor is it directed to archaic Greek poetry, nor does his praise of Horace as noble suit my purpose. But his remarks on the *minimum* of signs, *maximum* of energy might direct a reading of the fragmentary, one that attempts, not romantically, not lamenting the loss that surrounds the fragment, not to restore its lacks, but to read the minimal signs of the fragment with a maximum of energy.

What follows is a reading of a necessarily fragmented poem of Sappho, one that attempts to recognize the fragmentary state of my own encounter with the poem.

This is Sappho's poem "31:"

> To me he seems like a god
> as he sits facing you and
> hears you near as you speak
> softly and laugh
>
> in a sweet echo that jolts
> the heart in my ribs. For now
> as I look at you my voice
> is empty and
>
> can say nothing as my tongue
> cracks and slender fire is quick
> under my skin. My eyes are dead
> to light, my ears
>
> pound, and sweat pours over me.
> I convulse, greener than grass,
> and feel my mind slip as I
>   go close to death.[10]

> φαίνεταί μοι κῆνος ἴσος θέοισιν
> ἔμμεν' ὤνηρ, ὄττις ἐνάντιός τοι
> ἰσδάνει καὶ πλάσιον ἀδυ φωνεί-
> σας ὐπακούει
>
> καὶ γελαίσας ἰμέροεν, τό μ' ἦμὰν
> καρδίαν ἐν στήθεσιν ἐπτόαισεν
> ὠς γὰρ ἔς σ' ἴδω βρόχε', ὤς με φώναι-
> σσ' οὐδ' ἔν ἔτ' εἴκει,
>
> ἀλλὰ κὰμ μὲν γλῶσσά μ' ἔαγε, λέπτον
> δ' αὔτικα χρῷ πῦρ ὐπαδεδρόμηκεν,
> ὀππάτεσσι δ' οὐδ' ἔν ὄρημμ', ἐπιρρόμ-
> βεισι δ' ἄκουαι,
>
> κὰδ δέ μ' ἴδρως κακχέεται, τρόμος δὲ
> παῖσαν ἄγρει, χλωροτσρα δὲ ποίας
> ἔμμι, τεθνάκην δ' ὀλίγω σιδεύης
> φαίνομ' ἔμ' αὔτ[α.
>
> ἀλλὰ πὰν τόλματον, ἐπεὶ †καὶ πένητα†[11]

The lines break off here, into fragments. This poem was much admired in antiquity; Plato seems to echo it in the *Phaedrus* when Socrates describes the symptoms of love as beauty enters through the eyes:

> . . . first there come upon him a shuddering and a measuring of . . . awe. . . . Next, with the passing of the shudder, a strange sweating and fever seizes him.[12]

Catullus translated this poem, retaining the gender markers of the object of desire and transforming it into a heterosexual text. Longinus, in citing the poem in his work, speaks of the skill with which Sappho picks out and binds together the most striking and intense of the symptoms of love.[13]

Sappho's selection of *akra,* of high moments, is a fragmentation of experience, in that it must perforce break up the flow of lived time. Poetry performs such a splitting up of experience through selection. But piled on top of this sense of fragmentation is another, one peculiar to the thematics of this particular poem, in which the body is represented as falling into fragments, seen as a series of discrete, unconnected, disjunctive responses. As Longinus points out in remarks that have been found inadequate in the twentieth century but that suit my purpose admirably:

> Is it not wonderful [literally, *ou thaumazdeis?* are you not amazed?] how she summons at the same time soul body hearing tongue sight colour, all as though they had wandered off apart from herself?[14]

Longinus says that the poet constructs of all these things a *sunodos,* a meeting, a junction. The poem is a crossroads of emotions, a reassembly of the fragmented, disparate parts of the poetic "I" that have "wandered off apart from herself." These parts are her heart, which is given a separate existence in her breast, her voice, which escapes her, her broken tongue, her skin, over which fire runs, her blinded eyes, her humming ears. This is Eros the limb-loosener, *lusimelēs,* the one that unstrings the assembly of the body and brings the "I" here close to death.

Much has been written about this poem, some of it illustrating my view that classicists perpetuate a certain kind of subject, one rooted in reason, deciphering the cryptic fragments of the past, speculating endlessly about contexts about which evidence can never be regained. This is true of the argument about whether Sappho's bodily disintegration is caused by jealousy or fear, whether the occasion of the poem is a wedding feast, Sappho an observer overcome by envy of the bridegroom, or full of awestruck praise for the magnificence of the newly married. One particularly obfuscating debate concerns the issue of Sappho's homosexuality,[15] as in George Devereux's essay, "The Nature of Sappho's Seizure in Fr. 31 as Evidence of Her Inversion" (1970).[16] A belief in the tragedy of homosexual existence colors Thomas McEvilley's otherwise helpful reading of the poem in a way that seems postromantic to me; his essay is subtitled "The Face behind the Mask"! He argues that the beginning of the poem suggests a hymeneal occasion, but that then the poem veers into a private voice. As he describes what he terms the "dramatic situation," "Sappho has been asked to write or sing the wedding song, and she has begun nicely; then the sight of the beauty of the bride sends her out of control, calling up her very ambivalent feelings about homosexuality and married happiness." I actually find this rather unpersuasive and irreconcilable with the reading that argues that the fear and disintegration produced by the sight of the beloved are elements of praise, of suggesting the divine beauty of the beloved woman. It is not clear to me that Sappho's desire for girls produced ambivalence about homosexuality at all; we could read her songs of regret and longing as her ontological situation, her aesthetic response to the separation from the beloved that almost all overs experience.[17]

As Charles Segal points out, this poem is saturated with reference to the world of oral poetry. In a fascinating essay, he writes in detail about the poem's patterns of alliteration and assonance, features that contribute to its incantatory quality, and that link it with the oral tradition.[18] Jesper Svenbro reads it as Sappho's allegory about reading:

> Coming as she did from the oral tradition, she set up the disappearance of the writer in a new way—not by using the third person for herself, but by giving an allegorical description of her own death by writing.[19]

Leah Rissman, in *Love as War,* discusses fragment **"31"** in terms of the "application of Homeric battle simile and terminology to lovers."[20] Her argument supports the view that Sappho's symptoms suggest not jealousy of the man who is her beloved's companion, but rather that the whole poem is in some sense a poem of praise, that the poet is stunned by the woman's beauty, which has the kind of effect on her that the aegis of Athena had on Penelope's suitors in the *Odyssey.* The woman in this scene is divine, the man heroic. Rissman says: "Both Sappho and the poet of the *Iliad* are concerned with contrasting the behavior of winners and losers. Sappho's catalogue of her own reactions to a woman is similar to the Homeric catalogue of the coward's response to the stress of ambush: both lists include pallor and unsteadiness of heart."[21] Fragment **"31"** is, therefore, a marriage poem in her view, a poem of praise in which the man is presented as godlike, the woman as divine; the poem elevates marriage by investing it with the heroic grandeur of the Homeric situation.[22]

More persuasive than McEvilley's remarks on Sappho's homosexual alienation are his observations on the diction of fragment **"31,"** which support Rissman's commentary about the profoundly Homeric quality of Sapphic reference. He points out that *kardia,* "heart," does not occur elsewhere in our fragments; that *glōssa* is unusual, since Sappho usually refers not to tongue but to voice, that "fire" does not occur elsewhere. "Only in fr. **"31"** are the unpleasant physical sensations of heat and cold a part of Sappho's poetic world. They are . . . intrusions from the uncontrollable realm of physical circumstance from which Sappho's poetry usually provides escape." Ears do not appear elsewhere, and sweat too is Homeric, and inelegant. McEvilley points out that "in Sappho's general practice, parts of the body are mentioned only as containers of erotic beauty." He argues that all this diction is meant to "make explicit the difference between the real and the poetic worlds." "Now for once the grim facts of bodily death become overwhelmingly clear and close: she is mortal; her tongue of songs is broken, sweat pours down her body."[23] The poem alludes to the Homeric descriptions of the body, using cruder, more corporeal language than that of other poems in its depiction of the poet's collapse.

In a particularly startling image, for example, Sappho says: *glōssa eage,* variously translated "my tongue broke," "my tongue shivered," "my tongue cracked." Denys Page complains that the hiatus would be irregular, and the meaning "my tongue is broken" unsatisfactory; David Campbell nonetheless points out that Lucretius 3.155 seems to echo this passage in *infringi linguam,* and in the invocation to the catalog of ships in *Iliad* 2, the poet asks for the Muses' help with the words, "I could not tell over the multitude of them nor name them, not if I had ten tongues and ten mouths, not if I had a voice never to be broken [*phonē d'arrēktos*] (*Iliad* 2.488-90).[24] Sappho here alludes to this curious feature of the Homeric body, the frangible tongue, and in her poem the hiatus, the two vowels coming together, could be seen to "break" the tongue, to force an awkward, dysphonious phrase, a stumbling into the gap between the two vowels that produces a simulacrum of the poetic "I"'s distress in the reader.

Nancy Vickers has written brilliantly about the ways in which Renaissance lyric, the poems of Petrarch and his imitators perform a sort of dismemberment of the female body, how in their blazons and ekphrases, their descriptions of the physical appearance of the beloved, their lines anatomize, "cut up" the limbs, the parts of women.[25] Such an observation recalls the feminist critiques of contemporary advertising and pornography, which similarly dismember and commodify the parts of women's bodies. Such dismemberment produces not disorder but the control of anatomization. What is particularly fascinating about Sappho's poem is that here the woman herself sees the disorder in the body in love, sees herself objectified as a body in pieces, disjointed, a broken set of organs, limbs, bodily functions.

Whether or not the poem depicts envy or praise expressed as fear—both seem simultaneously possible—

readers interested in psychoanalysis might see this poem as an ideal text to demonstrate the universal value of psychoanalytic theory. Such work would point to the universality of the human condition and to the capacity of psychoanalysis to describe and illuminate all human desire.[26] Sappho's poem is an important example of a poetics based on recollection, the conscious mind recalling a moment of bodily alienation of a sort that might be thought to exemplify the Lacanian dialectic of imaginary and symbolic. Can we use the work of Lacan to describe the effects on Sappho of the sight of her lover? Lacan speaks, for example, in terms that might seem familiar to the reader of Sappho, of a body in pieces:

> This fragmented body . . . usually manifests itself in dreams when the movement of the analysis encounters a certain level of aggressive disintegration in the individual. It then appears in the form of disjointed limbs, or of those organs presented in exoscopy, growing wings and taking up arms for intestinal persecutions—the very same that the visionary Hieronymus Bosch has fixed, for all time, in painting, in their ascent from the fifteenth century to the imaginary zenith of modern man.[27]

Although Sappho's fragment **"31"** seems beautifully to exemplify Lacan's description of the Boschian vision, what follows is an argument against the view that Sappho's catalog of broken body parts proves the universal descriptive value of Lacanian psychoanalysis. This poem, I argue, reveals not transcendent human nature, not universal human psychic structures, but rather historical difference, a moment in the constitution of the aristocratic self, perhaps even before the theorization of gender per se. The "I" that speaks and writes, the "I" that is produced in that moment, regards the past, a disordered, fragmented past, from a present in which the poem itself and the fiction of subjectivity represented in it are constituted against the backdrop of fragmentation. The "I" of the poem comes out of that fragmentation, is constructed from it. The *sunodos,* the junction, must be read historically, neither generalized to describe some absolute and general proposition of feminine composition, nor used to prove the universality of our postmodern ideas of split subjectivity.

I would argue instead for a historicist understanding of this poem, recalling Bruno Snell's pages on the Homeric body. He argues that the Homeric authors and audience understood the body as such not to exist, but rather to be an assembly of parts, of functions, of disparate organs loosely allied, commanded independently by gods and men. Snell says:

> Of course the Homeric man had a body exactly like the later Greeks, but he did not know it *qua* body, but merely as the sum total of his limbs. This is another

way of saying that the Homeric Greeks did not yet have a body in the modern sense of the word; body, *sōma,* is a later interpretation of what was originally comprehended as *melē,* or *guia,* limbs."[28]

Snell makes a connection between this conception of the human form and its representation in early Greek art:

> Not until the classical art of the fifth century do we find attempts to depict the body as an organic unity whose parts are mutually correlated. In the preceding period the body is a mere construct of independent parts variously put together.[29]

The tribal, collective, prepolitical world of the Homeric heroes represents the body, or rather what will become the body, as similar to its own social organization, a loose confederation, a tenuous grouping of parts.

Although Snell's work has been called into question by some, the arguments of such scholars as Robert Renehan, in his essay on *sōma,* do not seem to me to discredit Snell's point.[30] I appreciate the objections made to the orthodoxy following Snell, who contended that the word *sōma* never refers to a living body. Furthermore, there are problems with seeing lyric poetry in relation to Homeric epic in such a way that we see only a Hegelian, nineteenth-century evolution, an inevitable progression, a Lévy-Bruhlian passage from myth to reason. I share many scholars' objections to these versions of historical inevitability. But I do not have the same difficulty with the notion that there is a difference, a *historical* difference, between Sappho and Homer and that their views of the body may differ. Snell's argument seems to me to be a particularly valuable intervention in the question of the *historicity* of the body.

Set against the background of this understanding of human beings' physical existence, Sappho's disordered, fragmented body takes on a different resonance than if it were to be understood only as figuring in the Lacanian imaginary. The subject, the "I" of archaic lyric, is generated in the earliest urban, that is, literally "political" setting, internal to the voice of a dominant aristocracy. According to Snell, these poems record the beginning of the historical evolution of selfhood, of individuality, the aristocratic origins of what will become the male citizens of the ancient *polis,* the city-state, and Michel Foucault's subject of philosophy in the Platonic tradition. Although I do not suggest that Sappho read Bruno Snell, or that she had a historical sense of distance from the Homeric past, Sappho's poem nonetheless recalls the relatively archaic view of the body represented for her in Homeric poetry. There is no historical consciousness for Sappho equal to Snell's in its formal grasp of a shift in consciousness between Homer's day and her own; rather, Sappho adopts here a traditional, conventional, epic description of the body, familiar to her and her audience from the traditional poetry, to express what appears to be a disintegration of her own body. If the relation of Sappho's description of her own physical distress to the earlier Homeric sense of the body may not be conscious for Sappho, it has definite consequences nonetheless. Sappho's view of eros *lusimelēs,* that love that disunites the only recently constituted body, suggests that eros returns that body to a past state, to an alliance of functions, a loose set of organic capacities; what she represents is a turning back from a tenuously held subjectivity, that new sense of the poet as an "I," back to an archaic sense of identity.

Lacan's work on the relationship between the body in pieces and the ego, though not directly applicable to Sappho's poetic universe, might . . . shed light on the question of what we make of the fragments, literal fragments, of ancient poetry. Who are we, these supposed agents of integrity and coherence, who desire to mend that past? I find especially useful, when considering these texts, Lacan's way of thinking about the alternation between the fictional whole, the "I," and the fragmentary past, as an ongoing dialectic; we are always conscious of the possibility of dismemberment, of the fragility of wholeness, of corporeal and psychic integrity, even as our identity is fashioned against the background of such dismemberment.

In approaching the Greeks in this way, fragmentation stands as a figure that both illuminates a contemporary relationship to the past and that recognizes in the Greeks themselves a certain contestation of figures of integrity and coherence. Such an approach might be seen to differ from a more traditional classicist drive for wholeness and integrity, recognition of origin and continuity, or from the need to fragment, to atomize, to render manageable and not-yet-interpretable the data we receive from antiquity.

It is crucial to understand that the pleasure Sappho's poem **"31"** affords us, in our positions as psychoanalytic subjects of the twentieth century, is not the same as that of the audience of Sappho's day. If Sappho's listeners heard an account of historical archaism, of dissolution back into undifferentiated collectivity, we may project a psychological state described by Lacan. And we recognize Sappho's distance from Homer, our distance from both. The richer reading of this poem would acknowledge all these dimensions, historical and contemporary, and would measure the distance between one pleasure and another. And this poem, in its evocation of distress, even of anguish, of the exaggerated pains of love, is a pleasure for us to read. The "I" as contemporary reader can appreciate Sappho's recollection of suffering because the poem has constructed

coherence from disorder, reconstituted subjectivity out of a body in pieces. The pleasure of this reconstitution is what allows for readerly transference, to refer to a psychoanalytic model. If the male lover, who sits across from, *enantios,* vis-à-vis Sappho's object of desire, is caught in a specular, dyadic relationship to her, gazing at her, the voice of the poet has entered the domain of language, acknowledges the passage of time and the possibility of a linguistic recovery of her fragmented body. The reader's pleasure comes from an appreciation of the disintegration the poet describes, the undeniable pain of eros, of a disordering desire that shatters the tongue, that brings the "I" to a place near death, but also from the security of that "I" that speaks the poem, the voice that gazes retrospectively at the experience of fragmentation, and from it creates a crossroads, a poem, and a self. And there is further the historical dimension of our reading, a sense of distance from the fragments of Sappho's work, a sense of another distance, internal to the poem, in which the Homeric body serves as a figure for the lover. If, as Shoshana Felman argues, we are both analyst and analysand as we read, if therefore we experience both transference and countertransference, if we see ourselves as authority and as subject to the authority of the text, then such readings might take account of the contradictory drives for integrity and for atomization, for mastery of a disturbing past.[31] The self constituted against a background of disorder can be a self of pleasure and authority that recognizes its construction of itself out of fragmentation, that acknowledges its own fictionality, its own historicity. And we as its readers can recognize our implication in its drama and our own situation in the late twentieth century, gazing at the fragments of the past, trying to work them into a story about ourselves, a story that enables action in the present, for the future. We can use the pleasures of that story, rethinking our relationship to the Greeks, to their privileged position in our history, countering the inherited vision of ancient society inhabited by disembodied, philosophical, male citizens.

I would argue for a historical materialist historicism, one that is not content merely to contemplate the past from the point of view of an autonomous subject in the present, who comes into contact with the collective past, but that rather engages with the past in order to generate some vision of historical difference. The ancient Greeks, and Sappho in particular, provide particularly suggestive material for historicist work, in part because we so often name the Greeks as our origin, in part because Sappho is in fact so radically different from us, even in such a "natural" domain as life in the body. And if Benjamin, in his vision of the aestheticizing, contemplative version of historicism, uses the image of the whore in historicism's bordello, feminism needs not only to resist such imagery but also to incorporate a materialist theory of history to see historical difference, to have a richer sense of possibility, to put into question our assumptions about the natural body.

Notes

1. Walter Benjamin, "Theses on the Philosophy of History," in *Illuminations: Essays and Reflections,* ed. Hannah Arendt, trans. Harry Zohn (New York, 1969), 262.

2. Fredric Jameson, "Marxism and Historicism," in *Syntax of History,* vol. 2 of *The Ideologies of Theory: Essays, 1971-1986* (Minneapolis, 1988), 157.

3. On Thebes and Athens, see Froma Zeitlin, "Thebes: Theater of Self and Society in Athenian Drama," in *Nothing To Do with Dionysos? Athenian Drama in Its Social Context,* ed. John J. Winkler and Froma I. Zeitlin (Princeton, N.J., 1990), 130-67.

4. *The Iliad of Homer,* trans. Richmond Lattimore (Chicago, 1951), 6.146-50.

5. On ostracism, see also Jean-Pierre Vernant, "Ambiguity and Reversal: On the Enigmatic Structure of *Oedipus Rex,*" trans. Page duBois, *New Literary History* 9:3 (1978): 475-501. "It [ostracism] was all organised so as to make it possible for the popular feeling that the Greeks called *phthonos* (a mixture of envy and religious distrust of anyone who rose too high or was too successful) to manifest itself in the most spontaneous and unanimous fashion (there had to be at least 6,000 voters) regardless of any rule of law or rational justification. The only things held against the ostracised man were the very superior qualities which had raised him above the common herd, and his exaggerated good luck which might call down the wrath of the gods upon the town" (488).

6. Cf. *sparganon,* in plural "swaddling clothes," "and so, in Trag., remembrances of one's childhood, tokens by which a person's extraction is discovered" (LSJ.). Presumably Oedipus' scarred ankles would be such tokens, Oedipus also of the house of Thebes.

7. Euripides, *The Bacchae,* trans. William Arrowsmith, *The Complete Greek Tragedies,* ed. David Grene and Richmond Lattimore (Chicago, 1959), ll. 1124-42.

8. Donald Preziosi, *Rethinking Art History: Meditations on a Coy Science* (New Haven, Conn., and London, 1989), 52.

9. Friedrich Nietzsche, *The Twilight of the Idols: or, How to Philosophise with the Hammer,* trans. Anthony M. Ludovici (New York, 1964), 113.

10. Willis Barnstone, trans., *Sappho and the Greek Lyric Poets* (New York, 1988), fr. 31.

11. David A. Campbell, *Greek Lyric Poetry: A Selection of Early Greek Lyric, Elegiac and Iambic Poetry* (Basingstoke and London, 1967), 44.

12. Plato, *Collected Dialogues,* ed. Edith Hamilton and Huntington Cairns (Princeton, N.J., 1961), 497.

13. See David A. Campbell, *The Golden Lyre: The Themes of the Greek Lyric Poets* (London, 1983), 13-14.

14. "Longinus," *On the Sublime,* in Aristotle, *The Poetics,* "Longinus," *On the Sublime,* Demetrius, *On Style* (Cambridge, Mass., and London, 1932), 10.3.

15. For a valuable corrective, see André Lardinois, "Lesbian Sappho and Sappho of Lesbos," in *From Sappho to De Sade: Moments in the History of Sexuality,* ed. Jan Bremmer (London and New York, 1989), 15-35.

16. George Devereux, "The Nature of Sappho's Seizure in Fr. 31 as Evidence of Her Inversion," *Classical Quarterly* 20 (1970): 17ff. For a response, see Miroslav Marcovich, "Sappho Fr. 31: Anxiety Attack or Love Declaration," in *Studies in Greek Poetry,* Illinois Classical Studies Suppl. 1 (Atlanta, 1991), 29-46. Other more illuminating studies are Eva Stehle Stigers, "Sappho's Private World," in *Reflections of Women in Antiquity,* ed. Helene P. Foley (New York, 1981), 45-61, and John J. Winkler, "Gardens of Nymphs: Public and Private in Sappho's Lyrics," in ibid., 63-89.

17. Thomas McEvilley, "Sappho, Fragment Thirty-One: The Face behind the Mask," *Phoenix* 32 (1978): 14. "She is showing us the extreme disharmony which she must have felt inwardly on such occasions. She seems to be the first poet who has left us a record of what has since become a familiar situation: the poet as a sensitive soul suffering feelings of frustration and alienation from the problems of relating his or her work to conventional social realities. Needless to say, in this case the situation was aggravated by Sappho's homosexuality" (15). McEvilley's tragic homosexual, like the "tragic mulatto" or the tormented Romantic poet, seems a highly ideological figure.

18. Charles Segal, "Eros and Incantation: Sappho and Oral Poetry," *Arethusa* 7 (1974): 139-57.

19. Jesper Svenbro, "Death by Writing: Sappho, the Poem, and the Reader," in *Phrasikleia: An Anthropology of Reading in Ancient Greece,* trans. Janet Lloyd (1988; Ithaca, N.Y., 1993), 152.

20. Leah Rissman, *Love as War: Homeric Allusion in the Poetry of Sappho* (Konigstein, 1983), 72.

21. Ibid., 89.

22. Anne Pippin Burnett shares this view, seeing the singer of fr. 31 as fearful, approaching someone who has aroused her desire. *Three Archaic Poets: Archilochus, Alcaeus, Sappho* (Cambridge, Mass., 1983), 219; see 230ff. for a useful bibliography of work on fr. 31.

23. McEvilley, "Sappho, Fragment Thirty-One," 16, 17, 18.

24. Page, *Sappho and Alcaeus;* Campbell, *Greek Lyric Poetry,* 272.

25. Nancy J. Vickers, "The Body Re-Membered: Petrarchan Lyrics and the Strategies of Description," in *Mimesis: From Mirror to Method, Augustine to Descartes,* ed. J. D. Lyons and S. G. Nichols (Hanover, N.H., 1982), 100-109.

26. For a psychoanalytic reading of a classical corpus, see Micaela Janan, *When the Lamp Is Shattered: Desire and Narrative in Catullus* (Carbondale, Ill., 1994).

27. Jacques Lacan, *Ecrits: A Selection,* trans. Alan Sheridan (New York and London, 1977), 4-5.

28. Bruno Snell, *The Discovery of the Mind: The Greek Origins of European Thought,* trans. T. G. Rosenmeyer (Cambridge, Mass., 1953), 8.

29. Ibid., 6.

30. Robert Renehan, "The Meaning of *Sōma* in Homer," *California Studies in Classical Antiquity* 12 (1981), 269-82.

31. "With respect to the text, the literary critic occupies thus at once the place of the psychoanalyst (in the relation of interpretation) and the place of the patient (in the relation of transference)." Shoshana Felman, "To Open the Question," in *Literature and Psychoanalysis: The Question of Reading: Otherwise* (Baltimore and London, 1982), 7.

Jane McIntosh Snyder (essay date 1997)

SOURCE: Snyder, Jane McIntosh. "Sappho's Challenge to the Homeric Inheritance" and "Sappho's Other Lyric Themes." In *Lesbian Desire in the Lyrics of Sappho,* pp. 63-77, 97-121. New York: Columbia University Press, 1997.

[*In the following excerpts, Snyder examines how Sappho's lyric poetry recontextualizes the patriarchal and heterosexual world of the Homeric epic, also surveying several of her lesser-known poetic fragments.*]

Despite obvious differences in scope, purpose, and tone, scholars have frequently noted the similarities between Homer's epics and Sappho's lyrics. Remarking on echoes in diction, phraseology, and themes, one critic inquires, "Why does [Sappho] use a pseudo-Homeric 'mode of writing'?"[1] He goes on to explain the parallels on the basis of social history, claiming that Sappho must have turned to the language of Homer's epics in an attempt to recover the lost heroic world of the old aristocracy, which was rapidly crumbling away during the period of political chaos in which she lived.

Here I would like to pose the question differently. Rather than viewing Sappho as a "pseudo-Homer," I ask instead, "In what ways can Sappho's allusions to and echoes of Homer be seen as a challenge to the epic tradition?" In other words, to what extent does Sappho present herself as a *new* Homer? Can she not be read as modifying and supplanting the old epics rather than as clinging to them? May Sappho perhaps be presenting herself as a "consciously 'antiheroic' persona"?[2] These seem particularly important questions in view of the poet's explicit statement in a programmatic song, fragment **"16"** V., where she emphatically declares—using Helen of Troy as an example to prove her point—that contrary to what "some" say, the most beautiful thing on earth is "what one loves."

Sappho refashions the legendary Helen, the bane of all Greeks, as a positive figure in pursuit of her own erotic fulfillment, and in so doing transforms the Homeric material to suit her own purposes. In fragment **"44"** V., as we will see, she writes her own mini-epic, focusing on the vignette of the wedding reception at Troy for Hektor and his bride, Andromache. Although the subject matter of the piece is based on part of the overall narrative of the *Iliad,* it is really more reminiscent of the *Odyssey* in its attention to domestic detail and to a female-oriented world. Although the traditional cast of Trojan characters is present in the narrative—Hektor, Andromache, and Priam—and although the language of the poem is more heavily laden with Homeric epithets ("far-shooting" Apollo, and the like) than is usually the case, the piece is completely removed from the battle context that so constantly informs its Iliadic model. In fact the festive occasion described, in which the various roles of younger and older women are detailed, could perhaps almost be said to reflect Sappho's own society (if we knew what that was) as much as Homeric society. In other words, Sappho is producing her own new version of Homer—minus the warriors carrying on warfare—rather than merely reproducing epic themes in a lyric mode.

Seen in this light, Sappho's songs may be read as challenges to the patriarchal and heterosexually focused stories of earlier epic, particularly the *Iliad.* They reflect a strong female authorial self who offers the audience a new way of seeing the world, through a female-centered perspective. In challenging the old Homeric tradition in both subtle and obvious ways, Sappho presents a fresh alternative to Homer, not merely recycled epic. At the same time, she does not really reject Homer material so much as make use of it for her own purposes. Ironically, her ties with Homer have most typically interested (male) critics of her work and have in effect contributed to the view of her (especially in the nineteenth century) as a "mainstream" poet. The Homeric garb she chooses to wear from time to time has no doubt protected her from the fate of other women poets whose iconoclastic language has contributed to their marginal status.

Helen and Eros

Fragment "16" V.

Some say that the most beautiful thing
upon the black earth is an army of horsemen;
others, of infantry, still others, of ships;
but I say it is what one loves.
It is completely easy to make this
intelligible to everyone; for the woman
who far surpassed all mortals in beauty,
Helen, left her most brave husband

And sailed off to Troy, nor did she
remember at all her child
or her dear parents; but [the Cyprian]
led her away. . . .

[All of which] has now reminded me
of Anaktoria, who is not here.

Her lovely walk and the bright sparkle of her face
would rather look upon than
all the Lydian chariots
and full-armed infantry.
    [This may be the end of the poem.]

This song about beauty and desire is a striking example of Sappho's power to articulate a uniquely female, woman-centered definition of eros. Sappho's answer to the question "What is the most beautiful thing on earth?" is "what one *loves*," *eratai* (line 4), the verbal form of the noun *eros*. Although many have tried to deny that gender is a factor in this poem, arguing that Sappho is presenting her audience with universal truth, the appearance of the distinctly female Sappho figure in many of the songs that have already been discussed suggests that the "I" of this song must also be read as gendered.[3] The military focus of the opening and closing of the fragment, so obviously male-centered in terms of the Homeric background, may then be seen as contrasted with the female singer's point of view, as I argue further below.

The Priamel

Scholars in recent years have devoted an extraordinary amount of energy to an analysis of the poem's logic and of the exact import of its chief rhetorical device—the so-called priamel. Derived from a mediaeval Latin word, the term *priamel* refers to a catalogue or list in which several items are presented in succession, followed by a concluding statement that usually asserts the primacy of one item or otherwise ties the list together in some kind of concluding assertion.[4] An early example may be found in the Spartan poet Tyrtaios's definition of *arete* ("excellence," literally, "manliness"). Writing probably during about the same period as Sappho (second half of the seventh century B.C.), Tyrtaios claims (fragment 9 Diehl) that he would not consider a man truly worthy of account just on the basis of fleet-footedness, or of his wrestling skills, or strength, or good looks, or wealth, or persuasive powers; rather, he says, true "excellence" consists of steadfastness in the front lines of battle. Tyrtaios's catalogue of virtues is thus capped by his own statement of what is of the greatest value as far as he is concerned.

Turning to Sappho's priamel, which occupies the opening stanza of fragment **"16,"** we see that she lists three groups of unspecified people (*oi men,* "some," *oi de,* "others," and *oi de,* "still others") who have certain preferences involving, in turn, cavalry, infantry, and naval forces. The *oi* here is simply the definite article ("the," as in the expression *[h]oi polloi*), and the particles *men . . . de . . . de* are used to mark a series of contrasting ideas. In the Greek, the first-person statement beginning *ego de,* "But *I* [say]," follows immediately after the statement of what these unspecified groups of persons are attempting to define, namely, "the most beautiful thing upon the black earth." The use of the personal pronoun, *ego* ("I"), which carries emphatic force in a language such as Greek in which the personal endings are already contained within the verb forms themselves, marks a particularly strong contrast that is reinforced by the third occurrence of the particle *de:* some people say the cavalry is the most beautiful (*kalliston*) thing on the earth, others the infantry, others ships, *but I* [say] it is that which one loves/desires. (In the Greek, the verb going with "I" must be supplied on the basis of the earlier third-person form in line 2, *phais'* ["they say"].)

In what is clearly the opening stanza of the song (as both the papyrus source and the internal rhetorical structure of the fragment indicate), Sappho has boldly set forth a definition of beauty that is linked directly to *eros* and that prides itself on its alterity. The Sappho figure, or the female singer of the song, declares a different point of view, and not one that poses simply as an alternative to *one* other point of view; no—this point of view, like Tyrtaios', follows a *list* of views against which it is counterpoised. The single figure of the poet-singer stands against the numberless unnamed persons who make up the three unspecified groups of "somes" and "others."

Perhaps because the form of this song is controlled—at least initially—by the rhetorical strategies of the priamel, critics have often sought in fragment **"16"** some kind of formal—even Aristotelian—logic.[5] Scholars argue, for example, over whether the final alternative ("but *I* say") is inclusive or exclusive; when the poet says that "whatever one loves" is the most beautiful thing on earth, does she mean that if you love ships or armies the most, then they are *kalliston* for you? Or does she posit her fourth definition of beauty as excluding mere things, like armies and ships? Does she mean to say, in using the verb *eratai* (line 4), normally applied to people rather than objects, that only human relationships qualify for the prize of "fairest"?

SAPPHO'S DEFINITION OF BEAUTY

Perhaps the answers to such questions are not really very important to someone listening to this song, for the hearer's attention is immediately diverted in the next stanza to the singer's "proofs" of her generalization. I will examine these proofs (one mythological, one not) in detail below, but first it may be useful to look closely at exactly how the Sappho figure formulates her definition of beauty.

Although some translators render the fourth definition of the most beautiful thing on earth as "she whom one loves," the Greek word is actually a pronoun (*ken'*, or in Attic dialect, *ekeino*) that is neither masculine nor feminine in gender, but neuter, "that *thing* which one loves."[6] The fact that Sappho chooses a grammatically "neutral" expression does, of course, render the definition she offers more generalized, and certainly more open to multiple readings than if she had referred to "that man" or "that woman" whom one loves. There is a curious analogue here to modern gay discourse within a heterosexual context, in which a lesbian or gay speaker may render her or his language ungendered through the omission of all personal pronouns; in this way a man might recount events without overtly tipping off the audience that the trip last week to Bermuda, for example, was spent with another man. In the case of fragment **"16,"** Sappho seems to be taking some pains to cast her generalization about desire in broadly applicable terms. In the phrasing she uses, not only the subject (the one loving) but also the object (the thing loved) are left indefinite—"*what one* loves" rather than, for example, "she whom I-as-woman love."

With stunning economy, the song lays forth its bold assertion in the time it takes to sing the opening stanza.

The claim of the Sappho figure is immediately reasserted in the first line and a half of the next stanza by the further claim that "it is completely easy to make this intelligible to everyone." This adjunct claim is marked by the assonance and verbal play in the opening words of lines 5 and 6, *pagchu* ("completely") and *panti* ("everyone"), both from the root *pan-* ("all," as in "pan-Hellenic"). Sappho could have gone directly from the priamel to its "proofs," the examples of Helen and Anaktoria that follow, simply through the use of the particle *gar* ("for," line 6), which marks an explanation of what has preceded. The presence of the additional claim further emphasizes the authority of the Sappho figure, the *ego* of the priamel. Not only can the poet assert her own iconoclastic definition of beauty, but she can also prove it—with ease—to any and all! This is not a poem of self-doubt.

A pair of proofs now follows the pair of claims. In a song about beauty and desire, what could be a more appropriate first example than the archetypal fairest of all women, Helen of Troy? The theme of the song—what is "most beautiful" (*kalliston,* line 3)—is echoed in the allusion to Helen's own beauty (*kallos,* line 7). Yet as the example unfolds we begin to see that this Helen is cast in the role of neither helpless victim nor evil betrayer. Rather than being portrayed as the face that launched a thousand ships, this Helen (albeit under the influence of Aphrodite) seems to be captain of her own ship. She leaves behind her noble husband (Menelaus, evidently not named in the song) and sails off—remembering neither child nor parents—in pursuit of what she loves, that is, the (unnamed) Paris. As Page duBois was the first to point out, in this version of Helen's story she is a *subject* of desire, not merely its object.[7] Although she herself is beautiful, the emphasis in these lines is on her active seeking after what she regards as beautiful, that is, Paris. Sappho's Helen is not a passive victim but an active pursuer. Nor does Sappho's Helen seem to display the self-reproach evident in the *Iliad,* where even in the face of King Priam's kindly words toward her, as she recalls her own abandonment of home and child, she calls herself *kunopis,* "dog-faced" (*Iliad* 3.180).[8] Although the gap in the fourth stanza prevents certainty, it appears that this Helen simply forgets her past and goes off to Troy, "led" by someone or something, perhaps Aphrodite, or perhaps the ship in which she sailed.[9]

Those critics who have sought a kind of linear logic in this example of the story of Helen have of course been disappointed, and they complain that Sappho's account of Helen—as the most beautiful woman on earth—seems unclear in its focus. If the myth is cited to show how Helen found her own *kalliston* ("most beautiful thing") in her lover Paris, they say, why does Sappho begin the account with the allusion to Helen's own surpassing *kallos* ("beauty")?[10] In response we might argue that Helen provides the quintessential proof of the poet's thesis: even one who already possesses *kallos* within herself is still going to pursue what is *kalliston* to her—that which she loves. As in fragment **"22"** V., desire in Sappho has little to do with possession of anything.

Because of the gap at the beginning of stanza four, we cannot tell exactly how Sappho makes the transition from the mythological proof to the personal proof—that is, to a narrative that is part of the poet's own fictive world of the present rather than Homer's fictive world of the past. In any case, in line 15 the temporal adverb *nun* ("now") seems to bring us firmly into the present moment as the poet begins to sing of Anaktoria, who is for some unspecified reason absent.

ANAKTORIA AND THE SAPPHIC GAZE

In contrast to Helen, who no longer remembers (*oude . . . emnasthe*) those once dear to her, the poet-singer does recall (*onemnais'*, lines 15-16) her beloved, Anaktoria—and as a result of the telling of the myth of Helen. Given the connections between memory and desire that Sappho frequently makes, it is not surprising that the recollection of Anaktoria brings with it the desire, expressed in the first person, to behold her more than anything else in the world. The verb of desiring, *boulomai*, is here put into the optative mood of the Greek verb system, a mood that is itself often used to express a wish or some other conditional (as opposed to actual) form of action; along with the particle *ke*, the form *bolloiman* in line 17 (or in Attic Greek, *bouloimen*) conveys the notion "I would wish" rather than simply "I wish." In effect, the mood of the verb here (impossible to render in English except through vague equivalents involving auxiliary verbs like "would") renders the singer's statement a timeless one; she is not merely saying "I want to see Anaktoria now," but rather "I *would rather* see Anaktoria" even if I could look instead upon every war-chariot in Lydia. It is a statement of preference that is true without regard to time, despite the setting of the example within the fictive present.

Before we look more closely at how the desire to gaze upon Anaktoria is articulated, what about her name itself? Commentators note that it is an aristocratic name, but this fact is not surprising given Sappho's own evidently aristocratic status.[11] The name is related to the word *anax* (stem *anakt-*), meaning "lord" or "master." In Homer's *Iliad* the word is frequently used to describe Agamemnon as the chief general of the Greeks, the *anax andron* ("lord of men," as in *Iliad* 1.442). Curi-

ously, then, the name that Sappho chooses for the "real-world" example to prove the thesis of the song has a kind of Homeric echo to it. The Homeric overtones of this most beautiful thing on earth, this "Maestra," as it were (to render "Anaktoria" in Italian), link this example to the mythical exemplum of Helen with which the proofs began. The "real-world" example, both through its timeless reference and through its epic associations, takes on some of the same larger-than-life qualities as the story of Helen. Both stories, that of Helen's desire for Paris and that of the Sappho persona's desire for Anaktoria, prove the same point: whatever one loves is the most beautiful thing on earth.

A closer look at the language of desire in the song's fifth (and possibly final) stanza reveals several links both to the opening of the song and to the construction of desire elsewhere in Sappho's poetry. In the Greek for line 17, the verb of wanting, *bolloiman*, is immediately followed by the adjective *eraton* ("lovely"), which is from the same root as the verb *eratai* in the song's opening stanza. As we have already noted in connection with fragments **"31"** and **"22"** . . . , desire in Sappho's songs is often configured in connection with gazing upon the beloved woman. Here the speaker would wish to gaze upon—in particular—Anaktoria's "lovely walk" (*eraton . . . bama*) and the "bright sparkle of her face" (*amaruchma lampron . . . prosopo*). The emphasis is on the dynamic—rather than static—qualities of Anaktoria, on the effect she creates as she moves and on the sparkling aura that surrounds her face.[12] As I argued in connection with fragment 22 (chapter 2), it is not the dress itself but the *flow* of the dress as it is worn by the beloved woman that elicits desire from the beholder.

Ironically, the language that Sappho chooses here to describe Anaktoria's face also suggests the military imagery with which the song opens and (probably) closes.[13] Sappho's compatriot Alkaios describes weapons and armor as "bright" (*lampron*, fragments 383 V. and 357 V.), and in the *Iliad* (4.432) weapons "glitter" (*elampe*) on the Greek soldiers as they march toward battle against the Trojans. (The Greek words here are derived from the same Indo-European root that gives us "lamp" in English.) The way that Sappho describes the narrator's desire further strengthens the song's claim in revising the old Homeric values: it is not the flash of weaponry that the narrator would wish to behold. Sappho seems almost to say, "War and weapons may be beautiful to some, but not to me; for I am the new Homer, and I sing not of war but of *eros* and desire."

As is the case with most of Sappho's more sensual songs, critics have sometimes tried to set fragment **"16"** within a strictly heterosexual context. The most amusing attempt has involved the explanation that Anaktoria is "not present" because she has gone off to marry a Lydian soldier—hence the military frame of reference in stanzas 1 and 5.[14] Although this kind of approach cannot completely remove the element of desire on the part of the narrator, it certainly neutralizes it by adding the implication of rejection. We note that the song itself—at least what survives of it—makes no mention as to the reason for Anaktoria's absence, any more than fragments "94" and "96" offer an explanation as to the reason for the separation between lovers. It seems more to the point to concentrate on what is in the song than what is not; just as in fragment "31," the focus is on the narrator's gaze (in this case, would-be gaze) upon the beloved woman. Here the image of the beloved woman, just as in fragment "96," must be called to mind through memory, for she is not in fact present at the moment of the song. The military images surely have more significance than as mere props for some alleged biographical underpinning of the song. Rather, they provide the framework within which Sappho argues for a new set of values: the primacy of *eros* as the determining factor in defining the most beautiful thing on earth.

By concentrating all the alternative definitions in the realm of the military in stanza 1 (whether cavalry or infantry or naval forces) and by setting the example of Anaktoria in opposition to the Lydian forces in stanza 5, Sappho in effect creates an opposition between war and *eros*. The Sappho persona, although not identified by name as in the **"Hymn to Aphrodite"** and elsewhere, comes through clearly in the "I" of the narrator's voice, which is set against the anonymous "some" and "others" of the priamel. The "I" of the song confidently asserts that *everyone* can see the validity of the new values set forth here. The example of Helen appears at first to be traditional in its subject matter and in the technique of drawing on myth to prove a point, but in fact it offers a radical treatment of Helen's story in focusing on her subjectivity and her agency. Even more radically, the narrator of the poem jumps from myth into the narrative of the present—into the story of Anaktoria and the narrator's desire to gaze upon her. In this way, the narrator's desire, her *eros*, supplants the "masculine" way of seeing the world as a struggle for control through military might; the splendor that the Sappho figure celebrates is not of swords but of the beauty of a woman.

ANOTHER SONG ABOUT EROS AND HELEN

Fragment "23" V.

. . . of *eros* (hoped?)

For when I look upon you face to face,
[not even] Hermione [seems] such as

you,
[nor is it unfitting] to liken you
to fair-haired Helen.
. . . for mortal women, but know this,
that by your . . . [you would free me]
of all my cares. . . .

. . . river banks . . .
. . . all night long. . . .

Like fragment "22," found in the same Oxyrhynchus papyrus as this song, fragment "23" is composed in the four-line Sapphic stanza. The fragment opens with a reference to *eros* and proceeds in the next stanza to portray the narrator as being in much the same position as the man of the opening of fragment "31"—who sits opposite (*enantios*) a woman and hears her sweet laughter. Here the narrator is standing or sitting opposite (*antion*, line 3) the woman whose beauty she compares first to that of Hermione, the only child of Helen of Troy, and then to that of Helen herself.

The mention of *eros* in the first extant line of the fragment and the resemblance to the intimate proximity described in fragment "31" suggest an erotic context for this piece as well, but we cannot be sure exactly what shape the song took. However, the allusion to Helen is likely to have functioned less as a digression into old heroic tales of war and abduction and more as a way of illustrating the present moment of the lyric— the desire of the narrator for the woman who is at first compared to the daughter of the most beautiful woman in the world, and then to the most beautiful woman herself.

The reference to riverbanks (*dewy* riverbanks, according to the commonly accepted restoration of the partially missing adjective) is reminiscent of another short fragment ("95" V.) in which the lotus-covered dewy banks of the river Acheron in Hades are mentioned in connection with the narrator's desire (*imeros*, 95.11) to die. If this fragment about the likeness of a woman to Hermione and Helen is indeed erotic in nature, then the possible allusion to dying toward the end of the piece should perhaps be compared to the narrator's self-description in fragment "31" V., where the sensation of almost dying caps the list of the physical responses experienced by the singer as she gazes upon the woman whom she desires. Particularly in view of the apparent resemblance between the description of the narrator's proximity to the woman here and the opening scenario of fragment "31" V., we may not be too far wrong in imagining that the Hermione-Helen fragment began by mentioning the narrator's feelings inspired by *eros*, praised the beloved woman through the mythical comparisons, and went on to describe the narrator's own sensations resulting from the effects of the goddesslike woman on her.

THE WEDDING RECEPTION OF HEKTOR AND
ANDROMACHE

Fragment "44" V.

Cyprus . . .
The herald came,
Idaeus . . . swift messenger
[who said]:
". . . and of the rest of Asia . . . the fame is undying.
Hektor and his companions are bringing a quick-
  glancing girl
from holy Thebes and the river Plakia—
tender Andromache—in ships upon the salty
sea; many golden bracelets and purple garments
. . . many-colored adornments,
countless silver cups and ivory."
So he spoke. Quickly [Hektor's] dear father leaped
  up;
the word went out over the broad-plained city to his
  friends.
At once the sons of Ilos yoked mules
to the well-wheeled chariots. The whole throng
of women and . . . of maidens . . .
But apart, the daughters of Priam . . .
and unmarried men yoked horses to the chariots,
and greatly . . .
. . . charioteers . . .

[Several verses are missing here.]

. . . like to the gods . . .
. . . holy . . .
set forth . . . to Ilium
and the sweet-melodied aulos [and
  kitharis] were mingled,
and the noise of castanets. . . . Then
  the maidens
sang a holy song; the divine echo
  reached the sky . . .
and everywhere along the road . . .
libation vessels . . . ,

myrrh and cassia and frankincense
  were mingled.

But the women, as many as were older, cried out,
and all the men shouted a high-pitched lovely song,
calling upon Paean, the far-shooting and well-lyred;
they sang of Hektor and Andromache, like to the gods.

Fragment **"44,"** of which all or parts of thirty-four lines
have been preserved in another Oxyrhynchus papyrus,
describes the return of Hektor to Troy together with his
new bride, Andromache, as well as the preparations of
the Trojans to celebrate the arrival of the newlyweds.
Leaving aside the complete **"Hymn to Aphrodite,"** this
is the longest fragment of Sappho's poetry that we have.
From the evidence in the papyrus in which the piece is
preserved, we know that it was the last poem in Book 2
of the Alexandrian collection of Sappho's songs. Several
writers of late antiquity (including Athenaeus, second

century A.D.) also cite the song as they comment on
particular details, thus doubly confirming Sappho's authorship.[15]

In form fragment **"44"** is unusual in that it was not
written in stanzas but rather in a line-by-line arrangement, each line being in virtually identical rhythms.
The meter is usually described as glyconic but with a
dactylic expansion: $xx/$‿‿-‿‿-‿‿-$/$‿-. The dactylic element, a long syllable followed by two short syllables
(‿‿), is so named from the Greek word for finger, *dak-
tulos,* representing one long element from the first to
the second finger joint, followed by two short elements
on either side of the joint nearest the fingertip. The
long-short-short dactylic rhythms in this poem clearly
echo, although they do not precisely duplicate, the dactylic hexameter in which both the *Iliad* and the *Odyssey*
were composed. Thus even without the Trojan subject
matter, the hearers of the song would most likely have
been expecting something relating to epic.

The epic context would have been suggested as well by
the several Homeric epithets and by the number of
dialect forms in this song that are peculiar to the Homeric form of the Greek language, as opposed to the
dialect spoken on Lesbos (Lesbian-Aeolic dialect). To
give just one example, the word for "city" in line 12
takes the Homeric form *ptolin,* whereas in Sappho's
usual dialect the word would have been pronounced *po-
lin* (or, in the subject case, *polis,* from which the English
word "political" derives).

Although it is hard to say how much of the song is
missing, we may have the essential narrative elements
more or less intact: the herald Idaeus's announcement
of the impending arrival of Hektor and Andromache
along with his description of the bridal trousseau; the
reaction of Hektor's father, King Priam; the spread of
the news throughout Troy and the consequent preparations on the part of the women, girls, and young men;
and, finally, the scene of celebration at the end involving musical instruments, incense, and everyone singing
the praises of the bride and groom.

We note that in the course of the narrative as we have it
Hektor and Andromache still do not seem actually to
have arrived in Troy. It is their *impending* arrival, and
the busy preparations of everyone expecting it, that
gives this fragment a certain breathless excitement. The
Iliadic context of the war fought over Helen's abduction to Troy seems far from the scene. No weapons are
mentioned, nor war-chariots, but only the *satine* of line
13, a special kind of woman's carriage not mentioned
in Homer.

The self-referential quality of fragment **"44"** becomes
obvious when we realize that in the absence of the
actual narration of the arrival of the bride and groom

(at least in the extant portion), the piece is essentially a song about singing.[16] In fact the scene of singing at the end is so vividly presented that we almost sense the arrival of the subjects even though the extant narrative never actually says, "And then Hektor and Andromache disembarked and proceeded through Troy." Even if the actual arrival was narrated in the gap following line 20, as seems probable, the piece may still have focused more on the reaction of the townspeople and on their celebratory preparations than on the heroic couple themselves.

As I suggested earlier, the attention in this song to domestic details is really more reminiscent of the *Odyssey* than of the *Iliad,* except perhaps for the scene of domestic tranquillity that is part of the description of the decoration on Achilles' new shield (*Iliad* 18.561-72). The herald's report of Andromache's gold bracelets and purple garments and many-colored (*poikila*) adornments, the music of the *aulos* (a double-reed instrument of the oboe family), lyre (if the supplement *kitharis* is accepted in line 24), and castanets, and the myrrh, cassia, and frankincense: all these details appeal to our senses of sight, sound, and smell, and evoke a world of beauty and harmony. The setting may be superficially Homeric, but Homer, or at least the Iliadic Homer, seems to have exited the scene. Instead of war and strife, we hear of finery and music, of joyful sounds to celebrate the union of the happy couple.

TROY RECAST: AN OLD MYTH IN A NEW CONTEXT

Scholars have wondered whether this song about an epic bride and groom might not have been composed to be sung at an actual wedding on Lesbos.[17] While we have no way of knowing the answer to such a question for sure, it does seem relevant to point out that the Homeric subtext of fragment "44" suggests that such a function would have been unlikely.[18] After all, once the war begins (after the narrative time frame of Sappho's lyric piece), Hektor is eventually killed by Achilles (*Iliad* Book 22), young Astyanax (son of Hektor and Andromache) is thrown from the walls of Troy, and Andromache herself is taken captive and subjected to the life of a slave, as she herself foretells at the close of the *Iliad* (24.725-45). These tragic outcomes, although not directly alluded to in Sappho's song about the beginning of their relationship, cannot help but color the listener's perception of the joyful celebrations in honor of the two epic figures. Even though Sappho chooses to focus her song on celebration and joyful beginnings and a sense of eager anticipation, thus creating a mini-epic that provides a respite from the usual Iliadic themes of war and suffering and death, the vignette she creates represents only an initial moment of the story that is all too familiar in its unhappy outcome. In fact it is the inevitability of misfortune that gives Sappho's lyric version a special poignancy, for we know that the sounds of joy echoing among the people of Troy will one day be replaced by sounds of lamentation after Hektor meets his doom at the hands of Achilles. For the moment of the song itself, however, Hektor and Andromache are *ikeloi theois* (line 21, "like to the gods"), a theme echoed in the final word of the song describing them as *theoeikelois* (literally, "godlike").

If we consider this song without regard to its intended function (if any), we can turn our attention to the exquisitely colorful detail and the emphasis on women's roles that are characteristics of Sappho's other songs. The bride's dowry, for example, includes golden bracelets, purple robes, many-colored (*poikila*) adornments, and silver cups. The women and girls ride in mule-drawn carriages, whereas the young men are in horse-drawn chariots. The girls sing a holy song, while the older women (line 31) cry out and the men sing a song to Apollo, and everyone sings the praises of the bride and groom. Page is probably right in his conclusion that Sappho "is not at all concerned to portray a Homeric scene."[19] In addition to the lack of epic models for the type of scene she describes, the particular details such as the women's carriages (line 13), the castanets (line 25), and the myrrh, cassia, and frankincense (line 30) are not found anywhere in the *Iliad* or the *Odyssey*.

What are we to make of this un-Homeric scene drawn from the world of the Homeric heroes? Like fragment "16," fragment "44" offers us an old myth in a new context. Just as the Sapphic Helen of fragment 16 provides a positive example of erotic self-fulfillment, so here the celebratory scene of joyful anticipation suggests what the union of Hektor and Andromache might have been: a long and happy marriage unmarred by the scars of death and destruction. The sensual details of color, sound, and scent describe a delightful scene that is a far cry from the battlefields of Troy.[20] As I will suggest [elsewhere], the details in this song accord perfectly with the aesthetic ideal described elsewhere in Sappho's verses—a world in which delicate variegation (*poikilia*) is the hallmark of a beautiful and orderly microcosm. Here there is no need for heroic exploits, contests of strength, or battles of will, for none of these is critical to Sapphic *eros*.

It would be tempting to wonder—if we had more of Sappho's poetry on which to form a judgment—whether or not she tended to use Homeric and other traditional myths in the same way that the great choral lyric poets of the early fifth century did.[21] Writers like Pindar of Thebes or Bacchylides of Keos routinely include allusions to or retellings of the old myths in their odes in order to illustrate some maxim or suggest a connection between the old story and the subject of the song at hand, usually with a moralizing slant. Sappho's contemporary Alkaios—although it is hard to be certain in view of the fragmentary nature of his songs—also seems to have used the old tales to make moral statements, as in the contrast he draws between the destruction wrought by Helen and the heroic offspring produced by Thetis, mother of Achilles (fragment "**42**" V.).[22] I venture to hazard a guess that Sappho used the old myths as she saw fit to enhance her descriptions of her female-oriented world. The fragments of her songs suggest little concern with moral pronouncements. Instead, she freely adapts traditional material to suit her own purposes, whether to suggest an epic precedent for the primacy of *eros* as experienced by the archetypal woman, Helen, to compare female beauty to the legendary pulchritude of Hermione and Helen, or to narrate a scene of splendid nuptial celebration seemingly far removed from the epic context of the Trojan War.

. . . . .

Despite the unquestionable prominence of Aphrodite, Eros, and woman-centered passions in the songs she composed, Sappho's role as a lyric poet treated a wide range of other themes as well. The present [essay] provides an overview of most of the remaining fragments of any substance (i.e., more than three or four connected words) that have not been discussed earlier in this book in an attempt to illustrate what that range most likely was. If we were miraculously to discover a complete copy of the nine books of Sappho's lyrics, we would find songs of prayer, marriage songs, folk songs, festival songs, and no doubt a variety of other kinds of lyric musings on everything from the traditional Greek myths to events of daily life.

Although some of the shorter fragments discussed in this [essay] are preserved in tattered papyrus rolls, many of them come from quotations by ancient grammarians or commentators who wrote many centuries after Sappho's time and who were chiefly interested in some peculiarity of dialect or a metrical phenomenon illustrated by the words they chose to quote. Generally speaking, they provide little or no help as to the context of the words quoted. Short of grouping these fragments into five general categories, I have not attempted to supply any missing context. Tempting though it is to try to imagine in what sort of poem the phrase "the black sleep of night [covers] the eyes" (fragment "**151**" V.) might have occurred, for example, such speculative guesswork is perhaps not as productive as one's simple indulgence in the evocative nature of any fragment. Like the ruins of an ancient temple, these bits and pieces of song stand as hieroglyphic enigmas that stir the imagination without necessarily begging for actual reconstruction.[23] Unlike the ruins of the Parthenon, however, these literary ruins are in no danger of collapse should we choose to let them simply stand as

fragments of the original—in most cases no doubt unrecoverable—whole.

Prayers

Not surprisingly, many of the shorter fragments take the same general shape as the "**Hymn to Aphrodite,**" that is, a prayer addressed to some deity or deities. We have already seen that several fragments open with an address to the *Charites* or to the Muses, and other deities called upon include Hera, the Nereids, Eos (Dawn), and perhaps Apollo and Artemis.[24] The most substantial among these is the following prayer addressed to the Nereids (and Aphrodite, if, as is likely, the opening of the song has been correctly restored) for the safe return of the speaker's brother following an unspecified journey. We may assume that the poem's journey was by sea, for the daughters of Nereus are sea-goddesses who assist sailors, a role that the Cyprian Aphrodite (whose name reappears toward the end of the fragment), born from the sea, also took on:

Fragment "5" V.

O [Cyprian] and Nereids, grant
that my brother come hither unharmed
and that as many things as he wishes in his heart to
  come about
are all brought to pass,

And that he atones for all his former errors,
and is a joy to his [friends],
a [pain] to his enemies; but for us
let there be no misery.

May he wish to do honor to his sister
  . . . painful suffering . . .

. . . millet-seed . . . of the citizens . . .

. . . but you, Cyprian, setting aside . . .

Like the "**Hymn to Aphrodite**" and other songs that made up the opening book of the Alexandrian edition of Sappho's work, this prayer is composed in four-line Sapphic stanzas. Voigt and other scholars believe that what we have left is a skeletal version of the entire song, beginning with the opening address to Aphrodite and the Nereids in stanza one, and concluding with a repeated address to Aphrodite in stanza five. Traditionally, the poem has been read autobiographically in conjunction with the statements in the historian Herodotus (2.134 ff.) regarding Sappho's brother Charaxos. Herodotus reports that Charaxos went to Naucratis in Egypt, where he purchased the freedom of a famous courtesan named Rhodopis with whom he was enamored. When he got home, Herodotus continues, Sappho mocked him for his actions in one of her poems. Is fragment "**5**" that poem? If it is, is our understanding of the fragment likely to be helped much by the remark of a historian writing some one hundred and twenty-five years after Sappho's time?

Perhaps it is more to the point to examine the fragment—since we have a substantial portion of it left—in comparison with other ancient prayers for the safe return of someone from a journey at sea. Such a poem was known as a *propemptikon,* literally a "send-off" song in which the speaker pleads that a friend or relative will come home safely. If an example by the Roman poet Horace (65-8 B.C.), who was a great admirer and imitator of Sappho's poetry, is any indication, such a piece might use the allusion to the departed person's trip as a taking-off point for other themes as well. In *Odes* 1.3, Horace entreats Aphrodite and the twins Kastor and Pollux to grant a safe journey to Vergil on his way home to Italy from Athens. But after the first eight lines, the poem veers off into philosophical musings (for another thirty-two lines) on the audacity of human enterprise in seeking to conquer nature—as, for example, in Daedalus's use of wings for human flight.

In Sappho's song, although the gaps prevent us from knowing exactly what direction the poem took, it seems clear enough that the actual wish for the brother's safe return was accomplished within the two opening lines. The remaining eighteen lines seem to have enlarged on this wish by setting forth a program for various kinds of reciprocal actions: the speaker prays that the brother will accomplish whatever his heart (*thumos*) desires, but that he will also atone for past mistakes; in addition, according to the conventional Greek morality (along the lines of an eye for an eye), she hopes that he will be a "joy" (*chara*) to his friends and a pain to his enemies. The speaker prays further that no pain will come to themselves, and that the brother will somehow bring honor to his sister. The song thus focuses on the reciprocity of various relationships—between the speaker and the addressees, between them and the brother, between the brother and his friends (or enemies), and between the brother and the speaker herself. Like the **"Hymn to Aphrodite,"** the song emphasizes the bonds between human and divine—and, especially in this fragment, between one person and another.

Another, more broken fragment (also in Sapphic stanzas) has been closely linked by scholars to fragment **"5,"** for it appears to contain some of the same language for the notion of atonement, and it mentions a woman named Doricha, identified by the first-century A.D. historian Strabo (17.1.33) as the courtesan Rhodopis with whom Sappho's brother Charaxos was supposed to have fallen in love. Whether or not this is the case, like fragment **"15,"** this poem, too, seems to be addressed to Aphrodite:[25]

> Fragment "15" V.
>
> . . . blessed (goddess?) . . .
>
> [May (s)he atone for] as many errors as
>   (s)he made [before] . . .
>
> Cypris, and may Doricha find you most harsh,
> and may she not boast saying this,
> how (s)he came a second time [to]
> much-desired *eros.*

Aside from the mention of the feminine name Doricha, the gender of the subjects in this song is not apparent from what is left, but on the basis of Strabo's identification of Doricha with the courtesan Rhodopis, we may perhaps assume a heterosexual context. Evidently the speaker is praying that Aphrodite treat Doricha harshly and not give her assistance in matters of the heart—a plea exactly the opposite of the speaker's request for help in the **"Hymn to Aphrodite."** In that song, Aphrodite is requested to assist, as she has done many times in the past, with the repetitive, cyclical, and reciprocal aspects of *eros;* here, on the contrary, the goddess is to see to it that the flow of *eros* comes to a dead halt. There is to be no second time.

Another prayer that has survived in skeletal form is fragment **"17"** V., a five-stanza song (in Sapphic stanzas) that is addressed to the goddess Hera:

> Fragment "17" V.
>
> Near to me, lady Hera,
> [may your lovely form appear],
> whom (famous) kings, the sons of Atreus,
> entreated,
>
> When they had accomplished [many labors],
> first at Ilium [and then at sea]
> setting out to here, they were not able
> [to complete the journey],
>
> Until they [called upon] you and Zeus Antiaios
> and the lovely [son] of Thuone.
> But now kindly [come to my aid]
> according to the custom of old.
>
> Holy and beautiful . . .
> maidens . . .
> around . . .
>
> . . . to be . . .
> to come to . . .

Addressed to Zeus's consort Hera, this prayer reminds the goddess of her relationship with earlier Homeric entreaters, namely the Greek kings Agamemnon and Menelaus (the sons of Atreus). In the version told in Homer's *Odyssey* (3.130-83), the two brothers have quarreled and set out separately on the homeward trip after the Trojan War; only Menelaus stops at nearby Lesbos, where he prays to Zeus for guidance in choosing the best route home. In Sappho's account, however, if the supplement in line 3 is correct, both Menelaus and Agamemnon are present, and they pray not only to Zeus but also to Hera and to Dionysos (the son of Thuone, another name for Semele). In any case, it is clear that the allusion to the Homeric story is meant to serve as part of the "reminder" section of the prayer. . . .

The mere shreds of the final two stanzas of the song do not permit a reconstruction of what the request to Hera might have been, although the last word of the final line, "to come to" (if the supplement is correct), suggests a journey, perhaps a sea voyage like that of the sons of Atreus. Perhaps Hera is being asked to grant safe passage. Although the song mentions Hera within the context of a trinity of deities especially worshipped on Lesbos (Alkaios fragment 129 V. in all likelihood calls upon the same trinity), Hera is singled out for her especially close relationship to the singer. The goddess is evidently asked to make herself manifest in the singer's very presence—"Near to me." The woman-centered nature of Sappho's poetry is evident even in her theology, for although gods are mentioned, it is the female deities who seem to occupy center stage.

MARRIAGE SONGS

I have . . . mentioned [elsewhere] . . . a few examples of fragments from Sappho's marriage songs (*epithalamia*), but here it is appropriate to discuss other examples in more detail. Some of these fragments seem to center either on the marriage ritual itself, in allusions to the song sung in honor of Hymen (the god of marriage) or on the appearance of the bridegroom. Here is the beginning of one such song, made familiar in the twentieth century through J. D. Salinger's borrowing of the opening words as the title for one of his long short stories (published in 1963):

Fragment "111" V.

Rise high the roof-beams!
Sing the Hymeneal!
Raise it high, O carpenter men!
Sing the Hymeneal!
The bridegroom enters, like to Ares,
by far bigger than a big man.

Some readers have seen an element of risqué humor in the allusion to the size of the bridegroom as "far bigger than a big man," perhaps referring to his ithyphallic state of excitement.[26] Similar humorous exaggeration is evident in the opening of another marriage song that makes fun of the groom's attendant, the doorkeeper:

Fragment "110" V.

[At the wedding]
the doorkeeper's feet are seven fathoms long,
and his sandals are made of five oxhides,
and ten shoemakers worked away to make them.

Another example in which the groom's appearance is alluded to opens with the following line:

Fragment "115" V.

To what, dear bridegroom, may I suitably liken you?
I liken you most to a slender sapling. . . .

The description of the groom in this fragment attributed to Sappho by Hephaestion (the second-century A.D. author of a handbook on meter) seems somewhat less than fully heroic, alluding as it may to Odysseus's likening of Nausikaa to the young shoot of a palm tree (*Odyssey* 6.163) and to Thetis's description of her son Achilles "shooting up like a tree" when he was a young child (*Iliad* 18.56). If there is any element of risqué humor here in the possibly phallic overtones of the image, the emphasis on slenderness again reduces the groom to less than heroic proportions.

While such instances of bantering raillery may have been a common feature of Sappho's hymeneals (as indeed they are in later Greek examples of the genre), other scraps of the wedding songs seem to emphasize the beauty of the bride or the poignancy of the impending loss of her girlhood status. Perhaps the most vivid example is the following fragment, which was evidently once part of a song in which the groom was likened to the hero Achilles. The meter is appropriately the dactylic hexameter of Homeric epic:

Fragment "105"A V.

[the bride]
just like a sweet apple that ripens on the uppermost
   bough,
on the top of the topmost; but the apple-gatherers
   have forgotten it,
or rather, they haven't altogether forgotten it, but they
   could not reach it.

Here desire becomes on one level the reach for the unreachable.[27] The young woman is like a beautiful, ripe red apple enjoying privileged access to the rays of the sun high up at the very top of the tree. The apple is perfect—but has only been able to achieve and maintain such a beautiful state because it was just out of the reach of the apple-pickers, who could not fulfill their desire to pluck the ripened fruit. At least within the context of the fragment itself, then, the bride is suspended in time at a moment of utter perfection.

The image of the apple, so high up among apple boughs such as those in Aphrodite's sacred precinct described in fragment "2," almost makes us forget that the

Achilles-like groom is indeed about to accomplish what the apple-pickers had wanted, but been unable, to do. Indeed, as far as the simile itself is concerned there is no Achilles; at this moment the red apple remains safely on its bough, and desire becomes perhaps not so much the reach for the unreachable as the contemplation of perfect beauty. Even the applepickers, though they could not reach the beautiful apple itself, held on to its image. Sappho makes a point of this in the correction of the original statement in line 2 to the effect that they "have forgotten" (*lelathonto*) the apple; no, she emends, they really have not "entirely forgotten" (*eklelathonto*) it, for, she implies, they can still see it in the mind's eye.

The enduring significance of the image of the perfect apple in this small fragment of Sappho's work has been well captured in the title of a book by the contemporary American poet Judy Grahn, *The Highest Apple: Sappho and the Lesbian Poetic Tradition.* In her view, the apple stands for "the centrality of women to themselves, to each other, and to their society. That apple remained, intact, safe from colonization and suppression, on the topmost branch, and in the fragmented history of a Lesbian poet and her underground descendants."[28]

Another simile, one that has been attributed to Sappho by modern scholars, also seems to compare someone (possibly a bride) to the beauty of the natural world, in this instance to a mountain hyacinth:

Fragment "105"B V.

[the bride?]
like a hyacinth in the mountains which the shepherd
   men
trample with their feet, but the purple flower [flying]
   on the ground. . . .

In this case, not enough of the context remains for us to guess what Sappho's hexameter lines (if indeed they are hers) might have said about the fate of the trampled hyacinth. It is only the resemblance (in meter and general structure) to fragment **"105a,"** the highest apple simile, that has led scholars to presume that these lines, too, were once part of a wedding song by Sappho.

Critics have generally further assumed that the trampled hyacinth may have functioned similarly to the "deflowering" imagery in a wedding song by the Roman poet Catullus (62.39-47), in which the chorus of young girls compare themselves to a wonderful hidden flower nourished by rain and sun, a flower that is about to be plucked and stained, thereby losing all desirability.[29] While it is certainly possible that the flower in fragment **"105b"** functioned as an image of lost virginity (a common enough trope in classical literature), we could just as easily conjecture that it stood for resilience: the hyacinth has been stepped on and some of its blossoms lie on the ground, but after the shepherds have passed it by, its stem, nourished by the mountain air, regains its strength and rises again toward the sun to bloom once more. (If only the ancient grammarian who quoted the lines—without attribution—had quoted one or two more, we would have a better idea as to where the image led!) In other words, it is just possible that the image of the hyacinth, like the image of the perfect apple high up on the tree, performed in some way the role of celebrating a woman's beauty.

A fragment that clearly does belong to the genre of the wedding song, as the remarks of the ancient grammarian who preserved it indicate, is the following dialogue between a bride and her virginity:

Fragment "114" V.

Bride:

   Maidenhood, maidenhood, where have you gone and left me?

Maidenhood:

   No more will I come back to you, no more will I come back.

The bantering tone of this exchange, with its repetition of the address (*parthenia, parthenia*) for mock-pathetic effect, may suggest a certain disdain on Sappho's part for the conventional notion of the "deflowering" of the bride. "Maidenhood" is something that simply departs, never to return again. It was for this nicety of expression—whereby the figure of speech in the question posed by the bride, who refers metaphorically to *parthenia* as a traveler, is picked up again in *parthenia*'s reply—that the fragment was preserved for us by the ancient grammarian.[30]

Other fragments that can be connected with wedding songs are hardly more than scraps. An ancient commentator on Vergil, Servius, quotes a line from a poem that he says came from Sappho's book entitled **Epithalamia,** no doubt referring to the ninth book of the Alexandrian edition of her poetry, which contained the wedding songs excluded from the other books on the basis of meter:

Fragment "116" V.

   Farewell, bride, farewell, honored bridegroom, many
     . . .

Similarly, Hephaestion quotes what is likely to have been the opening line of a wedding song:

Fragment "117" V.

   May you fare well, bride, and may the bridegroom
    fare well, too.

The same Oxyrhynchus papyrus (1231) that has preserved several significant fragments of the Sapphic stanzas of the first book of Sappho's poems (including the previously discussed fragments **"15," "16," "17," "22," "23,"** and **"24a"**) also contains two rather more substantial, if mutilated, fragments of what appear to be *epithalamia*. These songs were the final two poems in Book 1 of the Alexandrian edition of Sappho's work. The incomplete state of the text leaves much open to guesswork in both cases:

Fragment "27" V.

For once you, too, [as] a child . . .
. . . come now, sing of these things . . .
. . . strive after . . . and from . . .
freely grant us *charis* [favor/grace].

For we are going to a wedding. And you, too,
[know?] this well, but as quickly as possible
send away the girls, may the gods have . . .

[there is no] road to great Olympus for mortals . . .

Fragment "30" V.

the night . . .

The girls . . .
all night long . . .
singing of your love for the
violet-bosomed bride.

But wake up and go [to find]
the unmarried youths of your own age.
Let us see as much sleep as
the clear-voiced [nightingale?].

The first of these songs (fragment **"27"** V.) seems to be addressed to someone, perhaps female (the gender is not apparent from the existing grammatical clues), who is bidden to carry out various instructions. In the first more-or-less extant stanza, we note the familiar association of singing with *charis* and its underlying implication of pleasurable exchange. The request for song seems somehow tied in to the context of a wedding, for the subsequent stanza includes in its opening phrase the conjuction *gar* ("for"), which serves to mark an explanation of what has just preceded. Too many gaps remain to allow the certainty of an explanation like that of one scholar, who argues that the song is addressed to Sappho's rival poet Andromeda; Andromeda, he thinks, is being asked to send back the maidens to Sappho so that they may join in public dance and song.[31]

The second example (fragment **"30"** V.), the one that concluded Book 1 of the Alexandrian edition, is almost as enigmatic. It appears to be addressed to the bridegroom, who is bidden to go off in search of his fellow bachelors. The song is again one about singing, in this case the all-night singing of the girls about the groom's love for the bride. In what Voigt takes to be the end of the piece, the singer implies further nocturnal celebrations, for she says that they will see as much sleep as some "clear-voiced" creature; the gap at the end of line 8 is usually filled in with *ornis,* "bird," and the allusion is then assumed to be to the proverbially wakeful nightingale. Like the nightingale, the celebrants will forego sleep in favor of singing. The fragment leaves us with only a glimpse of how this book of Sapphic stanzas came to a close—the book that had begun with the powerful **"Hymn to Aphrodite."** It seems unlikely that the Alexandrian editors, who chose to end Book 1 with two wedding songs, would have been so disparaging of their form and content as one modern editor, Denys Page. Page brands the fragments of the *epithalamia* as "trivial in subject and style."[32] While they may not have carried the emotional force of a song like the "Hymn to Aphrodite" certainly several of these fragments of wedding songs—particularly fragment 105a about the apple on the uppermost bough—suggest a poignant beauty that ought not to be so lightly dismissed.

One other papyrus scrap preserves the end of what could be an *epithalamium* but might also simply be another kind of song meant for nighttime performance, or at least alluding to such performance:

Fragment "43" V.

beautiful . . .
stirs up peaceful (waters) . . .
toil . . . the heart . . .
sits down . . .
But come, my dears,
. . . for day is near.

The speaker's address to *o philai* (literally, "O dear ones" [feminine gender]) makes clear that the participants in the nighttime ritual or festival (or whatever was described) are other women, who seem to be bidden to depart now that the sun is rising.

FOLK MOTIFS

Another group of short fragments besides the wedding songs are those that contain folk motifs. The beginning two lines of one such poem are preserved for us again by Hephaestion, who reports that the song was in Book 7 of Sappho's collected works:

Fragment "102" V.

Sweet mother, I am not able to weave at my loom,
overwhelmed with desire for a youth because of tender
Aphrodite.

Weaving was of course a standard occupation for women all over the Greek world, and in this song the narrator, presumably a girl or young woman, complains to her mother that overwhelming desire for a young man prevents her from carrying out her appointed task.[33] Despite the filial, domestic quality of the setting, with the girl addressing her mother, the language of desire is strong: the girl claims that she is "overwhelmed" or "mastered" by desire (*pothos*), the same word that Sappho uses of sexual desire in fragments **"22."**11 and **"94."**23. Thus the opening of the song seems to contain the seeds of both innocence and grand passion at once.

A similar kind of folk element appears in the following fragment addressed to the evening star:

Fragment "104"A V.

> Hesperus, you bring all that the shining Dawn scattered,
> you bring the sheep, you bring the goat, you bring the child back to its mother.

The evening star, described in a related fragment (fragment **"104b"** V.) as *asteron panton o kallistos,* "the most beautiful of all the stars," is here lauded for its reunificatory powers; under its idyllic light, the flocks and the children all return home from the activities of the day.

A tantalizingly brief quotation from an ancient work on figures of speech preserves the following remarkably alliterative bit from one of Sappho's songs; the sentiment expressed seems to be based on a Greek proverb:

Fragment "146" V.

> Neither the honey nor the bee for me

Although the context is unknown, the ancient commentators suggest that the proverb refers to the desire to avoid the bad things that inevitably come along with good things; to escape the bee-sting, one may have to give up the bees' honey as well. Might this sentiment have been part of a song about *eros?* We cannot really tell, but we can say that what little evidence remains indicates that folk motifs and proverbial material such as fragment **"146"** occupied a significant place in Sappho's repertoire of themes.

Mythological Motifs

Another group of short fragments contains mythological figures. In these instances, the fragments are usually too brief to allow any reasonable guesses as to how the myth may have functioned vis-à-vis the major theme of the whole song. In one such song, for example, preserved in a quotation, Sappho describes Hermes as the wine-pourer for the rest of the gods:

Fragment "141" V.

> There a mixing bowl of ambrosia had been mixed,
> while Hermes, taking up the jug,
> poured wine for the gods.

> These all held their cups and made libations.
> They prayed for all good things for the bridegroom.

Whether this description of a marriage on Olympus formed part of a wedding song, we cannot tell, despite the preservation of several lines of context. In other cases, we have little left beyond the name of a mythological figure, as in fragment **"124"** V. referring to the Muse Kalliope, or fragment **"123"** V. describing "golden-sandaled Dawn" (*chrusopedilos Auos*).

The second-century A.D. scholar Athenaeus preserves two possibly related fragments, the first of which clearly has to do with the story of Leda and the swan (the form taken on that occasion by Zeus), whose union according to some versions in Greek mythology produced two eggs, from which were hatched Kastor, Pollux, Klytemnestra, and Helen:

Fragment "166" V.

> Indeed, they say that once Leda found
> an egg, colored like a hyacinth, covered with . . .

Fragment "167" V.

> whiter by far than an egg . . .

Athenaeus preserves another mythological reference in a fragment whose context is known only to the extent that he points out that even in his time free (as opposed to slave) women and girls use the term *hetairai* (literally, "companions") in referring to each other, just as Sappho did in her line:

Fragment "142" V.

> Leto and Niobe were very dear friends

Perhaps the fragment went on to describe the rift between the goddess Leto (mother of the twins Apollo and Artemis) and the Theban queen Niobe, who rashly boasted that as the mother of seven sons and seven daughters, she had been far more productive than Leto. As punishment, Apollo and Artemis struck down all of Niobe's children with their deadly arrows, and Niobe herself was transformed into a perpetually weeping mountain of stone, forever lamenting her dead offspring.

Hephaestion, in his handbook on meter, preserves what is probably the opening line of a song (in ionic meter) addressed to a woman named Eirana (the name occurs also in fragment **"91"** V.):

Fragment "135" V.

> Why, Eirana, does the swallow, daughter of Pandion,
> [awaken?] me?

The verb in the question is missing, but the supplement "awaken" seems as likely as any. The myth referred to is the story of Philomela, whose brother-in-law, Tereus, raped her and then cut out her tongue to prevent her telling her sister Procne of his evil deeds. Philomela, however, cleverly wove the story into a tapestry, and when Procne understood what had happened, the two sisters took revenge on Tereus by serving him the flesh of his own son, Itys, for dinner. In the end, all were transformed into birds—Philomela into a swallow, Procne into a nightingale, and Tereus into a pursuing hawk. (In Latin and mediaeval literature, the birds with which the two sisters are identified are sometimes reversed.)

In fragment **"135,"** we note that Philomela (identified as "daughter of Pandion") is already transformed into the wordless swallow, who can communicate only through inarticulate musical sound. Sappho's Philomela-swallow seems even further removed from articulate expression than the Philomela of a lost play by Sophocles (called *Tereus*), in which he referred to her use of "the voice of the shuttle."[34] Unfortunately, however, since so little of Sappho's song remains, we cannot explore further the possibility raised by Patricia Klindienst Joplin that the poet may have given us here "an ominous sign of what threatens the woman's voiced existence in culture."[35] Exactly how the Philomela-swallow functioned in the rest of the song we really cannot tell, but it is certainly tempting to note the irony of the parallels between Philomela's tapestry and the shreds of Sappho's own work, the majority of which must now be read through signs and traces.

One last fragment dealing with mythological figures is more substantial than many, but it cannot be assigned to Sappho with absolute certainty. Although the editors who first published the fragment thought that it was perhaps by Alkaios, Voigt and others attribute the piece to Sappho. Treu, for example, notes the reference in section (b) of the fragment to the Muses and to the *Charites*, so characteristic of Sappho's verse:[36]

Fragment "44"a V.

a

[to golden-haired Phoibos], whom the daughter of
  Koios (Leto) bore
after she had slept with the great-named son of
  Cronos.
[But Artemis] swore a great oath [of the gods]:
[By your] head, always I will be a virgin
  . . . upon the tops of the mountains . . .
  . . . grant me this favor.
The father of the blessed gods nodded assent.
The gods [called her] far-shooting Huntress,
a great name.
    Eros never draws near to her. . . .

b

The splendid [gifts?] of the Muses . . .
makes . . . and of the Charites
slender. . . .

not to forget the wrath . . .
mortals . . .

How the story of Apollo and Artemis was tied into the remainder of the song must remain a mystery, but perhaps they were somehow linked to the Muses and the Graces (*Charites*) as inspirers of song. Artemis is mentioned by name in one other fragment of Sappho's (fragment **"84"** V.), which is otherwise almost totally unintelligible, and Apollo is referred to in fragment **"44."**33 V. in his roles as both hunter and musician. Neither deity seems to have occupied the place of central importance in Sappho's poetry, which as we have seen was unquestionably held by Aphrodite.

MISCELLANEOUS SHORT FRAGMENTS

We come finally to a small group of fragments that seem to treat a variety of subjects. The most controversial of these is a short papyrus fragment (P. Oxy. 2291, col. I.1-9) that Voigt prefers to assign to Alkaios. Others assign it to Sappho, sometimes with cautionary notes to the effect that the poem may in fact be by Alkaios.[37] The fragment is badly mutilated but does clearly contain at least one, if not two, references to the sons of Poly-anax ("Much-Ruler"), a name that recurs in the following punning line preserved for us in a quotation from Sappho:

Fragment "155" V.

I'm overjoyed to say farewell to you,
  Miss Overlord.

In addition to the repetition of the "p" sounds, the pun on *polla* ("much") and *Polu-anaktida* ("child of Mr. Much-Ruler") produces a sarcastic tone that occurs occasionally among Sappho's fragments.[38] In the papyrus fragment in question, however, the allusions to the house of Polyanax occur in far more obscure contexts, quite possibly within two separate poems:

Alkaios Fragment 303A V. (= Sappho Fragment "99 L.-P.")

a

After a little . . .

 . . . the son(s) of Polyanax . . .

to strum on the strings. . . .
receiving the dildo(?) . . .

 . . . kindly
it quivers. . . .

 . . .
 . . .

    [possibly the end of this poem]

b

[possibly the beginning of a new poem]
O child of (Leto) and Zeus,
come . . .

leaving wooded [Gryneia?]
. . . to the oracle
. . .
sing . . .
. . . sister
show (?) . . . again . . . the sons of Polyanax . . .
I want to expose the greedy [man?] . . .

The chief reason that these papyrus scraps have attracted so much scholarly attention, despite their wretched state of preservation, is the possible reference in line 5 of part (a) to the word *olisbos,* known from Greek comedy (e.g., Aristophanes, *Lysistrata* 109) to be a leather phallus, or dildo. To those eagerly seeking information about ancient lesbian sexual practices, however, it must be pointed out that even if these fragments could be definitely assigned to Sappho rather than Alkaios, the occurrence of the word *olisbos* here is far from certain; every letter of *olisb-* in line 5 is printed in the Greek editions with a dot underneath, a convention used by editors of papyri to indicate the uncertainty of decipherment. The Sapphic dildo may be a figment of papyrological imagination—and if so, the question then arises as to why scholars have been so eager to find it in an almost illegible fragment of dubious authorship and uncertain context. The elements of scandal and masquerade in the notion of the Sapphic dildo are worth exploring further ("WOMAN POET WEARS FAKE PENIS!"), but I will leave that project aside for now. In any case, we certainly cannot accept Giangrande's glib conclusion that this fragment "leaves us in no doubt as to what Sappho and her companions were up to."[39]

Several of the shorter fragments offer just enough intelligibility to enable us to admire the vividness of the Sapphic imagery while at the same time savoring the multiple range of possibilities of context that each might have come from. Here are four examples that refer in one way or another to the tender, flowerlike qualities of a girl or young woman; had we more context, we might well find that these songs would illustrate some of the qualities of Sapphic *habrosune.*[40] The first of these is the most famous, for many readers have interpreted it as an autobiographical reference on Sappho's part to her daughter Kleis; others, drawing on the analogy of a male homosexual context, see Sappho's description of Kleis (who is referred to as a *pais,* "child," "boy") as crotic rather than familial:[41]

Fragment "132" V.

I have a child whose beauty
resembles golden flowers: beloved Kleis,
whom [I would not exchange]
either for all of Lydia or a lovely . . .

Fragment "41" V.

Toward you, beautiful women, my thoughts
are not changeable

Fragment "122" V.

[I saw] an exceedingly tender girl plucking flowers

Fragment "126" V.

. . . [a woman]
sleeping on the bosom of a tender companion [hetaira]
. . .

Another vivid but tantalizingly incomplete fragment, whose metrical peculiarities perhaps indicate less than precise quotation on the part of the preserver (Athenaeus), seems to describe the opposite of the aesthetic ideals of *charis, habrosune,* and *poikilia.* Here the narrator appears to be rebuking someone (named Andromeda, according to Athenaeus) for succumbing to the charms of a hayseed, a country-bumpkin:

Fragment "57" V.

What bumpkin girl charms [your] mind . . .
wearing her bumpkin dress . . .
not knowing how to draw her rags over her ankles?

The insulting overtones of *agroïotis* are suggested by a fragment from Alkaios, a relatively lengthy piece complaining of the deprivations of life in exile away from the center of the action, which in Alkaios's view consists of the politics of the assembly and the council. The narrator of the song (Alkaios fragment 130b V.) complains, "I in my wretchedness live the life of a bumpkin's lot, while I long to hear the assembly being summoned." After complaining further of living among the "wolf-thickets" in the middle of nowhere, the narrator provides this curious example of what it means to be away from the urban activities of the male aristocracy: he keeps out of trouble by going to watch a beauty contest of the women of Lesbos!

Alkaios Fragment 130B. 16-20 V.

I survive and keep my feet out of trouble,
where the women of Lesbos with their trailing robes
go up and down as they are being judged for beauty,
while all around there rings the marvelous echo
of the women's sacred cries each year.

Ironically, the Alkaios-narrator illustrates the enforced rustic alienation from the urban political process of the male aristocracy with a description of his own "feminization" at what appears to be an annual religious ritual for women, which, according to various ancient commentators, took place at the precinct of the goddess Hera.[42] No doubt if Sappho alluded to this beauty contest in her songs, it would have been in quite a different context.[43]

Four brief fragments preserved in quotation present puzzles as to what their original context might have been. All are in the form of the first-person statements so characteristic of Sappho's poetry; whether any of these songs featured the named Sappho persona that we have observed in the case of longer pieces such as the **"Hymn to Aphrodite"** or fragment **"94"** V., we cannot tell:

Fragment "51" V.

I do not know what to do; my mind is split

Fragment "52" V.

I do not think that I will touch the sky with my two arms(?)

Fragment "121" V.

But since you are our friend, seek a younger bed.
For I would not dare to live with you, since I am older.

Fragment "120" V.

But I am not someone resentful in
my feelings; I have a gentle heart.

A fuller representation of Sappho's lyrics would surely reveal more songs that, like the following fragment, allude self-consciously to the art of song:

Fragment "118" V.

Come now, divine lyre, speak to me,
and sounding forth be [my companion?] . . .

Preserved (perhaps somewhat inaccurately) through quotation in a later Greek writer named Hermogenes, the lines were cited as an example of what we would call pathetic fallacy, or the attribution of feelings and the the power of judgment to inanimate objects. Evidently, according to Hermogenes, the poem went on to represent the voice of the tortoise-shell lyre actually responding to the poet's apostrophe. We have noted earlier Sappho's fondness for dialogue embedded in her lyrics, as in the **"Hymn to Aphrodite"** (between the Sappho-narrator and Aphrodite) and in fragment **"94"** V (between the Sappho-narrator and the departing woman) and fragment **"114"** V. (between a bride and her virginity). This song addressed to the speaking lyre may have been yet another example of Sappho's enlargement of the lyric scope through the introduction of multiple "voices" within a given poem.

Another short fragment, the text and meter of which are uncertain, seems to refer to "those who serve the Muses," possibly poets:

Fragment "150" V.

For it is not right for there to be lamentation
in the house of those who serve the Muses.
That would not be suitable for us.

As we have already noted, Sappho frequently opens a song with an address to the Muses, either in conjunction with the *Charites* or independently, as in the following beginning of a poem preserved in a quotation in Hephaestion's treatise:

Fragment "127" V.

Hither again, O Muses, leaving your golden [house]
. . .

Three other brief fragments also seem to have to do with the power of song, although the lack of surrounding context makes certainty impossible. In one (in a glyconic meter) Sappho is quoted as praising a young woman (*parthenon,* literally "virgin," or at least an unmarried woman) for her "wisdom" or "skill" (*sophia*), which might be taken to be poetic skill:

Fragment "56" V.

I do not think there will be at any time
a woman who looks on the light of the sun
with wisdom such as yours

Elsewhere, in a two-word quotation, Sappho describes someone as a *parthenon aduphonon* ("sweet-voiced woman," fragment **"153"** V.), and a papyrus scrap preserves bits of a poem that mentions someone named Mika, a reference to the women of the family of Penthilus (one of the aristocratic Mytilenean families alluded to as well in the poetry of Alkaios), and a "sweet song":[44]

Fragment "71" V.

Mika . . .
. . . but I will not allow you . . .
. . . you preferred the friendship of the Penthilidae
. . . o mischievous one . . . our . . .
. . . some sweet song . . .
. . . gentle-voiced . . .
. . . sweet-sounding [breezes?]
. . . covered with dew . . .

If only we had another papyrus copy of this poem that was torn in different places than in this copy, we might have a better idea of the context of these allusions to song. Those who view Sappho as an official music teacher of young women would regard the fragment as referring to a rival "school," to which Mika has decamped and in so doing has become the object of Sappho's rebuke for her desertion. Of course the fragment may also be interpreted as alluding simply to rival poets or to a rival aristocratic family or to a fiction thereof, without reference to any kind of institutionalized practice.

Another short fragment (again preserved via quotation) seems to promote a "nationalist" concept of the singers of Sappho's homeland. The line is quoted as an example of Sappho's comparison of someone's superior qualities, which surpass the qualities of others by as much as Lesbian singers surpass all other singers:

Fragment "106" V.

. . . superior, just as when a Lesbian
singer [outdoes] foreign ones . . .

Aoidos ("singer") is the Homeric word for "bard," a professional singer who (like Phemios and Demodokos in the *Odyssey*) serves as a court musician and can render the latest song for the entertainment of the assembled guests. Here Sappho seems to be claiming a special status for the post-Homeric tradition of singers of which she was a part, and of which we now know so little beyond the scraps of songs written by Sappho herself and by her compatriot Alkaios. "We are the best," she seems to say.

I end this [essay] with a beautiful short fragment whose uncertain authorship highlights the tentativeness of nearly everything that can be said about Sappho's poetry. The piece is quoted as a metrical example by Hephaestion, who does not mention the author's name. Since he usually quotes opening lines, we probably have here the beginning of the song. While some modern scholars have rejected the Renaissance attribution of it to Sappho (notably Wilamowitz as well as Lobel and Page), Voigt includes it along with the one complete poem and the two hundred or so fragments of Sappho's work:[45]

Fragment "168b" V.

The moon has set,
and the Pleiades. The night
is at its midpoint, the moment passes,
and I sleep alone.[46]

One of the arguments for Sapphic authorship is that the fragment seems to be faintly echoed in connection with Sappho in both Horace (*Satires* 1.5.82-83) and Ovid (*Heroides* 15.155-56), although not closely enough in either case to be conclusive. Certainly the piece has a Sapphic ring to it: the description of the natural setting, the allusion to two female-centered celestial phenomena, namely the moon (Selene, or in Sappho's dialect, Selanna) and the Pleiades (seven sisters transformed into the constellation), a dramatic sense of time, and, finally, an implicitly erotic tone centered around the song's narrator, the *ego* of the final extant line. The emphasis on the solitary state of the singer implies that she had perhaps hoped it would be otherwise. It is late at night, for the moon has set, and perhaps it is a cold winter's night to boot—if the reference to the setting of the Pleiades alludes not just to their nightly setting but also to their cosmical setting at the end of the sailing

season, in November. However we interpret *ora* at the end of line 3 ("moment," "hour," "season," etc.), the song seems to capture the feeling that *tempus fugit*. The sky turns inexorably onward as the solitary narrator watches. Did the narrator go on to describe her desire for an absent woman? Was this song composed by Sappho, or only by someone imitating Sappho's images and dialect? Like so many questions about the lyrics of this "tenth Muse" of the ancient world, these must remain open ones. But open questions lead to openings, and . . . the openings suggested by the remnants of Sappho's work continue to inspire women writers twenty-six centuries after Sappho's lifetime.

Notes

1. Jesper Svenbro, "Sappho and Diomedes: Some Notes on Sappho 1 LP and the Epic," *Museum Philologum Londieniense* 1 (1975) 37-49, esp. p. 46. The question of the exact relationship between epic and lyric has been a matter of considerable scholarly debate; see, for example, J. T. Hooker, *The Language and Text of the Lesbian Poets* (Innsbruck: Institut für Sprachwissenschaft, 1977), who argues that Sappho's poetry draws independently from the same source as epic.

2. Deborah Boedeker, "Sappho and Acheron," in *Arktouros: Hellenic Studies Presented to Bernard M. W. Knox,* edited by G. W. Bowersock, Walter Burkert, and Michael C. J. Putnam, p. 52 (Berlin: de Gruyter, 1979).

3. For an opposing view, see George L. Koniaris, "On Sappho, Fr. 16 (L.P.)," *Hermes* 95 (1967): 257-68, esp. p. 263: "That this ἔγω [*ego,* "I"] is physically speaking a woman we all understand, but I think that it is absolutely unwarranted to claim that Sappho, when she writes ἔγω, means to say 'I being a woman.'" Garry Wills, "The Sapphic 'Umwertung aller Werte,'" *American Journal of Philology* 88 (1967): 434-42, argues along similar lines: "She does not contrast woman's world with man's, as many think" (p. 442).

4. See William H. Race, *The Classical Priamel from Homer to Boethius, Mnemosyne* suppl. 74 (Leiden: Brill, 1982).

5. For a recent modification of the approach to the poem through logical principles, see the application of semiotic narrative theory offered by Claude Calame, "Sappho et Helene: Le Mythe comme argumentation narrative et parabolique" in *Parole, Figure, Parabole,* ed. Jean Delorme, pp. 209-29 (Lyon: Presses Universitaires de Lyon, 1987).

6. See, for example, Richmond Lattimore, trans., *Greek Lyrics* (Chicago: University of Chicago Press, 1971), p. 40; he renders line 4 as "but I say

/ she whom one loves best / is the loveliest." The most recent translations aim for a more literal rendering of the neutrality of the Greek text; compare Diane J. Rayor, trans., *Sappho's Lyre* (Berkeley: University of California Press, 1991), p. 55 ("I say it is whatever one loves"), and Jim Powell, trans., *Sappho: A Garland: The Poems and Fragments of Sappho* (New York: Farrar, Straus, Giroux, 1993), p. 28 ("but I say it's what-/ ever you love best").

7. Page duBois, "Sappho and Helen," *Arethusa* 11 (1978): 89-99. See also her chapter on Helen in *Sappho Is Burning* (Chicago: University of Chicago Press, 1995), pp. 98-126. As Joseph A. Dane, "Sappho Fr. 16: An Analysis," *Eos* 69 (1981): 185-92, observes, Helen's status as lover *and* beloved renders her a complex, multivocal figure whom Sappho uses to good advantage.

8. Might Sappho's choice of Helen as an illustrative example in this song be colored by the Homeric description of what she left behind as a *omelikien erateinen* (*Iliad* 3.175), that is, a "lovely" (the adjective deriving from the same root as *eros*) group of age-mates? Evidently, despite their loveliness, the *eros* that they inspired in Helen was not as great as that inspired by Paris. I am indebted to Judith Hallett for calling the details of this description to my attention.

9. But see John Winkler, The *Contraints of Desire* (New York: Routledge, 1990), p. 178, who proposes that the missing subject of the verb "led" might have been Helen herself.

10. See Denys Page, *Sappho and Alcaeus* (Oxford: Clarendon Press, 1955), p. 53. The comment of Synnøve des Bouvrie Thorsen, "The Interpretation of Sappho's Fragment 16 L.-P.," *Symbolae Osloenses* 53 (1978): 5-23, regarding the opening stanza of fr. 16, would seem to apply to the whole poem: "It cannot be judged by logical reasoning" (p. 9). John Winkler, "Gardens of Nymphs: Public and Private in Sappho's Lyrics," *Women's Studies* 8 (1981): 65-91, esp. p. 74, goes so far as to view the poem as a parody of logical argumentation. For an opposing point of view, see Glen W. Most, "Sappho Fr. 16.6-7 L-P," *Classical Quarterly* 31 (1981): 11-17, who applies a passage from Aristotle's *Rhetoric* to his analysis of the poem.

11. On the aristocratic name, see Enzo Degani and Gabriele Burzacchini, eds., *Lirici Greci* (Florence: La Nuova Italia, 1977), p. 136.

12. See Christopher Brown, "Anactoria and the Χαρίτων ἀμαρύγματα: Sappho fr. 16, 18 Voigt," *Quaderni Urbinati di Cultura Classica* 32 (1989):

7-15, who points out (p. 8) that *amaruchma* refers to a "flashing" or "sparkling," particularly with reference to the eyes. See also Eleanor Irwin, *Colour Terms in Greek Poetry* (Toronto: Hakkert, 1974), p. 216, for this and other Greek terms that suggest both brightness and movement.

13. Gregson Davis, *Polyhymnia: The Rhetoric of Horatian Lyric Discourse* (Berkeley: University of California Press, 1991), pp. 34-35, cites Sappho fr. 16 V. as an "elegant example of figurative assimilation," whereby Sappho incorporates the language of martial spectacles into her description of Anaktoria.

14. The most recent version of this theory may be found in Brown, "Anactoria," 14; see also Carl Theander, "Studia Sapphica," *Eranos* 32 (1934): 57-85.

15. Denys Page, "The Authorship of Sappho β2 (Lobel)," *Classical Quarterly* 30 (1936): 10-15, disputes Wilamowitz's 1914 attempt to deny Sappho's authorship.

16. See Herman Fränkel, *Early Greek Poetry and Philosophy,* trans. Moses Hadas and James Willis (New York: Harcourt Brace Jovanovich, 1973), p. 174: "The song of Hector and Andromache ends with an account of a song on Hector and Andromache; it leads into itself in a circle."

17. See, for example, Hermann Fränkel, *Wege und Formen frühgriechischen Denkens* (Munich: Beck, 1960), 41.

18. See Johannes T. Kakridis, "Zu Sappho 44 LP," *Wiener Studien* 79 (1966): 21-26, esp. p. 26.

19. Page, *Sappho and Alcaeus,* p. 71.

20. On the whole, modern critics have devoted relatively little attention to fr. 44, which is generally viewed as an aberrant poem within the corpus of Sappho's fragments. Here, for example, is the opinion of Richard Jenkyns, *Three Classical Poets: Sappho, Catullus, and Juvenal* (Cambridge, Massachusetts: Harvard University Press, 1982), p. 61: "So under the guise of mythological narrative she is really giving her audience a vivid picture of contemporary life. In any case, it cannot be said that this fragment adds to her reputation. Quaint, lively and fluent, it is the work of an able poet; but there is no subtlety in it, and no inspiration." For a counterargument to Jenkyns, see Lawrence P. Schrenk, "Sappho Frag. 44 and the 'Iliad'," *Hermes* 122 (1994): 144-50; he argues that allusions to *Iliad* 22.466-72 (Andromache's wedding to Hektor) and to *Iliad* 24.699-804 (Hektor's funeral) render the poem another example of Sappho's portrayal of love as *glukupikron,* "bittersweet."

21. For arguments against the view of Hermann Fränkel regarding what he saw as choral feaures of Sappho fr. 16 V., see E. M. Stern, "Sappho Fr. 16 L.P.: Zur Strukturellen Einheit ihrer Lyrik," *Mnemosyne* 23 (1970): 348-61.

22. See William H. Race, "Sappho, Fr. 16 L.-P. and Alkaios, Fr. 42 L.-P.: Romantic and Classical Strains in Lesbian Lyric," *Classical Journal* 85 (1989): 16-33; he views Sappho's concern as being with individuals, while Alkaios focuses more on the fate of a whole people and their city.

23. For an intriguing (if sometimes baffling) discussion of the preeminence of the fragment over the whole in modern aesthetic theory in the light of the work of Walter Benjamin, see Christine Buci-Glucksmann, *Baroque Reason: The Aesthetics of Modernity,* trans. Patrick Camiller (London: Sage, 1994), pp. 69-73. See also Page duBois, *Sappho Is Burning* (Chicago: University of Chicago Press, 1995), pp. 31-54 ("The Aesthetics of the Fragment"); as she points out (p. 39), "We can accept the fragmentary for what it is, appreciate the few words of Sappho that we have inherited, rather than setting them, for example, against the fuller, more adequate corpus of Pindar, and naming him the greater poet."

24. The fragment in which Apollo and Artemis are addressed is assigned by some scholars to Alkaios (as Alkaios fr. 303A by Voigt) and by others to Sappho (as Sappho fr. 99 by Lobel-Page); see discussion of this so-called *olisbos* fragment at the end of the present chapter.

25. Some scholars also attempt to connect fr. 3 V. with Charaxos, but it is so fragmentary that little sense can be made of it. In addition, fr. 7 V. appears to contain mention of the name Doricha.

26. See G. S. Kirk, "A Fragment of Sappho Reinterpreted," *Classical Quarterly* 13 (1963): 51-52, who was the first to propose that the hyperbole involves the notion that the bridegroom is "fantastically ithyphallic" (p. 51).

27. See Anne Carson, *Eros the Bittersweet: An Essay* (Princeton: Princeton University Press, 1986), p. 26.

28. Judy Grahn, *The Highest Apple: Sappho and the Lesbian Poetic Tradition* (San Franciso: Spinsters, Ink, 1985), p. 11. Despite some minor factual errors (e.g., regarding the mode of preservation of Sappho's one complete song, p. 10), this is a useful study of nine modern poets in the Sapphic tradition: Emily Dickinson, Amy Lowell, H.D., Gertrude Stein, Adrienne Rich, Audre Lorde, Olga Broumas, Paula Gunn Allen, and Judy Grahn.

29. See Kenneth Quinn, ed., *Catullus: The Poems* (London: MacMillan, 1970), p. 280: "There is almost certainly an allusion to a poem attributed to Sappho of which a fragment survives."

30. A similar treatment may have occurred in fr. 107 V., *er' eti parthenias epiballomai?* ("Indeed, do I still desire virginity?"), but the fragment is too short to be sure.

31. Carl Theander, "Atthis et Andromeda," *Eranos* 44 (1946): 62-67. He reads *es choron* ("to the dance") in place of *es gamon* ("to a wedding").

32. Denys Page, *Sappho and Alcaeus* (Oxford: Clarendon Press), p. 126.

33. On the importance of weaving as a female occupation in Greek society, see Robert James Forbes, "Fabrics and Weavers," in *Studies in Ancient Technology* (Leiden: Brill, 1955—), vol. 4, pp. 220-51; Jane McIntosh Snyder, "The Web of Song: Weaving Imagery in Homer and the Lyric Poets," *Classical Journal* 76 (1981): 193-96; and Elizabeth Wayland Barber, *Women's Work, the First 20,000 Years: Women, Cloth, and Society in Early Times* (New York: Norton, 1994).

34. The phrase is quoted by Aristotle, *Poetics* 1454b. 36-37.

35. Patricia Klindienst Joplin, "Epilogue: Philomela's Loom," in *Coming to Light: American Women Poets in the Twentieth Century,* ed. Diane Wood Middlebrook and Marilyn Yalom, p. 254 (Ann Arbor: University of Michigan Press, 1985).

36. Max Treu, ed., *Sappho* (Munich: Heimeran, 1954), p. 162. The fragment was first published by E. Lobel and D. Page, "A New Fragment of Aeolic Verse," *Classical Quarterly* 2 (1952): 1-3, who assign the fragment either to Sappho or to Alkaios.

37. Bruno Snell, "Der Anfang eines äolischen Gedichts," *Hermes* 81 (1953): 118-19, points out that the sentiment expressed at the very end of part (b) sounds more characteristic of Alkaios than of Sappho.

38. Another example may occur in fr. 144 V., *mala de kekoremenois / Gorgos,* where the reference seems to be to people who are "quite fed up with Gorgo."

39. Giuseppe Giangrande, "Sappho and the ὄλισβος," *Emerita* 48 (1980): 250.

40. See also the references to perfume and expensive gifts in fr. 101 V., to "adornments" (*athurmata,* as in Sappho fr. 44.9 V.) in fr. 63.8 V., and to soft cushions in fr. 46 V. as possible further examples of *habrosune.*

41. Judith P. Hallett, "Beloved Cleïs," *Quaderni Urbinati di Cultura Classica* 10 (1982): 21-31, argues that the adjective (*agapetos,* "beloved," "highly valued") that Sappho uses to describe Kleis rules out any erotic connotation, and points out that its use in the *Iliad* and the *Odyssey* is always with reference to biological offspring.

42. See Eva-Maria Voigt, ed., *Sappho et Alcaeus: Fragmenta* (Amsterdam: Athenaeum-Polak and Van Gennep), p. 239 (regarding line 17).

43. The question of the literary exchange of differing views between the two fellow Lesbian poets is raised by Sappho fr. 137 V. (preserved in Aristotle's *Rhetoric*); interpretation of the fragment is fraught with difficulties, but Aristotle seems to be implying that Sappho wrote a poem in answer to a poem written by Alkaios.

44. Cf. also Sappho fr. 185 V., *meliphonos* ("honey-voiced").

45. On the question of authorship, see Treu, *Sappho,* pp. 211-12; Diskin Clay, "Fragmentum Adespotum 976," *Transactions of the American Philological Association* 101 (1970): 119-29, who favors the attribution to Sappho.

46. Despite the apparent simplicity of the poetry, the interpretation of this fragment is the subject of much controversy. The word that I have translated as "night" is actually plural in the Greek, but such usage is attested elsewhere (e.g., Plato *Republic* 621b). The word that I have translated as "moment" (*ora*) is variously interpreted as "hour" or "time" or "right moment." For a summary of the arguments, see Enzo Degani and Gabriele Burzacchini, eds., *Lirici Greci* (Florence: La Nouva Italia), pp. 188-90. David Sider, "Sappho 168B Voigt: Δέδυκε μὲν ἀ Σελάννα," *Eranos* 84 (1986): 57-59, argues that all three senses of *ora* are felt.

FURTHER READING

Criticism

Andreadis, Harriette. *Sappho in Early Modern England: Female Same-Sex Literary Erotics 1550-1714.* Chicago: University of Chicago Press, 2001, 254 p.

> Invokes the status of Sappho as an icon of female same-sex eroticism to study aspects of this phenomena in sixteenth- through eighteenth-century England.

Bergmann, Emilie L. "Fictions of Sor Juana/Fictions of Sappho." *Confluencia: Revista Hispanica de Cultura y Literatura* 9, no. 2 (spring 1994): 9-15.

> Applies Joan DeJean's theories of the role of the feminine in male poetic discourse outlined in her *Fictions of Sappho, 1546-1937* to a study of works by Latin writers Octavio Paz and Sor Juana.

Bigwood, Carol. "Sappho: The She-Greek Heidegger Forgot." In *Feminist Interpretations of Martin Heidegger,* edited by Nancy J. Holland and Patricia Huntington, pp. 165-95. University Park: Pennsylvania State University Press, 2001.

> Considers unusual affinities between the poetry of Sappho and the thought of Martin Heidegger.

Blank, Paula. "Comparing Sappho to Philaenis: John Donne's 'Homopoetics.'" *PMLA* 110, no. 3 (May 1995): 358-68.

> Interprets Donne's poem "Sappho to Philaenis" in the context of homoerotic desire.

Bonnet, Marie-Jo. "Sappho, or the Importance of Culture in the Language of Love." In *Queerly Phrased: Language, Gender, and Sexuality,* edited by Anna Livia and Kira Hall, pp. 147-66. Oxford: Oxford University Press, 1997.

> Traces the development of the terminology and symbolism of female homosexuality from Sappho to the end of the twentieth century.

Christy, Angela. "The Mary Barnard Translation of Sappho." *Paideuma* 23, no. 1 (spring 1994): 25-63.

> Evaluates the accuracy and style of Mary Barnard's English translations of Sapphic verse in her *Sappho: A New Translation* (1958).

Collecott, Diana. *H.D. and Sapphic Modernism,.* Cambridge: Cambridge University Press, 1999, 350 p.

> Uses the Sapphic fragments as evocative intertexts in the study of the poetry of Hilda Doolittle.

DeJean, Joan. Introduction to *Fictions of Sappho, 1546-1937,* pp. 1-28. Chicago: University of Chicago Press, 1989.

> Surveys and analyzes the profound influence of Sappho on the French literary tradition.

Goldensohn, Lorrie. "'The Speech of Her Stringed Shell': Mary Barnard's Sappho." *Paideuma* 23, no. 1 (spring 1994): 13-22.

> Praises Barnard's translations of Sapphic verse in her *Sappho: A New Translation.*

Harvey, Elizabeth D. "Ventriloquizing Sappho: Ovid, Donne, and the Erotics of the Feminine Voice." *Criticism* 31, no. 2 (spring 1989): 115-38.

Studies John Donne's adaptation of Sappho's classical, feminine poetic voice in his "Sappho to Philaenis."

Kaminsky, Amy. "The Construction of Immortality: Sappho, Saint Theresa and Caroline Coronado." *Letras Femeninas* 19, no. 1-2 (spring-fall 1993): 1-13.

Highlights the resonance of Sapphic legend in nineteenth-century Spanish literary feminism.

Mason, Hugh J. "The Literature of Classical Lesbos and the Fiction of Stratis Myrivilis." *Classical and Modern Literature* 9, no. 4 (summer 1989): 347-57.

Explores echoes of Sapphic verse in the writings of the twentieth-century Greek novelist Stratis Myrivilis.

McGann, Jerome. "Mary Robinson and the Myth of Sappho." *Modern Language Quarterly* 56, no. 1 (March 1995): 55-76.

Examines how Mary Robinson's 1796 drama *Sappho and Phaon* introduces Sappho's writing and myth to the poetics of sensibility.

Moore, Lisa L. *Dangerous Intimacies: Toward a Sapphic History of the British Novel.* Durham, N.C.: Duke University Press, 1997, 191 p.

Uses Sappho as a cipher for female homoeroticism in studying fiction by British women writers.

Most, Glenn W. "Reflecting Sappho." In *Re-Reading Sappho: Reception and Transmission,* edited by Ellen Greene, pp. 11–35. Berkeley: University of California Press, 1996.

Chronicles shifting popular and literary perceptions about Sappho's work from antiquity to the contemporary era.

Naafs-Wilstra, Marianne C. "Indo-European 'Dichtersprache' in Sappho and Alcaeus." *Journal of Indo-European Studies* 15, no. 3-4 (fall-winter 1987): 273-83.

Probes the poetic diction of Sappho and her contemporary Alcaeus to find evidence of an Aeolian tradition independent of the Ionian epic mode of Homer.

O'Connor, Desmond. "From Venus to Proserpine: 'Sappho's Last Song.'" *Rivista di Studi Italiani* 14, no. 2 (December 1998): 438-53.

Investigates the influence of Sapphic poetry and legend on the nineteenth-century Italian writer Giacomo Leopardi.

Petropoulos, J. C. B. "Sappho the Sorceress—Another Look at Fr. 1 (LP)." *Zeischrift für Papyrologie und Epigraphik* 97 (1993): 43–56.

Analyzes Sappho's "Hymn to Aphrodite" as a magical prayer or incantation akin to a love spell.

Powell, Jim. "Afterwords." *TriQuarterly* 86 (winter 1992–93): 244–58.

Comments on the poet's life, versification, style, and the textual and critical history of her works.

Prins, Yopie. *Victorian Sappho.* Princeton, N.J.: Princeton University Press, 1999, 279 p.

Feminist study of the reception of Sappho's poetry in Victorian England, which claims that "Sappho influenced the gendering of lyric as a feminine genre."

Race, William H. "Sappho Fr. 16 L-P. and Alkaios Fr. 42 L-P.: Romantic and Classical Strains in Lesbian Poetry." *Classical Journal* 85, no. 1 (1989): 16-33.

Contrasts fragments of verse by Sappho and her contemporary Alcaeus (Alkaios), suggesting that Sappho's work prefigures aspects of English Romanticism, while that of Alcaeus evokes echoes of Homer and Pindar.

———. "Some Visual Priamels from Sappho to Richard Wilbur and Raymond Carver." *Classical and Modern Literature* 20, no. 4 (fall 2000): 3-17.

Defines the poetic priamel, a series of seemingly unrelated, often paradoxical statements brought together in verse, and mentions its famous use in Sappho's sixteenth fragment.

Reynolds, ed., Margaret. *The Sappho Companion,* edited by Margaret Reynolds. London: Chatto & Windus, 2000, 422 p.

Collects and investigates some of the myriad legends, references, and metaphors associated with Sappho from throughout the western tradition.

Richards, David. "Swinburne and Sappho." *Notes and Queries* 246, no. 2 (June 2001): 155-58.

Documents English poet Algernon Charles Swinburne's reverence for Sappho and her poetry.

Slings, S. R. "Sappho Fr. 1, 8 V.: Golden House or Golden Chariot?" *Mnemosyne* 44, no. 3-4 (1991): 404-10.

Comments on grammatical ambiguity in Sappho's ancient Greek verse.

Vanita, Ruth. "The Sapphic Sublime and Romantic Lyricism." In *Sappho and the Virgin Mary: Same-Sex Love and the English Literary Imagination,* pp. 37-61. New York: Columbia University Press, 1996.

Surveys Sappho's influence, as both poet and myth, on English Romantic poetry.

West, William N. "Thinking with the Body: Sappho's 'Sappho to Philaenis,' Donne's 'Sappho to Philaenis.'" *Renaissance Papers* (1994): 67-83.

Explicates John Donne's poem "Sappho to Philaenis" as part of the tradition of masculine appropriations of Sappho's poetic voice.

Additional coverage of Sappho's life and career is contained in the following sources published by the Gale Group: *Classical and Medieval Literature Criticism,* **Vol. 3;** *Concise Dictionary of World Literary Biography,* **Vol. 1;** *Dictionary of Literary Biography,* **Vol. 176;** *Discovering Authors 3.0; Discovering Authors Modules, Poetry Edition; Literature Resource Center; Poetry Criticism,* **Vol. 5;** *Reference Guide to World Literature* **(St. James Press, an imprint of Gale), eds. 2, 3;** *World Poets* **(Charles Scribner's Sons, an imprint of Gale).**

How to Use This Index

CMW = *St. James Guide to Crime & Mystery Writers*

CN = *Contemporary Novelists*

CP = *Contemporary Poets*

CPW = *Contemporary Popular Writers*

CSW = *Contemporary Southern Writers*

CWD = *Contemporary Women Dramatists*

CWP = *Contemporary Women Poets*

CWRI = *St. James Guide to Children's Writers*

CWW = *Contemporary World Writers*

DA = *DISCovering Authors*

DA3 = *DISCovering Authors 3.0*

DAB = *DISCovering Authors: British Edition*

DAC = *DISCovering Authors: Canadian Edition*

DAM = *DISCovering Authors: Modules*

   DRAM: *Dramatists Module;* **MST:** *Most-studied Authors Module;*

   MULT: *Multicultural Authors Module;* **NOV:** *Novelists Module;*

   POET: *Poets Module;* **POP:** *Popular Fiction and Genre Authors Module*

DFS = *Drama for Students*

DLB = *Dictionary of Literary Biography*

DLBD = *Dictionary of Literary Biography Documentary Series*

DLBY = *Dictionary of Literary Biography Yearbook*

DNFS = *Literature of Developing Nations for Students*

EFS = *Epics for Students*

EXPN = *Exploring Novels*

EXPP = *Exploring Poetry*

EXPS = *Exploring Short Stories*

EW = *European Writers*

FANT = *St. James Guide to Fantasy Writers*

FW = *Feminist Writers*

GFL = *Guide to French Literature,* Beginnings to 1789, 1798 to the Present

GLL = *Gay and Lesbian Literature*

HGG = *St. James Guide to Horror, Ghost & Gothic Writers*

HW = *Hispanic Writers*

IDFW = *International Dictionary of Films and Filmmakers: Writers and Production Artists*

IDTP = *International Dictionary of Theatre: Playwrights*

LAIT = *Literature and Its Times*

LAW = *Latin American Writers*

JRDA = *Junior DISCovering Authors*

MAICYA = *Major Authors and Illustrators for Children and Young Adults*

MAICYAS = *Major Authors and Illustrators for Children and Young Adults Supplement*

MAWW = *Modern American Women Writers*

MJW = *Modern Japanese Writers*

MTCW = *Major 20th-Century Writers*

NCFS = *Nonfiction Classics for Students*

NFS = *Novels for Students*

PAB = *Poets: American and British*

PFS = *Poetry for Students*

RGAL = *Reference Guide to American Literature*

RGEL = *Reference Guide to English Literature*

RGSF = *Reference Guide to Short Fiction*

RGWL = *Reference Guide to World Literature*

RHW = *Twentieth-Century Romance and Historical Writers*

SAAS = *Something about the Author Autobiography Series*

SATA = *Something about the Author*

SFW = *St. James Guide to Science Fiction Writers*

SSFS = *Short Stories for Students*

TCWW = *Twentieth-Century Western Writers*

WLIT = *World Literature and Its Times*

WP = *World Poets*

YABC = *Yesterday's Authors of Books for Children*

YAW = *St. James Guide to Young Adult Writers*

Literary Criticism Series
Cumulative Author Index

Agrippa von Nettesheim, Henry Cornelius
1486-1535 **LC 27**

Aguilera Malta, Demetrio 1909-1981 **HLCS 1**
See also CA 111; 124; CANR 87; DAM MULT, NOV; DLB 145; EWL 3; HW 1; RGWL 3

Agustini, Delmira 1886-1914 **HLCS 1**
See also CA 166; DLB 290; HW 1, 2; LAW

Aherne, Owen
See Cassill, R(onald) V(erlin)

Ai 1947- **CLC 4, 14, 69**
See also CA 85-88; CAAS 13; CANR 70; DLB 120; PFS 16

Aickman, Robert (Fordyce) 1914-1981 **CLC 57**
See also CA 5-8R; CANR 3, 72, 100; DLB 261; HGG; SUFW 1, 2

Aidoo, (Christina) Ama Ata 1942- **BLCS; CLC 177**
See also AFW; BW 1; CA 101; CANR 62; CD 5; CDWLB 3; CN 7; CWD; CWP; DLB 117; DNFS 1, 2; EWL 3; FW; WLIT 2

Aiken, Conrad (Potter) 1889-1973 **CLC 1, 3, 5, 10, 52; PC 26; SSC 9**
See also AMW; CA 5-8R; 45-48; CANR 4, 60; CDALB 1929-1941; DAM NOV, POET; DLB 9, 45, 102; EWL 3; EXPS; HGG; MTCW 1, 2; RGAL 4; RGSF 2; SATA 3, 30; SSFS 8; TUS

Aiken, Joan (Delano) 1924-2004 **CLC 35**
See also AAYA 1, 25; CA 9-12R, 182; CAAE 182; CANR 4, 23, 34, 64, 121; CLR 1, 19, 90; DLB 161; FANT; HGG; JRDA; MAICYA 1, 2; MTCW 1; RHW; SAAS 1; SATA 2, 30, 73; SATA-Essay 109; SUFW 2; WYA; YAW

Ainsworth, William Harrison 1805-1882 **NCLC 13**
See also DLB 21; HGG; RGEL 2; SATA 24; SUFW 1

Aitmatov, Chingiz (Torekulovich) 1928- **CLC 71**
See Aytmatov, Chingiz
See also CA 103; CANR 38; CWW 2; MTCW 1; RGSF 2; SATA 56

Akers, Floyd
See Baum, L(yman) Frank

Akhmadulina, Bella Akhatovna 1937- **CLC 53; PC 43**
See also CA 65-68; CWP; CWW 2; DAM POET; EWL 3

Akhmatova, Anna 1888-1966 **CLC 11, 25, 64, 126; PC 2, 55**
See also CA 19-20; 25-28R; CANR 35; CAP 1; DA3; DAM POET; DLB 295; EW 10; EWL 3; MTCW 1, 2; RGWL 2, 3

Aksakov, Sergei Timofeyvich 1791-1859 **NCLC 2**
See also DLB 198

Aksenov, Vasilii (Pavlovich)
See Aksyonov, Vassily (Pavlovich)
See also CWW 2

Aksenov, Vassily
See Aksyonov, Vassily (Pavlovich)

Akst, Daniel 1956- **CLC 109**
See also CA 161; CANR 110

Aksyonov, Vassily (Pavlovich) 1932- **CLC 22, 37, 101**
See Aksenov, Vasilii (Pavlovich)
See also CA 53-56; CANR 12, 48, 77; EWL 3

Akutagawa Ryunosuke 1892-1927 **SSC 44; TCLC 16**
See also CA 117; 154; DLB 180; EWL 3; MJW; RGSF 2; RGWL 2, 3

Alabaster, William 1568-1640 **LC 90**
See also DLB 132; RGEL 2

Alain 1868-1951 **TCLC 41**
See also CA 163; EWL 3; GFL 1789 to the Present

Alain de Lille c. 1116-c. 1203 **CMLC 53**
See also DLB 208

Alain-Fournier TCLC 6
See Fournier, Henri-Alban
See also DLB 65; EWL 3; GFL 1789 to the Present; RGWL 2, 3

Al-Amin, Jamil Abdullah 1943- **BLC 1**
See also BW 1, 3; CA 112; 125; CANR 82; DAM MULT

Alanus de Insluis
See Alain de Lille

Alarcon, Pedro Antonio de 1833-1891 **NCLC 1; SSC 64**

Alas (y Urena), Leopoldo (Enrique Garcia) 1852-1901 **TCLC 29**
See also CA 113; 131; HW 1; RGSF 2

Albee, Edward (Franklin) (III) 1928- **CLC 1, 2, 3, 5, 9, 11, 13, 25, 53, 86, 113; DC 11; WLC**
See also AAYA 51; AITN 1; AMW; CA 5-8R; CABS 3; CAD; CANR 8, 54, 74, 124; CD 5; CDALB 1941-1968; DA; DA3; DAB; DAC; DAM DRAM, MST; DFS 2, 3, 8, 10, 13, 14; DLB 7, 266; EWL 3; INT CANR-8; LAIT 4; LMFS 2; MTCW 1, 2; RGAL 4; TUS

Alberti (Merello), Rafael
See Alberti, Rafael
See also CWW 2

Alberti, Rafael 1902-1999 **CLC 7**
See Alberti (Merello), Rafael
See also CA 85-88; 185; CANR 81; DLB 108; EWL 3; HW 2; RGWL 2, 3

Albert the Great 1193(?)-1280 **CMLC 16**
See also DLB 115

Alcaeus c. 620B.C.- **CMLC 65**
See also DLB 176

Alcala-Galiano, Juan Valera y
See Valera y Alcala-Galiano, Juan

Alcayaga, Lucila Godoy
See Godoy Alcayaga, Lucila

Alcott, Amos Bronson 1799-1888 **NCLC 1**
See also DLB 1, 223

Alcott, Louisa May 1832-1888 **NCLC 6, 58, 83; SSC 27; WLC**
See also AAYA 20; AMWS 1; BPFB 1; BYA 2; CDALB 1865-1917; CLR 1, 38; DA; DA3; DAB; DAC; DAM MST, NOV; DLB 1, 42, 79, 223, 239, 242; DLBD 14; FW; JRDA; LAIT 2; MAICYA 1, 2; NFS 12; RGAL 4; SATA 100; TUS; WCH; WYA; YABC 1; YAW

Aldanov, M. A.
See Aldanov, Mark (Alexandrovich)

Aldanov, Mark (Alexandrovich) 1886(?)-1957 **TCLC 23**
See also CA 118; 181

Aldington, Richard 1892-1962 **CLC 49**
See also CA 85-88; CANR 45; DLB 20, 36, 100, 149; LMFS 2; RGEL 2

Aldiss, Brian W(ilson) 1925- **CLC 5, 14, 40; SSC 36**
See also AAYA 42; CA 5-8R, 190; CAAE 190; CAAS 2; CANR 5, 28, 64, 121; CN 7; DAM NOV; DLB 14, 261, 271; MTCW 1, 2; SATA 34; SFW 4

Aldrich, Bess Streeter 1881-1954 **TCLC 125**
See also CLR 70

Alegria, Claribel
See Alegria, Claribel
See also CWW 2; DLB 145, 283

Alegria, Claribel 1924- **CLC 75; HLCS 1; PC 26**
See Alegria, Claribel
See also CA 131; CAAS 15; CANR 66, 94; DAM MULT; EWL 3; HW 1; MTCW 1

Alegria, Fernando 1918- **CLC 57**
See also CA 9-12R; CANR 5, 32, 72; EWL 3; HW 1, 2

Aleichem, Sholom SSC 33; TCLC 1, 35
See Rabinovitch, Sholem
See also TWA

Aleixandre, Vicente 1898-1984 **HLCS 1; TCLC 113**
See also CANR 81; DLB 108; EWL 3; HW 2; RGWL 2, 3

Aleman, Mateo 1547-1615(?) **LC 81**

Alencon, Marguerite d'
See de Navarre, Marguerite

Alepoudelis, Odysseus
See Elytis, Odysseus
See also CWW 2

Aleshkovsky, Joseph 1929-
See Aleshkovsky, Yuz
See also CA 121; 128

Aleshkovsky, Yuz CLC 44
See Aleshkovsky, Joseph

Alexander, Lloyd (Chudley) 1924- **CLC 35**
See also AAYA 1, 27; BPFB 1; BYA 5, 6, 7, 9, 10, 11; CA 1-4R; CANR 1, 24, 38, 55, 113; CLR 1, 5, 48; CWRI 5; DLB 52; FANT; JRDA; MAICYA 1, 2; MAICYAS 1; MTCW 1; SAAS 19; SATA 3, 49, 81, 129, 135; SUFW; TUS; WYA; YAW

Alexander, Meena 1951- **CLC 121**
See also CA 115; CANR 38, 70; CP 7; CWP; FW

Alexander, Samuel 1859-1938 **TCLC 77**

Alexie, Sherman (Joseph, Jr.) 1966- **CLC 96, 154; NNAL; PC 53**
See also AAYA 28; BYA 15; CA 138; CANR 65, 95; DA3; DAM MULT; DLB 175, 206, 278; LATS 1; MTCW 1; NFS 17; SSFS 18

al-Farabi 870(?)-950 **CMLC 58**
See also DLB 115

Alfau, Felipe 1902-1999 **CLC 66**
See also CA 137

Alfieri, Vittorio 1749-1803 **NCLC 101**
See also EW 4; RGWL 2, 3

Alfred, Jean Gaston
See Ponge, Francis

Alger, Horatio, Jr. 1832-1899 **NCLC 8, 83**
See also CLR 87; DLB 42; LAIT 2; RGAL 4; SATA 16; TUS

Al-Ghazali, Muhammad ibn Muhammad 1058-1111 **CMLC 50**
See also DLB 115

Algren, Nelson 1909-1981 **CLC 4, 10, 33; SSC 33**
See also AMWS 9; BPFB 1; CA 13-16R; 103; CANR 20, 61; CDALB 1941-1968; DLB 9; DLBY 1981, 1982, 2000; EWL 3; MTCW 1, 2; RGAL 4; RGSF 2

al-Hariri, al-Qasim ibn 'Ali Abu Muhammad al-Basri 1054-1122 **CMLC 63**
See also RGWL 3

Ali, Ahmed 1908-1998 **CLC 69**
See also CA 25-28R; CANR 15, 34; EWL 3

Ali, Tariq 1943- **CLC 173**
See also CA 25-28R; CANR 10, 99

Alighieri, Dante
See Dante

Allan, John B.
See Westlake, Donald E(dwin)

Allan, Sidney
See Hartmann, Sadakichi

Allan, Sydney
See Hartmann, Sadakichi

Allard, Janet CLC 59

Allen, Edward 1948- **CLC 59**

Allen, Fred 1894-1956 **TCLC 87**

Allen, Paula Gunn 1939- **CLC 84; NNAL**
See also AMWS 4; CA 112; 143; CANR 63; CWP; DA3; DAM MULT; DLB 175; FW; MTCW 1; RGAL 4

Allen, Roland
See Ayckbourn, Alan

Allen, Sarah A.
See Hopkins, Pauline Elizabeth

Allen, Sidney H.
See Hartmann, Sadakichi

Allen, Woody 1935- **CLC 16, 52**
See also AAYA 10, 51; CA 33-36R; CANR 27, 38, 63, 128; DAM POP; DLB 44; MTCW 1

Allende, Isabel 1942- **CLC 39, 57, 97, 170; HLC 1; SSC 65; WLCS**
See also AAYA 18; CA 125; 130; CANR 51, 74, 129; CDWLB 3; CWW 2; DA3; DAM MULT, NOV; DLB 145; DNFS 1; EWL 3; FW; HW 1, 2; INT CA-130; LAIT 5; LAWS 1; LMFS 2; MTCW 1, 2; NCFS 1; NFS 6, 18; RGSF 2; RGWL 3; SSFS 11, 16; WLIT 1

Alleyn, Ellen
See Rossetti, Christina (Georgina)

Alleyne, Carla D. CLC 65

Allingham, Margery (Louise) 1904-1966 **CLC 19**
See also CA 5-8R; 25-28R; CANR 4, 58; CMW 4; DLB 77; MSW; MTCW 1, 2

Allingham, William 1824-1889 **NCLC 25**
See also DLB 35; RGEL 2

Allison, Dorothy E. 1949- **CLC 78, 153**
See also AAYA 53; CA 140; CANR 66, 107; CSW; DA3; FW; MTCW 1; NFS 11; RGAL 4

Alloula, Malek CLC 65

Allston, Washington 1779-1843 **NCLC 2**
See also DLB 1, 235

Almedingen, E. M. CLC 12
See Almedingen, Martha Edith von
See also SATA 3

Almedingen, Martha Edith von 1898-1971
See Almedingen, E. M.
See also CA 1-4R; CANR 1

Almodovar, Pedro 1949(?)- **CLC 114; HLCS 1**
See also CA 133; CANR 72; HW 2

Almqvist, Carl Jonas Love 1793-1866 **NCLC 42**

al-Mutanabbi, Ahmad ibn al-Husayn Abu al-Tayyib al-Jufi al-Kindi 915-965 **CMLC 66**
See also RGWL 3

Alonso, Damaso 1898-1990 **CLC 14**
See also CA 110; 131; 130; CANR 72; DLB 108; EWL 3; HW 1, 2

Alov
See Gogol, Nikolai (Vasilyevich)

Al Siddik
See Rolfe, Frederick (William Serafino Austin Lewis Mary)
See also GLL 1; RGEL 2

Alta 1942- **CLC 19**
See also CA 57-60

Alter, Robert B(ernard) 1935- **CLC 34**
See also CA 49-52; CANR 1, 47, 100

Alther, Lisa 1944- **CLC 7, 41**
See also BPFB 1; CA 65-68; CAAS 30; CANR 12, 30, 51; CN 7; CSW; GLL 2; MTCW 1

Althusser, L.
See Althusser, Louis

Althusser, Louis 1918-1990 **CLC 106**
See also CA 131; 132; CANR 102; DLB 242

Altman, Robert 1925- **CLC 16, 116**
See also CA 73-76; CANR 43

Alurista HLCS 1
See Urista (Heredia), Alberto (Baltazar)
See also DLB 82; LLW 1

Alvarez, A(lfred) 1929- **CLC 5, 13**
See also CA 1-4R; CANR 3, 33, 63, 101; CN 7; CP 7; DLB 14, 40

Alvarez, Alejandro Rodriguez 1903-1965
See Casona, Alejandro
See also CA 131; 93-96; HW 1

Alvarez, Julia 1950- **CLC 93; HLCS 1**
See also AAYA 25; AMWS 7; CA 147; CANR 69, 101; DA3; DLB 282; LATS 1; LLW 1; MTCW 1; NFS 5, 9; SATA 129; WLIT 1

Alvaro, Corrado 1896-1956 **TCLC 60**
See also CA 163; DLB 264; EWL 3

Amado, Jorge 1912-2001 **CLC 13, 40, 106; HLC 1**
See also CA 77-80; 201; CANR 35, 74; CWW 2; DAM MULT, NOV; DLB 113; EWL 3; HW 2; LAW; LAWS 1; MTCW 1, 2; RGWL 2, 3; TWA; WLIT 1

Ambler, Eric 1909-1998 **CLC 4, 6, 9**
See also BRWS 4; CA 9-12R; 171; CANR 7, 38, 74; CMW 4; CN 7; DLB 77; MSW; MTCW 1, 2; TEA

Ambrose, Stephen E(dward) 1936-2002 **CLC 145**
See also AAYA 44; CA 1-4R; 209; CANR 3, 43, 57, 83, 105; NCFS 2; SATA 40, 138

Amichai, Yehuda 1924-2000 **CLC 9, 22, 57, 116; PC 38**
See also CA 85-88; 189; CANR 46, 60, 99; CWW 2; EWL 3; MTCW 1

Amichai, Yehudah
See Amichai, Yehuda

Amiel, Henri Frederic 1821-1881 **NCLC 4**
See also DLB 217

Amis, Kingsley (William) 1922-1995 **CLC 1, 2, 3, 5, 8, 13, 40, 44, 129**
See also AITN 2; BPFB 1; BRWS 2; CA 9-12R; 150; CANR 8, 28, 54; CDBLB 1945-1960; CN 7; CP 7; DA; DA3; DAB; DAC; DAM MST, NOV; DLB 15, 27, 100, 139; DLBY 1996; EWL 3; HGG; INT CANR-8; MTCW 1, 2; RGEL 2; RGSF 2; SFW 4

Amis, Martin (Louis) 1949- **CLC 4, 9, 38, 62, 101**
See also BEST 90:3; BRWS 4; CA 65-68; CANR 8, 27, 54, 73, 95; CN 7; DA3; DLB 14, 194; EWL 3; INT CANR-27; MTCW 1

Ammianus Marcellinus c. 330-c. 395 **CMLC 60**
See also AW 2; DLB 211

Ammons, A(rchie) R(andolph) 1926-2001 **CLC 2, 3, 5, 8, 9, 25, 57, 108; PC 16**
See also AITN 1; AMWS 7; CA 9-12R; 193; CANR 6, 36, 51, 73, 107; CP 7; CSW; DAM POET; DLB 5, 165; EWL 3; MTCW 1, 2; PFS 19; RGAL 4

Amo, Tauraatua i
See Adams, Henry (Brooks)

Amory, Thomas 1691(?)-1788 **LC 48**
See also DLB 39

Anand, Mulk Raj 1905- **CLC 23, 93**
See also CA 65-68; CANR 32, 64; CN 7; DAM NOV; EWL 3; MTCW 1, 2; RGSF 2

Anatol
See Schnitzler, Arthur

Anaximander c. 611B.C.-c. 546B.C. **CMLC 22**

Anaya, Rudolfo A(lfonso) 1937- **CLC 23, 148; HLC 1**
See also AAYA 20; BYA 13; CA 45-48; CAAS 4; CANR 1, 32, 51, 124; CN 7; DAM MULT, NOV; DLB 82, 206, 278;

HW 1; LAIT 4; LLW 1; MTCW 1, 2; NFS 12; RGAL 4; RGSF 2; WLIT 1

Andersen, Hans Christian 1805-1875 **NCLC 7, 79; SSC 6, 56; WLC**
See also CLR 6; DA; DA3; DAB; DAC; DAM MST, POP; EW 6; MAICYA 1, 2; RGSF 2; RGWL 2, 3; SATA 100; TWA; WCH; YABC 1

Anderson, C. Farley
See Mencken, H(enry) L(ouis); Nathan, George Jean

Anderson, Jessica (Margaret) Queale 1916- **CLC 37**
See also CA 9-12R; CANR 4, 62; CN 7

Anderson, Jon (Victor) 1940- **CLC 9**
See also CA 25-28R; CANR 20; DAM POET

Anderson, Lindsay (Gordon) 1923-1994 **CLC 20**
See also CA 125; 128; 146; CANR 77

Anderson, Maxwell 1888-1959 **TCLC 2, 144**
See also CA 105; 152; DAM DRAM; DFS 16; DLB 7, 228; MTCW 2; RGAL 4

Anderson, Poul (William) 1926-2001 **CLC 15**
See also AAYA 5, 34; BPFB 1; BYA 6, 8, 9; CA 1-4R; 181; 199; CAAE 181; CAAS 2; CANR 2, 15, 34, 64, 110; CLR 58; DLB 8; FANT; INT CANR-15; MTCW 1, 2; SATA 90; SATA-Brief 39; SATA-Essay 106; SCFW 2; SFW 4; SUFW 1, 2

Anderson, Robert (Woodruff) 1917- **CLC 23**
See also AITN 1; CA 21-24R; CANR 32; DAM DRAM; DLB 7; LAIT 5

Anderson, Roberta Joan
See Mitchell, Joni

Anderson, Sherwood 1876-1941 **SSC 1, 46; TCLC 1, 10, 24, 123; WLC**
See also AAYA 30; AMW; AMWC 2; BPFB 1; CA 104; 121; CANR 61; CDALB 1917-1929; DA; DA3; DAB; DAC; DAM MST, NOV; DLB 4, 9, 86; DLBD 1; EWL 3; EXPS; GLL 2; MTCW 1, 2; NFS 4; RGAL 4; RGSF 2; SSFS 4, 10, 11; TUS

Andier, Pierre
See Desnos, Robert

Andouard
See Giraudoux, Jean(-Hippolyte)

Andrade, Carlos Drummond de CLC 18
See Drummond de Andrade, Carlos
See also EWL 3; RGWL 2, 3

Andrade, Mario de TCLC 43
See de Andrade, Mario
See also EWL 3; LAW; RGWL 2, 3; WLIT 1

Andreae, Johann V(alentin) 1586-1654 **LC 32**
See also DLB 164

Andreas Capellanus fl. c. 1185- **CMLC 45**
See also DLB 208

Andreas-Salome, Lou 1861-1937 **TCLC 56**
See also CA 178; DLB 66

Andreev, Leonid
See Andreyev, Leonid (Nikolaevich)
See also DLB 295; EWL 3

Andress, Lesley
See Sanders, Lawrence

Andrewes, Lancelot 1555-1626 **LC 5**
See also DLB 151, 172

Andrews, Cicily Fairfield
See West, Rebecca

Andrews, Elton V.
See Pohl, Frederik

Andreyev, Leonid (Nikolaevich) 1871-1919 **TCLC 3**
See Andreev, Leonid
See also CA 104; 185

Arp, Hans
    See Arp, Jean
Arp, Jean 1887-1966 **CLC 5; TCLC 115**
    See also CA 81-84; 25-28R; CANR 42, 77;
    EW 10
Arrabal
    See Arrabal, Fernando
Arrabal, Fernando 1932- **CLC 2, 9, 18, 58**
    See Arrabal (Teran), Fernando
    See also CA 9-12R; CANR 15; EWL 3;
    LMFS 2
Arrabal (Teran), Fernando 1932-
    See Arrabal, Fernando
    See also CWW 2
Arreola, Juan Jose 1918-2001 **CLC 147; HLC 1; SSC 38**
    See also CA 113; 131; 200; CANR 81;
    CWW 2; DAM MULT; DLB 113; DNFS
    2; EWL 3; HW 1, 2; LAW; RGSF 2
Arrian c. 89(?)-c. 155(?) **CMLC 43**
    See also DLB 176
Arrick, Fran CLC 30
    See Gaberman, Judie Angell
    See also BYA 6
Arriey, Richmond
    See Delany, Samuel R(ay), Jr.
Artaud, Antonin (Marie Joseph) 1896-1948 **DC 14; TCLC 3, 36**
    See also CA 104; 149; DA3; DAM DRAM;
    DLB 258; EW 11; EWL 3; GFL 1789 to
    the Present; MTCW 1; RGWL 2, 3
Arthur, Ruth M(abel) 1905-1979 **CLC 12**
    See also CA 9-12R; 85-88; CANR 4; CWRI
    5; SATA 7, 26
Artsybashev, Mikhail (Petrovich) 1878-1927 **TCLC 31**
    See also CA 170; DLB 295
Arundel, Honor (Morfydd) 1919-1973 **CLC 17**
    See also CA 21-22; 41-44R; CAP 2; CLR
    35; CWRI 5; SATA 4; SATA-Obit 24
Arzner, Dorothy 1900-1979 **CLC 98**
Asch, Sholem 1880-1957 **TCLC 3**
    See also CA 105; EWL 3; GLL 2
Ascham, Roger 1516(?)-1568 **LC 101**
    See also DLB 236
Ash, Shalom
    See Asch, Sholem
Ashbery, John (Lawrence) 1927- **CLC 2, 3, 4, 6, 9, 13, 15, 25, 41, 77, 125; PC 26**
    See Berry, Jonas
    See also AMWS 3; CA 5-8R; CANR 9, 37,
    66, 102; CP 7; DA3; DAM POET; DLB
    5, 165; DLBY 1981; EWL 3; INT
    CANR-9; MTCW 1, 2; PAB; PFS 11;
    RGAL 4; WP
Ashdown, Clifford
    See Freeman, R(ichard) Austin
Ashe, Gordon
    See Creasey, John
Ashton-Warner, Sylvia (Constance) 1908-1984 **CLC 19**
    See also CA 69-72; 112; CANR 29; MTCW
    1, 2
Asimov, Isaac 1920-1992 **CLC 1, 3, 9, 19, 26, 76, 92**
    See also AAYA 13; BEST 90:2; BPFB 1;
    BYA 4, 6, 7, 9; CA 1-4R; 137; CANR 2,
    19, 36, 60, 125; CLR 12, 79; CMW 4;
    CPW; DA3; DAM POP; DLB 8; DLBY
    1992; INT CANR-19; JRDA; LAIT 5;
    LMFS 2; MAICYA 1, 2; MTCW 1, 2;
    RGAL 4; SATA 1, 26, 74; SCFW 2; SFW
    4; SSFS 17; TUS; YAW
Askew, Anne 1521(?)-1546 **LC 81**
    See also DLB 136

Assis, Joaquim Maria Machado de
    See Machado de Assis, Joaquim Maria
Astell, Mary 1666-1731 **LC 68**
    See also DLB 252; FW
Astley, Thea (Beatrice May) 1925- **CLC 41**
    See also CA 65-68; CANR 11, 43, 78; CN
    7; DLB 289; EWL 3
Astley, William 1855-1911
    See Warung, Price
Aston, James
    See White, T(erence) H(anbury)
Asturias, Miguel Angel 1899-1974 **CLC 3, 8, 13; HLC 1**
    See also CA 25-28; 49-52; CANR 32; CAP
    2; CDWLB 3; DA3; DAM MULT, NOV;
    DLB 113, 290; EWL 3; HW 1; LAW;
    LMFS 2; MTCW 1, 2; RGWL 2, 3; WLIT
    1
Atares, Carlos Saura
    See Saura (Atares), Carlos
Athanasius c. 295-c. 373 **CMLC 48**
Atheling, William
    See Pound, Ezra (Weston Loomis)
Atheling, William, Jr.
    See Blish, James (Benjamin)
Atherton, Gertrude (Franklin Horn) 1857-1948 **TCLC 2**
    See also CA 104; 155; DLB 9, 78, 186;
    HGG; RGAL 4; SUFW 1; TCWW 2
Atherton, Lucius
    See Masters, Edgar Lee
Atkins, Jack
    See Harris, Mark
Atkinson, Kate 1951- **CLC 99**
    See also CA 166; CANR 101; DLB 267
Attaway, William (Alexander) 1911-1986 **BLC 1; CLC 92**
    See also BW 2, 3; CA 143; CANR 82;
    DAM MULT; DLB 76
Atticus
    See Fleming, Ian (Lancaster); Wilson,
    (Thomas) Woodrow
Atwood, Margaret (Eleanor) 1939- **CLC 2, 3, 4, 8, 13, 15, 25, 44, 84, 135; PC 8; SSC 2, 46; WLC**
    See also AAYA 12, 47; AMWS 13; BEST
    89:2; BPFB 1; CA 49-52; CANR 3, 24,
    33, 59, 95; CN 7; CP 7; CPW; CWP; DA;
    DA3; DAB; DAC; DAM MST, NOV,
    POET; DLB 53, 251; EWL 3; EXPN; FW;
    INT CANR-24; LAIT 5; MTCW 1, 2;
    NFS 4, 12, 13, 14; PFS 7; RGSF 2; SATA
    50; SSFS 3, 13; TWA; WWE 1; YAW
Aubigny, Pierre d'
    See Mencken, H(enry) L(ouis)
Aubin, Penelope 1685-1731(?) **LC 9**
    See also DLB 39
Auchincloss, Louis (Stanton) 1917- **CLC 4, 6, 9, 18, 45; SSC 22**
    See also AMWS 4; CA 1-4R; CANR 6, 29,
    55, 87; CN 7; DAM NOV; DLB 2, 244;
    DLBY 1980; EWL 3; INT CANR-29;
    MTCW 1; RGAL 4
Auden, W(ystan) H(ugh) 1907-1973 **CLC 1, 2, 3, 4, 6, 9, 11, 14, 43, 123; PC 1; WLC**
    See also AAYA 18; AMWS 2; BRW 7;
    BRWR 1; CA 9-12R; 45-48; CANR 5, 61,
    105; CDBLB 1914-1945; DA; DA3;
    DAB; DAC; DAM DRAM, MST, POET;
    DLB 10, 20; EWL 3; EXPP; MTCW 1, 2;
    PAB; PFS 1, 3, 4, 10; TUS; WP
Audiberti, Jacques 1900-1965 **CLC 38**
    See also CA 25-28R; DAM DRAM; EWL 3
Audubon, John James 1785-1851 **NCLC 47**
    See also ANW; DLB 248
Auel, Jean M(arie) 1936- **CLC 31, 107**
    See also AAYA 7, 51; BEST 90:4; BPFB 1;
    CA 103; CANR 21, 64, 115; CPW; DA3;
    DAM POP; INT CANR-21; NFS 11;
    RHW; SATA 91

Auerbach, Erich 1892-1957 **TCLC 43**
    See also CA 118; 155; EWL 3
Augier, Emile 1820-1889 **NCLC 31**
    See also DLB 192; GFL 1789 to the Present
August, John
    See De Voto, Bernard (Augustine)
Augustine, St. 354-430 **CMLC 6; WLCS**
    See also DA; DA3; DAB; DAC; DAM
    MST; DLB 115; EW 1; RGWL 2, 3
Aunt Belinda
    See Braddon, Mary Elizabeth
Aunt Weedy
    See Alcott, Louisa May
Aurelius
    See Bourne, Randolph S(illiman)
Aurelius, Marcus 121-180 **CMLC 45**
    See Marcus Aurelius
    See also RGWL 2, 3
Aurobindo, Sri
    See Ghose, Aurabinda
Aurobindo Ghose
    See Ghose, Aurabinda
Austen, Jane 1775-1817 **NCLC 1, 13, 19, 33, 51, 81, 95, 119; WLC**
    See also AAYA 19; BRW 4; BRWC 1;
    BRWR 2; BYA 3; CDBLB 1789-1832;
    DA; DA3; DAB; DAC; DAM MST, NOV;
    DLB 116; EXPN; LAIT 2; LATS 1; LMFS
    1; NFS 1, 14, 18; TEA; WLIT 3; WYAS
    1
Auster, Paul 1947- **CLC 47, 131**
    See also AMWS 12; CA 69-72; CANR 23,
    52, 75, 129; CMW 4; CN 7; DA3; DLB
    227; MTCW 1; SUFW 2
Austin, Frank
    See Faust, Frederick (Schiller)
    See also TCWW 2
Austin, Mary (Hunter) 1868-1934 **TCLC 25**
    See Stairs, Gordon
    See also ANW; CA 109; 178; DLB 9, 78,
    206, 221, 275; FW; TCWW 2
Averroes 1126-1198 **CMLC 7**
    See also DLB 115
Avicenna 980-1037 **CMLC 16**
    See also DLB 115
Avison, Margaret 1918- **CLC 2, 4, 97**
    See also CA 17-20R; CP 7; DAC; DAM
    POET; DLB 53; MTCW 1
Axton, David
    See Koontz, Dean R(ay)
Ayckbourn, Alan 1939- **CLC 5, 8, 18, 33, 74; DC 13**
    See also BRWS 5; CA 21-24R; CANR 31,
    59, 118; CBD; CD 5; DAB; DAM DRAM;
    DFS 7; DLB 13, 245; EWL 3; MTCW 1,
    2
Aydy, Catherine
    See Tennant, Emma (Christina)
Ayme, Marcel (Andre) 1902-1967 **CLC 11; SSC 41**
    See also CA 89-92; CANR 67; CLR 25;
    DLB 72; EW 12; EWL 3; GFL 1789 to
    the Present; RGSF 2; RGWL 2, 3; SATA
    91
Ayrton, Michael 1921-1975 **CLC 7**
    See also CA 5-8R; 61-64; CANR 9, 21
Aytmatov, Chingiz
    See Aitmatov, Chingiz (Torekulovich)
    See also EWL 3
Azorin CLC 11
    See Martinez Ruiz, Jose
    See also EW 9; EWL 3
Azuela, Mariano 1873-1952 **HLC 1; TCLC 3, 145**
    See also CA 104; 131; CANR 81; DAM
    MULT; EWL 3; HW 1, 2; LAW; MTCW
    1, 2

Ba, Mariama 1929-1981 **BLCS**
See also AFW; BW 2; CA 141; CANR 87; DNFS 2; WLIT 2

Baastad, Babbis Friis
See Friis-Baastad, Babbis Ellinor

Bab
See Gilbert, W(illiam) S(chwenck)

Babbis, Eleanor
See Friis-Baastad, Babbis Ellinor

Babel, Isaac
See Babel, Isaak (Emmanuilovich)
See also EW 11; SSFS 10

Babel, Isaak (Emmanuilovich) 1894-1941(?) **SSC 16; TCLC 2, 13**
See Babel, Isaac
See also CA 104; 155; CANR 113; DLB 272; EWL 3; MTCW 1; RGSF 2; RGWL 2, 3; TWA

Babits, Mihaly 1883-1941 **TCLC 14**
See also CA 114; CDWLB 4; DLB 215; EWL 3

Babur 1483-1530 **LC 18**

Babylas 1898-1962
See Ghelderode, Michel de

Baca, Jimmy Santiago 1952- **HLC 1; PC 41**
See also CA 131; CANR 81, 90; CP 7; DAM MULT; DLB 122; HW 1, 2; LLW 1

Baca, Jose Santiago
See Baca, Jimmy Santiago

Bacchelli, Riccardo 1891-1985 **CLC 19**
See also CA 29-32R; 117; DLB 264; EWL 3

Bach, Richard (David) 1936- **CLC 14**
See also AITN 1; BEST 89:2; BPFB 1; BYA 5; CA 9-12R; CANR 18, 93; CPW; DAM NOV, POP; FANT; MTCW 1; SATA 13

Bache, Benjamin Franklin 1769-1798 **LC 74**
See also DLB 43

Bachelard, Gaston 1884-1962 **TCLC 128**
See also CA 97-100; 89-92; DLB 296; GFL 1789 to the Present

Bachman, Richard
See King, Stephen (Edwin)

Bachmann, Ingeborg 1926-1973 **CLC 69**
See also CA 93-96; 45-48; CANR 69; DLB 85; EWL 3; RGWL 2, 3

Bacon, Francis 1561-1626 **LC 18, 32**
See also BRW 1; CDBLB Before 1660; DLB 151, 236, 252; RGEL 2; TEA

Bacon, Roger 1214(?)-1294 **CMLC 14**
See also DLB 115

Bacovia, George 1881-1957 **TCLC 24**
See Vasiliu, Gheorghe
See also CDWLB 4; DLB 220; EWL 3

Badanes, Jerome 1937- **CLC 59**

Bagehot, Walter 1826-1877 **NCLC 10**
See also DLB 55

Bagnold, Enid 1889-1981 **CLC 25**
See also BYA 2; CA 5-8R; 103; CANR 5, 40; CBD; CWD; CWRI 5; DAM DRAM; DLB 13, 160, 191, 245; FW; MAICYA 1, 2; RGEL 2; SATA 1, 25

Bagritsky, Eduard TCLC 60
See Dzyubin, Eduard Georgievich

Bagrjana, Elisaveta
See Belcheva, Elisaveta Lyubomirova

Bagryana, Elisaveta CLC 10
See Belcheva, Elisaveta Lyubomirova
See also CA 178; CDWLB 4; DLB 147; EWL 3

Bailey, Paul 1937- **CLC 45**
See also CA 21-24R; CANR 16, 62, 124; CN 7; DLB 14, 271; GLL 2

Baillie, Joanna 1762-1851 **NCLC 71**
See also DLB 93; RGEL 2

Bainbridge, Beryl (Margaret) 1934- **CLC 4, 5, 8, 10, 14, 18, 22, 62, 130**
See also BRWS 6; CA 21-24R; CANR 24, 55, 75, 88, 128; CN 7; DAM NOV; DLB 14, 231; EWL 3; MTCW 1, 2

Baker, Carlos (Heard) 1909-1987 **TCLC 119**
See also CA 5-8R; 122; CANR 3, 63; DLB 103

Baker, Elliott 1922- **CLC 8**
See also CA 45-48; CANR 2, 63; CN 7

Baker, Jean H. TCLC 3, 10
See Russell, George William

Baker, Nicholson 1957- **CLC 61, 165**
See also AMWS 13; CA 135; CANR 63, 120; CN 7; CPW; DA3; DAM POP; DLB 227

Baker, Ray Stannard 1870-1946 **TCLC 47**
See also CA 118

Baker, Russell (Wayne) 1925- **CLC 31**
See also BEST 89:4; CA 57-60; CANR 11, 41, 59; MTCW 1, 2

Bakhtin, M.
See Bakhtin, Mikhail Mikhailovich

Bakhtin, M. M.
See Bakhtin, Mikhail Mikhailovich

Bakhtin, Mikhail
See Bakhtin, Mikhail Mikhailovich

Bakhtin, Mikhail Mikhailovich 1895-1975 **CLC 83**
See also CA 128; 113; DLB 242; EWL 3

Bakshi, Ralph 1938(?)- **CLC 26**
See also CA 112; 138; IDFW 3

Bakunin, Mikhail (Alexandrovich) 1814-1876 **NCLC 25, 58**
See also DLB 277

Baldwin, James (Arthur) 1924-1987 **BLC 1; CLC 1, 2, 3, 4, 5, 8, 13, 15, 17, 42, 50, 67, 90, 127; DC 1; SSC 10, 33; WLC**
See also AAYA 4, 34; AFAW 1, 2; AMWR 2; AMWS 1; BPFB 1; BW 1; CA 1-4R; 124; CABS 1; CAD; CANR 3, 24; CDALB 1941-1968; CPW; DA; DA3; DAB; DAC; DAM MST, MULT, NOV, POP; DFS 11, 15; DLB 2, 7, 33, 249, 278; DLBY 1987; EWL 3; EXPS; LAIT 5; MTCW 1, 2; NCFS 4; NFS 4; RGAL 4; RGSF 2; SATA 9; SATA-Obit 54; SSFS 2, 18; TUS

Bale, John 1495-1563 **LC 62**
See also DLB 132; RGEL 2; TEA

Ball, Hugo 1886-1927 **TCLC 104**

Ballard, J(ames) G(raham) 1930- **CLC 3, 6, 14, 36, 137; SSC 1, 53**
See also AAYA 3, 52; BRWS 5; CA 5-8R; CANR 15, 39, 65, 107; CN 7; DA3; DAM NOV, POP; DLB 14, 207, 261; EWL 3; HGG; MTCW 1, 2; NFS 8; RGEL 2; RGSF 2; SATA 93; SFW 4

Balmont, Konstantin (Dmitriyevich) 1867-1943 **TCLC 11**
See also CA 109; 155; DLB 295; EWL 3

Baltausis, Vincas 1847-1910
See Mikszath, Kalman

Balzac, Honore de 1799-1850 **NCLC 5, 35, 53; SSC 5, 59; WLC**
See also DA; DA3; DAB; DAC; DAM MST, NOV; DLB 119; EW 5; GFL 1789 to the Present; LMFS 1; RGSF 2; RGWL 2, 3; SSFS 10; SUFW; TWA

Bambara, Toni Cade 1939-1995 **BLC 1; CLC 19, 88; SSC 35; TCLC 116; WLCS**
See also AAYA 5, 49; AFAW 2; AMWS 11; BW 2, 3; BYA 12, 14; CA 29-32R; 150; CANR 24, 49, 81; CDALBS; DA; DA3; DAC; DAM MST, MULT; DLB 38, 218; EXPS; MTCW 1, 2; RGAL 4; RGSF 2; SATA 112; SSFS 4, 7, 12

Bamdad, A.
See Shamlu, Ahmad

Bamdad, Alef
See Shamlu, Ahmad

Banat, D. R.
See Bradbury, Ray (Douglas)

Bancroft, Laura
See Baum, L(yman) Frank

Banim, John 1798-1842 **NCLC 13**
See also DLB 116, 158, 159; RGEL 2

Banim, Michael 1796-1874 **NCLC 13**
See also DLB 158, 159

Banjo, The
See Paterson, A(ndrew) B(arton)

Banks, Iain
See Banks, Iain M(enzies)

Banks, Iain M(enzies) 1954- **CLC 34**
See also CA 123; 128; CANR 61, 106; DLB 194, 261; EWL 3; HGG; INT CA-128; SFW 4

Banks, Lynne Reid CLC 23
See Reid Banks, Lynne
See also AAYA 6; BYA 7; CLR 86

Banks, Russell (Earl) 1940- **CLC 37, 72, 187; SSC 42**
See also AAYA 45; AMWS 5; CA 65-68; CAAS 15; CANR 19, 52, 73, 118; CN 7; DLB 130, 278; EWL 3; NFS 13

Banville, John 1945- **CLC 46, 118**
See also CA 117; 128; CANR 104; CN 7; DLB 14, 271; INT CA-128

Banville, Theodore (Faullain) de 1832-1891 **NCLC 9**
See also DLB 217; GFL 1789 to the Present

Baraka, Amiri 1934- **BLC 1; CLC 1, 2, 3, 5, 10, 14, 33, 115; DC 6; PC 4; WLCS**
See Jones, LeRoi
See also AFAW 1, 2; AMWS 2; BW 2, 3; CA 21-24R; CABS 3; CAD; CANR 27, 38, 61; CD 5; CDALB 1941-1968; CP 7; CPW; DA; DA3; DAC; DAM MST, MULT, POET, POP; DFS 3, 11, 16; DLB 5, 7, 16, 38; DLBD 8; EWL 3; MTCW 1, 2; PFS 9; RGAL 4; TUS; WP

Baratynsky, Evgenii Abramovich 1800-1844 **NCLC 103**
See also DLB 205

Barbauld, Anna Laetitia 1743-1825 **NCLC 50**
See also DLB 107, 109, 142, 158; RGEL 2

Barbellion, W. N. P. TCLC 24
See Cummings, Bruce F(rederick)

Barber, Benjamin R. 1939- **CLC 141**
See also CA 29-32R; CANR 12, 32, 64, 119

Barbera, Jack (Vincent) 1945- **CLC 44**
See also CA 110; CANR 45

Barbey d'Aurevilly, Jules-Amedee 1808-1889 **NCLC 1; SSC 17**
See also DLB 119; GFL 1789 to the Present

Barbour, John c. 1316-1395 **CMLC 33**
See also DLB 146

Barbusse, Henri 1873-1935 **TCLC 5**
See also CA 105; 154; DLB 65; EWL 3; RGWL 2, 3

Barclay, Bill
See Moorcock, Michael (John)

Barclay, William Ewert
See Moorcock, Michael (John)

Barea, Arturo 1897-1957 **TCLC 14**
See also CA 111; 201

Barfoot, Joan 1946- **CLC 18**
See also CA 105

Barham, Richard Harris 1788-1845 **NCLC 77**
See also DLB 159

Baring, Maurice 1874-1945 **TCLC 8**
See also CA 105; 168; DLB 34; HGG

Baring-Gould, Sabine 1834-1924 **TCLC 88**
See also DLB 156, 190

Author Index

Barker, Clive 1952- **CLC 52; SSC 53**
See also AAYA 10; BEST 90:3; BPFB 1; CA 121; 129; CANR 71, 111; CPW; DA3; DAM POP; DLB 261; HGG; INT CA-129; MTCW 1, 2; SUFW 2

Barker, George Granville 1913-1991 **CLC 8, 48**
See also CA 9-12R; 135; CANR 7, 38; DAM POET; DLB 20; EWL 3; MTCW 1

Barker, Harley Granville
See Granville-Barker, Harley
See also DLB 10

Barker, Howard 1946- **CLC 37**
See also CA 102; CBD; CD 5; DLB 13, 233

Barker, Jane 1652-1732 **LC 42, 82**
See also DLB 39, 131

Barker, Pat(ricia) 1943- **CLC 32, 94, 146**
See also BRWS 4; CA 117; 122; CANR 50, 101; CN 7; DLB 271; INT CA-122

Barlach, Ernst (Heinrich) 1870-1938 **TCLC 84**
See also CA 178; DLB 56, 118; EWL 3

Barlow, Joel 1754-1812 **NCLC 23**
See also AMWS 2; DLB 37; RGAL 4

Barnard, Mary (Ethel) 1909- **CLC 48**
See also CA 21-22; CAP 2

Barnes, Djuna 1892-1982 **CLC 3, 4, 8, 11, 29, 127; SSC 3**
See Steptoe, Lydia
See also AMWS 3; CA 9-12R; 107; CAD; CANR 16, 55; CWD; DLB 4, 9, 45; EWL 3; GLL 1; MTCW 1, 2; RGAL 4; TUS

Barnes, Jim 1933- **NNAL**
See also CA 108, 175; CAAE 175; CAAS 28; DLB 175

Barnes, Julian (Patrick) 1946- **CLC 42, 141**
See also BRWS 4; CA 102; CANR 19, 54, 115; CN 7; DAB; DLB 194; DLBY 1993; EWL 3; MTCW 1

Barnes, Peter 1931- **CLC 5, 56**
See also CA 65-68; CAAS 12; CANR 33, 34, 64, 113; CBD; CD 5; DFS 6; DLB 13, 233; MTCW 1

Barnes, William 1801-1886 **NCLC 75**
See also DLB 32

Baroja (y Nessi), Pio 1872-1956 **HLC 1; TCLC 8**
See also CA 104; EW 9

Baron, David
See Pinter, Harold

Baron Corvo
See Rolfe, Frederick (William Serafino Austin Lewis Mary)

Barondess, Sue K(aufman) 1926-1977 **CLC 8**
See Kaufman, Sue
See also CA 1-4R; 69-72; CANR 1

Baron de Teive
See Pessoa, Fernando (Antonio Nogueira)

Baroness Von S.
See Zangwill, Israel

Barres, (Auguste-)Maurice 1862-1923 **TCLC 47**
See also CA 164; DLB 123; GFL 1789 to the Present

Barreto, Afonso Henrique de Lima
See Lima Barreto, Afonso Henrique de

Barrett, Andrea 1954- **CLC 150**
See also CA 156; CANR 92

Barrett, Michele CLC 65

Barrett, (Roger) Syd 1946- **CLC 35**

Barrett, William (Christopher) 1913-1992 **CLC 27**
See also CA 13-16R; 139; CANR 11, 67; INT CANR-11

Barrie, J(ames) M(atthew) 1860-1937 **TCLC 2**
See also BRWS 3; BYA 4, 5; CA 104; 136; CANR 77; CDBLB 1890-1914; CLR 16;
CWRI 5; DA3; DAB; DAM DRAM; DFS 7; DLB 10, 141, 156; EWL 3; FANT; MAICYA 1, 2; MTCW 1; SATA 100; SUFW; WCH; WLIT 4; YABC 1

Barrington, Michael
See Moorcock, Michael (John)

Barrol, Grady
See Bograd, Larry

Barry, Mike
See Malzberg, Barry N(athaniel)

Barry, Philip 1896-1949 **TCLC 11**
See also CA 109; 199; DFS 9; DLB 7, 228; RGAL 4

Bart, Andre Schwarz
See Schwarz-Bart, Andre

Barth, John (Simmons) 1930- **CLC 1, 2, 3, 5, 7, 9, 10, 14, 27, 51, 89; SSC 10**
See also AITN 1, 2; AMW; BPFB 1; CA 1-4R; CABS 1; CANR 5, 23, 49, 64, 113; CN 7; DAM NOV; DLB 2, 227; EWL 3; FANT; MTCW 1; RGAL 4; RGSF 2; RHW; SSFS 6; TUS

Barthelme, Donald 1931-1989 **CLC 1, 2, 3, 5, 6, 8, 13, 23, 46, 59, 115; SSC 2, 55**
See also AMWS 4; BPFB 1; CA 21-24R; 129; CANR 20, 58; DA3; DAM NOV; DLB 2, 234; DLBY 1980, 1989; EWL 3; FANT; LMFS 2; MTCW 1, 2; RGAL 4; RGSF 2; SATA 7; SATA-Obit 62; SSFS 17

Barthelme, Frederick 1943- **CLC 36, 117**
See also AMWS 11; CA 114; 122; CANR 77; CN 7; CSW; DLB 244; DLBY 1985; EWL 3; INT CA-122

Barthes, Roland (Gerard) 1915-1980 **CLC 24, 83; TCLC 135**
See also CA 130; 97-100; CANR 66; DLB 296; EW 13; EWL 3; GFL 1789 to the Present; MTCW 1, 2; TWA

Barzun, Jacques (Martin) 1907- **CLC 51, 145**
See also CA 61-64; CANR 22, 95

Bashevis, Isaac
See Singer, Isaac Bashevis

Bashkirtseff, Marie 1859-1884 **NCLC 27**

Basho, Matsuo
See Matsuo Basho
See also PFS 18; RGWL 2, 3; WP

Basil of Caesaria c. 330-379 **CMLC 35**

Basket, Raney
See Edgerton, Clyde (Carlyle)

Bass, Kingsley B., Jr.
See Bullins, Ed

Bass, Rick 1958- **CLC 79, 143; SSC 60**
See also ANW; CA 126; CANR 53, 93; CSW; DLB 212, 275

Bassani, Giorgio 1916-2000 **CLC 9**
See also CA 65-68; 190; CANR 33; CWW 2; DLB 128, 177; EWL 3; MTCW 1; RGWL 2, 3

Bastian, Ann CLC 70

Bastos, Augusto (Antonio) Roa
See Roa Bastos, Augusto (Antonio)

Bataille, Georges 1897-1962 **CLC 29**
See also CA 101; 89-92; EWL 3

Bates, H(erbert) E(rnest) 1905-1974 **CLC 46; SSC 10**
See also CA 93-96; 45-48; CANR 34; DA3; DAB; DAM POP; DLB 162, 191; EWL 3; EXPS; MTCW 1, 2; RGSF 2; SSFS 7

Bauchart
See Camus, Albert

Baudelaire, Charles 1821-1867 **NCLC 6, 29, 55; PC 1; SSC 18; WLC**
See also DA; DA3; DAB; DAC; DAM MST, POET; DLB 217; EW 7; GFL 1789 to the Present; LMFS 2; RGWL 2, 3; TWA

Baudouin, Marcel
See Peguy, Charles (Pierre)

Baudouin, Pierre
See Peguy, Charles (Pierre)

Baudrillard, Jean 1929- **CLC 60**
See also DLB 296

Baum, L(yman) Frank 1856-1919 **TCLC 7, 132**
See also AAYA 46; BYA 16; CA 108; 133; CLR 15; CWRI 5; DLB 22; FANT; JRDA; MAICYA 1, 2; MTCW 1, 2; NFS 13; RGAL 4; SATA 18, 100; WCH

Baum, Louis F.
See Baum, L(yman) Frank

Baumbach, Jonathan 1933- **CLC 6, 23**
See also CA 13-16R; CAAS 5; CANR 12, 66; CN 7; DLBY 1980; INT CANR-12; MTCW 1

Bausch, Richard (Carl) 1945- **CLC 51**
See also AMWS 7; CA 101; CAAS 14; CANR 43, 61, 87; CSW; DLB 130

Baxter, Charles (Morley) 1947- **CLC 45, 78**
See also CA 57-60; CANR 40, 64, 104; CPW; DAM POP; DLB 130; MTCW 2

Baxter, George Owen
See Faust, Frederick (Schiller)

Baxter, James K(eir) 1926-1972 **CLC 14**
See also CA 77-80; EWL 3

Baxter, John
See Hunt, E(verette) Howard, (Jr.)

Bayer, Sylvia
See Glassco, John

Baynton, Barbara 1857-1929 **TCLC 57**
See also DLB 230; RGSF 2

Beagle, Peter S(oyer) 1939- **CLC 7, 104**
See also AAYA 47; BPFB 1; BYA 9, 10, 16; CA 9-12R; CANR 4, 51, 73, 110; DA3; DLBY 1980; FANT; INT CANR-4; MTCW 1; SATA 60, 130; SUFW 1, 2; YAW

Bean, Normal
See Burroughs, Edgar Rice

Beard, Charles A(ustin) 1874-1948 **TCLC 15**
See also CA 115; 189; DLB 17; SATA 18

Beardsley, Aubrey 1872-1898 **NCLC 6**

Beattie, Ann 1947- **CLC 8, 13, 18, 40, 63, 146; SSC 11**
See also AMWS 5; BEST 90:2; BPFB 1; CA 81-84; CANR 53, 73, 128; CN 7; CPW; DA3; DAM NOV, POP; DLB 218, 278; DLBY 1982; EWL 3; MTCW 1, 2; RGAL 4; RGSF 2; SSFS 9; TUS

Beattie, James 1735-1803 **NCLC 25**
See also DLB 109

Beauchamp, Kathleen Mansfield 1888-1923
See Mansfield, Katherine
See also CA 104; 134; DA; DA3; DAC; DAM MST; MTCW 2; TEA

Beaumarchais, Pierre-Augustin Caron de 1732-1799 **DC 4; LC 61**
See also DAM DRAM; DFS 14, 16; EW 4; GFL Beginnings to 1789; RGWL 2, 3

Beaumont, Francis 1584(?)-1616 **DC 6; LC 33**
See also BRW 2; CDBLB Before 1660; DLB 58; TEA

Beauvoir, Simone (Lucie Ernestine Marie Bertrand) de 1908-1986 **CLC 1, 2, 4, 8, 14, 31, 44, 50, 71, 124; SSC 35; WLC**
See also BPFB 1; CA 9-12R; 118; CANR 28, 61; DA; DA3; DAB; DAC; DAM MST, NOV; DLB 72; DLBY 1986; EW 12; EWL 3; FW; GFL 1789 to the Present; LMFS 2; MTCW 1, 2; RGSF 2; RGWL 2, 3; TWA

Becker, Carl (Lotus) 1873-1945 **TCLC 63**
See also CA 157; DLB 17

Becker, Jurek 1937-1997 **CLC 7, 19**
See also CA 85-88; 157; CANR 60, 117; CWW 2; DLB 75; EWL 3

Becker, Walter 1950- **CLC 26**

Beckett, Samuel (Barclay) 1906-1989 **CLC 1, 2, 3, 4, 6, 9, 10, 11, 14, 18, 29, 57, 59, 83; DC 22; SSC 16; TCLC 145; WLC**
See also BRWC 2; BRWR 1; BRWS 1; CA 5-8R; 130; CANR 33, 61; CBD; CDBLB 1945-1960; DA; DA3; DAB; DAC; DAM DRAM, MST, NOV; DFS 2, 7, 18; DLB 13, 15, 233; DLBY 1990; EWL 3; GFL 1789 to the Present; LATS 1; LMFS 2; MTCW 1, 2; RGSF 2; RGWL 2, 3; SSFS 15; TEA; WLIT 4

Beckford, William 1760-1844 **NCLC 16**
See also BRW 3; DLB 39, 213; HGG; LMFS 1; SUFW

Beckham, Barry (Earl) 1944- **BLC 1**
See also BW 1; CA 29-32R; CANR 26, 62; CN 7; DAM MULT; DLB 33

Beckman, Gunnel 1910- **CLC 26**
See also CA 33-36R; CANR 15, 114; CLR 25; MAICYA 1, 2; SAAS 9; SATA 6

Becque, Henri 1837-1899 **DC 21; NCLC 3**
See also DLB 192; GFL 1789 to the Present

Becquer, Gustavo Adolfo 1836-1870 **HLCS 1; NCLC 106**
See also DAM MULT

Beddoes, Thomas Lovell 1803-1849 **DC 15; NCLC 3**
See also DLB 96

Bede c. 673-735 **CMLC 20**
See also DLB 146; TEA

Bedford, Denton R. 1907-(?) **NNAL**

Bedford, Donald F.
See Fearing, Kenneth (Flexner)

Beecher, Catharine Esther 1800-1878 **NCLC 30**
See also DLB 1, 243

Beecher, John 1904-1980 **CLC 6**
See also AITN 1; CA 5-8R; 105; CANR 8

Beer, Johann 1655-1700 **LC 5**
See also DLB 168

Beer, Patricia 1924- **CLC 58**
See also CA 61-64; 183; CANR 13, 46; CP 7; CWP; DLB 40; FW

Beerbohm, Max
See Beerbohm, (Henry) Max(imilian)

Beerbohm, (Henry) Max(imilian) 1872-1956 **TCLC 1, 24**
See also BRWS 2; CA 104; 154; CANR 79; DLB 34, 100; FANT

Beer-Hofmann, Richard 1866-1945 **TCLC 60**
See also CA 160; DLB 81

Beg, Shemus
See Stephens, James

Begiebing, Robert J(ohn) 1946- **CLC 70**
See also CA 122; CANR 40, 88

Behan, Brendan (Francis) 1923-1964 **CLC 1, 8, 11, 15, 79**
See also BRWS 2; CA 73-76; CANR 33, 121; CBD; CDBLB 1945-1960; DAM DRAM; DFS 7; DLB 13, 233; EWL 3; MTCW 1, 2

Behn, Aphra 1640(?)-1689 **DC 4; LC 1, 30, 42; PC 13; WLC**
See also BRWS 3; DA; DA3; DAB; DAC; DAM DRAM, MST, NOV, POET; DFS 16; DLB 39, 80, 131; FW; TEA; WLIT 3

Behrman, S(amuel) N(athaniel) 1893-1973 **CLC 40**
See also CA 13-16; 45-48; CAD; CAP 1; DLB 7, 44; IDFW 3; RGAL 4

Belasco, David 1853-1931 **TCLC 3**
See also CA 104; 168; DLB 7; RGAL 4

Belcheva, Elisaveta Lyubomirova 1893-1991 **CLC 10**
See also Bagryana, Elisaveta

Beldone, Phil "Cheech"
See Ellison, Harlan (Jay)

Beleno
See Azuela, Mariano

Belinski, Vissarion Grigoryevich 1811-1848 **NCLC 5**
See also DLB 198

Belitt, Ben 1911- **CLC 22**
See also CA 13-16R; CAAS 4; CANR 7, 77; CP 7; DLB 5

Bell, Gertrude (Margaret Lowthian) 1868-1926 **TCLC 67**
See also CA 167; CANR 110; DLB 174

Bell, J. Freeman
See Zangwill, Israel

Bell, James Madison 1826-1902 **BLC 1; TCLC 43**
See also BW 1; CA 122; 124; DAM MULT; DLB 50

Bell, Madison Smartt 1957- **CLC 41, 102**
See also AMWS 10; BPFB 1; CA 111, 183; CAAE 183; CANR 28, 54, 73; CN 7; CSW; DLB 218, 278; MTCW 1

Bell, Marvin (Hartley) 1937- **CLC 8, 31**
See also CA 21-24R; CAAS 14; CANR 59, 102; CP 7; DAM POET; DLB 5; MTCW 1

Bell, W. L. D.
See Mencken, H(enry) L(ouis)

Bellamy, Atwood C.
See Mencken, H(enry) L(ouis)

Bellamy, Edward 1850-1898 **NCLC 4, 86**
See also DLB 12; NFS 15; RGAL 4; SFW 4

Belli, Gioconda 1949- **HLCS 1**
See also CA 152; CWW 2; DLB 290; EWL 3; RGWL 3

Bellin, Edward J.
See Kuttner, Henry

Bello, Andres 1781-1865 **NCLC 131**
See also LAW

Belloc, (Joseph) Hilaire (Pierre Sebastien Rene Swanton) 1870-1953 **PC 24; TCLC 7, 18**
See also CA 106; 152; CWRI 5; DAM POET; DLB 19, 100, 141, 174; EWL 3; MTCW 1; SATA 112; WCH; YABC 1

Belloc, Joseph Peter Rene Hilaire
See Belloc, (Joseph) Hilaire (Pierre Sebastien Rene Swanton)

Belloc, Joseph Pierre Hilaire
See Belloc, (Joseph) Hilaire (Pierre Sebastien Rene Swanton)

Belloc, M. A.
See Lowndes, Marie Adelaide (Belloc)

Belloc-Lowndes, Mrs.
See Lowndes, Marie Adelaide (Belloc)

Bellow, Saul 1915- **CLC 1, 2, 3, 6, 8, 10, 13, 15, 25, 33, 34, 63, 79; SSC 14; WLC**
See also AITN 2; AMW; AMWC 2; AMWR 2; BEST 89:3; BPFB 1; CA 5-8R; CABS 1; CANR 29, 53, 95; CDALB 1941-1968; CN 7; DA; DA3; DAB; DAC; DAM MST, NOV, POP; DLB 2, 28; DLBD 3; DLBY 1982; EWL 3; MTCW 1, 2; NFS 4, 14; RGAL 4; RGSF 2; SSFS 12; TUS

Belser, Reimond Karel Maria de 1929-
See Ruyslinck, Ward
See also CA 152

Bely, Andrey PC 11; TCLC 7
See Bugayev, Boris Nikolayevich
See also DLB 295; EW 9; EWL 3; MTCW 1

Belyi, Andrei
See Bugayev, Boris Nikolayevich
See also RGWL 2, 3

Bembo, Pietro 1470-1547 **LC 79**
See also RGWL 2, 3

Benary, Margot
See Benary-Isbert, Margot

Benary-Isbert, Margot 1889-1979 **CLC 12**
See also CA 5-8R; 89-92; CANR 4, 72; CLR 12; MAICYA 1, 2; SATA 2; SATA-Obit 21

Benavente (y Martinez), Jacinto 1866-1954 **HLCS 1; TCLC 3**
See also CA 106; 131; CANR 81; DAM DRAM, MULT; EWL 3; GLL 2; HW 1, 2; MTCW 1, 2

Benchley, Peter (Bradford) 1940- **CLC 4, 8**
See also AAYA 14; AITN 2; BPFB 1; CA 17-20R; CANR 12, 35, 66, 115; CPW; DAM NOV, POP; HGG; MTCW 1, 2; SATA 3, 89

Benchley, Robert (Charles) 1889-1945 **TCLC 1, 55**
See also CA 105; 153; DLB 11; RGAL 4

Benda, Julien 1867-1956 **TCLC 60**
See also CA 120; 154; GFL 1789 to the Present

Benedict, Ruth (Fulton) 1887-1948 **TCLC 60**
See also CA 158; DLB 246

Benedikt, Michael 1935- **CLC 4, 14**
See also CA 13-16R; CANR 7; CP 7; DLB 5

Benet, Juan 1927-1993 **CLC 28**
See also CA 143; EWL 3

Benet, Stephen Vincent 1898-1943 **SSC 10; TCLC 7**
See also AMWS 11; CA 104; 152; DA3; DAM POET; DLB 4, 48, 102, 249, 284; DLBY 1997; EWL 3; HGG; MTCW 1; RGAL 4; RGSF 2; SUFW; WP; YABC 1

Benet, William Rose 1886-1950 **TCLC 28**
See also CA 118; 152; DAM POET; DLB 45; RGAL 4

Benford, Gregory (Albert) 1941- **CLC 52**
See also BPFB 1; CA 69-72, 175; CAAE 175; CAAS 27; CANR 12, 24, 49, 95; CSW; DLBY 1982; SCFW 2; SFW 4

Bengtsson, Frans (Gunnar) 1894-1954 **TCLC 48**
See also CA 170; EWL 3

Benjamin, David
See Slavitt, David R(ytman)

Benjamin, Lois
See Gould, Lois

Benjamin, Walter 1892-1940 **TCLC 39**
See also CA 164; DLB 242; EW 11; EWL 3

Ben Jelloun, Tahar 1944-
See Jelloun, Tahar ben
See also CA 135; CWW 2; EWL 3; RGWL 3; WLIT 2

Benn, Gottfried 1886-1956 **PC 35; TCLC 3**
See also CA 106; 153; DLB 56; EWL 3; RGWL 2, 3

Bennett, Alan 1934- **CLC 45, 77**
See also BRWS 8; CA 103; CANR 35, 55, 106; CBD; CD 5; DAB; DAM MST; MTCW 1, 2

Bennett, (Enoch) Arnold 1867-1931 **TCLC 5, 20**
See also BRW 6; CA 106; 155; CDBLB 1890-1914; DLB 10, 34, 98, 135; EWL 3; MTCW 2

Bennett, Elizabeth
See Mitchell, Margaret (Munnerlyn)

Bennett, George Harold 1930-
See Bennett, Hal
See also BW 1; CA 97-100; CANR 87

Bennett, Gwendolyn B. 1902-1981 **HR 2**
See also BW 1; CA 125; DLB 51; WP

Bennett, Hal CLC 5
See Bennett, George Harold
See also DLB 33

Bennett, Jay 1912- **CLC 35**
See also AAYA 10; CA 69-72; CANR 11, 42, 79; JRDA; SAAS 4; SATA 41, 87; SATA-Brief 27; WYA; YAW

Bennett, Louise (Simone) 1919- **BLC 1; CLC 28**
See also BW 2, 3; CA 151; CDWLB 3; CP 7; DAM MULT; DLB 117; EWL 3

Benson, A. C. 1862-1925 **TCLC 123**
See also DLB 98

Benson, E(dward) F(rederic) 1867-1940 **TCLC 27**
See also CA 114; 157; DLB 135, 153; HGG; SUFW 1

Benson, Jackson J. 1930- **CLC 34**
See also CA 25-28R; DLB 111

Benson, Sally 1900-1972 **CLC 17**
See also CA 19-20; 37-40R; CAP 1; SATA 1, 35; SATA-Obit 27

Benson, Stella 1892-1933 **TCLC 17**
See also CA 117; 154, 155; DLB 36, 162; FANT; TEA

Bentham, Jeremy 1748-1832 **NCLC 38**
See also DLB 107, 158, 252

Bentley, E(dmund) C(lerihew) 1875-1956 **TCLC 12**
See also CA 108; DLB 70; MSW

Bentley, Eric (Russell) 1916- **CLC 24**
See also CA 5-8R; CAD; CANR 6, 67; CBD; CD 5; INT CANR-6

ben Uzair, Salem
See Horne, Richard Henry Hengist

Beranger, Pierre Jean de 1780-1857 **NCLC 34**

Berdyaev, Nicolas
See Berdyaev, Nikolai (Aleksandrovich)

Berdyaev, Nikolai (Aleksandrovich) 1874-1948 **TCLC 67**
See also CA 120; 157

Berdyayev, Nikolai (Aleksandrovich)
See Berdyaev, Nikolai (Aleksandrovich)

Berendt, John (Lawrence) 1939- **CLC 86**
See also CA 146; CANR 75, 93; DA3; MTCW 1

Beresford, J(ohn) D(avys) 1873-1947 **TCLC 81**
See also CA 112; 155; DLB 162, 178, 197; SFW 4; SUFW 1

Bergelson, David (Rafailovich) 1884-1952 **TCLC 81**
See Bergelson, Dovid
See also CA 220

Bergelson, Dovid
See Bergelson, David (Rafailovich)
See also EWL 3

Berger, Colonel
See Malraux, (Georges-)Andre

Berger, John (Peter) 1926- **CLC 2, 19**
See also BRWS 4; CA 81-84; CANR 51, 78, 117; CN 7; DLB 14, 207

Berger, Melvin H. 1927- **CLC 12**
See also CA 5-8R; CANR 4; CLR 32; SAAS 2; SATA 5, 88; SATA-Essay 124

Berger, Thomas (Louis) 1924- **CLC 3, 5, 8, 11, 18, 38**
See also BPFB 1; CA 1-4R; CANR 5, 28, 51, 128; CN 7; DAM NOV; DLB 2; DLBY 1980; EWL 3; FANT; INT CANR-28; MTCW 1, 2; RHW; TCWW 2

Bergman, (Ernst) Ingmar 1918- **CLC 16, 72**
See also CA 81-84; CANR 33, 70; CWW 2; DLB 257; MTCW 2

Bergson, Henri(-Louis) 1859-1941 **TCLC 32**
See also CA 164; EW 8; EWL 3; GFL 1789 to the Present

Bergstein, Eleanor 1938- **CLC 4**
See also CA 53-56; CANR 5

Berkeley, George 1685-1753 **LC 65**
See also DLB 31, 101, 252

Berkoff, Steven 1937- **CLC 56**
See also CA 104; CANR 72; CBD; CD 5

Berlin, Isaiah 1909-1997 **TCLC 105**
See also CA 85-88; 162

Bermant, Chaim (Icyk) 1929-1998 **CLC 40**
See also CA 57-60; CANR 6, 31, 57, 105; CN 7

Bern, Victoria
See Fisher, M(ary) F(rances) K(ennedy)

Bernanos, (Paul Louis) Georges 1888-1948 **TCLC 3**
See also CA 104; 130; CANR 94; DLB 72; EWL 3; GFL 1789 to the Present; RGWL 2, 3

Bernard, April 1956- **CLC 59**
See also CA 131

Berne, Victoria
See Fisher, M(ary) F(rances) K(ennedy)

Bernhard, Thomas 1931-1989 **CLC 3, 32, 61; DC 14**
See also CA 85-88; 127; CANR 32, 57; CDWLB 2; DLB 85, 124; EWL 3; MTCW 1; RGWL 2, 3

Bernhardt, Sarah (Henriette Rosine) 1844-1923 **TCLC 75**
See also CA 157

Bernstein, Charles 1950- **CLC 142,**
See also CA 129; CAAS 24; CANR 90; CP 7; DLB 169

Bernstein, Ingrid
See Kirsch, Sarah

Berriault, Gina 1926-1999 **CLC 54, 109; SSC 30**
See also CA 116; 129; 185; CANR 66; DLB 130; SSFS 7,11

Berrigan, Daniel 1921- **CLC 4**
See also CA 33-36R, 187; CAAE 187; CAAS 1; CANR 11, 43, 78; CP 7; DLB 5

Berrigan, Edmund Joseph Michael, Jr. 1934-1983
See Berrigan, Ted
See also CA 61-64; 110; CANR 14, 102

Berrigan, Ted CLC 37
See Berrigan, Edmund Joseph Michael, Jr.
See also DLB 5, 169; WP

Berry, Charles Edward Anderson 1931-
See Berry, Chuck
See also CA 115

Berry, Chuck CLC 17
See Berry, Charles Edward Anderson

Berry, Jonas
See Ashbery, John (Lawrence)
See also GLL 1

Berry, Wendell (Erdman) 1934- **CLC 4, 6, 8, 27, 46; PC 28**
See also AITN 1; AMWS 10; ANW; CA 73-76; CANR 50, 73, 101; CP 7; CSW; DAM POET; DLB 5, 6, 234, 275; MTCW 1

Berryman, John 1914-1972 **CLC 1, 2, 3, 4, 6, 8, 10, 13, 25, 62**
See also AMW; CA 13-16; 33-36R; CABS 2; CANR 35; CAP 1; CDALB 1941-1968; DAM POET; DLB 48; EWL 3; MTCW 1, 2; PAB; RGAL 4; WP

Bertolucci, Bernardo 1940- **CLC 16, 157**
See also CA 106; CANR 125

Berton, Pierre (Francis Demarigny) 1920- **CLC 104**
See also CA 1-4R; CANR 2, 56; CPW; DLB 68; SATA 99

Bertrand, Aloysius 1807-1841 **NCLC 31**
See Bertrand, Louis oAloysiusc

Bertrand, Louis oAloysiusc
See Bertrand, Aloysius
See also DLB 217

Bertran de Born c. 1140-1215 **CMLC 5**

Besant, Annie (Wood) 1847-1933 **TCLC 9**
See also CA 105; 185

Bessie, Alvah 1904-1985 **CLC 23**
See also CA 5-8R; 116; CANR 2, 80; DLB 26

Bestuzhev, Aleksandr Aleksandrovich 1797-1837 **NCLC 131**
See also DLB 198

Bethlen, T. D.
See Silverberg, Robert

Beti, Mongo BLC 1; CLC 27
See Biyidi, Alexandre
See also AFW; CANR 79; DAM MULT; EWL 3; WLIT 2

Betjeman, John 1906-1984 **CLC 2, 6, 10, 34, 43**
See also BRW 7; CA 9-12R; 112; CANR 33, 56; CDBLB 1945-1960; DA3; DAB; DAM MST, POET; DLB 20; DLBY 1984; EWL 3; MTCW 1, 2

Bettelheim, Bruno 1903-1990 **CLC 79; TCLC 143**
See also CA 81-84; 131; CANR 23, 61; DA3; MTCW 1, 2

Betti, Ugo 1892-1953 **TCLC 5**
See also CA 104; 155; EWL 3; RGWL 2, 3

Betts, Doris (Waugh) 1932- **CLC 3, 6, 28; SSC 45**
See also CA 13-16R; CANR 9, 66, 77; CN 7; CSW; DLB 218; DLBY 1982; INT CANR-9; RGAL 4

Bevan, Alistair
See Roberts, Keith (John Kingston)

Bey, Pilaff
See Douglas, (George) Norman

Bialik, Chaim Nachman 1873-1934 **TCLC 25**
See also CA 170; EWL 3

Bickerstaff, Isaac
See Swift, Jonathan

Bidart, Frank 1939- **CLC 33**
See also CA 140; CANR 106; CP 7

Bienek, Horst 1930- **CLC 7, 11**
See also CA 73-76; DLB 75

Bierce, Ambrose (Gwinett) 1842-1914(?) **SSC 9; TCLC 1, 7, 44; WLC**
See also AAYA 55; AMW; BYA 11; CA 104; 139; CANR 78; CDALB 1865-1917; DA; DA3; DAC; DAM MST; DLB 11, 12, 23, 71, 74, 186; EWL 3; EXPS; HGG; LAIT 2; RGAL 4; RGSF 2; SSFS 9; SUFW 1

Biggers, Earl Derr 1884-1933 **TCLC 65**
See also CA 108; 153

Billiken, Bud
See Motley, Willard (Francis)

Billings, Josh
See Shaw, Henry Wheeler

Billington, (Lady) Rachel (Mary) 1942- **CLC 43**
See also AITN 2; CA 33-36R; CANR 44; CN 7

Binchy, Maeve 1940- **CLC 153**
See also BEST 90:1; BPFB 1; CA 127; 134; CANR 50, 96; CN 7; CPW; DA3; DAM POP; INT CA-134; MTCW 1; RHW

Binyon, T(imothy) J(ohn) 1936- **CLC 34**
See also CA 111; CANR 28

Bion 335B.C.-245B.C. **CMLC 39**

Bioy Casares, Adolfo 1914-1999 **CLC 4, 8, 13, 88; HLC 1; SSC 17**
See Casares, Adolfo Bioy; Miranda, Javier; Sacastru, Martin
See also CA 29-32R; 177; CANR 19, 43, 66; CWW 2; DAM MULT; DLB 113; EWL 3; HW 1, 2; LAW; MTCW 1, 2

Birch, Allison CLC 65

Bird, Cordwainer
See Ellison, Harlan (Jay)

Bird, Robert Montgomery 1806-1854 **NCLC 1**
See also DLB 202; RGAL 4

Birkerts, Sven 1951- **CLC 116**
See also CA 128; 133, 176; CAAE 176; CAAS 29; INT CA-133

Boker, George Henry 1823-1890 **NCLC 125**
See also RGAL 4

Boland, Eavan (Aisling) 1944- **CLC 40, 67, 113**
See also BRWS 5; CA 143, 207; CAAE 207; CANR 61; CP 7; CWP; DAM POET; DLB 40; FW; MTCW 2; PFS 12

Boll, Heinrich
See Boell, Heinrich (Theodor)
See also BPFB 1; CDWLB 2; EW 13; EWL 3; RGSF 2; RGWL 2, 3

Bolt, Lee
See Faust, Frederick (Schiller)

Bolt, Robert (Oxton) 1924-1995 **CLC 14**
See also CA 17-20R; 147; CANR 35, 67; CBD; DAM DRAM; DFS 2; DLB 13, 233; EWL 3; LAIT 1; MTCW 1

Bombal, Maria Luisa 1910-1980 **HLCS 1; SSC 37**
See also CA 127; CANR 72; EWL 3; HW 1; LAW; RGSF 2

Bombet, Louis-Alexandre-Cesar
See Stendhal

Bomkauf
See Kaufman, Bob (Garnell)

Bonaventura NCLC 35
See also DLB 90

Bond, Edward 1934- **CLC 4, 6, 13, 23**
See also AAYA 50; BRWS 1; CA 25-28R; CANR 38, 67, 106; CBD; CD 5; DAM DRAM; DFS 3, 8; DLB 13; EWL 3; MTCW 1

Bonham, Frank 1914-1989 **CLC 12**
See also AAYA 1; BYA 1, 3; CA 9-12R; CANR 4, 36; JRDA; MAICYA 1, 2; SAAS 3; SATA 1, 49; SATA-Obit 62; TCWW 2; YAW

Bonnefoy, Yves 1923- **CLC 9, 15, 58**
See also CA 85-88; CANR 33, 75, 97; CWW 2; DAM MST, POET; DLB 258; EWL 3; GFL 1789 to the Present; MTCW 1, 2

Bonner, Marita HR 2
See Occomy, Marita (Odette) Bonner

Bonnin, Gertrude 1876-1938 **NNAL**
See Zitkala-Sa
See also CA 150; DAM MULT

Bontemps, Arna(ud Wendell) 1902-1973 **BLC 1; CLC 1, 18; HR 2**
See also BW 1; CA 1-4R; 41-44R; CANR 4, 35; CLR 6; CWRI 5; DA3; DAM MULT, NOV, POET; DLB 48, 51; JRDA; MAICYA 1, 2; MTCW 1, 2; SATA 2, 44; SATA-Obit 24; WCH; WP

Boot, William
See Stoppard, Tom

Booth, Martin 1944-2004 **CLC 13**
See also CA 93-96, 188; CAAE 188; CAAS 2; CANR 92

Booth, Philip 1925- **CLC 23**
See also CA 5-8R; CANR 5, 88; CP 7; DLBY 1982

Booth, Wayne C(layson) 1921- **CLC 24**
See also CA 1-4R; CAAS 5; CANR 3, 43, 117; DLB 67

Borchert, Wolfgang 1921-1947 **TCLC 5**
See also CA 104; 188; DLB 69, 124; EWL 3

Borel, Petrus 1809-1859 **NCLC 41**
See also DLB 119; GFL 1789 to the Present

Borges, Jorge Luis 1899-1986 **CLC 1, 2, 3, 4, 6, 8, 9, 10, 13, 19, 44, 48, 83; HLC 1; PC 22, 32; SSC 4, 41; TCLC 109; WLC**
See also AAYA 26; BPFB 1; CA 21-24R; CANR 19, 33, 75, 105; CDWLB 3; DA; DA3; DAB; DAC; DAM MST, MULT; DLB 113, 283; DLBY 1986; DNFS 1, 2;

EWL 3; HW 1, 2; LAW; LMFS 2; MSW; MTCW 1, 2; RGSF 2; RGWL 2, 3; SFW 4; SSFS 17; TWA; WLIT 1

Borowski, Tadeusz 1922-1951 **SSC 48; TCLC 9**
See also CA 106; 154; CDWLB 4; DLB 215; EWL 3; RGSF 2; RGWL 3; SSFS 13

Borrow, George (Henry) 1803-1881 **NCLC 9**
See also DLB 21, 55, 166

Bosch (Gavino), Juan 1909-2001 **HLCS 1**
See also CA 151; 204; DAM MST, MULT; DLB 145; HW 1, 2

Bosman, Herman Charles 1905-1951 **TCLC 49**
See Malan, Herman
See also CA 160; DLB 225; RGSF 2

Bosschere, Jean de 1878(?)-1953 **TCLC 19**
See also CA 115; 186

Boswell, James 1740-1795 **LC 4, 50; WLC**
See also BRW 3; CDBLB 1660-1789; DA; DAB; DAC; DAM MST; DLB 104, 142; TEA; WLIT 3

Bottomley, Gordon 1874-1948 **TCLC 107**
See also CA 120; 192; DLB 10

Bottoms, David 1949- **CLC 53**
See also CA 105; CANR 22; CSW; DLB 120; DLBY 1983

Boucicault, Dion 1820-1890 **NCLC 41**

Boucolon, Maryse
See Conde, Maryse

Bourget, Paul (Charles Joseph) 1852-1935 **TCLC 12**
See also CA 107; 196; DLB 123; GFL 1789 to the Present

Bourjaily, Vance (Nye) 1922- **CLC 8, 62**
See also CA 1-4R; CAAS 1; CANR 2, 72; CN 7; DLB 2, 143

Bourne, Randolph S(illiman) 1886-1918 **TCLC 16**
See also AMW; CA 117; 155; DLB 63

Bova, Ben(jamin William) 1932- **CLC 45**
See also AAYA 16; CA 5-8R; CAAS 18; CANR 11, 56, 94, 111; CLR 3, 96; DLBY 1981; INT CANR-11; MAICYA 1, 2; MTCW 1; SATA 6, 68, 133; SFW 4

Bowen, Elizabeth (Dorothea Cole) 1899-1973 **CLC 1, 3, 6, 11, 15, 22, 118; SSC 3, 28, 66; TCLC 148**
See also BRWS 2; CA 17-18; 41-44R; CANR 35, 105; CAP 2; CDBLB 1945-1960; DA3; DAM NOV; DLB 15, 162; EWL 3; EXPS; FW; HGG; MTCW 1, 2; NFS 13; RGSF 2; SSFS 5; SUFW 1; TEA; WLIT 4

Bowering, George 1935- **CLC 15, 47**
See also CA 21-24R; CAAS 16; CANR 10; CP 7; DLB 53

Bowering, Marilyn R(uthe) 1949- **CLC 32**
See also CA 101; CANR 49; CP 7; CWP

Bowers, Edgar 1924-2000 **CLC 9**
See also CA 5-8R; 188; CANR 24; CP 7; CSW; DLB 5

Bowers, Mrs. J. Milton 1842-1914
See Bierce, Ambrose (Gwinett)

Bowie, David CLC 17
See Jones, David Robert

Bowles, Jane (Sydney) 1917-1973 **CLC 3, 68**
See Bowles, Jane Auer
See also CA 19-20; 41-44R; CAP 2

Bowles, Jane Auer
See Bowles, Jane (Sydney)
See also EWL 3

Bowles, Paul (Frederick) 1910-1999 **CLC 1, 2, 19, 53; SSC 3**
See also AMWS 4; CA 1-4R; 186; CAAS 1; CANR 1, 19, 50, 75; CN 7; DA3; DLB 5, 6, 218; EWL 3; MTCW 1, 2; RGAL 4; SSFS 17

Bowles, William Lisle 1762-1850 **NCLC 103**
See also DLB 93

Box, Edgar
See Vidal, Gore
See also GLL 1

Boyd, James 1888-1944 **TCLC 115**
See also CA 186; DLB 9; DLBD 16; RGAL 4; RHW

Boyd, Nancy
See Millay, Edna St. Vincent
See also GLL 1

Boyd, Thomas (Alexander) 1898-1935 **TCLC 111**
See also CA 111; 183; DLB 9; DLBD 16

Boyd, William 1952- **CLC 28, 53, 70**
See also CA 114; 120; CANR 51, 71; CN 7; DLB 231

Boyesen, Hjalmar Hjorth 1848-1895 **NCLC 135**
See also DLB 12, 71; DLBD 13; RGAL 4

Boyle, Kay 1902-1992 **CLC 1, 5, 19, 58, 121; SSC 5**
See also CA 13-16R; 140; CAAS 1; CANR 29, 61, 110; DLB 4, 9, 48, 86; DLBY 1993; EWL 3; MTCW 1, 2; RGAL 4; RGSF 2; SSFS 10, 13, 14

Boyle, Mark
See Kienzle, William X(avier)

Boyle, Patrick 1905-1982 **CLC 19**
See also CA 127

Boyle, T. C.
See Boyle, T(homas) Coraghessan
See also AMWS 8

Boyle, T(homas) Coraghessan 1948- **CLC 36, 55, 90; SSC 16**
See Boyle, T. C.
See also AAYA 47; BEST 90:4; BPFB 1; CA 120; CANR 44, 76, 89; CN 7; CPW; DA3; DAM POP; DLB 218, 278; DLBY 1986; EWL 3; MTCW 2; SSFS 13, 19

Boz
See Dickens, Charles (John Huffam)

Brackenridge, Hugh Henry 1748-1816 **NCLC 7**
See also DLB 11, 37; RGAL 4

Bradbury, Edward P.
See Moorcock, Michael (John)
See also MTCW 2

Bradbury, Malcolm (Stanley) 1932-2000 **CLC 32, 61**
See also CA 1-4R; CANR 1, 33, 91, 98; CN 7; DA3; DAM NOV; DLB 14, 207; EWL 3; MTCW 1, 2

Bradbury, Ray (Douglas) 1920- **CLC 1, 3, 10, 15, 42, 98; SSC 29, 53; WLC**
See also AAYA 15; AITN 1, 2; AMWS 4; BPFB 1; BYA 4, 5, 11; CA 1-4R; CANR 2, 30, 75, 125; CDALB 1968-1988; CN 7; CPW; DA; DA3; DAB; DAC; DAM MST, NOV, POP; DLB 2, 8; EXPN; EXPS; HGG; LAIT 3, 5; LATS 1; LMFS 2; MTCW 1, 2; NFS 1; RGAL 4; RGSF 2; SATA 11, 64, 123; SCFW 2; SFW 4; SSFS 1; SUFW 1, 2; TUS; YAW

Braddon, Mary Elizabeth 1837-1915 **TCLC 111**
See also BRWS 8; CA 108; 179; CMW 4; DLB 18, 70, 156; HGG

Bradfield, Scott (Michael) 1955- **SSC 65**
See also CA 147; CANR 90; HGG; SUFW 2

Bradford, Gamaliel 1863-1932 **TCLC 36**
See also CA 160; DLB 17

Bradford, William 1590-1657 **LC 64**
See also DLB 24, 30; RGAL 4

Bradley, David (Henry), Jr. 1950- **BLC 1; CLC 23, 118**
See also BW 1, 3; CA 104; CANR 26, 81; CN 7; DAM MULT; DLB 33

Bradley, John Ed(mund, Jr.) 1958- **CLC 55**
See also CA 139; CANR 99; CN 7; CSW

Bradley, Marion Zimmer 1930-1999 **CLC 30**
See Chapman, Lee; Dexter, John; Gardner, Miriam; Ives, Morgan; Rivers, Elfrida
See also AAYA 40; BPFB 1; CA 57-60; 185; CAAS 10; CANR 7, 31, 51, 75, 107; CPW; DA3; DAM POP; DLB 8; FANT; FW; MTCW 1, 2; SATA 90, 139; SATA-Obit 116; SFW 4; SUFW 2; YAW

Bradshaw, John 1933- **CLC 70**
See also CA 138; CANR 61

Bradstreet, Anne 1612(?)-1672 **LC 4, 30; PC 10**
See also AMWS 1; CDALB 1640-1865; DA; DA3; DAC; DAM MST, POET; DLB 24; EXPP; FW; PFS 6; RGAL 4; TUS; WP

Brady, Joan 1939- **CLC 86**
See also CA 141

Bragg, Melvyn 1939- **CLC 10**
See also BEST 89:3; CA 57-60; CANR 10, 48, 89; CN 7; DLB 14, 271; RHW

Brahe, Tycho 1546-1601 **LC 45**

Braine, John (Gerard) 1922-1986 **CLC 1, 3, 41**
See also CA 1-4R; 120; CANR 1, 33; CD-BLB 1945-1960; DLB 15; DLBY 1986; EWL 3; MTCW 1

Braithwaite, William Stanley (Beaumont) 1878-1962 **BLC 1; HR 2; PC 52**
See also BW 1; CA 125; DAM MULT; DLB 50, 54

Bramah, Ernest 1868-1942 **TCLC 72**
See also CA 156; CMW 4; DLB 70; FANT

Brammer, William 1930(?)-1978 **CLC 31**
See also CA 77-80

Brancati, Vitaliano 1907-1954 **TCLC 12**
See also CA 109; DLB 264; EWL 3

Brancato, Robin F(idler) 1936- **CLC 35**
See also AAYA 9; BYA 6; CA 69-72; CANR 11, 45; CLR 32; JRDA; MAICYA 2; MAICYAS 1; SAAS 9; SATA 97; WYA; YAW

Brand, Max
See Faust, Frederick (Schiller)
See also BPFB 1; TCWW 2

Brand, Millen 1906-1980 **CLC 7**
See also CA 21-24R; 97-100; CANR 72

Branden, Barbara CLC 44
See also CA 148

Brandes, Georg (Morris Cohen) 1842-1927 **TCLC 10**
See also CA 105; 189

Brandys, Kazimierz 1916-2000 **CLC 62**
See also EWL 3

Branley, Franklyn M(ansfield) 1915-2002 **CLC 21**
See also CA 33-36R; 207; CANR 14, 39; CLR 13; MAICYA 1, 2; SAAS 16; SATA 4, 68, 136

Brant, Beth (E.) 1941- **NNAL**
See also CA 144; FW

Brathwaite, Edward Kamau 1930- **BLCS; CLC 11; PC 56**
See also BW 2, 3; CA 25-28R; CANR 11, 26, 47, 107; CDWLB 3; CP 7; DAM POET; DLB 125; EWL 3

Brathwaite, Kamau
See Brathwaite, Edward Kamau

Brautigan, Richard (Gary) 1935-1984 **CLC 1, 3, 5, 9, 12, 34, 42; TCLC 133**
See also BPFB 1; CA 53-56; 113; CANR 34; DA3; DAM NOV; DLB 2, 5, 206; DLBY 1980, 1984; FANT; MTCW 1; RGAL 4; SATA 56

Brave Bird, Mary NNAL
See Crow Dog, Mary (Ellen)

Braverman, Kate 1950- **CLC 67**
See also CA 89-92

Brecht, (Eugen) Bertolt (Friedrich) 1898-1956 **DC 3; TCLC 1, 6, 13, 35; WLC**
See also CA 104; 133; CANR 62; CDWLB 2; DA; DA3; DAB; DAC; DAM DRAM, MST; DFS 4, 5, 9; DLB 56, 124; EW 11; EWL 3; IDTP; MTCW 1, 2; RGWL 2, 3; TWA

Brecht, Eugen Berthold Friedrich
See Brecht, (Eugen) Bertolt (Friedrich)

Bremer, Fredrika 1801-1865 **NCLC 11**
See also DLB 254

Brennan, Christopher John 1870-1932 **TCLC 17**
See also CA 117; 188; DLB 230; EWL 3

Brennan, Maeve 1917-1993 **CLC 5; TCLC 124**
See also CA 81-84; CANR 72, 100

Brent, Linda
See Jacobs, Harriet A(nn)

Brentano, Clemens (Maria) 1778-1842 **NCLC 1**
See also DLB 90; RGWL 2, 3

Brent of Bin Bin
See Franklin, (Stella Maria Sarah) Miles (Lampe)

Brenton, Howard 1942- **CLC 31**
See also CA 69-72; CANR 33, 67; CBD; CD 5; DLB 13; MTCW 1

Breslin, James 1930-
See Breslin, Jimmy
See also CA 73-76; CANR 31, 75; DAM NOV; MTCW 1, 2

Breslin, Jimmy CLC 4, 43
See Breslin, James
See also AITN 1; DLB 185; MTCW 2

Bresson, Robert 1901(?)-1999 **CLC 16**
See also CA 110; 187; CANR 49

Breton, Andre 1896-1966 **CLC 2, 9, 15, 54; PC 15**
See also CA 19-20; 25-28R; CANR 40, 60; CAP 2; DLB 65, 258; EW 11; EWL 3; GFL 1789 to the Present; LMFS 2; MTCW 1, 2; RGWL 2, 3; TWA; WP

Breytenbach, Breyten 1939(?)- **CLC 23, 37, 126**
See also CA 113; 129; CANR 61, 122; CWW 2; DAM POET; DLB 225; EWL 3

Bridgers, Sue Ellen 1942- **CLC 26**
See also AAYA 8, 49; BYA 7, 8; CA 65-68; CANR 11, 36; CLR 18; DLB 52; JRDA; MAICYA 1, 2; SAAS 1; SATA 22, 90; SATA-Essay 109; WYA; YAW

Bridges, Robert (Seymour) 1844-1930 **PC 28; TCLC 1**
See also BRW 6; CA 104; 152; CDBLB 1890-1914; DAM POET; DLB 19, 98

Bridie, James TCLC 3
See Mavor, Osborne Henry
See also DLB 10; EWL 3

Brin, David 1950- **CLC 34**
See also AAYA 21; CA 102; CANR 24, 70, 125, 127; INT CANR-24; SATA 65; SCFW 2; SFW 4

Brink, Andre (Philippus) 1935- **CLC 18, 36, 106**
See also AFW; BRWS 6; CA 104; CANR 39, 62, 109; CN 7; DLB 225; EWL 3; INT CA-103; LATS 1; MTCW 1, 2; WLIT 2

Brinsmead, H. F(ay)
See Brinsmead, H(esba) F(ay)

Brinsmead, H. F.
See Brinsmead, H(esba) F(ay)

Brinsmead, H(esba) F(ay) 1922- **CLC 21**
See also CA 21-24R; CANR 10; CLR 47; CWRI 5; MAICYA 1, 2; SAAS 5; SATA 18, 78

Brittain, Vera (Mary) 1893(?)-1970 **CLC 23**
See also CA 13-16; 25-28R; CANR 58; CAP 1; DLB 191; FW; MTCW 1, 2

Broch, Hermann 1886-1951 **TCLC 20**
See also CA 117; 211; CDWLB 2; DLB 85, 124; EW 10; EWL 3; RGWL 2, 3

Brock, Rose
See Hansen, Joseph
See also GLL 1

Brod, Max 1884-1968 **TCLC 115**
See also CA 5-8R; 25-28R; CANR 7; DLB 81; EWL 3

Brodkey, Harold (Roy) 1930-1996 **CLC 56; TCLC 123**
See also CA 111; 151; CANR 71; CN 7; DLB 130

Brodsky, Iosif Alexandrovich 1940-1996
See Brodsky, Joseph
See also AITN 1; CA 41-44R; 151; CANR 37, 106; DA3; DAM POET; MTCW 1, 2; RGWL 2, 3

Brodsky, Joseph CLC 4, 6, 13, 36, 100; PC 9
See Brodsky, Iosif Alexandrovich
See also AMWS 8; CWW 2; DLB 285; EWL 3; MTCW 1

Brodsky, Michael (Mark) 1948- **CLC 19**
See also CA 102; CANR 18, 41, 58; DLB 244

Brodzki, Bella ed. CLC 65

Brome, Richard 1590(?)-1652 **LC 61**
See also DLB 58

Bromell, Henry 1947- **CLC 5**
See also CA 53-56; CANR 9, 115, 116

Bromfield, Louis (Brucker) 1896-1956 **TCLC 11**
See also CA 107; 155; DLB 4, 9, 86; RGAL 4; RHW

Broner, E(sther) M(asserman) 1930- **CLC 19**
See also CA 17-20R; CANR 8, 25, 72; CN 7; DLB 28

Bronk, William (M.) 1918-1999 **CLC 10**
See also CA 89-92; 177; CANR 23; CP 7; DLB 165

Bronstein, Lev Davidovich
See Trotsky, Leon

Bronte, Anne 1820-1849 **NCLC 4, 71, 102**
See also BRW 5; BRWR 1; DA3; DLB 21, 199; TEA

Bronte, (Patrick) Branwell 1817-1848 **NCLC 109**
See also BRW 5; BRWC 1; BRWR 1; BYA 2; CDBLB 1832-1890; DA; DA3; DAB; DAC; DAM MST, NOV; DLB 21, 159, 199; EXPN; LAIT 2; NFS 4; TEA; WLIT 4

Bronte, Charlotte 1816-1855 **NCLC 3, 8, 33, 58, 105; WLC**
See also AAYA 17; BRW 5; BRWC 1; BRWR 1; BYA 2; CDBLB 1832-1890; DA; DA3; DAB; DAC; DAM MST, NOV; DLB 21, 159, 199; EXPN; LAIT 2; NFS 4; TEA; WLIT 4

Bronte, Emily (Jane) 1818-1848 **NCLC 16, 35; PC 8; WLC**
See also AAYA 17; BPFB 1; BRW 5; BRWC 1; BRWR 1; BYA 3; CDBLB 1832-1890; DA; DA3; DAB; DAC; DAM MST, NOV, POET; DLB 21, 32, 199; EXPN; LAIT 1; TEA; WLIT 3

Brontes
See Bronte, Anne; Bronte, Charlotte; Bronte, Emily (Jane)

Brooke, Frances 1724-1789 **LC 6, 48**
See also DLB 39, 99

Brooke, Henry 1703(?)-1783 **LC 1**
See also DLB 39

Brooke, Rupert (Chawner) 1887-1915 **PC 24; TCLC 2, 7; WLC**
See also BRWS 3; CA 104; 132; CANR 61; CDBLB 1914-1945; DA; DAB; DAC; DAM MST, POET; DLB 19, 216; EXPP; GLL 2; MTCW 1, 2; PFS 7; TEA

Brooke-Haven, P.
See Wodehouse, P(elham) G(renville)

Brooke-Rose, Christine 1926(?)- **CLC 40, 184**
See also BRWS 4; CA 13-16R; CANR 58, 118; CN 7; DLB 14, 231; EWL 3; SFW 4

Brookner, Anita 1928- **CLC 32, 34, 51, 136**
See also BRWS 4; CA 114; 120; CANR 37, 56, 87; CN 7; CPW; DA3; DAB; DAM POP; DLB 194; DLBY 1987; EWL 3; MTCW 1, 2; TEA

Brooks, Cleanth 1906-1994 **CLC 24, 86, 110**
See also CA 17-20R; 145; CANR 33, 35; CSW; DLB 63; DLBY 1994; EWL 3; INT CANR-35; MTCW 1, 2

Brooks, George
See Baum, L(yman) Frank

Brooks, Gwendolyn (Elizabeth) 1917-2000 **BLC 1; CLC 1, 2, 4, 5, 15, 49, 125; PC 7; WLC**
See also AAYA 20; AFAW 1, 2; AITN 1; AMWS 3; BW 2, 3; CA 1-4R; 190; CANR 1, 27, 52, 75; CDALB 1941-1968; CLR 27; CP 7; CWP; DA; DA3; DAC; DAM MST, MULT, POET; DLB 5, 76, 165; EWL 3; EXPP; MAWW; MTCW 1, 2; PFS 1, 2, 4, 6; RGAL 4; SATA 6; SATA-Obit 123; TUS; WP

Brooks, Mel CLC 12
See Kaminsky, Melvin
See also AAYA 13, 48; DLB 26

Brooks, Peter (Preston) 1938- **CLC 34**
See also CA 45-48; CANR 1, 107

Brooks, Van Wyck 1886-1963 **CLC 29**
See also AMW; CA 1-4R; CANR 6; DLB 45, 63, 103; TUS

Brophy, Brigid (Antonia) 1929-1995 **CLC 6, 11, 29, 105**
See also CA 5-8R; 149; CAAS 4; CANR 25, 53; CBD; CN 7; CWD; DA3; DLB 14, 271; EWL 3; MTCW 1, 2

Brosman, Catharine Savage 1934- **CLC 9**
See also CA 61-64; CANR 21, 46

Brossard, Nicole 1943- **CLC 115, 169**
See also CA 122; CAAS 16; CCA 1; CWP; CWW 2; DLB 53; EWL 3; FW; GLL 2; RGWL 3

Brother Antoninus
See Everson, William (Oliver)

The Brothers Quay
See Quay, Stephen; Quay, Timothy

Broughton, T(homas) Alan 1936- **CLC 19**
See also CA 45-48; CANR 2, 23, 48, 111

Broumas, Olga 1949- **CLC 10, 73**
See also CA 85-88; CANR 20, 69, 110; CP 7; CWP; GLL 2

Broun, Heywood 1888-1939 **TCLC 104**
See also DLB 29, 171

Brown, Alan 1950- **CLC 99**
See also CA 156

Brown, Charles Brockden 1771-1810 **NCLC 22, 74, 122**
See also AMWS 1; CDALB 1640-1865; DLB 37, 59, 73; FW; HGG; LMFS 1; RGAL 4; TUS

Brown, Christy 1932-1981 **CLC 63**
See also BYA 13; CA 105; 104; CANR 72; DLB 14

Brown, Claude 1937-2002 **BLC 1; CLC 30**
See also AAYA 7; BW 1, 3; CA 73-76; 205; CANR 81; DAM MULT

Brown, Dee (Alexander) 1908-2002 **CLC 18, 47**
See also AAYA 30; CA 13-16R; 212; CAAS 6; CANR 11, 45, 60; CPW; CSW; DA3; DAM POP; DLBY 1980; LAIT 2; MTCW 1, 2; NCFS 5; SATA 5, 110; SATA-Obit 141; TCWW 2

Brown, George
See Wertmueller, Lina

Brown, George Douglas 1869-1902 **TCLC 28**
See Douglas, George
See also CA 162

Brown, George Mackay 1921-1996 **CLC 5, 48, 100**
See also BRWS 6; CA 21-24R; 151; CAAS 6; CANR 12, 37, 67; CN 7; CP 7; DLB 14, 27, 139, 271; MTCW 1; RGSF 2; SATA 35

Brown, (William) Larry 1951- **CLC 73**
See also CA 130; 134; CANR 117; CSW; DLB 234; INT CA-134

Brown, Moses
See Barrett, William (Christopher)

Brown, Rita Mae 1944- **CLC 18, 43, 79**
See also BPFB 1; CA 45-48; CANR 2, 11, 35, 62, 95; CN 7; CPW; CSW; DA3; DAM NOV, POP; FW; INT CANR-11; MTCW 1, 2; NFS 9; RGAL 4; TUS

Brown, Roderick (Langmere) Haig-
See Haig-Brown, Roderick (Langmere)

Brown, Rosellen 1939- **CLC 32, 170**
See also CA 77-80; CAAS 10; CANR 14, 44, 98; CN 7

Brown, Sterling Allen 1901-1989 **BLC 1; CLC 1, 23, 59; HR 2; PC 55**
See also AFAW 1, 2; BW 1, 3; CA 85-88; 127; CANR 26; DA3; DAM MULT, POET; DLB 48, 51, 63; MTCW 1, 2; RGAL 4; WP

Brown, Will
See Ainsworth, William Harrison

Brown, William Hill 1765-1793 **LC 93**
See also DLB 37

Brown, William Wells 1815-1884 **BLC 1; DC 1; NCLC 2, 89**
See also DAM MULT; DLB 3, 50, 183, 248; RGAL 4

Browne, (Clyde) Jackson 1948(?)- **CLC 21**
See also CA 120

Browning, Elizabeth Barrett 1806-1861 **NCLC 1, 16, 61, 66; PC 6; WLC**
See also BRW 4; CDBLB 1832-1890; DA; DA3; DAB; DAC; DAM MST, POET; DLB 32, 199; EXPP; PAB; PFS 2, 16; TEA; WLIT 4; WP

Browning, Robert 1812-1889 **NCLC 19, 79; PC 2; WLCS**
See also BRW 4; BRWC 2; BRWR 2; CD-BLB 1832-1890; CLR 97; DA; DA3; DAB; DAC; DAM MST, POET; DLB 32, 163; EXPP; LATS 1; PAB; PFS 1, 15; RGEL 2; TEA; WLIT 4; WP; YABC 1

Browning, Tod 1882-1962 **CLC 16**
See also CA 141; 117

Brownmiller, Susan 1935- **CLC 159**
See also CA 103; CANR 35, 75; DAM NOV; FW; MTCW 1, 2

Brownson, Orestes Augustus 1803-1876 **NCLC 50**
See also DLB 1, 59, 73, 243

Bruccoli, Matthew J(oseph) 1931- **CLC 34**
See also CA 9-12R; CANR 7, 87; DLB 103

Bruce, Lenny CLC 21
See Schneider, Leonard Alfred

Bruchac, Joseph III 1942- **NNAL**
See also AAYA 19; CA 33-36R; CANR 13, 47, 75, 94; CLR 46; CWRI 5; DAM MULT; JRDA; MAICYA 2; MAICYAS 1; MTCW 1; SATA 42, 89, 131

Bruin, John
See Brutus, Dennis

Brulard, Henri
See Stendhal

Brulls, Christian
See Simenon, Georges (Jacques Christian)

Brunner, John (Kilian Houston) 1934-1995 **CLC 8, 10**
See also CA 1-4R; 149; CAAS 8; CANR 2, 37; CPW; DAM POP; DLB 261; MTCW 1, 2; SCFW 2; SFW 4

Bruno, Giordano 1548-1600 **LC 27**
See also RGWL 2, 3

Brutus, Dennis 1924- **BLC 1; CLC 43; PC 24**
See also AFW; BW 2, 3; CA 49-52; CAAS 14; CANR 2, 27, 42, 81; CDWLB 3; CP 7; DAM MULT, POET; DLB 117, 225; EWL 3

Bryan, C(ourtlandt) D(ixon) B(arnes) 1936- **CLC 29**
See also CA 73-76; CANR 13, 68; DLB 185; INT CANR-13

Bryan, Michael
See Moore, Brian
See also CCA 1

Bryan, William Jennings 1860-1925 **TCLC 99**

Bryant, William Cullen 1794-1878 **NCLC 6, 46; PC 20**
See also AMWS 1; CDALB 1640-1865; DA; DAB; DAC; DAM MST, POET; DLB 3, 43, 59, 189, 250; EXPP; PAB; RGAL 4; TUS

Bryusov, Valery Yakovlevich 1873-1924 **TCLC 10**
See also CA 107; 155; EWL 3; SFW 4

Buchan, John 1875-1940 **TCLC 41**
See also CA 108; 145; CMW 4; DAB; DAM POP; DLB 34, 70, 156; HGG; MSW; MTCW 1; RGEL 2; RHW; YABC 2

Buchanan, George 1506-1582 **LC 4**
See also DLB 132

Buchanan, Robert 1841-1901 **TCLC 107**
See also CA 179; DLB 18, 35

Buchheim, Lothar-Guenther 1918- **CLC 6**
See also CA 85-88

Buchner, (Karl) Georg 1813-1837 **NCLC 26**
See also CDWLB 2; DLB 133; EW 6; RGSF 2; RGWL 2, 3; TWA

Buchwald, Art(hur) 1925- **CLC 33**
See also AITN 1; CA 5-8R; CANR 21, 67, 107; MTCW 1, 2; SATA 10

Buck, Pearl S(ydenstricker) 1892-1973 **CLC 7, 11, 18, 127**
See also AAYA 42; AITN 1; AMWS 2; BPFB 1; CA 1-4R; 41-44R; CANR 1, 34; CDALBS; DA; DA3; DAB; DAC; DAM MST, NOV; DLB 9, 102; EWL 3; LAIT 3; MTCW 1, 2; RGAL 4; RHW; SATA 1, 25; TUS

Buckler, Ernest 1908-1984 **CLC 13**
See also CA 11-12; 114; CAP 1; CCA 1; DAC; DAM MST; DLB 68; SATA 47

Buckley, Christopher (Taylor) 1952- **CLC 165**
See also CA 139; CANR 119

Buckley, Vincent (Thomas) 1925-1988 **CLC 57**
See also CA 101; DLB 289

Buckley, William F(rank), Jr. 1925- **CLC 7, 18, 37**
See also AITN 1; BPFB 1; CA 1-4R; CANR 1, 24, 53, 93; CMW 4; CPW; DA3; DAM POP; DLB 137; DLBY 1980; INT CANR-24; MTCW 1, 2; TUS

Buechner, (Carl) Frederick 1926- **CLC 2, 4, 6, 9**
See also AMWS 12; BPFB 1; CA 13-16R; CANR 11, 39, 64, 114; CN 7; DAM NOV; DLBY 1980; INT CANR-11; MTCW 1, 2

Buell, John (Edward) 1927- **CLC 10**
See also CA 1-4R; CANR 71; DLB 53

Buero Vallejo, Antonio 1916-2000 **CLC 15, 46, 139; DC 18**
See also CA 106; 189; CANR 24, 49, 75; CWW 2; DFS 11; EWL 3; HW 1; MTCW 1, 2

Bufalino, Gesualdo 1920-1996 **CLC 74**
See also CWW 2; DLB 196

Bugayev, Boris Nikolayevich 1880-1934 **PC 11; TCLC 7**
See Bely, Andrey; Belyi, Andrei
See also CA 104; 165; MTCW 1

Bukowski, Charles 1920-1994 **CLC 2, 5, 9, 41, 82, 108; PC 18; SSC 45**
See also CA 17-20R; 144; CANR 40, 62, 105; CPW; DA3; DAM NOV, POET; DLB 5, 130, 169; EWL 3; MTCW 1, 2

Bulgakov, Mikhail (Afanas'evich) 1891-1940 **SSC 18; TCLC 2, 16**
See also BPFB 1; CA 105; 152; DAM DRAM, NOV; DLB 272; EWL 3; NFS 8; RGSF 2; RGWL 2, 3; SFW 4; TWA

Bulgya, Alexander Alexandrovich 1901-1956 **TCLC 53**
See Fadeev, Aleksandr Aleksandrovich; Fadeev, Alexandr Alexandrovich; Fadeyev, Alexander
See also CA 117; 181

Bullins, Ed 1935- **BLC 1; CLC 1, 5, 7; DC 6**
See also BW 2, 3; CA 49-52; CAAS 16; CAD; CANR 24, 46, 73; CD 5; DAM DRAM, MULT; DLB 7, 38, 249; EWL 3; MTCW 1, 2; RGAL 4

Bulosan, Carlos 1911-1956 **AAL**
See also CA 216; RGAL 4

Bulwer-Lytton, Edward (George Earle Lytton) 1803-1873 **NCLC 1, 45**
See also DLB 21; RGEL 2; SFW 4; SUFW 1; TEA

Bunin, Ivan Alexeyevich 1870-1953 **SSC 5; TCLC 6**
See also CA 104; EWL 3; RGSF 2; RGWL 2, 3; TWA

Bunting, Basil 1900-1985 **CLC 10, 39, 47**
See also BRWS 7; CA 53-56; 115; CANR 7; DAM POET; DLB 20; EWL 3; RGEL 2

Bunuel, Luis 1900-1983 **CLC 16, 80; HLC 1**
See also CA 101; 110; CANR 32, 77; DAM MULT; HW 1

Bunyan, John 1628-1688 **LC 4, 69; WLC**
See also BRW 2; BYA 5; CDBLB 1660-1789; DA; DAB; DAC; DAM MST; DLB 39; RGEL 2; TEA; WCH; WLIT 3

Buravsky, Alexandr CLC 59

Burckhardt, Jacob (Christoph) 1818-1897 **NCLC 49**
See also EW 6

Burford, Eleanor
See Hibbert, Eleanor Alice Burford

Burgess, Anthony CLC 1, 2, 4, 5, 8, 10, 13, 15, 22, 40, 62, 81, 94
See Wilson, John (Anthony) Burgess
See also AAYA 25; AITN 1; BRWS 1; CD-BLB 1960 to Present; DAB; DLB 14, 194, 261; DLBY 1998; EWL 3; MTCW 1; RGEL 2; RHW; SFW 4; YAW

Burke, Edmund 1729(?)-1797 **LC 7, 36; WLC**
See also BRW 3; DA; DA3; DAB; DAC; DAM MST; DLB 104, 252; RGEL 2; TEA

Burke, Kenneth (Duva) 1897-1993 **CLC 2, 24**
See also AMW; CA 5-8R; 143; CANR 39, 74; DLB 45, 63; EWL 3; MTCW 1, 2; RGAL 4

Burke, Leda
See Garnett, David

Burke, Ralph
See Silverberg, Robert

Burke, Thomas 1886-1945 **TCLC 63**
See also CA 113; 155; CMW 4; DLB 197

Burney, Fanny 1752-1840 **NCLC 12, 54, 107**
See also BRWS 3; DLB 39; NFS 16; RGEL 2; TEA

Burney, Frances
See Burney, Fanny

Burns, Robert 1759-1796 **LC 3, 29, 40; PC 6; WLC**
See also AAYA 51; BRW 3; CDBLB 1789-1832; DA; DA3; DAB; DAC; DAM MST, POET; DLB 109; EXPP; PAB; RGEL 2; TEA; WP

Burns, Tex
See L'Amour, Louis (Dearborn)
See also TCWW 2

Burnshaw, Stanley 1906- **CLC 3, 13, 44**
See also CA 9-12R; CP 7; DLB 48; DLBY 1997

Burr, Anne 1937- **CLC 6**
See also CA 25-28R

Burroughs, Edgar Rice 1875-1950 **TCLC 2, 32**
See also AAYA 11; BPFB 1; BYA 4, 9; CA 104; 132; DA3; DAM NOV; DLB 8; FANT; MTCW 1, 2; RGAL 4; SATA 41; SCFW 2; SFW 4; TUS; YAW

Burroughs, William S(eward) 1914-1997 **CLC 1, 2, 5, 15, 22, 42, 75, 109; TCLC 121; WLC**
See Lee, William; Lee, Willy
See also AITN 2; AMWS 3; BG 2; BPFB 1; CA 9-12R; 160; CANR 20, 52, 104; CN 7; CPW; DA; DA3; DAB; DAC; DAM MST, NOV, POP; DLB 2, 8, 16, 152, 237; DLBY 1981, 1997; EWL 3; HGG; LMFS 2; MTCW 1, 2; RGAL 4; SFW 4

Burton, Sir Richard F(rancis) 1821-1890 **NCLC 42**
See also DLB 55, 166, 184

Burton, Robert 1577-1640 **LC 74**
See also DLB 151; RGEL 2

Buruma, Ian 1951- **CLC 163**
See also CA 128; CANR 65

Busch, Frederick 1941- **CLC 7, 10, 18, 47, 166**
See also CA 33-36R; CAAS 1; CANR 45, 73, 92; CN 7; DLB 6, 218

Bush, Barney (Furman) 1946- **NNAL**
See also CA 145

Bush, Ronald 1946- **CLC 34**
See also CA 136

Bustos, F(rancisco)
See Borges, Jorge Luis

Bustos Domecq, H(onorio)
See Bioy Casares, Adolfo; Borges, Jorge Luis

Butler, Octavia E(stelle) 1947- **BLCS; CLC 38, 121**
See also AAYA 18, 48; AFAW 2; AMWS 13; BPFB 1; BW 2, 3; CA 73-76; CANR 12, 24, 38, 73; CLR 65; CPW; DA3; DAM MULT, POP; DLB 33; LATS 1; MTCW 1, 2; NFS 8; SATA 84; SCFW 2; SFW 4; SSFS 6; YAW

Butler, Robert Olen, (Jr.) 1945- **CLC 81, 162**
See also AMWS 12; BPFB 1; CA 112; CANR 66; CSW; DAM POP; DLB 173; INT CA-112; MTCW 1; SSFS 11

Butler, Samuel 1612-1680 **LC 16, 43**
See also DLB 101, 126; RGEL 2

Butler, Samuel 1835-1902 **TCLC 1, 33; WLC**
See also BRWS 2; CA 143; CDBLB 1890-1914; DA; DA3; DAB; DAC; DAM MST, NOV; DLB 18, 57, 174; RGEL 2; SFW 4; TEA

Butler, Walter C.
See Faust, Frederick (Schiller)

Butor, Michel (Marie Francois) 1926- **CLC 1, 3, 8, 11, 15, 161**
See also CA 9-12R; CANR 33, 66; CWW 2; DLB 83; EW 13; EWL 3; GFL 1789 to the Present; MTCW 1, 2

Butts, Mary 1890(?)-1937 **TCLC 77**
See also CA 148; DLB 240

Buxton, Ralph
See Silverstein, Alvin; Silverstein, Virginia B(arbara Opshelor)

Buzo, Alex
See Buzo, Alexander (John)
See also DLB 289

Buzo, Alexander (John) 1944- **CLC 61**
See also CA 97-100; CANR 17, 39, 69; CD 5

Buzzati, Dino 1906-1972 **CLC 36**
See also CA 160; 33-36R; DLB 177; RGWL 2, 3; SFW 4

Byars, Betsy (Cromer) 1928- **CLC 35**
See also AAYA 19; BYA 3; CA 33-36R, 183; CAAE 183; CANR 18, 36, 57, 102; CLR 1, 16, 72; DLB 52; INT CANR-18; JRDA; MAICYA 1, 2; MAICYAS 1; MTCW 1; SAAS 1; SATA 4, 46, 80; SATA-Essay 108; WYA; YAW

Byatt, A(ntonia) S(usan Drabble) 1936- **CLC 19, 65, 136**
See also BPFB 1; BRWC 2; BRWS 4; CA 13-16R; CANR 13, 33, 50, 75, 96; DA3; DAM NOV, POP; DLB 14, 194; EWL 3; MTCW 1, 2; RGSF 2; RHW; TEA

Byrne, David 1952- **CLC 26**
See also CA 127

Byrne, John Keyes 1926-
See Leonard, Hugh
See also CA 102; CANR 78; INT CA-102

Byron, George Gordon (Noel) 1788-1824 **NCLC 2, 12, 109; PC 16; WLC**
See also BRW 4; BRWC 2; CDBLB 1789-1832; DA; DA3; DAB; DAC; DAM MST, POET; DLB 96, 110; EXPP; LMFS 1; PAB; PFS 1, 14; RGEL 2; TEA; WLIT 3; WP

Byron, Robert 1905-1941 **TCLC 67**
See also CA 160; DLB 195

C. 3. 3.
See Wilde, Oscar (Fingal O'Flahertie Wills)

Caballero, Fernan 1796-1877 **NCLC 10**

Cabell, Branch
See Cabell, James Branch

Cabell, James Branch 1879-1958 **TCLC 6**
See also CA 105; 152; DLB 9, 78; FANT; MTCW 1; RGAL 4; SUFW 1

Cabeza de Vaca, Alvar Nunez 1490-1557(?) **LC 61**

Cable, George Washington 1844-1925 **SSC 4; TCLC 4**
See also CA 104; 155; DLB 12, 74; DLBD 13; RGAL 4; TUS

Cabral de Melo Neto, Joao 1920-1999 **CLC 76**
See Melo Neto, Joao Cabral de
See also CA 151; DAM MULT; LAW; LAWS 1

Cabrera Infante, G(uillermo) 1929- **CLC 5, 25, 45, 120; HLC 1; SSC 39**
See also CA 85-88; CANR 29, 65, 110; CD-WLB 3; CWW 2; DA3; DAM MULT; DLB 113; EWL 3; HW 1, 2; LAW; LAWS 1; MTCW 1, 2; RGSF 2; WLIT 1

Cade, Toni
See Bambara, Toni Cade

Cadmus and Harmonia
See Buchan, John

Caedmon fl. 658-680 **CMLC 7**
See also DLB 146

Caeiro, Alberto
 See Pessoa, Fernando (Antonio Nogueira)
Caesar, Julius CMLC 47
 See Julius Caesar
 See also AW 1; RGWL 2, 3
Cage, John (Milton, Jr.) 1912-1992 CLC 41
 See also CA 13-16R; 169; CANR 9, 78;
 DLB 193; INT CANR-9
Cahan, Abraham 1860-1951 TCLC 71
 See also CA 108; 154; DLB 9, 25, 28;
 RGAL 4
Cain, G.
 See Cabrera Infante, G(uillermo)
Cain, Guillermo
 See Cabrera Infante, G(uillermo)
**Cain, James M(allahan) 1892-1977 CLC 3,
 11, 28**
 See also AITN 1; BPFB 1; CA 17-20R; 73-
 76; CANR 8, 34, 61; CMW 4; DLB 226;
 EWL 3; MSW; MTCW 1; RGAL 4
Caine, Hall 1853-1931 TCLC 97
 See also RHW
Caine, Mark
 See Raphael, Frederic (Michael)
Calasso, Roberto 1941- CLC 81
 See also CA 143; CANR 89
**Calderon de la Barca, Pedro 1600-1681 DC
 3; HLCS 1; LC 23**
 See also EW 2; RGWL 2, 3; TWA
**Caldwell, Erskine (Preston) 1903-1987 CLC
 1, 8, 14, 50, 60; SSC 19; TCLC 117**
 See also AITN 1; AMW; BPFB 1; CA 1-4R;
 121; CAAS 1; CANR 2, 33; DA3; DAM
 NOV; DLB 9, 86; EWL 3; MTCW 1, 2;
 RGAL 4; RGSF 2; TUS
**Caldwell, (Janet Miriam) Taylor (Holland)
 1900-1985 CLC 2, 28, 39**
 See also BPFB 1; CA 5-8R; 116; CANR 5;
 DA3; DAM NOV, POP; DLBD 17; RHW
Calhoun, John Caldwell 1782-1850 NCLC 15
 See also DLB 3, 248
**Calisher, Hortense 1911- CLC 2, 4, 8, 38,
 134; SSC 15**
 See also CA 1-4R; CANR 1, 22, 117; CN
 7; DA3; DAM NOV; DLB 2, 218; INT
 CANR-22; MTCW 1, 2; RGAL 4; RGSF
 2
**Callaghan, Morley Edward 1903-1990 CLC
 3, 14, 41, 65; TCLC 145**
 See also CA 9-12R; 132; CANR 33, 73;
 DAC; DAM MST; DLB 68; EWL 3;
 MTCW 1, 2; RGEL 2; RGSF 2; SSFS 19
Callimachus c. 305B.C.-c. 240B.C. CMLC 18
 See also AW 1; DLB 176; RGWL 2, 3
Calvin, Jean
 See Calvin, John
 See also GFL Beginnings to 1789
Calvin, John 1509-1564 LC 37
 See Calvin, Jean
**Calvino, Italo 1923-1985 CLC 5, 8, 11, 22,
 33, 39, 73; SSC 3, 48**
 See also CA 85-88; 116; CANR 23, 61;
 DAM NOV; DLB 196; EW 13; EWL 3;
 MTCW 1, 2; RGSF 2; RGWL 2, 3; SFW
 4; SSFS 12
Camara Laye
 See Laye, Camara
 See also EWL 3
Camden, William 1551-1623 LC 77
 See also DLB 172
Cameron, Carey 1952- CLC 59
 See also CA 135
Cameron, Peter 1959- CLC 44
 See also AMWS 12; CA 125; CANR 50,
 117; DLB 234; GLL 2
Camoens, Luis Vaz de 1524(?)-1580
 See Camoes, Luis de
 See also EW 2

**Camoes, Luis de 1524(?)-1580 HLCS 1; LC
 62; PC 31**
 See Camoens, Luis Vaz de
 See also DLB 287; RGWL 2, 3
Campana, Dino 1885-1932 TCLC 20
 See also CA 117; DLB 114; EWL 3
Campanella, Tommaso 1568-1639 LC 32
 See also RGWL 2, 3
**Campbell, John W(ood, Jr.) 1910-1971 CLC
 32**
 See also CA 21-22; 29-32R; CANR 34;
 CAP 2; DLB 8; MTCW 1; SCFW; SFW 4
**Campbell, Joseph 1904-1987 CLC 69; TCLC
 140**
 See also AAYA 3; BEST 89:2; CA 1-4R;
 124; CANR 3, 28, 61, 107; DA3; MTCW
 1, 2
Campbell, Maria 1940- CLC 85; NNAL
 See also CA 102; CANR 54; CCA 1; DAC
**Campbell, (John) Ramsey 1946- CLC 42;
 SSC 19**
 See also AAYA 51; CA 57-60; CANR 7,
 102; DLB 261; HGG; INT CANR-7;
 SUFW 1, 2
**Campbell, (Ignatius) Roy (Dunnachie)
 1901-1957 TCLC 5**
 See also AFW; CA 104; 155; DLB 20, 225;
 EWL 3; MTCW 2; RGEL 2
Campbell, Thomas 1777-1844 NCLC 19
 See also DLB 93, 144; RGEL 2
Campbell, Wilfred TCLC 9
 See Campbell, William
Campbell, William 1858(?)-1918
 See Campbell, Wilfred
 See also CA 106; DLB 92
Campion, Jane 1954- CLC 95
 See also AAYA 33; CA 138; CANR 87
Campion, Thomas 1567-1620 LC 78
 See also CDBLB Before 1660; DAM POET;
 DLB 58, 172; RGEL 2
**Camus, Albert 1913-1960 CLC 1, 2, 4, 9, 11,
 14, 32, 63, 69, 124; DC 2; SSC 9; WLC**
 See also AAYA 36; AFW; BPFB 1; CA 89-
 92; DA; DA3; DAB; DAC; DAM DRAM,
 MST, NOV; DLB 72; EW 13; EWL 3;
 EXPN; EXPS; GFL 1789 to the Present;
 LATS 1; LMFS 2; MTCW 1, 2; NFS 6,
 16; RGSF 2; RGWL 2, 3; SSFS 4; TWA
Canby, Vincent 1924-2000 CLC 13
 See also CA 81-84; 191
Cancale
 See Desnos, Robert
**Canetti, Elias 1905-1994 CLC 3, 14, 25, 75,
 86**
 See also CA 21-24R; 146; CANR 23, 61,
 79; CDWLB 2; CWW 2; DA3; DLB 85,
 124; EW 12; EWL 3; MTCW 1, 2; RGWL
 2, 3; TWA
Canfield, Dorothea F.
 See Fisher, Dorothy (Frances) Canfield
Canfield, Dorothea Frances
 See Fisher, Dorothy (Frances) Canfield
Canfield, Dorothy
 See Fisher, Dorothy (Frances) Canfield
Canin, Ethan 1960- CLC 55; SSC 70
 See also CA 131; 135
Cankar, Ivan 1876-1918 TCLC 105
 See also CDWLB 4; DLB 147; EWL 3
Cannon, Curt
 See Hunter, Evan
Cao, Lan 1961- CLC 109
 See also CA 165
Cape, Judith
 See Page, P(atricia) K(athleen)
 See also CCA 1
**Capek, Karel 1890-1938 DC 1; SSC 36;
 TCLC 6, 37; WLC**
 See also CA 104; 140; CDWLB 4; DA;
 DA3; DAB; DAC; DAM DRAM, MST,

NOV; DFS 7, 11; DLB 215; EW 10; EWL
 3; MTCW 1; RGSF 2; RGWL 2, 3; SCFW
 2; SFW 4
**Capote, Truman 1924-1984 CLC 1, 3, 8, 13,
 19, 34, 38, 58; SSC 2, 47; WLC**
 See also AMWS 3; BPFB 1; CA 5-8R; 113;
 CANR 18, 62; CDALB 1941-1968; CPW;
 DA; DA3; DAB; DAC; DAM MST, NOV,
 POP; DLB 2, 185, 227; DLBY 1980,
 1984; EWL 3; EXPS; GLL 1; LAIT 3;
 MTCW 1, 2; NCFS 2; RGAL 4; RGSF 2;
 SATA 91; SSFS 2; TUS
Capra, Frank 1897-1991 CLC 16
 See also AAYA 52; CA 61-64; 135
Caputo, Philip 1941- CLC 32
 See also CA 73-76; CANR 40; YAW
Caragiale, Ion Luca 1852-1912 TCLC 76
 See also CA 157
Card, Orson Scott 1951- CLC 44, 47, 50
 See also AAYA 11, 42; BPFB 1; BYA 5, 8;
 CA 102; CANR 27, 47, 73, 102, 106;
 CPW; DA3; DAM POP; FANT; INT
 CANR-27; MTCW 1, 2; NFS 5; SATA
 83, 127; SCFW 2; SFW 4; SUFW 2; YAW
**Cardenal, Ernesto 1925- CLC 31, 161; HLC
 1; PC 22**
 See also CA 49-52; CANR 2, 32, 66; CWW
 2; DAM MULT, POET; DLB 290; EWL
 3; HW 1, 2; LAWS 1; MTCW 1, 2;
 RGWL 2, 3
**Cardozo, Benjamin N(athan) 1870-1938
 TCLC 65**
 See also CA 117; 164
**Carducci, Giosue (Alessandro Giuseppe)
 1835-1907 PC 46; TCLC 32**
 See also CA 163; EW 7; RGWL 2, 3
Carew, Thomas 1595(?)-1640 LC 13; PC 29
 See also BRW 2; DLB 126; PAB; RGEL 2
Carey, Ernestine Gilbreth 1908- CLC 17
 See also CA 5-8R; CANR 71; SATA 2
Carey, Peter 1943- CLC 40, 55, 96, 183
 See also CA 123; 127; CANR 53, 76, 117;
 CN 7; DLB 289; EWL 3; INT CA-127;
 MTCW 1, 2; RGSF 2; SATA 94
Carleton, William 1794-1869 NCLC 3
 See also DLB 159; RGEL 2; RGSF 2
Carlisle, Henry (Coffin) 1926- CLC 33
 See also CA 13-16R; CANR 15, 85
Carlsen, Chris
 See Holdstock, Robert P.
Carlson, Ron(ald F.) 1947- CLC 54
 See also CA 105; 189; CAAE 189; CANR
 27; DLB 244
Carlyle, Thomas 1795-1881 NCLC 22, 70
 See also BRW 4; CDBLB 1789-1832; DA;
 DAB; DAC; DAM MST; DLB 55, 144,
 254; RGEL 2; TEA
**Carman, (William) Bliss 1861-1929 PC 34;
 TCLC 7**
 See also CA 104; 152; DAC; DLB 92;
 RGEL 2
Carnegie, Dale 1888-1955 TCLC 53
 See also CA 218
Carossa, Hans 1878-1956 TCLC 48
 See also CA 170; DLB 66; EWL 3
**Carpenter, Don(ald Richard) 1931-1995 CLC
 41**
 See also CA 45-48; 149; CANR 1, 71
Carpenter, Edward 1844-1929 TCLC 88
 See also CA 163; GLL 1
Carpenter, John (Howard) 1948- CLC 161
 See also AAYA 2; CA 134; SATA 58
Carpenter, Johnny
 See Carpenter, John (Howard)
**Carpentier (y Valmont), Alejo 1904-1980
 CLC 8, 11, 38, 110; HLC 1; SSC 35**
 See also CA 65-68; 97-100; CANR 11, 70;
 CDWLB 3; DAM MULT; DLB 113; EWL

3; HW 1, 2; LAW; LMFS 2; RGSF 2;
RGWL 2, 3; WLIT 1

Carr, Caleb 1955- **CLC 86**
See also CA 147; CANR 73; DA3

Carr, Emily 1871-1945 **TCLC 32**
See also CA 159; DLB 68; FW; GLL 2

Carr, John Dickson 1906-1977 **CLC 3**
See Fairbairn, Roger
See also CA 49-52; 69-72; CANR 3, 33,
60; CMW 4; MSW; MTCW 1, 2

Carr, Philippa
See Hibbert, Eleanor Alice Burford

Carr, Virginia Spencer 1929- **CLC 34**
See also CA 61-64; DLB 111

Carrere, Emmanuel 1957- **CLC 89**
See also CA 200

Carrier, Roch 1937- **CLC 13, 78**
See also CA 130; CANR 61; CCA 1; DAC;
DAM MST; DLB 53; SATA 105

Carroll, James Dennis
See Carroll, Jim

Carroll, James P. 1943(?)- **CLC 38**
See also CA 81-84; CANR 73; MTCW 1

Carroll, Jim 1951- **CLC 35, 143**
See Carroll, James Dennis
See also AAYA 17; CA 45-48; CANR 42,
115; NCFS 5

**Carroll, Lewis NCLC 2, 53, 139; PC 18;
WLC**
See Dodgson, Charles L(utwidge)
See also AAYA 39; BRW 5; BYA 5, 13; CD-
BLB 1832-1890; CLR 2, 18; DLB 18,
163, 178; DLBY 1998; EXPN; EXPP;
FANT; JRDA; LAIT 1; NFS 7; PFS 11;
RGEL 2; SUFW 1; TEA; WCH

Carroll, Paul Vincent 1900-1968 **CLC 10**
See also CA 9-12R; 25-28R; DLB 10; EWL
3; RGEL 2

Carruth, Hayden 1921- **CLC 4, 7, 10, 18, 84;
PC 10**
See also CA 9-12R; CANR 4, 38, 59, 110;
CP 7; DLB 5, 165; INT CANR-4; MTCW
1, 2; SATA 47

Carson, Anne 1950- **CLC 185**
See also AMWS 12; CA 203; DLB 193;
PFS 18

Carson, Rachel
See Carson, Rachel Louise
See also AAYA 49; DLB 275

Carson, Rachel Louise 1907-1964 **CLC 71**
See Carson, Rachel
See also AMWS 9; ANW; CA 77-80; CANR
35; DA3; DAM POP; FW; LAIT 4;
MTCW 1, 2; NCFS 1; SATA 23

Carter, Angela (Olive) 1940-1992 **CLC 5, 41,
76; SSC 13; TCLC 139**
See also BRWS 3; CA 53-56; 136; CANR
12, 36, 61, 106; DA3; DLB 14, 207, 261;
EXPS; FANT; FW; MTCW 1, 2; RGSF 2;
SATA 66; SATA-Obit 70; SFW 4; SSFS
4, 12; SUFW 2; WLIT 4

Carter, Nick
See Smith, Martin Cruz

Carver, Raymond 1938-1988 **CLC 22, 36, 53,
55, 126; PC 54; SSC 8, 51**
See also AAYA 44; AMWS 3; BPFB 1; CA
33-36R; 126; CANR 17, 34, 61, 103;
CPW; DA3; DAM NOV; DLB 130;
DLBY 1984, 1988; EWL 3; MTCW 1, 2;
PFS 17; RGAL 4; RGSF 2; SSFS 3, 6,
12, 13; TCWW 2; TUS

Cary, Elizabeth, Lady Falkland 1585-1639
LC 30

Cary, (Arthur) Joyce (Lunel) 1888-1957
TCLC 1, 29
See also BRW 7; CA 104; 164; CDBLB
1914-1945; DLB 15, 100; EWL 3; MTCW
2; RGEL 2; TEA

Casal, Julian del 1863-1893 **NCLC 131**
See also DLB 283; LAW

Casanova de Seingalt, Giovanni Jacopo
1725-1798 **LC 13**

Casares, Adolfo Bioy
See Bioy Casares, Adolfo
See also RGSF 2

Casas, Bartolome de las 1474-1566
See Las Casas, Bartolome de
See also WLIT 1

Casely-Hayford, J(oseph) E(phraim)
1866-1903 **BLC 1; TCLC 24**
See also BW 2; CA 123; 152; DAM MULT

Casey, John (Dudley) 1939- **CLC 59**
See also BEST 90:2; CA 69-72; CANR 23,
100

Casey, Michael 1947- **CLC 2**
See also CA 65-68; CANR 109; DLB 5

Casey, Patrick
See Thurman, Wallace (Henry)

Casey, Warren (Peter) 1935-1988 **CLC 12**
See also CA 101; 127; INT CA-101

Casona, Alejandro CLC 49
See Alvarez, Alejandro Rodriguez
See also EWL 3

Cassavetes, John 1929-1989 **CLC 20**
See also CA 85-88; 127; CANR 82

Cassian, Nina 1924- **PC 17**
See also CWP; CWW 2

Cassill, R(onald) V(erlin) 1919-2002 **CLC 4,
23**
See also CA 9-12R; 208; CAAS 1; CANR
7, 45; CN 7; DLB 6, 218; DLBY 2002

Cassiodorus, Flavius Magnus c. 490(?)-c.
583(?) **CMLC 43**

Cassirer, Ernst 1874-1945 **TCLC 61**
See also CA 157

Cassity, (Allen) Turner 1929- **CLC 6, 42**
See also CA 17-20R; CAAS 8; CANR 11;
CSW; DLB 105

Castaneda, Carlos (Cesar Aranha)
1931(?)-1998 **CLC 12, 119**
See also CA 25-28R; CANR 32, 66, 105;
DNFS 1; HW 1; MTCW 1

Castedo, Elena 1937- **CLC 65**
See also CA 132

Castedo-Ellerman, Elena
See Castedo, Elena

Castellanos, Rosario 1925-1974 **CLC 66;
HLC 1; SSC 39, 68**
See also CA 131; 53-56; CANR 58; CD-
WLB 3; DAM MULT; DLB 113, 290;
EWL 3; FW; HW 1; LAW; MTCW 1;
RGSF 2; RGWL 2, 3

Castelvetro, Lodovico 1505-1571 **LC 12**

Castiglione, Baldassare 1478-1529 **LC 12**
See Castiglione, Baldesar
See also LMFS 1; RGWL 2, 3

Castiglione, Baldesar
See Castiglione, Baldassare
See also EW 2

Castillo, Ana (Hernandez Del) 1953- **CLC
151**
See also AAYA 42; CA 131; CANR 51, 86,
128; CWP; DLB 122, 227; DNFS 2; FW;
HW 1; LLW 1

Castle, Robert
See Hamilton, Edmond

Castro (Ruz), Fidel 1926(?)- **HLC 1**
See also CA 110; 129; CANR 81; DAM
MULT; HW 2

Castro, Guillen de 1569-1631 **LC 19**

Castro, Rosalia de 1837-1885 **NCLC 3, 78;
PC 41**
See also DAM MULT

Cather, Willa (Sibert) 1873-1947 **SSC 2, 50;
TCLC 1, 11, 31, 99, 132; WLC**
See also AAYA 24; AMW; AMWC 1;
AMWR 1; BPFB 1; CA 104; 128; CDALB
1865-1917; DA; DA3; DAB; DAC; DAM
MST, NOV; DLB 9, 54, 78, 256; DLBD
1; EWL 3; EXPN; EXPS; LAIT 3; LATS
1; MAWW; MTCW 1, 2; NFS 2; RGAL
4; RGSF 2; RHW; SATA 30; SSFS 2, 7,
16; TCWW 2; TUS

Catherine II
See Catherine the Great
See also DLB 150

Catherine the Great 1729-1796 **LC 69**
See Catherine II

Cato, Marcus Porcius 234B.C.-149B.C.
CMLC 21
See Cato the Elder

Cato, Marcus Porcius, the Elder
See Cato, Marcus Porcius

Cato the Elder
See Cato, Marcus Porcius
See also DLB 211

Catton, (Charles) Bruce 1899-1978 **CLC 35**
See also AITN 1; CA 5-8R; 81-84; CANR
7, 74; DLB 17; SATA 2; SATA-Obit 24

Catullus c. 84B.C.-54B.C. **CMLC 18**
See also AW 2; CDWLB 1; DLB 211;
RGWL 2, 3

Cauldwell, Frank
See King, Francis (Henry)

Caunitz, William J. 1933-1996 **CLC 34**
See also BEST 89:3; CA 125; 130; 152;
CANR 73; INT CA-130

Causley, Charles (Stanley) 1917-2003 **CLC 7**
See also CA 9-12R; CANR 5, 35, 94; CLR
30; CWRI 5; DLB 27; MTCW 1; SATA
3, 66

Caute, (John) David 1936- **CLC 29**
See also CA 1-4R; CAAS 4; CANR 1, 33,
64, 120; CBD; CD 5; CN 7; DAM NOV;
DLB 14, 231

**Cavafy, C(onstantine) P(eter) PC 36; TCLC
2, 7**
See Kavafis, Konstantinos Petrou
See also CA 148; DA3; DAM POET; EW
8; EWL 3; MTCW 1; PFS 19; RGWL 2,
3; WP

Cavalcanti, Guido c. 1250-c. 1300 **CMLC 54**

Cavallo, Evelyn
See Spark, Muriel (Sarah)

Cavanna, Betty CLC 12
See Harrison, Elizabeth (Allen) Cavanna
See also JRDA; MAICYA 1; SAAS 4;
SATA 1, 30

Cavendish, Margaret Lucas 1623-1673 **LC
30**
See also DLB 131, 252, 281; RGEL 2

Caxton, William 1421(?)-1491(?) **LC 17**
See also DLB 170

Cayer, D. M.
See Duffy, Maureen

Cayrol, Jean 1911- **CLC 11**
See also CA 89-92; DLB 83; EWL 3

Cela (y Trulock), Camilo Jose
See Cela, Camilo Jose
See also CWW 2

Cela, Camilo Jose 1916-2002 **CLC 4, 13, 59,
122; HLC 1**
See Cela (y Trulock), Camilo Jose
See also BEST 90:2; CA 21-24R; 206;
CAAS 10; CANR 21, 32, 76; DAM
MULT; DLBY 1989; EW 13; EWL 3; HW
1; MTCW 1, 2; RGSF 2; RGWL 2, 3

Celan, Paul CLC 10, 19, 53, 82; PC 10
See Antschel, Paul
See also CDWLB 2; DLB 69; EWL 3;
RGWL 2, 3

Celine, Louis-Ferdinand CLC 1, 3, 4, 7, 9, 15, 47, 124
See Destouches, Louis-Ferdinand
See also DLB 72; EW 11; EWL 3; GFL 1789 to the Present; RGWL 2, 3

Cellini, Benvenuto 1500-1571 LC 7

Cendrars, Blaise CLC 18, 106
See Sauser-Hall, Frederic
See also DLB 258; EWL 3; GFL 1789 to the Present; RGWL 2, 3; WP

Centlivre, Susanna 1669(?)-1723 LC 65
See also DLB 84; RGEL 2

Cernuda (y Bidon), Luis 1902-1963 CLC 54
See also CA 131; 89-92; DAM POET; DLB 134; EWL 3; GLL 1; HW 1; RGWL 2, 3

Cervantes, Lorna Dee 1954- HLCS 1; PC 35
See also CA 131; CANR 80; CWP; DLB 82; EXPP; HW 1; LLW 1

Cervantes (Saavedra), Miguel de 1547-1616 HLCS; LC 6, 23, 93; SSC 12; WLC
See also BYA 1, 14; DA; DAB; DAC; DAM MST, NOV; EW 2; LAIT 1; LATS 1; LMFS 1; NFS 8; RGSF 2; RGWL 2, 3; TWA

Cesaire, Aime (Fernand) 1913- BLC 1; CLC 19, 32, 112; DC 22; PC 25
See also BW 2, 3; CA 65-68; CANR 24, 43, 81; CWW 2; DA3; DAM MULT, POET; EWL 3; GFL 1789 to the Present; MTCW 1, 2; WP

Chabon, Michael 1963- CLC 55, 149; SSC 59
See also AAYA 45; AMWS 11; CA 139; CANR 57, 96, 127; DLB 278; SATA 145

Chabrol, Claude 1930- CLC 16
See also CA 110

Chairil Anwar
See Anwar, Chairil
See also EWL 3

Challans, Mary 1905-1983
See Renault, Mary
See also CA 81-84; 111; CANR 74; DA3; MTCW 2; SATA 23; SATA-Obit 36; TEA

Challis, George
See Faust, Frederick (Schiller)
See also TCWW 2

Chambers, Aidan 1934- CLC 35
See also AAYA 27; CA 25-28R; CANR 12, 31, 58, 116; JRDA; MAICYA 1, 2; SAAS 12; SATA 1, 69, 108; WYA; YAW

Chambers, James 1948-
See Cliff, Jimmy
See also CA 124

Chambers, Jessie
See Lawrence, D(avid) H(erbert Richards)
See also GLL 1

Chambers, Robert W(illiam) 1865-1933 TCLC 41
See also CA 165; DLB 202; HGG; SATA 107; SUFW 1

Chambers, (David) Whittaker 1901-1961 TCLC 129
See also CA 89-92

Chamisso, Adelbert von 1781-1838 NCLC 82
See also DLB 90; RGWL 2, 3; SUFW 1

Chance, James T.
See Carpenter, John (Howard)

Chance, John T.
See Carpenter, John (Howard)

Chandler, Raymond (Thornton) 1888-1959 SSC 23; TCLC 1, 7
See also AAYA 25; AMWC 2; AMWS 4; BPFB 1; CA 104; 129; CANR 60, 107; CDALB 1929-1941; CMW 4; DA3; DLB 226, 253; DLBD 6; EWL 3; MSW; MTCW 1, 2; NFS 17; RGAL 4; TUS

Chang, Diana 1934- AAL
See also CWP; EXPP

Chang, Eileen 1921-1995 AAL; SSC 28
See Chang Ai-Ling; Zhang Ailing
See also CA 166

Chang, Jung 1952- CLC 71
See also CA 142

Chang Ai-Ling
See Chang, Eileen
See also EWL 3

Channing, William Ellery 1780-1842 NCLC 17
See also DLB 1, 59, 235; RGAL 4

Chao, Patricia 1955- CLC 119
See also CA 163

Chaplin, Charles Spencer 1889-1977 CLC 16
See Chaplin, Charlie
See also CA 81-84; 73-76

Chaplin, Charlie
See Chaplin, Charles Spencer
See also DLB 44

Chapman, George 1559(?)-1634 DC 19; LC 22
See also BRW 1; DAM DRAM; DLB 62, 121; LMFS 1; RGEL 2

Chapman, Graham 1941-1989 CLC 21
See Monty Python
See also CA 116; 129; CANR 35, 95

Chapman, John Jay 1862-1933 TCLC 7
See also CA 104; 191

Chapman, Lee
See Bradley, Marion Zimmer
See also GLL 1

Chapman, Walker
See Silverberg, Robert

Chappell, Fred (Davis) 1936- CLC 40, 78, 162
See also CA 5-8R, 198; CAAE 198; CAAS 4; CANR 8, 33, 67, 110; CN 7; CP 7; CSW; DLB 6, 105; HGG

Char, Rene(-Emile) 1907-1988 CLC 9, 11, 14, 55; PC 56
See also CA 13-16R; 124; CANR 32; DAM POET; DLB 258; EWL 3; GFL 1789 to the Present; MTCW 1, 2; RGWL 2, 3

Charby, Jay
See Ellison, Harlan (Jay)

Chardin, Pierre Teilhard de
See Teilhard de Chardin, (Marie Joseph) Pierre

Chariton fl. 1st cent. (?)- CMLC 49

Charlemagne 742-814 CMLC 37

Charles I 1600-1649 LC 13

Charriere, Isabelle de 1740-1805 NCLC 66

Chartier, Alain c. 1392-1430 LC 94
See also DLB 208

Chartier, Emile-Auguste
See Alain

Charyn, Jerome 1937- CLC 5, 8, 18
See also CA 5-8R; CAAS 1; CANR 7, 61, 101; CMW 4; CN 7; DLBY 1983; MTCW 1

Chase, Adam
See Marlowe, Stephen

Chase, Mary (Coyle) 1907-1981 DC 1
See also CA 77-80; 105; CAD; CWD; DFS 11; DLB 228; SATA 17; SATA-Obit 29

Chase, Mary Ellen 1887-1973 CLC 2; TCLC 124
See also CA 13-16; 41-44R; CAP 1; SATA 10

Chase, Nicholas
See Hyde, Anthony
See also CCA 1

Chateaubriand, Francois Rene de 1768-1848 NCLC 3, 134
See also DLB 119; EW 5; GFL 1789 to the Present; RGWL 2, 3; TWA

Chatterje, Sarat Chandra 1876-1936(?)
See Chatterji, Saratchandra
See also CA 109

Chatterji, Bankim Chandra 1838-1894 NCLC 19

Chatterji, Saratchandra TCLC 13
See Chatterje, Sarat Chandra
See also CA 186; EWL 3

Chatterton, Thomas 1752-1770 LC 3, 54
See also DAM POET; DLB 109; RGEL 2

Chatwin, (Charles) Bruce 1940-1989 CLC 28, 57, 59
See also AAYA 4; BEST 90:1; BRWS 4; CA 85-88; 127; CPW; DAM POP; DLB 194, 204; EWL 3

Chaucer, Daniel
See Ford, Ford Madox
See also RHW

Chaucer, Geoffrey 1340(?)-1400 LC 17, 56; PC 19; WLCS
See also BRW 1; BRWC 1; BRWR 2; CD-BLB Before 1660; DA; DA3; DAB; DAC; DAM MST, POET; DLB 146; LAIT 1; PAB; PFS 14; RGEL 2; TEA; WLIT 3; WP

Chavez, Denise (Elia) 1948- HLC 1
See also CA 131; CANR 56, 81; DAM MULT; DLB 122; FW; HW 1, 2; LLW 1; MTCW 2

Chaviaras, Strates 1935-
See Haviaras, Stratis
See also CA 105

Chayefsky, Paddy CLC 23
See Chayefsky, Sidney
See also CAD; DLB 7, 44; DLBY 1981; RGAL 4

Chayefsky, Sidney 1923-1981
See Chayefsky, Paddy
See also CA 9-12R; 104; CANR 18; DAM DRAM

Chedid, Andree 1920- CLC 47
See also CA 145; CANR 95; EWL 3

Cheever, John 1912-1982 CLC 3, 7, 8, 11, 15, 25, 64; SSC 1, 38, 57; WLC
See also AMWS 1; BPFB 1; CA 5-8R; 106; CABS 1; CANR 5, 27, 76; CDALB 1941-1968; CPW; DA; DA3; DAB; DAC; DAM MST, NOV, POP; DLB 2, 102, 227; DLBY 1980, 1982; EWL 3; EXPS; INT CANR-5; MTCW 1, 2; RGAL 4; RGSF 2; SSFS 2, 14; TUS

Cheever, Susan 1943- CLC 18, 48
See also CA 103; CANR 27, 51, 92; DLBY 1982; INT CANR-27

Chekhonte, Antosha
See Chekhov, Anton (Pavlovich)

Chekhov, Anton (Pavlovich) 1860-1904 DC 9; SSC 2, 28, 41, 51; TCLC 3, 10, 31, 55, 96; WLC
See also BYA 14; CA 104; 124; DA; DA3; DAB; DAC; DAM DRAM, MST; DFS 1, 5, 10, 12; DLB 277; EW 7; EWL 3; EXPS; LAIT 3; LATS 1; RGSF 2; RGWL 2, 3; SATA 90; SSFS 5, 13, 14; TWA

Cheney, Lynne V. 1941- CLC 70
See also CA 89-92; CANR 58, 117

Chernyshevsky, Nikolai Gavrilovich
See Chernyshevsky, Nikolay Gavrilovich
See also DLB 238

Chernyshevsky, Nikolay Gavrilovich 1828-1889 NCLC 1
See Chernyshevsky, Nikolai Gavrilovich

Cherry, Carolyn Janice 1942-
See Cherryh, C. J.
See also CA 65-68; CANR 10

Cherryh, C. J. CLC 35
See Cherry, Carolyn Janice
See also AAYA 24; BPFB 1; DLBY 1980; FANT; SATA 93; SCFW 2; SFW 4; YAW

Chesnutt, Charles W(addell) 1858-1932 BLC 1; SSC 7, 54; TCLC 5, 39
See also AFAW 1, 2; BW 1, 3; CA 106; 125; CANR 76; DAM MULT; DLB 12, 50, 78; EWL 3; MTCW 1, 2; RGAL 4; RGSF 2; SSFS 11

Chester, Alfred 1929(?)-1971 CLC 49
See also CA 196; 33-36R; DLB 130

Chesterton, G(ilbert) K(eith) 1874-1936 PC 28; SSC 1, 46; TCLC 1, 6, 64
See also BRW 6; CA 104; 132; CANR 73; CDBLB 1914-1945; CMW 4; DAM NOV, POET; DLB 10, 19, 34, 70, 98, 149, 178; EWL 3; FANT; MSW; MTCW 1, 2; RGEL 2; RGSF 2; SATA 27; SUFW 1

Chiang, Pin-chin 1904-1986
See Ding Ling
See also CA 118

Chief Joseph 1840-1904 NNAL
See also CA 152; DA3; DAM MULT

Chief Seattle 1786(?)-1866 NNAL
See also DA3; DAM MULT

Ch'ien, Chung-shu 1910-1998 CLC 22
See Qian Zhongshu
See also CA 130; CANR 73; MTCW 1, 2

Chikamatsu Monzaemon 1653-1724 LC 66
See also RGWL 2, 3

Child, L. Maria
See Child, Lydia Maria

Child, Lydia Maria 1802-1880 NCLC 6, 73
See also DLB 1, 74, 243; RGAL 4; SATA 67

Child, Mrs.
See Child, Lydia Maria

Child, Philip 1898-1978 CLC 19, 68
See also CA 13-14; CAP 1; DLB 68; RHW; SATA 47

Childers, (Robert) Erskine 1870-1922 TCLC 65
See also CA 113; 153; DLB 70

Childress, Alice 1920-1994 BLC 1; CLC 12, 15, 86, 96; DC 4; TCLC 116
See also AAYA 8; BW 2, 3; BYA 2; CA 45-48; 146; CAD; CANR 3, 27, 50, 74; CLR 14; CWD; DA3; DAM DRAM, MULT, NOV; DFS 2, 8, 14; DLB 7, 38, 249; JRDA; LAIT 5; MAICYA 1, 2; MAICYAS 1; MTCW 1, 2; RGAL 4; SATA 7, 48, 81; TUS; WYA; YAW

Chin, Frank (Chew, Jr.) 1940- CLC 135; DC 7
See also CA 33-36R; CANR 71; CD 5; DAM MULT; DLB 206; LAIT 5; RGAL 4

Chin, Marilyn (Mei Ling) 1955- PC 40
See also CA 129; CANR 70, 113; CWP

Chislett, (Margaret) Anne 1943- CLC 34
See also CA 151

Chitty, Thomas Willes 1926- CLC 11
See Hinde, Thomas
See also CA 5-8R; CN 7

Chivers, Thomas Holley 1809-1858 NCLC 49
See also DLB 3, 248; RGAL 4

Choi, Susan 1969- CLC 119

Chomette, Rene Lucien 1898-1981
See Clair, Rene
See also CA 103

Chomsky, (Avram) Noam 1928- CLC 132
See also CA 17-20R; CANR 28, 62, 110; DA3; DLB 246; MTCW 1, 2

Chona, Maria 1845(?)-1936 NNAL
See also CA 144

Chopin, Kate SSC 8, 68; TCLC 127; WLCS
See Chopin, Katherine
See also AAYA 33; AMWR 2; AMWS 1; BYA 11, 15; CDALB 1865-1917; DA; DAB; DAC; DLB 12, 78; EXPN; EXPS; FW; LAIT 3; MAWW; NFS 3; RGAL 4; RGSF 2; SSFS 17; TUS

Chopin, Katherine 1851-1904
See Chopin, Kate
See also CA 104; 122; DA3; DAC; DAM MST, NOV

Chretien de Troyes c. 12th cent. - CMLC 10
See also DLB 208; EW 1; RGWL 2, 3; TWA

Christie
See Ichikawa, Kon

Christie, Agatha (Mary Clarissa) 1890-1976 CLC 1, 6, 8, 12, 39, 48, 110
See also AAYA 9; AITN 1, 2; BPFB 1; BRWS 2; CA 17-20R; 61-64; CANR 10, 37, 108; CBD; CDBLB 1914-1945; CMW 4; CPW; CWD; DA3; DAB; DAC; DAM NOV; DFS 2; DLB 13, 77, 245; MSW; MTCW 1, 2; NFS 8; RGEL 2; RHW; SATA 36; TEA; YAW

Christie, Philippa CLC 21
See Pearce, Philippa
See also BYA 5; CANR 109; CLR 9; DLB 161; MAICYA 1; SATA 1, 67, 129

Christine de Pizan 1365(?)-1431(?) LC 9
See also DLB 208; RGWL 2, 3

Chuang Tzu c. 369B.C.-c. 286B.C. CMLC 57

Chubb, Elmer
See Masters, Edgar Lee

Chulkov, Mikhail Dmitrievich 1743-1792 LC 2
See also DLB 150

Churchill, Caryl 1938- CLC 31, 55, 157; DC 5
See Churchill, Chick
See also BRWS 4; CA 102; CANR 22, 46, 108; CBD; CWD; DFS 12, 16; DLB 13; EWL 3; FW; MTCW 1; RGEL 2

Churchill, Charles 1731-1764 LC 3
See also DLB 109; RGEL 2

Churchill, Chick 1938-
See Churchill, Caryl
See also CD 5

Churchill, Sir Winston (Leonard Spencer) 1874-1965 TCLC 113
See also BRW 6; CA 97-100; CDBLB 1890-1914; DA3; DLB 100; DLBD 16; LAIT 4; MTCW 1, 2

Chute, Carolyn 1947- CLC 39
See also CA 123

Ciardi, John (Anthony) 1916-1986 CLC 10, 40, 44, 129
See also CA 5-8R; 118; CAAS 2; CANR 5, 33; CLR 19; CWRI 5; DAM POET; DLB 5; DLBY 1986; INT CANR-5; MAICYA 1, 2; MTCW 1, 2; RGAL 4; SAAS 26; SATA 1, 65; SATA-Obit 46

Cibber, Colley 1671-1757 LC 66
See also DLB 84; RGEL 2

Cicero, Marcus Tullius 106B.C.-43B.C. CMLC 3
See also AW 1; CDWLB 1; DLB 211; RGWL 2, 3

Cimino, Michael 1943- CLC 16
See also CA 105

Cioran, E(mil) M. 1911-1995 CLC 64
See also CA 25-28R; 149; CANR 91; DLB 220; EWL 3

Cisneros, Sandra 1954- CLC 69, 118; HLC 1; PC 52; SSC 32
See also AAYA 9, 53; AMWS 7; CA 131; CANR 64, 118; CWP; DA3; DAM MULT; DLB 122, 152; EWL 3; EXPN; FW; HW 1, 2; LAIT 5; LATS 1; LLW 1; MAICYA 2; MTCW 2; NFS 2; PFS 19; RGAL 4; RGSF 2; SSFS 3, 13; WLIT 1; YAW

Cixous, Helene 1937- CLC 92
See also CA 126; CANR 55, 123; CWW 2; DLB 83, 242; EWL 3; FW; GLL 2; MTCW 1, 2; TWA

Clair, Rene CLC 20
See Chomette, Rene Lucien

Clampitt, Amy 1920-1994 CLC 32; PC 19
See also AMWS 9; CA 110; 146; CANR 29, 79; DLB 105

Clancy, Thomas L., Jr. 1947-
See Clancy, Tom
See also CA 125; 131; CANR 62, 105; DA3; INT CA-131; MTCW 1, 2

Clancy, Tom CLC 45, 112
See Clancy, Thomas L., Jr.
See also AAYA 9, 51; BEST 89:1, 90:1; BPFB 1; BYA 10, 11; CMW 4; CPW; DAM NOV, POP; DLB 227

Clare, John 1793-1864 NCLC 9, 86; PC 23
See also DAB; DAM POET; DLB 55, 96; RGEL 2

Clarin
See Alas (y Urena), Leopoldo (Enrique Garcia)

Clark, Al C.
See Goines, Donald

Clark, (Robert) Brian 1932- CLC 29
See also CA 41-44R; CANR 67; CBD; CD 5

Clark, Curt
See Westlake, Donald E(dwin)

Clark, Eleanor 1913-1996 CLC 5, 19
See also CA 9-12R; 151; CANR 41; CN 7; DLB 6

Clark, J. P.
See Clark Bekederemo, J(ohnson) P(epper)
See also CDWLB 3; DLB 117

Clark, John Pepper
See Clark Bekederemo, J(ohnson) P(epper)
See also AFW; CD 5; CP 7; RGEL 2

Clark, Kenneth (Mackenzie) 1903-1983 TCLC 147
See also CA 93-96; 109; CANR 36; MTCW 1, 2

Clark, M. R.
See Clark, Mavis Thorpe

Clark, Mavis Thorpe 1909-1999 CLC 12
See also CA 57-60; CANR 8, 37, 107; CLR 30; CWRI 5; MAICYA 1, 2; SAAS 5; SATA 8, 74

Clark, Walter Van Tilburg 1909-1971 CLC 28
See also CA 9-12R; 33-36R; CANR 63, 113; DLB 9, 206; LAIT 2; RGAL 4; SATA 8

Clark Bekederemo, J(ohnson) P(epper) 1935- BLC 1; CLC 38; DC 5
See Clark, J. P.; Clark, John Pepper
See also BW 1; CA 65-68; CANR 16, 72; DAM DRAM, MULT; DFS 13; EWL 3; MTCW 1

Clarke, Arthur C(harles) 1917- CLC 1, 4, 13, 18, 35, 136; SSC 3
See also AAYA 4, 33; BPFB 1; BYA 13; CA 1-4R; CANR 2, 28, 55, 74; CN 7; CPW; DA3; DAM POP; DLB 261; JRDA; LAIT 5; MAICYA 1, 2; MTCW 1, 2; SATA 13, 70, 115; SCFW; SFW 4; SSFS 4, 18; YAW

Clarke, Austin 1896-1974 CLC 6, 9
See also CA 29-32; 49-52; CAP 2; DAM POET; DLB 10, 20; EWL 3; RGEL 2

Clarke, Austin C(hesterfield) 1934- BLC 1; CLC 8, 53; SSC 45
See also BW 1; CA 25-28R; CAAS 16; CANR 14, 32, 68; CN 7; DAC; DAM MULT; DLB 53, 125; DNFS 2; RGSF 2

Clarke, Gillian 1937- CLC 61
See also CA 106; CP 7; CWP; DLB 40

Clarke, Marcus (Andrew Hislop) 1846-1881 NCLC 19
See also DLB 230; RGEL 2; RGSF 2

Clarke, Shirley 1925-1997 **CLC 16**
See also CA 189

Clash, The
See Headon, (Nicky) Topper; Jones, Mick; Simonon, Paul; Strummer, Joe

Claudel, Paul (Louis Charles Marie)
1868-1955 **TCLC 2, 10**
See also CA 104; 165; DLB 192, 258; EW 8; EWL 3; GFL 1789 to the Present; RGWL 2, 3; TWA

Claudian 370(?)-404(?) **CMLC 46**
See also RGWL 2, 3

Claudius, Matthias 1740-1815 **NCLC 75**
See also DLB 97

Clavell, James (duMaresq) 1925-1994 **CLC 6, 25, 87**
See also BPFB 1; CA 25-28R; 146; CANR 26, 48; CPW; DA3; DAM NOV, POP; MTCW 1, 2; NFS 10; RHW

Clayman, Gregory CLC 65

Cleaver, (Leroy) Eldridge 1935-1998 **BLC 1; CLC 30, 119**
See also BW 1, 3; CA 21-24R; 167; CANR 16, 75; DA3; DAM MULT; MTCW 2; YAW

Cleese, John (Marwood) 1939- **CLC 21**
See Monty Python
See also CA 112; 116; CANR 35; MTCW 1

Cleishbotham, Jebediah
See Scott, Sir Walter

Cleland, John 1710-1789 **LC 2, 48**
See also DLB 39; RGEL 2

Clemens, Samuel Langhorne 1835-1910
See Twain, Mark
See also CA 104; 135; CDALB 1865-1917; DA; DA3; DAB; DAC; DAM MST, NOV; DLB 12, 23, 64, 74, 186, 189; JRDA; LMFS 1; MAICYA 1, 2; NCFS 4; SATA 100; SSFS 16; YABC 2

Clement of Alexandria 150(?)-215(?) **CMLC 41**

Cleophil
See Congreve, William

Clerihew, E.
See Bentley, E(dmund) C(lerihew)

Clerk, N. W.
See Lewis, C(live) S(taples)

Cliff, Jimmy CLC 21
See Chambers, James
See also CA 193

Cliff, Michelle 1946- **BLCS; CLC 120**
See also BW 2; CA 116; CANR 39, 72; CD-WLB 3; DLB 157; FW; GLL 2

Clifford, Lady Anne 1590-1676 **LC 76**
See also DLB 151

Clifton, (Thelma) Lucille 1936- **BLC 1; CLC 19, 66, 162; PC 17**
See also AFAW 2; BW 2, 3; CA 49-52; CANR 2, 24, 42, 76, 97; CLR 5; CP 7; CSW; CWP; CWRI 5; DA3; DAM MULT, POET; DLB 5, 41; EXPP; MAICYA 1, 2; MTCW 1, 2; PFS 1, 14; SATA 20, 69, 128; WP

Clinton, Dirk
See Silverberg, Robert

Clough, Arthur Hugh 1819-1861 **NCLC 27**
See also BRW 5; DLB 32; RGEL 2

Clutha, Janet Paterson Frame 1924-2004
See Frame, Janet
See also CA 1-4R; CANR 2, 36, 76; MTCW 1, 2; SATA 119

Clyne, Terence
See Blatty, William Peter

Cobalt, Martin
See Mayne, William (James Carter)

Cobb, Irvin S(hrewsbury) 1876-1944 **TCLC 77**
See also CA 175; DLB 11, 25, 86

Cobbett, William 1763-1835 **NCLC 49**
See also DLB 43, 107, 158; RGEL 2

Coburn, D(onald) L(ee) 1938- **CLC 10**
See also CA 89-92

Cocteau, Jean (Maurice Eugene Clement)
1889-1963 **CLC 1, 8, 15, 16, 43; DC 17; TCLC 119; WLC**
See also CANR 40; CAP 2; DA; DA3; DAB; DAC; DAM DRAM, MST, NOV; DLB 65, 258; EW 10; EWL 3; GFL 1789 to the Present; MTCW 1, 2; RGWL 2, 3; TWA

Codrescu, Andrei 1946- **CLC 46, 121**
See also CA 33-36R; CAAS 19; CANR 13, 34, 53, 76, 125; DA3; DAM POET; MTCW 2

Coe, Max
See Bourne, Randolph S(illiman)

Coe, Tucker
See Westlake, Donald E(dwin)

Coen, Ethan 1958- **CLC 108**
See also CA 126; CANR 85

Coen, Joel 1955- **CLC 108**
See also CA 126; CANR 119

The Coen Brothers
See Coen, Ethan; Coen, Joel

Coetzee, J(ohn) M(axwell) 1940- **CLC 23, 33, 66, 117, 161, 162**
See also AAYA 37; AFW; BRWS 6; CA 77-80; CANR 41, 54, 74, 114; CN 7; DA3; DAM NOV; DLB 225; EWL 3; LMFS 2; MTCW 1, 2; WLIT 2; WWE 1

Coffey, Brian
See Koontz, Dean R(ay)

Coffin, Robert P(eter) Tristram 1892-1955 **TCLC 95**
See also CA 123; 169; DLB 45

Cohan, George M(ichael) 1878-1942 **TCLC 60**
See also CA 157; DLB 249; RGAL 4

Cohen, Arthur A(llen) 1928-1986 **CLC 7, 31**
See also CA 1-4R; 120; CANR 1, 17, 42; DLB 28

Cohen, Leonard (Norman) 1934- **CLC 3, 38**
See also CA 21-24R; CANR 14, 69; CN 7; CP 7; DAC; DAM MST; DLB 53; EWL 3; MTCW 1

Cohen, Matt(hew) 1942-1999 **CLC 19**
See also CA 61-64; 187; CAAS 18; CANR 40; CN 7; DAC; DLB 53

Cohen-Solal, Annie 19(?)- **CLC 50**

Colegate, Isabel 1931- **CLC 36**
See also CA 17-20R; CANR 8, 22, 74; CN 7; DLB 14, 231; INT CANR-22; MTCW 1

Coleman, Emmett
See Reed, Ishmael

Coleridge, Hartley 1796-1849 **NCLC 90**
See also DLB 96

Coleridge, M. E.
See Coleridge, Mary E(lizabeth)

Coleridge, Mary E(lizabeth) 1861-1907 **TCLC 73**
See also CA 116; 166; DLB 19, 98

Coleridge, Samuel Taylor 1772-1834 **NCLC 9, 54, 99, 111; PC 11, 39; WLC**
See also BRW 4; BRWR 2; BYA 4; CD-BLB 1789-1832; DA; DA3; DAB; DAC; DAM MST, POET; DLB 93, 107; EXPP; LATS 1; LMFS 1; PAB; PFS 4, 5; RGEL 2; TEA; WLIT 3; WP

Coleridge, Sara 1802-1852 **NCLC 31**
See also DLB 199

Coles, Don 1928- **CLC 46**
See also CA 115; CANR 38; CP 7

Coles, Robert (Martin) 1929- **CLC 108**
See also CA 45-48; CANR 3, 32, 66, 70; INT CANR-32; SATA 23

Colette, (Sidonie-Gabrielle) 1873-1954 **SSC 10; TCLC 1, 5, 16**
See Willy, Colette
See also CA 104; 131; DA3; DAM NOV; DLB 65; EW 9; EWL 3; GFL 1789 to the Present; MTCW 1, 2; RGWL 2, 3; TWA

Collett, (Jacobine) Camilla (Wergeland) 1813-1895 **NCLC 22**

Collier, Christopher 1930- **CLC 30**
See also AAYA 13; BYA 2; CA 33-36R; CANR 13, 33, 102; JRDA; MAICYA 1, 2; SATA 16, 70; WYA; YAW 1

Collier, James Lincoln 1928- **CLC 30**
See also AAYA 13; BYA 2; CA 9-12R; CANR 4, 33, 60, 102; CLR 3; DAM POP; JRDA; MAICYA 1, 2; SAAS 21; SATA 8, 70; WYA; YAW 1

Collier, Jeremy 1650-1726 **LC 6**

Collier, John 1901-1980 **SSC 19; TCLC 127**
See also CA 65-68; 97-100; CANR 10; DLB 77, 255; FANT; SUFW 1

Collier, Mary 1690-1762 **LC 86**
See also DLB 95

Collingwood, R(obin) G(eorge) 1889(?)-1943 **TCLC 67**
See also CA 117; 155; DLB 262

Collins, Hunt
See Hunter, Evan

Collins, Linda 1931- **CLC 44**
See also CA 125

Collins, Tom
See Furphy, Joseph
See also RGEL 2

Collins, (William) Wilkie 1824-1889 **NCLC 1, 18, 93**
See also BRWS 6; CDBLB 1832-1890; CMW 4; DLB 18, 70, 159; MSW; RGEL 2; RGSF 2; SUFW 1; WLIT 4

Collins, William 1721-1759 **LC 4, 40**
See also BRW 3; DAM POET; DLB 109; RGEL 2

Collodi, Carlo NCLC 54
See Lorenzini, Carlo
See also CLR 5; WCH

Colman, George
See Glassco, John

Colman, George, the Elder 1732-1794 **LC 98**
See also RGEL 2

Colonna, Vittoria 1492-1547 **LC 71**
See also RGWL 2, 3

Colt, Winchester Remington
See Hubbard, L(afayette) Ron(ald)

Colter, Cyrus J. 1910-2002 **CLC 58**
See also BW 1; CA 65-68; 205; CANR 10, 66; CN 7; DLB 33

Colton, James
See Hansen, Joseph
See also GLL 1

Colum, Padraic 1881-1972 **CLC 28**
See also BYA 4; CA 73-76; 33-36R; CANR 35; CLR 36; CWRI 5; DLB 19; MAICYA 1, 2; MTCW 1; RGEL 2; SATA 15; WCH

Colvin, James
See Moorcock, Michael (John)

Colwin, Laurie (E.) 1944-1992 **CLC 5, 13, 23, 84**
See also CA 89-92; 139; CANR 20, 46; DLB 218; DLBY 1980; MTCW 1

Comfort, Alex(ander) 1920-2000 **CLC 7**
See also CA 1-4R; 190; CANR 1, 45; CP 7; DAM POP; MTCW 1

Comfort, Montgomery
See Campbell, (John) Ramsey

Compton-Burnett, I(vy) 1892(?)-1969 **CLC 1, 3, 10, 15, 34**
See also BRW 7; CA 1-4R; 25-28R; CANR 4; DAM NOV; DLB 36; EWL 3; MTCW 1; RGEL 2

Cowan, Peter (Walkinshaw) 1914-2002 **SSC 28**
See also CA 21-24R; CANR 9, 25, 50, 83; CN 7; DLB 260; RGSF 2

Coward, Noel (Peirce) 1899-1973 **CLC 1, 9, 29, 51**
See also AITN 1; BRWS 2; CA 17-18; 41-44R; CANR 35; CAP 2; CDBLB 1914-1945; DA3; DAM DRAM; DFS 3, 6; DLB 10, 245; EWL 3; IDFW 3, 4; MTCW 1, 2; RGEL 2; TEA

Cowley, Abraham 1618-1667 **LC 43**
See also BRW 2; DLB 131, 151; PAB; RGEL 2

Cowley, Malcolm 1898-1989 **CLC 39**
See also AMWS 2; CA 5-8R; 128; CANR 3, 55; DLB 4, 48; DLBY 1981, 1989; EWL 3; MTCW 1, 2

Cowper, William 1731-1800 **NCLC 8, 94; PC 40**
See also BRW 3; DA3; DAM POET; DLB 104, 109; RGEL 2

Cox, William Trevor 1928-
See Trevor, William
See also CA 9-12R; CANR 4, 37, 55, 76, 102; DAM NOV; INT CANR-37; MTCW 1, 2; TEA

Coyne, P. J.
See Masters, Hilary

Cozzens, James Gould 1903-1978 **CLC 1, 4, 11, 92**
See also AMW; BPFB 1; CA 9-12R; 81-84; CANR 19; CDALB 1941-1968; DLB 9, 294; DLBD 2; DLBY 1984, 1997; EWL 3; MTCW 1, 2; RGAL 4

Crabbe, George 1754-1832 **NCLC 26, 121**
See also BRW 3; DLB 93; RGEL 2

Crace, Jim 1946- **CLC 157; SSC 61**
See also CA 128; 135; CANR 55, 70, 123; CN 7; DLB 231; INT CA-135

Craddock, Charles Egbert
See Murfree, Mary Noailles

Craig, A. A.
See Anderson, Poul (William)

Craik, Mrs.
See Craik, Dinah Maria (Mulock)
See also RGEL 2

Craik, Dinah Maria (Mulock) 1826-1887 **NCLC 38**
See Craik, Mrs.; Mulock, Dinah Maria
See also DLB 35, 163; MAICYA 1, 2; SATA 34

Cram, Ralph Adams 1863-1942 **TCLC 45**
See also CA 160

Cranch, Christopher Pearse 1813-1892 **NCLC 115**
See also DLB 1, 42, 243

Crane, (Harold) Hart 1899-1932 **PC 3; TCLC 2, 5, 80; WLC**
See also AMW; AMWR 2; CA 104; 127; CDALB 1917-1929; DA; DA3; DAB; DAC; DAM MST, POET; DLB 4, 48; EWL 3; MTCW 1, 2; RGAL 4; TUS

Crane, R(onald) S(almon) 1886-1967 **CLC 27**
See also CA 85-88; DLB 63

Crane, Stephen (Townley) 1871-1900 **SSC 7, 56, 70; TCLC 11, 17, 32; WLC**
See also AAYA 21; AMW; AMWC 1; BPFB 1; BYA 3; CA 109; 140; CANR 84; CDALB 1865-1917; DA; DA3; DAB; DAC; DAM MST, NOV, POET; DLB 12, 54, 78; EXPN; EXPS; LAIT 2; LMFS 2; NFS 4; PFS 9; RGAL 4; RGSF 2; SSFS 4; TUS; WYA; YABC 2

Cranmer, Thomas 1489-1556 **LC 95**
See also DLB 132, 213

Cranshaw, Stanley
See Fisher, Dorothy (Frances) Canfield

Crase, Douglas 1944- **CLC 58**
See also CA 106

Crashaw, Richard 1612(?)-1649 **LC 24**
See also BRW 2; DLB 126; PAB; RGEL 2

Cratinus c. 519B.C.-c. 422B.C. **CMLC 54**
See also LMFS 1

Craven, Margaret 1901-1980 **CLC 17**
See also BYA 2; CA 103; CCA 1; DAC; LAIT 5

Crawford, F(rancis) Marion 1854-1909 **TCLC 10**
See also CA 107; 168; DLB 71; HGG; RGAL 4; SUFW 1

Crawford, Isabella Valancy 1850-1887 **NCLC 12, 127**
See also DLB 92; RGEL 2

Crayon, Geoffrey
See Irving, Washington

Creasey, John 1908-1973 **CLC 11**
See Marric, J. J.
See also CA 5-8R; 41-44R; CANR 8, 59; CMW 4; DLB 77; MTCW 1

Crebillon, Claude Prosper Jolyot de (fils) 1707-1777 **LC 1, 28**
See also GFL Beginnings to 1789

Credo
See Creasey, John

Credo, Alvaro J. de
See Prado (Calvo), Pedro

Creeley, Robert (White) 1926- **CLC 1, 2, 4, 8, 11, 15, 36, 78**
See also AMWS 4; CA 1-4R; CAAS 10; CANR 23, 43, 89; CP 7; DA3; DAM POET; DLB 5, 16, 169; DLBD 17; EWL 3; MTCW 1, 2; RGAL 4; WP

Crevecoeur, Hector St. John de
See Crevecoeur, Michel Guillaume Jean de
See also ANW

Crevecoeur, Michel Guillaume Jean de 1735-1813 **NCLC 105**
See Crevecoeur, Hector St. John de
See also AMWS 1; DLB 37

Crevel, Rene 1900-1935 **TCLC 112**
See also GLL 2

Crews, Harry (Eugene) 1935- **CLC 6, 23, 49**
See also AITN 1; AMWS 11; BPFB 1; CA 25-28R; CANR 20, 57; CN 7; CSW; DA3; DLB 6, 143, 185; MTCW 1, 2; RGAL 4

Crichton, (John) Michael 1942- **CLC 2, 6, 54, 90**
See also AAYA 10, 49; AITN 2; BPFB 1; CA 25-28R; CANR 13, 40, 54, 76, 127; CMW 4; CN 7; CPW; DA3; DAM NOV, POP; DLB 292; DLBY 1981; INT CANR-13; JRDA; MTCW 1, 2; SATA 9, 88; SFW 4; YAW

Crispin, Edmund CLC 22
See Montgomery, (Robert) Bruce
See also DLB 87; MSW

Cristofer, Michael 1945(?)- **CLC 28**
See also CA 110; 152; CAD; CD 5; DAM DRAM; DFS 15; DLB 7

Criton
See Alain

Croce, Benedetto 1866-1952 **TCLC 37**
See also CA 120; 155; EW 8; EWL 3

Crockett, David 1786-1836 **NCLC 8**
See also DLB 3, 11, 183, 248

Crockett, Davy
See Crockett, David

Crofts, Freeman Wills 1879-1957 **TCLC 55**
See also CA 115; 195; CMW 4; DLB 77; MSW

Croker, John Wilson 1780-1857 **NCLC 10**
See also DLB 110

Crommelynck, Fernand 1885-1970 **CLC 75**
See also CA 189; 89-92; EWL 3

Cromwell, Oliver 1599-1658 **LC 43**

Cronenberg, David 1943- **CLC 143**
See also CA 138; CCA 1

Cronin, A(rchibald) J(oseph) 1896-1981 **CLC 32**
See also BPFB 1; CA 1-4R; 102; CANR 5; DLB 191; SATA 47; SATA-Obit 25

Cross, Amanda
See Heilbrun, Carolyn G(old)
See also BPFB 1; CMW; CPW; MSW

Crothers, Rachel 1878-1958 **TCLC 19**
See also CA 113; 194; CAD; CWD; DLB 7, 266; RGAL 4

Croves, Hal
See Traven, B.

Crow Dog, Mary (Ellen) (?)- **CLC 93**
See Brave Bird, Mary
See also CA 154

Crowfield, Christopher
See Stowe, Harriet (Elizabeth) Beecher

Crowley, Aleister TCLC 7
See Crowley, Edward Alexander
See also GLL 1

Crowley, Edward Alexander 1875-1947
See Crowley, Aleister
See also CA 104; HGG

Crowley, John 1942- **CLC 57**
See also BPFB 1; CA 61-64; CANR 43, 98; DLBY 1982; FANT; SATA 65, 140; SFW 4; SUFW 2

Crud
See Crumb, R(obert)

Crumarums
See Crumb, R(obert)

Crumb, R(obert) 1943- **CLC 17**
See also CA 106; CANR 107

Crumbum
See Crumb, R(obert)

Crumski
See Crumb, R(obert)

Crum the Bum
See Crumb, R(obert)

Crunk
See Crumb, R(obert)

Crustt
See Crumb, R(obert)

Crutchfield, Les
See Trumbo, Dalton

Cruz, Victor Hernandez 1949- **HLC 1; PC 37**
See also BW 2; CA 65-68; CAAS 17; CANR 14, 32, 74; CP 7; DAM MULT, POET; DLB 41; DNFS 1; EXPP; HW 1, 2; LLW 1; MTCW 1; PFS 16; WP

Cryer, Gretchen (Kiger) 1935- **CLC 21**
See also CA 114; 123

Csath, Geza 1887-1919 **TCLC 13**
See also CA 111

Cudlip, David R(ockwell) 1933- **CLC 34**
See also CA 177

Cullen, Countee 1903-1946 **BLC 1; HR 2; PC 20; TCLC 4, 37; WLCS**
See also AFAW 2; AMWS 4; BW 1; CA 108; 124; CDALB 1917-1929; DA; DA3; DAC; DAM MST, MULT, POET; DLB 4, 48, 51; EWL 3; EXPP; LMFS 2; MTCW 1, 2; PFS 3; RGAL 4; SATA 18; WP

Culleton, Beatrice 1949- **NNAL**
See also CA 120; CANR 83; DAC

Cum, R.
See Crumb, R(obert)

Cummings, Bruce F(rederick) 1889-1919
See Barbellion, W. N. P.
See also CA 123

Dixon, Paige
See Corcoran, Barbara (Asenath)

Dixon, Stephen 1936- **CLC 52; SSC 16**
See also AMWS 12; CA 89-92; CANR 17, 40, 54, 91; CN 7; DLB 130

Djebar, Assia 1936- **CLC 182**
See also CA 188; EWL 3; RGWL 3; WLIT 2

Doak, Annie
See Dillard, Annie

Dobell, Sydney Thompson 1824-1874 **NCLC 43**
See also DLB 32; RGEL 2

Doblin, Alfred TCLC 13
See Doeblin, Alfred
See also CDWLB 2; EWL 3; RGWL 2, 3

Dobroliubov, Nikolai Aleksandrovich
See Dobrolyubov, Nikolai Alexandrovich
See also DLB 277

Dobrolyubov, Nikolai Alexandrovich
1836-1861 **NCLC 5**
See Dobroliubov, Nikolai Aleksandrovich

Dobson, Austin 1840-1921 **TCLC 79**
See also DLB 35, 144

Dobyns, Stephen 1941- **CLC 37**
See also AMWS 13; CA 45-48; CANR 2, 18, 99; CMW 4; CP 7

Doctorow, E(dgar) L(aurence) 1931- **CLC 6, 11, 15, 18, 37, 44, 65, 113**
See also AAYA 22; AITN 2; AMWS 4; BEST 89:3; BPFB 1; CA 45-48; CANR 2, 33, 51, 76, 97; CDALB 1968-1988; CN 7; CPW; DA3; DAM NOV, POP; DLB 2, 28, 173; DLBY 1980; EWL 3; LAIT 3; MTCW 1, 2; NFS 6; RGAL 4; RHW; TUS

Dodgson, Charles L(utwidge) 1832-1898
See Carroll, Lewis
See also CLR 2; DA; DA3; DAB; DAC; DAM MST, NOV, POET; MAICYA 1, 2; SATA 100; YABC 2

Dodsley, Robert 1703-1764 **LC 97**
See also DLB 95; RGEL 2

Dodson, Owen (Vincent) 1914-1983 **BLC 1; CLC 79**
See also BW 1; CA 65-68; 110; CANR 24; DAM MULT; DLB 76

Doeblin, Alfred 1878-1957 **TCLC 13**
See Doblin, Alfred
See also CA 110; 141; DLB 66

Doerr, Harriet 1910-2002 **CLC 34**
See also CA 117; 122; 213; CANR 47; INT CA-122; LATS 1

Domecq, H(onorio Bustos)
See Bioy Casares, Adolfo

Domecq, H(onorio) Bustos
See Bioy Casares, Adolfo; Borges, Jorge Luis

Domini, Rey
See Lorde, Audre (Geraldine)
See also GLL 1

Dominique
See Proust, (Valentin-Louis-George-Eugene) Marcel

Don, A
See Stephen, Sir Leslie

Donaldson, Stephen R(eeder) 1947- **CLC 46, 138**
See also AAYA 36; BPFB 1; CA 89-92; CANR 13, 55, 99; CPW; DAM POP; FANT; INT CANR-13; SATA 121; SFW 4; SUFW 1, 2

Donleavy, J(ames) P(atrick) 1926- **CLC 1, 4, 6, 10, 45**
See also AITN 2; BPFB 1; CA 9-12R; CANR 24, 49, 62, 80, 124; CBD; CD 5; CN 7; DLB 6, 173; INT CANR-24; MTCW 1, 2; RGAL 4

Donnadieu, Marguerite
See Duras, Marguerite
See also CWW 2

Donne, John 1572-1631 **LC 10, 24, 91; PC 1, 43; WLC**
See also BRW 1; BRWC 1; BRWR 2; CD-BLB Before 1660; DA; DAB; DAC; DAM MST, POET; DLB 121, 151; EXPP; PAB; PFS 2, 11; RGEL 3; TEA; WLIT 3; WP

Donnell, David 1939(?)- **CLC 34**
See also CA 197

Donoghue, P. S.
See Hunt, E(verette) Howard, (Jr.)

Donoso (Yanez), Jose 1924-1996 **CLC 4, 8, 11, 32, 99; HLC 1; SSC 34; TCLC 133**
See also CA 81-84; 155; CANR 32, 73; CD-WLB 3; DAM MULT; DLB 113; EWL 3; HW 1, 2; LAW; LAWS 1; MTCW 1, 2; RGSF 2; WLIT 1

Donovan, John 1928-1992 **CLC 35**
See also AAYA 20; CA 97-100; 137; CLR 3; MAICYA 1, 2; SATA 72; SATA-Brief 29; YAW

Don Roberto
See Cunninghame Graham, Robert (Gallnigad) Bontine

Doolittle, Hilda 1886-1961 **CLC 3, 8, 14, 31, 34, 73; PC 5; WLC**
See H. D.
See also AMWS 1; CA 97-100; CANR 35; DA; DAC; DAM MST, POET; DLB 4, 45; EWL 3; FW; GLL 1; LMFS 2; MAWW; MTCW 1, 2; PFS 6; RGAL 4

Doppo, Kunikida TCLC 99
See Kunikida Doppo

Dorfman, Ariel 1942- **CLC 48, 77; HLC 1**
See also CA 124; 130; CANR 67, 70; CWW 2; DAM MULT; DFS 4; EWL 3; HW 1, 2; INT CA-130; WLIT 1

Dorn, Edward (Merton) 1929-1999 **CLC 10, 18**
See also CA 93-96; 187; CANR 42, 79; CP 7; DLB 5; INT CA-93-96; WP

Dor-Ner, Zvi CLC 70

Dorris, Michael (Anthony) 1945-1997 **CLC 109; NNAL**
See also AAYA 20; BEST 90:1; BYA 12; CA 102; 157; CANR 19, 46, 75; CLR 58; DA3; DAM MULT, NOV; DLB 175; LAIT 5; MTCW 2; NFS 3; RGAL 4; SATA 75; SATA-Obit 94; TCWW 2; YAW

Dorris, Michael A.
See Dorris, Michael (Anthony)

Dorsan, Luc
See Simenon, Georges (Jacques Christian)

Dorsange, Jean
See Simenon, Georges (Jacques Christian)

Dorset
See Sackville, Thomas

Dos Passos, John (Roderigo) 1896-1970 **CLC 1, 4, 8, 11, 15, 25, 34, 82; WLC**
See also AMW; BPFB 1; CA 1-4R; 29-32R; CANR 3; CDALB 1929-1941; DA; DA3; DAB; DAC; DAM MST, NOV; DLB 4, 9, 274; DLBD 1, 15; DLBY 1996; EWL 3; MTCW 1, 2; NFS 14; RGAL 4; TUS

Dossage, Jean
See Simenon, Georges (Jacques Christian)

Dostoevsky, Fedor Mikhailovich 1821-1881 **NCLC 2, 7, 21, 33, 43, 119; SSC 2, 33, 44; WLC**
See Dostoevsky, Fyodor
See also AAYA 40; DA; DA3; DAB; DAC; DAM MST, NOV; EW 7; EXPN; NFS 3, 8; RGSF 2; RGWL 2, 3; SSFS 8; TWA

Dostoevsky, Fyodor
See Dostoevsky, Fedor Mikhailovich
See also DLB 238; LATS 1; LMFS 1, 2

Doty, M. R.
See Doty, Mark (Alan)

Doty, Mark
See Doty, Mark (Alan)

Doty, Mark (Alan) 1953(?)- **CLC 176; PC 53**
See also AMWS 11; CA 161, 183; CAAE 183; CANR 110

Doty, Mark A.
See Doty, Mark (Alan)

Doughty, Charles M(ontagu) 1843-1926 **TCLC 27**
See also CA 115; 178; DLB 19, 57, 174

Douglas, Ellen CLC 73
See Haxton, Josephine Ayres; Williamson, Ellen Douglas
See also CN 7; CSW; DLB 292

Douglas, Gavin 1475(?)-1522 **LC 20**
See also DLB 132; RGEL 2

Douglas, George
See Brown, George Douglas
See also RGEL 2

Douglas, Keith (Castellain) 1920-1944 **TCLC 40**
See also BRW 7; CA 160; DLB 27; EWL 3; PAB; RGEL 2

Douglas, Leonard
See Bradbury, Ray (Douglas)

Douglas, Michael
See Crichton, (John) Michael

Douglas, (George) Norman 1868-1952 **TCLC 68**
See also BRW 6; CA 119; 157; DLB 34, 195; RGEL 2

Douglas, William
See Brown, George Douglas

Douglass, Frederick 1817(?)-1895 **BLC 1; NCLC 7, 55; WLC**
See also AAYA 48; AFAW 1, 2; AMWC 1; AMWS 3; CDALB 1640-1865; DA; DA3; DAC; DAM MST, MULT; DLB 1, 43, 50, 79, 243; FW; LAIT 2; NCFS 2; RGAL 4; SATA 29

Dourado, (Waldomiro Freitas) Autran 1926- **CLC 23, 60**
See also CA 25-28R; 179; CANR 34, 81; DLB 145; HW 2

Dourado, Waldomiro Autran
See Dourado, (Waldomiro Freitas) Autran
See also CA 179

Dove, Rita (Frances) 1952- **BLCS; CLC 50, 81; PC 6**
See also AAYA 46; AMWS 4; BW 2; CA 109; CAAS 19; CANR 27, 42, 68, 76, 97; CDALBS; CP 7; CSW; CWP; DA3; DAM MULT, POET; DLB 120; EWL 3; EXPP; MTCW 1; PFS 1, 15; RGAL 4

Doveglion
See Villa, Jose Garcia

Dowell, Coleman 1925-1985 **CLC 60**
See also CA 25-28R; 117; CANR 10; DLB 130; GLL 2

Dowson, Ernest (Christopher) 1867-1900 **TCLC 4**
See also CA 105; 150; DLB 19, 135; RGEL 2

Doyle, A. Conan
See Doyle, Sir Arthur Conan

Doyle, Sir Arthur Conan 1859-1930 **SSC 12; TCLC 7; WLC**
See Conan Doyle, Arthur
See also AAYA 14; BRWS 2; CA 104; 122; CDBLB 1890-1914; CMW 4; DA; DA3; DAB; DAC; DAM MST, NOV; DLB 18, 70, 156, 178; EXPS; HGG; LAIT 2; MSW; MTCW 1, 2; RGEL 2; RGSF 2; RHW; SATA 24; SCFW 2; SFW 4; SSFS 2; TEA; WCH; WLIT 4; WYA; YAW

Doyle, Conan
See Doyle, Sir Arthur Conan

Duras, Marguerite 1914-1996 **CLC 3, 6, 11, 20, 34, 40, 68, 100; SSC 40**
See Donnadieu, Marguerite
See also BPFB 1; CA 25-28R; 151; CANR 50; CWW 2; DLB 83; EWL 3; GFL 1789 to the Present; IDFW 4; MTCW 1, 2; RGWL 2, 3; TWA

Durban, (Rosa) Pam 1947- **CLC 39**
See also CA 123; CANR 98; CSW

Durcan, Paul 1944- **CLC 43, 70**
See also CA 134; CANR 123; CP 7; DAM POET; EWL 3

Durfey, Thomas 1653-1723 **LC 94**
See also DLB 80; RGEL 2

Durkheim, Emile 1858-1917 **TCLC 55**

Durrell, Lawrence (George) 1912-1990 **CLC 1, 4, 6, 8, 13, 27, 41**
See also BPFB 1; BRWS 1; CA 9-12R; 132; CANR 40, 77; CDBLB 1945-1960; DAM NOV; DLB 15, 27, 204; DLBY 1990; EWL 3; MTCW 1, 2; RGEL 2; SFW 4; TEA

Durrenmatt, Friedrich
See Duerrenmatt, Friedrich
See also CDWLB 2; EW 13; EWL 3; RGWL 2, 3

Dutt, Michael Madhusudan 1824-1873 **NCLC 118**

Dutt, Toru 1856-1877 **NCLC 29**
See also DLB 240

Dwight, Timothy 1752-1817 **NCLC 13**
See also DLB 37; RGAL 4

Dworkin, Andrea 1946- **CLC 43, 123**
See also CA 77-80; CAAS 21; CANR 16, 39, 76, 96; FW; GLL 1; INT CANR-16; MTCW 1, 2

Dwyer, Deanna
See Koontz, Dean R(ay)

Dwyer, K. R.
See Koontz, Dean R(ay)

Dybek, Stuart 1942- **CLC 114; SSC 55**
See also CA 97-100; CANR 39; DLB 130

Dye, Richard
See De Voto, Bernard (Augustine)

Dyer, Geoff 1958- **CLC 149**
See also CA 125; CANR 88

Dyer, George 1755-1841 **NCLC 129**
See also DLB 93

Dylan, Bob 1941- **CLC 3, 4, 6, 12, 77; PC 37**
See also CA 41-44R; CANR 108; CP 7; DLB 16

Dyson, John 1943- **CLC 70**
See also CA 144

Dzyubin, Eduard Georgievich 1895-1934
See Bagritsky, Eduard
See also CA 170

E. V. L.
See Lucas, E(dward) V(errall)

Eagleton, Terence (Francis) 1943- **CLC 63, 132**
See also CA 57-60; CANR 7, 23, 68, 115; DLB 242; LMFS 2; MTCW 1, 2

Eagleton, Terry
See Eagleton, Terence (Francis)

Early, Jack
See Scoppettone, Sandra
See also GLL 1

East, Michael
See West, Morris L(anglo)

Eastaway, Edward
See Thomas, (Philip) Edward

Eastlake, William (Derry) 1917-1997 **CLC 8**
See also CA 5-8R; 158; CAAS 1; CANR 5, 63; CN 7; DLB 6, 206; INT CANR-5; TCWW 2

Eastman, Charles A(lexander) 1858-1939 **NNAL; TCLC 55**
See also CA 179; CANR 91; DAM MULT; DLB 175; YABC 1

Eaton, Edith Maude 1865-1914 **AAL**
See Far, Sui Sin
See also CA 154; DLB 221; FW

Eaton, (Lillie) Winnifred 1875-1954 **AAL**
See also CA 217; DLB 221; RGAL 4

Eberhart, Richard (Ghormley) 1904- **CLC 3, 11, 19, 56**
See also AMW; CA 1-4R; CANR 2, 125; CDALB 1941-1968; CP 7; DAM POET; DLB 48; MTCW 1; RGAL 4

Eberstadt, Fernanda 1960- **CLC 39**
See also CA 136; CANR 69, 128

Echegaray (y Eizaguirre), Jose (Maria Waldo) 1832-1916 **HLCS 1; TCLC 4**
See also CA 104; CANR 32; EWL 3; HW 1; MTCW 1

Echeverria, (Jose) Esteban (Antonino) 1805-1851 **NCLC 18**
See also LAW

Echo
See Proust, (Valentin-Louis-George-Eugene) Marcel

Eckert, Allan W. 1931- **CLC 17**
See also AAYA 18; BYA 2; CA 13-16R; CANR 14, 45; INT CANR-14; MAICYA 2; MAICYAS 1; SAAS 21; SATA 29, 91; SATA-Brief 27

Eckhart, Meister 1260(?)-1327(?) **CMLC 9**
See also DLB 115; LMFS 1

Eckmar, F. R.
See de Hartog, Jan

Eco, Umberto 1932- **CLC 28, 60, 142**
See also BEST 90:1; BPFB 1; CA 77-80; CANR 12, 33, 55, 110; CPW; CWW 2; DA3; DAM NOV, POP; DLB 196, 242; EWL 3; MSW; MTCW 1, 2; RGWL 3

Eddison, E(ric) R(ucker) 1882-1945 **TCLC 15**
See also CA 109; 156; DLB 255; FANT; SFW 4; SUFW 1

Eddy, Mary (Ann Morse) Baker 1821-1910 **TCLC 71**
See also CA 113; 174

Edel, (Joseph) Leon 1907-1997 **CLC 29, 34**
See also CA 1-4R; 161; CANR 1, 22, 112; DLB 103; INT CANR-22

Eden, Emily 1797-1869 **NCLC 10**

Edgar, David 1948- **CLC 42**
See also CA 57-60; CANR 12, 61, 112; CBD; CD 5; DAM DRAM; DFS 15; DLB 13, 233; MTCW 1

Edgerton, Clyde (Carlyle) 1944- **CLC 39**
See also AAYA 17; CA 118; 134; CANR 64, 125; CSW; DLB 278; INT CA-134; YAW

Edgeworth, Maria 1768-1849 **NCLC 1, 51**
See also BRWS 3; DLB 116, 159, 163; FW; RGEL 2; SATA 21; TEA; WLIT 3

Edmonds, Paul
See Kuttner, Henry

Edmonds, Walter D(umaux) 1903-1998 **CLC 35**
See also BYA 2; CA 5-8R; CANR 2; CWRI 5; DLB 9; LAIT 1; MAICYA 1, 2; RHW; SAAS 4; SATA 1, 27; SATA-Obit 99

Edmondson, Wallace
See Ellison, Harlan (Jay)

Edson, Russell 1935- **CLC 13**
See also CA 33-36R; CANR 115; DLB 244; WP

Edwards, Bronwen Elizabeth
See Rose, Wendy

Edwards, G(erald) B(asil) 1899-1976 **CLC 25**
See also CA 201; 110

Edwards, Gus 1939- **CLC 43**
See also CA 108; INT CA-108

Edwards, Jonathan 1703-1758 **LC 7, 54**
See also AMW; DA; DAC; DAM MST; DLB 24, 270; RGAL 4; TUS

Edwards, Sarah Pierpont 1710-1758 **LC 87**
See also DLB 200

Efron, Marina Ivanovna Tsvetaeva
See Tsvetaeva (Efron), Marina (Ivanovna)

Egoyan, Atom 1960- **CLC 151**
See also CA 157

Ehle, John (Marsden, Jr.) 1925- **CLC 27**
See also CA 9-12R; CSW

Ehrenbourg, Ilya (Grigoryevich)
See Ehrenburg, Ilya (Grigoryevich)

Ehrenburg, Ilya (Grigoryevich) 1891-1967 **CLC 18, 34, 62**
See Erenburg, Il'ia Grigor'evich
See also CA 102; 25-28R; EWL 3

Ehrenburg, Ilyo (Grigoryevich)
See Ehrenburg, Ilya (Grigoryevich)

Ehrenreich, Barbara 1941- **CLC 110**
See also BEST 90:4; CA 73-76; CANR 16, 37, 62, 117; DLB 246; FW; MTCW 1, 2

Eich, Gunter
See Eich, Gunter
See also RGWL 2, 3

Eich, Gunter 1907-1972 **CLC 15**
See Eich, Gunter
See also CA 111; 93-96; DLB 69, 124; EWL 3

Eichendorff, Joseph 1788-1857 **NCLC 8**
See also DLB 90; RGWL 2, 3

Eigner, Larry CLC 9
See Eigner, Laurence (Joel)
See also CAAS 23; DLB 5; WP

Eigner, Laurence (Joel) 1927-1996
See Eigner, Larry
See also CA 9-12R; 151; CANR 6, 84; CP 7; DLB 193

Eilhart von Oberge c. 1140-c. 1195 **CMLC 67**
See also DLB 148

Einhard c. 770-840 **CMLC 50**
See also DLB 148

Einstein, Albert 1879-1955 **TCLC 65**
See also CA 121; 133; MTCW 1, 2

Eiseley, Loren
See Eiseley, Loren Corey
See also DLB 275

Eiseley, Loren Corey 1907-1977 **CLC 7**
See Eiseley, Loren
See also AAYA 5; ANW; CA 1-4R; 73-76; CANR 6; DLBD 17

Eisenstadt, Jill 1963- **CLC 50**
See also CA 140

Eisenstein, Sergei (Mikhailovich) 1898-1948 **TCLC 57**
See also CA 114; 149

Eisner, Simon
See Kornbluth, C(yril) M.

Ekeloef, (Bengt) Gunnar 1907-1968 **CLC 27; PC 23**
See Ekelof, (Bengt) Gunnar
See also CA 123; 25-28R; DAM POET

Ekelof, (Bengt) Gunnar 1907-1968
See Ekeloef, (Bengt) Gunnar
See also DLB 259; EW 12; EWL 3

Ekelund, Vilhelm 1880-1949 **TCLC 75**
See also CA 189; EWL 3

Ekwensi, C. O. D.
See Ekwensi, Cyprian (Odiatu Duaka)

Ekwensi, Cyprian (Odiatu Duaka) 1921- **BLC 1; CLC 4**
See also AFW; BW 2, 3; CA 29-32R; CANR 18, 42, 74, 125; CDWLB 3; CN 7; CWRI 5; DAM MULT; DLB 117; EWL 3; MTCW 1, 2; RGEL 2; SATA 66; WLIT 2

Elaine TCLC 18
See Leverson, Ada Esther

El Crummo
See Crumb, R(obert)

Elder, Lonne III 1931-1996 **BLC 1; DC 8**
See also BW 1, 3; CA 81-84; 152; CAD; CANR 25; DAM MULT; DLB 7, 38, 44

Eleanor of Aquitaine 1122-1204 **CMLC 39**

Elia
See Lamb, Charles

Eliade, Mircea 1907-1986 **CLC 19**
See also CA 65-68; 119; CANR 30, 62; CD-WLB 4; DLB 220; EWL 3; MTCW 1; RGWL 3; SFW 4

Eliot, A. D.
See Jewett, (Theodora) Sarah Orne

Eliot, Alice
See Jewett, (Theodora) Sarah Orne

Eliot, Dan
See Silverberg, Robert

Eliot, George 1819-1880 **NCLC 4, 13, 23, 41, 49, 89, 118; PC 20; WLC**
See also BRW 5; BRWC 1, 2; BRWR 2; CDBLB 1832-1890; CN 7; CPW; DA; DA3; DAB; DAC; DAM MST, NOV; DLB 21, 35, 55; LATS 1; LMFS 1; NFS 17; RGEL 2; RGSF 2; SSFS 8; TEA; WLIT 3

Eliot, John 1604-1690 **LC 5**
See also DLB 24

Eliot, T(homas) S(tearns) 1888-1965 **CLC 1, 2, 3, 6, 9, 10, 13, 15, 24, 34, 41, 55, 57, 113; PC 5, 31; WLC**
See also AAYA 28; AMW; AMWC 1; AMWR 1; BRW 7; BRWR 2; CA 5-8R; 25-28R; CANR 41; CDALB 1929-1941; DA; DA3; DAB; DAC; DAM DRAM, MST, POET; DFS 4, 13; DLB 7, 10, 45, 63, 245; DLBY 1988; EWL 3; EXPP; LAIT 3; LATS 1; LMFS 2; MTCW 1, 2; NCFS 5; PAB; PFS 1, 7; RGAL 4; RGEL 2; TUS; WLIT 4; WP

Elizabeth 1866-1941 **TCLC 41**

Elkin, Stanley L(awrence) 1930-1995 **CLC 4, 6, 9, 14, 27, 51, 91; SSC 12**
See also AMWS 6; BPFB 1; CA 9-12R; 148; CANR 8, 46; CN 7; CPW; DAM NOV, POP; DLB 2, 28, 218, 278; DLBY 1980; EWL 3; INT CANR-8; MTCW 1, 2; RGAL 4

Elledge, Scott CLC 34

Elliott, Don
See Silverberg, Robert

Elliott, George P(aul) 1918-1980 **CLC 2**
See also CA 1-4R; 97-100; CANR 2; DLB 244

Elliott, Janice 1931-1995 **CLC 47**
See also CA 13-16R; CANR 8, 29, 84; CN 7; DLB 14; SATA 119

Elliott, Sumner Locke 1917-1991 **CLC 38**
See also CA 5-8R; 134; CANR 2, 21; DLB 289

Elliott, William
See Bradbury, Ray (Douglas)

Ellis, A. E. CLC 7

Ellis, Alice Thomas CLC 40
See Haycraft, Anna (Margaret)
See also DLB 194; MTCW 1

Ellis, Bret Easton 1964- **CLC 39, 71, 117**
See also AAYA 2, 43; CA 118; 123; CANR 51, 74, 126; CN 7; CPW; DA3; DAM POP; DLB 292; HGG; INT CA-123; MTCW 1; NFS 11

Ellis, (Henry) Havelock 1859-1939 **TCLC 14**
See also CA 109; 169; DLB 190

Ellis, Landon
See Ellison, Harlan (Jay)

Ellis, Trey 1962- **CLC 55**
See also CA 146; CANR 92

Ellison, Harlan (Jay) 1934- **CLC 1, 13, 42, 139; SSC 14**
See also AAYA 29; BPFB 1; BYA 14; CA 5-8R; CANR 5, 46, 115; CPW; DAM POP; DLB 8; HGG; INT CANR-5; MTCW 1, 2; SCFW 2; SFW 4; SSFS 13, 14, 15; SUFW 1, 2

Ellison, Ralph (Waldo) 1914-1994 **BLC 1; CLC 1, 3, 11, 54, 86, 114; SSC 26; WLC**
See also AAYA 19; AFAW 1, 2; AMWC 2; AMWR 2; AMWS 2; BPFB 1; BW 1, 3; BYA 2; CA 9-12R; 145; CANR 24, 53; CDALB 1941-1968; CSW; DA; DA3; DAB; DAC; DAM MST, MULT, NOV; DLB 2, 76, 227; DLBY 1994; EWL 3; EXPN; EXPS; LAIT 4; MTCW 1, 2; NCFS 3; NFS 2; RGAL 4; RGSF 2; SSFS 1, 11; YAW

Ellmann, Lucy (Elizabeth) 1956- **CLC 61**
See also CA 128

Ellmann, Richard (David) 1918-1987 **CLC 50**
See also BEST 89:2; CA 1-4R; 122; CANR 2, 28, 61; DLB 103; DLBY 1987; MTCW 1, 2

Elman, Richard (Martin) 1934-1997 **CLC 19**
See also CA 17-20R; 163; CAAS 3; CANR 47

Elron
See Hubbard, L(afayette) Ron(ald)

Eluard, Paul PC 38; TCLC 7, 41
See Grindel, Eugene
See also EWL 3; GFL 1789 to the Present; RGWL 2, 3

Elyot, Thomas 1490(?)-1546 **LC 11**
See also DLB 136; RGEL 2

Elytis, Odysseus 1911-1996 **CLC 15, 49, 100; PC 21**
See Alepoudelis, Odysseus
See also CA 102; 151; CANR 94; CWW 2; DAM POET; EW 13; EWL 3; MTCW 1, 2; RGWL 2, 3

Emecheta, (Florence Onye) Buchi 1944- **BLC 2; CLC 14, 48, 128**
See also AFW; BW 2, 3; CA 81-84; CANR 27, 81, 126; CDWLB 3; CN 7; CWRI 5; DA3; DAM MULT; DLB 117; EWL 3; FW; MTCW 1, 2; NFS 12, 14; SATA 66; WLIT 2

Emerson, Mary Moody 1774-1863 **NCLC 66**

Emerson, Ralph Waldo 1803-1882 **NCLC 1, 38, 98; PC 18; WLC**
See also AMW; ANW; CDALB 1640-1865; DA; DA3; DAB; DAC; DAM MST, POET; DLB 1, 59, 73, 183, 223, 270; EXPP; LAIT 2; LMFS 1; NCFS 3; PFS 4, 17; RGAL 4; TUS; WP

Eminescu, Mihail 1850-1889 **NCLC 33, 131**

Empedocles 5th cent. B.C.- **CMLC 50**
See also DLB 176

Empson, William 1906-1984 **CLC 3, 8, 19, 33, 34**
See also BRWS 2; CA 17-20R; 112; CANR 31, 61; DLB 20; EWL 3; MTCW 1, 2; RGEL 2

Enchi, Fumiko (Ueda) 1905-1986 **CLC 31**
See Enchi Fumiko
See also CA 129; 121; FW; MJW

Enchi Fumiko
See Enchi, Fumiko (Ueda)
See also DLB 182; EWL 3

Ende, Michael (Andreas Helmuth) 1929-1995 **CLC 31**
See also BYA 5; CA 118; 124; 149; CANR 36, 110; CLR 14; DLB 75; MAICYA 1, 2; MAICYAS 1; SATA 61, 130; SATA-Brief 42; SATA-Obit 86

Endo, Shusaku 1923-1996 **CLC 7, 14, 19, 54, 99; SSC 48**
See Endo Shusaku
See also CA 29-32R; 153; CANR 21, 54; DA3; DAM NOV; MTCW 1, 2; RGSF 2; RGWL 2, 3

Endo Shusaku
See Endo, Shusaku
See also DLB 182; EWL 3

Engel, Marian 1933-1985 **CLC 36; TCLC 137**
See also CA 25-28R; CANR 12; DLB 53; FW; INT CANR-12

Engelhardt, Frederick
See Hubbard, L(afayette) Ron(ald)

Engels, Friedrich 1820-1895 **NCLC 85, 114**
See also DLB 129; LATS 1

Enright, D(ennis) J(oseph) 1920-2002 **CLC 4, 8, 31**
See also CA 1-4R; 211; CANR 1, 42, 83; CP 7; DLB 27; EWL 3; SATA 25; SATA-Obit 140

Enzensberger, Hans Magnus 1929- **CLC 43; PC 28**
See also CA 116; 119; CANR 103; EWL 3

Ephron, Nora 1941- **CLC 17, 31**
See also AAYA 35; AITN 2; CA 65-68; CANR 12, 39, 83

Epicurus 341B.C.-270B.C. **CMLC 21**
See also DLB 176

Epsilon
See Betjeman, John

Epstein, Daniel Mark 1948- **CLC 7**
See also CA 49-52; CANR 2, 53, 90

Epstein, Jacob 1956- **CLC 19**
See also CA 114

Epstein, Jean 1897-1953 **TCLC 92**

Epstein, Joseph 1937- **CLC 39**
See also CA 112; 119; CANR 50, 65, 117

Epstein, Leslie 1938- **CLC 27**
See also AMWS 12; CA 73-76, 215; CAAE 215; CAAS 12; CANR 23, 69

Equiano, Olaudah 1745(?)-1797 **BLC 2; LC 16**
See also AFAW 1, 2; CDWLB 3; DAM MULT; DLB 37, 50; WLIT 2

Erasmus, Desiderius 1469(?)-1536 **LC 16, 93**
See also DLB 136; EW 2; LMFS 1; RGWL 2, 3; TWA

Erdman, Paul E(mil) 1932- **CLC 25**
See also AITN 1; CA 61-64; CANR 13, 43, 84

Erdrich, Louise 1954- **CLC 39, 54, 120, 176; NNAL; PC 52**
See also AAYA 10, 47; AMWS 4; BEST 89:1; BPFB 1; CA 114; CANR 41, 62, 118; CDALBS; CN 7; CP 7; CPW; CWP; DA3; DAM MULT, NOV, POP; DLB 152, 175, 206; EWL 3; EXPP; LAIT 5; LATS 1; MTCW 1; NFS 5; PFS 14; RGAL 4; SATA 94, 141; SSFS 14; TCWW 2

Erenburg, Ilya (Grigoryevich)
See Ehrenburg, Ilya (Grigoryevich)

Erickson, Stephen Michael 1950-
See Erickson, Steve
See also CA 129; SFW 4

Erickson, Steve CLC 64
See Erickson, Stephen Michael
See also CANR 60, 68; SUFW 2

Erickson, Walter
See Fast, Howard (Melvin)

Ericson, Walter
See Fast, Howard (Melvin)

Eriksson, Buntel
See Bergman, (Ernst) Ingmar

Eriugena, John Scottus c. 810-877 **CMLC 65**
See also DLB 115

Ernaux, Annie 1940- **CLC 88, 184**
See also CA 147; CANR 93; NCFS 3, 5

Erskine, John 1879-1951 **TCLC 84**
See also CA 112; 159; DLB 9, 102; FANT

Eschenbach, Wolfram von
See Wolfram von Eschenbach
See also RGWL 3

Eseki, Bruno
See Mphahlele, Ezekiel

Esenin, Sergei (Alexandrovich) 1895-1925 **TCLC 4**
See Yesenin, Sergey
See also CA 104; RGWL 2, 3

Eshleman, Clayton 1935- **CLC 7**
See also CA 33-36R, 212; CAAE 212; CAAS 6; CANR 93; CP 7; DLB 5

Espriella, Don Manuel Alvarez
See Southey, Robert

Espriu, Salvador 1913-1985 **CLC 9**
See also CA 154; 115; DLB 134; EWL 3

Espronceda, Jose de 1808-1842 **NCLC 39**

Esquivel, Laura 1951(?)- **CLC 141; HLCS 1**
See also AAYA 29; CA 143; CANR 68, 113; DA3; DNFS 2; LAIT 3; LMFS 2; MTCW 1; NFS 5; WLIT 1

Esse, James
See Stephens, James

Esterbrook, Tom
See Hubbard, L(afayette) Ron(ald)

Estleman, Loren D. 1952- **CLC 48**
See also AAYA 27; CA 85-88; CANR 27, 74; CMW 4; CPW; DA3; DAM NOV, POP; DLB 226; INT CANR-27; MTCW 1, 2

Etherege, Sir George 1636-1692 **LC 78**
See also BRW 2; DAM DRAM; DLB 80; PAB; RGEL 2

Euclid 306B.C.-283B.C. **CMLC 25**

Eugenides, Jeffrey 1960(?)- **CLC 81**
See also AAYA 51; CA 144; CANR 120

Euripides c. 484B.C.-406B.C. **CMLC 23, 51; DC 4; WLCS**
See also AW 1; CDWLB 1; DA; DA3; DAB; DAC; DAM DRAM, MST; DFS 1, 4, 6; DLB 176; LAIT 1; LMFS 1; RGWL 2, 3

Evan, Evin
See Faust, Frederick (Schiller)

Evans, Caradoc 1878-1945 **SSC 43; TCLC 85**
See also DLB 162

Evans, Evan
See Faust, Frederick (Schiller)
See also TCWW 2

Evans, Marian
See Eliot, George

Evans, Mary Ann
See Eliot, George

Evarts, Esther
See Benson, Sally

Everett, Percival
See Everett, Percival L.
See also CSW

Everett, Percival L. 1956- **CLC 57**
See Everett, Percival
See also BW 2; CA 129; CANR 94

Everson, R(onald) G(ilmour) 1903-1992 **CLC 27**
See also CA 17-20R; DLB 88

Everson, William (Oliver) 1912-1994 **CLC 1, 5, 14**
See also BG 2; CA 9-12R; 145; CANR 20; DLB 5, 16, 212; MTCW 1

Evtushenko, Evgenii Aleksandrovich
See Yevtushenko, Yevgeny (Alexandrovich)
See also RGWL 2, 3

Ewart, Gavin (Buchanan) 1916-1995 **CLC 13, 46**
See also BRWS 7; CA 89-92; 150; CANR 17, 46; CP 7; DLB 40; MTCW 1

Ewers, Hanns Heinz 1871-1943 **TCLC 12**
See also CA 109; 149

Ewing, Frederick R.
See Sturgeon, Theodore (Hamilton)

Exley, Frederick (Earl) 1929-1992 **CLC 6, 11**
See also AITN 2; BPFB 1; CA 81-84; 138; CANR 117; DLB 143; DLBY 1981

Eynhardt, Guillermo
See Quiroga, Horacio (Sylvestre)

Ezekiel, Nissim (Moses) 1924-2004 **CLC 61**
See also CA 61-64; CP 7; EWL 3

Ezekiel, Tish O'Dowd 1943- **CLC 34**
See also CA 129

Fadeev, Aleksandr Aleksandrovich
See Bulgya, Alexander Alexandrovich
See also DLB 272

Fadeev, Alexandr Alexandrovich
See Bulgya, Alexander Alexandrovich
See also EWL 3

Fadeyev, A.
See Bulgya, Alexander Alexandrovich

Fadeyev, Alexander TCLC 53
See Bulgya, Alexander Alexandrovich

Fagen, Donald 1948- **CLC 26**

Fainzilberg, Ilya Arnoldovich 1897-1937
See Ilf, Ilya
See also CA 120; 165

Fair, Ronald L. 1932- **CLC 18**
See also BW 1; CA 69-72; CANR 25; DLB 33

Fairbairn, Roger
See Carr, John Dickson

Fairbairns, Zoe (Ann) 1948- **CLC 32**
See also CA 103; CANR 21, 85; CN 7

Fairfield, Flora
See Alcott, Louisa May

Fairman, Paul W. 1916-1977
See Queen, Ellery
See also CA 114; SFW 4

Falco, Gian
See Papini, Giovanni

Falconer, James
See Kirkup, James

Falconer, Kenneth
See Kornbluth, C(yril) M.

Falkland, Samuel
See Heijermans, Herman

Fallaci, Oriana 1930- **CLC 11, 110**
See also CA 77-80; CANR 15, 58; FW; MTCW 1

Faludi, Susan 1959- **CLC 140**
See also CA 138; CANR 126; FW; MTCW 1; NCFS 3

Faludy, George 1913- **CLC 42**
See also CA 21-24R

Faludy, Gyoergy
See Faludy, George

Fanon, Frantz 1925-1961 **BLC 2; CLC 74**
See also BW 1; CA 116; 89-92; DAM MULT; DLB 296; LMFS 2; WLIT 2

Fanshawe, Ann 1625-1680 **LC 11**

Fante, John (Thomas) 1911-1983 **CLC 60; SSC 65**
See also AMWS 11; CA 69-72; 109; CANR 23, 104; DLB 130; DLBY 1983

Far, Sui Sin SSC 62
See Eaton, Edith Maude
See also SSFS 4

Farah, Nuruddin 1945- **BLC 2; CLC 53, 137**
See also AFW; BW 2, 3; CA 106; CANR 81; CDWLB 3; CN 7; DAM MULT; DLB 125; EWL 3; WLIT 2

Fargue, Leon-Paul 1876(?)-1947 **TCLC 11**
See also CA 109; CANR 107; DLB 258; EWL 3

Farigoule, Louis
See Romains, Jules

Farina, Richard 1936(?)-1966 **CLC 9**
See also CA 81-84; 25-28R

Farley, Walter (Lorimer) 1915-1989 **CLC 17**
See also BYA 14; CA 17-20R; CANR 8, 29, 84; DLB 22; JRDA; MAICYA 1, 2; SATA 2, 43, 132; YAW

Farmer, Philip Jose 1918- **CLC 1, 19**
See also AAYA 28; BPFB 1; CA 1-4R; CANR 4, 35, 111; DLB 8; MTCW 1; SATA 93; SCFW 2; SFW 4

Farquhar, George 1677-1707 **LC 21**
See also BRW 2; DAM DRAM; DLB 84; RGEL 2

Farrell, J(ames) G(ordon) 1935-1979 **CLC 6**
See also CA 73-76; 89-92; CANR 36; DLB 14, 271; MTCW 1; RGEL 2; RHW; WLIT 4

Farrell, James T(homas) 1904-1979 **CLC 1, 4, 8, 11, 66; SSC 28**
See also AMW; BPFB 1; CA 5-8R; 89-92; CANR 9, 61; DLB 4, 9, 86; DLBD 2; EWL 3; MTCW 1, 2; RGAL 4

Farrell, Warren (Thomas) 1943- **CLC 70**
See also CA 146; CANR 120

Farren, Richard J.
See Betjeman, John

Farren, Richard M.
See Betjeman, John

Fassbinder, Rainer Werner 1946-1982 **CLC 20**
See also CA 93-96; 106; CANR 31

Fast, Howard (Melvin) 1914-2003 **CLC 23, 131**
See also AAYA 16; BPFB 1; CA 1-4R, 181; 214; CAAE 181; CAAS 18; CANR 1, 33, 54, 75, 98; CMW 4; CN 7; CPW; DAM NOV; DLB 9; INT CANR-33; LATS 1; MTCW 1; RHW; SATA 7; SATA-Essay 107; TCWW 2; YAW

Faulcon, Robert
See Holdstock, Robert P.

Faulkner, William (Cuthbert) 1897-1962 **CLC 1, 3, 6, 8, 9, 11, 14, 18, 28, 52, 68; SSC 1, 35, 42; TCLC 141; WLC**
See also AAYA 7; AMW; AMWR 1; BPFB 1; BYA 5, 15; CA 81-84; CANR 33; CDALB 1929-1941; DA; DA3; DAB; DAC; DAM MST, NOV; DLB 9, 11, 44, 102; DLBD 2; DLBY 1986, 1997; EWL 3; EXPN; EXPS; LAIT 2; LATS 1; LMFS 2; MTCW 1, 2; NFS 4, 8, 13; RGAL 4; RGSF 2; SSFS 2, 5, 6, 12; TUS

Fauset, Jessie Redmon 1882(?)-1961 **BLC 2; CLC 19, 54; HR 2**
See also AFAW 2; BW 1; CA 109; CANR 83; DAM MULT; DLB 51; FW; LMFS 2; MAWW

Faust, Frederick (Schiller) 1892-1944(?) **TCLC 49**
See Austin, Frank; Brand, Max; Challis, George; Dawson, Peter; Dexter, Martin; Evans, Evan; Frederick, John; Frost, Frederick; Manning, David; Silver, Nicholas
See also CA 108; 152; DAM POP; DLB 256; TUS

Faust, Irvin 1924- **CLC 8**
See also CA 33-36R; CANR 28, 67; CN 7; DLB 2, 28, 218, 278; DLBY 1980

Faustino, Domingo 1811-1888 **NCLC 123**

Fawkes, Guy
See Benchley, Robert (Charles)

Fearing, Kenneth (Flexner) 1902-1961 **CLC 51**
See also CA 93-96; CANR 59; CMW 4; DLB 9; RGAL 4

Fecamps, Elise
See Creasey, John

Federman, Raymond 1928- **CLC 6, 47**
See also CA 17-20R, 208; CAAE 208; CAAS 8; CANR 10, 43, 83, 108; CN 7; DLBY 1980

Federspiel, J(uerg) F. 1931- **CLC 42**
See also CA 146

Feiffer, Jules (Ralph) 1929- **CLC 2, 8, 64**
See also AAYA 3; CA 17-20R; CAD; CANR 30, 59, 129; CD 5; DAM DRAM; DLB 7, 44; INT CANR-30; MTCW 1; SATA 8, 61, 111

Feige, Hermann Albert Otto Maximilian
See Traven, B.

Feinberg, David B. 1956-1994 **CLC 59**
See also CA 135; 147

Feinstein, Elaine 1930- **CLC 36**
See also CA 69-72; CAAS 1; CANR 31, 68, 121; CN 7; CP 7; CWP; DLB 14, 40; MTCW 1

Feke, Gilbert David CLC 65

Feldman, Irving (Mordecai) 1928- **CLC 7**
See also CA 1-4R; CANR 1; CP 7; DLB 169

Felix-Tchicaya, Gerald
See Tchicaya, Gerald Felix

Fellini, Federico 1920-1993 **CLC 16, 85**
See also CA 65-68; 143; CANR 33

Felltham, Owen 1602(?)-1668 **LC 92**
See also DLB 126, 151

Felsen, Henry Gregor 1916-1995 **CLC 17**
See also CA 1-4R; 180; CANR 1; SAAS 2; SATA 1

Felski, Rita CLC 65

Fenno, Jack
See Calisher, Hortense

Fenollosa, Ernest (Francisco) 1853-1908 **TCLC 91**

Fenton, James Martin 1949- **CLC 32**
See also CA 102; CANR 108; CP 7; DLB 40; PFS 11

Ferber, Edna 1887-1968 **CLC 18, 93**
See also AITN 1; CA 5-8R; 25-28R; CANR 68, 105; DLB 9, 28, 86, 266; MTCW 1, 2; RGAL 4; RHW; SATA 7; TCWW 2

Ferdowsi, Abu'l Qasem 940-1020 **CMLC 43**
See also RGWL 2, 3

Ferguson, Helen
See Kavan, Anna

Ferguson, Niall 1964- **CLC 134**
See also CA 190

Ferguson, Samuel 1810-1886 **NCLC 33**
See also DLB 32; RGEL 2

Fergusson, Robert 1750-1774 **LC 29**
See also DLB 109; RGEL 2

Ferling, Lawrence
See Ferlinghetti, Lawrence (Monsanto)

Ferlinghetti, Lawrence (Monsanto) 1919(?)- **CLC 2, 6, 10, 27, 111; PC 1**
See also CA 5-8R; CANR 3, 41, 73, 125; CDALB 1941-1968; CP 7; DA3; DAM POET; DLB 5, 16; MTCW 1, 2; RGAL 4; WP

Fern, Fanny
See Parton, Sara Payson Willis

Fernandez, Vicente Garcia Huidobro
See Huidobro Fernandez, Vicente Garcia

Fernandez-Armesto, Felipe CLC 70

Fernandez de Lizardi, Jose Joaquin
See Lizardi, Jose Joaquin Fernandez de

Ferre, Rosario 1938- **CLC 139; HLCS 1; SSC 36**
See also CA 131; CANR 55, 81; CWW 2; DLB 145; EWL 3; HW 1, 2; LAWS 1; MTCW 1; WLIT 1

Ferrer, Gabriel (Francisco Victor) Miro
See Miro (Ferrer), Gabriel (Francisco Victor)

Ferrier, Susan (Edmonstone) 1782-1854 **NCLC 8**
See also DLB 116; RGEL 2

Ferrigno, Robert 1948(?)- **CLC 65**
See also CA 140; CANR 125

Ferron, Jacques 1921-1985 **CLC 94**
See also CA 117; 129; CCA 1; DAC; DLB 60; EWL 3

Feuchtwanger, Lion 1884-1958 **TCLC 3**
See also CA 104; 187; DLB 66; EWL 3

Feuerbach, Ludwig 1804-1872 **NCLC 139**
See also DLB 133

Feuillet, Octave 1821-1890 **NCLC 45**
See also DLB 192

Feydeau, Georges (Leon Jules Marie) 1862-1921 **TCLC 22**
See also CA 113; 152; CANR 84; DAM DRAM; DLB 192; EWL 3; GFL 1789 to the Present; RGWL 2, 3

Fichte, Johann Gottlieb 1762-1814 **NCLC 62**
See also DLB 90

Ficino, Marsilio 1433-1499 **LC 12**
See also LMFS 1

Fiedeler, Hans
See Doeblin, Alfred

Fiedler, Leslie A(aron) 1917-2003 **CLC 4, 13, 24**
See also AMWS 13; CA 9-12R; 212; CANR 7, 63; CN 7; DLB 28, 67; EWL 3; MTCW 1, 2; RGAL 4; TUS

Field, Andrew 1938- **CLC 44**
See also CA 97-100; CANR 25

Field, Eugene 1850-1895 **NCLC 3**
See also DLB 23, 42, 140; DLBD 13; MAICYA 1, 2; RGAL 4; SATA 16

Field, Gans T.
See Wellman, Manly Wade

Field, Michael 1915-1971 **TCLC 43**
See also CA 29-32R

Field, Peter
See Hobson, Laura Z(ametkin)
See also TCWW 2

Fielding, Helen 1958- **CLC 146**
See also CA 172; CANR 127; DLB 231

Fielding, Henry 1707-1754 **LC 1, 46, 85; WLC**
See also BRW 3; BRWR 1; CDBLB 1660-1789; DA; DA3; DAB; DAC; DAM DRAM, MST, NOV; DLB 39, 84, 101; NFS 18; RGEL 2; TEA; WLIT 3

Fielding, Sarah 1710-1768 **LC 1, 44**
See also DLB 39; RGEL 2; TEA

Fields, W. C. 1880-1946 **TCLC 80**
See also DLB 44

Fierstein, Harvey (Forbes) 1954- **CLC 33**
See also CA 123; 129; CAD; CD 5; CPW; DA3; DAM DRAM, POP; DFS 6; DLB 266; GLL

Figes, Eva 1932- **CLC 31**
See also CA 53-56; CANR 4, 44, 83; CN 7; DLB 14, 271; FW

Filippo, Eduardo de
See de Filippo, Eduardo

Finch, Anne 1661-1720 **LC 3; PC 21**
See also BRWS 9; DLB 95

Finch, Robert (Duer Claydon) 1900-1995 **CLC 18**
See also CA 57-60; CANR 9, 24, 49; CP 7; DLB 88

Findley, Timothy (Irving Frederick) 1930-2002 **CLC 27, 102**
See also CA 25-28R; 206; CANR 12, 42, 69, 109; CCA 1; CN 7; DAC; DAM MST; DLB 53; FANT; RHW

Fink, William
See Mencken, H(enry) L(ouis)

Firbank, Louis 1942-
See Reed, Lou
See also CA 117

Firbank, (Arthur Annesley) Ronald 1886-1926 **TCLC 1**
See also BRWS 2; CA 104; 177; DLB 36; EWL 3; RGEL 2

Fish, Stanley
See Fish, Stanley Eugene

Fish, Stanley E.
See Fish, Stanley Eugene

Fish, Stanley Eugene 1938- **CLC 142**
See also CA 112; 132; CANR 90; DLB 67

Fisher, Dorothy (Frances) Canfield 1879-1958 **TCLC 87**
See also CA 114; 136; CANR 80; CLR 71,; CWRI 5; DLB 9, 102, 284; MAICYA 1, 2; YABC 1

Fisher, M(ary) F(rances) K(ennedy) 1908-1992 **CLC 76, 87**
See also CA 77-80; 138; CANR 44; MTCW 1

Fisher, Roy 1930- **CLC 25**
See also CA 81-84; CAAS 10; CANR 16; CP 7; DLB 40

Fisher, Rudolph 1897-1934 **BLC 2; HR 2; SSC 25; TCLC 11**
See also BW 1, 3; CA 107; 124; CANR 80; DAM MULT; DLB 51, 102

Fisher, Vardis (Alvero) 1895-1968 **CLC 7; TCLC 140**
See also CA 5-8R; 25-28R; CANR 68; DLB 9, 206; RGAL 4; TCWW 2

Fiske, Tarleton
See Bloch, Robert (Albert)

Fitch, Clarke
See Sinclair, Upton (Beall)

Fitch, John IV
See Cormier, Robert (Edmund)

Fitzgerald, Captain Hugh
See Baum, L(yman) Frank

FitzGerald, Edward 1809-1883 **NCLC 9**
See also BRW 4; DLB 32; RGEL 2

Fitzgerald, F(rancis) Scott (Key) 1896-1940 **SSC 6, 31; TCLC 1, 6, 14, 28, 55; WLC**
See also AAYA 24; AITN 1; AMW; AMWC 2; AMWR 1; BPFB 1; CA 110; 123; CDALB 1917-1929; DA; DA3; DAB; DAC; DAM MST, NOV; DLB 4, 9, 86, 219, 273; DLBD 1, 15, 16; DLBY 1981, 1996; EWL 3; EXPN; EXPS; LAIT 3; MTCW 1, 2; NFS 2; RGAL 4; RGSF 2; SSFS 4, 15; TUS

Fitzgerald, Penelope 1916-2000 **CLC 19, 51, 61, 143**
See also BRWS 5; CA 85-88; 190; CAAS 10; CANR 56, 86; CN 7; DLB 14, 194; EWL 3; MTCW 2

Fitzgerald, Robert (Stuart) 1910-1985 **CLC 39**
See also CA 1-4R; 114; CANR 1; DLBY 1980

FitzGerald, Robert D(avid) 1902-1987 **CLC 19**
See also CA 17-20R; DLB 260; RGEL 2

Fitzgerald, Zelda (Sayre) 1900-1948 **TCLC 52**
See also AMWS 9; CA 117; 126; DLBY 1984

Flanagan, Thomas (James Bonner) 1923-2002 **CLC 25, 52**
See also CA 108; 206; CANR 55; CN 7; DLBY 1980; INT CA-108; MTCW 1; RHW

Flaubert, Gustave 1821-1880 **NCLC 2, 10, 19, 62, 66, 135; SSC 11, 60; WLC**
See also DA; DA3; DAB; DAC; DAM MST, NOV; DLB 119; EW 7; EXPS; GFL

1789 to the Present; LAIT 2; LMFS 1;
NFS 14; RGSF 2; RGWL 2, 3; SSFS 6;
TWA

Flavius Josephus
See Josephus, Flavius

Flecker, Herman Elroy
See Flecker, (Herman) James Elroy

Flecker, (Herman) James Elroy 1884-1915
TCLC 43
See also CA 109; 150; DLB 10, 19; RGEL
2

Fleming, Ian (Lancaster) 1908-1964 **CLC 3,
30**
See also AAYA 26; BPFB 1; CA 5-8R;
CANR 59; CDBLB 1945-1960; CMW 4;
CPW; DA3; DAM POP; DLB 87, 201;
MSW; MTCW 1, 2; RGEL 2; SATA 9;
TEA; YAW

Fleming, Thomas (James) 1927- **CLC 37**
See also CA 5-8R; CANR 10, 102; INT
CANR-10; SATA 8

Fletcher, John 1579-1625 **DC 6; LC 33**
See also BRW 2; CDBLB Before 1660;
DLB 58; RGEL 2; TEA

Fletcher, John Gould 1886-1950 **TCLC 35**
See also CA 107; 167; DLB 4, 45; LMFS
2; RGAL 4

Fleur, Paul
See Pohl, Frederik

Flooglebuckle, Al
See Spiegelman, Art

Flora, Fletcher 1914-1969
See Queen, Ellery
See also CA 1-4R; CANR 3, 85

Flying Officer X
See Bates, H(erbert) E(rnest)

Fo, Dario 1926- **CLC 32, 109; DC 10**
See also CA 116; 128; CANR 68, 114;
CWW 2; DA3; DAM DRAM; DLBY
1997; EWL 3; MTCW 1, 2

Fogarty, Jonathan Titulescu Esq.
See Farrell, James T(homas)

Follett, Ken(neth Martin) 1949- **CLC 18**
See also AAYA 6, 50; BEST 89:4; BPFB 1;
CA 81-84; CANR 13, 33, 54, 102; CMW
4; CPW; DA3; DAM NOV, POP; DLB
87; DLBY 1981; INT CANR-33; MTCW
1

Fontane, Theodor 1819-1898 **NCLC 26**
See also CDWLB 2; DLB 129; EW 6;
RGWL 2, 3; TWA

Fontenot, Chester CLC 65

Fonvizin, Denis Ivanovich 1744(?)-1792 **LC
81**
See also DLB 150; RGWL 2, 3

Foote, Horton 1916- **CLC 51, 91**
See also CA 73-76; CAD; CANR 34, 51,
110; CD 5; CSW; DA3; DAM DRAM;
DLB 26, 266; EWL 3; INT CANR-34

Foote, Mary Hallock 1847-1938 **TCLC 108**
See also DLB 186, 188, 202, 221

Foote, Shelby 1916- **CLC 75**
See also AAYA 40; CA 5-8R; CANR 3, 45,
74; CN 7; CPW; CSW; DA3; DAM NOV,
POP; DLB 2, 17; MTCW 2; RHW

Forbes, Cosmo
See Lewton, Val

Forbes, Esther 1891-1967 **CLC 12**
See also AAYA 17; BYA 2; CA 13-14; 25-
28R; CAP 1; CLR 27; DLB 22; JRDA;
MAICYA 1, 2; RHW; SATA 2, 100; YAW

Forche, Carolyn (Louise) 1950- **CLC 25, 83,
86; PC 10**
See also CA 109; 117; CANR 50, 74; CP 7;
CWP; DA3; DAM POET; DLB 5, 193;
INT CA-117; MTCW 1; PFS 18; RGAL 4

Ford, Elbur
See Hibbert, Eleanor Alice Burford

Ford, Ford Madox 1873-1939 **TCLC 1, 15,
39, 57**
See Chaucer, Daniel
See also BRW 6; CA 104; 132; CANR 74;
CDBLB 1914-1945; DA3; DAM NOV;
DLB 34, 98, 162; EWL 3; MTCW 1, 2;
RGEL 2; TEA

Ford, Henry 1863-1947 **TCLC 73**
See also CA 115; 148

Ford, Jack
See Ford, John

Ford, John 1586-1639 **DC 8; LC 68**
See also BRW 2; CDBLB Before 1660;
DA3; DAM DRAM; DFS 7; DLB 58;
IDTP; RGEL 2

Ford, John 1895-1973 **CLC 16**
See also CA 187; 45-48

Ford, Richard 1944- **CLC 46, 99**
See also AMWS 5; CA 69-72; CANR 11,
47, 86, 128; CN 7; CSW; DLB 227; EWL
3; MTCW 1; RGAL 4; RGSF 2

Ford, Webster
See Masters, Edgar Lee

Foreman, Richard 1937- **CLC 50**
See also CA 65-68; CAD; CANR 32, 63;
CD 5

Forester, C(ecil) S(cott) 1899-1966 **CLC 35**
See also CA 73-76; 25-28R; CANR 83;
DLB 191; RGEL 2; RHW; SATA 13

Forez
See Mauriac, Francois (Charles)

Forman, James
See Forman, James D(ouglas)

Forman, James D(ouglas) 1932- **CLC 21**
See also AAYA 17; CA 9-12R; CANR 4,
19, 42; JRDA; MAICYA 1, 2; SATA 8,
70; YAW

Forman, Milos 1932- **CLC 164**
See also CA 109

Fornes, Maria Irene 1930- **CLC 39, 61, 187;
DC 10; HLCS 1**
See also CA 25-28R; CAD; CANR 28, 81;
CD 5; CWD; DLB 7; HW 1, 2; INT
CANR-28; LLW 1; MTCW 1; RGAL 4

Forrest, Leon (Richard) 1937-1997 **BLCS;
CLC 4**
See also AFAW 2; BW 2; CA 89-92; 162;
CAAS 7; CANR 25, 52, 87; CN 7; DLB
33

Forster, E(dward) M(organ) 1879-1970 **CLC
1, 2, 3, 4, 9, 10, 13, 15, 22, 45, 77; SSC
27; TCLC 125; WLC**
See also AAYA 2, 37; BRW 6; BRWR 2;
BYA 12; CA 13-14; 25-28R; CANR 45;
CAP 1; CDBLB 1914-1945; DA; DA3;
DAB; DAC; DAM MST, NOV; DLB 34,
98, 162, 178, 195; DLBD 10; EWL 3;
EXPN; LAIT 3; LMFS 1; MTCW 1, 2;
NCFS 1; NFS 3, 10, 11; RGEL 2; RGSF
2; SATA 57; SUFW 1; TEA; WLIT 4

Forster, John 1812-1876 **NCLC 11**
See also DLB 144, 184

Forster, Margaret 1938- **CLC 149**
See also CA 133; CANR 62, 115; CN 7;
DLB 155, 271

Forsyth, Frederick 1938- **CLC 2, 5, 36**
See also BEST 89:4; CA 85-88; CANR 38,
62, 115; CMW 4; CN 7; CPW; DAM
NOV, POP; DLB 87; MTCW 1, 2

Forten, Charlotte L. 1837-1914 **BLC 2;
TCLC 16**
See Grimke, Charlotte L(ottie) Forten
See also DLB 50, 239

Fortinbras
See Grieg, (Johan) Nordahl (Brun)

Foscolo, Ugo 1778-1827 **NCLC 8, 97**
See also EW 5

Fosse, Bob CLC 20
See Fosse, Robert Louis

Fosse, Robert Louis 1927-1987
See Fosse, Bob
See also CA 110; 123

Foster, Hannah Webster 1758-1840 **NCLC
99**
See also DLB 37, 200; RGAL 4

Foster, Stephen Collins 1826-1864 **NCLC 26**
See also RGAL 4

Foucault, Michel 1926-1984 **CLC 31, 34, 69**
See also CA 105; 113; CANR 34; DLB 242;
EW 13; EWL 3; GFL 1789 to the Present;
GLL 1; LMFS 2; MTCW 1, 2; TWA

**Fouque, Friedrich (Heinrich Karl) de la
Motte** 1777-1843 **NCLC 2**
See also DLB 90; RGWL 2, 3; SUFW 1

Fourier, Charles 1772-1837 **NCLC 51**

Fournier, Henri-Alban 1886-1914
See Alain-Fournier
See also CA 104; 179

Fournier, Pierre 1916- **CLC 11**
See Gascar, Pierre
See also CA 89-92; CANR 16, 40

Fowles, John (Robert) 1926- **CLC 1, 2, 3, 4,
6, 9, 10, 15, 33, 87; SSC 33**
See also BPFB 1; BRWS 1; CA 5-8R;
CANR 25, 71, 103; CDBLB 1960 to
Present; CN 7; DA3; DAB; DAC; DAM
MST; DLB 14, 139, 207; EWL 3; HGG;
MTCW 1, 2; RGEL 2; RHW; SATA 22;
TEA; WLIT 4

Fox, Paula 1923- **CLC 2, 8, 121**
See also AAYA 3, 37; BYA 3, 8; CA 73-76;
CANR 20, 36, 62, 105; CLR 1, 44, 96;
DLB 52; JRDA; MAICYA 1, 2; MTCW
1; NFS 12; SATA 17, 60, 120; WYA;
YAW

Fox, William Price (Jr.) 1926- **CLC 22**
See also CA 17-20R; CAAS 19; CANR 11;
CSW; DLB 2; DLBY 1981

Foxe, John 1517(?)-1587 **LC 14**
See also DLB 132

Frame, Janet CLC 2, 3, 6, 22, 66, 96; SSC 29
See Clutha, Janet Paterson Frame
See also CN 7; CWP; EWL 3; RGEL 2;
RGSF 2; TWA

France, Anatole TCLC 9
See Thibault, Jacques Anatole Francois
See also DLB 123; EWL 3; GFL 1789 to
the Present; MTCW 1; RGWL 2, 3;
SUFW 1

Francis, Claude CLC 50
See also CA 192

Francis, Dick 1920- **CLC 2, 22, 42, 102**
See also AAYA 5, 21; BEST 89:3; BPFB 1;
CA 5-8R; CANR 9, 42, 68, 100; CDBLB
1960 to Present; CMW 4; CN 7; DA3;
DAM POP; DLB 87; INT CANR-9;
MSW; MTCW 1, 2

Francis, Robert (Churchill) 1901-1987 **CLC
15; PC 34**
See also AMWS 9; CA 1-4R; 123; CANR
1; EXPP; PFS 12

Francis, Lord Jeffrey
See Jeffrey, Francis
See also DLB 107

Frank, Anne(lies Marie) 1929-1945 **TCLC
17; WLC**
See also AAYA 12; BYA 1; CA 113; 133;
CANR 68; DA; DA3; DAB; DAC; DAM
MST; LAIT 4; MAICYA 2; MAICYAS 1;
MTCW 1, 2; NCFS 2; SATA 87; SATA-
Brief 42; WYA; YAW

Frank, Bruno 1887-1945 **TCLC 81**
See also CA 189; DLB 118; EWL 3

Frank, Elizabeth 1945- **CLC 39**
See also CA 121; 126; CANR 78; INT CA-
126

Frankl, Viktor E(mil) 1905-1997 **CLC 93**
See also CA 65-68; 161

Franklin, Benjamin
    See Hasek, Jaroslav (Matej Frantisek)
Franklin, Benjamin 1706-1790 **LC 25; WLCS**
    See also AMW; CDALB 1640-1865; DA;
        DA3; DAB; DAC; DAM MST; DLB 24,
        43, 73, 183; LAIT 1; RGAL 4; TUS
Franklin, (Stella Maria Sarah) Miles
        (Lampe) 1879-1954 **TCLC 7**
    See also CA 104; 164; DLB 230; FW;
        MTCW 2; RGEL 2; TWA
Fraser, Antonia (Pakenham) 1932- **CLC 32,**
        107
    See also CA 85-88; CANR 44, 65, 119;
        CMW; DLB 276; MTCW 1, 2; SATA-
        Brief 32
Fraser, George MacDonald 1925- **CLC 7**
    See also AAYA 48; CA 45-48, 180; CAAE
        180; CANR 2, 48, 74; MTCW 1; RHW
Fraser, Sylvia 1935- **CLC 64**
    See also CA 45-48; CANR 1, 16, 60; CCA
        1
Frayn, Michael 1933- **CLC 3, 7, 31, 47, 176**
    See also BRWC 2; BRWS 7; CA 5-8R;
        CANR 30, 69, 114; CBD; CD 5; CN 7;
        DAM DRAM, NOV; DLB 13, 14, 194,
        245; FANT; MTCW 1, 2; SFW 4
Fraze, Candida (Merrill) 1945- **CLC 50**
    See also CA 126
Frazer, Andrew
    See Marlowe, Stephen
Frazer, J(ames) G(eorge) 1854-1941 **TCLC**
        32
    See also BRWS 3; CA 118; NCFS 5
Frazer, Robert Caine
    See Creasey, John
Frazer, Sir James George
    See Frazer, J(ames) G(eorge)
Frazier, Charles 1950- **CLC 109**
    See also AAYA 34; CA 161; CANR 126;
        CSW; DLB 292
Frazier, Ian 1951- **CLC 46**
    See also CA 130; CANR 54, 93
Frederic, Harold 1856-1898 **NCLC 10**
    See also AMW; DLB 12, 23; DLBD 13;
        RGAL 4
Frederick, John
    See Faust, Frederick (Schiller)
    See also TCWW 2
Frederick the Great 1712-1786 **LC 14**
Fredro, Aleksander 1793-1876 **NCLC 8**
Freeling, Nicolas 1927-2003 **CLC 38**
    See also CA 49-52; 218; CAAS 12; CANR
        1, 17, 50, 84; CMW 4; CN 7; DLB 87
Freeman, Douglas Southall 1886-1953 **TCLC**
        11
    See also CA 109; 195; DLB 17; DLBD 17
Freeman, Judith 1946- **CLC 55**
    See also CA 148; CANR 120; DLB 256
Freeman, Mary E(leanor) Wilkins 1852-1930
        SSC 1, 47; TCLC 9
    See also CA 106; 177; DLB 12, 78, 221;
        EXPS; FW; HGG; MAWW; RGAL 4;
        RGSF 2; SSFS 4, 8; SUFW 1; TUS
Freeman, R(ichard) Austin 1862-1943 **TCLC**
        21
    See also CA 113; CANR 84; CMW 4; DLB
        70
French, Albert 1943- **CLC 86**
    See also BW 3; CA 167
French, Antonia
    See Kureishi, Hanif
French, Marilyn 1929- **CLC 10, 18, 60, 177**
    See also BPFB 1; CA 69-72; CANR 3, 31;
        CN 7; CPW; DAM DRAM, NOV, POP;
        FW; INT CANR-31; MTCW 1, 2
French, Paul
    See Asimov, Isaac

Freneau, Philip Morin 1752-1832 **NCLC 1,**
        111
    See also AMWS 2; DLB 37, 43; RGAL 4
Freud, Sigmund 1856-1939 **TCLC 52**
    See also CA 115; 133; CANR 69; DLB 296;
        EW 8; EWL 3; LATS 1; MTCW 1, 2;
        NCFS 3; TWA
Freytag, Gustav 1816-1895 **NCLC 109**
    See also DLB 129
Friedan, Betty (Naomi) 1921- **CLC 74**
    See also CA 65-68; CANR 18, 45, 74; DLB
        246; FW; MTCW 1, 2; NCFS 5
Friedlander, Saul 1932- **CLC 90**
    See also CA 117; 130; CANR 72
Friedman, B(ernard) H(arper) 1926- **CLC 7**
    See also CA 1-4R; CANR 3, 48
Friedman, Bruce Jay 1930- **CLC 3, 5, 56**
    See also CA 9-12R; CAD; CANR 25, 52,
        101; CD 5; CN 7; DLB 2, 28, 244; INT
        CANR-25; SSFS 18
Friel, Brian 1929- **CLC 5, 42, 59, 115; DC 8**
    See also BRWS 5; CA 21-24R; CANR 33,
        69; CBD; CD 5; DFS 11; DLB 13; EWL
        3; MTCW 1; RGEL 2; TEA
Friis-Baastad, Babbis Ellinor 1921-1970 **CLC**
        12
    See also CA 17-20R; 134; SATA 7
Frisch, Max (Rudolf) 1911-1991 **CLC 3, 9,**
        14, 18, 32, 44; TCLC 121
    See also CA 85-88; 134; CANR 32, 74; CD-
        WLB 2; DAM DRAM, NOV; DLB 69,
        124; EW 13; EWL 3; MTCW 1, 2; RGWL
        2, 3
Fromentin, Eugene (Samuel Auguste)
        1820-1876 **NCLC 10, 125**
    See also DLB 123; GFL 1789 to the Present
Frost, Frederick
    See Faust, Frederick (Schiller)
    See also TCWW 2
Frost, Robert (Lee) 1874-1963 **CLC 1, 3, 4,**
        9, 10, 13, 15, 26, 34, 44; PC 1, 39; WLC
    See also AAYA 21; AMW; AMWR 1; CA
        89-92; CANR 33; CDALB 1917-1929;
        CLR 67; DA; DA3; DAB; DAC; DAM
        MST, POET; DLB 54, 284; DLBD 7;
        EWL 3; EXPP; MTCW 1, 2; PAB; PFS 1,
        2, 3, 4, 5, 6, 7, 10, 13; RGAL 4; SATA
        14; TUS; WP; WYA
Froude, James Anthony 1818-1894 **NCLC 43**
    See also DLB 18, 57, 144
Froy, Herald
    See Waterhouse, Keith (Spencer)
Fry, Christopher 1907- **CLC 2, 10, 14**
    See also BRWS 3; CA 17-20R; CAAS 23;
        CANR 9, 30, 74; CBD; CD 5; CP 7; DAM
        DRAM; DLB 13; EWL 3; MTCW 1, 2;
        RGEL 2; SATA 66; TEA
Frye, (Herman) Northrop 1912-1991 **CLC**
        24, 70
    See also CA 5-8R; 133; CANR 8, 37; DLB
        67, 68, 246; EWL 3; MTCW 1, 2; RGAL
        4; TWA
Fuchs, Daniel 1909-1993 **CLC 8, 22**
    See also CA 81-84; 142; CAAS 5; CANR
        40; DLB 9, 26, 28; DLBY 1993
Fuchs, Daniel 1934- **CLC 34**
    See also CA 37-40R; CANR 14, 48
Fuentes, Carlos 1928- **CLC 3, 8, 10, 13, 22,**
        41, 60, 113; HLC 1; SSC 24; WLC
    See also AAYA 4, 45; AITN 2; BPFB 1;
        CA 69-72; CANR 10, 32, 68, 104; CD-
        WLB 3; CWW 2; DA; DA3; DAB; DAC;
        DAM MST, MULT, NOV; DLB 113;
        DNFS 2; EWL 3; HW 1, 2; LAIT 3; LATS
        1; LAW; LAWS 1; LMFS 2; MTCW 1, 2;
        NFS 8; RGSF 2; RGWL 2, 3; TWA;
        WLIT 1

Fuentes, Gregorio Lopez y
    See Lopez y Fuentes, Gregorio
Fuertes, Gloria 1918-1998 **PC 27**
    See also CA 178, 180; DLB 108; HW 2;
        SATA 115
Fugard, (Harold) Athol 1932- **CLC 5, 9, 14,**
        25, 40, 80; DC 3
    See also AAYA 17; AFW; CA 85-88; CANR
        32, 54, 118; CD 5; DAM DRAM; DFS 3,
        6, 10; DLB 225; DNFS 1, 2; EWL 3;
        LATS 1; MTCW 1; RGEL 2; WLIT 2
Fugard, Sheila 1932- **CLC 48**
    See also CA 125
Fukuyama, Francis 1952- **CLC 131**
    See also CA 140; CANR 72, 125
Fuller, Charles (H.), (Jr.) 1939- **BLC 2; CLC**
        25; DC 1
    See also BW 2; CA 108; 112; CAD; CANR
        87; CD 5; DAM DRAM, MULT; DFS 8;
        DLB 38, 266; EWL 3; INT CA-112;
        MTCW 1
Fuller, Henry Blake 1857-1929 **TCLC 103**
    See also CA 108; 177; DLB 12; RGAL 4
Fuller, John (Leopold) 1937- **CLC 62**
    See also CA 21-24R; CANR 9, 44; CP 7;
        DLB 40
Fuller, Margaret
    See Ossoli, Sarah Margaret (Fuller)
    See also AMWS 2; DLB 183, 223, 239
Fuller, Roy (Broadbent) 1912-1991 **CLC 4,**
        28
    See also BRWS 7; CA 5-8R; 135; CAAS
        10; CANR 53, 83; CWRI 5; DLB 15, 20;
        EWL 3; RGEL 2; SATA 87
Fuller, Sarah Margaret
    See Ossoli, Sarah Margaret (Fuller)
Fuller, Sarah Margaret
    See Ossoli, Sarah Margaret (Fuller)
    See also DLB 1, 59, 73
Fulton, Alice 1952- **CLC 52**
    See also CA 116; CANR 57, 88; CP 7;
        CWP; DLB 193
Furphy, Joseph 1843-1912 **TCLC 25**
    See Collins, Tom
    See also CA 163; DLB 230; EWL 3; RGEL
        2
Fuson, Robert H(enderson) 1927- **CLC 70**
    See also CA 89-92; CANR 103
Fussell, Paul 1924- **CLC 74**
    See also BEST 90:1; CA 17-20R; CANR 8,
        21, 35, 69; INT CANR-21; MTCW 1, 2
Futabatei, Shimei 1864-1909 **TCLC 44**
    See Futabatei Shimei
    See also CA 162; MJW
Futabatei Shimei
    See Futabatei, Shimei
    See also DLB 180; EWL 3
Futrelle, Jacques 1875-1912 **TCLC 19**
    See also CA 113; 155; CMW 4
Gaboriau, Emile 1835-1873 **NCLC 14**
    See also CMW 4; MSW
Gadda, Carlo Emilio 1893-1973 **CLC 11;**
        TCLC 144
    See also CA 89-92; DLB 177; EWL 3
Gaddis, William 1922-1998 **CLC 1, 3, 6, 8,**
        10, 19, 43, 86
    See also AMWS 4; BPFB 1; CA 17-20R;
        172; CANR 21, 48; CN 7; DLB 2, 278;
        EWL 3; MTCW 1, 2; RGAL 4
Gaelique, Moruen le
    See Jacob, (Cyprien-)Max
Gage, Walter
    See Inge, William (Motter)
Gaines, Ernest J(ames) 1933- **BLC 2; CLC**
        3, 11, 18, 86, 181; SSC 68
    See also AAYA 18; AFAW 1, 2; AITN 1;
        BPFB 1; BW 2, 3; BYA 6; CA 9-12R;
        CANR 6, 24, 42, 75, 126; CDALB 1968-
        1988; CLR 62; CN 7; CSW; DA3; DAM

MULT; DLB 2, 33, 152; DLBY 1980; EWL 3; EXPN; LAIT 5; LATS 1; MTCW 1, 2; NFS 5, 7, 16; RGAL 4; RGSF 2; RHW; SATA 86; SSFS 5; YAW

Gaitskill, Mary (Lawrence) 1954- **CLC 69**
See also CA 128; CANR 61; DLB 244

Gaius Suetonius Tranquillus c. 70-c. 130
See Suetonius

Galdos, Benito Perez
See Perez Galdos, Benito
See also EW 7

Gale, Zona 1874-1938 **TCLC 7**
See also CA 105; 153; CANR 84; DAM DRAM; DFS 17; DLB 9, 78, 228; RGAL 4

Galeano, Eduardo (Hughes) 1940- **CLC 72; HLCS 1**
See also CA 29-32R; CANR 13, 32, 100; HW 1

Galiano, Juan Valera y Alcala
See Valera y Alcala-Galiano, Juan

Galilei, Galileo 1564-1642 **LC 45**

Gallagher, Tess 1943- **CLC 18, 63; PC 9**
See also CA 106; CP 7; CWP; DAM POET; DLB 120, 212, 244; PFS 16

Gallant, Mavis 1922- **CLC 7, 18, 38, 172; SSC 5**
See also CA 69-72; CANR 29, 69, 117; CCA 1; CN 7; DAC; DAM MST; DLB 53; EWL 3; MTCW 1, 2; RGEL 2; RGSF 2

Gallant, Roy A(rthur) 1924- **CLC 17**
See also CA 5-8R; CANR 4, 29, 54, 117; CLR 30; MAICYA 1, 2; SATA 4, 68, 110

Gallico, Paul (William) 1897-1976 **CLC 2**
See also AITN 1; CA 5-8R; 69-72; CANR 23; DLB 9, 171; FANT; MAICYA 1, 2; SATA 13

Gallo, Max Louis 1932- **CLC 95**
See also CA 85-88

Gallois, Lucien
See Desnos, Robert

Gallup, Ralph
See Whitemore, Hugh (John)

Galsworthy, John 1867-1933 **SSC 22; TCLC 1, 45; WLC**
See also BRW 6; CA 104; 141; CANR 75; CDBLB 1890-1914; DA; DA3; DAB; DAC; DAM DRAM, MST, NOV; DLB 10, 34, 98, 162; DLBD 16; EWL 3; MTCW 1; RGEL 2; SSFS 3; TEA

Galt, John 1779-1839 **NCLC 1, 110**
See also DLB 99, 116, 159; RGEL 2; RGSF 2

Galvin, James 1951- **CLC 38**
See also CA 108; CANR 26

Gamboa, Federico 1864-1939 **TCLC 36**
See also CA 167; HW 2; LAW

Gandhi, M. K.
See Gandhi, Mohandas Karamchand

Gandhi, Mahatma
See Gandhi, Mohandas Karamchand

Gandhi, Mohandas Karamchand 1869-1948 **TCLC 59**
See also CA 121; 132; DA3; DAM MULT; MTCW 1, 2

Gann, Ernest Kellogg 1910-1991 **CLC 23**
See also AITN 1; BPFB 2; CA 1-4R; 136; CANR 1, 83; RHW

Gao Xingjian 1940- **CLC 167**
See Xingjian, Gao

Garber, Eric 1943(?)-
See Holleran, Andrew
See also CANR 89

Garcia, Cristina 1958- **CLC 76**
See also AMWS 11; CA 141; CANR 73; DLB 292; DNFS 1; EWL 3; HW 2; LLW 1

Garcia Lorca, Federico 1898-1936 **DC 2; HLC 2; PC 3; TCLC 1, 7, 49; WLC**
See Lorca, Federico Garcia
See also AAYA 46; CA 104; 131; CANR 81; DA; DA3; DAB; DAC; DAM DRAM, MST, MULT, POET; DFS 4, 10; DLB 108; EWL 3; HW 1, 2; LATS 1; MTCW 1, 2; TWA

Garcia Marquez, Gabriel (Jose) 1928- **CLC 2, 3, 8, 10, 15, 27, 47, 55, 68, 170; HLC 1; SSC 8; WLC**
See also AAYA 3, 33; BEST 89:1, 90:4; BPFB 2; BYA 12, 16; CA 33-36R; CANR 10, 28, 50, 75, 82, 128; CDWLB 3; CPW; DA; DA3; DAB; DAC; DAM MST, MULT, NOV, POP; DLB 113; DNFS 1, 2; EWL 3; EXPN; EXPS; HW 1, 2; LAIT 2; LATS 1; LAW; LAWS 1; LMFS 2; MTCW 1, 2; NCFS 3; NFS 1, 5, 10; RGSF 2; RGWL 2, 3; SSFS 1, 6, 16; TWA; WLIT 1

Garcilaso de la Vega, El Inca 1503-1536 **HLCS 1**
See also LAW

Gard, Janice
See Latham, Jean Lee

Gard, Roger Martin du
See Martin du Gard, Roger

Gardam, Jane (Mary) 1928- **CLC 43**
See also CA 49-52; CANR 2, 18, 33, 54, 106; CLR 12; DLB 14, 161, 231; MAICYA 1, 2; MTCW 1; SAAS 9; SATA 39, 76, 130; SATA-Brief 28; YAW

Gardner, Herb(ert George) 1934-2003 **CLC 44**
See also CA 149; 220; CAD; CANR 119; CD 5; DFS 18

Gardner, John (Champlin), Jr. 1933-1982 **CLC 2, 3, 5, 7, 8, 10, 18, 28, 34; SSC 7**
See also AAYA 45; AITN 1; AMWS 6; BPFB 2; CA 65-68; 107; CANR 33, 73; CDALBS; CPW; DA3; DAM NOV, POP; DLB 2; DLBY 1982; EWL 3; FANT; LATS 1; MTCW 1; NFS 3; RGAL 4; RGSF 2; SATA 40; SATA-Obit 31; SSFS 8

Gardner, John (Edmund) 1926- **CLC 30**
See also CA 103; CANR 15, 69, 127; CMW 4; CPW; DAM POP; MTCW 1

Gardner, Miriam
See Bradley, Marion Zimmer
See also GLL 1

Gardner, Noel
See Kuttner, Henry

Gardons, S. S.
See Snodgrass, W(illiam) D(e Witt)

Garfield, Leon 1921-1996 **CLC 12**
See also AAYA 8; BYA 1, 3; CA 17-20R; 152; CANR 38, 41, 78; CLR 21; DLB 161; JRDA; MAICYA 1, 2; MAICYAS 1; SATA 1, 32, 76; SATA-Obit 90; TEA; WYA; YAW

Garland, (Hannibal) Hamlin 1860-1940 **SSC 18; TCLC 3**
See also CA 104; DLB 12, 71, 78, 186; RGAL 4; RGSF 2; TCWW 2

Garneau, (Hector de) Saint-Denys 1912-1943 **TCLC 13**
See also CA 111; DLB 88

Garner, Alan 1934- **CLC 17**
See also AAYA 18; BYA 3, 5; CA 73-76; 178; CAAE 178; CANR 15, 64; CLR 20; CPW; DAB; DAM POP; DLB 161, 261; FANT; MAICYA 1, 2; MTCW 1, 2; SATA 18, 69; SATA-Essay 108; SUFW 1, 2; YAW

Garner, Hugh 1913-1979 **CLC 13**
See Warwick, Jarvis
See also CA 69-72; CANR 31; CCA 1; DLB 68

Garnett, David 1892-1981 **CLC 3**
See also CA 5-8R; 103; CANR 17, 79; DLB 34; FANT; MTCW 2; RGEL 2; SFW 4; SUFW 1

Garos, Stephanie
See Katz, Steve

Garrett, George (Palmer) 1929- **CLC 3, 11, 51; SSC 30**
See also AMWS 7; BPFB 2; CA 1-4R, 202; CAAE 202; CAAS 5; CANR 1, 42, 67, 109; CN 7; CP 7; CSW; DLB 2, 5, 130, 152; DLBY 1983

Garrick, David 1717-1779 **LC 15**
See also DAM DRAM; DLB 84, 213; RGEL 2

Garrigue, Jean 1914-1972 **CLC 2, 8**
See also CA 5-8R; 37-40R; CANR 20

Garrison, Frederick
See Sinclair, Upton (Beall)

Garro, Elena 1920(?)-1998 **HLCS 1**
See also CA 131; 169; CWW 2; DLB 145; EWL 3; HW 1; LAWS 1; WLIT 1

Garth, Will
See Hamilton, Edmond; Kuttner, Henry

Garvey, Marcus (Moziah, Jr.) 1887-1940 **BLC 2; HR 2; TCLC 41**
See also BW 1; CA 120; 124; CANR 79; DAM MULT

Gary, Romain CLC 25
See Kacew, Romain
See also DLB 83

Gascar, Pierre CLC 11
See Fournier, Pierre
See also EWL 3

Gascoyne, David (Emery) 1916-2001 **CLC 45**
See also CA 65-68; 200; CANR 10, 28, 54; CP 7; DLB 20; MTCW 1; RGEL 2

Gaskell, Elizabeth Cleghorn 1810-1865 **NCLC 5, 70, 97, 137; SSC 25**
See also BRW 5; CDBLB 1832-1890; DAB; DAM MST; DLB 21, 144, 159; RGEL 2; RGSF 2; TEA

Gass, William H(oward) 1924- **CLC 1, 2, 8, 11, 15, 39, 132; SSC 12**
See also AMWS 6; CA 17-20R; CANR 30, 71, 100; CN 7; DLB 2, 227; EWL 3; MTCW 1, 2; RGAL 4

Gassendi, Pierre 1592-1655 **LC 54**
See also GFL Beginnings to 1789

Gasset, Jose Ortega y
See Ortega y Gasset, Jose

Gates, Henry Louis, Jr. 1950- **BLCS; CLC 65**
See also BW 2, 3; CA 109; CANR 25, 53, 75, 125; CSW; DA3; DAM MULT; DLB 67; EWL 3; MTCW 1; RGAL 4

Gautier, Theophile 1811-1872 **NCLC 1, 59; PC 18; SSC 20**
See also DAM POET; DLB 119; EW 6; GFL 1789 to the Present; RGWL 2, 3; SUFW; TWA

Gawsworth, John
See Bates, H(erbert) E(rnest)

Gay, John 1685-1732 **LC 49**
See also BRW 3; DAM DRAM; DLB 84, 95; RGEL 2; WLIT 3

Gay, Oliver
See Gogarty, Oliver St. John

Gay, Peter (Jack) 1923- **CLC 158**
See also CA 13-16R; CANR 18, 41, 77; INT CANR-18

Gaye, Marvin (Pentz, Jr.) 1939-1984 **CLC 26**
See also CA 195; 112

Gebler, Carlo (Ernest) 1954- **CLC 39**
See also CA 119; 133; CANR 96; DLB 271

Gee, Maggie (Mary) 1948- **CLC 57**
See also CA 130; CANR 125; CN 7; DLB 207

Gee, Maurice (Gough) 1931- **CLC 29**
See also AAYA 42; CA 97-100; CANR 67, 123; CLR 56; CN 7; CWRI 5; EWL 3; MAICYA 2; RGSF 2; SATA 46, 101

Geiogamah, Hanay 1945- **NNAL**
See also CA 153; DAM MULT; DLB 175

Gelbart, Larry (Simon) 1928- **CLC 21, 61**
See Gelbart, Larry
See also CA 73-76; CANR 45, 94

Gelbart, Larry 1928-
See Gelbart, Larry (Simon)
See also CAD; CD 5

Gelber, Jack 1932-2003 **CLC 1, 6, 14, 79**
See also CA 1-4R; 216; CAD; CANR 2; DLB 7, 228

Gellhorn, Martha (Ellis) 1908-1998 **CLC 14, 60**
See also CA 77-80; 164; CANR 44; CN 7; DLBY 1982, 1998

Genet, Jean 1910-1986 **CLC 1, 2, 5, 10, 14, 44, 46; TCLC 128**
See also CA 13-16R; CANR 18; DA3; DAM DRAM; DFS 10; DLB 72; DLBY 1986; EW 13; EWL 3; GFL 1789 to the Present; GLL 1; LMFS 2; MTCW 1, 2; RGWL 2, 3; TWA

Gent, Peter 1942- **CLC 29**
See also AITN 1; CA 89-92; DLBY 1982

Gentile, Giovanni 1875-1944 **TCLC 96**
See also CA 119

Gentlewoman in New England, A
See Bradstreet, Anne

Gentlewoman in Those Parts, A
See Bradstreet, Anne

Geoffrey of Monmouth c. 1100-1155 **CMLC 44**
See also DLB 146; TEA

George, Jean
See George, Jean Craighead

George, Jean Craighead 1919- **CLC 35**
See also AAYA 8; BYA 2, 4; CA 5-8R; CANR 25; CLR 1; 80; DLB 52; JRDA; MAICYA 1, 2; SATA 2, 68, 124; WYA; YAW

George, Stefan (Anton) 1868-1933 **TCLC 2, 14**
See also CA 104; 193; EW 8; EWL 3

Georges, Georges Martin
See Simenon, Georges (Jacques Christian)

Gerald of Wales c. 1146-c. 1223 **CMLC 60**

Gerhardi, William Alexander
See Gerhardie, William Alexander

Gerhardie, William Alexander 1895-1977 **CLC 5**
See also CA 25-28R; 73-76; CANR 18; DLB 36; RGEL 2

Gerson, Jean 1363-1429 **LC 77**
See also DLB 208

Gersonides 1288-1344 **CMLC 49**
See also DLB 115

Gerstler, Amy 1956- **CLC 70**
See also CA 146; CANR 99

Gertler, T. CLC 34
See also CA 116; 121

Gertsen, Aleksandr Ivanovich
See Herzen, Aleksandr Ivanovich

Ghalib NCLC 39, 78
See Ghalib, Asadullah Khan

Ghalib, Asadullah Khan 1797-1869
See Ghalib
See also DAM POET; RGWL 2, 3

Ghelderode, Michel de 1898-1962 **CLC 6, 11; DC 15**
See also CA 85-88; CANR 40, 77; DAM DRAM; EW 11; EWL 3; TWA

Ghiselin, Brewster 1903-2001 **CLC 23**
See also CA 13-16R; CAAS 10; CANR 13; CP 7

Ghose, Aurabinda 1872-1950 **TCLC 63**
See Ghose, Aurobindo
See also CA 163

Ghose, Aurobindo
See Ghose, Aurabinda
See also EWL 3

Ghose, Zulfikar 1935- **CLC 42**
See also CA 65-68; CANR 67; CN 7; CP 7; EWL 3

Ghosh, Amitav 1956- **CLC 44, 153**
See also CA 147; CANR 80; CN 7; WWE 1

Giacosa, Giuseppe 1847-1906 **TCLC 7**
See also CA 104

Gibb, Lee
See Waterhouse, Keith (Spencer)

Gibbon, Edward 1737-1794 **LC 97**
See also BRW 3; DLB 104; RGEL 2

Gibbon, Lewis Grassic TCLC 4
See Mitchell, James Leslie
See also RGEL 2

Gibbons, Kaye 1960- **CLC 50, 88, 145**
See also AAYA 34; AMWS 10; CA 151; CANR 75, 127; CSW; DA3; DAM POP; DLB 292; MTCW 1; NFS 3; RGAL 4; SATA 117

Gibran, Kahlil 1883-1931 **PC 9; TCLC 1, 9**
See also CA 104; 150; DA3; DAM POET, POP; EWL 3; MTCW 2

Gibran, Khalil
See Gibran, Kahlil

Gibson, William 1914- **CLC 23**
See also CA 9-12R; CAD 2; CANR 9, 42, 75, 125; CD 5; DA; DAB; DAC; DAM DRAM, MST; DFS 2; DLB 7; LAIT 2; MTCW 2; SATA 66; YAW

Gibson, William (Ford) 1948- **CLC 39, 63, 186; SSC 52**
See also AAYA 12; BPFB 2; CA 126; 133; CANR 52, 90, 106; CN 7; CPW; DA3; DAM POP; DLB 251; MTCW 2; SCFW 2; SFW 4

Gide, Andre (Paul Guillaume) 1869-1951 **SSC 13; TCLC 5, 12, 36; WLC**
See also CA 104; 124; DA; DA3; DAB; DAC; DAM MST, NOV; DLB 65; EW 8; EWL 3; GFL 1789 to the Present; MTCW 1, 2; RGSF 2; RGWL 2, 3; TWA

Gifford, Barry (Colby) 1946- **CLC 34**
See also CA 65-68; CANR 9, 30, 40, 90

Gilbert, Frank
See De Voto, Bernard (Augustine)

Gilbert, W(illiam) S(chwenck) 1836-1911 **TCLC 3**
See also CA 104; 173; DAM DRAM, POET; RGEL 2; SATA 36

Gilbreth, Frank B(unker), Jr. 1911-2001 **CLC 17**
See also CA 9-12R; SATA 2

Gilchrist, Ellen (Louise) 1935- **CLC 34, 48, 143; SSC 14, 63**
See also BPFB 2; CA 113; 116; CANR 41, 61, 104; CN 7; CPW; CSW; DAM POP; DLB 130; EWL 3; EXPS; MTCW 1, 2; RGAL 4; RGSF 2; SSFS 9

Giles, Molly 1942- **CLC 39**
See also CA 126; CANR 98

Gill, Eric 1882-1940 **TCLC 85**
See Gill, (Arthur) Eric (Rowton Peter Joseph)

Gill, (Arthur) Eric (Rowton Peter Joseph) 1882-1940
See Gill, Eric
See also CA 120; DLB 98

Gill, Patrick
See Creasey, John

Gillette, Douglas CLC 70

Gilliam, Terry (Vance) 1940- **CLC 21, 141**
See Monty Python
See also AAYA 19; CA 108; 113; CANR 35; INT CA-113

Gillian, Jerry
See Gilliam, Terry (Vance)

Gilliatt, Penelope (Ann Douglass) 1932-1993 **CLC 2, 10, 13, 53**
See also AITN 2; CA 13-16R; 141; CANR 49; DLB 14

Gilman, Charlotte (Anna) Perkins (Stetson) 1860-1935 **SSC 13, 62; TCLC 9, 37, 117**
See also AMWS 11; BYA 11; CA 106; 150; DLB 221; EXPS; FW; HGG; LAIT 2; MAWW; MTCW 1; RGAL 4; RGSF 2; SFW 4; SSFS 1, 18

Gilmour, David 1946- **CLC 35**

Gilpin, William 1724-1804 **NCLC 30**

Gilray, J. D.
See Mencken, H(enry) L(ouis)

Gilroy, Frank D(aniel) 1925- **CLC 2**
See also CA 81-84; CAD; CANR 32, 64, 86; CD 5; DFS 17; DLB 7

Gilstrap, John 1957(?)- **CLC 99**
See also CA 160; CANR 101

Ginsberg, Allen 1926-1997 **CLC 1, 2, 3, 4, 6, 13, 36, 69, 109; PC 4, 47; TCLC 120; WLC**
See also AAYA 33; AITN 1; AMWC 1; AMWS 2; BG 2; CA 1-4R; 157; CANR 2, 41, 63, 95; CDALB 1941-1968; CP 7; DA; DA3; DAB; DAC; DAM MST, POET; DLB 5, 16, 169, 237; EWL 3; GLL 1; LMFS 2; MTCW 1, 2; PAB; PFS 5; RGAL 4; TUS; WP

Ginzburg, Eugenia CLC 59

Ginzburg, Natalia 1916-1991 **CLC 5, 11, 54, 70; SSC 65**
See also CA 85-88; 135; CANR 33; DFS 14; DLB 177; EW 13; EWL 3; MTCW 1, 2; RGWL 2, 3

Giono, Jean 1895-1970 **CLC 4, 11; TCLC 124**
See also CA 45-48; 29-32R; CANR 2, 35; DLB 72; EWL 3; GFL 1789 to the Present; MTCW 1; RGWL 2, 3

Giovanni, Nikki 1943- **BLC 2; CLC 2, 4, 19, 64, 117; PC 19; WLCS**
See also AAYA 22; AITN 1; BW 2, 3; CA 29-32R; CAAS 6; CANR 18, 41, 60, 91; CDALBS; CLR 6, 73; CP 7; CSW; CWP; CWRI 5; DA; DA3; DAB; DAC; DAM MST, MULT, POET; DLB 5, 41; EWL 3; EXPP; INT CANR-18; MAICYA 1, 2; MTCW 1, 2; PFS 17; RGAL 4; SATA 24, 107; TUS; YAW

Giovene, Andrea 1904-1998 **CLC 7**
See also CA 85-88

Gippius, Zinaida (Nikolaevna) 1869-1945
See Hippius, Zinaida (Nikolaevna)
See also CA 106; 212

Giraudoux, Jean(-Hippolyte) 1882-1944 **TCLC 2, 7**
See also CA 104; 196; DAM DRAM; DLB 65; EW 9; EWL 3; GFL 1789 to the Present; RGWL 2, 3; TWA

Gironella, Jose Maria (Pous) 1917-2003 **CLC 11**
See also CA 101; 212; EWL 3; RGWL 2, 3

Gissing, George (Robert) 1857-1903 **SSC 37; TCLC 3, 24, 47**
See also BRW 5; CA 105; 167; DLB 18, 135, 184; RGEL 2; TEA

Giurlani, Aldo
See Palazzeschi, Aldo

Gladkov, Fedor Vasil'evich
See Gladkov, Fyodor (Vasilyevich)
See also DLB 272

Gladkov, Fyodor (Vasilyevich) 1883-1958
TCLC 27
See Gladkov, Fedor Vasil'evich
See also CA 170; EWL 3
Glancy, Diane 1941- **NNAL**
See also CA 136; CAAS 24; CANR 87;
DLB 175
Glanville, Brian (Lester) 1931- **CLC 6**
See also CA 5-8R; CAAS 9; CANR 3, 70;
CN 7; DLB 15, 139; SATA 42
Glasgow, Ellen (Anderson Gholson)
1873-1945 **SSC 34; TCLC 2, 7**
See also AMW; CA 104; 164; DLB 9, 12;
MAWW; MTCW 2; RGAL 4; RHW;
SSFS 9; TUS
Glaspell, Susan 1882(?)-1948 **DC 10; SSC 41;
TCLC 55**
See also AMWS 3; CA 110; 154; DFS 8,
18; DLB 7, 9, 78, 228; MAWW; RGAL
4; SSFS 3; TCWW 2; TUS; YABC 2
Glassco, John 1909-1981 **CLC 9**
See also CA 13-16R; 102; CANR 15; DLB
68
Glasscock, Amnesia
See Steinbeck, John (Ernst)
Glasser, Ronald J. 1940(?)- **CLC 37**
See also CA 209
Glassman, Joyce
See Johnson, Joyce
Gleick, James (W.) 1954- **CLC 147**
See also CA 131; 137; CANR 97; INT CA-
137
Glendinning, Victoria 1937- **CLC 50**
See also CA 120; 127; CANR 59, 89; DLB
155
Glissant, Edouard (Mathieu) 1928- **CLC 10,
68**
See also CA 153; CANR 111; CWW 2;
DAM MULT; EWL 3; RGWL 3
Gloag, Julian 1930- **CLC 40**
See also AITN 1; CA 65-68; CANR 10, 70;
CN 7
Glowacki, Aleksander
See Prus, Boleslaw
Gluck, Louise (Elisabeth) 1943- **CLC 7, 22,
44, 81, 160; PC 16**
See also AMWS 5; CA 33-36R; CANR 40,
69, 108; CP 7; CWP; DA3; DAM POET;
DLB 5; MTCW 2; PFS 5, 15; RGAL 4
Glyn, Elinor 1864-1943 **TCLC 72**
See also DLB 153; RHW
Gobineau, Joseph-Arthur 1816-1882 **NCLC
17**
See also DLB 123; GFL 1789 to the Present
Godard, Jean-Luc 1930- **CLC 20**
See also CA 93-96
Godden, (Margaret) Rumer 1907-1998 **CLC
53**
See also AAYA 6; BPFB 2; BYA 2, 5; CA
5-8R; 172; CANR 4, 27, 36, 55, 80; CLR
20; CN 7; CWRI 5; DLB 161; MAICYA
1, 2; RHW; SAAS 12; SATA 3, 36; SATA-
Obit 109; TEA
Godoy Alcayaga, Lucila 1899-1957 **HLC 2;
PC 32; TCLC 2**
See Mistral, Gabriela
See also BW 2; CA 104; 131; CANR 81;
DAM MULT; DNFS; HW 1, 2; MTCW 1,
2
Godwin, Gail (Kathleen) 1937- **CLC 5, 8, 22,
31, 69, 125**
See also BPFB 2; CA 29-32R; CANR 15,
43, 69; CN 7; CPW; CSW; DA3; DAM
POP; DLB 6, 234; INT CANR-15;
MTCW 1, 2
Godwin, William 1756-1836 **NCLC 14, 130**
See also CDBLB 1789-1832; CMW 4; DLB
39, 104, 142, 158, 163, 262; HGG; RGEL
2

Goebbels, Josef
See Goebbels, (Paul) Joseph
Goebbels, (Paul) Joseph 1897-1945 **TCLC 68**
See also CA 115; 148
Goebbels, Joseph Paul
See Goebbels, (Paul) Joseph
Goethe, Johann Wolfgang von 1749-1832 **DC
20; NCLC 4, 22, 34, 90; PC 5; SSC 38;
WLC**
See also CDWLB 2; DA; DA3; DAB;
DAC; DAM DRAM, MST, POET; DLB
94; EW 5; LATS 1; LMFS 1; RGWL 2,
3; TWA
Gogarty, Oliver St. John 1878-1957 **TCLC
15**
See also CA 109; 150; DLB 15, 19; RGEL
2
Gogol, Nikolai (Vasilyevich) 1809-1852 **DC 1;
NCLC 5, 15, 31; SSC 4, 29, 52; WLC**
See also DA; DAB; DAC; DAM DRAM,
MST; DFS 12; DLB 198; EW 6; EXPS;
RGSF 2; RGWL 2, 3; SSFS 7; TWA
Goines, Donald 1937(?)-1974 **BLC 2; CLC
80**
See also AITN 1; BW 1, 3; CA 124; 114;
CANR 82; CMW 4; DA3; DAM MULT,
POP; DLB 33
Gold, Herbert 1924- **CLC 4, 7, 14, 42, 152**
See also CA 9-12R; CANR 17, 45, 125; CN
7; DLB 2; DLBY 1981
Goldbarth, Albert 1948- **CLC 5, 38**
See also AMWS 12; CA 53-56; CANR 6,
40; CP 7; DLB 120
Goldberg, Anatol 1910-1982 **CLC 34**
See also CA 131; 117
Goldemberg, Isaac 1945- **CLC 52**
See also CA 69-72; CAAS 12; CANR 11,
32; EWL 3; HW 1; WLIT 1
Golding, Arthur 1536-1606 **LC 101**
See also DLB 136
Golding, William (Gerald) 1911-1993 **CLC 1,
2, 3, 8, 10, 17, 27, 58, 81; WLC**
See also AAYA 5, 44; BPFB 2; BRWR 1;
BRWS 1; BYA 2; CA 5-8R; 141; CANR
13, 33, 54; CDBLB 1945-1960; CLR 94;
DA; DA3; DAB; DAC; DAM MST, NOV;
DLB 15, 100, 255; EWL 3; EXPN; HGG;
LAIT 4; MTCW 1, 2; NFS 2; RGEL 2;
RHW; SFW 4; TEA; WLIT 4; YAW
Goldman, Emma 1869-1940 **TCLC 13**
See also CA 110; 150; DLB 221; FW;
RGAL 4; TUS
Goldman, Francisco 1954- **CLC 76**
See also CA 162
Goldman, William (W.) 1931- **CLC 1, 48**
See also BPFB 2; CA 9-12R; CANR 29,
69, 106; CN 7; DLB 44; FANT; IDFW 3,
4
Goldmann, Lucien 1913-1970 **CLC 24**
See also CA 25-28; CAP 2
Goldoni, Carlo 1707-1793 **LC 4**
See also DAM DRAM; EW 4; RGWL 2, 3
Goldsberry, Steven 1949- **CLC 34**
See also CA 131
Goldsmith, Oliver 1730-1774 **DC 8; LC 2,
48; WLC**
See also BRW 3; CDBLB 1660-1789; DA;
DAB; DAC; DAM DRAM, MST, NOV,
POET; DFS 1; DLB 39, 89, 104, 109, 142;
IDTP; RGEL 2; SATA 26; TEA; WLIT 3
Goldsmith, Peter
See Priestley, J(ohn) B(oynton)
Gombrowicz, Witold 1904-1969 **CLC 4, 7,
11, 49**
See also CA 19-20; 25-28R; CANR 105;
CAP 2; CDWLB 4; DAM DRAM; DLB
215; EW 12; EWL 3; RGWL 2, 3; TWA

Gomez de Avellaneda, Gertrudis 1814-1873
NCLC 111
See also LAW
Gomez de la Serna, Ramon 1888-1963 **CLC
9**
See also CA 153; 116; CANR 79; EWL 3;
HW 1, 2
Goncharov, Ivan Alexandrovich 1812-1891
NCLC 1, 63
See also DLB 238; EW 6; RGWL 2, 3
Goncourt, Edmond (Louis Antoine Huot) de
1822-1896 **NCLC 7**
See also DLB 123; EW 7; GFL 1789 to the
Present; RGWL 2, 3
Goncourt, Jules (Alfred Huot) de 1830-1870
NCLC 7
See also DLB 123; EW 7; GFL 1789 to the
Present; RGWL 2, 3
Gongora (y Argote), Luis de 1561-1627 **LC
72**
See also RGWL 2, 3
Gontier, Fernande 19(?)- **CLC 50**
Gonzalez Martinez, Enrique
See Gonzalez Martinez, Enrique
See also DLB 290
Gonzalez Martinez, Enrique 1871-1952
TCLC 72
See Gonzalez Martinez, Enrique
See also CA 166; CANR 81; EWL 3; HW
1, 2
Goodison, Lorna 1947- **PC 36**
See also CA 142; CANR 88; CP 7; CWP;
DLB 157; EWL 3
Goodman, Paul 1911-1972 **CLC 1, 2, 4, 7**
See also CA 19-20; 37-40R; CAD; CANR
34; CAP 2; DLB 130, 246; MTCW 1;
RGAL 4
GoodWeather, Harley
See King, Thomas
Googe, Barnabe 1540-1594 **LC 94**
See also DLB 132; RGEL 2
Gordimer, Nadine 1923- **CLC 3, 5, 7, 10, 18,
33, 51, 70, 123, 160, 161; SSC 17;
WLCS**
See also AAYA 39; AFW; BRWS 2; CA
5-8R; CANR 3, 28, 56, 88; CN 7; DA;
DA3; DAB; DAC; DAM MST, NOV;
DLB 225; EWL 3; EXPS; INT CANR-28;
LATS 1; MTCW 1, 2; NFS 4; RGEL 2;
RGSF 2; SSFS 2, 14, 19; TWA; WLIT 2;
YAW
Gordon, Adam Lindsay 1833-1870 **NCLC 21**
See also DLB 230
Gordon, Caroline 1895-1981 **CLC 6, 13, 29,
83; SSC 15**
See also AMW; CA 11-12; 103; CANR 36;
CAP 1; DLB 4, 9, 102; DLBD 17; DLBY
1981; EWL 3; MTCW 1, 2; RGAL 4;
RGSF 2
Gordon, Charles William 1860-1937
See Connor, Ralph
See also CA 109
Gordon, Mary (Catherine) 1949- **CLC 13,
22, 128; SSC 59**
See also AMWS 4; BPFB 2; CA 102;
CANR 44, 92; CN 7; DLB 6; DLBY
1981; FW; INT CA-102; MTCW 1
Gordon, N. J.
See Bosman, Herman Charles
Gordon, Sol 1923- **CLC 26**
See also CA 53-56; CANR 4; SATA 11
Gordone, Charles 1925-1995 **CLC 1, 4; DC 8**
See also BW 1, 3; CA 93-96; 180; 150;
CAAE 180; CAD; CANR 55; DAM
DRAM; DLB 7; INT CA-93-96; MTCW
1
Gore, Catherine 1800-1861 **NCLC 65**
See also DLB 116; RGEL 2

Gorenko, Anna Andreevna
See Akhmatova, Anna

Gorky, Maxim SSC 28; TCLC 8; WLC
See Peshkov, Alexei Maximovich
See also DAB; DFS 9; DLB 295; EW 8;
EWL 3; MTCW 2; TWA

Goryan, Sirak
See Saroyan, William

Gosse, Edmund (William) 1849-1928 **TCLC 28**
See also CA 117; DLB 57, 144, 184; RGEL 2

Gotlieb, Phyllis (Fay Bloom) 1926- **CLC 18**
See also CA 13-16R; CANR 7; DLB 88, 251; SFW 4

Gottesman, S. D.
See Kornbluth, C(yril) M.; Pohl, Frederik

Gottfried von Strassburg fl. c. 1170-1215 **CMLC 10**
See also CDWLB 2; DLB 138; EW 1; RGWL 2, 3

Gotthelf, Jeremias 1797-1854 **NCLC 117**
See also DLB 133; RGWL 2, 3

Gottschalk, Laura Riding
See Jackson, Laura (Riding)

Gould, Lois 1932(?)-2002 **CLC 4, 10**
See also CA 77-80; 208; CANR 29; MTCW 1

Gould, Stephen Jay 1941-2002 **CLC 163**
See also AAYA 26; BEST 90:2; CA 77-80; 205; CANR 10, 27, 56, 75, 125; CPW; INT CANR-27; MTCW 1, 2

Gourmont, Remy(-Marie-Charles) de 1858-1915 **TCLC 17**
See also CA 109; 150; GFL 1789 to the Present; MTCW 2

Gournay, Marie le Jars de
See de Gournay, Marie le Jars

Govier, Katherine 1948- **CLC 51**
See also CA 101; CANR 18, 40, 128; CCA 1

Gower, John c. 1330-1408 **LC 76**
See also BRW 1; DLB 146; RGEL 2

Goyen, (Charles) William 1915-1983 **CLC 5, 8, 14, 40**
See also AITN 2; CA 5-8R; 110; CANR 6, 71; DLB 2, 218; DLBY 1983; EWL 3; INT CANR-6

Goytisolo, Juan 1931- **CLC 5, 10, 23, 133; HLC 1**
See also CA 85-88; CANR 32, 61; CWW 2; DAM MULT; EWL 3; GLL 2; HW 1, 2; MTCW 1, 2

Gozzano, Guido 1883-1916 **PC 10**
See also CA 154; DLB 114; EWL 3

Gozzi, (Conte) Carlo 1720-1806 **NCLC 23**

Grabbe, Christian Dietrich 1801-1836 **NCLC 2**
See also DLB 133; RGWL 2, 3

Grace, Patricia Frances 1937- **CLC 56**
See also CA 176; CANR 118; CN 7; EWL 3; RGSF 2

Gracian y Morales, Baltasar 1601-1658 **LC 15**

Gracq, Julien **CLC 11, 48**
See Poirier, Louis
See also CWW 2; DLB 83; GFL 1789 to the Present

Grade, Chaim 1910-1982 **CLC 10**
See also CA 93-96; 107; EWL 3

Graduate of Oxford, A
See Ruskin, John

Grafton, Garth
See Duncan, Sara Jeannette

Grafton, Sue 1940- **CLC 163**
See also AAYA 11, 49; BEST 90:3; CA 108; CANR 31, 55, 111; CMW 4; CPW; CSW; DA3; DAM POP; DLB 226; FW; MSW

Graham, John
See Phillips, David Graham

Graham, Jorie 1950- **CLC 48, 118**
See also CA 111; CANR 63, 118; CP 7; CWP; DLB 120; EWL 3; PFS 10, 17

Graham, R(obert) B(ontine) Cunninghame
See Cunninghame Graham, Robert (Gallnigad) Bontine
See also DLB 98, 135, 174; RGEL 2; RGSF 2

Graham, Robert
See Haldeman, Joe (William)

Graham, Tom
See Lewis, (Harry) Sinclair

Graham, W(illiam) S(idney) 1918-1986 **CLC 29**
See also BRWS 7; CA 73-76; 118; DLB 20; RGEL 2

Graham, Winston (Mawdsley) 1910-2003 **CLC 23**
See also CA 49-52; 218; CANR 2, 22, 45, 66; CMW 4; CN 7; DLB 77; RHW

Grahame, Kenneth 1859-1932 **TCLC 64, 136**
See also BYA 5; CA 108; 136; CANR 80; CLR 5; CWRI 5; DA3; DAB; DLB 34, 141, 178; FANT; MAICYA 1, 2; MTCW 2; RGEL 2; SATA 100; TEA; WCH; YABC 1

Granger, Darius John
See Marlowe, Stephen

Granin, Daniil **CLC 59**

Granovsky, Timofei Nikolaevich 1813-1855 **NCLC 75**
See also DLB 198

Grant, Skeeter
See Spiegelman, Art

Granville-Barker, Harley 1877-1946 **TCLC 2**
See Barker, Harley Granville
See also CA 104; 204; DAM DRAM; RGEL 2

Granzotto, Gianni
See Granzotto, Giovanni Battista

Granzotto, Giovanni Battista 1914-1985 **CLC 70**
See also CA 166

Grass, Guenter (Wilhelm) 1927- **CLC 1, 2, 4, 6, 11, 15, 22, 32, 49, 88; WLC**
See also BPFB 2; CA 13-16R; CANR 20, 75, 93; CDWLB 2; DA; DA3; DAB; DAC; DAM MST, NOV; DLB 75, 124; EW 13; EWL 3; MTCW 1, 2; RGWL 2, 3; TWA

Gratton, Thomas
See Hulme, T(homas) E(rnest)

Grau, Shirley Ann 1929- **CLC 4, 9, 146; SSC 15**
See also CA 89-92; CANR 22, 69; CN 7; CSW; DLB 2, 218; INT CA-89-92, CANR-22; MTCW 1

Gravel, Fern
See Hall, James Norman

Graver, Elizabeth 1964- **CLC 70**
See also CA 135; CANR 71, 129

Graves, Richard Perceval 1895-1985 **CLC 44**
See also CA 65-68; CANR 9, 26, 51

Graves, Robert (von Ranke) 1895-1985 **CLC 1, 2, 6, 11, 39, 44, 45; PC 6**
See also BPFB 2; BRW 7; BYA 4; CA 5-8R; 117; CANR 5, 36; CDBLB 1914-1945; DA3; DAB; DAC; DAM MST, POET; DLB 20, 100, 191; DLBD 18; DLBY 1985; EWL 3; LATS 1; MTCW 1, 2; NCFS 2; RGEL 2; RHW; SATA 45; TEA

Graves, Valerie
See Bradley, Marion Zimmer

Gray, Alasdair (James) 1934- **CLC 41**
See also BRWS 9; CA 126; CANR 47, 69, 106; CN 7; DLB 194, 261; HGG; INT CA-126; MTCW 1, 2; RGSF 2; SUFW 2

Gray, Amlin 1946- **CLC 29**
See also CA 138

Gray, Francine du Plessix 1930- **CLC 22, 153**
See also BEST 90:3; CA 61-64; CAAS 2; CANR 11, 33, 75, 81; DAM NOV; INT CANR-11; MTCW 1, 2

Gray, John (Henry) 1866-1934 **TCLC 19**
See also CA 119; 162; RGEL 2

Gray, Simon (James Holliday) 1936- **CLC 9, 14, 36**
See also AITN 1; CA 21-24R; CAAS 3; CANR 32, 69; CD 5; DLB 13; EWL 3; MTCW 1; RGEL 2

Gray, Spalding 1941-2004 **CLC 49, 112; DC 7**
See also CA 128; CAD; CANR 74; CD 5; CPW; DAM POP; MTCW 2

Gray, Thomas 1716-1771 **LC 4, 40; PC 2; WLC**
See also BRW 3; CDBLB 1660-1789; DA; DA3; DAB; DAC; DAM MST; DLB 109; EXPP; PAB; PFS 9; RGEL 2; TEA; WP

Grayson, David
See Baker, Ray Stannard

Grayson, Richard (A.) 1951- **CLC 38**
See also CA 85-88; 210; CAAE 210; CANR 14, 31, 57; DLB 234

Greeley, Andrew M(oran) 1928- **CLC 28**
See also BPFB 2; CA 5-8R; CAAS 7; CANR 7, 43, 69, 104; CMW 4; CPW; DA3; DAM POP; MTCW 1, 2

Green, Anna Katharine 1846-1935 **TCLC 63**
See also CA 112; 159; CMW 4; DLB 202, 221; MSW

Green, Brian
See Card, Orson Scott

Green, Hannah
See Greenberg, Joanne (Goldenberg)

Green, Hannah 1927(?)-1996 **CLC 3**
See also CA 73-76; CANR 59, 93; NFS 10

Green, Henry **CLC 2, 13, 97**
See Yorke, Henry Vincent
See also BRWS 2; CA 175; DLB 15; EWL 3; RGEL 2

Green, Julian (Hartridge) 1900-1998
See Green, Julien
See also CA 21-24R; 169; CANR 33, 87; DLB 4, 72; MTCW 1

Green, Julien **CLC 3, 11, 77**
See Green, Julian (Hartridge)
See also EWL 3; GFL 1789 to the Present; MTCW 2

Green, Paul (Eliot) 1894-1981 **CLC 25**
See also AITN 1; CA 5-8R; 103; CANR 3; DAM DRAM; DLB 7, 9, 249; DLBY 1981; RGAL 4

Greenaway, Peter 1942- **CLC 159**
See also CA 127

Greenberg, Ivan 1908-1973
See Rahv, Philip
See also CA 85-88

Greenberg, Joanne (Goldenberg) 1932- **CLC 7, 30**
See also AAYA 12; CA 5-8R; CANR 14, 32, 69; CN 7; SATA 25; YAW

Greenberg, Richard 1959(?)- **CLC 57**
See also CA 138; CAD; CD 5

Greenblatt, Stephen J(ay) 1943- **CLC 70**
See also CA 49-52; CANR 115

Greene, Bette 1934- **CLC 30**
See also AAYA 7; BYA 3; CA 53-56; CANR 4; CLR 2; CWRI 5; JRDA; LAIT 4; MAICYA 1, 2; NFS 10; SAAS 16; SATA 8, 102; WYA; YAW

Greene, Gael **CLC 8**
See also CA 13-16R; CANR 10

Gunn, William Harrison 1934(?)-1989
See Gunn, Bill
See also AITN 1; BW 1, 3; CA 13-16R;
128; CANR 12, 25, 76
Gunn Allen, Paula
See Allen, Paula Gunn
Gunnars, Kristjana 1948- **CLC 69**
See also CA 113; CCA 1; CP 7; CWP; DLB
60
Gunter, Erich
See Eich, Gunter
Gurdjieff, G(eorgei) I(vanovich)
1877(?)-1949 **TCLC 71**
See also CA 157
Gurganus, Allan 1947- **CLC 70**
See also BEST 90:1; CA 135; CANR 114;
CN 7; CPW; CSW; DAM POP; GLL 1
Gurney, A. R.
See Gurney, A(lbert) R(amsdell), Jr.
See also DLB 266
Gurney, A(lbert) R(amsdell), Jr. 1930- **CLC
32, 50, 54**
See Gurney, A. R.
See also AMWS 5; CA 77-80; CAD; CANR
32, 64, 121; CD 5; DAM DRAM; EWL 3
Gurney, Ivor (Bertie) 1890-1937 **TCLC 33**
See also BRW 6; CA 167; DLBY 2002;
PAB; RGEL 2
Gurney, Peter
See Gurney, A(lbert) R(amsdell), Jr.
Guro, Elena (Genrikhovna) 1877-1913 **TCLC
56**
See also DLB 295
Gustafson, James M(oody) 1925- **CLC 100**
See also CA 25-28R; CANR 37
Gustafson, Ralph (Barker) 1909-1995 **CLC
36**
See also CA 21-24R; CANR 8, 45, 84; CP
7; DLB 88; RGEL 2
Gut, Gom
See Simenon, Georges (Jacques Christian)
Guterson, David 1956- **CLC 91**
See also CA 132; CANR 73, 126; DLB 292;
MTCW 2; NFS 13
Guthrie, A(lfred) B(ertram), Jr. 1901-1991
CLC 23
See also CA 57-60; 134; CANR 24; DLB 6,
212; SATA 62; SATA-Obit 67
Guthrie, Isobel
See Grieve, C(hristopher) M(urray)
Guthrie, Woodrow Wilson 1912-1967
See Guthrie, Woody
See also CA 113; 93-96
Guthrie, Woody CLC 35
See Guthrie, Woodrow Wilson
See also LAIT 3
Gutierrez Najera, Manuel 1859-1895 **HLCS
2; NCLC 133**
See also DLB 290; LAW
Guy, Rosa (Cuthbert) 1925- **CLC 26**
See also AAYA 4, 37; BW 2; CA 17-20R;
CANR 14, 34, 83; CLR 13; DLB 33;
DNFS 1; JRDA; MAICYA 1, 2; SATA 14,
62, 122; YAW
Gwendolyn
See Bennett, (Enoch) Arnold
H. D. CLC 3, 8, 14, 31, 34, 73; PC 5
See Doolittle, Hilda
H. de V.
See Buchan, John
Haavikko, Paavo Juhani 1931- **CLC 18, 34**
See also CA 106; EWL 3
Habbema, Koos
See Heijermans, Herman
Habermas, Juergen 1929- **CLC 104**
See also CA 109; CANR 85; DLB 242
Habermas, Jurgen
See Habermas, Juergen

Hacker, Marilyn 1942- **CLC 5, 9, 23, 72, 91;
PC 47**
See also CA 77-80; CANR 68, 129; CP 7;
CWP; DAM POET; DLB 120, 282; FW;
GLL 2; PFS 19
Hadewijch of Antwerp fl. 1250- **CMLC 61**
See also RGWL 3
Hadrian 76-138 **CMLC 52**
Haeckel, Ernst Heinrich (Philipp August)
1834-1919 **TCLC 83**
See also CA 157
Hafiz c. 1326-1389(?) **CMLC 34**
See also RGWL 2, 3
Hagedorn, Jessica T(arahata) 1949- **CLC 185**
See also CA 139; CANR 69; CWP; RGAL
4
Haggard, H(enry) Rider 1856-1925 **TCLC 11**
See also BRWS 3; BYA 4, 5; CA 108; 148;
CANR 112; DLB 70, 156, 174, 178;
FANT; LMFS 1; MTCW 2; RGEL 2;
RHW; SATA 16; SCFW; SFW 4; SUFW
1; WLIT 4
Hagiosy, L.
See Larbaud, Valery (Nicolas)
Hagiwara, Sakutaro 1886-1942 **PC 18; TCLC
60**
See Hagiwara Sakutaro
See also CA 154; RGWL 3
Hagiwara Sakutaro
See Hagiwara, Sakutaro
See also EWL 3
Haig, Fenil
See Ford, Ford Madox
Haig-Brown, Roderick (Langmere)
1908-1976 **CLC 21**
See also CA 5-8R; 69-72; CANR 4, 38, 83;
CLR 31; CWRI 5; DLB 88; MAICYA 1,
2; SATA 12
Haight, Rip
See Carpenter, John (Howard)
Hailey, Arthur 1920- **CLC 5**
See also AITN 2; BEST 90:3; BPFB 2; CA
1-4R; CANR 2, 36, 75; CCA 1; CN 7;
CPW; DAM NOV, POP; DLB 88; DLBY
1982; MTCW 1, 2
Hailey, Elizabeth Forsythe 1938- **CLC 40**
See also CA 93-96, 188; CAAE 188; CAAS
1; CANR 15, 48; INT CANR-15
Haines, John (Meade) 1924- **CLC 58**
See also AMWS 12; CA 17-20R; CANR
13, 34; CSW; DLB 5, 212
Hakluyt, Richard 1552-1616 **LC 31**
See also DLB 136; RGEL 2
Haldeman, Joe (William) 1943- **CLC 61**
See Graham, Robert
See also AAYA 38; CA 53-56, 179; CAAE
179; CAAS 25; CANR 6, 70, 72; DLB 8;
INT CANR-6; SCFW 2; SFW 4
Hale, Janet Campbell 1947- **NNAL**
See also CA 49-52; CANR 45, 75; DAM
MULT; DLB 175; MTCW 2
Hale, Sarah Josepha (Buell) 1788-1879
NCLC 75
See also DLB 1, 42, 73, 243
Halevy, Elie 1870-1937 **TCLC 104**
Haley, Alex(ander Murray Palmer)
1921-1992 **BLC 2; CLC 8, 12, 76; TCLC
147**
See also AAYA 26; BPFB 2; BW 2, 3; CA
77-80; 136; CANR 61; CDALBS; CPW;
CSW; DA; DA3; DAB; DAC; DAM MST,
MULT, POP; DLB 38; LAIT 5; MTCW
1, 2; NFS 9
Haliburton, Thomas Chandler 1796-1865
NCLC 15
See also DLB 11, 99; RGEL 2; RGSF 2

Hall, Donald (Andrew, Jr.) 1928- **CLC 1, 13,
37, 59, 151**
See also CA 5-8R; CAAS 7; CANR 2, 44,
64, 106; CP 7; DAM POET; DLB 5;
MTCW 1; RGAL 4; SATA 23, 97
Hall, Frederic Sauser
See Sauser-Hall, Frederic
Hall, James
See Kuttner, Henry
Hall, James Norman 1887-1951 **TCLC 23**
See also CA 123; 173; LAIT 1; RHW 1;
SATA 21
Hall, Joseph 1574-1656 **LC 91**
See also DLB 121, 151; RGEL 2
Hall, (Marguerite) Radclyffe 1880-1943
TCLC 12
See also BRWS 6; CA 110; 150; CANR 83;
DLB 191; MTCW 2; RGEL 2; RHW
Hall, Rodney 1935- **CLC 51**
See also CA 109; CANR 69; CN 7; CP 7;
DLB 289
Hallam, Arthur Henry 1811-1833 **NCLC 110**
See also DLB 32
Halldor Kiljan Gudjonsson 1902-1998
See Halldor Laxness
See also CA 103; 164; CWW 2
Halldor Laxness CLC 25
See Halldor Kiljan Gudjonsson
See also DLB 293; EW 12; EWL 3; RGWL
2, 3
Halleck, Fitz-Greene 1790-1867 **NCLC 47**
See also DLB 3, 250; RGAL 4
Halliday, Michael
See Creasey, John
Halpern, Daniel 1945- **CLC 14**
See also CA 33-36R; CANR 93; CP 7
Hamburger, Michael (Peter Leopold) 1924-
CLC 5, 14
See also CA 5-8R, 196; CAAE 196; CAAS
4; CANR 2, 47; CP 7; DLB 27
Hamill, Pete 1935- **CLC 10**
See also CA 25-28R; CANR 18, 71, 127
Hamilton, Alexander 1755(?)-1804 **NCLC 49**
See also DLB 37
Hamilton, Clive
See Lewis, C(live) S(taples)
Hamilton, Edmond 1904-1977 **CLC 1**
See also CA 1-4R; CANR 3, 84; DLB 8;
SATA 118; SFW 4
Hamilton, Eugene (Jacob) Lee
See Lee-Hamilton, Eugene (Jacob)
Hamilton, Franklin
See Silverberg, Robert
Hamilton, Gail
See Corcoran, Barbara (Asenath)
Hamilton, Jane 1957- **CLC 179**
See also CA 147; CANR 85, 128
Hamilton, Mollie
See Kaye, M(ary) M(argaret)
Hamilton, (Anthony Walter) Patrick
1904-1962 **CLC 51**
See also CA 176; 113; DLB 10, 191
Hamilton, Virginia (Esther) 1936-2002 **CLC
26**
See also AAYA 2, 21; BW 2, 3; BYA 1, 2,
8; CA 25-28R; 206; CANR 20, 37, 73,
126; CLR 1, 11, 40; DAM MULT; DLB
33, 52; DLBY 01; INT CANR-20; JRDA;
LAIT 5; MAICYA 1, 2; MAICYAS 1;
MTCW 1, 2; SATA 4, 56, 79, 123; SATA-
Obit 132; WYA; YAW
Hammett, (Samuel) Dashiell 1894-1961 **CLC
3, 5, 10, 19, 47; SSC 17**
See also AITN 1; AMWS 4; BPFB 2; CA
81-84; CANR 42; CDALB 1929-1941;
CMW 4; DA3; DLB 226, 280; DLBD 6;
DLBY 1996; EWL 3; LAIT 3; MSW;
MTCW 1, 2; RGAL 4; RGSF 2; TUS

Hammon, Jupiter 1720(?)-1800(?) **BLC 2;**
NCLC 5; PC 16
See also DAM MULT, POET; DLB 31, 50

Hammond, Keith
See Kuttner, Henry

Hamner, Earl (Henry), Jr. 1923- **CLC 12**
See also AITN 2; CA 73-76; DLB 6

Hampton, Christopher (James) 1946- **CLC 4**
See also CA 25-28R; CD 5; DLB 13;
MTCW 1

Hamsun, Knut TCLC 2, 14, 49
See Pedersen, Knut
See also DLB 297; EW 8; EWL 3; RGWL
2, 3

Handke, Peter 1942- **CLC 5, 8, 10, 15, 38,**
134; DC 17
See also CA 77-80; CANR 33, 75, 104;
CWW 2; DAM DRAM, NOV; DLB 85,
124; EWL 3; MTCW 1, 2; TWA

Handy, W(illiam) C(hristopher) 1873-1958
TCLC 97
See also BW 3; CA 121; 167

Hanley, James 1901-1985 **CLC 3, 5, 8, 13**
See also CA 73-76; 117; CANR 36; CBD;
DLB 191; EWL 3; MTCW 1; RGEL 2

Hannah, Barry 1942- **CLC 23, 38, 90**
See also BPFB 2; CA 108; 110; CANR 43,
68, 113; CN 7; CSW; DLB 6, 234; INT
CA-110; MTCW 1; RGSF 2

Hannon, Ezra
See Hunter, Evan

Hansberry, Lorraine (Vivian) 1930-1965 **BLC**
2; CLC 17, 62; DC 2
See also AAYA 25; AFAW 1, 2; AMWS 4;
BW 1, 3; CA 109; 25-28R; CABS 3;
CAD; CANR 58; CDALB 1941-1968;
CWD; DA; DA3; DAB; DAC; DAM
DRAM, MST, MULT; DFS 2; DLB 7, 38;
EWL 3; FW; LAIT 4; MTCW 1, 2; RGAL
4; TUS

Hansen, Joseph 1923- **CLC 38**
See Brock, Rose; Colton, James
See also BPFB 2; CA 29-32R; CAAS 17;
CANR 16, 44, 66, 125; CMW 4; DLB
226; GLL 1; INT CANR-16

Hansen, Martin A(lfred) 1909-1955 **TCLC**
32
See also CA 167; DLB 214; EWL 3

Hansen and Philipson eds. CLC 65

Hanson, Kenneth O(stlin) 1922- **CLC 13**
See also CA 53-56; CANR 7

Hardwick, Elizabeth (Bruce) 1916- **CLC 13**
See also AMWS 3; CA 5-8R; CANR 3, 32,
70, 100; CN 7; CSW; DA3; DAM NOV;
DLB 6; MAWW; MTCW 1, 2

Hardy, Thomas 1840-1928 **PC 8; SSC 2, 60;**
TCLC 4, 10, 18, 32, 48, 53, 72, 143;
WLC
See also BRW 6; BRWC 1, 2; BRWR 1;
CA 104; 123; CDBLB 1890-1914; DA;
DA3; DAB; DAC; DAM MST, NOV,
POET; DLB 18, 19, 135, 284; EWL 3;
EXPN; EXPP; LAIT 2; MTCW 1, 2; NFS
3, 11, 15; PFS 3, 4, 18; RGEL 2; RGSF
2; TEA; WLIT 4

Hare, David 1947- **CLC 29, 58, 136**
See also BRWS 4; CA 97-100; CANR 39,
91; CBD; CD 5; DFS 4, 7, 16; DLB 13;
MTCW 1; TEA

Harewood, John
See Van Druten, John (William)

Harford, Henry
See Hudson, W(illiam) H(enry)

Hargrave, Leonie
See Disch, Thomas M(ichael)

Hariri, Al- al-Qasim ibn 'Ali Abu
Muhammad al-Basri
See al-Hariri, al-Qasim ibn 'Ali Abu Mu-
hammad al-Basri

Harjo, Joy 1951- **CLC 83; NNAL; PC 27**
See also AMWS 12; CA 114; CANR 35,
67, 91, 129; CP 7; CWP; DAM MULT;
DLB 120, 175; EWL 3; MTCW 2; PFS
15; RGAL 4

Harlan, Louis R(udolph) 1922- **CLC 34**
See also CA 21-24R; CANR 25, 55, 80

Harling, Robert 1951(?)- **CLC 53**
See also CA 147

Harmon, William (Ruth) 1938- **CLC 38**
See also CA 33-36R; CANR 14, 32, 35;
SATA 65

Harper, F. E. W.
See Harper, Frances Ellen Watkins

Harper, Frances E. W.
See Harper, Frances Ellen Watkins

Harper, Frances E. Watkins
See Harper, Frances Ellen Watkins

Harper, Frances Ellen
See Harper, Frances Ellen Watkins

Harper, Frances Ellen Watkins 1825-1911
BLC 2; PC 21; TCLC 14
See also AFAW 1, 2; BW 1, 3; CA 111; 125;
CANR 79; DAM MULT, POET; DLB 50,
221; MAWW; RGAL 4

Harper, Michael S(teven) 1938- **CLC 7, 22**
See also AFAW 2; BW 1; CA 33-36R;
CANR 24, 108; CP 7; DLB 41; RGAL 4

Harper, Mrs. F. E. W.
See Harper, Frances Ellen Watkins

Harpur, Charles 1813-1868 **NCLC 114**
See also DLB 230; RGEL 2

Harris, Christie
See Harris, Christie (Lucy) Irwin

Harris, Christie (Lucy) Irwin 1907-2002 **CLC**
12
See also CA 5-8R; CANR 6, 83; CLR 47;
DLB 88; JRDA; MAICYA 1; SAAS 10;
SATA 6, 74; SATA-Essay 116

Harris, Frank 1856-1931 **TCLC 24**
See also CA 109; 150; CANR 80; DLB 156,
197; RGEL 2

Harris, George Washington 1814-1869 **NCLC**
23
See also DLB 3, 11, 248; RGAL 4

Harris, Joel Chandler 1848-1908 **SSC 19;**
TCLC 2
See also CA 104; 137; CANR 80; CLR 49;
DLB 11, 23, 42, 78, 91; LAIT 2; MAI-
CYA 1, 2; RGSF 2; SATA 100; WCH;
YABC 1

Harris, John (Wyndham Parkes Lucas)
Beynon 1903-1969
See Wyndham, John
See also CA 102; 89-92; CANR 84; SATA
118; SFW 4

Harris, MacDonald CLC 9
See Heiney, Donald (William)

Harris, Mark 1922- **CLC 19**
See also CA 5-8R; CAAS 3; CANR 2, 55,
83; CN 7; DLB 2; DLBY 1980

Harris, Norman CLC 65

Harris, (Theodore) Wilson 1921- **CLC 25,**
159
See also BRWS 5; BW 2, 3; CA 65-68;
CAAS 16; CANR 11, 27, 69, 114; CD-
WLB 3; CN 7; CP 7; DLB 117; EWL 3;
MTCW 1; RGEL 2

Harrison, Barbara Grizzuti 1934-2002 **CLC**
144
See also CA 77-80; 205; CANR 15, 48; INT
CANR-15

Harrison, Elizabeth (Allen) Cavanna
1909-2001
See Cavanna, Betty
See also CA 9-12R; 200; CANR 6, 27, 85,
104, 121; MAICYA 2; SATA 142; YAW

Harrison, Harry (Max) 1925- **CLC 42**
See also CA 1-4R; CANR 5, 21, 84; DLB
8; SATA 4; SCFW 2; SFW 4

Harrison, James (Thomas) 1937- **CLC 6, 14,**
33, 66, 143; SSC 19
See Harrison, Jim
See also CA 13-16R; CANR 8, 51, 79; CN
7; CP 7; DLBY 1982; INT CANR-8

Harrison, Jim
See Harrison, James (Thomas)
See also AMWS 8; RGAL 4; TCWW 2;
TUS

Harrison, Kathryn 1961- **CLC 70, 151**
See also CA 144; CANR 68, 122

Harrison, Tony 1937- **CLC 43, 129**
See also BRWS 5; CA 65-68; CANR 44,
98; CBD; CD 5; CP 7; DLB 40, 245;
MTCW 1; RGEL 2

Harriss, Will(ard Irvin) 1922- **CLC 34**
See also CA 111

Hart, Ellis
See Ellison, Harlan (Jay)

Hart, Josephine 1942(?)- **CLC 70**
See also CA 138; CANR 70; CPW; DAM
POP

Hart, Moss 1904-1961 **CLC 66**
See also CA 109; 89-92; CANR 84; DAM
DRAM; DFS 1; DLB 7, 266; RGAL 4

Harte, (Francis) Bret(t) 1836(?)-1902 **SSC 8,**
59; TCLC 1, 25; WLC
See also AMWS 2; CA 104; 140; CANR
80; CDALB 1865-1917; DA; DA3; DAC;
DAM MST; DLB 12, 64, 74, 79, 186;
EXPS; LAIT 2; RGAL 4; RGSF 2; SATA
26; SSFS 3; TUS

Hartley, L(eslie) P(oles) 1895-1972 **CLC 2,**
22
See also BRWS 7; CA 45-48; 37-40R;
CANR 33; DLB 15, 139; EWL 3; HGG;
MTCW 1, 2; RGEL 2; RGSF 2; SUFW 1

Hartman, Geoffrey H. 1929- **CLC 27**
See also CA 117; 125; CANR 79; DLB 67

Hartmann, Sadakichi 1869-1944 **TCLC 73**
See also CA 157; DLB 54

Hartmann von Aue c. 1170-c. 1210 **CMLC**
15
See also CDWLB 2; DLB 138; RGWL 2, 3

Hartog, Jan de
See de Hartog, Jan

Haruf, Kent 1943- **CLC 34**
See also AAYA 44; CA 149; CANR 91

Harvey, Caroline
See Trollope, Joanna

Harvey, Gabriel 1550(?)-1631 **LC 88**
See also DLB 167, 213, 281

Harwood, Ronald 1934- **CLC 32**
See also CA 1-4R; CANR 4, 55; CBD; CD
5; DAM DRAM, MST; DLB 13

Hasegawa Tatsunosuke
See Futabatei, Shimei

Hasek, Jaroslav (Matej Frantisek)
1883-1923 **SSC 69; TCLC 4**
See also CA 104; 129; CDWLB 4; DLB
215; EW 9; EWL 3; MTCW 1, 2; RGSF
2; RGWL 2, 3

Hass, Robert 1941- **CLC 18, 39, 99; PC 16**
See also AMWS 6; CA 111; CANR 30, 50,
71; CP 7; DLB 105, 206; EWL 3; RGAL
4; SATA 94

Hastings, Hudson
See Kuttner, Henry

Hastings, Selina CLC 44

Hathorne, John 1641-1717 **LC 38**

Hatteras, Amelia
See Mencken, H(enry) L(ouis)

Hatteras, Owen TCLC 18
See Mencken, H(enry) L(ouis); Nathan,
George Jean

Henkin, Joshua CLC 119
See also CA 161
Henley, Beth CLC 23; DC 6, 14
See Henley, Elizabeth Becker
See also CABS 3; CAD; CD 5; CSW;
CWD; DFS 2; DLBY 1986; FW
Henley, Elizabeth Becker 1952-
See Henley, Beth
See also CA 107; CANR 32, 73; DA3;
DAM DRAM, MST; MTCW 1, 2
Henley, William Ernest 1849-1903 TCLC 8
See also CA 105; DLB 19; RGEL 2
Hennissart, Martha
See Lathen, Emma
See also CA 85-88; CANR 64
Henry VIII 1491-1547 LC 10
See also DLB 132
Henry, O. SSC 5, 49; TCLC 1, 19; WLC
See Porter, William Sydney
See also AAYA 41; AMWS 2; EXPS; RGAL
4; RGSF 2; SSFS 2, 18
Henry, Patrick 1736-1799 LC 25
See also LAIT 1
Henryson, Robert 1430(?)-1506(?) LC 20
See also BRWS 7; DLB 146; RGEL 2
Henschke, Alfred
See Klabund
Henson, Lance 1944- NNAL
See also CA 146; DLB 175
Hentoff, Nat(han Irving) 1925- CLC 26
See also AAYA 4, 42; BYA 6; CA 1-4R;
CAAS 6; CANR 5, 25, 77, 114; CLR 1,
52; INT CANR-25; JRDA; MAICYA 1,
2; SATA 42, 69, 133; SATA-Brief 27;
WYA; YAW
Heppenstall, (John) Rayner 1911-1981 CLC
10
See also CA 1-4R; 103; CANR 29; EWL 3
Heraclitus c. 540B.C.-c. 450B.C. CMLC 22
See also DLB 176
Herbert, Frank (Patrick) 1920-1986 CLC 12,
23, 35, 44, 85
See also AAYA 21; BPFB 2; BYA 4, 14;
CA 53-56; 118; CANR 5, 43; CDALBS;
CPW; DAM POP; DLB 8; INT CANR-5;
LAIT 5; MTCW 1, 2; NFS 17; SATA 9,
37; SATA-Obit 47; SCFW 2; SFW 4;
YAW
Herbert, George 1593-1633 LC 24; PC 4
See also BRW 2; BRWR 2; CDBLB Before
1660; DAB; DAM POET; DLB 126;
EXPP; RGEL 2; TEA; WP
Herbert, Zbigniew 1924-1998 CLC 9, 43; PC
50
See also CA 89-92; 169; CANR 36, 74; CD-
WLB 4; CWW 2; DAM POET; DLB 232;
EWL 3; MTCW 1
Herbst, Josephine (Frey) 1897-1969 CLC 34
See also CA 5-8R; 25-28R; DLB 9
Herder, Johann Gottfried von 1744-1803
NCLC 8
See also DLB 97; EW 4; TWA
Heredia, Jose Maria 1803-1839 HLCS 2
See also LAW
Hergesheimer, Joseph 1880-1954 TCLC 11
See also CA 109; 194; DLB 102, 9; RGAL
4
Herlihy, James Leo 1927-1993 CLC 6
See also CA 1-4R; 143; CAD; CANR 2
Herman, William
See Bierce, Ambrose (Gwinett)
Hermogenes fl. c. 175- CMLC 6
Hernandez, Jose 1834-1886 NCLC 17
See also LAW; RGWL 2, 3; WLIT 1
Herodotus c. 484B.C.-c. 420B.C. CMLC 17
See also AW 1; CDWLB 1; DLB 176;
RGWL 2, 3; TWA

Herrick, Robert 1591-1674 LC 13; PC 9
See also BRW 2; BRWC 2; DA; DAB;
DAC; DAM MST, POP; DLB 126; EXPP;
PFS 13; RGAL 4; RGEL 2; TEA; WP
Herring, Guilles
See Somerville, Edith Oenone
Herriot, James 1916-1995 CLC 12
See Wight, James Alfred
See also AAYA 1; BPFB 2; CA 148; CANR
40; CLR 80; CPW; DAM POP; LAIT 3;
MAICYA; MAICYAS 1; MTCW 2;
SATA 86, 135; TEA; YAW
Herris, Violet
See Hunt, Violet
Herrmann, Dorothy 1941- CLC 44
See also CA 107
Herrmann, Taffy
See Herrmann, Dorothy
Hersey, John (Richard) 1914-1993 CLC 1, 2,
7, 9, 40, 81, 97
See also AAYA 29; BPFB 2; CA 17-20R;
140; CANR 33; CDALBS; CPW; DAM
POP; DLB 6, 185, 278; MTCW 1, 2;
SATA 25; SATA-Obit 76; TUS
Herzen, Aleksandr Ivanovich 1812-1870
NCLC 10, 61
See Herzen, Alexander
Herzen, Alexander
See Herzen, Aleksandr Ivanovich
See also DLB 277
Herzl, Theodor 1860-1904 TCLC 36
See also CA 168
Herzog, Werner 1942- CLC 16
See also CA 89-92
Hesiod c. 8th cent. B.C.- CMLC 5
See also AW 1; DLB 176; RGWL 2, 3
Hesse, Hermann 1877-1962 CLC 1, 2, 3, 6,
11, 17, 25, 69; SSC 9, 49; TCLC 148;
WLC
See also AAYA 43; BPFB 2; CA 17-18;
CAP 2; CDWLB 2; DA; DA3; DAB;
DAC; DAM MST, NOV; DLB 66; EW 9;
EWL 3; EXPN; LAIT 1; MTCW 1, 2;
NFS 6, 15; RGWL 2, 3; SATA 50; TWA
Hewes, Cady
See De Voto, Bernard (Augustine)
Heyen, William 1940- CLC 13, 18
See also CA 33-36R, 220; CAAE 220;
CAAS 9; CANR 98; CP 7; DLB 5
Heyerdahl, Thor 1914-2002 CLC 26
See also CA 5-8R; 207; CANR 5, 22, 66,
73; LAIT 4; MTCW 1, 2; SATA 2, 52
Heym, Georg (Theodor Franz Arthur)
1887-1912 TCLC 9
See also CA 106; 181
Heym, Stefan 1913-2001 CLC 41
See also CA 9-12R; 203; CANR 4; CWW
2; DLB 69; EWL 3
Heyse, Paul (Johann Ludwig von) 1830-1914
TCLC 8
See also CA 104; 209; DLB 129
Heyward, (Edwin) DuBose 1885-1940 HR 2;
TCLC 59
See also CA 108; 157; DLB 7, 9, 45, 249;
SATA 21
Heywood, John 1497(?)-1580(?) LC 65
See also DLB 136; RGEL 2
Hibbert, Eleanor Alice Burford 1906-1993
CLC 7
See Holt, Victoria
See also BEST 90:4; CA 17-20R; 140;
CANR 9, 28, 59; CMW 4; CPW; DAM
POP; MTCW 2; RHW; SATA 2; SATA-
Obit 74
Hichens, Robert (Smythe) 1864-1950 TCLC
64
See also CA 162; DLB 153; HGG; RHW;
SUFW

Higgins, Aidan 1927- SSC 68
See also CA 9-12R; CANR 70, 115; CN 7;
DLB 14
Higgins, George V(incent) 1939-1999 CLC 4,
7, 10, 18
See also BPFB 2; CA 77-80; 186; CAAS 5;
CANR 17, 51, 89, 96; CMW 4; CN 7;
DLB 2; DLBY 1981, 1998; INT CANR-
17; MSW; MTCW 1
Higginson, Thomas Wentworth 1823-1911
TCLC 36
See also CA 162; DLB 1, 64, 243
Higgonet, Margaret ed. CLC 65
Highet, Helen
See MacInnes, Helen (Clark)
Highsmith, (Mary) Patricia 1921-1995 CLC
2, 4, 14, 42, 102
See Morgan, Claire
See also AAYA 48; BRWS 5; CA 1-4R; 147;
CANR 1, 20, 48, 62, 108; CMW 4; CPW;
DA3; DAM NOV, POP; MSW; MTCW 1,
2
Highwater, Jamake (Mamake) 1942(?)-2001
CLC 12
See also AAYA 7; BPFB 2; BYA 4; CA 65-
68; 199; CAAS 7; CANR 10, 34, 84; CLR
17; CWRI 5; DLB 52; DLBY 1985;
JRDA; MAICYA 1, 2; SATA 32, 69;
SATA-Brief 30
Highway, Tomson 1951- CLC 92; NNAL
See also CA 151; CANR 75; CCA 1; CD 5;
DAC; DAM MULT; DFS 2; MTCW 2
Hijuelos, Oscar 1951- CLC 65; HLC 1
See also AAYA 25; AMWS 8; BEST 90:1;
CA 123; CANR 50, 75, 125; CPW; DA3;
DAM MULT, POP; DLB 145; HW 1, 2;
LLW 1; MTCW 2; NFS 17; RGAL 4;
WLIT 1
Hikmet, Nazim 1902(?)-1963 CLC 40
See also CA 141; 93-96; EWL 3
Hildegard von Bingen 1098-1179 CMLC 20
See also DLB 148
Hildesheimer, Wolfgang 1916-1991 CLC 49
See also CA 101; 135; DLB 69, 124; EWL
3
Hill, Geoffrey (William) 1932- CLC 5, 8, 18,
45
See also BRWS 5; CA 81-84; CANR 21,
89; CDBLB 1960 to Present; CP 7; DAM
POET; DLB 40; EWL 3; MTCW 1; RGEL
2
Hill, George Roy 1921-2002 CLC 26
See also CA 110; 122; 213
Hill, John
See Koontz, Dean R(ay)
Hill, Susan (Elizabeth) 1942- CLC 4, 113
See also CA 33-36R; CANR 29, 69, 129;
CN 7; DAB; DAM MST, NOV; DLB 14,
139; HGG; MTCW 1; RHW
Hillard, Asa G. III CLC 70
Hillerman, Tony 1925- CLC 62, 170
See also AAYA 40; BEST 89:1; BPFB 2;
CA 29-32R; CANR 21, 42, 65, 97; CMW
4; CPW; DA3; DAM POP; DLB 206;
MSW; RGAL 4; SATA 6; TCWW 2; YAW
Hillesum, Etty 1914-1943 TCLC 49
See also CA 137
Hilliard, Noel (Harvey) 1929-1996 CLC 15
See also CA 9-12R; CANR 7, 69; CN 7
Hillis, Rick 1956- CLC 66
See also CA 134
Hilton, James 1900-1954 TCLC 21
See also CA 108; 169; DLB 34, 77; FANT;
SATA 34
Hilton, Walter (?)-1396 CMLC 58
See also DLB 146; RGEL 2
Himes, Chester (Bomar) 1909-1984 BLC 2;
CLC 2, 4, 7, 18, 58, 108; TCLC 139
See also AFAW 2; BPFB 2; BW 2; CA 25-
28R; 114; CANR 22, 89; CMW 4; DAM

MULT; DLB 2, 76, 143, 226; EWL 3;
MSW; MTCW 1, 2; RGAL 4

Hinde, Thomas CLC **6, 11**
See Chitty, Thomas Willes
See also EWL 3

Hine, (William) Daryl 1936- CLC **15**
See also CA 1-4R; CAAS 15; CANR 1, 20;
CP 7; DLB 60

Hinkson, Katharine Tynan
See Tynan, Katharine

Hinojosa(-Smith), Rolando (R.) 1929- HLC **1**
See Hinojosa-Smith, Rolando
See also CA 131; CAAS 16; CANR 62;
DAM MULT; DLB 82; HW 1, 2; LLW 1;
MTCW 2; RGAL 4

Hinton, S(usan) E(loise) 1950- CLC **30, 111**
See also AAYA 2, 33; BPFB 2; BYA 2, 3;
CA 81-84; CANR 32, 62, 92; CDALBS;
CLR 3, 23; CPW; DA; DA3; DAB; DAC;
DAM MST, NOV; JRDA; LAIT 5; MAI-
CYA 1, 2; MTCW 1, 2; NFS 5, 9, 15, 16;
SATA 19, 58, 115; WYA; YAW

Hippius, Zinaida (Nikolaevna) TCLC **9**
See Gippius, Zinaida (Nikolaevna)
See also DLB 295; EWL 3

Hiraoka, Kimitake 1925-1970
See Mishima, Yukio
See also CA 97-100; 29-32R; DA3; DAM
DRAM; GLL 1; MTCW 1, 2

Hirsch, E(ric) D(onald), Jr. 1928- CLC **79**
See also CA 25-28R; CANR 27, 51; DLB
67; INT CANR-27; MTCW 1

Hirsch, Edward 1950- CLC **31, 50**
See also CA 104; CANR 20, 42, 102; CP 7;
DLB 120

Hitchcock, Alfred (Joseph) 1899-1980 CLC **16**
See also AAYA 22; CA 159; 97-100; SATA
27; SATA-Obit 24

Hitchens, Christopher (Eric) 1949- CLC **157**
See also CA 152; CANR 89

Hitler, Adolf 1889-1945 TCLC **53**
See also CA 117; 147

Hoagland, Edward 1932- CLC **28**
See also ANW; CA 1-4R; CANR 2, 31, 57,
107; CN 7; DLB 6; SATA 51; TCWW 2

Hoban, Russell (Conwell) 1925- CLC **7, 25**
See also BPFB 2; CA 5-8R; CANR 23, 37,
66, 114; CLR 3, 69; CN 7; CWRI 5; DAM
NOV; DLB 52; FANT; MAICYA 1, 2;
MTCW 1, 2; SATA 1, 40, 78, 136; SFW
4; SUFW 2

Hobbes, Thomas 1588-1679 LC **36**
See also DLB 151, 252, 281; RGEL 2

Hobbs, Perry
See Blackmur, R(ichard) P(almer)

Hobson, Laura Z(ametkin) 1900-1986 CLC **7, 25**
See Field, Peter
See also BPFB 2; CA 17-20R; 118; CANR
55; DLB 28; SATA 52

Hoccleve, Thomas c. 1368-c. 1437 LC **75**
See also DLB 146; RGEL 2

Hoch, Edward D(entinger) 1930-
See Queen, Ellery
See also CA 29-32R; CANR 11, 27, 51, 97;
CMW 4; SFW 4

Hochhuth, Rolf 1931- CLC **4, 11, 18**
See also CA 5-8R; CANR 33, 75; CWW 2;
DAM DRAM; DLB 124; EWL 3; MTCW
1, 2

Hochman, Sandra 1936- CLC **3, 8**
See also CA 5-8R; DLB 5

Hochwaelder, Fritz 1911-1986 CLC **36**
See Hochwalder, Fritz
See also CA 29-32R; 120; CANR 42; DAM
DRAM; MTCW 1; RGWL 3

Hochwalder, Fritz
See Hochwaelder, Fritz
See also EWL 3; RGWL 2

Hocking, Mary (Eunice) 1921- CLC **13**
See also CA 101; CANR 18, 40

Hodgins, Jack 1938- CLC **23**
See also CA 93-96; CN 7; DLB 60

Hodgson, William Hope 1877(?)-1918 TCLC **13**
See also CA 111; 164; CMW 4; DLB 70,
153, 156, 178; HGG; MTCW 2; SFW 4;
SUFW 1

Hoeg, Peter 1957- CLC **95, 156**
See also CA 151; CANR 75; CMW 4; DA3;
DLB 214; EWL 3; MTCW 2; NFS 17;
RGWL 3; SSFS 18

Hoffman, Alice 1952- CLC **51**
See also AAYA 37; AMWS 10; CA 77-80;
CANR 34, 66, 100; CN 7; CPW; DAM
NOV; DLB 292; MTCW 1, 2

Hoffman, Daniel (Gerard) 1923- CLC **6, 13, 23**
See also CA 1-4R; CANR 4; CP 7; DLB 5

Hoffman, Eva 1945- CLC **182**
See also CA 132

Hoffman, Stanley 1944- CLC **5**
See also CA 77-80

Hoffman, William 1925- CLC **141**
See also CA 21-24R; CANR 9, 103; CSW;
DLB 234

Hoffman, William M(oses) 1939- CLC **40**
See Hoffman, William M.
See also CA 57-60; CANR 11, 71

Hoffmann, E(rnst) T(heodor) A(madeus) 1776-1822 NCLC **2; SSC 13**
See also CDWLB 2; DLB 90; EW 5; RGSF
2; RGWL 2, 3; SATA 27; SUFW 1; WCH

Hofmann, Gert 1931- CLC **54**
See also CA 128; EWL 3

Hofmannsthal, Hugo von 1874-1929 DC **4; TCLC 11**
See also CA 106; 153; CDWLB 2; DAM
DRAM; DFS 17; DLB 81, 118; EW 9;
EWL 3; RGWL 2, 3

Hogan, Linda 1947- CLC **73; NNAL; PC 35**
See also AMWS 4; ANW; BYA 12; CA 120;
CANR 45, 73, 129; CWP; DAM MULT;
DLB 175; SATA 132; TCWW 2

Hogarth, Charles
See Creasey, John

Hogarth, Emmett
See Polonsky, Abraham (Lincoln)

Hogg, James 1770-1835 NCLC **4, 109**
See also DLB 93, 116, 159; HGG; RGEL 2;
SUFW 1

Holbach, Paul Henri Thiry Baron 1723-1789 LC **14**

Holberg, Ludvig 1684-1754 LC **6**
See also RGWL 2, 3

Holcroft, Thomas 1745-1809 NCLC **85**
See also DLB 39, 89, 158; RGEL 2

Holden, Ursula 1921- CLC **18**
See also CA 101; CAAS 8; CANR 22

Holderlin, (Johann Christian) Friedrich 1770-1843 NCLC **16; PC 4**
See also CDWLB 2; DLB 90; EW 5; RGWL
2, 3

Holdstock, Robert
See Holdstock, Robert P.

Holdstock, Robert P. 1948- CLC **39**
See also CA 131; CANR 81; DLB 261;
FANT; HGG; SFW 4; SUFW 2

Holinshed, Raphael fl. 1580- LC **69**
See also DLB 167; RGEL 2

Holland, Isabelle (Christian) 1920-2002 CLC **21**
See also AAYA 11; CA 21-24R; 205; CAAE
181; CANR 10, 25, 47; CLR 57; CWRI
5; JRDA; LAIT 4; MAICYA 1, 2; SATA
8, 70; SATA-Essay 103; SATA-Obit 132;
WYA

Holland, Marcus
See Caldwell, (Janet Miriam) Taylor
(Holland)

Hollander, John 1929- CLC **2, 5, 8, 14**
See also CA 1-4R; CANR 1, 52; CP 7; DLB
5; SATA 13

Hollander, Paul
See Silverberg, Robert

Holleran, Andrew 1943(?)- CLC **38**
See Garber, Eric
See also CA 144; GLL 1

Holley, Marietta 1836(?)-1926 TCLC **99**
See also CA 118; DLB 11

Hollinghurst, Alan 1954- CLC **55, 91**
See also CA 114; CN 7; DLB 207; GLL 1

Hollis, Jim
See Summers, Hollis (Spurgeon, Jr.)

Holly, Buddy 1936-1959 TCLC **65**
See also CA 213

Holmes, Gordon
See Shiel, M(atthew) P(hipps)

Holmes, John
See Souster, (Holmes) Raymond

Holmes, John Clellon 1926-1988 CLC **56**
See also BG 2; CA 9-12R; 125; CANR 4;
DLB 16, 237

Holmes, Oliver Wendell, Jr. 1841-1935 TCLC **77**
See also CA 114; 186

Holmes, Oliver Wendell 1809-1894 NCLC **14, 81**
See also AMWS 1; CDALB 1640-1865;
DLB 1, 189, 235; EXPP; RGAL 4; SATA
34

Holmes, Raymond
See Souster, (Holmes) Raymond

Holt, Victoria
See Hibbert, Eleanor Alice Burford
See also BPFB 2

Holub, Miroslav 1923-1998 CLC **4**
See also CA 21-24R; 169; CANR 10; CD-
WLB 4; CWW 2; DLB 232; EWL 3;
RGWL 3

Holz, Detlev
See Benjamin, Walter

Homer c. 8th cent. B.C.- CMLC **1, 16, 61; PC 23; WLCS**
See also AW 1; CDWLB 1; DA; DA3;
DAB; DAC; DAM MST, POET; DLB
176; EFS 1; LAIT 1; LMFS 1; RGWL 2,
3; TWA; WP

Hongo, Garrett Kaoru 1951- PC **23**
See also CA 133; CAAS 22; CP 7; DLB
120; EWL 3; EXPP; RGAL 4

Honig, Edwin 1919- CLC **33**
See also CA 5-8R; CAAS 8; CANR 4, 45;
CP 7; DLB 5

Hood, Hugh (John Blagdon) 1928- CLC **15, 28; SSC 42**
See also CA 49-52; CAAS 17; CANR 1,
33, 87; CN 7; DLB 53; RGSF 2

Hood, Thomas 1799-1845 NCLC **16**
See also BRW 4; DLB 96; RGEL 2

Hooker, (Peter) Jeremy 1941- CLC **43**
See also CA 77-80; CANR 22; CP 7; DLB
40

Hooker, Richard 1554-1600 LC **95**
See also BRW 1; DLB 132; RGEL 2

hooks, bell
See Watkins, Gloria Jean

Hope, A(lec) D(erwent) 1907-2000 CLC **3, 51; PC 56**
See also BRWS 7; CA 21-24R; 188; CANR
33, 74; DLB 289; EWL 3; MTCW 1, 2;
PFS 8; RGEL 2

Hope, Anthony 1863-1933 **TCLC 83**
See also CA 157; DLB 153, 156; RGEL 2;
RHW

Hope, Brian
See Creasey, John

Hope, Christopher (David Tully) 1944- **CLC 52**
See also AFW; CA 106; CANR 47, 101;
CN 7; DLB 225; SATA 62

Hopkins, Gerard Manley 1844-1889 **NCLC 17; PC 15; WLC**
See also BRW 5; BRWR 2; CDBLB 1890-
1914; DA; DA3; DAB; DAC; DAM MST,
POET; DLB 35, 57; EXPP; PAB; RGEL
2; TEA; WP

Hopkins, John (Richard) 1931-1998 **CLC 4**
See also CA 85-88; 169; CBD; CD 5

Hopkins, Pauline Elizabeth 1859-1930 **BLC 2; TCLC 28**
See also AFAW 2; BW 2, 3; CA 141; CANR
82; DAM MULT; DLB 50

Hopkinson, Francis 1737-1791 **LC 25**
See also DLB 31; RGAL 4

Hopley-Woolrich, Cornell George 1903-1968
See Woolrich, Cornell
See also CA 13-14; CANR 58; CAP 1;
CMW 4; DLB 226; MTCW 2

Horace 65B.C.-8B.C. **CMLC 39; PC 46**
See also AW 2; CDWLB 1; DLB 211;
RGWL 2, 3

Horatio
See Proust, (Valentin-Louis-George-Eugene)
Marcel

Horgan, Paul (George Vincent O'Shaughnessy) 1903-1995 **CLC 9, 53**
See also BPFB 2; CA 13-16R; 147; CANR
9, 35; DAM NOV; DLB 102, 212; DLBY
1985; INT CANR-9; MTCW 1, 2; SATA
13; SATA-Obit 84; TCWW 2

Horkheimer, Max 1895-1973 **TCLC 132**
See also CA 216; 41-44R; DLB 296

Horn, Peter
See Kuttner, Henry

Horne, Frank (Smith) 1899-1974 **HR 2**
See also BW 1; CA 125; 53-56; DLB 51;
WP

Horne, Richard Henry Hengist 1802(?)-1884 **NCLC 127**
See also DLB 32; SATA 29

Hornem, Horace Esq.
See Byron, George Gordon (Noel)

Horney, Karen (Clementine Theodore Danielsen) 1885-1952 **TCLC 71**
See also CA 114; 165; DLB 246; FW

Hornung, E(rnest) W(illiam) 1866-1921 **TCLC 59**
See also CA 108; 160; CMW 4; DLB 70

Horovitz, Israel (Arthur) 1939- **CLC 56**
See also CA 33-36R; CAD; CANR 46, 59;
CD 5; DAM DRAM; DLB 7

Horton, George Moses 1797(?)-1883(?) **NCLC 87**
See also DLB 50

Horvath, odon von 1901-1938
See von Horvath, Odon
See also EWL 3

Horvath, Oedoen von -1938
See von Horvath, Odon

Horwitz, Julius 1920-1986 **CLC 14**
See also CA 9-12R; 119; CANR 12

Hospital, Janette Turner 1942- **CLC 42, 145**
See also CA 108; CANR 48; CN 7; DLBY
2002; RGSF 2

Hostos, E. M. de
See Hostos (y Bonilla), Eugenio Maria de

Hostos, Eugenio M. de
See Hostos (y Bonilla), Eugenio Maria de

Hostos, Eugenio Maria
See Hostos (y Bonilla), Eugenio Maria de

Hostos (y Bonilla), Eugenio Maria de 1839-1903 **TCLC 24**
See also CA 123; 131; HW 1

Houdini
See Lovecraft, H(oward) P(hillips)

Houellebecq, Michel 1958- **CLC 179**
See also CA 185

Hougan, Carolyn 1943- **CLC 34**
See also CA 139

Household, Geoffrey (Edward West) 1900-1988 **CLC 11**
See also CA 77-80; 126; CANR 58; CMW
4; DLB 87; SATA 14; SATA-Obit 59

Housman, A(lfred) E(dward) 1859-1936 **PC 2, 43; TCLC 1, 10; WLCS**
See also BRW 6; CA 104; 125; DA; DA3;
DAB; DAC; DAM MST, POET; DLB 19,
284; EWL 3; EXPP; MTCW 1, 2; PAB;
PFS 4, 7; RGEL 2; TEA; WP

Housman, Laurence 1865-1959 **TCLC 7**
See also CA 106; 155; DLB 10; FANT;
RGEL 2; SATA 25

Houston, Jeanne (Toyo) Wakatsuki 1934- **AAL**
See also AAYA 49; CA 103; CAAS 16;
CANR 29, 123; LAIT 4; SATA 78

Howard, Elizabeth Jane 1923- **CLC 7, 29**
See also CA 5-8R; CANR 8, 62; CN 7

Howard, Maureen 1930- **CLC 5, 14, 46, 151**
See also CA 53-56; CANR 31, 75; CN 7;
DLBY 1983; INT CANR-31; MTCW 1, 2

Howard, Richard 1929- **CLC 7, 10, 47**
See also AITN 1; CA 85-88; CANR 25, 80;
CP 7; DLB 5; INT CANR-25

Howard, Robert E(rvin) 1906-1936 **TCLC 8**
See also BPFB 2; BYA 5; CA 105; 157;
FANT; SUFW 1

Howard, Warren F.
See Pohl, Frederik

Howe, Fanny (Quincy) 1940- **CLC 47**
See also CA 117, 187; CAAE 187; CAAS
27; CANR 70, 116; CP 7; CWP; SATA-
Brief 52

Howe, Irving 1920-1993 **CLC 85**
See also AMWS 6; CA 9-12R; 141; CANR
21, 50; DLB 67; EWL 3; MTCW 1, 2

Howe, Julia Ward 1819-1910 **TCLC 21**
See also CA 117; 191; DLB 1, 189, 235;
FW

Howe, Susan 1937- **CLC 72, 152; PC 54**
See also AMWS 4; CA 160; CP 7; CWP;
DLB 120; FW; RGAL 4

Howe, Tina 1937- **CLC 48**
See also CA 109; CAD; CANR 125; CD 5;
CWD

Howell, James 1594(?)-1666 **LC 13**
See also DLB 151

Howells, W. D.
See Howells, William Dean

Howells, William D.
See Howells, William Dean

Howells, William Dean 1837-1920 **SSC 36; TCLC 7, 17, 41**
See also AMW; CA 104; 134; CDALB
1865-1917; DLB 12, 64, 74, 79, 189;
LMFS 1; MTCW 2; RGAL 4; TUS

Howes, Barbara 1914-1996 **CLC 15**
See also CA 9-12R; 151; CAAS 3; CANR
53; CP 7; SATA 5

Hrabal, Bohumil 1914-1997 **CLC 13, 67**
See also CA 106; 156; CAAS 12; CANR
57; CWW 2; DLB 232; EWL 3; RGSF 2

Hrotsvit of Gandersheim c. 935-c. 1000 **CMLC 29**
See also DLB 148

Hsi, Chu 1130-1200 **CMLC 42**

Hsun, Lu
See Lu Hsun

Hubbard, L(afayette) Ron(ald) 1911-1986 **CLC 43**
See also CA 77-80; 118; CANR 52; CPW;
DA3; DAM POP; FANT; MTCW 2; SFW
4

Huch, Ricarda (Octavia) 1864-1947 **TCLC 13**
See also CA 111; 189; DLB 66; EWL 3

Huddle, David 1942- **CLC 49**
See also CA 57-60; CAAS 20; CANR 89;
DLB 130

Hudson, Jeffrey
See Crichton, (John) Michael

Hudson, W(illiam) H(enry) 1841-1922 **TCLC 29**
See also CA 115; 190; DLB 98, 153, 174;
RGEL 2; SATA 35

Hueffer, Ford Madox
See Ford, Ford Madox

Hughart, Barry 1934- **CLC 39**
See also CA 137; FANT; SFW 4; SUFW 2

Hughes, Colin
See Creasey, John

Hughes, David (John) 1930- **CLC 48**
See also CA 116; 129; CN 7; DLB 14

Hughes, Edward James
See Hughes, Ted
See also DA3; DAM MST, POET

Hughes, (James Mercer) Langston 1902-1967 **BLC 2; CLC 1, 5, 10, 15, 35, 44, 108; DC 3; HR 2; PC 1, 53; SSC 6; WLC**
See also AAYA 12; AFAW 1, 2; AMWR 1;
AMWS 1; BW 1, 3; CA 1-4R; 25-28R;
CANR 1, 34, 82; CDALB 1929-1941;
CLR 17; DA; DA3; DAB; DAC; DAM
DRAM, MST, MULT, POET; DFS 6, 18;
DLB 4, 7, 48, 51, 86, 228; EWL 3; EXPP;
EXPS; JRDA; LAIT 3; LMFS 2; MAI-
CYA 1, 2; MTCW 1, 2; PAB; PFS 1, 3, 6,
10, 15; RGAL 4; RGSF 2; SATA 4, 33;
SSFS 4, 7; TUS; WCH; WP; YAW

Hughes, Richard (Arthur Warren) 1900-1976 **CLC 1, 11**
See also CA 5-8R; 65-68; CANR 4; DAM
NOV; DLB 15, 161; EWL 3; MTCW 1;
RGEL 2; SATA 8; SATA-Obit 25

Hughes, Ted 1930-1998 **CLC 2, 4, 9, 14, 37, 119; PC 7**
See Hughes, Edward James
See also BRWC 2; BRWR 2; BRWS 1; CA
1-4R; 171; CANR 1, 33, 66, 108; CLR 3;
CP 7; DAB; DAC; DLB 40, 161; EWL 3;
EXPP; MAICYA 1, 2; MTCW 1, 2; PAB;
PFS 4, 19; RGEL 2; SATA 49; SATA-
Brief 27; SATA-Obit 107; TEA; YAW

Hugo, Richard
See Huch, Ricarda (Octavia)

Hugo, Richard F(ranklin) 1923-1982 **CLC 6, 18, 32**
See also AMWS 6; CA 49-52; 108; CANR
3; DAM POET; DLB 5, 206; EWL 3; PFS
17; RGAL 4

Hugo, Victor (Marie) 1802-1885 **NCLC 3, 10, 21; PC 17; WLC**
See also AAYA 28; DA; DA3; DAB; DAC;
DAM DRAM, MST, POET; DLB
119, 192, 217; EFS 2; EW 6; EXPN; GFL
1789 to the Present; LAIT 1, 2; NFS 5;
RGWL 2, 3; SATA 47; TWA

Huidobro, Vicente
See Huidobro Fernandez, Vicente Garcia
See also DLB 283; EWL 3; LAW

Huidobro Fernandez, Vicente Garcia 1893-1948 **TCLC 31**
See Huidobro, Vicente
See also CA 131; HW 1

Hulme, Keri 1947- **CLC 39, 130**
See also CA 125; CANR 69; CN 7; CP 7;
CWP; EWL 3; FW; INT CA-125

Hulme, T(homas) E(rnest) 1883-1917 TCLC 21
See also BRWS 6; CA 117; 203; DLB 19

Humboldt, Wilhelm von 1767-1835 NCLC 134
See also DLB 90

Hume, David 1711-1776 LC 7, 56
See also BRWS 3; DLB 104, 252; LMFS 1; TEA

Humphrey, William 1924-1997 CLC 45
See also AMWS 9; CA 77-80; 160; CANR 68; CN 7; CSW; DLB 6, 212, 234, 278; TCWW 2

Humphreys, Emyr Owen 1919- CLC 47
See also CA 5-8R; CANR 3, 24; CN 7; DLB 15

Humphreys, Josephine 1945- CLC 34, 57
See also CA 121; 127; CANR 97; CSW; DLB 292; INT CA-127

Huneker, James Gibbons 1860-1921 TCLC 65
See also CA 193; DLB 71; RGAL 4

Hungerford, Hesba Fay
See Brinsmead, H(esba) F(ay)

Hungerford, Pixie
See Brinsmead, H(esba) F(ay)

Hunt, E(verette) Howard, (Jr.) 1918- CLC 3
See also AITN 1; CA 45-48; CANR 2, 47, 103; CMW 4

Hunt, Francesca
See Holland, Isabelle (Christian)

Hunt, Howard
See Hunt, E(verette) Howard, (Jr.)

Hunt, Kyle
See Creasey, John

Hunt, (James Henry) Leigh 1784-1859 NCLC 1, 70
See also DAM POET; DLB 96, 110, 144; RGEL 2; TEA

Hunt, Marsha 1946- CLC 70
See also BW 2, 3; CA 143; CANR 79

Hunt, Violet 1866(?)-1942 TCLC 53
See also CA 184; DLB 162, 197

Hunter, E. Waldo
See Sturgeon, Theodore (Hamilton)

Hunter, Evan 1926- CLC 11, 31
See McBain, Ed
See also AAYA 39; BPFB 2; CA 5-8R; CANR 5, 38, 62, 97; CMW 4; CN 7; CPW; DAM POP; DLBY 1982; INT CANR-5; MSW; MTCW 1; SATA 25; SFW 4

Hunter, Kristin 1931-
See Lattany, Kristin (Elaine Eggleston) Hunter

Hunter, Mary
See Austin, Mary (Hunter)

Hunter, Mollie 1922- CLC 21
See McIlwraith, Maureen Mollie Hunter
See also AAYA 13; BYA 6; CANR 37, 78; CLR 25; DLB 161; JRDA; MAICYA 1, 2; SAAS 7; SATA 54, 106, 139; SATA-Essay 139; WYA; YAW

Hunter, Robert (?)-1734 LC 7

Hurston, Zora Neale 1891-1960 BLC 2; CLC 7, 30, 61; DC 12; HR 2; SSC 4; TCLC 121, 131; WLCS
See also AAYA 15; AFAW 1, 2; AMWS 6; BW 1, 3; BYA 12; CA 85-88; CANR 61; CDALBS; DA; DA3; DAC; DAM MST, MULT, NOV; DFS 6; DLB 51, 86; EWL 3; EXPN; EXPS; FW; LAIT 3; LATS 1; LMFS 2; MAWW; MTCW 1, 2; NFS 3; RGAL 4; RGSF 2; SSFS 1, 6, 11, 19; TUS; YAW

Husserl, E. G.
See Husserl, Edmund (Gustav Albrecht)

Husserl, Edmund (Gustav Albrecht) 1859-1938 TCLC 100
See also CA 116; 133; DLB 296

Huston, John (Marcellus) 1906-1987 CLC 20
See also CA 73-76; 123; CANR 34; DLB 26

Hustvedt, Siri 1955- CLC 76
See also CA 137

Hutten, Ulrich von 1488-1523 LC 16
See also DLB 179

Huxley, Aldous (Leonard) 1894-1963 CLC 1, 3, 4, 5, 8, 11, 18, 35, 79; SSC 39; WLC
See also AAYA 11; BPFB 2; BRW 7; CA 85-88; CANR 44, 99; CDBLB 1914-1945; DA; DA3; DAB; DAC; DAM MST, NOV; DLB 36, 100, 162, 195, 255; EWL 3; EXPN; LAIT 5; LMFS 2; MTCW 1, 2; NFS 6; RGEL 2; SATA 63; SCFW 2; SFW 4; TEA; YAW

Huxley, T(homas) H(enry) 1825-1895 NCLC 67
See also DLB 57; TEA

Huysmans, Joris-Karl 1848-1907 TCLC 7, 69
See also CA 104; 165; DLB 123; EW 7; GFL 1789 to the Present; LMFS 2; RGWL 2, 3

Hwang, David Henry 1957- CLC 55; DC 4
See also CA 127; 132; CAD; CANR 76, 124; CD 5; DA3; DAM DRAM; DFS 11, 18; DLB 212, 228; INT CA-132; MTCW 2; RGAL 4

Hyde, Anthony 1946- CLC 42
See Chase, Nicholas
See also CA 136; CCA 1

Hyde, Margaret O(ldroyd) 1917- CLC 21
See also CA 1-4R; CANR 1, 36; CLR 23; JRDA; MAICYA 1, 2; SAAS 8; SATA 1, 42, 76, 139

Hynes, James 1956(?)- CLC 65
See also CA 164; CANR 105

Hypatia c. 370-415 CMLC 35

Ian, Janis 1951- CLC 21
See also CA 105; 187

Ibanez, Vicente Blasco
See Blasco Ibanez, Vicente

Ibarbourou, Juana de 1895-1979 HLCS 2
See also DLB 290; HW 1; LAW

Ibarguengoitia, Jorge 1928-1983 CLC 37; TCLC 148
See also CA 124; 113; EWL 3; HW 1

Ibn Battuta, Abu Abdalla 1304-1368(?) CMLC 57
See also WLIT 2

Ibn Hazm 994-1064 CMLC 64

Ibsen, Henrik (Johan) 1828-1906 DC 2; TCLC 2, 8, 16, 37, 52; WLC
See also AAYA 46; CA 104; 141; DA; DA3; DAB; DAC; DAM DRAM, MST; DFS 1, 6, 8, 10, 11, 15, 16; EW 7; LAIT 1; LATS 1; RGWL 2, 3

Ibuse, Masuji 1898-1993 CLC 22
See Ibuse Masuji
See also CA 127; 141; MJW; RGWL 3

Ibuse Masuji
See Ibuse, Masuji
See also DLB 180; EWL 3

Ichikawa, Kon 1915- CLC 20
See also CA 121

Ichiyo, Higuchi 1872-1896 NCLC 49
See also MJW

Idle, Eric 1943- CLC 21
See Monty Python
See also CA 116; CANR 35, 91

Ignatow, David 1914-1997 CLC 4, 7, 14, 40; PC 34
See also CA 9-12R; 162; CAAS 3; CANR 31, 57, 96; CP 7; DLB 5; EWL 3

Ignotus
See Strachey, (Giles) Lytton

Ihimaera, Witi (Tame) 1944- CLC 46
See also CA 77-80; CN 7; RGSF 2; SATA 148

Ilf, Ilya TCLC 21
See Fainzilberg, Ilya Arnoldovich
See also EWL 3

Illyes, Gyula 1902-1983 PC 16
See also CA 114; 109; CDWLB 4; DLB 215; EWL 3; RGWL 2, 3

Imalayen, Fatima-Zohra
See Djebar, Assia

Immermann, Karl (Lebrecht) 1796-1840 NCLC 4, 49
See also DLB 133

Ince, Thomas H. 1882-1924 TCLC 89
See also IDFW 3, 4

Inchbald, Elizabeth 1753-1821 NCLC 62
See also DLB 39, 89; RGEL 2

Inclan, Ramon (Maria) del Valle
See Valle-Inclan, Ramon (Maria) del

Infante, G(uillermo) Cabrera
See Cabrera Infante, G(uillermo)

Ingalls, Rachel (Holmes) 1940- CLC 42
See also CA 123; 127

Ingamells, Reginald Charles
See Ingamells, Rex

Ingamells, Rex 1913-1955 TCLC 35
See also CA 167; DLB 260

Inge, William (Motter) 1913-1973 CLC 1, 8, 19
See also CA 9-12R; CDALB 1941-1968; DA3; DAM DRAM; DFS 1, 3, 5, 8; DLB 7, 249; EWL 3; MTCW 1, 2; RGAL 4; TUS

Ingelow, Jean 1820-1897 NCLC 39, 107
See also DLB 35, 163; FANT; SATA 33

Ingram, Willis J.
See Harris, Mark

Innaurato, Albert (F.) 1948(?)- CLC 21, 60
See also CA 115; 122; CAD; CANR 78; CD 5; INT CA-122

Innes, Michael
See Stewart, J(ohn) I(nnes) M(ackintosh)
See also DLB 276; MSW

Innis, Harold Adams 1894-1952 TCLC 77
See also CA 181; DLB 88

Insluis, Alanus de
See Alain de Lille

Iola
See Wells-Barnett, Ida B(ell)

Ionesco, Eugene 1912-1994 CLC 1, 4, 6, 9, 11, 15, 41, 86; DC 12; WLC
See also CA 9-12R; 144; CANR 55; CWW 2; DA; DA3; DAB; DAC; DAM DRAM, MST; DFS 4, 9; EW 13; EWL 3; GFL 1789 to the Present; LMFS 2; MTCW 1, 2; RGWL 2, 3; SATA 7; SATA-Obit 79; TWA

Iqbal, Muhammad 1877-1938 TCLC 28
See also CA 215; EWL 3

Ireland, Patrick
See O'Doherty, Brian

Irenaeus St. 130- CMLC 42

Irigaray, Luce 1930- CLC 164
See also CA 154; CANR 121; FW

Iron, Ralph
See Schreiner, Olive (Emilie Albertina)

Irving, John (Winslow) 1942- CLC 13, 23, 38, 112, 175
See also AAYA 8; AMWS 6; BEST 89:3; BPFB 2; CA 25-28R; CANR 28, 73, 112; CN 7; CPW; DA3; DAM NOV, POP; DLB 6, 278; DLBY 1982; EWL 3; MTCW 1, 2; NFS 12, 14; RGAL 4; TUS

Irving, Washington 1783-1859 **NCLC 2, 19, 95; SSC 2, 37; WLC**
See also AMW; CDALB 1640-1865; CLR 97; DA; DA3; DAB; DAC; DAM MST; DLB 3, 11, 30, 59, 73, 74, 183, 186, 250, 254; EXPS; LAIT 1; RGAL 4; RGSF 2; SSFS 1, 8, 16; SUFW 1; TUS; WCH; YABC 2

Irwin, P. K.
See Page, P(atricia) K(athleen)

Isaacs, Jorge Ricardo 1837-1895 **NCLC 70**
See also LAW

Isaacs, Susan 1943- **CLC 32**
See also BEST 89:1; BPFB 2; CA 89-92; CANR 20, 41, 65, 112; CPW; DA3; DAM POP; INT CANR-20; MTCW 1, 2

Isherwood, Christopher (William Bradshaw) 1904-1986 **CLC 1, 9, 11, 14, 44; SSC 56**
See also BRW 7; CA 13-16R; 117; CANR 35, 97; DA3; DAM DRAM, NOV; DLB 15, 195; DLBY 1986; EWL 3; IDTP; MTCW 1, 2; RGAL 4; RGEL 2; TUS; WLIT 4

Ishiguro, Kazuo 1954- **CLC 27, 56, 59, 110**
See also BEST 90:2; BPFB 2; BRWS 4; CA 120; CANR 49, 95; CN 7; DA3; DAM NOV; DLB 194; EWL 3; MTCW 1, 2; NFS 13; WLIT 4; WWE 1

Ishikawa, Hakuhin
See Ishikawa, Takuboku

Ishikawa, Takuboku 1886(?)-1912 **PC 10; TCLC 15**
See Ishikawa Takuboku
See also CA 113; 153; DAM POET

Iskander, Fazil (Abdulovich) 1929- **CLC 47**
See also CA 102; EWL 3

Isler, Alan (David) 1934- **CLC 91**
See also CA 156; CANR 105

Ivan IV 1530-1584 **LC 17**

Ivanov, Vyacheslav Ivanovich 1866-1949 **TCLC 33**
See also CA 122; EWL 3

Ivask, Ivar Vidrik 1927-1992 **CLC 14**
See also CA 37-40R; 139; CANR 24

Ives, Morgan
See Bradley, Marion Zimmer
See also GLL 1

Izumi Shikibu c. 973-c. 1034 **CMLC 33**

J. R. S.
See Gogarty, Oliver St. John

Jabran, Kahlil
See Gibran, Kahlil

Jabran, Khalil
See Gibran, Kahlil

Jackson, Daniel
See Wingrove, David (John)

Jackson, Helen Hunt 1830-1885 **NCLC 90**
See also DLB 42, 47, 186, 189; RGAL 4

Jackson, Jesse 1908-1983 **CLC 12**
See also BW 1; CA 25-28R; 109; CANR 27; CLR 28; CWRI 5; MAICYA 1, 2; SATA 2, 29; SATA-Obit 48

Jackson, Laura (Riding) 1901-1991 **PC 44**
See Riding, Laura
See also CA 65-68; 135; CANR 28, 89; DLB 48

Jackson, Sam
See Trumbo, Dalton

Jackson, Sara
See Wingrove, David (John)

Jackson, Shirley 1919-1965 **CLC 11, 60, 87; SSC 9, 39; WLC**
See also AAYA 9; AMWS 9; BPFB 2; CA 1-4R; 25-28R; CANR 4, 52; CDALB 1941-1968; DA; DA3; DAC; DAM MST; DLB 6, 234; EXPS; HGG; LAIT 4; MTCW 2; RGAL 4; RGSF 2; SATA 2; SSFS 1; SUFW 1, 2

Jacob, (Cyprien-)Max 1876-1944 **TCLC 6**
See also CA 104; 193; DLB 258; EWL 3; GFL 1789 to the Present; GLL 2; RGWL 2, 3

Jacobs, Harriet A(nn) 1813(?)-1897 **NCLC 67**
See also AFAW 1, 2; DLB 239; FW; LAIT 2; RGAL 4

Jacobs, Jim 1942- **CLC 12**
See also CA 97-100; INT CA-97-100

Jacobs, W(illiam) W(ymark) 1863-1943 **TCLC 22**
See also CA 121; 167; DLB 135; EXPS; HGG; RGEL 2; RGSF 2; SSFS 2; SUFW 1

Jacobsen, Jens Peter 1847-1885 **NCLC 34**

Jacobsen, Josephine (Winder) 1908-2003 **CLC 48, 102**
See also CA 33-36R; 218; CAAS 18; CANR 23, 48; CCA 1; CP 7; DLB 244

Jacobson, Dan 1929- **CLC 4, 14**
See also AFW; CA 1-4R; CANR 2, 25, 66; CN 7; DLB 14, 207, 225; EWL 3; MTCW 1; RGSF 2

Jacqueline
See Carpentier (y Valmont), Alejo

Jacques de Vitry c. 1160-1240 **CMLC 63**
See also DLB 208

Jagger, Mick 1944- **CLC 17**

Jahiz, al- c. 780-c. 869 **CMLC 25**

Jakes, John (William) 1932- **CLC 29**
See also AAYA 32; BEST 89:4; BPFB 2; CA 57-60, 214; CAAE 214; CANR 10, 43, 66, 111; CPW; CSW; DA3; DAM NOV, POP; DLB 278; DLBY 1983; FANT; INT CANR-10; MTCW 1, 2; RHW; SATA 62; SFW 4; TCWW 2

James I 1394-1437 **LC 20**
See also RGEL 2

James, Andrew
See Kirkup, James

James, C(yril) L(ionel) R(obert) 1901-1989 **BLCS; CLC 33**
See also BW 2; CA 117; 125; 128; CANR 62; DLB 125; MTCW 1

James, Daniel (Lewis) 1911-1988
See Santiago, Danny
See also CA 174; 125

James, Dynely
See Mayne, William (James Carter)

James, Henry Sr. 1811-1882 **NCLC 53**

James, Henry 1843-1916 **SSC 8, 32, 47; TCLC 2, 11, 24, 40, 47, 64; WLC**
See also AMW; AMWC 1; AMWR 1; BPFB 2; BRW 6; CA 104; 132; CDALB 1865-1917; DA; DA3; DAB; DAC; DAM MST, NOV; DLB 12, 71, 74, 189; DLBD 13; EWL 3; EXPS; HGG; LAIT 2; MTCW 1, 2; NFS 12, 16; RGAL 4; RGEL 2; RGSF 2; SSFS 9; SUFW 1; TUS

James, M. R.
See James, Montague (Rhodes)
See also DLB 156, 201

James, Montague (Rhodes) 1862-1936 **SSC 16; TCLC 6**
See James, M. R.
See also CA 104; 203; HGG; RGEL 2; RGSF 2; SUFW 1

James, P. D. CLC 18, 46, 122
See White, Phyllis Dorothy James
See also BEST 90:2; BPFB 2; BRWS 4; CDBLB 1960 to Present; DLB 87, 276; DLBD 17; MSW

James, Philip
See Moorcock, Michael (John)

James, Samuel
See Stephens, James

James, Seumas
See Stephens, James

James, Stephen
See Stephens, James

James, William 1842-1910 **TCLC 15, 32**
See also AMW; CA 109; 193; DLB 270, 284; NCFS 5; RGAL 4

Jameson, Anna 1794-1860 **NCLC 43**
See also DLB 99, 166

Jameson, Fredric (R.) 1934- **CLC 142**
See also CA 196; DLB 67; LMFS 2

Jami, Nur al-Din 'Abd al-Rahman 1414-1492 **LC 9**

Jammes, Francis 1868-1938 **TCLC 75**
See also CA 198; EWL 3; GFL 1789 to the Present

Jandl, Ernst 1925-2000 **CLC 34**
See also CA 200; EWL 3

Janowitz, Tama 1957- **CLC 43, 145**
See also CA 106; CANR 52, 89, 129; CN 7; CPW; DAM POP; DLB 292

Japrisot, Sebastien 1931- **CLC 90**
See Rossi, Jean-Baptiste
See also CMW 4; NFS 18

Jarrell, Randall 1914-1965 **CLC 1, 2, 6, 9, 13, 49; PC 41**
See also AMW; BYA 5; CA 5-8R; 25-28R; CABS 2; CANR 6, 34; CDALB 1941-1968; CLR 6; CWRI 5; DAM POET; DLB 48, 52; EWL 3; EXPP; MAICYA 1, 2; MTCW 1, 2; PAB; PFS 2; RGAL 4; SATA 7

Jarry, Alfred 1873-1907 **SSC 20; TCLC 2, 14, 147**
See also CA 104; 153; DA3; DAM DRAM; DFS 8; DLB 192, 258; EW 9; EWL 3; GFL 1789 to the Present; RGWL 2, 3; TWA

Jarvis, E. K.
See Ellison, Harlan (Jay)

Jawien, Andrzej
See John Paul II, Pope

Jaynes, Roderick
See Coen, Ethan

Jeake, Samuel, Jr.
See Aiken, Conrad (Potter)

Jean Paul 1763-1825 **NCLC 7**

Jefferies, (John) Richard 1848-1887 **NCLC 47**
See also DLB 98, 141; RGEL 2; SATA 16; SFW 4

Jeffers, (John) Robinson 1887-1962 **CLC 2, 3, 11, 15, 54; PC 17; WLC**
See also AMWS 2; CA 85-88; CANR 35; CDALB 1917-1929; DA; DAC; DAM MST, POET; DLB 45, 212; EWL 3; MTCW 1, 2; PAB; PFS 3, 4; RGAL 4

Jefferson, Janet
See Mencken, H(enry) L(ouis)

Jefferson, Thomas 1743-1826 **NCLC 11, 103**
See also ANW; CDALB 1640-1865; DA3; DLB 31, 183; LAIT 1; RGAL 4

Jeffrey, Francis 1773-1850 **NCLC 33**
See Francis, Lord Jeffrey

Jelakowitch, Ivan
See Heijermans, Herman

Jelinek, Elfriede 1946- **CLC 169**
See also CA 154; DLB 85; FW

Jellicoe, (Patricia) Ann 1927- **CLC 27**
See also CA 85-88; CBD; CD 5; CWD; CWRI 5; DLB 13, 233; FW

Jelloun, Tahar ben 1944- **CLC 180**
See Ben Jelloun, Tahar
See also CA 162; CANR 100

Jemyma
See Holley, Marietta

Jen, Gish AAL; CLC 70
See Jen, Lillian
See also AMWC 2

Jen, Lillian 1956(?)-
See Jen, Gish
See also CA 135; CANR 89

Jenkins, (John) Robin 1912- **CLC 52**
See also CA 1-4R; CANR 1; CN 7; DLB 14, 271

Jennings, Elizabeth (Joan) 1926-2001 **CLC 5, 14, 131**
See also BRWS 5; CA 61-64; 200; CAAS 5; CANR 8, 39, 66, 127; CP 7; CWP; DLB 27; EWL 3; MTCW 1; SATA 66

Jennings, Waylon 1937- **CLC 21**

Jensen, Johannes V(ilhelm) 1873-1950 **TCLC 41**
See also CA 170; DLB 214; EWL 3; RGWL 3

Jensen, Laura (Linnea) 1948- **CLC 37**
See also CA 103

Jerome, Saint 345-420 **CMLC 30**
See also RGWL 3

Jerome, Jerome K(lapka) 1859-1927 **TCLC 23**
See also CA 119; 177; DLB 10, 34, 135; RGEL 2

Jerrold, Douglas William 1803-1857 **NCLC 2**
See also DLB 158, 159; RGEL 2

Jewett, (Theodora) Sarah Orne 1849-1909 **SSC 6, 44; TCLC 1, 22**
See also AMW; AMWC 2; AMWR 2; CA 108; 127; CANR 71; DLB 12, 74, 221; EXPS; FW; MAWW; NFS 15; RGAL 4; RGSF 2; SATA 15; SSFS 4

Jewsbury, Geraldine (Endsor) 1812-1880 **NCLC 22**
See also DLB 21

Jhabvala, Ruth Prawer 1927- **CLC 4, 8, 29, 94, 138**
See also BRWS 5; CA 1-4R; CANR 2, 29, 51, 74, 91, 128; CN 7; DAB; DAM NOV; DLB 139, 194; EWL 3; IDFW 3, 4; INT CANR-29; MTCW 1, 2; RGSF 2; RGWL 2; RHW; TEA

Jibran, Kahlil
See Gibran, Kahlil

Jibran, Khalil
See Gibran, Kahlil

Jiles, Paulette 1943- **CLC 13, 58**
See also CA 101; CANR 70, 124; CWP

Jimenez (Mantecon), Juan Ramon 1881-1958 **HLC 1; PC 7; TCLC 4**
See also CA 104; 131; CANR 74; DAM MULT, POET; DLB 134; EW 9; EWL 3; HW 1; MTCW 1, 2; RGWL 2, 3

Jimenez, Ramon
See Jimenez (Mantecon), Juan Ramon

Jimenez Mantecon, Juan
See Jimenez (Mantecon), Juan Ramon

Jin, Ha CLC 109
See Jin, Xuefei
See also CA 152; DLB 244, 292; SSFS 17

Jin, Xuefei 1956-
See Jin, Ha
See also CANR 91; SSFS 17

Joel, Billy CLC 26
See Joel, William Martin

Joel, William Martin 1949-
See Joel, Billy
See also CA 108

Johann Sigurjonsson 1880-1919 **TCLC 27**
See also CA 170; DLB 293; EWL 3

John, Saint 10(?)-100 **CMLC 27, 63**

John of Salisbury c. 1115-1180 **CMLC 63**

John of the Cross, St. 1542-1591 **LC 18**
See also RGWL 2, 3

John Paul II, Pope 1920- **CLC 128**
See also CA 106; 133

Johnson, B(ryan) S(tanley William) 1933-1973 **CLC 6, 9**
See also CA 9-12R; 53-56; CANR 9; DLB 14, 40; EWL 3; RGEL 2

Johnson, Benjamin F., of Boone
See Riley, James Whitcomb

Johnson, Charles (Richard) 1948- **BLC 2; CLC 7, 51, 65, 163**
See also AFAW 2; AMWS 6; BW 2, 3; CA 116; CAAS 18; CANR 42, 66, 82, 129; CN 7; DAM MULT; DLB 33, 278; MTCW 2; RGAL 4; SSFS 16

Johnson, Charles S(purgeon) 1893-1956 **HR 3**
See also BW 1, 3; CA 125; CANR 82; DLB 51, 91

Johnson, Denis 1949- **CLC 52, 160; SSC 56**
See also CA 117; 121; CANR 71, 99; CN 7; DLB 120

Johnson, Diane 1934- **CLC 5, 13, 48**
See also BPFB 2; CA 41-44R; CANR 17, 40, 62, 95; CN 7; DLBY 1980; INT CANR-17; MTCW 1

Johnson, E. Pauline 1861-1913 **NNAL**
See also CA 150; DAC; DAM MULT; DLB 92, 175

Johnson, Eyvind (Olof Verner) 1900-1976 **CLC 14**
See also CA 73-76; 69-72; CANR 34, 101; DLB 259; EW 12; EWL 3

Johnson, Fenton 1888-1958 **BLC 2**
See also BW 1; CA 118; 124; DAM MULT; DLB 45, 50

Johnson, Georgia Douglas (Camp) 1880-1966 **HR 3**
See also BW 1; CA 125; DLB 51, 249; WP

Johnson, Helene 1907-1995 **HR 3**
See also CA 181; DLB 51; WP

Johnson, J. R.
See James, C(yril) L(ionel) R(obert)

Johnson, James Weldon 1871-1938 **BLC 2; HR 3; PC 24; TCLC 3, 19**
See also AFAW 1, 2; BW 1, 3; CA 104; 125; CANR 82; CDALB 1917-1929; CLR 32; DA3; DAM MULT; DLB 51; EWL 3; EXPP; LMFS 2; MTCW 1, 2; PFS 1; RGAL 4; SATA 31; TUS

Johnson, Joyce 1935- **CLC 58**
See also BG 3; CA 125; 129; CANR 102

Johnson, Judith (Emlyn) 1936- **CLC 7, 15**
See Sherwin, Judith Johnson
See also CA 25-28R; 153; CANR 34

Johnson, Lionel (Pigot) 1867-1902 **TCLC 19**
See also CA 117; 209; DLB 19; RGEL 2

Johnson, Marguerite Annie
See Angelou, Maya

Johnson, Mel
See Malzberg, Barry N(athaniel)

Johnson, Pamela Hansford 1912-1981 **CLC 1, 7, 27**
See also CA 1-4R; 104; CANR 2, 28; DLB 15; MTCW 1, 2; RGEL 2

Johnson, Paul (Bede) 1928- **CLC 147**
See also BEST 89:4; CA 17-20R; CANR 34, 62, 100

Johnson, Robert CLC 70

Johnson, Robert 1911(?)-1938 **TCLC 69**
See also BW 3; CA 174

Johnson, Samuel 1709-1784 **LC 15, 52; WLC**
See also BRW 3; BRWR 1; CDBLB 1660-1789; DA; DAB; DAC; DAM MST; DLB 39, 95, 104, 142, 213; LMFS 1; RGEL 2; TEA

Johnson, Uwe 1934-1984 **CLC 5, 10, 15, 40**
See also CA 1-4R; 112; CANR 1, 39; CDWLB 2; DLB 75; EWL 3; MTCW 1; RGWL 2, 3

Johnston, Basil H. 1929- **NNAL**
See also CA 69-72; CANR 11, 28, 66; DAC; DAM MULT; DLB 60

Johnston, George (Benson) 1913- **CLC 51**
See also CA 1-4R; CANR 5, 20; CP 7; DLB 88

Johnston, Jennifer (Prudence) 1930- **CLC 7, 150**
See also CA 85-88; CANR 92; CN 7; DLB 14

Joinville, Jean de 1224(?)-1317 **CMLC 38**

Jolley, (Monica) Elizabeth 1923- **CLC 46; SSC 19**
See also CA 127; CAAS 13; CANR 59; CN 7; EWL 3; RGSF 2

Jones, Arthur Llewellyn 1863-1947
See Machen, Arthur
See also CA 104; 179; HGG

Jones, D(ouglas) G(ordon) 1929- **CLC 10**
See also CA 29-32R; CANR 13, 90; CP 7; DLB 53

Jones, David (Michael) 1895-1974 **CLC 2, 4, 7, 13, 42**
See also BRW 6; BRWS 7; CA 9-12R; 53-56; CANR 28; CDBLB 1945-1960; DLB 20, 100; EWL 3; MTCW 1; PAB; RGEL 2

Jones, David Robert 1947-
See Bowie, David
See also CA 103; CANR 104

Jones, Diana Wynne 1934- **CLC 26**
See also AAYA 12; BYA 6, 7, 9, 11, 13, 16; CA 49-52; CANR 4, 26, 56, 120; CLR 23; DLB 161; FANT; JRDA; MAICYA 1, 2; SAAS 7; SATA 9, 70, 108; SFW 4; SUFW 2; YAW

Jones, Edward P. 1950- **CLC 76**
See also BW 2, 3; CA 142; CANR 79; CSW

Jones, Gayl 1949- **BLC 2; CLC 6, 9, 131**
See also AFAW 1, 2; BW 2, 3; CA 77-80; CANR 27, 66, 122; CN 7; CSW; DA3; DAM MULT; DLB 33, 278; MTCW 1, 2; RGAL 4

Jones, James 1921-1977 **CLC 1, 3, 10, 39**
See also AITN 1, 2; AMWS 11; BPFB 2; CA 1-4R; 69-72; CANR 6; DLB 2, 143; DLBD 17; DLBY 1998; EWL 3; MTCW 1; RGAL 4

Jones, John J.
See Lovecraft, H(oward) P(hillips)

Jones, LeRoi CLC 1, 2, 3, 5, 10, 14
See Baraka, Amiri
See also MTCW 2

Jones, Louis B. 1953- **CLC 65**
See also CA 141; CANR 73

Jones, Madison (Percy, Jr.) 1925- **CLC 4**
See also CA 13-16R; CAAS 11; CANR 7, 54, 83; CN 7; CSW; DLB 152

Jones, Mervyn 1922- **CLC 10, 52**
See also CA 45-48; CAAS 5; CANR 1, 91; CN 7; MTCW 1

Jones, Mick 1956(?)- **CLC 30**

Jones, Nettie (Pearl) 1941- **CLC 34**
See also BW 2; CA 137; CAAS 20; CANR 88

Jones, Peter 1802-1856 **NNAL**

Jones, Preston 1936-1979 **CLC 10**
See also CA 73-76; 89-92; DLB 7

Jones, Robert F(rancis) 1934-2003 **CLC 7**
See also CA 49-52; CANR 2, 61, 118

Jones, Rod 1953- **CLC 50**
See also CA 128

Jones, Terence Graham Parry 1942- **CLC 21**
See Jones, Terry; Monty Python
See also CA 112; 116; CANR 35, 93; INT CA-116; SATA 127

Jones, Terry
See Jones, Terence Graham Parry
See also SATA 67; SATA-Brief 51

Jones, Thom (Douglas) 1945(?)- **CLC 81; SSC 56**
See also CA 157; CANR 88; DLB 244

Jong, Erica 1942- **CLC 4, 6, 8, 18, 83**
See also AITN 1; AMWS 5; BEST 90:2; BPFB 2; CA 73-76; CANR 26, 52, 75; CN 7; CP 7; CPW; DA3; DAM NOV, POP; DLB 2, 5, 28, 152; FW; INT CANR-26; MTCW 1, 2

Jonson, Ben(jamin) 1572(?)-1637 **DC 4; LC 6, 33; PC 17; WLC**
See also BRW 1; BRWC 1; BRWR 1; CD-BLB Before 1660; DA; DAB; DAC; DAM DRAM, MST, POET; DFS 4, 10; DLB 62, 121; LMFS 1; RGEL 2; TEA; WLIT 3

Jordan, June (Meyer) 1936-2002 **BLCS; CLC 5, 11, 23, 114; PC 38**
See also AAYA 2; AFAW 1, 2; BW 2, 3; CA 33-36R; 206; CANR 25, 70, 114; CLR 10; CP 7; CWP; DAM MULT, POET; DLB 38; GLL 2; LAIT 5; MAICYA 1, 2; MTCW 1; SATA 4, 136; YAW

Jordan, Neil (Patrick) 1950- **CLC 110**
See also CA 124; 130; CANR 54; CN 7; GLL 2; INT CA-130

Jordan, Pat(rick M.) 1941- **CLC 37**
See also CA 33-36R; CANR 121

Jorgensen, Ivar
See Ellison, Harlan (Jay)

Jorgenson, Ivar
See Silverberg, Robert

Joseph, George Ghevarughese CLC 70

Josephson, Mary
See O'Doherty, Brian

Josephus, Flavius c. 37-100 **CMLC 13**
See also AW 2; DLB 176

Josiah Allen's Wife
See Holley, Marietta

Josipovici, Gabriel (David) 1940- **CLC 6, 43, 153**
See also CA 37-40R; CAAS 8; CANR 47, 84; CN 7; DLB 14

Joubert, Joseph 1754-1824 **NCLC 9**

Jouve, Pierre Jean 1887-1976 **CLC 47**
See also CA 65-68; DLB 258; EWL 3

Jovine, Francesco 1902-1950 **TCLC 79**
See also DLB 264; EWL 3

Joyce, James (Augustine Aloysius) 1882-1941 **DC 16; PC 22; SSC 3, 26, 44, 64; TCLC 3, 8, 16, 35, 52; WLC**
See also AAYA 42; BRW 7; BRWC 1; BRWR 1; BYA 11, 13; CA 104; 126; CD-BLB 1914-1945; DA; DA3; DAB; DAC; DAM MST, NOV, POET; DLB 10, 19, 36, 162, 247; EWL 3; EXPN; EXPS; LAIT 3; LMFS 1, 2; MTCW 1, 2; NFS 7; RGSF 2; SSFS 1, 19; TEA; WLIT 4

Jozsef, Attila 1905-1937 **TCLC 22**
See also CA 116; CDWLB 4; DLB 215; EWL 3

Juana Ines de la Cruz, Sor 1651(?)-1695 **HLCS 1; LC 5; PC 24**
See also FW; LAW; RGWL 2, 3; WLIT 1

Juana Inez de La Cruz, Sor
See Juana Ines de la Cruz, Sor

Judd, Cyril
See Kornbluth, C(yril) M.; Pohl, Frederik

Juenger, Ernst 1895-1998 **CLC 125**
See Junger, Ernst
See also CA 101; 167; CANR 21, 47, 106; DLB 56

Julian of Norwich 1342(?)-1416(?) **LC 6, 52**
See also DLB 146; LMFS 1

Julius Caesar 100B.C.-44B.C.
See Caesar, Julius
See also CDWLB 1; DLB 211

Junger, Ernst
See Juenger, Ernst
See also CDWLB 2; EWL 3; RGWL 2, 3

Junger, Sebastian 1962- **CLC 109**
See also AAYA 28; CA 165

Juniper, Alex
See Hospital, Janette Turner

Junius
See Luxemburg, Rosa

Just, Ward (Swift) 1935- **CLC 4, 27**
See also CA 25-28R; CANR 32, 87; CN 7; INT CANR-32

Justice, Donald (Rodney) 1925- **CLC 6, 19, 102**
See also AMWS 7; CA 5-8R; CANR 26, 54, 74, 121, 122; CP 7; CSW; DAM POET; DLBY 1983; EWL 3; INT CANR-26; MTCW 2; PFS 14

Juvenal c. 60-c. 130 **CMLC 8**
See also AW 2; CDWLB 1; DLB 211; RGWL 2, 3

Juvenis
See Bourne, Randolph S(illiman)

K., Alice
See Knapp, Caroline

Kabakov, Sasha CLC 59

Kabir 1398(?)-1448(?) **PC 56**
See also RGWL 2, 3

Kacew, Romain 1914-1980
See Gary, Romain
See also CA 108; 102

Kadare, Ismail 1936- **CLC 52**
See also CA 161; EWL 3; RGWL 3

Kadohata, Cynthia 1956(?)- **CLC 59, 122**
See also CA 140; CANR 124

Kafka, Franz 1883-1924 **SSC 5, 29, 35, 60; TCLC 2, 6, 13, 29, 47, 53, 112; WLC**
See also AAYA 31; BPFB 2; CA 105; 126; CDWLB 2; DA; DA3; DAB; DAC; DAM MST, NOV; DLB 81; EW 9; EWL 3; EXPS; LATS 1; LMFS 2; MTCW 1, 2; NFS 7; RGSF 2; RGWL 2, 3; SFW 4; SSFS 3, 7, 12; TWA

Kahanovitsch, Pinkhes
See Der Nister

Kahn, Roger 1927- **CLC 30**
See also CA 25-28R; CANR 44, 69; DLB 171; SATA 37

Kain, Saul
See Sassoon, Siegfried (Lorraine)

Kaiser, Georg 1878-1945 **TCLC 9**
See also CA 106; 190; CDWLB 2; DLB 124; EWL 3; LMFS 2; RGWL 2, 3

Kaledin, Sergei CLC 59

Kaletski, Alexander 1946- **CLC 39**
See also CA 118; 143

Kalidasa fl. c. 400-455 **CMLC 9; PC 22**
See also RGWL 2, 3

Kallman, Chester (Simon) 1921-1975 **CLC 2**
See also CA 45-48; 53-56; CANR 3

Kaminsky, Melvin 1926-
See Brooks, Mel
See also CA 65-68; CANR 16

Kaminsky, Stuart M(elvin) 1934- **CLC 59**
See also CA 73-76; CANR 29, 53, 89; CMW 4

Kamo no Chomei 1153(?)-1216 **CMLC 66**
See also DLB 203

Kamo no Nagaakira
See Kamo no Chomei

Kandinsky, Wassily 1866-1944 **TCLC 92**
See also CA 118; 155

Kane, Francis
See Robbins, Harold

Kane, Henry 1918-
See Queen, Ellery
See also CA 156; CMW 4

Kane, Paul
See Simon, Paul (Frederick)

Kanin, Garson 1912-1999 **CLC 22**
See also AITN 1; CA 5-8R; 177; CAD; CANR 7, 78; DLB 7; IDFW 3, 4

Kaniuk, Yoram 1930- **CLC 19**
See also CA 134

Kant, Immanuel 1724-1804 **NCLC 27, 67**
See also DLB 94

Kantor, MacKinlay 1904-1977 **CLC 7**
See also CA 61-64; 73-76; CANR 60, 63; DLB 9, 102; MTCW 2; RHW; TCWW 2

Kanze Motokiyo
See Zeami

Kaplan, David Michael 1946- **CLC 50**
See also CA 187

Kaplan, James 1951- **CLC 59**
See also CA 135; CANR 121

Karadzic, Vuk Stefanovic 1787-1864 **NCLC 115**
See also CDWLB 4; DLB 147

Karageorge, Michael
See Anderson, Poul (William)

Karamzin, Nikolai Mikhailovich 1766-1826 **NCLC 3**
See also DLB 150; RGSF 2

Karapanou, Margarita 1946- **CLC 13**
See also CA 101

Karinthy, Frigyes 1887-1938 **TCLC 47**
See also CA 170; DLB 215; EWL 3

Karl, Frederick R(obert) 1927-2004 **CLC 34**
See also CA 5-8R; CANR 3, 44

Karr, Mary 1955- **CLC 188**
See also AMWS 11; CA 151; CANR 100; NCFS 5

Kastel, Warren
See Silverberg, Robert

Kataev, Evgeny Petrovich 1903-1942
See Petrov, Evgeny
See also CA 120

Kataphusin
See Ruskin, John

Katz, Steve 1935- **CLC 47**
See also CA 25-28R; CAAS 14, 64; CANR 12; CN 7; DLBY 1983

Kauffman, Janet 1945- **CLC 42**
See also CA 117; CANR 43, 84; DLB 218; DLBY 1986

Kaufman, Bob (Garnell) 1925-1986 **CLC 49**
See also BG 3; BW 1; CA 41-44R; 118; CANR 22; DLB 16, 41

Kaufman, George S. 1889-1961 **CLC 38; DC 17**
See also CA 108; 93-96; DAM DRAM; DFS 1, 10; DLB 7; INT CA-108; MTCW 2; RGAL 4; TUS

Kaufman, Sue CLC 3, 8
See Barondess, Sue K(aufman)

Kavafis, Konstantinos Petrou 1863-1933
See Cavafy, C(onstantine) P(eter)
See also CA 104

Kavan, Anna 1901-1968 **CLC 5, 13, 82**
See also BRWS 7; CA 5-8R; CANR 6, 57; DLB 255; MTCW 1; RGEL 2; SFW 4

Kavanagh, Dan
See Barnes, Julian (Patrick)

Kavanagh, Julie 1952- **CLC 119**
See also CA 163

Kavanagh, Patrick (Joseph) 1904-1967 **CLC 22; PC 33**
See also BRWS 7; CA 123; 25-28R; DLB 15, 20; EWL 3; MTCW 1; RGEL 2

Kawabata, Yasunari 1899-1972 **CLC 2, 5, 9, 18, 107; SSC 17**
See Kawabata Yasunari
See also CA 93-96; 33-36R; CANR 88; DAM MULT; MJW; MTCW 2; RGSF 2; RGWL 2, 3

Kawabata Yasunari
See Kawabata, Yasunari
See also DLB 180; EWL 3

Kaye, M(ary) M(argaret) 1908-2004 **CLC 28**
See also CA 89-92; CANR 24, 60, 102;
MTCW 1, 2; RHW; SATA 62

Kaye, Mollie
See Kaye, M(ary) M(argaret)

Kaye-Smith, Sheila 1887-1956 **TCLC 20**
See also CA 118; 203; DLB 36

Kaymor, Patrice Maguilene
See Senghor, Leopold Sedar

Kazakov, Yuri Pavlovich 1927-1982 **SSC 43**
See Kazakov, Yury
See also CA 5-8R; CANR 36; MTCW 1;
RGSF 2

Kazakov, Yury
See Kazakov, Yuri Pavlovich
See also EWL 3

Kazan, Elia 1909-2003 **CLC 6, 16, 63**
See also CA 21-24R; 220; CANR 32, 78

Kazantzakis, Nikos 1883(?)-1957 **TCLC 2, 5, 33**
See also BPFB 2; CA 105; 132; DA3; EW
9; EWL 3; MTCW 1, 2; RGWL 2, 3

Kazin, Alfred 1915-1998 **CLC 34, 38, 119**
See also AMWS 8; CA 1-4R; CAAS 7;
CANR 1, 45, 79; DLB 67; EWL 3

Keane, Mary Nesta (Skrine) 1904-1996
See Keane, Molly
See also CA 108; 114; 151; CN 7; RHW

Keane, Molly CLC 31
See Keane, Mary Nesta (Skrine)
See also INT CA-114

Keates, Jonathan 1946(?)- **CLC 34**
See also CA 163; CANR 126

Keaton, Buster 1895-1966 **CLC 20**
See also CA 194

Keats, John 1795-1821 **NCLC 8, 73, 121; PC 1; WLC**
See also BRW 4; BRWR 1; CDBLB 1789-
1832; DA; DA3; DAB; DAC; DAM MST,
POET; DLB 96, 110; EXPP; LMFS 1;
PAB; PFS 1, 2, 3, 9, 17; RGEL 2; TEA;
WLIT 3; WP

Keble, John 1792-1866 **NCLC 87**
See also DLB 32, 55; RGEL 2

Keene, Donald 1922- **CLC 34**
See also CA 1-4R; CANR 5, 119

Keillor, Garrison CLC 40, 115
See Keillor, Gary (Edward)
See also AAYA 2; BEST 89:3; BPFB 2;
DLBY 1987; EWL 3; SATA 58; TUS

Keillor, Gary (Edward) 1942-
See Keillor, Garrison
See also CA 111; 117; CANR 36, 59, 124;
CPW; DA3; DAM POP; MTCW 1, 2

Keith, Carlos
See Lewton, Val

Keith, Michael
See Hubbard, L(afayette) Ron(ald)

Keller, Gottfried 1819-1890 **NCLC 2; SSC 26**
See also CDWLB 2; DLB 129; EW; RGSF
2; RGWL 2, 3

Keller, Nora Okja 1965- **CLC 109**
See also CA 187

Kellerman, Jonathan 1949- **CLC 44**
See also AAYA 35; BEST 90:1; CA 106;
CANR 29, 51; CMW 4; CPW; DA3;
DAM POP; INT CANR-29

Kelley, William Melvin 1937- **CLC 22**
See also BW 1; CA 77-80; CANR 27, 83;
CN 7; DLB 33; EWL 3

Kellogg, Marjorie 1922- **CLC 2**
See also CA 81-84

Kellow, Kathleen
See Hibbert, Eleanor Alice Burford

Kelly, M(ilton) T(errence) 1947- **CLC 55**
See also CA 97-100; CAAS 22; CANR 19,
43, 84; CN 7

Kelly, Robert 1935- **SSC 50**
See also CA 17-20R; CAAS 19; CANR 47;
CP 7; DLB 5, 130, 165

Kelman, James 1946- **CLC 58, 86**
See also BRWS 5; CA 148; CANR 85; CN
7; DLB 194; RGSF 2; WLIT 4

Kemal, Yashar 1923- **CLC 14, 29**
See also CA 89-92; CANR 44; CWW 2

Kemble, Fanny 1809-1893 **NCLC 18**
See also DLB 32

Kemelman, Harry 1908-1996 **CLC 2**
See also AITN 1; BPFB 2; CA 9-12R; 155;
CANR 6, 71; CMW 4; DLB 28

Kempe, Margery 1373(?)-1440(?) **LC 6, 56**
See also DLB 146; RGEL 2

Kempis, Thomas a 1380-1471 **LC 11**

Kendall, Henry 1839-1882 **NCLC 12**
See also DLB 230

Keneally, Thomas (Michael) 1935- **CLC 5, 8, 10, 14, 19, 27, 43, 117**
See also BRWS 4; CA 85-88; CANR 10,
50, 74; CN 7; CPW; DA3; DAM NOV;
DLB 289; EWL 3; MTCW 1, 2; NFS 17;
RGEL 2; RHW

Kennedy, A(lison) L(ouise) 1965- **CLC 188**
See also CA 168, 213; CAAE 213; CANR
108; CD 5; CN 7; DLB 271; RGSF 2

Kennedy, Adrienne (Lita) 1931- **BLC 2; CLC 66; DC 5**
See also AFAW 2; BW 2, 3; CA 103; CAAS
20; CABS 3; CANR 26, 53, 82; CD 5;
DAM MULT; DFS 9; DLB 38; FW

Kennedy, John Pendleton 1795-1870 **NCLC 2**
See also DLB 3, 248, 254; RGAL 4

Kennedy, Joseph Charles 1929-
See Kennedy, X. J.
See also CA 1-4R, 201; CAAE 201; CANR
4, 30, 40; CP 7; CWRI 5; MAICYA 2;
MAICYAS 1; SATA 14, 86, 130; SATA-
Essay 130

Kennedy, William 1928- **CLC 6, 28, 34, 53**
See also AAYA 1; AMWS 7; BPFB 2; CA
85-88; CANR 14, 31, 76; CN 7; DA3;
DAM NOV; DLB 143; DLBY 1985; EWL
3; INT CANR-31; MTCW 1, 2; SATA 57

Kennedy, X. J. CLC 8, 42
See Kennedy, Joseph Charles
See also CAAS 9; CLR 27; DLB 5; SAAS
22

Kenny, Maurice (Francis) 1929- **CLC 87; NNAL**
See also CA 144; CAAS 22; DAM MULT;
DLB 175

Kent, Kelvin
See Kuttner, Henry

Kenton, Maxwell
See Southern, Terry

Kenyon, Robert O.
See Kuttner, Henry

Kepler, Johannes 1571-1630 **LC 45**

Ker, Jill
See Conway, Jill K(er)

Kerkow, H. C.
See Lewton, Val

Kerouac, Jack 1922-1969 **CLC 1, 2, 3, 5, 14, 29, 61; TCLC 117; WLC**
See Kerouac, Jean-Louis Lebris de
See also AAYA 25; AMWC 1; AMWS 3;
BG 3; BPFB 2; CDALB 1941-1968;
CPW; DLB 2, 16, 237; DLBD 3; DLBY
1995; EWL 3; GLL 1; LATS 1; LMFS 2;
MTCW 2; NFS 8; RGAL 4; TUS; WP

Kerouac, Jean-Louis Lebris de 1922-1969
See Kerouac, Jack
See also AITN 1; CA 5-8R; 25-28R; CANR
26, 54, 95; DA; DA3; DAB; DAC; DAM
MST, NOV, POET, POP; MTCW 1, 2

Kerr, (Bridget) Jean (Collins) 1923(?)-2003 **CLC 22**
See also CA 5-8R; 212; CANR 7; INT
CANR-7

Kerr, M. E. CLC 12, 35
See Meaker, Marijane (Agnes)
See also AAYA 2, 23; BYA 1, 7, 8; CLR
29; SAAS 1; WYA

Kerr, Robert CLC 55

Kerrigan, (Thomas) Anthony 1918- **CLC 4, 6**
See also CA 49-52; CAAS 11; CANR 4

Kerry, Lois
See Duncan, Lois

Kesey, Ken (Elton) 1935-2001 **CLC 1, 3, 6, 11, 46, 64, 184; WLC**
See also AAYA 25; BG 3; BPFB 2; CA
1-4R; 204; CANR 22, 38, 66, 124;
CDALB 1968-1988; CN 7; CPW; DA;
DA3; DAB; DAC; DAM MST, NOV,
POP; DLB 2, 16, 206; EWL 3; EXPN;
LAIT 4; MTCW 1, 2; NFS 2; RGAL 4;
SATA 66; SATA-Obit 131; TUS; YAW

Kesselring, Joseph (Otto) 1902-1967 **CLC 45**
See also CA 150; DAM DRAM, MST

Kessler, Jascha (Frederick) 1929- **CLC 4**
See also CA 17-20R; CANR 8, 48, 111

Kettelkamp, Larry (Dale) 1933- **CLC 12**
See also CA 29-32R; CANR 16; SAAS 3;
SATA 2

Key, Ellen (Karolina Sofia) 1849-1926 **TCLC 65**
See also DLB 259

Keyber, Conny
See Fielding, Henry

Keyes, Daniel 1927- **CLC 80**
See also AAYA 23; BYA 11; CA 17-20R,
181; CAAE 181; CANR 10, 26, 54, 74;
DA; DA3; DAC; DAM MST, NOV;
EXPN; LAIT 4; MTCW 2; NFS 2; SATA
37; SFW 4

Keynes, John Maynard 1883-1946 **TCLC 64**
See also CA 114; 162, 163; DLBD 10;
MTCW 2

Khanshendel, Chiron
See Rose, Wendy

Khayyam, Omar 1048-1131 **CMLC 11; PC 8**
See Omar Khayyam
See also DA3; DAM POET

Kherdian, David 1931- **CLC 6, 9**
See also AAYA 42; CA 21-24R, 192; CAAE
192; CANR 2; CANR 39, 78; CLR 24;
JRDA; LAIT 3; MAICYA 1, 2; SATA 16,
74; SATA-Essay 125

Khlebnikov, Velimir TCLC 20
See Khlebnikov, Viktor Vladimirovich
See also DLB 295; EW 10; EWL 3; RGWL
2, 3

Khlebnikov, Viktor Vladimirovich 1885-1922
See Khlebnikov, Velimir
See also CA 117; 217

Khodasevich, Vladislav (Felitsianovich) 1886-1939 **TCLC 15**
See also CA 115; EWL 3

Kielland, Alexander Lange 1849-1906 **TCLC 5**
See also CA 104

Kiely, Benedict 1919- **CLC 23, 43; SSC 58**
See also CA 1-4R; CANR 2, 84; CN 7;
DLB 15

Kienzle, William X(avier) 1928-2001 **CLC 25**
See also CA 93-96; 203; CAAS 1; CANR
9, 31, 59, 111; CMW 4; DA3; DAM POP;
INT CANR-31; MSW; MTCW 1, 2

Kogawa, Joy Nozomi 1935- **CLC 78, 129**
See also AAYA 47; CA 101; CANR 19, 62, 126; CN 7; CWP; DAC; DAM MST, MULT; FW; MTCW 2; NFS 3; SATA 99

Kohout, Pavel 1928- **CLC 13**
See also CA 45-48; CANR 3

Koizumi, Yakumo
See Hearn, (Patricio) Lafcadio (Tessima Carlos)

Kolmar, Gertrud 1894-1943 **TCLC 40**
See also CA 167; EWL 3

Komunyakaa, Yusef 1947- **BLCS; CLC 86, 94; PC 51**
See also AFAW 2; AMWS 13; CA 147; CANR 83; CP 7; CSW; DLB 120; EWL 3; PFS 5; RGAL 4

Konrad, George
See Konrad, Gyorgy
See also CWW 2

Konrad, Gyorgy 1933- **CLC 4, 10, 73**
See Konrad, George
See also CA 85-88; CANR 97; CDWLB 4; CWW 2; DLB 232; EWL 3

Konwicki, Tadeusz 1926- **CLC 8, 28, 54, 117**
See also CA 101; CAAS 9; CANR 39, 59; CWW 2; DLB 232; EWL 3; IDFW 3; MTCW 1

Koontz, Dean R(ay) 1945- **CLC 78**
See also AAYA 9, 31; BEST 89:3, 90:2; CA 108; CANR 19, 36, 52, 95; CMW 4; CPW; DA3; DAM NOV, POP; DLB 292; HGG; MTCW 1; SATA 92; SFW 4; SUFW 2; YAW

Kopernik, Mikolaj
See Copernicus, Nicolaus

Kopit, Arthur (Lee) 1937- **CLC 1, 18, 33**
See also AITN 1; CA 81-84; CABS 3; CD 5; DAM DRAM; DFS 7, 14; DLB 7; MTCW 1; RGAL 4

Kopitar, Jernej (Bartholomaus) 1780-1844 **NCLC 117**

Kops, Bernard 1926- **CLC 4**
See also CA 5-8R; CANR 84; CBD; CN 7; CP 7; DLB 13

Kornbluth, C(yril) M. 1923-1958 **TCLC 8**
See also CA 105; 160; DLB 8; SFW 4

Korolenko, V. G.
See Korolenko, Vladimir Galaktionovich

Korolenko, Vladimir
See Korolenko, Vladimir Galaktionovich

Korolenko, Vladimir G.
See Korolenko, Vladimir Galaktionovich

Korolenko, Vladimir Galaktionovich 1853-1921 **TCLC 22**
See also CA 121; DLB 277

Korzybski, Alfred (Habdank Skarbek) 1879-1950 **TCLC 61**
See also CA 123; 160

Kosinski, Jerzy (Nikodem) 1933-1991 **CLC 1, 2, 3, 6, 10, 15, 53, 70**
See also AMWS 7; BPFB 2; CA 17-20R; 134; CANR 9, 46; DA3; DAM NOV; DLB 2; DLBY 1982; EWL 3; HGG; MTCW 1, 2; NFS 12; RGAL 4; TUS

Kostelanetz, Richard (Cory) 1940- **CLC 28**
See also CA 13-16R; CAAS 8; CANR 38, 77; CN 7; CP 7

Kostrowitzki, Wilhelm Apollinaris de 1880-1918
See Apollinaire, Guillaume
See also CA 104

Kotlowitz, Robert 1924- **CLC 4**
See also CA 33-36R; CANR 36

Kotzebue, August (Friedrich Ferdinand) von 1761-1819 **NCLC 25**
See also DLB 94

Kotzwinkle, William 1938- **CLC 5, 14, 35**
See also BPFB 2; CA 45-48; CANR 3, 44, 84, 129; CLR 6; DLB 173; FANT; MAICYA 1, 2; SATA 24, 70, 146; SFW 4; SUFW 2; YAW

Kowna, Stancy
See Szymborska, Wislawa

Kozol, Jonathan 1936- **CLC 17**
See also AAYA 46; CA 61-64; CANR 16, 45, 96

Kozoll, Michael 1940(?)- **CLC 35**

Kramer, Kathryn 19(?)- **CLC 34**

Kramer, Larry 1935- **CLC 42; DC 8**
See also CA 124; 126; CANR 60; DAM POP; DLB 249; GLL 1

Krasicki, Ignacy 1735-1801 **NCLC 8**

Krasinski, Zygmunt 1812-1859 **NCLC 4**
See also RGWL 2, 3

Kraus, Karl 1874-1936 **TCLC 5**
See also CA 104; 216; DLB 118; EWL 3

Kreve (Mickevicius), Vincas 1882-1954 **TCLC 27**
See also CA 170; DLB 220; EWL 3

Kristeva, Julia 1941- **CLC 77, 140**
See also CA 154; CANR 99; DLB 242; EWL 3; FW; LMFS 2

Kristofferson, Kris 1936- **CLC 26**
See also CA 104

Krizanc, John 1956- **CLC 57**
See also CA 187

Krleza, Miroslav 1893-1981 **CLC 8, 114**
See also CA 97-100; 105; CANR 50; CDWLB 4; DLB 147; EW 11; RGWL 2, 3

Kroetsch, Robert 1927- **CLC 5, 23, 57, 132**
See also CA 17-20R; CANR 8, 38; CCA 1; CN 7; CP 7; DAC; DAM POET; DLB 53; MTCW 1

Kroetz, Franz
See Kroetz, Franz Xaver

Kroetz, Franz Xaver 1946- **CLC 41**
See also CA 130; EWL 3

Kroker, Arthur (W.) 1945- **CLC 77**
See also CA 161

Kropotkin, Peter (Aleksieevich) 1842-1921 **TCLC 36**
See Kropotkin, Petr Alekseevich
See also CA 119; 219

Kropotkin, Petr Alekseevich
See Kropotkin, Peter (Aleksieevich)
See also DLB 277

Krotkov, Yuri 1917-1981 **CLC 19**
See also CA 102

Krumb
See Crumb, R(obert)

Krumgold, Joseph (Quincy) 1908-1980 **CLC 12**
See also BYA 1, 2; CA 9-12R; 101; CANR 7; MAICYA 1, 2; SATA 1, 48; SATA-Obit 23; YAW

Krumwitz
See Crumb, R(obert)

Krutch, Joseph Wood 1893-1970 **CLC 24**
See also ANW; CA 1-4R; 25-28R; CANR 4; DLB 63, 206, 275

Krutzch, Gus
See Eliot, T(homas) S(tearns)

Krylov, Ivan Andreevich 1768(?)-1844 **NCLC 1**
See also DLB 150

Kubin, Alfred (Leopold Isidor) 1877-1959 **TCLC 23**
See also CA 112; 149; CANR 104; DLB 81

Kubrick, Stanley 1928-1999 **CLC 16; TCLC 112**
See also AAYA 30; CA 81-84; 177; CANR 33; DLB 26

Kumin, Maxine (Winokur) 1925- **CLC 5, 13, 28, 164; PC 15**
See also AITN 2; AMWS 4; ANW; CA 1-4R; CAAS 8; CANR 1, 21, 69, 115; CP 7; CWP; DA3; DAM POET; DLB 5; EWL 3; EXPP; MTCW 1, 2; PAB; PFS 18; SATA 12

Kundera, Milan 1929- **CLC 4, 9, 19, 32, 68, 115, 135; SSC 24**
See also AAYA 2; BPFB 2; CA 85-88; CANR 19, 52, 74; CDWLB 4; CWW 2; DA3; DAM NOV; DLB 232; EW 13; EWL 3; MTCW 1, 2; NFS 18; RGSF 2; RGWL 3; SSFS 10

Kunene, Mazisi (Raymond) 1930- **CLC 85**
See also BW 1, 3; CA 125; CANR 81; CP 7; DLB 117

Kung, Hans CLC 130
See Kung, Hans

Kung, Hans 1928-
See Kung, Hans
See also CA 53-56; CANR 66; MTCW 1, 2

Kunikida Doppo 1869(?)-1908
See Doppo, Kunikida
See also DLB 180; EWL 3

Kunitz, Stanley (Jasspon) 1905- **CLC 6, 11, 14, 148; PC 19**
See also AMWS 3; CA 41-44R; CANR 26, 57, 98; CP 7; DA3; DLB 48; INT CANR-26; MTCW 1, 2; PFS 11; RGAL 4

Kunze, Reiner 1933- **CLC 10**
See also CA 93-96; CWW 2; DLB 75; EWL 3

Kuprin, Aleksander Ivanovich 1870-1938 **TCLC 5**
See Kuprin, Aleksandr Ivanovich; Kuprin, Alexandr Ivanovich
See also CA 104; 182

Kuprin, Aleksandr Ivanovich
See Kuprin, Aleksander Ivanovich
See also DLB 295

Kuprin, Alexandr Ivanovich
See Kuprin, Aleksander Ivanovich
See also EWL 3

Kureishi, Hanif 1954(?)- **CLC 64, 135**
See also CA 139; CANR 113; CBD; CD 5; CN 7; DLB 194, 245; GLL 2; IDFW 4; WLIT 4; WWE 1

Kurosawa, Akira 1910-1998 **CLC 16, 119**
See also AAYA 11; CA 101; 170; CANR 46; DAM MULT

Kushner, Tony 1957(?)- **CLC 81; DC 10**
See also AMWS 9; CA 144; CAD; CANR 74; CD 5; DA3; DAM DRAM; DFS 5; DLB 228; EWL 3; GLL 1; LAIT 5; MTCW 2; RGAL 4

Kuttner, Henry 1915-1958 **TCLC 10**
See also CA 107; 157; DLB 8; FANT; SCFW 2; SFW 4

Kutty, Madhavi
See Das, Kamala

Kuzma, Greg 1944- **CLC 7**
See also CA 33-36R; CANR 70

Kuzmin, Mikhail (Alekseevich) 1872(?)-1936 **TCLC 40**
See also CA 170; DLB 295; EWL 3

Kyd, Thomas 1558-1594 **DC 3; LC 22**
See also BRW 1; DAM DRAM; DLB 62; IDTP; LMFS 1; RGEL 2; TEA; WLIT 3

Kyprianos, Iossif
See Samarakis, Antonis

L. S.
See Stephen, Sir Leslie

Labrunie, Gerard
See Nerval, Gerard de

La Bruyere, Jean de 1645-1696 **LC 17**
See also DLB 268; EW 3; GFL Beginnings to 1789

Leger, Saintleger
See Leger, (Marie-Rene Auguste) Alexis Saint-Leger

Le Guin, Ursula K(roeber) 1929- **CLC 8, 13, 22, 45, 71, 136; SSC 12, 69**
See also AAYA 9, 27; AITN 1; BPFB 2; BYA 5, 8, 11, 14; CA 21-24R; CANR 9, 32, 52, 74; CDALB 1968-1988; CLR 3, 28, 91; CN 7; CPW; DA3; DAB; DAC; DAM MST, POP; DLB 8, 52, 256, 275; EXPS; FANT; FW; INT CANR-32; JRDA; LAIT 5; MAICYA 1, 2; MTCW 1, 2; NFS 6, 9; SATA 4, 52, 99; SCFW; SFW 4; SSFS 2; SUFW 1, 2; WYA; YAW

Lehmann, Rosamond (Nina) 1901-1990 **CLC 5**
See also CA 77-80; 131; CANR 8, 73; DLB 15; MTCW 2; RGEL 2; RHW

Leiber, Fritz (Reuter, Jr.) 1910-1992 **CLC 25**
See also BPFB 2; CA 45-48; 139; CANR 2, 40, 86; DLB 8; FANT; HGG; MTCW 1, 2; SATA 45; SATA-Obit 73; SCFW 2; SFW 4; SUFW 1, 2

Leibniz, Gottfried Wilhelm von 1646-1716 **LC 35**
See also DLB 168

Leimbach, Martha 1963-
See Leimbach, Marti
See also CA 130

Leimbach, Marti CLC 65
See Leimbach, Martha

Leino, Eino TCLC 24
See Lonnbohm, Armas Eino Leopold
See also EWL 3

Leiris, Michel (Julien) 1901-1990 **CLC 61**
See also CA 119; 128; 132; EWL 3; GFL 1789 to the Present

Leithauser, Brad 1953- **CLC 27**
See also CA 107; CANR 27, 81; CP 7; DLB 120, 282

le Jars de Gournay, Marie
See de Gournay, Marie le Jars

Lelchuk, Alan 1938- **CLC 5**
See also CA 45-48; CAAS 20; CANR 1, 70; CN 7

Lem, Stanislaw 1921- **CLC 8, 15, 40, 149**
See also CA 105; CAAS 1; CANR 32; CWW 2; MTCW 1; SCFW 2; SFW 4

Lemann, Nancy (Elise) 1956- **CLC 39**
See also CA 118; 136; CANR 121

Lemonnier, (Antoine Louis) Camille 1844-1913 **TCLC 22**
See also CA 121

Lenau, Nikolaus 1802-1850 **NCLC 16**

L'Engle, Madeleine (Camp Franklin) 1918- **CLC 12**
See also AAYA 28; AITN 2; BPFB 2; BYA 2, 4, 5, 7; CA 1-4R; CANR 3, 21, 39, 66, 107; CLR 1, 14, 57; CPW; CWRI 5; DA3; DAM POP; DLB 52; JRDA; MAICYA 1, 2; MTCW 1, 2; SAAS 15; SATA 1, 27, 75, 128; SFW 4; WYA; YAW

Lengyel, Jozsef 1896-1975 **CLC 7**
See also CA 85-88; 57-60; CANR 71; RGSF 2

Lenin 1870-1924
See Lenin, V. I.
See also CA 121; 168

Lenin, V. I. TCLC 67
See Lenin

Lennon, John (Ono) 1940-1980 **CLC 12, 35**
See also CA 102; SATA 114

Lennox, Charlotte Ramsay 1729(?)-1804 **NCLC 23, 134**
See also DLB 39; RGEL 2

Lentricchia, Frank, (Jr.) 1940- **CLC 34**
See also CA 25-28R; CANR 19, 106; DLB 246

Lenz, Gunter CLC 65

Lenz, Jakob Michael Reinhold 1751-1792 **LC 100**
See also DLB 94; RGWL 2, 3

Lenz, Siegfried 1926- **CLC 27; SSC 33**
See also CA 89-92; CANR 80; CWW 2; DLB 75; EWL 3; RGSF 2; RGWL 2, 3

Leon, David
See Jacob, (Cyprien-)Max

Leonard, Elmore (John, Jr.) 1925- **CLC 28, 34, 71, 120**
See also AAYA 22; AITN 1; BEST 89:1, 90:4; BPFB 2; CA 81-84; CANR 12, 28, 53, 76, 96; CMW 4; CN 7; CPW; DA3; DAM POP; DLB 173, 226; INT CANR-28; MSW; MTCW 1, 2; RGAL 4; TCWW 2

Leonard, Hugh CLC 19
See Byrne, John Keyes
See also CBD; CD 5; DFS 13; DLB 13

Leonov, Leonid (Maximovich) 1899-1994 **CLC 92**
See Leonov, Leonid Maksimovich
See also CA 129; CANR 74, 76; DAM NOV; EWL 3; MTCW 1, 2

Leonov, Leonid Maksimovich
See Leonov, Leonid (Maximovich)
See also DLB 272

Leopardi, (Conte) Giacomo 1798-1837 **NCLC 22, 129; PC 37**
See also EW 5; RGWL 2, 3; WP

Le Reveler
See Artaud, Antonin (Marie Joseph)

Lerman, Eleanor 1952- **CLC 9**
See also CA 85-88; CANR 69, 124

Lerman, Rhoda 1936- **CLC 56**
See also CA 49-52; CANR 70

Lermontov, Mikhail Iur'evich
See Lermontov, Mikhail Yuryevich
See also DLB 205

Lermontov, Mikhail Yuryevich 1814-1841 **NCLC 5, 47, 126; PC 18**
See Lermontov, Mikhail Iur'evich
See also EW 6; RGWL 2, 3; TWA

Leroux, Gaston 1868-1927 **TCLC 25**
See also CA 108; 136; CANR 69; CMW 4; SATA 65

Lesage, Alain-Rene 1668-1747 **LC 2, 28**
See also EW 3; GFL Beginnings to 1789; RGWL 2, 3

Leskov, N(ikolai) S(emenovich) 1831-1895
See Leskov, Nikolai (Semyonovich)

Leskov, Nikolai (Semyonovich) 1831-1895 **NCLC 25; SSC 34**
See Leskov, Nikolai Semenovich

Leskov, Nikolai Semenovich
See Leskov, Nikolai (Semyonovich)
See also DLB 238

Lesser, Milton
See Marlowe, Stephen

Lessing, Doris (May) 1919- **CLC 1, 2, 3, 6, 10, 15, 22, 40, 94, 170; SSC 6, 61; WLCS**
See also AFW; BRWS 1; CA 9-12R; CAAS 14; CANR 33, 54, 76, 122; CD 5; CDBLB 1960 to Present; CN 7; DA; DA3; DAB; DAC; DAM MST, NOV; DLB 15, 139; DLBY 1985; EWL 3; EXPS; FW; LAIT 4; MTCW 1, 2; RGEL 2; RGSF 2; SFW 4; SSFS 1, 12; TEA; WLIT 2, 4

Lessing, Gotthold Ephraim 1729-1781 **LC 8**
See also CDWLB 2; DLB 97; EW 4; RGWL 2, 3

Lester, Richard 1932- **CLC 20**

Levenson, Jay CLC 70

Lever, Charles (James) 1806-1872 **NCLC 23**
See also DLB 21; RGEL 2

Leverson, Ada Esther 1862(?)-1933(?) **TCLC 18**
See Elaine
See also CA 117; 202; DLB 153; RGEL 2

Levertov, Denise 1923-1997 **CLC 1, 2, 3, 5, 8, 15, 28, 66; PC 11**
See also AMWS 3; CA 1-4R, 178; 163; CAAE 178; CAAS 19; CANR 3, 29, 50, 108; CDALBS; CP 7; CWP; DAM POET; DLB 5, 165; EWL 3; EXPP; FW; INT CANR-29; MTCW 1, 2; PAB; PFS 7, 17; RGAL 4; TUS; WP

Levi, Carlo 1902-1975 **TCLC 125**
See also CA 65-68; 53-56; CANR 10; EWL 3; RGWL 2, 3

Levi, Jonathan CLC 76
See also CA 197

Levi, Peter (Chad Tigar) 1931-2000 **CLC 41**
See also CA 5-8R; 187; CANR 34, 80; CP 7; DLB 40

Levi, Primo 1919-1987 **CLC 37, 50; SSC 12; TCLC 109**
See also CA 13-16R; 122; CANR 12, 33, 61, 70; DLB 177; EWL 3; MTCW 1, 2; RGWL 2, 3

Levin, Ira 1929- **CLC 3, 6**
See also CA 21-24R; CANR 17, 44, 74; CMW 4; CN 7; CPW; DA3; DAM POP; HGG; MTCW 1, 2; SATA 66; SFW 4

Levin, Meyer 1905-1981 **CLC 7**
See also AITN 1; CA 9-12R; 104; CANR 15; DAM POP; DLB 9, 28; DLBY 1981; SATA 21; SATA-Obit 27

Levine, Norman 1924- **CLC 54**
See also CA 73-76; CAAS 23; CANR 14, 70; DLB 88

Levine, Philip 1928- **CLC 2, 4, 5, 9, 14, 33, 118; PC 22**
See also AMWS 5; CA 9-12R; CANR 9, 37, 52, 116; CP 7; DAM POET; DLB 5; EWL 3; PFS 8

Levinson, Deirdre 1931- **CLC 49**
See also CA 73-76; CANR 70

Levi-Strauss, Claude 1908- **CLC 38**
See also CA 1-4R; CANR 6, 32, 57; DLB 242; EWL 3; GFL 1789 to the Present; MTCW 1, 2; TWA

Levitin, Sonia (Wolff) 1934- **CLC 17**
See also AAYA 13, 48; CA 29-32R; CANR 14, 32, 79; CLR 53; JRDA; MAICYA 1, 2; SAAS 2; SATA 4, 68, 119, 131; SATA-Essay 131; YAW

Levon, O. U.
See Kesey, Ken (Elton)

Levy, Amy 1861-1889 **NCLC 59**
See also DLB 156, 240

Lewes, George Henry 1817-1878 **NCLC 25**
See also DLB 55, 144

Lewis, Alun 1915-1944 **SSC 40; TCLC 3**
See also BRW 7; CA 104; 188; DLB 20, 162; PAB; RGEL 2

Lewis, C. Day
See Day Lewis, C(ecil)

Lewis, C(live) S(taples) 1898-1963 **CLC 1, 3, 6, 14, 27, 124; WLC**
See also AAYA 3, 39; BPFB 2; BRWS 3; BYA 15, 16; CA 81-84; CANR 33, 71; CDBLB 1945-1960; CLR 3, 27; CWRI 5; DA; DA3; DAB; DAC; DAM MST, NOV, POP; DLB 15, 100, 160, 255; EWL 3; FANT; JRDA; LMFS 2; MAICYA 1, 2; MTCW 1, 2; RGEL 2; SATA 13, 100; SCFW; SFW 4; SUFW 1; TEA; WCH; WYA; YAW

Lewis, Cecil Day
See Day Lewis, C(ecil)

Lewis, Janet 1899-1998 **CLC 41**
See Winters, Janet Lewis
See also CA 9-12R; 172; CANR 29, 63;
CAP 1; CN 7; DLBY 1987; RHW;
TCWW 2

Lewis, Matthew Gregory 1775-1818 **NCLC
11, 62**
See also DLB 39, 158, 178; HGG; LMFS
1; RGEL 2; SUFW

Lewis, (Harry) Sinclair 1885-1951 **TCLC 4,
13, 23, 39; WLC**
See also AMW; AMWC 1; BPFB 2; CA
104; 133; CDALB 1917-1929; DA; DA3;
DAB; DAC; DAM MST, NOV; DLB 9,
102, 284; DLBD 1; EWL 3; LAIT 3;
MTCW 1, 2; NFS 15; RGAL 4; TUS

Lewis, (Percy) Wyndham 1884(?)-1957 **SSC
34; TCLC 2, 9, 104**
See also BRW 7; CA 104; 157; DLB 15;
EWL 3; FANT; MTCW 2; RGEL 2

Lewisohn, Ludwig 1883-1955 **TCLC 19**
See also CA 107; 203; DLB 4, 9, 28, 102

Lewton, Val 1904-1951 **TCLC 76**
See also CA 199; IDFW 3, 4

Leyner, Mark 1956- **CLC 92**
See also CA 110; CANR 28, 53; DA3; DLB
292; MTCW 2

Lezama Lima, Jose 1910-1976 **CLC 4, 10,
101; HLCS 2**
See also CA 77-80; CANR 71; DAM
MULT; DLB 113, 283; EWL 3; HW 1, 2;
LAW; RGWL 2, 3

L'Heureux, John (Clarke) 1934- **CLC 52**
See also CA 13-16R; CANR 23, 45, 88;
DLB 244

Liddell, C. H.
See Kuttner, Henry

Lie, Jonas (Lauritz Idemil) 1833-1908(?)
TCLC 5
See also CA 115

Lieber, Joel 1937-1971 **CLC 6**
See also CA 73-76; 29-32R

Lieber, Stanley Martin
See Lee, Stan

Lieberman, Laurence (James) 1935- **CLC 4,
36**
See also CA 17-20R; CANR 8, 36, 89; CP
7

Lieh Tzu fl. 7th cent. B.C.-5th cent. B.C.
CMLC 27

Lieksman, Anders
See Haavikko, Paavo Juhani

Li Fei-kan 1904-
See Pa Chin
See also CA 105; TWA

Lifton, Robert Jay 1926- **CLC 67**
See also CA 17-20R; CANR 27, 78; INT
CANR-27; SATA 66

Lightfoot, Gordon 1938- **CLC 26**
See also CA 109

Lightman, Alan P(aige) 1948- **CLC 81**
See also CA 141; CANR 63, 105

Ligotti, Thomas (Robert) 1953- **CLC 44; SSC
16**
See also CA 123; CANR 49; HGG; SUFW
2

Li Ho 791-817 **PC 13**

Li Ju-chen c. 1763-c. 1830 **NCLC 137**

**Liliencron, (Friedrich Adolf Axel) Detlev
von** 1844-1909 **TCLC 18**
See also CA 117

Lille, Alain de
See Alain de Lille

Lilly, William 1602-1681 **LC 27**

Lima, Jose Lezama
See Lezama Lima, Jose

Lima Barreto, Afonso Henrique de
1881-1922 **TCLC 23**
See also CA 117; 181; LAW

Lima Barreto, Afonso Henriques de
See Lima Barreto, Afonso Henrique de

Limonov, Edward 1944- **CLC 67**
See also CA 137

Lin, Frank
See Atherton, Gertrude (Franklin Horn)

Lin, Yutang 1895-1976 **TCLC 149**
See also CA 45-48; 65-68; CANR 2; RGAL
4

Lincoln, Abraham 1809-1865 **NCLC 18**
See also LAIT 2

Lind, Jakov CLC 1, 2, 4, 27, 82
See Landwirth, Heinz
See also CAAS 4; EWL 3

Lindbergh, Anne (Spencer) Morrow
1906-2001 **CLC 82**
See also BPFB 2; CA 17-20R; 193; CANR
16, 73; DAM NOV; MTCW 1, 2; SATA
33; SATA-Obit 125; TUS

Lindsay, David 1878(?)-1945 **TCLC 15**
See also CA 113; 187; DLB 255; FANT;
SFW 4; SUFW 1

Lindsay, (Nicholas) Vachel 1879-1931 **PC 23;
TCLC 17; WLC**
See also AMWS 1; CA 114; 135; CANR
79; CDALB 1865-1917; DA; DA3; DAC;
DAM MST, POET; DLB 54; EWL 3;
EXPP; RGAL 4; SATA 40; WP

Linke-Poot
See Doeblin, Alfred

Linney, Romulus 1930- **CLC 51**
See also CA 1-4R; CAD; CANR 40, 44,
79; CD 5; CSW; RGAL 4

Linton, Eliza Lynn 1822-1898 **NCLC 41**
See also DLB 18

Li Po 701-763 **CMLC 2; PC 29**
See also WP

Lipsius, Justus 1547-1606 **LC 16**

Lipsyte, Robert (Michael) 1938- **CLC 21**
See also AAYA 7, 45; CA 17-20R; CANR
8, 57; CLR 23, 76; DA; DAC; DAM
MST, NOV; JRDA; LAIT 5; MAICYA 1,
2; SATA 5, 68, 113; WYA; YAW

Lish, Gordon (Jay) 1934- **CLC 45; SSC 18**
See also CA 113; 117; CANR 79; DLB 130;
INT CA-117

Lispector, Clarice 1925(?)-1977 **CLC 43;
HLCS 2; SSC 34**
See also CA 139; 116; CANR 71; CDWLB
3; DLB 113; DNFS 1; EWL 3; FW; HW
2; LAW; RGSF 2; RGWL 2, 3; WLIT 1

Littell, Robert 1935(?)- **CLC 42**
See also CA 109; 112; CANR 64, 115;
CMW 4

Little, Malcolm 1925-1965
See Malcolm X
See also BW 1, 3; CA 125; 111; CANR 82;
DA; DA3; DAB; DAC; DAM MST,
MULT; MTCW 1, 2

Littlewit, Humphrey Gent.
See Lovecraft, H(oward) P(hillips)

Litwos
See Sienkiewicz, Henryk (Adam Alexander
Pius)

Liu, E. 1857-1909 **TCLC 15**
See also CA 115; 190

Lively, Penelope (Margaret) 1933- **CLC 32,
50**
See also BPFB 2; CA 41-44R; CANR 29,
67, 79; CLR 7; CN 7; CWRI 5; DAM
NOV; DLB 14, 161, 207; FANT; JRDA;
MAICYA 1, 2; MTCW 1, 2; SATA 7, 60,
101; TEA

Livesay, Dorothy (Kathleen) 1909-1996 **CLC
4, 15, 79**
See also AITN 2; CA 25-28R; CAAS 8;
CANR 36, 67; DAC; DAM MST, POET;
DLB 68; FW; MTCW 1; RGEL 2; TWA

Livy c. 59B.C.-c. 12 **CMLC 11**
See also AW 2; CDWLB 1; DLB 211;
RGWL 2, 3

Lizardi, Jose Joaquin Fernandez de
1776-1827 **NCLC 30**
See also LAW

Llewellyn, Richard
See Llewellyn Lloyd, Richard Dafydd Viv-
ian
See also DLB 15

Llewellyn Lloyd, Richard Dafydd Vivian
1906-1983 **CLC 7, 80**
See Llewellyn, Richard
See also CA 53-56; 111; CANR 7, 71;
SATA 11; SATA-Obit 37

Llosa, (Jorge) Mario (Pedro) Vargas
See Vargas Llosa, (Jorge) Mario (Pedro)
See also RGWL 3

Llosa, Mario Vargas
See Vargas Llosa, (Jorge) Mario (Pedro)

Lloyd, Manda
See Mander, (Mary) Jane

Lloyd Webber, Andrew 1948-
See Webber, Andrew Lloyd
See also AAYA 1, 38; CA 116; 149; DAM
DRAM; SATA 56

Llull, Ramon c. 1235-c. 1316 **CMLC 12**

Lobb, Ebenezer
See Upward, Allen

Locke, Alain (Le Roy) 1886-1954 **BLCS; HR
3; TCLC 43**
See also BW 1, 3; CA 106; 124; CANR 79;
DLB 51; LMFS 2; RGAL 4

Locke, John 1632-1704 **LC 7, 35**
See also DLB 31, 101, 213, 252; RGEL 2;
WLIT 3

Locke-Elliott, Sumner
See Elliott, Sumner Locke

Lockhart, John Gibson 1794-1854 **NCLC 6**
See also DLB 110, 116, 144

Lockridge, Ross (Franklin), Jr. 1914-1948
TCLC 111
See also CA 108; 145; CANR 79; DLB 143;
DLBY 1980; RGAL 4; RHW

Lockwood, Robert
See Johnson, Robert

Lodge, David (John) 1935- **CLC 36, 141**
See also BEST 90:1; BRWS 4; CA 17-20R;
CANR 19, 53, 92; CN 7; CPW; DAM
POP; DLB 14, 194; EWL 3; INT CANR-
19; MTCW 1, 2

Lodge, Thomas 1558-1625 **LC 41**
See also DLB 172; RGEL 2

Loewinsohn, Ron(ald William) 1937- **CLC
52**
See also CA 25-28R; CANR 71

Logan, Jake
See Smith, Martin Cruz

Logan, John (Burton) 1923-1987 **CLC 5**
See also CA 77-80; 124; CANR 45; DLB 5

Lo Kuan-chung 1330(?)-1400(?) **LC 12**

Lombard, Nap
See Johnson, Pamela Hansford

London, Jack 1876-1916 **SSC 4, 49; TCLC 9,
15, 39; WLC**
See London, John Griffith
See also AAYA 13; AITN 2; AMW; BPFB
2; BYA 4, 13; CDALB 1865-1917; DLB
8, 12, 78, 212; EWL 3; EXPS; LAIT 3;
NFS 8; RGAL 4; RGSF 2; SATA 18; SFW
4; SSFS 7; TCWW 2; TUS; WYA; YAW

London, John Griffith 1876-1916
　　See London, Jack
　　See also CA 110; 119; CANR 73; DA; DA3;
　　DAB; DAC; DAM MST, NOV; JRDA;
　　MAICYA 1, 2; MTCW 1, 2
Long, Emmett
　　See Leonard, Elmore (John, Jr.)
Longbaugh, Harry
　　See Goldman, William (W.)
Longfellow, Henry Wadsworth 1807-1882
　　NCLC 2, 45, 101, 103; PC 30; WLCS
　　See also AMW; AMWR 2; CDALB 1640-
　　1865; DA; DA3; DAB; DAC; DAM MST,
　　POET; DLB 1, 59, 235; EXPP; PAB; PFS
　　2, 7, 17; RGAL 4; SATA 19; TUS; WP
Longinus c. 1st cent. - **CMLC 27**
　　See also AW 2; DLB 176
Longley, Michael 1939- **CLC 29**
　　See also BRWS 8; CA 102; CP 7; DLB 40
Longus fl. c. 2nd cent. - **CMLC 7**
Longway, A. Hugh
　　See Lang, Andrew
Lonnbohm, Armas Eino Leopold 1878-1926
　　See Leino, Eino
　　See also CA 123
Lonnrot, Elias 1802-1884 **NCLC 53**
　　See also EFS 1
Lonsdale, Roger ed. CLC 65
Lopate, Phillip 1943- **CLC 29**
　　See also CA 97-100; CANR 88; DLBY
　　1980; INT CA-97-100
Lopez, Barry (Holstun) 1945- **CLC 70**
　　See also AAYA 9; ANW; CA 65-68; CANR
　　7, 23, 47, 68, 92; DLB 256, 275; INT
　　CANR-7, -23; MTCW 1; RGAL 4; SATA
　　67
Lopez Portillo (y Pacheco), Jose 1920-2004
　　CLC 46
　　See also CA 129; HW 1
Lopez y Fuentes, Gregorio 1897(?)-1966 **CLC
　　32**
　　See also CA 131; EWL 3; HW 1
Lorca, Federico Garcia
　　See Garcia Lorca, Federico
　　See also DFS 4; EW 11; RGWL 2, 3; WP
Lord, Audre
　　See Lorde, Audre (Geraldine)
　　See also EWL 3
Lord, Bette Bao 1938- **AAL; CLC 23**
　　See also BEST 90:3; BPFB 2; CA 107;
　　CANR 41, 79; INT CA-107; SATA 58
Lord Auch
　　See Bataille, Georges
Lord Brooke
　　See Greville, Fulke
Lord Byron
　　See Byron, George Gordon (Noel)
Lorde, Audre (Geraldine) 1934-1992 **BLC 2;
　　CLC 18, 71; PC 12**
　　See Domini, Rey; Lord, Audre
　　See also AFAW 1, 2; BW 1, 3; CA 25-28R;
　　142; CANR 16, 26, 46, 82; DA3; DAM
　　MULT, POET; DLB 41; FW; MTCW 1,
　　2; PFS 16; RGAL 4
Lord Houghton
　　See Milnes, Richard Monckton
Lord Jeffrey
　　See Jeffrey, Francis
Loreaux, Nichol CLC 65
Lorenzini, Carlo 1826-1890
　　See Collodi, Carlo
　　See also MAICYA 1, 2; SATA 29, 100
Lorenzo, Heberto Padilla
　　See Padilla (Lorenzo), Heberto
Loris
　　See Hofmannsthal, Hugo von
Loti, Pierre TCLC 11
　　See Viaud, (Louis Marie) Julien
　　See also DLB 123; GFL 1789 to the Present

Lou, Henri
　　See Andreas-Salome, Lou
Louie, David Wong 1954- **CLC 70**
　　See also CA 139; CANR 120
Louis, Adrian C. NNAL
Louis, Father M.
　　See Merton, Thomas (James)
Louise, Heidi
　　See Erdrich, Louise
Lovecraft, H(oward) P(hillips) 1890-1937
　　SSC 3, 52; TCLC 4, 22
　　See also AAYA 14; BPFB 2; CA 104; 133;
　　CANR 106; DA3; DAM POP; HGG;
　　MTCW 1, 2; RGAL 4; SCFW; SFW 4;
　　SUFW
Lovelace, Earl 1935- **CLC 51**
　　See also BW 2; CA 77-80; CANR 41, 72,
　　114; CD 5; CDWLB 3; CN 7; DLB 125;
　　EWL 3; MTCW 1
Lovelace, Richard 1618-1657 **LC 24**
　　See also BRW 2; DLB 131; EXPP; PAB;
　　RGEL 2
Lowe, Pardee 1904- **AAL**
Lowell, Amy 1874-1925 **PC 13; TCLC 1, 8**
　　See also AMW; CA 104; 151; DAM POET;
　　DLB 54, 140; EWL 3; EXPP; LMFS 2;
　　MAWW; MTCW 2; RGAL 4; TUS
Lowell, James Russell 1819-1891 **NCLC 2,
　　90**
　　See also AMWS 1; CDALB 1640-1865;
　　DLB 1, 11, 64, 79, 189, 235; RGAL 4
Lowell, Robert (Traill Spence, Jr.)
　　1917-1977 **CLC 1, 2, 3, 4, 5, 8, 9, 11, 15,
　　37, 124; PC 3; WLC**
　　See also AMW; AMWC 2; AMWR 2; CA
　　9-12R; 73-76; CABS 2; CANR 26, 60;
　　CDALBS; DA; DA3; DAB; DAC; DAM
　　MST, NOV; DLB 5, 169; EWL 3; MTCW
　　1, 2; PAB; PFS 6, 7; RGAL 4; WP
Lowenthal, Michael (Francis) 1969- **CLC 119**
　　See also CA 150; CANR 115
Lowndes, Marie Adelaide (Belloc) 1868-1947
　　TCLC 12
　　See also CA 107; CMW 4; DLB 70; RHW
Lowry, (Clarence) Malcolm 1909-1957 **SSC
　　31; TCLC 6, 40**
　　See also BPFB 2; BRWS 3; CA 105; 131;
　　CANR 62, 105; CDBLB 1945-1960; DLB
　　15; EWL 3; MTCW 1, 2; RGEL 2
Lowry, Mina Gertrude 1882-1966
　　See Loy, Mina
　　See also CA 113
Loxsmith, John
　　See Brunner, John (Kilian Houston)
Loy, Mina CLC 28; PC 16
　　See Lowry, Mina Gertrude
　　See also DAM POET; DLB 4, 54
Loyson-Bridet
　　See Schwob, Marcel (Mayer Andre)
Lucan 39-65 **CMLC 33**
　　See also AW 2; DLB 211; EFS 2; RGWL 2,
　　3
Lucas, Craig 1951- **CLC 64**
　　See also CA 137; CAD; CANR 71, 109;
　　CD 5; GLL 2
Lucas, E(dward) V(errall) 1868-1938 **TCLC
　　73**
　　See also CA 176; DLB 98, 149, 153; SATA
　　20
Lucas, George 1944- **CLC 16**
　　See also AAYA 1, 23; CA 77-80; CANR
　　30; SATA 56
Lucas, Hans
　　See Godard, Jean-Luc
Lucas, Victoria
　　See Plath, Sylvia
Lucian c. 125-c. 180 **CMLC 32**
　　See also AW 2; DLB 176; RGWL 2, 3

Lucretius c. 94B.C.-c. 49B.C. **CMLC 48**
　　See also AW 2; CDWLB 1; DLB 211; EFS
　　2; RGWL 2, 3
Ludlam, Charles 1943-1987 **CLC 46, 50**
　　See also CA 85-88; 122; CAD; CANR 72,
　　86; DLB 266
Ludlum, Robert 1927-2001 **CLC 22, 43**
　　See also AAYA 10; BEST 89:1, 90:3; BPFB
　　2; CA 33-36R; 195; CANR 25, 41, 68,
　　105; CMW 4; CPW; DA3; DAM NOV,
　　POP; DLBY 1982; MSW; MTCW 1, 2
Ludwig, Ken CLC 60
　　See also CA 195; CAD
Ludwig, Otto 1813-1865 **NCLC 4**
　　See also DLB 129
Lugones, Leopoldo 1874-1938 **HLCS 2;
　　TCLC 15**
　　See also CA 116; 131; CANR 104; DLB
　　283; EWL 3; HW 1; LAW
Lu Hsun SSC 20; TCLC 3
　　See Shu-Jen, Chou
　　See also EWL 3
Lukacs, George CLC 24
　　See Lukacs, Gyorgy (Szegeny von)
Lukacs, Gyorgy (Szegeny von) 1885-1971
　　See Lukacs, George
　　See also CA 101; 29-32R; CANR 62; CD-
　　WLB 4; DLB 215, 242; EW 10; EWL 3;
　　MTCW 2
Luke, Peter (Ambrose Cyprian) 1919-1995
　　CLC 38
　　See also CA 81-84; 147; CANR 72; CBD;
　　CD 5; DLB 13
Lunar, Dennis
　　See Mungo, Raymond
Lurie, Alison 1926- **CLC 4, 5, 18, 39, 175**
　　See also BPFB 2; CA 1-4R; CANR 2, 17,
　　50, 88; CN 7; DLB 2; MTCW 1; SATA
　　46, 112
Lustig, Arnost 1926- **CLC 56**
　　See also AAYA 3; CA 69-72; CANR 47,
　　102; CWW 2; DLB 232; EWL 3; SATA
　　56
Luther, Martin 1483-1546 **LC 9, 37**
　　See also CDWLB 2; DLB 179; EW 2;
　　RGWL 2, 3
Luxemburg, Rosa 1870(?)-1919 **TCLC 63**
　　See also CA 118
Luzi, Mario 1914- **CLC 13**
　　See also CA 61-64; CANR 9, 70; CWW 2;
　　DLB 128; EWL 3
L'vov, Arkady CLC 59
Lydgate, John c. 1370-1450(?) **LC 81**
　　See also BRW 1; DLB 146; RGEL 2
Lyly, John 1554(?)-1606 **DC 7; LC 41**
　　See also BRW 1; DAM DRAM; DLB 62,
　　167; RGEL 2
L'Ymagier
　　See Gourmont, Remy(-Marie-Charles) de
Lynch, B. Suarez
　　See Borges, Jorge Luis
Lynch, David (Keith) 1946- **CLC 66, 162**
　　See also AAYA 55; CA 124; 129; CANR
　　111
Lynch, James
　　See Andreyev, Leonid (Nikolaevich)
Lyndsay, Sir David 1485-1555 **LC 20**
　　See also RGEL 2
Lynn, Kenneth S(chuyler) 1923-2001 **CLC
　　50**
　　See also CA 1-4R; 196; CANR 3, 27, 65
Lynx
　　See West, Rebecca
Lyons, Marcus
　　See Blish, James (Benjamin)
Lyotard, Jean-Francois 1924-1998 **TCLC 103**
　　See also DLB 242; EWL 3

Lyre, Pinchbeck
See Sassoon, Siegfried (Lorraine)

Lytle, Andrew (Nelson) 1902-1995 **CLC 22**
See also CA 9-12R; 150; CANR 70; CN 7;
CSW; DLB 6; DLBY 1995; RGAL 4;
RHW

Lyttelton, George 1709-1773 **LC 10**
See also RGEL 2

Lytton of Knebworth, Baron
See Bulwer-Lytton, Edward (George Earle
Lytton)

Maas, Peter 1929-2001 **CLC 29**
See also CA 93-96; 201; INT CA-93-96;
MTCW 2

Macaulay, Catherine 1731-1791 **LC 64**
See also DLB 104

Macaulay, (Emilie) Rose 1881(?)-1958 **TCLC
7, 44**
See also CA 104; DLB 36; EWL 3; RGEL
2; RHW

Macaulay, Thomas Babington 1800-1859
NCLC 42
See also BRW 4; CDBLB 1832-1890; DLB
32, 55; RGEL 2

MacBeth, George (Mann) 1932-1992 **CLC 2,
5, 9**
See also CA 25-28R; 136; CANR 61, 66;
DLB 40; MTCW 1; PFS 8; SATA 4;
SATA-Obit 70

MacCaig, Norman (Alexander) 1910-1996
CLC 36
See also BRWS 6; CA 9-12R; CANR 3, 34;
CP 7; DAB; DAM POET; DLB 27; EWL
3; RGEL 2

MacCarthy, Sir (Charles Otto) Desmond
1877-1952 **TCLC 36**
See also CA 167

MacDiarmid, Hugh **CLC 2, 4, 11, 19, 63; PC
9**
See Grieve, C(hristopher) M(urray)
See also CDBLB 1945-1960; DLB 20;
EWL 3; RGEL 2

MacDonald, Anson
See Heinlein, Robert A(nson)

Macdonald, Cynthia 1928- **CLC 13, 19**
See also CA 49-52; CANR 4, 44; DLB 105

MacDonald, George 1824-1905 **TCLC 9, 113**
See also BYA 5; CA 106; 137; CANR 80;
CLR 67; DLB 18, 163, 178; FANT; MAI-
CYA 1, 2; RGEL 2; SATA 33, 100; SFW
4; SUFW; WCH

Macdonald, John
See Millar, Kenneth

MacDonald, John D(ann) 1916-1986 **CLC 3,
27, 44**
See also BPFB 2; CA 1-4R; 121; CANR 1,
19, 60; CMW 4; CPW; DAM NOV, POP;
DLB 8; DLBY 1986; MSW; MTCW 1, 2;
SFW 4

Macdonald, John Ross
See Millar, Kenneth

Macdonald, Ross **CLC 1, 2, 3, 14, 34, 41**
See Millar, Kenneth
See also AMWS 4; BPFB 2; DLBD 6;
MSW; RGAL 4

MacDougal, John
See Blish, James (Benjamin)

MacDougal, John
See Blish, James (Benjamin)

MacDowell, John
See Parks, Tim(othy Harold)

MacEwen, Gwendolyn (Margaret)
1941-1987 **CLC 13, 55**
See also CA 9-12R; 124; CANR 7, 22; DLB
53, 251; SATA 50; SATA-Obit 55

Macha, Karel Hynek 1810-1846 **NCLC 46**

Machado (y Ruiz), Antonio 1875-1939 **TCLC
3**
See also CA 104; 174; DLB 108; EW 9;
EWL 3; HW 2; RGWL 2, 3

Machado de Assis, Joaquim Maria
1839-1908 **BLC 2; HLCS 2; SSC 24;
TCLC 10**
See also CA 107; 153; CANR 91; LAW;
RGSF 2; RGWL 2, 3; TWA; WLIT 1

Machaut, Guillaume de c. 1300-1377 **CMLC
64**
See also DLB 208

Machen, Arthur **SSC 20; TCLC 4**
See Jones, Arthur Llewellyn
See also CA 179; DLB 156, 178; RGEL 2;
SUFW 1

Machiavelli, Niccolo 1469-1527 **DC 16; LC 8,
36; WLCS**
See also DA; DAB; DAC; DAM MST; EW
2; LAIT 1; LMFS 1; NFS 9; RGWL 2, 3;
TWA

MacInnes, Colin 1914-1976 **CLC 4, 23**
See also CA 69-72; 65-68; CANR 21; DLB
14; MTCW 1, 2; RGEL 2; RHW

MacInnes, Helen (Clark) 1907-1985 **CLC 27,
39**
See also BPFB 2; CA 1-4R; 117; CANR 1,
28, 58; CMW 4; CPW; DAM POP; DLB
87; MSW; MTCW 1, 2; SATA 22; SATA-
Obit 44

Mackay, Mary 1855-1924
See Corelli, Marie
See also CA 118; 177; FANT; RHW

Mackenzie, Compton (Edward Montague)
1883-1972 **CLC 18; TCLC 116**
See also CA 21-22; 37-40R; CAP 2; DLB
34, 100; RGEL 2

Mackenzie, Henry 1745-1831 **NCLC 41**
See also DLB 39; RGEL 2

Mackey, Nathaniel (Ernest) 1947- **PC 49**
See also CA 153; CANR 114; CP 7; DLB
169

MacKinnon, Catharine A. 1946- **CLC 181**
See also CA 128; 132; CANR 73; FW;
MTCW 2

Mackintosh, Elizabeth 1896(?)-1952
See Tey, Josephine
See also CA 110; CMW 4

MacLaren, James
See Grieve, C(hristopher) M(urray)

Mac Laverty, Bernard 1942- **CLC 31**
See also CA 116; 118; CANR 43, 88; CN
7; DLB 267; INT CA-118; RGSF 2

MacLean, Alistair (Stuart) 1922(?)-1987 **CLC
3, 13, 50, 63**
See also CA 57-60; 121; CANR 28, 61;
CMW 4; CPW; DAM POP; DLB 276;
MTCW 1; SATA 23; SATA-Obit 50;
TCWW 2

Maclean, Norman (Fitzroy) 1902-1990 **CLC
78; SSC 13**
See also CA 102; 132; CANR 49; CPW;
DAM POP; DLB 206; TCWW 2

MacLeish, Archibald 1892-1982 **CLC 3, 8,
14, 68; PC 47**
See also AMW; CA 9-12R; 106; CAD;
CANR 33, 63; CDALBS; DAM POET;
DFS 15; DLB 4, 7, 45; DLBY 1982; EWL
3; EXPP; MTCW 1, 2; PAB; PFS 5;
RGAL 4; TUS

MacLennan, (John) Hugh 1907-1990 **CLC 2,
14, 92**
See also CA 5-8R; 142; CANR 33; DAC;
DAM MST; DLB 68; EWL 3; MTCW 1,
2; RGEL 2; TWA

MacLeod, Alistair 1936- **CLC 56, 165**
See also CA 123; CCA 1; DAC; DAM
MST; DLB 60; MTCW 2; RGSF 2

Macleod, Fiona
See Sharp, William
See also RGEL 2; SUFW

MacNeice, (Frederick) Louis 1907-1963 **CLC
1, 4, 10, 53**
See also BRW 7; CA 85-88; CANR 61;
DAB; DAM POET; DLB 10, 20; EWL 3;
MTCW 1, 2; RGEL 2

MacNeill, Dand
See Fraser, George MacDonald

Macpherson, James 1736-1796 **LC 29**
See Ossian
See also BRWS 8; DLB 109; RGEL 2

Macpherson, (Jean) Jay 1931- **CLC 14**
See also CA 5-8R; CANR 90; CP 7; CWP;
DLB 53

Macrobius fl. 430- **CMLC 48**

MacShane, Frank 1927-1999 **CLC 39**
See also CA 9-12R; 186; CANR 3, 33; DLB
111

Macumber, Mari
See Sandoz, Mari(e Susette)

Madach, Imre 1823-1864 **NCLC 19**

Madden, (Jerry) David 1933- **CLC 5, 15**
See also CA 1-4R; CAAS 3; CANR 4, 45;
CN 7; CSW; DLB 6; MTCW 1

Maddern, Al(an)
See Ellison, Harlan (Jay)

Madhubuti, Haki R. 1942- **BLC 2; CLC 6,
73; PC 5**
See Lee, Don L.
See also BW 2, 3; CA 73-76; CANR 24,
51, 73; CP 7; CSW; DAM MULT, POET;
DLB 5, 41; DLBD 8; EWL 3; MTCW 2;
RGAL 4

Madison, James 1751-1836 **NCLC 126**
See also DLB 37

Maepenn, Hugh
See Kuttner, Henry

Maepenn, K. H.
See Kuttner, Henry

Maeterlinck, Maurice 1862-1949 **TCLC 3**
See also CA 104; 136; CANR 80; DAM
DRAM; DLB 192; EW 8; EWL 3; GFL
1789 to the Present; LMFS 2; RGWL 2,
3; SATA 66; TWA

Maginn, William 1794-1842 **NCLC 8**
See also DLB 110, 159

Mahapatra, Jayanta 1928- **CLC 33**
See also CA 73-76; CAAS 9; CANR 15,
33, 66, 87; CP 7; DAM MULT

Mahfouz, Naguib (Abdel Aziz Al-Sabilgi)
1911(?)- **CLC 153; SSC 66**
See Mahfuz, Najib (Abdel Aziz al-Sabilgi)
See also AAYA 49; BEST 89:2; CA 128;
CANR 55, 101; CWW 2; DA3; DAM
NOV; MTCW 1, 2; RGWL 2, 3; SSFS 9

Mahfuz, Najib (Abdel Aziz al-Sabilgi) **CLC
52, 55**
See Mahfouz, Naguib (Abdel Aziz Al-
Sabilgi)
See also AFW; DLBY 1988; EWL 3; RGSF
2; WLIT 2

Mahon, Derek 1941- **CLC 27**
See also BRWS 6; CA 113; 128; CANR 88;
CP 7; DLB 40; EWL 3

Maiakovskii, Vladimir
See Mayakovski, Vladimir (Vladimirovich)
See also IDTP; RGWL 2, 3

Mailer, Norman 1923- **CLC 1, 2, 3, 4, 5, 8,
11, 14, 28, 39, 74, 111**
See also AAYA 31; AITN 2; AMW; AMWC
2; AMWR 2; BPFB 2; CA 9-12R; CABS
1; CANR 28, 74, 77; CDALB 1968-1988;
CN 7; CPW; DA; DA3; DAB; DAC;
DAM MST, NOV, POP; DLB 2, 16, 28,
185, 278; DLBD 3; DLBY 1980, 1983;
EWL 3; MTCW 1, 2; NFS 10; RGAL 4;
TUS

Maillet, Antonine 1929- **CLC 54, 118**
See also CA 115; 120; CANR 46, 74, 77;
CCA 1; CWW 2; DAC; DLB 60; INT CA-
120; MTCW 2

Mais, Roger 1905-1955 **TCLC 8**
See also BW 1, 3; CA 105; 124; CANR 82;
CDWLB 3; DLB 125; EWL 3; MTCW 1;
RGEL 2

Maistre, Joseph 1753-1821 **NCLC 37**
See also GFL 1789 to the Present

Maitland, Frederic William 1850-1906 **TCLC 65**

Maitland, Sara (Louise) 1950- **CLC 49**
See also CA 69-72; CANR 13, 59; DLB 271; FW

Major, Clarence 1936- **BLC 2; CLC 3, 19, 48**
See also AFAW 2; BW 2, 3; CA 21-24R;
CAAS 6; CANR 13, 25, 53, 82; CN 7;
CP 7; CSW; DAM MULT; DLB 33; EWL
3; MSW

Major, Kevin (Gerald) 1949- **CLC 26**
See also AAYA 16; CA 97-100; CANR 21,
38, 112; CLR 11; DAC; DLB 60; INT
CANR-21; JRDA; MAICYA 1, 2; MAIC-
YAS 1; SATA 32, 82, 134; WYA; YAW

Maki, James
See Ozu, Yasujiro

Malabaila, Damiano
See Levi, Primo

Malamud, Bernard 1914-1986 **CLC 1, 2, 3,
5, 8, 9, 11, 18, 27, 44, 78, 85; SSC 15;
TCLC 129; WLC**
See also AAYA 16; AMWS 1; BPFB 2;
BYA 15; CA 5-8R; 118; CABS 1; CANR
28, 62, 114; CDALB 1941-1968; CPW;
DA; DA3; DAB; DAC; DAM MST, NOV,
POP; DLB 2, 28, 152; DLBY 1980, 1986;
EWL 3; EXPS; LAIT 4; LATS 1; MTCW
1, 2; NFS 4, 9; RGAL 4; RGSF 2; SSFS
8, 13, 16; TUS

Malan, Herman
See Bosman, Herman Charles; Bosman,
Herman Charles

Malaparte, Curzio 1898-1957 **TCLC 52**
See also DLB 264

Malcolm, Dan
See Silverberg, Robert

Malcolm X BLC 2; CLC 82, 117; WLCS
See Little, Malcolm
See also LAIT 5; NCFS 3

Malherbe, Francois de 1555-1628 **LC 5**
See also GFL Beginnings to 1789

Mallarme, Stephane 1842-1898 **NCLC 4, 41;
PC 4**
See also DAM POET; DLB 217; EW 7;
GFL 1789 to the Present; LMFS 2; RGWL
2, 3; TWA

Mallet-Joris, Francoise 1930- **CLC 11**
See also CA 65-68; CANR 17; DLB 83;
EWL 3; GFL 1789 to the Present

Malley, Ern
See McAuley, James Phillip

Mallon, Thomas 1951- **CLC 172**
See also CA 110; CANR 29, 57, 92

Mallowan, Agatha Christie
See Christie, Agatha (Mary Clarissa)

Maloff, Saul 1922- **CLC 5**
See also CA 33-36R

Malone, Louis
See MacNeice, (Frederick) Louis

Malone, Michael (Christopher) 1942- **CLC 43**
See also CA 77-80; CANR 14, 32, 57, 114

Malory, Sir Thomas 1410(?)-1471(?) **LC 11,
88; WLCS**
See also BRW 1; BRWR 2; CDBLB Before
1660; DA; DAB; DAC; DAM MST; DLB
146; EFS 2; RGEL 2; SATA 59; SATA-
Brief 33; TEA; WLIT 3

Malouf, (George Joseph) David 1934- **CLC
28, 86**
See also CA 124; CANR 50, 76; CN 7; CP
7; DLB 289; EWL 3; MTCW 2

Malraux, (Georges-)Andre 1901-1976 **CLC
1, 4, 9, 13, 15, 57**
See also BPFB 2; CA 21-22; 69-72; CANR
34, 58; CAP 2; DA3; DAM NOV; DLB
72; EW 12; EWL 3; GFL 1789 to the
Present; MTCW 1, 2; RGWL 2, 3; TWA

Malzberg, Barry N(athaniel) 1939- **CLC 7**
See also CA 61-64; CAAS 4; CANR 16;
CMW 4; DLB 8; SFW 4

Mamet, David (Alan) 1947- **CLC 9, 15, 34,
46, 91, 166; DC 4**
See also AAYA 3; CA 81-84; CABS 3;
CANR 15, 41, 67, 72, 129; CD 5; DA3;
DAM DRAM; DFS 2, 3, 6, 12, 15; DLB
7; EWL 3; IDFW 4; MTCW 1, 2; RGAL
4

Mamoulian, Rouben (Zachary) 1897-1987
CLC 16
See also CA 25-28R; 124; CANR 85

Mandelshtam, Osip
See Mandelstam, Osip (Emilievich)
See also EW 10; EWL 3; RGWL 2, 3

Mandelstam, Osip (Emilievich)
1891(?)-1943(?) **PC 14; TCLC 2, 6**
See Mandelshtam, Osip
See also CA 104; 150; MTCW 2; TWA

Mander, (Mary) Jane 1877-1949 **TCLC 31**
See also CA 162; RGEL 2

Mandeville, Bernard 1670-1733 **LC 82**
See also DLB 101

Mandeville, Sir John fl. 1350- **CMLC 19**
See also DLB 146

Mandiargues, Andre Pieyre de CLC 41
See Pieyre de Mandiargues, Andre
See also DLB 83

Mandrake, Ethel Belle
See Thurman, Wallace (Henry)

Mangan, James Clarence 1803-1849 **NCLC
27**
See also RGEL 2

Maniere, J.-E.
See Giraudoux, Jean(-Hippolyte)

Mankiewicz, Herman (Jacob) 1897-1953
TCLC 85
See also CA 120; 169; DLB 26; IDFW 3, 4

Manley, (Mary) Delariviere 1672(?)-1724 **LC
1, 42**
See also DLB 39, 80; RGEL 2

Mann, Abel
See Creasey, John

Mann, Emily 1952- **DC 7**
See also CA 130; CAD; CANR 55; CD 5;
CWD; DLB 266

Mann, (Luiz) Heinrich 1871-1950 **TCLC 9**
See also CA 106; 164, 181; DLB 66, 118;
EW 8; EWL 3; RGWL 2, 3

Mann, (Paul) Thomas 1875-1955 **SSC 5, 70;
TCLC 2, 8, 14, 21, 35, 44, 60; WLC**
See also BPFB 2; CA 104; 128; CDWLB 2;
DA; DA3; DAB; DAC; DAM MST, NOV;
DLB 66; EW 9; EWL 3; GLL 1; LATS 1;
LMFS 1; MTCW 1, 2; NFS 17; RGSF 2;
RGWL 2, 3; SSFS 4, 9; TWA

Mannheim, Karl 1893-1947 **TCLC 65**
See also CA 204

Manning, David
See Faust, Frederick (Schiller)
See also TCWW 2

Manning, Frederic 1882-1935 **TCLC 25**
See also CA 124; 216; DLB 260

Manning, Olivia 1915-1980 **CLC 5, 19**
See also CA 5-8R; 101; CANR 29; EWL 3;
FW; MTCW 1; RGEL 2

Mano, D. Keith 1942- **CLC 2, 10**
See also CA 25-28R; CAAS 6; CANR 26,
57; DLB 6

**Mansfield, Katherine SSC 9, 23, 38; TCLC
2, 8, 39; WLC**
See Beauchamp, Kathleen Mansfield
See also BPFB 2; BRW 7; DAB; DLB 162;
EWL 3; EXPS; FW; GLL 1; RGEL 2;
RGSF 2; SSFS 2, 8, 10, 11; WWE 1

Manso, Peter 1940- **CLC 39**
See also CA 29-32R; CANR 44

Mantecon, Juan Jimenez
See Jimenez (Mantecon), Juan Ramon

Mantel, Hilary (Mary) 1952- **CLC 144**
See also CA 125; CANR 54, 101; CN 7;
DLB 271; RHW

Manton, Peter
See Creasey, John

Man Without a Spleen, A
See Chekhov, Anton (Pavlovich)

Manzoni, Alessandro 1785-1873 **NCLC 29,
98**
See also EW 5; RGWL 2, 3; TWA

Map, Walter 1140-1209 **CMLC 32**

Mapu, Abraham (ben Jekutiel) 1808-1867
NCLC 18

Mara, Sally
See Queneau, Raymond

Maracle, Lee 1950- **NNAL**
See also CA 149

Marat, Jean Paul 1743-1793 **LC 10**

Marcel, Gabriel Honore 1889-1973 **CLC 15**
See also CA 102; 45-48; EWL 3; MTCW 1,
2

March, William 1893-1954 **TCLC 96**
See also CA 216

Marchbanks, Samuel
See Davies, (William) Robertson
See also CCA 1

Marchi, Giacomo
See Bassani, Giorgio

Marcus Aurelius
See Aurelius, Marcus
See also AW 2

Marguerite
See de Navarre, Marguerite

Marguerite d'Angouleme
See de Navarre, Marguerite
See also GFL Beginnings to 1789

Marguerite de Navarre
See de Navarre, Marguerite
See also RGWL 2, 3

Margulies, Donald 1954- **CLC 76**
See also CA 200; DFS 13; DLB 228

Marie de France c. 12th cent. - **CMLC 8; PC
22**
See also DLB 208; FW; RGWL 2, 3

Marie de l'Incarnation 1599-1672 **LC 10**

Marier, Captain Victor
See Griffith, D(avid Lewelyn) W(ark)

Mariner, Scott
See Pohl, Frederik

Marinetti, Filippo Tommaso 1876-1944
TCLC 10
See also CA 107; DLB 114, 264; EW 9;
EWL 3

Marivaux, Pierre Carlet de Chamblain de
1688-1763 **DC 7; LC 4**
See also GFL Beginnings to 1789; RGWL
2, 3; TWA

Markandaya, Kamala CLC 8, 38
See Taylor, Kamala (Purnaiya)
See also BYA 13; CN 7; EWL 3

Markfield, Wallace 1926-2002 **CLC 8**
See also CA 69-72; 208; CAAS 3; CN 7;
DLB 2, 28; DLBY 2002

Markham, Edwin 1852-1940 **TCLC 47**
See also CA 160; DLB 54, 186; RGAL 4

Markham, Robert
See Amis, Kingsley (William)
Markoosie NNAL
See Patsauq, Markoosie
See also CLR 23; DAM MULT
Marks, J
See Highwater, Jamake (Mamake)
Marks, J.
See Highwater, Jamake (Mamake)
Marks-Highwater, J
See Highwater, Jamake (Mamake)
Marks-Highwater, J.
See Highwater, Jamake (Mamake)
Markson, David M(errill) 1927- **CLC 67**
See also CA 49-52; CANR 1, 91; CN 7
Marlatt, Daphne (Buckle) 1942- **CLC 168**
See also CA 25-28R; CANR 17, 39; CN 7;
CP 7; CWP; DLB 60; FW
Marley, Bob CLC 17
See Marley, Robert Nesta
Marley, Robert Nesta 1945-1981
See Marley, Bob
See also CA 107; 103
Marlowe, Christopher 1564-1593 **DC 1; LC
22, 47; WLC**
See also BRW 1; BRWR 1; CDBLB Before
1660; DA; DA3; DAB; DAC; DAM
DRAM, MST; DFS 1, 5, 13; DLB 62;
EXPP; LMFS 1; RGEL 2; TEA; WLIT 3
Marlowe, Stephen 1928- **CLC 70**
See Queen, Ellery
See also CA 13-16R; CANR 6, 55; CMW
4; SFW 4
Marmion, Shakerley 1603-1639 **LC 89**
See also DLB 58; RGEL 2
Marmontel, Jean-Francois 1723-1799 **LC 2**
Maron, Monika 1941- **CLC 165**
See also CA 201
Marquand, John P(hillips) 1893-1960 **CLC
2, 10**
See also AMW; BPFB 2; CA 85-88; CANR
73; CMW 4; DLB 9, 102; EWL 3; MTCW
2; RGAL 4
Marques, Rene 1919-1979 **CLC 96; HLC 2**
See also CA 97-100; 85-88; CANR 78;
DAM MULT; DLB 113; EWL 3; HW 1,
2; LAW; RGSF 2
Marquez, Gabriel (Jose) Garcia
See Garcia Marquez, Gabriel (Jose)
Marquis, Don(ald Robert Perry) 1878-1937
TCLC 7
See also CA 104; 166; DLB 11, 25; RGAL
4
Marquis de Sade
See Sade, Donatien Alphonse Francois
Marric, J. J.
See Creasey, John
See also MSW
Marryat, Frederick 1792-1848 **NCLC 3**
See also DLB 21, 163; RGEL 2; WCH
Marsden, James
See Creasey, John
Marsh, Edward 1872-1953 **TCLC 99**
Marsh, (Edith) Ngaio 1895-1982 **CLC 7, 53**
See also CA 9-12R; CANR 6, 58; CMW 4;
CPW; DAM POP; DLB 77; MSW;
MTCW 1, 2; RGEL 2; TEA
Marshall, Garry 1934- **CLC 17**
See also AAYA 3; CA 111; SATA 60
Marshall, Paule 1929- **BLC 3; CLC 27, 72;
SSC 3**
See also AFAW 1, 2; AMWS 11; BPFB 2;
BW 2, 3; CA 77-80; CANR 25, 73, 129;
CN 7; DA3; DAM MULT; DLB 33, 157,
227; EWL 3; LATS 1; MTCW 1, 2;
RGAL 4; SSFS 15
Marshallik
See Zangwill, Israel

Marsten, Richard
See Hunter, Evan
Marston, John 1576-1634 **LC 33**
See also BRW 2; DAM DRAM; DLB 58,
172; RGEL 2
Martha, Henry
See Harris, Mark
Marti, Jose
See Marti (y Perez), Jose (Julian)
See also DLB 290
Marti (y Perez), Jose (Julian) 1853-1895 **HLC
2; NCLC 63**
See Marti, Jose
See also DAM MULT; HW 2; LAW; RGWL
2, 3; WLIT 1
Martial c. 40-c. 104 **CMLC 35; PC 10**
See also AW 2; CDWLB 1; DLB 211;
RGWL 2, 3
Martin, Ken
See Hubbard, L(afayette) Ron(ald)
Martin, Richard
See Creasey, John
Martin, Steve 1945- **CLC 30**
See also AAYA 53; CA 97-100; CANR 30,
100; MTCW 1
Martin, Valerie 1948- **CLC 89**
See also BEST 90:2; CA 85-88; CANR 49,
89
Martin, Violet Florence 1862-1915 **SSC 56;
TCLC 51**
Martin, Webber
See Silverberg, Robert
Martindale, Patrick Victor
See White, Patrick (Victor Martindale)
Martin du Gard, Roger 1881-1958 **TCLC 24**
See also CA 118; CANR 94; DLB 65; EWL
3; GFL 1789 to the Present; RGWL 2, 3
Martineau, Harriet 1802-1876 **NCLC 26, 137**
See also DLB 21, 55, 159, 163, 166, 190;
FW; RGEL 2; YABC 2
Martines, Julia
See O'Faolain, Julia
Martinez, Enrique Gonzalez
See Gonzalez Martinez, Enrique
Martinez, Jacinto Benavente y
See Benavente (y Martinez), Jacinto
Martinez de la Rosa, Francisco de Paula
1787-1862 **NCLC 102**
See also TWA
Martinez Ruiz, Jose 1873-1967
See Azorin; Ruiz, Jose Martinez
See also CA 93-96; HW 1
Martinez Sierra, Gregorio 1881-1947 **TCLC
6**
See also CA 115; EWL 3
Martinez Sierra, Maria (de la O'LeJarraga)
1874-1974 **TCLC 6**
See also CA 115; EWL 3
Martinsen, Martin
See Follett, Ken(neth Martin)
Martinson, Harry (Edmund) 1904-1978 **CLC
14**
See also CA 77-80; CANR 34; DLB 259;
EWL 3
Martyn, Edward 1859-1923 **TCLC 131**
See also CA 179; DLB 10; RGEL 2
Marut, Ret
See Traven, B.
Marut, Robert
See Traven, B.
Marvell, Andrew 1621-1678 **LC 4, 43; PC
10; WLC**
See also BRW 2; BRWR 2; CDBLB 1660-
1789; DA; DAB; DAC; DAM MST,
POET; DLB 131; EXPP; PFS 5; RGEL 2;
TEA; WP
Marx, Karl (Heinrich) 1818-1883 **NCLC 17,
114**
See also DLB 129; LATS 1; TWA

Masaoka, Shiki -1902 **TCLC 18**
See Masaoka, Tsunenori
See also RGWL 3
Masaoka, Tsunenori 1867-1902
See Masaoka, Shiki
See also CA 117; 191; TWA
Masefield, John (Edward) 1878-1967 **CLC
11, 47**
See also CA 19-20; 25-28R; CANR 33;
CAP 2; CDBLB 1890-1914; DAM POET;
DLB 10, 19, 153, 160; EWL 3; EXPP;
FANT; MTCW 1, 2; PFS 5; RGEL 2;
SATA 19
Maso, Carole 19(?)- **CLC 44**
See also CA 170; GLL 2; RGAL 4
Mason, Bobbie Ann 1940- **CLC 28, 43, 82,
154; SSC 4**
See also AAYA 5, 42; AMWS 8; BPFB 2;
CA 53-56; CANR 11, 31, 58, 83, 125;
CDALBS; CN 7; CSW; DA3; DLB 173;
DLBY 1987; EWL 3; EXPS; INT CANR-
31; MTCW 1, 2; NFS 4; RGAL 4; RGSF
2; SSFS 3,8; YAW
Mason, Ernst
See Pohl, Frederik
Mason, Hunni B.
See Sternheim, (William Adolf) Carl
Mason, Lee W.
See Malzberg, Barry N(athaniel)
Mason, Nick 1945- **CLC 35**
Mason, Tally
See Derleth, August (William)
Mass, Anna CLC 59
Mass, William
See Gibson, William
Massinger, Philip 1583-1640 **LC 70**
See also DLB 58; RGEL 2
Master Lao
See Lao Tzu
Masters, Edgar Lee 1868-1950 **PC 1, 36;
TCLC 2, 25; WLCS**
See also AMWS 1; CA 104; 133; CDALB
1865-1917; DA; DAC; DAM MST,
POET; DLB 54; EWL 3; EXPP; MTCW
1, 2; RGAL 4; TUS; WP
Masters, Hilary 1928- **CLC 48**
See also CA 25-28R, 217; CAAE 217;
CANR 13, 47, 97; CN 7; DLB 244
Mastrosimone, William 19(?)- **CLC 36**
See also CA 186; CAD; CD 5
Mathe, Albert
See Camus, Albert
Mather, Cotton 1663-1728 **LC 38**
See also AMWS 2; CDALB 1640-1865;
DLB 24, 30, 140; RGAL 4; TUS
Mather, Increase 1639-1723 **LC 38**
See also DLB 24
Matheson, Richard (Burton) 1926- **CLC 37**
See also AAYA 31; CA 97-100; CANR 88,
99; DLB 8, 44; HGG; INT CA-97-100;
SCFW 2; SFW 4; SUFW 2
Mathews, Harry 1930- **CLC 6, 52**
See also CA 21-24R; CAAS 6; CANR 18,
40, 98; CN 7
Mathews, John Joseph 1894-1979 **CLC 84;
NNAL**
See also CA 19-20; 142; CANR 45; CAP 2;
DAM MULT; DLB 175
Mathias, Roland (Glyn) 1915- **CLC 45**
See also CA 97-100; CANR 19, 41; CP 7;
DLB 27
Matsuo Basho 1644-1694 **LC 62; PC 3**
See Basho, Matsuo
See also DAM POET; PFS 2, 7
Mattheson, Rodney
See Creasey, John
Matthews, (James) Brander 1852-1929 **TCLC
95**
See also DLB 71, 78; DLBD 13

Matthews, Greg 1949- **CLC 45**
　　See also CA 135
Matthews, William (Procter III) 1942-1997
　　CLC 40
　　See also AMWS 9; CA 29-32R; 162; CAAS
　　18; CANR 12, 57; CP 7; DLB 5
Matthias, John (Edward) 1941- **CLC 9**
　　See also CA 33-36R; CANR 56; CP 7
Matthiessen, F(rancis) O(tto) 1902-1950
　　TCLC 100
　　See also CA 185; DLB 63
Matthiessen, Peter 1927- **CLC 5, 7, 11, 32, 64**
　　See also AAYA 6, 40; AMWS 5; ANW;
　　BEST 90:4; BPFB 2; CA 9-12R; CANR
　　21, 50, 73, 100; CN 7; DA3; DAM NOV;
　　DLB 6, 173, 275; MTCW 1, 2; SATA 27
Maturin, Charles Robert 1780(?)-1824 **NCLC**
　　6
　　See also BRWS 8; DLB 178; HGG; LMFS
　　1; RGEL 2; SUFW
Matute (Ausejo), Ana Maria 1925- **CLC 11**
　　See also CA 89-92; CANR 129; EWL 3;
　　MTCW 1; RGSF 2
Maugham, W. S.
　　See Maugham, W(illiam) Somerset
Maugham, W(illiam) Somerset 1874-1965
　　CLC 1, 11, 15, 67, 93; SSC 8; WLC
　　See also AAYA 55; BPFB 2; BRW 6; CA
　　5-8R; 25-28R; CANR 40, 127; CDBLB
　　1914-1945; CMW 4; DA; DA3; DAB;
　　DAC; DAM DRAM, MST, NOV; DLB
　　10, 36, 77, 100, 162, 195; EWL 3; LAIT
　　3; MTCW 1, 2; RGEL 2; RGSF 2; SATA
　　54; SSFS 17
Maugham, William Somerset
　　See Maugham, W(illiam) Somerset
Maupassant, (Henri Rene Albert) Guy de
　　1850-1893 **NCLC 1, 42, 83; SSC 1, 64;**
　　WLC
　　See also BYA 14; DA; DA3; DAB; DAC;
　　DAM MST; DLB 123; EW 7; EXPS; GFL
　　1789 to the Present; LAIT 2; LMFS 1;
　　RGSF 2; RGWL 2, 3; SSFS 4; SUFW;
　　TWA
Maupin, Armistead (Jones, Jr.) 1944- **CLC**
　　95
　　See also CA 125; 130; CANR 58, 101;
　　CPW; DA3; DAM POP; DLB 278; GLL
　　1; INT CA-130; MTCW 2
Maurhut, Richard
　　See Traven, B.
Mauriac, Claude 1914-1996 **CLC 9**
　　See also CA 89-92; 152; CWW 2; DLB 83;
　　EWL 3; GFL 1789 to the Present
Mauriac, Francois (Charles) 1885-1970 **CLC**
　　4, 9, 56; SSC 24
　　See also CA 25-28; CAP 2; DLB 65; EW
　　10; EWL 3; GFL 1789 to the Present;
　　MTCW 1, 2; RGWL 2, 3; TWA
Mavor, Osborne Henry 1888-1951
　　See Bridie, James
　　See also CA 104
Maxwell, William (Keepers, Jr.) 1908-2000
　　CLC 19
　　See also AMWS 8; CA 93-96; 189; CANR
　　54, 95; CN 7; DLB 218, 278; DLBY
　　1980; INT CA-93-96; SATA-Obit 128
May, Elaine 1932- **CLC 16**
　　See also CA 124; 142; CAD; CWD; DLB
　　44
Mayakovski, Vladimir (Vladimirovich)
　　1893-1930 **TCLC 4, 18**
　　See Maiakovskii, Vladimir; Mayakovsky,
　　Vladimir
　　See also CA 104; 158; EWL 3; MTCW 2;
　　SFW 4; TWA
Mayakovsky, Vladimir
　　See Mayakovski, Vladimir (Vladimirovich)
　　See also EW 11; WP

Mayhew, Henry 1812-1887 **NCLC 31**
　　See also DLB 18, 55, 190
Mayle, Peter 1939(?)- **CLC 89**
　　See also CA 139; CANR 64, 109
Maynard, Joyce 1953- **CLC 23**
　　See also CA 111; 129; CANR 64
Mayne, William (James Carter) 1928- **CLC**
　　12
　　See also AAYA 20; CA 9-12R; CANR 37,
　　80, 100; CLR 25; FANT; JRDA; MAI-
　　CYA 1, 2; MAICYAS 1; SAAS 11; SATA
　　6, 68, 122; SUFW 2; YAW
Mayo, Jim
　　See L'Amour, Louis (Dearborn)
　　See also TCWW 2
Maysles, Albert 1926- **CLC 16**
　　See also CA 29-32R
Maysles, David 1932-1987 **CLC 16**
　　See also CA 191
Mazer, Norma Fox 1931- **CLC 26**
　　See also AAYA 5, 36; BYA 1, 8; CA 69-72;
　　CANR 12, 32, 66, 129; CLR 23; JRDA;
　　MAICYA 1, 2; SAAS 1; SATA 24, 67,
　　105; WYA; YAW
Mazzini, Guiseppe 1805-1872 **NCLC 34**
McAlmon, Robert (Menzies) 1895-1956
　　TCLC 97
　　See also CA 107; 168; DLB 4, 45; DLBD
　　15; GLL 1
McAuley, James Phillip 1917-1976 **CLC 45**
　　See also CA 97-100; DLB 260; RGEL 2
McBain, Ed
　　See Hunter, Evan
　　See also MSW
McBrien, William (Augustine) 1930- **CLC 44**
　　See also CA 107; CANR 90
McCabe, Patrick 1955- **CLC 133**
　　See also BRWS 9; CA 130; CANR 50, 90;
　　CN 7; DLB 194
McCaffrey, Anne (Inez) 1926- **CLC 17**
　　See also AAYA 6, 34; AITN 2; BEST 89:2;
　　BPFB 2; BYA 5; CA 25-28R; CANR 15,
　　35, 55, 96; CLR 49; CPW; DA3; DAM
　　NOV, POP; DLB 8; JRDA; MAICYA 1,
　　2; MTCW 1, 2; SAAS 11; SATA 8, 70,
　　116; SFW 4; SUFW 2; WYA; YAW
McCall, Nathan 1955(?)- **CLC 86**
　　See also BW 3; CA 146; CANR 88
McCann, Arthur
　　See Campbell, John W(ood, Jr.)
McCann, Edson
　　See Pohl, Frederik
McCarthy, Charles, Jr. 1933-
　　See McCarthy, Cormac
　　See also CANR 42, 69, 101; CN 7; CPW;
　　CSW; DA3; DAM POP; MTCW 2
McCarthy, Cormac CLC 4, 57, 101
　　See McCarthy, Charles, Jr.
　　See also AAYA 41; AMWS 8; BPFB 2; CA
　　13-16R; CANR 10; DLB 6, 143, 256;
　　EWL 3; LATS 1; TCWW 2
McCarthy, Mary (Therese) 1912-1989 **CLC**
　　1, 3, 5, 14, 24, 39, 59; SSC 24
　　See also AMW; BPFB 2; CA 5-8R; 129;
　　CANR 16, 50, 64; DA3; DLB 2; DLBY
　　1981; EWL 3; FW; INT CANR-16;
　　MAWW; MTCW 1, 2; RGAL 4; TUS
McCartney, (James) Paul 1942- **CLC 12, 35**
　　See also CA 146; CANR 111
McCauley, Stephen (D.) 1955- **CLC 50**
　　See also CA 141
McClaren, Peter CLC 70
McClure, Michael (Thomas) 1932- **CLC 6,**
　　10
　　See also BG 3; CA 21-24R; CAD; CANR
　　17, 46, 77; CD 5; CP 7; DLB 16; WP
McCorkle, Jill (Collins) 1958- **CLC 51**
　　See also CA 121; CANR 113; CSW; DLB
　　234; DLBY 1987

McCourt, Frank 1930- **CLC 109**
　　See also AMWS 12; CA 157; CANR 97;
　　NCFS 1
McCourt, James 1941- **CLC 5**
　　See also CA 57-60; CANR 98
McCourt, Malachy 1931- **CLC 119**
　　See also SATA 126
McCoy, Horace (Stanley) 1897-1955 **TCLC**
　　28
　　See also AMWS 13; CA 108; 155; CMW 4;
　　DLB 9
McCrae, John 1872-1918 **TCLC 12**
　　See also CA 109; DLB 92; PFS 5
McCreigh, James
　　See Pohl, Frederik
McCullers, (Lula) Carson (Smith) 1917-1967
　　CLC 1, 4, 10, 12, 48, 100; SSC 9, 24;
　　WLC
　　See also AAYA 21; AMW; AMWC 2; BPFB
　　2; CA 5-8R; 25-28R; CABS 1, 3; CANR
　　18; CDALB 1941-1968; DA; DA3; DAB;
　　DAC; DAM MST, NOV; DFS 5, 18; DLB
　　2, 7, 173, 228; EWL 3; EXPS; FW; GLL
　　1; LAIT 3, 4; MAWW; MTCW 1, 2; NFS
　　6, 13; RGAL 4; RGSF 2; SATA 27; SSFS
　　5; TUS; YAW
McCulloch, John Tyler
　　See Burroughs, Edgar Rice
McCullough, Colleen 1938(?)- **CLC 27, 107**
　　See also AAYA 36; BPFB 2; CA 81-84;
　　CANR 17, 46, 67, 98; CPW; DA3; DAM
　　NOV, POP; MTCW 1, 2; RHW
McCunn, Ruthanne Lum 1946- **AAL**
　　See also CA 119; CANR 43, 96; LAIT 2;
　　SATA 63
McDermott, Alice 1953- **CLC 90**
　　See also CA 109; CANR 40, 90, 126; DLB
　　292
McElroy, Joseph 1930- **CLC 5, 47**
　　See also CA 17-20R; CN 7
McEwan, Ian (Russell) 1948- **CLC 13, 66,**
　　169
　　See also BEST 90:4; BRWS 4; CA 61-64;
　　CANR 14, 41, 69, 87; CN 7; DAM NOV;
　　DLB 14, 194; HGG; MTCW 1, 2; RGSF
　　2; SUFW 2; TEA
McFadden, David 1940- **CLC 48**
　　See also CA 104; CP 7; DLB 60; INT CA-
　　104
McFarland, Dennis 1950- **CLC 65**
　　See also CA 165; CANR 110
McGahern, John 1934- **CLC 5, 9, 48, 156;**
　　SSC 17
　　See also CA 17-20R; CANR 29, 68, 113;
　　CN 7; DLB 14, 231; MTCW 1
McGinley, Patrick (Anthony) 1937- **CLC 41**
　　See also CA 120; 127; CANR 56; INT CA-
　　127
McGinley, Phyllis 1905-1978 **CLC 14**
　　See also CA 9-12R; 77-80; CANR 19;
　　CWRI 5; DLB 11, 48; PFS 9, 13; SATA
　　2, 44; SATA-Obit 24
McGinniss, Joe 1942- **CLC 32**
　　See also AITN 2; BEST 89:2; CA 25-28R;
　　CANR 26, 70; CPW; DLB 185; INT
　　CANR-26
McGivern, Maureen Daly
　　See Daly, Maureen
McGrath, Patrick 1950- **CLC 55**
　　See also CA 136; CANR 65; CN 7; DLB
　　231; HGG; SUFW 2
McGrath, Thomas (Matthew) 1916-1990
　　CLC 28, 59
　　See also AMWS 10; CA 9-12R; 132; CANR
　　6, 33, 95; DAM POET; MTCW 1; SATA
　　41; SATA-Obit 66

McGuane, Thomas (Francis III) 1939- **CLC 3, 7, 18, 45, 127**
See also AITN 2; BPFB 2; CA 49-52; CANR 5, 24, 49, 94; CN 7; DLB 2, 212; DLBY 1980; EWL 3; INT CANR-24; MTCW 1; TCWW 2

McGuckian, Medbh 1950- **CLC 48, 174; PC 27**
See also BRWS 5; CA 143; CP 7; CWP; DAM POET; DLB 40

McHale, Tom 1942(?)-1982 **CLC 3, 5**
See also AITN 1; CA 77-80; 106

McIlvanney, William 1936- **CLC 42**
See also CA 25-28R; CANR 61; CMW 4; DLB 14, 207

McIlwraith, Maureen Mollie Hunter
See Hunter, Mollie
See also SATA 2

McInerney, Jay 1955- **CLC 34, 112**
See also AAYA 18; BPFB 2; CA 116; 123; CANR 45, 68, 116; CN 7; CPW; DA3; DAM POP; DLB 292; INT CA-123; MTCW 2

McIntyre, Vonda N(eel) 1948- **CLC 18**
See also CA 81-84; CANR 17, 34, 69; MTCW 1; SFW 4; YAW

McKay, Claude BLC 3; HR 3; PC 2; TCLC 7, 41; WLC
See McKay, Festus Claudius
See also AFAW 1, 2; AMWS 10; DAB; DLB 4, 45, 51, 117; EWL 3; EXPP; GLL 2; LAIT 3; LMFS 2; PAB; PFS 4; RGAL 4; WP

McKay, Festus Claudius 1889-1948
See McKay, Claude
See also BW 1, 3; CA 104; 124; CANR 73; DA; DAC; DAM MST, MULT, NOV, POET; MTCW 1, 2; TUS

McKuen, Rod 1933- **CLC 1, 3**
See also AITN 1; CA 41-44R; CANR 40

McLoughlin, R. B.
See Mencken, H(enry) L(ouis)

McLuhan, (Herbert) Marshall 1911-1980 **CLC 37, 83**
See also CA 9-12R; 102; CANR 12, 34, 61; DLB 88; INT CANR-12; MTCW 1, 2

McManus, Declan Patrick Aloysius
See Costello, Elvis

McMillan, Terry (L.) 1951- **BLCS; CLC 50, 61, 112**
See also AAYA 21; AMWS 13; BPFB 2; BW 2, 3; CA 140; CANR 60, 104; CPW; DA3; DAM MULT, NOV, POP; MTCW 2; RGAL 4; YAW

McMurtry, Larry (Jeff) 1936- **CLC 2, 3, 7, 11, 27, 44, 127**
See also AAYA 15; AITN 2; AMWS 5; BEST 89:2; BPFB 2; CA 5-8R; CANR 19, 43, 64, 103; CDALB 1968-1988; CN 7; CPW; CSW; DA3; DAM NOV, POP; DLB 2, 143, 256; DLBY 1980, 1987; EWL 3; MTCW 1, 2; RGAL 4; TCWW 2

McNally, T. M. 1961- **CLC 82**

McNally, Terrence 1939- **CLC 4, 7, 41, 91**
See also AMWS 13; CA 45-48; CAD; CANR 2, 56, 116; CD 5; DA3; DAM DRAM; DFS 16; DLB 7, 249; EWL 3; GLL 1; MTCW 2

McNamer, Deirdre 1950- **CLC 70**

McNeal, Tom CLC 119

McNeile, Herman Cyril 1888-1937
See Sapper
See also CA 184; CMW 4; DLB 77

McNickle, (William) D'Arcy 1904-1977 **CLC 89; NNAL**
See also CA 9-12R; 85-88; CANR 5, 45; DAM MULT; DLB 175, 212; RGAL 4; SATA-Obit 22

McPhee, John (Angus) 1931- **CLC 36**
See also AMWS 3; ANW; BEST 90:1; CA 65-68; CANR 20, 46, 64, 69, 121; CPW; DLB 185, 275; MTCW 1, 2; TUS

McPherson, James Alan 1943- **BLCS; CLC 19, 77**
See also BW 1, 3; CA 25-28R; CAAS 17; CANR 24, 74; CN 7; CSW; DLB 38, 244; EWL 3; MTCW 1, 2; RGAL 4; RGSF 2

McPherson, William (Alexander) 1933- **CLC 34**
See also CA 69-72; CANR 28; INT CANR-28

McTaggart, J. McT. Ellis
See McTaggart, John McTaggart Ellis

McTaggart, John McTaggart Ellis 1866-1925 **TCLC 105**
See also CA 120; DLB 262

Mead, George Herbert 1863-1931 **TCLC 89**
See also CA 212; DLB 270

Mead, Margaret 1901-1978 **CLC 37**
See also AITN 1; CA 1-4R; 81-84; CANR 4; DA3; FW; MTCW 1, 2; SATA-Obit 20

Meaker, Marijane (Agnes) 1927-
See Kerr, M. E.
See also CA 107; CANR 37, 63; INT CA-107; JRDA; MAICYA 1, 2; MAICYAS 1; MTCW 1; SATA 20, 61, 99; SATA-Essay 111; YAW

Medoff, Mark (Howard) 1940- **CLC 6, 23**
See also AITN 1; CA 53-56; CAD; CANR 5; CD 5; DAM DRAM; DFS 4; DLB 7; INT CANR-5

Medvedev, P. N.
See Bakhtin, Mikhail Mikhailovich

Meged, Aharon
See Megged, Aharon

Meged, Aron
See Megged, Aharon

Megged, Aharon 1920- **CLC 9**
See also CA 49-52; CAAS 13; CANR 1; EWL 3

Mehta, Gita 1943- **CLC 179**
See also DNFS 2

Mehta, Ved (Parkash) 1934- **CLC 37**
See also CA 1-4R; 212; CAAE 212; CANR 2, 23, 69; MTCW 1

Melanchthon, Philipp 1497-1560 **LC 90**
See also DLB 179

Melanter
See Blackmore, R(ichard) D(oddridge)

Meleager c. 140B.C.-c. 70B.C. **CMLC 53**

Melies, Georges 1861-1938 **TCLC 81**

Melikow, Loris
See Hofmannsthal, Hugo von

Melmoth, Sebastian
See Wilde, Oscar (Fingal O'Flahertie Wills)

Melo Neto, Joao Cabral de
See Cabral de Melo Neto, Joao
See also CWW 2; EWL 3

Meltzer, Milton 1915- **CLC 26**
See also AAYA 8, 45; BYA 2, 6; CA 13-16R; CANR 38, 92, 107; CLR 13; DLB 61; JRDA; MAICYA 1, 2; SAAS 1; SATA 1, 50, 80, 128; SATA-Essay 124; WYA; YAW

Melville, Herman 1819-1891 **NCLC 3, 12, 29, 45, 49, 91, 93, 123; SSC 1, 17, 46; WLC**
See also AAYA 25; AMW; AMWR 1; CDALB 1640-1865; DA; DA3; DAB; DAC; DAM MST, NOV; DLB 3, 74, 250, 254; EXPN; EXPS; LAIT 1, 2; NFS 7, 9; RGAL 4; RGSF 2; SATA 59; SSFS 3; TUS

Members, Mark
See Powell, Anthony (Dymoke)

Membreno, Alejandro CLC 59

Menander c. 342B.C.-c. 293B.C. **CMLC 9, 51; DC 3**
See also AW 1; CDWLB 1; DAM DRAM; DLB 176; LMFS 1; RGWL 2, 3

Menchu, Rigoberta 1959- **CLC 160; HLCS 2**
See also CA 175; DNFS 1; WLIT 1

Mencken, H(enry) L(ouis) 1880-1956 **TCLC 13**
See also AMW; CA 105; 125; CDALB 1917-1929; DLB 11, 29, 63, 137, 222; EWL 3; MTCW 1, 2; NCFS 4; RGAL 4; TUS

Mendelsohn, Jane 1965- **CLC 99**
See also CA 154; CANR 94

Menton, Francisco de
See Chin, Frank (Chew, Jr.)

Mercer, David 1928-1980 **CLC 5**
See also CA 9-12R; 102; CANR 23; CBD; DAM DRAM; DLB 13; MTCW 1; RGEL 2

Merchant, Paul
See Ellison, Harlan (Jay)

Meredith, George 1828-1909 **TCLC 17, 43**
See also CA 117; 153; CANR 80; CDBLB 1832-1890; DAM POET; DLB 18, 35, 57, 159; RGEL 2; TEA

Meredith, William (Morris) 1919- **CLC 4, 13, 22, 55; PC 28**
See also CA 9-12R; CAAS 14; CANR 6, 40, 129; CP 7; DAM POET; DLB 5

Merezhkovsky, Dmitrii Sergeevich
See Merezhkovsky, Dmitry Sergeyevich
See also DLB 295

Merezhkovsky, Dmitry Sergeevich
See Merezhkovsky, Dmitry Sergeyevich
See also EWL 3

Merezhkovsky, Dmitry Sergeyevich 1865-1941 **TCLC 29**
See Merezhkovsky, Dmitrii Sergeevich; Merezhkovsky, Dmitry Sergeevich
See also CA 169

Merimee, Prosper 1803-1870 **NCLC 6, 65; SSC 7**
See also DLB 119, 192; EW 6; EXPS; GFL 1789 to the Present; RGSF 2; RGWL 2, 3; SSFS 8; SUFW

Merkin, Daphne 1954- **CLC 44**
See also CA 123

Merlin, Arthur
See Blish, James (Benjamin)

Mernissi, Fatima 1940- **CLC 171**
See also CA 152; FW

Merrill, James (Ingram) 1926-1995 **CLC 2, 3, 6, 8, 13, 18, 34, 91; PC 28**
See also AMWS 3; CA 13-16R; 147; CANR 10, 49, 63, 108; DA3; DAM POET; DLB 5, 165; DLBY 1985; EWL 3; INT CANR-10; MTCW 1, 2; PAB; RGAL 4

Merriman, Alex
See Silverberg, Robert

Merriman, Brian 1747-1805 **NCLC 70**

Merritt, E. B.
See Waddington, Miriam

Merton, Thomas (James) 1915-1968 **CLC 1, 3, 11, 34, 83; PC 10**
See also AMWS 8; CA 5-8R; 25-28R; CANR 22, 53, 111; DA3; DLB 48; DLBY 1981; MTCW 1, 2

Merwin, W(illiam) S(tanley) 1927- **CLC 1, 2, 3, 5, 8, 13, 18, 45, 88; PC 45**
See also AMWS 3; CA 13-16R; CANR 15, 51, 112; CP 7; DA3; DAM POET; DLB 5, 169; EWL 3; INT CANR-15; MTCW 1, 2; PAB; PFS 5, 15; RGAL 4

Metcalf, John 1938- **CLC 37; SSC 43**
See also CA 113; CN 7; DLB 60; RGSF 2; TWA

Metcalf, Suzanne
See Baum, L(yman) Frank

Mew, Charlotte (Mary) 1870-1928 **TCLC 8**
See also CA 105; 189; DLB 19, 135; RGEL 2

Mewshaw, Michael 1943- **CLC 9**
See also CA 53-56; CANR 7, 47; DLBY 1980

Meyer, Conrad Ferdinand 1825-1898 **NCLC 81**
See also DLB 129; EW; RGWL 2, 3

Meyer, Gustav 1868-1932
See Meyrink, Gustav
See also CA 117; 190

Meyer, June
See Jordan, June (Meyer)

Meyer, Lynn
See Slavitt, David R(ytman)

Meyers, Jeffrey 1939- **CLC 39**
See also CA 73-76, 186; CAAE 186; CANR 54, 102; DLB 111

Meynell, Alice (Christina Gertrude Thompson) 1847-1922 **TCLC 6**
See also CA 104; 177; DLB 19, 98; RGEL 2

Meyrink, Gustav TCLC 21
See Meyer, Gustav
See also DLB 81; EWL 3

Michaels, Leonard 1933-2003 **CLC 6, 25; SSC 16**
See also CA 61-64; 216; CANR 21, 62, 119; CN 7; DLB 130; MTCW 1

Michaux, Henri 1899-1984 **CLC 8, 19**
See also CA 85-88; 114; DLB 258; EWL 3; GFL 1789 to the Present; RGWL 2, 3

Micheaux, Oscar (Devereaux) 1884-1951 **TCLC 76**
See also BW 3; CA 174; DLB 50; TCWW 2

Michelangelo 1475-1564 **LC 12**
See also AAYA 43

Michelet, Jules 1798-1874 **NCLC 31**
See also EW 5; GFL 1789 to the Present

Michels, Robert 1876-1936 **TCLC 88**
See also CA 212

Michener, James A(lbert) 1907(?)-1997 **CLC 1, 5, 11, 29, 60, 109**
See also AAYA 27; AITN 1; BEST 90:1; BPFB 2; CA 5-8R; 161; CANR 21, 45, 68; CN 7; CPW; DA3; DAM NOV, POP; DLB 6; MTCW 1, 2; RHW

Mickiewicz, Adam 1798-1855 **NCLC 3, 101; PC 38**
See also EW 5; RGWL 2, 3

Middleton, (John) Christopher 1926- **CLC 13**
See also CA 13-16R; CANR 29, 54, 117; CP 7; DLB 40

Middleton, Richard (Barham) 1882-1911 **TCLC 56**
See also CA 187; DLB 156; HGG

Middleton, Stanley 1919- **CLC 7, 38**
See also CA 25-28R; CAAS 23; CANR 21, 46, 81; CN 7; DLB 14

Middleton, Thomas 1580-1627 **DC 5; LC 33**
See also BRW 2; DAM DRAM, MST; DFS 18; DLB 58; RGEL 2

Migueis, Jose Rodrigues 1901-1980 **CLC 10**
See also DLB 287

Mikszath, Kalman 1847-1910 **TCLC 31**
See also CA 170

Miles, Jack CLC 100
See also CA 200

Miles, John Russiano
See Miles, Jack

Miles, Josephine (Louise) 1911-1985 **CLC 1, 2, 14, 34, 39**
See also CA 1-4R; 116; CANR 2, 55; DAM POET; DLB 48

Militant
See Sandburg, Carl (August)

Mill, Harriet (Hardy) Taylor 1807-1858 **NCLC 102**
See also FW

Mill, John Stuart 1806-1873 **NCLC 11, 58**
See also CDBLB 1832-1890; DLB 55, 190, 262; FW 1; RGEL 2; TEA

Millar, Kenneth 1915-1983 **CLC 14**
See Macdonald, Ross
See also CA 9-12R; 110; CANR 16, 63, 107; CMW 4; CPW; DA3; DAM POP; DLB 2, 226; DLBD 6; DLBY 1983; MTCW 1, 2

Millay, E. Vincent
See Millay, Edna St. Vincent

Millay, Edna St. Vincent 1892-1950 **PC 6; TCLC 4, 49; WLCS**
See Boyd, Nancy
See also AMW; CA 104; 130; CDALB 1917-1929; DA; DA3; DAB; DAC; DAM MST, POET; DLB 45, 249; EWL 3; EXPP; MAWW; MTCW 1, 2; PAB; PFS 3, 17; RGAL 4; TUS; WP

Miller, Arthur 1915- **CLC 1, 2, 6, 10, 15, 26, 47, 78, 179; DC 1; WLC**
See also AAYA 15; AITN 1; AMW; AMWC 1; CA 1-4R; CABS 3; CAD; CANR 2, 30, 54, 76; CD 5; CDALB 1941-1968; DA; DA3; DAB; DAC; DAM MST, DFS 1, 3, 8; DLB 7, 266; EWL 3; LAIT 1, 4; LATS 1; MTCW 1, 2; RGAL 4; TUS; WYAS 1

Miller, Henry (Valentine) 1891-1980 **CLC 1, 2, 4, 9, 14, 43, 84; WLC**
See also AMW; BPFB 2; CA 9-12R; 97-100; CANR 33, 64; CDALB 1929-1941; DA; DA3; DAB; DAC; DAM MST, NOV; DLB 4, 9; DLBY 1980; EWL 3; MTCW 1, 2; RGAL 4; TUS

Miller, Jason 1939(?)-2001 **CLC 2**
See also AITN 1; CA 73-76; 197; CAD; DFS 12; DLB 7

Miller, Sue 1943- **CLC 44**
See also AMWS 12; BEST 90:3; CA 139; CANR 59, 91, 128; DA3; DAM POP; DLB 143

Miller, Walter M(ichael, Jr.) 1923-1996 **CLC 4, 30**
See also BPFB 2; CA 85-88; CANR 108; DLB 8; SCFW; SFW 4

Millett, Kate 1934- **CLC 67**
See also AITN 1; CA 73-76; CANR 32, 53, 76, 110; DA3; DLB 246; FW; GLL 1; MTCW 1, 2

Millhauser, Steven (Lewis) 1943- **CLC 21, 54, 109; SSC 57**
See also CA 110; 111; CANR 63, 114; CN 7; DA3; DLB 2; FANT; INT CA-111; MTCW 2

Millin, Sarah Gertrude 1889-1968 **CLC 49**
See also CA 102; 93-96; DLB 225; EWL 3

Milne, A(lan) A(lexander) 1882-1956 **TCLC 6, 88**
See also BRWS 5; CA 104; 133; CLR 1, 26; CMW 4; CWRI 5; DA3; DAB; DAC; DAM MST; DLB 10, 77, 100, 160; FANT; MAICYA 1, 2; MTCW 1, 2; RGEL 2; SATA 100; WCH; YABC 1

Milner, Ron(ald) 1938- **BLC 3; CLC 56**
See also AITN 1; BW 1; CA 73-76; CAD; CANR 24, 81; CD 5; DAM MULT; DLB 38; MTCW 1

Milnes, Richard Monckton 1809-1885 **NCLC 61**
See also DLB 32, 184

Milosz, Czeslaw 1911- **CLC 5, 11, 22, 31, 56, 82; PC 8; WLCS**
See also CA 81-84; CANR 23, 51, 91, 126; CDWLB 4; CWW 2; DA3; DAM MST, POET; DLB 215; EW 13; EWL 3; MTCW 1, 2; PFS 16; RGWL 2, 3

Milton, John 1608-1674 **LC 9, 43, 92; PC 19, 29; WLC**
See also BRW 2; BRWR 2; CDBLB 1660-1789; DA; DA3; DAB; DAC; DAM MST, POET; DLB 131, 151, 281; EFS 1; EXPP; LAIT 1; PAB; PFS 3, 17; RGEL 2; TEA; WLIT 3; WP

Min, Anchee 1957- **CLC 86**
See also CA 146; CANR 94

Minehaha, Cornelius
See Wedekind, (Benjamin) Frank(lin)

Miner, Valerie 1947- **CLC 40**
See also CA 97-100; CANR 59; FW; GLL 2

Minimo, Duca
See D'Annunzio, Gabriele

Minot, Susan 1956- **CLC 44, 159**
See also AMWS 6; CA 134; CANR 118; CN 7

Minus, Ed 1938- **CLC 39**
See also CA 185

Mirabai 1498(?)-1550(?) **PC 48**

Miranda, Javier
See Bioy Casares, Adolfo
See also CWW 2

Mirbeau, Octave 1848-1917 **TCLC 55**
See also CA 216; DLB 123, 192; GFL 1789 to the Present

Mirikitani, Janice 1942- **AAL**
See also CA 211; RGAL 4

Miro (Ferrer), Gabriel (Francisco Victor) 1879-1930 **TCLC 5**
See also CA 104; 185; EWL 3

Misharin, Alexandr CLC 59

Mishima, Yukio CLC 2, 4, 6, 9, 27; DC 1; SSC 4
See Hiraoka, Kimitake
See also AAYA 50; BPFB 2; GLL 1; MJW; MTCW 2; RGSF 2; RGWL 2, 3; SSFS 5, 12

Mistral, Frederic 1830-1914 **TCLC 51**
See also CA 122; 213; GFL 1789 to the Present

Mistral, Gabriela
See Godoy Alcayaga, Lucila
See also DLB 283; DNFS 1; EWL 3; LAW; RGWL 2, 3; WP

Mistry, Rohinton 1952- **CLC 71**
See also CA 141; CANR 86, 114; CCA 1; CN 7; DAC; SSFS 6

Mitchell, Clyde
See Ellison, Harlan (Jay)

Mitchell, Emerson Blackhorse Barney 1945- **NNAL**
See also CA 45-48

Mitchell, James Leslie 1901-1935
See Gibbon, Lewis Grassic
See also CA 104; 188; DLB 15

Mitchell, Joni 1943- **CLC 12**
See also CA 112; CCA 1

Mitchell, Joseph (Quincy) 1908-1996 **CLC 98**
See also CA 77-80; 152; CANR 69; CN 7; CSW; DLB 185; DLBY 1996

Mitchell, Margaret (Munnerlyn) 1900-1949 **TCLC 11**
See also AAYA 23; BPFB 2; BYA 1; CA 109; 125; CANR 55, 94; CDALBS; DA3; DAM NOV, POP; DLB 9; LAIT 2; MTCW 1, 2; NFS 9; RGAL 4; RHW; TUS; WYAS 1; YAW

Mitchell, Peggy
See Mitchell, Margaret (Munnerlyn)

Mitchell, S(ilas) Weir 1829-1914 **TCLC 36**
See also CA 165; DLB 202; RGAL 4

Mitchell, W(illiam) O(rmond) 1914-1998 **CLC 25**
See also CA 77-80; 165; CANR 15, 43; CN 7; DAC; DAM MST; DLB 88

Mitchell, William (Lendrum) 1879-1936 **TCLC 81**
See also CA 213

Mitford, Mary Russell 1787-1855 **NCLC 4**
See also DLB 110, 116; RGEL 2

Mitford, Nancy 1904-1973 **CLC 44**
See also CA 9-12R; DLB 191; RGEL 2

Miyamoto, (Chujo) Yuriko 1899-1951 **TCLC 37**
See Miyamoto Yuriko
See also CA 170, 174

Miyamoto Yuriko
See Miyamoto, (Chujo) Yuriko
See also DLB 180

Miyazawa, Kenji 1896-1933 **TCLC 76**
See Miyazawa Kenji
See also CA 157; RGWL 3

Miyazawa Kenji
See Miyazawa, Kenji
See also EWL 3

Mizoguchi, Kenji 1898-1956 **TCLC 72**
See also CA 167

Mo, Timothy (Peter) 1950(?)- **CLC 46, 134**
See also CA 117; CANR 128; CN 7; DLB 194; MTCW 1; WLIT 4; WWE 1

Modarressi, Taghi (M.) 1931-1997 **CLC 44**
See also CA 121; 134; INT CA-134

Modiano, Patrick (Jean) 1945- **CLC 18**
See also CA 85-88; CANR 17, 40, 115; CWW 2; DLB 83; EWL 3

Mofolo, Thomas (Mokopu) 1875(?)-1948 **BLC 3; TCLC 22**
See also AFW; CA 121; 153; CANR 83; DAM MULT; DLB 225; EWL 3; MTCW 2; WLIT 2

Mohr, Nicholasa 1938- **CLC 12; HLC 2**
See also AAYA 8, 46; CA 49-52; CANR 1, 32, 64; CLR 22; DAM MULT; DLB 145; HW 1, 2; JRDA; LAIT 5; LLW 1; MAICYA 2; MAICYAS 1; RGAL 4; SAAS 8; SATA 8, 97; SATA-Essay 113; WYA; YAW

Moi, Toril 1953- **CLC 172**
See also CA 154; CANR 102; FW

Mojtabai, A(nn) G(race) 1938- **CLC 5, 9, 15, 29**
See also CA 85-88; CANR 88

Moliere 1622-1673 **DC 13; LC 10, 28, 64; WLC**
See also DA; DA3; DAB; DAC; DAM DRAM, MST; DFS 13, 18; DLB 268; EW 3; GFL Beginnings to 1789; LATS 1; RGWL 2, 3; TWA

Molin, Charles
See Mayne, William (James Carter)

Molnar, Ferenc 1878-1952 **TCLC 20**
See also CA 109; 153; CANR 83; CDWLB 4; DAM DRAM; DLB 215; EWL 3; RGWL 2, 3

Momaday, N(avarre) Scott 1934- **CLC 2, 19, 85, 95, 160; NNAL; PC 25; WLCS**
See also AAYA 11; AMWS 4; ANW; BPFB 2; BYA 12; CA 25-28R; CANR 14, 34, 68; CDALBS; CN 7; CPW; DA; DA3; DAB; DAC; DAM MST, MULT, NOV, POP; DLB 143, 175, 256; EWL 3; EXPP; INT CANR-14; LAIT 4; LATS 1; MTCW 1, 2; NFS 10; PFS 2, 11; RGAL 4; SATA 48; SATA-Brief 30; WP; YAW

Monette, Paul 1945-1995 **CLC 82**
See also AMWS 10; CA 139; 147; CN 7; GLL 1

Monroe, Harriet 1860-1936 **TCLC 12**
See also CA 109; 204; DLB 54, 91

Monroe, Lyle
See Heinlein, Robert A(nson)

Montagu, Elizabeth 1720-1800 **NCLC 7, 117**
See also FW

Montagu, Mary (Pierrepont) Wortley 1689-1762 **LC 9, 57; PC 16**
See also DLB 95, 101; RGEL 2

Montagu, W. H.
See Coleridge, Samuel Taylor

Montague, John (Patrick) 1929- **CLC 13, 46**
See also CA 9-12R; CANR 9, 69, 121; CP 7; DLB 40; EWL 3; MTCW 1; PFS 12; RGEL 2

Montaigne, Michel (Eyquem) de 1533-1592 **LC 8; WLC**
See also DA; DAB; DAC; DAM MST; EW 2; GFL Beginnings to 1789; LMFS 1; RGWL 2, 3; TWA

Montale, Eugenio 1896-1981 **CLC 7, 9, 18; PC 13**
See also CA 17-20R; 104; CANR 30; DLB 114; EW 11; EWL 3; MTCW 1; RGWL 2, 3; TWA

Montesquieu, Charles-Louis de Secondat 1689-1755 **LC 7, 69**
See also EW 3; GFL Beginnings to 1789; TWA

Montessori, Maria 1870-1952 **TCLC 103**
See also CA 115; 147

Montgomery, (Robert) Bruce 1921(?)-1978
See Crispin, Edmund
See also CA 179; 104; CMW 4

Montgomery, L(ucy) M(aud) 1874-1942 **TCLC 51, 140**
See also AAYA 12; BYA 1; CA 108; 137; CLR 8, 91; DA3; DAC; DAM MST; DLB 92; DLBD 14; JRDA; MAICYA 1, 2; MTCW 2; RGEL 2; SATA 100; TWA; WCH; WYA; YABC 1

Montgomery, Marion H., Jr. 1925- **CLC 7**
See also AITN 1; CA 1-4R; CANR 3, 48; CSW; DLB 6

Montgomery, Max
See Davenport, Guy (Mattison, Jr.)

Montherlant, Henry (Milon) de 1896-1972 **CLC 8, 19**
See also CA 85-88; 37-40R; DAM DRAM; DLB 72; EW 11; EWL 3; GFL 1789 to the Present; MTCW 1

Monty Python
See Chapman, Graham; Cleese, John (Marwood); Gilliam, Terry (Vance); Idle, Eric; Jones, Terence Graham Parry; Palin, Michael (Edward)
See also AAYA 7

Moodie, Susanna (Strickland) 1803-1885 **NCLC 14, 113**
See also DLB 99

Moody, Hiram (F. III) 1961-
See Moody, Rick
See also CA 138; CANR 64, 112

Moody, Minerva
See Alcott, Louisa May

Moody, Rick CLC 147
See Moody, Hiram (F. III)

Moody, William Vaughan 1869-1910 **TCLC 105**
See also CA 110; 178; DLB 7, 54; RGAL 4

Mooney, Edward 1951-
See Mooney, Ted
See also CA 130

Mooney, Ted CLC 25
See Mooney, Edward

Moorcock, Michael (John) 1939- **CLC 5, 27, 58**
See Bradbury, Edward P.
See also AAYA 26; CA 45-48; CAAS 5; CANR 2, 17, 38, 64, 122; CN 7; DLB 14, 231, 261; FANT; MTCW 1, 2; SATA 93; SCFW 2; SFW 4; SUFW 1, 2

Moore, Brian 1921-1999 **CLC 1, 3, 5, 7, 8, 19, 32, 90**
See Bryan, Michael
See also BRWS 9; CA 1-4R; 174; CANR 1, 25, 42, 63; CCA 1; CN 7; DAB; DAC; DAM MST; DLB 251; EWL 3; FANT; MTCW 1, 2; RGEL 2

Moore, Edward
See Muir, Edwin
See also RGEL 2

Moore, G. E. 1873-1958 **TCLC 89**
See also DLB 262

Moore, George Augustus 1852-1933 **SSC 19; TCLC 7**
See also BRW 6; CA 104; 177; DLB 10, 18, 57, 135; EWL 3; RGEL 2; RGSF 2

Moore, Lorrie CLC 39, 45, 68
See Moore, Marie Lorena
See also AMWS 10; DLB 234; SSFS 19

Moore, Marianne (Craig) 1887-1972 **CLC 1, 2, 4, 8, 10, 13, 19, 47; PC 4, 49; WLCS**
See also AMW; CA 1-4R; 33-36R; CANR 3, 61; CDALB 1929-1941; DA; DA3; DAB; DAC; DAM MST; POET; DLB 45; DLBD 7; EWL 3; EXPP; MAWW; MTCW 1, 2; PAB; PFS 14, 17; RGAL 4; SATA 20; TUS; WP

Moore, Marie Lorena 1957- **CLC 165**
See Moore, Lorrie
See also CA 116; CANR 39, 83; CN 7; DLB 234

Moore, Thomas 1779-1852 **NCLC 6, 110**
See also DLB 96, 144; RGEL 2

Moorhouse, Frank 1938- **SSC 40**
See also CA 118; CANR 92; CN 7; DLB 289; RGSF 2

Mora, Pat(ricia) 1942- **HLC 2**
See also AMWS 13; CA 129; CANR 57, 81, 112; CLR 58; DAM MULT; DLB 209; HW 1, 2; LLW 1; MAICYA 2; SATA 92, 134

Moraga, Cherrie 1952- **CLC 126; DC 22**
See also CA 131; CANR 66; DAM MULT; DLB 82, 249; FW; GLL 1; HW 1, 2; LLW 1

Morand, Paul 1888-1976 **CLC 41; SSC 22**
See also CA 184; 69-72; DLB 65; EWL 3

Morante, Elsa 1918-1985 **CLC 8, 47**
See also CA 85-88; 117; CANR 35; DLB 177; EWL 3; MTCW 1, 2; RGWL 2, 3

Moravia, Alberto CLC 2, 7, 11, 27, 46; SSC 26
See Pincherle, Alberto
See also DLB 177; EW 12; EWL 3; MTCW 2; RGSF 2; RGWL 2, 3

More, Hannah 1745-1833 **NCLC 27**
See also DLB 107, 109, 116, 158; RGEL 2

More, Henry 1614-1687 **LC 9**
See also DLB 126, 252

More, Sir Thomas 1478(?)-1535 **LC 10, 32**
See also BRWC 1; BRWS 7; DLB 136, 281; LMFS 1; RGEL 2; TEA

Moreas, Jean TCLC 18
See Papadiamantopoulos, Johannes
See also GFL 1789 to the Present

Moreton, Andrew Esq.
See Defoe, Daniel

Morgan, Berry 1919-2002 **CLC 6**
See also CA 49-52; 208; DLB 6

Morgan, Claire
See Highsmith, (Mary) Patricia
See also GLL 1

Morgan, Edwin (George) 1920- **CLC 31**
See also BRWS 9; CA 5-8R; CANR 3, 43, 90; CP 7; DLB 27

Morgan, (George) Frederick 1922-2004 **CLC 23**
See also CA 17-20R; CANR 21; CP 7

Morgan, Harriet
　See Mencken, H(enry) L(ouis)
Morgan, Jane
　See Cooper, James Fenimore
Morgan, Janet 1945- **CLC 39**
　See also CA 65-68
Morgan, Lady 1776(?)-1859 **NCLC 29**
　See also DLB 116, 158; RGEL 2
Morgan, Robin (Evonne) 1941- **CLC 2**
　See also CA 69-72; CANR 29, 68; FW;
　　GLL 2; MTCW 1; SATA 80
Morgan, Scott
　See Kuttner, Henry
Morgan, Seth 1949(?)-1990 **CLC 65**
　See also CA 185; 132
Morgenstern, Christian (Otto Josef
　　Wolfgang) 1871-1914 **TCLC 8**
　See also CA 105; 191; EWL 3
Morgenstern, S.
　See Goldman, William (W.)
Mori, Rintaro
　See Mori Ogai
　See also CA 110
Moricz, Zsigmond 1879-1942 **TCLC 33**
　See also CA 165; DLB 215; EWL 3
Morike, Eduard (Friedrich) 1804-1875
　　NCLC 10
　See also DLB 133; RGWL 2, 3
Mori Ogai 1862-1922 **TCLC 14**
　See Ogai
　See also CA 164; DLB 180; EWL 3; RGWL
　　3; TWA
Moritz, Karl Philipp 1756-1793 **LC 2**
　See also DLB 94
Morland, Peter Henry
　See Faust, Frederick (Schiller)
Morley, Christopher (Darlington) 1890-1957
　　TCLC 87
　See also CA 112; DLB 9; RGAL 4
Morren, Theophil
　See Hofmannsthal, Hugo von
Morris, Bill 1952- **CLC 76**
Morris, Julian
　See West, Morris L(anglo)
Morris, Steveland Judkins 1950(?)-
　See Wonder, Stevie
　See also CA 111
Morris, William 1834-1896 **NCLC 4; PC 55**
　See also BRW 5; CDBLB 1832-1890; DLB
　　18, 35, 57, 156, 178, 184; FANT; RGEL
　　2; SFW 4; SUFW
Morris, Wright 1910-1998 **CLC 1, 3, 7, 18,**
　　37; TCLC 107
　See also AMW; CA 9-12R; 167; CANR 21,
　　81; CN 7; DLB 2, 206, 218; DLBY 1981;
　　EWL 3; MTCW 1, 2; RGAL 4; TCWW 2
Morrison, Arthur 1863-1945 **SSC 40; TCLC**
　　72
　See also CA 120; 157; CMW 4; DLB 70,
　　135, 197; RGEL 2
Morrison, Chloe Anthony Wofford
　See Morrison, Toni
Morrison, James Douglas 1943-1971
　See Morrison, Jim
　See also CA 73-76; CANR 40
Morrison, Jim CLC 17
　See Morrison, James Douglas
Morrison, Toni 1931- **BLC 3; CLC 4, 10, 22,**
　　55, 81, 87, 173
　See also AAYA 1, 22; AFAW 1, 2; AMWC
　　1; AMWS 3; BPFB 2; BW 2, 3; CA 29-
　　32R; CANR 27, 42, 67, 113, 124; CDALB
　　1968-1988; CN 7; CPW; DA; DA3; DAB;
　　DAC; DAM MST, MULT, NOV, POP;
　　DLB 6, 33, 143; DLBY 1981; EWL 3;
　　EXPN; FW; LAIT 2, 4; LATS 1; LMFS
　　2; MAWW; MTCW 1, 2; NFS 1, 6, 8, 14;
　　RGAL 4; RHW; SATA 57, 144; SSFS 5;
　　TUS; YAW

Morrison, Van 1945- **CLC 21**
　See also CA 116; 168
Morrissy, Mary 1957- **CLC 99**
　See also CA 205; DLB 267
Mortimer, John (Clifford) 1923- **CLC 28, 43**
　See also CA 13-16R; CANR 21, 69, 109;
　　CD 5; CDBLB 1960 to Present; CMW 4;
　　CN 7; CPW; DA3; DAM DRAM, POP;
　　DLB 13, 245, 271; INT CANR-21; MSW;
　　MTCW 1, 2; RGEL 2
Mortimer, Penelope (Ruth) 1918-1999 **CLC 5**
　See also CA 57-60; 187; CANR 45, 88; CN
　　7
Mortimer, Sir John
　See Mortimer, John (Clifford)
Morton, Anthony
　See Creasey, John
Morton, Thomas 1579(?)-1647(?) **LC 72**
　See also DLB 24; RGEL 2
Mosca, Gaetano 1858-1941 **TCLC 75**
Moses, Daniel David 1952- **NNAL**
　See also CA 186
Mosher, Howard Frank 1943- **CLC 62**
　See also CA 139; CANR 65, 115
Mosley, Nicholas 1923- **CLC 43, 70**
　See also CA 69-72; CANR 41, 60, 108; CN
　　7; DLB 14, 207
Mosley, Walter 1952- **BLCS; CLC 97, 184**
　See also AAYA 17; AMWS 13; BPFB 2;
　　BW 2; CA 142; CANR 57, 92; CMW 4;
　　CPW; DA3; DAM MULT, POP; MSW;
　　MTCW 2
Moss, Howard 1922-1987 **CLC 7, 14, 45, 50**
　See also CA 1-4R; 123; CANR 1, 44; DAM
　　POET; DLB 5
Mossgiel, Rab
　See Burns, Robert
Motion, Andrew (Peter) 1952- **CLC 47**
　See also BRWS 7; CA 146; CANR 90; CP
　　7; DLB 40
Motley, Willard (Francis) 1909-1965 **CLC 18**
　See also BW 1; CA 117; 106; CANR 88;
　　DLB 76, 143
Motoori, Norinaga 1730-1801 **NCLC 45**
Mott, Michael (Charles Alston) 1930- **CLC**
　　15, 34
　See also CA 5-8R; CAAS 7; CANR 7, 29
Mountain Wolf Woman 1884-1960 **CLC 92;**
　　NNAL
　See also CA 144; CANR 90
Moure, Erin 1955- **CLC 88**
　See also CA 113; CP 7; CWP; DLB 60
Mourning Dove 1885(?)-1936 **NNAL**
　See also CA 144; CANR 90; DAM MULT;
　　DLB 175, 221
Mowat, Farley (McGill) 1921- **CLC 26**
　See also AAYA 1, 50; BYA 2; CA 1-4R;
　　CANR 4, 24, 42, 68, 108; CLR 20; CPW;
　　DAC; DAM MST; DLB 68; INT CANR-
　　24; JRDA; MAICYA 1, 2; MTCW 1, 2;
　　SATA 3, 55; YAW
Mowatt, Anna Cora 1819-1870 **NCLC 74**
　See also RGAL 4
Moyers, Bill 1934- **CLC 74**
　See also AITN 2; CA 61-64; CANR 31, 52
Mphahlele, Es'kia
　See Mphahlele, Ezekiel
　See also AFW; CDWLB 3; DLB 125, 225;
　　RGSF 2; SSFS 11
Mphahlele, Ezekiel 1919- **BLC 3; CLC 25,**
　　133
　See Mphahlele, Es'kia
　See also BW 2, 3; CA 81-84; CANR 26,
　　76; CN 7; DA3; DAM MULT; EWL 3;
　　MTCW 2; SATA 119
Mqhayi, S(amuel) E(dward) K(rune Loliwe)
　　1875-1945 **BLC 3; TCLC 25**
　See also CA 153; CANR 87; DAM MULT

Mrozek, Slawomir 1930- **CLC 3, 13**
　See also CA 13-16R; CAAS 10; CANR 29;
　　CDWLB 4; CWW 2; DLB 232; EWL 3;
　　MTCW 1
Mrs. Belloc-Lowndes
　See Lowndes, Marie Adelaide (Belloc)
Mrs. Fairstar
　See Horne, Richard Henry Hengist
M'Taggart, John M'Taggart Ellis
　See McTaggart, John McTaggart Ellis
Mtwa, Percy (?)- CLC 47
Mueller, Lisel 1924- **CLC 13, 51; PC 33**
　See also CA 93-96; CP 7; DLB 105; PFS 9,
　　13
Muggeridge, Malcolm (Thomas) 1903-1990
　　TCLC 120
　See also AITN 1; CA 101; CANR 33, 63;
　　MTCW 1, 2
Muhammad 570-632 **WLCS**
　See also DA; DAB; DAC; DAM MST
Muir, Edwin 1887-1959 **PC 49; TCLC 2, 87**
　See Moore, Edward
　See also BRWS 6; CA 104; 193; DLB 20,
　　100, 191; EWL 3; RGEL 2
Muir, John 1838-1914 **TCLC 28**
　See also AMWS 9; ANW; CA 165; DLB
　　186, 275
Mujica Lainez, Manuel 1910-1984 **CLC 31**
　See Lainez, Manuel Mujica
　See also CA 81-84; 112; CANR 32; EWL
　　3; HW 1
Mukherjee, Bharati 1940- **AAL; CLC 53,**
　　115; SSC 38
　See also AAYA 46; BEST 89:2; CA 107;
　　CANR 45, 72, 128; CN 7; DAM NOV;
　　DLB 60, 218; DNFS 1, 2; EWL 3; FW;
　　MTCW 1, 2; RGAL 4; RGSF 2; SSFS 7;
　　TUS; WWE 1
Muldoon, Paul 1951- **CLC 32, 72, 166**
　See also BRWS 4; CA 113; 129; CANR 52,
　　91; CP 7; DAM POET; DLB 40; INT CA-
　　129; PFS 7
Mulisch, Harry 1927- **CLC 42**
　See also CA 9-12R; CANR 6, 26, 56, 110;
　　EWL 3
Mull, Martin 1943- **CLC 17**
　See also CA 105
Muller, Wilhelm NCLC 73
Mulock, Dinah Maria
　See Craik, Dinah Maria (Mulock)
　See also RGEL 2
Munday, Anthony 1560-1633 **LC 87**
　See also DLB 62, 172; RGEL 2
Munford, Robert 1737(?)-1783 **LC 5**
　See also DLB 31
Mungo, Raymond 1946- **CLC 72**
　See also CA 49-52; CANR 2
Munro, Alice 1931- **CLC 6, 10, 19, 50, 95;**
　　SSC 3; WLCS
　See also AITN 2; BPFB 2; CA 33-36R;
　　CANR 33, 53, 75, 114; CCA 1; CN 7;
　　DA3; DAC; DAM MST, NOV; DLB 53;
　　EWL 3; MTCW 1, 2; RGEL 2; RGSF 2;
　　SATA 29; SSFS 5, 13, 19; WWE 1
Munro, H(ector) H(ugh) 1870-1916 **WLC**
　See Saki
　See also CA 104; 130; CANR 104; CDBLB
　　1890-1914; DA; DA3; DAB; DAC; DAM
　　MST, NOV; DLB 34, 162; EXPS; MTCW
　　1, 2; RGEL 2; SSFS 15
Murakami, Haruki 1949- **CLC 150**
　See Murakami Haruki
　See also CA 165; CANR 102; MJW; RGWL
　　3; SFW 4
Murakami Haruki
　See Murakami, Haruki
　See also DLB 182; EWL 3

Murasaki, Lady
See Murasaki Shikibu
Murasaki Shikibu 978(?)-1026(?) **CMLC 1**
See also EFS 2; LATS 1; RGWL 2, 3
Murdoch, (Jean) Iris 1919-1999 **CLC 1, 2, 3, 4, 6, 8, 11, 15, 22, 31, 51**
See also BRWS 1; CA 13-16R; 179; CANR 8, 43, 68, 103; CDBLB 1960 to Present; CN 7; CWD; DA3; DAB; DAC; DAM MST, NOV; DLB 14, 194, 233; EWL 3; INT CANR-8; MTCW 1, 2; NFS 18; RGEL 2; TEA; WLIT 4
Murfree, Mary Noailles 1850-1922 **SSC 22; TCLC 135**
See also CA 122; 176; DLB 12, 74; RGAL 4
Murnau, Friedrich Wilhelm
See Plumpe, Friedrich Wilhelm
Murphy, Richard 1927- **CLC 41**
See also BRWS 5; CA 29-32R; CP 7; DLB 40; EWL 3
Murphy, Sylvia 1937- **CLC 34**
See also CA 121
Murphy, Thomas (Bernard) 1935- **CLC 51**
See also CA 101
Murray, Albert L. 1916- **CLC 73**
See also BW 2; CA 49-52; CANR 26, 52, 78; CSW; DLB 38
Murray, James Augustus Henry 1837-1915 **TCLC 117**
Murray, Judith Sargent 1751-1820 **NCLC 63**
See also DLB 37, 200
Murray, Les(lie Allan) 1938- **CLC 40**
See also BRWS 7; CA 21-24R; CANR 11, 27, 56, 103; CP 7; DAM POET; DLB 289; DLBY 2001; EWL 3; RGEL 2
Murry, J. Middleton
See Murry, John Middleton
Murry, John Middleton 1889-1957 **TCLC 16**
See also CA 118; 217; DLB 149
Musgrave, Susan 1951- **CLC 13, 54**
See also CA 69-72; CANR 45, 84; CCA 1; CP 7; CWP
Musil, Robert (Edler von) 1880-1942 **SSC 18; TCLC 12, 68**
See also CA 109; CANR 55, 84; CDWLB 2; DLB 81, 124; EW 9; EWL 3; MTCW 2; RGSF 2; RGWL 2, 3
Muske, Carol CLC 90
See Muske-Dukes, Carol (Anne)
Muske-Dukes, Carol (Anne) 1945-
See Muske, Carol
See also CA 65-68, 203; CAAE 203; CANR 32, 70; CWP
Musset, (Louis Charles) Alfred de 1810-1857 **NCLC 7**
See also DLB 192, 217; EW 6; GFL 1789 to the Present; RGWL 2, 3; TWA
Mussolini, Benito (Amilcare Andrea) 1883-1945 **TCLC 96**
See also CA 116
Mutanabbi, Al-
See al-Mutanabbi, Ahmad ibn al-Husayn Abu al-Tayyib al-Jufi al-Kindi
My Brother's Brother
See Chekhov, Anton (Pavlovich)
Myers, L(eopold) H(amilton) 1881-1944 **TCLC 59**
See also CA 157; DLB 15; EWL 3; RGEL 2
Myers, Walter Dean 1937- **BLC 3; CLC 35**
See also AAYA 4, 23; BW 2; BYA 6, 8, 11; CA 33-36R; CANR 20, 42, 67, 108; CLR 4, 16, 35; DAM MULT, NOV; DLB 33; INT CANR-20; JRDA; LAIT 5; MAICYA 1, 2; MAICYAS 1; MTCW 2; SAAS 2; SATA 41, 71, 109; SATA-Brief 27; WYA; YAW

Myers, Walter M.
See Myers, Walter Dean
Myles, Symon
See Follett, Ken(neth Martin)
Nabokov, Vladimir (Vladimirovich) 1899-1977 **CLC 1, 2, 3, 6, 8, 11, 15, 23, 44, 46, 64; SSC 11; TCLC 108; WLC**
See also AAYA 45; AMW; AMWC 1; AMWR 1; BPFB 2; CA 5-8R; 69-72; CANR 20, 102; CDALB 1941-1968; DA; DA3; DAB; DAC; DAM MST, NOV; DLB 2, 244, 278; DLBD 3; DLBY 1980, 1991; EWL 3; EXPS; LATS 1; MTCW 1, 2; NCFS 4; NFS 9; RGAL 4; RGSF 2; SSFS 6, 15; TUS
Naevius c. 265B.C.-201B.C. **CMLC 37**
See also DLB 211
Nagai, Kafu TCLC 51
See Nagai, Sokichi
See also DLB 180
Nagai, Sokichi 1879-1959
See Nagai, Kafu
See also CA 117
Nagy, Laszlo 1925-1978 **CLC 7**
See also CA 129; 112
Naidu, Sarojini 1879-1949 **TCLC 80**
See also EWL 3; RGEL 2
Naipaul, Shiva(dhar Srinivasa) 1945-1985 **CLC 32, 39**
See also CA 110; 112; 116; CANR 33; DA3; DAM NOV; DLB 157; DLBY 1985; EWL 3; MTCW 1, 2
Naipaul, V(idiadhar) S(urajprasad) 1932- **CLC 4, 7, 9, 13, 18, 37, 105; SSC 38**
See also BPFB 2; BRWS 1; CA 1-4R; CANR 1, 33, 51, 91, 126; CDBLB 1960 to Present; CDWLB 3; CN 7; DA3; DAB; DAC; DAM MST, NOV; DLB 125, 204, 207; DLBY 1985, 2001; EWL 3; LATS 1; MTCW 1, 2; RGEL 2; RGSF 2; TWA; WLIT 4; WWE 1
Nakos, Lilika 1903(?)-1989 **CLC 29**
Napoleon
See Yamamoto, Hisaye
Narayan, R(asipuram) K(rishnaswami) 1906-2001 **CLC 7, 28, 47, 121; SSC 25**
See also BPFB 2; CA 81-84; 196; CANR 33, 61, 112; CN 7; DA3; DAM NOV; DNFS 1; EWL 3; MTCW 1, 2; RGEL 2; RGSF 2; SATA 62; SSFS 5; WWE 1
Nash, (Frediric) Ogden 1902-1971 **CLC 23; PC 21; TCLC 109**
See also CA 13-14; 29-32R; CANR 34, 61; CAP 1; DAM POET; DLB 11; MAICYA 1, 2; MTCW 1, 2; RGAL 4; SATA 2, 46; WP
Nashe, Thomas 1567-1601(?) **LC 41, 89**
See also DLB 167; RGEL 2
Nathan, Daniel
See Dannay, Frederic
Nathan, George Jean 1882-1958 **TCLC 18**
See Hatteras, Owen
See also CA 114; 169; DLB 137
Natsume, Kinnosuke
See Natsume, Soseki
Natsume, Soseki 1867-1916 **TCLC 2, 10**
See Natsume Soseki; Soseki
See also CA 104; 195; RGWL 2, 3; TWA
Natsume Soseki
See Natsume, Soseki
See also DLB 180; EWL 3
Natti, (Mary) Lee 1919-
See Kingman, Lee
See also CA 5-8R; CANR 2
Navarre, Marguerite de
See de Navarre, Marguerite

Naylor, Gloria 1950- **BLC 3; CLC 28, 52, 156; WLCS**
See also AAYA 6, 39; AFAW 1, 2; AMWS 8; BW 2, 3; CA 107; CANR 27, 51, 74; CN 7; CPW; DA; DA3; DAC; DAM MST, MULT, NOV; POP; DLB 173; EWL 3; FW; MTCW 1, 2; NFS 4, 7; RGAL 4; TUS
Neff, Debra CLC 59
Neihardt, John Gneisenau 1881-1973 **CLC 32**
See also CA 13-14; CANR 65; CAP 1; DLB 9, 54, 256; LAIT 2
Nekrasov, Nikolai Alekseevich 1821-1878 **NCLC 11**
See also DLB 277
Nelligan, Emile 1879-1941 **TCLC 14**
See also CA 114; 204; DLB 92; EWL 3
Nelson, Willie 1933- **CLC 17**
See also CA 107; CANR 114
Nemerov, Howard (Stanley) 1920-1991 **CLC 2, 6, 9, 36; PC 24; TCLC 124**
See also AMW; CA 1-4R; 134; CABS 2; CANR 1, 27, 53; DAM POET; DLB 5, 6; DLBY 1983; EWL 3; INT CANR-27; MTCW 1, 2; PFS 10, 14; RGAL 4
Neruda, Pablo 1904-1973 **CLC 1, 2, 5, 7, 9, 28, 62; HLC 2; PC 4; WLC**
See also CA 19-20; 45-48; CAP 2; DA; DA3; DAB; DAC; DAM MST, MULT, POET; DLB 283; DNFS 2; EWL 3; HW 1; LAW; MTCW 1, 2; PFS 11; RGWL 2, 3; TWA; WLIT 1; WP
Nerval, Gerard de 1808-1855 **NCLC 1, 67; PC 13; SSC 18**
See also DLB 217; EW 6; GFL 1789 to the Present; RGSF 2; RGWL 2, 3
Nervo, (Jose) Amado (Ruiz de) 1870-1919 **HLCS 2; TCLC 11**
See also CA 109; 131; DLB 290; EWL 3; HW 1; LAW
Nesbit, Malcolm
See Chester, Alfred
Nessi, Pio Baroja y
See Baroja (y Nessi), Pio
Nestroy, Johann 1801-1862 **NCLC 42**
See also DLB 133; RGWL 2, 3
Netterville, Luke
See O'Grady, Standish (James)
Neufeld, John (Arthur) 1938- **CLC 17**
See also AAYA 11; CA 25-28R; CANR 11, 37, 56; CLR 52; MAICYA 1, 2; SAAS 3; SATA 6, 81, 131; SATA-Essay 131; YAW
Neumann, Alfred 1895-1952 **TCLC 100**
See also CA 183; DLB 56
Neumann, Ferenc
See Molnar, Ferenc
Neville, Emily Cheney 1919- **CLC 12**
See also BYA 2; CA 5-8R; CANR 3, 37, 85; JRDA; MAICYA 1, 2; SAAS 2; SATA 1; YAW
Newbound, Bernard Slade 1930-
See Slade, Bernard
See also CA 81-84; CANR 49; CD 5; DAM DRAM
Newby, P(ercy) H(oward) 1918-1997 **CLC 2, 13**
See also CA 5-8R; 161; CANR 32, 67; CN 7; DAM NOV; DLB 15; MTCW 1; RGEL 2
Newcastle
See Cavendish, Margaret Lucas
Newlove, Donald 1928- **CLC 6**
See also CA 29-32R; CANR 25
Newlove, John (Herbert) 1938- **CLC 14**
See also CA 21-24R; CANR 9, 25; CP 7
Newman, Charles 1938- **CLC 2, 8**
See also CA 21-24R; CANR 84; CN 7

Newman, Edwin (Harold) 1919- **CLC 14**
See also AITN 1; CA 69-72; CANR 5
Newman, John Henry 1801-1890 **NCLC 38, 99**
See also BRWS 7; DLB 18, 32, 55; RGEL 2
Newton, (Sir) Isaac 1642-1727 **LC 35, 53**
See also DLB 252
Newton, Suzanne 1936- **CLC 35**
See also BYA 7; CA 41-44R; CANR 14; JRDA; SATA 5, 77
New York Dept. of Ed. CLC 70
Nexo, Martin Andersen 1869-1954 **TCLC 43**
See also CA 202; DLB 214; EWL 3
Nezval, Vitezslav 1900-1958 **TCLC 44**
See also CA 123; CDWLB 4; DLB 215; EWL 3
Ng, Fae Myenne 1957(?)- **CLC 81**
See also BYA 11; CA 146
Ngema, Mbongeni 1955- **CLC 57**
See also BW 2; CA 143; CANR 84; CD 5
Ngugi, James T(hiong'o) CLC 3, 7, 13, 182
See Ngugi wa Thiong'o
Ngugi wa Thiong'o
See Ngugi wa Thiong'o
See also DLB 125; EWL 3
Ngugi wa Thiong'o 1938- **BLC 3; CLC 36, 182**
See Ngugi, James T(hiong'o); Ngugi wa Thiong'o
See also AFW; BRWS 8; BW 2; CA 81-84; CANR 27, 58; CDWLB 3; DAM MULT, NOV; DNFS 2; MTCW 1, 2; RGEL 2; WWE 1
Niatum, Duane 1938- **NNAL**
See also CA 41-44R; CANR 21, 45, 83; DLB 175
Nichol, B(arrie) P(hillip) 1944-1988 **CLC 18**
See also CA 53-56; DLB 53; SATA 66
Nicholas of Cusa 1401-1464 **LC 80**
See also DLB 115
Nichols, John (Treadwell) 1940- **CLC 38**
See also AMWS 13; CA 9-12R, 190; CAAE 190; CAAS 2; CANR 6, 70, 121; DLBY 1982; LATS 1; TCWW 2
Nichols, Leigh
See Koontz, Dean R(ay)
Nichols, Peter (Richard) 1927- **CLC 5, 36, 65**
See also CA 104; CANR 33, 86; CBD; CD 5; DLB 13, 245; MTCW 1
Nicholson, Linda ed. CLC 65
Ni Chuilleanain, Eilean 1942- **PC 34**
See also CA 126; CANR 53, 83; CP 7; CWP; DLB 40
Nicolas, F. R. E.
See Freeling, Nicolas
Niedecker, Lorine 1903-1970 **CLC 10, 42; PC 42**
See also CA 25-28; CAP 2; DAM POET; DLB 48
Nietzsche, Friedrich (Wilhelm) 1844-1900 **TCLC 10, 18, 55**
See also CA 107; 121; CDWLB 2; DLB 129; EW 7; RGWL 2, 3; TWA
Nievo, Ippolito 1831-1861 **NCLC 22**
Nightingale, Anne Redmon 1943-
See Redmon, Anne
See also CA 103
Nightingale, Florence 1820-1910 **TCLC 85**
See also CA 188; DLB 166
Nijo Yoshimoto 1320-1388 **CMLC 49**
See also DLB 203
Nik. T. O.
See Annensky, Innokenty (Fyodorovich)
Nin, Anais 1903-1977 **CLC 1, 4, 8, 11, 14, 60, 127; SSC 10**
See also AITN 2; AMWS 10; BPFB 2; CA 13-16R; 69-72; CANR 22, 53; DAM

NOV, POP; DLB 2, 4, 152; EWL 3; GLL 2; MAWW; MTCW 1, 2; RGAL 4; RGSF 2
Nisbet, Robert A(lexander) 1913-1996 **TCLC 117**
See also CA 25-28R; 153; CANR 17; INT CANR-17
Nishida, Kitaro 1870-1945 **TCLC 83**
Nishiwaki, Junzaburo
See Nishiwaki, Junzaburo
See also CA 194
Nishiwaki, Junzaburo 1894-1982 **PC 15**
See Nishiwaki, Junzaburo; Nishiwaki Junzaburo
See also CA 194; 107; MJW; RGWL 3
Nishiwaki Junzaburo
See Nishiwaki, Junzaburo
See also EWL 3
Nissenson, Hugh 1933- **CLC 4, 9**
See also CA 17-20R; CANR 27, 108; CN 7; DLB 28
Nister, Der
See Der Nister
See also EWL 3
Niven, Larry CLC 8
See Niven, Laurence Van Cott
See also AAYA 27; BPFB 2; BYA 10; DLB 8; SCFW 2
Niven, Laurence Van Cott 1938-
See Niven, Larry
See also CA 21-24R, 207; CAAE 207; CAAS 12; CANR 14, 44, 66, 113; CPW; DAM POP; MTCW 1, 2; SATA 95; SFW 4
Nixon, Agnes Eckhardt 1927- **CLC 21**
See also CA 110
Nizan, Paul 1905-1940 **TCLC 40**
See also CA 161; DLB 72; EWL 3; GFL 1789 to the Present
Nkosi, Lewis 1936- **BLC 3; CLC 45**
See also BW 1, 3; CA 65-68; CANR 27, 81; CBD; CD 5; DAM MULT; DLB 157, 225; WWE 1
Nodier, (Jean) Charles (Emmanuel) 1780-1844 **NCLC 19**
See also DLB 119; GFL 1789 to the Present
Noguchi, Yone 1875-1947 **TCLC 80**
Nolan, Christopher 1965- **CLC 58**
See also CA 111; CANR 88
Noon, Jeff 1957- **CLC 91**
See also CA 148; CANR 83; DLB 267; SFW 4
Norden, Charles
See Durrell, Lawrence (George)
Nordhoff, Charles Bernard 1887-1947 **TCLC 23**
See also CA 108; 211; DLB 9; LAIT 1; RHW 1; SATA 23
Norfolk, Lawrence 1963- **CLC 76**
See also CA 144; CANR 85; CN 7; DLB 267
Norman, Marsha 1947- **CLC 28, 186; DC 8**
See also CA 105; CABS 3; CAD; CANR 41; CD 5; CSW; CWD; DAM DRAM; DFS 2; DLB 266; DLBY 1984; FW
Normyx
See Douglas, (George) Norman
Norris, (Benjamin) Frank(lin, Jr.) 1870-1902 **SSC 28; TCLC 24**
See also AMW; AMWC 2; BPFB 2; CA 110; 160; CDALB 1865-1917; DLB 12, 71, 186; LMFS 2; NFS 12; RGAL 4; TCWW 2; TUS
Norris, Leslie 1921- **CLC 14**
See also CA 11-12; CANR 14, 117; CAP 1; CP 7; DLB 27, 256
North, Andrew
See Norton, Andre

North, Anthony
See Koontz, Dean R(ay)
North, Captain George
See Stevenson, Robert Louis (Balfour)
North, Captain George
See Stevenson, Robert Louis (Balfour)
North, Milou
See Erdrich, Louise
Northrup, B. A.
See Hubbard, L(afayette) Ron(ald)
North Staffs
See Hulme, T(homas) E(rnest)
Northup, Solomon 1808-1863 **NCLC 105**
Norton, Alice Mary
See Norton, Andre
See also MAICYA 1; SATA 1, 43
Norton, Andre 1912- **CLC 12**
See Norton, Alice Mary
See also AAYA 14; BPFB 2; BYA 4, 10, 12; CA 1-4R; CANR 68; CLR 50; DLB 8, 52; JRDA; MAICYA 2; MTCW 1; SATA 91; SUFW 1, 2; YAW
Norton, Caroline 1808-1877 **NCLC 47**
See also DLB 21, 159, 199
Norway, Nevil Shute 1899-1960
See Shute, Nevil
See also CA 102; 93-96; CANR 85; MTCW 2
Norwid, Cyprian Kamil 1821-1883 **NCLC 17**
See also RGWL 3
Nosille, Nabrah
See Ellison, Harlan (Jay)
Nossack, Hans Erich 1901-1978 **CLC 6**
See also CA 93-96; 85-88; DLB 69; EWL 3
Nostradamus 1503-1566 **LC 27**
Nosu, Chuji
See Ozu, Yasujiro
Notenburg, Eleanora (Genrikhovna) von
See Guro, Elena (Genrikhovna)
Nova, Craig 1945- **CLC 7, 31**
See also CA 45-48; CANR 2, 53, 127
Novak, Joseph
See Kosinski, Jerzy (Nikodem)
Novalis 1772-1801 **NCLC 13**
See also CDWLB 2; DLB 90; EW 5; RGWL 2, 3
Novick, Peter 1934- **CLC 164**
See also CA 188
Novis, Emile
See Weil, Simone (Adolphine)
Nowlan, Alden (Albert) 1933-1983 **CLC 15**
See also CA 9-12R; CANR 5; DAC; DAM MST; DLB 53; PFS 12
Noyes, Alfred 1880-1958 **PC 27; TCLC 7**
See also CA 104; 188; DLB 20; EXPP; FANT; PFS 4; RGEL 2
Nugent, Richard Bruce 1906(?)-1987 **HR 3**
See also BW 1; CA 125; DLB 51; GLL 2
Nunn, Kem CLC 34
See also CA 159
Nwapa, Flora (Nwanzuruaha) 1931-1993 **BLCS; CLC 133**
See also BW 2; CA 143; CANR 83; CD-WLB 3; CWRI 5; DLB 125; EWL 3; WLIT 2
Nye, Robert 1939- **CLC 13, 42**
See also CA 33-36R; CANR 29, 67, 107; CN 7; CP 7; CWRI 5; DAM NOV; DLB 14, 271; FANT; HGG; MTCW 1; RHW; SATA 6
Nyro, Laura 1947-1997 **CLC 17**
See also CA 194
Oates, Joyce Carol 1938- **CLC 1, 2, 3, 6, 9, 11, 15, 19, 33, 52, 108, 134; SSC 6, 70; WLC**
See also AAYA 15, 52; AITN 1; AMWS 2; BEST 89:2; BPFB 2; BYA 11; CA 5-8R; CANR 25, 45, 74, 113, 129; CDALB

O Nuallain, Brian 1911-1966
See O'Brien, Flann
See also CA 21-22; 25-28R; CAP 2; DLB 231; FANT; TEA

Ophuls, Max 1902-1957 **TCLC 79**
See also CA 113

Opie, Amelia 1769-1853 **NCLC 65**
See also DLB 116, 159; RGEL 2

Oppen, George 1908-1984 **CLC 7, 13, 34; PC 35; TCLC 107**
See also CA 13-16R; 113; CANR 8, 82; DLB 5, 165

Oppenheim, E(dward) Phillips 1866-1946 **TCLC 45**
See also CA 111; 202; CMW 4; DLB 70

Opuls, Max
See Ophuls, Max

Origen c. 185-c. 254 **CMLC 19**

Orlovitz, Gil 1918-1973 **CLC 22**
See also CA 77-80; 45-48; DLB 2, 5

Orris
See Ingelow, Jean

Ortega y Gasset, Jose 1883-1955 **HLC 2; TCLC 9**
See also CA 106; 130; DAM MULT; EW 9; EWL 3; HW 1, 2; MTCW 1, 2

Ortese, Anna Maria 1914-1998 **CLC 89**
See also DLB 177; EWL 3

Ortiz, Simon J(oseph) 1941- **CLC 45; NNAL; PC 17**
See also AMWS 4; CA 134; CANR 69, 118; CP 7; DAM MULT, POET; DLB 120, 175, 256; EXPP; PFS 4, 16; RGAL 4

Orton, Joe CLC 4, 13, 43; DC 3
See Orton, John Kingsley
See also BRWS 5; CBD; CDBLB 1960 to Present; DFS 3, 6; DLB 13; GLL 1; MTCW 2; RGEL 2; TEA; WLIT 4

Orton, John Kingsley 1933-1967
See Orton, Joe
See also CA 85-88; CANR 35, 66; DAM DRAM; MTCW 1, 2

Orwell, George SSC 68; TCLC 2, 6, 15, 31, 51, 128, 129; WLC
See Blair, Eric (Arthur)
See also BPFB 3; BRW 7; BYA 5; CDBLB 1945-1960; CLR 68; DAB; DLB 15, 98, 195, 255; EWL 3; EXPN; LAIT 4, 5; LATS 1; NFS 3, 7; RGEL 2; SCFW 2; SFW 4; SSFS 4; TEA; WLIT 4; YAW

Osborne, David
See Silverberg, Robert

Osborne, George
See Silverberg, Robert

Osborne, John (James) 1929-1994 **CLC 1, 2, 5, 11, 45; WLC**
See also BRWS 1; CA 13-16R; 147; CANR 21, 56; CDBLB 1945-1960; DA; DAB; DAC; DAM DRAM, MST; DFS 4; DLB 13; EWL 3; MTCW 1, 2; RGEL 2

Osborne, Lawrence 1958- **CLC 50**
See also CA 189

Osbourne, Lloyd 1868-1947 **TCLC 93**

Oshima, Nagisa 1932- **CLC 20**
See also CA 116; 121; CANR 78

Oskison, John Milton 1874-1947 **NNAL; TCLC 35**
See also CA 144; CANR 84; DAM MULT; DLB 175

Ossian c. 3rd cent. - **CMLC 28**
See Macpherson, James

Ossoli, Sarah Margaret (Fuller) 1810-1850 **NCLC 5, 50**
See Fuller, Margaret; Fuller, Sarah Margaret
See also CDALB 1640-1865; FW; LMFS 1; SATA 25

Ostriker, Alicia (Suskin) 1937- **CLC 132**
See also CA 25-28R; CAAS 24; CANR 10, 30, 62, 99; CWP; DLB 120; EXPP; PFS 19

Ostrovsky, Aleksandr Nikolaevich
See Ostrovsky, Alexander
See also DLB 277

Ostrovsky, Alexander 1823-1886 **NCLC 30, 57**
See Ostrovsky, Aleksandr Nikolaevich

Otero, Blas de 1916-1979 **CLC 11**
See also CA 89-92; DLB 134; EWL 3

O'Trigger, Sir Lucius
See Horne, Richard Henry Hengist

Otto, Rudolf 1869-1937 **TCLC 85**

Otto, Whitney 1955- **CLC 70**
See also CA 140; CANR 120

Ouida TCLC 43
See De la Ramee, Marie Louise (Ouida)
See also DLB 18, 156; RGEL 2

Ouologuem, Yambo 1940- **CLC 146**
See also CA 111; 176

Ousmane, Sembene 1923- **BLC 3; CLC 66**
See Sembene, Ousmane
See also BW 1, 3; CA 117; 125; CANR 81; CWW 2; MTCW 1

Ovid 43B.C.-17 **CMLC 7; PC 2**
See also AW 2; CDWLB 1; DA3; DAM POET; DLB 211; RGWL 2, 3; WP

Owen, Hugh
See Faust, Frederick (Schiller)

Owen, Wilfred (Edward Salter) 1893-1918 **PC 19; TCLC 5, 27; WLC**
See also BRW 6; CA 104; 141; CDBLB 1914-1945; DA; DAB; DAC; DAM MST, POET; DLB 20; EWL 3; EXPP; MTCW 2; PFS 10; RGEL 2; WLIT 4

Owens, Louis (Dean) 1948-2002 **NNAL**
See also CA 137, 179; 207; CAAE 179; CAAS 24; CANR 71

Owens, Rochelle 1936- **CLC 8**
See also CA 17-20R; CAAS 2; CAD; CANR 39; CD 5; CP 7; CWD; CWP

Oz, Amos 1939- **CLC 5, 8, 11, 27, 33, 54; SSC 66**
See also CA 53-56; CANR 27, 47, 65, 113; CWW 2; DAM NOV; EWL 3; MTCW 1, 2; RGSF 2; RGWL 3

Ozick, Cynthia 1928- **CLC 3, 7, 28, 62, 155; SSC 15, 60**
See also AMWS 5; BEST 90:1; CA 17-20R; CANR 23, 58, 116; CN 7; CPW; DA3; DAM NOV, POP; DLB 28, 152; DLBY 1982; EWL 3; EXPS; INT CANR-23; MTCW 1, 2; RGAL 4; RGSF 2; SSFS 3, 12

Ozu, Yasujiro 1903-1963 **CLC 16**
See also CA 112

Pabst, G. W. 1885-1967 **TCLC 127**

Pacheco, C.
See Pessoa, Fernando (Antonio Nogueira)

Pacheco, Jose Emilio 1939- **HLC 2**
See also CA 111; 131; CANR 65; DAM MULT; DLB 290; EWL 3; HW 1, 2; RGSF 2

Pa Chin CLC 18
See Li Fei-kan
See also EWL 3

Pack, Robert 1929- **CLC 13**
See also CA 1-4R; CANR 3, 44, 82; CP 7; DLB 5; SATA 118

Padgett, Lewis
See Kuttner, Henry

Padilla (Lorenzo), Heberto 1932-2000 **CLC 38**
See also AITN 1; CA 123; 131; 189; EWL 3; HW 1

Page, James Patrick 1944-
See Page, Jimmy
See also CA 204

Page, Jimmy 1944- **CLC 12**
See Page, James Patrick

Page, Louise 1955- **CLC 40**
See also CA 140; CANR 76; CBD; CD 5; CWD; DLB 233

Page, P(atricia) K(athleen) 1916- **CLC 7, 18; PC 12**
See Cape, Judith
See also CA 53-56; CANR 4, 22, 65; CP 7; DAC; DAM MST; DLB 68; MTCW 1; RGEL 2

Page, Stanton
See Fuller, Henry Blake

Page, Stanton
See Fuller, Henry Blake

Page, Thomas Nelson 1853-1922 **SSC 23**
See also CA 118; 177; DLB 12, 78; DLBD 13; RGAL 4

Pagels, Elaine Hiesey 1943- **CLC 104**
See also CA 45-48; CANR 2, 24, 51; FW; NCFS 4

Paget, Violet 1856-1935
See Lee, Vernon
See also CA 104; 166; GLL 1; HGG

Paget-Lowe, Henry
See Lovecraft, H(oward) P(hillips)

Paglia, Camille (Anna) 1947- **CLC 68**
See also CA 140; CANR 72; CPW; FW; GLL 2; MTCW 2

Paige, Richard
See Koontz, Dean R(ay)

Paine, Thomas 1737-1809 **NCLC 62**
See also AMWS 1; CDALB 1640-1865; DLB 31, 43, 73, 158; LAIT 1; RGAL 4; RGEL 2; TUS

Pakenham, Antonia
See Fraser, Antonia (Pakenham)

Palamas, Costis
See Palamas, Kostes

Palamas, Kostes 1859-1943 **TCLC 5**
See Palamas, Kostis
See also CA 105; 190; RGWL 2, 3

Palamas, Kostis
See Palamas, Kostes
See also EWL 3

Palazzeschi, Aldo 1885-1974 **CLC 11**
See also CA 89-92; 53-56; DLB 114, 264; EWL 3

Pales Matos, Luis 1898-1959 **HLCS 2**
See Pales Matos, Luis
See also DLB 290; HW 1; LAW

Paley, Grace 1922- **CLC 4, 6, 37, 140; SSC 8**
See also AMWS 6; CA 25-28R; CANR 13, 46, 74, 118; CN 7; CPW; DA3; DAM POP; DLB 28, 218; EWL 3; EXPS; FW; INT CANR-13; MAWW; MTCW 1, 2; RGAL 4; RGSF 2; SSFS 3

Palin, Michael (Edward) 1943- **CLC 21**
See Monty Python
See also CA 107; CANR 35, 109; SATA 67

Palliser, Charles 1947- **CLC 65**
See also CA 136; CANR 76; CN 7

Palma, Ricardo 1833-1919 **TCLC 29**
See also CA 168; LAW

Pamuk, Orhan 1952- **CLC 185**
See also CA 142; CANR 75, 127; CWW 2

Pancake, Breece Dexter 1952-1979
See Pancake, Breece D'J
See also CA 123; 109

Pancake, Breece D'J CLC 29; SSC 61
See Pancake, Breece Dexter
See also DLB 130

Panchenko, Nikolai CLC 59

Pankhurst, Emmeline (Goulden) 1858-1928 **TCLC 100**
See also CA 116; FW

Author Index

Peckinpah, (David) Sam(uel) 1925-1984 **CLC 20**
See also CA 109; 114; CANR 82
Pedersen, Knut 1859-1952
See Hamsun, Knut
See also CA 104; 119; CANR 63; MTCW 1, 2
Peeslake, Gaffer
See Durrell, Lawrence (George)
Peguy, Charles (Pierre) 1873-1914 **TCLC 10**
See also CA 107; 193; DLB 258; EWL 3; GFL 1789 to the Present
Peirce, Charles Sanders 1839-1914 **TCLC 81**
See also CA 194; DLB 270
Pellicer, Carlos 1900(?)-1977 **HLCS 2**
See also CA 153; 69-72; DLB 290; EWL 3; HW 1
Pena, Ramon del Valle y
See Valle-Inclan, Ramon (Maria) del
Pendennis, Arthur Esquir
See Thackeray, William Makepeace
Penn, William 1644-1718 **LC 25**
See also DLB 24
PEPECE
See Prado (Calvo), Pedro
Pepys, Samuel 1633-1703 **LC 11, 58; WLC**
See also BRW 2; CDBLB 1660-1789; DA; DA3; DAB; DAC; DAM MST; DLB 101, 213; NCFS 4; RGEL 2; TEA; WLIT 3
Percy, Thomas 1729-1811 **NCLC 95**
See also DLB 104
Percy, Walker 1916-1990 **CLC 2, 3, 6, 8, 14, 18, 47, 65**
See also AMWS 3; BPFB 3; CA 1-4R; 131; CANR 1, 23, 64; CPW; CSW; DA3; DAM NOV, POP; DLB 2; DLBY 1980, 1990; EWL 3; MTCW 1, 2; RGAL 4; TUS
Percy, William Alexander 1885-1942 **TCLC 84**
See also CA 163; MTCW 2
Perec, Georges 1936-1982 **CLC 56, 116**
See also CA 141; DLB 83; EWL 3; GFL 1789 to the Present; RGWL 3
Pereda (y Sanchez de Porrua), Jose Maria de 1833-1906 **TCLC 16**
See also CA 117
Pereda y Porrua, Jose Maria de
See Pereda (y Sanchez de Porrua), Jose Maria de
Peregoy, George Weems
See Mencken, H(enry) L(ouis)
Perelman, S(idney) J(oseph) 1904-1979 **CLC 3, 5, 9, 15, 23, 44, 49; SSC 32**
See also AITN 1, 2; BPFB 3; CA 73-76; 89-92; CANR 18; DAM DRAM; DLB 11, 44; MTCW 1, 2; RGAL 4
Peret, Benjamin 1899-1959 **PC 33; TCLC 20**
See also CA 117; 186; GFL 1789 to the Present
Peretz, Isaac Leib 1851(?)-1915
See Peretz, Isaac Loeb
See also CA 201
Peretz, Isaac Loeb 1851(?)-1915 **SSC 26; TCLC 16**
See Peretz, Isaac Leib
See also CA 109
Peretz, Yitzhok Leibush
See Peretz, Isaac Loeb
Perez Galdos, Benito 1843-1920 **HLCS 2; TCLC 27**
See Galdos, Benito Perez
See also CA 125; 153; EWL 3; HW 1; RGWL 2, 3
Peri Rossi, Cristina 1941- **CLC 156; HLCS 2**
See also CA 131; CANR 59, 81; DLB 145, 290; EWL 3; HW 1, 2

Perlata
See Peret, Benjamin
Perloff, Marjorie G(abrielle) 1931- **CLC 137**
See also CA 57-60; CANR 7, 22, 49, 104
Perrault, Charles 1628-1703 **DC 12; LC 2, 56**
See also BYA 4; CLR 79; DLB 268; GFL Beginnings to 1789; MAICYA 1, 2; RGWL 2, 3; SATA 25; WCH
Perry, Anne 1938- **CLC 126**
See also CA 101; CANR 22, 50, 84; CMW 4; CN 7; CPW; DLB 276
Perry, Brighton
See Sherwood, Robert E(mmet)
Perse, St.-John
See Leger, (Marie-Rene Auguste) Alexis Saint-Leger
Perse, Saint-John
See Leger, (Marie-Rene Auguste) Alexis Saint-Leger
See also DLB 258; RGWL 3
Perutz, Leo(pold) 1882-1957 **TCLC 60**
See also CA 147; DLB 81
Peseenz, Tulio F.
See Lopez y Fuentes, Gregorio
Pesetsky, Bette 1932- **CLC 28**
See also CA 133; DLB 130
Peshkov, Alexei Maximovich 1868-1936
See Gorky, Maxim
See also CA 105; 141; CANR 83; DA; DAC; DAM DRAM, MST, NOV; MTCW 2
Pessoa, Fernando (Antonio Nogueira) 1888-1935 **HLC 2; PC 20; TCLC 27**
See also CA 125; 183; DAM MULT; DLB 287; EW 10; EWL 3; RGWL 2, 3; WP
Peterkin, Julia Mood 1880-1961 **CLC 31**
See also CA 102; DLB 9
Peters, Joan K(aren) 1945- **CLC 39**
See also CA 158; CANR 109
Peters, Robert L(ouis) 1924- **CLC 7**
See also CA 13-16R; CAAS 8; CP 7; DLB 105
Petofi, Sandor 1823-1849 **NCLC 21**
See also RGWL 2, 3
Petrakis, Harry Mark 1923- **CLC 3**
See also CA 9-12R; CANR 4, 30, 85; CN 7
Petrarch 1304-1374 **CMLC 20; PC 8**
See also DA3; DAM POET; EW 2; LMFS 1; RGWL 2. 3
Petronius c. 20-66 **CMLC 34**
See also AW 2; CDWLB 1; DLB 211; RGWL 2, 3
Petrov, Evgeny TCLC 21
See Kataev, Evgeny Petrovich
Petry, Ann (Lane) 1908-1997 **CLC 1, 7, 18; TCLC 112**
See also AFAW 1, 2; BPFB 3; BW 1, 3; BYA 2; CA 5-8R; 157; CAAS 6; CANR 4, 46; CLR 12; CN 7; DLB 76; EWL 3; JRDA; LAIT 1; MAICYA 1, 2; MAICYAS 1; MTCW 1; RGAL 4; SATA 5; SATA-Obit 94; TUS
Petursson, Halligrimur 1614-1674 **LC 8**
Peychinovich
See Vazov, Ivan (Minchov)
Phaedrus c. 15B.C.-c. 50 **CMLC 25**
See also DLB 211
Phelps (Ward), Elizabeth Stuart
See Phelps, Elizabeth Stuart
See also FW
Phelps, Elizabeth Stuart 1844-1911 **TCLC 113**
See Phelps (Ward), Elizabeth Stuart
See also DLB 74
Philips, Katherine 1632-1664 **LC 30; PC 40**
See also DLB 131; RGEL 2
Philipson, Morris H. 1926- **CLC 53**
See also CA 1-4R; CANR 4

Phillips, Caryl 1958- **BLCS; CLC 96**
See also BRWS 5; BW 2; CA 141; CANR 63, 104; CBD; CD 5; CN 7; DA3; DAM MULT; DLB 157; EWL 3; MTCW 2; WLIT 4; WWE 1
Phillips, David Graham 1867-1911 **TCLC 44**
See also CA 108; 176; DLB 9, 12; RGAL 4
Phillips, Jack
See Sandburg, Carl (August)
Phillips, Jayne Anne 1952- **CLC 15, 33, 139; SSC 16**
See also BPFB 3; CA 101; CANR 24, 50, 96; CN 7; CSW; DLBY 1980; INT CANR-24; MTCW 1, 2; RGAL 4; RGSF 2; SSFS 4
Phillips, Richard
See Dick, Philip K(indred)
Phillips, Robert (Schaeffer) 1938- **CLC 28**
See also CA 17-20R; CAAS 13; CANR 8; DLB 105
Phillips, Ward
See Lovecraft, H(oward) P(hillips)
Philostratus, Flavius c. 179-c. 244 **CMLC 62**
Piccolo, Lucio 1901-1969 **CLC 13**
See also CA 97-100; DLB 114; EWL 3
Pickthall, Marjorie L(owry) C(hristie) 1883-1922 **TCLC 21**
See also CA 107; DLB 92
Pico della Mirandola, Giovanni 1463-1494 **LC 15**
See also LMFS 1
Piercy, Marge 1936- **CLC 3, 6, 14, 18, 27, 62, 128; PC 29**
See also BPFB 3; CA 21-24R; 187; CAAE 187; CAAS 1; CANR 13, 43, 66, 111; CN 7; CP 7; CWP; DLB 120, 227; EXPP; FW; MTCW 1, 2; PFS 9; SFW 4
Piers, Robert
See Anthony, Piers
Pieyre de Mandiargues, Andre 1909-1991
See Mandiargues, Andre Pieyre de
See also CA 103; 136; CANR 22, 82; EWL 3; GFL 1789 to the Present
Pilnyak, Boris 1894-1938 **SSC 48; TCLC 23**
See Vogau, Boris Andreyevich
See also EWL 3
Pinchback, Eugene
See Toomer, Jean
Pincherle, Alberto 1907-1990 **CLC 11, 18**
See Moravia, Alberto
See also CA 25-28R; 132; CANR 33, 63; DAM NOV; MTCW 1
Pinckney, Darryl 1953- **CLC 76**
See also BW 2, 3; CA 143; CANR 79
Pindar 518(?)B.C.-438(?)B.C. **CMLC 12; PC 19**
See also AW 1; CDWLB 1; DLB 176; RGWL 2
Pineda, Cecile 1942- **CLC 39**
See also CA 118; DLB 209
Pinero, Arthur Wing 1855-1934 **TCLC 32**
See also CA 110; 153; DAM DRAM; DLB 10; RGEL 2
Pinero, Miguel (Antonio Gomez) 1946-1988 **CLC 4, 55**
See also CA 61-64; 125; CAD; CANR 29, 90; DLB 266; HW 1; LLW 1
Pinget, Robert 1919-1997 **CLC 7, 13, 37**
See also CA 85-88; 160; CWW 2; DLB 83; EWL 3; GFL 1789 to the Present
Pink Floyd
See Barrett, (Roger) Syd; Gilmour, David; Mason, Nick; Waters, Roger; Wright, Rick
Pinkney, Edward 1802-1828 **NCLC 31**
See also DLB 248

Pinkwater, Daniel
See Pinkwater, Daniel Manus
Pinkwater, Daniel Manus 1941- **CLC 35**
See also AAYA 1, 46; BYA 9; CA 29-32R;
CANR 12, 38, 89; CLR 4; CSW; FANT;
JRDA; MAICYA 1, 2; SAAS 3; SATA 8,
46, 76, 114; SFW 4; YAW
Pinkwater, Manus
See Pinkwater, Daniel Manus
Pinsky, Robert 1940- **CLC 9, 19, 38, 94, 121;
PC 27**
See also AMWS 6; CA 29-32R; CAAS 4;
CANR 58, 97; CP 7; DA3; DAM POET;
DLBY 1982, 1998; MTCW 2; PFS 18;
RGAL 4
Pinta, Harold
See Pinter, Harold
Pinter, Harold 1930- **CLC 1, 3, 6, 9, 11, 15,
27, 58, 73; DC 15; WLC**
See also BRWR 1; BRWS 1; CA 5-8R;
CANR 33, 65, 112; CBD; CD 5; CDBLB
1960 to Present; DA; DA3; DAB; DAC;
DAM DRAM, MST; DFS 3, 5, 7, 14;
DLB 13; EWL 3; IDFW 3, 4; LMFS 2;
MTCW 1, 2; RGEL 2; TEA
Piozzi, Hester Lynch (Thrale) 1741-1821
NCLC 57
See also DLB 104, 142
Pirandello, Luigi 1867-1936 **DC 5; SSC 22;
TCLC 4, 29; WLC**
See also CA 104; 153; CANR 103; DA;
DA3; DAB; DAC; DAM DRAM, MST;
DFS 4, 9; DLB 264; EW 8; EWL 3;
MTCW 2; RGSF 2; RGWL 2, 3
Pirsig, Robert M(aynard) 1928- **CLC 4, 6, 73**
See also CA 53-56; CANR 42, 74; CPW 1;
DA3; DAM POP; MTCW 1, 2; SATA 39
Pisarev, Dmitrii Ivanovich
See Pisarev, Dmitry Ivanovich
See also DLB 277
Pisarev, Dmitry Ivanovich 1840-1868 **NCLC
25**
See also Pisarev, Dmitrii Ivanovich
Pix, Mary (Griffith) 1666-1709 **LC 8**
See also DLB 80
Pixerecourt, (Rene Charles) Guilbert de
1773-1844 **NCLC 39**
See also DLB 192; GFL 1789 to the Present
Plaatje, Sol(omon) T(shekisho) 1878-1932
BLCS; TCLC 73
See also BW 2, 3; CA 141; CANR 79; DLB
125, 225
Plaidy, Jean
See Hibbert, Eleanor Alice Burford
Planche, James Robinson 1796-1880 **NCLC
42**
See also RGEL 2
Plant, Robert 1948- **CLC 12**
Plante, David (Robert) 1940- **CLC 7, 23, 38**
See also CA 37-40R; CANR 12, 36, 58, 82;
CN 7; DAM NOV; DLBY 1983; INT
CANR-12; MTCW 1
Plath, Sylvia 1932-1963 **CLC 1, 2, 3, 5, 9, 11,
14, 17, 50, 51, 62, 111; PC 1, 37; WLC**
See also AAYA 13; AMWR 2; AMWS 1;
BPFB 3; CA 19-20; CANR 34; CAP
2; CDALB 1941-1968; DA; DA3; DAB;
DAC; DAM MST, POET; DLB 5, 6, 152;
EWL 3; EXPN; EXPP; FW; LAIT 4;
MAWW; MTCW 1, 2; NFS 1; PAB; PFS
1, 15; RGAL 4; SATA 96; TUS; WP;
YAW
Plato c. 428B.C.-347B.C. **CMLC 8; WLCS**
See also AW 1; CDWLB 1; DA; DA3;
DAB; DAC; DAM MST; DLB 176; LAIT
1; LATS 1; RGWL 2, 3
Platonov, Andrei
See Klimentov, Andrei Platonovich

Platonov, Andrei Platonovich
See Klimentov, Andrei Platonovich
See also DLB 272
Platonov, Andrey Platonovich
See Klimentov, Andrei Platonovich
See also EWL 3
Platt, Kin 1911- **CLC 26**
See also AAYA 11; CA 17-20R; CANR 11;
JRDA; SAAS 17; SATA 21, 86; WYA
Plautus c. 254B.C.-c. 184B.C. **CMLC 24; DC
6**
See also AW 1; CDWLB 1; DLB 211;
RGWL 2, 3
Plick et Plock
See Simenon, Georges (Jacques Christian)
Plieksans, Janis
See Rainis, Janis
Plimpton, George (Ames) 1927-2003 **CLC 36**
See also AITN 1; CA 21-24R; CANR 32,
70, 103; DLB 185, 241; MTCW 1, 2;
SATA 10
Pliny the Elder c. 23-79 **CMLC 23**
See also DLB 211
Pliny the Younger c. 61-c. 112 **CMLC 62**
See also AW 2; DLB 211
Plomer, William Charles Franklin 1903-1973
CLC 4, 8
See also AFW; CA 21-22; CANR 34; CAP
2; DLB 20, 162, 191, 225; EWL 3;
MTCW 1; RGEL 2; RGSF 2; SATA 24
Plotinus 204-270 **CMLC 46**
See also CDWLB 1; DLB 176
Plowman, Piers
See Kavanagh, Patrick (Joseph)
Plum, J.
See Wodehouse, P(elham) G(renville)
Plumly, Stanley (Ross) 1939- **CLC 33**
See also CA 108; 110; CANR 97; CP 7;
DLB 5, 193; INT CA-110
Plumpe, Friedrich Wilhelm 1888-1931 **TCLC
53**
See also CA 112
Plutarch c. 46-c. 120 **CMLC 60**
See also AW 2; CDWLB 1; DLB 176;
RGWL 2, 3; TWA
Po Chu-i 772-846 **CMLC 24**
Poe, Edgar Allan 1809-1849 **NCLC 1, 16, 55,
78, 94, 97, 117; PC 1, 54; SSC 1, 22, 34,
35, 54; WLC**
See also AAYA 14; AMW; AMWC 1;
AMWR 2; BPFB 3; BYA 5, 11; CDALB
1640-1865; CMW 4; DA; DA3; DAB;
DAC; DAM MST, POET; DLB 3, 59, 73,
74, 248, 254; EXPP; EXPS; HGG; LAIT
2; LATS 1; LMFS 1; MSW; PAB; PFS 1,
3, 9; RGAL 4; RGSF 2; SATA 23; SCFW
2; SFW 4; SSFS 2, 4, 7, 8, 16; SUFW;
TUS; WP; WYA
Poet of Titchfield Street, The
See Pound, Ezra (Weston Loomis)
Pohl, Frederik 1919- **CLC 18; SSC 25**
See also AAYA 24; CA 61-64, 188; CAAE
188; CAAS 1; CANR 11, 37, 81; CN 7;
DLB 8; INT CANR-11; MTCW 1, 2;
SATA 24; SCFW 2; SFW 4
Poirier, Louis 1910-
See Gracq, Julien
See also CA 122; 126; CWW 2
Poitier, Sidney 1927- **CLC 26**
See also BW 1; CA 117; CANR 94
Pokagon, Simon 1830-1899 **NNAL**
See also DAM MULT
Polanski, Roman 1933- **CLC 16, 178**
See also CA 77-80
Poliakoff, Stephen 1952- **CLC 38**
See also CA 106; CANR 116; CBD; CD 5;
DLB 13

Police, The
See Copeland, Stewart (Armstrong); Sum-
mers, Andrew James
Polidori, John William 1795-1821 **NCLC 51**
See also DLB 116; HGG
Pollitt, Katha 1949- **CLC 28, 122**
See also CA 120; 122; CANR 66, 108;
MTCW 1, 2
Pollock, (Mary) Sharon 1936- **CLC 50**
See also CA 141; CD 5; CWD; DAC; DAM
DRAM, MST; DFS 3; DLB 60; FW
Pollock, Sharon 1936- **DC 20**
Polo, Marco 1254-1324 **CMLC 15**
Polonsky, Abraham (Lincoln) 1910-1999
CLC 92
See also CA 104; 187; DLB 26; INT CA-
104
Polybius c. 200B.C.-c. 118B.C. **CMLC 17**
See also AW 1; DLB 176; RGWL 2, 3
Pomerance, Bernard 1940- **CLC 13**
See also CA 101; CAD; CANR 49; CD 5;
DAM DRAM; DFS 9; LAIT 2
Ponge, Francis 1899-1988 **CLC 6, 18**
See also CA 85-88; 126; CANR 40, 86;
DAM POET; DLBY 2002; EWL 3; GFL
1789 to the Present; RGWL 2, 3
Poniatowska, Elena 1933- **CLC 140; HLC 2**
See also CA 101; CANR 32, 66, 107; CD-
WLB 3; DAM MULT; DLB 113; EWL 3;
HW 1, 2; LAWS 1; WLIT 1
Pontoppidan, Henrik 1857-1943 **TCLC 29**
See also CA 170
Poole, Josephine CLC 17
See Helyar, Jane Penelope Josephine
See also SAAS 2; SATA 5
Popa, Vasko 1922-1991 **CLC 19**
See also CA 112; 148; CDWLB 4; DLB
181; EWL 3; RGWL 2, 3
Pope, Alexander 1688-1744 **LC 3, 58, 60, 64;
PC 26; WLC**
See also BRW 3; BRWC 1; BRWR 1; CD-
BLB 1660-1789; DA; DA3; DAB; DAC;
DAM MST, POET; DLB 95, 101, 213;
EXPP; PAB; PFS 12; RGEL 2; WLIT 3;
WP
Popov, Evgenii Anatol'evich
See Popov, Yevgeny
See also DLB 285
Popov, Yevgeny CLC 59
See Popov, Evgenii Anatol'evich
Poquelin, Jean-Baptiste
See Moliere
Porter, Connie (Rose) 1959(?)- **CLC 70**
See also BW 2, 3; CA 142; CANR 90, 109;
SATA 81, 129
Porter, Gene(va Grace) Stratton TCLC 21
See Stratton-Porter, Gene(va Grace)
See also BPFB 3; CA 112; CWRI 5; RHW
Porter, Katherine Anne 1890-1980 **CLC 1, 3,
7, 10, 13, 15, 27, 101; SSC 4, 31, 43**
See also AAYA 42; AITN 2; AMW; BPFB
3; CA 1-4R; 101; CANR 1, 65; CDALBS;
DA; DA3; DAB; DAC; DAM MST, NOV;
DLB 4, 9, 102; DLBD 12; DLBY 1980;
EWL 3; EXPS; LAIT 3; MAWW; MTCW
1, 2; NFS 14; RGAL 4; RGSF 2; SATA
39; SATA-Obit 23; SSFS 1, 8, 11, 16;
TUS
Porter, Peter (Neville Frederick) 1929- **CLC
5, 13, 33**
See also CA 85-88; CP 7; DLB 40, 289;
WWE 1
Porter, William Sydney 1862-1910
See Henry, O.
See also CA 104; 131; CDALB 1865-1917;
DA; DA3; DAB; DAC; DAM MST; DLB
12, 78, 79; MTCW 1, 2; TUS; YABC 2

Portillo (y Pacheco), Jose Lopez
See Lopez Portillo (y Pacheco), Jose
Portillo Trambley, Estela 1927-1998 **HLC 2**
See Trambley, Estela Portillo
See also CANR 32; DAM MULT; DLB
209; HW 1
Posey, Alexander (Lawrence) 1873-1908
NNAL
See also CA 144; CANR 80; DAM MULT;
DLB 175
Posse, Abel CLC 70
Post, Melville Davisson 1869-1930 **TCLC 39**
See also CA 110; 202; CMW 4
Potok, Chaim 1929-2002 **CLC 2, 7, 14, 26,
112**
See also AAYA 15, 50; AITN 1, 2; BPFB 3;
BYA 1; CA 17-20R; 208; CANR 19, 35,
64, 98; CLR 92; CN 7; DA3; DAM NOV;
DLB 28, 152; EXPN; INT CANR-19;
LAIT 4; MTCW 1, 2; NFS 4; SATA 33,
106; SATA-Obit 134; TUS; YAW
Potok, Herbert Harold -2002
See Potok, Chaim
Potok, Herman Harold
See Potok, Chaim
Potter, Dennis (Christopher George)
1935-1994 **CLC 58, 86, 123**
See also CA 107; 145; CANR 33, 61; CBD;
DLB 233; MTCW 1
Pound, Ezra (Weston Loomis) 1885-1972
**CLC 1, 2, 3, 4, 5, 7, 10, 13, 18, 34, 48,
50, 112; PC 4; WLC**
See also AAYA 47; AMW; AMWR 1; CA
5-8R; 37-40R; CANR 40; CDALB 1917-
1929; DA; DA3; DAB; DAC; DAM MST,
POET; DLB 4, 45, 63; DLBD 15; EFS 2;
EWL 3; EXPP; LMFS 2; MTCW 1, 2;
PAB; PFS 2, 8, 16; RGAL 4; TUS; WP
Povod, Reinaldo 1959-1994 **CLC 44**
See also CA 136; 146; CANR 83
Powell, Adam Clayton, Jr. 1908-1972 **BLC 3;
CLC 89**
See also BW 1, 3; CA 102; 33-36R; CANR
86; DAM MULT
Powell, Anthony (Dymoke) 1905-2000 **CLC
1, 3, 7, 9, 10, 31**
See also BRW 7; CA 1-4R; 189; CANR 1,
32, 62, 107; CDBLB 1945-1960; CN 7;
DLB 15; EWL 3; MTCW 1, 2; RGEL 2;
TEA
Powell, Dawn 1896(?)-1965 **CLC 66**
See also CA 5-8R; CANR 121; DLBY 1997
Powell, Padgett 1952- **CLC 34**
See also CA 126; CANR 63, 101; CSW;
DLB 234; DLBY 01
Powell, (Oval) Talmage 1920-2000
See Queen, Ellery
See also CA 5-8R; CANR 2, 80
Power, Susan 1961- **CLC 91**
See also BYA 14; CA 160; NFS 11
Powers, J(ames) F(arl) 1917-1999 **CLC 1, 4,
8, 57; SSC 4**
See also CA 1-4R; 181; CANR 2, 61; CN
7; DLB 130; MTCW 1; RGAL 4; RGSF
2
Powers, John J(ames) 1945-
See Powers, John R.
See also CA 69-72
Powers, John R. CLC 66
See Powers, John J(ames)
Powers, Richard (S.) 1957- **CLC 93**
See also AMWS 9; BPFB 3; CA 148;
CANR 80; CN 7
Pownall, David 1938- **CLC 10**
See also CA 89-92, 180; CAAS 18; CANR
49, 101; CBD; CD 5; CN 7; DLB 14

Powys, John Cowper 1872-1963 **CLC 7, 9,
15, 46, 125**
See also CA 85-88; CANR 106; DLB 15,
255; EWL 3; FANT; MTCW 1, 2; RGEL
2; SUFW
Powys, T(heodore) F(rancis) 1875-1953
TCLC 9
See also BRWS 8; CA 106; 189; DLB 36,
162; EWL 3; FANT; RGEL 2; SUFW
Prado (Calvo), Pedro 1886-1952 **TCLC 75**
See also CA 131; DLB 283; HW 1; LAW
Prager, Emily 1952- **CLC 56**
See also CA 204
Pratolini, Vasco 1913-1991 **TCLC 124**
See also CA 211; DLB 177; EWL 3; RGWL
2, 3
Pratt, E(dwin) J(ohn) 1883(?)-1964 **CLC 19**
See also CA 141; 93-96; CANR 77; DAC;
DAM POET; DLB 92; EWL 3; RGEL 2;
TWA
Premchand TCLC 21
See Srivastava, Dhanpat Rai
See also EWL 3
Preseren, France 1800-1849 **NCLC 127**
See also CDWLB 4; DLB 147
Preussler, Otfried 1923- **CLC 17**
See also CA 77-80; SATA 24
Prevert, Jacques (Henri Marie) 1900-1977
CLC 15
See also CA 77-80; 69-72; CANR 29, 61;
DLB 258; EWL 3; GFL 1789 to the
Present; IDFW 3, 4; MTCW 1; RGWL 2,
3; SATA-Obit 30
Prevost, (Antoine Francois) 1697-1763 **LC 1**
See also EW 4; GFL Beginnings to 1789;
RGWL 2, 3
Price, (Edward) Reynolds 1933- **CLC 3, 6,
13, 43, 50, 63; SSC 22**
See also AMWS 6; CA 1-4R; CANR 1, 37,
57, 87, 128; CN 7; CSW; DAM NOV;
DLB 2, 218, 278; EWL 3; INT CANR-
37; NFS 18
Price, Richard 1949- **CLC 6, 12**
See also CA 49-52; CANR 3; DLBY 1981
Prichard, Katharine Susannah 1883-1969
CLC 46
See also CA 11-12; CANR 33; CAP 1; DLB
260; MTCW 1; RGEL 2; RGSF 2; SATA
66
Priestley, J(ohn) B(oynton) 1894-1984 **CLC
2, 5, 9, 34**
See also BRW 7; CA 9-12R; 113; CANR
33; CDBLB 1914-1945; DA3; DAM
DRAM, NOV; DLB 10, 34, 77, 100, 139;
DLBY 1984; EWL 3; MTCW 1, 2; RGEL
2; SFW 4
Prince 1958- **CLC 35**
See also CA 213
Prince, F(rank) T(empleton) 1912-2003 **CLC
22**
See also CA 101; 219; CANR 43, 79; CP 7;
DLB 20
Prince Kropotkin
See Kropotkin, Peter (Alekseievich)
Prior, Matthew 1664-1721 **LC 4**
See also DLB 95; RGEL 2
Prishvin, Mikhail 1873-1954 **TCLC 75**
See Prishvin, Mikhail Mikhailovich
Prishvin, Mikhail Mikhailovich
See Prishvin, Mikhail
See also DLB 272; EWL 3
Pritchard, William H(arrison) 1932- **CLC 34**
See also CA 65-68; CANR 23, 95; DLB
111
Pritchett, V(ictor) S(awdon) 1900-1997 **CLC
5, 13, 15, 41; SSC 14**
See also BPFB 3; BRWS 3; CA 61-64; 157;
CANR 31, 63; CN 7; DA3; DAM NOV;
DLB 15, 139; EWL 3; MTCW 1, 2;
RGEL 2; RGSF 2; TEA

Private 19022
See Manning, Frederic
Probst, Mark 1925- **CLC 59**
See also CA 130
Prokosch, Frederic 1908-1989 **CLC 4, 48**
See also CA 73-76; 128; CANR 82; DLB
48; MTCW 2
Propertius, Sextus c. 50B.C.-c. 16B.C. **CMLC
32**
See also AW 2; CDWLB 1; DLB 211;
RGWL 2, 3
Prophet, The
See Dreiser, Theodore (Herman Albert)
Prose, Francine 1947- **CLC 45**
See also CA 109; 112; CANR 46, 95; DLB
234; SATA 101
Proudhon
See Cunha, Euclides (Rodrigues Pimenta)
da
Proulx, Annie
See Proulx, E(dna) Annie
Proulx, E(dna) Annie 1935- **CLC 81, 158**
See also AMWS 7; BPFB 3; CA 145;
CANR 65, 110; CN 7; CPW 1; DA3;
DAM POP; MTCW 2; SSFS 18
**Proust, (Valentin-Louis-George-Eugene)
Marcel** 1871-1922 **TCLC 7, 13, 33;
WLC**
See also BPFB 3; CA 104; 120; CANR 110;
DA; DA3; DAB; DAC; DAM MST, NOV;
DLB 65; EW 8; EWL 3; GFL 1789 to the
Present; MTCW 1, 2; RGWL 2, 3; TWA
Prowler, Harley
See Masters, Edgar Lee
Prus, Boleslaw 1845-1912 **TCLC 48**
See also RGWL 2, 3
Pryor, Richard (Franklin Lenox Thomas)
1940- **CLC 26**
See also CA 122; 152
Przybyszewski, Stanislaw 1868-1927 **TCLC
36**
See also CA 160; DLB 66; EWL 3
Pteleon
See Grieve, C(hristopher) M(urray)
See also DAM POET
Puckett, Lute
See Masters, Edgar Lee
Puig, Manuel 1932-1990 **CLC 3, 5, 10, 28,
65, 133; HLC 2**
See also BPFB 3; CA 45-48; CANR 2, 32,
63; CDWLB 3; DA3; DAM MULT; DLB
113; DNFS 1; EWL 3; GLL 1; HW 1, 2;
LAW; MTCW 1, 2; RGWL 2, 3; TWA;
WLIT 1
Pulitzer, Joseph 1847-1911 **TCLC 76**
See also CA 114; DLB 23
Purchas, Samuel 1577(?)-1626 **LC 70**
See also DLB 151
Purdy, A(lfred) W(ellington) 1918-2000 **CLC
3, 6, 14, 50**
See also CA 81-84; 189; CAAS 17; CANR
42, 66; CP 7; DAC; DAM MST, POET;
DLB 88; PFS 5; RGEL 2
Purdy, James (Amos) 1923- **CLC 2, 4, 10, 28,
52**
See also AMWS 7; CA 33-36R; CAAS 1;
CANR 19, 51; CN 7; DLB 2, 218; EWL
3; INT CANR-19; MTCW 1; RGAL 4
Pure, Simon
See Swinnerton, Frank Arthur
Pushkin, Aleksandr Sergeevich
See Pushkin, Alexander (Sergeyevich)
See also DLB 205
Pushkin, Alexander (Sergeyevich) 1799-1837
**NCLC 3, 27, 83; PC 10; SSC 27, 55;
WLC**
See Pushkin, Aleksandr Sergeevich
See also DA; DA3; DAB; DAC; DAM
DRAM, MST, POET; EW 5; EXPS; RGSF
2; RGWL 2, 3; SATA 61; SSFS 9; TWA

P'u Sung-ling 1640-1715 **LC 49; SSC 31**
Putnam, Arthur Lee
  See Alger, Horatio, Jr.
Puzo, Mario 1920-1999 **CLC 1, 2, 6, 36, 107**
  See also BPFB 3; CA 65-68; 185; CANR 4,
  42, 65, 99; CN 7; CPW; DA3; DAM
  NOV, POP; DLB 6; MTCW 1, 2; NFS 16;
  RGAL 4
Pygge, Edward
  See Barnes, Julian (Patrick)
Pyle, Ernest Taylor 1900-1945
  See Pyle, Ernie
  See also CA 115; 160
Pyle, Ernie **TCLC 75**
  See Pyle, Ernest Taylor
  See also DLB 29; MTCW 2
Pyle, Howard 1853-1911 **TCLC 81**
  See also BYA 2, 4; CA 109; 137; CLR 22;
  DLB 42, 188; DLBD 13; LAIT 1; MAI-
  CYA 1, 2; SATA 16, 100; WCH; YAW
Pym, Barbara (Mary Crampton) 1913-1980
  CLC 13, 19, 37, 111
  See also BPFB 3; BRWS 2; CA 13-14; 97-
  100; CANR 13, 34; CAP 1; DLB 14, 207;
  DLBY 1987; EWL 3; MTCW 1, 2; RGEL
  2; TEA
Pynchon, Thomas (Ruggles, Jr.) 1937- **CLC
2, 3, 6, 9, 11, 18, 33, 62, 72, 123; SSC
14; WLC**
  See also AMWS 2; BEST 90:2; BPFB 3;
  CA 17-20R; CANR 22, 46, 73; CN 7;
  CPW 1; DA; DA3; DAB; DAC; DAM
  MST, NOV, POP; DLB 2, 173; EWL 3;
  MTCW 1, 2; RGAL 4; SFW 4; TUS
Pythagoras c. 582B.C.-c. 507B.C. **CMLC 22**
  See also DLB 176
Q
  See Quiller-Couch, Sir Arthur (Thomas)
Qian, Chongzhu
  See Ch'ien, Chung-shu
Qian Zhongshu
  See Ch'ien, Chung-shu
  See also CWW 2
Qroll
  See Dagerman, Stig (Halvard)
Quarrington, Paul (Lewis) 1953- **CLC 65**
  See also CA 129; CANR 62, 95
Quasimodo, Salvatore 1901-1968 **CLC 10;
PC 47**
  See also CA 13-16; 25-28R; CAP 1; DLB
  114; EW 12; EWL 3; MTCW 1; RGWL
  2, 3
Quatermass, Martin
  See Carpenter, John (Howard)
Quay, Stephen 1947- **CLC 95**
  See also CA 189
Quay, Timothy 1947- **CLC 95**
  See also CA 189
Queen, Ellery **CLC 3, 11**
  See Dannay, Frederic; Davidson, Avram
  (James); Deming, Richard; Fairman, Paul
  W.; Flora, Fletcher; Hoch, Edward
  D(entinger); Kane, Henry; Lee, Manfred
  B(ennington); Marlowe, Stephen; Powell,
  (Oval) Talmage; Sheldon, Walter J(ames);
  Sturgeon, Theodore (Hamilton); Tracy,
  Don(ald Fiske); Vance, John Holbrook
  See also BPFB 3; CMW 4; MSW; RGAL 4
Queen, Ellery, Jr.
  See Dannay, Frederic; Lee, Manfred
  B(ennington)
Queneau, Raymond 1903-1976 **CLC 2, 5, 10,
42**
  See also CA 77-80; 69-72; CANR 32; DLB
  72, 258; EW 12; EWL 3; GFL 1789 to
  the Present; MTCW 1, 2; RGWL 2, 3
Quevedo, Francisco de 1580-1645 **LC 23**

Quiller-Couch, Sir Arthur (Thomas)
  1863-1944 **TCLC 53**
  See also CA 118; 166; DLB 135, 153, 190;
  HGG; RGEL 2; SUFW 1
Quin, Ann (Marie) 1936-1973 **CLC 6**
  See also CA 9-12R; 45-48; DLB 14, 231
Quincey, Thomas de
  See De Quincey, Thomas
Quinn, Martin
  See Smith, Martin Cruz
Quinn, Peter 1947- **CLC 91**
  See also CA 197
Quinn, Simon
  See Smith, Martin Cruz
Quintana, Leroy V. 1944- **HLC 2; PC 36**
  See also CA 131; CANR 65; DAM MULT;
  DLB 82; HW 1, 2
Quiroga, Horacio (Sylvestre) 1878-1937 **HLC
2; TCLC 20**
  See also CA 117; 131; DAM MULT; EWL
  3; HW 1; LAW; MTCW 1; RGSF 2;
  WLIT 1
Quoirez, Francoise 1935- **CLC 9**
  See Sagan, Francoise
  See also CA 49-52; CANR 6, 39, 73; CWW
  2; MTCW 1, 2; TWA
Raabe, Wilhelm (Karl) 1831-1910 **TCLC 45**
  See also CA 167; DLB 129
Rabe, David (William) 1940- **CLC 4, 8, 33;
DC 16**
  See also CA 85-88; CABS 3; CAD; CANR
  59, 129; CD 5; DAM DRAM; DFS 3, 8,
  13; DLB 7, 228; EWL 3
Rabelais, Francois 1494-1553 **LC 5, 60; WLC**
  See also DA; DAB; DAC; DAM MST; EW
  2; GFL Beginnings to 1789; LMFS 1;
  RGWL 2, 3; TWA
Rabinovitch, Sholem 1859-1916
  See Aleichem, Sholom
  See also CA 104
Rabinyan, Dorit 1972- **CLC 119**
  See also CA 170
Rachilde
  See Vallette, Marguerite Eymery; Vallette,
  Marguerite Eymery
  See also EWL 3
Racine, Jean 1639-1699 **LC 28**
  See also DA3; DAB; DAM MST; DLB 268;
  EW 3; GFL Beginnings to 1789; LMFS
  1; RGWL 2, 3; TWA
Radcliffe, Ann (Ward) 1764-1823 **NCLC 6,
55, 106**
  See also DLB 39, 178; HGG; LMFS 1;
  RGEL 2; SUFW; WLIT 3
Radclyffe-Hall, Marguerite
  See Hall, (Marguerite) Radclyffe
Radiguet, Raymond 1903-1923 **TCLC 29**
  See also CA 162; DLB 65; EWL 3; GFL
  1789 to the Present; RGWL 2, 3
Radnoti, Miklos 1909-1944 **TCLC 16**
  See also CA 118; 212; CDWLB 4; DLB
  215; EWL 3; RGWL 2, 3
Rado, James 1939- **CLC 17**
  See also CA 105
Radvanyi, Netty 1900-1983
  See Seghers, Anna
  See also CA 85-88; 110; CANR 82
Rae, Ben
  See Griffiths, Trevor
Raeburn, John (Hay) 1941- **CLC 34**
  See also CA 57-60
Ragni, Gerome 1942-1991 **CLC 17**
  See also CA 105; 134
Rahv, Philip **CLC 24**
  See Greenberg, Ivan
  See also DLB 137
Raimund, Ferdinand Jakob 1790-1836
  NCLC 69
  See also DLB 90

Raine, Craig (Anthony) 1944- **CLC 32, 103**
  See also CA 108; CANR 29, 51, 103; CP 7;
  DLB 40; PFS 7
Raine, Kathleen (Jessie) 1908-2003 **CLC 7,
45**
  See also CA 85-88; 218; CANR 46, 109;
  CP 7; DLB 20; EWL 3; MTCW 1; RGEL
  2
Rainis, Janis 1865-1929 **TCLC 29**
  See also CA 170; CDWLB 4; DLB 220;
  EWL 3
Rakosi, Carl **CLC 47**
  See Rawley, Callman
  See also CAAS 5; CP 7; DLB 193
Ralegh, Sir Walter
  See Raleigh, Sir Walter
  See also BRW 1; RGEL 2; WP
Raleigh, Richard
  See Lovecraft, H(oward) P(hillips)
Raleigh, Sir Walter 1554(?)-1618 **LC 31, 39;
PC 31**
  See Ralegh, Sir Walter
  See also CDBLB Before 1660; DLB 172;
  EXPP; PFS 14; TEA
Rallentando, H. P.
  See Sayers, Dorothy L(eigh)
Ramal, Walter
  See de la Mare, Walter (John)
Ramana Maharshi 1879-1950 **TCLC 84**
Ramoacn y Cajal, Santiago 1852-1934 **TCLC
93**
Ramon, Juan
  See Jimenez (Mantecon), Juan Ramon
Ramos, Graciliano 1892-1953 **TCLC 32**
  See also CA 167; EWL 3; HW 2; LAW;
  WLIT 1
Rampersad, Arnold 1941- **CLC 44**
  See also BW 2, 3; CA 127; 133; CANR 81;
  DLB 111; INT CA-133
Rampling, Anne
  See Rice, Anne
  See also GLL 2
Ramsay, Allan 1686(?)-1758 **LC 29**
  See also DLB 95; RGEL 2
Ramsay, Jay
  See Campbell, (John) Ramsey
Ramuz, Charles-Ferdinand 1878-1947 **TCLC
33**
  See also CA 165; EWL 3
Rand, Ayn 1905-1982 **CLC 3, 30, 44, 79;
WLC**
  See also AAYA 10; AMWS 4; BPFB 3;
  BYA 12; CA 13-16R; 105; CANR 27, 73;
  CDALBS; CPW; DA; DA3; DAC; DAM
  MST, NOV, POP; DLB 227, 279; MTCW
  1, 2; NFS 10, 16; RGAL 4; SFW 4; TUS;
  YAW
Randall, Dudley (Felker) 1914-2000 **BLC 3;
CLC 1, 135**
  See also BW 1, 3; CA 25-28R; 189; CANR
  23, 82; DAM MULT; DLB 41; PFS 5
Randall, Robert
  See Silverberg, Robert
Ranger, Ken
  See Creasey, John
Rank, Otto 1884-1939 **TCLC 115**
Ransom, John Crowe 1888-1974 **CLC 2, 4, 5,
11, 24**
  See also AMW; CA 5-8R; 49-52; CANR 6,
  34; CDALBS; DA3; DAM POET; DLB
  45, 63; EWL 3; EXPP; MTCW 1, 2;
  RGAL 4; TUS
Rao, Raja 1909- **CLC 25, 56**
  See also CA 73-76; CANR 51; CN 7; DAM
  NOV; EWL 3; MTCW 1, 2; RGEL 2;
  RGSF 2

Raphael, Frederic (Michael) 1931- **CLC 2, 14**
See also CA 1-4R; CANR 1, 86; CN 7; DLB 14

Ratcliffe, James P.
See Mencken, H(enry) L(ouis)

Rathbone, Julian 1935- **CLC 41**
See also CA 101; CANR 34, 73

Rattigan, Terence (Mervyn) 1911-1977 **CLC 7; DC 18**
See also BRWS 7; CA 85-88; 73-76; CBD; CDBLB 1945-1960; DAM DRAM; DFS 8; DLB 13; IDFW 3, 4; MTCW 1, 2; RGEL 2

Ratushinskaya, Irina 1954- **CLC 54**
See also CA 129; CANR 68; CWW 2

Raven, Simon (Arthur Noel) 1927-2001 **CLC 14**
See also CA 81-84; 197; CANR 86; CN 7; DLB 271

Ravenna, Michael
See Welty, Eudora (Alice)

Rawley, Callman 1903-
See Rakosi, Carl
See also CA 21-24R; CANR 12, 32, 91

Rawlings, Marjorie Kinnan 1896-1953 **TCLC 4**
See also AAYA 20; AMWS 10; ANW; BPFB 3; BYA 3; CA 104; 137; CANR 74; CLR 63; DLB 9, 22, 102; DLBD 17; JRDA; MAICYA 1, 2; MTCW 2; RGAL 4; SATA 100; WCH; YABC 1; YAW

Ray, Satyajit 1921-1992 **CLC 16, 76**
See also CA 114; 137; DAM MULT

Read, Herbert Edward 1893-1968 **CLC 4**
See also BRW 6; CA 85-88; 25-28R; DLB 20, 149; EWL 3; PAB; RGEL 2

Read, Piers Paul 1941- **CLC 4, 10, 25**
See also CA 21-24R; CANR 38, 86; CN 7; DLB 14; SATA 21

Reade, Charles 1814-1884 **NCLC 2, 74**
See also DLB 21; RGEL 2

Reade, Hamish
See Gray, Simon (James Holliday)

Reading, Peter 1946- **CLC 47**
See also BRWS 8; CA 103; CANR 46, 96; CP 7; DLB 40

Reaney, James 1926- **CLC 13**
See also CA 41-44R; CAAS 15; CANR 42; CD 5; CP 7; DAC; DAM MST; DLB 68; RGEL 2; SATA 43

Rebreanu, Liviu 1885-1944 **TCLC 28**
See also CA 165; DLB 220; EWL 3

Rechy, John (Francisco) 1934- **CLC 1, 7, 14, 18, 107; HLC 2**
See also CA 5-8R, 195; CAAE 195; CAAS 4; CANR 6, 32, 64; CN 7; DAM MULT; DLB 122, 278; DLBY 1982; HW 1, 2; INT CANR-6; LLW 1; RGAL 4

Redcam, Tom 1870-1933 **TCLC 25**

Reddin, Keith **CLC 67**
See also CAD

Redgrove, Peter (William) 1932-2003 **CLC 6, 41**
See also BRWS 6; CA 1-4R; 217; CANR 3, 39, 77; CP 7; DLB 40

Redmon, Anne **CLC 22**
See Nightingale, Anne Redmon
See also DLBY 1986

Reed, Eliot
See Ambler, Eric

Reed, Ishmael 1938- **BLC 3; CLC 2, 3, 5, 6, 13, 32, 60, 174**
See also AFAW 1, 2; AMWS 10; BPFB 3; BW 2, 3; CA 21-24R; CANR 25, 48, 74, 128; CN 7; CP 7; CSW; DA3; DAM MULT; DLB 2, 5, 33, 169, 227; DLBD 8; EWL 3; LMFS 2; MSW; MTCW 1, 2; PFS 6; RGAL 4; TCWW 2

Reed, John (Silas) 1887-1920 **TCLC 9**
See also CA 106; 195; TUS

Reed, Lou **CLC 21**
See Firbank, Louis

Reese, Lizette Woodworth 1856-1935 **PC 29**
See also CA 180; DLB 54

Reeve, Clara 1729-1807 **NCLC 19**
See also DLB 39; RGEL 2

Reich, Wilhelm 1897-1957 **TCLC 57**
See also CA 199

Reid, Christopher (John) 1949- **CLC 33**
See also CA 140; CANR 89; CP 7; DLB 40; EWL 3

Reid, Desmond
See Moorcock, Michael (John)

Reid Banks, Lynne 1929-
See Banks, Lynne Reid
See also AAYA 49; CA 1-4R; CANR 6, 22, 38, 87; CLR 24; CN 7; JRDA; MAICYA 1, 2; SATA 22, 75, 111; YAW

Reilly, William K.
See Creasey, John

Reiner, Max
See Caldwell, (Janet Miriam) Taylor (Holland)

Reis, Ricardo
See Pessoa, Fernando (Antonio Nogueira)

Reizenstein, Elmer Leopold
See Rice, Elmer (Leopold)
See also EWL 3

Remarque, Erich Maria 1898-1970 **CLC 21**
See also AAYA 27; BPFB 3; CA 77-80; 29-32R; CDWLB 2; DA; DA3; DAB; DAC; DAM MST, NOV; DLB 56; EWL 3; EXPN; LAIT 3; MTCW 1, 2; NFS 4; RGWL 2, 3

Remington, Frederic 1861-1909 **TCLC 89**
See also CA 108; 169; DLB 12, 186, 188; SATA 41

Remizov, A.
See Remizov, Aleksei (Mikhailovich)

Remizov, A. M.
See Remizov, Aleksei (Mikhailovich)

Remizov, Aleksei (Mikhailovich) 1877-1957 **TCLC 27**
See Remizov, Alexey Mikhaylovich
See also CA 125; 133; DLB 295

Remizov, Alexey Mikhaylovich
See Remizov, Aleksei (Mikhailovich)
See also EWL 3

Renan, Joseph Ernest 1823-1892 **NCLC 26**
See also GFL 1789 to the Present

Renard, Jules(-Pierre) 1864-1910 **TCLC 17**
See also CA 117; 202; GFL 1789 to the Present

Renault, Mary **CLC 3, 11, 17**
See Challans, Mary
See also BPFB 3; BYA 2; DLBY 1983; EWL 3; GLL 1; LAIT 1; MTCW 2; RGEL 2; RHW

Rendell, Ruth (Barbara) 1930- **CLC 28, 48**
See Vine, Barbara
See also BPFB 3; BRWS 9; CA 109; CANR 32, 52, 74, 127; CN 7; CPW; DAM POP; DLB 87, 276; INT CANR-32; MSW; MTCW 1, 2

Renoir, Jean 1894-1979 **CLC 20**
See also CA 129; 85-88

Resnais, Alain 1922- **CLC 16**

Revard, Carter (Curtis) 1931- **NNAL**
See also CA 144; CANR 81; PFS 5

Reverdy, Pierre 1889-1960 **CLC 53**
See also CA 97-100; 89-92; DLB 258; EWL 3; GFL 1789 to the Present

Rexroth, Kenneth 1905-1982 **CLC 1, 2, 6, 11, 22, 49, 112; PC 20**
See also BG 3; CA 5-8R; 107; CANR 14, 34, 63; CDALB 1941-1968; DAM POET; DLB 16, 48, 165, 212; DLBY 1982; EWL 3; INT CANR-14; MTCW 1, 2; RGAL 4

Reyes, Alfonso 1889-1959 **HLCS 2; TCLC 33**
See also CA 131; EWL 3; HW 1; LAW

Reyes y Basoalto, Ricardo Eliecer Neftali
See Neruda, Pablo

Reymont, Wladyslaw (Stanislaw) 1868(?)-1925 **TCLC 5**
See also CA 104; EWL 3

Reynolds, Jonathan 1942- **CLC 6, 38**
See also CA 65-68; CANR 28

Reynolds, Joshua 1723-1792 **LC 15**
See also DLB 104

Reynolds, Michael S(hane) 1937-2000 **CLC 44**
See also CA 65-68; 189; CANR 9, 89, 97

Reznikoff, Charles 1894-1976 **CLC 9**
See also CA 33-36; 61-64; CAP 2; DLB 28, 45; WP

Rezzori (d'Arezzo), Gregor von 1914-1998 **CLC 25**
See also CA 122; 136; 167

Rhine, Richard
See Silverstein, Alvin; Silverstein, Virginia B(arbara Opshelor)

Rhodes, Eugene Manlove 1869-1934 **TCLC 53**
See also CA 198; DLB 256

R'hoone, Lord
See Balzac, Honore de

Rhys, Jean 1894(?)-1979 **CLC 2, 4, 6, 14, 19, 51, 124; SSC 21**
See also BRWS 2; CA 25-28R; 85-88; CANR 35, 62; CDBLB 1945-1960; CDWLB 3; DA3; DAM NOV; DLB 36, 117, 162; DNFS 2; EWL 3; LATS 1; MTCW 1, 2; RGEL 2; RGSF 2; RHW; TEA; WWE 1

Ribeiro, Darcy 1922-1997 **CLC 34**
See also CA 33-36R; 156; EWL 3

Ribeiro, Joao Ubaldo (Osorio Pimentel) 1941- **CLC 10, 67**
See also CA 81-84; EWL 3

Ribman, Ronald (Burt) 1932- **CLC 7**
See also CA 21-24R; CAD; CANR 46, 80; CD 5

Ricci, Nino (Pio) 1959- **CLC 70**
See also CA 137; CCA 1

Rice, Anne 1941- **CLC 41, 128**
See Rampling, Anne
See also AAYA 9, 53; AMWS 7; BEST 89:2; BPFB 3; CA 65-68; CANR 12, 36, 53, 74, 100; CN 7; CPW; CSW; DA3; DAM POP; DLB 292; GLL 2; HGG; MTCW 2; SUFW 2; YAW

Rice, Elmer (Leopold) 1892-1967 **CLC 7, 49**
See Reizenstein, Elmer Leopold
See also CA 21-22; 25-28R; CAP 2; DAM DRAM; DFS 12; DLB 4, 7; MTCW 1, 2; RGAL 4

Rice, Tim(othy Miles Bindon) 1944- **CLC 21**
See also CA 103; CANR 46; DFS 7

Rich, Adrienne (Cecile) 1929- **CLC 3, 6, 7, 11, 18, 36, 73, 76, 125; PC 5**
See also AMWR 2; AMWS 1; CA 9-12R; CANR 20, 53, 74, 128; CDALBS; CP 7; CSW; CWP; DA3; DAM POET; DLB 5, 67; EWL 3; EXPP; FW; MAWW; MTCW 1, 2; PAB; PFS 15; RGAL 4; WP

Rich, Barbara
See Graves, Robert (von Ranke)

Rich, Robert
See Trumbo, Dalton

Richard, Keith **CLC 17**
See Richards, Keith

Richards, David Adams 1950- **CLC 59**
See also CA 93-96; CANR 60, 110; DAC; DLB 53

Richards, I(vor) A(rmstrong) 1893-1979 **CLC 14, 24**
See also BRWS 2; CA 41-44R; 89-92; CANR 34, 74; DLB 27; EWL 3; MTCW 2; RGEL 2

Richards, Keith 1943-
See Richard, Keith
See also CA 107; CANR 77

Richardson, Anne
See Roiphe, Anne (Richardson)

Richardson, Dorothy Miller 1873-1957 **TCLC 3**
See also CA 104; 192; DLB 36; EWL 3; FW; RGEL 2

Richardson (Robertson), Ethel Florence Lindesay 1870-1946
See Richardson, Henry Handel
See also CA 105; 190; DLB 230; RHW

Richardson, Henry Handel TCLC 4
See Richardson (Robertson), Ethel Florence Lindesay
See also DLB 197; EWL 3; RGEL 2; RGSF 2

Richardson, John 1796-1852 **NCLC 55**
See also CCA 1; DAC; DLB 99

Richardson, Samuel 1689-1761 **LC 1, 44; WLC**
See also BRW 3; CDBLB 1660-1789; DA; DAB; DAC; DAM MST, NOV; DLB 39; RGEL 2; TEA; WLIT 3

Richardson, Willis 1889-1977 **HR 3**
See also BW 1; CA 124; DLB 51; SATA 60

Richler, Mordecai 1931-2001 **CLC 3, 5, 9, 13, 18, 46, 70, 185**
See also AITN 1; CA 65-68; 201; CANR 31, 62, 111; CCA 1; CLR 17; CWRI 5; DAC; DAM MST, NOV; DLB 53; EWL 3; MAICYA 1, 2; MTCW 1, 2; RGEL 2; SATA 44, 98; SATA-Brief 27; TWA

Richter, Conrad (Michael) 1890-1968 **CLC 30**
See also AAYA 21; BYA 2; CA 5-8R; 25-28R; CANR 23; DLB 9, 212; LAIT 1; MTCW 1, 2; RGAL 4; SATA 3; TCWW 2; TUS; YAW

Ricostranza, Tom
See Ellis, Trey

Riddell, Charlotte 1832-1906 **TCLC 40**
See Riddell, Mrs. J. H.
See also CA 165; DLB 156

Riddell, Mrs. J. H.
See Riddell, Charlotte
See also HGG; SUFW

Ridge, John Rollin 1827-1867 **NCLC 82; NNAL**
See also CA 144; DAM MULT; DLB 175

Ridgeway, Jason
See Marlowe, Stephen

Ridgway, Keith 1965- **CLC 119**
See also CA 172

Riding, Laura CLC 3, 7
See Jackson, Laura (Riding)
See also RGAL 4

Riefenstahl, Berta Helene Amalia 1902-2003
See Riefenstahl, Leni
See also CA 108; 220

Riefenstahl, Leni CLC 16
See Riefenstahl, Berta Helene Amalia

Riffe, Ernest
See Bergman, (Ernst) Ingmar

Riggs, (Rolla) Lynn 1899-1954 **NNAL; TCLC 56**
See also CA 144; DAM MULT; DLB 175

Riis, Jacob A(ugust) 1849-1914 **TCLC 80**
See also CA 113; 168; DLB 23

Riley, James Whitcomb 1849-1916 **PC 48; TCLC 51**
See also CA 118; 137; DAM POET; MAICYA 1, 2; RGAL 4; SATA 17

Riley, Tex
See Creasey, John

Rilke, Rainer Maria 1875-1926 **PC 2; TCLC 1, 6, 19**
See also CA 104; 132; CANR 62, 99; CDWLB 2; DA3; DAM POET; DLB 81; EW 9; EWL 3; MTCW 1, 2; PFS 19; RGWL 2, 3; TWA; WP

Rimbaud, (Jean Nicolas) Arthur 1854-1891 **NCLC 4, 35, 82; PC 3; WLC**
See also DA; DA3; DAB; DAC; DAM MST, POET; DLB 217; EW 7; GFL 1789 to the Present; LMFS 2; RGWL 2, 3; TWA; WP

Rinehart, Mary Roberts 1876-1958 **TCLC 52**
See also BPFB 3; CA 108; 166; RGAL 4; RHW

Ringmaster, The
See Mencken, H(enry) L(ouis)

Ringwood, Gwen(dolyn Margaret) Pharis 1910-1984 **CLC 48**
See also CA 148; 112; DLB 88

Rio, Michel 1945(?)- **CLC 43**
See also CA 201

Ritsos, Giannes
See Ritsos, Yannis

Ritsos, Yannis 1909-1990 **CLC 6, 13, 31**
See also CA 77-80; 133; CANR 39, 61; EW 12; EWL 3; MTCW 1; RGWL 2, 3

Ritter, Erika 1948(?)- **CLC 52**
See also CD 5; CWD

Rivera, Jose Eustasio 1889-1928 **TCLC 35**
See also CA 162; EWL 3; HW 1, 2; LAW

Rivera, Tomas 1935-1984 **HLCS 2**
See also CA 49-52; CANR 32; DLB 82; HW 1; LLW 1; RGAL 4; SSFS 15; TCWW 2; WLIT 1

Rivers, Conrad Kent 1933-1968 **CLC 1**
See also BW 1; CA 85-88; DLB 41

Rivers, Elfrida
See Bradley, Marion Zimmer
See also GLL 1

Riverside, John
See Heinlein, Robert A(nson)

Rizal, Jose 1861-1896 **NCLC 27**

Roa Bastos, Augusto (Antonio) 1917- **CLC 45; HLC 2**
See also CA 131; CWW 2; DAM MULT; DLB 113; EWL 3; HW 1; LAW; RGSF 2; WLIT 1

Robbe-Grillet, Alain 1922- **CLC 1, 2, 4, 6, 8, 10, 14, 43, 128**
See also BPFB 3; CA 9-12R; CANR 33, 65, 115; DLB 83; EW 13; EWL 3; GFL 1789 to the Present; IDFW 3, 4; MTCW 1, 2; SSFS 15

Robbins, Harold 1916-1997 **CLC 5**
See also BPFB 3; CA 73-76; 162; CANR 26, 54, 112; DA3; DAM NOV; MTCW 1, 2

Robbins, Thomas Eugene 1936-
See Robbins, Tom
See also CA 81-84; CANR 29, 59, 95; CN 7; CPW; CSW; DA3; DAM NOV, POP; MTCW 1, 2

Robbins, Tom CLC 9, 32, 64
See Robbins, Thomas Eugene
See also AAYA 32; AMWS 10; BEST 90:3; BPFB 3; DLBY 1980; MTCW 2

Robbins, Trina 1938- **CLC 21**
See also CA 128

Roberts, Charles G(eorge) D(ouglas) 1860-1943 **TCLC 8**
See also CA 105; 188; CLR 33; CWRI 5; DLB 92; RGEL 2; RGSF 2; SATA 88; SATA-Brief 29

Roberts, Elizabeth Madox 1886-1941 **TCLC 68**
See also CA 111; 166; CWRI 5; DLB 9, 54, 102; RGAL 4; RHW; SATA 33; SATA-Brief 27; WCH

Roberts, Kate 1891-1985 **CLC 15**
See also CA 107; 116

Roberts, Keith (John Kingston) 1935-2000 **CLC 14**
See also CA 25-28R; CANR 46; DLB 261; SFW 4

Roberts, Kenneth (Lewis) 1885-1957 **TCLC 23**
See also CA 109; 199; DLB 9; RGAL 4; RHW

Roberts, Michele (Brigitte) 1949- **CLC 48, 178**
See also CA 115; CANR 58, 120; CN 7; DLB 231; FW

Robertson, Ellis
See Ellison, Harlan (Jay); Silverberg, Robert

Robertson, Thomas William 1829-1871 **NCLC 35**
See Robertson, Tom
See also DAM DRAM

Robertson, Tom
See Robertson, Thomas William
See also RGEL 2

Robeson, Kenneth
See Dent, Lester

Robinson, Edwin Arlington 1869-1935 **PC 1, 35; TCLC 5, 101**
See also AMW; CA 104; 133; CDALB 1865-1917; DA; DAC; DAM MST, POET; DLB 54; EWL 3; EXPP; MTCW 1, 2; PAB; PFS 4; RGAL 4; WP

Robinson, Henry Crabb 1775-1867 **NCLC 15**
See also DLB 107

Robinson, Jill 1936- **CLC 10**
See also CA 102; CANR 120; INT CA-102

Robinson, Kim Stanley 1952- **CLC 34**
See also AAYA 26; CA 126; CANR 113; CN 7; SATA 109; SCFW 2; SFW 4

Robinson, Lloyd
See Silverberg, Robert

Robinson, Marilynne 1944- **CLC 25, 180**
See also CA 116; CANR 80; CN 7; DLB 206

Robinson, Smokey CLC 21
See Robinson, William, Jr.

Robinson, William, Jr. 1940-
See Robinson, Smokey
See also CA 116

Robison, Mary 1949- **CLC 42, 98**
See also CA 113; 116; CANR 87; CN 7; DLB 130; INT CA-116; RGSF 2

Rochester
See Wilmot, John
See also RGEL 2

Rod, Edouard 1857-1910 **TCLC 52**

Roddenberry, Eugene Wesley 1921-1991
See Roddenberry, Gene
See also CA 110; 135; CANR 37; SATA 45; SATA-Obit 69

Roddenberry, Gene CLC 17
See Roddenberry, Eugene Wesley
See also AAYA 5; SATA-Obit 69

Rodgers, Mary 1931- **CLC 12**
See also BYA 5; CA 49-52; CANR 8, 55, 90; CLR 20; CWRI 5; INT CANR-8; JRDA; MAICYA 1, 2; SATA 8, 130

Rodgers, W(illiam) R(obert) 1909-1969 **CLC 7**
See also CA 85-88; DLB 20; RGEL 2

Rodman, Eric
See Silverberg, Robert

Rodman, Howard 1920(?)-1985 **CLC 65**
See also CA 118

Rodman, Maia
See Wojciechowska, Maia (Teresa)
Rodo, Jose Enrique 1871(?)-1917 **HLCS 2**
See also CA 178; EWL 3; HW 2; LAW
Rodolph, Utto
See Ouologuem, Yambo
Rodriguez, Claudio 1934-1999 **CLC 10**
See also CA 188; DLB 134
Rodriguez, Richard 1944- **CLC 155; HLC 2**
See also CA 110; CANR 66, 116; DAM
MULT; DLB 82, 256; HW 1, 2; LAIT 5;
LLW 1; NCFS 3; WLIT 1
Roelvaag, O(le) E(dvart) 1876-1931
See Rolvaag, O(le) E(dvart)
See also CA 117; 171
Roethke, Theodore (Huebner) 1908-1963
CLC 1, 3, 8, 11, 19, 46, 101; PC 15
See also AMW; CA 81-84; CABS 2;
CDALB 1941-1968; DA3; DAM POET;
DLB 5, 206; EWL 3; EXPP; MTCW 1, 2;
PAB; PFS 3; RGAL 4; WP
Rogers, Carl R(ansom) 1902-1987 **TCLC 125**
See also CA 1-4R; 121; CANR 1, 18;
MTCW 1
Rogers, Samuel 1763-1855 **NCLC 69**
See also DLB 93; RGEL 2
Rogers, Thomas Hunton 1927- **CLC 57**
See also CA 89-92; INT CA-89-92
Rogers, Will(iam Penn Adair) 1879-1935
NNAL; TCLC 8, 71
See also CA 105; 144; DA3; DAM MULT;
DLB 11; MTCW 2
Rogin, Gilbert 1929- **CLC 18**
See also CA 65-68; CANR 15
Rohan, Koda
See Koda Shigeyuki
Rohlfs, Anna Katharine Green
See Green, Anna Katharine
Rohmer, Eric CLC 16
See Scherer, Jean-Marie Maurice
Rohmer, Sax TCLC 28
See Ward, Arthur Henry Sarsfield
See also DLB 70; MSW; SUFW
Roiphe, Anne (Richardson) 1935- **CLC 3, 9**
See also CA 89-92; CANR 45, 73; DLBY
1980; INT CA-89-92
Rojas, Fernando de 1475-1541 **HLCS 1, 2;
LC 23**
See also DLB 286; RGWL 2, 3
Rojas, Gonzalo 1917- **HLCS 2**
See also CA 178; HW 2; LAWS 1
Roland, Marie-Jeanne 1754-1793 **LC 98**
**Rolfe, Frederick (William Serafino Austin
Lewis Mary)** 1860-1913 **TCLC 12**
See Al Siddik
See also CA 107; 210; DLB 34, 156; RGEL
2
Rolland, Romain 1866-1944 **TCLC 23**
See also CA 118; 197; DLB 65, 284; EWL
3; GFL 1789 to the Present; RGWL 2, 3
Rolle, Richard c. 1300-c. 1349 **CMLC 21**
See also DLB 146; LMFS 1; RGEL 2
Rolvaag, O(le) E(dvart) **TCLC 17**
See Roelvaag, O(le) E(dvart)
See also DLB 9, 212; NFS 5; RGAL 4
Romain Arnaud, Saint
See Aragon, Louis
Romains, Jules 1885-1972 **CLC 7**
See also CA 85-88; CANR 34; DLB 65;
EWL 3; GFL 1789 to the Present; MTCW
1
Romero, Jose Ruben 1890-1952 **TCLC 14**
See also CA 114; 131; EWL 3; HW 1; LAW
Ronsard, Pierre de 1524-1585 **LC 6, 54; PC
11**
See also EW 2; GFL Beginnings to 1789;
RGWL 2, 3; TWA

Rooke, Leon 1934- **CLC 25, 34**
See also CA 25-28R; CANR 23, 53; CCA
1; CPW; DAM POP
Roosevelt, Franklin Delano 1882-1945 **TCLC
93**
See also CA 116; 173; LAIT 3
Roosevelt, Theodore 1858-1919 **TCLC 69**
See also CA 115; 170; DLB 47, 186, 275
Roper, William 1498-1578 **LC 10**
Roquelaure, A. N.
See Rice, Anne
Rosa, Joao Guimaraes 1908-1967 **CLC 23;
HLCS 1**
See Guimaraes Rosa, Joao
See also CA 89-92; DLB 113; EWL 3;
WLIT 1
Rose, Wendy 1948- **CLC 85; NNAL; PC 13**
See also CA 53-56; CANR 5, 51; CWP;
DAM MULT; DLB 175; PFS 13; RGAL
4; SATA 12
Rosen, R. D.
See Rosen, Richard (Dean)
Rosen, Richard (Dean) 1949- **CLC 39**
See also CA 77-80; CANR 62, 120; CMW
4; INT CANR-30
Rosenberg, Isaac 1890-1918 **TCLC 12**
See also BRW 6; CA 107; 188; DLB 20,
216; EWL 3; PAB; RGEL 2
Rosenblatt, Joe CLC 15
See Rosenblatt, Joseph
Rosenblatt, Joseph 1933-
See Rosenblatt, Joe
See also CA 89-92; CP 7; INT CA-89-92
Rosenfeld, Samuel
See Tzara, Tristan
Rosenstock, Sami
See Tzara, Tristan
Rosenstock, Samuel
See Tzara, Tristan
Rosenthal, M(acha) L(ouis) 1917-1996 **CLC
28**
See also CA 1-4R; 152; CAAS 6; CANR 4,
51; CP 7; DLB 5; SATA 59
Ross, Barnaby
See Dannay, Frederic
Ross, Bernard L.
See Follett, Ken(neth Martin)
Ross, J. H.
See Lawrence, T(homas) E(dward)
Ross, John Hume
See Lawrence, T(homas) E(dward)
Ross, Martin 1862-1915
See Martin, Violet Florence
See also DLB 135; GLL 2; RGEL 2; RGSF
2
Ross, (James) Sinclair 1908-1996 **CLC 13;
SSC 24**
See also CA 73-76; CANR 81; CN 7; DAC;
DAM MST; DLB 88; RGEL 2; RGSF 2;
TCWW 2
Rossetti, Christina (Georgina) 1830-1894
NCLC 2, 50, 66; PC 7; WLC
See also AAYA 51; BRW 5; BYA 4; DA;
DA3; DAB; DAC; DAM MST, POET;
DLB 35, 163, 240; EXPP; LATS 1; MAI-
CYA 1, 2; PFS 10, 14; RGEL 2; SATA
20; TEA; WCH
Rossetti, Dante Gabriel 1828-1882 **NCLC 4,
77; PC 44; WLC**
See also AAYA 51; BRW 5; CDBLB 1832-
1890; DA; DAB; DAC; DAM MST,
POET; DLB 35; EXPP; RGEL 2; TEA
Rossi, Cristina Peri
See Peri Rossi, Cristina
Rossi, Jean-Baptiste 1931-2003
See Japrisot, Sebastien
See also CA 201; 215

Rossner, Judith (Perelman) 1935- **CLC 6, 9,
29**
See also AITN 2; BEST 90:3; BPFB 3; CA
17-20R; CANR 18, 51, 73; CN 7; DLB 6;
INT CANR-18; MTCW 1, 2
Rostand, Edmond (Eugene Alexis)
1868-1918 **DC 10; TCLC 6, 37**
See also CA 104; 126; DA; DA3; DAB;
DAC; DAM DRAM, MST; DFS 1; DLB
192; LAIT 1; MTCW 1; RGWL 2, 3;
TWA
Roth, Henry 1906-1995 **CLC 2, 6, 11, 104**
See also AMWS 9; CA 11-12; 149; CANR
38, 63; CAP 1; CN 7; DA3; DLB 28;
EWL 3; MTCW 1, 2; RGAL 4
Roth, (Moses) Joseph 1894-1939 **TCLC 33**
See also CA 160; DLB 85; EWL 3; RGWL
2, 3
Roth, Philip (Milton) 1933- **CLC 1, 2, 3, 4, 6,
9, 15, 22, 31, 47, 66, 86, 119; SSC 26;
WLC**
See also AMWR 2; AMWS 3; BEST 90:3;
BPFB 3; CA 1-4R; CANR 1, 22, 36, 55,
89; CDALB 1968-1988; CN 7; CPW 1;
DA; DA3; DAB; DAC; DAM MST, NOV,
POP; DLB 2, 28, 173; DLBY 1982; EWL
3; MTCW 1, 2; RGAL 4; RGSF 2; SSFS
12, 18; TUS
Rothenberg, Jerome 1931- **CLC 6, 57**
See also CA 45-48; CANR 1, 106; CP 7;
DLB 5, 193
Rotter, Pat ed. CLC 65
Roumain, Jacques (Jean Baptiste) 1907-1944
BLC 3; TCLC 19
See also BW 1; CA 117; 125; DAM MULT;
EWL 3
Rourke, Constance Mayfield 1885-1941
TCLC 12
See also CA 107; 200; YABC 1
Rousseau, Jean-Baptiste 1671-1741 **LC 9**
Rousseau, Jean-Jacques 1712-1778 **LC 14,
36; WLC**
See also DA; DA3; DAB; DAC; DAM
MST; EW 4; GFL Beginnings to 1789;
LMFS 1; RGWL 2, 3; TWA
Roussel, Raymond 1877-1933 **TCLC 20**
See also CA 117; 201; EWL 3; GFL 1789
to the Present
Rovit, Earl (Herbert) 1927- **CLC 7**
See also CA 5-8R; CANR 12
Rowe, Elizabeth Singer 1674-1737 **LC 44**
See also DLB 39, 95
Rowe, Nicholas 1674-1718 **LC 8**
See also DLB 84; RGEL 2
Rowlandson, Mary 1637(?)-1678 **LC 66**
See also DLB 24, 200; RGAL 4
Rowley, Ames Dorrance
See Lovecraft, H(oward) P(hillips)
Rowley, William 1585(?)-1626 **LC 100**
See also DLB 58; RGEL 2
Rowling, J(oanne) K(athleen) 1966- **CLC 137**
See also AAYA 34; BYA 11, 13, 14; CA
173; CANR 128; CLR 66, 80; MAICYA
2; SATA 109; SUFW 2
Rowson, Susanna Haswell 1762(?)-1824
NCLC 5, 69
See also DLB 37, 200; RGAL 4
Roy, Arundhati 1960(?)- **CLC 109**
See also CA 163; CANR 90, 126; DLBY
1997; EWL 3; LATS 1; WWE 1
Roy, Gabrielle 1909-1983 **CLC 10, 14**
See also CA 53-56; 110; CANR 5, 61; CCA
1; DAB; DAC; DAM MST; DLB 68;
EWL 3; MTCW 1; RGWL 2, 3; SATA 104
Royko, Mike 1932-1997 **CLC 109**
See also CA 89-92; 157; CANR 26, 111;
CPW

Rozanov, Vasilii Vasil'evich
See Rozanov, Vassili
See also DLB 295
Rozanov, Vasily Vasilyevich
See Rozanov, Vassili
See also EWL 3
Rozanov, Vassili 1856-1919 **TCLC 104**
See Rozanov, Vasilii Vasil'evich; Rozanov, Vasily Vasilyevich
Rozewicz, Tadeusz 1921- **CLC 9, 23, 139**
See also CA 108; CANR 36, 66; CWW 2; DA3; DAM POET; DLB 232; EWL 3; MTCW 1, 2; RGWL 3
Ruark, Gibbons 1941- **CLC 3**
See also CA 33-36R; CAAS 23; CANR 14, 31, 57; DLB 120
Rubens, Bernice (Ruth) 1923- **CLC 19, 31**
See also CA 25-28R; CANR 33, 65, 128; CN 7; DLB 14, 207; MTCW 1
Rubin, Harold
See Robbins, Harold
Rudkin, (James) David 1936- **CLC 14**
See also CA 89-92; CBD; CD 5; DLB 13
Rudnik, Raphael 1933- **CLC 7**
See also CA 29-32R
Ruffian, M.
See Hasek, Jaroslav (Matej Frantisek)
Ruiz, Jose Martinez CLC 11
See Martinez Ruiz, Jose
Ruiz, Juan c. 1283-c. 1350 **CMLC 66**
Rukeyser, Muriel 1913-1980 **CLC 6, 10, 15, 27; PC 12**
See also AMWS 6; CA 5-8R; 93-96; CANR 26, 60; DA3; DAM POET; DLB 48; EWL 3; FW; GLL 2; MTCW 1, 2; PFS 10; RGAL 4; SATA-Obit 22
Rule, Jane (Vance) 1931- **CLC 27**
See also CA 25-28R; CAAS 18; CANR 12, 87; CN 7; DLB 60; FW
Rulfo, Juan 1918-1986 **CLC 8, 80; HLC 2; SSC 25**
See also CA 85-88; 118; CANR 26; CD-WLB 3; DAM MULT; DLB 113; EWL 3; HW 1, 2; LAW; MTCW 1, 2; RGSF 2; RGWL 2, 3; WLIT 1
Rumi, Jalal al-Din 1207-1273 **CMLC 20; PC 45**
See also RGWL 2, 3; WP
Runeberg, Johan 1804-1877 **NCLC 41**
Runyon, (Alfred) Damon 1884(?)-1946 **TCLC 10**
See also CA 107; 165; DLB 11, 86, 171; MTCW 2; RGAL 4
Rush, Norman 1933- **CLC 44**
See also CA 121; 126; INT CA-126
Rushdie, (Ahmed) Salman 1947- **CLC 23, 31, 55, 100; WLCS**
See also BEST 89:3; BPFB 3; BRWS 4; CA 108; 111; CANR 33, 56, 108; CN 7; CPW 1; DA3; DAB; DAC; DAM MST, NOV, POP; DLB 194; EWL 3; FANT; INT CA-111; LATS 1; LMFS 2; MTCW 1, 2; RGEL 2; RGSF 2; TEA; WLIT 4; WWE 1
Rushforth, Peter (Scott) 1945- **CLC 19**
See also CA 101
Ruskin, John 1819-1900 **TCLC 63**
See also BRW 5; BYA 5; CA 114; 129; CD-BLB 1832-1890; DLB 55, 163, 190; RGEL 2; SATA 24; TEA; WCH
Russ, Joanna 1937- **CLC 15**
See also BPFB 3; CA 5-28R; CANR 11, 31, 65; CN 7; DLB 8; FW; GLL 1; MTCW 1; SCFW 2; SFW 4
Russ, Richard Patrick
See O'Brian, Patrick

Russell, George William 1867-1935
See A.E.; Baker, Jean H.
See also BRWS 8; CA 104; 153; CDBLB 1890-1914; DAM POET; EWL 3; RGEL 2
Russell, Jeffrey Burton 1934- **CLC 70**
See also CA 25-28R; CANR 11, 28, 52
Russell, (Henry) Ken(neth Alfred) 1927- **CLC 16**
See also CA 105
Russell, William Martin 1947-
See Russell, Willy
See also CA 164; CANR 107
Russell, Willy CLC 60
See Russell, William Martin
See also CBD; CD 5; DLB 233
Russo, Richard 1949- **CLC 181**
See also AMWS 12; CA 127; 133; CANR 87, 114
Rutherford, Mark TCLC 25
See White, William Hale
See also DLB 18; RGEL 2
Ruyslinck, Ward CLC 14
See Belser, Reimond Karel Maria de
Ryan, Cornelius (John) 1920-1974 **CLC 7**
See also CA 69-72; 53-56; CANR 38
Ryan, Michael 1946- **CLC 65**
See also CA 49-52; CANR 109; DLBY 1982
Ryan, Tim
See Dent, Lester
Rybakov, Anatoli (Naumovich) 1911-1998 **CLC 23, 53**
See also CA 126; 135; 172; SATA 79; SATA-Obit 108
Ryder, Jonathan
See Ludlum, Robert
Ryga, George 1932-1987 **CLC 14**
See also CA 101; 124; CANR 43, 90; CCA 1; DAC; DAM MST; DLB 60
S. H.
See Hartmann, Sadakichi
S. S.
See Sassoon, Siegfried (Lorraine)
Saba, Umberto 1883-1957 **TCLC 33**
See also CA 144; CANR 79; DLB 114; EWL 3; RGWL 2, 3
Sabatini, Rafael 1875-1950 **TCLC 47**
See also BPFB 3; CA 162; RHW
Sabato, Ernesto (R.) 1911- **CLC 10, 23; HLC 2**
See also CA 97-100; CANR 32, 65; CD-WLB 3; DAM MULT; DLB 145; EWL 3; HW 1, 2; LAW; MTCW 1, 2
Sa-Carneiro, Mario de 1890-1916 **TCLC 83**
See also DLB 287; EWL 3
Sacastru, Martin
See Bioy Casares, Adolfo
See also CWW 2
Sacher-Masoch, Leopold von 1836(?)-1895 **NCLC 31**
Sachs, Hans 1494-1576 **LC 95**
See also CDWLB 2; DLB 179; RGWL 2, 3
Sachs, Marilyn (Stickle) 1927- **CLC 35**
See also AAYA 2; BYA 6; CA 17-20R; CANR 13, 47; CLR 2; JRDA; MAICYA 1, 2; SAAS 2; SATA 3, 68; SATA-Essay 110; WYA; YAW
Sachs, Nelly 1891-1970 **CLC 14, 98**
See also CA 17-18; 25-28R; CANR 87; CAP 2; EWL 3; MTCW 2; RGWL 2, 3
Sackler, Howard (Oliver) 1929-1982 **CLC 14**
See also CA 61-64; 108; CAD; CANR 30; DFS 15; DLB 7
Sacks, Oliver (Wolf) 1933- **CLC 67**
See also CA 53-56; CANR 28, 50, 76; CPW; DA3; INT CANR-28; MTCW 1, 2

Sackville, Thomas 1536-1608 **LC 98**
See also DAM DRAM; DLB 62, 132; RGEL 2
Sadakichi
See Hartmann, Sadakichi
Sade, Donatien Alphonse Francois 1740-1814 **NCLC 3, 47**
See also EW 4; GFL Beginnings to 1789; RGWL 2, 3
Sade, Marquis de
See Sade, Donatien Alphonse Francois
Sadoff, Ira 1945- **CLC 9**
See also CA 53-56; CANR 5, 21, 109; DLB 120
Saetone
See Camus, Albert
Safire, William 1929- **CLC 10**
See also CA 17-20R; CANR 31, 54, 91
Sagan, Carl (Edward) 1934-1996 **CLC 30, 112**
See also AAYA 2; CA 25-28R; 155; CANR 11, 36, 74; CPW; DA3; MTCW 1, 2; SATA 58; SATA-Obit 94
Sagan, Francoise CLC 3, 6, 9, 17, 36
See Quoirez, Francoise
See also CWW 2; DLB 83; EWL 3; GFL 1789 to the Present; MTCW 2
Sahgal, Nayantara (Pandit) 1927- **CLC 41**
See also CA 9-12R; CANR 11, 88; CN 7
Said, Edward W. 1935-2003 **CLC 123**
See also CA 21-24R; 220; CANR 45, 74, 107; DLB 67; MTCW 2
Saint, H(arry) F. 1941- **CLC 50**
See also CA 127
St. Aubin de Teran, Lisa 1953-
See Teran, Lisa St. Aubin de
See also CA 118; 126; CN 7; INT CA-126
Saint Birgitta of Sweden c. 1303-1373 **CMLC 24**
Sainte-Beuve, Charles Augustin 1804-1869 **NCLC 5**
See also DLB 217; EW 6; GFL 1789 to the Present
Saint-Exupery, Antoine (Jean Baptiste Marie Roger) de 1900-1944 **TCLC 2, 56; WLC**
See also BPFB 3; BYA 3; CA 108; 132; CLR 10; DA3; DAM NOV; DLB 72; EW 12; EWL 3; GFL 1789 to the Present; LAIT 3; MAICYA 1, 2; MTCW 1, 2; RGWL 2, 3; SATA 20; TWA
St. John, David
See Hunt, E(verette) Howard, (Jr.)
St. John, J. Hector
See Crevecoeur, Michel Guillaume Jean de
Saint-John Perse
See Leger, (Marie-Rene Auguste) Alexis Saint-Leger
See also EW 10; EWL 3; GFL 1789 to the Present; RGWL 2
Saintsbury, George (Edward Bateman) 1845-1933 **TCLC 31**
See also CA 160; DLB 57, 149
Sait Faik TCLC 23
See Abasiyanik, Sait Faik
Saki SSC 12; TCLC 3
See Munro, H(ector) H(ugh)
See also BRWS 6; BYA 11; LAIT 2; MTCW 2; RGEL 2; SSFS 1; SUFW
Sala, George Augustus 1828-1895 **NCLC 46**
Saladin 1138-1193 **CMLC 38**
Salama, Hannu 1936- **CLC 18**
See also EWL 3
Salamanca, J(ack) R(ichard) 1922- **CLC 4, 15**
See also CA 25-28R, 193; CAAE 193

Seferis, George CLC 5, 11
See Seferiades, Giorgos Stylianou
See also EW 12; EWL 3; RGWL 2, 3

Segal, Erich (Wolf) 1937- CLC 3, 10
See also BEST 89:1; BPFB 3; CA 25-28R;
CANR 20, 36, 65, 113; CPW; DAM POP;
DLBY 1986; INT CANR-20; MTCW 1

Seger, Bob 1945- CLC 35

Seghers, Anna CLC 7
See Radvanyi, Netty
See also CDWLB 2; DLB 69; EWL 3

Seidel, Frederick (Lewis) 1936- CLC 18
See also CA 13-16R; CANR 8, 99; CP 7;
DLBY 1984

**Seifert, Jaroslav 1901-1986 CLC 34, 44, 93;
PC 47**
See also CA 127; CDWLB 4; DLB 215;
EWL 3; MTCW 1, 2

Sei Shonagon c. 966-1017(?) CMLC 6

Sejour, Victor 1817-1874 DC 10
See also DLB 50

Sejour Marcou et Ferrand, Juan Victor
See Sejour, Victor

**Selby, Hubert, Jr. 1928-2004 CLC 1, 2, 4, 8;
SSC 20**
See also CA 13-16R; CANR 33, 85; CN 7;
DLB 2, 227

Selzer, Richard 1928- CLC 74
See also CA 65-68; CANR 14, 106

Sembene, Ousmane
See Ousmane, Sembene
See also AFW; CWW 2; EWL 3; WLIT 2

**Senancour, Etienne Pivert de 1770-1846
NCLC 16**
See also DLB 119; GFL 1789 to the Present

**Sender, Ramon (Jose) 1902-1982 CLC 8;
HLC 2; TCLC 136**
See also CA 5-8R; 105; CANR 8; DAM
MULT; EWL 3; HW 1; MTCW 1; RGWL
2, 3

**Seneca, Lucius Annaeus c. 4B.C.-c. 65 CMLC
6; DC 5**
See also AW 2; CDWLB 1; DAM DRAM;
DLB 211; RGWL 2, 3; TWA

**Senghor, Leopold Sedar 1906-2001 BLC 3;
CLC 54, 130; PC 25**
See also AFW; BW 2; CA 116; 125; 203;
CANR 47, 74; DAM MULT, POET;
DNFS 2; EWL 3; GFL 1789 to the
Present; MTCW 1, 2; TWA

Senna, Danzy 1970- CLC 119
See also CA 169

**Serling, (Edward) Rod(man) 1924-1975 CLC
30**
See also AAYA 14; AITN 1; CA 162; 57-
60; DLB 26; SFW 4

Serna, Ramon Gomez de la
See Gomez de la Serna, Ramon

Serpieres
See Guillevic, (Eugene)

Service, Robert
See Service, Robert W(illiam)
See also BYA 4; DAB; DLB 92

**Service, Robert W(illiam) 1874(?)-1958
TCLC 15; WLC**
See Service, Robert
See also CA 115; 140; CANR 84; DA;
DAC; DAM MST, POET; PFS 10; RGEL
2; SATA 20

Seth, Vikram 1952- CLC 43, 90
See also CA 121; 127; CANR 50, 74; CN
7; CP 7; DA3; DAM MULT; DLB 120,
271, 282; EWL 3; INT CA-127; MTCW
2; WWE 1

Seton, Cynthia Propper 1926-1982 CLC 27
See also CA 5-8R; 108; CANR 7

**Seton, Ernest (Evan) Thompson 1860-1946
TCLC 31**
See also ANW; BYA 3; CA 109; 204; CLR
59; DLB 92; DLBD 13; JRDA; SATA 18

Seton-Thompson, Ernest
See Seton, Ernest (Evan) Thompson

Settle, Mary Lee 1918- CLC 19, 61
See also BPFB 3; CA 89-92; CAAS 1;
CANR 44, 87, 126; CN 7; CSW; DLB 6;
INT CA-89-92

Seuphor, Michel
See Arp, Jean

**Sevigne, Marie (de Rabutin-Chantal)
1626-1696 LC 11**
See Sevigne, Marie de Rabutin Chantal
See also GFL Beginnings to 1789; TWA

Sevigne, Marie de Rabutin Chantal
See Sevigne, Marie (de Rabutin-Chantal)
See also DLB 268

Sewall, Samuel 1652-1730 LC 38
See also DLB 24; RGAL 4

**Sexton, Anne (Harvey) 1928-1974 CLC 2, 4,
6, 8, 10, 15, 53, 123; PC 2; WLC**
See also AMWS 2; CA 1-4R; 53-56; CABS
2; CANR 3, 36; CDALB 1941-1968; DA;
DA3; DAB; DAC; DAM MST, POET;
DLB 5, 169; EWL 3; EXPP; FW;
MAWW; MTCW 1, 2; PAB; PFS 4, 14;
RGAL 4; SATA 10; TUS

Shaara, Jeff 1952- CLC 119
See also CA 163; CANR 109

**Shaara, Michael (Joseph, Jr.) 1929-1988 CLC
15**
See also AITN 1; BPFB 3; CA 102; 125;
CANR 52, 85; DAM POP; DLBY 1983

Shackleton, C. C.
See Aldiss, Brian W(ilson)

Shacochis, Bob CLC 39
See Shacochis, Robert G.

Shacochis, Robert G. 1951-
See Shacochis, Bob
See also CA 119; 124; CANR 100; INT CA-
124

**Shaffer, Anthony (Joshua) 1926-2001 CLC
19**
See also CA 110; 116; 200; CBD; CD 5;
DAM DRAM; DFS 13; DLB 13

**Shaffer, Peter (Levin) 1926- CLC 5, 14, 18,
37, 60; DC 7**
See also BRWS 1; CA 25-28R; CANR 25,
47, 74, 118; CBD; CD 5; CDBLB 1960 to
Present; DA3; DAB; DAM DRAM, MST;
DFS 5, 13; DLB 13, 233; EWL 3; MTCW
1, 2; RGEL 2; TEA

Shakespeare, William 1564-1616 WLC
See also AAYA 35; BRW 1; CDBLB Before
1660; DA; DA3; DAB; DAC; DAM
DRAM, MST, POET; DLB 62, 172, 263;
EXPP; LAIT 1; LATS 1; LMFS 1; PAB;
PFS 1, 2, 3, 4, 5, 8, 9; RGEL 2; TEA;
WLIT 3; WP; WS; WYA

Shakey, Bernard
See Young, Neil

**Shalamov, Varlam (Tikhonovich)
1907(?)-1982 CLC 18**
See also CA 129; 105; RGSF 2

Shamloo, Ahmad
See Shamlu, Ahmad

Shamlou, Ahmad
See Shamlu, Ahmad

Shamlu, Ahmad 1925-2000 CLC 10
See also CA 216; CWW 2

Shammas, Anton 1951- CLC 55
See also CA 199

Shandling, Arline
See Berriault, Gina

**Shange, Ntozake 1948- BLC 3; CLC 8, 25,
38, 74, 126; DC 3**
See also AAYA 9; AFAW 1, 2; BW 2; CA
85-88; CABS 3; CAD; CANR 27, 48, 74;
CD 5; CP 7; CWD; CWP; DA3; DAM
DRAM, MULT; DFS 2, 11; DLB 38, 249;
FW; LAIT 5; MTCW 1, 2; NFS 11;
RGAL 4; YAW

Shanley, John Patrick 1950- CLC 75
See also CA 128; 133; CAD; CANR 83;
CD 5

Shapcott, Thomas W(illiam) 1935- CLC 38
See also CA 69-72; CANR 49, 83, 103; CP
7; DLB 289

Shapiro, Jane 1942- CLC 76
See also CA 196

**Shapiro, Karl (Jay) 1913-2000 CLC 4, 8, 15,
53; PC 25**
See also AMWS 2; CA 1-4R; 188; CAAS
6; CANR 1, 36, 66; CP 7; DLB 48; EWL
3; EXPP; MTCW 1, 2; PFS 3; RGAL 4

Sharp, William 1855-1905 TCLC 39
See Macleod, Fiona
See also CA 160; DLB 156; RGEL 2

Sharpe, Thomas Ridley 1928-
See Sharpe, Tom
See also CA 114; 122; CANR 85; INT CA-
122

Sharpe, Tom CLC 36
See Sharpe, Thomas Ridley
See also CN 7; DLB 14, 231

Shatrov, Mikhail CLC 59

Shaw, Bernard
See Shaw, George Bernard
See also DLB 190

Shaw, G. Bernard
See Shaw, George Bernard

**Shaw, George Bernard 1856-1950 TCLC 3,
9, 21, 45; WLC**
See Shaw, Bernard
See also BRW 6; BRWC 1; BRWR 2; CA
104; 128; CDBLB 1914-1945; DA; DA3;
DAB; DAC; DAM DRAM, MST; DFS 1,
3, 6, 11; DLB 10, 57; EWL 3; LAIT 3;
LATS 1; MTCW 1, 2; RGEL 2; TEA;
WLIT 4

Shaw, Henry Wheeler 1818-1885 NCLC 15
See also DLB 11; RGAL 4

Shaw, Irwin 1913-1984 CLC 7, 23, 34
See also AITN 1; BPFB 3; CA 13-16R; 112;
CANR 21; CDALB 1941-1968; CPW;
DAM DRAM, POP; DLB 6, 102; DLBY
1984; MTCW 1, 21

Shaw, Robert 1927-1978 CLC 5
See also AITN 1; CA 1-4R; 81-84; CANR
4; DLB 13, 14

Shaw, T. E.
See Lawrence, T(homas) E(dward)

Shawn, Wallace 1943- CLC 41
See also CA 112; CAD; CD 5; DLB 266

Shchedrin, N.
See Saltykov, Mikhail Evgrafovich

Shea, Lisa 1953- CLC 86
See also CA 147

**Sheed, Wilfrid (John Joseph) 1930- CLC 2,
4, 10, 53**
See also CA 65-68; CANR 30, 66; CN 7;
DLB 6; MTCW 1, 2

Sheehy, Gail 1937- CLC 171
See also CA 49-52; CANR 1, 33, 55, 92;
CPW; MTCW 1

**Sheldon, Alice Hastings Bradley
1915(?)-1987**
See Tiptree, James, Jr.
See also CA 108; 122; CANR 34; INT CA-
108; MTCW 1

Sheldon, John
See Bloch, Robert (Albert)

Sheldon, Walter J(ames) 1917-1996
See Queen, Ellery
See also AITN 1; CA 25-28R; CANR 10

Shelley, Mary Wollstonecraft (Godwin)
1797-1851 **NCLC 14, 59, 103; WLC**
See also AAYA 20; BPFB 3; BRW 3;
BRWC 2; BRWS 3; BYA 5; CDBLB
1789-1832; DA; DA3; DAB; DAC; DAM
MST, NOV; DLB 110, 116, 159, 178;
EXPN; HGG; LAIT 1; LMFS 1, 2; NFS
1; RGEL 2; SATA 29; SCFW; SFW 4;
TEA; WLIT 3

Shelley, Percy Bysshe 1792-1822 NCLC 18,
93; PC 14; WLC
See also BRW 4; BRWR 1; CDBLB 1789-
1832; DA; DA3; DAB; DAC; DAM MST,
POET; DLB 96, 110, 158; EXPP; LMFS
1; PAB; PFS 2; RGEL 2; TEA; WLIT 3;
WP

Shepard, Jim 1956- CLC 36
See also CA 137; CANR 59, 104; SATA 90

Shepard, Lucius 1947- CLC 34
See also CA 128; 141; CANR 81, 124;
HGG; SCFW 2; SFW 4; SUFW 2

Shepard, Sam 1943- CLC 4, 6, 17, 34, 41, 44,
169; DC 5
See also AAYA 1; AMWS 3; CA 69-72;
CABS 3; CAD; CANR 22, 120; CD 5;
DA3; DAM DRAM; DFS 3, 6, 7, 14;
DLB 7, 212; EWL 3; IDFW 3, 4; MTCW
1, 2; RGAL 4

Shepherd, Michael
See Ludlum, Robert

Sherburne, Zoa (Lillian Morin) 1912-1995
CLC 30
See also AAYA 13; CA 1-4R; 176; CANR
3, 37; MAICYA 1, 2; SAAS 18; SATA 3;
YAW

Sheridan, Frances 1724-1766 LC 7
See also DLB 39, 84

Sheridan, Richard Brinsley 1751-1816 DC 1;
NCLC 5, 91; WLC
See also BRW 3; CDBLB 1660-1789; DA;
DAB; DAC; DAM DRAM, MST; DFS
15; DLB 89; WLIT 3

Sherman, Jonathan Marc CLC 55

Sherman, Martin 1941(?)- CLC 19
See also CA 116; 123; CAD; CANR 86;
CD 5; DLB 228; GLL 1; IDTP

Sherwin, Judith Johnson
See Johnson, Judith (Emlyn)
See also CANR 85; CP 7; CWP

Sherwood, Frances 1940- CLC 81
See also CA 146, 220; CAAE 220

Sherwood, Robert E(mmet) 1896-1955 TCLC
3
See also CA 104; 153; CANR 86; DAM
DRAM; DFS 11, 15, 17; DLB 7, 26, 249;
IDFW 3, 4; RGAL 4

Shestov, Lev 1866-1938 TCLC 56

Shevchenko, Taras 1814-1861 NCLC 54

Shiel, M(atthew) P(hipps) 1865-1947 TCLC
8
See Holmes, Gordon
See also CA 106; 160; DLB 153; HGG;
MTCW 2; SFW 4; SUFW

Shields, Carol (Ann) 1935-2003 CLC 91, 113
See also AMWS 7; CA 81-84; 218; CANR
51, 74, 98; CCA 1; CN 7; CPW; DA3;
DAC; MTCW 2

Shields, David (Jonathan) 1956- CLC 97
See also CA 124; CANR 48, 99, 112

Shiga, Naoya 1883-1971 CLC 33; SSC 23
See Shiga Naoya
See also CA 101; 33-36R; MJW; RGWL 3

Shiga Naoya
See Shiga, Naoya
See also DLB 180; EWL 3; RGWL 3

Shilts, Randy 1951-1994 CLC 85
See also AAYA 19; CA 115; 127; 144;
CANR 45; DA3; GLL 1; INT CA-127;
MTCW 2

Shimazaki, Haruki 1872-1943
See Shimazaki Toson
See also CA 105; 134; CANR 84; RGWL 3

Shimazaki Toson TCLC 5
See Shimazaki, Haruki
See also DLB 180; EWL 3

Shirley, James 1596-1666 LC 96
See also DLB 58; RGEL 2

Sholokhov, Mikhail (Aleksandrovich)
1905-1984 **CLC 7, 15**
See also CA 101; 112; DLB 272; EWL 3;
MTCW 1, 2; RGWL 2, 3; SATA-Obit 36

Shone, Patric
See Hanley, James

Showalter, Elaine 1941- CLC 169
See also CA 57-60; CANR 58, 106; DLB
67; FW; GLL 2

Shreve, Susan Richards 1939- CLC 23
See also CA 49-52; CAAS 5; CANR 5, 38,
69, 100; MAICYA 1, 2; SATA 46, 95;
SATA-Brief 41

Shue, Larry 1946-1985 CLC 52
See also CA 145; 117; DAM DRAM; DFS
7

Shu-Jen, Chou 1881-1936
See Lu Hsun
See also CA 104

Shulman, Alix Kates 1932- CLC 2, 10
See also CA 29-32R; CANR 43; FW; SATA
7

Shusaku, Endo
See Endo, Shusaku

Shuster, Joe 1914-1992 CLC 21
See also AAYA 50

Shute, Nevil CLC 30
See Norway, Nevil Shute
See also BPFB 3; DLB 255; NFS 9; RHW;
SFW 4

Shuttle, Penelope (Diane) 1947- CLC 7
See also CA 93-96; CANR 39, 84, 92, 108;
CP 7; CWP; DLB 14, 40

Shvarts, Elena 1948- PC 50
See also CA 147

Sidhwa, Bapsy (N.) 1938- CLC 168
See also CA 108; CANR 25, 57; CN 7; FW

Sidney, Mary 1561-1621 LC 19, 39
See Sidney Herbert, Mary

Sidney, Sir Philip 1554-1586 LC 19, 39; PC
32
See also BRW 1; BRWR 2; CDBLB Before
1660; DA; DA3; DAB; DAC; DAM MST,
POET; DLB 167; EXPP; PAB; RGEL 2;
TEA; WP

Sidney Herbert, Mary
See Sidney, Mary
See also DLB 167

Siegel, Jerome 1914-1996 CLC 21
See Siegel, Jerry
See also CA 116; 169; 151

Siegel, Jerry
See Siegel, Jerome
See also AAYA 50

Sienkiewicz, Henryk (Adam Alexander Pius)
1846-1916 **TCLC 3**
See also CA 104; 134; CANR 84; EWL 3;
RGSF 2; RGWL 2, 3

Sierra, Gregorio Martinez
See Martinez Sierra, Gregorio

Sierra, Maria (de la O'LeJarraga) Martinez
See Martinez Sierra, Maria (de la
O'LeJarraga)

Sigal, Clancy 1926- CLC 7
See also CA 1-4R; CANR 85; CN 7

Sigourney, Lydia H.
See Sigourney, Lydia Howard (Huntley)
See also DLB 73, 183

Sigourney, Lydia Howard (Huntley)
1791-1865 **NCLC 21, 87**
See Sigourney, Lydia H.; Sigourney, Lydia
Huntley
See also DLB 1

Sigourney, Lydia Huntley
See Sigourney, Lydia Howard (Huntley)
See also DLB 42, 239, 243

Siguenza y Gongora, Carlos de 1645-1700
HLCS 2; LC 8
See also LAW

Sigurjonsson, Johann
See Johann Sigurjonsson

Sikelianos, Angelos 1884-1951 PC 29; TCLC
39
See also EWL 3; RGWL 2, 3

Silkin, Jon 1930-1997 CLC 2, 6, 43
See also CA 5-8R; CAAS 5; CANR 89; CP
7; DLB 27

Silko, Leslie (Marmon) 1948- CLC 23, 74,
114; NNAL; SSC 37, 66; WLCS
See also AAYA 14; AMWS 4; ANW; BYA
12; CA 115; 122; CANR 45, 65, 118; CN
7; CP 7; CWP; DA; DA3; DAC;
DAM MST, MULT, POP; DLB 143, 175,
256, 275; EWL 3; EXPP; EXPS; LAIT 4;
MTCW 2; NFS 4; PFS 9, 16; RGAL 4;
RGSF 2; SSFS 4, 8, 10, 11

Sillanpaa, Frans Eemil 1888-1964 CLC 19
See also CA 129; 93-96; EWL 3; MTCW 1

Sillitoe, Alan 1928- CLC 1, 3, 6, 10, 19, 57,
148
See also AITN 1; BRWS 5; CA 9-12R, 191;
CAAE 191; CAAS 2; CANR 8, 26, 55;
CDBLB 1960 to Present; CN 7; DLB 14,
139; EWL 3; MTCW 1, 2; RGEL 2;
RGSF 2; SATA 61

Silone, Ignazio 1900-1978 CLC 4
See also CA 25-28; 81-84; CANR 34; CAP
2; DLB 264; EW 12; EWL 3; MTCW 1;
RGSF 2; RGWL 2, 3

Silone, Ignazione
See Silone, Ignazio

Silver, Joan Micklin 1935- CLC 20
See also CA 114; 121; INT CA-121

Silver, Nicholas
See Faust, Frederick (Schiller)
See also TCWW 2

Silverberg, Robert 1935- CLC 7, 140
See also AAYA 24; BPFB 3; BYA 7, 9; CA
1-4R, 186; CAAE 186; CAAS 3; CANR
1, 20, 36, 85; CLR 59; CN 7; CPW; DAM
POP; DLB 8; INT CANR-20; MAICYA
1, 2; MTCW 1, 2; SATA 13, 91; SATA-
Essay 104; SCFW 2; SFW 4; SUFW 2

Silverstein, Alvin 1933- CLC 17
See also CA 49-52; CANR 2; CLR 25;
JRDA; MAICYA 1, 2; SATA 8, 69, 124

Silverstein, Shel(don Allan) 1932-1999 PC 49
See also AAYA 40; BW 3; CA 107; 179;
CANR 47, 74, 81; CLR 5, 96; CWRI 5;
JRDA; MAICYA 1, 2; MTCW 2; SATA
33, 92; SATA-Brief 27; SATA-Obit 116

Silverstein, Virginia B(arbara Opshelor)
1937- **CLC 17**
See also CA 49-52; CANR 2; CLR 25;
JRDA; MAICYA 1, 2; SATA 8, 69, 124

Sim, Georges
See Simenon, Georges (Jacques Christian)

Simak, Clifford D(onald) 1904-1988 CLC 1,
55
See also CA 1-4R; 125; CANR 1, 35; DLB
8; MTCW 1; SATA-Obit 56; SFW 4

Simenon, Georges (Jacques Christian)
1903-1989 **CLC 1, 2, 3, 8, 18, 47**
See also BPFB 3; CA 85-88; 129; CANR
35; CMW 4; DA3; DAM POP; DLB 72;

DLBY 1989; EW 12; EWL 3; GFL 1789
to the Present; MSW; MTCW 1, 2; RGWL
2, 3

Simic, Charles 1938- **CLC 6, 9, 22, 49, 68, 130**
See also AMWS 8; CA 29-32R; CAAS 4;
CANR 12, 33, 52, 61, 96; CP 7; DA3;
DAM POET; DLB 105; MTCW 2; PFS 7;
RGAL 4; WP

Simmel, Georg 1858-1918 **TCLC 64**
See also CA 157; DLB 296

Simmons, Charles (Paul) 1924- **CLC 57**
See also CA 89-92; INT CA-89-92

Simmons, Dan 1948- **CLC 44**
See also AAYA 16; CA 138; CANR 53, 81,
126; CPW; DAM POP; HGG; SUFW 2

Simmons, James (Stewart Alexander) 1933-
CLC 43
See also CA 105; CAAS 21; CP 7; DLB 40

Simms, William Gilmore 1806-1870 **NCLC 3**
See also DLB 3, 30, 59, 73, 248, 254;
RGAL 4

Simon, Carly 1945- **CLC 26**
See also CA 105

Simon, Claude (Henri Eugene) 1913-1984
CLC 4, 9, 15, 39
See also CA 89-92; CANR 33, 117; DAM
NOV; DLB 83; EW 13; EWL 3; GFL
1789 to the Present; MTCW 1

Simon, Myles
See Follett, Ken(neth Martin)

Simon, (Marvin) Neil 1927- **CLC 6, 11, 31, 39, 70; DC 14**
See also AAYA 32; AITN 1; AMWS 4; CA
21-24R; CANR 26, 54, 87, 126; CD 5;
DA3; DAM DRAM; DFS 2, 6, 12, 18;
DLB 7, 266; LAIT 4; MTCW 1, 2; RGAL
4; TUS

Simon, Paul (Frederick) 1941(?)- **CLC 17**
See also CA 116; 153

Simonon, Paul 1956(?)- **CLC 30**

Simonson, Rick ed. **CLC 70**

Simpson, Harriette
See Arnow, Harriette (Louisa) Simpson

Simpson, Louis (Aston Marantz) 1923- **CLC 4, 7, 9, 32, 149**
See also AMWS 9; CA 1-4R; CAAS 4;
CANR 1, 61; CP 7; DAM POET; DLB 5;
MTCW 1, 2; PFS 7, 11, 14; RGAL 4

Simpson, Mona (Elizabeth) 1957- **CLC 44, 146**
See also CA 122; 135; CANR 68, 103; CN
7; EWL 3

Simpson, N(orman) F(rederick) 1919- **CLC 29**
See also CA 13-16R; CBD; DLB 13; RGEL
2

Sinclair, Andrew (Annandale) 1935- **CLC 2, 14**
See also CA 9-12R; CAAS 5; CANR 14,
38, 91; CN 7; DLB 14; FANT; MTCW 1

Sinclair, Emil
See Hesse, Hermann

Sinclair, Iain 1943- **CLC 76**
See also CA 132; CANR 81; CP 7; HGG

Sinclair, Iain MacGregor
See Sinclair, Iain

Sinclair, Irene
See Griffith, D(avid Lewelyn) W(ark)

Sinclair, Mary Amelia St. Clair 1865(?)-1946
See Sinclair, May
See also CA 104; HGG; RHW

Sinclair, May **TCLC 3, 11**
See Sinclair, Mary Amelia St. Clair
See also CA 166; DLB 36, 135; EWL 3;
RGEL 2; SUFW

Sinclair, Roy
See Griffith, D(avid Lewelyn) W(ark)

Sinclair, Upton (Beall) 1878-1968 **CLC 1, 11, 15, 63; WLC**
See also AMWS 5; BPFB 3; BYA 2; CA
5-8R; 25-28R; CANR 7; CDALB 1929-
1941; DA; DA3; DAB; DAC; DAM MST,
NOV; DLB 9; EWL 3; INT CANR-7;
LAIT 3; MTCW 1, 2; NFS 6; RGAL 4;
SATA 9; TUS; YAW

Singe, (Edmund) J(ohn) M(illington)
1871-1909 **WLC**

Singer, Isaac
See Singer, Isaac Bashevis

Singer, Isaac Bashevis 1904-1991 **CLC 1, 3, 6, 9, 11, 15, 23, 38, 69, 111; SSC 3, 53; WLC**
See also AAYA 32; AITN 1, 2; AMW;
AMWR 2; BPFB 1, 4; BYA 1, 4; CA 1-4R;
134; CANR 1, 39, 106; CDALB 1941-
1968; CLR 1; CWRI 5; DA; DA3; DAB;
DAC; DAM MST, NOV; DLB 6, 28, 52,
278; DLBY 1991; EWL 3; EXPS; HGG;
JRDA; LAIT 3; MAICYA 1, 2; MTCW 1,
2; RGAL 4; RGSF 2; SATA 3, 27; SATA-
Obit 68; SSFS 2, 12, 16; TUS; TWA

Singer, Israel Joshua 1893-1944 **TCLC 33**
See also CA 169; EWL 3

Singh, Khushwant 1915- **CLC 11**
See also CA 9-12R; CAAS 9; CANR 6, 84;
CN 7; EWL 3; RGEL 2

Singleton, Ann
See Benedict, Ruth (Fulton)

Singleton, John 1968(?)- **CLC 156**
See also AAYA 50; BW 2, 3; CA 138;
CANR 67, 82; DAM MULT

Sinjohn, John
See Galsworthy, John

Sinyavsky, Andrei (Donatevich) 1925-1997
CLC 8
See Sinyavsky, Andrey Donatovich; Tertz,
Abram
See also CA 85-88; 159

Sinyavsky, Andrey Donatovich
See Sinyavsky, Andrei (Donatevich)
See also EWL 3

Sirin, V.
See Nabokov, Vladimir (Vladimirovich)

Sissman, L(ouis) E(dward) 1928-1976 **CLC 9, 18**
See also CA 21-24R; 65-68; CANR 13;
DLB 5

Sisson, C(harles) H(ubert) 1914-2003 **CLC 8**
See also CA 1-4R; 220; CAAS 3; CANR 3,
48, 84; CP 7; DLB 27

Sitting Bull 1831(?)-1890 **NNAL**
See also DA3; DAM MULT

Sitwell, Dame Edith 1887-1964 **CLC 2, 9, 67; PC 3**
See also BRW 7; CA 9-12R; CANR 35;
CDBLB 1945-1960; DAM POET; DLB
20; EWL 3; MTCW 1, 2; RGEL 2; TEA

Siwaarmill, H. P.
See Sharp, William

Sjoewall, Maj 1935- **CLC 7**
See Sjowall, Maj
See also CA 65-68; CANR 73

Sjowall, Maj
See Sjoewall, Maj
See also BPFB 3; CMW 4; MSW

Skelton, John 1460(?)-1529 **LC 71; PC 25**
See also BRW 1; DLB 136; RGEL 2

Skelton, Robin 1925-1997 **CLC 13**
See Zuk, Georges
See also AITN 2; CA 5-8R; 160; CAAS 5;
CANR 28, 89; CCA 1; CP 7; DLB 27, 53

Skolimowski, Jerzy 1938- **CLC 20**
See also CA 128

Skram, Amalie (Bertha) 1847-1905 **TCLC 25**
See also CA 165

Skvorecky, Josef (Vaclav) 1924- **CLC 15, 39, 69, 152**
See also CA 61-64; CAAS 1; CANR 10,
34, 63, 108; CDWLB 4; DA3; DAC;
DAM NOV; DLB 232; EWL 3; MTCW
1, 2

Slade, Bernard **CLC 11, 46**
See Newbound, Bernard Slade
See also CAAS 9; CCA 1; DLB 53

Slaughter, Carolyn 1946- **CLC 56**
See also CA 85-88; CANR 85; CN 7

Slaughter, Frank G(ill) 1908-2001 **CLC 29**
See also AITN 2; CA 5-8R; 197; CANR 5,
85; INT CANR-5; RHW

Slavitt, David R(ytman) 1935- **CLC 5, 14**
See also CA 21-24R; CAAS 3; CANR 41,
83; CP 7; DLB 5, 6

Slesinger, Tess 1905-1945 **TCLC 10**
See also CA 107; 199; DLB 102

Slessor, Kenneth 1901-1971 **CLC 14**
See also CA 102; 89-92; DLB 260; RGEL
2

Slowacki, Juliusz 1809-1849 **NCLC 15**
See also RGWL 3

Smart, Christopher 1722-1771 **LC 3; PC 13**
See also DAM POET; DLB 109; RGEL 2

Smart, Elizabeth 1913-1986 **CLC 54**
See also CA 81-84; 118; DLB 88

Smiley, Jane (Graves) 1949- **CLC 53, 76, 144**
See also AMWS 6; BPFB 3; CA 104;
CANR 30, 50, 74, 96; CN 7; CPW 1;
DA3; DAM POP; DLB 227, 234; EWL 3;
INT CANR-30; SSFS 19

Smith, A(rthur) J(ames) M(arshall)
1902-1980 **CLC 15**
See also CA 1-4R; 102; CANR 4; DAC;
DLB 88; RGEL 2

Smith, Adam 1723(?)-1790 **LC 36**
See also DLB 104, 252; RGEL 2

Smith, Alexander 1829-1867 **NCLC 59**
See also DLB 32, 55

Smith, Anna Deavere 1950- **CLC 86**
See also CA 133; CANR 103; CD 5; DFS 2

Smith, Betty (Wehner) 1904-1972 **CLC 19**
See also BPFB 3; BYA 3; CA 5-8R; 33-
36R; DLBY 1982; LAIT 3; RGAL 4;
SATA 6

Smith, Charlotte (Turner) 1749-1806 **NCLC 23, 115**
See also DLB 39, 109; RGEL 2; TEA

Smith, Clark Ashton 1893-1961 **CLC 43**
See also CA 143; CANR 81; FANT; HGG;
MTCW 2; SCFW 2; SFW 4; SUFW

Smith, Dave **CLC 22, 42**
See Smith, David (Jeddie)
See also CAAS 7; DLB 5

Smith, David (Jeddie) 1942-
See Smith, Dave
See also CA 49-52; CANR 1, 59, 120; CP
7; CSW; DAM POET

Smith, Florence Margaret 1902-1971
See Smith, Stevie
See also CA 17-18; 29-32R; CANR 35;
CAP 2; DAM POET; MTCW 1, 2; TEA

Smith, Iain Crichton 1928-1998 **CLC 64**
See also BRWS 9; CA 21-24R; 171; CN 7;
CP 7; DLB 40, 139; RGSF 2

Smith, John 1580(?)-1631 **LC 9**
See also DLB 24, 30; TUS

Smith, Johnston
See Crane, Stephen (Townley)

Smith, Joseph, Jr. 1805-1844 **NCLC 53**

Smith, Lee 1944- **CLC 25, 73**
See also CA 114; 119; CANR 46, 118;
CSW; DLB 143; DLBY 1983; EWL 3;
INT CA-119; RGAL 4

Smith, Martin
See Smith, Martin Cruz
Smith, Martin Cruz 1942- **CLC 25; NNAL**
See also BEST 89:4; BPFB 3; CA 85-88;
CANR 6, 23, 43, 65, 119; CMW 4; CPW;
DAM MULT, POP; HGG; INT CANR-
23; MTCW 2; RGAL 4
Smith, Patti 1946- **CLC 12**
See also CA 93-96; CANR 63
Smith, Pauline (Urmson) 1882-1959 **TCLC
25**
See also DLB 225; EWL 3
Smith, Rosamond
See Oates, Joyce Carol
Smith, Sheila Kaye
See Kaye-Smith, Sheila
Smith, Stevie CLC 3, 8, 25, 44; PC 12
See Smith, Florence Margaret
See also BRWS 2; DLB 20; EWL 3; MTCW
2; PAB; PFS 3; RGEL 2
Smith, Wilbur (Addison) 1933- **CLC 33**
See also CA 13-16R; CANR 7, 46, 66;
CPW; MTCW 1, 2
Smith, William Jay 1918- **CLC 6**
See also AMWS 13; CA 5-8R; CANR 44,
106; CP 7; CSW; CWRI 5; DLB 5; MAI-
CYA 1, 2; SAAS 22; SATA 2, 68
Smith, Woodrow Wilson
See Kuttner, Henry
Smith, Zadie 1976- **CLC 158**
See also AAYA 50; CA 193
Smolenskin, Peretz 1842-1885 **NCLC 30**
Smollett, Tobias (George) 1721-1771 **LC 2,
46**
See also BRW 3; CDBLB 1660-1789; DLB
39, 104; RGEL 2; TEA
Snodgrass, W(illiam) D(e Witt) 1926- **CLC 2,
6, 10, 18, 68**
See also AMWS 6; CA 1-4R; CANR 6, 36,
65, 85; CP 7; DAM POET; DLB 5;
MTCW 1, 2; RGAL 4
Snorri Sturluson 1179-1241 **CMLC 56**
See also RGWL 2, 3
Snow, C(harles) P(ercy) 1905-1980 **CLC 1, 4,
6, 9, 13, 19**
See also BRW 7; CA 5-8R; 101; CANR 28;
CDBLB 1945-1960; DAM NOV; DLB 15,
77; DLBD 17; EWL 3; MTCW 1, 2;
RGEL 2; TEA
Snow, Frances Compton
See Adams, Henry (Brooks)
Snyder, Gary (Sherman) 1930- **CLC 1, 2, 5,
9, 32, 120; PC 21**
See also AMWS 8; ANW; BG 3; CA 17-
20R; CANR 30, 60, 125; CP 7; DA3;
DAM POET; DLB 5, 16, 165, 212, 237,
275; EWL 3; MTCW 2; PFS 9, 19; RGAL
4; WP
Snyder, Zilpha Keatley 1927- **CLC 17**
See also AAYA 15; BYA 1; CA 9-12R;
CANR 38; CLR 31; JRDA; MAICYA 1,
2; SAAS 2; SATA 1, 28, 75, 110; SATA-
Essay 112; YAW
Soares, Bernardo
See Pessoa, Fernando (Antonio Nogueira)
Sobh, A.
See Shamlu, Ahmad
Sobh, Alef
See Shamlu, Ahmad
Sobol, Joshua 1939- **CLC 60**
See Sobol, Yehoshua
See also CA 200; CWW 2
Sobol, Yehoshua 1939-
See Sobol, Joshua
See also CWW 2
Socrates 470B.C.-399B.C. **CMLC 27**
Soderberg, Hjalmar 1869-1941 **TCLC 39**
See also DLB 259; EWL 3; RGSF 2

Soderbergh, Steven 1963- **CLC 154**
See also AAYA 43
Sodergran, Edith (Irene) 1892-1923
See Soedergran, Edith (Irene)
See also CA 202; DLB 259; EW 11; EWL
3; RGWL 2, 3
Soedergran, Edith (Irene) 1892-1923 **TCLC
31**
See Sodergran, Edith (Irene)
Softly, Edgar
See Lovecraft, H(oward) P(hillips)
Softly, Edward
See Lovecraft, H(oward) P(hillips)
Sokolov, Alexander V(sevolodovich) 1943-
See Sokolov, Sasha
See also CA 73-76
Sokolov, Raymond 1941- **CLC 7**
See also CA 85-88
Sokolov, Sasha CLC 59
See Sokolov, Alexander V(sevolodovich)
See also CWW 2; DLB 285; EWL 3; RGWL
2, 3
Sokolov, Sasha CLC 59
Solo, Jay
See Ellison, Harlan (Jay)
Sologub, Fyodor TCLC 9
See Teternikov, Fyodor Kuzmich
See also EWL 3
Solomons, Ikey Esquir
See Thackeray, William Makepeace
Solomos, Dionysios 1798-1857 **NCLC 15**
Solwoska, Mara
See French, Marilyn
Solzhenitsyn, Aleksandr I(sayevich) 1918-
**CLC 1, 2, 4, 7, 9, 10, 18, 26, 34, 78, 134;
SSC 32; WLC**
See Solzhenitsyn, Aleksandr Isaevich
See also AAYA 49; AITN 1; BPFB 3; CA
69-72; CANR 40, 65, 116; DA; DA3;
DAB; DAC; DAM MST, NOV; EW 13;
EXPS; LAIT 4; MTCW 1, 2; NFS 6;
RGSF 2; RGWL 2, 3; SSFS 9; TWA
Solzhenitsyn, Aleksandr Isaevich
See Solzhenitsyn, Aleksandr I(sayevich)
See also EWL 3
Somers, Jane
See Lessing, Doris (May)
Somerville, Edith Oenone 1858-1949 **SSC 56;
TCLC 51**
See also CA 196; DLB 135; RGEL 2; RGSF
2
Somerville & Ross
See Martin, Violet Florence; Somerville,
Edith Oenone
Sommer, Scott 1951- **CLC 25**
See also CA 106
Sondheim, Stephen (Joshua) 1930- **CLC 30,
39, 147; DC 22**
See also AAYA 11; CA 103; CANR 47, 67,
125; DAM DRAM; LAIT 4
Sone, Monica 1919- **AAL**
Song, Cathy 1955- **AAL; PC 21**
See also CA 154; CANR 118; CWP; DLB
169; EXPP; FW; PFS 5
Sontag, Susan 1933- **CLC 1, 2, 10, 13, 31,
105**
See also AMWS 3; CA 17-20R; CANR 25,
51, 74, 97; CN 7; CPW; DA3; DAM POP;
DLB 2, 67; EWL 3; MAWW; MTCW 1,
2; RGAL 4; RHW; SSFS 10
Sophocles 496(?)B.C.-406(?)B.C. **CMLC 2,
47, 51; DC 1; WLCS**
See also AW 1; CDWLB 1; DA; DA3;
DAB; DAC; DAM DRAM, MST; DFS 1,
4, 8; DLB 176; LAIT 1; LATS 1; LMFS
1; RGWL 2, 3; TWA
Sordello 1189-1269 **CMLC 15**
Sorel, Georges 1847-1922 **TCLC 91**
See also CA 118; 188

Sorel, Julia
See Drexler, Rosalyn
Sorokin, Vladimir CLC 59
See Sorokin, Vladimir Georgievich
Sorokin, Vladimir Georgievich
See Sorokin, Vladimir
See also DLB 285
Sorrentino, Gilbert 1929- **CLC 3, 7, 14, 22,
40**
See also CA 77-80; CANR 14, 33, 115; CN
7; CP 7; DLB 5, 173; DLBY 1980; INT
CANR-14
Soseki
See Natsume, Soseki
See also MJW
Soto, Gary 1952- **CLC 32, 80; HLC 2; PC 28**
See also AAYA 10, 37; BYA 11; CA 119;
125; CANR 50, 74, 107; CLR 38; CP 7;
DAM MULT; DLB 82; EWL 3; EXPP;
HW 1, 2; INT CA-125; JRDA; LLW 1;
MAICYA 2; MAICYAS 1; MTCW 2; PFS
7; RGAL 4; SATA 80, 120; WYA; YAW
Soupault, Philippe 1897-1990 **CLC 68**
See also CA 116; 147; 131; EWL 3; GFL
1789 to the Present; LMFS 2
Souster, (Holmes) Raymond 1921- **CLC 5, 14**
See also CA 13-16R; CAAS 14; CANR 13,
29, 53; CP 7; DA3; DAC; DAM POET;
DLB 88; RGEL 2; SATA 63
Southern, Terry 1924(?)-1995 **CLC 7**
See also AMWS 11; BPFB 3; CA 1-4R;
150; CANR 1, 55, 107; CN 7; DLB 2;
IDFW 3, 4
Southerne, Thomas 1660-1746 **LC 99**
See also DLB 80; RGEL 2
Southey, Robert 1774-1843 **NCLC 8, 97**
See also BRW 4; DLB 93, 107, 142; RGEL
2; SATA 54
Southworth, Emma Dorothy Eliza Nevitte
1819-1899 **NCLC 26**
See also DLB 239
Souza, Ernest
See Scott, Evelyn
Soyinka, Wole 1934- **BLC 3; CLC 3, 5, 14,
36, 44, 179; DC 2; WLC**
See also AFW; BW 2, 3; CA 13-16R;
CANR 27, 39, 82; CD 5; CDWLB 3; CN
7; CP 7; DA; DA3; DAB; DAC; DAM
DRAM, MST, MULT; DFS 10; DLB 125;
EWL 3; MTCW 1, 2; RGEL 2; TWA;
WLIT 2; WWE 1
Spackman, W(illiam) M(ode) 1905-1990 **CLC
46**
See also CA 81-84; 132
Spacks, Barry (Bernard) 1931- **CLC 14**
See also CA 154; CANR 33, 109; CP 7;
DLB 105
Spanidou, Irini 1946- **CLC 44**
See also CA 185
Spark, Muriel (Sarah) 1918- **CLC 2, 3, 5, 8,
13, 18, 40, 94; SSC 10**
See also BRWS 1; CA 5-8R; CANR 12, 36,
76, 89; CDBLB 1945-1960; CN 7; CP 7;
DA3; DAB; DAC; DAM MST, NOV;
DLB 15, 139; EWL 3; FW; INT CANR-
12; LAIT 4; MTCW 1, 2; RGEL 2; TEA;
WLIT 4; YAW
Spaulding, Douglas
See Bradbury, Ray (Douglas)
Spaulding, Leonard
See Bradbury, Ray (Douglas)
Speght, Rachel 1597-c. 1630 **LC 97**
See also DLB 126
Spelman, Elizabeth CLC 65
Spence, J. A. D.
See Eliot, T(homas) S(tearns)
Spencer, Anne 1882-1975 **HR 3**
See also BW 2; CA 161; DLB 51, 54

Spencer, Elizabeth 1921- **CLC 22; SSC 57**
See also CA 13-16R; CANR 32, 65, 87; CN 7; CSW; DLB 6, 218; EWL 3; MTCW 1; RGAL 4; SATA 14

Spencer, Leonard G.
See Silverberg, Robert

Spencer, Scott 1945- **CLC 30**
See also CA 113; CANR 51; DLBY 1986

Spender, Stephen (Harold) 1909-1995 **CLC 1, 2, 5, 10, 41, 91**
See also BRWS 2; CA 9-12R; 149; CANR 31, 54; CDBLB 1945-1960; CP 7; DA3; DAM POET; DLB 20; EWL 3; MTCW 1, 2; PAB; RGEL 2; TEA

Spengler, Oswald (Arnold Gottfried) 1880-1936 **TCLC 25**
See also CA 118; 189

Spenser, Edmund 1552(?)-1599 **LC 5, 39; PC 8, 42; WLC**
See also BRW 1; CDBLB Before 1660; DA; DA3; DAB; DAC; DAM MST, POET; DLB 167; EFS 2; EXPP; PAB; RGEL 2; TEA; WLIT 3; WP

Spicer, Jack 1925-1965 **CLC 8, 18, 72**
See also BG 3; CA 85-88; DAM POET; DLB 5, 16, 193; GLL 1; WP

Spiegelman, Art 1948- **CLC 76, 178**
See also AAYA 10, 46; CA 125; CANR 41, 55, 74, 124; MTCW 2; SATA 109; YAW

Spielberg, Peter 1929- **CLC 6**
See also CA 5-8R; CANR 4, 48; DLBY 1981

Spielberg, Steven 1947- **CLC 20, 188**
See also AAYA 8, 24; CA 77-80; CANR 32; SATA 32

Spillane, Frank Morrison 1918-
See Spillane, Mickey
See also CA 25-28R; CANR 28, 63, 125; DA3; MTCW 1, 2; SATA 66

Spillane, Mickey CLC 3, 13
See Spillane, Frank Morrison
See also BPFB 3; CMW 4; DLB 226; MSW; MTCW 2

Spinoza, Benedictus de 1632-1677 **LC 9, 58**

Spinrad, Norman (Richard) 1940- **CLC 46**
See also BPFB 3; CA 37-40R; CAAS 19; CANR 20, 91; DLB 8; INT CANR-20; SFW 4

Spitteler, Carl (Friedrich Georg) 1845-1924 **TCLC 12**
See also CA 109; DLB 129; EWL 3

Spivack, Kathleen (Romola Drucker) 1938- **CLC 6**
See also CA 49-52

Spoto, Donald 1941- **CLC 39**
See also CA 65-68; CANR 11, 57, 93

Springsteen, Bruce (F.) 1949- **CLC 17**
See also CA 111

Spurling, (Susan) Hilary 1940- **CLC 34**
See also CA 104; CANR 25, 52, 94

Spyker, John Howland
See Elman, Richard (Martin)

Squared, A.
See Abbott, Edwin A.

Squires, (James) Radcliffe 1917-1993 **CLC 51**
See also CA 1-4R; 140; CANR 6, 21

Srivastava, Dhanpat Rai 1880(?)-1936
See Premchand
See also CA 118; 197

Stacy, Donald
See Pohl, Frederik

Stael
See Stael-Holstein, Anne Louise Germaine Necker
See also EW 5; RGWL 2, 3

Stael, Germaine de
See Stael-Holstein, Anne Louise Germaine Necker
See also DLB 119, 192; FW; GFL 1789 to the Present; TWA

Stael-Holstein, Anne Louise Germaine Necker 1766-1817 **NCLC 3, 91**
See Stael; Stael, Germaine de

Stafford, Jean 1915-1979 **CLC 4, 7, 19, 68; SSC 26**
See also CA 1-4R; 85-88; CANR 3, 65; DLB 2, 173; MTCW 1, 2; RGAL 4; RGSF 2; SATA-Obit 22; TCWW 2; TUS

Stafford, William (Edgar) 1914-1993 **CLC 4, 7, 29**
See also AMWS 11; CA 5-8R; 142; CAAS 3; CANR 5, 22; DAM POET; DLB 5, 206; EXPP; INT CANR-22; PFS 2, 8, 16; RGAL 4; WP

Stagnelius, Eric Johan 1793-1823 **NCLC 61**

Staines, Trevor
See Brunner, John (Kilian Houston)

Stairs, Gordon
See Austin, Mary (Hunter)
See also TCWW 2

Stalin, Joseph 1879-1953 **TCLC 92**

Stampa, Gaspara c. 1524-1554 **PC 43**
See also RGWL 2, 3

Stampflinger, K. A.
See Benjamin, Walter

Stancykowna
See Szymborska, Wislawa

Standing Bear, Luther 1868(?)-1939(?) **NNAL**
See also CA 113; 144; DAM MULT

Stannard, Martin 1947- **CLC 44**
See also CA 142; DLB 155

Stanton, Elizabeth Cady 1815-1902 **TCLC 73**
See also CA 171; DLB 79; FW

Stanton, Maura 1946- **CLC 9**
See also CA 89-92; CANR 15, 123; DLB 120

Stanton, Schuyler
See Baum, L(yman) Frank

Stapledon, (William) Olaf 1886-1950 **TCLC 22**
See also CA 111; 162; DLB 15, 255; SFW 4

Starbuck, George (Edwin) 1931-1996 **CLC 53**
See also CA 21-24R; 153; CANR 23; DAM POET

Stark, Richard
See Westlake, Donald E(dwin)

Staunton, Schuyler
See Baum, L(yman) Frank

Stead, Christina (Ellen) 1902-1983 **CLC 2, 5, 8, 32, 80**
See also BRWS 4; CA 13-16R; 109; CANR 33, 40; DLB 260; EWL 3; FW; MTCW 1, 2; RGEL 2; RGSF 2; WWE 1

Stead, William Thomas 1849-1912 **TCLC 48**
See also CA 167

Stebnitsky, M.
See Leskov, Nikolai (Semyonovich)

Steele, Sir Richard 1672-1729 **LC 18**
See also BRW 3; CDBLB 1660-1789; DLB 84, 101; RGEL 2; WLIT 3

Steele, Timothy (Reid) 1948- **CLC 45**
See also CA 93-96; CANR 16, 50, 92; CP 7; DLB 120, 282

Steffens, (Joseph) Lincoln 1866-1936 **TCLC 20**
See also CA 117; 198

Stegner, Wallace (Earle) 1909-1993 **CLC 9, 49, 81; SSC 27**
See also AITN 1; AMWS 4; ANW; BEST 90:3; BPFB 3; CA 1-4R; 141; CAAS 9; CANR 1, 21, 46; DAM NOV; DLB 9,

206, 275; DLBY 1993; EWL 3; MTCW 1, 2; RGAL 4; TCWW 2; TUS

Stein, Gertrude 1874-1946 **DC 19; PC 18; SSC 42; TCLC 1, 6, 28, 48; WLC**
See also AMW; AMWC 2; CA 104; 132; CANR 108; CDALB 1917-1929; DA; DA3; DAB; DAC; DAM MST, NOV, POET; DLB 4, 54, 86, 228; DLBD 15; EWL 3; EXPS; GLL 1; MAWW; MTCW 1, 2; NCFS 4; RGAL 4; RGSF 2; SSFS 5; TUS; WP

Steinbeck, John (Ernst) 1902-1968 **CLC 1, 5, 9, 13, 21, 34, 45, 75, 124; SSC 11, 37; TCLC 135; WLC**
See also AAYA 12; AMW; BPFB 3; BYA 2, 3, 13; CA 1-4R; 25-28R; CANR 1, 35; CDALB 1929-1941; DA; DA3; DAB; DAC; DAM DRAM, MST, NOV; DLB 7, 9, 212, 275; DLBD 2; EWL 3; EXPS; LAIT 3; MTCW 1, 2; NFS 1, 5, 7, 17; RGAL 4; RGSF 2; RHW; SATA 9; SSFS 3, 6; TCWW 2; TUS; WYA; YAW

Steinem, Gloria 1934- **CLC 63**
See also CA 53-56; CANR 28, 51; DLB 246; FW; MTCW 1, 2

Steiner, George 1929- **CLC 24**
See also CA 73-76; CANR 31, 67, 108; DAM NOV; DLB 67; EWL 3; MTCW 1, 2; SATA 62

Steiner, K. Leslie
See Delany, Samuel R(ay), Jr.

Steiner, Rudolf 1861-1925 **TCLC 13**
See also CA 107

Stendhal 1783-1842 **NCLC 23, 46; SSC 27; WLC**
See also DA; DA3; DAB; DAC; DAM MST, NOV; DLB 119; EW 5; GFL 1789 to the Present; RGWL 2, 3; TWA

Stephen, Adeline Virginia
See Woolf, (Adeline) Virginia

Stephen, Sir Leslie 1832-1904 **TCLC 23**
See also BRW 5; CA 123; DLB 57, 144, 190

Stephen, Sir Leslie
See Stephen, Sir Leslie

Stephen, Virginia
See Woolf, (Adeline) Virginia

Stephens, James 1882(?)-1950 **SSC 50; TCLC 4**
See also CA 104; 192; DLB 19, 153, 162; EWL 3; FANT; RGEL 2; SUFW

Stephens, Reed
See Donaldson, Stephen R(eeder)

Steptoe, Lydia
See Barnes, Djuna
See also GLL 1

Sterchi, Beat 1949- **CLC 65**
See also CA 203

Sterling, Brett
See Bradbury, Ray (Douglas); Hamilton, Edmond

Sterling, Bruce 1954- **CLC 72**
See also CA 119; CANR 44; SCFW 2; SFW 4

Sterling, George 1869-1926 **TCLC 20**
See also CA 117; 165; DLB 54

Stern, Gerald 1925- **CLC 40, 100**
See also AMWS 9; CA 81-84; CANR 28, 94; CP 7; DLB 105; RGAL 4

Stern, Richard (Gustave) 1928- **CLC 4, 39**
See also CA 1-4R; CANR 1, 25, 52, 120; CN 7; DLB 218; DLBY 1987; INT CANR-25

Sternberg, Josef von 1894-1969 **CLC 20**
See also CA 81-84

Sterne, Laurence 1713-1768 **LC 2, 48; WLC**
See also BRW 3; BRWC 1; CDBLB 1660-1789; DA; DAB; DAC; DAM MST, NOV; DLB 39; RGEL 2; TEA

Sternheim, (William Adolf) Carl 1878-1942
TCLC 8
See also CA 105; 193; DLB 56, 118; EWL
3; RGWL 2, 3

Stevens, Mark 1951- **CLC 34**
See also CA 122

Stevens, Wallace 1879-1955 **PC 6; TCLC 3,
12, 45; WLC**
See also AMW; AMWR 1; CA 104; 124;
CDALB 1929-1941; DA; DA3; DAB;
DAC; DAM MST, POET; DLB 54; EWL
3; EXPP; MTCW 1, 2; PAB; PFS 13, 16;
RGAL 4; TUS; WP

Stevenson, Anne (Katharine) 1933- **CLC 7,
33**
See also BRWS 6; CA 17-20R; CAAS 9;
CANR 9, 33, 123; CP 7; CWP; DLB 40;
MTCW 1; RHW

Stevenson, Robert Louis (Balfour)
1850-1894 **NCLC 5, 14, 63; SSC 11, 51;
WLC**
See also AAYA 24; BPFB 3; BRW 5;
BRWC 1; BRWR 1; BYA 1, 2, 4, 13; CD-
BLB 1890-1914; CLR 10, 11; DA; DA3;
DAB; DAC; DAM MST, NOV; DLB 18,
57, 141, 156, 174; DLBD 13; HGG;
JRDA; LAIT 1, 3; MAICYA 1, 2; NFS
11; RGEL 2; RGSF 2; SATA 100; SUFW;
TEA; WCH; WLIT 4; WYA; YABC 2;
YAW

Stewart, J(ohn) I(nnes) M(ackintosh)
1906-1994 **CLC 7, 14, 32**
See Innes, Michael
See also CA 85-88; 147; CAAS 3; CANR
47; CMW 4; MTCW 1, 2

Stewart, Mary (Florence Elinor) 1916- **CLC
7, 35, 117**
See also AAYA 29; BPFB 3; CA 1-4R;
CANR 1, 59; CMW 4; CPW; DAB;
FANT; RHW; SATA 12; YAW

Stewart, Mary Rainbow
See Stewart, Mary (Florence Elinor)

Stifle, June
See Campbell, Maria

Stifter, Adalbert 1805-1868 **NCLC 41; SSC
28**
See also CDWLB 2; DLB 133; RGSF 2;
RGWL 2, 3

Still, James 1906-2001 **CLC 49**
See also CA 65-68; 195; CAAS 17; CANR
10, 26; CSW; DLB 9; DLBY 01; SATA
29; SATA-Obit 127

Sting 1951-
See Sumner, Gordon Matthew
See also CA 167

Stirling, Arthur
See Sinclair, Upton (Beall)

Stitt, Milan 1941- **CLC 29**
See also CA 69-72

Stockton, Francis Richard 1834-1902
See Stockton, Frank R.
See also CA 108; 137; MAICYA 1, 2; SATA
44; SFW 4

Stockton, Frank R. TCLC 47
See Stockton, Francis Richard
See also BYA 4, 13; DLB 42, 74; DLBD
13; EXPS; SATA-Brief 32; SSFS 3;
SUFW; WCH

Stoddard, Charles
See Kuttner, Henry

Stoker, Abraham 1847-1912
See Stoker, Bram
See also CA 105; 150; DA; DA3; DAC;
DAM MST, NOV; HGG; SATA 29

Stoker, Bram SSC 62; TCLC 8, 144; WLC
See Stoker, Abraham
See also AAYA 23; BPFB 3; BRWS 3; BYA
5; CDBLB 1890-1914; DAB; DLB 36, 70,
178; LATS 1; NFS 18; RGEL 2; SUFW;
TEA; WLIT 4

Stolz, Mary (Slattery) 1920- **CLC 12**
See also AAYA 8; AITN 1; CA 5-8R;
CANR 13, 41, 112; JRDA; MAICYA 1,
2; SAAS 3; SATA 10, 71, 133; YAW

Stone, Irving 1903-1989 **CLC 7**
See also AITN 1; BPFB 3; CA 1-4R; 129;
CAAS 3; CANR 1, 23; CPW; DA3; DAM
POP; INT CANR-23; MTCW 1, 2; RHW;
SATA 3; SATA-Obit 64

Stone, Oliver (William) 1946- **CLC 73**
See also AAYA 15; CA 110; CANR 55, 125

Stone, Robert (Anthony) 1937- **CLC 5, 23,
42, 175**
See also AMWS 5; BPFB 3; CA 85-88;
CANR 23, 66, 95; CN 7; DLB 152; EWL
3; INT CANR-23; MTCW 1

Stone, Ruth 1915- **PC 53**
See also CA 45-48; CANR 2, 91; CP 7;
CSW; DLB 105; PFS 19

Stone, Zachary
See Follett, Ken(neth Martin)

Stoppard, Tom 1937- **CLC 1, 3, 4, 5, 8, 15,
29, 34, 63, 91; DC 6; WLC**
See also BRWC 1; BRWR 2; BRWS 1; CA
81-84; CANR 39, 67, 125; CBD; CD 5;
CDBLB 1960 to Present; DA; DA3;
DAB; DAC; DAM DRAM, MST; DFS 2,
5, 8, 11, 13, 16; DLB 13, 233; DLBY
1985; EWL 3; LATS 1; MTCW 1, 2;
RGEL 2; TEA; WLIT 4

Storey, David (Malcolm) 1933- **CLC 2, 4, 5,
8**
See also BRWS 1; CA 81-84; CANR 36;
CBD; CD 5; CN 7; DAM DRAM; DLB
13, 14, 207, 245; EWL 3; MTCW 1;
RGEL 2

Storm, Hyemeyohsts 1935- **CLC 3; NNAL**
See also CA 81-84; CANR 45; DAM MULT

Storm, (Hans) Theodor (Woldsen) 1817-1888
NCLC 1; SSC 27
See also CDWLB 2; DLB 129; EW; RGSF
2; RGWL 2, 3

Storni, Alfonsina 1892-1938 **HLC 2; PC 33;
TCLC 5**
See also CA 104; 131; DAM MULT; DLB
283; HW 1; LAW

Stoughton, William 1631-1701 **LC 38**
See also DLB 24

Stout, Rex (Todhunter) 1886-1975 **CLC 3**
See also AITN 2; BPFB 3; CA 61-64;
CANR 71; CMW 4; MSW; RGAL 4

Stow, (Julian) Randolph 1935- **CLC 23, 48**
See also CA 13-16R; CANR 33; CN 7;
DLB 260; MTCW 1; RGEL 2

Stowe, Harriet (Elizabeth) Beecher
1811-1896 **NCLC 3, 50, 133; WLC**
See also AAYA 53; AMWS 1; CDALB
1865-1917; DA; DA3; DAB; DAC; DAM
MST, NOV; DLB 1, 12, 42, 74, 189, 239,
243; EXPN; JRDA; LAIT 2; MAICYA 1,
2; NFS 6; RGAL 4; TUS; YABC 1

Strabo c. 64B.C.-c. 25 **CMLC 37**
See also DLB 176

Strachey, (Giles) Lytton 1880-1932 **TCLC 12**
See also BRWS 2; CA 110; 178; DLB 149;
DLBD 10; EWL 3; MTCW 2; NCFS 4

Stramm, August 1874-1915 **PC 50**
See also CA 195; EWL 3

Strand, Mark 1934- **CLC 6, 18, 41, 71**
See also AMWS 4; CA 21-24R; CANR 40,
65, 100; CP 7; DAM POET; DLB 5; EWL
3; PAB; PFS 9, 18; RGAL 4; SATA 41

Stratton-Porter, Gene(va Grace) 1863-1924
See Porter, Gene(va Grace) Stratton
See also ANW; CA 137; CLR 87; DLB 221;
DLBD 14; MAICYA 1, 2; SATA 15

Straub, Peter (Francis) 1943- **CLC 28, 107**
See also BEST 89:1; BPFB 3; CA 85-88;
CANR 28, 65, 109; CPW; DAM POP;
DLBY 1984; HGG; MTCW 1, 2; SUFW
2

Strauss, Botho 1944- **CLC 22**
See also CA 157; CWW 2; DLB 124

Strauss, Leo 1899-1973 **TCLC 141**
See also CA 101; 45-48; CANR 122

Streatfeild, (Mary) Noel 1897(?)-1986 **CLC
21**
See also CA 81-84; 120; CANR 31; CLR
17, 83; CWRI 5; DLB 160; MAICYA 1,
2; SATA 20; SATA-Obit 48

Stribling, T(homas) S(igismund) 1881-1965
CLC 23
See also CA 189; 107; CMW 4; DLB 9;
RGAL 4

Strindberg, (Johan) August 1849-1912 **DC
18; TCLC 1, 8, 21, 47; WLC**
See also CA 104; 135; DA; DA3; DAB;
DAC; DAM DRAM, MST; DFS 4, 9;
DLB 259; EW 7; EWL 3; IDTP; LMFS
2; MTCW 2; RGWL 2, 3; TWA

Stringer, Arthur 1874-1950 **TCLC 37**
See also CA 161; DLB 92

Stringer, David
See Roberts, Keith (John Kingston)

Stroheim, Erich von 1885-1957 **TCLC 71**

Strugatskii, Arkadii (Natanovich) 1925-1991
CLC 27
See also CA 106; 135; SFW 4

Strugatskii, Boris (Natanovich) 1933- **CLC
27**
See also CA 106; SFW 4

Strummer, Joe 1953(?)- **CLC 30**

Strunk, William, Jr. 1869-1946 **TCLC 92**
See also CA 118; 164; NCFS 5

Stryk, Lucien 1924- **PC 27**
See also CA 13-16R; CANR 10, 28, 55,
110; CP 7

Stuart, Don A.
See Campbell, John W(ood, Jr.)

Stuart, Ian
See MacLean, Alistair (Stuart)

Stuart, Jesse (Hilton) 1906-1984 **CLC 1, 8,
11, 14, 34; SSC 31**
See also CA 5-8R; 112; CANR 31; DLB 9,
48, 102; DLBY 1984; SATA 2; SATA-
Obit 36

Stubblefield, Sally
See Trumbo, Dalton

Sturgeon, Theodore (Hamilton) 1918-1985
CLC 22, 39
See Queen, Ellery
See also AAYA 51; BPFB 3; BYA 9, 10;
CA 81-84; 116; CANR 32, 103; DLB 8;
DLBY 1985; HGG; MTCW 1, 2; SCFW;
SFW 4; SUFW

Sturges, Preston 1898-1959 **TCLC 48**
See also CA 114; 149; DLB 26

Styron, William 1925- **CLC 1, 3, 5, 11, 15,
60; SSC 25**
See also AMW; AMWC 2; BEST 90:4;
BPFB 3; CA 5-8R; CANR 6, 33, 74, 126;
CDALB 1968-1988; CN 7; CPW; CSW;
DA3; DAM NOV, POP; DLB 2, 143;
DLBY 1980; EWL 3; INT CANR-6;
LAIT 2; MTCW 1, 2; NCFS 1; RGAL 4;
RHW; TUS

Su, Chien 1884-1918
See Su Man-shu
See also CA 123

Suarez Lynch, B.
See Bioy Casares, Adolfo; Borges, Jorge
Luis

Suassuna, Ariano Vilar 1927- **HLCS 1**
See also CA 178; HW 2; LAW

Suckert, Kurt Erich
   See Malaparte, Curzio
Suckling, Sir John 1609-1642 **LC 75; PC 30**
   See also BRW 2; DAM POET; DLB 58, 126; EXPP; PAB; RGEL 2
Suckow, Ruth 1892-1960 **SSC 18**
   See also CA 193; 113; DLB 9, 102; RGAL 4; TCWW 2
Sudermann, Hermann 1857-1928 **TCLC 15**
   See also CA 107; 201; DLB 118
Sue, Eugene 1804-1857 **NCLC 1**
   See also DLB 119
Sueskind, Patrick 1949- **CLC 44, 182**
   See Suskind, Patrick
Suetonius c. 70-c. 130 **CMLC 60**
   See also AW 2; DLB 211; RGWL 2, 3
Sukenick, Ronald 1932- **CLC 3, 4, 6, 48**
   See also CA 25-28R; 209; CAAE 209; CAAS 8; CANR 32, 89; CN 7; DLB 173; DLBY 1981
Suknaski, Andrew 1942- **CLC 19**
   See also CA 101; CP 7; DLB 53
Sullivan, Vernon
   See Vian, Boris
Sully Prudhomme, Rene-Francois-Armand 1839-1907 **TCLC 31**
   See also GFL 1789 to the Present
Su Man-shu **TCLC 24**
   See Su, Chien
   See also EWL 3
Summerforest, Ivy B.
   See Kirkup, James
Summers, Andrew James 1942- **CLC 26**
Summers, Andy
   See Summers, Andrew James
Summers, Hollis (Spurgeon, Jr.) 1916- **CLC 10**
   See also CA 5-8R; CANR 3; DLB 6
Summers, (Alphonsus Joseph-Mary Augustus) Montague 1880-1948 **TCLC 16**
   See also CA 118; 163
Sumner, Gordon Matthew **CLC 26**
   See Police, The; Sting
Sun Tzu c. 400B.C.-c. 320B.C. **CMLC 56**
Surtees, Robert Smith 1805-1864 **NCLC 14**
   See also DLB 21; RGEL 2
Susann, Jacqueline 1921-1974 **CLC 3**
   See also AITN 1; BPFB 3; CA 65-68; 53-56; MTCW 1, 2
Su Shi
   See Su Shih
   See also RGWL 2, 3
Su Shih 1036-1101 **CMLC 15**
   See Su Shi
Suskind, Patrick **CLC 182**
   See Sueskind, Patrick
   See also BPFB 3; CA 145; CWW 2
Sutcliff, Rosemary 1920-1992 **CLC 26**
   See also AAYA 10; BYA 1, 4; CA 5-8R; 139; CANR 37; CLR 1, 37; CPW; DAB; DAC; DAM MST, POP; JRDA; LATS 1; MAICYA 1, 2; MAICYAS 1; RHW; SATA 6, 44, 78; SATA-Obit 73; WYA; YAW
Sutro, Alfred 1863-1933 **TCLC 6**
   See also CA 105; 185; DLB 10; RGEL 2
Sutton, Henry
   See Slavitt, David R(ytman)
Suzuki, D. T.
   See Suzuki, Daisetz Teitaro
Suzuki, Daisetz T.
   See Suzuki, Daisetz Teitaro
Suzuki, Daisetz Teitaro 1870-1966 **TCLC 109**
   See also CA 121; 111; MTCW 1, 2

Suzuki, Teitaro
   See Suzuki, Daisetz Teitaro
Svevo, Italo **SSC 25; TCLC 2, 35**
   See Schmitz, Aron Hector
   See also DLB 264; EW 8; EWL 3; RGWL 2, 3
Swados, Elizabeth (A.) 1951- **CLC 12**
   See also CA 97-100; CANR 49; INT CA-97-100
Swados, Harvey 1920-1972 **CLC 5**
   See also CA 5-8R; 37-40R; CANR 6; DLB 2
Swan, Gladys 1934- **CLC 69**
   See also CA 101; CANR 17, 39
Swanson, Logan
   See Matheson, Richard (Burton)
Swarthout, Glendon (Fred) 1918-1992 **CLC 35**
   See also AAYA 55; CA 1-4R; 139; CANR 1, 47; LAIT 5; SATA 26; TCWW 2; YAW
Sweet, Sarah C.
   See Jewett, (Theodora) Sarah Orne
Swenson, May 1919-1989 **CLC 4, 14, 61, 106; PC 14**
   See also AMWS 4; CA 5-8R; 130; CANR 36, 61; DA; DAB; DAC; DAM MST, POET; DLB 5; EXPP; GLL 2; MTCW 1, 2; PFS 16; SATA 15; WP
Swift, Augustus
   See Lovecraft, H(oward) P(hillips)
Swift, Graham (Colin) 1949- **CLC 41, 88**
   See also BRWC 2; BRWS 5; CA 117; 122; CANR 46, 71, 128; CN 7; DLB 194; MTCW 2; NFS 18; RGSF 2
Swift, Jonathan 1667-1745 **LC 1, 42, 101; PC 9; WLC**
   See also AAYA 41; BRW 3; BRWC 1; BRWR 1; BYA 5, 14; CDBLB 1660-1789; CLR 53; DA; DA3; DAB; DAC; DAM MST, NOV, POET; DLB 39, 95, 101; EXPN; LAIT 1; NFS 6; RGEL 2; SATA 19; TEA; WCH; WLIT 3
Swinburne, Algernon Charles 1837-1909 **PC 24; TCLC 8, 36; WLC**
   See also BRW 5; CA 105; 140; CDBLB 1832-1890; DA; DA3; DAB; DAC; DAM MST, POET; DLB 35, 57; PAB; RGEL 2; TEA
Swinfen, Ann **CLC 34**
   See also CA 202
Swinnerton, Frank Arthur 1884-1982 **CLC 31**
   See also CA 108; DLB 34
Swithen, John
   See King, Stephen (Edwin)
Sylvia
   See Ashton-Warner, Sylvia (Constance)
Symmes, Robert Edward
   See Duncan, Robert (Edward)
Symonds, John Addington 1840-1893 **NCLC 34**
   See also DLB 57, 144
Symons, Arthur 1865-1945 **TCLC 11**
   See also CA 107; 189; DLB 19, 57, 149; RGEL 2
Symons, Julian (Gustave) 1912-1994 **CLC 2, 14, 32**
   See also CA 49-52; 147; CAAS 3; CANR 3, 33, 59; CMW 4; DLB 87, 155; DLBY 1992; MSW; MTCW 1
Synge, (Edmund) J(ohn) M(illington) 1871-1909 **DC 2; TCLC 6, 37**
   See also BRW 6; BRWR 1; CA 104; 141; CDBLB 1890-1914; DAM DRAM; DFS 18; DLB 10, 19; EWL 3; RGEL 2; TEA; WLIT 4
Syruc, J.
   See Milosz, Czeslaw
Szirtes, George 1948- **CLC 46; PC 51**
   See also CA 109; CANR 27, 61, 117; CP 7

Szymborska, Wislawa 1923- **CLC 99; PC 44**
   See also CA 154; CANR 91; CDWLB 4; CWP; CWW 2; DA3; DLB 232; DLBY 1996; EWL 3; MTCW 2; PFS 15; RGWL 3
T. O., Nik
   See Annensky, Innokenty (Fyodorovich)
Tabori, George 1914- **CLC 19**
   See also CA 49-52; CANR 4, 69; CBD; CD 5; DLB 245
Tacitus c. 55-c. 117 **CMLC 56**
   See also AW 2; CDWLB 1; DLB 211; RGWL 2, 3
Tagore, Rabindranath 1861-1941 **PC 8; SSC 48; TCLC 3, 53**
   See also CA 104; 120; DA3; DAM DRAM, POET; EWL 3; MTCW 1, 2; PFS 18; RGEL 2; RGSF 2; RGWL 2, 3; TWA
Taine, Hippolyte Adolphe 1828-1893 **NCLC 15**
   See also EW 7; GFL 1789 to the Present
Talayesva, Don C. 1890-(?) **NNAL**
Talese, Gay 1932- **CLC 37**
   See also AITN 1; CA 1-4R; CANR 9, 58; DLB 185; INT CANR-9; MTCW 1, 2
Tallent, Elizabeth (Ann) 1954- **CLC 45**
   See also CA 117; CANR 72; DLB 130
Tallmountain, Mary 1918-1997 **NNAL**
   See also CA 146; 161; DLB 193
Tally, Ted 1952- **CLC 42**
   See also CA 120; 124; CAD; CANR 125; CD 5; INT CA-124
Talvik, Heiti 1904-1947 **TCLC 87**
   See also EWL 3
Tamayo y Baus, Manuel 1829-1898 **NCLC 1**
Tammsaare, A(nton) H(ansen) 1878-1940 **TCLC 27**
   See also CA 164; CDWLB 4; DLB 220; EWL 3
Tam'si, Tchicaya U
   See Tchicaya, Gerald Felix
Tan, Amy (Ruth) 1952- **AAL; CLC 59, 120, 151**
   See also AAYA 9, 48; AMWS 10; BEST 89:3; BPFB 3; CA 136; CANR 54, 105; CDALBS; CN 7; CPW 1; DA3; DAM MULT, NOV, POP; DLB 173; EXPN; FW; LAIT 3, 5; MTCW 2; NFS 1, 13, 16; RGAL 4; SATA 75; SSFS 9; YAW
Tandem, Felix
   See Spitteler, Carl (Friedrich Georg)
Tanizaki, Jun'ichiro 1886-1965 **CLC 8, 14, 28; SSC 21**
   See Tanizaki Jun'ichiro
   See also CA 93-96; 25-28R; MJW; MTCW 2; RGSF 2; RGWL 2
Tanizaki Jun'ichiro
   See Tanizaki, Jun'ichiro
   See also DLB 180; EWL 3
Tanner, William
   See Amis, Kingsley (William)
Tao Lao
   See Storni, Alfonsina
Tapahonso, Luci 1953- **NNAL**
   See also CA 145; CANR 72, 127; DLB 175
Tarantino, Quentin (Jerome) 1963- **CLC 125**
   See also CA 171; CANR 125
Tarassoff, Lev
   See Troyat, Henri
Tarbell, Ida M(inerva) 1857-1944 **TCLC 40**
   See also CA 122; 181; DLB 47
Tarkington, (Newton) Booth 1869-1946 **TCLC 9**
   See also BPFB 3; BYA 3; CA 110; 143; CWRI 5; DLB 9, 102; MTCW 2; RGAL 4; SATA 17
Tarkovskii, Andrei Arsen'evich
   See Tarkovsky, Andrei (Arsenyevich)

Thomas, Ross (Elmore) 1926-1995 **CLC 39**
See also CA 33-36R; 150; CANR 22, 63;
CMW 4

Thompson, Francis (Joseph) 1859-1907
TCLC 4
See also BRW 5; CA 104; 189; CDBLB
1890-1914; DLB 19; RGEL 2; TEA

Thompson, Francis Clegg
See Mencken, H(enry) L(ouis)

Thompson, Hunter S(tockton) 1937(?)- **CLC
9, 17, 40, 104**
See also AAYA 45; BEST 89:1; BPFB 3;
CA 17-20R; CANR 23, 46, 74, 77, 111;
CPW; CSW; DA3; DAM POP; DLB 185;
MTCW 1, 2; TUS

Thompson, James Myers
See Thompson, Jim (Myers)

Thompson, Jim (Myers) 1906-1977(?) **CLC
69**
See also BPFB 3; CA 140; CMW 4; CPW;
DLB 226; MSW

Thompson, Judith CLC 39
See also CWD

Thomson, James 1700-1748 **LC 16, 29, 40**
See also BRWS 3; DAM POET; DLB 95;
RGEL 2

Thomson, James 1834-1882 **NCLC 18**
See also DAM POET; DLB 35; RGEL 2

Thoreau, Henry David 1817-1862 **NCLC 7,
21, 61, 138; PC 30; WLC**
See also AAYA 42; AMW; ANW; BYA 3;
CDALB 1640-1865; DA; DA3; DAB;
DAC; DAM MST; DLB 1, 183, 223, 270,
298; LAIT 2; LMFS 1; NCFS 3; RGAL
4; TUS

Thorndike, E. L.
See Thorndike, Edward L(ee)

Thorndike, Edward L(ee) 1874-1949 **TCLC
107**
See also CA 121

Thornton, Hall
See Silverberg, Robert

Thorpe, Adam 1956- **CLC 176**
See also CA 129; CANR 92; DLB 231

Thubron, Colin (Gerald Dryden) 1939- **CLC
163**
See also CA 25-28R; CANR 12, 29, 59, 95;
CN 7; DLB 204, 231

Thucydides c. 455B.C.-c. 395B.C. **CMLC 17**
See also AW 1; DLB 176; RGWL 2, 3

Thumboo, Edwin Nadason 1933- **PC 30**
See also CA 194

Thurber, James (Grover) 1894-1961 **CLC 5,
11, 25, 125; SSC 1, 47**
See also AMWS 1; BPFB 3; BYA 5; CA
73-76; CANR 17, 39; CDALB 1929-1941;
CWRI 5; DA; DA3; DAB; DAC; DAM
DRAM, MST, NOV; DLB 4, 11, 22, 102;
EWL 3; EXPS; FANT; LAIT 3; MAICYA
1, 2; MTCW 1, 2; RGAL 4; RGSF 2;
SATA 13; SSFS 1, 10, 19; SUFW; TUS

Thurman, Wallace (Henry) 1902-1934 **BLC
3; HR 3; TCLC 6**
See also BW 1, 3; CA 104; 124; CANR 81;
DAM MULT; DLB 51

Tibullus c. 54B.C.-c. 18B.C. **CMLC 36**
See also AW 2; DLB 211; RGWL 2, 3

Ticheburn, Cheviot
See Ainsworth, William Harrison

Tieck, (Johann) Ludwig 1773-1853 **NCLC 5,
46; SSC 31**
See also CDWLB 2; DLB 90; EW 5; IDTP;
RGSF 2; RGWL 2, 3; SUFW

Tiger, Derry
See Ellison, Harlan (Jay)

Tilghman, Christopher 1946- **CLC 65**
See also CA 159; CSW; DLB 244

Tillich, Paul (Johannes) 1886-1965 **CLC 131**
See also CA 5-8R; 25-28R; CANR 33;
MTCW 1, 2

Tillinghast, Richard (Williford) 1940- **CLC
29**
See also CA 29-32R; CAAS 23; CANR 26,
51, 96; CP 7; CSW

Timrod, Henry 1828-1867 **NCLC 25**
See also DLB 3, 248; RGAL 4

Tindall, Gillian (Elizabeth) 1938- **CLC 7**
See also CA 21-24R; CANR 11, 65, 107;
CN 7

Tiptree, James, Jr. CLC 48, 50
See Sheldon, Alice Hastings Bradley
See also DLB 8; SCFW 2; SFW 4

Tirone Smith, Mary-Ann 1944- **CLC 39**
See also CA 118; 136; CANR 113; SATA
143

Tirso de Molina 1580(?)-1648 **DC 13; HLCS
2; LC 73**
See also RGWL 2, 3

Titmarsh, Michael Angelo
See Thackeray, William Makepeace

**Tocqueville, Alexis (Charles Henri Maurice
Clerel Comte) de** 1805-1859 **NCLC 7,
63**
See also EW 6; GFL 1789 to the Present;
TWA

Toer, Pramoedya Ananta 1925- **CLC 186**
See also CA 197; RGWL 3

Toffler, Alvin 1928- **CLC 168**
See also CA 13-16R; CANR 15, 46, 67;
CPW; DAM POP; MTCW 1, 2

Toibin, Colm
See Toibin, Colm
See also DLB 271

Toibin, Colm 1955- **CLC 162**
See Toibin, Colm
See also CA 142; CANR 81

Tolkien, J(ohn) R(onald) R(euel) 1892-1973
CLC 1, 2, 3, 8, 12, 38; TCLC 137; WLC
See also AAYA 10; AITN 1; BPFB 3;
BRWC 2; BRWS 2; CA 17-18; 45-48;
CANR 36; CAP 2; CDBLB 1914-1945;
CLR 56; CPW 1; CWRI 5; DA; DA3;
DAB; DAC; DAM MST, NOV, POP;
DLB 15, 160, 255; EFS 2; EWL 3; FANT;
JRDA; LAIT 1; LATS 1; LMFS 2; MAI-
CYA 1, 2; MTCW 1, 2; NFS 8; RGEL 2;
SATA 2, 32, 100; SATA-Obit 24; SFW 4;
SUFW; TEA; WCH; WYA; YAW

Toller, Ernst 1893-1939 **TCLC 10**
See also CA 107; 186; DLB 124; EWL 3;
RGWL 2, 3

Tolson, M. B.
See Tolson, Melvin B(eaunorus)

Tolson, Melvin B(eaunorus) 1898(?)-1966
BLC 3; CLC 36, 105
See also AFAW 1, 2; BW 1, 3; CA 124; 89-
92; CANR 80; DAM MULT, POET; DLB
48, 76; RGAL 4

Tolstoi, Aleksei Nikolaevich
See Tolstoy, Alexey Nikolaevich

Tolstoi, Lev
See Tolstoy, Leo (Nikolaevich)
See also RGSF 2; RGWL 2, 3

Tolstoy, Aleksei Nikolaevich
See Tolstoy, Alexey Nikolaevich
See also DLB 272

Tolstoy, Alexey Nikolaevich 1882-1945 **TCLC
18**
See also Tolstoi, Aleksei Nikolaevich
See also CA 107; 158; EWL 3; SFW 4

Tolstoy, Leo (Nikolaevich) 1828-1910 **SSC 9,
30, 45, 54; TCLC 4, 11, 17, 28, 44, 79;
WLC**
See Tolstoi, Lev
See also CA 104; 123; DA; DA3; DAB;
DAC; DAM MST, NOV; DLB 238; EFS

2; EW 7; EXPS; IDTP; LAIT 2; LATS 1;
LMFS 1; NFS 10; SATA 26; SSFS 5;
TWA

Tolstoy, Count Leo
See Tolstoy, Leo (Nikolaevich)

Tomalin, Claire 1933- **CLC 166**
See also CA 89-92; CANR 52, 88; DLB
155

Tomasi di Lampedusa, Giuseppe 1896-1957
See Lampedusa, Giuseppe (Tomasi) di
See also CA 111; DLB 177; EWL 3

Tomlin, Lily CLC 17
See Tomlin, Mary Jean

Tomlin, Mary Jean 1939(?)-
See Tomlin, Lily
See also CA 117

Tomline, F. Latour
See Gilbert, W(illiam) S(chwenck)

Tomlinson, (Alfred) Charles 1927- **CLC 2, 4,
6, 13, 45; PC 17**
See also CA 5-8R; CANR 33; CP 7; DAM
POET; DLB 40

Tomlinson, H(enry) M(ajor) 1873-1958
TCLC 71
See also CA 118; 161; DLB 36, 100, 195

Tonna, Charlotte Elizabeth 1790-1846 **NCLC
135**
See also DLB 163

Tonson, Jacob fl. 1655(?)-1736 **LC 86**
See also DLB 170

Toole, John Kennedy 1937-1969 **CLC 19, 64**
See also BPFB 3; CA 104; DLBY 1981;
MTCW 2

Toomer, Eugene
See Toomer, Jean

Toomer, Eugene Pinchback
See Toomer, Jean

Toomer, Jean 1894-1967 **BLC 3; CLC 1, 4,
13, 22; HR 3; PC 7; SSC 1, 45; WLCS**
See also AFAW 1, 2; AMWS 3, 9; BW 1;
CA 85-88; CDALB 1917-1929; DA3;
DAM MULT; DLB 45, 51; EWL 3; EXPP;
EXPS; LMFS 2; MTCW 1, 2; NFS 11;
RGAL 4; RGSF 2; SSFS 5

Toomer, Nathan Jean
See Toomer, Jean

Toomer, Nathan Pinchback
See Toomer, Jean

Torley, Luke
See Blish, James (Benjamin)

Tornimparte, Alessandra
See Ginzburg, Natalia

Torre, Raoul della
See Mencken, H(enry) L(ouis)

Torrence, Ridgely 1874-1950 **TCLC 97**
See also DLB 54, 249

Torrey, E(dwin) Fuller 1937- **CLC 34**
See also CA 119; CANR 71

Torsvan, Ben Traven
See Traven, B.

Torsvan, Benno Traven
See Traven, B.

Torsvan, Berick Traven
See Traven, B.

Torsvan, Berwick Traven
See Traven, B.

Torsvan, Bruno Traven
See Traven, B.

Torsvan, Traven
See Traven, B.

Tourneur, Cyril 1575(?)-1626 **LC 66**
See also BRW 2; DAM DRAM; DLB 58;
RGEL 2

Tournier, Michel (Edouard) 1924- **CLC 6,
23, 36, 95**
See also CA 49-52; CANR 3, 36, 74; DLB
83; EWL 3; GFL 1789 to the Present;
MTCW 1, 2; SATA 23

Tournimparte, Alessandra
See Ginzburg, Natalia
Towers, Ivar
See Kornbluth, C(yril) M.
Towne, Robert (Burton) 1936(?)- **CLC 87**
See also CA 108; DLB 44; IDFW 3, 4
Townsend, Sue CLC 61
See Townsend, Susan Lilian
See also AAYA 28; CA 119; 127; CANR 65, 107; CBD; CD 5; CPW; CWD; DAB; DAC; DAM MST; DLB 271; INT CA-127; SATA 55, 93; SATA-Brief 48; YAW
Townsend, Susan Lilian 1946-
See Townsend, Sue
Townshend, Pete
See Townshend, Peter (Dennis Blandford)
Townshend, Peter (Dennis Blandford) 1945- **CLC 17, 42**
See also CA 107
Tozzi, Federigo 1883-1920 **TCLC 31**
See also CA 160; CANR 110; DLB 264; EWL 3
Tracy, Don(ald Fiske) 1905-1970(?)
See Queen, Ellery
See also CA 1-4R; 176; CANR 2
Trafford, F. G.
See Riddell, Charlotte
Traherne, Thomas 1637(?)-1674 **LC 99**
See also BRW 2; DLB 131; PAB; RGEL 2
Traill, Catharine Parr 1802-1899 **NCLC 31**
See also DLB 99
Trakl, Georg 1887-1914 **PC 20; TCLC 5**
See also CA 104; 165; EW 10; EWL 3; LMFS 2; MTCW 2; RGWL 2, 3
Tranquilli, Secondino
See Silone, Ignazio
Transtroemer, Tomas Gosta
See Transtromer, Tomas (Goesta)
Transtromer, Tomas
See Transtromer, Tomas (Goesta)
Transtromer, Tomas (Goesta) 1931- **CLC 52, 65**
See also CA 117; 129; CAAS 17; CANR 115; DAM POET; DLB 257; EWL 3
Transtromer, Tomas Gosta
See Transtromer, Tomas (Goesta)
Traven, B. 1882(?)-1969 **CLC 8, 11**
See also CA 19-20; 25-28R; CAP 2; DLB 9, 56; EWL 3; MTCW 1; RGAL 4
Trediakovsky, Vasilii Kirillovich 1703-1769 **LC 68**
See also DLB 150
Treitel, Jonathan 1959- **CLC 70**
See also CA 210; DLB 267
Trelawny, Edward John 1792-1881 **NCLC 85**
See also DLB 110, 116, 144
Tremain, Rose 1943- **CLC 42**
See also CA 97-100; CANR 44, 95; CN 7; DLB 14, 271; RGSF 2; RHW
Tremblay, Michel 1942- **CLC 29, 102**
See also CA 116; 128; CCA 1; CWW 2; DAC; DAM MST; DLB 60; EWL 3; GLL 1; MTCW 1, 2
Trevanian CLC 29
See Whitaker, Rod(ney)
Trevor, Glen
See Hilton, James
Trevor, William CLC 7, 9, 14, 25, 71, 116; SSC 21, 58
See Cox, William Trevor
See also BRWS 4; CBD; CD 5; CN 7; DLB 14, 139; EWL 3; LATS 1; MTCW 2; RGEL 2; RGSF 2; SSFS 10
Trifonov, Iurii (Valentinovich)
See Trifonov, Yuri (Valentinovich)
See also RGWL 2, 3

Trifonov, Yuri (Valentinovich) 1925-1981 **CLC 45**
See Trifonov, Iurii (Valentinovich); Trifonov, Yury Valentinovich
See also CA 126; 103; MTCW 1
Trifonov, Yury Valentinovich
See Trifonov, Yuri (Valentinovich)
See also EWL 3
Trilling, Diana (Rubin) 1905-1996 **CLC 129**
See also CA 5-8R; 154; CANR 10, 46; INT CANR-10; MTCW 1, 2
Trilling, Lionel 1905-1975 **CLC 9, 11, 24**
See also AMWS 3; CA 9-12R; 61-64; CANR 10, 105; DLB 28, 63; EWL 3; INT CANR-10; MTCW 1, 2; RGAL 4; TUS
Trimball, W. H.
See Mencken, H(enry) L(ouis)
Tristan
See Gomez de la Serna, Ramon
Tristram
See Housman, A(lfred) E(dward)
Trogdon, William (Lewis) 1939-
See Heat-Moon, William Least
See also CA 115; 119; CANR 47, 89; CPW; INT CA-119
Trollope, Anthony 1815-1882 **NCLC 6, 33, 101; SSC 28; WLC**
See also BRW 5; CDBLB 1832-1890; DA; DA3; DAB; DAC; DAM MST, NOV; DLB 21, 57, 159; RGEL 2; RGSF 2; SATA 22
Trollope, Frances 1779-1863 **NCLC 30**
See also DLB 21, 166
Trollope, Joanna 1943- **CLC 186**
See also CA 101; CANR 58, 95; CPW; DLB 207; RHW
Trotsky, Leon 1879-1940 **TCLC 22**
See also CA 118; 167
Trotter (Cockburn), Catharine 1679-1749 **LC 8**
See also DLB 84, 252
Trotter, Wilfred 1872-1939 **TCLC 97**
Trout, Kilgore
See Farmer, Philip Jose
Trow, George W. S. 1943- **CLC 52**
See also CA 126; CANR 91
Troyat, Henri 1911- **CLC 23**
See also CA 45-48; CANR 2, 33, 67, 117; GFL 1789 to the Present; MTCW 1
Trudeau, G(arretson) B(eekman) 1948-
See Trudeau, Garry B.
See also CA 81-84; CANR 31; SATA 35
Trudeau, Garry B. CLC 12
See Trudeau, G(arretson) B(eekman)
See also AAYA 10; AITN 2
Truffaut, Francois 1932-1984 **CLC 20, 101**
See also CA 81-84; 113; CANR 34
Trumbo, Dalton 1905-1976 **CLC 19**
See also CA 21-24R; 69-72; CANR 10; DLB 26; IDFW 3, 4; YAW
Trumbull, John 1750-1831 **NCLC 30**
See also DLB 31; RGAL 4
Trundlett, Helen B.
See Eliot, T(homas) S(tearns)
Truth, Sojourner 1797(?)-1883 **NCLC 94**
See also DLB 239; FW; LAIT 2
Tryon, Thomas 1926-1991 **CLC 3, 11**
See also AITN 1; BPFB 3; CA 29-32R; 135; CANR 32, 77; CPW; DA3; DAM POP; HGG; MTCW 1
Tryon, Tom
See Tryon, Thomas
Ts'ao Hsueh-ch'in 1715(?)-1763 **LC 1**
Tsushima, Shuji 1909-1948
See Dazai Osamu
See also CA 107

Tsvetaeva (Efron), Marina (Ivanovna) 1892-1941 **PC 14; TCLC 7, 35**
See also CA 104; 128; CANR 73; DLB 295; EW 11; MTCW 1, 2; RGWL 2, 3
Tuck, Lily 1938- **CLC 70**
See also CA 139; CANR 90
Tu Fu 712-770 **PC 9**
See Du Fu
See also DAM MULT; TWA; WP
Tunis, John R(oberts) 1889-1975 **CLC 12**
See also BYA 1; CA 61-64; CANR 62; DLB 22, 171; JRDA; MAICYA 1, 2; SATA 37; SATA-Brief 30; YAW
Tuohy, Frank CLC 37
See Tuohy, John Francis
See also DLB 14, 139
Tuohy, John Francis 1925-
See Tuohy, Frank
See also CA 5-8R; 178; CANR 3, 47; CN 7
Turco, Lewis (Putnam) 1934- **CLC 11, 63**
See also CA 13-16R; CAAS 22; CANR 24, 51; CP 7; DLBY 1984
Turgenev, Ivan (Sergeevich) 1818-1883 **DC 7; NCLC 21, 37, 122; SSC 7, 57; WLC**
See also DA; DAB; DAC; DAM MST, NOV; DFS 6; DLB 238, 284; EW 6; LATS 1; NFS 16; RGSF 2; RGWL 2, 3; TWA
Turgot, Anne-Robert-Jacques 1727-1781 **LC 26**
Turner, Frederick 1943- **CLC 48**
See also CA 73-76; CAAS 10; CANR 12, 30, 56; DLB 40, 282
Turton, James
See Crace, Jim
Tutu, Desmond M(pilo) 1931- **BLC 3; CLC 80**
See also BW 1, 3; CA 125; CANR 67, 81; DAM MULT
Tutuola, Amos 1920-1997 **BLC 3; CLC 5, 14, 29**
See also AFW; BW 2, 3; CA 9-12R; 159; CANR 27, 66; CDWLB 3; CN 7; DA3; DAM MULT; DLB 125; DNFS 2; EWL 3; MTCW 1, 2; RGEL 2; WLIT 2
Twain, Mark SSC 34; TCLC 6, 12, 19, 36, 48, 59; WLC
See Clemens, Samuel Langhorne
See also AAYA 20; AMW; AMWC 1; BPFB 3; BYA 2, 3, 11, 14; CLR 58, 60, 66; DLB 11; EXPN; EXPS; FANT; LAIT 2; NCFS 4; NFS 1, 6; RGAL 4; RGSF 2; SFW 4; SSFS 1, 7; SUFW; TUS; WCH; WYA; YAW
Tyler, Anne 1941- **CLC 7, 11, 18, 28, 44, 59, 103**
See also AAYA 18; AMWS 4; BEST 89:1; BPFB 3; BYA 12; CA 9-12R; CANR 11, 33, 53, 109; CDALBS; CN 7; CPW; CSW; DAM NOV, POP; DLB 6, 143; DLBY 1982; EWL 3; EXPN; LATS 1; MAWW; MTCW 1, 2; NFS 2, 7, 10; RGAL 4; SATA 7, 90; SSFS 17; TUS; YAW
Tyler, Royall 1757-1826 **NCLC 3**
See also DLB 37; RGAL 4
Tynan, Katharine 1861-1931 **TCLC 3**
See also CA 104; 167; DLB 153, 240; FW
Tyutchev, Fyodor 1803-1873 **NCLC 34**
Tzara, Tristan 1896-1963 **CLC 47; PC 27**
See also CA 153; 89-92; DAM POET; EWL 3; MTCW 2
Uchida, Yoshiko 1921-1992 **AAL**
See also AAYA 16; BYA 2, 3; CA 13-16R; 139; CANR 6, 22, 47, 61; CDALBS; CLR 6, 56; CWRI 5; JRDA; MAICYA 1, 2; MTCW 1, 2; SAAS 1; SATA 1, 53; SATA-Obit 72
Udall, Nicholas 1504-1556 **LC 84**
See also DLB 62; RGEL 2

Ueda Akinari 1734-1809 **NCLC 131**

Uhry, Alfred 1936- **CLC 55**
See also CA 127; 133; CAD; CANR 112; CD 5; CSW; DA3; DAM DRAM, POP; DFS 11, 15; INT CA-133

Ulf, Haerved
See Strindberg, (Johan) August

Ulf, Harved
See Strindberg, (Johan) August

Ulibarri, Sabine R(eyes) 1919-2003 **CLC 83; HLCS 2**
See also CA 131; 214; CANR 81; DAM MULT; DLB 82; HW 1, 2; RGSF 2

Unamuno (y Jugo), Miguel de 1864-1936 **HLC 2; SSC 11, 69; TCLC 2, 9, 148**
See also CA 104; 131; CANR 81; DAM MULT, NOV; DLB 108; EW 8; EWL 3; HW 1, 2; MTCW 1, 2; RGSF 2; RGWL 2, 3; TWA

Uncle Shelby
See Silverstein, Shel(don Allan)

Undercliffe, Errol
See Campbell, (John) Ramsey

Underwood, Miles
See Glassco, John

Undset, Sigrid 1882-1949 **TCLC 3; WLC**
See also CA 104; 129; DA; DA3; DAB; DAC; DAM MST, NOV; DLB 293; EW 9; EWL 3; FW; MTCW 1, 2; RGWL 2, 3

Ungaretti, Giuseppe 1888-1970 **CLC 7, 11, 15**
See also CA 19-20; 25-28R; CAP 2; DLB 114; EW 10; EWL 3; RGWL 2, 3

Unger, Douglas 1952- **CLC 34**
See also CA 130; CANR 94

Unsworth, Barry (Forster) 1930- **CLC 76, 127**
See also BRWS 7; CA 25-28R; CANR 30, 54, 125; CN 7; DLB 194

Updike, John (Hoyer) 1932- **CLC 1, 2, 3, 5, 7, 9, 13, 15, 23, 34, 43, 70, 139; SSC 13, 27; WLC**
See also AAYA 36; AMW; AMWC 1; AMWR 1; BPFB 3; BYA 12; CA 1-4R; CABS 1; CANR 4, 33, 51, 94; CDALB 1968-1988; CN 7; CP 7; CPW 1; DA; DA3; DAB; DAC; DAM MST, NOV, POET, POP; DLB 2, 5, 143, 218, 227; DLBD 3; DLBY 1980, 1982, 1997; EWL 3; EXPP; HGG; MTCW 1, 2; NFS 12; RGAL 4; RGSF 2; SSFS 3, 19; TUS

Upshaw, Margaret Mitchell
See Mitchell, Margaret (Munnerlyn)

Upton, Mark
See Sanders, Lawrence

Upward, Allen 1863-1926 **TCLC 85**
See also CA 117; 187; DLB 36

Urdang, Constance (Henriette) 1922-1996 **CLC 47**
See also CA 21-24R; CANR 9, 24; CP 7; CWP

Uriel, Henry
See Faust, Frederick (Schiller)

Uris, Leon (Marcus) 1924-2003 **CLC 7, 32**
See also AITN 1, 2; BEST 89:2; BPFB 3; CA 1-4R; 217; CANR 1, 40, 65, 123; CN 7; CPW 1; DA3; DAM NOV, POP; MTCW 1, 2; SATA 49; SATA-Obit 146

Urista (Heredia), Alberto (Baltazar) 1947- **HLCS 1; PC 34**
See Alurista
See also CA 45-48, 182; CANR 2, 32; HW 1

Urmuz
See Codrescu, Andrei

Urquhart, Guy
See McAlmon, Robert (Menzies)

Urquhart, Jane 1949- **CLC 90**
See also CA 113; CANR 32, 68, 116; CCA 1; DAC

Usigli, Rodolfo 1905-1979 **HLCS 1**
See also CA 131; EWL 3; HW 1; LAW

Ustinov, Peter (Alexander) 1921-2004 **CLC 1**
See also AITN 1; CA 13-16R; CANR 25, 51; CBD; CD 5; DLB 13; MTCW 2

U Tam'si, Gerald Felix Tchicaya
See Tchicaya, Gerald Felix

U Tam'si, Tchicaya
See Tchicaya, Gerald Felix

Vachss, Andrew (Henry) 1942- **CLC 106**
See also CA 118, 214; CAAE 214; CANR 44, 95; CMW 4

Vachss, Andrew H.
See Vachss, Andrew (Henry)

Vaculik, Ludvik 1926- **CLC 7**
See also CA 53-56; CANR 72; CWW 2; DLB 232; EWL 3

Vaihinger, Hans 1852-1933 **TCLC 71**
See also CA 116; 166

Valdez, Luis (Miguel) 1940- **CLC 84; DC 10; HLC 2**
See also CA 101; CAD; CANR 32, 81; CD 5; DAM MULT; DFS 5; DLB 122; EWL 3; HW 1; LAIT 4; LLW 1

Valenzuela, Luisa 1938- **CLC 31, 104; HLCS 2; SSC 14**
See also CA 101; CANR 32, 65, 123; CD-WLB 3; CWW 2; DAM MULT; DLB 113; EWL 3; FW; HW 1, 2; LAW; RGSF 2; RGWL 3

Valera y Alcala-Galiano, Juan 1824-1905 **TCLC 10**
See also CA 106

Valerius Maximus fl. 20- **CMLC 64**
See also DLB 211

Valery, (Ambroise) Paul (Toussaint Jules) 1871-1945 **PC 9; TCLC 4, 15**
See also CA 104; 122; DA3; DAM POET; DLB 258; EW 8; EWL 3; GFL 1789 to the Present; MTCW 1, 2; RGWL 2, 3; TWA

Valle-Inclan, Ramon (Maria) del 1866-1936 **HLC 2; TCLC 5**
See also CA 106; 153; CANR 80; DAM MULT; DLB 134; EW 8; EWL 3; HW 2; RGSF 2; RGWL 2, 3

Vallejo, Antonio Buero
See Buero Vallejo, Antonio

Vallejo, Cesar (Abraham) 1892-1938 **HLC 2; TCLC 3, 56**
See also CA 105; 153; DAM MULT; DLB 290; EWL 3; HW 1; LAW; RGWL 2, 3

Valles, Jules 1832-1885 **NCLC 71**
See also DLB 123; GFL 1789 to the Present

Vallette, Marguerite Eymery 1860-1953 **TCLC 67**
See Rachilde
See also CA 182; DLB 123, 192

Valle Y Pena, Ramon del
See Valle-Inclan, Ramon (Maria) del

Van Ash, Cay 1918-1994 **CLC 34**
See also CA 220

Vanbrugh, Sir John 1664-1726 **LC 21**
See also BRW 2; DAM DRAM; DLB 80; IDTP; RGEL 2

Van Campen, Karl
See Campbell, John W(ood, Jr.)

Vance, Gerald
See Silverberg, Robert

Vance, Jack CLC 35
See Vance, John Holbrook
See also DLB 8; FANT; SCFW 2; SFW 4; SUFW 1, 2

Vance, John Holbrook 1916-
See Queen, Ellery; Vance, Jack
See also CA 29-32R; CANR 17, 65; CMW 4; MTCW 1

Van Den Bogarde, Derek Jules Gaspard Ulric Niven 1921-1999 **CLC 14**
See Bogarde, Dirk
See also CA 77-80; 179

Vandenburgh, Jane CLC 59
See also CA 168

Vanderhaeghe, Guy 1951- **CLC 41**
See also BPFB 3; CA 113; CANR 72

van der Post, Laurens (Jan) 1906-1996 **CLC 5**
See also AFW; CA 5-8R; 155; CANR 35; CN 7; DLB 204; RGEL 2

van de Wetering, Janwillem 1931- **CLC 47**
See also CA 49-52; CANR 4, 62, 90; CMW 4

Van Dine, S. S. TCLC 23
See Wright, Willard Huntington
See also MSW

Van Doren, Carl (Clinton) 1885-1950 **TCLC 18**
See also CA 111; 168

Van Doren, Mark 1894-1972 **CLC 6, 10**
See also CA 1-4R; 37-40R; CANR 3; DLB 45, 284; MTCW 1, 2; RGAL 4

Van Druten, John (William) 1901-1957 **TCLC 2**
See also CA 104; 161; DLB 10; RGAL 4

Van Duyn, Mona (Jane) 1921- **CLC 3, 7, 63, 116**
See also CA 9-12R; CANR 7, 38, 60, 116; CP 7; CWP; DAM POET; DLB 5

Van Dyne, Edith
See Baum, L(yman) Frank

van Itallie, Jean-Claude 1936- **CLC 3**
See also CA 45-48; CAAS 2; CAD; CANR 1, 48; CD 5; DLB 7

Van Loot, Cornelius Obenchain
See Roberts, Kenneth (Lewis)

van Ostaijen, Paul 1896-1928 **TCLC 33**
See also CA 163

Van Peebles, Melvin 1932- **CLC 2, 20**
See also BW 2, 3; CA 85-88; CANR 27, 67, 82; DAM MULT

van Schendel, Arthur(-Francois-Emile) 1874-1946 **TCLC 56**
See also EWL 3

Vansittart, Peter 1920- **CLC 42**
See also CA 1-4R; CANR 3, 49, 90; CN 7; RHW

Van Vechten, Carl 1880-1964 **CLC 33; HR 3**
See also AMWS 2; CA 183; 89-92; DLB 4, 9, 51; RGAL 4

van Vogt, A(lfred) E(lton) 1912-2000 **CLC 1**
See also BPFB 3; BYA 13, 14; CA 21-24R; 190; CANR 28; DLB 8, 251; SATA 14; SATA-Obit 124; SCFW; SFW 4

Vara, Madeleine
See Jackson, Laura (Riding)

Varda, Agnes 1928- **CLC 16**
See also CA 116; 122

Vargas Llosa, (Jorge) Mario (Pedro) 1939- **CLC 3, 6, 9, 10, 15, 31, 42, 85, 181; HLC 2**
See Llosa, (Jorge) Mario (Pedro) Vargas
See also BPFB 3; CA 73-76; CANR 18, 32, 42, 67, 116; CDWLB 3; DA; DA3; DAB; DAC; DAM MST, MULT, NOV; DLB 145; DNFS 2; EWL 3; HW 1, 2; LAIT 5; LATS 1; LAW; LAWS 1; MTCW 1, 2; RGWL 2, 3; SSFS 14; TWA; WLIT 1

Varnhagen von Ense, Rahel 1771-1833 **NCLC 130**
See also DLB 90

Vasiliu, George
See Bacovia, George

Vasiliu, Gheorghe
See Bacovia, George
See also CA 123; 189

Vassa, Gustavus
  See Equiano, Olaudah
Vassilikos, Vassilis 1933- **CLC 4, 8**
  See also CA 81-84; CANR 75; EWL 3
Vaughan, Henry 1621-1695 **LC 27**
  See also BRW 2; DLB 131; PAB; RGEL 2
Vaughn, Stephanie CLC 62
Vazov, Ivan (Minchov) 1850-1921 **TCLC 25**
  See also CA 121; 167; CDWLB 4; DLB 147
Veblen, Thorstein B(unde) 1857-1929 **TCLC 31**
  See also AMWS 1; CA 115; 165; DLB 246
Vega, Lope de 1562-1635 **HLCS 2; LC 23**
  See also EW 2; RGWL 2, 3
Vendler, Helen (Hennessy) 1933- **CLC 138**
  See also CA 41-44R; CANR 25, 72; MTCW 1, 2
Venison, Alfred
  See Pound, Ezra (Weston Loomis)
Ventsel, Elena Sergeevna 1907-
  See Grekova, I.
  See also CA 154
Verdi, Marie de
  See Mencken, H(enry) L(ouis)
Verdu, Matilde
  See Cela, Camilo Jose
Verga, Giovanni (Carmelo) 1840-1922 **SSC 21; TCLC 3**
  See also CA 104; 123; CANR 101; EW 7; EWL 3; RGSF 2; RGWL 2, 3
Vergil 70B.C.-19B.C. **CMLC 9, 40; PC 12; WLCS**
  See Virgil
  See also AW 2; DA; DA3; DAB; DAC; DAM MST, POET; EFS 1; LMFS 1
Verhaeren, Emile (Adolphe Gustave) 1855-1916 **TCLC 12**
  See also CA 109; EWL 3; GFL 1789 to the Present
Verlaine, Paul (Marie) 1844-1896 **NCLC 2, 51; PC 2, 32**
  See also DAM POET; DLB 217; EW 7; GFL 1789 to the Present; LMFS 2; RGWL 2, 3; TWA
Verne, Jules (Gabriel) 1828-1905 **TCLC 6, 52**
  See also AAYA 16; BYA 4; CA 110; 131; CLR 88; DA3; DLB 123; GFL 1789 to the Present; JRDA; LAIT 2; LMFS 2; MAICYA 1, 2; RGWL 2, 3; SATA 21; SCFW; SFW 4; TWA; WCH
Verus, Marcus Annius
  See Aurelius, Marcus
Very, Jones 1813-1880 **NCLC 9**
  See also DLB 1, 243; RGAL 4
Vesaas, Tarjei 1897-1970 **CLC 48**
  See also CA 190; 29-32R; DLB 297; EW 11; EWL 3; RGWL 3
Vialis, Gaston
  See Simenon, Georges (Jacques Christian)
Vian, Boris 1920-1959(?) **TCLC 9**
  See also CA 106; 164; CANR 111; DLB 72; EWL 3; GFL 1789 to the Present; MTCW 2; RGWL 2, 3
Viaud, (Louis Marie) Julien 1850-1923
  See Loti, Pierre
  See also CA 107
Vicar, Henry
  See Felsen, Henry Gregor
Vicente, Gil 1465-c. 1536 **LC 99**
  See also DLB 287; RGWL 2, 3
Vicker, Angus
  See Felsen, Henry Gregor
Vidal, Gore 1925- **CLC 2, 4, 6, 8, 10, 22, 33, 72, 142**
  See Box, Edgar
  See also AITN 1; AMWS 4; BEST 90:2; BPFB 3; CA 5-8R; CAD; CANR 13, 45, 65, 100; CD 5; CDALBS; CN 7; CPW;

DA3; DAM NOV, POP; DFS 2; DLB 6, 152; EWL 3; INT CANR-13; MTCW 1, 2; RGAL 4; RHW; TUS
Viereck, Peter (Robert Edwin) 1916- **CLC 4; PC 27**
  See also CA 1-4R; CANR 1, 47; CP 7; DLB 5; PFS 9, 14
Vigny, Alfred (Victor) de 1797-1863 **NCLC 7, 102; PC 26**
  See also DAM POET; DLB 119, 192, 217; EW 5; GFL 1789 to the Present; RGWL 2, 3
Vilakazi, Benedict Wallet 1906-1947 **TCLC 37**
  See also CA 168
Villa, Jose Garcia 1914-1997 **AAL; PC 22**
  See also CA 25-28R; CANR 12, 118; EWL 3; EXPP
Villa, Jose Garcia 1914-1997
  See Villa, Jose Garcia
Villarreal, Jose Antonio 1924- **HLC 2**
  See also CA 133; CANR 93; DAM MULT; DLB 82; HW 1; LAIT 4; RGAL 4
Villaurrutia, Xavier 1903-1950 **TCLC 80**
  See also CA 192; EWL 3; HW 1; LAW
Villaverde, Cirilo 1812-1894 **NCLC 121**
  See also LAW
Villehardouin, Geoffroi de 1150(?)-1218(?) **CMLC 38**
Villiers de l'Isle Adam, Jean Marie Mathias Philippe Auguste 1838-1889 **NCLC 3; SSC 14**
  See also DLB 123, 192; GFL 1789 to the Present; RGSF 2
Villon, Francois 1431-1463(?) **LC 62; PC 13**
  See also DLB 208; EW 2; RGWL 2, 3; TWA
Vine, Barbara CLC 50
  See Rendell, Ruth (Barbara)
  See also BEST 90:4
Vinge, Joan (Carol) D(ennison) 1948- **CLC 30**
  See also AAYA 32; BPFB 3; CA 93-96; CANR 72; SATA 36, 113; SFW 4; YAW
Viola, Herman J(oseph) 1938- **CLC 70**
  See also CA 61-64; CANR 8, 23, 48, 91; SATA 126
Violis, G.
  See Simenon, Georges (Jacques Christian)
Viramontes, Helena Maria 1954- **HLCS 2**
  See also CA 159; DLB 122; HW 2; LLW 1
Virgil
  See Vergil
  See also CDWLB 1; DLB 211; LAIT 1; RGWL 2, 3; WP
Visconti, Luchino 1906-1976 **CLC 16**
  See also CA 81-84; 65-68; CANR 39
Vitry, Jacques de
  See Jacques de Vitry
Vittorini, Elio 1908-1966 **CLC 6, 9, 14**
  See also CA 133; 25-28R; DLB 264; EW 12; EWL 3; RGWL 2, 3
Vivekananda, Swami 1863-1902 **TCLC 88**
Vizenor, Gerald Robert 1934- **CLC 103; NNAL**
  See also CA 13-16R, 205; CAAE 205; CAAS 22; CANR 5, 21, 44, 67; DAM MULT; DLB 175, 227; MTCW 2; TCWW 2
Vizinczey, Stephen 1933- **CLC 40**
  See also CA 128; CCA 1; INT CA-128
Vliet, R(ussell) G(ordon) 1929-1984 **CLC 22**
  See also CA 37-40R; 112; CANR 18
Vogau, Boris Andreyevich 1894-1938
  See Pilnyak, Boris
  See also CA 123; 218
Vogel, Paula A(nne) 1951- **CLC 76; DC 19**
  See also CA 108; CAD; CANR 119; CD 5; CWD; DFS 14; RGAL 4

Voigt, Cynthia 1942- **CLC 30**
  See also AAYA 3, 30; BYA 1, 3, 6, 7, 8; CA 106; CANR 18, 37, 40, 94; CLR 13, 48; INT CANR-18; JRDA; LAIT 5; MAICYA 1, 2; MAICYAS 1; SATA 48, 79, 116; SATA-Brief 33; WYA; YAW
Voigt, Ellen Bryant 1943- **CLC 54**
  See also CA 69-72; CANR 11, 29, 55, 115; CP 7; CSW; CWP; DLB 120
Voinovich, Vladimir (Nikolaevich) 1932- **CLC 10, 49, 147**
  See also CA 81-84; CAAS 12; CANR 33, 67; MTCW 1
Vollmann, William T. 1959- **CLC 89**
  See also CA 134; CANR 67, 116; CPW; DA3; DAM NOV, POP; MTCW 2
Voloshinov, V. N.
  See Bakhtin, Mikhail Mikhailovich
Voltaire 1694-1778 **LC 14, 79; SSC 12; WLC**
  See also BYA 13; DA; DA3; DAB; DAC; DAM DRAM, MST; EW 4; GFL Beginnings to 1789; LATS 1; LMFS 1; NFS 7; RGWL 2, 3; TWA
von Aschendrof, Baron Ignatz
  See Ford, Ford Madox
von Chamisso, Adelbert
  See Chamisso, Adelbert von
von Daeniken, Erich 1935- **CLC 30**
  See also AITN 1; CA 37-40R; CANR 17, 44
von Daniken, Erich
  See von Daeniken, Erich
von Hartmann, Eduard 1842-1906 **TCLC 96**
von Hayek, Friedrich August
  See Hayek, F(riedrich) A(ugust von)
von Heidenstam, (Carl Gustaf) Verner
  See Heidenstam, (Carl Gustaf) Verner von
von Heyse, Paul (Johann Ludwig)
  See Heyse, Paul (Johann Ludwig von)
von Hofmannsthal, Hugo
  See Hofmannsthal, Hugo von
von Horvath, Odon
  See von Horvath, Odon
von Horvath, Odon
  See von Horvath, Odon
von Horvath, Odon 1901-1938 **TCLC 45**
  See von Horvath, Oedoen
  See also CA 118; 194; DLB 85, 124; RGWL 2, 3
von Horvath, Oedoen
  See von Horvath, Odon
  See also CA 184
von Kleist, Heinrich
  See Kleist, Heinrich von
von Liliencron, (Friedrich Adolf Axel) Detlev
  See Liliencron, (Friedrich Adolf Axel) Detlev von
Vonnegut, Kurt, Jr. 1922- **CLC 1, 2, 3, 4, 5, 8, 12, 22, 40, 60, 111; SSC 8; WLC**
  See also AAYA 6, 44; AITN 1; AMWS 2; BEST 90:4; BPFB 3; BYA 3, 14; CA 1-4R; CANR 1, 25, 49, 75, 92; CDALB 1968-1988; CN 7; CPW 1; DA; DA3; DAB; DAC; DAM MST, NOV, POP; DLB 2, 8, 152; DLBD 3; DLBY 1980; EWL 3; EXPN; EXPS; LAIT 4; LMFS 2; MTCW 1, 2; NFS 3; RGAL 4; SCFW; SFW 4; SSFS 5; TUS; YAW
Von Rachen, Kurt
  See Hubbard, L(afayette) Ron(ald)
von Rezzori (d'Arezzo), Gregor
  See Rezzori (d'Arezzo), Gregor von
von Sternberg, Josef
  See Sternberg, Josef von
Vorster, Gordon 1924- **CLC 34**
  See also CA 133
Vosce, Trudie
  See Ozick, Cynthia

Voznesensky, Andrei (Andreievich) 1933-
CLC 1, 15, 57
See Voznesensky, Andrey
See also CA 89-92; CANR 37; CWW 2;
DAM POET; MTCW 1

Voznesensky, Andrey
See Voznesensky, Andrei (Andreievich)
See also EWL 3

Wace, Robert c. 1100-c. 1175 **CMLC 55**
See also DLB 146

Waddington, Miriam 1917- **CLC 28**
See also CA 21-24R; CANR 12, 30; CCA
1; CP 7; DLB 68

Wagman, Fredrica 1937- **CLC 7**
See also CA 97-100; INT CA-97-100

Wagner, Linda W.
See Wagner-Martin, Linda (C.)

Wagner, Linda Welshimer
See Wagner-Martin, Linda (C.)

Wagner, Richard 1813-1883 **NCLC 9, 119**
See also DLB 129; EW 6

Wagner-Martin, Linda (C.) 1936- **CLC 50**
See also CA 159

Wagoner, David (Russell) 1926- **CLC 3, 5,
15; PC 33**
See also AMWS 9; CA 1-4R; CAAS 3;
CANR 2, 71; CN 7; CP 7; DLB 5, 256;
SATA 14; TCWW 2

Wah, Fred(erick James) 1939- **CLC 44**
See also CA 107; 141; CP 7; DLB 60

Wahloo, Per 1926-1975 **CLC 7**
See also BPFB 3; CA 61-64; CANR 73;
CMW 4; MSW

Wahloo, Peter
See Wahloo, Per

Wain, John (Barrington) 1925-1994 **CLC 2,
11, 15, 46**
See also CA 5-8R; 145; CAAS 4; CANR
23, 54; CDBLB 1960 to Present; DLB 15,
27, 139, 155; EWL 3; MTCW 1, 2

Wajda, Andrzej 1926- **CLC 16**
See also CA 102

Wakefield, Dan 1932- **CLC 7**
See also CA 21-24R; 211; CAAE 211;
CAAS 7; CN 7

Wakefield, Herbert Russell 1888-1965 **TCLC
120**
See also CA 5-8R; CANR 77; HGG; SUFW

Wakoski, Diane 1937- **CLC 2, 4, 7, 9, 11, 40;
PC 15**
See also CA 13-16R; 216; CAAE 216;
CAAS 1; CANR 9, 60, 106; CP 7; CWP;
DAM POET; DLB 5; INT CANR-9;
MTCW 2

Wakoski-Sherbell, Diane
See Wakoski, Diane

Walcott, Derek (Alton) 1930- **BLC 3; CLC 2,
4, 9, 14, 25, 42, 67, 76, 160; DC 7; PC
46**
See also BW 2; CA 89-92; CANR 26, 47,
75, 80; CBD; CD 5; CDWLB 3; CP 7;
DA3; DAB; DAC; DAM MST, MULT,
POET; DLB 117; DLBY 1981; DNFS 1;
EFS 1; EWL 3; LMFS 2; MTCW 1, 2;
PFS 6; RGEL 2; TWA; WWE 1

Waldman, Anne (Lesley) 1945- **CLC 7**
See also BG 3; CA 37-40R; CAAS 17;
CANR 34, 69, 116; CP 7; CWP; DLB 16

Waldo, E. Hunter
See Sturgeon, Theodore (Hamilton)

Waldo, Edward Hamilton
See Sturgeon, Theodore (Hamilton)

Walker, Alice (Malsenior) 1944- **BLC 3; CLC
5, 6, 9, 19, 27, 46, 58, 103, 167; PC 30;
SSC 5; WLCS**
See also AAYA 3, 33; AFAW 1, 2; AMWS
3; BEST 89:4; BPFB 3; BW 2, 3; CA 37-
40R; CANR 9, 27, 49, 66, 82; CDALB
1968-1988; CN 7; CPW; CSW; DA; DA3;

DAB; DAC; DAM MST, MULT, NOV,
POET, POP; DLB 6, 33, 143; EWL 3;
EXPN; EXPS; FW; INT CANR-27; LAIT
3; MAWW; MTCW 1, 2; NFS 5; RGAL
4; RGSF 2; SATA 31; SSFS 2, 11; TUS;
YAW

Walker, David Harry 1911-1992 **CLC 14**
See also CA 1-4R; 137; CANR 1; CWRI 5;
SATA 8; SATA-Obit 71

Walker, Edward Joseph 1934-2004
See Walker, Ted
See also CA 21-24R; CANR 12, 28, 53; CP
7

Walker, George F. 1947- **CLC 44, 61**
See also CA 103; CANR 21, 43, 59; CD 5;
DAB; DAC; DAM MST; DLB 60

Walker, Joseph A. 1935- **CLC 19**
See also BW 1, 3; CA 89-92; CAD; CANR
26; CD 5; DAM DRAM, MST; DFS 12;
DLB 38

Walker, Margaret (Abigail) 1915-1998 **BLC;
CLC 1, 6; PC 20; TCLC 129**
See also AFAW 1, 2; BW 2, 3; CA 73-76;
172; CANR 26, 54, 76; CN 7; CP 7;
CSW; DAM MULT; DLB 76, 152; EXPP;
FW; MTCW 1, 2; RGAL 4; RHW

Walker, Ted **CLC 13**
See Walker, Edward Joseph
See also DLB 40

Wallace, David Foster 1962- **CLC 50, 114;
SSC 68**
See also AAYA 50; AMWS 10; CA 132;
CANR 59; DA3; MTCW 2

Wallace, Dexter
See Masters, Edgar Lee

Wallace, (Richard Horatio) Edgar 1875-1932
TCLC 57
See also CA 115; 218; CMW 4; DLB 70;
MSW; RGEL 2

Wallace, Irving 1916-1990 **CLC 7, 13**
See also AITN 1; BPFB 3; CA 1-4R; 132;
CAAS 1; CANR 1, 27; CPW; DAM NOV,
POP; INT CANR-27; MTCW 1, 2

Wallant, Edward Lewis 1926-1962 **CLC 5,
10**
See also CA 1-4R; CANR 22; DLB 2, 28,
143; EWL 3; MTCW 1, 2; RGAL 4

Wallas, Graham 1858-1932 **TCLC 91**

Waller, Edmund 1606-1687 **LC 86**
See also BRW 2; DAM POET; DLB 126;
PAB; RGEL 2

Walley, Byron
See Card, Orson Scott

Walpole, Horace 1717-1797 **LC 2, 49**
See also BRW 3; DLB 39, 104, 213; HGG;
LMFS 1; RGEL 2; SUFW 1; TEA

Walpole, Hugh (Seymour) 1884-1941 **TCLC
5**
See also CA 104; 165; DLB 34; HGG;
MTCW 2; RGEL 2; RHW

Walrond, Eric (Derwent) 1898-1966 **HR 3**
See also BW 1; CA 125; DLB 51

Walser, Martin 1927- **CLC 27, 183**
See also CA 57-60; CANR 8, 46; CWW 2;
DLB 75, 124; EWL 3

Walser, Robert 1878-1956 **SSC 20; TCLC 18**
See also CA 118; 165; CANR 100; DLB
66; EWL 3

Walsh, Gillian Paton
See Paton Walsh, Gillian

Walsh, Jill Paton **CLC 35**
See Paton Walsh, Gillian
See also CLR 2, 65; WYA

Walter, Villiam Christian
See Andersen, Hans Christian

Walters, Anna L(ee) 1946- **NNAL**
See also CA 73-76

Walther von der Vogelweide c. 1170-1228
CMLC 56

Walton, Izaak 1593-1683 **LC 72**
See also BRW 2; CDBLB Before 1660;
DLB 151, 213; RGEL 2

Wambaugh, Joseph (Aloysius), Jr. 1937- **CLC
3, 18**
See also AITN 1; BEST 89:3; BPFB 3; CA
33-36R; CANR 42, 65, 115; CMW 4;
CPW 1; DA3; DAM NOV, POP; DLB 6;
DLBY 1983; MSW; MTCW 1, 2

Wang Wei 699(?)-761(?) **PC 18**
See also TWA

Warburton, William 1698-1779 **LC 97**
See also DLB 104

Ward, Arthur Henry Sarsfield 1883-1959
See Rohmer, Sax
See also CA 108; 173; CMW 4; HGG

Ward, Douglas Turner 1930- **CLC 19**
See also BW 1; CA 81-84; CAD; CANR
27; CD 5; DLB 7, 38

Ward, E. D.
See Lucas, E(dward) V(errall)

Ward, Mrs. Humphry 1851-1920
See Ward, Mary Augusta
See also RGEL 2

Ward, Mary Augusta 1851-1920 **TCLC 55**
See Ward, Mrs. Humphry
See also DLB 18

Ward, Peter
See Faust, Frederick (Schiller)

Warhol, Andy 1928(?)-1987 **CLC 20**
See also AAYA 12; BEST 89:4; CA 89-92;
121; CANR 34

Warner, Francis (Robert le Plastrier) 1937-
CLC 14
See also CA 53-56; CANR 11

Warner, Marina 1946- **CLC 59**
See also CA 65-68; CANR 21, 55, 118; CN
7; DLB 194

Warner, Rex (Ernest) 1905-1986 **CLC 45**
See also CA 89-92; 119; DLB 15; RGEL 2;
RHW

Warner, Susan (Bogert) 1819-1885 **NCLC 31**
See also DLB 3, 42, 239, 250, 254

Warner, Sylvia (Constance) Ashton
See Ashton-Warner, Sylvia (Constance)

Warner, Sylvia Townsend 1893-1978 **CLC 7,
19; SSC 23; TCLC 131**
See also BRWS 7; CA 61-64; 77-80; CANR
16, 60, 104; DLB 34, 139; EWL 3; FANT;
FW; MTCW 1, 2; RGEL 2; RGSF 2;
RHW

Warren, Mercy Otis 1728-1814 **NCLC 13**
See also DLB 31, 200; RGAL 4; TUS

Warren, Robert Penn 1905-1989 **CLC 1, 4,
6, 8, 10, 13, 18, 39, 53, 59; PC 37; SSC
4, 58; WLC**
See also AITN 1; AMW; AMWC 2; BPFB
3; BYA 1; CA 13-16R; 129; CANR 10,
47; CDALB 1968-1988; DA; DA3; DAB;
DAC; DAM MST, NOV, POET; DLB 2,
48, 152; DLBY 1980, 1989; EWL 3; INT
CANR-10; MTCW 1, 2; NFS 13; RGAL
4; RGSF 2; RHW; SATA 46; SATA-Obit
63; SSFS 8; TUS

Warrigal, Jack
See Furphy, Joseph

Warshofsky, Isaac
See Singer, Isaac Bashevis

Warton, Joseph 1722-1800 **NCLC 118**
See also DLB 104, 109; RGEL 2

Warton, Thomas 1728-1790 **LC 15, 82**
See also DAM POET; DLB 104, 109;
RGEL 2

Waruk, Kona
See Harris, (Theodore) Wilson

Warung, Price **TCLC 45**
See Astley, William
See also DLB 230; RGEL 2

Warwick, Jarvis
See Garner, Hugh
See also CCA 1

Washington, Alex
See Harris, Mark

Washington, Booker T(aliaferro) 1856-1915
BLC 3; TCLC 10
See also BW 1; CA 114; 125; DA3; DAM
MULT; LAIT 2; RGAL 4; SATA 28

Washington, George 1732-1799 **LC 25**
See also DLB 31

Wassermann, (Karl) Jakob 1873-1934 **TCLC 6**
See also CA 104; 163; DLB 66; EWL 3

Wasserstein, Wendy 1950- **CLC 32, 59, 90, 183; DC 4**
See also CA 121; 129; CABS 3; CAD;
CANR 53, 75, 128; CD 5; CWD; DA3;
DAM DRAM; DFS 5, 17; DLB 228;
EWL 3; FW; INT CA-129; MTCW 2;
SATA 94

Waterhouse, Keith (Spencer) 1929- **CLC 47**
See also CA 5-8R; CANR 38, 67, 109;
CBD; CN 7; DLB 13, 15; MTCW 1, 2

Waters, Frank (Joseph) 1902-1995 **CLC 88**
See also CA 5-8R; 149; CAAS 13; CANR
3, 18, 63, 121; DLB 212; DLBY 1986;
RGAL 4; TCWW 2

Waters, Mary C. CLC 70

Waters, Roger 1944- **CLC 35**

Watkins, Frances Ellen
See Harper, Frances Ellen Watkins

Watkins, Gerrold
See Malzberg, Barry N(athaniel)

Watkins, Gloria Jean 1952(?)- **CLC 94**
See also BW 2; CA 143; CANR 87, 126;
DLB 246; MTCW 2; SATA 115

Watkins, Paul 1964- **CLC 55**
See also CA 132; CANR 62, 98

Watkins, Vernon Phillips 1906-1967 **CLC 43**
See also CA 9-10; 25-28R; CAP 1; DLB
20; EWL 3; RGEL 2

Watson, Irving S.
See Mencken, H(enry) L(ouis)

Watson, John H.
See Farmer, Philip Jose

Watson, Richard F.
See Silverberg, Robert

Watts, Ephraim
See Horne, Richard Henry Hengist

Watts, Isaac 1674-1748 **LC 98**
See also DLB 95; RGEL 2; SATA 52

Waugh, Auberon (Alexander) 1939-2001
CLC 7
See also CA 45-48; 192; CANR 6, 22, 92;
DLB 14, 194

Waugh, Evelyn (Arthur St. John) 1903-1966
**CLC 1, 3, 8, 13, 19, 27, 44, 107; SSC
41; WLC**
See also BPFB 3; BRW 7; CA 85-88; 25-
28R; CANR 22; CDBLB 1914-1945; DA;
DA3; DAB; DAC; DAM MST, NOV,
POP; DLB 15, 162, 195; EWL 3; MTCW
1, 2; NFS 13, 17; RGEL 2; RGSF 2; TEA;
WLIT 4

Waugh, Harriet 1944- **CLC 6**
See also CA 85-88; CANR 22

Ways, C. R.
See Blount, Roy (Alton), Jr.

Waystaff, Simon
See Swift, Jonathan

Webb, Beatrice (Martha Potter) 1858-1943
TCLC 22
See also CA 117; 162; DLB 190; FW

Webb, Charles (Richard) 1939- **CLC 7**
See also CA 25-28R; CANR 114

Webb, James H(enry), Jr. 1946- **CLC 22**
See also CA 81-84

Webb, Mary Gladys (Meredith) 1881-1927
TCLC 24
See also CA 182; 123; DLB 34; FW

Webb, Mrs. Sidney
See Webb, Beatrice (Martha Potter)

Webb, Phyllis 1927- **CLC 18**
See also CA 104; CANR 23; CCA 1; CP 7;
CWP; DLB 53

Webb, Sidney (James) 1859-1947 **TCLC 22**
See also CA 117; 163; DLB 190

Webber, Andrew Lloyd CLC 21
See Lloyd Webber, Andrew
See also DFS 7

Weber, Lenora Mattingly 1895-1971 **CLC 12**
See also CA 19-20; 29-32R; CAP 1; SATA
2; SATA-Obit 26

Weber, Max 1864-1920 **TCLC 69**
See also CA 109; 189; DLB 296

Webster, John 1580(?)-1634(?) **DC 2; LC 33, 84; WLC**
See also BRW 2; CDBLB Before 1660; DA;
DAB; DAC; DAM DRAM, MST; DFS
17; DLB 58; IDTP; RGEL 2; WLIT 3

Webster, Noah 1758-1843 **NCLC 30**
See also DLB 1, 37, 42, 43, 73, 243

Wedekind, (Benjamin) Frank(lin) 1864-1918
TCLC 7
See also CA 104; 153; CANR 121, 122;
CDWLB 2; DAM DRAM; DLB 118; EW
8; EWL 3; LMFS 2; RGWL 2, 3

Wehr, Demaris CLC 65

Weidman, Jerome 1913-1998 **CLC 7**
See also AITN 2; CA 1-4R; 171; CAD;
CANR 1; DLB 28

Weil, Simone (Adolphine) 1909-1943 **TCLC
23**
See also CA 117; 159; EW 12; EWL 3; FW;
GFL 1789 to the Present; MTCW 2

Weininger, Otto 1880-1903 **TCLC 84**

Weinstein, Nathan
See West, Nathanael

Weinstein, Nathan von Wallenstein
See West, Nathanael

Weir, Peter (Lindsay) 1944- **CLC 20**
See also CA 113; 123

Weiss, Peter (Ulrich) 1916-1982 **CLC 3, 15, 51**
See also CA 45-48; 106; CANR 3; DAM
DRAM; DFS 3; DLB 69, 124; EWL 3;
RGWL 2, 3

Weiss, Theodore (Russell) 1916-2003 **CLC 3, 8, 14**
See also CA 9-12R; 189; 216; CAAE 189;
CAAS 2; CANR 46, 94; CP 7; DLB 5

Welch, (Maurice) Denton 1915-1948 **TCLC
22**
See also BRWS 8, 9; CA 121; 148; RGEL
2

Welch, James (Phillip) 1940-2003 **CLC 6, 14, 52; NNAL**
See also CA 85-88; 219; CANR 42, 66, 107;
CN 7; CP 7; CPW; DAM MULT, POP;
DLB 175, 256; LATS 1; RGAL 4; TCWW
2

Weldon, Fay 1931- **CLC 6, 9, 11, 19, 36, 59, 122**
See also BRWS 4; CA 21-24R; CANR 16,
46, 63, 97; CDBLB 1960 to Present; CN
7; CPW; DAM POP; DLB 14, 194; EWL
3; FW; HGG; INT CANR-16; MTCW 1,
2; RGEL 2; RGSF 2

Wellek, Rene 1903-1995 **CLC 28**
See also CA 5-8R; 150; CAAS 7; CANR 8;
DLB 63; EWL 3; INT CANR-8

Weller, Michael 1942- **CLC 10, 53**
See also CA 85-88; CAD; CD 5

Weller, Paul 1958- **CLC 26**

Wellershoff, Dieter 1925- **CLC 46**
See also CA 89-92; CANR 16, 37

Welles, (George) Orson 1915-1985 **CLC 20, 80**
See also AAYA 40; CA 93-96; 117

Wellman, John McDowell 1945-
See Wellman, Mac
See also CA 166; CD 5

Wellman, Mac CLC 65
See Wellman, John McDowell; Wellman,
John McDowell
See also CAD; RGAL 4

Wellman, Manly Wade 1903-1986 **CLC 49**
See also CA 1-4R; 118; CANR 6, 16, 44;
FANT; SATA 6; SATA-Obit 47; SFW 4;
SUFW

Wells, Carolyn 1869(?)-1942 **TCLC 35**
See also CA 113; 185; CMW 4; DLB 11

Wells, H(erbert) G(eorge) 1866-1946 **SSC 6, 70; TCLC 6, 12, 19, 133; WLC**
See also AAYA 18; BPFB 3; BRW 6; CA
110; 121; CDBLB 1914-1945; CLR 64;
DA; DA3; DAB; DAC; DAM MST, NOV;
DLB 34, 70, 156, 178; EWL 3; EXPS;
HGG; LAIT 3; LMFS 2; MTCW 1, 2;
NFS 17; RGEL 2; RGSF 2; SATA 20;
SCFW; SFW 4; SSFS 3; SUFW; TEA;
WCH; WLIT 4; YAW

Wells, Rosemary 1943- **CLC 12**
See also AAYA 13; BYA 7, 8; CA 85-88;
CANR 48, 120; CLR 16, 69; CWRI 5;
MAICYA 1, 2; SAAS 1; SATA 18, 69,
114; YAW

Wells-Barnett, Ida B(ell) 1862-1931 **TCLC
125**
See also CA 182; DLB 23, 221

Welsh, Irvine 1958- **CLC 144**
See also CA 173; DLB 271

Welty, Eudora (Alice) 1909-2001 **CLC 1, 2, 5, 14, 22, 33, 105; SSC 1, 27, 51; WLC**
See also AAYA 48; AMW; AMWR 1; BPFB
3; CA 9-12R; 199; CABS 1; CANR 32,
65, 128; CDALB 1941-1968; CN 7; CSW;
DA; DA3; DAB; DAC; DAM MST, NOV;
DLB 2, 102, 143; DLBD 12; DLBY 1987,
2001; EWL 3; EXPS; HGG; LAIT 3;
MAWW; MTCW 1, 2; NFS 13, 15; RGAL
4; RGSF 2; RHW; SSFS 2, 10; TUS

Wen I-to 1899-1946 **TCLC 28**
See also EWL 3

Wentworth, Robert
See Hamilton, Edmond

Werfel, Franz (Viktor) 1890-1945 **TCLC 8**
See also CA 104; 161; DLB 81, 124; EWL
3; RGWL 2, 3

Wergeland, Henrik Arnold 1808-1845 **NCLC
5**

Wersba, Barbara 1932- **CLC 30**
See also AAYA 2, 30; BYA 6, 12, 13; CA
29-32R, 182; CAAE 182; CANR 16, 38;
CLR 3, 78; DLB 52; JRDA; MAICYA 1,
2; SAAS 2; SATA 1, 58; SATA-Essay 103;
WYA; YAW

Wertmueller, Lina 1928- **CLC 16**
See also CA 97-100; CANR 39, 78

Wescott, Glenway 1901-1987 **CLC 13; SSC
35**
See also CA 13-16R; 121; CANR 23, 70;
DLB 4, 9, 102; RGAL 4

Wesker, Arnold 1932- **CLC 3, 5, 42**
See also CA 1-4R; CAAS 7; CANR 1, 33;
CBD; CD 5; CDBLB 1960 to Present;
DAB; DAM DRAM; DLB 13; EWL 3;
MTCW 1; RGEL 2; TEA

Wesley, John 1703-1791 **LC 88**
See also DLB 104

Wesley, Richard (Errol) 1945- **CLC 7**
See also BW 1; CA 57-60; CAD; CANR
27; CD 5; DLB 38

Wessel, Johan Herman 1742-1785 **LC 7**

West, Anthony (Panther) 1914-1987 **CLC 50**
See also CA 45-48; 124; CANR 3, 19; DLB 15

West, C. P.
See Wodehouse, P(elham) G(renville)

West, Cornel (Ronald) 1953- **BLCS; CLC 134**
See also CA 144; CANR 91; DLB 246

West, Delno C(loyde), Jr. 1936- **CLC 70**
See also CA 57-60

West, Dorothy 1907-1998 **HR 3; TCLC 108**
See also BW 2; CA 143; 169; DLB 76

West, (Mary) Jessamyn 1902-1984 **CLC 7, 17**
See also CA 9-12R; 112; CANR 27; DLB 6; DLBY 1984; MTCW 1, 2; RGAL 4; RHW; SATA-Obit 37; TCWW 2; TUS; YAW

West, Morris
See West, Morris L(anglo)
See also DLB 289

West, Morris L(anglo) 1916-1999 **CLC 6, 33**
See West, Morris
See also BPFB 3; CA 5-8R; 187; CANR 24, 49, 64; CN 7; CPW; MTCW 1, 2

West, Nathanael 1903-1940 **SSC 16; TCLC 1, 14, 44**
See also AMW; AMWR 2; BPFB 3; CA 104; 125; CDALB 1929-1941; DA3; DLB 4, 9, 28; EWL 3; MTCW 1, 2; NFS 16; RGAL 4; TUS

West, Owen
See Koontz, Dean R(ay)

West, Paul 1930- **CLC 7, 14, 96**
See also CA 13-16R; CAAS 7; CANR 22, 53, 76, 89; CN 7; DLB 14; INT CANR-22; MTCW 2

West, Rebecca 1892-1983 **CLC 7, 9, 31, 50**
See also BPFB 3; BRWS 3; CA 5-8R; 109; CANR 19; DLB 36; DLBY 1983; EWL 3; FW; MTCW 1, 2; NCFS 4; RGEL 2; TEA

Westall, Robert (Atkinson) 1929-1993 **CLC 17**
See also AAYA 12; BYA 2, 6, 7, 8, 9, 15; CA 69-72; 141; CANR 18, 68; CLR 13; FANT; JRDA; MAICYA 1, 2; MAICYAS 1; SAAS 2; SATA 23, 69; SATA-Obit 75; WYA; YAW

Westermarck, Edward 1862-1939 **TCLC 87**

Westlake, Donald E(dwin) 1933- **CLC 7, 33**
See also BPFB 3; CA 17-20R; CAAS 13; CANR 16, 44, 65, 94; CMW 4; CPW; DAM POP; INT CANR-16; MSW; MTCW 2

Westmacott, Mary
See Christie, Agatha (Mary Clarissa)

Weston, Allen
See Norton, Andre

Wetcheek, J. L.
See Feuchtwanger, Lion

Wetering, Janwillem van de
See van de Wetering, Janwillem

Wetherald, Agnes Ethelwyn 1857-1940 **TCLC 81**
See also CA 202; DLB 99

Wetherell, Elizabeth
See Warner, Susan (Bogert)

Whale, James 1889-1957 **TCLC 63**

Whalen, Philip (Glenn) 1923-2002 **CLC 6, 29**
See also BG 3; CA 9-12R; 209; CANR 5, 39; CP 7; DLB 16; WP

Wharton, Edith (Newbold Jones) 1862-1937 **SSC 6; TCLC 3, 9, 27, 53, 129, 149; WLC**
See also AAYA 25; AMW; AMWC 2; AMWR 1; BPFB 3; CA 104; 132; CDALB 1865-1917; DA; DA3; DAB; DAC; DAM MST, NOV; DLB 4, 9, 12, 78, 189; DLBD

13; EWL 3; EXPS; HGG; LAIT 2, 3; LATS 1; MAWW; MTCW 1, 2; NFS 5, 11, 15; RGAL 4; RGSF 2; RHW; SSFS 6, 7; SUFW; TUS

Wharton, James
See Mencken, H(enry) L(ouis)

Wharton, William (a pseudonym) **CLC 18, 37**
See also CA 93-96; DLBY 1980; INT CA-93-96

Wheatley (Peters), Phillis 1753(?)-1784 **BLC 3; LC 3, 50; PC 3; WLC**
See also AFAW 1, 2; CDALB 1640-1865; DA; DA3; DAC; DAM MST, MULT, POET; DLB 31, 50; EXPP; PFS 13; RGAL 4

Wheelock, John Hall 1886-1978 **CLC 14**
See also CA 13-16R; 77-80; CANR 14; DLB 45

Whim-Wham
See Curnow, (Thomas) Allen (Monro)

White, Babington
See Braddon, Mary Elizabeth

White, E(lwyn) B(rooks) 1899-1985 **CLC 10, 34, 39**
See also AITN 2; AMWS 1; CA 13-16R; 116; CANR 16, 37; CDALBS; CLR 1, 21; CPW; DA3; DAM POP; DLB 11, 22; EWL 3; FANT; MAICYA 1, 2; MTCW 1, 2; NCFS 5; RGAL 4; SATA 2, 29, 100; SATA-Obit 44; TUS

White, Edmund (Valentine III) 1940- **CLC 27, 110**
See also AAYA 7; CA 45-48; CANR 3, 19, 36, 62, 107; CN 7; DA3; DAM POP; DLB 227; MTCW 1, 2

White, Hayden V. 1928- **CLC 148**
See also CA 128; DLB 246

White, Patrick (Victor Martindale) 1912-1990 **CLC 3, 4, 5, 7, 9, 18, 65, 69; SSC 39**
See also BRWS 1; CA 81-84; 132; CANR 43; DLB 260; EWL 3; MTCW 1; RGEL 2; RGSF 2; RHW; TWA; WWE 1

White, Phyllis Dorothy James 1920-
See James, P. D.
See also CA 21-24R; CANR 17, 43, 65, 112; CMW 4; CN 7; CPW; DA3; DAM POP; MTCW 1, 2; TEA

White, T(erence) H(anbury) 1906-1964 **CLC 30**
See also AAYA 22; BPFB 3; BYA 4, 5; CA 73-76; CANR 37; DLB 160; FANT; JRDA; LAIT 1; MAICYA 1, 2; RGEL 2; SATA 12; SUFW 1; YAW

White, Terence de Vere 1912-1994 **CLC 49**
See also CA 49-52; 145; CANR 3

White, Walter
See White, Walter F(rancis)

White, Walter F(rancis) 1893-1955 **BLC 3; HR 3; TCLC 15**
See also BW 1; CA 115; 124; DAM MULT; DLB 51

White, William Hale 1831-1913
See Rutherford, Mark
See also CA 121; 189

Whitehead, Alfred North 1861-1947 **TCLC 97**
See also CA 117; 165; DLB 100, 262

Whitehead, E(dward) A(nthony) 1933- **CLC 5**
See also CA 65-68; CANR 58, 118; CBD; CD 5

Whitehead, Ted
See Whitehead, E(dward) A(nthony)

Whiteman, Roberta J. Hill 1947- **NNAL**
See also CA 146

Whitemore, Hugh (John) 1936- **CLC 37**
See also CA 132; CANR 77; CBD; CD 5; INT CA-132

Whitman, Sarah Helen (Power) 1803-1878 **NCLC 19**
See also DLB 1, 243

Whitman, Walt(er) 1819-1892 **NCLC 4, 31, 81; PC 3; WLC**
See also AAYA 42; AMW; AMWR 1; CDALB 1640-1865; DA; DA3; DAB; DAC; DAM MST, POET; DLB 3, 64, 224, 250; EXPP; LAIT 2; LMFS 1; PAB; PFS 2, 3, 13; RGAL 4; SATA 20; TUS; WP; WYAS 1

Whitney, Phyllis A(yame) 1903- **CLC 42**
See also AAYA 36; AITN 2; BEST 90:3; CA 1-4R; CANR 3, 25, 38, 60; CLR 59; CMW 4; CPW; DA3; DAM POP; JRDA; MAICYA 1, 2; MTCW 2; RHW; SATA 1, 30; YAW

Whittemore, (Edward) Reed, Jr. 1919- **CLC 4**
See also CA 9-12R; 219; CAAE 219; CAAS 8; CANR 4, 119; CP 7; DLB 5

Whittier, John Greenleaf 1807-1892 **NCLC 8, 59**
See also AMWS 1; DLB 1, 243; RGAL 4

Whittlebot, Hernia
See Coward, Noel (Peirce)

Wicker, Thomas Grey 1926-
See Wicker, Tom
See also CA 65-68; CANR 21, 46

Wicker, Tom **CLC 7**
See Wicker, Thomas Grey

Wideman, John Edgar 1941- **BLC 3; CLC 5, 34, 36, 67, 122; SSC 62**
See also AFAW 1, 2; AMWS 10; BPFB 4; BW 2, 3; CA 85-88; CANR 14, 42, 67, 109; CN 7; DAM MULT; DLB 33, 143; MTCW 2; RGAL 4; RGSF 2; SSFS 6, 12

Wiebe, Rudy (Henry) 1934- **CLC 6, 11, 14, 138**
See also CA 37-40R; CANR 42, 67, 123; CN 7; DAC; DAM MST; DLB 60; RHW

Wieland, Christoph Martin 1733-1813 **NCLC 17**
See also DLB 97; EW 4; LMFS 1; RGWL 2, 3

Wiene, Robert 1881-1938 **TCLC 56**

Wieners, John 1934- **CLC 7**
See also BG 3; CA 13-16R; CP 7; DLB 16; WP

Wiesel, Elie(zer) 1928- **CLC 3, 5, 11, 37, 165; WLCS**
See also AAYA 7; AITN 1; CA 5-8R; CAAS 4; CANR 8, 40, 65, 125; CDALBS; DA; DA3; DAB; DAC; DAM MST, NOV; DLB 83; DLBY 1987; EWL 3; INT CANR-8; LAIT 4; MTCW 1, 2; NCFS 4; NFS 4; RGWL 3; SATA 56; YAW

Wiggins, Marianne 1947- **CLC 57**
See also BEST 89:3; CA 130; CANR 60

Wiggs, Susan **CLC 70**
See also CA 201

Wight, James Alfred 1916-1995
See Herriot, James
See also CA 77-80; SATA 55; SATA-Brief 44

Wilbur, Richard (Purdy) 1921- **CLC 3, 6, 9, 14, 53, 110; PC 51**
See also AMWS 3; CA 1-4R; CABS 2; CANR 2, 29, 76, 93; CDALBS; CP 7; DA; DAB; DAC; DAM MST, POET; DLB 5, 169; EWL 3; EXPP; INT CANR-29; MTCW 1, 2; PAB; PFS 11, 12, 16; RGAL 4; SATA 9, 108; WP

Wild, Peter 1940- **CLC 14**
See also CA 37-40R; CP 7; DLB 5

Wilde, Oscar (Fingal O'Flahertie Wills)
  1854(?)-1900 **DC 17; SSC 11; TCLC 1,
  8, 23, 41; WLC**
  See also AAYA 49; BRW 5; BRWC 1, 2;
  BRWR 2; BYA 15; CA 104; 119; CANR
  112; CDBLB 1890-1914; DA; DA3;
  DAB; DAC; DAM DRAM, MST, NOV;
  DFS 4, 8, 9; DLB 10, 19, 34, 57, 141,
  156, 190; EXPS; FANT; LATS 1; RGEL
  2; RGSF 2; SATA 24; SSFS 7; SUFW;
  TEA; WCH; WLIT 4
Wilder, Billy CLC 20
  See Wilder, Samuel
  See also DLB 26
Wilder, Samuel 1906-2002
  See Wilder, Billy
  See also CA 89-92; 205
Wilder, Stephen
  See Marlowe, Stephen
**Wilder, Thornton (Niven) 1897-1975 CLC 1,
  5, 6, 10, 15, 35, 82; DC 1; WLC**
  See also AAYA 29; AITN 2; AMW; CA 13-
  16R; 61-64; CAD; CANR 40; CDALBS;
  DA; DA3; DAB; DAC; DAM DRAM,
  MST, NOV; DFS 1, 4, 16; DLB 4, 7, 9,
  228; DLBY 1997; EWL 3; LAIT 3;
  MTCW 1, 2; RGAL 4; RHW; WYAS 1
Wilding, Michael 1942- CLC 73; SSC 50
  See also CA 104; CANR 24, 49, 106; CN
  7; RGSF 2
Wiley, Richard 1944- CLC 44
  See also CA 121; 129; CANR 71
Wilhelm, Kate CLC 7
  See Wilhelm, Katie (Gertrude)
  See also AAYA 20; BYA 16; CAAS 5; DLB
  8; INT CANR-17; SCFW 2
Wilhelm, Katie (Gertrude) 1928-
  See Wilhelm, Kate
  See also CA 37-40R; CANR 17, 36, 60, 94;
  MTCW 1; SFW 4
Wilkins, Mary
  See Freeman, Mary E(leanor) Wilkins
Willard, Nancy 1936- CLC 7, 37
  See also BYA 5; CA 89-92; CANR 10, 39,
  68, 107; CLR 5; CWP; CWRI 5; DLB 5,
  52; FANT; MAICYA 1, 2; MTCW 1;
  SATA 37, 71, 127; SATA-Brief 30; SUFW
  2
**William of Malmesbury c. 1090B.C.-c.
  1140B.C. CMLC 57**
William of Ockham 1290-1349 CMLC 32
Williams, Ben Ames 1889-1953 TCLC 89
  See also CA 183; DLB 102
**Williams, C(harles) K(enneth) 1936- CLC
  33, 56, 148**
  See also CA 37-40R; CAAS 26; CANR 57,
  106; CP 7; DAM POET; DLB 5
Williams, Charles
  See Collier, James Lincoln
**Williams, Charles (Walter Stansby)
  1886-1945 TCLC 1, 11**
  See also BRWS 9; CA 104; 163; DLB 100,
  153, 255; FANT; RGEL 2; SUFW 1
Williams, Ella Gwendolen Rees
  See Rhys, Jean
**Williams, (George) Emlyn 1905-1987 CLC
  15**
  See also CA 104; 123; CANR 36; DAM
  DRAM; DLB 10, 77; IDTP; MTCW 1
Williams, Hank 1923-1953 TCLC 81
  See Williams, Hiram King
Williams, Helen Maria 1761-1827 NCLC 135
  See also DLB 158
Williams, Hiram Hank
  See Williams, Hank
Williams, Hiram King
  See Williams, Hank
  See also CA 188

Williams, Hugo (Mordaunt) 1942- CLC 42
  See also CA 17-20R; CANR 45, 119; CP 7;
  DLB 40
Williams, J. Walker
  See Wodehouse, P(elham) G(renville)
**Williams, John A(lfred) 1925- BLC 3; CLC
  5, 13**
  See also AFAW 2; BW 2, 3; CA 53-56, 195;
  CAAE 195; CAAS 3; CANR 6, 26, 51,
  118; CN 7; CSW; DAM MULT; DLB 2,
  33; EWL 3; INT CANR-6; RGAL 4; SFW
  4
**Williams, Jonathan (Chamberlain) 1929-
  CLC 13**
  See also CA 9-12R; CAAS 12; CANR 8,
  108; CP 7; DLB 5
Williams, Joy 1944- CLC 31
  See also CA 41-44R; CANR 22, 48, 97
Williams, Norman 1952- CLC 39
  See also CA 118
**Williams, Sherley Anne 1944-1999 BLC 3;
  CLC 89**
  See also AFAW 2; BW 2, 3; CA 73-76; 185;
  CANR 25, 82; DAM MULT, POET; DLB
  41; INT CANR-25; SATA 78; SATA-Obit
  116
Williams, Shirley
  See Williams, Sherley Anne
**Williams, Tennessee 1911-1983 CLC 1, 2, 5,
  7, 8, 11, 15, 19, 30, 39, 45, 71, 111; DC
  4; WLC**
  See also AAYA 31; AITN 1, 2; AMW;
  AMWC 1; CA 5-8R; 108; CABS 3; CAD;
  CANR 31; CDALB 1941-1968; DA;
  DA3; DAB; DAC; DAM DRAM, MST;
  DFS 17; DLB 7; DLBD 4; DLBY 1983;
  EWL 3; GLL 1; LAIT 4; LATS 1; MTCW
  1, 2; RGAL 4; TUS
**Williams, Thomas (Alonzo) 1926-1990 CLC
  14**
  See also CA 1-4R; 132; CANR 2
Williams, William C.
  See Williams, William Carlos
**Williams, William Carlos 1883-1963 CLC 1,
  2, 5, 9, 13, 22, 42, 67; PC 7; SSC 31**
  See also AAYA 46; AMW; AMWR 1; CA
  89-92; CANR 34; CDALB 1917-1929;
  DA; DA3; DAB; DAC; DAM MST,
  POET; DLB 4, 16, 54, 86; EWL 3; EXPP;
  MTCW 1, 2; NCFS 4; PAB; PFS 1, 6, 11;
  RGAL 4; RGSF 2; TUS; WP
Williamson, David (Keith) 1942- CLC 56
  See also CA 103; CANR 41; CD 5; DLB
  289
Williamson, Ellen Douglas 1905-1984
  See Douglas, Ellen
  See also CA 17-20R; 114; CANR 39
Williamson, Jack CLC 29
  See Williamson, John Stewart
  See also CAAS 8; DLB 8; SCFW 2
Williamson, John Stewart 1908-
  See Williamson, Jack
  See also CA 17-20R; CANR 23, 70; SFW 4
Willie, Frederick
  See Lovecraft, H(oward) P(hillips)
**Willingham, Calder (Baynard, Jr.)
  1922-1995 CLC 5, 51**
  See also CA 5-8R; 147; CANR 3; CSW;
  DLB 2, 44; IDFW 3, 4; MTCW 1
Willis, Charles
  See Clarke, Arthur C(harles)
Willy
  See Colette, (Sidonie-Gabrielle)
Willy, Colette
  See Colette, (Sidonie-Gabrielle)
  See also GLL 1
Wilmot, John 1647-1680 LC 75
  See Rochester
  See also BRW 2; DLB 131; PAB

Wilson, A(ndrew) N(orman) 1950- CLC 33
  See also BRWS 6; CA 112; 122; CN 7;
  DLB 14, 155, 194; MTCW 2
**Wilson, Angus (Frank Johnstone) 1913-1991
  CLC 2, 3, 5, 25, 34; SSC 21**
  See also BRWS 1; CA 5-8R; 134; CANR
  21; DLB 15, 139, 155; EWL 3; MTCW 1,
  2; RGEL 2; RGSF 2
**Wilson, August 1945- BLC 3; CLC 39, 50,
  63, 118; DC 2; WLCS**
  See also AAYA 16; AFAW 2; AMWS 8; BW
  2, 3; CA 115; 122; CAD; CANR 42, 54,
  76, 128; CD 5; DA; DA3; DAB; DAC;
  DAM DRAM, MST, MULT; DFS 3, 7,
  15, 17; DLB 228; EWL 3; LAIT 4; LATS
  1; MTCW 1, 2; RGAL 4
Wilson, Brian 1942- CLC 12
Wilson, Colin 1931- CLC 3, 14
  See also CA 1-4R; CAAS 5; CANR 1, 22,
  33, 77; CMW 4; CN 7; DLB 14, 194;
  HGG; MTCW 1; SFW 4
Wilson, Dirk
  See Pohl, Frederik
**Wilson, Edmund 1895-1972 CLC 1, 2, 3, 8,
  24**
  See also AMW; CA 1-4R; 37-40R; CANR
  1, 46, 110; DLB 63; EWL 3; MTCW 1, 2;
  RGAL 4; TUS
**Wilson, Ethel Davis (Bryant) 1888(?)-1980
  CLC 13**
  See also CA 102; DAC; DAM POET; DLB
  68; MTCW 1; RGEL 2
Wilson, Harriet
  See Wilson, Harriet E. Adams
  See also DLB 239
Wilson, Harriet E.
  See Wilson, Harriet E. Adams
  See also DLB 243
**Wilson, Harriet E. Adams 1827(?)-1863(?)
  BLC 3; NCLC 78**
  See Wilson, Harriet; Wilson, Harriet E.
  See also DAM MULT; DLB 50
Wilson, John 1785-1854 NCLC 5
Wilson, John (Anthony) Burgess 1917-1993
  See Burgess, Anthony
  See also CA 1-4R; 143; CANR 2, 46; DA3;
  DAC; DAM NOV; MTCW 1, 2; NFS 15;
  TEA
Wilson, Lanford 1937- CLC 7, 14, 36; DC 19
  See also CA 17-20R; CABS 3; CAD; CANR
  45, 96; CD 5; DAM DRAM; DFS 4, 9,
  12, 16; DLB 7; EWL 3; TUS
Wilson, Robert M. 1941- CLC 7, 9
  See also CA 49-52; CAD; CANR 2, 41; CD
  5; MTCW 1
Wilson, Robert McLiam 1964- CLC 59
  See also CA 132; DLB 267
Wilson, Sloan 1920-2003 CLC 32
  See also CA 1-4R; 216; CANR 1, 44; CN 7
Wilson, Snoo 1948- CLC 33
  See also CA 69-72; CBD; CD 5
Wilson, William S(mith) 1932- CLC 49
  See also CA 81-84
**Wilson, (Thomas) Woodrow 1856-1924
  TCLC 79**
  See also CA 166; DLB 47
Wilson and Warnke eds. CLC 65
**Winchilsea, Anne (Kingsmill) Finch
  1661-1720**
  See Finch, Anne
  See also RGEL 2
Windham, Basil
  See Wodehouse, P(elham) G(renville)
Wingrove, David (John) 1954- CLC 68
  See also CA 133; SFW 4
**Winnemucca, Sarah 1844-1891 NCLC 79;
  NNAL**
  See also DAM MULT; DLB 175; RGAL 4
Winstanley, Gerrard 1609-1676 LC 52

Wintergreen, Jane
See Duncan, Sara Jeannette
Winters, Janet Lewis CLC 41
See Lewis, Janet
See also DLBY 1987
Winters, (Arthur) Yvor 1900-1968 CLC 4, 8, 32
See also AMWS 2; CA 11-12; 25-28R; CAP 1; DLB 48; EWL 3; MTCW 1; RGAL 4
Winterson, Jeanette 1959- CLC 64, 158
See also BRWS 4; CA 136; CANR 58, 116; CN 7; CPW; DA3; DAM POP; DLB 207, 261; FANT; FW; GLL 1; MTCW 2; RHW
Winthrop, John 1588-1649 LC 31
See also DLB 24, 30
Wirth, Louis 1897-1952 TCLC 92
See also CA 210
Wiseman, Frederick 1930- CLC 20
See also CA 159
Wister, Owen 1860-1938 TCLC 21
See also BPFB 3; CA 108; 162; DLB 9, 78, 186; RGAL 4; SATA 62; TCWW 2
Wither, George 1588-1667 LC 96
See also DLB 121; RGEL 2
Witkacy
See Witkiewicz, Stanislaw Ignacy
Witkiewicz, Stanislaw Ignacy 1885-1939 TCLC 8
See also CA 105; 162; CDWLB 4; DLB 215; EW 10; EWL 3; RGWL 2, 3; SFW 4
Wittgenstein, Ludwig (Josef Johann) 1889-1951 TCLC 59
See also CA 113; 164; DLB 262; MTCW 2
Wittig, Monique 1935(?)-2003 CLC 22
See also CA 116; 135; 212; CWW 2; DLB 83; EWL 3; FW; GLL 1
Wittlin, Jozef 1896-1976 CLC 25
See also CA 49-52; 65-68; CANR 3; EWL 3
Wodehouse, P(elham) G(renville) 1881-1975 CLC 1, 2, 5, 10, 22; SSC 2; TCLC 108
See also AITN 2; BRWS 3; CA 45-48; 57-60; CANR 3, 33; CDBLB 1914-1945; CPW 1; DA3; DAB; DAC; DAM NOV; DLB 34, 162; EWL 3; MTCW 1, 2; RGEL 2; RGSF 2; SATA 22; SSFS 10
Woiwode, L.
See Woiwode, Larry (Alfred)
Woiwode, Larry (Alfred) 1941- CLC 6, 10
See also CA 73-76; CANR 16, 94; CN 7; DLB 6; INT CANR-16
Wojciechowska, Maia (Teresa) 1927-2002 CLC 26
See also AAYA 8, 46; BYA 3; CA 9-12R, 183; 209; CAAE 183; CANR 4, 41; CLR 1; JRDA; MAICYA 1, 2; SAAS 1; SATA 1, 28, 83; SATA-Essay 104; SATA-Obit 134; YAW
Wojtyla, Karol
See John Paul II, Pope
Wolf, Christa 1929- CLC 14, 29, 58, 150
See also CA 85-88; CANR 45, 123; CD-WLB 2; CWW 2; DLB 75; EWL 3; FW; MTCW 1; RGWL 2, 3; SSFS 14
Wolf, Naomi 1962- CLC 157
See also CA 141; CANR 110; FW
Wolfe, Gene (Rodman) 1931- CLC 25
See also AAYA 35; CA 57-60; CAAS 9; CANR 6, 32, 60; CPW; DAM POP; DLB 8; FANT; MTCW 2; SATA 118; SCFW 2; SFW 2; SUFW 2
Wolfe, George C. 1954- BLCS; CLC 49
See also CA 149; CAD; CD 5
Wolfe, Thomas (Clayton) 1900-1938 SSC 33; TCLC 4, 13, 29, 61; WLC
See also AMW; BPFB 3; CA 104; 132; DA3; DAB; DAC; DAM MST, NOV;

DLB 9, 102, 229; DLBD 2, 16; DLBY 1985, 1997; EWL 3; MTCW 1, 2; NFS 18; RGAL 4; TUS
Wolfe, Thomas Kennerly, Jr. 1931- CLC 147
See Wolfe, Tom
See also CA 13-16R; CANR 9, 33, 70, 104; DA3; DAM POP; DLB 185; EWL 3; INT CANR-9; MTCW 1, 2; SSFS 18; TUS
Wolfe, Tom CLC 1, 2, 9, 15, 35, 51
See Wolfe, Thomas Kennerly, Jr.
See also AAYA 8; AITN 2; AMWS 3; BEST 89:1; BPFB 3; CN 7; CPW; CSW; DLB 152; LAIT 5; RGAL 4
Wolff, Geoffrey (Ansell) 1937- CLC 41
See also CA 29-32R; CANR 29, 43, 78
Wolff, Sonia
See Levitin, Sonia (Wolff)
Wolff, Tobias (Jonathan Ansell) 1945- CLC 39, 64, 172; SSC 63
See also AAYA 16; AMWS 7; BEST 90:2; BYA 12; CA 114; 117; CAAS 22; CANR 54, 76, 96; CN 7; CSW; DA3; DLB 130; EWL 3; INT CA-117; MTCW 2; RGAL 4; RGSF 2; SSFS 4, 11
Wolfram von Eschenbach c. 1170-c. 1220 CMLC 5
See Eschenbach, Wolfram von
See also CDWLB 2; DLB 138; EW 1; RGWL 2
Wolitzer, Hilma 1930- CLC 17
See also CA 65-68; CANR 18, 40; INT CANR-18; SATA 31; YAW
Wollstonecraft, Mary 1759-1797 LC 5, 50, 90
See also BRWS 3; CDBLB 1789-1832; DLB 39, 104, 158, 252; FW; LAIT 1; RGEL 2; TEA; WLIT 3
Wonder, Stevie CLC 12
See Morris, Steveland Judkins
Wong, Jade Snow 1922- CLC 17
See also CA 109; CANR 91; SATA 112
Woodberry, George Edward 1855-1930 TCLC 73
See also CA 165; DLB 71, 103
Woodcott, Keith
See Brunner, John (Kilian Houston)
Woodruff, Robert W.
See Mencken, H(enry) L(ouis)
Woolf, (Adeline) Virginia 1882-1941 SSC 7; TCLC 1, 5, 20, 43, 56, 101, 123, 128; WLC
See also AAYA 44; BPFB 3; BRW 7; BRWC 2; BRWR 1; CA 104; 130; CANR 64; CDBLB 1914-1945; DA; DA3; DAB; DAC; DAM MST, NOV; DLB 36, 100, 162; DLBD 10; EWL 3; EXPS; FW; LAIT 3; LATS 1; LMFS 2; MTCW 1, 2; NCFS 2; NFS 8, 12; RGEL 2; RGSF 2; SSFS 4, 12; TEA; WLIT 4
Woollcott, Alexander (Humphreys) 1887-1943 TCLC 5
See also CA 105; 161; DLB 29
Woolrich, Cornell CLC 77
See Hopley-Woolrich, Cornell George
See also MSW
Woolson, Constance Fenimore 1840-1894 NCLC 82
See also DLB 12, 74, 189, 221; RGAL 4
Wordsworth, Dorothy 1771-1855 NCLC 25, 138
See also DLB 107
Wordsworth, William 1770-1850 NCLC 12, 38, 111; PC 4; WLC
See also BRW 4; BRWC 1; CDBLB 1789-1832; DA; DA3; DAB; DAC; DAM MST, POET; DLB 93, 107; EXPP; LATS 1; LMFS 1; PAB; PFS 2; RGEL 2; TEA; WLIT 3; WP
Wotton, Sir Henry 1568-1639 LC 68
See also DLB 121; RGEL 2

Wouk, Herman 1915- CLC 1, 9, 38
See also BPFB 2, 3; CA 5-8R; CANR 6, 33, 67; CDALBS; CN 7; CPW; DA3; DAM NOV, POP; DLBY 1982; INT CANR-6; LAIT 4; MTCW 1, 2; NFS 7; TUS
Wright, Charles (Penzel, Jr.) 1935- CLC 6, 13, 28, 119, 146
See also AMWS 5; CA 29-32R; CAAS 7; CANR 23, 36, 62, 88; CP 7; DLB 165; DLBY 1982; EWL 3; MTCW 1, 2; PFS 10
Wright, Charles Stevenson 1932- BLC 3; CLC 49
See also BW 1; CA 9-12R; CANR 26; CN 7; DAM MULT, POET; DLB 33
Wright, Frances 1795-1852 NCLC 74
See also DLB 73
Wright, Frank Lloyd 1867-1959 TCLC 95
See also AAYA 33; CA 174
Wright, Jack R.
See Harris, Mark
Wright, James (Arlington) 1927-1980 CLC 3, 5, 10, 28; PC 36
See also AITN 2; AMWS 3; CA 49-52; 97-100; CANR 4, 34, 64; CDALBS; DAM POET; DLB 5, 169; EWL 3; EXPP; MTCW 1, 2; PFS 7, 8; RGAL 4; TUS; WP
Wright, Judith (Arundell) 1915-2000 CLC 11, 53; PC 14
See also CA 13-16R; 188; CANR 31, 76, 93; CP 7; CWP; DLB 260; EWL 3; MTCW 1, 2; PFS 8; RGEL 2; SATA 14; SATA-Obit 121
Wright, L(aurali) R. 1939- CLC 44
See also CA 138; CMW 4
Wright, Richard (Nathaniel) 1908-1960 BLC 3; CLC 1, 3, 4, 9, 14, 21, 48, 74; SSC 2; TCLC 136; WLC
See also AAYA 5, 42; AFAW 1, 2; AMW; BPFB 3; BW 1; BYA 2; CA 108; CANR 64; CDALB 1929-1941; DA; DA3; DAB; DAC; DAM MST, MULT, NOV; DLB 76, 102; DLBD 2; EWL 3; EXPN; LAIT 3, 4; MTCW 1, 2; NCFS 1; NFS 1, 7; RGAL 4; RGSF 2; SSFS 3, 9, 15; TUS; YAW
Wright, Richard B(ruce) 1937- CLC 6
See also CA 85-88; CANR 120; DLB 53
Wright, Rick 1945- CLC 35
Wright, Rowland
See Wells, Carolyn
Wright, Stephen 1946- CLC 33
Wright, Willard Huntington 1888-1939
See Van Dine, S. S.
See also CA 115; 189; CMW 4; DLBD 16
Wright, William 1930- CLC 44
See also CA 53-56; CANR 7, 23
Wroth, Lady Mary 1587-1653(?) LC 30; PC 38
See also DLB 121
Wu Ch'eng-en 1500(?)-1582(?) LC 7
Wu Ching-tzu 1701-1754 LC 2
Wulfstan c. 10th cent. -1023 CMLC 59
Wurlitzer, Rudolph 1938(?)- CLC 2, 4, 15
See also CA 85-88; CN 7; DLB 173
Wyatt, Sir Thomas c. 1503-1542 LC 70; PC 27
See also BRW 1; DLB 132; EXPP; RGEL 2; TEA
Wycherley, William 1640-1716 LC 8, 21
See also BRW 2; CDBLB 1660-1789; DAM DRAM; DLB 80; RGEL 2
Wylie, Elinor (Morton Hoyt) 1885-1928 PC 23; TCLC 8
See also AMWS 1; CA 105; 162; DLB 9, 45; EXPP; RGAL 4

Zorrilla y Moral, Jose 1817-1893 NCLC 6

Zoshchenko, Mikhail (Mikhailovich)
   1895-1958 SSC 15; TCLC 15
      See also CA 115; 160; EWL 3; RGSF 2;
      RGWL 3

Zuckmayer, Carl 1896-1977 CLC 18
      See also CA 69-72; DLB 56, 124; EWL 3;
      RGWL 2, 3

Zuk, Georges
      See Skelton, Robin
      See also CCA 1

Zukofsky, Louis 1904-1978 CLC 1, 2, 4, 7,
   11, 18; PC 11
      See also AMWS 3; CA 9-12R; 77-80;
      CANR 39; DAM POET; DLB 5, 165;
      EWL 3; MTCW 1; RGAL 4

Zweig, Paul 1935-1984 CLC 34, 42
      See also CA 85-88; 113

Zweig, Stefan 1881-1942 TCLC 17
      See also CA 112; 170; DLB 81, 118; EWL
      3

Zwingli, Huldreich 1484-1531 LC 37
      See also DLB 179

Literary Criticism Series
Cumulative Topic Index

This index lists all topic entries in Gale's *Classical and Medieval Literature Criticism* (CMLC), *Contemporary Literary Criticism* (CLC), *Drama Criticism* (DC), *Literature Criticism from 1400 to 1800* (LC), *Nineteenth-Century Literature Criticism* (NCLC), *Short Story Criticism* (SSC), and *Twentieth-Century Literary Criticism* (TCLC). The index also lists topic entries in the Gale Critical Companion Collection, which includes the following publications: *The Beat Generation* (BG), and *Harlem Renaissance* (HR).

CMLC Cumulative Nationality Index

CMLC Cumulative Title Index

Title Index

Title Index

Title Index

Title Index

ISBN 0-7876-6770-6

9 780787 667702